JEFFREY WAYBRIGHT LIANG-HSUAN CHEN RHONDA PYPER CANADIAN EDITION

Spokane Community College   University of Toronto Scarborough   University of Ottawa

FINANCIAL ACCOUNTING

PEARSON

Toronto

Vice-President, Editorial Director: Gary Bennett
Editor-in-Chief: Nicole Lukach
Acquisitions Editor: Megan Farrell
Marketing Managers: Cas Shields, Jenna Wulff
Developmental Editor: Catherine Belshaw
Project Managers: Marissa Lok, Jessica Hellen
Manufacturing Manager: Susan Johnson
Production Editor: Susan Bindernagel
Copy Editor: Cat Haggert

Proofreader: Susan Bindernagel
Cold Reader: Anita Smale
Compositor: Nelson Gonzalez
Photo Researcher: Tara Smith
Permissions Researcher: Tara Smith
Art Director: Julia Hall
Cover and Interior Designer: Anthony Leung
Cover Image: Martin Barraud/GettyImages

Credits and acknowledgments for material borrowed from other sources and reproduced, with permission, in this textbook appear on the appropriate page within text or on page 795.

10 9 8 7 6 5 4 3 2 1 [QG]

Library and Archives Canada Cataloguing in Publication

Waybright, Jeffrey
    Financial accounting / Jeffrey Waybright, Liang-Hsuan Chen, Rhonda Pyper.—Canadian ed.

Includes bibliographical references and index.
ISBN 978-0-13-214753-8

    1. Accounting—Canada.   2. Accounting—Canada—Textbooks.
I. Chen, Liang-Hsuan, 1962– II. Pyper, Rhonda, 1968– III. Title.

HF5636.W39 2012   657'.044   C2011-905076-5

ISBN 978-0-13-214753-8

Dedication

My family—I couldn't have done this without their
support and encouragement

Jim Kahl—Jim has been a mentor, a colleague, and above all,
a tremendous friend for my entire teaching career

My students, past, present, and future—without them I would not be
doing that which I love to do, teaching accounting

Jeffrey Waybright

My husband, Dr. Louis Florence—thank you for your support in this
project and in the many new exciting endeavours in my career

Liang-Hsuan Chen

For my daughter Michelle and my husband René

Rhonda Pyper

About the Authors

Jeffrey Waybright teaches accounting at Spokane Community College, which is part of a multi-college district in eastern Washington. He has been a full-time, tenured, community college instructor for over 16 years. In addition to teaching at the community college level, he has taught upper division courses for Linfield College. Jeffrey is a recent co-recipient of the Washington Society of CPA's Outstanding Educator Award.

Jeffrey received his BA in business administration (emphasis in accounting) and MBA from Eastern Washington University. Before becoming a professor, Jeffrey spent eight years as a practicing CPA in Washington State and still holds his licence. During his teaching career, he has taught in many disciplines of accounting including financial, managerial, computerized, and payroll accounting as well as in the disciplines of economics, business math, and general business. Jeffrey developed online courses in accounting, teaches online and traditional courses for financial and managerial accounting, and advises students. Jeffrey is passionate about teaching students the subject of accounting.

Liang-Hsuan Chen, BA, MSEd, MBA, PhD, FCGA, is a Senior Lecturer in Accounting who holds an administrative leadership position as the Associate Dean – Registrarial and Student Services at the University of Toronto Scarborough, and has served as a board member of the Certified General Accountants of Ontario. Dr. Chen is also an Associate Member of the School of Graduate Studies with the Department of Theory and Policy Studies in Education at OISE/UT. Prior to her current position, Liang-Hsuan was an Accounting Professor and Program Coordinator for three Business programs at Humber College. She has extensive teaching experience, ranging from preschool to graduate school, in Taiwan, the US, and Canada. She has also worked in the private sector in Accounting and Marketing functions. Her research interests include issues in higher education, such as university/college choice, marketing of higher education, international education and internationalization of higher education, graduate and professional education, teaching/learning, and student experience. Liang-Hsuan was one of two recipients of the Alice L. Beeman Research Award in Communications and Marketing for Educational Advancement, Council for Advancement and Support of Education (CASE), based in Washington DC, in 2007. The award was for her doctoral thesis entitled "Choosing Canadian Graduate Schools from Afar: East-Asian International Students' Perspectives." Her publications related to international students' choice of Canadian graduate schools and marketing of higher education can be seen in *Higher Education*, the *Canadian Journal of Higher Education*, the *International Journal of Educational Advancement*, and the *Journal of Marketing for Higher Education*. She also co-authored a Cost Management textbook.

Dr. Chen received her BA in English Language and Literature from Soochow University in Taiwan, a Master of Science in Education from the University of Pennsylvania, and obtained an MBA and later a PhD in Higher Education, both from the University of Toronto.

Rhonda Pyper is a professor of accounting at the University of Ottawa. She is a member of the Society of Certified Management Accountants and an entrepreneur. Her research interests are varied and include investigating the impact of expertise and risk-taking on careers, the image of accountants, and the connection between leadership characteristics and the financial results of organizations. Professor Pyper has presented her research internationally and has been published in journals such as the *Canadian Journal of Administrative Sciences* and the Ontario Institute for Studies in Education's *Higher Education Perspectives.*

Professor Pyper has received research grants for her ongoing study on leadership and has been recognized for her volunteering by the province of Ontario. She has also received an award from the wing commander of Canadian Forces Base North Bay for volunteering as a musician and vocalist for the military band. She has performed with the band for ceremonial functions, military events, and as a representative of Canada at international festivals.

Professor Pyper and her husband have three daughters and they own and manage an equestrian facility. Most of her spare time is spent with her family on the farm.

Brief Contents

Contents

Chapter 8

Long-Term Assets 452

Chapter 9

Current Liabilities and Long-Term Debt 516

Chapter 10

Corporations: Share Capital and Retained Earnings 576

Chapter 11

The Cash Flow Statement   628

Chapter 12

Financial Statement Analysis   700

Appendix A

Bombardier Annual Report for Year Ended January 31, 2011   761

Appendix B

Time Value of Money—Future and Present Value Concepts   762

Preface

Financial Accounting, Canadian Edition, in combination with MyAccountingLab, translates the essentials of accounting to students so they understand "why" and "when" financially sound decisions are made in business today. *Financial Accounting* and MyAccountingLab work together to solidify students' understanding of the language of business, leading them to success.

THE CANADIAN EDITION

Financial Accounting, Canadian Edition, has been adapted from the first edition of an innovative text published in the United States. We took on the project of adapting this book for a Canadian audience because we found in the original text a solid foundation on which to build a Canadian financial accounting textbook. The features of the text, such as its focus on decision making, the clarity of its writing style, its innovative pedagogical features and approach to the visuals and, of course, MyAccountingLab, provided an excellent starting point for the Canadian edition.

We have been teaching financial accounting for many years and have prepared this text so that it highlights the relevance of accounting to all students, whether or not they are planning a career in accounting. The text is written in a way that provides students with coverage of the essential financial accounting concepts and in a way that will help them relate these concepts to their everyday lives:

- **Focus on Decision Making**

  Beginning with Chapter 1, an emphasis is placed on the importance of making financially sound business decisions. This emphasis helps students determine how much risk and impact is involved in the types of decisions they may encounter in their future careers. Ethics and ratio coverage are also woven throughout the text to continually support this decision-making focus.

- **Coverage of IFRS and Canadian ASPE**

  IFRS and Canadian ASPE are used in Canada for different business sectors—publicly accountable entities and private enterprises. There are many similarities in IFRS and Canadian ASPE; therefore, this textbook focuses its discussion on IFRS. There are a few specific topics that are treated differently in IFRS and Canadian ASPE, and in these situations, the differences are described and highlighted.

- **Balanced coverage**

  It is important for students to understand how financial accounting applies in small business scenarios as well as corporate ones. *Financial Accounting*, Canadian Edition, provides a straightforward look at the way many different types of organizations use accounting to ensure students are equipped with the knowledge they need.

  Students also need to understand both the "how" and the "why" of accounting. This text offers an appropriate blend of two perspectives—the preparer of accounting information and the user of accounting information—and uses this balanced approach to provide students with a solid grasp of accounting fundamentals and a clear understanding of how accounting information is used to make good business decisions. By demonstrating not only how to create information that communicates the activities of an organization but also why this information is important to a wide variety of users, the reader will see the relevance of financial accounting for anyone in society.

This text would be appropriate for any introductory financial accounting course. The book covers the concepts needed for accounting majors pursuing an accounting designation, but it is also appropriate for non-accounting students due to the interactive and user-friendly approach. The end-of-chapter problems cover a range of levels of difficulty, which, when combined with the the Demo Doc problems in each chapter and the unlimited problems available in MyAccountingLab, will enable students who have never been exposed to accounting to work their way up to the more challenging problems, and ensure that those students who excel in the concepts will still be able to work on challenging problems.

This adaptation started with an American text that had many of the necessary elements for a Canadian market. We made a number of important changes to make the text relevant to a Canadian audience. Most importantly, coverage in the Canadian text is based on the International Financial Reporting Standards and the Accounting Standards for Private Enterprises. Concepts that were not relevant to Canada, such as LIFO, were replaced with complete coverage of concepts that are relevant. Chapter 1 now incorporates an introduction to the careers in accounting that are available in Canada, both IFRS and ASPE are described and introduced, and terminology changes (for example, from stockholder to shareholder) are implemented. Chapter 4, which details the relationship between ethics and accounting, required significant adaptations to make the material relevant to Canadian students. Canadian accounting scandals and the impact of international accounting scandals on the Canadian accounting system are presented. Both the periodic and perpetual inventory systems are shown side by side to highlight the similarities and differences in the two systems in Chapter 5, while the LIFO cost flow assumption is removed from Chapter 6. The concept of par value shares is removed from the discussion of shares in Chapter 10. The Canadian edition is also full of Canadian examples and stories, which will help to create an interest among students in the Canadian business environment.

ORGANIZATION

The Canadian edition of *Financial Accounting* takes a cumulative approach to the concepts. Each topic builds on the knowledge of the previous chapters. The placement of a brief look at the financial statements in the first chapter helps to tie each of the following chapters together. The text also incorporates a blend of theory and application. Readers are provided with the tools necessary for understanding the creation of the financial statements through technical details and resources such as the Demo Doc problems and end-of-chapter questions. At the same time, readers are able to see how the concepts are relevant to all users of financial statements through examples, the presentation of various perspectives, and features such as the Focus on Users Box.

Financial Accounting, Canadian Edition, begins with the introduction of accounting as the language of organizations. This is followed by what a career in accounting might be like, then a brief description of financial statements. This description of the financial statements is used to link the chapters together as each chapter delves deeper into specific elements of the financial statements.

Next, the text demonstrates the accounting equation and works through the accounting cycle, continuously referring back to the accounting equation. Concepts are built one on top of the other in layers that will eventually result in a complete picture of the financial statements including a wide breadth of knowledge along with significant depth of detail.

Once the fundamentals have been presented, a full chapter is devoted to examining how ethics and accounting merge together. This chapter is filled with real-life examples that will ground the discussion and provide students with an idea of how significant an issue ethics can be.

Chapters 5 through 10 tackle the various groups of accounts (assets, liabilities, shareholders' equity). Each chapter covers the most important concepts for each type of account in enough depth to prepare students for subsequent financial and managerial accounting courses.

The text then returns to the financial statements by demonstrating the creation of the Cash Flow Statement and its uses, followed by an in-depth look at financial statement analysis in the final chapter. This brings the text full circle from starting with the financial statements, then breaking them down into their various elements, and returning back to the statements in full detail with a view to describing what the financial statements tell us, the users.

ENHANCEMENTS FOR LEARNING

PRESENTING CONCEPTS WITH CLARITY AND PURPOSE

The first thing that will distract students is jargon and difficult language, especially when it comes to understanding accounting concepts. Waybright, Chen, and Pyper have crafted a text that is written the way a great teacher would speak in class, with both clarity and purpose. Examples that are engaging and easy to understand are used throughout, facilitating the reader-friendly style of the text.

QUESTION AND ANSWER FORMAT

Some of the most teachable moments happen when a student asks a key question that gets straight to the heart of a topic. This text mirrors that approach by providing key questions in the headers, followed by clear, direct, and detailed explanations.

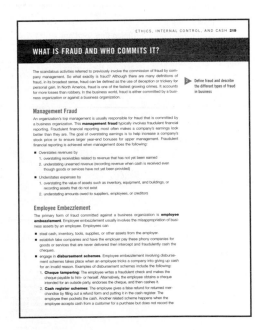

SEEING IT ALL TOGETHER

Waybright, Chen, and Pyper effectively illustrate the connection between accounting equations and big picture concepts by introducing a slight twist on the visuals used in the text. Instead of presenting the details of the journal entries, general ledger, and T-accounts in isolation, *Financial Accounting*, Canadian Edition, shows these details within the context of the accounting equation and financial statements. This approach helps students appreciate the steps involved in preparing and interpreting financial statements, which is critical to their understanding of the material and success in the course.

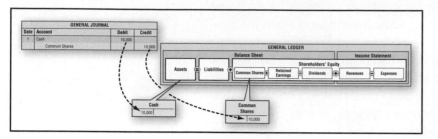

DEMO DOCS

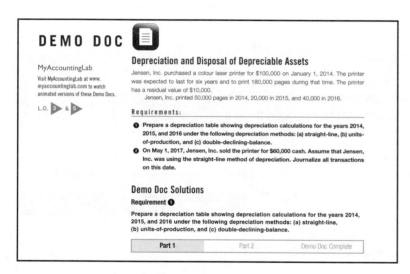

The **Demo Doc** examples consist of entire problems, worked through step by step, from start to finish, narrated with the kind of comments that instructors would say in class. The Demo Docs are available in most chapters of the text. In addition to the printed Demo Docs, Flash-animated versions are available so that students can watch the problems as they are worked through while listening to the explanations and details. Demo Docs will aid students when they are trying to solve exercises and problems on their own, duplicating the classroom experience outside of class.

DECISION GUIDELINES

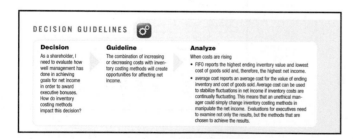

Decision Guidelines summarize the chapter's key terms, concepts, and formulas in the context of business decisions. Found throughout and at the end of each chapter, Decision Guidelines show students each decision and how to evaluate it so they can readily see the value in, and for, a business. Overall, these guidelines continue to reinforce how accounting information is used to make decisions in business.

ACCOUNTING IN YOUR WORLD

Found in every chapter, the **Accounting in Your World** boxed feature personalizes accounting challenges, issues, and ethical situations for students to evaluate from their own perspective.

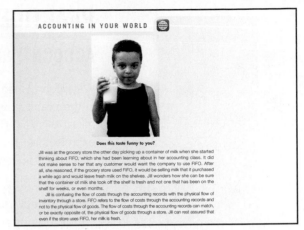

CRITICAL THINKING

Critical Thinking questions appear throughout the chapter, providing students with the opportunity to think about the impact of the accounting treatment on the accounts, the financial statements, as well as on the company's financial objectives and shareholders' objectives. Critical thinking reinforces how accounting information is used to impact decision-makers and their respective objectives.

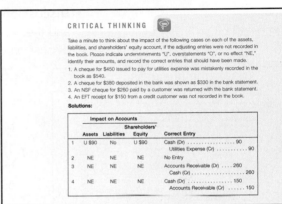

CONCEPT CHECKS

Concept Checks appear throughout the chapter so that students can review their understanding and interpretation of the material. By showing "what it is" and "why and when it matters" together, these checks allow students a place to pause and interpret what they've just learned.

FOCUS ON USERS

The **Focus on Users** feature shows the links between the concepts covered in each chapter and how that accounting information is used by a wide variety of individuals, whether they are inside an organization or outside, accountants or not. The main concepts of each chapter are examined from the viewpoints of various users, such as shareholders and investors, management, competitors, and unions. By demonstrating not only how to create information that communicates the activities of an organization, but also why this information is important to a wide variety of users, the reader will see the relevance of financial accounting for anyone in society. By highlighting these differing viewpoints, the reader also gets a sense of the difficulty in pleasing all users with one set of financial accounting statements and the challenges that arise during the preparation of these statements.

PRACTICE MAKES PERFECT
ACCOUNTING PRACTICE

Waybright, Chen, and Pyper understand that the key to students' accounting success is in the practice and work completed in the end-of-chapter problem material. With this in mind, this text presents the material so that students progress from simple calculative exercises, to a mixture of calculative and conceptual exercises, and finally on to more complex, conceptual analysis problems, and cases. This progression allows students to build confidence and achieve mastery of the material.

- **Self Check questions** quickly audit the students' understanding of the chapter concepts by presenting them with a series of multiple choice questions.

- **Discussion Questions** help students make the connections between the "how" and the "why" of financial accounting information through a guided series of in-class discussion questions.

- **"A" and "B" Sets of Exercises and Problems.** Students and instructors have two sets of exercises and problems provided for them in the text. Three sets of alternative exercises and problems are also available in MyAccountingLab to give students more practice opportunities.

- **The Continuing Exercise** highlights the same small business from chapter to chapter, allowing students to apply their understanding of chapter concepts in a business context. As students move through the text, they complete additional steps in this comprehensive exercise. Students are able to see the big picture and learn how the topics build on one another. The Continuing Exercise can be assigned and completed within MyAccountingLab.

- **The Continuing Problem** is a more comprehensive version of the Continuing Exercise, featuring a different small business. Once again, students learn how accounting is a process and the Continuing Problem helps them put it all together.

The questions in the **Know Your Business** section demonstrate how accounting is applicable in real life. Featuring **Financial Analysis**, **Industry Analysis**, and **Small Business Analysis** questions, students learn how to apply the concepts of each chapter to help them understand the significance of financial statement and industry analysis as a means to evaluate the financial health of a company. The financial and industry analysis questions feature one company, Bombardier, allowing students to see how chapter concepts are connected. The financial statements for Bombardier can be found at www.myaccountinglab.com.

KNOW YOUR BUSINESS
FINANCIAL ANALYSIS

Purpose: To help familiarize you with the financial reporting of a real company to further your understanding of the chapter material you are learning.

This case will help you to better understand the effect of adjusting journal entries on the financial statements. We do not have access to the journals and ledgers used by Bombardier Inc., but we can see some of the adjusted accounts on the company's financial statements. Refer to the Bombardier Inc. income statements, "Consolidated Statements of Income," and the Bombardier Inc. balance sheets in MyAccountingLab. Also, Note 7 titled "Property, Plant and Equipment" on page 184 of the Bombardier Annual Report uses the term amortization instead of depreciation. You can consider these two terms to mean the same thing at this point.

Requirements

1. Open T-accounts for the following accounts and their balances as of January 31, 2011 prior to closing. (All amounts in millions of US$.)

PP&E	$1,930.25
Accounts Payable and Accrued Liabilities	$7,835
Advances and progress billings in excess of related long-term contract costs....	$1,638
Long-Term Debt	$6,210

2. Using the following information for Bombardier Inc.'s 2011 operations, make the appropriate year-end journal entries.
   a. Payment of Accrued Liabilities of $1,021.
   b. Amortization expense, $13.75.
   c. Accrue Accounts Payable and Accrued Liabilities, $1,213.
   d. Additional Advances and progress billings in excess of related long-term contract costs, $783.
   e. Principal repayments on the Long-Term Debt of $1,575.

3. Post the journal entries to the T-accounts you set up. Check the updated ending balances in each account against the balances reported by iBombardier Inc. as of January 31, 2011. You can determine the total Accumulated Amortization account by taking the difference between Cost and Net Book Value from Note 7.

INDUSTRY ANALYSIS

Purpose: To help you understand and compare the performance of two companies in the same industry.

Go to the Bombardier Annual Report located in MyAccountingLab. Now access the Annual Report for The Boeing Company. To do this from the internet, go to the company's web page for Investor Relations at *http://www.boeing.com/companyoffices/financial/quarterly.htm* and download the annual report for the year ended December 31, 2010.

Requirement

1. Identify three accounts for each company that indicate that both Bombardier and Boeing use the accrual basis of accounting. Why do you think using the accrual basis of accounting would be more helpful for analysis purposes than the cash basis for these two companies?

SMALL BUSINESS ANALYSIS

Purpose: To help you understand the importance of cash flows in the operation of a small business.

Your business has been doing pretty well since you first opened the doors five years ago. You've been thinking for the last six months or so about expanding the business. There is some property right next door that will work well into your expansion plans. It would take some renovations to the building, but to continue to grow, you know you're going to need more room. But here's the problem. How are you going to pay for the building and the renovations? Your cash account is in pretty good shape, but you remember the sage advice of the business consultant who helped you when you were just getting started. That advice was to always have enough available cash to cover three months' worth of expenses just in case of some unexpected business interruption. Your available cash and short term investments of $100,000 is right at that benchmark.

Some preliminary investigation into the property next door indicates that the existing owner would probably be willing to accept $200,000 for the property. You also have a discussion with a contractor associate who tells you that the renovations to your specifications would cost about $50,000. So your dilemma is how are you going to come up with $250,000? You figure the best place to start is with a visit to your banker.

At that meeting with the banker, he tells you something like this:

"Frank, we would be pleased to help you out with your expansion plans. We would require you to take out a mortgage on the building and we would need a 20% down payment of the total amount up front. So the balance that we would be lending you would be 80% of the total you need, or $200,000. Your down payment amount would be $50,000. At 8% for 20 years, your monthly payments would be $1,672.88."

You are somewhat pleased with the outcome of the meeting, but you tell the banker you will get back to him in a day or two. You know that this is big step and a long-term investment for the business.

Requirements

1. After thinking through the details of the plan the banker gave you, what are your thoughts? Since the down payment is going to use up about half of your available cash, how does that concern you? What about the long-term commitment of 20 years?

2. Assuming you go ahead with the mortgage and the purchase and renovation of the property, journalize the transactions to acquire the property and make the renovations. Where will the building and the renovations show up on your financial statements? Where will the mortgage show up on your financial statements? If the interest portion of your first payment is going to be $1,333.33, journalize the transaction to make your first mortgage payment.

MYACCOUNTINGLAB

The moment you know.

Educators know it. Students know it. It's that inspired moment when something that was difficult to understand suddenly makes perfect sense. Our MyLab products have been designed and refined with a single purpose in mind—to help educators create that moment of understanding with their students.

MyAccountingLab delivers proven results in helping individual students succeed. It provides engaging experiences that personalize, stimulate, and measure learning for each student. And it comes from a trusted partner with educational expertise and an eye on the future.

MyAccountingLab can be used by itself or linked to any learning management system. To learn more about how MyAccountingLab combines proven learning applications with powerful assessment, visit **www.myaccountinglab.com**.

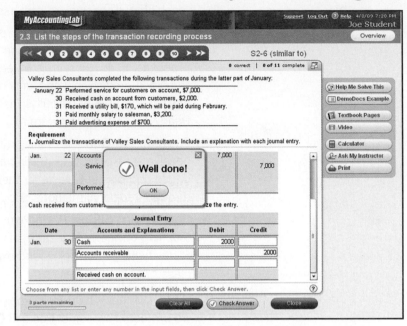

STUDY ON THE GO

At the end of each chapter, you will find a unique QR code providing access to Study on the Go, an unprecedented mobile integration between text and online content. Students link to Pearson's unique Study on the Go content directly from their smartphones, allowing them to study whenever and wherever they wish! Go to one of the sites below to see how you can download an app to your smartphone for free. Once the app is installed, your phone will scan the code and link to a website containing Pearson's Study on the Go content, including the popular study tools Glossary Flashcards, Audio Summaries, and Quizzes, which can be accessed anytime.

SCAN THIS

ScanLife
http://getscanlife.com/

NeoReader
http://get.neoreader.com/

QuickMark
http://www.quickmark.com.tw/

INSTRUCTOR RESOURCES

Supplements available to instructors include the following:

- **Instructor's Resource CD-ROM** (0-13-261031-0) This resource CD includes the following instructor supplements:
- **The Instructor's Solutions Manual:** Contains thoroughly worked-through solutions to every question, exercise, problem, and case in the text. All solutions were prepared by the authors and technically checked twice by professional accountants.

- **The Instructor's Manual:** Offers course-specific content, including useful information on how to best manage your course when using the text in class, and content-specific material linked to the PowerPoint Slides, including chapter overviews, teaching outlines, lecture tips, assignment grids, quizzes, and more!

- **Test Item File:** Available in Microsoft Word format, this test bank includes approximately 1400 questions, including true/false and multiple choice questions, and problems. Each question is linked to the learning objectives in each chapter and to Canadian professional accounting standards, and is accompanied by the correct answer and level of difficulty. The test bank for *Financial Accounting* is also offered in Pearson's TestGen Software.

- **Pearson TestGen:** The TestGen test bank for *Financial Accounting* offers a comprehensive suite of tools for testing and assessment. TestGen allows educators to easily create and distribute tests for their courses, either by printing and distributing through traditional methods or by online delivery.

- **PowerPoint Slides:** PowerPoint slides are provided for each chapter. Linked to the teaching outlines and lecture tips found in the Instructor's Manual, the PowerPoint Slides highlight key points and examples from the text, providing a framework for in-class or online lectures.

Most of these instructor supplements are also available for download from a password protected section of Pearson Canada's online catalogue (catalogue.pearsoned.ca). Navigate to your book's catalogue page to view a list of those supplements that are available. See your local sales representative for details and access.

CourseSmart

CourseSmart goes beyond traditional expectations—providing instant, online access to the textbooks and course materials you need at a lower cost for students. And even as students save money, you can save time and hassle with a digital eTextbook that allows you to search for the most relevant content at the very moment you need it. Whether it's evaluating textbooks or creating lecture notes to help students with difficult concepts, CourseSmart can make life a little easier. See how when you visit www.coursesmart.com/instructors.

Technology Specialists

Pearson's Technology Specialists work with faculty and campus course designers to ensure that Pearson technology products, assessment tools, and online course materials are tailored to meet your specific needs. This highly qualified team is dedicated to helping schools take full advantage of a wide range of educational resources, by assisting in the integration of a variety of instructional materials and media formats. Your local Pearson Education sales representative can provide you with more details on this service program.

Pearson Custom Library

For enrollments of at least 25 students, you can create your own textbook by choosing the chapters that best suit your own course needs. To begin building your custom text, visit www.pearsoncustomlibrary.com. You may also work with a dedicated Pearson Custom editor to create your ideal text—publishing your own original content or mixing and matching Pearson content. *Contact your local Pearson Representative to get started.*

ACKNOWLEDGMENTS

For the Canadian edition of *Financial Accounting*, we had the help of instructors from across the country who participated in chapter reviews. Their comments and suggestions for the text have been a great help in planning and carrying out the vision of this textbook, and we thank them for their contributions.

Bharat Aggarwal, Professional Programs, CMA
Mina Ally, Seneca College
Ron Baker, University of Guelph
Maria Belanger, Algonquin College
Stephen L. Bergstrom, SAIT Polytechnic
W. Peter Blake, Sheridan College
Maria Blazkiewicz, Dawson College
Dianne Davis, Nipissing University
Meredith Delaney, Seneca College
Robert G. Ducharme, University of Waterloo
John Harris, Centennial College
David Hoffman, Seneca College of Applied Arts and Technology
Gordon Holyer, Vancouver Island University
Ian Hutchinson, Acadia University
Gerry La Rocca, Vanier College
Howard Leaman, University of Guelph/Humber
Camillo Lento, Lakehead University
Sheila McGillis, Laurentian University
Carol A. Meissner, Georgian College
Ann Clarke-Okah, Carleton University
Clifton Philpott, Kwantlen Polytechnic University
Brad Sacho, Kwantlen Polytechnic University
Barrie Tober, Niagara College
Cindy Trudel, Acadia University
Valerie Warren, Kwantlen Polytechnic University
Brad Witt, Humber ITAL
Patricia Zima, Mohawk College

Liang-Hsuan Chen would like to thank Jerry Kong for his assistance in this project.

Rhonda Pyper would like to send a sincere thank you to the team at Pearson for their encouragement and support.

CHAPTER 1

Business, Accounting, and You

Learning objectives are a "roadmap" showing what will be covered and what is especially important in each chapter.

▼

LEARNING OBJECTIVES:

 1 Describe the major types of business organizations

2 Identify career opportunities in accounting and related fields

3 Explain the key accounting principles and the conceptual framework

4 Analyze transactions using the basic accounting equation

5 Understand and be able to prepare basic financial statements

Do you want to open your own business some day, or perhaps work for a large, multinational company? Whether your goal is to start your own business or to work for another company, the study of financial accounting can help you reach that goal. Accounting will help you answer questions such as "How much money is the business making?" or "Where does the business stand financially?" Knowing the answers to these and other important questions gives you a competitive advantage in the business world.

Each chapter opens with questions about why the chapter is important. The questions are answered throughout the chapter and summarized in the Decision Guidelines found throughout the chapter. ▶

WHY STUDY ACCOUNTING?

Accounting Teaches the Language of Business

Many students who enrol in accounting classes often ask the question "Why do I have to take accounting anyway? I am not going to be an accountant." Perhaps the most compelling reason for taking an accounting course, especially if you do not plan on becoming an accountant, is that accounting teaches "the language of business." No matter what your intended area of study, if you want to be successful in business, you need to know how to speak the language of business.

Consider a patient in the hospital. Many health-care professionals, in addition to the doctor, are responsible for ensuring the overall health and welfare of the patient. There are nurses, nursing assistants, x-ray technicians, and others involved in the treatment and care of the patient. Additionally, many pieces of equipment monitor the patient's condition. If the doctor is the only person able to speak "the language of medicine" and read and interpret information provided about the patient's health, the ability of the other health-care professionals to provide quality care to the patient is severely limited. Therefore, all individuals in the health-care profession are required to speak "the language of medicine." They must understand how to speak, read, and interpret information relative to the health of the patients they serve to provide the highest level of care. Similarly, if only the accountants in a business organization are able to speak, read, and interpret financial information regarding the health of the business, the ability of others within the organization to manage the affairs of the business in a manner that ensures the health of the business will be limited. Whether your intended area of study is marketing or management, or even cosmetology or automotive, an understanding of accounting will allow you to monitor and manage the health of the organization for which you work.

Accounting Emphasizes the Importance of Ethical Business Behaviour

Boldfaced words are new terms that are explained here and defined in the Accounting Vocabulary at the end of each chapter and in the Glossary at the end of the book.

Proper ethical behaviour has taken on renewed importance in the wake of recent accounting scandals, such as Enron, that have occurred in the United States as well as in other countries. **Ethics** refers to the principles of right behaviour that guide decision making. Individuals from top management to front-line workers may be confronted with ethical dilemmas in their jobs. Ethical dilemmas often arise when the actions that most benefit an individual differ from the actions that most benefit the organization. Ethical dilemmas are also created when personal beliefs or organizational culture differ from ethical principles.

The study of accounting will help individuals better identify situations that create ethical dilemmas within an organization. More importantly, it helps them discern the proper course of action to take in these situations.

ACCOUNTING IN YOUR WORLD

How would you respond to the following situations?

1 The company CEO asks you to falsify the company's accounting records. He or she says that the company cannot afford to report that it is performing poorly. If it does, some stores will likely have to be closed and people will lose their jobs. The CEO implies that if you are not a "team player" and falsify the records that it will be your fault these people are unemployed.

2 At the end of the month, your supervisor asks you to create fictitious sales invoices. He or she tells you that your department is just a little bit shy of reaching the sales goal necessary for each member of the department to receive a quarterly bonus. Your supervisor says that you can just delete the fictitious sales at the beginning of the next month and that no one will ever know.

3 A co-worker of yours confides in you that he or she has stolen several MP3 players from the store at which you both work. Your co-worker offers to give you one of the players. He or she says that you both deserve it for all of the long hours you have worked for the company lately.

You may find yourself faced with an ethical dilemma at any time during your career. You only have one chance to make the right decision. In Chapter 4 we take a closer look at ethics and reveal the consequences of other people's poor choices.

An Understanding of Accounting Helps Individuals Ensure That the Business Is Healthy and Profitable

Many small business owners and managers within larger businesses are very knowledgeable with regards to many aspects of their position but often fail due to a lack of accounting knowledge. Individuals in these positions often know a lot about the products they sell but are unable to answer questions such as the following:

- What is the true cost of what I am selling?
- Am I being "ripped off" by my employees or my customers?
- How much will it cost my company (or department) to achieve the growth that has been projected for the upcoming quarter?

An understanding of accounting will allow an individual to answer these and other questions, and monitor the operations that will help the company be profitable.

WHAT IS ACCOUNTING?

Have you noticed how many kids play little league sports these days, and wondered why so many kids compete in these sports? Some kids play to get into better shape and some kids play just for the fun, but most kids play because they want to win. If you think about it, we live in a very competitive world. This competitiveness makes the job of the scorekeeper very important, because without the scorekeeper, nobody would know which team won the contest. In addition to keeping track of who wins, the scorekeeper in an athletic contest tracks many other statistics, which help the coach and the players judge individual performances. It also allows individuals outside of the team, such as spectators, team owners, journalists, and others, follow along and keep track of how the team is doing.

The world of business is very much like little league sports. **Businesses** exist to win, which is usually defined as making money. The scorekeepers in the world of business are the accountants. Their job is to "keep score" to determine if the business has won or lost through a process known as financial accounting. An accountant also tracks other types of information in addition to whether the company made or lost money to help employees and managers judge individual performance. It is the job of the accountant to provide useful information to various users regarding the performance of the organization. The information is used mostly to determine whether or not to invest capital or lend money to a business. Financial accounting produces reports called **financial statements** that show financial information about a business. These reports are "historical" reports that communicate financial information about a business to people or organizations outside the company (such as the fans, journalists, etc.). The external users of financial statements include those who are not directly involved in the business operations, such as shareholders, potential investors, creditors, suppliers, customers, regulators, government, financial analysts, and the public, while internal users of the financial statements include the CEO, CFO, controller, and managers who run the business. Financial statements

- allow investors and creditors to make investment and credit decisions.
- enable suppliers and customers to determine the financial condition of a business.
- report results, if needed, to regulatory agencies such as the Ontario Securities Commission (OSC) and the Canada Revenue Agency.
- allow managers to make operating decisions, and provide feedback for learning and improvement.

Ultimately, the financial statements are the responsibility of the company's managers (the users of the financial statements) rather than the responsibility of the bookkeepers or internal accounting team (the preparers of the statements). This book teaches students the process of **accounting**, or "scorekeeping," for a business organization and the analysis of business performance. This textbook will examine financial accounting with a balanced perspective: focused on users of financial information as well as the preparers of financial information. This balanced approach demonstrates that a solid understanding of accounting is needed regardless of whether or not you pursue a career in accounting. Therefore, answering the question "Why is this important?" will be highlighted as well as the question "How do we do this?" Understanding how the processes of accounting work is necessary for understanding what the output tells us. For example, if we want to be an expert race car driver, understanding the mechanics of automotives will improve our ability to use the vehicle to maximize its performance. This same concept applies to accounting and businesses. To maximize the performance or understand the performance of an organization, it is important to know how the information on which we are relying was created.

Throughout the book, the "How" will be demonstrated and then followed up with the "Why," or the element of what this information tells us. The Decision Guidelines, Accounting in the Real World, and the Focus on Users boxes, along with other features, are incorporated in this text to assist in demonstrating the relevance of these concepts to all users of financial information.

HOW ARE BUSINESSES ORGANIZED?

Types of Businesses

The three types of business are a **service business**, a **merchandising business**, and a **manufacturing business**.

- A service business provides services to its customers. In other words, what it sells is time and knowledge or skills. Common types of service businesses are law firms, accounting firms, physical therapy offices, painting companies, etc.

- A merchandise business sells physical goods or products to its customers. Common types of merchandise businesses are automobile dealerships, department stores, grocery stores, sporting goods stores, etc. A merchandise business may be either a **wholesale business** or a **retail business**. A retailer sells directly to the final customer whereas a wholesaler buys from manufacturers and sells to retailers.

- Manufacturing businesses produce the physical goods that they sell to their customers. Common types of manufacturing businesses are automobile manufacturers, the makers of clothing, soft drink manufacturers, etc.

- A business can also be a blend of different types, or a hybrid. For example, an automotive repair shop provides a service, but also sells parts similar to a retail business.

Bombardier Inc. is a well-known Canadian manufacturer of aerospace and transportations vehicles, but it also provides services such as repair and maintenance, software development, and technical support.

 Describe the major types of business organizations

 Learning Objectives in the margin signal the beginning of the section that covers the learning objective topic. Look for the Learning Objective when you want to review this topic.

Choice of Business Organizations

A business can be organized as a sole proprietorship, partnership, or corporation. But how do you know what type of business organization is best for your business?

- A **sole proprietorship** is a business entity that has one owner. For legal purposes and for tax purposes, the business and the owner are considered the same. The business is not a separate legal entity, and the owner is personally responsible for all of the debts and obligations of the business. If somebody wants to sue the business, he or she would have to sue the owner. In addition, all of the income or loss generated by the business is reported on the owner's personal tax return and taxed at individual tax rates.

- A **partnership** is very similar to a sole proprietorship except that it has two or more owners. For legal purposes, the owners (partners) and the business are considered the same. If somebody sues the business, he or she would need to sue one or more of the business owners. For tax purposes, the partners divide all of the income or loss of the partnership among themselves and report it on their personal tax returns. Therefore, it is taxed at individual tax rates just like a sole proprietorship. One advantage of a partnership is flexibility regarding the division of the business income between the partners.

- A **corporation** differs from a sole proprietorship or a partnership because it is a separate legal entity from the owners. This legal separation is very attractive to the business owners because it limits their personal liability to what they have invested in the corporation. The corporation may sue another person or business and it may be sued by another person or business. For tax purposes, the corporation is a separate entity from the owners. Therefore, income tax is imposed on the income of the corporation at corporate tax rates. Any remaining income that is distributed to the owners, or **shareholders**, in the form of dividends is then taxed at the shareholder's individual income tax rates. However, shareholders can claim an enhanced dividend tax credit to reduce the income taxes.

Public versus Private Corporations

A corporation can be publicly held or privately held. A privately held corporation has very few owners and is not traded on the stock exchange. Quite often, corporations start out as privately held organizations and then through the process of an initial public offering, shares are then bought and sold on the stock market by shareholders. Once this takes place, the organization becomes a publicly held company.

Due to the different ways a business can be organized, the preparation and presentation of the owners' claims in different business organizations vary. For example, the injection of money or properties from owners in exchange for the ownership of the business is called **owner(s)'s capital** for sole proprietorships and partnerships, and is called share capital for corporations. The income distributed to owner(s) is called **withdrawals** for sole proprietorships and partnerships, and is called dividends for corporations. Corporations are required to prepare a statement to describe the changes in shareholders' equity, including the changes in the number of shares issued and the amount of share capital and earnings.

The Business Entity Concept

The most basic concept in accounting is that of the business **entity**. The business entity concept dictates that the financial affairs of a business organization must be kept separate from the personal financial affairs of the business owners. This separation is necessary because if the owners of a business choose to place personal assets into the business, then those assets are now considered to belong to the business and no longer to the owners. For example, if a business owner invests a used car into his or her business, that car should no longer be used by the business owner for personal purposes.

Exhibit 1-1 summarizes the different types of business organizations:

Type of Business	Legal Status	Tax Status	Benefits	Drawbacks
Sole Proprietorship	Business and owner are considered to be the same entity	Business income is allocated to the owner and taxed at owner's personal tax rate	• Ease of formation	• Unlimited liability of owner • Difficult to raise capital • Limited life
Partnership	Business and owners are considered to be the same entity	Business income is allocated to the owners and taxed at owners' personal tax rates	• Ease of formation • Shared investment/knowledge	• Unlimited liability of owners • Disagreements between partners • Limited life
Corporation	Business and owners are considered to be **separate** entities	Business income is taxed at corporate tax rates.	• Limited liability of owners • Easier to raise capital • Unlimited life	• More difficult and costly to form • More paperwork • More regulations

Exhibit 1-1 ▲

Exhibits summarize key ideas in a visual way.

Although the process of accounting for the different types of business organizations is similar, there are slight variations depending on the type of organization. In this book, we will focus our attention on accounting for corporations.

DECISION GUIDELINES

Decision

I am planning to start a new business. What form of business organization should be chosen?

Guideline

There are many ways to organize a business including the following: a sole proprietorship, partnership, or corporation. Each type of business organization has different advantages and disadvantages.

Analyze

Know the tax and legal treatments of each type of organization. Weigh the best treatment of taxes and legal liability of each type and pick the format that is most advantageous for the business owners.

Decision Guidelines show why accounting principles and concepts are important to business people, not just accountants. They are also an excellent summary of the chapter topics.

WHAT ARE THE CAREER OPPORTUNITIES IN ACCOUNTING-RELATED FIELDS?

2 ▶ Identify career opportunities in accounting and related fields

Careers in accounting and related fields provide rewarding opportunities for professional and personal development and growth, as well as job security and social prestige. There are several broad areas of expertise that accounting professionals build their careers on: financial accounting, managerial accounting, taxation, and banking and financial services.

Exhibit 1-2 illustrates careers in the field of accounting, the types of tasks typically undertaken, and some examples of common job titles. **Financial accounting** is a branch of accounting that focuses on serving the needs of external users who need to make sound economic decisions. Major tasks involved in financial accounting are financial statement preparation, financial analysis, auditing, criminal investigation, etc. Financial statement preparation is guided by a set of accounting standards, such as International Financial Reporting Standards (IFRS) or Canadian Accounting Standards for Private Enterprises (ASPE). The information gathered is past-oriented, meaning events have occurred, and the information is gathered from the business entity as a whole.

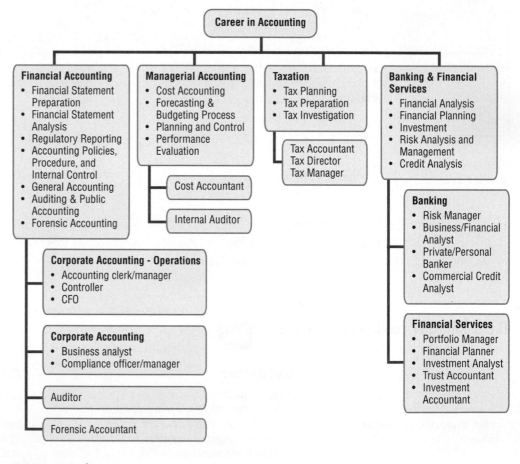

Exhibit 1-2 ▲

Managerial accounting is a branch of accounting that provides accounting information for internal users to help make business decisions. Major tasks involved in managerial accounting are cost accounting, budgeting, planning and control, performance evaluation, internal auditing, etc. Performing these tasks is not guided by external accounting standards. The information gathered is future-oriented, and is gathered from the various segments of the business entity.

With accounting knowledge, accounting professionals can choose to work in the field of taxation by providing tax planning, tax preparation, and tax audit to individuals and business taxpayers. Many accountants work in the banking or financial services fields. They help banks and investment companies assess and analyze client risks and credit ratings, and they may work as investment advisor to help individuals or companies manage and invest their funds.

There are three professional accounting bodies in Canada: the Certified General Accountants Association of Canada, the Society of Management Accountants of Canada, and the Canadian Institute of Chartered Accountants. Each accounting body is a self-regulated body to grant the qualifying members its respective designation (i.e. CGA, CMA, and CA) and public accounting license. These professional accounting designations increase the confidence of employers and the general public in accounting professionals who provide accounting-related services.

WHAT ACCOUNTING PRINCIPLES AND CONCEPTS GOVERN THE FIELD OF ACCOUNTING?

What Are the Applicable Accounting Reporting Standards in Canada?

In sports there are established rules and principles that dictate how each game is to be played and how the score is to be kept. In accounting, there are reporting standards that guide how business activities should be recognized, measured, and recorded, and how financial information should be reported.

 3 Explain the key accounting principles and the conceptual framework

There are several accounting reporting standards in Canada for various types of entities, such as publicly accountable enterprises, private enterprises, not-for-profit organizations, public sector organizations, etc. Canadian publicly accountable enterprises are required to adopt **International Financial Reporting Standards (IFRS)** effective January 1, 2011. Canadian private enterprises, on the other hand, have the option to adopt IFRS or to adopt a new set of "made in Canada" financial reporting standards— the **Accounting Standards for Private Enterprises (ASPE)**—developed by the Accounting Standards Board (AcSB). Some significant differences between IFRS and **Canadian Accounting Standards for Private Enterprises** lie in the areas of how events that take place are measured and presented, what information needs to be disclosed to people outside of the company, and when certain elements need to be recorded.

The Accounting Standards Board has prepared a five-part *CICA Handbook— Accounting* for the Canadian Institute of Chartered Accountants (CICA), that allows different sectors to adopt the appropriate standards to suit their needs. The five parts include:

Part I—International Financial Reporting Standards
Part II—Accounting Standards for Private Enterprises
Part III—Accounting Standards for Not-for-Profit Organizations
Part IV—Accounting Standards for Pension Plans, and
Part V—A complete set of the existing *CICA Handbook* contents

Since we will be examining corporations and their financial accounting processes throughout this text, this textbook is based on IFRS and, where applicable, addresses the Canadian Accounting Standards for Private Enterprises (ASPE) as they will be the most applicable and relevant. This is due to the fact that publicly accountable enterprises must use IFRS. In addition, some private enterprises may elect to adopt IFRS as a result of having a plan to eventually become public companies or to access capital, funding, and investment opportunities internationally.

International Financial Reporting Standards

In the 1970s a set of accounting standards was developed for use primarily by companies located in countries that did not have their own accounting standards. These standards, originally called International Accounting Standards (IAS), evolved into what is currently known as International Financial Reporting Standards, or IFRS. IFRS are created by the International Accounting Standards Board. The members of the International Accounting Standards Board are appointed by the International Accounting Standards Committee. Both the International Accounting Standards Board and the International Accounting Standards Committee have members from many different regions throughout the world. This ensures that the IFRS are the result of input from many different countries throughout the entire world. The goal of the International Accounting Standards Board is to create a set of global, high-quality, enforceable accounting standards. The set of IFRS is referred to as a principles-based system. Instead of creating countless rules that need to be followed, IFRS relies on a **conceptual framework** and a small number of overriding principles coupled with sound decision making and good ethical behaviour.

IFRS has become widespread throughout the world. As a matter of fact, many countries that have their own accounting standards have started to allow the use of IFRS in addition to, or instead of, their own standards. Currently, IFRS is used by more than 100 countries in the world, and a number of economically important countries, such as Japan and the United States, have convergence plans to adopt IFRS in 2015 or 2016.

The Conceptual Framework

The conceptual framework is a theoretical foundation that helps accounting standard setters develop consistent and coherent standards, and helps accountants determine the appropriate treatment of events in the absence of specific guidance, so that financial information can be properly communicated to the users. The main objective of financial reporting is to provide information that is useful for making economic (e.g., investment and lending) decisions. To be useful, information about the financial position, performance, and changes in financial position of an entity, which are the elements of the financial statements, must be understandable, relevant, reliable, and comparable. These are the four main qualitative characteristics of financial statements. However, to achieve these objectives, there are three constraints—**timeliness**, **cost–benefit**, and **materiality**. Accountants need to use their professional judgment and balance the three to provide quality information to users. For example, accountants need to balance the benefit of timely reporting and providing relevant and reliable information. In addition, accountants have to balance between the costs and benefits of obtaining very complete information. In other words, the benefits of obtaining complete information should outweigh the costs of obtaining it. It is important that accountants exercise professional judgement to assess the amount of information to be reported. If the information is material and will impact decision-making, then it should be included for completeness.

In essence, IFRS provides a general framework and accountants are required to make sound professional judgement in various situations. When in doubt, accountants need to refer to the framework and consider whether the financial information to be provided is understandable, comparable, and relevant to users, and whether the financial information can be relied on for users to make economic decisions.

Exhibit 1-3 depicts the IFRS conceptual framework for financial reporting. IFRS puts the users in the centre, as all the financial information preparation and presentation is geared towards the users' need for decision-making. Accountants should possess a set of comprehensive core competencies, including a clear understanding of (1) the elements of financial statements, (2) accounting principles, and (3) assumptions. With all these comprehensive core competencies, accountants are at the outside of the core, because in addition to possessing core competencies, they have to exercise professional judgement and find a balance between respecting the qualitative characteristics of the financial information while abiding by the constraints. Professional judgement is needed in the area between the core competencies and users. The information presented to the users needs to possess the qualities of **understandability**, **relevance**, **reliability**, and **comparability**. Understandability means that financial statements must be presented in a clear and understandable manner for users. Relevance means that information has predictive value and has been prepared in a timely manner. Reliability means that

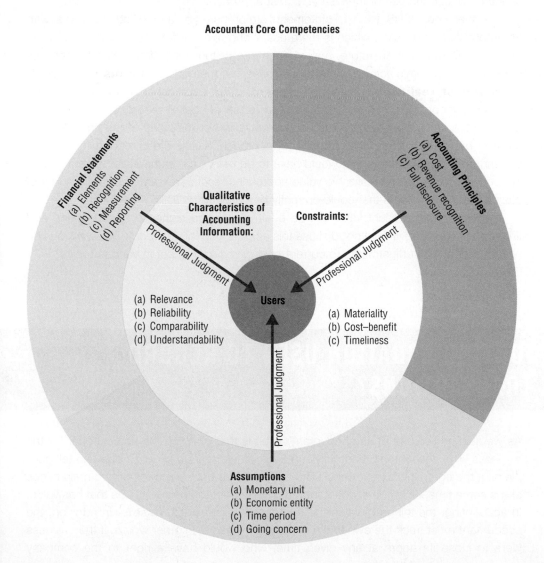

Exhibit 1-3 ▲

financial information should be represented faithfully. It should be neutral, free of biases, prudent, complete, and should emphasize economic substance over legal form. Comparability ensures that users will be able to compare the financial information with previous periods or compare it to other companies operating in the same industry. Accountants need to balance these qualities of the information with the above mentioned constraints in preparing useful financial information for users.

Two underlying assumptions of the conceptual framework are the **accrual basis** and the **going-concern principle**. Financial statements are prepared on the accrual basis, meaning that the business transactions are recognized and recorded when they occur, not when cash is exchanged. Furthermore, financial statements are prepared based on the assumption that the business entity is a going concern and will continue in operation for the foreseeable future.

When assets (the items that an organization owns or controls, for example, buildings, equipment, inventory of goods that are sold, etc.) or services are measured and recorded at cost, where cash or cash equivalents were paid to acquire them at the time of their acquisition, this is called historical cost basis measurement. Using the historical cost approach, businesses will keep the historical cost of an asset throughout its useful life because this cost is a reliable measure. This is the most common method of recording the cost of assets. Canadian Accounting Standards for Private Enterprises (ASPE) continues to require the use of the historical cost approach.

However, under IFRS, financial statements are prepared on a modified cost basis, with an emphasis on fair value, which is more useful and relevant for users' decision-making purposes. Businesses, therefore, may choose one of four recording methods that best reflects their economic activities and reality. These four methods are the **historical cost**, **current cost**, **realizable value,** and **present value** approaches. For example, when a business records a purchase of an asset at historical cost, it records the value of the asset as the amount of cash or cash equivalents paid or fair value of the consideration given to purchase it. Using the current cost approach, assets are carried at the amount of cash or cash equivalents that would have to be paid if the same asset were acquired currently; while using the realizable value approach, assets are carried at the amount of cash or cash equivalents that could currently be obtained by selling the asset.

The concept of present value will be dealt with in the higher level accounting and finance courses, and we will not discuss this approach in this textbook. We will focus on historical cost with adjustments to current cost or realizable cost in various topics.

HOW IS THE ACCOUNTING EQUATION USED TO RECORD BUSINESS TRANSACTIONS?

 Analyze transactions using the basic accounting equation

As we said earlier, one of an accountant's jobs is that of being the scorekeeper for the business. The accountant needs to keep track of information so he or she can tell people how the company is performing. The accountant must keep track of two main things at the same time. First, the accountant must track what the company has that has value. In accounting, the things of value the company has are called **assets**. In addition, the accountant must track the ownership rights to the assets. In other words, if the business were to close its doors at any given time, who would have a right to the company assets? Two possibilities for rights to the company's assets are people other than the owners of the company (called a **third party** or creditors) and the owners of the company themselves (called the shareholders). In accounting terminology, the amount a business owes to third parties is called **liabilities**. Assets not owned by third parties must belong to the shareholders, and the amount of assets owned by the shareholders of the company is called **shareholders' equity**. The amount of assets that a company has must always equal the total rights to those assets. This concept can be expressed as an equation, referred to as the **fundamental accounting equation:**

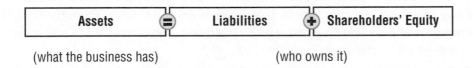

| Assets | = | Liabilities | + | Shareholders' Equity |

(what the business has)   (who owns it)

CONCEPT CHECK

At the end of its first month of operations, Patel Consulting, Inc. has assets totalling $57,000 and liabilities totalling $25,000. What is the amount of Patel Consulting's total shareholders' equity at the end of the month?

Answer:

We can use the fundamental accounting equation to figure out what Patel Consulting's total shareholders' equity are. First, it helps to restate the equation in a different format by subtracting liabilities from both sides of the equation as follows:

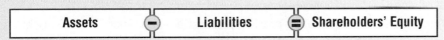

| Assets | − | Liabilities | = | Shareholders' Equity |

Next, insert the amount of Patel Consulting's total assets and the total liabilities into the restated formula.

$$\$57,000 - \$25,000 = \text{Shareholders' Equity}$$

Finally, solve the equation to get the total shareholder's equity of $32,000.

$$\$57,000 - \$25,000 = \$32,000$$

Concept Check questions appear throughout the chapter, giving you the chance to test your mastery of the concepts you just covered before moving on to the next one.

Shareholders' equity is also called net assets, the residual interest in the assets of the entity after deducting all its liabilities.

Transaction Analysis

Accountants will record the effects of transactions in this equation. A **transaction** is any event that has a financial impact on the business. If something changes either what the company has or who owns it, it must be recorded in the accounting equation. When the accountant records a transaction that affects the business, he or she will record what effect the transaction has on the assets of the business and he or she will record what effect it has on the ownership of those assets. This process is called transaction analysis.

Shareholders' Equity

Before we start looking at how transactions affect the accounting equation, let's take a closer look at the shareholders' equity section of the equation. To provide more useful information to various users, the shareholders' equity section of the equation can be broken down into smaller subcategories:

- **Share capital** is used to reflect shareholders' equity that is the result of the owners of the business investing assets or injecting cash into the business. In other words, the assets of the company increased because the shareholders invested those assets into the company. In general, there are two types of share capital: **common shares** and preferred shares. The difference between these two types of shares will be discussed in Chapter 10.

- **Retained earnings** is used to reflect shareholders' equity that is the result of the business having earnings that have not been distributed to shareholders but have been retained in the business. As we will see shortly, earnings are created when the business provides goods or services to customers.

An expanded version of the accounting equation would look like this:

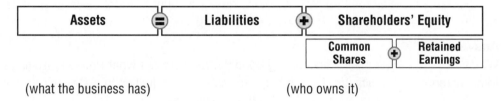

(what the business has)   (who owns it)

The retained earnings subcategory can now be further broken down into smaller subcategories to help the accountant provide even better information. These subcategories and what they reflect are as follows:

- **Revenue** is an increase in retained earnings that is the result of the business providing goods and services.

- **Expenses** are used to reflect a decrease in retained earnings that is the result of the business incurring costs related to providing goods and services.

- **Dividends** are used to reflect a decrease in retained earnings that is the result of the owners receiving assets (usually cash) from the business.

An expanded version of the accounting equation would now look like this:

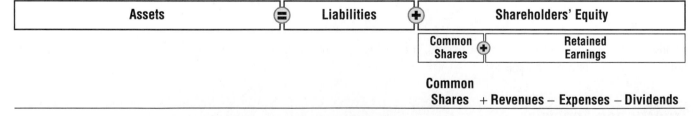

Retained Earnings and, therefore, Shareholders' Equity is increased by adding amounts to Revenues, and is decreased by adding amounts to Expenses and Dividends. These subcategories will make more sense as we see how they are used to record the effects of business transactions. To illustrate, let us analyze the effects of several transactions on the accounting equation for the month of January 2013 for Hooray Consulting, Inc., a new computer consulting business started by Ray Hu.

1. **Sale of shares.** Ray Hu invests $10,000 to start the business. Hooray Consulting, Inc. sells Ray 1,000 common shares for $10,000 in exchange for his cash investment. The effect of this transaction on the accounting equation is to increase Hooray Consulting's Assets and Shareholders' Equity as follows:

	Assets	=	Liabilities	+	Shareholders' Equity	
					Common Shares +	Retained Earnings
	Cash	=			Common Shares	+ Revenues − Expenses − Dividends
(1)	+ $10,000				+ $10,000	
Bal	$10,000	=			$10,000	

Remember for each transaction that the amount on the left side of the equation must equal the amount on the right side. The amount of assets will be increased by $10,000 because the business now has $10,000 of cash that it did not have before. To keep track of what type of assets the business has, the accountant will create a subcategory under assets for each different type of asset that the business has, so a subcategory for Cash was created. Since the assets have increased, there is now a need to increase the ownership side of the equation. The business does not owe the $10,000 to a creditor so the $10,000 ownership interest must belong to Ray and must be entered in the Shareholders' Equity section of the equation. If we look at the Shareholders' Equity side of the equation, we can see that there are two possible places the $10,000 can be entered to increase Shareholders' Equity: Common Shares and Retained Earnings. Based on the definitions as discussed previously, we see that the $10,000 should be entered in the Common Shares section of Shareholders' Equity because this increase in Shareholders' Equity was the result of Ray investing assets into the business.

2. **Purchase supplies on credit.** Hooray Consulting purchases office supplies, agreeing to pay $350 within 30 days. The effect of this transaction on the accounting equation is to increase Assets and increase Liabilities as follows:

	Assets			=	Liabilities	+	Shareholders' Equity	
							Common Shares +	Retained Earnings
	Cash	+	Supplies	=	Accounts Payable	+	Common Shares	+ Revenues − Expenses − Dividends
Bal	$10,000			=			$10,000	
(2)			+ $350		+ $350			
Bal	$10,000	+	$350	=	$350	+	$10,000	

The Supplies account is an asset because the supplies that were purchased have not been used yet. Supplies are an example of what we call **prepaid expenses**. A prepaid expense is considered an asset until it has been used up in the business operations. The agreement to pay for them later creates an **account payable**, a liability, because the business owes $350 to a creditor.

3. Purchase equipment for cash. The business purchases equipment, paying cash of $4,000. The effect of this transaction on the accounting equation is to increase one asset and decrease another asset as follows:

	Assets						=	Liabilities		+		Shareholders' Equity			
											Common Shares +		**Retained Earnings**		
	Cash	+	Supplies	+	Equipment	=		Accounts Payable		+	Common Shares	+ Revenues	– Expenses	– Dividends	
Bal	$10,000	+	$350			=		$350		+	$10,000				
(3)	– $ 4,000				+ $4,000										
Bal	$ 6,000	+	$350	+	$4,000	=		$350		+	$10,000				

The cash purchase of equipment increases one asset, Equipment, and decreases another asset, Cash, by the same amount. After the transaction is completed, Hooray Consulting has total assets of $10,350, liabilities of $350 and shareholders' equity of $10,000. Because there has been no change in the total amount of assets, there should be no change in ownership; therefore, there will be no change in the amount of Shareholders' Equity.

4. Borrow cash from the bank. Hooray Consulting borrows $12,000 cash from the bank and signs a two-year note payable to the bank. The effect of this transaction on the accounting equation is to increase Assets and increase Liabilities as follows:

	Assets						=	Liabilities			+		Shareholders' Equity			
													Common Shares +		**Retained Earnings**		
	Cash	+	Supplies	+	Equipment	=	Accounts Payable	+	Notes Payable	+	Common Shares	+ Revenues	– Expenses	– Dividends			
Bal	$ 6,000	+	$350	+	$4,000	=	$350			+	$10,000						
(4)	+ $12,000							+ $12,000									
Bal	$18,000	+	$350	+	$4,000	=	$350	+	$12,000	+	$10,000						

A **note payable** is a written promise to pay a specified amount in the future. Often businesses will borrow money from the bank to purchase assets or to make sure enough cash is available to operate the business. Borrowing cash from the bank increases the asset Cash because the business has $12,000 that it did not have before. It also increases the liability, Notes Payable, by $12,000 because the business owes $12,000 to the bank. In other words, the bank has an ownership interest for $12,000 of Hooray Consulting's assets. Note that total assets of $22,350 still equal the total liabilities of $12,350 plus the shareholders' equity of $10,000.

5. Provide services for cash. Hooray Consulting earns service revenue by providing consulting services for clients. Hooray collects $1,200 cash for services provided. The effect of this transaction on the accounting equation is to increase Assets and increase Shareholders' Equity as follows:

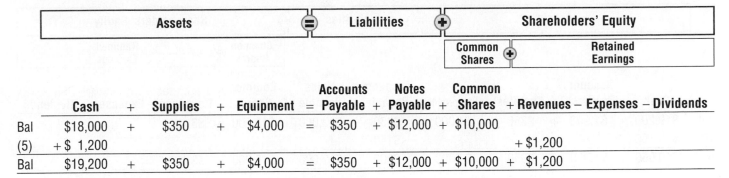

	Cash	+	Supplies	+	Equipment	=	Accounts Payable	+	Notes Payable	+	Common Shares	+ Revenues	– Expenses	– Dividends
Bal	$18,000	+	$350	+	$4,000	=	$350	+	$12,000	+	$10,000			
(5)	+$ 1,200											+$1,200		
Bal	$19,200	+	$350	+	$4,000	=	$350	+	$12,000	+	$10,000	+ $1,200		

Providing services increases both Cash and Revenues by $1,200. Cash is increased because the business has $1,200 that it did not have before and Revenues is increased because Shareholders' Equity must be increased to reflect the fact that Ray, the sole shareholder, has an ownership interest in the increased assets. As was previously discussed, the specific subcategory that is used to increase Retained Earnings (and, therefore, Shareholders' Equity) because of providing goods and services is Revenues.

6. Provide services on credit. A business can also earn service revenue even if it has not yet received cash for these services. Hooray Consulting performs $1,900 of services and, in return, receives customers' promises to pay this $1,900 within one month. In accounting, we say that Hooray performed this service **on account**. A client's promise to pay is called an **account receivable**. It is an asset because the business has the right to collect the cash in the future. The effect on the accounting equation is to increase Assets and increase Shareholders' Equity as follows:

	Cash	+	Accounts Receivable	+	Supplies	+	Equipment	=	Accounts Payable	+	Notes Payable	+	Common Shares	+ Revenues	– Expenses	– Dividends
Bal	$19,200			+	$350	+	$4,000	=	$350	+	$12,000	+	$10,000	+ $1,200		
(6)			+$1,900											+$1,900		
Bal	$19,200	+	$1,900	+	$350	+	$4,000	=	$350	+	$12,000	+	$10,000	+ $3,100		

Notice the Revenue account was increased just as it was in the previous transaction when Hooray Consulting performed services and received cash. The Revenue account was increased to reflect the fact that there has been an increase in the shareholders' ownership interest in the assets of the business.

In Transaction 5, the assets increased because the business received cash, and in Transaction 6, the assets increased because the business received an account receivable.

7. Partial payment of accounts payable. Hooray Consulting pays $150 to the store where it purchased $350 worth of supplies in Transaction 2. In accounting this is referred to as "paying on account." The effect on the accounting equation is to decrease Assets and decrease Liabilities as follows:

	Assets					=	Liabilities		+	Shareholders' Equity		
										Common Shares +		Retained Earnings
	Cash	+ Accounts Receivable	+ Supplies	+ Equipment	=	Accounts Payable	+ Notes Payable	+ Common Shares	+ Revenues	− Expenses	− Dividends
Bal	$19,200	+ $1,900	+ $350	+ $4,000	=	$350	+ $12,000	+ $10,000	+ $3,100		
(7)	− $ 150					− $150					
Bal	$19,050	+ $1,900	+ $350	+ $4,000	=	$200	+ $12,000	+ $10,000	+ $3,100		

The payment of cash on account has no effect on Supplies because the payment does not affect the amount of supplies that the business has. Likewise, the payment on account does not affect Expenses because the business is paying off an amount owed, not using those supplies. The Cash account decreases because the business has less cash and the Accounts Payable account decreases because the business owes less to a creditor by paying down a portion of the accounts payable.

8. Payment of expenses. During the month, Hooray Consulting paid $1,700 cash for expenses incurred such as wages, building rent, and utilities. Later on we will see that each different type of expense will be shown separately in the accounting equation, but for now we will lump them all together under the heading Expenses. The effect on the accounting equation is to decrease Assets and decrease Shareholders' Equity as follows:

	Assets					=	Liabilities		+	Shareholders' Equity		
										Common Shares +		Retained Earnings
	Cash	+ Accounts Receivable	+ Supplies	+ Equipment	=	Accounts Payable	+ Notes Payable	+ Common Shares	+ Revenues	− Expenses	− Dividends
Bal	$19,050	+ $1,900	+ $350	+ $4,000	=	$200	+ $12,000	+ $10,000	+ $3,100		
(8)	− $ 1,700									+ $1,700	
Bal	$17,350	+ $1,900	+ $350	+ $4,000	=	$200	+ $12,000	+ $10,000	+ $3,100	− $1,700	

For this transaction, Cash decreases and Expenses increase. Because Expenses are subtracted from Retained Earnings, Retained Earnings (and, therefore, Shareholders' Equity) will decrease. This decrease in Shareholders' Equity reflects that the assets for the business have decreased and, therefore, there has to be less ownership reported. Remember that Expenses are used to decrease Retained Earnings when needed as the result of the business incurring costs related to providing goods and services.

9. Cash dividends. Hooray Consulting pays $500 of cash dividends to Ray Hu, the shareholder. The effect on the accounting equation is to decrease Assets and decrease Shareholders' Equity as follows:

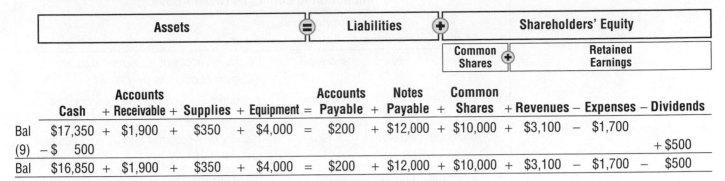

	Cash	+ Receivable	+ Supplies	+ Equipment =	Payable	+ Payable	+ Shares	+ Revenues	− Expenses	− Dividends
		Accounts			Accounts	Notes	Common			
Bal	$17,350	+ $1,900	+ $350	+ $4,000 =	$200	+ $12,000	+ $10,000	+ $3,100	− $1,700	
(9)	− $ 500									+ $500
Bal	$16,850	+ $1,900	+ $350	+ $4,000 =	$200	+ $12,000	+ $10,000	+ $3,100	− $1,700	− $500

The payment of dividends causes a decrease in Cash of $500 and an increase in Dividends of $500. Because Dividends are subtracted from Retained Earnings, Retained Earnings (and, therefore, Shareholders' Equity) will decrease. This decrease in Shareholders' Equity reflects that the assets (i.e., Cash) for the business have decreased and, therefore, there has to be less ownership reported. Dividends are different from expenses because the cash is paid directly to the owners rather than being paid for costs that were related to providing goods or services. Once again we can see that the total assets of $23,100 still equal the total liabilities of $12,200, plus shareholders' equity of $10,900 so the accounting equation continues to balance. Remember that total Shareholders' Equity equals the Common Shares of $10,000 plus the Retained Earnings of $900 and that the Retained Earnings was arrived at by calculating earnings of $1,400 (subtracting the Expenses from the Revenues) and then subtracting the Dividends of $500.

CRITICAL THINKING

Take a minute to think about the impact of the following independent cases on each of the Assets, Liabilities, and Shareholders' Equity accounts. What is the error, if any?

1. A payment of Dividends, $5,000, was recorded as a decrease in Cash and in Expenses.

2. A receipt of $2,500 from a customer who pays her debt was recorded as an increase in Cash and in Service Revenue.

3. A receipt of $12,000 from shareholders in exchange for company's shares was recorded as an increase in Cash and in Liabilities.

4. A purchase of supplies on account for $250 was recorded as an increase in Supplies and in Accounts Payable.

Critical Thinking questions appear throughout the chapter, challenging you to think about the real-world implications of accounting issues and challenges raised in the chapter.

Solution:

| | | | Shareholders' | |
	Assets	Liabilities	Equity	Error
		Impact on Accounts as Given Above		
1.	Decrease	No	Increase	Dividends account is understated and expense account is overstated.
2.	Increase	No	Increase	Accounts Receivable and Revenue are both overstated.
3.	Increase	Increase	No	Liability is overstated and Share Capital is understated.
4.	Increase	Increase	No	No error

	Impact on Accounts as Corrected		
	Assets	Liabilities	Shareholders' Equity
1.	Decrease	No	Decrease
2.	Increase and Decrease equally, net effect is No Change	No	No
3.	Increase	No	Increase
4.	Increase	Increase	No

WHAT DO FINANCIAL STATEMENTS REPORT, AND HOW ARE THEY PREPARED?

5 Understand and be able to prepare basic financial statements

To present the results of a business's transactions for a period, financial statements need to be prepared. These reports show the entity's financial information to interested stakeholders both inside and outside the organization. Under IFRS, four basic financial statements are prepared by most organizations:

- Statement of comprehensive income (the income statement is the basis for the statement of comprehensive income; additional details are then added for gains and losses)
- Statement of changes in equity (the statement of retained earnings is the basis for the statement of changes in equity; additional details are then added for the capital stock elements)
- Statement of financial position or balance sheet (both names are interchangeable and it is fine to use either one)
- Statement of cash flows

The Statement of Comprehensive Income

A **statement of comprehensive income** is prepared to answer the question, "Is the organization making a **profit**?" Just as a scoreboard shows how many points a team earned and whether the team is winning or losing, for a specific period of time, a business prepares a statement of comprehensive income to show, for a specific time period, whether the business had **net income** (total revenues were greater than total expenses) or a **net loss** (total revenues are less than total expenses), as well as to show any unrealized gains or losses from holding certain assets, such as investments. Companies can prepare a single statement of comprehensive income or two statements including (1) an income statement ending with net income or net loss, and (2) a statement beginning with the net income or net loss and showing components of other comprehensive income. For the time being, we will focus on the business operations with net income or net loss in an income statement, and in later chapters, we will introduce the statement of comprehensive income.

The Income Statement

To prepare an **income statement**, we set up a format that includes a heading and the body of the statement. The heading of all financial statements should show "who," "what," and "when." The "who" is the name of the business, the "what" is the name of the financial statement, and the "when" is the time period covered by the statement. The body of the income statement lists the revenues, then the expenses, and finally the net income or net loss. When revenues are greater than expenses, the business earns net income, or profit. When expenses are greater than revenues, the business has a net loss. Expenses should be listed based on either their nature or their function in the income statement. Since most Canadian companies prepared their income statement by function in the past and companies are permitted to continue with this practice, we will show the income statement classified by function in this textbook.

We can prepare an income statement for Hooray Consulting for the month of January 2013 by referring to the ending balances in the accounting equation that we recently completed.

If we look at **Exhibit 1-4** we can see what the income statement for Hooray Consulting looks like. In the first month of operations, Hooray Consulting, Inc. earned $3,100 in revenue and had $1,700 in expenses, which resulted in net income of $1,400, ignoring taxes for the time being. This amount can remain part of the shareholders' equity in the business and can be used to "grow" or expand the business, or the business can use all or part of these funds to pay dividends to the shareholders.

Hooray Consulting, Inc.
Income Statement
Month Ended January 31, 2013

Revenue	$3,100
Expenses	(1,700)
Net Income	$1,400

Hooray Consulting, Inc.
Statement of Changes in Shareholders' Equity
Month Ended January 31, 2013

	Common Shares		Retained Earnings	Total
	Number of Shares	$		
Balance, January 1, 2013	—	$ 0	$ 0	$ 0
Issued Common Shares	1,000	$10,000		10,000
Net Income			$1,400	1,400
Dividends			(500)	(500)
Balance, January 31, 2013	1,000	$10,000	$ 900	$10,900

Hooray Consulting, Inc.
Statement of Financial Position
As of January 31, 2013

ASSETS		LIABILITIES	
Cash	$16,850	Accounts Payable	$ 200
Accounts Receivable	1,900	Note Payable	12,000
Supplies	350	Total Liabilities	12,200
Equipment	4,000		
		SHAREHOLDERS' EQUITY	
		Common Shares	10,000
		Retained Earnings	900
		Total Shareholders' Equity	10,900
		Total Liabilities &	
Total Assets	$23,100	Shareholders' Equity	$23,100

Exhibit 1-4 ▲

Notice the dollar signs on the first and last amounts and the double underline under the last amount, net income, presented on the statement. It is common practice to place a dollar sign on the first number and the last number in each column on a financial statement and to double underline the final amount.

Decision	**Guideline**	**Analyze**
I need to determine if a business is profitable. Which financial statement do I use?	Use the income statement to determine the profitability of a business. The income statement reports the revenues and expenses of a business. Revenues represent what a business earns as a result of providing goods or services. Expenses represent the cost to the business of providing those goods or services.	If revenues exceed expenses, the business is profitable and has earned net income. However, if expenses exceed revenue, the business has incurred a net loss and is not profitable.

The Statement of Changes in Equity

"How many shares has the corporation issued in exchange for assets, such as cash or equipment?" "How much has the corporation made and kept during the current accounting period?" The **statement of changes in equity** answers these questions by presenting the amount of the share capital, the retained earnings, and the changes to these accounts during a specific time period, such as a month or a year. Increases in common shares are due to issuing more shares and decreases are due to share buy-backs. Likewise, increases in retained earnings come from net income and decreases result from either a net loss or the payment of dividends.

To prepare the statement of changes in equity, we set up a format that includes a heading and body similar to what we did for the income statement. The heading includes the name of the business, the name of the financial statement, and the time period covered by the statement. The body of the statement lists the beginning of each account that belongs to shareholders' equity, for example, common shares and retained earnings balances, any new shares issued, net income earned or net loss incurred, any dividends paid, and the ending balance of Common Shares and Retained Earnings. Using the information from the income statement that we just prepared and the dividend information from our accounting equation, we can prepare the portion of the changes in the retained earnings account in the statement of changes in equity.

Exhibit 1-4 shows what Hooray Consulting's statement of changes in equity looks like. Because this is the first month that Hooray Consulting has been in business, there is a zero balance in beginning common shares and retained earnings. During the first month of operations, Hooray Consulting, Inc. issued $10,000 of common shares to Ray Hu and paid dividends of $500, which when combined with the $1,400 of net income for January leaves an ending retained earnings balance at January 31 of $900. We can see that of the $1,400 that Hooray Consulting earned during January, $900 was retained in the business.

Under Canadian Accounting Standards for Private Enterprises, a business is not required to prepare a statement of changes in equity. Instead, a business is required to prepare a statement of retained earnings, which is one of the components in the statement of changes in equity. The statement of retained earnings shows the changes in the retained earnings account. **Exhibit 1-5** shows what Hooray Consulting's statement of retained earnings looks like.

Hooray Consulting, Inc. Statement of Retained Earnings Month Ended January 31, 2013	
Retained Earnings, January 1, 2013	$ 0
Add: Net Income for the month	1,400
Subtotal	1,400
Less: Dividends	500
Retained Earnings, January 31, 2013	$ 900

Exhibit 1-5 ▲

DECISION GUIDELINES

Decision	**Guideline**	**Analyze**
I want to know if a company was profitable, and if it was, what it did with the profits. Which financial statement do I use?	Use the statement of changes in equity to find out. The retained earnings account in the statement of changes in equity shows whether the net income of a business was paid out as dividends or retained in the business.	If a business is planning on growth, it will often issue low or no dividends to shareholders. This way, it retains the income in the business.

The Statement of Financial Position or the Balance Sheet

"What assets does the company have and who has ownership rights to those assets?" The **statement of financial position** is also known as the **balance sheet**, and answers this question by listing all of an entity's assets, liabilities, and shareholders' equity as of a specific date, usually the end of a month or a year. Since the balance of each account may change from one day to the next, the amount of each account in the statement of financial position shows the balance on a specific date, not for a period of time. Basically the balance sheet shows the accounting equation for a business and reflects the fact that assets equal liabilities plus shareholders' equity. Using the information from the statement of changes in equity that we just prepared and information from our accounting equation, we can prepare a statement of financial position for Hooray Consulting. Exhibit 1-4 shows what Hooray Consulting's statement of financial position will look like. Notice that total assets equal total liabilities and shareholders' equity. When a statement of financial position is presented in side-by-side format so that assets are listed on the left-hand side and liabilities and shareholders' equity are the right-hand side, it is said to be in account format. It may be more convenient to list assets, then liabilities, and shareholders' equity vertically in a computer spreadsheet. This vertical format is called report format. Companies can use either title of the financial statement—either "Statement of Financial Position" or "Balance Sheet."

DECISION GUIDELINES

Decision	Guideline	Analyze
I want to know who would get its assets if a business were to close its doors. Which financial statement would I use?	Use the statement of financial position to determine who has claims to the company's assets.	The liabilities of a business reflect the claims of creditors to the assets of the business. Once those claims are settled, the remaining assets (called "net assets") belong to the shareholders (the owners) of the business. This amount is reflected by the shareholders' equity on the balance sheet.

The Statement of Cash Flows

"Where did the business get the money it needed to operate and where did it spend its money?" The **statement of cash flows** answers this question by showing stakeholders all of the sources and all of the uses of cash by a business for a specified period of time. Businesses can get cash and use cash through three business activities—operating activities, investing activities, and financing activities. The statement of cash flows is a complex statement to prepare; therefore, we will postpone the coverage of the statement of cash flows until Chapter 11.

DECISION GUIDELINES

Decision	Guideline	Analyze
I want to know where a business get its cash and where it is spent. Which financial statement would I use?	Use the statement of cash flows to see all of the sources and uses of cash for a business.	You can see whether a company's operations generated cash for the business and how much cash the business invested in the purchase of assets such as buildings and equipment. If a company's operations generated insufficient funds to finance its investments in assets, you can determine how the business financed these acquisitions.

Relationships Among the Financial Statements

The financial statements are prepared in the following order:

1 Income statement and statement of comprehensive income

2 Statement of changes in equity

3 Statement of financial position (balance sheet)

4 Statement of cash flows

The reason for this order is that the net income figure from the income statement is needed to prepare the comprehensive income, and then the retained earnings in the statement of changes in equity. Likewise, the ending share capital and retained earnings balances from the statement of changes in equity are needed to prepare the statement of financial position (balance sheet). Finally, information from both the statement of comprehensive income and the statement of financial position is needed to prepare the statement of cash flows.

FOCUS ON USERS

The Focus on Users box found at the end of each chapter shows you who the users of the financial statements are, and why the concepts discussed in the chapter are important to them. This box demonstrates the relevance of accounting concepts to everyone, regardless of their career choices.

These boxes will be presented in each chapter to demonstrate the relevance of accounting concepts to everyone, regardless of their career choices. Each Focus on Users box will feature concepts covered in each chapter and will discuss why they might be important to the users of financial statements. Some of the users of financial statements include:

❶ Bookkeepers —as the preparers of financial statements, the bookkeepers will be interested in seeing the completed output, preparing internal audits to check their own work, and preparing the work for the next set of financial statements.

❷ Managers —the managers of organizations need to be able to evaluate the performance of the organization, make recommendations for improvement, and plan for the future. All of these elements will require financial statements, which are indications of the past performance of the organization.

❸ Shareholders and Potential Investors —this group of individuals (or other organizations) will be looking to evaluate the performance of the organization to determine if it is a sound investment, if it is providing them with an appropriate return on their investment (are they getting something out of being an investor), and if the company is showing signs that may indicate that it is time to sell, or perhaps time to invest even further. This is a section that many people will be able to relate to in their lifetime as they invest their own personal funds for their retirement or for "playing" on the stock market.

❹ Creditors —individuals and institutions that loan funds to organizations will want to examine the financial statements of an organization to determine whether they are an appropriate risk to lend to and if they have the ability to repay their debt.

❺ Competitors —individuals and other organizations that compete with a company can examine the financial statements of competitors to compare the performance of each company and assess the strengths and weaknesses.

6 Government and regulatory bodies —governments and regulatory organizations will examine financial statements to determine the amount of taxes to be paid, or to ensure that specific regulations are being followed.

7 Unions —employee unions will be interested in the financial statements of the organization to assess whether or not the employees are receiving appropriate levels of pay and benefits, etc.

This list of users of financial statements is not exhaustive and could also include people such as financial advisors, venture capitalists, journalists, customers, suppliers, etc.

The Focus on Users Box at the end of each chapter will discuss the perspectives of a variety of users and how the concepts of the chapter relate to them. Not all users of financial statements will be included in each discussion, but some will be highlighted. It is important to recognize that the organization creates one set of financial statements that needs to satisfy all of these users. For the organization, this can create a problem as there may be conflicting images that the organization wants to portray. For example, an organization would want the financial statements to show as profitable an image as possible when communicating with creditors to obtain loans; however, the organization, to minimize taxes to the government, would need to show a minimal amount of profit. It is impossible to both minimize and maximize profit at the same time; therefore, the organization needs to make decisions regarding the reporting of activities that will balance the needs of all users. As you read through this text and come across areas where there are a variety of ways to report the same activity, try to keep in mind the variety of users of the financial statements and how the decisions that are made will influence the message that is conveyed to them.

FOCUS ON USERS

Concept	User	Why is this Important to this User?
Guidelines (IFRS, Accounting Standards for Private Enterprises, etc.)		All users of financial statements need to understand what guidelines were used to know what types of decisions have been made in the creation of the statements. Managers, in particular, will need to pay close attention to the decision of which set of guidelines should be used to facilitate the most effective communication with the users of financial statements.
Conceptual Framework		All users of financial statements are at the core of the conceptual framework. The users need to be aware of the balance between the qualitative characteristics of accounting and the constraints on what is feasible to include in the presentation of the financial statements.
Financial Statements		Managers need to be able to organize, plan, control, and evaluate the performance of individuals, departments, and the organization as a whole. The financial statements assist the managers in all of these functions. The income statement or statement of comprehensive income will demonstrate whether or not the organization has been profitable, in what areas, and how revenues and expenses have changed from one period to the next. The balance sheet will highlight what is owned, what the organization owes to third parties, and the rights to ownership held by shareholders. This statement will assist managers in understanding whether they can take on more debt or perhaps raise funds through bringing on more shareholders.
		Shareholders and potential investors are looking to ensure that their investment is in a good position to provide returns on their investment. Dividends are the way that the profits of the organization are distributed to the owners, so shareholders and potential investors will specifically examine the statement of changes in equity to evaluate the changes in the areas that are most important to them.
		Creditors will be examining the financial statements for the organization's ability to repay debts. The cash flow statement will show where the cash comes from and how it is used, which will demonstrate if the organization has the capacity to repay debt. The income statement will demonstrate if the organization is profitable and how much of the profits are taken up with interest (the cost of borrowing). The balance sheet can be used to highlight what the company owns that may be able to be used as collateral for a loan, and how much cash is actually held by the organization.
		Competitors may examine financial statements to assess the strengths and weaknesses of an organization. This could provide the competitor with areas on which to capitalize.

DEMO DOC

Demo Docs walk you through an extensive, challenging review problem that pulls together the chapter concepts. The worked solution provides a full solution so you can check progress, and provides some reminders and hints for how to find the solution.

Transaction Analysis Using the Accounting Equation/Financial Statement Preparation

On June 1, 2013, Raj Chopra started a webpage design business named MyWeb, Inc. The business is organized as a corporation. During June 2013 MyWeb, Inc. engaged in the following transactions:

a. Raj invested $25,000 in exchange for 5,000 shares to start the business.

b. The business paid $7,500 cash to acquire computer equipment.

c. Supplies costing $350 were purchased on account.

d. Performed design services and received $1,100 cash.

e. Performed $1,800 of design services for a customer. The customer agreed to pay next week.

f. Paid $200 cash toward the supplies purchased in Transaction c.

g. Paid $600 for employee salaries for the month.

h. Paid $500 of dividends to Raj, the only shareholder.

i. Collected $1,000 from the customer in Transaction e.

MyAccountingLab

Visit MyAccountingLab at www. myaccountinglab.com to watch animated versions of these Demo Docs.

These references to MyAccountingLab are reminders that you can review animated versions of the Demo docs on MyAccountingLab.

REQUIREMENTS:

❶ Enter these transactions in the expanded accounting equation of MyWeb, Inc.

❷ Prepare the income statement, statement of changes in equity, and statement of financial position of MyWeb, Inc. after recording the transactions.

Demo Doc Solutions

Requirement ❶

Enter these transactions in the expanded accounting equation of MyWeb, Inc.

Part 1	Part 2	Demo Doc Complete

a. Raj invested $25,000 in exchange for 5,000 shares to start the business.

Raj is using his own money, but he is paying it *to the business*. Because the business is involved, it is a recordable transaction. From the business's perspective, this transaction will increase Cash (an asset) by $25,000 and increase Common Shares (shareholders' equity) by $25,000.

The effect of this transaction on the accounting equation is as follows:

Assets				=	Liabilities	+	Shareholders' Equity			
							Common Shares	+	Retained Earnings	
Cash	+ Accounts Receivable	+ Supplies	+ Equipment =		Accounts Payable	+	Common Shares	+ Service Revenue	− Salaries Expense	− Dividends
a) + $25,000							+ $25,000			
Bal $25,000			=				$25,000			

To record this transaction in the equation, we add $25,000 to Cash and add $25,000 to Common Shares. Before we move on, we bring down the account balances and check to see that the left side of the equation equals the right side. It is important to remember that the equation must balance after each transaction is recorded.

b. The business paid $7,500 cash to acquire computer equipment.

Equipment (an asset) is increased by $7,500, while Cash (an asset) is decreased by $7,500.

The effect of this transaction on the accounting equation is as follows:

	Assets				=	Liabilities +		Shareholders' Equity				
								Common Shares +		Retained Earnings		
	Cash	+ Accounts Receivable +	Supplies	+ Equipment =		Accounts Payable +	Common Shares	+	Service Revenue –	Salaries Expense	– Dividends
Bal	$25,000			=			$25,000				
b)	– $ 7,500			+ $7,500							
Bal	$17,500	+		$7,500	=		$25,000				

Notice that transactions do not have to affect both sides of the equation. However, the accounting equation *must always balance*.

c. Supplies costing $350 were purchased on account.

Supplies is an asset that is increased by $350. However, the supplies were not paid for in cash, but instead *on account*. This transaction involves accounts *pay*able (because it will have to be *paid* later). Because we now have *more* money that has to be paid later, it is an increase in Accounts Payable (a liability) of $350.

The effect of this transaction on the accounting equation is as follows:

	Assets				=	Liabilities +		Shareholders' Equity				
								Common Shares +		Retained Earnings		
	Cash	+ Accounts Receivable +	Supplies	+ Equipment =		Accounts Payable +	Common Shares	+	Service Revenue –	Salaries Expense	– Dividends
Bal	$17,500			+ $7,500 =			$25,000				
c)			+ $350			+ $350					
Bal	$17,500	+	$350	+ $7,500 =		$350 +	$25,000				

Remember that the supplies will be recorded as an asset until the time that they are used by the business (we will learn how to adjust for supplies used in a later chapter). The obligation to pay the $350 will remain in Accounts Payable until it is paid.

d. Performed design services and received $1,100 cash.

When the business designs webpages, it is doing work for customers. Doing work for customers (or performing services) is the way that the business makes money. By performing these services, the business is earning service revenues. This means that Service Revenue increases (which increases retained earnings) by $1,100. Because the customer paid in cash, this transaction also results in an increase in Cash (an asset) of $1,100.

The effect of this transaction on the accounting equation is as follows:

		Assets			=	Liabilities	+		Shareholders' Equity			
	Cash	+ Accounts Receivable +	Supplies	+ Equipment =		Accounts Payable	+	Common Shares	+ Service Revenue	− Salaries Expense	− Dividends
Bal	$17,500		+ $350	+ $7,500 =		$350	+	$25,000			
d)	+ $ 1,100								+ $1,100		
Bal	$18,600		+ $350	+ $7,500 =		$350	+	$25,000	+ $1,100		

e. **Performed $1,800 of design services for a customer. The customer agreed to pay next week.**

Again, the business is performing services for customers, which means that it is earning service revenues. This transaction results in an increase in Service Revenue (retained earnings) of $1,800.

This transaction is similar to Transaction d, except that the business is not receiving the cash immediately. Should we wait to record the revenue until the cash is received? Now, refer to the IFRS underlying assumptions and the conceptual framework. Accrual basis accounting specifies that businesses should record transactions based on when they occur, not when cash is exchanged. Therefore, the answer is no, because MyWeb, Inc. should recognize the revenue when the service is performed, regardless of whether or not it has received the cash.

However, this time the client did not pay in cash but instead agreed to pay later, which is the same as charging the services *on account*. The business will *receive* this money in the future (when the customer eventually pays), so it is called an accounts *receiv*able. Accounts Receivable (an asset) is increased by $1,800. Accounts Receivable represents amounts owed to the business and decreases when a customer pays.

The effect of this transaction on the accounting equation is as follows:

		Assets			=	Liabilities	+		Shareholders' Equity			
	Cash	+ Accounts Receivable +	Supplies	+ Equipment =		Accounts Payable	+	Common Shares	+ Service Revenue	− Salaries Expense	− Dividends
Bal	$18,600		+ $350	+ $7,500 =		$350	+	$25,000	$1,100		
e)		+ $1,800							+ $1,800		
Bal	$18,600 +	$1,800 +	$350	+ $7,500 =		$350	+	$25,000	+ $2,900		

f. **Paid $200 cash toward the supplies purchased in Transaction c.**

Think of Accounts Payable (a liability) as a list of companies to which the business owes money. In other words, it is a list of companies to which the business will *pay* money. In this particular problem, the business owes money to the company from which it purchased supplies on account in Transaction c. When the business *pays* the money in full, it can cross this company off of the list. Right now, the business is paying only *part* of the money owed.

This transaction results in a decrease to Accounts Payable (a liability) of $200 and a decrease to Cash (an asset) of $200. Because the business is only paying part of the money it owes to the supply store, the balance to Accounts Payable is still $150 ($350−$200).

You should note that this transaction does not affect Supplies because we are not buying more supplies. We are simply paying off a liability, not acquiring more assets or incurring a new expense.

The effect of this transaction on the accounting equation is as follows:

	Assets				=	Liabilities	+	Shareholders' Equity				
								Common Shares +			Retained Earnings	
	Cash	+ Accounts Receivable +	Supplies	+ Equipment =		Accounts Payable	+	Common Shares	+	Service Revenue	− Salaries Expense	− Dividends
Bal	$18,600 +	$1,800 +	$350 +	$7,500 =		$350	+	$25,000	+	$2,900		
f)	− $ 200					− $200						
Bal	$18,400 +	$1,800 +	$350 +	$7,500 =		$150	+	$25,000	+	$2,900		

g. Paid $600 for employee salaries for the month.

The work the employees have given to the business has *already been used*. By the end of June, MyWeb's employees have worked for the entire month. Therefore, the *benefit* of the employees' work has *already been received*, which means that it is a salary *expense*. Salary Expense increases by $600, which is a decrease to retained earnings. Remember, expenses *decrease* retained earnings.

The salaries were paid in cash, so Cash (an asset) also decreases by $600.

The effect of this transaction on the accounting equation is as follows:

	Assets				=	Liabilities	+	Shareholders' Equity				
								Common Shares +			Retained Earnings	
	Cash	+ Accounts Receivable +	Supplies	+ Equipment =		Accounts Payable	+	Common Shares	+	Service Revenue	− Salaries Expense	− Dividends
Bal	$18,400 +	$1,800 +	$350 +	$7,500 =		$150	+	$25,000	+	$2,900		
g)	− $ 600										+ $600	
Bal	$17,800 +	$1,800 +	$350 +	$7,500 =		$150	+	$25,000	+	$2,900	− $600	

h. Paid $500 of dividends to Raj, the only shareholder.

A decrease to Cash (an asset) is recorded because the business paid Raj $500. This transaction also results in a $500 increase to the Dividend account, which results in a decrease of $500 to Retained Earnings. You should note that *the dividend is not an expense* because the cash is not used by the business. A dividend is a distribution of the profit of a business in that the business pays part of its profit to the shareholder for his or her investment in the business.

The effect of this transaction on the accounting equation is as follows:

	Assets				=	Liabilities	+	Shareholders' Equity				
								Common Shares +			Retained Earnings	
	Cash	+ Accounts Receivable +	Supplies	+ Equipment =		Accounts Payable	+	Common Shares	+	Service Revenue	− Salaries Expense	− Dividends
Bal	$17,800 +	$1,800 +	$350 +	$7,500 =		$150	+	$25,000	+	$2,900	− $600	
h)	− $ 500											+ $500
Bal	$17,300 +	$1,800 +	$350 +	$7,500 =		$150	+	$25,000	+	$2,900	− $600	− $500

i. Collected $1,000 from the customer in Transaction e.

Think of Accounts Receivable (an asset) as a list of people/companies from which the business will *receive* money at some point in the future. Later, when the business collects (receives) the cash in full from any particular customer, it can cross that customer off the list.

In Transaction e, MyWeb, Inc. performed services for a client who did not pay at that time. Now MyWeb, Inc. is receiving *part* of the money owed ($1,000). Because cash is received, this is an increase to Cash (an asset) of $1,000. This collection also decreases Accounts Receivable (an asset) by $1,000 because the customer no longer owes this amount to MyWeb, Inc.

The effect of this transaction on the accounting equation is as follows:

		Assets				= Liabilities +		Shareholders' Equity				
								Common Shares +		Retained Earnings		
	Cash	+ Accounts Receivable +	Supplies	+ Equipment =	Accounts Payable +		Common Shares +	Service Revenue −	Salaries Expense −		Dividends	
Bal	$17,300 +	$1,800 +	$350	+ $7,500 =	$150	+	$25,000 +	$2,900 −	$600 −		$500	
i)	+ $ 1,000	− $1,000										
Bal	$18,300 +	$ 800 +	$350	+ $7,500 =	$150	+	$25,000 +	$2,900 −	$600 −		$500	

Requirement ❷

Prepare the income statement, statement of changes in equity, and balance sheet of MyWeb, Inc. after recording the transactions.

Part 1	**Part 2**	Demo Doc Complete

Income Statement

The income statement is the first statement that should be prepared because the other financial statements rely upon the net income number calculated on the income statement.

The income statement reports the profitability of the business. To prepare an income statement, begin with the proper heading. A proper heading includes the name of the company (MyWeb, Inc.), the name of the statement (Income Statement), and the time period covered (Month Ended June 30, 2013). Notice that we are reporting income for a period of time, rather than a single date.

The income statement lists all revenues and expenses. It uses the following formula to calculate net income (ignoring taxes for this case):

$$\text{Revenues} - \text{Expenses} = \text{Net Income or Net Loss}$$

First, you should list revenues. Secondly, list the expenses. After you have listed and totalled the revenues and expenses, you subtract the total expenses from total revenues to determine net income or net loss. If you have a positive number, then you report net income. A negative number indicates that expenses exceeded revenues, and you will report a net loss.

In the case of MyWeb, Inc., transactions d and e increased service revenue (by $1,100 and $1,800, respectively). These transactions mean that total service revenue for the month was $2,900 ($1,100 + 1,800).

The only expenses incurred were in Transaction g, which resulted in a salary expense of $600. The income statement for MyWeb, Inc. is presented next:

MyWeb, Inc.			
Income Statement			
Month Ended June 30, 2013			
	Revenue		$2,900
	Expenses		(600)
	Net Income		$2,300

You will use the $2,300 net income on the statement of changes in equity.

Statement of Changes in Equity

The statement of changes in equity shows the changes in common shares and retained earnings for a period of time. To prepare a statement of changes in equity, begin with the proper heading. A proper heading includes the name of the company (MyWeb, Inc.), the name of the statement (Statement of Changes in Equity), and the time period covered (Month Ended June 30, 2013). As with the income statement, we are reporting changes for a period of time, rather than a single date.

Net income is used on the statement of changes in equity to calculate the new balance in the Retained Earnings account. This calculation uses the following formula:

> Beginning Retained Earnings
> + Net Income or − Net Loss
> − Dividends
> _____
> = Ending Retained Earnings

You will begin the body of the statement by reporting each account that belongs to the shareholders' equity—common shares and the retained earnings—at the beginning of the period (June 1). List each account on the top of the statement and show the date on the left column. Then, list the events that caused the change in each account, for example, net income increases the retained earnings, net loss and dividends decrease the retained earnings. You should notice that the amount of net income comes directly from the income statement.

In this case, because the company is new, the beginning balances of common shares and retained earnings are both zero. New shares worth $25,000 are issued and added to the zero balance in common shares, and the net income of $2,300 is added to the zero balance in retained earnings for a subtotal of $2,300. The $500 of dividends is subtracted from the $2,300 subtotal to arrive at the ending balance in retained earnings of $1,800. MyWeb's statement of changes in equity would appear as follows:

	Common Shares			
	Number of Shares	**$**	**Retained Earnings**	**Total**
MyWeb, Inc. **Statement of Changes in Shareholders' Equity** Month Ended June 30, 2013				
Balance, June 1, 2013	—	$ 0	$ 0	$ 0
Issued Common Shares	5,000	$25,000		25,000
Net Income			$2,300	2,300
Dividends			(500)	(500)
Balance, June 30, 2013	5,000	$25,000	$1,800	$26,800

You will use the $25,000 and $1,800 ending balance in common shares and retained earnings on the balance sheet.

Statement of Financial Position (Balance Sheet)

The statement of financial position or balance sheet reports the financial position of the business. To prepare a balance sheet, begin with the proper heading. A proper heading includes the name of the company (MyWeb, Inc.), the name of the statement (Statement of Financial Position), and the date (June 30, 2013). Unlike the income statement and statement of changes in equity, we are reporting the financial position of the company for a *specific date*, rather than a period of time.

The statement of financial position is just a listing of all assets, liabilities, and equity, with the equality of the accounting equation verified at the bottom.

To prepare the body of the statement, begin by listing assets. Next, list the liabilities and shareholders' equity. Notice that the balance sheet is organized in the same order as the accounting equation. You should also note that the amount of common shares and retained earnings come from the ending common shares and retained earnings on your statement of changes in equity. You should then total both sides to make sure that they are equal. If they are not equal, you need to look for an error.

The figures for assets and liabilities come directly from the accounting equation. In this case, assets include the total cash balance of $18,300, accounts receivable of $800, supplies worth $350, and the equipment's value of $7,500, for a total of $26,950 in assets. Liabilities total $150: the balance in the Accounts Payable account. The $25,000 common shares balance is added to the ending retained earnings of $1,800 (from the statement of changes in equity) to give us total shareholders' equity of $26,800. The shareholders' equity is then added to the liabilities to get total liabilities and shareholders' equity of $26,950. The $26,950 of total assets equals the $26,950 of total liabilities plus shareholders' equity, which confirms the accounting equation: Assets = Liabilities + Shareholders' Equity.

MyWeb, Inc. Statement of Financial Position As of June 30, 2013			
ASSETS		**LIABILITIES**	
Cash	$18,300	Accounts Payable	$ 150
Accounts Receivable	800		
Supplies	350		
Equipment	7,500		
		SHAREHOLDERS' EQUITY	
		Common Shares	25,000
		Retained Earnings	1,800
		Total Shareholders' Equity	$26,800
		Total Liabilities &	
Total Assets	$26,950	Shareholders' Equity	$26,950

Demo Doc Complete

Part 1	Part 2	**Demo Doc Complete**

DECISION GUIDELINES

Accounting and the Business Environment

Suppose you open a business. Here are some questions you should consider:

Decision	Guideline	Analyze
I am planning to start a new business. What form of business organization is the best?	There are many ways to organize a business including the following: a sole proprietorship, partnership, or corporation. Each type of business organization has different advantages and disadvantages.	Know the tax and legal treatments of each type of organization. Weigh the best treatment of taxes and legal liability of each type and pick the format that is most advantageous for the business owners.
I need to determine if a business is profitable. Which financial statement do I use?	Use the income statement to determine the profitability of a business. The income statement reports the revenues and expenses of a business. Revenues represent what a business earns as a result of providing goods or services. Expenses represent the cost to the business of providing those goods or services.	If revenues exceed expenses, the business is profitable and has earned net income. However, if expenses exceed revenue, the business has incurred a net loss and is not profitable.
I want to know if a company was profitable, and if it was, what it did with the profits. Which financial statement do I use?	Use the statement of changes in equity to find out. The statement of changes in equity shows whether the net income of a business was paid out as dividends or retained in the business.	If a business is planning on growth, it will often issue low or no dividends to shareholders. This way, it retains the income in the business.
I want to know who would get its assets if a business were to close its doors. Which financial statement would I use?	Use the statement of financial position (balance sheet) to determine who has claims to the company's assets.	The liabilities of a business reflect the claims of third parties to the assets of the business. Once those claims are settled, the remaining assets belong to the shareholders (the owners) of the business. This amount is reflected by the shareholders' equity on the statement of financial position.
I want to know where a business get its cash and where it is spent. Which financial statement would I use?	Use the statement of cash flows to see all of the sources and all of the uses of cash for a business.	You can see whether a company's operations generated cash for the business and how much cash the business invested in the purchase of assets such as buildings and equipment. If a company's operations generated insufficient funds to finance its investments in assets, you can determine how the business financed these acquisitions.

ACCOUNTING VOCABULARY
THE LANGUAGE OF BUSINESS

 Accounting Vocabulary lists all the new boldfaced terms that were explained in the chapter along with their definitions. Page references help you to review the terms.

Accounts payable (p. 17) A liability backed by the general reputation and credit standing of the debtor.

Accounts receivable (p. 19) An asset representing amounts due from customers to whom the business has sold goods or for whom the business has performed services.

Accounting (p. 7) The information system that measures business activity, processes the results of activities into reports, and communicates the results to decision makers.

Accounting Standards for Private Enterprises (ASPE) (p. 11) A set of guidelines that have replaced the original Canadian Generally Accepted Accounting Principles (GAAP), but specifically used for private enterprises.

Accrual basis accounting (p. 14) An accounting system that records the business event based on when it occurs, not when cash is exchanged.

Assets (p. 14) Items of value that a business possesses; also referred to as the economic resources or properties owned by the business that will provide future benefits to the business.

Balance sheet (p. 26) Summary of an entity's assets, liabilities, and shareholders' equity as of a specific date; also called the *statement of financial position*.

Businesses (p. 6) Organizations that sell products or services to customers.

Canadian Accounting Standards for Private Enterprises (p. 11) Accounting rules, created by the Accounting Standards Board (AcSB), that govern how accountants measure, process, and communicate financial information for Canadian private enterprises.

Common shares (p. 16) Represents the investment of assets made by shareholders into a corporation.

Comparability (p. 13) One of the qualitative characteristics of accounting information that should enable users to compare one company's accounting information to another company's accounting information and to its own previous years' results.

Conceptual framework (p. 12) A theoretical foundation that helps accounting standard setters develop consistent and coherent standards, and helps accountants determine the appropriate treatment of the events in the absence of specific guidance, so that financial information can be properly communicated to the users.

Corporation (p. 8) A business owned by shareholders that is an entity legally separate from its owners.

Cost–benefit (p. 12) An analysis of what one option costs and what its benefits are to determine whether to implement the action or not.

Current cost (p. 14) The amount required to purchase the asset today.

Dividends (p. 16) Distribution of earnings by a corporation to its shareholders.

Entity (p. 9) An organization or a section of an organization that, for accounting purposes, stands apart as a separate economic unit.

Ethics (p. 4) Principles of socially responsible behaviour.

Expenses (p. 16) Decreases to retained earnings caused by using resources to deliver goods or provide services to customers.

Financial accounting (p. 10) A process used to track business transactions and to provide financial information about a business to external users.

Financial statements (p. 6) Financial information prepared according to IFRS or Canadian Accounting Standards for Private Enterprises, that communicate an entity's performance or financial position.

Fundamental accounting equation (p. 15) The basic tool of accounting that measures the resources of a business and the claims to those resources: Assets = Liabilities + Shareholders' Equity.

Going-concern principle (p. 14) The assumption that the business entity will continue in operation for the foreseeable future.

Historical cost (p. 14) The actual cost of goods and assets acquired.

Income statement (p. 23) Summary of a business's revenues, expenses, and net income or net loss for a specific period. It is a component of the statement of comprehensive income.

International Financial Reporting Standards (IFRS) (p. 11) A set of internationally accepted reporting standards that guide how business activities should be recognized, measured, and recorded, and how financial information should be reported. IFRS were developed by the International Accounting Standards Board.

Liabilities (p. 15) Third party or creditor claims to the assets of a business; the debts owed by the business entity to third parties, which will reduce the future assets of a business or require future services or products.

Managerial accounting (p. 10) A branch of accounting involved in the process of gathering cost information, budgeting, planning, performance evaluation, etc. for internal users.

Manufacturing business (p. 7) A business that makes its own products that are sold to the final customer or to other companies.

Materiality (p. 12) This is a measure of whether or not something is relevant to a decision. If an analysis leads to a response that something is significant or that it will change an opinion, then this is material, or of enough significance or size to matter.

Merchandising business (p. 7) A business that sells products made by another company; also called *wholesale* and *retail companies*.

Net income (p. 23) The excess of total revenues over total expenses; also called *profit*.

Net loss (p. 23) The excess of total expenses over total revenues.

Note payable (p. 18) A written promise of future payment made by the business.

On account (p. 19) Buying or selling on credit.

Owner(s)'s capital (p. 8) The amount invested in a sole proprietorship or a partnership by an individual in exchange for ownership of the business.

Partnership (p. 8) A business with two or more owners.

Prepaid expenses (p. 17) Amounts that are assets of a business because they represent items that have been paid for but will be used later.

Present value (p. 14) The value on a given date of a future amount, adjusted to reflect the time value of a single amount or of an annuity.

Profit (p. 23) The difference between the revenues (the sales price of the goods or services sold by the business) and expenses (the cost of the resources used to provide these goods and services); also called *net income*.

Realizable value (p. 14) The amount that is likely to be received in exchange for an asset, factoring in any cash or other benefit, less any costs or expenses to sell or distribute the asset.

Relevance (p. 13) One of the qualitative characteristics of accounting information that makes a difference in a decision-making process. The information should be predictable and provide feedback in a timely manner.

Reliability (p. 13) One of the qualitative characteristics of accounting information that it be verifiable, confirmable by any independent observer.

Retail business (p. 7) A business that sells products purchased from another company to the final consumer.

Retained earnings (p. 16) Earnings of a business that are kept, or retained, in the business.

Revenue (p. 16) Increases to retained earnings created by delivering goods or providing services to customers.

Service business (p. 7) A business that provides services to customers.

Share capital (p. 16) Funds raised by the business entity in either cash or other consideration, and in exchange, the business entity issues ownership rights (preferred shares or common shares in a corporation) to the owner(s) who provided the funds.

Shareholder (p. 8) A person who owns shares in a corporation.

Shareholders' equity (p. 15) Represents the shareholders' ownership interest in the assets of a corporation.

Sole proprietorship (p. 8) A business with a single owner.

Statement of cash flows (p. 27) Summary of the changes in a business's cash balance for a specific period.

Statement of changes in equity (p. 25) Summary of the changes in shareholders' equity during a period by providing information on common shares, retained earnings, and other comprehensive income.

Statement of comprehensive income (p. 23) Summary of a business's revenues, expenses, and net income or net loss for a specific period, as well as other comprehensive income, such as unrealized gains or losses from holding assets. The income statement is one of the components included in the statement of comprehensive income.

Statement of financial position (p. 26) Summary of business's assets, liabilities, and shareholders' equity as of a specific date; also called the *balance sheet*.

Third party (p. 15) Person or organization unrelated to the organization.

Timeliness (p. 12) Having something done or information provided fast enough to make a difference in a decision.

Transaction (p. 15) An event that has a financial impact on a business entity.

Understandability (p. 13) One of the qualitative characteristics of accounting information, that it be understandable for users.

Wholesale business (p. 7) A business that purchases products from a manufacturer and sells them to a retail business.

Withdrawals (p. 8) Income that is removed from the company and distributed to the owner(s).

ACCOUNTING PRACTICE

DISCUSSION QUESTIONS

1. The text states that accounting is the "language of business." What does this mean? Why is it important to know the language?

2. Would you describe accounting as being primarily a technical discipline or primarily an ethical discipline? Why?

3. What are the streams of accounting career opportunities available for accounting professionals? What tasks do financial accountants do? What tasks do management accountants do?

4. What are some reasons why accounting has adopted "historical" financial statements as the model? What are some disadvantages associated with presenting "historical" financial statements?

5. What are some of the uses of financial statements?

6. What is the primary way in which corporations differ from proprietorships and partnerships? What are some of the factors that might affect a person's decision about the form of organization that would be best in a given situation?

7. What is the fundamental accounting equation? Define each of the components of this equation.

8. How is the accounting equation affected by each of the following transactions?
   a. Owners contribute cash to start the business.
   b. The company borrows money from the bank.
   c. The company provides services for a client who promises to pay later.
   d. The company collects from the customer in option c.

9. In what order would the financial statements be prepared? Why?

10. Which financial statement would be most useful to answer each of the following questions?
    a. Does the corporation have enough resources to pay its short-term debts?
    b. What is the corporation's policy toward "growing the company" versus distributing its wealth to owners?
    c. Did the corporation pay its operating costs with resources generated from operations, money borrowed from banks, or money generated from selling off its buildings and equipment?
    d. Did the corporation make a profit last year?

SELF CHECK

1. Which type of business organization is owned by its shareholders?
   a. Proprietorship
   b. Partnership
   c. Corporation
   d. All the above are owned by shareholders.

2. International Financial Reporting Standards (IFRS) are created by the
   a. Ontario Securities Commission
   b. Canadian Revenue Agency
   c. Accounting Standards Board
   d. International Accounting Standards Board

MyAccountingLab

Make the grade with MyAccountingLab. The exercises and problems in this chapter can be found on MyAccountingLab at **www.myaccountinglab.com**. You can practise them as often as you want, and they feature step-by-step guided solutions to help you find the right answer.

This reference to MyAccountingLab reminds you that all of the Exercises and Problems in this chapter can also be found on MyAccountingLab.

Test your understanding with these multiple choice questions. The answers are given at the end of each chapter.

3. Which accounting concept or principle specifically states that we should record transactions at amounts that can be verified?

    a. Entity concept
    b. Reliability
    c. Relevance
    d. Going-concern concept

4. Boardmaster is famous for custom skateboards. At the end of a recent year, Boardmaster's total assets added up to $622 million, and shareholders' equity was $487 million. How much did Boardmaster owe creditors?

    a. $1,109 million
    b. $622 million
    c. $135 million
    d. $487 million

5. Assume that Boardmaster sold skateboards to a department store for $35,000 cash. How would this transaction affect Boardmaster's accounting equation?

    a. Increase both assets and shareholders' equity by $35,000
    b. Increase both assets and liabilities by $35,000
    c. Increase both liabilities and shareholders' equity by $35,000
    d. It will not affect the accounting equation because the effects cancel out.

6. Assume that Boardmaster sold skateboards to another department store for $22,000 on account. Which parts of the accounting equation does a sale on account affect?

    a. Accounts Receivable and Accounts Payable
    b. Accounts Payable and Cash
    c. Accounts Payable and Retained Earnings
    d. Accounts Receivable and Retained Earnings

7. Assume that Boardmaster paid expenses totalling $38,000. How does this transaction affect Boardmaster's accounting equation?

    a. Increases assets and decreases liabilities
    b. Increases both assets and shareholders' equity
    c. Decreases both assets and shareholders' equity
    d. Decreases assets and increases liabilities

8. Consider the overall effects of transactions in questions 5, 6, and 7 on Boardmaster. What is Boardmaster's net income or net loss?

    a. Net income of $57,000
    b. Net loss of $3,000
    c. Net income of $19,000
    d. It cannot be determined from the data given.

9. The balance sheet reports

    a. financial position on a specific date.
    b. results of operations on a specific date.
    c. financial position for a specific period.
    d. results of operations for a specific period.

10. The income statement reports

    a. financial position on a specific date.
    b. results of operations on a specific date.
    c. financial position for a specific period.
    d. results of operations for a specific period.

    Answers are given after Written Communication.

SHORT EXERCISES

S1-1. Accounting principles and conceptual framework (*Learning Objective 3*) 5–10 min.

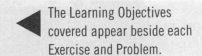

The Learning Objectives covered appear beside each Exercise and Problem.

Place the corresponding letter of the definition next to the term.

   a. An organization that stands as a separate economic unit must not have its financial affairs confused with that of other entities.

   b. Data must be verifiable.

   c. Standards developed by IASB.

   d. Acquired assets and services should be recorded at their actual cost.

_____ 1. Historical cost method

_____ 2. Entity concept

_____ 3. International Financial Reporting Standards

_____ 4. Reliability

S1-2. Accounting principles and conceptual framework (*Learning Objective 3*) 5–10 min.

Jill Riggins owns and operates Jill's Java coffee shop. She proposes to account for the shop's revenue when she receives cash. Which accounting concept or principle does Jill violate?

   a. Accrual basis accounting

   b. Entity concept

   c. Going-concern concept

   d. Comparability

S1-3. Types of accounting (*Learning Objective 2*) 5–10 min.

Place the corresponding letter next to the appropriate term.

___ **1.** Cost accounting

___ **2.** Accounts receivable and accounts payable management

___ **3.** Auditing

___ **4.** Budget and planning

___ **5.** Investment and financial planning

___ **6.** Financial statement preparation

___ **7.** Tax planning

   a. Financial Accounting

   b. Managerial Accounting

   c. Taxation

   d. Banking and Financial Services

S1-4. Conceptual framework and qualitative financial information (*Learning Objective 3*) 5–10 min.

Place the corresponding letter next to the appropriate term.

___ **1.** Financial information should provide predictable value for decision making.

___ **2.** The value of financial information obtained should outweigh the cost of obtaining it.

___ **3.** Financial statements are prepared using the same accounting standards consistently from year to year.

___ **4.** Financial information is included in the financial statement for completeness, as a lack of information will likely impact the decision making.

___ **5.** Financial information should verifiable, neutral, and complete.

a. Comparability

b. Cost–Benefit

c. Reliability

d. Materiality

e. Relevance

S1-5. Accounting terminology (*Learning Objectives 1 & 4*) 10–15 min.

Place the corresponding letter of the definition next to the term.

___ **1.** Liabilities

___ **2.** Assets

___ **3.** Corporation

___ **4.** Dividends

___ **5.** Sole proprietorship

___ **6.** Partnership

___ **7.** Transaction

a. Any event that affects financial position.

b. Organization form with a single owner.

c. Organization form with two or more owners.

d. Organization form that can have an indefinite life.

e. Debts owed to outsiders.

f. Economic resources of the business.

g. Payment of cash to the owners of a corporation.

S1-6. Basic accounting equation (*Learning Objective 4*) 5–10 min

Determine the missing amounts in the following accounting equations.

	Assets	=	Liabilities	+	Shareholders' Equity
a.	$75,000	=	$32,000	+	?
b.	?	=	$43,000	+	$37,000
c.	$92,000	=	?	+	$60,000

S1-7. Basic accounting equation (*Learning Objective 4*) 5–10 min

Ming An owns Ming's Lawncare Service. The business has cash of $3,000 and equipment that costs $12,000. Debts of the business include accounts payable of $6,000 and a $5,000 note payable. Determine the amount of shareholders' equity Ming has in the business. Write the accounting equation for Ming's Lawncare Service.

S1-8. Basic accounting equation (*Learning Objective 4*) 5–10 min.

Apex Financial Services, Inc. has cash of $2,000, supplies costing $800, and shareholders' equity of $1,300. Determine the liabilities of the business. Write the accounting equation for Apex Financial Services, Inc.

S1-9. Basic accounting equation (*Learning Objective 4*) 5–10 min.

Syed Foods, Inc. started as a business when Mr. Syed purchased $8,000 of shares in the business. Before starting operations, Syed Foods, Inc. borrowed $5,000 cash by signing a note payable to First National Bank. Account for these two transactions in the accounting equation.

**S1-10. Entering transactions in the accounting equation (*Learning Objective 4*)
5–10 min.**

T & T Towing Service, Inc. earns service revenue by towing vehicles for CAA. T & T
Towing Service's main expenses are the salaries paid to its employees. Account for
the following transactions in the expanded accounting equation:

a. T & T Towing Service, Inc. earned $14,000 of service revenue on account.

b. T & T Towing Service, Inc. paid $8,000 in salaries expense.

S1-11. Basic accounting equation (*Learning Objective 4*) 5–10 min.

Match each of the following items with its location in the accounting equation. Use
the most detailed category appropriate:

a. Assets

b. Liabilities

c. Shareholders' Equity

d. Revenues

e. Expenses

___ **1.** Utilities Expense

___ **2.** Accounts Receivable

___ **3.** Common Shares

___ **4.** Office Supplies

___ **5.** Lease Expense, Computer

___ **6.** Salary Expense

___ **7.** Cash

___ **8.** Rent Expense, Office

___ **9.** Service Revenue

___ **10.** Accounts Payable

___ **11.** Land

S1-12. Basic financial statements (*Learning Objective 4*) 5–10 min.

Label each of the items listed with the abbreviation of the financial statement on
which it appears. Items may appear on more than one statement.

- Income Statement (IS)
- Statement of Changes in Equity (SCE)
- Statement of Financial Position (SFP)

___ **1.** Accounts Receivable

___ **2.** Notes Payable

___ **3.** Advertising Expense

___ **4.** Service Revenue

___ **5.** Retained Earnings

___ **6.** Office Supplies

___ **7.** Common Shares

___ **8.** Cash

___ **9.** Salary Expense

___ **10.** Dividends

S1-13. Entering transactions in the accounting equation (*Learning Objective 4*) 5–10 min.

As a manager of a department store, you must deal with a variety of business transactions. Place the letter of each of the following transactions next to the effect it has on the accounting equation.

a. Paid cash to the shareholders as a distribution of earnings.

b. Purchased land for building site.

c. Paid cash on an account payable.

d. Sold shares to shareholders.

e. Received cash from the bank in exchange for a note payable.

___ **1.** Increase an asset and increase shareholders' equity.

___ **2.** Increase an asset and increase a liability.

___ **3.** Increase one asset and decrease another asset.

___ **4.** Decrease an asset and decrease shareholders' equity.

___ **5.** Decrease an asset and decrease a liability.

S1-14. Transaction analysis (*Learning Objective 4*) 5–10 min.

PWC Motorsports, Inc., a corporation, sells and services personal watercraft. The business experienced the following events. State whether each event (a) increased, (b) decreased, or (c) had no effect on the total assets of the business, and identify the asset(s) involved in each transaction.

1. PWC Motorsports, Inc. sold additional shares to shareholders.

2. Purchased land as a building site for cash.

3. Paid cash on accounts payable.

4. Purchased machinery and equipment; signed a promissory note in payment.

5. Performed service for a customer on account.

6. Paid cash to the shareholders as a distribution of earnings.

7. Received cash from a customer on accounts receivable.

8. Sold land for a price equal to the cost of the land; received cash.

9. Borrowed money from the bank.

S1-15. Transaction analysis (*Learning Objective 4*) 5–10 min.

Presented here are nine transactions and the analysis used to account for them. Evaluate each of the suggested accounting treatments and indicate whether it is true or false.

1. Received cash of $38,000 from the shareholders, who bought shares in the business.

  Answer: Increase asset, increase shareholders' equity. _____ True _____ False

2. Paid $450 cash to purchase supplies.

  Answer: Increase asset, increase shareholders' equity. _____ True _____ False

3. Earned service revenue on account, $500.

  Answer: Increase asset, increase retained earnings. _____ True _____ False

4. Purchased office furniture on account at a cost of $850.

  Answer: Increase asset, increase liability. _____ True _____ False

5. Received cash on account, $1,400.

  Answer: Increase asset, decrease asset. _____ True _____ False

6. Paid cash on account, $675.

  Answer: Increase asset, increase liability. _____ True _____ False

7. Sold land for $38,000, which was the cost of the land.

    Answer: Increase asset, decrease asset. _____ True _____ False

8. Serviced automobiles and received cash of $680.

    Answer: Increase asset, increase revenue. _____ True _____ False

9. Paid monthly office rent of $1,200.

    Answer: Decrease asset, increase shareholders' equity. _____ True _____ False

S1-16. Transaction analysis and calculating net income (*Learning Objectives 4 & 5*)
5–10 min.

The analysis of Nelson's Painting Service's first seven transactions follows. The business only sold shares once and paid no dividends.

	Assets			=	Liabilities			+	Shareholders' Equity	
	Cash	+ Accounts Receivable	+ Equipment =		Accounts Payable	+	Notes Payable	+	Common Shares	+ Retained Earnings
1.	+ $40,000		=						+ $40,000	
2.	– 1,200		+ $ 1,200 =							
3.			+ 25,000 =				+ $25,000			
4.		+ $400	=							+ 400
5.	– 750		=							– 750
6.	+ 1,800		=							+ 1,800
7.	+ 200	– 200	=							

1. Label each of the transactions in the preceding analysis with the corresponding letter of the description that best fits it:

    a. Earned revenue for painting services provided, but customer will pay later.

    b. Customers paid cash for painting services completed earlier in the month.

    c. Received cash for revenue earned by providing painting services.

    d. Paid cash for expenses incurred to operate the business.

    e. Paid cash to purchase painting equipment.

    f. Sold shares to start the painting service business.

    g. Borrowed money from the bank to purchase painting equipment.

2. If these transactions fully describe the operations of Nelson's Painting Service, Inc. during the month, what was the amount of its net income or net loss?

EXERCISES (GROUP A)

E1-1A. Basic accounting equation (*Learning Objective 4*) 10–15 min.

Determine the missing amounts in the following accounting equations.

	Assets	=	Liabilities	+	Shareholders' Equity
Inland Equipment, Corp.	?	=	$52,700	+	$18,000
Peter's Hardware, Inc.	$ 96,000	=	?	+	$42,000
Sparky's Electric, Inc.	$107,400	=	$88,200	+	?

Quick solution:

$37,000 increase.

Quick Solutions appear in the margin when applicable to help you make sure you are "on track"

E1-2A. Basic accounting equation (*Learning Objective 4*) 10–15 min.

Styles Salon had $87,000 of total assets and $52,000 of total shareholders' equity at December 31, 2013. At December 31, 2014, Styles Salon had assets totalling $153,000 and shareholders' equity totalling $81,000.

After analyzing the data, answer the following questions:

1. What was the amount of the increase or decrease in liabilities?
2. Identify a possible reason for the change in liabilities during the year.

E1-3A. Basic accounting equation (*Learning Objective 4*) 10–15 min.

Anthony's Consulting, Inc. started business in 2013 with total assets of $32,000 and total liabilities of $14,000. At the end of 2013, Anthony's total assets were $42,000 and total liabilities were $18,500.

After analyzing the data, answer the following questions:

1. What was the amount of the increase or decrease in shareholders' equity?
2. Identify two possible reasons for the change in shareholders' equity during the year.

E1-4A. Using the accounting equation to determine net income (*Learning Objectives 4 & 5*) 15–20 min.

The balance sheet data for Quick Care, Inc. at August 31, 2013, and September 30, 2013, follow:

	Aug 31, 2013	Sep 30, 2013
Total Assets	$130,000	$165,000
Total Liabilities	87,000	131,000
Common Shares	15,000	15,000
Total Shareholders' Equity	?	?

Requirement

1. The following are three *independent* assumptions about the business during September. For each assumption, compute the amount of net income or net loss during September 2013. Find the solution by preparing the statement of changes in equity. First, use the amounts of total assets, total liabilities, and common shares given previously and the accounting equation to determine the beginning and ending retained earnings amounts. Then plug those and the other amounts given in each assumption into the statement of changes in equity to determine the net income or net loss.

   a. The business paid no dividends.
   b. The business paid $8,000 of dividends.
   c. The business paid $14,000 of dividends.

E1-5A. Transaction analysis (*Learning Objective 4*) 15–20 min.

Suzuka Ito opened a massage practice titled Suzuka Ito Health, Inc. During March, the first month of operations, the business experienced the following events:

Mar 2	Ito bought $65,000 of stock in the business by opening a bank account in the name of Suzuka Ito Health, Inc.
6	The business paid $55,000 cash for land with the intention of building an office building on the land.
11	The business purchased supplies for $1,000 on account.
15	The business officially opened for business.
17	The business treated patients and earned service revenue of $7,000, receiving cash.
19	The business paid office rent, $1,800.
22	The business sold supplies to another massage therapist for the cost of those supplies, $250.
30	The business paid $500 on account related to the March 11 purchase.

Requirement

1. Analyze the effects of these events on the accounting equation of the massage practice of Suzuka Ito Health, Inc. Use headings for Cash, Clinic Supplies, Land, Accounts Payable, Common Shares, Service Revenue, and Rent Expense.

E1-6A. Types of business organizations and balance sheet preparation (*Learning Objectives 1 & 4*) 10–15 min.

The following are the balances of the assets, liabilities, and equity of Hair Today Salon at July 31, 2013:

Cash	$3,500	Office Equipment	$6,300
Retained Earnings	2,200	Common Shares	3,000
Accounts Payable	2,500	Note Payable	4,000
Accounts Receivable	1,200	Supplies	700

Requirements

1. What type of business organization is Hair Today Salon?
2. Prepare the balance sheet of the business at July 31, 2013.
3. What does the balance sheet report?

E1-7A. Transaction analysis and statement of changes in equity (*Learning Objective 5*) 10–15 min.

Yuan Spa Inc.'s statement of changes in equity shows the following information:

	Common Shares	Retained Earnings	Total
Balance, Jan. 1, 2013	$12,000	?	$18,000
Issued Common Shares	?		?
Net Income (Loss)		?	?
Dividends		$(3,000)	?
Balance, Dec. 31, 2013	$20,000	?	$42,000

Requirement

1. Calculate the missing amounts.
2. If Yuan Spa's revenue was $45,000, what were the expenses for the year?

E1-8A. Types of accounts and income statement preparation (*Learning Objectives 4 & 5*) 15–20 min.

Selected accounts of Armstrong Consulting, Inc., a financial services business, have the following balances at December 31, 2013, the end of its first year of operations. During the year, Lori Armstrong, the only shareholder, bought $20,000 of shares in the business.

Office Furniture	$ 28,000	Rent Expense	$36,000
Utilities Expense	12,600	Cash	5,400
Accounts Payable	3,800	Office Supplies	800
Note Payable	21,500	Salary Expense	43,000
Service Revenue	141,500	Salaries Payable	2,000
Accounts Receivable	9,500	Property Tax Expense	2,300
Supplies Expense	4,200	Equipment	22,000

Requirements

1. Identify each as an asset, liability, revenue, or expense.

2. Prepare the income statement of Armstrong Consulting, Inc. for the year ended December 31, 2013. What is the result of operations for 2013?

3. Assuming the balance in Retained Earnings on December 31, 2013, was $18,400, what was the amount of the Dividends during the year? Answer by preparing a statement of retained earnings to solve for the dividends. Recall that the business has just completed its first year and has no beginning balance for retained earnings.

E1-9A. Using the accounting equation to determine net income (*Learning Objectives 4 & 5*) 15–20 min.

Presented here is information for Telco, Inc. for the year ended December 31, 2013.

Telco, Inc.	
Beginning:	
Assets	$66,000
Liabilities	15,000
Ending:	
Assets	$94,000
Liabilities	28,000
Shareholders' Equity:	
Sale of Shares	$ 7,000
Payment of Dividends	20,000

Requirements

1. What is the beginning shareholders' equity of Telco, Inc.?

2. What is the ending shareholders' equity of Telco, Inc.?

3. What is the net income or net loss for the year?

EXERCISES (GROUP B)

E1-1B. Basic accounting equation (*Learning Objective 4*) 10–15 min.

Determine the missing amounts in the following accounting equations.

	Assets	=	Liabilities	+	Shareholders' Equity
Style Cuts Corp.	?	=	$52,700	+	$ 2,500
Your Basket, Inc.	$102,000	=	?	+	$48,000
Perfect Cleaners, Inc.	$108,800	=	$87,100	+	?

E1-2B. Basic accounting equation (*Learning Objective 4*) 10–15 min.

Great Wall Chinese Cuisine had $93,000 of total assets and $31,000 of total shareholders' equity at May 31, 2013. At May 31, 2014, Great Wall Chinese Cuisine had assets totalling $147,000 and shareholders' equity totalling $87,000.

After analyzing the data, answer the following questions:

1. What was the amount of the increase or decrease in liabilities?

2. Identify a possible reason for the change in liabilities during the year.

E1-3B. Basic accounting equation (*Learning Objective 4*) 10–15 min.

Kablossom started business in 2013 with total assets of $35,000 and total liabilities of $32,000. At the end of 2013, Kablossom's total assets were $65,000, and total liabilities were $20,000.

After analyzing the data, answer the following questions:

1. What was the amount of the increase or decrease in shareholders' equity?

2. Identify three possible reasons for the change in shareholders' equity during the year.

E1-4B. Using the accounting equation to determine net income (*Learning Objectives 4 & 5*) 15–20 min.

The balance sheet data for Bob's Electronics, Corp. at October 31, 2013, and November 30, 2013, follow:

	Oct 31, 2013	Nov 30, 2013
Total Assets	$140,000	$175,000
Total Liabilities..	75,000	117,000
Common Shares	45,000	45,000
Total Shareholders' Equity	?	?

Requirement

1. The following are three *independent* assumptions about the business during November. For each assumption, compute the amount of net income or net loss during November 2013. Find the solution by preparing the statement of changes in equity. First, use the amounts of total assets, total liabilities, and common shares given previously and the accounting equation to determine the beginning and ending retained earnings amounts. Then plug those and the other amounts given in each assumption into the statement of changes in equity to determine the net income or net loss.

a. The business paid no dividends.

b. The business paid $17,000 of dividends.

c. The business paid $25,000 of dividends.

E1-5B. Transaction analysis (*Learning Objective 4*) 15–20 min.

Shuo Lin opened a yoga centre titled Shuo Lin Yoga, Inc. During January, the first month of operations, the business experienced the following events:

Jan 2	Shuo Lin bought $80,000 of shares in the business by opening a bank account in the name of Shuo Lin Yoga, Inc.
6	The business paid $30,000 cash for land with the intention of building an office building on the land.
11	The business purchased supplies for $600 on account.
15	The business officially opened for business.
17	The business earned revenue of $13,000, receiving cash.
19	The business paid office rent, $1,100.
22	The business sold supplies to another yoga studio for the cost of those supplies, $400.
30	The business paid $150 on account related to the January 11 purchase.

Requirement

1. Analyze the effects of these events on the accounting equation of the yoga centre of Shuo Lin Yoga, Inc. Use headings for Cash, Supplies, Land, Accounts Payable, Common Shares, Service Revenue, and Rent Expense.

E1-6B. Types of business organizations and balance sheet preparation (*Learning Objectives 1 & 5*) 10–15 min.

The following are the balances of the assets, liabilities, and equity of Kite Runner, Inc. at August 31, 2013:

Cash..	$24,000	Office Equipment........................	$4,100
Retained Earnings.....................	18,400	Common Shares	5,000
Accounts Payable......................	5,000	Note Payable..............................	1,000
Accounts Receivable................	600	Supplies......................................	700

Requirements

1. What type of business organization is Kite Runner, Inc.?
2. Prepare the balance sheet of the business at August 31, 2013.
3. What does the balance sheet report?

E1-7B. Transaction analysis and statement of changes in equity (*Learning Objective 5*) 10–15 min.

Omar Fitness Inc.'s statement of changes in equity shows the following information:

	Common Shares	Retained Earnings	Total
Balance, Jan. 1, 2013	?	$28,000	?
Issued Common Shares	$24,000		$24,000
Net Income		?	?
Dividends		$(5,000)	$(5,000)
Balance, Dec. 31, 2013	$34,000	?	$48,000

Requirements

1. Calculate the missing amounts.
2. If Omar Fitness Inc.'s revenue was $26,000, what were the expenses for the year?

E1-8B. Types of accounts and income statement preparation (*Learning Objectives 4 & 5*) 15–20 min.

Selected accounts of Albright Consulting, Inc., a financial services business, have the following balances at January 31, 2013, the end of its first year of operations. During the year, Lilly Albright, the only shareholder, bought $49,700 of shares in the business.

Office Furniture	$ 20,000	Rent Expense	$36,000
Utilities Expense	13,500	Cash	15,600
Accounts Payable	9,500	Office Supplies	1,400
Notes Payable	21,500	Salary Expense	43,000
Service Revenue	155,000	Salaries Payable	1,000
Accounts Receivable	10,500	Property Tax Expense	3,000
Supplies Expense	3,700	Equipment	40,000

Requirements

1. Identify each as an asset, liability, revenue, or expense.

2. Prepare the income statement of Albright Consulting, Inc. for the year ended January 31, 2013. What is the result of operations for 2013?

3. Assuming the balance in Retained Earnings on January 31, 2013, was $5,800, what was the amount of the dividends during the year? Answer by preparing a statement of changes in retained earnings to solve for the dividends. Recall that the business has just completed its first year and has no beginning balance for retained earnings.

F1-9B. Using the accounting equation to determine net income (*Learning Objectives 4 & 5*) 15–20 min.

Presented here is information for Edo, Inc. for the year ended August 31, 2013.

Edo, Inc.	
Beginning:	
Assets	$ 99,000
Liabilities	15,000
Ending:	
Assets	$164,000
Liabilities	70,000
Shareholders' Equity:	
Sale of Shares	$ 17,000
Payment of Dividends	55,000

Requirements

1. What is the beginning shareholders' equity of Edo, Inc.?

2. What is the ending shareholders' equity of Edo, Inc.?

3. What is the net income or net loss for the year?

EXERCISES (ALTERNATES 1, 2, AND 3)

These alternative exercise sets are available for your practice benefit at
www.myaccountinglab.com

PROBLEMS (GROUP A)

P1-1A. Transaction analysis and the calculation of net income (*Learning Objectives 4 & 5*) 20–25 min.

Dan Oliver worked as an accountant at a local accounting firm for five years after graduating from university. Recently, he opened his own accounting practice, which he operates as a corporation. The name of the new entity is Oliver and Associates, Inc. Dan experienced the following events during the first month of operations. Some of the events were personal and did not affect the accounting practice. Others were business transactions and should be accounted for by the business.

Jun	3	Received $30,000 cash proceeds from refinancing his house.
	5	$60,000 of shares in the business were sold to Dan Oliver. The cash proceeds were deposited in a new business bank account titled Oliver and Associates, Inc.
	7	Paid $450 cash for office supplies for the new accounting practice.
	9	Purchased $3,800 of office furniture for the accounting practice and agreed to pay the vendor within three months.
	10	Dan sold 500 shares of General Motors stock, which he had owned for several years, receiving $48,000 cash. The cash from the sale of shares was deposited in his personal bank account.
	14	A representative of a large company telephoned Dan and told him of the company's intention to hire Oliver and Associates, Inc. as its accountants.
	20	Finished accounting work for a client and sent the client a bill for $3,800. The client is expected to pay within two weeks.
	27	Paid office rent, $1,600.
	30	Paid $1,000 of dividends to Oliver and Associates, Inc. shareholders.

Requirements

1. Enter each transaction in the expanded accounting equation of Oliver and Associates, Inc. as needed, calculating new balances after each transaction.

2. Determine the following items:

   a. Total assets

   b. Total liabilities

   c. Total shareholders' equity

   d. Net income or net loss for June

P1-2A. Income statement and statement of financial position transactions; prepare the income statement and statement of financial position (*Learning Objectives 4 & 5*) 25–30 min.

Donna Au started an interior design company called Interiors by Donna, Inc. on September 1, 2013. The following amounts summarize the financial position of her business on September 14, 2013, after the first two weeks of operations:

Assets				= Liabilities +	Shareholders' Equity			
					Common Shares +	Retained Earnings		
Cash	+ Accounts Receivable +	Supplies +	Equipment =	Accounts Payable +	Common Shares +	Service Revenue –	Salaries Expense –	Dividends
$1,540 +	$3,680 +	+	$24,000 =	$5,100 +	$21,000 +	$5,100 –	$1,980	

During the remainder of September, the following events occurred:

a. Au received $10,000 as a gift and used it to buy 5,000 shares in the business.

b. Paid off the beginning balance of Accounts Payable.

c. Performed services for a client and received cash of $2,500.

d. Collected cash from a customer on account, $850.

e. Purchased supplies on account, $600.

f. Consulted on the interior design of a major office building and billed the client for services performed, $5,000.

g. Sold an additional 1,000 shares for $2,500 in the business.

h. Paid salaries of $2,400.

i. Sold supplies at cost to another interior designer for $110 cash.

j. Paid dividends of $1,500 to Au.

Requirements

1. Enter the remaining transactions for the month of September into the expanded accounting equation, calculating new balances after each transaction.

2. Prepare the income statement of Interiors by Donna, Inc. for the month ended September 30, 2013.

3. Prepare the statement of changes in equity of Interiors by Donna, Inc. for the month ended September 30, 2013.

4. Prepare the statement of financial position of Interiors by Donna, Inc. at September 30, 2013.

P1-3A. Prepare the income statement, statement of changes in equity, and statement of financial position (*Learning Objective 5*) 20–25 mln.

Gear Heads, Inc. restores antique automobiles. The common shares and retained earnings balances of the corporation were $20,000 and $32,000 respectively at December 31, 2012. During 2013, the corporation paid $40,000 in dividends to its shareholders. At December 31, 2013, the business's accounting records show these balances:

Accounts Receivable	$ 5,000	Cash	$ 7,000
Note Payable	25,000	Accounts Payable	2,000
Retained Earnings	?	Advertising Expense	3,000
Salary Expense	14,000	Service Revenue	72,000
Equipment	78,000	Common Shares	20,000
Insurance Expense	4,000		

Requirement

1. Prepare the following financial statements for Gear Heads, Inc.:

   a. Income statement for the year ended December 31, 2013

   b. Statement of retained earnings for the year ended December 31, 2013

   c. Statement of financial position at December 31, 2013

Quick solution:

a. Net income = $51,000
b. Ending Retained earnings = $43,000
c. Total assets = $90,000

P1-4A. Prepare the income statement and statement of financial position; identify certain financial information (*Learning Objective 5*) 25–30 min.

Presented here are the amounts of Assets, Liabilities, Shareholders' Equity, Revenues, and Expenses of The Better Body, Inc. at December 31, 2013. The items are listed in alphabetical order.

Accounts Payable	$ 15,000	Interest Expense	$ 9,000
Accounts Receivable	14,000	Land	40,000
Advertising Expense	13,000	Note Payable	65,000
Building	130,000	Property Tax Expense	3,000
Cash	16,000	Rent Expense	24,000
Common Shares	40,000	Salary Expense	71,000
Dividends	36,000	Salary Payable	2,000
Equipment	45,000	Service Revenue	185,000
Insurance Expense	1,000	Supplies	2,000

The common shares and retained earnings balances of the business were $40,000 and $97,000 respectively at December 31, 2012.

Requirements

1. Identify each amount shown as an asset, liability, or shareholders' equity.
2. Prepare the company's income statement and statement of changes in equity for the year ended December 31, 2013.
3. Prepare the company's statement of financial position at December 31, 2013.
4. Answer these questions about the company:
   a. What was the profit or loss for the year?
   b. What was the increase or decrease of retained earnings for the year?
   c. What is the amount of economic resources on December 31, 2013?
   d. What is the amount owed on December 31, 2013?

P1-5A. Error analysis and preparation of statement of financial position (*Learning Objective 5*) 20–25 min.

The IT manager of Aztec Realty, Inc. prepared the statement of financial position of the company while the accountant was ill. The statement of financial position contains numerous errors. In particular, the IT manager knew that the statement of financial position should balance, so she plugged in the retained earnings amount to achieve this balance. The retained earnings amount, however, is not correct. All other amounts are accurate, but some are out of place.

Aztec Realty, Inc.			
Balance Sheet			
Month Ended June 30, 2013			
ASSETS		**LIABILITIES**	
Cash	$ 9,000	Accounts Payable	$ 200
Rent Expense	1,000	Utilities Expense	900
Supplies Expense	350	Accounts Receivable	1,400
Salaries Payable	1,750	Notes Payable	5,700
Equipment	7,500		
		SHAREHOLDERS' EQUITY	
		Common Shares	8,000
		Supplies	800
		Retained Earnings	2,600
		Total Shareholders' Equity	11,400
		Total Liabilities &	
Total Assets	$19,600	Shareholders' Equity	$19,600

Requirement

1. Prepare a new, corrected statement of financial position for Aztec Realty, Inc.

PROBLEMS (GROUP B)

P1-1B. Transaction analysis and the calculation of net income (*Learning Objectives 4 & 5*) 20–25 min.

Don Griffin worked as an accountant at a local accounting firm for five years after graduating from university. Recently, he opened his own accounting practice, which he operates as a corporation. The name of the new entity is Griffin and Associates, Inc. Don experienced the following events during the first month of operations. Some of the events were personal and did not affect the accounting practice. Others were business transactions and should be accounted for by the business.

Apr 3	Received $20,000 cash proceeds from refinancing his house.
5	$90,000 of shares in the business were sold to Don Griffin. The cash proceeds were deposited in a new business bank account titled Griffin and Associates, Ir
7	Paid $600 cash for office supplies for the new accounting practice.
9	Purchased $4,000 of office furniture for the accounting practice and agreed to pay the vendor within three months.
10	Don sold 1,200 Mercedes shares, which he had owned for several years, receiv $22,000 cash. The cash from the sale of shares was deposited in his personal bank account.
14	A representative of a large company telephoned Don and told him of the compan intention to hire Griffin and Associates, Inc. as its accountants.
20	Finished accounting work for a client and sent the client a bill for $3,900. The client is expected to pay within two weeks.
27	Paid office rent, $1,200.
30	Paid $500 of dividends to Griffin and Associates, Inc. shareholders.

Requirements

1. Enter each transaction in the expanded accounting equation of Griffin and Associates, Inc. as needed, calculating new balances after each transaction.

2. Determine the following items:

a. Total assets

b. Total liabilities

c. Total shareholders' equity

d. Net income or net loss for April

P1-2B. Income statement and statement of financial position transactions; prepare the income statement and statement of financial position (*Learning Objectives 4 & 5*) 25–30 min.

Daiyi Gong started a renovation company called Reno by Daiyi, Inc. on November 1, 2013. The following amounts summarize the financial position of her business on November 14, 2013, after the first two weeks of operations:

Assets				= Liabilities +	Shareholders' Equity			
					Common Shares +		Retained Earnings	
Cash	+ Accounts Receivable +	Supplies	+ Equipment =	Accounts Payable +	Common Shares +	Service Revenue −	Salaries Expense −	Dividends
$1,750 +	$3,210 +		+ $24,000 =	$5,400 +	$18,020 +	$6,900 −	$1,360	

During the remainder of November, the following events occurred:

a. Gong received $6,900 as a gift and used it to buy 3,000 shares in the business.

b. Paid off the beginning balance of Accounts Payable.

c. Performed services for a client and received cash of $1,500.

d. Collected cash from a customer on account, $850.

e. Purchased supplies on account, $400.

f. Consulted on the renovation of a major office building and billed the client for services performed, $9,000.

g. Sold an additional 2,200 shares for $5,500 in the business.

h. Paid salaries of $2,550.

i. Sold supplies at cost to a renovation company for $250 cash.

j. Paid dividends of $1,200 to Gong.

Requirements

1. Enter the remaining transactions for the month of November into the expanded accounting equation, calculating new balances after each transaction.

2. Prepare the income statement of Reno by Daiyi, Inc. for the month ended November 30, 2013.

3. Prepare the statement of retained earnings of Reno by Daiyi, Inc. for the month ended November 30, 2013.

4. Prepare the balance sheet for Reno by Daiyi, Inc. at November 30, 2013.

P1-3B. Prepare the income statement, statement of changes in equity, and statement of financial position (_Learning Objective 5_) 20–25 min.

Barrett, Inc. restores antique automobiles. The common shares and retained earnings balances of the corporation were $32,000 and $28,500 respectively at December 31, 2012. During 2013, the corporation paid $35,000 in dividends to its shareholders. At December 31, 2013, the business's accounting records show these balances:

Accounts Receivable	$ 5,000	Cash	$10,000
Note Payable	16,000	Accounts Payable	2,000
Retained Earnings	?	Advertising Expense	3,500
Salary Expense	16,000	Service Revenue	70,000
Equipment	70,000	Common Shares	32,000
Insurance Expense	9,000		

Requirement

1. Prepare the following financial statements for Barrett, Inc.:

a. Income statement for the year ended December 31, 2013

b. Statement of changes in equity for the year ended December 31, 2013

c. Statement of financial position at December 31, 2013

P1-4B. **Prepare the income statement and statement of financial position; identify certain financial information (Learning Objective 5) 25–30 min.**

Presented here are the amounts of Assets, Liabilities, Shareholders' Equity, Revenues, and Expenses of Camp Out, Inc. at October 31, 2013. The items are listed in alphabetical order.

Accounts Payable..................	$ 13,000	Interest Expense	$ 7,000
Accounts Receivable..............	21,000	Land..	36,000
Advertising Expense...............	17,000	Note Payable	64,000
Building...................................	150,000	Property Tax Expense	2,500
Cash.......................................	17,000	Rent Expense	22,000
Common Shares	75,000	Salary Expense......................	71,000
Dividends	33,000	Salary Payable.......................	1,900
Equipment..............................	50,000	Service Revenue	195,000
Insurance Expense................	1,000	Supplies.................................	1,100

The common shares and retained earnings balance of the business were $75,000 and $79,700 respectively at October 31, 2012.

Requirements

1. Identify each amount shown as an asset, liability, or shareholders' equity.
2. Prepare the company's income statement and statement of changes in equity for the year ended October 31, 2013.
3. Prepare the company's statement of financial position at October 31, 2013.
4. Answer these questions about the company:
   a. What was the profit or loss for the year?
   b. What was the increase or decrease of retained earnings for the year?
   c. What is the amount of economic resources on October 31, 2013?
   d. What is the amount owed on October 31, 2013?

P1-5B. **Error analysis and preparation of statement of financial position (Learning Objective 5) 20–25 min.**

The IT manager of Right Away Realty, Inc. prepared the statement of financial position of the company while the accountant was ill. The statement of financial position contains numerous errors. In particular, the IT manager knew that the statement of financial position should balance, so she plugged in the retained earnings amount to achieve this balance. The retained earnings amount, however, is not correct. All other amounts are accurate, but some are out of place.

Right Away Realty, Inc. Balance Sheet Month Ended September 30, 2013			
ASSETS		**LIABILITIES**	
Cash	$14,000	Accounts Payable	$ 300
Rent Expense	1,600	Utilities Expense	700
Supplies Expense	100	Accounts Receivable	2,200
Salaries Payable	1,950	Notes Payable	7,000
Equipment	8,300		
		SHAREHOLDERS' EQUITY	
		Common Shares	12,000
		Supplies	600
		Retained Earnings	3,150
		Total Shareholders' Equity	15,750
		Total Liabilities &	
Total Assets	$25,950	Shareholders' Equity	$25,950

Requirement

1. Prepare a new, corrected statement of financial position for Right Away Realty, Inc.

PROBLEMS (ALTERNATES 1, 2, AND 3)

These alternative problem sets are available for your practice benefit at **www.myaccountinglab.com**

CONTINUING EXERCISE

This exercise is the first exercise in a sequence that begins an accounting cycle. The cycle is continued in Chapter 2 and completed in Chapter 3.

Graham's Yard Care, Inc. began operations and completed the following transactions during June:

Jun	1	Received $1,000 and issued 100 common shares. Deposited this amount in bank account titled Graham's Yard Care, Inc.
	3	Purchased on account a mower, $1,000, and weed whacker, $400. The equipment is expected to remain in service for four years.
	5	Purchased $20 of gas. Wrote cheque #1 from the new bank account.
	6	Performed lawn services for client on account, $200.
	8	Purchased $50 of fertilizer from the lawn store. Wrote cheque #2 from the new bank account.
	17	Completed landscaping job for client, received cash $500.
	30	Received $50 on account from June 6 sale.

Requirement

1. Analyze the effects of Graham's Yard Care, Inc.'s transactions on the accounting equation. Include these headings: Cash, Accounts Receivable, Lawn Supplies, Equipment, Accounts Payable, Common Shares, Retained Earnings, Dividends, Service Revenue, and Fuel Expense.

CONTINUING PROBLEM

This problem is the first problem in a sequence that begins an accounting cycle. The cycle is continued in Chapter 2 and completed in Chapter 3.

Mike Han recently left his job at a local pool company to open his own pool and spa maintenance business. Mike Han took all of the money he and his wife had in their personal savings account and used it to open Aqua Elite, Inc. on May 1, 2013. Presented next are the transactions for the first month of operations for Aqua Elite, Inc.:

May	1	Mike invested $15,000 cash and a used truck worth $13,500 in the business in exchange for 2,000 company shares.
	3	Paid $4,700 cash to purchase office equipment.
	7	Purchased $860 of supplies on account.
	12	Performed services for cash customers and received $850.
	15	Paid salaries of $675 to the office receptionist.
	16	Sold the company truck for $13,500.
	18	Signed a note payable for $31,000 to purchase a new truck.
	21	Performed $3,200 of services on account for a local hotel chain.
	27	Paid $500 of the amount owed from the purchase of supplies on May 7.
	30	Received $2,000 on account from credit customers.
	31	Received the utility bill for the month of May, $480. The bill is not due until the 15th of June.
	31	Paid $1,000 dividends to the shareholder, Mike Han.

Requirements

1. Enter the transactions for Aqua Elite, Inc. for the month of May into the expanded accounting equation. Calculate the ending balances at the end of May.

2. Prepare the income statement for Aqua Elite, Inc. for the first month of operations.

3. Prepare the statement of changes in equity for Aqua Elite, Inc. for the first month of operations.

4. Prepare the statement of financial position for Aqua Elite, Inc. for the first month of operations.

5. Did Mike make a wise decision leaving his job to start Aqua Elite, Inc.?

APPLY YOUR KNOWLEDGE

ETHICS IN ACTION

Case 1. Wen Bai and her husband Jung were the owners of WJ Enterprises, Inc. They applied for a small business loan, and the bank requested the most recent business financial statements. When Wen compiled the statement of financial position, she noticed that the business assets and related owner's equity were small. Accordingly, she told Jung that they should contribute some of their personal assets to the business so that the assets and equity would appear much larger and thus the bank would more likely agree to the business loan. Jung agreed that the statement of financial position would appear stronger with more assets and equity but his concern was with the income statement. The sales for the latest period were low, which resulted in a slight net loss because expenses were slightly higher than revenues. Jung reasoned that contributing assets would show a stronger statement of financial position but felt something had to be done to also improve the income statement. He then told Wen that their business could "sell" back some of the assets they had contributed and report higher sales on the income statement, which would result in net income rather than the actual net loss. Wen did not feel comfortable buying back assets from their business just to increase reported sales.

Discuss any ethical concerns you may have with Wen's proposal. Discuss any ethical concerns you may have with Jung's proposal. Do you think it is ethical for a business to "dress up" its financial statements when applying for a loan?

Case 2. Eagle Ridge, Inc. was in the final phase of completing a land development project it started earlier in the year. Eagle Ridge, Inc. had acquired 100 acres of raw land for $250,000 and then spent an additional $1,650,000 in land development costs to create a new subdivision with 200 residential lots. With a total cost of $1,900,000 and 200 lots, each lot had a cost of $9,500; however, the lots were listed for sale at $32,000 per lot. Eagle Ridge, Inc. was applying for a business loan and needed to provide current financial statements to the bank. Jill Hamilton, the company president, wanted to include the total current value of the lots, $6,400,000 (200 lots × $32,000 per lot), rather than the total cost currently listed on the statement of financial position, $1,900,000. Dave Jamison, the company accountant, told Jill that the lots were inventory and the cost principle required that they be included on the statement of financial position at the $1,900,000 rather than the fair market value. Furthermore, even though the lots were listed for sale at $32,000 each, there was no guarantee that they would actually all sell at this value, and according to the objectivity principle, the more reliable cost figure should be used for this reason, too.

Is the accountant right about recording the lots using historical cost? What alternative approaches could be used to measure the cost of assets? Should the statement of financial position for Eagle Ridge, Inc. list the lots at their total cost of $1,900,000 or their total selling price of $6,400,000? If Eagle Ridge, Inc. records the realizable value of the assets, where should this unrealized gain be reported?

KNOW YOUR BUSINESS

FINANCIAL ANALYSIS

Purpose: To help familiarize you with the financial reporting of a real company to further your understanding of the chapter material you are learning.

Each chapter will have a financial statement case that will focus on material contained in that chapter. You will be asked questions and you will then refer to MyAccountingLab where you will find the Bombardier Annual Report, Year Ended January 31, 2011. Bombardier Inc. is a Canadian company that operates in the aerospace and rail transportation industries. In aerospace, the company designs and manufactures aircraft and provides support services to the business and commercial sectors. In rail transportation, Bombardier manufactures and sells rail cars in addition to systems and support services. Use the annual report to answer these questions. As you progress through each chapter, you will gain a real understanding of actual corporate financial reporting in addition to the basic accounting concepts you are learning within each textbook chapter. This added learning experience will further reinforce your understanding of accounting.

Note that Bombardier reports in U.S. dollars, so all of your answers may be given in U.S. dollars. There is no need to convert these to Canadian dollars.

Requirements

1. Look at all the financial statements starting on page 166 of the annual report and see whether you can identify the balance sheet income statement, statement of comprehensive income and statement of cash flows. (Note that the term *consolidated* simply means combined.)

2. What was the total amount of assets Bombardier reported as of January 31, 2011? Did the total assets increase or decrease from January 31, 2010?

3. What was the total amount of revenues Bombardier reported for the year ended January 31, 2011? Did the revenues increase or decrease from the previous years presented?

4. What was the total cash flow provided from operating activities reported for Bombardier? Did this increase or decrease from January 31, 2010?

INDUSTRY ANALYSIS

Purpose: To help you understand and compare the performance of two companies in the same industry.

Go to the Bombardier Inc. annual report located in MyAccountingLab and find the Consolidated Balance Sheets on page 166. Now access the December 31, 2010 annual report for The Boeing Company. To do this from the internet, go to their webpage for the Investor Relations at http://www.boeing.com/companyoffices/financial/quarterly.htm and under annual reports go to the 2010 Annual Report. (Hint: you can search using a key term such as "annual report," which will make finding this report much easier). Their Consolidated Balance Sheet is located on page 51.

Bombardier Inc. and The Boeing Company are in similar industries, that is, the design and manufacturing of aircraft for the commercial sector. However, Boeing also designs and manufactures aircraft for the defence sector, and Bombardier designs and manufactures rail cars. To gauge a company's performance, it is often helpful to compare a company's financial data against other companies in its industry.

Requirement

1. Look at the data from the Consolidated Balance Sheets for each of the companies. Which company's shareholders have a higher percentage claim to their company's assets? To find out, divide the total shareholders' equity for each company by its total liabilities and shareholders' equity.

SMALL BUSINESS ANALYSIS

Purpose: To help you understand the importance of cash flows in the operation of a small business.

You have just received your year-end financial statements from your accountant and you notice one very disturbing item. The net income from your income statement shows $40,000! Your very first thought is "Where is it?" Then you look at your cash balance and see that it decreased $10,000 from last year to this year. You're thinking there has to be something wrong here. So you call up your accountant and ask for a meeting to discuss this obvious error. After all, how can you possibly have a positive net income and have your cash balance *decrease*?

At the meeting, the accountant lays out the financial statements in front of you and begins to explain how this would have happened. The following is a condensed income statement, statement of changes in equity, and statement of financial position.

BCS Consultants, Inc.
Income Statement
For Year Ended December 31, 2013

Revenue		$150,000
Expenses		(110,000)
Net Income		$ 40,000

BCS Consultants, Inc.
Statement of Changes in Equity
For Year Ended December 31, 2013

	Common Shares		Retained Earnings	Total
	Number of Shares	$		
Balance, December 31, 2013	—	$ 0	$ 91,000	$ 91,000
Issued Common Shares	2,000	$20,000		20,000
Net Income			40,000	40,000
Dividends			(13,000)	(13,000)
Balance, December 31, 2013	2,000	$20,000	$118,000	$138,000

BCS Consultants, Inc.
Statement of Financial Position
As of December 31, 2014 & 2013

	2014	2013
Assets:		
Cash	$ 30,000	$ 40,000
Equipment	158,000	146,000
Total Assets	$188,000	$186,000
Liabilities:		
Notes Payable—Bank	$ 50,000	$ 75,000
Shareholders' Equity:		
Common Shares	20,000	20,000
Retained Earnings	118,000	91,000
Total Shareholders' Equity	$138,000	$111,000
Total Liabilities and Shareholders' Equity	$188,000	$186,000

Requirement

1. By looking at the three financial statements, can you anticipate what the accountant is going to tell you about why the cash decreased even though you had net income for the year? What changed from 2013 to 2014? And are transactions that affect the income statement the only transactions that affect your cash balance?

WRITTEN COMMUNICATION

You just got an email from a potential new client who contacted you from your Web site. This client has indicated to you that he or she is planning to start a new business. The client would like to find out from you what different types of business organizations are available. And also, he or she is wondering exactly what role an accountant would have in the running of the client's business.

Requirement

1. Prepare an email back to this potential client addressing his or her questions about the different types of business organizations and why he or she needs to have an accountant involved in the business.

Self Check Answers
1. c 2. d 3. b 4. c 5. a 6. d 7. c 8. c 9. a 10. d

◀ Check how well you answered the Self Check questions.

SCAN THIS

CHAPTER 2

Analyzing and Recording Business Transactions

1 Define accounts and understand how they are used in accounting

2 Explain debits, credits, and the double entry system of accounting

3 Demonstrate the use of the general journal and the general ledger to record business transactions

4 Use a trial balance to prepare financial statements

ow that you know why an understanding of accounting is important to everyone, you might ask yourself "How is accounting done in the real world?" You may wonder how to determine if a transaction has occurred, and if it has, how is it recorded? Maybe you have heard that accountants use things called debits and credits, and wondered what they are. In this chapter, we will explore these questions as we learn about the process of accounting.

HOW ARE ACCOUNTS USED TO KEEP BUSINESS TRANSACTIONS ORGANIZED?

> **1** Define accounts and understand how they are used in accounting

As we discussed in Chapter 1, accounting provides useful information to various users. For the information to be useful for decision makers, it has to be detailed information, which has four qualitative characteristics: (1) understandability, (2) relevance, (3) reliability, and (4) comparability. Therefore, to facilitate the detail required, accountants will create many categories to track information in. These categories are referred to as **accounts**. We have already seen accounts in use. When recording transactions in the accounting equation in Chapter 1, we created accounts such as Cash, Equipment, and Accounts Payable.

Organizing Accounts

Numbering helps keep the accounts organized. Account numbers usually have two or more digits. The first digit indicates the type of account. Generally, if an account starts with:

- 1, it is an asset account.
- 2, it is a liability account.
- 3, it is a shareholders' equity account other than a revenue or expense account.
- 4, it is a revenue account.
- 5, it is an expense account.

Accounts that start with 6, 7, 8, or 9 are used by some businesses to record special types of accounts such as other revenues and expenses.

The remaining digits in an account number are used to specify the exact account. For example, Cash may be numbered 1010 and Accounts Receivable may be numbered 1030. A gap in numbers is usually left between the different accounts to allow for additional accounts to be added later. A listing of all of the accounts is referred to as a **chart of accounts**. The accounts are typically listed in the chart of accounts in the order that they appear in the accounting equation. Therefore, assets would be listed first, followed by the liabilities, and then the shareholders' equity accounts. Typical types of accounts for many businesses are as follows:

Assets

As described in Chapter 1, assets represent things of value that a business has. They are economic resources or properties owned by a business that will generate future benefits to the business. Most businesses use the following asset accounts:

- **Cash.** Cash typically includes the business's bank account balance, paper currency, coins, and cheques.
- **Accounts Receivable.** A business may sell goods or services in exchange for a promise of a future cash receipt. Such sales are said to be made on credit or on account. The Accounts Receivable account reflects the amounts that customers owe the business for goods or services that have already been provided. In other words, it shows how much money the company can expect to *receive* from customers in the future. Along with the Accounts Receivable account, the business will

also keep an Accounts Receivable subledger. The subledger is a group of individual accounts that track each customer's amount owing, the amounts that are paid, and any new amounts sold to these customers.

■ **Inventory.** A business may purchase merchandise for resale or purchase raw materials to produce goods as a part of business operation.

■ **Notes Receivable.** A business may sell goods or services or loan money and receive a promissory note. A note receivable is a written promise that the customer or borrower will pay a fixed amount of money by a certain date. Notes Receivable reflects the amount of the **promissory notes** that the business expects to collect in cash at a later date. Interest fees are associated with Notes Receivable; however, they are calculated and recorded separately and at a different time.

■ **Prepaid Expenses.** A business often pays certain expenses, such as rent and insurance, in advance. A prepaid expense is an asset because the prepayment provides a future benefit for the business. A separate asset account is used for each prepaid expense. Prepaid Rent and Prepaid Insurance are examples of prepaid expense accounts.

■ **Land.** The Land account is used to track of the cost of land a business owns and uses in its operations.

■ **Buildings.** The cost of a business's buildings, offices, warehouses, etc. is recorded in the Buildings account.

■ **Equipment, Furniture, and Fixtures.** A business typically has a separate asset account for each type of equipment. Examples include Computer Equipment, Office Equipment, Store Equipment, and Furniture and Fixtures.

Depending on the nature and timing of the use of assets, assets can be grouped or *classified* into different categories to help users understand the company's financial position. Assets can be grouped into two classifications: current assets and non-current assets. **Current assets** are the ones that are expected to be converted to cash, sold, or consumed either within a year or within the operating cycle. For example, cash, accounts receivable, inventory, and prepaid expenses are current assets. **Non-current assets** are those that the business will hold for more than one year or longer than the operating cycle, and depending on the nature of the assets, they may be grouped into (1) long-term investments, (2) property, plant, and equipment, and (3) intangible assets (assets such as patents and copyrights—things that are typically not physical items but still have future value for the business). Non-current assets are also sometimes referred to as long-term assets, fixed assets, or capital assets.

Liabilities

As defined in Chapter 1, liabilities are amounts owed to third parties. A business's liabilities can be summarized in categories such as the following:

■ **Accounts Payable.** A business may purchase goods or services in exchange for a promise of future payment. Such purchases are said to be made on credit or on account. The Accounts Payable account reflects how much cash the business must pay to suppliers for goods or services that have already been received.

■ **Unearned Revenue. Unearned revenue** is created when customers pay in advance or make a deposit for goods or services to be delivered in the future. At the point when cash is received, the company has an obligation to fulfill and has not earned the revenue. The rules for when revenues are earned will be discussed in Chapter 7, but it is important to note that when revenue is earned and when the cash is received do not necessarily have to happen at the same time.

- **Notes Payable.** Notes Payable represents amounts the business must pay because it signed promissory notes to borrow money or to purchase goods or services.

- **Accrued Liabilities.** An accrued liability is a liability for an expense that has been incurred but has not yet been paid. An incurred expense means that a resource has been used. For example, a company will use electricity for a month but the invoice for this will not be received until the following month. Since the electricity has been used, it has been incurred. The same is true for salaries of employees. Employees will work throughout a certain time frame and as they work, the salaries payable accrues until the employees are paid for their work. Taxes Payable, Interest Payable, and Wages Payable are also examples of accrued liability accounts.

Depending on the timing of the debt or obligation repayment, liabilities can also be grouped or *classified* into two different categories. **Current liabilities** are the ones that are expected to be paid or obligations fulfilled either within a year or within the operating cycle. For example, accounts payable, accrued liabilities, and short-term bank loans are current liabilities. **Non-current liabilities** are those expected to be paid after more than one year or at a point in time longer than the operating cycle, such as a mortgage payable. Non-current liabilities (or long-term debt) will be discussed further in later chapters.

Shareholders' Equity

As we saw in Chapter 1, the owners' claim to the assets of the business is called Shareholders' Equity. We have already discussed the different types of shareholders' equity accounts and what they're used for but they are listed here again for review.

- **Share Capital.** The share capital account represents the investment of assets, usually cash, the shareholders have invested into a business in exchange for the company's shares. A business may issue different classes of shares, for example, preferred shares and/or common shares.

- **Retained Earnings.** The Retained Earnings account tracks the cumulative earnings of the business since it began, less any dividends given to shareholders.

- **Revenues.** Increases in retained earnings (and, therefore, Shareholders' Equity) created by selling goods or services to customers are called revenues. Review the conceptual framework related to accrual-basis accounting discussed in Chapter 1. This account represents amounts *earned* by the company even if the company has not yet received payment for the goods and services provided. A business may have several revenue accounts depending on how many ways it earns its revenue.

- **Expenses.** Expenses are decreases in retained earnings (and, therefore, Shareholders' Equity) from using resources to deliver goods and services to customers. Again, based on accrual accounting, expenses are incurred when resources or services are consumed, not when they are paid. A business needs a separate account for each type of expense, such as Insurance Expense, Rent Expense, Wages Expense, and Utilities Expense. Businesses often have numerous expense accounts because many different types of costs are associated with providing goods and services to customers.

- **Dividends.** This account reflects the amount of earnings that have been distributed to the shareholders. Dividends decrease retained earnings (and, therefore, Shareholders' Equity).

WHAT ARE DEBITS, CREDITS, AND T-ACCOUNTS?

In Chapter 1, we learned that every time we entered a transaction in the accounting equation, it affected at least two accounts. In accounting, the requirement that every transaction impact at least two accounts is called **double-entry accounting**. To simplify the process of accounting, each account is broken down into two sides. This can be visualized as a large T. For each account, one side of the T will represent an increase to the account, while the other side represents a decrease. Whether it is the left side of the T or the right side that increases the account depends on the type of account and on which side of the accounting equation it can be found. Some accounts will increase on the left side and some will increase on the right side. For example, the Cash account is on the left side of the accounting equation (A = L + SE) and when Cash increases the total amount of assets increases; therefore, cash is increased on the left side of the T account. The Accounts Payable account is on the right side of the accounting equation (A = L + SE) and since total liabilities increase when accounts payable increases (if the amount that you owe a supplier increases, then the total amount that you owe to third parties increases), accounts payable is increased on the right side of its T account. In accounting terms, the left side of an account is referred to as the **debit** side. The right side of an account is referred to as the **credit** side. An example of a **T-account** is as follows:

2 Explain debits, credits, and the double entry system of accounting

Account Title	
Debit = left side Dr.	Credit = right side Cr.

Although T-accounts are not an official accounting tool, some accounting professors and accounting practitioners use them to help visualize and analyze accounts. When first learning accounting, it can be very confusing to understand why some accounts are increased with debits (on the left side) while other accounts are increased with credits (on the right side). However confusing this might be, it was designed this way for a purpose. In addition to the rule that states that assets must always equal liabilities plus shareholders' equity, another accounting rule states that in every transaction the dollar amount of debits must equal the dollar amount of credits. By requiring that the amount of debits always equals the amount of credits and having some accounts increase with debits and other accounts increase with credits, the accounting equation is automatically kept in balance. **Exhibit 2-1** shows the accounting equation with T-accounts under each type of account along with which side of the account increases it or decreases it.

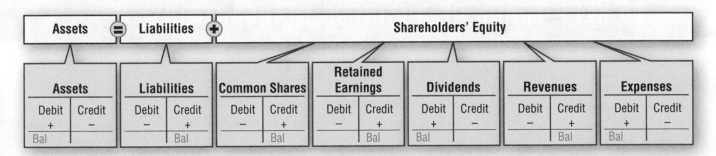

Exhibit 2-1 ▲

When trying to learn which accounts are increased with debits and which accounts are increased with credits, you may create your own memory tool, but it can be helpful to think of the acronym ADE and the acronym LCR. In the acronym ADE, the A stands for Assets, the D for Dividends, and the E for Expenses. These accounts are increased on the debit side (think of the DE in ADE). In the acronym LCR, the L stands for Liabilities, the C stands for Common Shares, and the R stands for both Revenues and Retained Earnings. These accounts are increased on the credit side (think of the CR in LCR). The rules of using T-accounts to record an increase or decrease of each type of account are shown below.

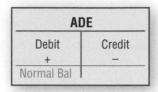
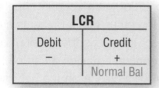

Normal Balance

The increase side is called the **normal balance** of the account, meaning normally, the account balance should be either 0 or positive on that side. The normal balance of an account is on the increase side of an account:

- Assets increase on the debit side, so the normal balance of an asset is on the debit side.

- Liabilities increase on the credit side, so the normal balance of a liability is on the credit side.

- Common Shares increase on the credit side, so the normal balance of this account is on the credit side.

- Retained Earnings increase on the credit side, so the normal balance of this account is on the credit side.

- Dividends increase on the debit side, so the normal balance of the Dividends account is on the debit side.

- Revenues increase on the credit side, so the normal balance of a revenue is on the credit side.

- Expenses increase on the debit side, so the normal balance of an expense is on the debit side.

HOW ARE THE GENERAL JOURNAL AND GENERAL LEDGER USED TO KEEP TRACK OF BUSINESS TRANSACTIONS?

 Demonstrate the use of the general journal and the general ledger to record business transactions

Although it would be possible to enter transactions directly into the T-accounts, if we were to try to do this for a real company, it would become very cumbersome and inefficient. Accountants need to enter transactions efficiently and in a timely manner. To do this, the **general journal** was created. The general journal is a chronological, or date order, record of the transactions of a business. The general journal can be compared to an individual person's diary. Like an individual person's diary, the general journal is a

ACCOUNTING IN YOUR WORLD

Jung recently purchased a train ticket online from Via Rail and used her debit card to pay for it. When she checked her bank account activity online, the bank "debited" her account when it took money out of her account to pay for the purchase. Jung read in the textbook that a debit would increase her cash account. Now Jung is really confused.

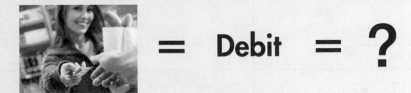

Many students feel this way when first introduced to debits and credits. It is really just a matter of perspective. You see, your bank account is an asset to you because it represents cash that is yours. However, your account is a liability to the bank because it represents money that the bank owes you. So, when the bank removes money from your account, it will debit the account to lower the liability because it no longer owes you the money. This is why it is called a *debit* card. You would actually need to credit your cash account, an asset, to show a decrease to your cash. Because you view your account as an asset and the bank views it as a liability, what you do (debit or credit) to the account to increase or decrease it will be exactly opposite of what the bank does.

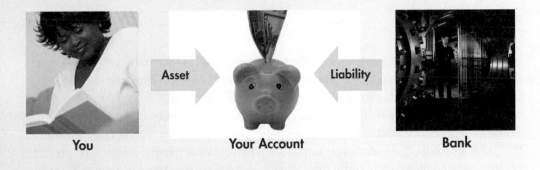

You   Your Account   Bank

place to **record** events that have affected the business. Recording a transaction in the general journal is referred to as **journalizing** the transaction. To record a journal entry:

❶ Record the date.

❷ Record the debit entry (or entries) by entering the account title and then entering the amount in the debit column.

❸ Record the credit entry (or entries) on the next line by indenting the account title and then entering the amount in the credit column.

❹ Write an explanation describing the entry.

Exhibit 2-2, Panel A, describes a transaction, and Panel B shows how this transaction is entered in the journal. The page number of the journal appears in its upper right corner.

Because the information in the general journal is organized by date and not by account, the information that it provides is not very useful. For example, if you want to find out how much cash you have at the end of the month, you may not be able to find it from the general journal, unless you add all the debits (increases) and credits

PANEL A—Illustrative Transaction:

DATE	TRANSACTION
Jan 1, 2013	Hooray Consulting, Inc., sold $10,000 of shares to Ray Hu, who was investing in the business.

PANEL B—Journal:

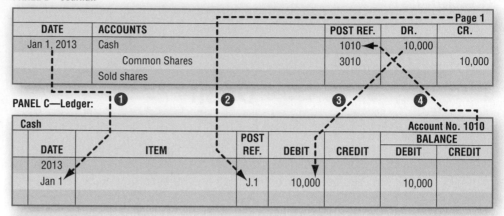

Page 1

DATE	ACCOUNTS	POST REF.	DR.	CR.
Jan 1, 2013	Cash	1010	10,000	
	Common Shares	3010		10,000
	Sold shares			

PANEL C—Ledger: ❶ ❷ ❸ ❹

Cash — Account No. 1010

DATE	ITEM	POST REF.	DEBIT	CREDIT	BALANCE DEBIT	BALANCE CREDIT
2013						
Jan 1		J.1	10,000		10,000	

Common Shares — Account No. 3010

DATE	ITEM	POST REF.	DEBIT	CREDIT	BALANCE DEBIT	BALANCE CREDIT
2013						
Jan 1		J.1		10,000		10,000

Exhibit 2-2 ▲

(decreases) in the cash account. In order to be more useful, information must be organized by account. Therefore, the **general ledger** was created. The general ledger is a grouping of all the accounts of a business with their balances in the order of the statement of financial position. It shows the amount of Assets, Liabilities, and the Shareholders' Equity accounts on a given date. Once transactions have been entered in the general journal, the information is then transferred to the general ledger. The process of transferring information from the general journal to the general ledger is called **posting**. Posting simply means copying the amounts from the journal to the ledger. Debits in the journal are posted as debits in the ledger, and credits in the journal are posted as credits in the ledger. In essence, all the increases and decreases of every account are now grouped or *posted* into each individual account, and then, we can easily figure out the balance of each account. Exhibit 2-2, Panel C, demonstrates how an entry is posted from the journal to the ledger.

The posting process demonstrated in Exhibit 2-2 includes four steps. The four steps required to post the first part of the journal entry are as follows:

Arrow ❶ Copy the transaction date from the journal to the Cash account in the ledger.

Arrow ❷ Copy the journal page number from the journal to the **Posting Reference** column in the Cash account in the ledger. "J.1" refers to Journal page 1. Since there may be more than one type of Journal, sometimes GJ1 (for General Journal page 1) or another acronym may be used to be as clear as possible about where to find the entry. This provides a reference that links the entry in the ledger back to the journal.

Arrow ❸ Copy the dollar amount of the debit, $10,000, from the journal as a debit into the Cash account in the ledger.

Arrow ❹ Copy the account number, 1010, from the Cash account in the ledger back to the Posting Reference column in the journal. This step indicates that the $10,000 debit to Cash was posted to the Cash account in the ledger.

The journal entry is posted to Cash first because this is the first account listed in the entry. Once posting to Cash is complete, repeat the process to post the entry to Common Shares. The account format that is utilized in Exhibit 2-2 is called a four-column account. The first pair of debit and credit columns contains the individual transaction amounts that have been posted from journal entries, such as the $10,000 debit. The second pair of debit and credit columns is used to show the cumulative effect on the account's balance after each entry. Posting used to be performed on a periodic basis, such as daily or weekly. However, most modern computerized accounting systems post transactions immediately after they have been entered.

Transaction Analysis

To properly record, or journalize, transactions in the general journal, it is helpful to complete a five-step process. Steps 1 through 4 analyze the transaction for the journal entry and Step 5 reflects the journalizing of the transaction and the posting from the journal into the accounts. The five-step process is as follows:

Step 1 Ask what accounts are involved? *Example*: Cash, Accounts Payable, Salary Expense, etc. If you have difficulty identifying the accounts, try to find the nouns, such as computer, equipment, or salary; otherwise, try to find the verbs, such as paid (cash) or borrowed (from a bank loan or note payable).

Step 2 For each account involved, what type of account is it? Is it an asset, liability, or one of the shareholders' equity accounts? *Example*: Cash is an asset.

Step 3 Is the account balance increasing or decreasing? *Example*: If you receive cash, then that account increases.

Step 4 Should the account be debited or credited? *Example*: Cash is an asset and it increases; increases in assets are recorded as debits.

Step 5 Record the entry and post to the accounts in the general ledger.

The five-step analysis looks like the following in chart form:

Step 1	Step 2	Step 3	Step 4	Step 5
Accounts Affected	Type	↑↓	Dr. or Cr.	Journalize entry and post to ledger

Applying Transaction Analysis

Check out how the transactions for the first month of operations for Hooray Consulting, Inc. are analyzed and recorded. *For illustration purposes, journal entries are shown being posted to T-accounts within the accounting equation. In actual practice, the journal entries would be posted to four-column accounts in the general ledger.*

1. Sale of stock. The business sold Ray Hu 1,000 common shares for $10,000.

Analysis of Transaction (1)

Step 1 What accounts are involved? The business received cash in exchange for shares so the accounts involved are Cash and Common Shares.

Step 2 What type of account is it? Cash is an asset. Common Shares is an account within shareholders' equity.

Step 3 Does the account balance increase or decrease? Because cash was received, Cash is increased. Common Shares also increased because there have been more shares issued.

Step 4 Do you debit or credit the account in the journal entry? According to the rules of debits and credits, an increase in an asset is recorded with a debit. An increase in Common Shares is recorded with a credit.

The first four steps can be summarized as follows:

1 Accounts Affected	2 Type	3 ↑↓	4 Dr. or Cr.
Cash	Asset	↑	Dr.
Common Shares	Shareholders' Equity	↑	Cr.

Step 5 Journalize and post the transactions as follows:

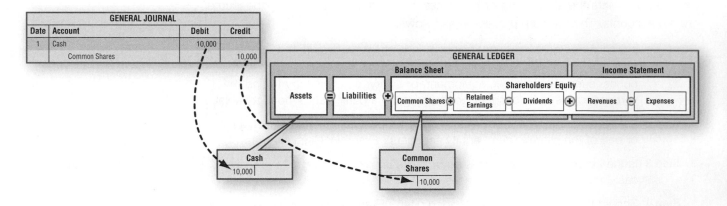

Notice that the name of the account being credited is indented in the journal. This format is a standard way to differentiate the accounts that are credited from the accounts that are debited. Also, note again that every transaction affects at least two accounts and that the total amount added to the debit side equals the total amount added to the credit side. This demonstrates double-entry accounting, which keeps the accounting equation in balance.

2. Purchase supplies on credit. Hooray Consulting purchases office supplies, agreeing to pay $350 within 30 days.

Analysis of Transaction (2)

Step 1 The business received supplies in exchange for a promise to pay cash to the supplier next month. The accounts involved in the transaction are Supplies and Accounts Payable.

Step 2 Supplies is an asset; Accounts Payable is a liability.

Step 3 The asset Supplies is increased. The liability Accounts Payable is increased because the business owes more than it did before this transaction.

Step 4 An increase in the asset Supplies is a debit; an increase in the liability Accounts Payable is a credit.

1 Accounts Affected	2 Type	3 ↑↓	4 Dr. or Cr.
Supplies	Asset	↑	Dr.
Accounts Payable	Liability	↑	Cr.

Step 5 Journalize and post the transaction as follows:

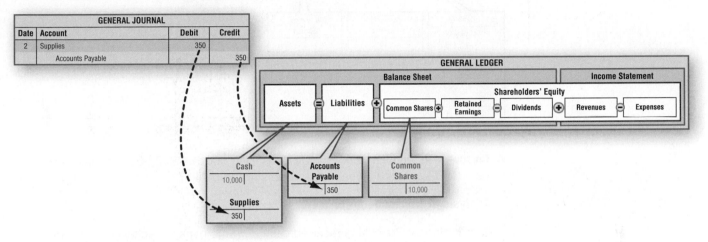

3. **Purchase equipment for cash.** The business purchases equipment, paying cash of $4,000.

Analysis of Transaction (3)

Step 1 The business received equipment in exchange for cash paid to the equipment manufacturing company. The accounts involved in the transaction are Equipment and Cash.

Step 2 Equipment and Cash are both assets.

Step 3 The asset Equipment is increased. The asset Cash is decreased because a cheque was written to pay for the equipment.

Step 4 An increase in the asset Equipment is a debit; a decrease in the asset Cash is a credit.

1 Accounts Affected	2 Type	3 ↑↓	4 Dr. or Cr.
Equipment	Asset	↑	Dr.
Cash	Asset	↓	Cr.

Step 5 Journalize and post the transaction as follows:

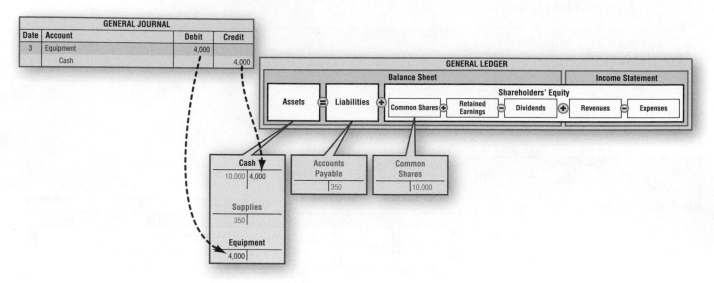

4. Borrow cash from the bank. Hooray Consulting borrows $12,000 cash from the bank and signs a two-year note payable to the bank.

Analysis of Transaction (4)

Step 1 Hooray Consulting received cash from the bank in exchange for a signed note agreeing to pay the cash back in two years. The accounts involved in the transaction are Cash and Notes Payable.

Step 2 Cash is an asset; Notes Payable is a liability.

Step 3 The asset Cash is increased. The liability Notes Payable is also increased because it represents an obligation owed to the bank.

Step 4 An increase in the asset Cash is a debit; an increase in the liability Notes Payable is a credit.

1 Accounts Affected	2 Type	3 ↑↓	4 Dr. or Cr.
Cash	Asset	↑	Dr.
Notes Payable	Liability	↑	Cr.

Step 5 Journalize and post the transaction as follows:

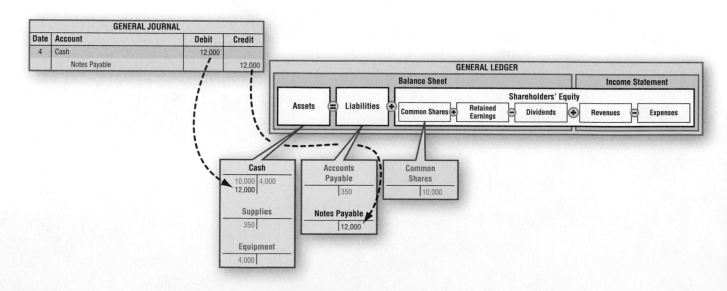

5. Provide services for cash. Hooray collects $1,200 of cash for services provided.

Analysis of Transaction (5)

Step 1 The business received cash in exchange for computer consulting services. The accounts involved in the transaction are Cash and Service Revenue.

Step 2 Cash is an asset; Service Revenue is a revenue.

Step 3 The asset Cash is increased. The revenue Service Revenue is increased also because the business has earned revenue by providing services.

Step 4 An increase in the asset Cash is a debit; an increase in the revenue, Service Revenue, is a credit.

1 Accounts Affected	2 Type	3 ↑↓	4 Dr. or Cr.
Cash	Asset	↑	Dr.
Service Revenue	Revenue	↑	Cr.

Step 5 Journalize and post the transaction as follows:

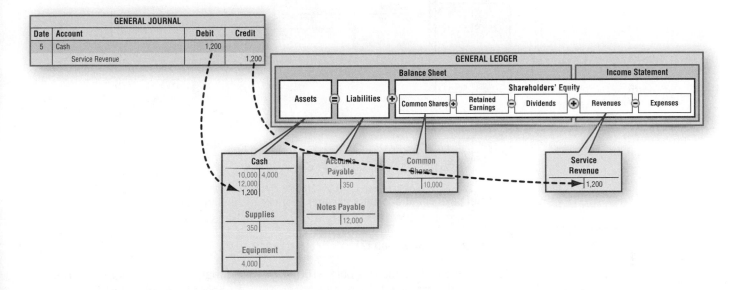

6. Provide services on credit. Hooray Consulting performs $1,900 of services on account.

Analysis of Transaction (6)

Step 1 Hooray Consulting received promises from customers to send cash next month in exchange for consulting services provided. Again, the business *earned* this money, although it has not received it yet. The accounts involved in the transaction are Accounts Receivable and Service Revenue.

Step 2 Accounts Receivable is an asset; Service Revenue is a revenue.

Step 3 The asset Accounts Receivable and the revenue Service Revenue are both increased.

Step 4 An increase in the asset Accounts Receivable is a debit; an increase in the revenue Service Revenue is a credit.

1 Accounts Affected	2 Type	3 ↑↓	4 Dr. or Cr.
Accounts Receivable	Asset	↑	Dr.
Service Revenue	Revenue	↑	Cr.

Step 5 Journalize and post the transaction as follows:

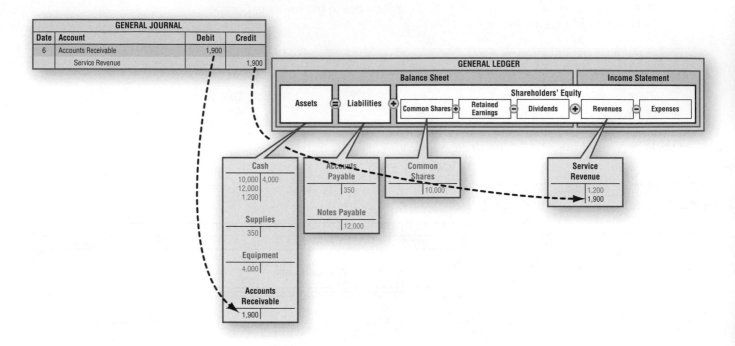

GENERAL JOURNAL			
Date	Account	Debit	Credit
6	Accounts Receivable	1,900	
	Service Revenue		1,900

7. Partial payment of accounts payable. Hooray Consulting pays $150 to the store where it purchased $350 worth of supplies in Transaction (2).

Analysis of Transaction (7)

Step 1 Hooray Consulting paid $150 of the $350 that it owed to a supplier. The accounts involved in the transaction are Accounts Payable and Cash.

Step 2 Accounts Payable is a liability; Cash is an asset.

Step 3 The liability Accounts Payable is decreased because in total we now owe less. The asset Cash is also decreased.

Step 4 A decrease in the liability Accounts Payable is a debit; a decrease in the asset Cash is a credit.

1 Accounts Affected	2 Type	3 ↑↓	4 Dr. or Cr.
Accounts Payable	Liability	↓	Dr.
Cash	Asset	↓	Cr.

Step 5 Journalize and post the transaction as follows:

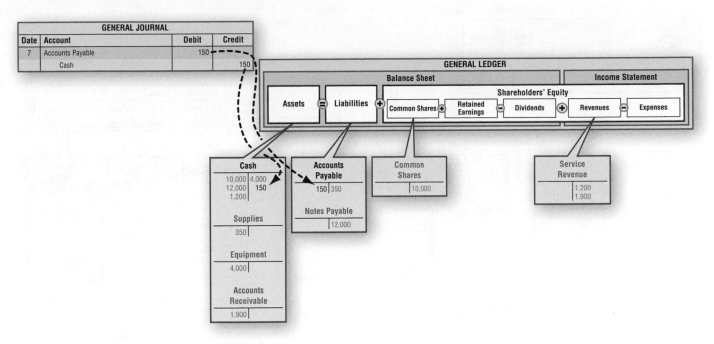

8. **Payment of expenses.** During the month, Hooray Consulting paid cash of $1,700 for expenses incurred such as wages ($600), building rent ($900), and utilities ($200).

Analysis of Transaction (8)

Step 1 The business paid $1,700 in exchange for employee services, the use of the building, and for utilities consumed as part of operating the business. The accounts involved in the transaction are Wages Expense, Rent Expense, Utilities Expense, and Cash. (This will be the first journal entry that we will see that has more than two accounts involved in the entry.)

Step 2 Wages Expense, Rent Expense, and Utilities Expense are expenses; Cash is an asset.

Step 3 The expense accounts are increased (more resources have been used so the total expenses increases). The asset Cash is decreased.

Step 4 An increase in an expense is a debit; a decrease in the asset Cash is a credit.

1 Accounts Affected	2 Type	3 ↑↓	4 Dr. or Cr.
Wages Expense	Expense	↑	Dr.
Rent Expense	Expense	↑	Dr.
Utilities Expense	Expense	↑	Dr.
Cash	Asset	↓	Cr.

Step 5 Journalize and post the transaction as follows:

GENERAL JOURNAL

Date	Account	Debit	Credit
8	Wages Expense	600	
	Rent Expense	900	
	Utilities Expense	200	
	Cash		1,700

GENERAL LEDGER

Balance Sheet

Assets = Liabilities +

Shareholders' Equity

Common Shares + Retained Earnings – Dividends +

Income Statement

Revenues = Expenses

Cash

10,000	4,000
12,000	150
1,200	1,700

Supplies

350

Equipment

4,000

Accounts Receivable

1,900

Accounts Payable

| 150 | 350 |

Notes Payable

12,000

Common Shares

10,000

Service Revenue

| 1,200 |
| 1,900 |

Wages Expense

600

Rent Expense

900

Utilities Expense

200

As we can see by this entry, it is possible to have more than two accounts utilized in an entry. This is referred to as a **compound journal entry**. Note that the total amount of debits must still equal the total amount of credits.

9. Cash dividends. Hooray Consulting pays $500 of cash dividends to Ray Hu, the shareholder.

Analysis of Transaction (9)

Step 1 The shareholder received cash dividends because the business has distributed some of the accumulated earnings of the business to the owners. The business reduced the shareholders' equity interest because of dividends paid to the shareholder. The accounts involved in the transaction are Dividends and Cash.

Step 2 Dividends is an account within shareholders' equity and Cash is an asset.

Step 3 The Dividends account is increased because the amount of money distributed to the shareholder increased. The asset Cash is decreased.

Step 4 An increase in Dividends is a debit; a decrease in the asset Cash is a credit.

1 **Accounts Affected**	2 **Type**	3 ↑↓	4 **Dr. or Cr.**
Dividends	Shareholders' Equity	↑	Dr.
Cash	Asset	↓	Cr.

Step 5 Journalize and post the transaction as follows:

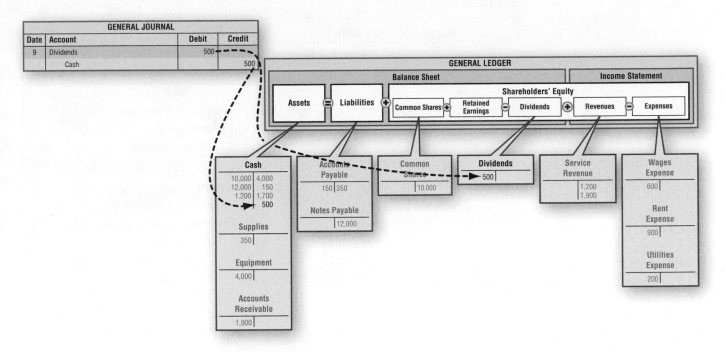

DECISION GUIDELINES

Decision	Guideline	Analyze
How do I know if an event should be entered into a company's accounting records?	Examine the effect of the event on the company's accounting equation.	If the event increases or decreases the assets, liabilities, or shareholders' equity of the business, it represents a transaction that should be recorded in the company's accounting records. If the event doesn't impact the assets, liabilities, or shareholders' equity of the company, then a recordable transaction has not occurred.

CRITICAL THINKING

Take a minute to think about the impact of the following independent cases on each of the Assets, Liabilities, and Shareholders' Equity accounts. Should each of the events be entered into a company's accounting records?

- Ordered a computer system costing $12,000, which will be delivered by the vendor early next month.
- Received a deposit of $2,000 from a customer, for a service to be provided next month.
- Signed a contract of $5,000 with a customer for a service to be provided next month.
- Received a shipment of supplies costing $500. The payment will be made by the end of the month.

Solution:

	Assets	Liabilities	Shareholders' Equity	Entry in Accounting Record
			Impact on Accounts	
1.	No	No	No	No Entry—the item was ordered but not paid for, so cash is not affected and the item has not been used yet, so no expense has been incurred.
2.	+ 2,000	+ 2,000	No	Yes: Cash (Dr); Unearned Revenue (Cr)
3.	No	No	No	No Entry—the contract was signed, but no cash was received and the business has not earned the revenues yet because it has not actually done the work.
4.	+ 500	+ 500	No	Yes: Supplies (Dr); Accounts Payable (Cr)

Balancing the T-Accounts

After the transactions are recorded and posted to the T-accounts, you will calculate each account's **balance**. The balance is the difference between the account's total debits and its total credits. Every account has a balance as shown as "Bal" in the following T-account:

Cash			1010
(1) Bal	0	(3)	300
(2)	1,000		
(4) Bal	700		

❶ The beginning balance for the current accounting period is the ending balance brought forward from the previous period. In this example, the business is new, so its beginning balance is $0.

❷ If, for example, the business receives $1,000 from the sale of shares during the first accounting period, this transaction will show up as a debit to the Cash account.

❸ If the company then pays $300 cash for supplies purchased, the amount will be entered on the credit side of the account.

❹ Because the company just started, this account had a beginning debit balance of $0. Add increases of $1,000 that appear on the debit side, and subtract decreases of $300 that appear on the credit side. The resulting ending balance of Cash is $700. The Cash account normally has a debit balance because debits increase this account.

A horizontal line separates the transaction amounts from the account balance at the end of an accounting period. The "Bal 700" under the horizontal line shows that the balance in Cash at the end of the accounting period was $700. In the next accounting period, this balance will be the new beginning balance and will change as the business receives more cash and pays out more cash.

If an account's total debits are more than its total credits, then that account has a debit balance. If an account's total credits are more than its total debits, then that account has a credit balance. The ending balance of any T-account can be found in the same way that we just did for the Cash account.

The ending balances for Hooray Consulting would be as follows:

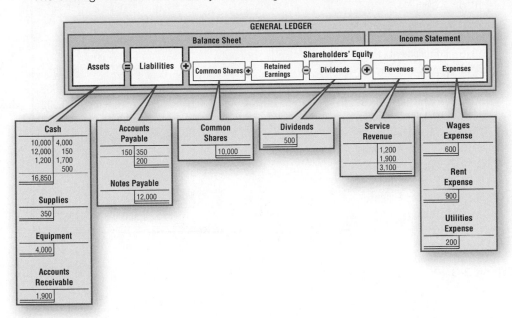

HOW IS A TRIAL BALANCE PREPARED, AND WHAT IS IT USED FOR?

Once transactions have been recorded in the journal and posted to accounts in the ledger, a **trial balance** is prepared. The first step in preparing a trial balance is to complete the heading. Similar to the financial statements that were prepared in Chapter 1, the heading should show the company name, the statement name, and the period covered by the statement. Next, the account number and name of each account are entered into the first two columns of the trial balance in the order that the account appears in the general ledger. Then, two columns are created labelled "debit" and "credit" and the balance of each account is entered into the correct column. Finally, the debit and credit columns are totalled. As was done when preparing the financial statements in Chapter 1, the first and last amount in each column has a dollar sign placed before it and the last amounts in both columns are double underlined. It should be noted that the trial balance is not an "official" financial statement. Its purpose is to summarize all account balances to be certain that total debits equal total credits after the entries have been journalized and posted. A trial balance can be prepared at any time, but is most commonly done at the end of the **accounting period**. An accounting period is usually defined as a month, a quarter, or a year, etc. **Exhibit 2-3** shows the trial balance for Hooray Consulting, Inc. after all transactions have been journalized and posted for January 2013.

4 ▶ Use a trial balance to prepare financial statements

		Hooray Consulting, Inc. Trial Balance January 31, 2013		
ACCT #	**ACCOUNT**		**DEBIT**	**CREDIT**
1010	Cash		$16,850	
1020	Accounts Receivable		1,900	
1030	Supplies		350	
1040	Equipment		4,000	
2010	Accounts Payable			$ 200
2050	Notes Payable			12,000
3010	Common Shares			10,000
3030	Retained Earnings			0
3040	Dividends		500	
4010	Service Revenues			3,100
5010	Wages Expense		900	
5020	Rent Expense		600	
5030	Utilities Expense		200	
	Total		$25,300	$25,300

Exhibit 2-3 ▲

CONCEPT CHECK

Jung just completed a problem that was assigned in her accounting class. She told Alan, one of her classmates, that she was confident that she did the problem correctly because the debits equal the credits on the trial balance. According to Alan, just because the debits equal the credits on the trial balance does not mean that everything was done correctly. Who is right, Jung or Alan?

Answer:

Alan is correct. The following are some of the errors that can occur and yet the trial balance will still be in balance:

■ A transaction can be recorded for the wrong amount in a journal entry.

■ An entire journal entry can be recorded twice, or not recorded at all.

■ The wrong accounts can be debited or credited in a journal entry. For example, when recording a payment on an account payable it is possible to debit accounts receivable instead of accounts payable.

Correcting Errors

If an error has occurred, the steps required to correct it depends on the type of error that was made. If a journal entry has been made to the wrong accounts or for the wrong amount, it is easiest to reverse, or undo, the incorrect entry. A new entry should then be prepared that contains the correct accounts or amount. To correct an entry that has been made twice, one of the entries should be reversed. If an entry was erroneously omitted, it simply needs to be entered.

If the trial balance does not balance, you will need to check all entries and postings to find the errors and correct them. Otherwise, the financial statements are not accurate. Three frequent errors are (1) transposition error, where two digits are reversed or transposed, (2) adding or dropping a zero (0), and (3) entering the amount in the wrong column (for example the debit column instead of the credit column). If you only make one of the errors, then there are a couple of things that you can do to help you identify the error. First, take the difference between the total debits and credits. Second, divide the difference by 9. If the number can be divided evenly, then there is a possibility of a transposition error or an adding/dropping zero error.

Transposition Error:	$530 - 350 = 180$	$180 \div 9 = 20$
Adding/Dropping "0" Error:	$5,000 - 500 = 4,500$	$4,500 \div 9 = 500$

If this does not help you identify the error, then once again take the difference between the total debits and credits. Instead of dividing the difference by 9, divide the difference by 2. Check for this number in the debit column and credit column to ensure the number is entered in the proper column. For example, if Utilities Expense of $200 were incorrectly entered in the credit column, then the total debit balance would be $25,100, and the total credit balance would be $25,500.

$25,500 - $25,100 = 400	$400 \div 2 - 200

CRITICAL THINKING

Take a minute to think about the impact of the following errors on the trial balance. What are the correct debit and credit balances? Does each error change the overall debit and credit balance? What is the impact on each of the Assets, Liabilities, and Shareholders' Equity accounts due to the errors?

Mehta Company's trial balance shows $116,000 on both the debit and credit sides. Mehta's accountant found the following three mistakes:

1. Cash dividends of $2,000 were incorrectly recorded as salary expense.

2. A $3,000 deposit from a customer for services to be delivered in the following month was incorrectly recorded as revenue.

3. Cash paid for equipment of $1,000 was incorrectly recorded as purchase on account.

Solution:

Corrections needed:	DR	CR		Impact on Accounts:		
				Assets	Liabilities	SE
Dividends	$2,000					+2000
Salary Expense		$2,000				−2000
Revenue	$3,000					−3000
Unearned Revenue		$3,000			+3000	
Accounts Payable	$1,000				−1000	
Cash		$1,000		−1000		

Only the third error will affect the total debits and credits. Let's assume that the trial balance (before the corrections are made) appeared as follows in the box on the left. If we now make the corrections to the balances of the accounts, we will see that the totals of the debits and the credits in the box on the right change by only $1,000.

	DR	CR
Cash	$12,000	
A/P		$6,000
Unearned Revenue		7,000
Revenue		12,000
Salary Expense	9,000	
Dividends	4,000	
Total	$25,000	$25,000

	DR	CR
Cash	$11,000	
A/P		$5,000
Unearned Revenue		10,000
Revenue		9,000
Salary Expense	7,000	
Dividends	6,000	
Total	$24,000	$24,000

DECISION GUIDELINES

Decision

As the manager of a department, I am responsible for the budget for the department and for evaluating how well the department has performed. When looking at the financial statements for my department, some of the numbers do not feel right and I'm wondering if something was perhaps recorded incorrectly (for example, perhaps someone else's expenses were recorded in my department's records by mistake). I need to check the detail of these accounts that do not seem right. Where can I find more detail?

Guideline

Review the trial balance or the general ledger.

Analyze

The trial balance is a summary of all of a company's accounts with their respective balances on a given day. The general ledger provides the detail of all of the transactions that have impacted an account along with a running balance of the account. Having quick access to the account balances often allows managers and owners to make better decisions.

Preparation of Financial Statements

After completing the trial balance, you can use it to prepare the financial statements because it shows all of the accounts with their balances. First, set up the financial statements as we did in Chapter 1, starting with the titles to the financial statements. Now, using the account balances from the trial balance, insert the account names and their balances into the financial statements, starting with the income statement, then the statement of changes in equity, and finishing with the statement of financial position. Make sure the statement of financial position is in balance! That is, total assets equal total liabilities plus shareholders' equity.

Exhibit 2-4 shows the income statement, statement of changes in equity, and statement of financial position for Hooray Consulting, Inc. at January 31, 2013. You can see once again how the information flows from one statement to another.

These statements look the same as they did in Chapter 1, except now on the income statement we see detailed information for revenues and expenses. Also, notice that the income statement now has two columns. Many students assume, erroneously, that these columns represent debits and credits as they did on the trial balance. Debits and

Hooray Consulting, Inc.
Income Statement
Month Ended January 31, 2013

Revenue:		
Service Revenues		$3,100
Expenses:		
Wages Expense	$900	
Rent Expense	600	
Utilities Expense	200	
Total Expenses		1,700
Net Income		$1,400

Hooray Consulting, Inc.
Statement of Changes in Equity
Month Ended January 31, 2013

	Common Shares		Retained Earnings	Total
	Number of Shares	$		
Balance, January 1, 2013	—	$ 0	$ 0	$ 0
Issued Common Shares	1,000	$10,000		10,000
Net Income			$1,400	1,400
Dividends			(500)	(500)
Balance, January 31, 2013	1,000	$10,000	$ 900	$10,900

Hooray Consulting, Inc.
Statement of Financial Position
As of January 31, 2013

ASSETS		LIABILITIES	
Cash	$16,850	Accounts Payable	$ 200
Accounts Receivable	1,900	Note Payable	12,000
Supplies	350	Total Liabilities	12,200
Equipment	4,000		
		SHAREHOLDERS' EQUITY	
		Common Shares	10,000
		Retained Earnings	900
		Total Shareholders' Equity	10,900
		Total Liabilities &	
Total Assets	$23,100	Shareholders' Equity	$23,100

Exhibit 2-4 ▲

credits are used to *record* increases and decreases of accounts due to the business transaction. Financial statements are used to *report* the balance of each account. On financial statements, the company reports its performance for the period and its financial position at the end of the period. Columns are used to make the statement more organized and easier to read; they are not used to signify debits and credits.

DECISION GUIDELINES

Decision	**Guideline**	**Analyze**
I am considering changing the companies that I'm invested in for my pension. Where do I find feedback on the performance of the companies in order to decide where best to invest my funds?	A company's financial statements will provide feedback regarding the performance of the company.	The income statement reflects how profitable a business has been for a specified period of time. The statement of changes in equity shows the amount of the share capital, the retained earnings, including the earnings that have been distributed to the shareholders, and the changes to these accounts during the time period. The statement of financial position shows the assets that a business owns, the liabilities it owes, and owners' claims on the business on a given date. In other words, it shows what assets the business has and who has rights to those assets.

The process of analyzing transactions, entering them into the journal, posting them to the ledger, preparing a trial balance, and preparing financial statements is only a part of what is called the **accounting cycle**. This accounting cycle is completed by a business for every accounting period and then it is repeated for the next accounting period, and the next, and the next, and so on. Shown next is a visual representation of the accounting cycle:

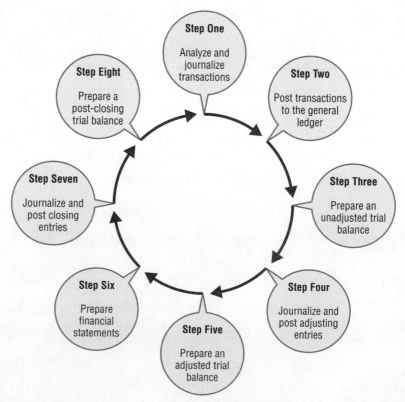

In the next chapter, you will learn the remaining steps in the accounting cycle, which includes preparing adjusting and closing entries.

FOCUS ON USERS

Concept	User	Why is this Important to this User?
Recording and Posting Transactions		Bookkeepers need to understand the process of accounting to be able to complete their jobs. The analysis of transactions is an important element of what they do. Even in a computerized environment it is important to understand the process because if something goes wrong technically, you need to be able to continue, fix the problem, and understand any hidden issues.
		Managers need to understand the process of accounting particularly for internal auditing and control purposes. For example, management needs to be able to verify the accuracy of what is recorded to be able to have confidence in what the financial statements are presenting.
		Regulators are interested in the ways in which transactions are recorded and the impact of the choices made in recording transactions on the financial statements to make any necessary changes to regulations and guidelines.
Trial Balance		A bookkeeper will use the trial balance as a tool to double-check that the transactions in the general journal have been recorded properly. A balanced trial balance does not guarantee that the transactions are error-free, but it does provide a check-point where the accounting department can assess the transactions prior to creating the financial statements.

DEMO DOC

Debit/Credit Transaction Analysis

On June 1, 2013, Jean Dion opened PaintPro, Inc., a company that provides residential and commercial painting services. During the month of June, the business incurred the following transactions:

a. To begin operations, the business sold Jean 1,000 shares for $8,000. The business received the cash from the sale and gave Jean an ownership interest.

b. Purchased equipment for $4,800 on account.

c. Purchased office supplies for $500 cash.

d. Performed $1,600 of services for a customer on account.

e. Paid $2,000 cash toward the equipment purchased on account in Transaction b.

f. Received $2,300 in cash for services provided to a new customer.

g. Paid $350 cash to repair equipment.

h. Paid $1,150 cash in salary expense.

MyAccountingLab

Visit MyAccountingLab at www. myaccountinglab.com to watch animated versions of these Demo Docs.

L.O.

i. Received $700 cash from customers on account.

j. Paid $1,000 of dividends to its only shareholder, Jean Dion.

REQUIREMENTS

❶ **Create blank T-accounts for the following accounts:** Cash, 1010; Accounts Receivable, 1020; Supplies, 1030; Equipment, 1040; Accounts Payable, 2010; Common Shares, 3010; Dividends, 3020; Service Revenue, 4010; Salary Expense, 5010; and Repairs Expense, 5020.

❷ **Journalize the transactions and show how they are posted in T-accounts.**

❸ **Total all the T-accounts to determine their balances at the end of the month.**

Demo Doc Solutions

Requirement ❶

Create blank T-accounts for the following accounts:

Cash, 1010; Accounts Receivable, 1020; Supplies, 1030; Equipment, 1040; Accounts Payable, 2010; Common Shares, 3010; Dividends, 3020; Service Revenue, 4010; Salary Expense, 5010; and Repairs Expense, 5020.

Part 1	Part 2	Part 3	Demo Doc Complete

Opening a T-account simply means drawing a blank account (the T) and putting the account title (and the account number, if used) on top. To help find the accounts later, they are usually organized into assets, liabilities, shareholders' equity, revenue, and expenses (in that order). Note that the account numbers also follow this order.

Draw empty T-accounts for every account listed in the question.

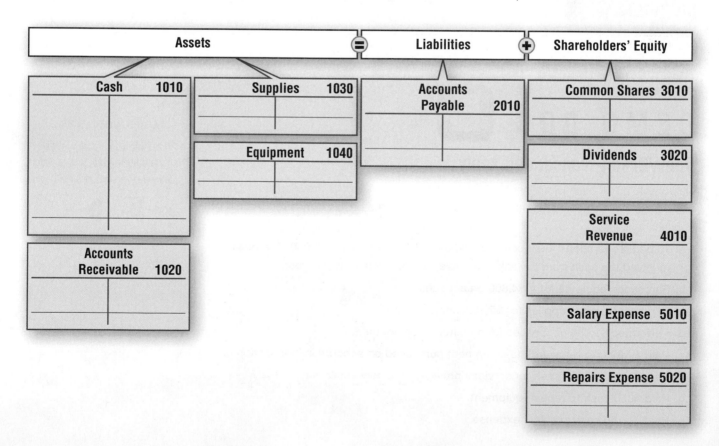

Requirement ❷

Journalize the transactions and show how they are posted in T-accounts.

Part 1	**Part 2**	Part 3	Demo Doc Complete

a. To begin operations, the business sold Jean 1,000 shares for $8,000. The business received the cash from the sale and gave Jean an ownership interest.

Remember the transaction analysis steps listed earlier in the chapter. First, we must determine which accounts are affected.

The business received $8,000 cash when it sold Jean 1,000 shares. In exchange, Jean received an equity interest in the business. So, the accounts involved are Cash and Common Shares.

The next step is to determine what type of accounts they are. Cash is an asset, while Common Shares is part of shareholders' equity.

The next step is to determine whether these accounts increased or decreased. From *the business's* point of view, Cash (an asset) increased. Common Shares (equity) also increased.

Now we must determine whether these accounts should be debited or credited. According to the rules of debits and credits, an increase in assets is a debit, while an increase in common shares (equity) is a credit.

So, Cash (an asset) increases, which is a debit. Common Shares (equity) also increases, which is a credit.

1 Accounts Affected	2 Type	3 ↑↓	4 Dr. or Cr.
Cash	Asset	↑	Dr.
Common Shares	Shareholders' Equity	↑	Cr.

The journal entry would be as follows:

DATE	ACCOUNTS	POST REF.	DR.	CR.
a.	Cash		8,000	
	Common Shares			8,000
	Sold shares			

Note that the total dollar amounts of debits will equal the total dollar amounts of credits. Remember to use the transaction letters for references. This will help when we post this entry to the T-accounts.

Posting to the T-accounts is the last step in transaction analysis.

To post the transaction to the T-accounts, simply transfer the amount of each debit to its correct account as a debit (left side) entry, and transfer the amount of each credit to its correct account as a credit (right side) entry.

For this transaction, a debit of $8,000 to Cash means that we enter $8,000 on the left side of the Cash T-account. A credit of $8,000 to Common Shares means that we enter $8,000 on the right side of the Common Shares T-account:

Cash	1010		Common Shares	3010
(a) 8,000			(a) 8,000	

b. Purchased equipment for $4,800 on account.

Because it is a new transaction, we perform the transaction analysis steps again.

The business received equipment in exchange for a promise to pay for the cost ($4,800) at a future date. So the accounts involved in the transaction are Equipment and Accounts Payable.

Equipment is an asset, and Accounts Payable is a liability. Equipment (an asset) increased. Accounts Payable (a liability) also increased.

According to the debit and credit rules, an increase in assets is a debit, while an increase in liabilities is a credit.

So, Equipment (an asset) increases, which is a debit. Accounts Payable (a liability) also increases, which is a credit.

1 Accounts Affected	2 Type	3 ↑↓	4 Dr. or Cr.
Equipment	Asset	↑	Dr.
Accounts Payable	Liability	↑	Cr.

The journal entry would be as follows:

DATE	ACCOUNTS	POST REF.	DR.	CR.
b.	Equipment		4,800	
	Accounts Payable			4,800
	Purchased equipment on account.			

We enter $4,800 on the debit (left) side of the Equipment T-account and $4,800 on the credit (right) side of the Accounts Payable T-account.

Equipment	1040		Accounts Payable	2010
(b)	4,800		(b)	4,800

c. Purchased office supplies for $500 cash.

The business purchased supplies in exchange for cash ($500). The accounts involved in the transaction are Supplies and Cash.

Supplies and Cash are both assets. Supplies (an asset) increased. Cash (an asset) decreased.

An increase in assets is a debit, while a decrease in assets is a credit.

So, Supplies (an asset) increases, which is a debit. Cash (an asset) decreases, which is a credit.

1 Accounts Affected	2 Type	3 ↑↓	4 Dr. or Cr.
Supplies	Asset	↑	Dr.
Cash	Asset	↓	Cr.

The journal entry would be as follows:

DATE	ACCOUNTS	POST REF.	DR.	CR.
c.	Supplies		500	
	Cash			500
	Purchased supplies for cash.			

We enter $500 on the debit (left) side of the Supplies T-account and $500 on the credit (right) side of the Cash T-account.

Cash		1010
(a)	8,000	(c) 500

Supplies	1030
(c) 500	

d. Performed $1,600 of services for a customer on account.

The business received promises from customers to send cash ($1,600) next month in exchange for painting services rendered. So the accounts involved in the transaction are Accounts Receivable and Service Revenue.

Accounts Receivable is an asset and Service Revenue is a revenue. Accounts Receivable (an asset) increased. Service Revenue (revenue) also increased.

An increase in assets is a debit, while an increase in a revenue is a credit.

So, Accounts Receivable (an asset) increases, which is a debit. Service Revenue (revenue) increases, which is a credit.

1 Accounts Affected	2 Type	3 ↑↓	4 Dr. or Cr.
Accounts Receivable	Asset	↑	Dr.
Service Revenue	Revenue	↑	Cr.

The journal entry is as follows:

DATE	ACCOUNTS	POST REF.	DR.	CR.
d.	Accounts Receivable		1,600	
	Service Revenue			1,600
	Performed services on account.			

We enter $1,600 on the debit (left) side of the Accounts Receivable T-account and $1,600 on the credit (right) side of the Service Revenue T-account.

Accounts Receivable 1020	
(d) 1,600	

Service Revenue	4010
	(d) 1,600

e. Paid $2,000 cash toward the equipment purchased on account in Transaction b.

The business paid *some* of the money that was owed on the purchase of equipment in Transaction b. The accounts involved in the transaction are Accounts Payable and Cash.

Accounts Payable is a liability, and Cash is an asset. Accounts Payable (a liability) decreased. Cash (an asset) also decreased.

Remember, the Accounts Payable account is the total amount owed to creditors to which the business will have to make payments in the future (a liability). When the business makes these payments to the creditors, the amount of this account decreases, because the business now owes less (in this case, it reduces from $4,800—in Transaction b—to $2,800).

A decrease in liabilities is a debit, while a decrease in assets is a credit.

So, Accounts Payable (a liability) decreases, which is a debit. Cash (an asset) decreases, which is a credit.

1 Accounts Affected	2 Type	3 ↑↓	4 Dr. or Cr.
Accounts Payable	Liability	↓	Dr.
Cash	Asset	↓	Cr.

The journal entry is as follows:

DATE	ACCOUNTS	POST REF.	DR.	CR.
e.	Accounts Payable		2,000	
	Cash			2,000
	Made a partial payment on account.			

We enter $2,000 on the debit (left) side of the Accounts Payable T-account and $2,000 on the credit (right) side of the Cash T-account.

Cash		1010		Accounts Payable		2010
(a)	8,000	(c) 500		(e) 2,000	(b)	4,800
		(e) 2,000				

f. Received $2,300 in cash for services provided to a new customer.

The business received cash ($2,300) in exchange for painting services rendered to a client. The accounts involved in the transaction are Cash and Service Revenue.

Cash is an asset, and Service Revenue is a revenue. Cash (an asset) increased. Service Revenue (revenue) also increased.

An increase in assets is a debit, while an increase in a revenue is a credit.

So, Cash (an asset) increases, which is a debit. Service Revenue (revenue) increases, which is a credit.

1 Accounts Affected	2 Type	3 ↑↓	4 Dr. or Cr.
Cash	Asset	↑	Dr.
Service Revenue	Revenue	↑	Cr.

The journal entry is as follows:

DATE	ACCOUNTS	POST REF.	DR.	CR.
f.	Cash		2,300	
	Service Revenue			2,300
	Received cash for services performed.			

We enter $2,300 on the debit (left) side of the Cash T-account and $2,300 on the credit (right) side of the Service Revenue T-account.

Cash		1010		Service Revenue		4010
(a)	8,000	(c) 500			(d)	1,600
(f)	2,300	(e) 2,000			(f)	2,300

Notice how we keep adding onto the T-accounts. The values from previous transactions are already in place.

g. Paid $350 cash to repair equipment.

The business paid $350 cash to repair equipment. Because the benefit of the repairs has already been used, the repairs are recorded as Repairs Expense. Because the repairs were paid in cash, the Cash account is also involved.

Repairs Expense is an expense and Cash is an asset. Repairs Expense (an expense) increased. Cash (an asset) decreased.

An increase in expenses is a debit, while a decrease in an asset is a credit.

So, Repairs Expense (an expense) increases, which is a debit. Cash (an asset) decreases, which is a credit.

1 Accounts Affected	2 Type	3 ↑↓	4 Dr. or Cr.
Repairs Expense	Expense	↑	Dr.
Cash	Asset	↓	Cr.

The journal entry is as follows:

DATE	ACCOUNTS	POST REF.	DR.	CR.
g.	Repairs Expense		350	
	Cash			350
	Paid cash for repairs.			

We enter $350 on the debit (left) side of the Repairs Expense T-account and $350 on the credit (right) side of the Cash T-account.

	Cash		**1010**		**Repairs Expense**	**5020**
(a)	8,000	(c)	500	(g)	350	
(f)	2,300	(e)	2,000			
		(g)	350			

h. Paid $1,150 cash in salary expense.

The business paid employees $1,150 in cash. Because the benefit of the employee's work has already been used, the salary is recorded as Salary Expense. Because the salary was paid in cash, the Cash account is also involved.

Salary Expense is an expense, and Cash is an asset. Salary Expense (an expense) increased. Cash (an asset) decreased.

An increase in expenses is a debit, while a decrease in an asset is a credit.

So, Salary Expense (an expense) increases, which is a debit. Cash (an asset) decreases, which is a credit.

1 Accounts Affected	2 Type	3 ↑↓	4 Dr. or Cr.
Salary Expense	Expense	↑	Dr.
Cash	Asset	↓	Cr.

The journal entry is as follows:

DATE	ACCOUNTS	POST REF.	DR.	CR.
h.	Salary Expense		1,150	
	Cash			1,150
	Paid salary with cash.			

We enter $1,150 on the debit (left) side of the Salary Expense T-account and $1,150 on the credit (right) side of the Cash T-account.

	Cash		**1010**		**Salary Expense**	**5010**
(a)	8,000	(c)	500	(h)	1,150	
(f)	2,300	(e)	2,000			
		(g)	350			
		(h)	1,150			

i. Received $700 cash from customers on account

The business received payments ($700) from customers for services previously provided in Transaction d. The accounts involved in this transaction are Cash and Accounts Receivable.

Cash and Accounts Receivable are both assets. Cash (an asset) increased. Accounts Receivable (an asset) decreased.

Remember, accounts receivable is the total amount due from customers from which the business will receive money. When the business receives these payments from its customers, the amount of this account decreases, because the business now has less to receive in the future (in this case, it reduces from $1,600—in Transaction d—to $900).

An increase in assets is a debit, while a decrease in assets is a credit.

So Cash (an asset) increases, which is a debit. Accounts Receivable (an asset) decreases, which is a credit.

1 Accounts Affected	2 Type	3 ↑↓	4 Dr. or Cr.
Cash	Asset	↑	Dr.
Accounts Receivable	Asset	↓	Cr.

The journal entry is as follows:

DATE	ACCOUNTS	POST REF.	DR.	CR.
i.	Cash		700	
	Accounts Receivable			700
	Collected cash from customers on account.			

We enter $700 on the debit (left) side of the Cash T-account and $700 on the credit (right) side of the Accounts Receivable account.

	Cash		1010
(a)	8,000	(c)	500
(f)	2,300	(e)	2,000
(i)	700	(g)	350
		(h)	1,150

	Accounts Receivable		1020
(d)	1,600	(i)	700

j. Paid $1,000 of dividends to its only shareholder, Jean Dion.

The business distributed $1,000 of earnings to Jean by paying him dividends. The business paid cash to Jean, whose ownership interest (equity) decreased. The accounts involved in the transaction are Dividends and Cash.

Dividends is a shareholders' equity account, and Cash is an asset. Dividends increased and Cash (an asset) decreased.

An increase in dividends is a debit, while a decrease in an asset is a credit.

1 Accounts Affected	2 Type	3 ↑↓	4 Dr. or Cr.
Dividends	Shareholders' Equity	↑	Dr.
Cash	Asset	↓	Cr.

The journal entry is as follows:

DATE	ACCOUNTS	POST REF.	DR.	CR.
j.	Dividends		1,000	
	Cash			1,000
	Paid dividends.			

We enter $1,000 on the debit (left) side of the Dividends T-account and $1,000 on the credit (right) side of the Cash account.

Cash			1010
(a)	8,000	(c)	500
(f)	2,300	(e)	2,000
(i)	700	(g)	350
		(h)	1,150
		(j)	1,000

Dividends		3020
(j)	1,000	

Now we will summarize the journal entries for the month.

DATE	ACCOUNTS	POST REF.	DR.	CR.
a.	Cash	1010	8,000	
	Common Shares	3010		8,000
	Sold 1,000 shares.			
b.	Equipment	1040	4,800	
	Accounts Payable	2010		4,800
	Purchased equipment on account.			
c.	Supplies	1030	500	
	Cash	1010		500
	Purchased supplies for cash.			
d.	Accounts Receivable	1020	1,600	
	Service Revenue	4010		1,600
	Performed services on account.			
e.	Accounts Payable	2010	2,000	
	Cash	1010		2,000
	Made a partial payment on account.			
f.	Cash	1010	2,300	
	Service Revenue	4010		2,300
	Received cash for services performed.			
g.	Repairs Expense	5020	350	
	Cash	1010		350
	Paid cash for repairs.			
h.	Salary Expense	5010	1,150	
	Cash	1010		1,150
	Paid salary with cash.			
i.	Cash	1010	700	
	Accounts Receivable	1020		700
	Collected cash from customers on account.			
j.	Dividends	3020	1,000	
	Cash	1010		1,000
	Paid dividends.			

Notice how the posting reference field now contains the account number that indicates that the entries have been posted to the general ledger (or in this case, the T-accounts).

Requirement ❸

Total all the T-accounts to determine their balances at the end of the month.

Part 1	Part 2	**Part 3**	Demo Doc Complete

To compute the balance in a T-account (total the T-account), add up the numbers on the debit/left side of the account and (separately) the credit/right side of the account. Subtract the smaller number from the bigger number and put the difference on the side of the bigger number. This procedure gives the balance in the T-account (the net total of both sides combined). For example, for the Cash account, the numbers on the left side total $8,000 + $2,300 + $700 = $11,000. The credit/right side = $500 + $2,000 + $350 + $1,150 + $1,000 = $5,000. The difference is $11,000 - $5,000 = $6,000. We put the $6,000 on the debit side because it is the side of the bigger number of $11,000.

Another way to think of adding up (totalling) T-accounts is the following:

> Beginning Balance in T-account
> + Increases to T-account
> − Decreases to T-account
> = Ending Balance in T-account

The T-accounts should look like the following after posting all transactions and totalling each account:

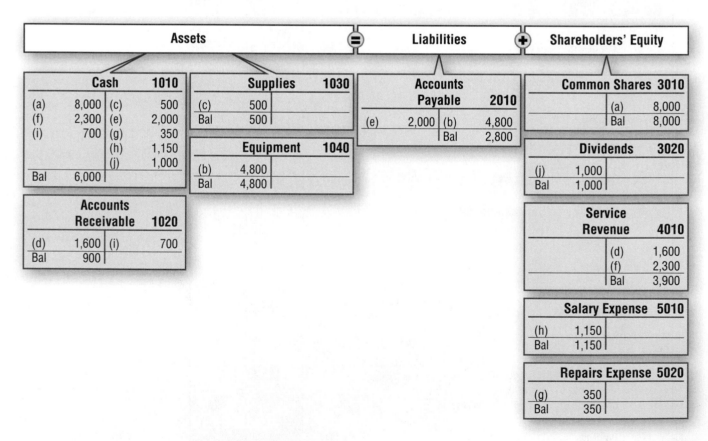

Demo Doc Complete

DECISION GUIDELINES

Recording Business Transactions

Here are some decisions that you would make as you record and summarize transactions in your business:

Decision	**Guideline**	**Analyze**
How do I know if an event should be entered into a company's accounting records?	Examine the effect of the event on the company's accounting equation.	If the event increases or decreases the assets, liabilities, or shareholders' equity of the business, it represents a transaction that should be recorded in the company's accounting records. If the event doesn't impact the assets, liabilities, or shareholders' equity of the company, then a recordable transaction has not occurred.
As the manager of a department, I am responsible for the budget for the department and for evaluating how well the department has performed. When looking at the financial statements for my department, some of the numbers do not feel right and I'm wondering if something was perhaps recorded incorrectly (for example, perhaps someone else's expenses were recorded in my department's records by mistake). I need to check the detail of these accounts that do not seem right. Where can I find more detail?	Review the trial balance or the general ledger.	The trial balance is a summary of all of a company's accounts with their respective balances on a given day. The general ledger provides the detail of all of the transactions that have impacted an account along with a running balance of the account. Having quick access to the account balances often allows managers and owners to make better decisions.
I am considering changing the companies that I'm invested in for my pension. Where do I find feedback on the performance of the companies in order to decide where best to invest my funds?	A company's financial statements will provide feedback regarding the performance of the company.	The income statement reflects how profitable a business has been for a specified period of time. The statement of changes in equity shows the amount of the share capital, the retained earnings, including the earnings that have been distributed to the shareholders, and the changes to these accounts during the time period. And, the statement of financial position shows the assets that a business owns, the liabilities it owes and the owners' claims in the business on a given date. In other words, it shows what assets the business has and who has rights to those assets.

ACCOUNTING VOCABULARY
THE LANGUAGE OF BUSINESS

Account (p. 68) The basic summary device of accounting; the detailed record of all the changes in a specific asset, liability, or shareholders' equity item as a result of transactions.

Accounting cycle (p. 90) The sequence of steps used to record and report business transactions.

Accounting period (p. 85) Generally, the time period reflected by a set of financial statements.

Balance (p. 84) The difference between an account's total debit and total credit amounts; the ending value of an account.

Chart of accounts (p. 68) A list of all the accounts of a business and the numbers assigned to those accounts.

Compound journal entry (p. 82) A journal entry affecting more than two accounts; an entry that has more than one debit and/or more than one credit.

Credit (p. 71) The right side of any account; an entry made to the right side of an account.

Current assets (p. 69) Assets that are expected to be converted to cash, sold, or consumed within one year or the business's operating cycle if the cycle is longer than a year.

Current liabilities (p. 70) Debts due to be paid with cash or fulfilled with goods and services within one year or the entity's operating cycle if the cycle is longer than a year.

Debit (p. 71) The left side of any account; an entry made to the left side of an account.

Double-entry accounting (p. 71) The rule of accounting that specifies that every transaction involves at least two accounts and is recorded with equal amounts of debits and credits.

General journal (p. 72) The chronological accounting record of the transactions of a business.

General ledger (p. 74) The accounting record summarizing, in accounts, the transactions of a business and showing the resulting account balances.

Journalize (p. 73) Entering a transaction in a journal; also called *record*.

Non-current asset (p. 69) An asset that will be held for more than one year or longer than the operating cycle.

Non-current liability (p. 70) A liability that is expected to be paid after more than one year or after the period of one operating cycle.

Normal balance (p. 72) The balance that appears on the side of an account where increases are recorded; the expected balance of an account.

Posting (p. 74) Copying information from the general journal to accounts in the general ledger.

Posting reference (p. 74) A notation in the journal and ledger that links these two accounting records together.

Promissory note (p.69) A written pledge to pay a fixed amount of money at a later date.

Record (p. 73) Entering a transaction in a journal; also called *journalize*.

T-account (p. 71) An informal account form used to summarize transactions, where the top of the T holds the account title and the base divides the debit and credit sides of the account.

Trial balance (p. 85) A list of all the accounts of a business and their balances in the order of the statement of financial position; its purpose is to verify that total debits equal total credits.

Unearned revenue (p. 69) A liability created when customers pay in advance for goods and services to be delivered in the future. At the point when cash is received, the company has an obligation to fulfill and has not earned the revenue.

MyAccountingLab

Make the grade with MyAccountingLab. The exercises and problems in this chapter can be found on MyAccountingLab at www.myaccountinglab.com. You can practise them as often as you want, and they feature step-by-step guided solutions to help you find the right answer.

ACCOUNTING PRACTICE
DISCUSSION QUESTIONS

1. The order in which assets were listed and described in the text is the order in which you will see them listed on the statement of financial position. What is the organizing principle behind the order in which assets are listed?

2. What type of transaction would result in the recording of a prepaid asset? What do you think will happen to that prepaid asset eventually?

3. How is revenue related to retained earnings?

4. Distinguish between an event and a transaction. Are all transactions events? Are all events transactions? Why or why not? What are the implications of your answers with respect to journal entries?

5. What is a "normal balance"? What are normal balances for the following accounts?
   a. Accounts Receivable
   b. Prepaid Expenses
   c. Notes Payable
   d. Retained Earnings
   e. Salaries Expense

6. You learned in this chapter that cash is increased with a debit. When you deposit your paycheque in your account, however, the teller might say that he or she is going to credit your account. Why?

7. What would be the implications of a credit balance in the cash account?

8. Distinguish between journalizing and posting.

9. True or false: If the trial balance is in balance, the financial statements will be accurate. Why or why not?

10. When it comes time to prepare the financial statements, from where do the financial statement numbers come?

SELF CHECK

1. Which sequence of actions correctly summarizes the accounting process?
   a. Prepare a trial balance, journalize transactions, post to the accounts
   b. Post to the accounts, journalize transactions, prepare a trial balance
   c. Journalize transactions, post to the accounts, prepare a trial balance
   d. Journalize transactions, prepare a trial balance, post to the accounts

2. The left side of an account is used to record
   a. debits.
   b. credits.
   c. debits or credits, depending on the type of account.
   d. increases.

3. Suppose Sunshine Florists, Inc. has cash of $40,000, receivables of $30,000, and furniture and fixtures totalling $170,000. Sunshine Florists, Inc. owes $60,000 on account and has a $120,000 note payable. How much is the shareholders' equity?
   a. $240,000
   b. $120,000
   c. $180,000
   d. $60,000

4. Lori's Catering, Inc. purchased $400 of supplies on account. The journal entry to record this transaction is denoted by which of the following?

DATE	ACCOUNTS	POST REF.	DR.	CR.
a.	Inventory		400	
	Accounts Payable			400
b.	Accounts Payable		400	
	Supplies			400
c.	Supplies		400	
	Accounts Payable			400
d.	Supplies		400	
	Accounts Receivable			400

5. Posting a $800 purchase of supplies on account appears as which of the following?

a.

Supplies	Accounts Receivable
800	800

c.

Supplies	Accounts Payable
800	800

b.

Supplies	Accounts Payable
800	800

d.

Cash	Supplies
800	800

6. Which journal entry records obtaining a bank loan of $15,000?

DATE	ACCOUNTS	POST REF.	DR.	CR.
a.	Notes Payable		15,000	
	Accounts Receivable			15,000
b.	Notes Payable		15,000	
	Cash			15,000
c.	Cash		15,000	
	Notes Payable			15,000
d.	Cash		15,000	
	Accounts Payable			15,000

7. S & S Janitorial, Inc. paid $600 for supplies and purchased additional supplies on account for $800. S & S Janitorial, Inc. also paid $300 of the accounts payable. What is the balance in the Supplies account?

   a. $800
   b. $1,100
   c. $1,400
   d. $1,700

8. The Blue Ox Restaurant recorded a cash collection on account by debiting Cash and crediting Accounts Payable. What will the trial balance show for this error?

   a. Too much for liabilities
   b. Too much for assets
   c. The trial balance will not balance
   d. Both a and b

9. TingTing Wu, an interior designer, has a corporation, TTW Design, Inc., that began the year with total assets of $110,000, total liabilities of $80,000, and shareholders' equity of $30,000. During the year, TTW Design, Inc. earned revenue of $90,000 and paid expenses of $40,000. TTW Design, Inc. also sold an additional $10,000 of shares and paid $20,000 in dividends. How much is the shareholders' equity in TTW Design, Inc. at year-end?

   a. $70,000
   b. $110,000
   c. $130,000
   d. $160,000

10. The entry to record the payment of $1,200 rent expense would be which of the following?

DATE	ACCOUNTS	POST REF.	DR.	CR.
a.	Rent Expense		1,200	
	Accounts Payable			1,200
b.	Cash		1,200	
	Rent Expense			1,200
c.	Rent Expense		1,200	
	Cash			1,200
d.	Accounts Payable		1,200	
	Rent Expense			1,200

Answers are given after Written Communication.

SHORT EXERCISES

S2-1. Accounting terms (*Learning Objective 1*) 5–10 min.

Match the accounting terms at the left with the corresponding definitions at the right.

_____ 1. Account   a. Any economic event that has a financial impact on the business

_____ 2. Assets   b. The detailed record of the changes in a particular asset, liability, or shareholders' equity

_____ 3. Shareholders' Equity   c. Economic resources that provide a future benefit for a business

_____ 4. Expenses   d. Debts or obligations of a business

_____ 5. Liabilities   e. Shareholders' claim to the assets of a corporation

_____ 6. Revenues   f. Increases in shareholders' equity from selling goods or services to customers

_____ 7. Transactions   g. Decreases in shareholders' equity from using resources to sell goods or services

S2-2. Account types (*Learning Objective 1*) 5–10 min.

For each of the following accounts, place the corresponding letter(s) of its account type in the space provided. Use the most detailed account type appropriate.

(A) Asset (L) Liability (SE) Shareholders' Equity (R) Revenue (E) Expense

__SE__   Dividends

_____ 1. Accounts Payable

_____ 2. Cash

_____ 3. Service Revenue

_____ 4. Prepaid Rent

_____ 5. Rent Expense

_____ 6. Common Shares

S2-3. Accounting cycle steps (*Learning Objectives 2, 3, & 4*) 5–10 min.

The following list names the activities involved in the accounting process of recording and summarizing business transactions. Place the number corresponding with the order the activity occurs next to the activity, starting with 1.

__1__ Transaction occurs.

_____ Prepare the financial statements.

_____ Prepare the trial balance.

_____ Post the transactions from the journal to the ledger.

_____ Record the transactions in the journal.

S2-4. Account types (*Learning Objective 1*) 5–10 min.

For each of the following accounts, indicate the account type by labelling it as an asset (A), liability (L), shareholders' equity (SE), revenue (R), or expense (E). Also give the digit each account number would begin with in the chart of accounts. Use the most detailed account type appropriate.

__A,1__ Land

_____ 1. Service Revenue

_____ 2. Dividends

_____ 3. Accounts Receivable

_____ 4. Salary Expense

_____ 5. Notes Payable

_____ 6. Common Shares

_____ 7. Rent Expense

S2-5. Accounting terminology (*Learning Objective 2, 3, & 4*) 5–10 min.

Demonstrate your knowledge of accounting terminology by filling in the blanks to review some key definitions.

Dillon Baker is describing the accounting process for a friend who is a psychology major. Dillon states, "The basic summary device in accounting is the _____. The left side of an account is called the _____ side, and the right side is called the _____ side. We record transactions first in a _____. Then we post, or copy, the data to the _____. It is helpful to list all the accounts with their balances on a _____ __ _____."

S2-6. Effects of debits and credits on accounts (*Learning Objective 2*) 5–10 min.

For each of the following accounts, indicate if the account's normal balance is a debit balance (DR) or a credit balance (CR).

__DR__ Cash

_____ 1. Rent Expense

_____ 2. Accounts Payable

_____ 3. Service Revenue

_____ 4. Office Furniture

_____ 5. Common Shares

_____ 6. Land

_____ 7. Dividends

S2-7. Balancing accounts and normal balances (*Learning Objective 2*) 5–10 min.

Calculate each account balance.

	Supplies		1030		Note Payable		2030
3/8	400	3/27	600	3/20	2,000	3/5	10,000
3/17	500			3/31	4,000		

S2-8. Types of accounts and effects of debits and credits (*Learning Objective 2*) 5–10 min.

Complete the following table. For each account listed, identify the type of account, how the account is increased (debit or credit), and how the account is decreased (debit or credit). Use the most detailed account type appropriate.

Account	Type	↑	↓
Office Equipment	Asset	Dr.	Cr.
Dividends			
Service Revenue			
Accounts Payable			
Rent Expense			
Cash			

S2-9. Recreating journal entries from T-account postings (*Learning Objective 2*) 15–20 min.

IPW, Inc. began operations on January 1, 2013. The seven transactions recorded during January by the company accountant are shown in the following T-accounts:

	Cash		1010
(1)	15,000	(2)	3,000
		(5)	250
		(6)	2,300
		(7)	1,000
Bal	8,450		

	Accounts Receivable		1020
(4)	4,500		
Bal	4,500		

	Supplies		1030
(3)	600		
Bal	600		

	Equipment		1040
(2)	3,000		
Bal	3,000		

	Accounts Payable		2010
(5)	250	(3)	600
		Bal	350

	Common Shares		3010
		(1)	15,000
		Bal	15,000

	Dividends		3020
(7)	1,000		
Bal	1,000		

	Service Revenue		4010
		(4)	4,500
		Bal	4,500

	Operating Expenses		5010–5040
(6)	2,300		
Bal	2,300		

Complete the following table. For each transaction shown, determine the accounts affected, the type of account, whether the account increases or decreases, and whether it would be recorded in the journal on the debit or credit side.

Transaction	Accounts Affected	Type	↑↓	Dr. or Cr.
(1)	Cash	Asset	Increase	Dr.
	Common Shares	Shareholders' Equity	Increase	Cr.

S2-10. Journalizing transactions (*Learning Objective 3*) 10–15 min.

Shohei Oda opened a DJ service in Vancouver, British Columbia as a corporation. The following transactions took place in June:

Jun	1	Sold $20,000 of shares to Shohei to start the business.
	5	Purchased party supplies on account, $4,600.
	7	Paid monthly office rent of $2,400.
	10	Provided $4,000 of DJ services to customers. Received cash of $1,700 for these services and sent bills to clients for the remainder.

Using the steps outlined in the five-step transaction analysis, record the transactions in the journal.

S2-11. Journalizing transactions (*Learning Objective 3*) 10–15 min.

After operating for a month Shohei Oda's DJ services completed the following transactions during July:

Jul	3	The business borrowed $25,000 from the bank, signing a note payable.
	9	Performed DJ service for clients on account, $2,900.
	16	Received cash on account from clients, $1,200.
	22	Received a utility bill, $550, which will be paid during August.
	31	Paid the monthly salary to its employee, $1,900.
	31	Paid interest expense of $125 on the bank loan.

Using the steps outlined in the five-step transaction analysis, record the transactions in the journal.

S2-12. Prepare trial balance (*Learning Objective 4*) 10–15 min.

The accounting records for Airborne Services contain the following amounts on December 31, 2013. The accounts appear in no particular order.

Service Revenues	$79,000	Utilities Expense	$24,000
Prepaid Rent	4,000	Note Payable	15,000
Accounts Payable	1,000	Cash	14,000
Equipment	18,000	Rent Expense	36,000
Dividends	6,000	Common Shares	7,000

Prepare the trial balance for Airborne Services, Inc. at December 31, 2013. List the accounts in proper order.

**S2-13. Preparation of financial statements from a trial balance (*Learning Objective 4*)
5–10 min.**

To the left of each account listed on the trial balance, indicate the financial statement that will include the account: income statement (IS), statement of changes in equity (SCE), or statement of financial position (SFP).

		ACCOUNT	DEBIT	CREDIT
		Wirt's Dirt, Inc.		
		Trial Balance		
		December 31, 2013		
		Cash	$13,900	
		Accounts Receivable	2,100	
		Supplies	400	
		Equipment	5,200	
		Accounts Payable		$ 1,900
		Notes Payable		11,000
		Common Shares		8,000
		Dividends	500	
		Service Revenues		3,300
		Wages Expense	1,300	
		Rent Expense	600	
		Utilities Expense	200	
		Total	$24,200	$24,200

S2-14. Accounting terminology (*Learning Objectives 1, 2, & 3*) 5–10 min.

Accounting has its own vocabulary and basic relationships. Match the accounting terms at the left with the corresponding phrase at the right.

_____ 1. Posting a. Chronological record of transactions

_____ 2. Normal balance b. An asset

_____ 3. Payable c. Left side of an account

_____ 4. Journal d. Side of an account where increases are recorded

_____ 5. Receivable e. Copying data from the journal to the ledger

_____ 6. Chart of accounts f. List of all accounts with their balances

_____ 7. Debit g. A liability

_____ 8. Trial balance h. List of all of the accounts of a business

_____ 9. Credit i. Right side of an account

**S2-15. Types of accounts and effects of debits and credits (*Learning Objective 2*)
10–15 min.**

Fill in the chart using the first line as an example. The account that is listed on the right column has specific features that you are to list in the chart. For example, Accounts Payable is a liability (account classification), it is increased by a credit (second column), decreased by a debit (third column), has a normal balance as a credit, and it is found on the balance sheet or statement of financial position (financial statement).

Account Classification	Increase	Decrease	Normal Balance	Normal Financial	Statement Account
Liability	Credit	Debit	Credit	SFP	Accounts Payable
_____	_____	_____	_____	_____	Accounts Receivable
_____	_____	_____	_____	_____	Dividends
_____	_____	_____	_____	_____	Building
_____	_____	_____	_____	_____	Consulting Revenue
_____	_____	_____	_____	_____	Inventory
_____	_____	_____	_____	_____	Licence
_____	_____	_____	_____	_____	Preferred Shares
_____	_____	_____	_____	_____	Salary Expense
_____	_____	_____	_____	_____	Unearned Revenue
_____	_____	_____	_____	_____	Prepaid Rent

EXERCISES (GROUP A)

E2-1A. Journalizing transactions (*Learning Objective 2 & 3*) 10–15 min.

The following are six transactions for Gonzalez Engineering, Inc. during the month of July.

Jul	1	Paid advertising expense, $275.
	3	Performed service for customers and received cash, $3,000.
	5	Purchased supplies on account, $450.
	9	Received cash of $1,200 from credit customers on account.
	12	Paid $900 on accounts payable.
	17	Performed service for customers on account, $2,800.

Requirement

1. Complete the following table. For each transaction shown, determine the accounts affected, the type of account, whether the account increases or decreases, and whether it would be recorded in the journal on the debit or credit side.

Transaction	Accounts Affected	Account Type	↑↓	Dr. or Cr.
(1)	Advertising Expense	Shareholders' Equity	↑	Dr.
	Cash	Asset	↓	Cr.

E2-2A. Journalizing transactions (*Learning Objective 3*) 15–20 min.

Using the steps outlined in the five-step transaction analysis, record the following transactions in the general journal for Alread Plumbing, Inc. Explanations are not required.

Feb	1	Paid interest expense, $300.
	5	Purchased office furniture on account, $2,200.
	10	Performed service on account for a customer, $1,700.
	12	Borrowed $4,500 cash, signing a note payable.
	19	Sold for $85,000 land that had cost the company $85,000.
	21	Purchased building for $290,000; signed a note payable.
	27	Paid $1,500 on account.

E2-3A. Journalizing transactions (*Learning Objective 3*) 15–20 min.

Williams & Associates, Inc. completed the following transactions during October 2013, its first month of operations:

Oct	1	Sold 2,000 shares for $50,000 to Kirsten Williams to start the business.
	3	Purchased supplies on account, $300.
	5	Paid cash for a building to use for storage, $42,000.
	6	Performed service for customers and received cash, $1,600.
	11	Paid on accounts payable, $200.
	18	Performed service for customers on account, $2,400.
	24	Received cash from a customer on account, $800.
	31	Paid the following expenses: salary, $500; and rent, $1,200.

Requirement

1. Using the steps outlined in the five-step transaction analysis, journalize the transactions of Williams & Associates, Inc. List transactions by date. Use the following accounts: Cash, Accounts Receivable, Supplies, Building, Accounts Payable, Common Shares, Service Revenue, Salary Expense, and Rent Expense.

E2-4A. Balance accounts and prepare trial balance (*Learning Objectives 3 & 4*) 10–15 min.

The transactions for Little Tykes Daycare, Inc. for the month of January 2013 are posted in the following T-accounts.

Cash			1010
Jan 1	25,000	Jan 4	6,800
6	3,000	9	100
23	1,200	29	700
Bal			

Accounts Receivable			1020
Jan 17	1,600	Jan 23	1,200
Bal			

Supplies			1030
Jan 2	200		
Bal			

Equipment			1040
Jan 4	6,800		
Bal			

Accounts Payable			2010
Jan 9	100	Jan 2	200
		Bal	

Common Shares			3010
		Jan 1	25,000
		Bal	

Service Revenue			4010
		Jan 6	3,000
		17	1,600
		Bal	

Salary Expense			5010
Jan 29	700		
Bal			

Requirements

1. Calculate account balances.
2. Prepare the trial balance for Little Tykes Daycare, Inc. at January 31, 2013.

Quick solution:

1. Cash balance = $21,600;
2. Trial balance totals = $29,700

E2-5A. Record transactions and prepare a trial balance (Learning Objectives 3 & 4) 15–20 min.

Baldwin Realty, Inc. had the following transactions for the month of May, 2013.

May	2	Paid Rent Expense, $600.
	4	Performed service for a customer and received cash, $1,000.
	8	Purchased supplies on account, $400.
	11	Received cash from credit customers on account, $1,200.
	15	Sold an additional $5,000 of common shares.
	19	Paid $500 on account.
	27	Performed service for customers on account, $1,600.
	31	Made a payment on the Notes Payable, $3,000.

The following T-accounts have been set up for Baldwin Realty, Inc. with their beginning balances as of May 1, 2013.

Cash		1010
May 1	3,000	

Accounts Payable		2010
	May 1	800

Accounts Receivable		1020
May 1	1,800	

Notes Payable		2030
	May 1	10,000

Supplies		1030
May 1	300	

Common Shares		3010
	May 1	30,000

Office Furniture		1050
May 1	1,200	

Service Revenue		4010
	May 1	2,100

Building		1060
May 1	36,000	

Rent Expense		5050
May 1	600	

Requirements

1. Journalize the transactions for the month of May.
2. Post the journal entries to the appropriate T-accounts. Identify all items by date.
3. Calculate the balance of each account at May 31, 2013.
4. Prove that the total of all the debit balances equals the total of all of the credit balances by preparing a trial balance.

E2-6A. Journalize transactions, prepare a trial balance and statement of financial position (*Learning Objectives 3 & 4*) 20–25 min.

The transactions for Crazy Curlz, Inc. for the month of June 2013 have been posted to the accounts as follows:

Cash			
(1)	16,000	(4)	8,000
		(5)	5,000
		(6)	300

Supplies	
(2)	800

Equipment	
(4)	8,000

Building	
(3)	60,000

Accounts Payable			
(6)	300	(2)	800

Notes Payable			
(5)	5,000	(3)	60,000

Common Shares	
(1)	16,000

Requirements

1. Prepare the journal entries that served as the sources for the six transactions.
2. Calculate the balance in each account.
3. Prepare the trial balance for Crazy Curlz, Inc. at June 30, 2013.
4. Prepare a statement of financial position for Crazy Curlz, Inc. as of June 30, 2013.

E2-7A. Explaining the effects of transactions on accounts using T-accounts and inferring the missing amount (*Learning Objectives 2 & 3*) 10–15 min.

The following transactions occurred during April 2013 in Sion, Inc.'s operations:

1. Salary Expense for the month of April was $4,600. Sion made a monthly payment to employees on the 15th of the month.

2. Sales on account were $8,270.

3. The Cash, Accounts Receivable, and Salary Payable beginning and ending balances were:

Cash		Accounts Receivable		Salary Payable	
8,650	(2)	3,780	(4)	(2)	4,200
(4)		(3)			(1)
(5)		4,350			3,600

Requirements

1. What was the amount paid for salaries in April?

2. What was the amount received from customers in April?

3. What do (1) and (3) represent?

4. What was the Cash ending balance?

E2-8A. Journalizing, posting, trial balance, income statement, and statement of financial position (*Learning Objectives 3 & 4*) 25–30 min.

McDonald Consulting, Inc. completed the following transactions during December 2013, its first month of operations:

Dec 2	Sold $10,000 of shares to Dan McDonald to start the consulting practice.
3	Paid monthly office rent, $800.
6	Paid cash for a new computer, $1,600.
8	Purchased office furniture on account, $2,100.
11	Purchased supplies on account, $200.
19	Performed consulting service for a client on account, $900.
20	Paid utility expenses, $300.
28	Performed service for a client and received cash for the full amount of $1,100.

Requirements

1. Open, or set up, T-accounts in the ledger: Cash, Accounts Receivable; Supplies; Equipment; Furniture; Accounts Payable; Common Shares; Service Revenue; Rent Expense; Utilities Expense.

2. Record transactions in the journal. Explanations are not required.

3. Post the transactions to the T-accounts, identify all items by date. Calculate the balance in each account.

4. Prepare a trial balance at December 31, 2013.

5. Prepare the income statement, statement of changes in equity, and statement of financial position.

E2-9A. Error correction (*Learning Objective 4*) 20–25 min.

Julie Palmer has trouble keeping her debits and credits equal. During a recent month, Julie made the following errors:

a. Julie recorded a $750 payment of rent by debiting Rent Expense for $75 and crediting Cash for $75.

b. In recording a $250 payment on account, Julie debited Accounts Receivable and credited Cash.

   c. Julie recorded the receipt of cash for service revenue by debiting Cash for $130 instead of the correct amount of $310. Julie also credited Service Revenue for $130, the incorrect amount.

   d. Julie recorded a $120 purchase of supplies on account by debiting Accounts Payable and crediting Supplies.

   e. In preparing the trial balance, Julie omitted a $15,000 note payable.

Requirements

1. For each of these errors, state whether Julie's mistake would cause the total debits and total credits on the trial balance to be unequal.

2. Identify each account with an incorrect balance, and indicate the amount and direction of the error.

Use the following format:

Effect on Trial Balance	Account(s) Misstated
Total debits = Total credits	Cash $675 too high Rent Expense $675 too low

---

E2-10A. Error correction (*Learning Objective 4*) 20–25 min.

Kwik Klean, Inc.'s trial balance shows $96,000 on both debit and credit sides. Kwik Klean's accountant found the following mistakes:

1. Purchase of supplies $2,000 on account was incorrectly recorded as supplies expense.

2. A $560 deposit from a customer for services to be delivered in the following month was incorrectly recorded as $650.

3. Cash paid for salary expense of $2,500 was incorrectly recorded as salary payable.

4. Borrowed $10,000 from one of the shareholders that was incorrectly recorded as common shares.

5. Paid $3,500 for salary expense was incorrectly recorded as dividends.

Requirements

1. What are the correct debit and credit balances?

2. Does each error change the overall debit and credit balance?

3. What is the impact on each of the Assets, Liabilities, and Shareholders' Equity accounts due to these errors?

EXERCISES (GROUP B)

E2-1B. Journalizing transactions (*Learning Objective 2 & 3*) 10–15 min.

The following are six journal entries Keene Engineering, Inc. made during the month of April.

Apr	1	Paid advertising expense, $275.
	3	Paid $4,000 cash to purchase a new piece of equipment.
	5	Issued shares in exchange for $7,000 cash.
	9	Borrowed $5,000 on a note payable from the bank.
	12	Paid monthly telephone bill, $325.
	17	Purchased supplies for $175, paid cash.

Requirement

1. For each transaction shown, determine the accounts affected, the type of account, whether the account increases or decreases, and whether it would be recorded in the journal on the debit or credit side. The first transaction has been analyzed for you.

Transaction	Accounts Affected	Type	Increase/Decrease	Dr. or Cr.
(1)	Advertising Expense	Shareholders' Equity	Increase	Dr.
	Cash	Asset	Decrease	Cr.

E2-2B. Journalizing transactions (*Learning Objective 3*) 15–20 min.

Using the steps outlined in the five-step transaction analysis, record the following transactions in the general journal for Laverden Plumbing, Inc. Explanations are not required.

May	1	Paid interest expense, $500.
	5	Purchased office furniture on account, $2,500.
	10	Performed service on account for a customer, $2,700.
	12	Borrowed $4,500 cash, signing a note payable.
	19	Sold for $50,000 land that had cost the company $50,000.
	21	Purchased building for $800,000; signed a note payable.
	27	Paid $700 on account.

E2-3B. Journalizing transactions (*Learning Objective 3*) 15–20 min.

Welch & Associates, Inc. completed the following transactions during September 2013, its first month of operations:

Sep	1	Sold $40,000 of shares to Katie Welch to start the business.
	3	Purchased supplies on account, $200.
	5	Paid cash for a building to use for storage, $32,000.
	6	Performed service for customers and received cash, $3,000.
	11	Paid on accounts payable, $100.
	18	Performed service for customers on account, $2,900.
	24	Received cash from a customer on account, $1,500.
	30	Paid the following expenses: salary, $650; and rent, $1,100.

Requirement

1. Using the steps outlined in the five-step transaction analysis, journalize the transactions of Welch & Associates, Inc. List transactions by date.

E2-4B. Balancing accounts and prepare trial balance (*Learning Objectives 3 & 4*) 10–15 min.

The transactions for Learning Fun Daycare, Inc. for the month of May 2013 are posted in the following T-accounts.

Cash			1010
May 1	45,000	May 4	12,700
6	7,500	9	200
23	900	29	1,100
Bal			

Equipment			1040
May 4	12,700		
Bal			

Service Revenue			4010
		May 6	7,500
		17	3,600
		Bal	

Accounts Receivable			1020
May 17	3,600	May 23	900
Bal			

Accounts Payable			2010
May 9	200	May 2	700
		Bal	

Salary Expense			5010
May 29	1,100		
Bal			

Supplies			1030
May 2	700		
Bal			

Common Shares			3010
		May 1	45,000
		Bal	

Requirements

1. Calculate account balances.

2. Prepare the trial balance for Learning Fun Daycare, Inc. at May 31, 2013.

E2-5B. Record transactions and prepare a trial balance (*Learning Objectives 3 & 4*) 15–20 min.

Spadina Realty, Inc. had the following transactions for the month of June 2013.

Jun	2	Paid Rent Expense, $900.
	4	Performed service for a customer and received cash, $1,500.
	8	Purchased supplies on account, $900.
	11	Received cash from credit customers on account, $1,100.
	15	Sold an additional $15,000 of common shares.
	19	Paid $600 on account.
	27	Performed service for customers on account, $3,000.
	30	Made a payment on the Notes Payable, $3,500.

The following T-accounts have been set up for Spadina Realty, Inc. with their beginning balances as of June 1, 2013.

Cash			1010
Jun 1	9,000		

Accounts Payable			2010
		Jun 1	2,600

Accounts Receivable			1020
Jun 1	1,800		

Notes Payable			2030
		Jun 1	10,000

Supplies			1030
Jun 1	600		

Common Shares			3010
		Jun 1	34,500

Office Furniture			1050
Jun 1	1,900		

Service Revenue			4010
		Jun 1	3,700

Building			1060
Jun 1	36,000		

Rent Expense			5050
Jun 1	1,500		

Requirements

1. Journalize the transactions for the month of June.
2. Post the journal entries to the appropriate T-accounts. Identify all items by date.
3. Calculate the balance of each account at June 30, 2013.
4. Prove that the total of all the debit balances equals the total of all of the credit balances by preparing a trial balance.

E2-6B. **Journalize transactions, prepare a trial balance and statement of financial position (*Learning Objectives 3 & 4*) 20–25 min.**

The transactions for Dancing Antz, Inc. for the month of September 2013 have been posted to the accounts as follows:

Cash				Supplies		Equipment		Building	
(1)	28,000	(4)	2,000	(2)	600	(4)	2,000	(3)	80,000
		(5)	6,000						
		(6)	150						

Accounts Payable			Notes Payable			Common Shares		
(6)	150	(2) 600	(5)	6,000	(3) 80,000		(1)	28,000

Requirements

1. Prepare the journal entries that served as the sources for the six transactions.
2. Calculate the balance in each account.
3. Prepare the trial balance for Dancing Antz, Inc. at September 30, 2013.
4. Prepare a statement of financial position for Dancing Antz, Inc. as of September 30, 2013.

E2-7B. **Explaining the effects of transactions on accounts using T-accounts and inferring the missing amount (*Learning Objective 3*) 10–15 min.**

The following transactions occurred during May 2013 of the Lion, Inc.'s operations:

1. Sales on account were $5,700.
2. Interest Expense for the month of May was $1,600. Lion made a monthly interest payment on the 20th of the month.
3. The Cash, Accounts Receivable, and Interest Payable beginning and ending balances were:

Cash		Accounts Receivable		Interest Payable	
4,850	(2)	2,480	(4)	(2)	2,200
(4)		(3)			(1)
(5)		1,730			1,400

Requirements

1. What was the amount paid for interest in May?
2. What was the amount received from customers in May?
3. What do (1) and (3) represent?
4. What was the Cash ending balance?

E2-8B. Journalizing, posting, trial balance, income statement, and statement of financial position (*Learning Objectives 3 & 4*) 25–30 min.

Meo Consulting, Inc. completed the following transactions during February 2013, its first month of operations:

Feb	2	Sold 6,500 shares for $65,000 to DaPing Meo to start the consulting practice.
	3	Paid monthly office rent, $800.
	6	Paid cash for a new computer, $1,900.
	8	Purchased office furniture on account, $2,500.
	11	Purchased supplies on account, $500.
	19	Performed consulting service for a client on account, $2,700.
	20	Paid utility expenses, $450.
	28	Performed service for a client and received cash for the full amount of $2,000.

Requirements

1. Record transactions in the journal. Explanations are not required.

2. Create the necessary T-accounts and post the transactions to the T-accounts. Identify all items by date. Calculate the balance in each account.

3. Prepare a trial balance at February 28, 2013.

4. Prepare the income statement, statement of changes in equity, and statement of financial position.

E2-9B. Error correction (*Learning Objective 4*) 20–25 min.

Chester Hinkson has trouble keeping his debits and credits equal. During a recent month, Chester made the following errors:

a. Chester recorded a $850 payment of rent by debiting Rent Expense for $85 and crediting Cash for $85.

b. In recording a $600 payment on account, Chester debited Accounts Receivable and credited Cash.

c. Chester recorded the receipt of cash for service revenue by debiting Cash for $280 instead of the correct amount of $820. Chester also credited Service Revenue for the $280, the incorrect amount.

d. Chester posted a $350 purchase of supplies on account by debiting Accounts Payable and crediting Supplies.

e. In preparing the trial balance, Chester omitted a $50,000 note payable.

Requirements

1. For each of these errors, state whether Chester's mistake would cause the total debits and total credits on the trial balance to be unequal.

2. Identify each account with an incorrect balance, and indicate the amount and direction of the error.

E2-10B. Error correction (*Learning Objective 4*) 20–25 min.

Top Cut, Inc.'s trial balance shows $42,000 on both debit and credit sides. Top Cut's accountant found the following mistakes:

1. Purchase of Equipment $2,000 on account was incorrectly recorded as cash payment.

2. A payment of $1,200 to a supplier on account was incorrectly recorded as $2,100.

3. Cash paid for dividends of $1,500 was incorrectly recorded as salary expense.

4. Issued 2,000 shares for $6,000 to shareholders, which was incorrectly recorded as Revenue.

5. Paid $750 for an insurance policy that was incorrectly recorded as insurance expense.

Requirements

1. What are the correct debit and credit balances?

2. Does each error change the overall debit and credit balance?

3. What is the impact on each of the Assets, Liabilities, and Shareholders' Equity accounts due to the errors?

EXERCISES (ALTERNATES 1, 2, AND 3)

These alternative exercise sets are available for your practice benefit at
www.myaccountinglab.com.

PROBLEMS (GROUP A)

P2-1A. Journalizing transactions (*Learning Objective 3*) 15–20 min.

Yuming Ma provides immigration services under the business title YMM Immigration, Inc. During June, her business engaged in the following transactions:

Jun 1	Sold $60,000 shares to Yuming Ma to start the business.
3	Paid $500 for the purchase of office supplies.
8	Paid $34,000 cash to purchase land for an office site.
12	Purchased office equipment on account, $3,800.
17	Borrowed $15,000 from the bank. Ma signed a note payable to the bank in the name of the business.
26	Paid $2,500 on account.
30	Revenues earned during the month included $7,000 cash and $9,000 on account.
30	Paid employees' salaries, $2,800; office rent, $3,600; and utilities, $600.
30	Paid $6,000 of dividends to shareholder, Ma.

Ma's business uses the following accounts: Cash, Accounts Receivable, Supplies, Land, Office Equipment, Accounts Payable, Notes Payable, Common Shares, Dividends, Service Revenue, Salary Expense, Rent Expense, and Utilities Expense.

Requirements

1. Journalize each transaction. Omit explanations.

P2-2A. Journalizing transactions (*Learning Objective 3*) 15–20 min.

Advantage Advertising, Inc. engaged in the following business transactions during November of 2013:

Nov 1	Borrowed $200,000 from First National Bank. The company president signed a note payable to the bank in the name of Advantage Advertising, Inc.
3	Paid $145,000 cash to purchase an office building.
6	Provided services to customers on account, $14,700.
9	Purchased $1,600 of office supplies on account.
13	Provided services to cash customers, $8,100.
15	Paid $6,000 of dividends to company shareholders.
17	Received payment on account from credit customers, $6,600.
18	Paid property tax expense on office building, $1,600.
22	Paid employee salaries, $2,800.
26	Paid cash to purchase supplies, $700.
30	Paid $2,000 on account.

Advantage Advertising, Inc. uses the following accounts: Cash, Accounts Receivable, Supplies, Building, Accounts Payable, Notes Payable, Common Shares, Dividends, Sales Revenue, Salary Expense, and Property Tax Expense.

Requirement

1. Journalize each transaction. Omit explanations.

P2-3A. Journalizing, posting, and trial balance preparation (Learning Objectives 3 & 4) 20–25 min.

Fang Sun opened a financial services firm on March 1, 2013. During the month of March, the business completed the following transactions:

Mar	1	The business sold $40,000 shares to open the firm, Sun & Associates, Inc.
	3	Purchased supplies, $400, and furniture, $2,100, on account.
	5	Performed financial service for a client and received cash, $1,700.
	8	Paid cash to acquire land for a future office site, $18,000.
	11	Prepared tax returns for a client on account, $500.
	14	Paid assistant's salary, $1,100.
	16	Paid for the furniture purchased March 3 on account.
	19	Received $800 cash for accounting services performed.
	23	Billed a client for $1,300 of accounting services.
	28	Received $300 from client on account.
	31	Paid assistant's salary, $900.
	31	Paid rent expense, $1,200.
	31	Paid $1,800 of dividends.

Requirements

1. Open, or set up, the following T-accounts: Cash, Accounts Receivable, Supplies, Furniture, Land, Accounts Payable, Common Shares, Dividends, Service Revenue, Salary Expense, and Rent Expense.

2. Journalize transactions. Explanations are not required.

3. Post the transactions to the T-accounts, using transaction dates as posting references.

4. Calculate the balance in each account.

5. Prepare the trial balance for Sun & Associates, Inc. at the end of March.

P2-4A. Journalizing, posting, and trial balance preparation (Learning Objectives 3 & 4) 25–30 min.

The trial balance for TDR Systems, Inc. at July 15, 2013, follows:

TDR Systems, Inc.
Trial Balance
July 15, 2013

ACCT #	ACCOUNT	DEBIT	CREDIT
110	Cash	$ 3,500	
112	Accounts Receivable	7,700	
115	Supplies	700	
140	Equipment	13,200	
210	Accounts Payable		$ 4,500
311	Common Shares		20,000
315	Dividends	2,600	
411	Service Revenues		6,700
511	Salary Expense	2,200	
515	Rent Expense	1,300	
	Total	$31,200	$31,200

During the remainder of July, TDR Systems, Inc. completed the following transactions:

Jul 16	Collected $2,500 cash from a client on account.
18	Performed services on account, $1,900.
21	Received $1,700 cash for services performed.
23	Purchased supplies on account, $600.
25	Paid $1,400 in dividends.
27	Paid $3,200 on account.
29	Received $2,900 cash for services performed.
30	Paid rent, $1,200.
30	Paid employees' salaries, $2,500.

Requirements

1. Journalize the transactions that occurred July 16 to July 30.

2. Open the ledger accounts listed in the trial balance together with their beginning balances at July 15. Use the four-column account format illustrated in the chapter. Enter "Bal" for the previous balance in the Item column. Post the transactions to the ledger using dates, account numbers, and posting references. Calculate the new account balances.

3. Prepare the trial balance for TDR Systems, Inc. at the end of July.

Quick solution:

2. Cash balance = $2,300;

3. Trial balance totals = $35,100

P2-5A. **Prepare a trial balance, income statement, statement of changes in equity, and statement of financial position (*Learning Objective 4*) 20–25 min.**

The accounts of Cascade Consulting, Inc. follow with their normal balances at December 31, 2013. The accounts are listed in no particular order.

Account	Balance
Common Shares	$ 65,000
Insurance Expense	1,700
Accounts Payable	3,700
Service Revenue	83,000
Land	24,000
Supplies Expense	2,800
Cash	8,300
Salary Expense	51,000
Building	110,000
Rent Expense	12,800
Dividends	13,500
Utilities Expense	6,400
Retained Earnings	9,700
Accounts Receivable	6,500
Notes Payable	76,000
Supplies	400

Requirements

1. Prepare the company's trial balance at December 31, 2013, listing accounts in the proper order. List the largest expense first, the second-largest expense next, and so on.

2. Prepare the financial statements: income statement, statement of changes in equity, and statement of financial position. The retained earnings balance of $9,700 is the beginning balance for the year; it has not been updated for the current year's income or loss.

3. Was it a profitable year for Cascade Consulting, Inc.? Why or why not?

P2-6A. Error correction (*Learning Objective 4*) 15–20 min.

The following errors occurred in the accounting records of Pacific Outfitters, Inc.:

a. The company accountant recorded the receipt of cash for service revenue by debiting Cash for $890 instead of the correct amount of $980. Service Revenue was also credited for $890, the incorrect amount.

b. A $270 purchase of supplies on account was recorded by debiting Accounts Payable and crediting Supplies.

c. The company accountant recorded a $1,200 payment of rent by debiting rent expense for $12,000 and crediting Cash for $12,000.

d. In recording a $850 payment on account, Accounts Receivable was debited and Cash was credited.

Requirements

1. Prepare the necessary journal entries to correct each of these errors.

2. For each of the errors, determine if the error would cause net income to be overstated, understated, or unchanged.

P2-7A. Explaining the effects of transactions on accounts using T-accounts, inferring the missing amount, and preparing a trial balance (*Learning Objectives 3 & 4*) 20–25 min.

The following transactions occurred during March 2013 from KopyKat, Inc.'s operations:

Cash			Accounts Payable			Revenue	
5,000	2,500		900	2,400			(2)
(1)	900			(4)			
4,100				2,700			

Accounts Receivable			Unearned Revenue			Utilities Expense	
2,400				(1)		(4)	
(2)	5,000						
2,300							

Equipment			Note Payable	
3,200			2,500	3,200
(3)				(3)
?				4,700

Requirements

1. For each T-account, calculate the missing amount.

2. Explain transactions (1) to (4), which resulted in the entries in the T-accounts.

3. Prepare the trial balance for KopyKat, Inc. at the end of March.

P2-8A. Journalizing, trial balance, income statement, statement of changes in equity preparation (*Learning Objectives 3 & 4*) 30–40 min.

Gleaner Advertising, Inc.'s trial balance on September 30, 2013, shows the following:

ACCT #	ACCOUNT TITLE	DEBIT	CREDIT
	Gleaner Advertising, Inc.		
	Trial Balance		
	September 30, 2013		
1010	Cash	$ 8,600	
1020	Accounts Receivable	4,200	
1030	Prepaid Insurance	1,200	
1040	Prepaid Rent		
1400	Equipment	42,000	
2010	Accounts Payable		$ 5,000
2020	Unearned Advertising Revenue		3,000
2100	Long-term Note Payable		32,000
3010	Preferred Shares		
3015	Common Shares (5,000 shares)		10,000
3030	Retained Earnings		6,000
3040	Dividends		
4010	Advertising Revenue		
5010	Advertising Expense		
5020	Salary Expense		
5030	Rent Expense		
	Total	$56,000	$56,000

Gleaner completed the following transactions in October:

Oct	2	Paid 3 months rent for $1,200/month.
	3	Signed a contract for $1,800/month for 4 months with a local radio station for radio ads.
	10	Sold 2,000 common shares for $5,000 and 3,000 preferred shares for $9,000.
	14	Paid half of the accounts payable owed to suppliers.
	20	Received $6,500 cash for advertising project from a client. The project will be completed in November.
	30	The advertising revenue for October was $9,300, of which two-thirds was on account.
	31	Received an invoice for $1,800 from the local radio station for the radio ads for October. The payment is due on November 7.
	31	Paid $4,300 for employee salaries.
	31	Paid $2,400 dividends to shareholders.

Requirements

1. Set up T-accounts with the beginning balances for each account.
2. Journalize the above transactions and post to the appropriate T-accounts.
3. Prepare the trial balance on October 31, 2013.
4. Prepare the income statement and the statement of changes in equity for the month of October.

PROBLEMS (GROUP B)

P2-1B. Journalizing transactions (*Learning Objective 3*) 15–20 min.

Miko Ohara provides consulting services under the business title MO Consulting, Inc. During November, her business engaged in the following transactions:

Nov	1	Sold $55,000 of shares to Ohara to start the business.
	3	Paid $200 for the purchase of office supplies.
	8	Paid $28,000 cash to purchase land for an office site.
	12	Purchased office equipment on account, $2,800.
	17	Borrowed $50,000 from the bank. Ohara signed a note payable to the bank in the name of the business.
	26	Paid $2,700 on account.
	30	Revenues earned during the month included $12,000 cash and $23,000 on account.
	30	Paid employees' salaries, $2,100; office rent, $2,500; and utilities, $300.
	30	Paid $2,000 of dividends to shareholder, Ohara.

Ohara's business uses the following accounts: Cash, Accounts Receivable, Supplies, Land, Office Equipment, Accounts Payable, Notes Payable, Common Shares, Dividends, Service Revenue, Salary Expense, Rent Expense, and Utilities Expense.

Requirement

1. Journalize each transaction. Omit explanations.

P2-2B. Journalizing transactions (*Learning Objective 3*) 15–20 min.

Tip Top Advertising, Inc. engaged in the following business transactions during July of 2013:

Jul	1	Borrowed $190,000 from Oakville Bank. The company president signed a note payable to the bank in the name of Tip Top Advertising, Inc.
	3	Paid $110,000 cash to purchase an office building.
	6	Provided services to customers on account, $18,400.
	9	Purchased $1,200 of office supplies on account.
	13	Provided services to cash customers, $8,500.
	15	Paid $3,000 of dividends to company shareholders.
	17	Received payment on account from credit customers, $2,900.
	18	Paid property tax expense on office building, $1,400.
	22	Paid employee salaries, $3,150.
	26	Paid cash to purchase supplies, $500.
	31	Paid $2,200 on account.

Tip Top Advertising, Inc. uses the following accounts: Cash, Accounts Receivable, Supplies, Building, Accounts Payable, Notes Payable, Common Shares, Dividends, Sales Revenue, Salary Expense, and Property Tax Expense.

Requirement

1. Journalize each transaction. Omit explanations.

P2-3B. Journalizing, posting, and trial balance preparation (*Learning Objectives 3 & 4*) 20–25 min.

Teddy Sargent opened an accounting firm on May 1, 2013. During the month of May the business completed the following transactions:

May	1	The business sold $80,000 of shares to open the firm, Sargent & Associates, Inc.
	3	Purchased supplies, $500, and furniture, $1,200, on account.
	5	Performed accounting service for a client and received cash, $2,700.
	8	Paid cash to acquire land for a future office site, $22,000.
	11	Prepared tax returns for a client on account, $2,500.
	14	Paid assistant's salary, $1,200.
	16	Paid for the furniture purchased May 3 on account.
	19	Received $700 cash for accounting services performed.
	23	Billed a client for $1,300 of accounting services.
	28	Received $400 from client on account.
	31	Paid assistant's salary, $1,200.
	31	Paid rent expense, $1,700.
	31	Paid $1,200 of dividends.

Requirements

1. Open, or set up, the following T-accounts: Cash, Accounts Receivable, Supplies, Furniture, Land, Accounts Payable, Common Shares, Dividends, Service Revenue, Salary Expense, and Rent Expense.

2. Journalize transactions. Explanations are not required.

3. Post the transactions to the T-accounts, using transaction dates as posting references.

4. Calculate the balance in each account.

5. Prepare the trial balance for Sargent & Associates, Inc. at the end of May.

P2-4B. Journalizing, posting, and trial balance preparation (*Learning Objectives 3 & 4*) 25–30 min.

The trial balance for BFF Systems, Inc. at March 15, 2013, follows:

<table>
<tr><td colspan="4" align="center">BFF Systems, Inc.
Trial Balance
March 15, 2013</td></tr>
<tr><th>ACCT #</th><th>ACCOUNT</th><th>DEBIT</th><th>CREDIT</th></tr>
<tr><td>1010</td><td>Cash</td><td>$ 4,400</td><td></td></tr>
<tr><td>1020</td><td>Accounts Receivable</td><td>8,900</td><td></td></tr>
<tr><td>1030</td><td>Supplies</td><td>100</td><td></td></tr>
<tr><td>1040</td><td>Equipment</td><td>16,000</td><td></td></tr>
<tr><td>2010</td><td>Accounts Payable</td><td></td><td>$ 4,100</td></tr>
<tr><td>3010</td><td>Common Shares</td><td></td><td>23,900</td></tr>
<tr><td>3020</td><td>Dividends</td><td>2,800</td><td></td></tr>
<tr><td>4010</td><td>Service Revenue</td><td></td><td>7,700</td></tr>
<tr><td>5010</td><td>Salary Expense</td><td>2,200</td><td></td></tr>
<tr><td>5050</td><td>Rent Expense</td><td>1,300</td><td></td></tr>
<tr><td></td><td>Total</td><td>$35,700</td><td>$35,700</td></tr>
</table>

During the remainder of March, BFF Systems, Inc. completed the following transactions:

Mar 16	Collected $1,700 cash from a client on account.
18	Performed services on account, $1,900.
21	Received $1,500 cash for services performed.
23	Purchased supplies on account, $700.
25	Paid $1,300 in dividends.
27	Paid $3,300 on account.
29	Received $2,500 cash for services performed.
30	Paid rent, $1,600.
30	Paid employees' salaries, $2,600.

Requirements

1. Journalize the transactions that occurred March 16 to March 30 in the journal.

2. Open the ledger accounts listed in the trial balance together with their beginning balances at March 15, 2013. Use the four-column account format illustrated in the chapter. Enter "Bal." for the previous balance in the Item column. Post the transactions to the ledger, using dates, account numbers, and posting references. Calculate the new account balances.

3. Prepare the trial balance for BFF Systems, Inc. at the end of March.

P2-5B. Prepare a trial balance, income statement, statement of changes in equity, and statement of financial position (*Learning Objective 4*) 20–25 min.

The accounts of Highland Consulting, Inc. follow with their normal balances at August 31, 2013. The accounts are listed in no particular order.

Account	Balance
Common Shares	$107,700
Insurance Expense	1,300
Accounts Payable	4,000
Service Revenue	86,500
Land	89,000
Supplies Expense	3,100
Cash	9,200
Salary Expense	56,000
Building	91,000
Rent Expense	8,700
Dividends	10,000
Utilities Expense	5,400
Retained Earnings	13,600
Accounts Receivable	5,500
Notes Payable	68,000
Supplies	600

Requirements

1. Prepare the company's trial balance at August 31, 2013, listing accounts in the proper order. For the expenses, list the largest expense first, the second-largest expense next, and so on.

2. Prepare the financial statements: income statement, statement of changes in equity, and statement of financial position. The retained earnings balance of $13,600 is the beginning balance for the year; it has not been updated for the current year's net income or loss.

3. Was it a profitable year for Highland Consulting, Inc.? Why or why not?

P2-6B. Error correction (*Learning Objective 4*) 15–20 min.

The following errors occurred in the accounting records of Over Side, Inc.:

a. The company accountant recorded the receipt of cash for service revenue by debiting Cash for $1,140 instead of the correct amount of $1,410. Service revenue was also credited for $1,140, the incorrect amount.

b. A $150 purchase of supplies on account was recorded by debiting Accounts Payable and crediting Supplies.

c. The company accountant recorded an $800 payment of rent by debiting Rent Expense for $8,000 and crediting Cash for $8,000.

d. In recording an $815 payment on account, Accounts Receivable was debited and Cash was credited.

Requirements

1. Prepare the necessary journal entries to correct each of these errors.

2. For each of the errors, determine if the error would cause net income to be overstated, understated, or unchanged.

P2-7B. Explaining the effects of transactions on accounts using T-accounts, inferring the missing amount, and preparing a trial balance (*Learning Objectives 3 & 4*) 20–25 min.

The following transactions occurred during July 2013 from Dragon Boat, Inc.'s operations:

Cash			Accounts Payable		Revenue	
2,000	2,500		800	1,300		(1)
5,900	800			(2)		
	(4)			2,100		
1,600						

Accounts Receivable			Salary Payable		Salary Expense	
2,400			2,500	4,400	(3)	
(1)	5,900			(3)		
2,300				6,100		

Supplies			Dividends	
1,300			(4)	
(2)				
2,900				

Requirements

1. For each T-account, calculate the missing amount.

2. Explain transactions (1) to (4), which resulted in the entries in the T-accounts.

3. Prepare the trial balance for Dragon Boat, Inc. at the end of July.

P2-8B. Journalizing, trial balance, income statement, statement of changes in equity preparation (*Learning Objectives 3 & 4*) 30–40 min.

Smile Maids, Inc.'s trial balance on February 28, 2013, shows the following:

	Smile Maids, Inc. Trial Balance February 28, 2013		
ACCT #	**ACCOUNT TITLE**	**DEBIT**	**CREDIT**
1010	Cash	$ 7,200	
1020	Accounts Receivable	3,800	
1030	Cleaning Supplies	500	
1040	Prepaid Rent		
1400	Truck	52,000	
2010	Accounts Payable		$ 6,600
2020	Unearned Cleaning Revenue		4,400
2100	Long-term Note Payable		34,000
3010	Preferred Shares		
3015	Common Shares (4,000 shares)		12,000
3030	Retained Earnings		6,500
3040	Dividends		
4010	Cleaning Revenue		
5010	Cleaning Supplies Expense		
5020	Salary Expense		
5030	Rent Expense		
	Total	$63,500	$63,500

Smile Maids, Inc. completed the following transactions in March:

Mar	2	Signed a contract worth $1,200/month for a year to provide cleaning service to an office building.
	3	Paid one third of amount owing to the suppliers.
	4	Paid 4 months rent in advance, $1,500 per month.
	10	Sold 2,000 common shares for $6,800, and 2,500 preferred shares for $10,000.
	14	Ordered cleaning supplies, $3,400.
	20	Received $4,800 cash from a client for cleaning services starting in April for 3 months.
	25	Received cleaning supplies ordered on the 14th; half of the supplies were used. The invoice will be paid on April 7th.
	30	The cleaning revenue for March was $8,400, of which one quarter was on account.
	31	Paid $3,600 for employee salaries.
	31	Paid $1,800 dividends to shareholders.

Requirements

1. Set up T-accounts with the beginning balances for each account.

2. Journalize the above transactions and post to the appropriate T-accounts.

3. Prepare the trial balance on March 31, 2013.

4. Prepare the income statement and the statement of changes in equity for the month of March.

PROBLEMS (ALTERNATES 1, 2, AND 3)

These alternative problem sets are available for your practice benefit at
www.myaccountinglab.com.

CONTINUING EXERCISE

This exercise continues with the business of Graham's Yard Care, Inc. begun in the Continuing Exercise in Chapter 1. Here you will account for Graham's Yard Care, Inc.'s transactions in the general journal. Graham's Yard Care, Inc. completed the following transactions during June:

Jun	1	Received $1,000 and issued 100 common shares. Deposited this amount in bank account titled Graham's Yard Care, Inc.
	3	Purchased on account a mower, $1,000, and weed whacker, $400. The equipment is expected to remain in service for four years.
	5	Purchased $20 of gas. Wrote cheque #1 from the new bank account.
	6	Performed lawn services for client on account, $200.
	8	Purchased $50 of fertilizer from the lawn store. Wrote cheque #2 from the new bank account.
	17	Completed landscaping job for client, received cash $500.
	30	Received $50 on account from June 6 sale.

Requirements

1. Open T-accounts in the ledger: Cash, Accounts Receivable, Lawn Supplies, Equipment, Accounts Payable, Common Shares, Retained Earnings, Service Revenue, and Fuel Expense.

2. Journalize the transactions. Explanations are not required.

3. Post to the T-accounts. Key all items by date and denote an account balance as "Bal." Formal posting references are not required.

4. Prepare a trial balance at June 30, 2013.

CONTINUING PROBLEM

This problem continues with the business of Aqua Elite, Inc. begun in the Continuing Problem in Chapter 1. Here you will account for Aqua Elite, Inc.'s transactions using formal accounting practices. The trial balance for Aqua Elite, Inc. as of May 31, 2013, is presented below.

		Aqua Elite, Inc. Trial Balance May 31, 2013		
		ACCOUNT	**DEBIT**	**CREDIT**
		Cash	$24,475	
		Accounts Receivable	1,200	
		Supplies	860	
		Equipment	4,700	
		Vehicles	31,000	
		Accounts Payable		$ 840
		Notes Payable		31,000
		Common Shares		28,500
		Dividends	1,000	
		Service Revenues		4,050
		Salary Expense	675	
		Utilities Expense	480	
		Total	$64,390	$64,390

During June the following transactions occurred:

Jun	1	Paid receptionist's salary, $675.
	2	Paid cash to acquire land for a future office site, $15,000.
	3	Moved into a new location for the business and paid the first month's rent, $1,800
	4	Performed service for a customer and received cash, $1,700.
	5	Received $500 on account.
	8	Purchased $750 of supplies on account.
	11	Billed customers for services performed, $3,800.
	13	Sold an additional $10,000 of common shares to Mike Hanson.
	16	Paid receptionist's salary, $675.
	17	Received $1,350 cash for services performed.
	18	Received $1,500 from customers on account.
	19	Paid $325 to be listed in the Yellow Pages telephone directory.
	21	Paid $1,000 on account.
	22	Purchased office furniture on account, $3,300.
	24	Paid miscellaneous expenses, $275.
	26	Billed customers for services provided, $1,100.
	28	Received $300 from customers on account.
	30	Paid utility bill, $745.
	30	Paid receptionist's salary, $675.
	30	Paid $1,800 of dividends.

Requirements

1. Journalize the transactions that occurred in June. Omit explanations.

2. Open the ledger accounts listed in the trial balance together with their beginning balances at May 31. Use the four-column account format illustrated in the chapter. Enter "Bal" for the previous balance in the Item column. Post the transactions to the ledger creating new ledger accounts as necessary, omitting posting references. Calculate the new account balances.

3. Prepare the trial balance for Aqua Elite, Inc. at the end of June.

APPLY YOUR KNOWLEDGE

ETHICS IN ACTION

Case 1. Jamie Hanson was recording the daily transactions of Alpine Physical Therapy, Inc. into the accounting records so she could prepare financial statements and apply for a bank loan. Some of the business expenses were higher than she had expected, and Jamie was worried about the effect of these expenses on net income. Jamie was recording a $5,000 payment for legal fees incurred by the business by debiting Legal Expense and crediting Cash to properly record the journal entry. She then thought that, rather than debiting the expense account for the $5,000 payment, she could debit the Dividends account, which also had a normal debit balance. Jamie knew that debits had to equal credits so debiting the Dividends account instead of the Legal Expense account would not affect the trial balance. Further, the net income would be $5,000 higher because now no legal expense would be recorded. She thought that either way the retained earnings would be lower, and besides, it really didn't matter how the $5,000 payment was shown as long as she showed it somewhere.

Should Jamie debit the Dividends account rather than the Legal Expense account? Do you agree with her thought that it really doesn't matter how the $5,000 payment is shown as long as it is shown somewhere? Considering that Jamie owns all of Alpine Physical Therapy, Inc.'s common shares, does she have any ethical responsibilities to properly record each business transaction?

Case 2. Jim Peterson is the accountant for ProCare Lawnservice, Inc. During the month, numerous payments were made for wages, and therefore, he was properly debiting the Wage Expense account and crediting Cash. Jim became concerned that if he kept debiting the Wage Expense account it would end up with a balance much higher than any of the other expense accounts. Accordingly, he began debiting other expense accounts for some of the wage payments and thus, "spread the expenses around" to other expense accounts. When he was done posting all the journal entries to the ledger accounts, he printed a trial balance. He saw that the Wage Expense debit balance was $38,000 and the total of all the other expense accounts was $24,000. Had he properly posted all the wage expense transactions, Wage Expense would have totalled $52,000 and the other expense accounts would have totalled $10,000. Jim reasoned that his actions provided for "more balanced" expense account totals and, regardless of his postings, the total expenses were still $62,000, so the overall net income would be the same.

Were Jim's actions justified? Do they cause any ethical concerns? If you were the owner of ProCare Lawnservice, Inc. would you have a problem with what Jim did?

KNOW YOUR BUSINESS

FINANCIAL ANALYSIS

Purpose: To help familiarize you with the financial reporting of companies to further your understanding of the chapter material you are learning.

Although we do not have access to the journals used by Bombardier Inc., we can still understand various business transactions that Bombardier Inc. had as seen on the financial statements in its annual report. Refer to Bombardier's income statements, (Consolidated Earnings), and Bombardier's balance sheet in MyAccountingLab. Assume Bombardier completed the following transactions during January, 2012:

Jan	3	Purchased $485,000 of equipment for cash.
	7	Paid cash for $45,000 of employee wages.
	10	Purchased materials to be used directly in the manufacturing of aircraft inventory of $500,000 on account.
	15	Made $642,000 of sales on account.
	29	Paid $16,750,000 on account from the January 10 purchase.

Requirements

1. Prepare journal entries to record the transactions listed. Use the account titles found in the Bombardier Inc. financial statements: Cash and Cash Equivalents; Receivables; PP&E (Plant, Property and Equipment); Accounts Payable and Accrued Liabilities; and Revenues.

2. Look at the financial statements and locate the accounts that you included in your journal entries. Note that the balances Bombardier Inc. reported include millions of dollars in transactions for the year. Imagine how much activity and how many transactions Bombardier has every day!

INDUSTRY ANALYSIS

Purpose: To help you understand and compare the performance of two companies in the same industry.

Go to the Bombardier Inc. annual report located in MyAccountingLab. Now access the 2010 Annual Report for The Boeing Company. To do this from the internet, go to their webpage for the Investor Relations at http://www.boeing.com/companyoffices/financial/quarterly.htm and under Annual Reports, download the annual report for the year ended December 31, 2010.

Requirements

Answer these questions about the two companies:

1. In terms of total revenue, which is the larger company? Which financial statement did you look at to find that information?

2. In terms of total assets, which is the larger company? Which financial statement did you look at to find that information?

3. Which company has more total debt? Which financial statement did you look at to find that information?

4. Which company has the higher gross profit percentage? Don't know that one? On the Consolidated Statements of Income, calculate the Gross Profit by taking Total Revenues minus Total Cost of Sales for Bombardier. For Boeing, Gross Profit is represented by the Income from Operating Investments. Determine the gross profit percentage of taking Gross Profit divided by Total Revenues. What does it mean to have a higher gross profit percentage? What might affect this percentage for these two companies?

5. Who paid more cash dividends to its shareholders in the past year? Which financial statement did you look at to find that information?

6. Based on this preliminary information, which company's shares would you prefer to own? Why?

SMALL BUSINESS ANALYSIS

Purpose: To help you understand the importance of cash flows in the operation of a small business.

You're sitting in your CA office late on a Friday afternoon when you get an email from a friend. You know that she has been working on setting up a new accounting system in her office for a new business that she just started. You figured that this would eventually generate some communication between the two of you because you know that she has relatively limited accounting knowledge. Here's her email to you.

"Jerry, I'm pretty frustrated right now! As you know, I've been installing this new accounting system here in the office and I've run into a problem. I don't understand this cash account. I have purchased some items on my debit card and I've purchased some items on my credit card. So logically, when I purchased the items on my debit card, I debited the cash account. But when I used my credit card, it made sense to credit my cash account. And to make things even worse, my cash account ends up with a credit balance, and I'm pretty sure that's not right. This is too confusing and it's Friday afternoon; I'm going home!"

The following journal entries were attached to your friend's email.

DATE	ACCOUNTS	POST REF.	DR.	CR.
May 5	Cash		400	
	Supplies			400
	Purchased supplies using debit card.			

DATE	ACCOUNTS	POST REF.	DR.	CR.
May 6	Utilities Expense		250	
	Cash			250
	Paid utilities bill using credit card.			

Requirement

1. Since cash is the lifeblood of any business, having a correct balance in the cash account is of utmost importance. Correctly entering cash transactions is equally as important. Suggest to your friend the corrections that need to be made to the journal entries she made.

WRITTEN COMMUNICATION

Consider the situation that was presented in the Small Business Analysis. Your friend had two concerns that she asked you about. The first one is that she was concerned that her cash balance was showing as a credit balance instead of a debit balance. And even after the corrections were made, the cash balance was still a credit. The second concern she had was how to record transactions when she uses her debit card as opposed to transactions when she uses her credit card.

Write a short memo or letter to your friend addressing these two situations and what you would consider to be the proper accounting treatment for each of the two. More specifically, if the cash account was showing as a credit balance, how would that have happened? Is it possible for that to happen? And regarding the use of the debit card versus the credit card, from the information contained in the chapter, explain the difference between the two types of cards and how each transaction should be recorded from an accounting point of view.

Self Check Answers
1. c 2. a 3. d 4. c 5. b 6. c 7. c 8. d 9. a 10. c

SCAN THIS

CHAPTER 3

Adjusting and Closing Entries

Now that you have an understanding of how to analyze and record transactions, it is time to explore a couple more important questions. The first question is "How does a company make sure that it is reporting its income accurately?" And, the second question is "How does a company prepare for a new accounting period?" In this chapter, we will see the answers to these questions when discussing adjusting and closing entries.

CHAPTER OUTLINE:

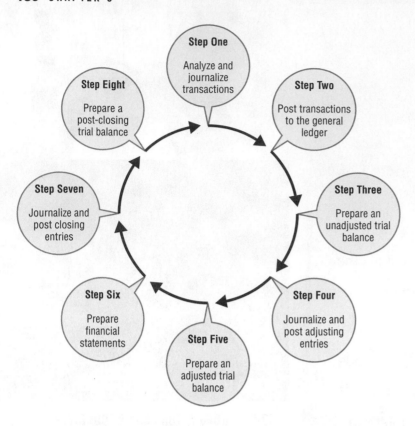

In Chapter 2, we learned about journalizing and posting transactions for a business as well as how to prepare a trial balance and financial statements. These were steps one, two, three, and six of the accounting cycle, as you can see in the visual representation.

Here in Chapter 3, we will learn how to prepare steps four, five, seven, and eight. The accounting cycle is repeated for every accounting period. The accounting period can be defined as a month, a quarter, or a year. The annual accounting period for most large companies runs the calendar year from January 1 through December 31, although some companies use a fiscal year that does not coincide with the calendar year. A **fiscal year** is any consecutive 12-month period that a business chooses. It may begin on any day of the year and end 12 months later. Usually, the fiscal year-end date is the low point in business activity for the year. Although we will focus primarily on an annual time period, financial statements are usually also prepared monthly, quarterly, or semiannually so that businesses have an idea of how they are doing before the year ends.

HOW DOES A COMPANY ACCURATELY REPORT ITS INCOME?

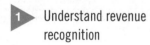 **1** Understand revenue recognition

Revenue Recognition

In Chapter 1 we learned that financial statements are prepared to provide useful information to various users. However, for financial statements to be useful, they must be accurate and up to date. To ensure that financial statements are up to date, various accounting standards, such as IFRS and the Canadian Accounting Standards for Private Enterprises, require the use of accrual accounting. To practise accrual accounting, a business must follow this accounting principle:

■ The **revenue recognition principle** states that revenues should be recognized, or recorded, when they are earned regardless of when cash is received.

Accruals and Deferrals

It is possible for a business to record revenues only when cash is received and record expenses only when cash is paid. This is referred to as **cash-basis accounting**. In many instances, when a company uses cash-basis accounting, its financial statements do not present an accurate picture of how the company is performing. This is because a business may provide goods and services to customers "on account." In this case, the business has earned revenue prior to receiving cash from the customer. A business may also purchase goods and services from suppliers on account. In this case, expenses are incurred before cash is paid. When revenues are earned before cash is received, or expenses are incurred before cash is paid, it is called an **accrual**. We have already seen accruals in Chapters 1 and 2 when we recorded transactions in Accounts Receivable and Accounts Payable.

Businesses may also receive cash from customers prior to the delivery of goods or services to the customer. In this case, cash is received before revenue is earned, and therefore, the revenue is deferred until it is earned. In addition, businesses may pay for goods or services prior to receiving those goods or services from the supplier. In this case, cash is paid before an expense is incurred, and therefore, the expense is deferred until it is consumed. When cash is received for goods or services prior to the recognition of a revenue, or cash is paid for goods or services prior to the recognition of the expense, it is called a **deferral**. We have also seen deferrals in Chapters 1 and 2 when we purchased supplies and equipment. Accruals and deferrals can be summarized as follows:

	Now	Later
Accrued Revenue	Revenue is recognized	Cash is received
Accrued Expense	Expense is recognized	Cash is paid
Deferred Revenue	Cash is received	Revenue is recognized
Deferred Expense	Cash is paid	Expense is recognized

As we saw in Chapter 2, a business records transactions throughout the accounting period as the transactions occur. At the end of the period, the accountant prepares a trial balance and uses it to prepare financial statements. However, before most businesses can prepare accurate, up-to-date financial statements, the accountant will have to prepare **adjusting entries**.

WHAT IS THE ROLE OF ADJUSTING ENTRIES, AND WHEN ARE THEY PREPARED?

Adjusting entries are journal entries used to ensure the revenue recognition principle is followed. Adjustments may be needed for accruals when revenues have been earned, or expenses have been incurred, before cash is exchanged. Since cash has not been exchanged, it is possible that the revenue or expense has not been recorded, so an adjusting entry is needed to record the revenue or expense.

 2 Understand the four types of adjustments and prepare adjusting entries

- Two types of adjustments are made for accruals:
  1. Accrue, or record, unrecorded revenues. Revenues are recorded in the current period by debiting a receivable and crediting revenue.
  2. Accrue, or record, unrecorded expenses. Record the expenses in the current period by debiting an expense and crediting a liability.

A deferral is created when cash is exchanged before the related revenue or expense is recognized. Examples include receiving cash from customers prior to providing services or purchasing supplies that are not used immediately.

- Two types of adjustments are made for deferrals:
    1. Divide **unearned revenues** between periods. When payment is received in advance from a customer for goods or services, cash is debited. The liability account, Unearned Revenues, is credited because the customer is owed the goods or services. Once the customer receives the goods or services, an adjusting entry is prepared in which the Unearned Revenue account is debited to reduce it and a revenue is credited.
    2. Divide prepaid expenses, supplies, buildings, equipment, and other assets between periods. These items are recorded as assets when they are purchased because the item that was paid for has not yet been used up. Therefore, an asset account is debited and Cash is credited to record the purchase. Once part, or all, of the item is used up, an adjusting entry is prepared in which an expense account is debited and the related asset is credited to reduce it.

At the end of the accounting period, the accountant prepares a trial balance from the account information contained in the general ledger. This trial balance lists most of the revenues and expenses of the business, but these amounts are incomplete because the adjusting entries have not yet been prepared. Therefore, this trial balance is called an **unadjusted trial balance** (step three in the accounting cycle). Remember Hooray Consulting, Inc. from Chapter 2? **Exhibit 3-1** shows the unadjusted trial balance for Hooray Consulting, Inc. at the end of its first quarter of operations, at March 31, 2013.

Remember from Chapter 2 that transactions are recorded in the journal and posted to accounts in the general ledger. This process is still used when adjusting the accounts. In this chapter, we will show how to record adjusting entries and how to post them to accounts. However, instead of using the real ledger account form, we will post adjustments to T-accounts. We use this method because it is easier to see how these entries affect the specific accounts as well as the accounting equation.

Hooray Consulting, Inc.
(Unadjusted) Trial Balance
March 31, 2013

			BALANCE	
		ACCOUNT TITLE	**DEBIT**	**CREDIT**
		Cash	$26,300	
		Accounts Receivable	3,100	
		Supplies	900	
		Prepaid Rent	3,000	
		Equipment	12,600	
		Accounts Payable		$13,100
		Unearned Service Revenue		450
		Common Shares		20,000
		Retained Earnings		9,500
		Dividends	3,200	
		Service Revenue		7,000
		Salary Expense	550	
		Utilities Expense	400	
		Total	$50,050	$50,050

Exhibit 3-1 ▲

Accruing Revenues

Accounts Receivable Businesses sometimes earn revenue by providing goods or services before they receive cash. Assume that a local car dealership hires Hooray Consulting, Inc. on March 15 as a computer consultant. Hooray Consulting agrees to a monthly fee of $500, which the car dealership pays on the 15th of each month beginning on April 15. During March, Hooray earns half a month's fee, $250 ($500 × 1/2 month), for consulting work performed March 15 through March 31. On March 31, Hooray makes the following adjusting entry to reflect the accrual of the revenue earned during March (the beginning balance of each account is found on the unadjusted trial balance presented in Exhibit 3-1):

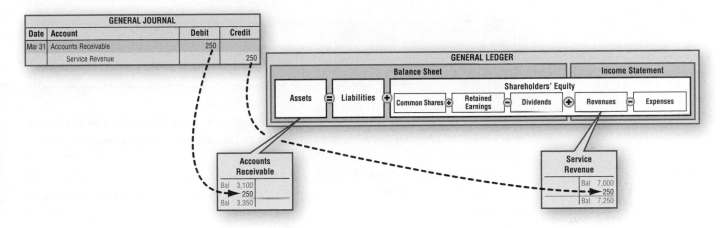

Without the adjustment, Hooray Consulting's financial statements are inaccurate because they would understate both Accounts Receivable and Service Revenue.

Accruing Expenses

Salary Payable Suppose Hooray Consulting pays its employee a monthly salary of $550. Hooray pays the employee on the 15th of each month for the past month's work. On March 31, the following adjustment must be made to record the salary expense for the month of March:

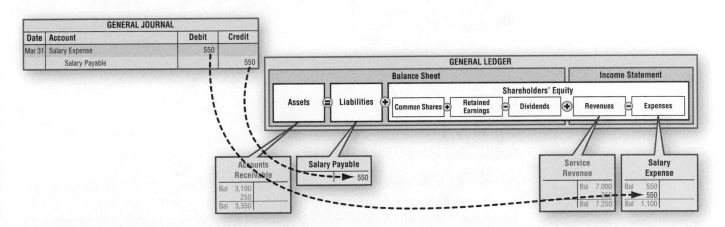

This is referred to as accruing the expense. **Accrued expenses**, such as the accrual for salary expense, are expenses that the business has incurred but not paid. The adjusting entry to accrue the expense always creates a liability, such as Salary Payable, Taxes Payable, or Interest Payable.

Adjusting Deferred Revenues

Unearned Revenues It is possible for a business to collect cash from customers prior to providing goods or services. Receiving cash from a customer before earning it creates a liability called unearned revenue, or **deferred revenue**. It is classified as a liability because the company owes a product or service to the customer. Even though the account has the word "revenue" in its title, it is not a revenue account because the amounts in the account represent what has *not* yet been earned.

Suppose a local real estate agency hires Hooray Consulting to provide consulting services, agreeing to pay $450 monthly, beginning immediately. Hooray Consulting collects the first amount from the real estate agency on March 21. Hooray Consulting records the cash receipt and a liability as follows:

DATE	ACCOUNTS	POST REF.	DR.	CR.
Mar 21	Cash		450	
	Unearned Service Revenue			450
	Collected revenue in advance.			

The liability account Unearned Service Revenue now shows that Hooray Consulting owes $450 of services because of its obligation to provide consulting services to the real estate agency.

During the last 10 days of March, Hooray Consulting earned one-third of the $450, or $150 ($450 × 1/3). Therefore, Hooray Consulting makes the following adjustment to record earning $150 of the revenue:

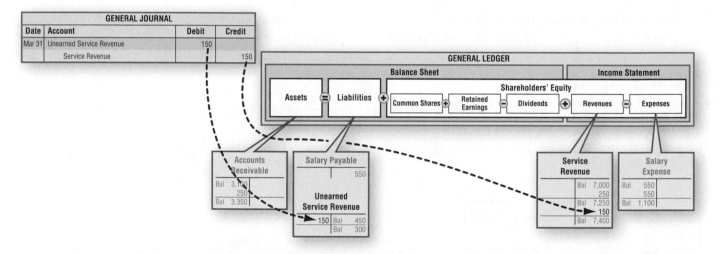

Service Revenue increases by $150, and Unearned Service Revenue decreases by $150. Now both accounts are up to date at March 31.

Adjusting Deferred Expenses

Prepaid Rent Prepaid rent and prepaid insurance are examples of prepaid expenses, also called **deferred expenses**. Prepaid expenses represent items that are paid for before they are used. Often, renters are required to pay rent in advance. This prepayment creates an asset for the renter. Suppose Hooray Consulting, Inc. moves to a new office and prepays three months' office rent on March 1, 2013. If the lease specifies a monthly rental of $1,000, the amount of cash paid is $3,000 ($1,000 × 3 months). The entry to record the payment is as follows:

DATE	ACCOUNTS	POST REF.	DR.	CR.
Mar 1	Prepaid Rent		3,000	
	Cash			3,000
	Paid three months' rent in advance.			

After posting, Prepaid Rent has a $3,000 debit balance. During March, Hooray Consulting uses the rented space for one month; therefore, the balance in Prepaid Rent is reduced by $1,000 (one month's rent). The required adjusting entry is as follows:

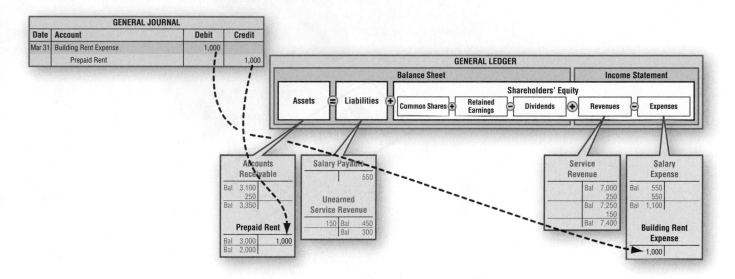

The Building Rent Expense account is increased with a debit, which reduces Retained Earnings and, therefore, Shareholders' Equity. The asset account Prepaid Rent is decreased with a credit for the same amount. After posting, Prepaid Rent and Building Rent Expense show the correct ending balances. If Hooray Consulting, Inc. had prepaid insurance, the same analysis would also apply to this asset account. The difference in the adjusting entry would be in the account titles, which would be Prepaid Insurance instead of Prepaid Rent, and Insurance Expense instead of Building Rent Expense. The amount of the entry would also be different.

Supplies Supplies receive the same treatment as prepaid expenses. On March 5, Hooray Consulting pays $900 for office supplies. The asset accounts, Supplies and Cash, are both affected. Supplies increased by $900, while Cash decreased by $900, as shown here:

DATE	ACCOUNTS	POST REF.	DR.	CR.
Mar 5	Supplies		900	
	Cash			900
	Purchased office supplies.			

The March 31 trial balance, as shown in Exhibit 3-1 on page 138, shows Supplies with a $900 debit balance. During March, Hooray Consulting uses some of these supplies to conduct business. Therefore, Hooray Consulting's March 31 Balance Sheet should *not* report supplies of $900. To figure out the amount of supplies used, Hooray Consulting counts the supplies on hand at the end of March. The supplies on hand are still an asset to the business. Assume that Hooray Consulting has supplies costing $600

ACCOUNTING IN YOUR WORLD

To better understand the difference between a prepaid expense and an unearned revenue, consider this example:

At the start of this semester in school, you paid your school the tuition that was due for the upcoming term. Your tuition will ultimately be an expense to you. However, before the term began, the amount you paid was not yet an expense to you because the school had not yet provided any classes. In other words, you had not yet received anything for your payment. Instead, the amount you paid represented an asset known as a prepaid expense. It was an asset because the school owes you either the classes or your money back.

Once classes started, you began to incur an expense. Technically, the amount of your asset, prepaid expense, would have decreased and the amount of your expenses would have increased every day. By the end of the semester, none of the tuition you paid would be considered to be a prepaid expense. Instead, it becomes an expense.

Now, let's look at the same example from the perspective of your school. When your school received the tuition payment from you, it did not have the right to record it as a revenue because it had not provided you with any classes. Instead, the school would record your tuition as a liability called unearned revenue. Unearned revenue represents a liability to the school because the school owes you either the classes or your money back.

Once classes started, your school began to earn revenue. The amount of its unearned revenue would have decreased and the amount of its revenue would have increased every day. By the end of the semester, the entire amount of tuition you paid would be considered to be revenue to your school. As you can see, one entity's prepaid expense is another entity's unearned revenue and vice versa.

at March 31st. The supplies purchased ($900) minus the supplies on hand at the end of March ($600) equals the value of the supplies used during the month ($300). The amount of supplies used during the month will become supplies expense. The March 31 adjusting entry updates the Supplies account and records Supplies Expense for the month:

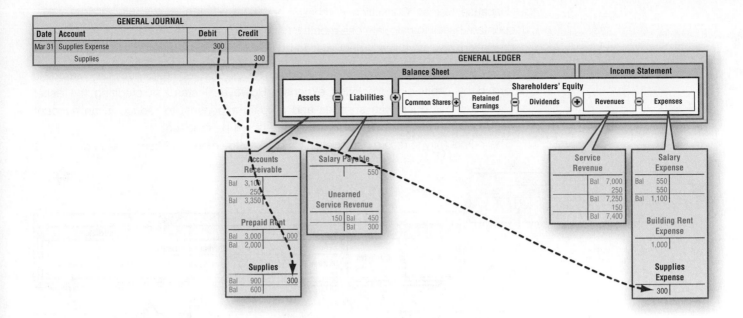

After the entry is posted to the general ledger, the correct account balances for Supplies and Supplies Expense will be reflected.

Depreciation of long-term assets **Long-term assets**, or fixed assets, are assets that last for more than one year. Examples include land, buildings, equipment, and furniture. All of these assets, except land, are used up over time. As a long-term asset is used up, part of the asset's cost becomes an expense, just as supplies become supplies expense when they are used up. The expensing of a long-term asset's cost over its useful life is called **depreciation**. No depreciation is recorded for land because it is never really used up.

We account for long-term assets in the same way as prepaid expenses and supplies because they are all assets. The major difference is the length of time it takes for the asset to be used up. Prepaid expenses and supplies are typically used within a year, while most long-term assets remain functional for several years. Suppose that on March 8, Hooray Consulting purchases equipment on account for $12,600 and makes this journal entry:

DATE	ACCOUNTS	POST REF.	DR.	CR.
Mar 8	Equipment		12,600	
	Accounts Payable			12,600
	Purchased equipment on account.			

After posting the entry, the Equipment account has a $12,600 balance. It is difficult to measure the amount of a long-term asset that has been used up over time, so the amount must be estimated. Several methods can be used to estimate the amount of depreciation. The most common method, which Hooray Consulting utilizes, is called the **straight-line depreciation** method. Hooray Consulting believes the equipment will be useful for three years and will be worthless and have no **salvage (or residual) value** at the end of its life. Depreciation of this equipment is calculated using the straight-line method as follows:

$$\text{Depreciation Expense per Year} = \frac{\text{Cost of Asset} - \text{Salvage Value of Asset}}{\text{Useful Life of Asset}} = \frac{\$12,600}{3} = \$4,200$$

Because Hooray Consulting purchased the equipment in the month of March, the accountant needs to calculate one month's depreciation expense. To calculate one month's depreciation, divide the yearly depreciation by twelve ($4,200/12 months = $350).

The Accumulated Depreciation Account Depreciation expense for March is recorded by debiting depreciation expense. However, instead of crediting the asset account (as was done with supplies and prepaid expenses) to reduce it, an account called **Accumulated Depreciation**, Equipment will be credited.

The journal entry to record depreciation expense for the month of March is as follows:

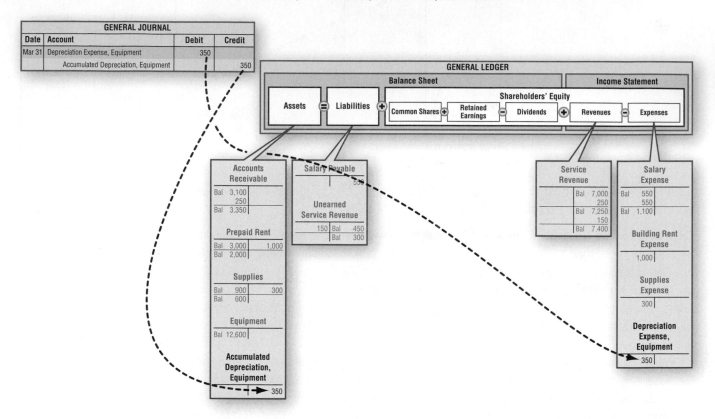

Accumulated Depreciation, Equipment, is a contra-asset. A **contra-account** has three main characteristics:

- A contra-account is linked to another account and will always appear with this account in the financial statements.
- A contra-account's normal balance is always opposite of the account it is linked to.
- The balance in a contra-account is subtracted from the balance of the account it is linked to in order to find the **net value** of the two accounts.

Because it is linked to Equipment, an asset account, Accumulated Depreciation, Equipment will appear on the statement of financial position or balance sheet. Being an asset, the Equipment account has a debit balance, so the Accumulated Depreciation, Equipment account will have a credit balance because it is a contra-asset. Since it's a contra-account, the balance of Accumulated Depreciation, Equipment is subtracted from Equipment. The net amount of a long-term asset is called its **book value**, or **carrying value**, and is calculated as follows:

Book Value of a Long-Term Asset		
Cost	Equipment...	$12,600
− Accumulated Depreciation	Less: Accumulated Depreciation, Equipment..............	350
= Book (or Carrying) Value	Book Value...	$12,250

Accumulated Depreciation, Equipment increases over the life of the asset as the asset is used up, which reduces the book value of the equipment. By keeping the cost of the equipment separate from its accumulated depreciation, financial statement users can look at the Equipment account to see how much the asset originally cost and also look at the Accumulated Depreciation, Equipment account to see how much of the original cost has been used up. A business usually keeps an accumulated depreciation account for each type of depreciable long-term asset. If Hooray Consulting, Inc. had both buildings and equipment, it would use two accumulated depreciation accounts, Accumulated Depreciation, Buildings, and Accumulated Depreciation, Equipment. Depreciation will be covered in more depth in Chapter 8.

CONCEPT CHECK

Jim Oda is the accountant for Crazy Critters, Inc., a local veterinary clinic. After Jim finished preparing the financial statements for the year, he realized that he had failed to make an adjusting entry to record $1,800 of depreciation expense for the year. What effect did this error have on Crazy Critter's financial statements?

Answer

To determine the effects of omitting an adjusting entry, we must examine what the adjusting entry should have been. The adjusting entry Jim should have made is as follows:

DATE	ACCOUNTS	POST REF.	DR.	CR.
	Depreciation Expense		1,800	
	Accumulated Depreciation			1,800

As we can see from the journal entry, Depreciation Expense should have been debited (increased), which would have increased total expenses for the year. An increase in total expenses causes a decrease in net income. So, the omission of the adjusting entry for depreciation expense causes net income, and therefore, retained earnings, to be overstated. We also see that the Accumulated Depreciation account should have been credited (increased), which would cause total assets to decrease because Accumulated Depreciation is a contra-asset account. So, the omission of the adjusting entry for depreciation expense also causes the total assets to be overstated.

DECISION GUIDELINES

Decision	Guideline	Analyze
I would like to invest in a company. Can I trust that the statements are accurate?	To produce accurate financial information the revenue recognition principle should be followed.	The revenue recognition principle requires that revenues be recorded only when they are earned regardless of when cash is received. When the revenue recognition principle is followed it is referred to as *accrual accounting*. The auditors check a random selection of entries to help verify that the guidelines and principles have been followed appropriately.

HOW ARE FINANCIAL STATEMENTS PREPARED FROM AN ADJUSTED TRIAL BALANCE?

The Adjusted Trial Balance

3 Prepare financial statements from an adjusted trial balance

Earlier in the chapter, the unadjusted trial balance in Exhibit 3-1 on page 138 showed the account balances for Hooray Consulting, Inc. before the adjustments had been made. After adjustment, Hooray Consulting's accounts would appear as presented in **Exhibit 3-2**.

Assets = Liabilities + Shareholders' Equity

Cash
| 26,300 | |

Accounts Receivable
3,100	
250	
3,350	

Supplies
| 900 | 300 |
| 600 | |

Prepaid Rent
| 3,000 | 1,000 |
| 2,000 | |

Equipment
| 12,600 | |

Accum. Depreciation Equipment
| | 350 |

Accounts Payable
| | 13,100 |

Salary Payable
| | 550 |
| | 550 |

Unearned Service Revenue
| 150 | 450 |
| | 300 |

Common Shares
| | 20,000 |

Retained Earnings
| | 9,500 |

Dividends
| 3,200 | |

Service Revenue
	7,000
	250
	150
	7,400

Salary Expense
550	
550	
1,100	

Building Rent Expense
| 1,000 | |

Supplies Expense
| 300 | |

Depreciation Expense, Equipment
| 350 | |

Utilities Expense
| 400 | |

Exhibit 3-2 ▲

CRITICAL THINKING

Take a minute to think about the impact of the errors in the following independent cases on each of the assets, liabilities, and shareholders' equity accounts, based on each of the scenarios. What are the entries required to make the account balance correct? Who might have found these errors?

- Depreciation of $1,000 on a delivery truck was debited Depreciation Expense $1,000, and credited Delivery Truck $1,000.
- An annual insurance premium of $1,200 was originally recorded in the Insurance Expense account. Four months of insurance premium have expired. No adjusting entry was made at the year end.
- A receipt of $6,000 from a customer for a three-month service contract was originally recorded in the Service Revenue account. One month of service has been provided. No adjusting entry was made at the year end.

Solution:

Impact on Accounts

	Assets	Liabilities	Shareholders' Equity	Required entries to correct account balances	Debit	Credit
1	No	No	No	1 (a) Delivery Truck	1,000	
	There is no impact on the Assets account since the error involved recording the increase in the Accumulated Depreciation account as a reduction in the Delivery Truck account instead. The net effect on the total assets is the same.			Depreciation Expense		1,000
				1 (b) Depreciation Expense	1,000	
				Accumulated Depreciation, Delivery Truck		1,000
				or		
				2. Delivery Truck	1,000	
				Accumulated Depreciation, Delivery Truck		1,000
2	Understated	No	Understated	1 (a) Prepaid Insurance	1,200	
	The Shareholders' Equity account is understated because the expenses are recorded too high, which reduced Retained Earnings and in turn reduces Shareholders' Equity.			Insurance Expense		1,200
				1 (b) Insurance Expense	400	
				Prepaid Insurance		400
				or		
				2. Prepaid Insurance	800	
				Insurance Expense		800
3	No	Understated	Overstated			
	Liabilities are understated because the Unearned Revenue account should have been increased, but wasn't.			1 (a) Service Revenue	6,000	
				Unearned Revenue		6,000
				1 (b) Unearned Revenue	2,000	
				Service Revenue		2,000

The first error may have been noticed by the manager responsible for the fleet of delivery trucks. The manager would notice that the recorded value of the trucks decreased for no reason. The second error would be spotted by the manager responsible for organizing the insurance. In a comparison from the previous year and the current year, there would be a noticeable increase in the insurance costs for the current year. The last error would be noticed by an internal auditor. The list of jobs that are not complete yet would not balance with the Unearned Revenue account since this job was not set up as a liability.

Prior to preparing the financial statements, an **adjusted trial balance** is prepared to make sure total debits still equal total credits after adjusting entries have been recorded and posted. The adjusted trial balance for Hooray Consulting is presented in Exhibit 3-3.

	Hooray Consulting, Inc. Adjusted Trial Balance March 31, 2013		
ACCT #	ACCOUNT	DEBIT	CREDIT
1010	Cash	$26,300	
1020	Accounts Receivable	3,350	
1030	Supplies	600	
1035	Prepaid Rent	2,000	
1040	Equipment	12,600	
1041	Accumulated Depreciation, Equipment		$ 350
2010	Accounts Payable		13,100
2015	Salary Payable		550
2020	Unearned Service Revenue		300
3010	Common Shares		20,000
3030	Retained Earnings		9,500
3040	Dividends	3,200	
4010	Service Revenue		7,400
5010	Salary Expense	1,100	
5015	Building Rent Expense	1,000	
5030	Utilities Expense	400	
5040	Depreciation Expense, Equipment	350	
5050	Supplies Expense	300	
	Total	$51,200	$51,200

Exhibit 3-3 ▲

Preparing the Financial Statements

The March financial statements of Hooray Consulting, Inc. are prepared from the adjusted trial balance in Exhibit 3-3. The financial statements should be prepared in the same order that we used in previous chapters:

❶ The income statement (Exhibit 3-4) reports the revenues and the expenses to determine net income or net loss for a period of time. Assume Hooray Consulting, Inc. pays 30% income tax on its profit.

❷ The statement of retained earnings (Exhibit 3-5, a component of the Statement of Changes in Equity) shows the changes in retained earnings during the period and computes the ending balance of retained earnings. Notice that the Retained Earnings balance of $9,500 on the adjusted trial balance does *not* represent the ending Retained Earnings balance because the account has not yet been updated for the current period's earnings or dividends.

❸ The classified statement of financial position or balance sheet (Exhibit 3-6) reports the assets, liabilities, and shareholders' equity to see the financial position of the business at a specific point in time. There are two classes of assets: (a) current assets, which are assets that will be used or converted to cash within one year or one operating cycle, and (b) non-current assets, which will be kept for more than one year or one operating cycle.

Hooray Consulting, Inc.
Income Statement
Month Ended March 31, 2013

Revenue:			
Service Revenue			$7,400
Expenses:			
Salary Expense		$1,100	
Building Rent Expense		1,000	
Utilities Expense		400	
Depreciation Expense, Equipment		350	
Supplies Expense		300	
Total Operating Expenses			3,150
Operating Income			4,250
Income Tax (30%)			1,275
Net Income			$2,975

Exhibit 3-4 ▲

Hooray Consulting, Inc.
Statement of Retained Earnings
Month Ended March 31, 2013

Retained Earnings, March 1, 2013			$9,500
Add: Net Income			2,975
Subtotal			12,475
Less: Dividends			3,200
Retained Earnings, March 31, 2013			$9,275

Exhibit 3-5 ▲

Hooray Consulting, Inc.
Statement of Financial Position
March 31, 2013

ASSETS			LIABILITIES	
Current Assets			Accounts Payable	$13,100
Cash	$26,300		Salary Payable	550
Accounts Receivable	3,350		Unearned Service Revenue	300
Supplies	600		Income Tax Payable	1,275
Prepaid Rent	2,000		Total Liabilities	$15,225
Total Current Assets		$32,250		
			SHAREHOLDERS' EQUITY	
Equipment	$12,600		Common Shares	$20,000
Less: Accumulated				
Depreciation, Equipment	350	12,250	Retained Earnings	9,275
			Total Shareholders' Equity	$29,275
			Total Liabilities &	
Total Assets		$44,500	Shareholders' Equity	$44,500

Exhibit 3-6 ▲

As we first discussed in Chapter 1, all financial statements include these elements:

- Heading
    1. Name of the entity, such as Hooray Consulting, Inc.
    2. Title of the statement: income statement, statement of retained earnings, statement of financial position, or balance sheet
    3. Date or period covered by the statement: Month ended March 31, 2013, or March 31, 2013
- Body of the statement

On the income statement, expenses may be listed in descending order from the largest amount to the smallest amount, as Hooray Consulting did, or they may be listed in some other order, such as alphabetical order. Note that once the income statement is prepared, we know the amount of income tax that Hooray needs to pay to the government. However, Hooray will not make the income tax payment to the government on March 31. Therefore, Hooray needs to prepare another adjusting entry to record the income tax expense incurred for the month and income tax payable to government. As a result, both the income statement and liabilities section show an additional item—income tax expense and income tax payable.

During the creation of the income statement, income taxes need to be recorded. At 30% of the income before taxes, the income tax expense becomes $4250 \times 30\% = \$1,275$. This expense would need to be recorded in the General Journal as shown.

GENERAL JOURNAL			
Date	Account	Debit	Credit
Mar 31	Income Tax Expense	1,275	
	Income Tax Payable		1,275

HOW DOES A COMPANY PREPARE FOR A NEW ACCOUNTING PERIOD?

Completing the Accounting Cycle

4 ▶ Prepare closing entries and a post-closing trial balance

We have now seen steps one through six in the accounting cycle completed for Hooray Consulting. The entire accounting cycle can be completed by finishing steps seven and eight. Step seven of the accounting cycle is the journalizing and posting of the closing entries, and step eight is the preparation of a post-closing trial balance.

In order to complete the accounting cycle, **closing entries** must be journalized and posted. Earlier in the chapter, we processed the transactions for Hooray Consulting and prepared the financial statements for the month of March. If we continue recording information in the revenue, expense, and dividend accounts, we will lose track of what activity happened in March compared to what happens in April, making it impossible to prepare accurate financial statements for the month of April.

In order to not confuse the transactions from the two different months, the revenue, expense, and dividend accounts must be reset back to zero before we start recording transactions for April. It is similar to resetting the scoreboard at the end of a game before you start a new game. Since we must keep the accounting equation in balance, we cannot just erase the balances in the revenue, expense, and dividend accounts. To keep the accounting equation in balance and still be able to zero out these accounts, we will use closing entries. Closing entries are utilized to accomplish two things:

- The revenue, expense, and dividend account balances from the current accounting period are set back to zero so that accounting for the next period can begin.
- The revenue, expense, and dividend account balances from the current accounting period are transferred into Retained Earnings so that the accounting equation stays in balance. Transferring the revenue and expense account balances into retained earnings actually transfers the net income, or net loss, for the current period into Retained Earnings. Transferring the dividend account balance into Retained Earnings decreases Retained Earnings by the amount of dividends for the period.

The revenue, expense, and dividend accounts are known as **temporary accounts**. They are called temporary because they are used temporarily to record activity for a specific period, the accounting period, and then they are closed into Retained Earnings. It is easy to remember the temporary accounts if you think of the color RED. The R in RED stands for revenues, the E stands for expenses, and the D stands for dividends. The RED accounts are closed at the end of each accounting period.

Before closing the accounts, the accounting equation for a corporation would be as follows:

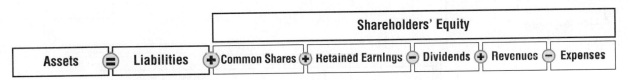

After closing the accounts, the accounting equation would be as follows:

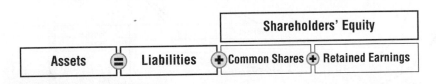

The accounts that remain in the accounting equation after closing are called **permanent accounts**. Assets, liabilities, common shares, and retained earnings are *not* closed at the end of the period because they are not used to measure activity for a specific period. Consider Cash, Accounts Receivable, Accounts Payable, and Common Shares. These accounts do not represent business activity for a single period, so they are not closed at the end of the period. Their balances carry over to the next period. For example, the Cash balance at March 31, 2013, becomes the beginning balance on April 1, 2013.

The Three Closing Entries: Revenues, Expenses, and Dividends

To journalize closing entries, complete the following steps:

Step 1 Close the revenue accounts and move their balances into the Retained Earnings account. To close revenues, debit each revenue account for the amount of its credit balance. Transfer the revenue balances to Retained Earnings by crediting the Retained Earnings account for the total amount of the revenues. This closing entry transfers total revenues to the credit side of Retained Earnings.

Step 2 Close the expense accounts and move their balances into the Retained Earnings account. To close expenses, credit each expense account for the amount of its debit balance. Transfer the expense balances to Retained Earnings by debiting the Retained Earnings account for the total amount of the expenses. This closing entry transfers total expenses to the debit side of Retained Earnings.

Step 3 Close the Dividends account and move its balance into the Retained Earnings account. To close the Dividends account, credit it for the amount of its debit balance and debit the Retained Earnings account. This entry transfers the dividends to the debit side of Retained Earnings.

Remember that net income is equal to revenues minus expenses. So, closing the revenues and expenses into retained earnings, Steps 1 and 2, has the effect of adding net income for the period to, or deducting a net loss for the period from, retained earnings. Once the Dividends account has been subtracted from retained earnings, Step 3, the balance in the retained earnings account should match ending retained earnings on the statement of retained earnings.

The process for making closing entries is the same as it is for making any entry: record the entries in the journal and post them to the proper accounts in the ledger.

Now, let's apply this process to Hooray Consulting, Inc. for the month of March:

Step 1

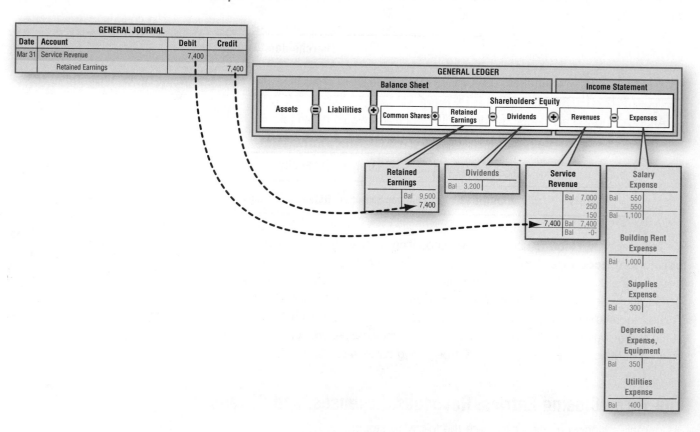

Step 2

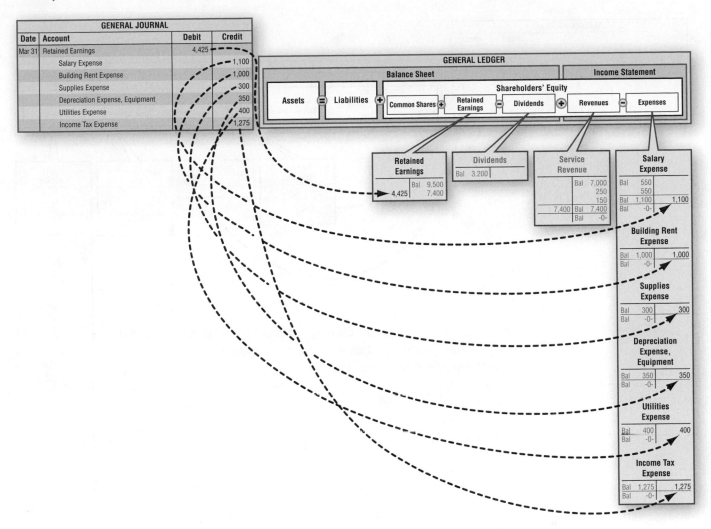

GENERAL JOURNAL			
Date	Account	Debit	Credit
Mar 31	Retained Earnings	4,425	
	Salary Expense		1,100
	Building Rent Expense		1,000
	Supplies Expense		300
	Depreciation Expense, Equipment		350
	Utilities Expense		400
	Income Tax Expense		1,275

Step 3

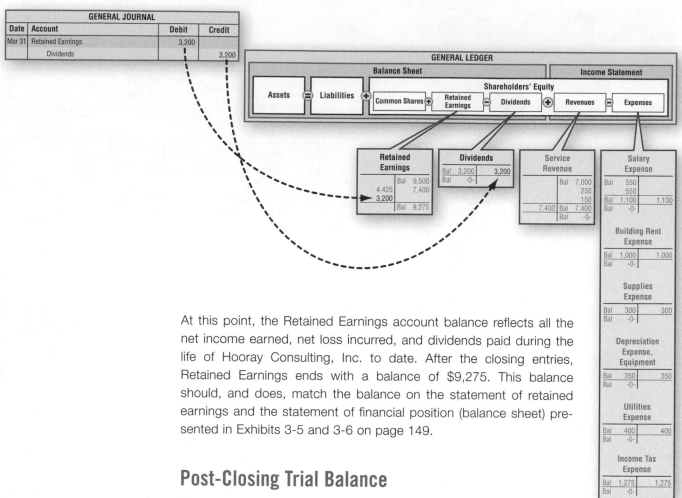

At this point, the Retained Earnings account balance reflects all the net income earned, net loss incurred, and dividends paid during the life of Hooray Consulting, Inc. to date. After the closing entries, Retained Earnings ends with a balance of $9,275. This balance should, and does, match the balance on the statement of retained earnings and the statement of financial position (balance sheet) presented in Exhibits 3-5 and 3-6 on page 149.

Post-Closing Trial Balance

The accounting cycle ends with the preparation of a **post-closing trial balance**, as seen in **Exhibit 3-7**. This trial balance lists the

ACCT #	ACCOUNT	DEBIT	CREDIT
	Hooray Consulting, Inc.		
	Post-Closing Trial Balance		
	March 31, 2013		
1010	Cash	$26,300	
1020	Accounts Receivable	3,350	
1030	Supplies	600	
1035	Prepaid Rent	2,000	
1040	Equipment	12,600	
1041	Accumulated Depreciation, Equipment		$ 350
2010	Accounts Payable		13,100
2015	Salary Payable		550
2020	Unearned Service Revenue		300
2030	Income Tax Payable		1,275
3010	Common Shares		20,000
3030	Retained Earnings		9,275
	Total	$44,850	$44,850

Exhibit 3-7 ▲

accounts and their adjusted balances after closing. Only assets, liabilities, and shareholders' equity appear on the post-closing trial balance. No temporary accounts—revenues, expenses, or dividends—are included because they have been closed. The accounts in the ledger are now up to date and ready for the next period's transactions.

DECISION GUIDELINES

Decision	**Guideline**	**Analyze**
As the bookkeeper for a company, how do I ensure that my accounting records are ready to start a new period?	Prepare *closing entries* for the *temporary accounts*: • Revenues • Expenses • Dividends	The *temporary accounts* have balances that relate only to one accounting period and need to be reset to $0 before accounting for the next period can begin. To reset the temporary accounts, closing entries are made that close the account balances into Retained Earnings. This ensures that the net income for the following period can be tracked accurately. Assets, Liabilities, Common Shares, and Retained Earnings do not get closed. These accounts are referred to as *permanent accounts*. Their balances are carried forward into the next period. After temporary accounts have been closed, a post-closing trial balance is prepared to ensure that all of the temporary accounts were properly closed.

Summary of the Adjusting and Closing Process

Businesses record adjusting entries at the *end* of the accounting period to accomplish two purposes:

❶ Report net income or net loss accurately on the income statement.

❷ Reflect the correct account balances on the balance sheet.

Each adjusting entry will always affect one income statement account, a revenue or an expense, and one balance sheet account, an asset or a liability. *Cash is never included in a period-end adjusting entry because cash should always be recorded accurately at the time it is received or paid.*

Deferrals and accruals can be summarized as follows:

❶ A *deferred revenue or expense* is paid first, and recorded as a revenue or expense later as the revenue is earned or the expense is incurred.

❷ An *accrued revenue or expense* is recorded as a revenue or expense first as the revenue is earned or the expense is incurred, and paid later.

Exhibit 3-8 summarizes the accrual and deferral adjustments.

Businesses record closing entries at the *end* of the accounting period to accomplish two purposes:

■ Zero out the revenue, expense, and dividend accounts.

■ Transfer the balance of the revenue, expense, and dividend accounts into Retained Earnings.

Closing entries are the end-of-period journal entries that get the temporary accounts—revenues, expenses, and dividends—ready for the next accounting period by

Adjusting Entries

Deferrals: Cash transaction comes first.

	First	Dr.	Cr.	Later	Dr.	Cr.
Prepaid Expenses, Depreciable Assets	*Pay cash and record an asset:*			*Record an expense and decrease the asset:*		
	Prepaid Rent	XXX		Rent Expense	XXX	
	Cash		XXX	Prepaid Rent		XXX
Unearned Revenues	*Receive cash and record a liability:*			*Record a revenue and decrease the liability:*		
	Cash	XXX		Unearned Service Revenue	XXX	
	Unearned Service Revenue		XXX	Service Revenue		XXX

Accruals: Cash transaction comes later.

	First	Dr.	Cr.	Later	Dr.	Cr.
Accrued Expenses	*Accrue an expense and the related liability:*			*Pay cash and decrease the liability:*		
	Salary Expense	XXX		Salary Payable	XXX	
	Salary Payable		XXX	Cash		XXX
Accrued Revenues	*Accrue a revenue and the related asset:*			*Receive cash and decrease the asset:*		
	Accounts Receivable	XXX		Cash	XXX	
	Service Revenue		XXX	Accounts Receivable		XXX

Exhibit 3-8 ▲

FOCUS ON USERS

Concept	User	Why is this Important to this User?
Adjusting Entries		Creditors are interested in the effect of adjusting entries because the adjusting entries highlight the difference between the timing of when cash is paid or received and when the revenues or expenses are recorded. This may have an impact on the ability of a company to pay its debts.
		Managers need to understand the adjusting entries because adjusting entries are quite often based on estimations. For example, an adjusting entry to change unearned revenue to revenue may be based on an estimate of how much of the work has been completed for the job that has been prepaid by the customer. What this means is that the adjusting entry is subjective and those in charge of making the estimations may be able to exaggerate situations for their own reasons. For example, a sales manager who receives a bonus based on the amount of revenues recorded would be interested in estimating as high an amount of revenues as possible to maximize his or her bonus.
Depreciation		Shareholders watch the balance sheet for the value of assets, the accumulated depreciation, and the net book value of long-term assets. Since the accumulated depreciation is an indication of the usage of the assets, the smaller the value of the net book assets, the more likely it is that the organization will need to invest in additional long-term assets.

zeroing them out. Closing entries also transfer the balances from the temporary accounts into the Retained Earnings account. The post-closing trial balance is the final step in the accounting cycle. The post-closing trial balance is prepared to ensure that debits still equal credits before a new accounting period is started.

One optional step that accountants may choose to include is to prepare adjusting entries and closing entries using a worksheet. A worksheet can be easily set up in a spreadsheet program, such as Excel. One of the benefits of preparing a worksheet is that it provides a bird's-eye view of the accounting process and adjusting and closing transactions. **Exhibit 3-9** shows a worksheet for Hooray Consulting, Inc. There are five sets of double columns of debit and credit: the first set of columns shows the unadjusted trial balance, the next set shows the six adjusting entries that updated the account balances, the third set is the adjusted trial balance, the fourth set shows the three closing entries that are required to zero out the temporary accounts, and the last set shows the post-closing trial balance. The only change occurring in the permanent accounts from the adjusted trial balance to the post-closing trial balance is in the retained earnings account. The net income and dividends have been closed to the retained earnings account, and therefore, the new balance of the retained earnings account reflects these changes.

5 ▶ Prepare a worksheet

Hooray Consulting, Inc.
Worksheet
For the Month Ended March 31, 2013

		UNADJUSTED TRIAL BALANCE		ADJUSTMENTS		ADJUSTED TRIAL BALANCE		CLOSING ENTRIES		POST-CLOSING TRIAL BALANCE	
ACCT #	ACCOUNT	DR.	CR.	DR.	CR.	DR.	CR.	DR.	CR.	DR.	CR.
1010	Cash	$26,300				$26,300				$26,300	
1020	Accounts Receivable	3,100		① 250		3,350				3,350	
1030	Supplies	900			⑤ 300	600				600	
1035	Prepaid Rent	3,000			④ 1,000	2,000				2,000	
1040	Equipment	12,600				12,600				12,600	
1041	Accumulated Depreciation, Equipment				⑥ 350		$ 350				$ 350
2010	Accounts Payable		$13,100				13,100				13,100
2015	Salary Payable				② 550		550				550
2020	Unearned Service Revenue		450	③ 150			300				300
2030	Income Tax Payable				⑦ 1,275		1,275				1,275
3010	Common Shares		20,000				20,000				20,000
3030	Retained Earnings		9,500				9,500	② 4,425	① 7,400		9,275
								③ 3,200			
3040	Dividends	3,200				3,200			③ 3,200		
4010	Service Revenue		7,000		① 250		7,400	① 7,400			
					③ 150						
5010	Salary Expense	550		② 550		1,100			② 1,100		
5015	Building Rent Expense			④ 1,000		1,000			② 1,000		
5030	Utilities Expense	400				400			② 400		
5040	Depreciation Expense, Equipment			⑥ 350		350			② 350		
5050	Supplies Expense			⑤ 300		300			② 300		
5060	Income Tax Expense			⑦ 1,275		1,275			② 1,275		
	Total	$50,050	$50,050	$3,875	$3,875	$52,475	$52,475	$15,025	$15,025	$44,850	$44,850

Exhibit 3-9 ▲

DEMO DOC

MyAccountingLab

Visit MyAccountingLab at **www. myaccountinglab.com** to watch animated versions of these Demo Docs.

L.O.

Preparation of Adjusting Entries, Adjusted Trial Balance, Financial Statements, Closing Entries, and Post-Closing Trial Balance

Apex Architects, Inc. has the following unadjusted trial balance at December 31, 2013:

Apex Architects, Inc. Unadjusted Trial Balance December 31, 2013		
ACCOUNT	**DEBIT**	**CREDIT**
Cash	$124,000	
Accounts Receivable	96,000	
Supplies	3,500	
Prepaid Rent	24,000	
Land	48,000	
Building	270,000	
Accumulated Depreciation, Building		$135,000
Accounts Payable		118,000
Unearned Service Revenue		36,000
Common Shares		50,000
Retained Earnings		64,700
Dividends	46,000	
Service Revenue		486,000
Salary Expense	245,000	
Rent Expense	32,000	
Miscellaneous Expense	1,200	
Total	$889,700	$889,700

Apex Architects, Inc. must make adjusting entries related to the following items:

a. Supplies on hand at year-end, $800.

b. Six months of rent ($24,000) was paid in advance on September 1, 2013. No rent expense has been recorded since that date.

c. Depreciation expense has not been recorded on the building for 2013. The building has a useful life of 30 years.

d. Employees work Monday through Friday. The weekly payroll is $3,500 and is paid every Friday. December 31, 2013, is a Wednesday.

e. Service revenue of $18,000 must be accrued.

f. A client paid $36,000 in advance on August 1, 2013, for services to be provided evenly from August 1, 2013, through January 31, 2014. None of the revenue from this client has been recorded.

g. Apex's tax rate is 30%.

REQUIREMENTS:

1. Open the ledger T-accounts with their unadjusted balances.
2. Journalize Apex Architects' adjusting entries at December 31, 2013, and post the entries to the T-accounts.
3. Total all the T-accounts in the ledger.
4. Prepare an adjusted trial balance.
5. Prepare the income statement, the statement of retained earnings, and the statement of financial position. Draw arrows linking the three financial statements.
6. Journalize and post Apex Architects' closing entries.
7. Prepare a post-closing trial balance.

Demo Doc Solution

Requirement 1

Open the ledger T-accounts with their unadjusted balances.

Part 1	Part 2	Part 3	Part 4	Part 5	Part 6	Part 7	Demo Doc Complete

Remember from Chapter 2 that opening a T-account means drawing a blank account that looks like a capital T and putting the account title across the top. To help find the accounts later, they are usually organized into assets, liabilities, shareholders' equity, revenue, and expenses (in that order). If the account has a beginning balance, it **must** be put in on the correct side.

Remember that debits are always on the left side of the T-account and credits are always on the right side. This rule is true for *every* account.

The correct side to enter each account's beginning balance is the side of *increase* in the account. We expect all accounts to have a *positive* balance, or more increases than decreases.

For assets, an increase is a debit, so we would expect all assets to have a debit balance. For liabilities and shareholders' equity, an increase is a credit, so we would expect all of these accounts to have a credit balance. By the same reasoning, we expect revenues to have a credit balance and expenses and dividends to have a debit balance.

The unadjusted balances to be posted into the T-accounts are simply the amounts from the unadjusted trial balance.

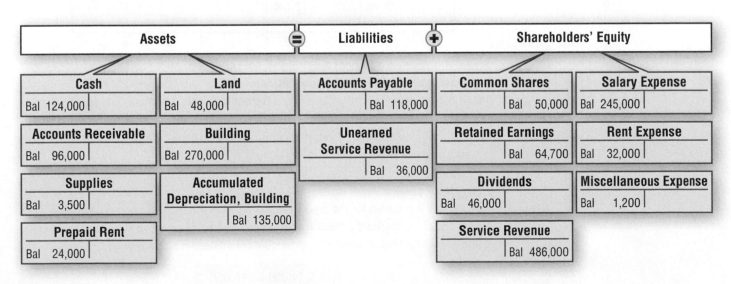

Requirement ❷

Journalize Apex Architects' adjusting entries at December 31, 2013, and post the entries to the T-accounts.

Part 1	**Part 2**	Part 3	Part 4	Part 5	Part 6	Part 7	Demo Doc Complete

a. Supplies on hand at year-end, $800.

On December 31, 2013, the unadjusted balance in supplies was $3,500. However, a count shows that only $800 of supplies actually remains on hand. The supplies that are no longer there have been used. When assets/benefits are used, an expense is created.

Apex Architects, Inc. will need to make an adjusting journal entry to reflect the correct amount of supplies on the balance sheet. The amount to be shown on the balance sheet is the actual amount of supplies on hand of $800. However, right now the Supplies account shows $3,500 (as we can see from the trial balance). This $3,500 is the "cost of asset available."

Cost of asset available	−	Cost of asset on hand at the end of the period	=	Cost of asset used (expense) during the period
$3,500	−	$800	=	$2,700

The supplies have decreased because they have been used up. The $2,700 of supplies expense must be recorded to show the value of supplies that were used.

DATE	ACCOUNTS	POST REF.	DR.	CR.
Dec 31	Supplies Expense		2,700	
	Supplies			2,700
	Record supply expense.			

After posting, Supplies and Supplies Expense reflect correct ending balances:

ASSETS   **EXPENSES**

Supplies			
Bal	3,500	(a)	2,700
Bal	800		

Supplies Expense		
(a)	2,700	
Bal	2,700	

b. Six months of rent ($24,000) was paid in advance on September 1, 2013. No rent expense has been recorded since that date.

When something is prepaid, it is a *future* benefit (an asset) because the business is now entitled to receive goods or services. Once those goods or services are received (in this case, once Apex Architects, Inc. has occupied the building being rented), they become a *past* benefit, and therefore an expense.

Apex Architects, Inc. prepaid $24,000 for six months of rent on September 1, which means that Apex Architects, Inc. pays $24,000/6 = $4,000 a month for rent. At December 31, prepaid rent is adjusted for the amount of the asset that has been used up. Because Apex Architects, Inc. occupied the building being rented for four months, we know that four months of the prepayment has been used. The amount of rent used is as follows:

$$4 \times \$4,000 = \$16,000$$

The amount of prepaid rent that will appear on the balance sheet is the amount of prepaid rent that has not been used. In this case, two months' worth of prepaid rent has not been used. $2 \times \$4,000 = \$8,000$. However, right now the Prepaid Rent account shows \$24,000 (as we can see from the trial balance). This \$24,000 is the "total asset to account for."

$$\text{Total asset to account for} - \frac{\text{Asset remaining}}{\text{at end of period}} = \frac{\text{Cost of asset used (expense)}}{\text{during the period}}$$

$$\$24,000 \quad - \quad \$8,000 \quad = \quad \$16,000$$

Because the \$16,000 of prepaid rent is a *past* benefit, an expense is recorded. Rent Expense must be increased (a debit) and Prepaid Rent (an asset) must be decreased (a credit).

DATE	ACCOUNTS	POST REF.	DR.	CR.
Dec 31	Rent Expense		16,000	
	Prepaid Rent			16,000
	Record rent expense.			

ASSETS   **EXPENSES**

Prepaid Rent			
Bal	24,000	(b)	16,000
Bal	8,000		

Rent Expense		
Bal	32,000	
(b)	16,000	
Bal	48,000	

c. **Depreciation expense has not been recorded on the building for 2013. The building has a useful life of 30 years.**

Depreciation expense per year is calculated as follows:

$$\text{Depreciation Expense per Year} = \frac{(\text{Cost of Asset} - \text{Salvage Value of Asset})}{\text{Useful Life of Asset}}$$

The cost principle compels us to keep the original cost of a plant asset in that asset account. Because the Building account has a balance of \$270,000, we know that this is the original cost of the building. No salvage value is mentioned in the question, so we assume it is \$0. We are told in the question that the building's useful life is 30 years.

$$\text{Depreciation Expense per Year} = \frac{(\$270,000 - \$0)}{30 \text{ Years}}$$

$$= \$9,000 \text{ per Year}$$

We will record depreciation of \$9,000 in the adjusting journal entry.

The journal entry to record depreciation expense is *always* the same. It is only the *number* (dollar amount) in the entry that changes. It always involves an increase to Depreciation Expense (a debit) and an increase to the contra-asset account of Accumulated Depreciation (a credit).

DATE	ACCOUNTS	POST REF.	DR.	CR.
Dec 31	Depreciation Expense		9,000	
	Accumulated Depreciation, Building			9,000
	Record depreciation expense.			

ASSETS			EXPENSES
ASSET		**CONTRA-ASSET**	

Building			**Accumulated Depreciation, Building**			**Depreciation Expense, Building**	
Bal	270,000					(c)	9,000
Bal	270,000		Bal	135,000			
			(c)	9,000		Bal	9,000
			Bal	144,000			

The book value of the building is its original cost (the amount in the Building T-account) minus the accumulated depreciation on the building:

Book Value of Plant Assets	
Building..	$ 270,000
Less: Accumulated Depreciation, Building..............	(144,000)
Book Value of the Building....................................	$ 126,000

d. **Employees work Monday through Friday. The weekly payroll is $3,500 and is paid every Friday. December 31, 2013, is a Wednesday.**

Salary is an accrued expense. That is, it is a liability that incurs from an *expense* that hasn't been paid yet. Most employers pay their employees *after* the work has been done, which means that the work is a *past* benefit. This is salary expense, and it grows each pay period until payday.

Apex Architects' employees are paid $3,500 for five days of work (Monday through Friday), which means they earn $3,500/5 = $700 per day. By the end of the day on Wednesday, December 31, the employees have worked for three days and have not been paid. Therefore, Apex Architects, Inc. owes employees $700 × 3 = $2,100 of salary at December 31.

If the salaries have not been paid, then they are pay*able* (or in other words, they are *owed*). They must be recorded in a payable account. We might be tempted to use Accounts Payable, but this account is usually reserved for *bills* received. Employees do not typically send their employers a bill. They simply expect to be paid and Apex Architects, Inc. knows that the salaries are owed. For this reason, we put this amount into another payable account. In this case, Salary Payable is most appropriate.

Salary is not owed until work is performed, and we know that Apex Architects' employees have already worked for three days. We therefore need to record an expense (in this case, Salary Expense) for the past benefit Apex Architects, Inc. received from its employees.

We record an increase to Salary Expense (a debit) and an increase to the liability Salary Payable (a credit) of $2,100.

DATE	ACCOUNTS	POST REF.	DR.	CR.
Dec 31	Salary Expense		2,100	
	Salary Payable			2,100
	Accrue salary expense.			

EXPENSES		LIABILITIES	

Salary Expense			**Salary Payable**	
Bal	245,000		(d)	2,100
(d)	2,100		Bal	2,100
Bal	247,100			

e. Service revenue of $18,000 must be accrued.

Accrued revenue is another way of saying "receivable" (or receipt in the future). If *accrued* revenue is recorded, it means that a receivable is also recorded. Customers have received goods or services from the business, but the business has not yet received the cash. The business is entitled to these receivables because the revenue has been earned.

Service Revenue must be increased by $18,000 (a credit) and the Accounts Receivable asset must be increased by $18,000 (a debit).

DATE	ACCOUNTS	POST REF.	DR.	CR.
Dec 31	Accounts Receivable		18,000	
	Service Revenue			18,000
	Accrue service revenue.			

ASSETS

Accounts Receivable			
Bal	96,000		
(e)	18,000		
Bal	114,000		

REVENUES

Service Revenue			
		Bal	486,000
		(e)	18,000
		Bal	504,000

f. A client paid $36,000 in advance on August 1, 2013, for services to be provided evenly from August 1, 2013, through January 31, 2014. None of the revenue from this client has been recorded.

Apex Architects, Inc. received cash in advance for work not yet performed for the client. By accepting the cash, Apex Architects, Inc. also accepted the obligation to porform that work (or provide a refund if it did not). In accounting, an obligation is a liability. We call this liability "unearned revenue" because it *will* be revenue (after the work is performed) but it is not revenue *yet*.

The $36,000 paid in advance is still in the Unearned Service Revenue account. However, some of the revenue has been earned as of December 31. Five months of the earnings period have passed (August 1 through December 31), so five months' worth of the revenue have been earned.

The entire revenue earnings period is six months (August 1 through January 31), so the revenue earned per month is $36,000/6 = $6,000. The five months of revenue earned total:

$$5 \times \$6,000 = \$30,000$$

The amount of unearned revenue that will appear on the balance sheet is the amount of unearned revenue that remains at the end of the period. In this case, one month of unearned revenue remains: $1 \times \$6,000 = \$6,000$. However, right now the Unearned Service Revenue account shows a balance of $36,000 (as we can see from the trial balance). This $36,000 is the "total to account for."

Total unearned revenue to account for	−	Unearned revenue remaining at the end of period	=	Revenue earned during the period
$36,000	−	$6,000	=	$30,000

So Unearned Service Revenue, a liability, must be decreased by $30,000 (a debit). Because the revenue is now earned, it can be recorded as normal service revenue. Therefore, Service Revenue also increases by $30,000 (a credit).

DATE	ACCOUNTS	POST REF.	DR.	CR.
Dec 31	Unearned Service Revenue		30,000	
	Service Revenue			30,000
	Record unearned service revenue that has been earned.			

Essentially, the $30,000 has been shifted from "unearned" to "earned" revenue.

LIABILITIES　　　　　　　　　　**REVENUES**

Unearned Service Revenue				Service Revenue	
(f)	30,000	Bal	36,000	Bal	486,000
		Bal	6,000	(e)	18,000
				(f)	30,000
				Bal	534,000

Now we will summarize all of the adjusting journal entries:

DATE	ACCOUNTS	POST REF.	DR.	CR.
Dec 31	Supplies Expense		2,700	
	Supplies			2,700
	Record supply expense.			
Dec 31	Rent Expense		16,000	
	Prepaid Rent			16,000
	Record rent expense.			
Dec 31	Depreciation Expense, Building		9,000	
	Accumulated Depreciation, Building			9,000
	Record depreciation expense.			
Dec 31	Salary Expense		2,100	
	Salary Payable			2,100
	Accrue salary expense.			
Dec 31	Accounts Receivable		18,000	
	Service Revenue			18,000
	Accrue service revenue.			
Dec 31	Unearned Service Revenue		30,000	
	Service Revenue			30,000
	Record unearned service revenue that has been earned.			

Requirement ❸

Total all the T-accounts in the ledger.

Part 1	Part 2	**Part 3**	Part 4	Part 5	Part 6	Part 7	Demo Doc Complete

After posting all of these entries and totalling all of the T-accounts, we have the following:

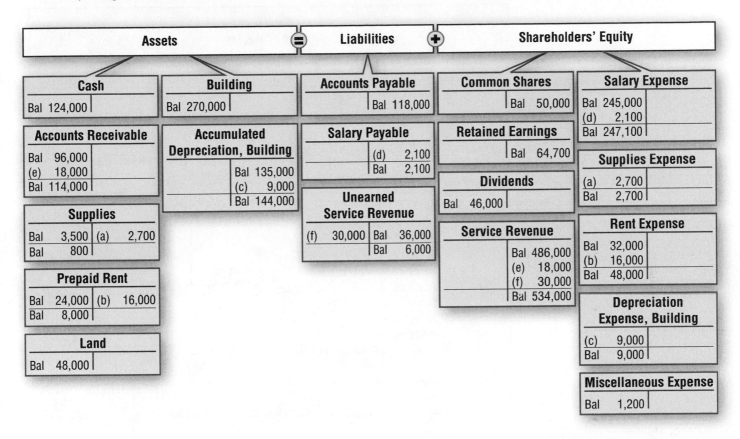

Assets = **Liabilities** + **Shareholders' Equity**

Cash
Bal 124,000 |

Building
Bal 270,000 |

Accounts Payable
| Bal 118,000

Common Shares
| Bal 50,000

Salary Expense
Bal 245,000 |
(d) 2,100 |
Bal 247,100 |

Accounts Receivable
Bal 96,000 |
(e) 18,000 |
Bal 114,000 |

Accumulated Depreciation, Building
| Bal 135,000
| (c) 9,000
| Bal 144,000

Salary Payable
| (d) 2,100
| Bal 2,100

Retained Earnings
| Bal 64,700

Supplies Expense
(a) 2,700 |
Bal 2,700 |

Dividends
Bal 46,000 |

Supplies
Bal 3,500 | (a) 2,700
Bal 800 |

Unearned Service Revenue
(f) 30,000 | Bal 36,000
| Bal 6,000

Service Revenue
| Bal 486,000
| (e) 18,000
| (f) 30,000
| Bal 534,000

Rent Expense
Bal 32,000 |
(b) 16,000 |
Bal 48,000 |

Prepaid Rent
Bal 24,000 | (b) 16,000
Bal 8,000 |

Depreciation Expense, Building
(c) 9,000 |
Bal 9,000 |

Land
Bal 48,000 |

Miscellaneous Expense
Bal 1,200 |

Requirement ❹

Prepare an adjusted trial balance.

| Part 1 | Part 2 | Part 3 | **Part 4** | Part 5 | Part 6 | Part 7 | Demo Doc Complete |

<table>
<tr><th colspan="4" align="center">Apex Architects, Inc.
Adjusted Trial Balance
December 31, 2013</th></tr>
<tr><th colspan="2">ACCOUNT</th><th>DEBIT</th><th>CREDIT</th></tr>
<tr><td colspan="2">Cash</td><td>$124,000</td><td></td></tr>
<tr><td colspan="2">Accounts Receivable</td><td>114,000</td><td></td></tr>
<tr><td colspan="2">Supplies</td><td>800</td><td></td></tr>
<tr><td colspan="2">Prepaid Rent</td><td>8,000</td><td></td></tr>
<tr><td colspan="2">Land</td><td>48,000</td><td></td></tr>
<tr><td colspan="2">Building</td><td>270,000</td><td></td></tr>
<tr><td colspan="2">Accumulated Depreciation, Building</td><td></td><td>$144,000</td></tr>
<tr><td colspan="2">Accounts Payable</td><td></td><td>118,000</td></tr>
<tr><td colspan="2">Salary Payable</td><td></td><td>2,100</td></tr>
<tr><td colspan="2">Unearned Service Revenue</td><td></td><td>6,000</td></tr>
<tr><td colspan="2">Common Shares</td><td></td><td>50,000</td></tr>
<tr><td colspan="2">Retained Earnings</td><td></td><td>64,700</td></tr>
<tr><td colspan="2">Dividends</td><td>46,000</td><td></td></tr>
<tr><td colspan="2">Service Revenue</td><td></td><td>534,000</td></tr>
<tr><td colspan="2">Salary Expense</td><td>247,100</td><td></td></tr>
<tr><td colspan="2">Rent Expense</td><td>48,000</td><td></td></tr>
<tr><td colspan="2">Depreciation Expense, Building</td><td>9,000</td><td></td></tr>
<tr><td colspan="2">Supplies Expense</td><td>2,700</td><td></td></tr>
<tr><td colspan="2">Miscellaneous Expense</td><td>1,200</td><td></td></tr>
<tr><td colspan="2">Total</td><td>$918,800</td><td>$918,800</td></tr>
</table>

Requirement ❺

Prepare the income statement, the statement of retained earnings, and the statement of financial position. Draw arrows linking the three financial statements.

Part 1	Part 2	Part 3	Part 4	**Part 5**	Part 6	Part 7	Demo Doc Complete

Apex Architects, Inc.
Income Statement
Year Ended December 31, 2013

Revenue:		
Service Revenue		$534,000
Expenses:		
Salary Expense	$247,100	
Rent Expense	48,000	
Depreciation Expense, Building	9,000	
Supplies Expense	2,700	
Miscellaneous Expense	1,200	
Total Operating Expenses		308,000
Operating Income		226,000
Income Tax (30%)		67,800
Net Income		$158,200

Apex Architects, Inc.
Statement of Retained Earnings
Year Ended December 31, 2013

Retained Earnings, January 1, 2013	$ 64,700
Add: Net Income	158,200
Subtotal	222,900
Less: Dividends	46,000
Retained Earnings, December 31, 2013	$176,900

Apex Architects, Inc.
Statement of Financial Position
December 31, 2013

ASSETS			LIABILITIES	
Current Assets			Accounts Payable	$118,000
Cash	$124,000		Salary Payable	2,100
Accounts Receivable	114,000		Unearned Service Revenue	6,000
Supplies	800		Income Tax Payable	67,800
Prepaid Rent	8,000		Total Liabilities	$193,900
Total Current Assets		$246,800		
			SHAREHOLDERS' EQUITY	
Land		48,000	Common Shares	$ 50,000
Equipment	$270,000		Retained Earnings	176,900
Less: Accumulated			Total Shareholders'	
Depreciation	144,000	$126,000	Equity	$226,900
			Total Liabilities &	
Total Assets		$420,800	Shareholders' Equity	$420,800

g. Apex's tax rate is 30%.

Once the income statement is prepared, Apex knows the amount of tax expense incurred, which will need to be paid to the government shortly after the year-end. The income tax expense, $67,800, is calculated based on the income before taxes. Apex Architects, Inc. will need to make one additional adjusting entry to reflect the income tax incurred but not yet paid on December 31.

DATE	ACCOUNTS	POST REF.	DR.	CR.
Dec 31	Income Tax Expense		67,800	
	Income Tax Payable			67,800

After posting, Income Tax Payable and Income Tax Expense reflect correct ending balances:

<table>
<tr><th colspan="3">LIABILITIES</th><th colspan="3">EXPENSES</th></tr>
<tr><th colspan="3">Income Tax Payable</th><th colspan="3">Income Tax Expense</th></tr>
<tr><td></td><td>(g)</td><td>67,800</td><td>(g)</td><td>67,800</td><td></td></tr>
<tr><td></td><td>Bal</td><td>67,800</td><td>Bal</td><td>67,800</td><td></td></tr>
</table>

Requirement ⑥

Journalize and post Apex Architects' closing entries.

Part 1	Part 2	Part 3	Part 4	Part 5	**Part 6**	Part 7	Demo Doc Complete

We prepare closing entries for two reasons. First, we need to clear out the temporary accounts (the revenue, expense, and dividends accounts) to a zero balance. They need to begin the next period empty so that the next period's income statement can begin fresh. Second, we need to update the Retained Earnings account.

The first step in the closing process is to close the revenue accounts. Apex Architects, Inc. only has one revenue account, Service Revenue. Because the Service Revenue account has a credit balance we will need to debit it to bring its balance to zero. The credit side of the entry is to Retained Earnings. The effect of this entry is to move the revenues into the Retained Earnings account.

DATE	ACCOUNTS	POST REF.	DR.	CR.
Dec 31	Service Revenue		534,000	
	Retained Earnings			534,000
	Close revenue accounts.			

<table>
<tr><th colspan="4">Service Revenue</th><th colspan="3">Retained Earnings</th></tr>
<tr><td></td><td></td><td>Bal</td><td>486,000</td><td></td><td>Bal</td><td>64,700</td></tr>
<tr><td></td><td></td><td>(e)</td><td>18,000</td><td></td><td>Clo</td><td>534,000</td></tr>
<tr><td></td><td></td><td>(f)</td><td>30,000</td><td></td><td></td><td></td></tr>
<tr><td>Clo</td><td>534,000</td><td>Bal</td><td>534,000</td><td></td><td></td><td></td></tr>
<tr><td></td><td></td><td>Bal</td><td>-0-</td><td></td><td></td><td></td></tr>
</table>

The next step in the closing process is to close the expenses into the Retained Earnings account.

Each of the expenses has a *debit* balance. To bring the accounts to zero, we must *credit* them. The debit side of the entry will go to the Retained Earnings account:

DATE	ACCOUNTS	POST REF.	DR.	CR.
Dec 31	Retained Earnings		375,800	
	Salary Expense			247,100
	Rent Expense			48,000
	Depreciation Expense, Building			9,000
	Supplies Expense			2,700
	Miscellaneous Expense			1,200
	Income Tax Expense			67,800
	Close expense accounts.			

Salary Expense

Bal	245,000		
(d)	2,100		
Bal	247,100	Clo	247,100
Bal	0		

Rent Expense

Bal	32,000		
(b)	16,000		
Bal	48,000	Clo	48,000
Bal	0		

Depreciation Expense, Building

(c)	9,000		
Bal	9,000	Clo	9,000
Bal	0		

Supplies Expense

(a)	2,700		
Bal	2,700	Clo	2,700
Bal	0		

Miscellaneous Expense

Bal	1,200	Clo	1,200
Bal	0		

Retained Earnings

Clo	308,000	Bal	64,700
		Clo	534,000

Income Tax Expense

(g)	67,800		
Bal	67,800	Clo	67,800
Bal	0		

The final step in the closing process is to close the Dividends account to the Retained Earnings account, which moves the amount from Dividends to Retained Earnings. The Dividends account has a debit balance of $46,000, so to bring that to zero, we *credit* the Dividends account for $46,000. The balancing debit goes to the Retained Earnings account:

DATE	ACCOUNTS	POST REF.	DR.	CR.
Dec 31	Retained Earnings		46,000	
	Dividends			46,000
	Close Dividends account.			

Dividends

Bal	46,000	Clo	46,000
Bal	0		

Retained Earnings

Clo	375,800	Bal	64,700
Clo	46,000	Clo	534,000
		Bal	176,900

Notice that all temporary accounts (that is the revenue, the expense, and the dividends accounts) now return to a zero balance and are ready to begin the next year.

Requirement ❼

Prepare a post-closing trial balance.

Part 1	Part 2	Part 3	Part 4	Part 5	Part 6	**Part 7**	Demo Doc Complete

<table>
<tr><td colspan="3" align="center">Apex Architects, Inc.
Post-Closing Trial Balance
December 31, 2013</td></tr>
<tr><td>ACCOUNT</td><td>DEBIT</td><td>CREDIT</td></tr>
<tr><td>Cash</td><td>$124,000</td><td></td></tr>
<tr><td>Accounts Receivable</td><td>114,000</td><td></td></tr>
<tr><td>Supplies</td><td>800</td><td></td></tr>
<tr><td>Prepaid Rent</td><td>8,000</td><td></td></tr>
<tr><td>Land</td><td>48,000</td><td></td></tr>
<tr><td>Building</td><td>270,000</td><td></td></tr>
<tr><td>Accumulated Depreciation, Building</td><td></td><td>$144,000</td></tr>
<tr><td>Accounts Payable</td><td></td><td>118,000</td></tr>
<tr><td>Salary Payable</td><td></td><td>2,100</td></tr>
<tr><td>Unearned Service Revenue</td><td></td><td>6,000</td></tr>
<tr><td>Income Tax Payable</td><td></td><td>67,800</td></tr>
<tr><td>Common Shares</td><td></td><td>50,000</td></tr>
<tr><td>Retained Earnings</td><td></td><td>176,900</td></tr>
<tr><td>Total</td><td>$564,800</td><td>$564,800</td></tr>
</table>

Notice that the post-closing trial balance only contains permanent accounts. This is because all of the temporary accounts have been closed and have zero balances.

Demo Doc Complete

Part 1	Part 2	Part 3	Part 4	Part 5	Part 6	Part 7	**Demo Doc Complete**

DECISION GUIDELINES

Completing the Accounting Cycle

In completing the accounting cycle for your business, you might encounter the following decisions:

Decision	Guideline	Analyze
I would like to invest in a company. Can I trust that the statements are accurate?	To produce accurate financial information, the revenue recognition principle should be followed.	The revenue recognition principle requires that revenues be recorded only when they are earned regardless of when cash is received. When the revenue recognition principle is followed, it is referred to as *accrual accounting*. The auditors check a random selection of entries to help verify that the guidelines and principles have been used appropriately.
As the bookkeeper for a company, how do I ensure that my accounting records are ready to start a new period?	Prepare *closing entries* for the *temporary accounts*: • Revenues • Expenses • Dividends	The *temporary accounts* have balances that relate only to one accounting period and need to be reset to $0 before accounting for the next period can begin. To reset the temporary accounts, closing entries are made that close the account balances into Retained Earnings. This ensures that the net income for the following period can be tracked accurately. Assets, Liabilities, Common Shares, and Retained Earnings do not get closed. These accounts are referred to as *permanent accounts*. Their balances are carried forward into the next period. After temporary accounts have been closed, a post-closing trial balance is prepared to ensure that all of the temporary accounts were properly closed.

ACCOUNTING VOCABULARY

THE LANGUAGE OF BUSINESS

Accruals (p. 137) Revenues earned or expenses incurred before cash has been exchanged.

Accrued expenses (p. 139) Expenses that have been incurred prior to being paid for.

Accumulated depreciation (p. 144) A contra-asset account that reflects all of the depreciation recorded for an asset to date.

Adjusted trial balance (p. 148) A list of all the accounts of a business with their adjusted balances.

Adjusting entries (p. 137) Journal entries made at the end of the accounting period to measure the period's income accurately and bring the related asset and liability accounts to correct balances before the financial statements are prepared.

Book value (p. 144) The asset's cost minus its accumulated depreciation; also called *carrying value*.

Carrying value (p. 144) The asset's cost minus its accumulated depreciation; also called *book value*.

Cash-basis accounting (p. 136) Accounting method that records revenues when cash is received and expenses when cash is paid.

Closing entries (p. 150) Journal entries that are prepared at the end of the accounting period. Closing entries zero out the revenue, expense, and dividends accounts so that accounting can begin for the next period.

Contra-account (p. 144) An account that is linked to another account. A contra-account will have a normal balance opposite of the account it is linked to.

Deferrals (p. 137) Cash received or paid before revenues have been earned or expenses have been incurred.

Deferred expenses (p. 140) Amounts that are assets of a business because they represent items that have been paid for but will be used later. Also called *prepaid expenses*.

Deferred revenue (p. 140) A liability created when a business collects cash from customers in advance of providing goods or services; also called *unearned revenue*.

Depreciation (p. 143) Allocation of the cost of a long-term asset to expense over its useful life.

Fiscal year (p. 136) Any consecutive, 12-month period that a business adopts as its accounting year.

Long-term assets (p. 143) Long-lived, tangible assets such as land, buildings, equipment, and furniture lasting for more than a year used in the operation of a business.

Net value (p. 144) The amount found by subtracting the balance of a contra-account from the balance of the account it is linked to.

Permanent accounts (p. 151) The asset, liability, and share-holders' equity accounts; these accounts are not closed at the end of the period.

Post-closing trial balance (p. 154) A list of the accounts and their balances at the end of the accounting period after closing entries have been journalized and posted.

Revenue recognition principle (p. 136) Recording revenues when they are earned by providing goods or services to customers.

Salvage value (p. 143) The estimated value at the end of a long-term asset's useful life.

Straight-line depreciation (p. 143) A method of estimating depreciation: (Cost of the Asset – Salvage Value)/Useful Life of the Asset.

Temporary accounts (p. 151) The revenue, expense, and dividend accounts; these accounts are closed at the end of the period.

Unadjusted trial balance (p. 138) A trial balance that is prepared prior to the adjusting entries being made.

Unearned revenue (p. 138) A liability created when a business collects cash from customers in advance of providing goods or services; also called *deferred revenue*.

MyAccountingLab

Make the grade with MyAccountingLab. The exercises and problems in this chapter can be found on MyAccountingLab at **www.myaccountinglab.com**. You can practise them as often as you want, and they feature step-by-step guided solutions to help you find the right answer.

ACCOUNTING PRACTICE

DISCUSSION QUESTIONS

1. If XYZ Consulting performs a consulting service and bills the customer on June 28 and receives payment from the customer on July 19, on what date would revenue be recorded if
   a. XYZ uses the cash basis of accounting?
   b. XYZ uses the accrual basis of accounting?

2. Why does the time period in which revenue is recognized matter?

3. What is a deferral? Under which basis of accounting, cash or accrual, would deferrals come into play? Under what circumstances would a company record a deferral?

4. Why do companies prepare adjusting entries?

5. What are some similarities and differences between assets and expenses?

6. What type of account (asset, liability, revenue, or expense) would Joe's Towing debit when it pays (credits) cash for each of the following transactions?
   a. Pays $100 to fill tow truck with gas
   b. Pays $1,000 to have a gas company deliver gas for its on-site refueling station
   Did you choose the same type of account or different ones? Why?

7. Describe the type of transaction that gives rise to a deferred revenue journal entry during the year. Why might deferred revenues require adjustment?

8. What kind of account is Accumulated Depreciation? How is it reported on the financial statements?

9 What are the objectives of the closing process? Which kind of accounts get closed? What is the only account that is affected by the closing process but not closed?

SELF CHECK

1. The revenue recognition principle says

  a. record revenue only after you have earned it.
  b. record revenue only when you receive cash.
  c. match revenues and expenses to compute net income.
  d. divide time into equal periods to measure net income or net loss properly.

2. Adjusting the accounts is the process of

  a. recording transactions as they occur during the period.
  b. updating the accounts at the end of the period.
  c. zeroing out account balances to prepare for the next period.
  d. subtracting expenses from revenues to measure net income.

3. Which of the following terms describe the types of adjusting entries?

  a. Deferrals and depreciation
  b. Expenses and revenues
  c. Deferrals and accruals
  d. Prepaid expenses and prepaid revenues

4. Assume that the weekly payroll of IDT, Inc. is $3,500. December 31, the end of the year, falls on Tuesday, but the company won't pay employees for the full week until its usual pay-day, Friday. What adjusting entry will IDT, Inc. make on Tuesday, December 31?

DATE	ACCOUNTS	POST REF.	DR.	CR.
a.	Salary Expense		1,400	
	Accumulated Salary			1,400
b.	Salary Expense		1,400	
	Cash			1,400
c.	Salary Payable		1,400	
	Salary Expense			1,400
d.	Salary Expense		1,400	
	Salary Payable			1,400

5. Unearned Revenue is always

  a. a liability.
  b. revenue.
  c. an asset.
  d. shareholders' equity.

6. The adjusted trial balance shows

  a. amounts that may be out of balance.
  b. revenues and expenses only.
  c. assets, liabilities, and common shares only.
  d. amounts that are ready for the financial statements.

7. Which of the following accounts is not closed?

  a. Salary Expense
  b. Service Revenue
  c. Accumulated Depreciation, Equipment
  d. Dividends

8. What do closing entries accomplish?

    a. Transfer revenues, expenses, and dividends to retained earnings

    b. Zero out the revenues, expenses, and dividends to prepare them for the next period

    c. Bring the Retained Earnings account to its correct ending balance

    d. All of the above

9. Which of the following is not a closing entry?

DATE	ACCOUNTS	POST REF.	DR.	CR.
a.	Retained Earnings		300	
	Building Rent Expense			300
b.	Salary Payable		700	
	Retained Earnings			700
c.	Service Revenue		1,100	
	Retained Earnings			1,100
d.	Retained Earnings		600	
	Dividends			600

10. Which correctly represents the flow of information from one financial statement to another?

    a. Income statement to the statement of retained earnings

    b. Statement of retained earnings to the statement of financial position

    c. Both a and b are correct

    d. None of the above is correct

Answers are given after Written Communication.

SHORT EXERCISES

S3-1. Accounting principles (*Learning Objective 1*) 5–10 min.

Match the accounting term with the corresponding definition.

    ____ 1. Accrual basis accounting

    ____ 2. Revenue recognition principle

    ____ 3. Fiscal period

    a. Any consecutive 12-month period.

    b. Records the impact of a business event as it occurs regardless of whether the transaction affected cash.

    c. Records revenue when it is earned.

S3-2. Accounting terminology (*Learning Objectives 2 & 3*) 5–10 min.

Match the accounting term with the corresponding definition.

____ 1. Accumulated depreciation	a. An account whose normal balance is opposite that of its companion account.
____ 2. Adjusted trial balance	b. Entry made to assign revenues to the period in which they are earned and expenses to the period incurred.
____ 3. Adjusting entry	c. A list of accounts with their adjusted balances.
____ 4. Book value	d. The cumulative sum of all depreciation recorded for an asset.
____ 5. Contra-account	e. The allocation of a long-term asset's cost to expense over its useful life.
____ 6. Depreciation	f. The asset's cost less its accumulated depreciation.
____ 7. Long-term asset	g. Long-lived asset used to operate the business.

S3-3. Types of adjusting entries (*Learning Objective 2*) 5–10 min.

The trial balance of Sampson & Associates includes the following balance sheet accounts. For each account, identify the type of adjusting entry that is typically made for the account (deferred expense, deferred revenue, accrued expense, or accrued revenue), and give the related income statement account used in that adjustment. Example: Prepaid Insurance: deferred expense; Insurance Expense

a. Interest Payable

b. Unearned Service Revenue

c. Accounts Receivable

d. Supplies

e. Accumulated Depreciation

S3-4. Adjusting journal entry—prepaid rent (*Learning Objective 2*) 5–10 min.

Alpine Ski Shop's Prepaid Rent balance is $4,500 on June 1. This prepaid rent represents six months' rent. Journalize and post the adjusting entry on June 30 to record one month's rent. Compute the balances of the two accounts involved.

S3-5. Adjusting journal entry—supplies (*Learning Objective 2*) 5–10 min.

Alpine Ski Shop's Office Supplies balance on September 1 is $1,200 and the balance in Office Supplies Expense is $0. On September 30, there is $500 of supplies on hand. Journalize and post the adjusting entry on September 30 for the supplies used. Compute the balances of the two accounts involved.

S3-6. Adjusting journal entry—interest expense (*Learning Objective 2*) 5–10 min.

To purchase equipment and supplies, ProPaint, Inc. borrowed $30,000 on August 1 by signing a note payable to First Nations Bank. Interest expense for ProPaint, Inc. is $200 per month. Journalize an adjusting entry to accrue interest expense at December 31, assuming no other adjusting entries have been made for the year. Use T-accounts to post to the two accounts affected by the adjustment.

S3-7. Adjusting journal entry—magazine subscriptions (*Learning Objective 2*) 5–10 min.

Wild Wonders, an outdoor magazine, collected $2,400 on April 1 for one-year subscriptions from subscribers in advance. Journalize and use T-accounts to post the adjusting entry on December 31 to record the revenue that *Wild Wonders* has earned, assuming no other adjusting entries have been made for the year. Compute the balances of the two accounts involved.

S3-8. Adjusting journal entry—salaries, accrued revenue, interest expense (*Learning Objective 2*) 5–10 min.

Journalize the following adjusting entries at December 31:

1. Services provided but not recorded, $1,500.
2. Salaries earned by employees but not recorded, $2,300.
3. Accrued interest on a note payable, $375.

S3-9. Adjusting journal entry—accrued service revenue (*Learning Objective 2*) 5–10 min.

Suppose you work summers mowing yards. Most of your customers pay you immediately after their lawn is mowed, but a few customers ask you to bill them at the end of the month. It is now September 30 and you have collected $1,200 from cash-paying customers. Your remaining customers owe you $150. How much service revenue would you record according to accrual basis accounting?

S3-10. Closing entries (*Learning Objective 4*) 5–10 min.

From the following list of accounts from the adjusted trial balance, identify each as an asset, liability, shareholders' equity, revenue, or expense. Use the most detailed account type appropriate. Also state whether each account is a permanent or temporary account, and if it is an account that gets closed at the end of the accounting period. Following the accounts is a sample of the format to use.

1. Depreciation Expense
2. Sales Revenue
3. Building
4. Cash
5. Unearned Service Revenue
6. Prepaid Rent
7. Dividends

Account	Type of Account	Permanent/Temporary	Closed
Supplies	Asset	Permanent	No

S3-11. Financial statements and closing entries (*Learning Objectives 3 & 4*) 10–15 min.

The following selected accounts and balances appear on the adjusted trial balance for Ray Service, Inc. on December 31, 2013:

Service Revenue	$1,200
Building Rent Expense	200
Salary Expense	300
Dividends	500
Common Shares	4,000
Retained Earnings	3,500

1. What is the net income or net loss?
2. What is the change in Retained Earnings?
3. Journalize the closing entries required.

S3-12. Adjusting and closing entries (*Learning Objectives 2 & 4*) 5–10 min.

For the following series of journal entries, indicate whether each is an adjusting entry (ADJ) or a closing entry (CL).

TYPE OF ENTRY (ADJ OR CL)	ACCOUNTS	POST REF.	DR.	CR.
	Salary Expense		400	
	Salary Payable			400
	Service Revenue		900	
	Retained Earnings			900
	Retained Earnings		1,500	
	Dividends			1,500
	Unearned Revenue		800	
	Service Revenue			800

S3-13. Preparing a post-closing trial balance (*Learning Objective 4*) 5–10 min.

After closing its accounts at October 31, 2013, Simmons Realty, Inc. had the following account balances:

Notes Payable	$2,000	Cash	$1,850
Prepaid Rent	975	Service Revenue	0
Accounts Receivable	2,450	Retained Earnings	1,075
Prepaid Insurance	1,300	Common Shares	5,000
Accounts Payable	300	Salary Expense	0
Equipment	1,800		

Prepare Simmons Realty's post-closing trial balance at October 31, 2013. List accounts in proper order.

EXERCISES (GROUP A)

E3-1A. Adjusting journal entries—unearned revenue and accrued revenue (*Learning Objective 2*) 10–15 min.

Suppose you started up your own landscaping business. A customer paid you $175 in advance to mow his or her lawn while he or she was on vacation. You performed landscaping services for a local business but the business hasn't paid you the $340 fee yet. A customer pays you $150 cash for landscaping services. Answer the following questions about the correct way to account for your revenue under accrual basis accounting:

1. Name the accounts used to record these events.

2. Prepare the journal entries to record the three transactions.

E3-2A. Adjusting journal entry—prepaid advertising (*Learning Objective 2*) 5–10 min.

Calculate the missing amounts for each of the following Prepaid Insurance situations. For situation A, journalize the adjusting entry. Consider each situation separately.

	Situation			
	A	B	C	D
Beginning Prepaid Insurance	$ 300	$ 600	$?	$ 400
Payments for Prepaid Insurance during the year..........	1,200	?	1,300	?
Total amount to account for	?	?	2,000	1,900
Ending Prepaid Insurance	400	500	?	?
Insurance Expense...	$?	$1,000	$1,200	$ 800

E3-3A. Common adjusting journal entries (*Learning Objective 2*) 10–15 min.

Journalize the adjusting entries for the following adjustments at December 31, the end of the accounting period, omitting explanations.

a. Employee salaries owed for Monday through Thursday of a five-day workweek equals $6,000.

b. Unearned service revenue now earned, $750.

c. Depreciation, $1,800.

d. Prepaid rent expired, $450.

e. Interest revenue accrued, $875.

E3-4A. Error analysis (*Learning Objective 2*) 10–15 min.

The adjusting entries for the following adjustments were omitted at year-end:

a. Prepaid insurance expired, $2,400.

b. Depreciation, $1,800.

c. Employee salaries owed for Monday through Wednesday of a five-day work-week, $2,700.

d. Supplies used during the year, $700.

e. Unearned service revenue now earned, $3,500.

Requirement

1. Compute the amount that net income for the year is overstated or understated by for each omitted entry. Use the following format to help analyze the transactions.

Transaction	Overstated/Understated	Amount
Sample a., b., etc.	Overstated	$5,000

E3-5A. Common adjusting journal entries (*Learning Objective 2*) 15–20 min.

Journalize the adjusting entry needed at October 31, the fiscal year-end, for each of the following independent situations. No other adjusting entries have been made for the year.

a. On September 1, we collected $4,800 rent in advance. We debited Cash and credited Unearned Rent Revenue. The tenant was paying six months' rent in advance.

b. The business holds a $30,000 note receivable. Interest revenue of $650 has been earned on the note but not yet received.

c. Salary expense is $1,700 per day, Monday through Friday, and the business pays employees each Friday. This year, October 31 falls on a Thursday.

d. The unadjusted balance of the Supplies account is $2,200. Supplies on hand total $700.

e. Equipment was purchased last year at a cost of $18,000. The equipment's useful life is four years.

f. On June 1, when we prepaid $1,500 for a one-year insurance policy, we debited Prepaid Insurance and credited Cash.

E3-6A. Common adjusting journal entries (*Learning Objective 2*) 15–20 min.

The accounting records of Vacations Unlimited include the following unadjusted balances at June 30: Accounts Receivable, $1,500; Supplies, $800; Salary Payable, $0; Unearned Service Revenue, $900; Service Revenue, $3,900; Salary Expense, $1,700; and Supplies Expense, $0. The following data pertain to the June 30 adjusting entries:

a. Service revenue accrued, $1,200.

b. Unearned service revenue that has been earned, $500.

c. Supplies on hand, $150.

d. Salary owed to employees, $1,100.

Requirement

1. Record the adjustments, then post them to T-accounts, labelling each adjustment by letter. Calculate each account's adjusted balance.

E3-7A. Income statement preparation (*Learning Objective 3*) 15–20 min.

The accountant for Henderson Roofing, Inc. posted adjusting entries (a) through (e) to the accounts at December 31, 2013. Selected balance sheet accounts and all the revenues and expenses of the entity follow in T-account form.

Accounts Receivable			Supplies			Accumulated Depreciation, Equipment			Accumulated Depreciation, Building	
21,000			2,800	(a)	1,200		5,600			28,000
(e) 1,500						(b) 1,400		(c)		2,000

Salary Payable									Service Revenue	
	(d) 2,900									97,000
									(e)	1,500

Salary Expense		Supplies Expense		Depreciation Expense, Equipment		Depreciation Expense, Building	
14,000		(a) 1,200		(b) 1,400		(c) 2,000	
(d) 2,900							

Requirements

1. Calculate balances in the accounts and use the appropriate accounts to prepare the income statement of Henderson Roofing, Inc. for the year ended December 31, 2013. List expenses in order from largest to smallest.

2. Were the 2013 operations successful? Give the reason for your answer.

Quick solution:

Net Income = $77,000

E3-8A. Statement of retained earnings preparation (*Learning Objective 3*) 10–15 min.

Sigma Security, Inc. began the year with $15,000 of common shares and $32,000 of retained earnings. On May 5, investors bought $12,000 of additional shares in the business. On August 22, the business purchased land valued at $65,000. The income statement for the year ended December 31, 2013, reported a net loss of $11,000. During this fiscal year, the business paid $800 each month for dividends.

Requirements

1. Prepare Sigma Security's statement of retained earnings for the year ended December 31, 2013.

2. Did the retained earnings of the business increase or decrease during the year? What caused this change?

E3-9A. Recreating adjusting journal entries (*Learning Objective 2*) 10–15 min.

The adjusted trial balances of PDQ, Inc. at December 31, 2013 and December 31, 2014 include these amounts:

	2013	2014
Supplies	$ 2,800	$ 1,700
Salary Payable	2,800	3,700
Unearned Service Revenue	18,000	16,300

Analysis of the accounts at December 31, 2014 reveals these transactions for 2014:

Purchase of supplies	$ 8,700
Cash payments for salaries	52,300
Cash receipts in advance for services revenue	106,400

Requirement

1. Compute the amount of supplies expense, salary expense, and service revenue PDQ, Inc. will report for the year ended December 31, 2014. Solve by making T-accounts and posting the information to solve for the unknown amounts.

E3-10A. Financial statement preparation (*Learning Objective 3*) 15–20 min.

The adjusted trial balance for Country Cookin Catering, Inc. is presented next. Prepare the income statement, statement of retained earnings, and balance sheet for Country Cookin Catering, Inc. for the month ended March 31, 2013.

Country Cookin Catering, Inc. Adjusted Trial Balance March 31, 2013		
ACCOUNT	**DEBIT**	**CREDIT**
Cash	$ 4,000	
Accounts Receivable	8,000	
Supplies	1,300	
Equipment	22,500	
Accumulated Depreciation, Equipment		$ 8,800
Accounts Payable		2,100
Salary Payable		600
Unearned Service Revenue		1,400
Common Shares		5,000
Retained Earnings		5,800
Dividends	800	
Service Revenues		18,600
Salary Expense	3,600	
Rent Expense	1,200	
Depreciation Expense, Equipment	600	
Supplies Expense	300	
Total	$42,300	$42,300

E3-11A. Prepare closing entries (*Learning Objective 1*) 10–15 min.

Requirements

1. Using the following selected accounts of A to Z Electrical, Inc. at April 30, 2013, prepare the entity's closing entries:

Common Shares	$ 18,000	Accounts Receivable	$ 9,000
Service Revenue	127,000	Retained Earnings	6,500
Unearned Revenues	1,800	Salary Payable	800
Salary Expense	18,500	Depreciation Expense	8,200
Accumulated Depreciation	32,600	Building Rent Expense	5,100
Supplies Expense	1,700	Dividends	18,000
Interest Revenue	800	Supplies	1,800
Interest Expense	2,300		

2. What is A to Z Electrical's ending retained earnings balance at April 30, 2013?

E3-12A. Statement of retained earnings preparation (*Learning Objective 3*) 10–15 min.

From the following accounts of Kurlz Salon, Inc., prepare the business's statement of retained earnings for the year ended December 31, 2013:

Retained Earnings					Dividends		
Clo	95,000	Jan 1	188,000	Mar 31	18,000		
Clo	76,000	Clo	234,000	Jun 30	14,000		
		Bal	251,000	Sep 30	23,000		
				Dec 31	21,000		
				Bal	76,000	Clo	76,000

E3-13A. Prepare a post-closing trial balance (*Learning Objective 4*) 10–15 min.

The following post-closing trial balance was prepared for Cunningham Photography, Inc. Prepare a corrected post-closing trial balance. Assume all accounts have normal balances and the amounts are correct.

	ACCOUNT	DEBIT	CREDIT
	Cunningham Photography, Inc.		
	Post-Closing Trial Balance		
	December 31, 2013		
	Cash	$ 9,450	
	Accounts Receivable	33,100	
	Supplies		$ 1,900
	Equipment		68,000
	Accumulated Depreciation, Equipment	19,700	
	Accounts Payable	11,450	
	Salary Payable		2,500
	Unearned Service Revenue	5,600	
	Common Shares		30,000
	Retained Earnings	43,200	
	Total	$122,500	$102,400

E3-14A. Prepare closing entries (*Learning Objective 4*) 10–15 min.

The following is the adjusted trial balance of Qwik Care Clinic, Inc. for December 31, 2013.

Requirement

1. Journalize the closing entries at December 31.

	ACCOUNT	DEBIT	CREDIT
	Qwik Care Clinic, Inc.		
	Adjusted Trial Balance		
	December 31, 2013		
	Cash	$ 7,400	
	Accounts Receivable	8,700	
	Supplies	200	
	Furniture	4,800	
	Accumulated Depreciation, Furniture		$ 1,200
	Equipment	32,000	
	Accumulated Depreciation, Equipment		8,800
	Accounts Payable		1,300
	Salary Payable		3,500
	Unearned Service Revenue		3,100
	Common Shares		10,000
	Retained Earnings		18,500
	Dividends	14,000	
	Service Revenues		73,000
	Salary Expense	31,000	
	Rent Expense	18,600	
	Depreciation Expense, Equipment	1,600	
	Depreciation Expense, Furniture	400	
	Supplies Expense	700	
	Total	$119,400	$119,400

E3-15A. Common adjusting journal entries and financial statement reporting (*Learning Objectives 2 & 3*) 15–20 min.

Chen Financial Services (CFS) is making adjusting entries for the year ended June 30, 2013. The accounting clerk gathered the following information:

a. Paid one-year insurance premium of $2,400 on December 1, 2012, for coverage beginning on January 1, 2013.

b. Office Supplies account showed a balance of $480 and $270 on June 30, 2012 and 2013, respectively. During the year, CFS purchased $860 of office supplies.

c. Received $3,600 from a customer who paid for a three-month financial service contract starting on June 1. Financial Services Revenue account was credited on June 1.

d. An employee borrowed $12,000 by signing a one-year, 5% interest-bearing note from CFS on September 1. The note specified that interest was payable on the 5th of each month, starting October 2013.

e. Signed a contract on June 1 with a local advertising company for $1,500 monthly advertising fee. The advertising service started immediately after signing the contract, and the payment was to be made on the 2nd of each month, starting July 2013.

Requirements

1. Prepare the adjusting entry for each item (a) to (e).

2. What amount should be reported for revenue and expense accounts, from (a) to (e) on the income statement, for the year ended June 30, 2013?

3. What amount should be reported for each asset and liability account in the statement of financial position?

E3-16A. Analyzing the effects of errors on accounts and adjusting entries (*Learning Objective 2*) 10–15 min.

Patel Instruments, Inc. made the following errors in the year-end account adjustments on December 31:

a. Did not record $1,200 salary owed to employees for 4 days of work.

b. Did not adjust $1,600 of revenue earned from the Unearned Revenue account for the second half of December.

c. Recorded a full year of depreciation, based on an equipment cost of $26,000 and salvage value of $2,000, with a useful life of 4 years. The equipment was purchased on October 1.

d. Did not adjust $600 of unused office supplies that was originally recorded in the Office Supplies Expense account.

Requirements

1. What is the impact that each item has had on net income, and on the asset, liability, and shareholders' equity accounts? Show understatements by "U," overstatements by "O," and no effect by "NE," and identify their amounts.

2. Based on each item (a) to (d) described above, prepare the appropriate adjusting entry for each item to reflect the correct account balance.

E3-17A. Identify the type of adjustment and adjusting entries (*Learning Objectives 1 & 2*) 10–15 min.

Techco Computer Services had the following transactions during the year. Its year-end is on September 30.

a. One-year insurance premium $1,800 was purchased on April 30. Coverage began on May 1.

b. The monthly payroll was $4,200, and the payment to employees was on the 1st of the following month.

c. A server was purchased on February 1 for $16,000. Techco estimated that the server could last 5 years, with a salvage value of $1,000 at the end of the 5th year.

d. Computer maintenance service was performed for a client on September 28 for $2,600. The invoice was sent on October 5, after the year-end date.

e. The Unearned Service Revenue account showed a balance of $5,200, which represents a four-month service contract. Three-quarters of the service was performed by the end of September.

Requirements

1. Identify each of the above transactions as accrued revenue, accrued expense, deferred revenue, or deferred expense.

2. Record the adjusting entry for each transaction.

E3-18A. Adjusting entries and inferring transactions (*Learning Objectives 2 & 3*)
10–15 min.

Park Management Ltd's selected account balances are presented below.

Account Title	November 30	December 31
Rent Receivable	$8,200	$5,600
Prepaid Insurance	1,300	900
Unearned Rent Revenue	3,800	2,500
Salary Payable	3,000	5,000

Additional information regarding transactions that occurred in December:

1. Collection from rent receivable was $12,500.

2. Additional insurance purchased was $600.

3. Cash paid in advance from customers was $1,600.

4. Salary paid to employee was $4,000.

Requirements

1. Record the transactions that occurred during December.

2. Record the adjusting entries on December 31.

3. What amount should be reported for revenue and expense accounts on the income statement for the month ended December 31?

EXERCISES (GROUP B)

E3-1B. Adjusting journal entries—unearned revenue and accrued revenue (*Learning Objective 2*) 10–15 min.

Suppose you started up your own landscaping business. A customer paid you $120 in advance to mow his or her lawn while he or she was on vacation. You performed landscaping services for a local business but the business hasn't paid you the $425 fee yet. A customer pays you $110 cash for landscaping services. Answer the following questions about the correct way to account for your revenue under accrual basis accounting:

1. Name the accounts used to record these events.
2. Prepare the journal entries to record the three transactions.

E3-2B. Adjusting journal entry—prepaid advertising (*Learning Objective 2*) 5–10 min.

Calculate the missing amounts for each of the Prepaid Insurance situations.

For situation A, journalize the adjusting entry. Consider each situation separately.

	Situation			
	A	B	C	D
Beginning Prepaid Insurance	$ 800	$1,100	?	$ 300
Payments for Prepaid Insurance during the year	1,500	?	1,600	?
Total amount to account for	?	?	3,200	2,700
Ending Prepaid Insurance	700	1,200	?	?
Insurance Expense	$?	$ 500	$2,600	$1,400

E3-3B. Common adjusting journal entries (*Learning Objective 2*) 10–15 min.

Journalize the adjusting entries at May 31, the end of the accounting period. Omit explanations.

a. Employee salaries owed for Monday through Thursday of a five-day work week equals $7,500.

b. Unearned service revenue now earned, $1,250.

c. Depreciation, $1,900.

d. Prepaid rent expired, $550.

e. Interest revenue accrued, $980.

E3-4B. Error analysis (*Learning Objective 2*) 10–15 min.

The adjusting entries for the following adjustments were omitted at year-end:

a. Prepaid rent expired, $2,500.

b. Depreciation, $1,000.

c. Employee salaries owed for Monday through Wednesday of a five-day work-week, $3,100.

d. Supplies used during the year, $800.

e. Unearned service revenue now earned, $4,500.

Requirement

1. Compute the amount that net income for the year is overstated or understated for each omitted entry. Use the following format to help analyze the transactions.

Transaction	Overstated/Understated	Amount
Sample a., b., etc.	Overstated	$5,000

E3-5B. Common adjusting journal entries (*Learning Objective 2*) 15–20 min.

Journalize the adjusting entry needed at August 31, the fiscal year-end, for each of the following independent situations. No other adjusting entries have been made for the year.

a. On July 1, we collected $3,000 rent in advance. We debited Cash and credited Unearned Rent Revenue. The tenant was paying six months' rent in advance.

b. The business holds a $35,000 note receivable. Interest revenue of $520 has been earned on the note but not yet received.

c. Salary expense is $2,900 per day, Monday through Friday, and the business pays employees each Friday. This year, August 31 falls on a Tuesday.

d. The unadjusted balance of the Supplies account is $1,400. Supplies on hand total $200.

e. Equipment was purchased last year at a cost of $8,000. The equipment's useful life is 10 years.

f. On April 1, when we prepaid $1,560 for a one-year insurance policy, we debited Prepaid Insurance and credited Cash.

E3-6B. Common adjusting journal entries (*Learning Objective 2*) 15–20 min.

The accounting records of Weddings Unlimited include the following unadjusted balances at April 30: Accounts Receivable, $1,900; Supplies, $1,100; Salary Payable, $0; Unearned Service Revenue, $1,300; Service Revenue, $5,300; Salary Expense, $3,100; and Supplies Expense, $0. The following data pertains to April 30 adjusting entries:

a. Service revenue accrued, $2,200.

b. Unearned service revenue that has been earned, $300.

c. Supplies on hand, $150.

d. Salary owed to employees, $700.

Requirement

1. Record the adjustments, then post them to T-accounts, labelling each adjustment by letter. Calculate each account's adjusted balance.

E3-7B. Income statement preparation (*Learning Objective 3*) 15–20 min.

The accountant for Metal Main, Inc. posted adjusting entries (a) through (e) to the accounts at August 31, 2013. Selected balance sheet accounts and all the revenues and expenses of the entity follow in T-account form.

Accounts Receivable	
19,200	
(e) 2,250	

Supplies		
2,200	(a)	1,600

Accumulated Depreciation, Equipment		
		4,200
	(b)	1,400

Accumulated Depreciation, Building		
		46,000
	(c)	1,000

Salary Payable		
	(d)	2,500

Service Revenue		
		6,400
	(e)	2,250

Salary Expense	
13,500	
(d) 2,500	

Supplies Expense		
(a)	1,600	

Depreciation Expense, Equipment		
(b)	1,400	

Depreciation Expense, Building		
(c)	1,000	

Requirements

1. Calculate balances in the accounts and use the appropriate accounts to prepare the income statement of Metal Main, Inc. for the year ended August 31, 2013. List expenses in order from largest to smallest.

2. Were the 2013 operations successful? Give the reason for your answer.

E3-8B. Statement of retained earnings preparation (*Learning Objective 3*) 10–15 min.

Zeta Safety, Inc. began the year with $15,000 of common shares and $34,000 of retained earnings. On August 5, investors bought $19,000 of additional shares in the business. On October 22, the business purchased land valued at $45,000. The income statement for the year ended December 31, 2013, reported a net loss of $5,000. During this fiscal year, the business paid $550 each month for dividends.

Requirements

1. Prepare Zeta Safety's statement of retained earnings for the year ended December 31, 2013.

2. Did the retained earnings of the business increase or decrease during the year? What caused this change?

E3-9B. Recreating adjusting journal entries (*Learning Objective 2*) 10–15 min.

The adjusted trial balances of CAS, Inc. at March 31, 2013, and March 31, 2014, include these amounts:

	2013	2014
Supplies	$ 1,700	$ 1,200
Salary Payable	4,000	4,500
Unearned Service Revenue	17,000	15,100

Analysis of the accounts at March 31, 2014, reveals these transactions for 2014:

Purchases of supplies	$ 9,000
Cash payments for salaries	55,500
Cash receipts in advance for service revenue	58,000

Requirement

1. Compute the amount of supplies expense, salary expense, and service revenue CAS, Inc. will report for the year ended March 31, 2014. Solve by making T-accounts and posting the information to solve for the unknown amounts.

E3-10B. Financial statement preparation (*Learning Objective 3*) 15–20 min.

The adjusted trial balance for Spruce Up Catering, Inc. is presented next. Prepare the income statement, statement of retained earnings, and balance sheet for Spruce Up Catering, Inc. for the month ended January 31, 2013.

Spruce Up Catering, Inc.			
Adjusted Trial Balance			
January 31, 2013			
ACCOUNT		**DEBIT**	**CREDIT**
Cash		$ 6,500	
Accounts Receivable		6,000	
Supplies		400	
Equipment		26,600	
Accumulated Depreciation, Equipment			$ 6,800
Accounts Payable			2,300
Salary Payable			1,100
Unearned Service Revenue			1,900
Common Shares			5,200
Retained Earnings			11,100
Dividends		1,100	
Service Revenue			20,100
Salary Expense		3,800	
Rent Expense		1,700	
Depreciation Expense, Equipment		1,500	
Supplies Expense		900	
Total		$48,500	$48,500

E3-11B. Prepare closing entries (*Learning Objective 4*) 10–15 min.

Requirements

1. Using the following selected accounts of Juba Electrical, Inc. at September 30, 2013, prepare the entity's closing entries:

Common Shares	$17,000	Accounts Receivable	$14,000
Service Revenue	49,000	Retained Earnings	7,900
Unearned Revenues	2,500	Salary Payable	700
Salary Expense	21,900	Depreciation Expense	5,000
Accumulated Depreciation	32,600	Building Rent Expense	5,600
Supplies Expense	2,300	Dividends	14,000
Interest Revenue	300	Supplies	2,300
Interest Expense	2,400		

2. What is Juba Electrical's ending retained earnings balance at September 30, 2013?

E3-12B. Statement of retained earnings preparation (*Learning Objective 3*) 10–15 min.

From the following accounts of Resch Restore, Inc. prepare the business's statement of retained earnings for the year ended January 31, 2013:

Retained Earnings			
Clo	110,000	Feb 1	77,000
Clo	82,000	Clo	299,000
		Bal	184,000

Dividends			
Apr 30	17,000		
Jul 31	14,000		
Oct 31	24,000		
Jan 31	27,000		
Bal	82,000	Clo	82,000

E3-13B. Prepare a post-closing trial balance (*Learning Objective 4*) 10–15 min.

The following post-closing trial balance was prepared for Fonzarelli Photo, Inc. Prepare a corrected post-closing trial balance. Assume all accounts have normal balances and the amounts are correct.

Fonzarelli Photo, Inc.
Post-Closing Trial Balance
March 31, 2013

ACCOUNT	DEBIT	CREDIT
Cash	$10,250	
Accounts Receivable	25,000	
Supplies		$ 600
Equipment		17,000
Accumulated Depreciation, Equip.	5,000	
Accounts Payable	8,800	
Salary Payable		5,200
Unearned Service Revenue	2,200	
Common Shares		20,000
Retained Earnings	11,650	
Total	$62,900	$42,800

E3-14B. Prepare closing entries (*Learning Objective 4*) 10–15 min.

The following is the adjusted trial balance of Happy Health, Inc. for August 31, 2013.

		ACCOUNT	DEBIT	CREDIT
		Happy Health, Inc. **Adjusted Trial Balance** **August 31, 2013**		
		Cash	$ 9,000	
		Accounts Receivable	11,000	
		Supplies	170	
		Furniture	5,200	
		Accumulated Depreciation, Furniture		$ 1,800
		Equipment	39,000	
		Accumulated Depreciation, Equipment		4,500
		Accounts Payable		1,200
		Salary Payable		3,500
		Unearned Service Revenue		2,200
		Common Shares		18,000
		Retained Earnings		7,970
		Dividends	14,000	
		Service Revenue		77,000
		Salary Expense	27,000	
		Rent Expense	6,000	
		Depreciation Expense, Equipment	1,500	
		Depreciation Expense, Furniture	1,300	
		Supplies Expense	2,000	
		Total	$116,170	$116,170

Requirement

1. Journalize the closing entries at August 31.

E3-15B. Common adjusting journal entries and financial statement reporting (*Learning Objectives 2 & 3*) 15–20 min.

Fung Cleaning Services (FCS) is making adjusting entries for the year ended September 30, 2013. The accounting clerk gathered the following information:

a. Paid one-year insurance premium of $1,800 on January 21, 2013, for coverage beginning on February 1, 2013.

b. Cleaning Supplies account showed a balance of $520 and $430 on September 30, 2012 and 2013, respectively. During the year, FCS purchased $780 of cleaning supplies.

c. Received $3,600 from a restaurant customer who paid for a six-month cleaning service contract starting on July 1. Cleaning Services Revenue account was credited on July 1.

d. An employee borrowed $9,000 by signing a one-year, 4% interest-bearing note from FCS on September 1. The note specified that interest was payable on the 5th of each month, starting October 2013.

e. Signed a contract on July 1 with a local advertising company for $1,750 monthly advertising fee. The advertising service started immediately after signing the contract, and the payment was to be made on the 2nd of each month, starting August 2013.

Requirements

1. Prepare the adjusting entry for each item (a) to (e).

2. What amount should be reported for revenue and expense accounts, from (a) to (e) on the income statement, for the year ended September 30, 2013?

3. What amount should be reported for each asset and liability account on the statement of financial position? (You can assume that interest payments have been received on time and payments for advertising have been made on time.)

E3-16B. Analyzing the effects of errors on accounts and adjusting entries (*Learning Objective 2*) 10–15 min.

Rupinder Delivery Services made the following errors in the year-end account adjustments on June 30:

a. Did not record $1,800 gasoline charges on the credit card for the week of June 26.

b. Did not adjust $900 of delivery services provided to a client for the second half of June. The invoice for the service was sent out on July 3rd.

c. Recorded a full year of depreciation, based on a delivery truck cost of $27,000 and salvage value of $2,000, with a useful life of 5 years. The delivery truck was purchased on April 1.

d. Did not adjust for unexpired insurance. A one-year insurance premium of $2,400 was paid on February 1 and the coverage started immediately. The transaction was recorded in the Insurance Expense account.

Requirements

1. What is the impact that each item has had on net income, and asset, liability, and shareholders' equity accounts? Show understatements by "U," overstatements by "O," and no effect by "NE," and identify their amounts.

2. Based on each item described above, prepare the appropriate adjusting entry to reflect the correct account balance.

E3-17B. Identify the type of adjustment and adjusting entries (*Learning Objectives 1 & 2)* 10–15 min.

BT Spa had the following transactions during the year. Its year-end is on June 30.

a. The Unearned Revenue account showed a balance of $800, which represented four gift certificates of $200 each sold in June. Three gift certificates had been redeemed in June.

b. The Prepaid Rent account showed a balance of $6,000, which represented six months' rent paid on April 1.

c. An exercise machine was purchased on March 1 for $7,500. BT estimated that the machine could last 8 years, with a salvage value of $300 at the end of the 8th year.

d. Five employees each earned $100/day. Salary for the last seven days of June would be paid on July 2nd.

e. A fitness service was performed for a business client on June 30 for $350. The invoice was sent on July 5th, after the year-end date.

Requirements

1. Identify each of the above transactions as accrued revenue, accrued expense, deferred revenue, or deferred expense.

2. Record the adjusting entry for each transaction.

E3-18B. Adjusting entries and inferring transactions (*Learning Objectives 2 & 3*)
10–15 min.

Giuseppe Landscaping Ltd's selected account balances are presented below.

Account Title	May 31	June 30
Accounts Receivable	$4,200	$6,300
Landscaping Supplies	1,200	1,400
Unearned Revenue	2,100	2,400
Salary Payable	4,000	3,500

Additional information regarding transactions that occurred in June:

1. Collection from accounts receivable was $7,500.
2. Additional landscaping supplies purchased were $1,000.
3. Cash paid in advance from customers was $1,800.
4. Salary paid to employee that was owing from the previous month was $4,000.

Requirements

1. Record the transactions that occurred during June.
2. Record the adjusting entries on June 30.
3. What amount should be reported for revenue and expense accounts on the income statement for the month ended June 30?

EXERCISES (ALTERNATES 1, 2, AND 3)

MyAccountingLab

These alternative exercise sets are available for your practice benefit at
www.myaccountinglab.com

PROBLEMS (GROUP A)

P3-1A. Common adjusting journal entries (*Learning Objective 2*) 15–20 min.

Journalize the adjusting entry needed on December 31, the end of the current accounting year, for each of the following independent cases affecting Outdoor Adventures, Inc. No other adjusting entries have been made for the year.

a. Prior to making the adjusting entry on December 31, the balance in Prepaid Insurance is $2,400. Outdoor Adventures, Inc. pays liability insurance each year on April 30.

b. Outdoor Adventures, Inc. pays employees each Friday. The amount of the weekly payroll is $6,500 for a five-day workweek. December 31, the fiscal year-end, is a Tuesday.

c. Outdoor Adventures, Inc. received notes receivable from some customers for services provided. For the current year, accrued interest amounts to $350 and will be collected next year.

d. The beginning balance of Supplies was $1,800. During the year, $3,700 of supplies were purchased. At December 31, the supplies on hand total $2,200.

e. During the year, Outdoor Adventures, Inc. received $8,800 in advance for services to be provided at a later date. As of December 31, Outdoor Adventures, Inc. earned $5,100 of the total fees received during the current year.

f. Depreciation for the current year includes Vehicles, $2,850, and Equipment, $1,200.

P3-2A. Recreating adjusting journal entries from trial balances (*Learning Objective 2*) 15–20 min.

Assume the unadjusted and adjusted trial balances for Kristy's Consulting, Inc. at June 30, 2013, show the following data:

			UNADJUSTED TRIAL BALANCE		ADJUSTED TRIAL BALANCE	
		ACCOUNT	**DR.**	**CR.**	**DR.**	**CR.**
		Cash	$ 6,200		$ 6,200	
		Accounts Receivable	5,800		5,800	
		Supplies	1,400		300	
		Prepaid Rent	2,800		2,100	
		Equipment	18,000		18,000	
		Accumulated Depreciation, Equipment		$ 7,500		$ 7,750
		Accounts Payable		1,800		1,800
		Salary Payable				1,250
		Interest Payable				150
		Unearned Service Revenue		2,600		900
		Notes Payable		7,000		7,000
		Common Shares		5,000		5,000
		Retained Earnings		4,900		4,900
		Dividends	13,600		13,600	
		Service Revenues		47,400		49,100
		Salary Expense	23,400		24,650	
		Rent Expense	3,500		4,200	
		Depreciation Expense, Equipment	1,250		1,500	
		Interest Expense	250		400	
		Supplies Expense			1,100	
		Total	$76,200	$76,200	$77,850	$77,850

Kristy's Consulting, Inc. / Trial Balance / June 30, 2013

Requirement

1. Journalize the adjusting entries that account for the differences between the two trial balances.

P3-3A. Prepare adjusting journal entries and an adjusted trial balance (*Learning Objectives 2 & 3*) 25–30 min.

The trial balance of Alpha Advertising, Inc. at November 30, 2013, and the data needed for the month-end adjustments follow:

		ACCOUNT	DEBIT	CREDIT
		Alpha Advertising, Inc. **Trial Balance** November 30, 2013		
		Cash	$ 22,800	
		Accounts Receivable	39,400	
		Prepaid Insurance	2,700	
		Supplies	900	
		Equipment	83,800	
		Accumulated Depreciation, Equipment		$ 64,300
		Accounts Payable		1,900
		Salary Payable		
		Unearned Service Revenue		2,200
		Common Shares		50,000
		Retained Earnings		29,300
		Dividends	3,600	
		Service Revenues		8,400
		Salary Expense	2,900	
		Insurance Expense		
		Depreciation Expense, Equipment		
		Utilities Expense		
		Supplies Expense		
		Total	$156,100	$156,100

a. Insurance coverage still remaining at November 30, $300.

b. Supplies used during the month, $250.

c. Depreciation for the month, $1,200.

d. Accrued utilities expense at November 30, $300. (Use Accounts Payable as the liability account needed.)

e. Accrued salaries at November 30, $450.

f. Service revenue still unearned at November 30, $800.

Requirements

1. Open T-accounts for the accounts listed in the trial balance and insert their November 30 unadjusted balances.

2. Journalize the adjusting entries and post them to the T-accounts. Reference the posted amounts by letters (a) through (f). Calculate the adjusted balance in each account.

3. Prepare the adjusted trial balance.

4. How will the company use the adjusted trial balance?

P3-4A. Effects of adjusting journal entries on income statement accounts (*Learning Objectives 2 & 3*) 20–25 min.

Helgeson Enterprises, Corp. completed the following selected transactions and prepared these adjusting entries during January:

Jan	1	Prepaid insurance for January through March, $750.
	3	Performed service on account, $1,800.
	6	Purchased office furniture on account, $350.
	8	Paid property tax expense, $600.
	12	Purchased office equipment for cash, $1,400.
	18	Performed services and received cash, $4,700.
	23	Collected $900 on account.
	26	Paid the account payable from the January 6 transaction.
	30	Paid salary expense, $2,400.
	31	Recorded an adjusting entry for January insurance expense related to the January 1 transaction.
	31	Recorded an adjusting entry for unearned revenue now earned, $400.

Requirements

1. State whether the transaction would increase revenues, decrease revenues, increase expenses, decrease expenses, or have no effect on revenues or expenses. If revenues or expenses are affected, give the amount of the impact on revenues or expenses for January. Use the following format for your answer.

Revenues and Expenses for January		
Date	**Impact on Revenues or Expenses**	**$ Effect on Revenues or Expenses**
Jan XX	Increase Revenues	$500

2. Compute January net income or net loss under the accrual basis of accounting.

3. State why the accrual basis of accounting results in an accurate measurement of income.

P3-5A. Prepare financial statements (*Learning Objective 3*) 20–25 min.

The adjusted trial balance of Lighthouse Realty, Inc. at December 31, 2013, follows:

ACCOUNT	DEBIT	CREDIT
Lighthouse Realty, Inc.		
Adjusted Trial Balance		
December 31, 2013		
Cash	$ 6,300	
Accounts Receivable	11,600	
Prepaid Rent	1,200	
Supplies	900	
Equipment	48,000	
Accumulated Depreciation, Equipment		$ 12,000
Accounts Payable		5,400
Unearned Service Revenue		2,100
Interest Payable		750
Salary Payable		1,800
Notes Payable		12,000
Common Shares		20,000
Retained Earnings		8,200
Dividends	14,000	
Service Revenue		97,000
Interest Revenue		650
Salary Expense	51,000	
Rent Expense	18,000	
Depreciation Expense, Equipment	4,200	
Utilities Expense	2,700	
Interest Expense	1,300	
Supplies Expense	700	
Total	$159,900	$159,900

Requirements

1. Prepare Lighthouse Realty's 2013 income statement, statement of retained earnings, and year-end balance sheet. List expenses in decreasing order on the income statement.

2. a. Which financial statement reports Lighthouse Realty's results of operations? Were operations successful during 2013? Cite specifics from the financial statements to support your evaluation.

   b. Which statement reports the company's financial position?

P3-6A. Prepare closing entries and a post-closing trial balance (*Learning Objective 4*)
20–25 min.

The June 30, 2013, adjusted trial balance of Energized Espresso, Inc. is shown next.

Energized Espresso, Inc. Adjusted Trial Balance June 30, 2013		
ACCOUNT	**DEBIT**	**CREDIT**
Cash	$ 4,900	
Accounts Receivable	9,600	
Prepaid Rent	1,800	
Supplies	600	
Equipment	26,000	
Accumulated Depreciation, Equipment		$ 4,200
Accounts Payable		2,400
Unearned Service Revenue		1,100
Salary Payable		1,800
Notes Payable		3,000
Common Shares		10,000
Retained Earnings		11,950
Dividends	2,000	
Service Revenue		43,000
Interest Revenue		400
Salary Expense	24,500	
Rent Expense	6,000	
Depreciation Expense, Equipment	1,200	
Utilities Expense	700	
Supplies Expense	550	
Total	$77,850	$77,850

Requirements

1. Prepare the June closing entries for Energized Espresso, Inc.
2. Calculate the ending balance in retained earnings.
3. Prepare a post-closing trial balance.

Quick solution:

2. Retained Earnings = $20,400
3. Trial balance totals = $42,900

P3-7A. Effects of errors on assets, liabilities, shareholders' equity, and net income (*Learning Objectives 2 & 3*) 15–20 min.

The following errors were made in the accounting records of Garceau Corp. in 2013 and were not discovered until 2014.

a. The journal entry to record a receipt of $3,170 for Consulting Revenue was incorrectly recorded as $7,310.

b. A $2,400 credit to Accumulated Amortization, Automobile account was incorrectly credited to Automobile account.

c. A payment of $2,800 for dividends was incorrectly debited to Salary Expense account.

d. Salary expense for 2013 of $1,650 was not recorded. It was recorded as Salary Expense in 2014 when it was paid.

e A $1,850 credit to Unearned Revenue was posted to Accounts Receivable.

Requirements

For each of the independent errors in parts (a) through (e), identify the net effect on assets, liabilities, shareholders' equity, and net income for 2013 and 2014. Show understatements by "U," overstatements by "O," and no effect by "NE," and identify their amounts.

	Assets		Liabilities		Shareholders' Equity		Net Income	
	2013	2014	2013	2014	2013	2014	2013	2014
a								
b								
c								
d								
e								

P3-8A. Adjusting entries using a worksheet (*Learning Objectives 1, 2, 3 & 5*) 35–40 min.

Klean Laundry Services (KLS) has been providing commercial laundry services to restaurants and hotels for several years. KLS's year-end is on June 30. The unadjusted trial balance on June 30, 2013, was as follows:

Klean Laundry Services
Worksheet
For Month Ended June 30, 2013

ACCT #	ACCOUNT	UNADJUSTED TRIAL BALANCE DR.	UNADJUSTED TRIAL BALANCE CR.	ADJUSTMENTS DR.	ADJUSTMENTS CR.	ADJUSTED TRIAL BALANCE DR.	ADJUSTED TRIAL BALANCE CR.
1010	Cash	$ 5,100					
1020	Accounts Receivable	9,300					
1030	Laundry Supplies	8,600					
1035	Prepaid Insurance	3,600					
1040	Laundry Machines	50,000					
1041	Accumulated Depreciation, Laundry Machines		$ 15,000				
2010	Accounts Payable		3,700				
2015	Salary Payable						
2020	Unearned Laundry Revenue		2,100				
2025	Interest Payable						
2030	Income Tax Payable						
2100	Note Payable – 3 years		21,000				
3010	Common Shares		10,000				
3030	Retained Earnings		18,500				
3040	Dividends	4,500					
4010	Laundry Revenue		98,000				
5010	Salary Expense	62,000					
5015	Insurance Expense	9,000					
5030	Utilities Expense	8,400					
5040	Depreciation Expense, Laundry Machines						
5050	Laundry Supplies Expense	7,800					
5060	Interest Expense						
5070	Income Tax Expense						
	Total	$168,300	$168,300				

Additional information about several transactions that occurred during the year:

a. Laundry services provided to hotels amounted to $7,500 in June. The client would pay on July 5.

b. A physical count of laundry supplies showed that there was $3,200 of cleaning supplies on hand on June 30. The balance of Laundry Supplies Expense, $7,800 on June 30, represents laundry supplies purchased during the year.

c. The balance of Prepaid Insurance represents one-year insurance premium paid on February 1.

d. Laundry machines were estimated to last for 8 years, with a salvage value of $2,000 at the end of the 8th year. No adjustment was made for this fiscal year.

e. Four workers each earned $60/day. Six days of wages were earned by employees, but not paid by June 30.

f. Seventy percent of the unearned revenue was earned in June.

g. On March 1, KLS borrowed $21,000 from the RBC bank by signing a three-year note with a 5% interest rate. KLS was required to make annual interest payments at the end of each year.

h. The utilities expense for June was estimated at $1,200. The utility bill usually arrived during the first week of the following month.

i. KLS's income tax rate was 30%.

Requirements

1. Indicate the type of adjustments for each transaction.

2. Prepare the adjusting entry and enter the amount for each transaction in the worksheet.

3. Prepare the adjusted trial balance in the worksheet.

4. What is the age of the laundry machines?

5. Prepare the income statement, statement of retained earnings, and statement of financial position.

6. Record the adjusting entry for the income tax.

P3-9A. Closing entries using a worksheet (*Learning Objectives 4 & 5*) 10–15 min.

Refer to P3-8A.

Requirement

Using the adjusted trial balance from P3-8A, prepare the closing entries for 2013 and the post-closing trial balance in the worksheet.

PROBLEMS (GROUP B)

P3-1B. Common adjusting journal entries (*Learning Objective 2*) 15–20 min.

Journalize the adjusting entries needed at December 31, the end of the current accounting year, for each of the following independent cases affecting Waterfall Heights, Inc. No other adjusting entries have been made for the year.

a. Prior to making the adjusting entry on December 31, the balance in Prepaid Insurance is $3,000. Waterfall Heights, Inc. pays liability insurance each year on September 30.

b. Waterfall Heights, Inc. pays employees each Friday. The amount of the weekly payroll is $19,000 for a five-day workweek. December 31, the fiscal year-end, is a Thursday.

c. Waterfall Heights, Inc. received notes receivable from some customers for services provided. For the current year, accrued interest amounts to $875 and will be collected next year.

d. The beginning balance of Supplies was $1,600. During the year, $4,400 of supplies were purchased. At December 31, the supplies on hand total $2,500.

e. During the year, Waterfall Heights, Inc. received $14,500 in advance for services to be provided at a later date. As of December 31, Waterfall Heights, Inc. earned $5,100 of the total fees received during the current year.

f. Depreciation for the current year includes Vehicles, $2,170, and Equipment, $1,300.

P3-2B. Recreating adjusting journal entries from trial balances (*Learning Objective 2*)
15–20 min.

Assume the unadjusted and adjusted trial balances for Milky Way Theater, Inc. at November 30, 2013, show the following data:

			UNADJUSTED TRIAL BALANCE		ADJUSTED TRIAL BALANCE	
		ACCOUNT	**DR.**	**CR.**	**DR.**	**CR.**
		Cash	$ 9,200		$ 9,200	
		Accounts Receivable	6,200		6,200	
		Supplies	2,200		800	
		Prepaid Rent	3,600		2,700	
		Equipment	26,000		26,000	
		Accumulated Depreciation, Equipment		$ 4,700		$ 6,200
		Accounts Payable		2,600		2,600
		Salary Payable				1,250
		Interest Payable				290
		Unearned Service Revenue		3,000		2,100
		Notes Payable		7,000		7,000
		Common Shares		15,000		15,000
		Retained Earnings		2,900		2,900
		Dividends	12,000		12,000	
		Service Revenue		53,400		54,300
		Salary Expense	23,600		24,850	
		Rent Expense	4,800		5,700	
		Depreciation Expense, Equipment	750		2,250	
		Interest Expense	250		540	
		Supplies Expense			1,400	
		Total	$88,600	$88,600	$91,640	$91,640

Milky Way Theater, Inc.
Trial Balance
November 30, 2013

Requirement

1. Journalize the adjusting entries that account for the differences between the two trial balances.

P3-3B. Prepare adjusting journal entries and an adjusted trial balance (*Learning Objectives 2 & 3*) 25–30 min.

The trial balance of Nina's Novelty, Inc. at September 30, 2013, and the data needed for the month-end adjustments follow:

		ACCOUNT	DEBIT	CREDIT
		Nina's Novelty, Inc.		
		Trial Balance		
		September 30, 2013		
		Cash	$ 25,000	
		Accounts Receivable	17,400	
		Prepaid Insurance	2,400	
		Supplies	1,200	
		Equipment	59,000	
		Accumulated Depreciation, Equipment		$ 50,000
		Accounts Payable		2,000
		Salary Payable		
		Unearned Service Revenue		2,400
		Common Shares		25,000
		Retained Earnings		22,800
		Dividends	9,700	
		Service Revenue		16,200
		Salary Expense	3,700	
		Insurance Expense		
		Depreciation Expense		
		Utilities Expense		
		Supplies Expense		
		Total	$118,400	$118,400

a. Insurance coverage still remaining at September 30, $800.

b. Supplies used during the month, $900.

c. Depreciation for the month, $2,200.

d. Accrued utilities expense at September 30, $1,000. (Use Accounts Payable as the liability account needed.)

e. Accrued salaries at September 30, $800.

f. Service revenue still unearned at September 30, $1,600.

Requirements

1. Journalize the adjusting entries.

2. Open T-accounts for the accounts listed in the trial balance and insert their September 30 unadjusted balances. Post the adjusting entries to the T-accounts. Reference the posted amounts by letters (a) through (f). Calculate the adjusted balance in each account.

3. Prepare the adjusted trial balance.

4. How will the company use the adjusted trial balance?

P3-4B. Effects of adjusting journal entries on income statement accounts (*Learning Objectives 2 & 3*) 20–25 min.

Moore, Corp. completed the following selected transactions and prepared these adjusting entries during May:

May 1	Prepaid insurance for May through July, $2,700.
3	Performed service on account, $2,500.
6	Purchased office furniture on account, $900.
8	Paid property tax expense, $500.
12	Purchased office equipment for cash, $1,500.
18	Performed services and received cash, $3,500.
23	Collected $800 on account.
26	Paid the account payable from the May 6 transaction.
30	Paid salary expense, $1,300.
31	Recorded an adjusting entry for May insurance expense related to the May 1 transaction.
31	Recorded an adjusting entry for unearned revenue now earned, $1,100.

Requirements

1. State whether the transaction would increase revenues, decrease revenues, increase expenses, decrease expenses, or have no effect on revenues or expenses. If revenues or expenses are affected, give the amount of the impact on revenues or expenses for May. Use the following format for your answer.

Revenues and Expenses for May		
Date	**Impact on Revenues or Expenses**	**$ Effect on Revenues or Expenses**
May XX	Increase Revenues	$XXX

2. Compute May net income or net loss under the accrual basis of accounting.

3. State why the accrual basis of accounting results in an accurate measurement of income.

P3-5B. Prepare financial statements (*Learning Objective 3*) 20–25 min.

The adjusted trial balance for Destination Realty, Inc. at October 31, 2013, follows:

		Destination Realty, Inc. Adjusted Trial Balance October 31, 2013		
		ACCOUNT	**DEBIT**	**CREDIT**
		Cash	$ 6,500	
		Accounts Receivable	12,100	
		Prepaid Rent	2,500	
		Supplies	500	
		Equipment	42,500	
		Accumulated Depreciation, Equipment		$ 11,300
		Accounts Payable		4,300
		Unearned Service Revenue		2,800
		Interest Payable		720
		Salary Payable		9,000
		Notes Payable		8,000
		Common Shares		3,960
		Retained Earnings		9,700
		Dividends	5,000	
		Service Revenue		85,000
		Interest Revenue		420
		Salary Expense	40,000	
		Rent Expense	20,000	
		Depreciation Expense, Equipment	2,500	
		Utilities Expense	1,800	
		Interest Expense	1,100	
		Supplies Expense	700	
		Total	$135,200	$135,200

Requirements

1. Prepare Destination Realty's income statement, statement of retained earnings, and year-end balance sheet. List expenses in decreasing order on the income statement.

2. **a.** Which financial statement reports Destination Realty's results of operations? Were operations successful during 2013? Cite specifics from the financial statements to support your evaluation.

   b. Which statement reports the company's financial position?

P3-6B. Prepare closing entries and a post-closing trial balance (*Learning Objective 4*) 20–25 min.

The September 30, 2013, adjusted trial balance of Java Jolt, Inc. is shown next.

		ACCOUNT	DEBIT	CREDIT
		Java Jolt, Inc.		
		Adjusted Trial Balance		
		June 30, 2013		
		Cash	$ 5,800	
		Accounts Receivable	7,000	
		Prepaid Rent	2,300	
		Supplies	300	
		Equipment	30,000	
		Accumulated Depreciation, Equipment		$ 3,800
		Accounts Payable		3,000
		Unearned Service Revenue		1,900
		Salary Payable		1,400
		Notes Payable		10,000
		Common Shares		3,100
		Retained Earnings		11,200
		Dividends	4,000	
		Service Revenue		41,000
		Interest Revenue		1,000
		Salary Expense	18,500	
		Rent Expense	5,400	
		Depreciation Expense, Equipment	1,700	
		Utilities Expense	800	
		Supplies Expense	600	
		Total	$76,400	$76,400

Requirements

1. Prepare the September closing entries for Java Jolt, Inc.
2. Calculate the ending balance in retained earnings.
3. Prepare a post-closing trial balance.

P3-7B. Effects of errors on assets, liabilities, shareholders' equity, and net income (*Learning Objectives 2 & 3*) 15–20 min.

The following errors were made in the accounting records of Gagnon Corp. in 2013 and were not discovered until 2014.

a. Management revenue of $3,750 earned in 2013 was not recorded until it was collected in 2014.

b. One year of Amortization Expense, $4,200, was recorded instead of three-quarters of the amount.

c. A deposit of $4,000 for Management Service to be delivered in 2014 was recorded as Management Revenue in 2013.

d One-year insurance premium of $3,300 for 2014 was recorded as Insurance Expense for 2013 when it was paid.

e. Half of the unearned revenue of $4,500 was earned in 2013, but was not recorded.

Requirements

1. For each of the independent errors in parts (a) through (e), identify the net effect on assets, liabilities, shareholders' equity, and net income for 2013 and 2014. Show understatements by "U," overstatements by "O," and no effect by "NE," and identify their amounts.

	Assets		Liabilities		Shareholders' Equity		Net Income	
	2013	2014	2013	2014	2013	2014	2013	2014
a								
b								
c								
d								
e								

P3-8B. Adjusting entries using a worksheet (*Learning Objective 1, 2, 3 & 5*) 35–40 min.

Muse Daycare Centre (MDC) has been providing daycare services to its local community for several years. MDC's year-end is on December 31. The unadjusted trial balance on December 31, 2013 was as follows:

		UNADJUSTED TRIAL BALANCE		ADJUSTMENTS		ADJUSTED TRIAL BALANCE	
ACCT #	ACCOUNT	DR.	CR.	DR.	CR.	DR.	CR.
1010	Cash	$ 6,200					
1020	Accounts Receivable	2,700					
1030	Art Supplies	3,200					
1035	Prepaid Rent	3,600					
1040	Playground Equipment	43,000					
1041	Accumulated Depreciation, Playground Equipment		$ 7,800				
2010	Accounts Payable		2,450				
2015	Salary Payable						
2020	Unearned Daycare Revenue		2,100				
2030	Income Tax Payable						
3010	Common Shares		25,000				
3030	Retained Earnings		10,500				
3040	Dividends	5,000					
4010	Daycare Revenue		95,000				
5010	Salary Expense	60,000					
5015	Rent Expense	9,000					
5030	Utilities Expense	5,350					
5040	Depreciation Expense, Playground Equipment						
5050	Art Supplies Expense	4,800					
5060	Income Tax Expense						
	Total	$142,850	$142,850				

Muse Daycare Centre
Worksheet
For Year Ended December 31, 2013

Additional information about several transactions that occurred during the year:

a. Several parents did not pay the fee for the last week of daycare. These parents would pay $1,400 (which included $700 owed in December) in the first week of January.

b. A physical count of art supplies showed that there was $1,500 of art supplies on hand on December 31. The balance of Art Supplies Expense, $4,800 on December 31, represents art supplies purchased during the year.

c. The balance of Prepaid Rent represents the 4 months of rent paid on November 1.

d. Playground Equipment was estimated to last for 10 years, with a salvage value of $4,000 at the end of 10th year. No adjustment was made in 2013.

e. Three daycare workers each earned $80/day. Seven days of wages were earned by employees, but not paid on December 31.

f. Half of the unearned revenue was earned in December.

g. The utilities expense for December was estimated at $480. The utility bill usually arrived during the first week of the following month.

h. MDC's income tax rate was 30%.

Requirements

1. Indicate the type of adjustments for each transaction.

2. Prepare the adjusting entry and enter the amount for each transaction in the worksheet.

3. Prepared the adjusted trial balance in the worksheet.

4. What is the age of the playground equipment?

5. Prepare the income statement, statement of retained earnings, and classified statement of financial position.

6. Record the adjusting entry for the income tax.

P3-9B. Closing entries using a worksheet (*Learning Objectives 4 & 5*) 10–15 min.

Refer to P3-8B.

Requirements

Using the adjusted trial balance from P3-8B, prepare the closing entries for 2013 and the post-closing trial balance in the worksheet.

PROBLEMS (ALTERNATES 1, 2, AND 3)

MyAccountingLab

These alternative problem sets are available for your practice benefit at
www.myaccountinglab.com

CONTINUING EXERCISE

This exercise continues the accounting process for Graham's Yard Care, Inc. from the Continuing Exercise in Chapter 2. Refer to the T-accounts and the trial balance that you prepared for Graham's Yard Care, Inc. at June 30, 2013.

Requirements

1. Open these additional T-accounts: Accumulated Depreciation, Equipment; Depreciation Expense, Equipment; Supplies Expense.

2. A physical count shows $20 of lawn supplies on hand at June 30, 2013. Depreciation on equipment for the month totals $30. Journalize any required adjusting journal entries and post to the T-accounts, identifying all items by date.

3. Prepare the adjusted trial balance.

4. Journalize and post the closing entries at June 30. Denote each closing amount as *Clo* and an account balance as *Bal*.

5. Prepare a post-closing trial balance.

CONTINUING PROBLEM

This problem continues the accounting process for Aqua Elite, Inc. from the Continuing Problem in Chapter 2. The trial balance for Aqua Elite, Inc. at June 30, 2013, should look like this:

		Aqua Elite, Inc. Trial Balance June 30, 2013		
	ACCOUNT		**DEBIT**	**CREDIT**
	Cash		$16,855	
	Accounts Receivable		3,800	
	Supplies		1,610	
	Land		15,000	
	Furniture		3,300	
	Equipment		4,700	
	Vehicles		31,000	
	Accounts Payable			$ 3,890
	Notes Payable			31,000
	Common Shares			38,500
	Dividends		2,800	
	Service Revenue			12,000
	Salary Expense		2,700	
	Rent Expense		1,800	
	Utilities Expense		1,225	
	Advertising Expense		325	
	Miscellaneous Expense		275	
	Total		$85,390	$85,390

During July, the following transactions occurred:

Jul	1	Paid three months' rent, $5,400.
	4	Performed service for a customer and received cash, $2,100.
	9	Received $3,600 from customers for services to be performed later.
	12	Purchased $750 of supplies on account.
	15	Billed customers for services performed, $2,800.
	16	Paid receptionist's salary, $675.
	22	Received $3,100 on account.
	25	Paid $2,800 on account.
	28	Received $1,200 cash for services performed.
	30	Paid $600 of dividends.

Requirements

1. Journalize the transactions that occurred in July. Omit explanations.

2. Using the four-column accounts from the Continuing Problem in Chapter 2, post the transactions to the ledger creating new ledger accounts as necessary; omit posting references. Calculate the new account balances.

3. Prepare the unadjusted trial balance for Aqua Elite, Inc. at the end of July.

4. Journalize and post the adjusting entries for July based on the following adjustment information.

    a. Record the expired rent.

    b. Supplies on hand, $350.

    c. Depreciation; $400 equipment, $210 furniture, $650 vehicles.

    d. Services performed but unbilled, $1,900.

    e. Accrued salaries, $675.

    f. Unearned service revenue earned as of July 31, $800.

5. Prepare an adjusted trial balance for Aqua Elite, Inc. at the end of July.

6. Prepare the income statement, statement of retained earnings, and balance sheet for the three-month period May through July, 2013.

7. Prepare and post closing entries.

8. Prepare a post-closing trial balance for the end of the period.

APPLY YOUR KNOWLEDGE

ETHICS IN ACTION

Case 1. Jennifer Baxter was preparing the adjusting journal entries for Jennifer's Java, a business that uses the accrual basis of accounting, to prepare the adjusted trial balance and financial statements. She knew that $750 of salaries related to the current accounting period had accrued but wouldn't be paid until the next period. Jennifer thought that simply not including the adjustment for these salaries would mean that salary expense would be lower, and reported net income would be higher than it would have been if she had made the adjustment. Further, she knew that the Salary Payable account would be zero, so the liabilities reported on the balance sheet would be less, and her business would look even better. Besides, she reasoned that these salaries would be reported eventually, so it was merely a matter of showing them in one period instead of another. Dismissing the reporting as just a timing issue, she ignored the adjustment for the additional salary expense.

Is Jennifer acting unethically by failing to record the adjustment for accrued salaries? Does it matter that, shortly into the new accounting period, the salaries will ultimately be paid? Is it really simply a matter of timing? What are the potential problems of failing to include all the adjusting journal entries?

Case 2. Jim Anderson and his banker were reviewing the quarterly income statements for his consulting business, Anderson and Associates, Inc. The banker was impressed with the growth of sales revenue and net income for the second quarter this year as compared to the second quarter of last year. Jim knew it had been a good quarter, but didn't think it had been spectacular. Suddenly, Jim realized that he failed to close out the revenue and expense accounts for the prior quarter, which ended in March. Because those temporary accounts were not closed out, their balances were included in the second quarter amounts for the current year. Jim then realized that the banker had the financial statements but not the general ledger or any trial balances. Thus, the banker would not be able to see that the accounting cycle was not properly closed and that this failure was creating a misstated income statement for the second quarter of the current year. The banker then commented that the business appeared to be performing so well that he would approve a line of credit for the business. Jim decided to not say anything because he did not want to lose the line of credit. Besides, he thought, it really did not matter that the income statement was misstated because his business would be sure to repay any amounts borrowed.

Should Jim have informed the banker of the mistake made and should he have redone the second quarter's income statement? Was Jim's failure to close the prior quarter's revenue and expense accounts unethical? Does the fact that the business will repay the loan matter?

KNOW YOUR BUSINESS

FINANCIAL ANALYSIS

Purpose: To help familiarize you with the financial reporting of a real company to further your understanding of the chapter material you are learning.

This case will help you to better understand the effect of adjusting journal entries on the financial statements. We do not have access to the journals and ledgers used by Bombardier Inc., but we can see some of the adjusted accounts on the company's financial statements. Refer to the Bombardier Inc. income statements, "Consolidated Statements of Income," and the Bombardier Inc. balance sheets in MyAccountingLab. Also, Note 7 titled "Property, Plant and Equipment" on page 184 of the Bombardier Annual Report uses the term amortization instead of depreciation. You can consider these two terms to mean the same thing at this point.

Requirements

1. Open T-accounts for the following accounts and their balances as of January 31, 2011 prior to closing. (All amounts in millions of US$.)

PP&E	$1,930.25
Accounts Payable and Accrued Liabilities	$7,835
Advances and progress billings in excess of related long-term contract costs	$1,638
Long-Term Debt..	$6,210

2. Using the following information for Bombardier Inc.'s 2011 operations, make the appropriate year-end journal entries.

   a. Payment of Accrued Liabilities of $1,021.

   b. Amortization expense, $13.75.

   c. Accrue Accounts Payable and Accrued Liabilities, $1,213.

   d. Additional Advances and progress billings in excess of related long-term contract costs, $783.

   e. Principal repayments on the Long-Term Debt of $1,575.

3. Post the journal entries to the T-accounts you set up. Check the updated ending balances in each account against the balances reported by iBombardier Inc. as of January 31, 2011. You can determine the total Accumulated Amortization account by taking the difference between Cost and Net Book Value from Note 7.

INDUSTRY ANALYSIS

Purpose: To help you understand and compare the performance of two companies in the same industry.

Go to the Bombardier Annual Report located in MyAccountingLab. Now access the Annual Report for The Boeing Company. To do this from the internet, go to the company's web page for Investor Relations at *http://www.boeing.com/companyoffices/financial/quarterly.htm* and download the annual report for the year ended December 31, 2010.

Requirement

1. Identify three accounts for each company that indicate that both Bombardier and Boeing use the accrual basis of accounting. Why do you think using the accrual basis of accounting would be more helpful for analysis purposes than the cash basis for these two companies?

SMALL BUSINESS ANALYSIS

Purpose: To help you understand the importance of cash flows in the operation of a small business.

It's the end of the month and cash flow has been a little slow, as it usually is during this time of the accounting period. It just seems to be a little slower this month. You know that Wednesday the 31st is payday, which always requires a large cash outlay. However, you also know that your bank is looking for a set of financial statements as of the end of the month because the loan on your building is coming up for renewal soon. In some of the previous meetings with your bankers, you know that they were always concerned with the cash balance, so you want to have your cash balance as high as possible.

You come up with a tentative plan to not only preserve some of your cash balance at the end of the month, but you believe it will also help your bottom line, your net income. That's the other thing that the bankers are always concerned about. You don't want to make any mistakes with your financial statements at this crucial point, so you decide to contact your accountant to run the idea by her. The conversation goes something like this:

"Good morning, Linda. This is Jerry from BCS Consultants, Inc. Our financial statements have to look really good this month because the bank is going to be scrutinizing them pretty closely for our pending loan renewal. I know that the two things they concentrate on are the cash balance and the net income. So, I've got a plan to help in both of those areas. I'm going to hold off paying my employees until after the first of the month. Plus, last month, I made a big insurance payment to cover me for the next six months, so I won't need to show any insurance expense this month. Both of those will help my net income because I won't be showing those expenses on my income statement. Plus, by not writing the paycheques until the first of the month, I'll be helping to show a higher cash balance. It's really only one day, but the bank won't know that my cash balance should be lower. These certainly sound like some good ideas that would help with my situation, but just in case, I wanted to check with you to see what you thought. Any comments?"

The first words out of the accountant's mouth are "Jerry, you know that your financial statements are prepared using the accrual basis of accounting."

Requirement

1. Complete the thought process of the accountant concerning Jerry's plan. What does she mean by the accrual basis of accounting? What effect will that have on the net income? Is Jerry correct in his assessment of the big insurance payment he made last month covering the next six months? What effect will that have on the net income? And in regard to the last item, what about Jerry's plan to keep the cash balance as high as possible and his statement "the bank won't know that my cash balance should be lower"?

WRITTEN COMMUNICATION

You received a letter from a disgruntled client concerning this year's tax return that you just completed for his or her company. The client's business is in the second year of operations, and you remembered that it seemed to be much more profitable this year than during the first year of operations. You also recall that this particular client's year-end work was assigned to a relatively new staff accountant, which might be part of the problem. The gist of the letter is that last year's taxable net income was about $25,000, and according to the company's calculations, the net income from this year should have been about $50,000. And so the client is wondering why the company is showing taxable net income of $75,000 on this year's return and paying income tax on that amount. You retrieve the file to review it and immediately see the problem. The staff accountant failed to make the closing entries at the end of the first year of operations!

Requirement

1. Prepare a letter to this client explaining the situation and, most importantly, explaining the importance of doing closing entries at the end of each and every year. Also, suggest a solution to this problem for the client, knowing that just explaining the accounting issue might not be enough to retain this client in the future.

Self Check Answers
1. a 2. b 3. c 4. d 5. a 6. d 7. c 8. d 9. b 10. c

COMPREHENSIVE PROBLEM

JOURNALIZING, POSTING, ADJUSTING, PREPARING FINANCIAL STATEMENTS, AND CLOSING

Waters Landscaping, Inc. completed the following transactions during its first month of operations for January 2013:

a. Gary Waters invested $7,500 cash and a truck valued at $15,000 to start Waters Landscaping, Inc. The business issued common shares in exchange for these assets.

b. Purchased $300 of supplies on account.

c. Paid $1,200 for a six-month insurance policy.

d. Performed landscape services for a customer and received $800 cash.

e. Completed a $4,500 landscaping job on account.

f. Paid employee salary, $600.

g. Received $1,100 cash for performing landscaping services.

h. Collected $1,500 in advance for landscaping service to be performed later.

i. Collected $2,500 cash from a customer on account.

j. Purchased fuel for the truck, paying $80 with a company credit card. Credit Accounts Payable.

k. Performed landscaping services on account, $1,600.

l. Paid the current month's office rent, $750.

m. Paid $50 on account.

n. Paid cash dividends of $500.

Requirements

1. Record each transaction in the general journal. Use the letter corresponding to each transaction as the transaction date. Explanations are not required.

2. Post the transactions that you recorded in Requirement 1 in the following T-accounts.

Cash	Salary Payable	Service Revenue
Accounts Receivable	Unearned Service Revenue	Salary Expense
Supplies	Common Shares	Depreciation Expense
Prepaid Insurance	Retained Earnings	Insurance Expense
Truck	Dividends	Fuel Expense
Accumulated Depreciation		Rent Expense
Accounts Payable		Supplies Expense

3. Prepare an unadjusted trial balance as of January 31, 2013.

4. Journalize and post the adjusting journal entries based on the following information:

    a. Accrued salary expense, $600.

    b. Depreciation expense, $375.

    c. Record the expiration of one month's insurance.

    d. Supplies on hand, $75.

    e. Earned 1/3 of the Unearned Service Revenue during January.

    f. Waters Landscaping's income tax rate is 30%.

5. Prepare an adjusted trial balance as of January 31, 2013. Use the adjusted trial balance to prepare Waters Landscaping's income statement, statement of retained earnings, and balance sheet for January. On the income statement list expenses in decreasing order by amount—that is, the largest expense first, the smallest expense last.

6. Journalize and post the closing entries.

7. Prepare a post-closing trial balance at January 31, 2013.

SCAN THIS

CHAPTER 4

Ethics, Internal Control, and Cash

LEARNING OBJECTIVES:

1. ▶ Understand the role of ethics in business and accounting

2. ▶ Define fraud and describe the different types of fraud in business

3. ▶ Identify the three elements of the fraud triangle

4. ▶ Define *internal control* and describe the objectives of an internal control system

5. ▶ Identify the elements of a good internal control system

6. ▶ Describe the major requirements of the Sarbanes-Oxley Act and how they impacted Canadian provincial regulations

7. ▶ Discuss internal controls for cash and prepare a bank reconciliation

8. ▶ Report cash on the balance sheet

9. ▶ (Appendix 4A) Account for the petty cash fund

M ost likely you have heard of Enron and the accounting firm of Arthur Andersen because of the major accounting fraud that both companies played a part in back in 2002. In light of this and other financial scandals that took place around the same time, perhaps you wonder what measures companies use to prevent and detect fraud. Or you may wonder, how did these scandals affect Canadian companies? In Chapter 4, we will explore what fraud is and how businesses try to prevent it by implementing internal controls. We will examine the Sarbanes-Oxley Act, which was the American response to all of the scandals of the early 2000s and the driving force behind changes in Canadian provincial securities exchanges' regulations. We will also learn how cash and other assets are protected as part of internal control measures.

CHAPTER OUTLINE:

In the early part of the 1990s, the management of a company called Phar-Mor committed an accounting **fraud** that amounted to somewhere between 350 and 500 million dollars. Unfortunately, this pales in comparison to some of the more recent scandals that have affected North American businesses. The recent fraudulent activities of companies such as Enron, Livent, Nortel, and Hollinger International have resulted in losses of hundreds of millions of dollars, but that is only a portion of the impact of the activities of a small group of people. **Exhibit 4-1** outlines these recent scandals.

These and other scandals rocked the business community and eroded investor confidence. Innocent people lost their jobs, and the stock market suffered when stock prices dropped. Therefore, it is no surprise that these scandals ushered in a new era in the field of accounting and business in general—the need for higher ethical standards and improved internal controls.

Company and Year Detected	Type of Company	Who Perpetrated Fraud?	Nature of Fraud	Fallout
Enron 2001	Enron was an American company that was formed in 1985 from the merger of two gas and pipeline companies. By 1999, the company was enjoying many successes, including being highly ranked on the Fortune 500 and having its stock price at $90 per share. In October 2001, the company reported its first ever quarterly loss. By November the company's stock was below $1 per share and in December, the company filed for bankruptcy.	The Chairman of the Board, Ken Lay, the Chief Executive Officer, Jeffrey Skilling, the Chief Financial Officer, Andrew Fastow, as well as others under their direction.	Complex relationships with offshore partnerships along with questionable accounting practices were used to overstate revenues, understate expenses, and hide the true amount of Enron's liabilities.	Enron filed for bankruptcy. Lay, Skilling, Fastow, and other top executives were convicted of fraud and/or other related charges. Numerous individuals were also convicted of insider trading. Enron's auditor, Arthur Andersen, was convicted of obstruction of justice for shredding documents related to the audit. Arthur Andersen dissolved its U.S. operations despite the conviction being overturned by the U.S. Supreme Court. Around 5,600 Enron employees lost their jobs with the company's collapse.
Conrad Black and Hollinger International 2003	Conrad Black started buying newspaper companies while he was in his twenties and by 1985 Hollinger Inc. was formed through an amalgamation of three companies. In 2003, Black was called to testify in front of the U.S. Securities and Exchange Commission. Early in 2004, Hollinger International removed Black as chairman and announced a lawsuit against Black and another executive for $200 million, based on alleged financial irregularities. A criminal investigation began in March 2005 and Black was charged with racketeering, money laundering, fraud, and obstruction of justice. By the end of 2007 Conrad Black was sentenced to 6.5 years in jail for obstruction of justice and mail fraud.	Conrad Black, David Radler (former executive), and two other executives of Hollinger International.	Diversion of funds from Hollinger International to reduce assets, understatement of income to evade paying taxes, violations of securities laws, and obstruction of justice through the removal of 12 boxes of unknown content assumed to be evidence from Black's Toronto offices.	David Radler pleaded guilty to mail fraud for a reduced sentence and testified against Conrad Black. Conrad Black was sentenced to 6.5 years in jail. In October 2010, Black won an appeal and two fraud convictions were thrown out. The remaining convictions were not overturned.

Exhibit 4-1 ▲

Company and Year Detected	Type of Company	Who Perpetrated Fraud?	Nature of Fraud	Fallout
Livent 1998	Garth Drabinsky and Myron Gottlieb founded Cineplex Odeon in 1979. Drabinsky and Gottlieb were forced by the shareholders to resign from Cineplex Odeon after accounting irregularities were discovered in 1989. In the negotiations to leave the company, Drabinsky and Gottlieb acquired the Pantages Theatre in Toronto and by 1993, Livent, a live theatrical production company, was formed. By 1998 the productions performed in their theatres had earned twenty Tony Awards. In the summer of 1998, shareholders discovered significant financial irregularities and trading in the company's stock was suspended and lawsuits were filed against the company and its officers. In 1998 Livent was under investigation by a number of agencies including the RCMP, the Ontario Securities Commission, the American Securities Exchange Commission, the U.S. Department of Justice, and others.	Maria Messina, CA (CFO of Livent and former audit manager and partner at Deloitte & Touche)	Kickback schemes where suppliers would overcharge Livent for services and then the extra payments would be given directly to Gottlieb and Drabinsky to the amount of $7 million. Accounting manipulations (such as just eliminating expenses from the records) to hide losses and achieve targeted goals.	Messina pleaded guilty to a federal felony charge. Livent filed for bankruptcy citing debts of $334 million and the remaining assets were bought by SFX Entertainment. Both Gottlieb and Drabinsky were found guilty of fraud and forgery. Drabinsky was sentenced to seven years while Gottlieb was sentenced to six years.
Nortel 2004	Nortel began in 1895 as Northern Electric and Manufacturing and supplied telecommunications equipment and services globally. The company grew to an organization valued at over $300 billion and in January 2009 dropped to a low of about $200 million. In 2004, the company delayed publishing financial statements for 2003 and fired a number of executives including the CEO and CFO.	CEO Frank Dunn, CFO, controller, at least 4 more executives, and at least 7 additional people from the finance department.	Overstating earnings so much that the earnings for 2003 needed to be restated at less than 50% of the original reported amount.	More than 60,000 jobs were lost. In March 2007, Dunn and three former executives were charged with civil fraud from making "material misstatements" by the Securities and Exchange Commission (U.S.) and the Ontario Securities Commission. In 2008, the RCMP charged Dunn and two former executives with fraud. The first quarter financial results for 2011 showed revenues of $20 million, which was drastically reduced from previous quarters due to "the sale of substantially all of its businesses" (www.nortel.com).

Exhibit 4-1 ▲ (cont.)

WHY IS ETHICS IMPORTANT IN BUSINESS AND ACCOUNTING?

Some accounting professionals contend that the accounting rules (for example, IFRS or Accounting Standards for Private Enterprises) may have contributed to the recent accounting scandals. How could that be, you might wonder? Well, accounting rules do not always

1 Understand the role of ethics in business and accounting

have many specific rules but instead consist of a small number of overriding principles. Accountants were expected to exercise their professional judgment to ensure that proper accounting treatment was being applied to adhere to these overriding principles. Over time, accounting rules and guidelines have evolved into a system with numerous rules that have been adopted to address very specific accounting situations. With this evolution of the rules, some feel, has come an attitude that "if the rules don't prohibit a specific accounting treatment, then it must be acceptable and, therefore, I am not acting unethically if I utilize this accounting treatment." This attitude may encourage some individuals to search for unique ways of accounting for certain transactions that, although not specifically prohibited, most likely would have been considered to violate the original overriding accounting principles. It is impossible to write enough rules to cover every situation. To promote ethical behaviour, the accounting profession may need to return to a system with a small number of overriding principles and the expectation that sound judgment be applied to ensure that the principles are followed.

Whether or not the current system of accounting rules contributed to the recent accounting scandals is a topic for debate. What is certain is that most, if not all, of these scandals were the result of poor ethical behaviour on the part of one or more individuals. In Chapter 1, ethics was defined as principles of right behaviour that guide decision making. Scandals, such as those that have occurred in the last decade, do not result from decision making based on proper ethical behaviour. Proper ethical behaviour is more than just following the rules or doing what is legal; it is characterized by honesty, fairness, and integrity. Proper ethical behaviour can be summarized by the "golden rule," which says "treat others the same way that you would want to be treated in the same situation." For organizations to earn and keep the public's trust, they must practise good ethical behaviour at every level within the organization. Some of the steps that many organizations utilize to accomplish this include, but are not limited to, the following:

- Develop a written **code of ethics**. A code of ethics defines standards of behaviour all members of an organization are expected to follow.
- Communicate the code of ethics to all members of the organization. A good idea is to distribute the code of ethics in written format to all employees at least annually. Then, have employees acknowledge in writing that they have received, read, and understand what is expected of them.
- Ensure top management within the organization models good ethical behaviour at all times because ethics is better "caught than taught." As any parent can tell you, expecting your children to "do as I say, not as I do" does not work very well.
- Establish a method that allows for ethics violations to be reported anonymously. A person who reports unethical behaviour, a **whistleblower**, must be able to make a report without fear of punishment or retaliation.
- Enforce the ethics code. Ethics violations should always be addressed in a timely fashion. This helps ensure that the ethics code is taken seriously.

The three Canadian Accounting Associations, CA, CGA, and CMA, have their own codes of ethics to guide their members' conduct and ethical standards. Some code of ethics principles include responsibility to society, trust and duties, due care and professional judgment, deceptive information, and responsibilities to the Profession. You can access the code of ethics of the CGA at http://www.cga-canada.org/en-ca/StandardsLib/ca_ceproc.pdf, and the CMA at http://www.cma-ontario.org/index.cfm?ci_id=7406&la_id=1.

WHAT IS FRAUD AND WHO COMMITS IT?

The scandalous activities referred to previously involve the commission of fraud by company management. So what exactly is fraud? Although there are many definitions of fraud, in its broadest sense fraud can be defined as the use of deception or trickery for personal gain. In North America, fraud is one of the fastest growing crimes. It accounts for more losses than robbery. In the business world, fraud is either committed by a business organization or against a business organization.

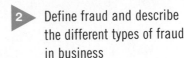

2 Define fraud and describe the different types of fraud in business

Management Fraud

An organization's top management is usually responsible for fraud that is committed by a business organization. This **management fraud** typically involves fraudulent financial reporting. Fraudulent financial reporting most often makes a company's earnings look better than they are. The goal of overstating earnings is to help increase a company's stock price or to ensure larger year-end bonuses for upper management. Fraudulent financial reporting is achieved when management does the following:

- Overstates revenues by
    1. overstating receivables related to revenue that has not yet been earned
    2. understating unearned revenue (recording revenue when cash is received even though goods or services have not yet been provided)

- Understates expenses by
    1. overstating the value of assets such as inventory, equipment, and buildings, or recording assets that do not exist
    2. understating amounts owed to suppliers, employees, or creditors

Employee Embezzlement

The primary form of fraud committed against a business organization is **employee embezzlement**. Employee embezzlement usually involves the misappropriation of business assets by an employee. Employees can

- steal cash, inventory, tools, supplies, or other assets from the employer.
- establish fake companies and have the employer pay these phony companies for goods or services that are never delivered, then intercept and fraudulently cash the cheques.
- engage in **disbursement schemes**. Employee embezzlement involving disbursement schemes takes place when an employee tricks a company into giving up cash for an invalid reason. Examples of disbursement schemes include the following:
    1. **Cheque tampering**: The employee writes a fraudulent cheque and makes the cheque payable to him- or herself. Alternatively, the employee obtains a cheque intended for an outside party, endorses the cheque, and then cashes it.
    2. **Cash register schemes**: The employee gives a false refund for returned merchandise by filling out a refund form and putting it in the cash register. The employee then pockets the cash. Another related scheme happens when the employee accepts cash from a customer for a purchase but does not record the

transaction in the cash register. The employee then keeps the cash for personal use.

3. **Expense schemes**: The employee overbills the company for travel or other business-related expenses, such as lunches, hotels, air travel, parking fees, and cab fares.

Another form of employee embezzlement occurs when an employee takes **bribes** or **kickbacks** from

- suppliers in exchange for the employee turning a blind eye to a supplier charging the employer higher purchase prices.
- suppliers in exchange for the employee turning a blind eye to delivery of inferior goods.
- suppliers in exchange for the employee authorizing payments to the supplier for goods not delivered to the employer.
- customers in exchange for granting the customer a lower sales price.
- customers in exchange for giving the customer goods or services for which the employer is never paid.

DECISION GUIDELINES

Decision

As the credit manager for a bank, do I need to be concerned about fraud?

Guideline

Fraud is *deceit or trickery causing financial harm*. It may be perpetrated by management or by employees.

Analyze

Management fraud typically involves fraudulent financial reporting. Fraudulent financial reporting occurs when financial information is manipulated so that the business looks more profitable than it really is. Managers may record revenues prematurely or fictitiously, or understate expenses.

Employee embezzlement usually involves the misappropriation of assets. Employee embezzlement can include stealing cash or other assets; taking kickbacks from suppliers or customers; or using cheque tampering, cash register schemes, and expense schemes that result in improper payment from the employer.

Both management fraud and employee embezzlement can cause financial ruin for a company as well as result in criminal prosecution for the perpetrators. Therefore, as a credit manager for a bank, you will need to understand fraud and the signs of fraud to protect the bank from companies that engage in fraud, such as by borrowing funds and then going out of business without repaying the debt.

WHAT FACTORS ARE USUALLY PRESENT WHEN FRAUD IS COMMITTED?

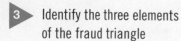 Identify the three elements of the fraud triangle

Anyone who has done much camping knows that it takes three things to build a fire: fuel, oxygen, and ignition. For fraud to occur, three factors must also exist: perceived pressure, rationalization, and perceived opportunity. **Exhibit 4-2** on the following page presents the

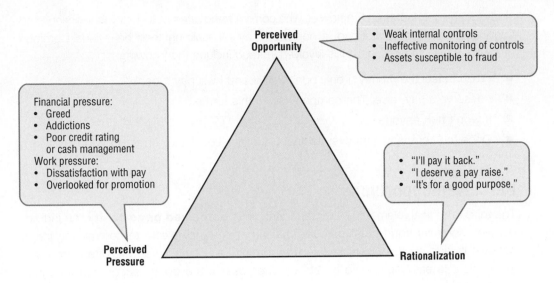

Exhibit 4-2 ▲

fraud triangle, which shows the connection of the three factors necessary to commit fraud.

Let us take a closer look at the three elements of the fraud triangle.

Perceived Pressure

Numerous reasons exist that could cause an individual to feel pressured to commit fraud. However, the most likely sources of **perceived pressure** are usually financial pressure or work-related pressure. Financial pressure can be caused by, but is not limited to, the following:

■ Unexpected financial needs, such as medical bills

■ A drug or alcohol habit

■ Living beyond one's means

■ A gambling addiction

■ Unanticipated financial losses

■ Excessive bills or personal debt

Work-related pressure also has several possible causes. An employee might feel dissatisfied with his or her job because of a sense of being underpaid or underappreciated. An employee might have recently been overlooked for a promotion. Either of these things can motivate an employee to "get even" with the company by committing fraud. Also, if a company is performing poorly, it is possible for people within management to feel they are personally responsible. The perceived pressure caused by this feeling of personal responsibility can lead them to commit management fraud by falsifying the financial statements.

Rationalization

The next element of the fraud triangle that must be present for fraud to occur is **rationalization**. Rationalization is simply finding good reasons for doing things that we really know are wrong. Rationalization is human nature and very few people, if any, do not rationalize their behaviour at some time or another. For example, you may have rationalized going out to a movie with your friends last night when you knew that you really needed to study for an important quiz. Employees who commit fraud attempt to justify their actions and convince themselves that fraud is not wrong by rationalizing their behaviour. Common rationalizations used by individuals involved in fraud include the following:

- "I didn't steal the money; I only borrowed it and I will pay it back."
- "I deserve a pay raise. The company owes this to me."
- "It won't hurt anyone."
- "Once the company gets over its financial difficulties, I will correct the books."

Perceived Opportunity

The third, and final, element of the fraud triangle is **perceived opportunity**. An individual who commits fraud must perceive that an opportunity exists to commit the fraud, conceal it, and avoid punishment. An opportunity to commit fraud is often perceived when there is easy access to assets or when assets are poorly accounted for by an organization.

Removing any one of the three elements of the fraud triangle makes it much less likely that fraud will occur. Consider the following examples:

- No perceived pressure: An employee may see an opportunity to steal a company computer. He or she may even be able to justify taking the computer by telling him- or herself that the computer is an older one the company no longer uses. However, if he or she can afford to purchase a new computer, the employee will have a low incentive to commit fraud.
- No rationalization: An employee may desperately need cash to pay overdue bills and may see a way to steal money without detection. However, the employee's moral beliefs may make it impossible for him or her to justify taking the money.
- No perceived opportunity: An employee may feel pressured to steal money to cover a gambling debt. He or she may rationalize the theft by convincing him- or herself that he or she will repay the company next month. However, if it is not possible for the employee to steal money without detection, it is unlikely that he or she will commit fraud. This situation arises because the employee sees no opportunity to engage in fraudulent activity without discovery.

Out of the three elements of the fraud triangle, a business can have the most influence over the element of perceived opportunity. A business generally has limited control over perceived pressure felt by an employee or an employee's ability to rationalize unethical behaviour. The most effective way for a business to prevent fraud is to reduce, or eliminate, the perceived opportunity for an employee to misappropriate company assets or for a manager to falsify financial information. Perceived opportunity can be reduced through a good system of **internal control**.

DECISION GUIDELINES

Decision

As the owner of my own company, I have some cash to invest in deterring fraudulent activities by my employees. How should I spend my money?

Guideline

When all three "legs," or elements, of the fraud triangle are present, fraud is more likely to occur. These elements are as follows:

- Perceived pressure
- Rationalization
- Perceived opportunity

Analyze

If you remove one of the legs from a three-legged stool, the stool will fall down. In a similar manner, if you can remove one of the elements of the fraud triangle, it is much less likely that fraud will occur. Perceived pressure and rationalization are influenced more by a perpetrator of fraud and are, therefore, very hard to remove. However, it is possible to control the element of perceived opportunity and, therefore, reduce the risk of fraud occurring.

WHAT IS AN INTERNAL CONTROL SYSTEM?

Internal control is a comprehensive system that helps an organization do the following:

- Safeguard assets
- Operate efficiently and effectively
- Ensure proper reporting of financial information
- Ensure compliance with applicable laws and regulations

An organization's management is responsible for the design and implementation of the internal control system. Internal control systems vary from one company to another. Usually, large companies have better developed, more complex internal control systems than small companies. Despite being less formal and less structured, the internal control systems of small companies can still be effective.

4 Define *internal control* and describe the objectives of an internal control system

5 Identify the elements of a good internal control system

Elements of an Internal Control System

There are five key elements that affect an organization's internal control system. The complexity of, and the effectiveness of, the internal control system depends upon these elements. These elements are as follows:

- The control environment
- Risk assessment
- Control activities
- Information and communication
- Monitoring

Control Environment

The **control environment** is the foundation for all other components of internal control. The control environment reflects management and staff attitudes regarding internal control and sets the tone for the entire organization. Control environment factors include the following:

- Leadership philosophy and operating style (an effective control environment cannot exist if management has a "do as I say, not as I do" attitude)
- The competency of the employees within an organization
- The integrity and ethical values of the company personnel
- The organizational structure of the company, namely the delegation of authority and responsibility

Risk Assessment

Risk is a fact of life. Every day, a company will face a variety of risks from both internal and external sources. **Risk assessment** is an ongoing process that identifies and analyzes risks and takes steps to reduce them. For example, a fast food restaurant that hires predominately younger workers would be at a higher risk of violating "child labour laws." Also, a company that has a large amount of cash on hand will have a higher risk of having cash stolen from it.

Control Activities

There are two elements related to **control activities**: policies establishing what should be done and the procedures that should be followed to implement the policies. The types of control activities used by an organization vary from company to company. Control activities occur at all levels and in all functions throughout the entire organization. Generally, the controls chosen for an organization are based on its control environment, its assessment of risk, the size and structure of the organization, and the nature of its operations. Examples of common control activities include the following:

- Employment of competent personnel: Employees must be competent and trustworthy. They should have written job descriptions and be properly trained and adequately supervised.
- Separation of duties: Responsibility for more than one of the following functions should not be given to any one employee:
  1. Authorizing transactions
  2. Maintaining custody of assets
  3. Keeping accounting records

  Assigning an individual responsibility for more than one of these duties creates an opportunity for fraud. For example, if an employee has access to cash or other assets and he or she can record transactions, that employee can steal from the company and falsify financial information to hide the theft.
- Mandatory vacations: Employees should be required to take annual vacations. If an employee knows that another person will be performing his or her duties during the vacation, there is less perceived opportunity to commit fraud. The vacationing employee will be concerned that any improper activities will be detected.
- Restricted access: Limit the number of employees who have access to company assets, such as cash, inventory, and supplies. For instance, use cash registers, vaults, and locked storage units to control access to assets. Also, access to computerized accounting records should be restricted to authorized personnel through the use of passwords. Allowing too many people access to assets and records

creates opportunity for fraud to occur. It also makes it more difficult to find the perpetrator should fraud occur.

- Security measures: Proper security measures should be implemented to deter theft. These measures can include the use of security cameras and alarm systems. Cash registers that print a receipt should also be utilized with a requirement that all customers receive a receipt.

- Proper authorization: Requiring proper authorization for certain activities. For example, requiring proper authorization for all sales returns can help prevent improper refunds from being issued.

- Maintain adequate documents and records: A trail of business documents and records, called an **audit trail**, should be maintained. The audit trail provides evidence of, and the details supporting, business transactions. Documents should be pre-numbered so gaps in the numbered sequence draw attention. Creating an effective audit trail lowers the chance that inappropriate activity will go unnoticed.

ACCOUNTING IN YOUR WORLD

Who says there's no free lunch?

Have you ever eaten at a food court in a mall and seen a sign that says "If you do not get a receipt, your meal is free"? Why would the business care if you get a receipt? This is actually part of the business's internal control activities. You see, the company doesn't really care if you get a receipt, they just care that a receipt is printed. This practice prevents an employee from taking your money and pocketing it because once the receipt is printed, the sale is recorded. If the employee pockets your payment, the daily cash count will not match the daily record of sales and the theft will be detected. This example is just one of many control activities that businesses utilize as part of their internal control systems.

Information and Communication

To maximize the effectiveness of an internal control system, information about the control environment, the risk assessment, and the control activities must be communicated at all levels of the organization. This information should be communicated up, down, and across the organizational structure of the company. It is also critical that management communicates to all personnel that internal control must be taken seriously.

Monitoring

The internal control system must be continually monitored to locate weaknesses in the system. Monitoring can be accomplished through ongoing activities or through separate evaluations. Ongoing monitoring activities include regular management and supervisory activities. It also includes the assessment of the performance of the internal control system by employees as they perform their required duties. The need for separate evaluations depends on the effectiveness of the ongoing monitoring procedures.

Internal Control Limitations

A good internal control system reduces the risk of undetected errors and irregularities. However, an internal control system cannot provide absolute assurance that no errors will occur. It also does not guarantee that fraud will be prevented or detected. The effectiveness of an internal control system is limited because of the following:

- Employees can become tired, careless, or distracted and make mistakes. They may also use poor judgment or misunderstand policies and procedures.
- Controls can be poorly designed.
- Staff size limitations may hinder efforts to properly segregate duties.
- Two or more people can work together to circumvent controls. This is known as **collusion**.
- Management can override controls.
- The cost of implementing some internal controls may exceed the benefits of these controls.

Some examples of these limitations are as follows:

- An employee may forget to check authorization for the extension of credit to a customer when the phone rings in the middle of the transaction.
- A disgruntled employee may convince another employee to help steal from the company.
- Management may override controls and direct the accounting staff to record revenue for services that have not yet been performed.
- In small businesses, the cost of employing enough people for separation of duties may exceed the benefits of the segregation.

CONCEPT CHECK

Goodguys Tire Company is a small retail tire outlet located in Aurora, Ontario. Bill Han, the president of Goodguys Tire Company, has assigned the bookkeeper the responsibility of processing all cash receipts as well as all cash disbursements. The bookkeeper also prepares the daily cash deposits and takes them to the bank. Bill knows that he has not achieved a very good separation of duties, but the limited number of employees (due to the size of the company) did not allow it. Is there anything Bill can do in light of the fact that there is not a good separation of duties to help prevent fraud from occurring?

Answer

Yes, although there is no substitute for proper separation of duties, some of the steps Bill could take to help detect/deter fraud include, but are not limited to, the following:

- Ensure that someone other than the bookkeeper receives the unopened bank statement and prepares a bank reconciliation on a monthly basis.

- Require that all adjustments to customer accounts be authorized by someone other than the bookkeeper. A periodic review of the customer account detail should also be performed by someone other than the bookkeeper. Any unauthorized adjustments to the accounts should be noted and investigated.

- Require that someone other than the bookkeeper authorize all cash disbursements. The cash disbursement detail should also be reviewed for unusual disbursements periodically by someone other than the bookkeeper.

DECISION GUIDELINES

Decision	**Guideline**	**Analyze**
As the owner of my own small business, I know I need to incorporate internal controls, but I don't know where to start. What do I need to consider to make an effective internal control system?	A good system of internal control must achieve the following objectives: • Safeguard assets • Operate efficiently and effectively • Ensure proper reporting of financial information • Ensure compliance with applicable laws and regulations	The internal control system consists of all of the policies and procedures that a business has in place to achieve these objectives. One of the most important things that can be done to help prevent fraud is to ensure that there is adequate separation of duties within the organization. However, no matter how good a system of internal controls is, there are still limitations. For example, two or more employees can work together (collude) to commit fraud even though there is adequate separation of duties.

WHO IS RESPONSIBLE FOR INTERNAL CONTROL?

6 ▶ Describe the major requirements of the Sarbanes-Oxley Act and how they impacted Canadian provincial regulations

Audits confirm, or validate, the accounting records and reports of a business. Auditors examine the company's financial statements and the accounting system that produces them. Audits may be internal or external. Employees conduct **internal audits** of a business. These employees, or internal auditors, verify that company personnel are following policies and procedures, and that operations are running efficiently. Internal auditors also determine whether the company is following applicable legal requirements.

Public Accountants are the auditors who are licensed to perform **external audits** of an organization's financial statements. Public accountants are independent of the organization. The provincial securities commissions require that all companies that sell shares and bonds to the general public be audited by independent public accountants. This audit includes an assessment of the company's financial statements to determine whether they are fairly presented in accordance with the appropriate guidelines, whether the company uses IFRS or Accounting Standards for Private Enterprises, as well as an examination of the company's internal control system. **Exhibit 4-3** illustrates a typical organizational chart.

Audit Opinions

The outcome of an external audit is the issuance of an opinion by the independent public accountant. **Exhibit 4-4** on the next page describes the four different types of audit opinions:

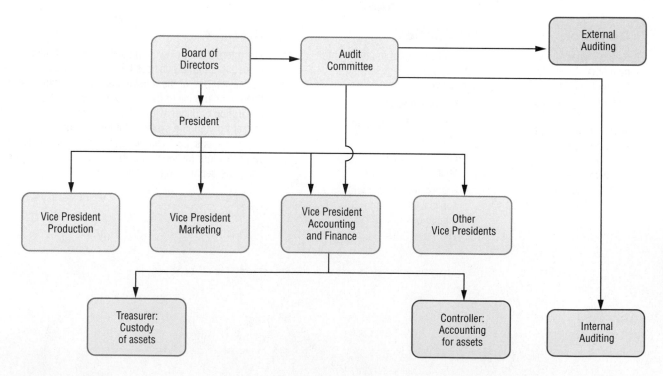

Exhibit 4-3 ▲

Type of Opinion	Reason Supporting the Opinion	Impact as a Result of the Opinion
Unqualified (also called a "clean" opinion)	An unqualified opinion means that, in the auditors' opinion, the financial statements are fairly presented. In addition, they are free of material misstatements, and have been prepared in accordance with the appropriate accounting guidelines, unless otherwise noted.	This is the best type of opinion. It gives the financial statement users assurance that the financial statements can be relied upon.
Qualified (also called an "except for" opinion)	A qualified opinion is issued when one of the following occurs: • The auditors have taken exception to an accounting application or treatment the company being audited used • The auditors were unable to gather the information they felt was necessary to issue an unqualified opinion • The auditors were unable to determine the outcome of an uncertainty, which could have an effect on the financial statements	A qualified opinion includes a separate paragraph outlining the reason for the qualification. A qualified opinion is used to help financial statement users make more informed decisions about the company. It allows the auditor to bring to the attention of the users circumstances or situations that may affect the user's reliance on the financial statements.
Adverse	By issuing an adverse opinion, the auditors are stating that in their opinion one of the following situations exists: • The financial statements are not fairly presented in accordance with appropriate accounting guidelines • There are material misstatements in the financial statements	An adverse opinion will be accompanied by a paragraph explaining the reason for the negative opinion. An adverse opinion is very detrimental to a company as it basically informs users that the financial statements should not be relied upon.
Disclaimer	A disclaimer indicates that the auditors are unable to express an opinion based on their audit. A disclaimer of opinion may be issued because of the following: • A lack of independence on the auditors' part • The inability to obtain the evidence needed to support a different type of opinion • The existence of substantial doubts regarding the business's ability to continue as a "going concern" • Material uncertainties for which the auditors are unable to determine the outcome	Since the auditors are unable, or unwilling, to express an opinion on the financial statements, investors will give considerable thought before investing in a company that has been issued a disclaimer of opinion.

Exhibit 4-4 ▲

The Sarbanes-Oxley Act

As discussed earlier in the chapter, an unprecedented number of accounting frauds perpetrated by upper management have occurred in North America in recent years. This is despite the fact that the financial statements of the companies involved were all audited by independent auditors. As a response to these frauds, the United States developed the **Sarbanes-Oxley Act** in 2002, commonly referred to as **SOX**. The Sarbanes-Oxley Act

- applies to publicly traded companies.
- established the Public Company Accounting Oversight Board (PCAOB). The PCAOB is a private sector, nonprofit corporation that oversees the auditors of public companies. The PCAOB protects the interests of investors by helping ensure fair, independent audit reports.

- requires that external auditors report to an audit committee, rather than to an organization's management. Prior to Sarbanes-Oxley, the external auditors often reported to a company's upper management.

- requires that a company's Chief Executive Officer (CEO) and Chief Financial Officer (CFO) certify all annual, or quarterly, reports filed by an organization. By signing the reports, the executives certify the following:

  1. They have reviewed the report

  2. The report does not contain any materially untrue statements

  3. The financial statements and related information contained in the report fairly present the financial condition and the results of operations in all material respects of the organization

  4. The signing officers are responsible for internal controls and have evaluated these internal controls within the previous 90 days and have reported on their findings

  5. They have disclosed

     a. a list of all deficiencies in the internal controls and information on any fraud that involves employees who are involved with internal activities.

     b. any significant changes in internal controls or related factors that could have a negative impact on the internal controls.

While SOX has been costly to implement for many companies, it has had a definite impact on improving internal controls in corporate America. SOX has also had an impact on Canadian regulations. Canadian regulators were able to learn from the implementation of the Sarbanes-Oxley Act in America as the Canadian regulations began to be implemented in 2005. The Canadian system is substantially different from the American system in that each province in Canada has its own securities commission. The Canadian Securities Administrators (CSA) is an umbrella organization that makes recommendations for each of the provincial bodies. The CSA, in combination with the Ontario Securities Commission, drafted recommendations based on the Sarbanes-Oxley Act that incorporated CEO/CFO certification of annual reports, new rules for more independence of the audit committee, the implementation and testing of new internal controls, and the formation of a new accounting supervisory body, the Canadian Public Accountability Board. The recommendations are not mandatory for each province, but most recommendations have been adopted by each province. In addition to these recommendations for corporate reporting, the Ontario government implemented tougher penalties for public companies that do not adhere to the regulations, and the federal government made changes to the Criminal Code to toughen the rules against insider trading, to protect from threatening against whistleblowing, and to increase the penalties for public market-related offences.

WHAT INTERNAL CONTROL PROCEDURES SHOULD BE USED FOR CASH?

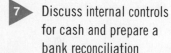

7 Discuss internal controls for cash and prepare a bank reconciliation

Regardless of whether sales are cash sales, credit/debit card sales, or sales on account, ultimately a business will collect cash from the transaction. Cash is one of the most vulnerable assets a business has. Cash is easy to conceal and has no identifying marks that link it to its owner, making it relatively easy to steal. Transactions that affect the cash account also impact other accounts, so misstatements of cash can result in misstatements of other items. As a result, it is important to have good internal controls over cash.

Internal Controls over Cash Receipts

Companies typically receive cash over the counter and through the mail. Good internal control dictates that all cash receipts be deposited in the bank quickly. Each source of cash needs its own security measures.

Over the Counter Cash Receipts

The cash register provides control over the cash receipts for a retail business. Consider a Shoppers Drug Mart store. Shoppers Drug Mart issues a receipt for each transaction to ensure that every sale is recorded; a customer cannot receive a receipt unless the register records the transaction. When the sales associate enters a transaction in the register, the machine records it and the cash drawer opens to receive cash. At the end of the day, the cash in the drawer is reconciled against the machine's record of cash sales to ensure the proper amount of cash is on hand. The machine's record of sales is then used as the source for the journal entry to record sales.

At the end of the day, or several times daily if the company is making a lot of sales, cash should be deposited in the bank. Any cash not in a cash register should be kept in a locked location within the business, such as a safe, until it can be deposited in the bank. These measures, coupled with oversight by management, help discourage theft.

Cash Receipts by Mail

Many companies receive payments by mail, especially if they sell products or services on credit. **Exhibit 4-5** shows how companies can control cash received by mail. Generally, an employee who has no other involvement in the sales or collection process, often a mailroom employee, opens all incoming mail and prepares a control listing of amounts received. At this time a remittance advice is prepared if one did not accompany the payment. The mailroom then sends all customer cheques to the treasurer, who oversees having the money deposited in the bank. The remittance advices, often cheque stubs, go to the Accounting Department and serve as a basis for making journal entries to Cash and the customer accounts receivable. As a final step, the controller compares the bank deposit amount from the treasurer with the debit to Cash from the Accounting Department.

The payments received according to the mailroom should match the debit to Cash and should equal the amount deposited in the bank. This procedure ensures that cash receipts are safe in the bank, and the company accounting records are up to date.

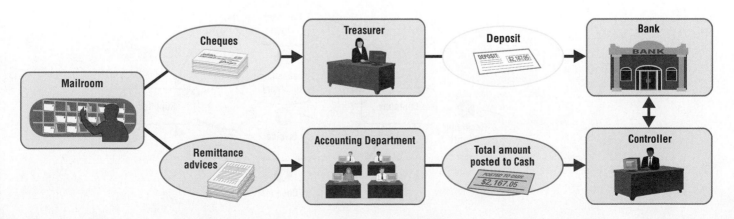

Exhibit 4-5 ▲

Internal Control over Cash Payments

A good separation of duties between operations and cash payments provides internal control over those payments. Also, making payments by cheque is another important control for several reasons:

- The cheque provides a written record of the payment.
- An authorized official studies the evidence supporting the payment.
- The official approves the payment by signing the cheque.

Purchase and Payment Process

To illustrate the internal control over cash payments by cheque in a company large enough to separate duties, suppose Joe's Sporting Goods buys snowboard inventory from Burton Snowboards. This purchase and payment process will generally follow steps similar to those shown in **Exhibit 4-6**:

① Joe's Sporting Goods sends a **purchase order** to Burton Snowboards, its supplier. By preparing this document, Joe's is placing an order to buy snowboards.

② Burton Snowboards ships the goods and sends an invoice back to Joe's.

③ Joe's receives the snowboards and prepares a **receiving report** as evidence that it received the goods.

④ After matching the information on these documents, Joe's sends a cheque to Burton Snowboards to pay for the goods.

For good internal control, the **purchasing agent**, the individual who places the order, should neither receive the goods nor approve the payment. Otherwise, the purchasing agent could buy goods and have them shipped to his or her home. Or he or she could receive kickbacks from suppliers by having the supplier bill his or her employer too much, approving the payment and splitting the excess with the supplier. The **controller**, as the person responsible for the accounting function, should not sign the cheques for similar reasons; he or she could sign a cheque payable to him- or herself and then manipulate the accounting records to hide this improper payment.

Before signing the cheque, the **treasurer**, who usually assumes responsibility for the custody of cash, should examine each set of documents including the purchase order, receiving report, purchase invoice, and cheque to prove that they agree. This helps the company ensure that

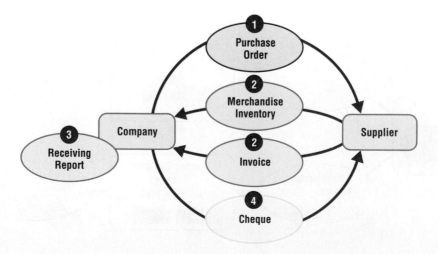

Exhibit 4-6 ▲

❶ the goods it received were the goods it ordered, as proved by the purchase order and receiving report.

❷ it is paying only for the goods ordered and received, as proved by the purchase order, receiving report, invoice, and cheque.

The payment should be issued using pre-numbered cheques. After payment, the cheque signer should deface the set of documents. This can be accomplished by punching a hole through the payment packet or stamping the documents "PAID." This hole or stamp confirms the bill has been paid and prevents the documents from being used to generate a second payment.

Streamlined Payment Procedures

For many companies, the purchase and payment process is made more efficient through the use of **electronic data interchange (EDI)**. EDI is a streamlined process that bypasses people and documents altogether. For example, in electronic data interchange, Walmart's computers communicate directly with the computers of suppliers such as Proctor & Gamble and Hershey Foods. When Walmart's inventory of Hershey chocolate candy reaches a low level, the computer sends a purchase order to Hershey. Hershey ships the candy and invoices Walmart electronically. Then an **electronic funds transfer (EFT)** sends Walmart's payment to Hershey via electronic communication.

The Bank Reconciliation

Preparing a **bank reconciliation** is an important internal control that should be performed regularly. On a monthly basis a company will receive a **bank statement** from its bank that shows the **bank balance**, the cash balance in the company's account according to the bank. This balance usually does not agree to the **book balance**, the cash balance according to the company's records. Differences between the bank balance and the book balance arise because of

■ differences, called timing differences, between the time when the bank records a transaction and when the business records it.

■ errors made by either the bank or the business.

The bank reconciliation identifies and explains the differences between the bank balance and the book balance and is used to arrive at the actual "true" balance of cash. The bank reconciliation serves as an internal control because it allows the correct amount of cash to be arrived at according to both bank and book records.

Preparing the Bank Reconciliation

The basic format, showing items that typically appear on a bank reconciliation, is illustrated in **Exhibit 4-7** on the next page. The bank reconciliation is divided into two sides, the bank side and the book side. When establishing the procedures for a bank reconciliation, keep in mind our discussion of separation of duties: the person who prepares the bank reconciliation should have no other responsibilities related to cash. Otherwise, the bank reconciler could steal cash and manipulate the reconciliation to conceal the theft. The ultimate goal of the bank reconciliation is to ensure that after the adjustments, the bank balance will equal the book balance.

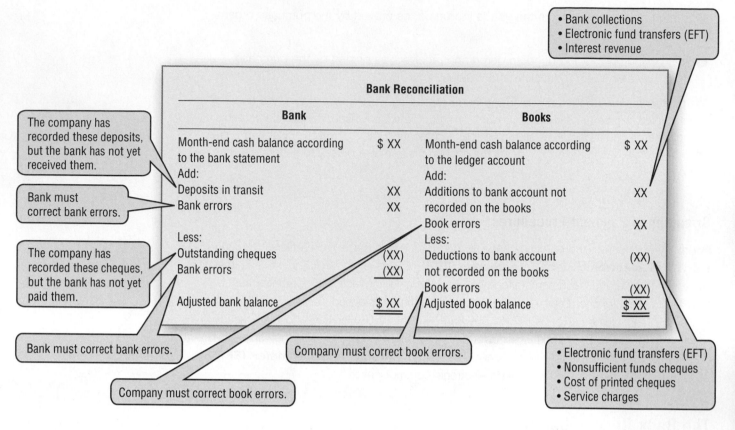

Exhibit 4-7 ▲

Bank Side of the Reconciliation

When preparing a bank reconciliation, the following items are included on the bank side of the reconciliation:

❶ Deposits in transit are deposits that the business has recorded but the bank has not. Deposits in transit are added to the bank balance.

❷ Outstanding cheques are cheques that the business has recorded but the bank has not yet paid. Outstanding cheques are subtracted from the bank balance.

❸ Bank errors include the bank recording a deposit or a cheque for the wrong amount. The bank may also record a deposit or cheque that belongs in another bank customer's account. The bank must correct the errors that it has made. Adjust the bank balance for the amount of the error, adding or subtracting as necessary depending on the nature of the error.

Book Side of the Reconciliation

When preparing a bank reconciliation, the following items are included on the book side of the reconciliation:

❶ Bank collections are cash collections made by the bank on behalf of the business. Many businesses have their customers pay their bank directly. One way customers make payment is through a **lock-box system** in which they send their payments to a business's post office box. The bank then collects payments from the box and deposits them in the business's account, thus reducing the chance of theft. Another example is a bank collection of a depositor's note receivable. Because the bank statement is often the first communication that cash was received, the business has not yet recorded the receipt. These collections are added to the book balance.

2 Electronic fund transfers occur when the bank receives or pays cash on the depositor's behalf electronically. Because the bank statement is often the first communication of the transactions, the book balance may need to be adjusted accordingly for the cash receipt or cash payment.

3 Interest revenue may be earned on an account depending on the balance in that account. Interest revenue is added to the book balance.

4 **Nonsufficient funds (NSF) cheques** represent customer cheques that the business has previously deposited that have turned out to be worthless. In other words, there were not sufficient funds in the customers' bank accounts to pay the cheques. These amounts are subtracted from the book balance to reverse the deposit amount made earlier.

5 Service charges represent bank fees for processing transactions, printing cheques, etc. These amounts are subtracted from the book balance.

6 Book errors include mistakes made in recording cash transactions. For example, an error might involve recording a cheque in the accounting records for a different amount than what the cheque was written for. Another mistake might be failing to record a deposit that was made. The book balance is adjusted for the amount of the error, adding or subtracting as necessary depending on the nature of the error.

ACCOUNTING IN YOUR WORLD

I don't need a cheque register; I use online banking.

Jean-Paul got a job his senior year in high school and opened a bank account to keep the money he earns. Jean-Paul deposits his paycheques into the account and then uses a debit card to make purchases. Jean-Paul's dad encouraged him to keep track of his finances using a cheque register and to reconcile his account balance each month when his bank statement arrived. Instead, Jean-Paul decided to just check his account activity every few days online to see that the deductions from his account agree with what he remembers purchasing. A few days after going out for pizza with a couple of friends, Jean-Paul was looking at his account activity online. Jean-Paul happened to have his receipt from the pizza parlor in his wallet, which was unusual as he normally throws them away, and decided to check it against his account activity. The receipt from the pizza parlor showed that the cost of the pizza was $18.53 and that Jean-Paul had added a $2 tip bringing the total amount to $20.53. However, the amount deducted from Jean-Paul's account was $22.53. It appears that the amount of the tip was, accidentally or purposefully, added into the total amount charged twice. Jean-Paul feels lucky that he caught this mistake but wonders how many mistakes like this have occurred in the past that he didn't catch. Now Jean-Paul understands why it is important to maintain a cheque register and to reconcile the account activity each month when he gets his bank statement.

Bank Reconciliation Illustrated

The January bank statement of Acrofab, Inc. is presented in **Exhibit 4-8**. The summary at the top shows the beginning balance, total deposits, total withdrawals, service

INWNB
INLAND NORTHWEST NATIONAL BANK.

Acrofab, Inc.
161 Bay St
Toronto, Ontario M5J 2S4

CHEQUING ACCOUNT 136-213733

CHEQUING ACCOUNT SUMMARY AS OF 1/31/2013

BEGINNING BALANCE	TOTAL DEPOSITS	TOTAL WITHDRAWALS	SERVICE CHARGES	ENDING BALANCE
6,500	4,362	4,972	15	5,875

DEPOSITS	DATE	AMOUNT
Deposits	4-Jan	1,000
Deposits	4-Jan	112
Deposits	8-Jan	200
EFT-Rent	17-Jan	905
Bank collection	26-Jan	2,115
Interest	31-Jan	30

CHARGES	DATE	AMOUNT
Service charges	31-Jan	15

CHEQUES		DAILY BALANCE				
Number	Amount	Date	Balance		Date	Balance
956	100	31-Dec	6,500		20-Jan	4,845
732	3,000	4-Jan	7,560		26-Jan	6,960
733	160	6-Jan	7,360		31-Jan	5,875
734	100	8-Jan	7,560			
735	100	10-Jan	7,460			
736	1,100	17-Jan	5,205			

OTHER CHARGES	DATE	AMOUNT
NSF	4-Jan	52
EFT-Insurance	20-Jan	360

MONTHLY SUMMARY

Withdrawals: 8	Minimum Balance: 4,845	Average Balance: 6,085

Exhibit 4-8 ▲

charges, and the resulting ending balance. Details of the transactions for the month appear on the statement following this summary. The statement shows that the January 31 bank balance of Acrofab, Inc. is $5,875.

Acrofab's Cash account has a balance of $3,147, as shown in **Exhibit 4-9**. Notice that the cash payments appear as one deduction, or credit, to the Cash account in the general ledger to make the process more efficient because businesses often write and record many cheques at once.

General Ledger:							
Cash						Account No. 1010	
		POST			BALANCE		
DATE	ITEM	REF.	DEBIT	CREDIT	DEBIT	CREDIT
2013						
Jan 1	Balance				6,500	
2		J. 30	1,112		7,612	
7		J. 30	200		7,812	
31		J. 32		6,265*	1,547	
31		J. 32	1,600		3,147	

Cash Payments: *Supporting Detail for Jan 31 Credit to Cash				
CHEQUE NO.	AMOUNT	CHEQUE NO.	AMOUNT	
732	$3,000	738	$ 320	
733	610	739	85	
734	100	740	205	
735	100	741	460	
736	1,100			
737	285	Total	$6,265	

Exhibit 4-9 ▲

The bank reconciliation in **Exhibit 4-10** on the next page identifies and explains the differences between the balance according to the bank statement and the balance according to Acrofab's records, thus determining the correct Cash balance at the end of January. Exhibit 4-10, Panel A, lists the reconciling items, and Panel B shows the completed reconciliation.

PANEL A—Reconciling Items

a. Deposit in transit: $1,600
b. Bank error: The bank mistakenly deducted $100 for a cheque written by another company. Add $100 to bank balance because this balance will be $100 higher once the bank fixes its error.
c. Outstanding cheques:

Cheque No.	Amount
737	$285
738	320
739	85
740	205
741	460

d. EFT receipt of rent revenue: $905
e. Bank collection of a note receivable: $2,115, which includes interest revenue of $115
f. Interest revenue earned on bank balance: $30
g. Book error: Cheque no. 733 for $160 paid to Brown Company on account was recorded as $610; add $450 to the book balance.
h. Bank service charge: $15
i. NSF cheque from L. Ross: $52
j. EFT payment of insurance expense: $360

PANEL B—Completed Reconciliation

Acrofab, Inc.
Bank Reconciliation
January 31, 2013

BANK		BOOKS	
Bal, Jan 31	$5,875	Bal, Jan 31	$3,147
Add:		Add:	
a. Deposit of January 31 in transit	1,600	d. EFT receipt of rent revenue	905
b. Correction of bank error	100	e. Bank collection of note receivable,	
	7,575	$2,000 plus interest revenue of $115	2,115
		f. Interest revenue earned on bank balance	30
Less:		g. Correction of book error—overstated	
c. Outstanding cheques		our cheque no. 733 ($610 – $160)	450
No. 737	(285)		6,647
No. 738	(320)	Less:	
No. 739	(85)	h. Service charge	(15)
No. 740	(205)	i. NSF cheque	(52)
No. 741	(460)	j. EFT payment of insurance expense	(360)
Adjusted bank balance	$6,220	Adjusted book balance	$6,220

These amounts must agree, or the reconciliation is not complete.

Here is a summary of how to treat the reconciling items encountered most often:

Bank Balance—Always:

- *Add* deposits in transit.
- *Subtract* outstanding cheques.
- *Add* or *subtract* corrections of bank errors.

Book Balance—Always:

- *Add* bank collections, interest revenue, and EFT receipts.
- *Subtract* NSF cheques, the cost of printed cheques, service charges, and EFT payments.
- *Add* or *subtract* corrections of book errors.

Exhibit 4-10▲

Journalizing Transactions from the Reconciliation

Once the bank reconciliation has been prepared, the true balance of cash is known. However, the Cash account in the general ledger still reflects the original book balance if we do not update the book records. Therefore, journal entries must be made and posted to the general ledger so that it reflects the updated cash balance. *All items on the book side of the bank reconciliation require journal entries; whereas, none of the items on the bank side require journal entries since those are all things that the company has already recorded*.

The journal entries listed here bring the Cash account up to date as a result of completing the reconciliation. The letters of the entries correspond to the letters of the reconciling items listed in Exhibit 4-10, Panel A. Entry (i), the entry for the NSF cheque, needs explanation. When L. Ross's cheque was first deposited, Inland Northwest National Bank added $52 to Acrofab's account. When L. Ross's cheque was returned to Inland Northwest National Bank due to insufficient funds, the bank deducted $52 from Acrofab's account. Because the funds are still receivable from Ross, Accounts Receivable—L. Ross is debited to reestablish the amount due from Ross.

DATE	ACCOUNTS	POST REF.	DR.	CR.
d.	Cash		905	
	Rent Revenue			905
	Record receipt of monthly rent.			
e.	Cash		2,115	
	Notes Receivable			2,000
	Interest Revenue			115
	Record note receivable and interest collected by bank.			
f.	Cash		30	
	Interest Revenue			30
	Record interest earned on bank balance.			
g.	Cash		450	
	Accounts Payable—Brown, Co.			450
	Correct recording of cheque no. 733			
h.	Bank Charges Expense		15	
	Cash			15
	Record bank service charge.			
i.	Accounts Receivable—L. Ross		52	
	Cash			52
	Record NSF cheque returned by bank.			
j.	Insurance Expense		360	
	Cash			360
	Record payment of monthly insurance premium.			

Online Banking

Online banking allows businesses to pay bills and view account activity electronically. The company doesn't have to wait until the end of the month to get a bank statement. The account history is like a bank statement since it lists all transactions including deposits, cheques, EFT receipts and payments, ATM withdrawals, and interest earned on the bank balance. Because of this, it can be used instead of a bank statement to reconcile the bank account at any time.

DECISION GUIDELINES

Decision

As a manager of a business, I would like to complete some renovations for my retail space. I do not want a loan for this, so I am limited by the amount of cash I have available. But the amount of cash on the bank statement is different from the cash in my general ledger cash account. Which amount is the amount that I can spend?

Guideline

Neither. The correct cash balance can only be obtained by preparing a bank reconciliation.

Analyze

The bank reconciliation identifies differences that arise from the following:

- *Timing differences* resulting from items that have been recorded by the business but not yet by the bank or vice-versa
- *Errors* that have been made by the business or by the bank

Once the bank reconciliation has been completed, journal entries are made to adjust the business's cash account balance to the balance according to the bank reconciliation. This is the correct cash balance.

CRITICAL THINKING

Take a minute to think about the impact of the following cases on each of the assets, liabilities, and shareholders' equity accounts, if the adjusting entries were not recorded in the books. Please indicate understatements "U", overstatements "O", or no effect "NE," identify their amounts, and record the correct entries that should have been made.

1. A cheque for $450 issued to pay for utilities expense was mistakenly recorded in the books as $540.
2. A cheque for $380 deposited in the bank was shown as $330 on the bank statement.
3. An NSF cheque for $260 paid by a customer was returned with the bank statement.
4. An EFT receipt for $150 from a credit customer was not recorded in the book.

Solutions:

		Impact on Accounts		
	Assets	Liabilities	Shareholders' Equity	Correct Entry
1	U $90	No	U $90	Cash (Dr) . . . . 90 Utilities Expense (Cr) 90
2	NE	NE	NE	No Entry
3	NE	NE	NE	Accounts Receivable (Dr) . . . . 260 Cash (Cr) 260
4	NE	NE	NE	Cash (Dr) . . . . 150 Accounts Receivable (Cr) 150

HOW IS CASH REPORTED ON THE BALANCE SHEET?

Remember from our discussion of the balance sheet in Chapter 2 that Cash is the first asset listed because it's the most liquid. Businesses often have several bank accounts but they customarily combine all cash amounts into a single total. On the balance sheet, this total may be called Cash, or it may be called **Cash and Cash Equivalents**.

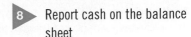 Report cash on the balance sheet

Cash on the balance sheet includes coin, currency, cheques on hand, **petty cash** (discussed in Appendix 4A), chequing accounts, money orders, and traveller's cheques. In short, cash consists of anything that a bank will take as a deposit.

Cash equivalents include very liquid, very safe short-term investments. They include time deposits, money market funds, certificates of deposit, and Treasury bills and Treasury notes. Although Treasury bills and Treasury notes and other cash equivalents can have maturity dates, they are considered cash equivalents if they mature within 90 days of the balance sheet date. These items are liquid because they can readily be converted into cash, and are safe because they have little risk of losing their value. Cash equivalents so closely resemble cash that they are included with cash on the balance sheet.

FOCUS ON USERS

Concept	User	Why Is this Important to this User?
Ethical behaviour		A bookkeeper will need to have a strong sense of the code of ethics for an organization and how to report unethical behaviour. The bookkeeper may be the first person to notice irregularities since the bookkeeper is typically quite knowledgeable about the accounts of the organization.
		Shareholders are the people with the ability to set the ethical standard for the company and to ensure that the top executives fulfill their roles in managing the organization while adhering to the ethical code.
Audit Opinions		All users should pay close attention to the audit opinions in the annual report. The audit opinion will identify any concerns regarding the creation and reporting of the financial statements. There are no guarantees that there are no errors or misstatements because the auditors cannot possibly check every transaction, but there is reasonable assurance that the financial statements represent the actual actions of the organization. It is important to remember that ultimately it is management's responsibility to ensure that the financial statements are accurate and fairly represent the accounts of the organization.

ACCOUNTING VOCABULARY
THE LANGUAGE OF BUSINESS

Audit (p. 228) An examination of a company's financial statements performed to determine their fairness.

Audit trail (p. 225) A trail of business documents and records that provides evidence of transactions.

Bank balance (p. 233) The balance in the company's bank account according to the bank.

Bank collection (p. 234) Collection of money by the bank on behalf of a depositor.

Bank reconciliation (p. 233) A document that identifies and explains the differences between a depositor's record of a cash account and a bank's record of the same cash account.

Bank statement (p. 233) A document the bank prepares to report the changes in the depositor's cash account for a period of time. It shows the beginning bank account balance, lists the month's cash transactions, and shows the ending bank account balance.

Book balance (p. 233) The balance in a company's bank account according to the company's accounting records, or books.

Bribe (p. 220) The payment of money to influence the conduct of a person.

Cash (p. 241) Coin, currency, cheques, petty cash, chequing accounts, payroll accounts, money orders, traveller's cheques, and anything the bank will accept as a deposit.

Cash and cash equivalents (p. 241) The balance sheet item used to describe cash and items so closely resembling cash that they are presented as cash.

Cash equivalents (p. 241) Highly liquid, highly safe investments that so closely resemble cash that they may be shown with cash on the balance sheet.

Cash register scheme (p. 219) A fraud scheme in which an employee steals cash by processing false refunds.

Cheque tampering (p. 219) A fraud scheme in which an employee writes a fraudulent cheque and makes the cheque payable to him- or herself, or obtains a cheque intended for an outside party, endorses the cheque, and then cashes it.

Code of ethics (p. 218) A formal written document that contains broad statements intended to guide proper ethical decision making.

Collusion (p. 226) Two or more individuals working together to commit fraud.

Control activities (p. 224) The policies and procedures implemented in an internal control system.

Control environment (p. 223) The overall attitude, awareness, and actions of management and staff regarding the internal control system and its importance to the business.

Controller (p. 232) The individual in an organization responsible for the accounting system and financial statements.

Deposits in transit (p. 234) Deposits that have been recorded by a company but not yet by its bank.

Disbursement scheme (p. 219) A form of employee embezzlement in which an employee tricks a company into giving up cash for an invalid reason. Examples include cheque tampering, cash register schemes, and expense schemes.

Electronic data interchange (EDI) (p. 233) Direct electronic communication between suppliers and retailers.

Electronic funds transfer (EFT) (p. 233) System that transfers cash by electronic communication rather than by paper documents.

Employee embezzlement (p. 219) Fraud where employees steal from employers by taking assets, bribes, or kickbacks, or engaging in disbursement schemes to steal cash.

Expense scheme (p. 220) A fraud scheme in which an employee overcharges the company for travel and other business-related expenses, such as lunches, hotels, air travel, parking fees, and cab fares.

External audit (p. 228) An audit of financial statements performed by public accountants.

Fraud (p. 216) Deceit or trickery involving intentional actions that cause harm to a business, its stakeholders, or both.

Fraud triangle (p. 221) The combination of perceived pressure, rationalization, and perceived opportunity necessary to commit fraud.

Internal audit (p. 228) Assessment of a company's compliance with laws and regulations, operations, and policies and procedures performed by employees of the company.

Internal control (p. 222) A system implemented within an organization to safeguard assets, operate efficiently and effectively, report financial information properly, and comply with applicable laws and regulations.

Kickback (p. 220) The return of part of a sum received because of a confidential agreement.

Lock-box system (p. 234) A system in which customers send payments to a post office box of a business. The bank collects payments from the box and deposits them into the business's account.

Management fraud (p. 219) Management's intentional misstatement of the financial statements, driven by greed or the pressure to show that a business is more profitable than it really is.

Nonsufficient funds (NSF) cheque (p. 235) A cheque drawn against a bank account that has insufficient money to pay the cheque.

Outstanding cheques (p. 234) Cheques that have been issued by a company and recorded in its books but have not yet been paid by its bank.

Perceived opportunity (p. 222) An element of the fraud triangle in which the employee believes a chance exists to commit fraud, conceal it, and avoid punishment.

Perceived pressure (p. 221) An element of the fraud triangle in which the employee feels a need to obtain cash or other assets.

Petty cash (p. 241) Fund containing a small amount of cash that is used to pay for minor expenditures.

Public Accountant (p. 228) A licensed accountant who serves the general public rather than one particular company.

Purchase order (p. 232) A document showing details of merchandise being ordered from a supplier.

Purchasing agent (p. 232) The individual in an organization responsible for buying items for that organization.

Rationalization (p. 221) An element of the fraud triangle in which the employee justifies his or her actions and convinces him- or herself that fraud is not wrong.

Receiving report (p. 232) A document evidencing the receipt of goods purchased.

Risk assessment (p. 224) The process of identifying risks and gauging the probability that they will occur.

Sarbanes-Oxley Act (p. 229) A law passed in 2002 by the U.S. Congress in response to large-scale fraud in publicly owned companies.

SOX (p. 229) Acronym for the Sarbanes-Oxley Act.

Treasurer (p. 232) The individual in an organization responsible for the custody of assets, such as cash.

Whistleblower (p. 218) A person who reports unethical behaviour.

ACCOUNTING PRACTICE

DISCUSSION QUESTIONS

1. Can ethics be taught in the college or university classroom? Why or why not?

2. Is there a distinction between personal and professional ethics? What are the implications for the study of ethics in the college or university classroom?

3. What is management fraud? What is employee fraud? Give some examples of each.

4. What are the three components of the fraud triangle? How can they be helpful in fighting fraud in an organization?

5. Do you think the risk factors for management fraud are the same as the risk factors for employee fraud? Why or why not?

6. What is the control environment? Discuss how the control environment had a strong influence over a situation with which you are personally familiar (e.g., a place where you work, your family, your living group in college or university, a classroom, etc.).

7. What part of the fraud triangle is most closely associated with the control activities component of internal control? That is, if control activities are improved, which corner of the fraud triangle is most affected? Why?

8. What are the implications of the fact that every internal control structure has inherent limitations? That is, how does the knowledge that no internal control structure is perfect help management run the organization more effectively?

9. What effect does the Sarbanes-Oxley Act have on the role and influence of the CEO in the corporation?

10. What duties should be segregated in the purchasing process? Why? That is, what could go wrong if two or more of those duties are not segregated?

11 After preparing a bank reconciliation, which reconciling items will require journal entries? Why?

MyAccountingLab

Make the grade with MyAccountingLab. The exercises and problems in this chapter can be found on MyAccountingLab at **www.myaccountinglab.com**. You can practise them as often as you want, and they feature step-by-step guided solutions to help you find the right answer.

SELF CHECK

1. On what element of the fraud triangle do most organizations usually focus their fraud prevention efforts?

   a. Perceived pressure
   b. Perceived opportunity
   c. Rationalization
   d. All three are targeted.

2. Internal control is

   a. the act of stealing a business's assets.
   b. the preparation of fraudulent financial statements.
   c. the process that helps a business achieve its objectives, such as operating efficiently and effectively.
   d. the reconciliation of the bank's cash balance to the book's cash balance.

3. Which of the following is *not* an element of an internal control system?

   a. Auditing
   b. The control environment
   c. Monitoring
   d. Information and communication

4. Separation of duties refers to separating all of these functions *except* which of the following?

   a. Authorizing transactions
   b. Keeping accounting records
   c. Hiring personnel
   d. Maintaining custody of assets

5. Darice Goodrich receives cash from customers as part of her job duties. Her other duty is to post the receipts to customer accounts receivable. Based on these duties, her company has weak

   a. ethics.
   b. fraud triangle.
   c. separation of duties.
   d. disbursement schemes.

6. The document that identifies and explains all differences between the company's record of cash and the bank's record of that cash is the

   a. bank reconciliation.
   b. bank collection.
   c. bank statement.
   d. electronic fund transfer.

7. Which item(s) appears as a reconciling item(s) to the book balance in a bank reconciliation?

   a. Outstanding cheques
   b. Deposits in transit
   c. Both a and b
   d. None of the above

8. Which item(s) appears as a reconciling item(s) to the bank balance in a bank reconciliation?

   a. Outstanding cheques
   b. Deposits in transit
   c. Both a and b
   d. None of the above

9. On its books, Nobu Company's Cash account shows an ending balance of $770. The bank statement for the current period shows a $20 service charge and an NSF cheque for $100. A $250 deposit is in transit, and outstanding cheques total $400. What is Nobu's adjusted book balance for Cash?

   a. $530   b. $650   c. $680   d. $1,050

10. After performing a bank reconciliation, journal entries are required for

a. all items on the bank side of the reconciliation.

b. all items on the book side of the reconciliation.

c. all items on the reconciliation.

d. no items from the reconciliation because the Cash account needs no adjustment.

SHORT EXERCISES

S4-1. Internal controls (*Learning Objective 2*) 5–10 min.

Indicate by letters the type of fraud committed:

Cheque tampering (CT)

Cash register scheme (CR)

Expense scheme (E)

Bribe (B)

Fraudulent financial reporting (F)

Here is an example:

<u>CT</u>   Employee writes a fraudulent cheque making it payable to herself.

_____ 1. At the end of the year, the chief financial officer for Electra International recorded $100,000 in sales that had not been made.

_____ 2. Carrie is a cashier at a local restaurant. Once a day, she leaves the cash register open and does not record the sale in the cash register when she takes the customer's cash.

_____ 3. Harry's major customer in Iowa asked Harry to take 20% off of the sales price on the next shipment of jeans to his stores. In return, the customer will give him part of the money saved from the reduced sales price. Harry agrees to lower the price.

_____ 4. Frank Farmer, owner of Farmer Real Estate, asked the accountant to ignore any depreciation that should be recorded on assets owned.

_____ 5. Judson submits a cash reimbursement request form for a cab ride he never took.

S4-2. Fraud triangle (*Learning Objective 3*) 5–10 min.

Identify each of the following as an example of a perceived pressure (P), perceived opportunity (O), or rationalization (R) in the fraud triangle:

_____ 1. Job dissatisfaction

_____ 2. Greed

_____ 3. "It's for a good purpose."

_____ 4. Weak internal control

_____ 5. Gambling addiction

S4-3. Internal controls (*Learning Objective 4*) 5–10 min.

Internal controls are designed to safeguard assets, encourage employees to follow company policies, promote operational efficiency, and ensure accurate records.

Which objective is most important? Which must the internal controls accomplish for the business to survive? Give your reason.

S4-4. Internal controls (*Learning Objective 5*) 5–10 min.

Indicate by letters which of the following control activities match with the following descriptions:

Separation of duties (SD)

Restricted access (RA)

Proper authorization (PA)

Adequate documents and records (ADR)

_____ 1. Prenumbered invoices

_____ 2. Locking inventory in a warehouse

_____ 3. Manager approval of sales returns

_____ 4. Password protection of accounting software

_____ 5. Not allowing the accounts payable clerk to sign cheques

S4-5. Internal controls (*Learning Objective 5*) 10–15 min.

Explain in your own words why separation of duties is often described as the cornerstone of internal control for safeguarding assets. Describe what can happen if the same person has custody of an asset and also accounts for the asset.

S4-6. Fraud triangle (*Learning Objective 3*) 5–10 min.

Look at each of the following employees of Agetro's Restaurant. Which of the elements of the fraud triangle apply?

Perceived pressure (P)

Perceived opportunity (O)

Rationalization (R)

_____ 1. As the bartender puts $100 in tips in his pocket, he thinks, "Nobody will get hurt."

_____ 2. Tina uses the stolen money to pay for her mother's high medical bills.

_____ 3. Hector knows he will be fired if he doesn't record some fictitious sales.

_____ 4. Roxanne, the night shift manager, knows that upper management does not monitor internal control.

_____ 5. Leo, a waiter, drove to work in a BMW and bragged about his recent vacation to the French Riviera.

_____ 6. Victoria, a cashier for the past five years, was caught stealing cash. When questioned about the theft, she said that she had not received a promotion and deserved more pay.

S4-7. Internal controls (*Learning Objectives 4 & 5*) 5–10 min.

Identify each of the following as an internal control objective (O), an internal control activity (A), or a limitation of internal control (L).

_____ 1. Separation of duties

_____ 2. Collusion

_____ 3. Proper authorization

_____ 4. Reports financial information properly

_____ 5. Mandatory vacations

_____ 6. Management override

_____ 7. Complies with laws and regulations

_____ 8. Adequate documents and records

_____ 9. Poor design

_____10. Operates efficiently and effectively

S4-8. Internal controls (*Learning Objective* 5) 5–10 min.

Hazel's Video Store maintains the following policies/procedures with regard to internal control. Indicate by letter which of the following control activities applies to each of the following policies/procedures:

_____ 1. Every day, all cheques written are recorded in the accounting records, using the information on the cheque stubs.

_____ 2. All stores utilize electronic theft detection systems.

_____ 3. Purchases of new DVDs must be approved by the store manager.

_____ 4. Daily sales are recorded in the accounting records by someone other than the sales associates.

_____ 5. The company maintains passwords that limit access to its computerized accounting records.

a. Proper authorization

b. Adequate documents and records

c. Restricted access

d. Security measures

e. Separation of duties

S4-9. Internal controls (*Learning Objective* 5) 5–10 min.

The following situations suggest a strength or a weakness in internal control. Identify each as a strength or weakness, and give the reason for your answer.

a. All employees must take at least five consecutive days off each year.

b. The accounting department orders merchandise and approves invoices for payment.

c. Cash received over the counter is controlled by the sales clerk, who rings up the sale and places the cash in the register. The daily sales are recorded in the accounting records by the accounting department.

d. The officer who signs the cheques need not examine the payment packet because he is confident the amounts are correct.

S4-10. Internal controls (*Learning Objective* 5) 5–10 min.

Identify the missing internal control in the following situations. Select from these activities:

- Proper authorization
- Separation of duties
- Adequate documents and records

a. While reviewing the records of Discount Pharmacy, you find that the same employee orders merchandise and approves invoices for payment.

b. Business is slow at Fun City Amusement Park on Tuesday, Wednesday, and Thursday nights. To reduce expenses, the owner decides not to use a ticket taker on those nights. The ticket seller is told to keep the tickets as a record of the number sold.

c. When business is brisk, Stop-n-Go does not give customers a written receipt unless they ask for it.

d. Jim has worked for Peter's hardware for over 10 years. Due to his length of employment, he has been allowed to grant sales returns at his discretion.

e. At a grocery store, the manager decides to reduce paperwork. She eliminates the requirement that the receiving department prepare a receiving report.

S4-11. Fraud and internal controls (*Learning Objectives 2, 4, & 5*) 15-20 min.

Each of the following situations has an internal control weakness.

a. Betty Grable has been your trusted employee for 30 years. She performs all cash-handling and accounting duties. Betty Grable just purchased a new Lexus and a new home in an expensive suburb. As owner of the company you wonder how she can afford these luxuries because you pay her only $35,000 a year and she has no sources of outside income.

b. Sanchez Hardwoods, a private company, falsified sales and inventory figures to get an important loan. The loan went through, but Sanchez Hardwoods later went bankrupt and couldn't repay the bank.

c. The office supply company where Champ's Sporting Goods purchases its business forms recently notified Champ's Sporting Goods that its documents were no longer going to be prenumbered. Alex Champ, the owner, replied that he never uses the receipt numbers anyway.

d. Discount stores such as Giant Tiger make most of their sales in cash, with the remainder in credit card sales. To reduce expenses, one store manager allows the cashiers to record sales in the accounting records.

Identify the missing internal control in each situation. Answers should include audit, documentation, and separation of duties. Identify the possible problem caused by each control weakness. Answers should include theft and unreliable financial statements. Propose a solution to each internal control problem.

S4-12. Sarbanes-Oxley Act (*Learning Objective 6*) 20–25 min.

What are the main provisions of the Sarbanes-Oxley Act? Be specific.

S4-13. Bank reconciliation adjustments (*Learning Objective 7*) 5–10 min.

For each of the following, indicate whether the item is an adjustment to the bank balance or the book balance:

_____ 1. Bank service charge

_____ 2. Deposit in transit

_____ 3. Bank collection of amount due from customer

_____ 4. Interest revenue on bank balance

_____ 5. Outstanding cheque

S4-14. Bank reconciliation adjustments (*Learning Objective 7*) 10–15 min.

Classify each of the following items as one of the following:

Addition to the book balance (+ Book)

Subtraction from the book balance (– Book)

Addition to the bank balance (+ Bank)

Subtraction from the bank balance (– Bank)

_____ 1. Outstanding cheques

_____ 2. Deposits in transit

_____ 3. NSF cheque

_____ 4. Bank collection of our note receivable

_____ 5. Interest earned on bank balance

_____ 6. Bank service charge

_____ 7. Book error: We credited Cash for $200. The correct amount of the cheque was $2,000.

_____ 8. Bank error: The bank decreased our account for a cheque written by another customer.

S4-15. Prepare a bank reconciliation (*Learning Objective 7*) 5–10 min.

The T-account for cash and the bank statement of Mee Auto Services for the month of March 2013 follows:

Cash			
Mar 1	3,200	Cheque #704	540
Mar 10 deposit	750	Cheque #705	210
Mar 31 deposit	200	Cheque #706	900
Pre-adjusted Bal @ Mar 31	2,500		

Bank Statement:

Bal, Mar 1			$3,200
Deposits:			
Deposits		$750	
Bank collection		710	
Interest		10	1,470
Cheques:	No.	Amount	
	704	540	
	705	210	(750)
Other Charges:			
Service charge		$ 20	(20)
Bal, Mar 31			$3,900

Prepare Mee Auto Services' bank reconciliation at March 31.

S4-16. Prepare bank reconciliation journal entries (*Learning Objective 7*) 5–10 min.

Make the necessary journal entries arising from Dee Zee Motor's bank reconciliation presented next. Date each entry March 31 and include an explanation with each entry.

Dee Zee Motors Bank Reconciliation March			
BANK		**BOOKS**	
Bal, Mar 31	$ 500	Bal, Mar 31	$ 740
Add:		Add:	
Deposit in transit	300	Interest revenue	10
	800		750
		Less:	
Less:		Service charge	(20)
Outstanding cheques	(250)	NSF cheques	(180)
Adjusted bank balance	$ 550	Adjusted book balance	$ 550

S4-17. Balance sheet presentation of cash (*Learning Objective 8*) 5–10 min.

Prepare the current assets section of the balance sheet as of December 31, 2013, for Lipton, Inc. using the following information:

Accounts Receivable	$63,000
Petty Cash	500
Cash in Bank Accounts	22,000
Inventory	55,500

S4-18. Bank reconciliation adjustments (*Learning Objective 7*) 10–15 min.

Assess each of the following items and indicate the proper treatment of each case as one of the following:

Addition to the book balance (+ Book)

Subtraction from the book balance (– Book)

Addition to the bank balance (+ Bank)

Subtraction from the bank balance (– Bank)

_____ 1. A cheque for $680 received from a customer was recorded as $860 in the books.

_____ 2. A deposit for $580 was shown in the bank statement as $530.

_____ 3. A cheque for $1,250 issued to pay a supplier was not cleared from the bank.

_____ 4. An NSF cheque for $720 was returned with the bank statement

_____ 5. An EFT receipt for $50 from a purchase rebate.

EXERCISES (GROUP A)

E4-1A. Bank reconciliation adjustments (*Learning Objective 7*) 10–15 min.

Calculate the answers for the missing data:

BANK		BOOKS	
Bal, Jan 31	$1,000	Bal, Jan 31	(c)
Add:		Add:	
Deposit in transit	600	Bank collection	425
	(a)	Interest revenue	15
			(d)
Less:		Less:	
Outstanding cheques	(b)	Service charge	(30)
Adjusted bank balance	$1,200	Adjusted book balance	$1,200

E4-2A. Prepare a bank reconciliation and journal entries (*Learning Objective 7*) 20–25 min.

Dirk Cole's chequebook lists the following:

Date	Cheque No.	Item	Amount	Deposit	Balance
9/ 1					$1,425
5	922	Mesilla Kitchen	$ 22		1,403
10		Dividends received		$ 115	1,518
14	923	Best Products	25		1,493
15	924	Fina (payment on account)	60		1,433
19	925	Cash	200		1,233
27	926	Staples	175		1,058
29	927	Hobart Properties	1,000		58
30		Paycheque		4,095	4,153

Dirk Cole's September bank statement shows the following:

Bal, Sep 1			$1,425
Deposits:			115
Cheques:	No.	Amount	
	922	$ 22	
	923	25	
	924	70*	
	925	200	(317)
Other Charges:			
Printed cheques		$20	
Service charge		15	(35)
Bal, Sep 30			$1,188

*This amount is correct for cheque no. 924.

Requirements

1. Prepare Dirk Cole's bank reconciliation on September 30. How much cash does Dirk Cole actually have on September 30?

2. Prepare all necessary journal entries for Dirk Cole to update the Cash account as a result of the bank reconciliation.

E4-3A. Prepare a bank reconciliation (*Learning Objective 7*) 20–25 min.

Information from Goddard Picture Frames' Cash account as well as the January bank statement is presented next.

Cash			
Jan 1	1,400	Cheque #210	30
Jan 30	2,700	Cheque #211	400
		Cheque #212	110
		Cheque #213	325
		Cheque #214	200
Pre-adjusted			
Bal @ Jan 31	3,035		

Bank Statement:			
Bal, Jan 1			$1,400
Deposits:			
EFT—rent			500
Cheques:	No.	Amount	
	210	300	
	211	400	
	212	110	(810)
Other Charges:			
Service charge		$ 15	
Cheque printing		10	
NSF cheque #201		65	(90)
Bal, Jan 31			$1,000

Quick solution: *1. Adjusted cash balance = $3,175*

Cheque #210 was written for $300 to pay salaries.

Requirements

1. Prepare the bank reconciliation on January 31.

2. Prepare all necessary journal entries for Goddard Picture Frames to update the Cash account as a result of the bank reconciliation.

E4-4A. Bank reconciliation adjustments (*Learning Objective 7*) 15–20 min.

MiThai's new accounting clerk could not get the bank reconciliation balanced. She needs your help and has provided you with her bank reconciliation and all the information she used to prepare the bank reconciliation:

Bank	7,610	Book	8,620
Deposit	2,100	Cheque No. 125 (outstanding)	1,680
EFT – Collection	1,200		
Subtotal	10,910	Subtotal	10,300
Subtract		Subtract	
Interest charges	24	NSF cheque	1,735
Bank service charges	16	NSF fee	15
Total	40	Total	1,750
Reconciled bank balance	10,870	Reconciled book balance	8,550

Additional Information:

1. The July 31st bank statement showed a cash balance of $7,610, EFT collection of $1,200, interest charges of $24, bank service charges of $16, NSF cheque of $1,735, and NSF fee of $15.

2. The book ledger showed a cash balance of $8,620. In addition, the book records showed that both cheque #125 for the amount of $1,680 and a deposit of $2,100 were not included in the bank statement.

Requirement

1. Prepare MiThai's bank reconciliation on July 31. What is the reconciled book balance?

E4-5A. Bank reconciliation adjustments (*Learning Objective 7*) 20–25 min.

The following information is for Jae Kim, Ltd. in June:

1. Cash balance on June 30 in the ledger was $12,450, and cash balance on June 30's bank statement was $14,860.

2. Deposit in transit for the amount of $1,500 from May 31 was recorded in the bank statement on June 1. Deposit in transit for the amount of $1,800 from June 30 was not recorded in the June bank statement.

3. Cheque 103 for the amount of $1,720 was outstanding on May 31 and was still outstanding on June 30.

4. Cheque 125 for the amount of $680 was outstanding on June 30.

5. EFT collection of $1,200 from a tenant for his rent payment was shown on June 2 in the bank statement.

6. NSF cheque for the amount of $760 and an NSF fee of $20 were included in the bank statement.

7. Interest and bank service charges for June were $15 and $35 respectively.

8. A cheque for cash sales for the amount of $1,600 was mistakenly recorded as $160 in the books.

Requirements

1. Prepare Jae Kim's bank reconciliation on June 30. What is the reconciled book balance?

2. Record the entries to update the Cash account balance. Include an explanation for each entry.

3. If the entries were not recorded in (2), what is the impact on each of the assets, liabilities, and shareholders' equity accounts?

EXERCISES (GROUP B)

E4-1B. Bank reconciliation adjustments (*Learning Objective 7*) 10–15 min.

Calculate the answers for the missing data:

BANK		BOOKS	
Bal, Mar 31	$ 990	Bal, Mar 31	(c)
Add:		Add:	
Deposit in transit	680	Bank collection	420
	(a)	Interest revenue	100
			(d)
Less:		Less:	
Outstanding cheques	(b)	Service charge	(40)
Adjusted bank balance	$1,240	Adjusted book balance	$1,240

E4-2B. Prepare a bank reconciliation and journal entries (*Learning Objective 7*) 20–25 min.

Dan Cryer's chequebook lists the following:

Date	Cheque No.	Item	Amount	Deposit	Balance
10/ 1					$1,435
5	922	Rivertown Kitchen	$ 40		1,395
10		Dividends received		$ 125	1,520
14	923	Everyday Products	37		1,483
15	924	Fauna (payment on account)	63		1,420
19	925	Cash	200		1,220
27	926	Office Supply	117		1,103
28	927	North East Properties	984		119
31		Paycheque		5,285	5,404

Dan Cryer's October bank statement shows the following:

Bal, Oct 1				$1,435
Deposits:				125
Cheques:	No.	Amount		
	922	$ 40		
	923	37		
	924	163*		
	925	200		(440)
Other Charges:				
Printed cheques			$25	
Service charge			10	(35)
Bal, Oct 31				$1,085

*This amount is correct for cheque no. 924.

Requirements

1. Prepare Dan Cryer's bank reconciliation on October 31. How much cash does Dan Cryer actually have on October 31?

2. Prepare all necessary journal entries for Dan Cryer to update the Cash account as a result of the bank reconciliation.

E4-3B. Prepare a bank reconciliation (*Learning Objective 7*) 20–25 min.

Information from Sheppard Picture Frames' cash account as well as the November bank statement is presented next.

Cash				
Nov 1	2,100	Cheque #210	60	
Nov 30	2,000	Cheque #211	400	
		Cheque #212	137	
		Cheque #213	310	
		Cheque #214	180	
Pre-adjusted				
Bal @ Nov 30	3,013			

Bank Statement:				
Bal, Nov 1				$ 2,100
Deposits:				
EFT—rent				750
Cheques:	No.	Amount		
	210	600		
	211	400		
	212	137		(1,137)
Other Charges:				
Service charge			$ 30	
Cheque printing			16	
NSF cheque #201			80	(126)
Bal, Nov 30				$ 1,587

Cheque #210 was written for $600 to pay salaries.

Requirements

1. Prepare the bank reconciliation on November 30.

2. Prepare all necessary journal entries for Sheppard Picture Frames to update the Cash account as a result of the bank reconciliation.

E4-4B. Bank reconciliation adjustments (*Learning Objective 7*) 15–20 min.

Patel Ltd.'s new accounting clerk could not get the bank reconciliation balanced. He needs your help and provided you with his bank reconciliation and all the information he used to prepare the bank reconciliation:

Bank	6,750	Book	7,520
Deposit	1,650	Cheque No. 578 (outstanding)	1,320
EFT – Collection	1,040		
Subtotal	9,440	Subtotal	8,840
Subtract		Subtract	
NSF cheque	1,400	Interest charges	25
NSF fee	20	Bank service charges	35
Total	1,420	Total	60
Reconciled bank balance	8,020	Reconciled book balance	8,780

Additional Information:

1. The May 31 bank statement showed a cash balance of $6,750, EFT collection of $1,040, interest charges of $25, bank service charges of $35, an NSF cheque of $1,400, and an NSF fee of $20.

2. The book ledger showed a cash balance of $7,520. In addition, the book records showed that both cheque no. 578 for the amount of $1,320 and a deposit of $1,650 were not included in the bank statement.

Requirement

1. Prepare Patel Ltd.'s bank reconciliation on May 31. What is the reconciled book balance?

E4-5B. Bank reconciliation adjustments (*Learning Objective 7*) 20–25 min.

The following information is for Yamada, Ltd. in April:

1. Cash balance on April 30 in the ledger was $8,645, and cash balance on April 30's bank statement was $10,750.

2. Deposit in transit for the amount of $1,180 from February 28 was recorded in the bank statement on March 1. Deposit in transit for the amount of $720 from April 30 was not recorded in the April bank statement.

3. Cheque 683 for the amount of $1,400 was outstanding on March 31 and was still outstanding on April 30.

4. Cheque 705 for the amount of $1,020 was outstanding on April 30.

5. EFT collection of $620 from a tenant for his rent payment was shown on April 2 in the bank statement.

6. A cheque for cash sales for the amount of $630 was mistakenly recorded as $360 in the book.

7. An NSF cheque for the amount of $425 together with an NSF fee of $15 were included in the bank statement.

8. Interest and bank service charges for April were $30 and $15 respectively.

Requirements

1. Prepare Yamada's bank reconciliation on April 30. What is the reconciled book balance?

2. Record the entries to update the Cash account balance. Include an explanation for each entry.

3. If the entries were not recorded in (2), what is the impact on each of the assets, liabilities, and shareholders' equity accounts?

EXERCISES (ALTERNATES 1, 2, AND 3)

These alternative exercise sets are available for your practice benefit at
www.myaccountinglab.com

PROBLEMS (GROUP A)

P4-1A. Prepare a bank reconciliation (*Learning Objective 7*) 20–25 min.

The May cash records of Nielson, Inc. follow:

Cash Receipts (CR)		Cash Payments (CP)	
Date	Cash Debit	Cheque No.	Cash Credit
May 4	$2,716	1416	$ 8
9	544	1417	775
14	896	1418	88
17	367	1419	126
31	2,037	1420	970
		1421	200
		1422	2,267

Nielson's Cash account shows the balance of $6,171 on May 31. On May 31, Nielson, Inc. received the following bank statement:

Bank Statement for May		
Beginning Balance		$ 4,045
Deposits and other additions		
May 1	$ 625 EFT	
5	2,716	
10	544	
15	896	
18	367	
31	1,000 BC	6,148
Cheques and other deductions		
May 8	$ 441 NSF	
15 (Cheque #1416)	8	
19	340 EFT	
22 (Cheque #1417)	775	
29 (Cheque #1418)	88	
31 (Cheque #1419)	216	
31	25 SC	(1,893)
Ending Balance		$ 8,300

Explanations: BC—bank collection; EFT—electronic funds transfer; NSF—nonsufficient funds cheque; SC—service charge.

Additional data for the bank reconciliation:

a. The EFT deposit was a receipt of rent revenue. The EFT debit was payment of insurance expense.

b. The NSF cheque was received from a customer.

c. The $1,000 bank collection was for a note receivable.

d. The correct amount of cheque 1419 is $216. Nielson, Inc. mistakenly recorded the cheque for $126.

Requirement

1. Prepare Nielson's bank reconciliation at May 31.

P4-2A. Prepare a bank reconciliation (*Learning Objective 7*) 20–25 min.

The October bank statement of Blake's Hamburger just arrived from First National Bank.

October Bank Statement:				
Bal, Oct 1				$12,769
Deposits:				
EFT—rent			$900	
EFT—deposit			200	
Interest			16	1,116
Cheques:	No.	Amount		
	807	600		
	808	400		
	1668	410		(1,410)
Other Charges:				
Service charge			$ 7	
NSF cheque #998			67	
NSF cheque #201			192	(266)
Bal, Oct 31				$12,209

To prepare the bank reconciliation, you gather the following additional data:

a. The following cheques are outstanding at October 31:

Cheque No.	Amount
800	$402
802	74
806	36
809	161
810	229
811	48

b. On October 31, Blake's Hamburger's treasurer deposited $381, but this deposit does not appear on the bank statement.

c. The bank statement includes a $410 deduction for cheque #1668 written by Danson Freight rather than Blake's Hamburger. Blake's Hamburger notified the bank of this bank error.

d. Blake's Hamburger's Cash account shows a balance of $11,200 on October 31.

Requirements

1. Prepare the bank reconciliation for October 31.

2. Record the entries called for by the reconciliation. Include an explanation for each entry.

P4-3A. Prepare a bank reconciliation (*Learning Objective 7*) 25–30 min.

The following is Oishi Sushi's bank statement:

Date	Description	Debit	Credit	Balance
May 31				12,650
Jun 1	Deposit		4,250	16,900
3	Cheque #144	780		16,120
4	Cheque #162	2,705		13,415
7	Deposit		3,480	16,895
10	Cheque #183	625		16,270
12	Cheque #184	1,680		14,590
15	EFT - Salaries	3,600		10,990
16	Deposit		1,720	12,710
16	Cheque #185	840		11,870
18	Cheque #188	550		11,320
20	NSF Cheque - Fundy Bay FishMart	620		10,700
20	NSF Fee	15		10,685
24	EFT - Collection Dalhousie Inc.		1,425	12,110
27	Cheque #190	630		11,480
30	Deposit		2,430	13,910
30	EFT - Salaries	3,600		10,310
30	Bank Service Charges	35		10,275
30	Interest Charges	25		10,250

Oishi Sushi's ledger shows the following transactions in the Cash account in June:

Date	Description	Debit	Credit	Balance
May 31				12,650
Jun 1	Deposit	3,480		16,130
Jun 8	Cheque #183		625	15,505
Jun 9	Cheque #184		1,680	13,825
Jun 10	Cheque #185		840	12,985
Jun 12	Cheque #186		1,360	11,625
Jun 12	Cheque #187		950	10,675
Jun 16	Deposit	1,720		12,395
Jun 16	Cheque #188		550	11,845
Jun 20	Cheque #189		365	11,480
Jun 22	Cheque #190		680	10,800
Jun 28	Deposit	2,340		13,140
Jun 30	Deposit	4,520		17,660

Additional information:

1. Deposit of $4,250 on May 31st was deposited in the bank on June 1.
2. Cheque 178 for $140 and cheque 180 for $625 were issued in May, and they were not cashed in June.
3. Oishi Sushi made an error in recording cheque 190 and the June 28 deposit. Cheque 190 was for an advertisement and the deposit was a collection from ABC Corp.

Requirements

1. Prepare Oishi Sushi's bank reconciliation at June 30.
2. Record the entries to update the cash account balance. Include an explanation for each entry.

3. If the entries were not recorded in (2), what is the impact on each of the assets, liabilities, and shareholders' equity accounts?

P4-4A. Prepare a bank reconciliation (*Learning Objective 7*) 20–25 min.

Dion Ltd's ledger showed a cash balance of $12,134 on December 31. In preparing the bank reconciliation, the following information was determined:

a. EFT collection by bank from a credit customer was $5,620.

b. A deposit of $2,600 was correctly recorded in the books, but it showed as $26.00 on the bank statement.

c. Cheque 205 issued by Dion Ltd. in the amount of $550, for the payment of the bank loan $500 and 10% of interest, had been incorrectly recorded in the books as $55.

d. Cheque 221 issued by Dion Ltd. in the amount of $2,460, for the purchase of a computer, had been incorrectly paid by the bank as $246.

e. A cheque for $521 paid by a customer for his purchase was incorrectly recorded in the books as $125.

f. An NSF cheque for $2,850 was returned with the bank statement, with a bank charge of $15 for this transaction.

g. Cheque #201 issued by Dion Ltd. in the amount of $1,250 was not included in the bank statement.

h. The bank statement showed interest charges and bank service charges were $52 and $28 respectively.

Requirements

1. Prepare Dion's bank reconciliation at December 31.

2. What was the reconciled book balance? What was the bank statement balance before reconciliation?

3. Record the entries to update the Cash account balance. Include an explanation for each entry.

4. If the entries were not recorded in (3), what is the impact on each of the assets, liabilities, and shareholders' equity accounts?

PROBLEMS (GROUP B)

P4-1B. Prepare a bank reconciliation (*Learning Objective 7*) 20–25 min.

The November cash records of Stenback, Inc. follow:

Cash Receipts (CR)		Cash Payments (CP)	
Date	Cash Debit	Cheque No.	Cash Credit
Nov 4	$2,725	1416	$ 9
9	530	1417	750
14	880	1418	93
17	353	1419	124
31	2,040	1420	960
		1421	210
		1422	2,250

Stenback's Cash account shows the balance of $6,172 on November 30. On November 30, Stenback received the following bank statement:

Bank Statement for November		
Beginning Balance		$ 4,040
Deposits and other additions:		
Nov 1	$ 635 EFT	
5	2,725	
10	530	
15	880	
18	353	
31	1,800 BC	6,923
Cheques and other deductions:		
Nov 8	$ 452 NSF	
15 (Cheque no. 1416)	9	
19	350 EFT	
22 (Cheque no. 1417)	750	
29 (Cheque no. 1418)	93	
31 (Cheque no. 1419)	214	
31	45 SC	(1,913)
Ending Balance		$ 9,050

Explanations: BC—bank collection; EFT—electronic funds transfer; NSF—nonsufficient funds cheque; SC—service charge.

Additional data for the bank reconciliation:

a. The EFT deposit was a receipt of rent revenue. The EFT debit was payment of insurance expense.

b. The NSF cheque was received from a customer.

c. The $1,800 bank collection was for a note receivable.

d. The correct amount of cheque 1419 is $214. Stenback, Inc. mistakenly recorded the cheque for $124.

Requirement

1. Prepare Stenback's bank reconciliation on November 30.

P4-2B. Prepare a bank reconciliation (*Learning Objective 7*) 20–25 min.

The December 31, bank statement of Billy's Hamburger just arrived from Safety Bank.

Bank Statement for December			
Bal, Dec 1			$13,384
Deposits:			
EFT—rent		$700	
EFT—deposit		400	
Interest		12	1,112
Cheques:	No.	Amount	
	807	$600	
	808	200	
	1668	410	(1,210)
Other Charges:			
Service charge		$ 19	
NSF cheque #998		60	
NSF cheque #201		205	(284)
Bal, Dec 31			$13,002

To prepare the bank reconciliation, you gather the following additional data:

a. The following cheques are outstanding on December 31:

Cheque No.	Amount
800	$415
802	75
806	34
809	123
810	228
811	39

b. On December 31, Billy's Hamburger's treasurer deposited $330, but this deposit does not appear on the bank statement.

c. The bank statement includes a $410 deduction for a cheque written by Jenny's Jump Ropes rather than Billy's Hamburger. Billy's Hamburger notified the bank of this bank error.

d. Billy's Cash account shows a balance of $12,000 on December 31.

Requirements

1. Prepare the bank reconciliation for December 31.

2. Record the journal entries called for by the reconciliation. Include an explanation for each entry.

P4-3B. Prepare a bank reconciliation (*Learning Objective 7*) 25–30 min.

The following is the MaMa Pizza's bank statement:

Date	Description	Debit	Credit	Balance
July 31				14,220
August 1	Deposit		2,560	16,780
3	Cheque #264	860		15,920
4	Cheque #283	180		15,740
7	Deposit		3,165	18,905
10	Cheque #303	865		18,040
12	Cheque #304	1,460		16,580
15	EFT - Salaries	2,400		14,180
16	Deposit		1,580	15,760
16	Cheque #305	1,250		14,510
18	Cheque #308	2,120		12,390
20	NSF cheque -Toni Ltd.	1,680		10,710
20	NSF Fee	15		10,695
24	EFT - Collection Roma Inc.		3,080	13,775
27	Cheque #310	830		12,945
28	Deposit		2,160	15,105
30	EFT - Salaries	2,400		12,705
30	Bank service charges	60		12,645
30	Interest charges	105		12,540

MaMa Pizza's ledger shows the following transactions in the Cash account in June:

Date	Description	Debit	Credit	Balance
July 31				14,220
August 1	Deposit	3,165		17,385
8	Cheque #303		865	16,520
9	Cheque #304		1,460	15,060
10	Cheque #305		1,250	13,810
12	Cheque #306		970	12,840
12	Cheque #307		655	12,185
16	Deposit	1,580		13,765
16	Cheque #308		212	13,553
20	Cheque #309		1,040	12,513
22	Cheque #310		830	11,683
28	Deposit	1,260		12,943
30	Deposit	5,250		18,193

Additional information:

1. Deposit of $2,560 on July 31 was deposited in the bank on August 1.

2. Cheque 278 for $260 and cheque 298 for $1,260 were issued in July, and they were not cashed in August.

3. MaMa Pizza made an error in recording cheque 308 and the August 28 deposit. Cheque 308 was for delivery car rental fees and the deposit was a collection from a catering event.

Requirements

1. Prepare MaMa Pizza's bank reconciliation at August 31.

2. Record the entries to update the cash account balance. Include an explanation for each entry.

3. If the entries were not recorded in (2), what is the impact on each of the assets, liabilities, and shareholders' equity accounts?

P4-4B. Prepare a bank reconciliation (*Learning Objective 7*) 20–25 min.

Vihn Ltd's ledger showed a cash balance of $22,680 on March 31. In preparing the bank reconciliation, the following information was determined:

a. EFT collection by bank from a credit customer was $3,280.

b. A deposit of $1,800 was correctly recorded in the books, but it showed as $18.00 on the bank statement.

c. Cheque 725 issued by Vihn Ltd. in the amount of $880, for the payment of the bank loan $800 and 10% of interest, had been incorrectly recorded in the books as $88.

d. Cheque 741 issued by Vihn Ltd. in the amount of $2,580, for the purchase of a computer, had been incorrectly paid by the bank as $258.

e. A cheque of $425 paid by a customer for his purchase was incorrectly recorded in the books as $245.

f. An NSF cheque for $1,370 was returned with the bank statement, with a bank charge of $18 for this transaction.

g. Cheque 701 issued by Vihn Ltd. in the amount of $1,680 was not included in the bank statement.

h. The bank statement showed interest charges and bank service charges were $26 and $54 respectively.

Requirements

1. Prepare Vihn's bank reconciliation at March 31.

2. What was the reconciled book balance? What was the bank statement balance before reconciliation?

3. Record the entries to update the Cash account balance. Include an explanation for each entry.

4. If the entries were not recorded in (2), what is the impact on each of the assets, liabilities, and shareholders' equity accounts?

PROBLEMS (ALTERNATES 1, 2, AND 3)

These alternative problem sets are available for your practice benefit at
www.myaccountinglab.com

APPLY YOUR KNOWLEDGE

ETHICS IN ACTION

Case 1. Jake needed a summer job and was lucky enough to land a job as a ticket collector at a local amusement park. On his first day, he was assigned to work alongside Tim, who had worked at the park for the past two summers. Tim explained to Jake that tickets are purchased from the box office outside the gate, and that park-goers present their tickets at the gate when they are ready to enter. Each ticket has a stub that is torn off and given back to the park-goer so they can leave and return the same day.

Jake decided this was not going to be a bad summer job considering that one of the "perks" of working at the park was that on his days off he could enter the park free. However, he had remembered from reading the employee handbook that only employees were admitted free. Any friends or family accompanying the employee must pay full price. Tim showed Jake the gate that employees used on their days off. He said, "just swipe your employee ID card through the card reader on the outside of the gate and you are in the park."

Soon after Jake started working at the park, he began to notice that many of the employees would hold the employee gate open while their friends and family entered without purchasing a ticket. One day Jake asked Tim about what he had saw. Tim replied, "Oh, nobody around here follows that policy. Last week I even saw the park superintendent come in with his entire family without paying."

A few weeks later on one of his days off, Jake was hanging out with his friends when one of them said, "Hey Jake, since you are working at the amusement park, can't you get us all in free today?" Jake thought about how much more fun it would be to go to the park with his friends and he began to reason "Why should I follow the rules if no one else does, not even the park superintendent? Anyway, it's not like I would really be stealing anything."

Requirement

1. What are the ethical considerations in this case?

Case 2. Marybeth Jones is the controller at Patterson Supply Company, a publicly traded distributor of floral supplies. It is the end of the third quarter and Marybeth is working under a deadline to get the quarterly financial statements prepared before the board of directors meeting at 2 P.M. The board of directors approves the quarterly financial statements before they are sent to the provincial securities commission.

Unfortunately, Marybeth has a bit of a problem. The debit and credit columns of the general ledger trial balance do not balance. She is certain that this is a simple mistake that someone made in recording a journal entry, but she just doesn't have time to look for the mistake. To make the deadline, Marybeth decides to force the trial balance into balance by adding the

$200,000 that she is out-of-balance to the Inventory account. Since inventory is the company's largest asset, Marybeth justified her actions by thinking that this wouldn't make a difference to anyone looking at the financial statements. She wished she had more time to look for the mistake, but the clock is ticking away.

Requirement

1. Is there any evidence of unethical behaviour in this case? Explain your answer.

Case 3. Rex Banner is the manager of a Stop Mart convenience store. He has been employed by the company for 12 years, the last 9 years of which was as a store manager. Rex applied for a promotion to regional manager, which oversees all 30 locations, but was once again denied promotion. Had he been promoted, the regional manager salary would have given Rex $14,000 more per year.

Rex was upset and decided that if the company would not give him the additional compensation he deserved then he would give himself a raise at the expense of the company. He knew that whenever he hired a new employee, the required paperwork sent to the corporate headquarters was simply filed without being reviewed. Thus, Rex completed all the company employment forms for a fictitious new employee he named "Sam Jones." He figured that, when the company was notified by Service Canada that the Social Insurance Number for "Sam Jones" was fraudulent, Rex would simply report that the employee had just quit and that Rex had no way to contact him. Rex's scheme involved the following actions:

- He put "Sam" on the schedule.
- Every week, he submitted a signed time card for "Sam" along with all the other legitimate employee time cards.
- Every two weeks when Rex received the employee paycheques, he pulled "Sam's" paycheque and hid it in his briefcase.
- He then cashed the paycheque for "Sam" and enjoyed the extra money.

Requirement

1. While Rex's actions are clearly unethical, were they justified, given that he was again denied a promotion and therefore undercompensated? Will Rex be caught? Does the company bear some responsibility too? If the company required direct deposit of its employee paycheques, could this type of fraud be prevented? Can you recommend any other procedures the company could adopt that would help to prevent Rex's fraud?

Case 4. RAS, Inc. is a supplier of residence alarm systems to building contractors. Sam Jennings, the company's new CEO, is out to make a name for himself and makes it known to his management team that he plans for the company to meet, if not exceed, its sales target each quarter.

Sam begins to realize that the company is falling short of its goal and he quickly calls a management meeting to announce his new plan. He says he has arranged sweet deals with several of the company's largest customers. RAS will pay the contractors a 1% fee to buy a large quantity of alarm systems just before the end of each quarter, with the understanding that RAS will buy the alarm systems back shortly after the beginning of the next quarter. Sam uses the term "buy" loosely since there is no plan for an exchange of cash. RAS will record the sales transaction by debiting Accounts Receivable and crediting Sales Revenue. When the alarm systems are bought back, RAS will debit Inventory and credit Accounts Receivable, which, of course, will have no impact on the income statement.

Lisa Barlow, the company's accountant, tells Sam that there is a problem with his plan. She explains that under International Financial Reporting Standards (IFRS), RAS has not earned revenue until inventory is delivered to customers. Sam quickly responds that he has everything under control. He explains to Lisa that the contractors have agreed to accept automatic shipments of the alarm systems and carry them in the company's inventory as of quarter-end. Sam says this is a "win-win" situation for everyone.

The plan did exactly what Sam hoped it would do. The company reported sales that consistently exceeded expectations. These inflated sales figures helped to boost the company's stock price to an all-time high. Sam considered himself a true winner. His compensation package included a lucrative stock bonus plan tied to the company's sales growth. As a result of the company's reported sales revenue, Sam received shares in the company that he was able to sell for thousands of dollars at the inflated stock price.

Requirements

1. Is there any evidence of unethical behaviour in this case? Explain your answer.

2. Other than Sam and the contractors, who could be harmed by Sam's plan?

Case 5. Mary Rel was hired as the new store manager for the Bargain Bin. The store used four cash registers, and 10 cashiers worked various shifts in the store. Store operations include the following procedures:

- At the start of each shift, a cashier counts the beginning cash balance in the drawer, which is supposed to be $550.
- At the end of each shift, the cashier then does the following:

1. Counts the ending cash balance in the drawer and adds to it any amounts dropped in the safe.

2. Completes the shift cash form that reconciles the cash received to the total register sales tape.

3. Reports any difference between the cash on hand and the cash that should be on hand based on receipts.

As a manager, Mary was responsible for preparing the cash drawers for each shift. She decided to test the honesty of the cashiers so she added an additional $50 to the beginning balance of one cash drawer. Mary planned to look at the shift cash form to see whether the cashier reported the extra $50 that was part of the beginning balance or just reported the $550 expected balance, taking the $50 for personal use.

Mary also tested her assistant manager. She gave him the bank deposit bag containing $5,246.24, but included a deposit ticket that was exactly $100 less, listing $5,146.24 as the deposit amount. Mary wanted to see whether the assistant manager would report the extra $100 in the deposit bag.

Mary planned to never let her employees or even her assistant manager know that she had tested them; instead she would just say that she made a simple mistake in counting the cash if they questioned her.

Requirement

1. Should Mary distrust her employees? Is it ethical for a manager to test employees without their knowledge? Should Mary ever inform the employees that they had been tested? Was it unethical for Mary to test an assistant manager?

Case 6. Assume that you were recently hired as a staff accountant for Environmental Solutions, Inc. You report to Karen, the director of financial reporting, who in turn reports to the CFO. One of your first assignments is to prepare the adjusting entries for the end of the second quarter and to draft the income statement. Karen instructs you to let her know as soon as you have the estimated earnings for the quarter. She says she will need to review the adjusting entries and earnings calculation with the CFO.

After reviewing your work with the CFO, Karen tells you to change the entry that you recorded for depreciation expense on the company's fleet of trucks from $229,000 to $184,000. At first you thought that you must have made some mistake in calculating the amount of depreciation, so you re-check your calculations. Surprisingly, you come up with the same amount again. So tactfully you ask Karen for an explanation for the change. She tells you that depreciation is only an estimate and that the CFO will change his mind about estimates based on earnings.

Requirements

1. What is the effect of the change in the amount of the depreciation expense on the company's second-quarter earnings?

2. What is the ethical dilemma that you face?

3. What are the alternatives that you might consider and what are the potential consequences of each alternative?

4. What are some of the common pitfalls used to rationalize unethical behaviour?

Case 7. Marvin Silverstein, a trusted employee of Progressive Supply Company, found himself in a difficult financial situation. His son's college tuition had to be paid in full by the end of the month. The family had experienced some unexpected expenses and the money was just not there to pay the tuition. Marvin knew his son could not register for classes until the tuition was paid, and classes filled quickly, so this could cause his son not to get the classes that he needed to graduate on time.

Marvin considered himself a "true company man" who never missed work and was always willing to work until the job was finished. Although he had been with the company for 10 years and was entitled to two weeks vacation per year, Marvin never found time to take vacation. Because of his loyalty to the company over the years, he knew that his boss would probably loan him the money that he needed for his son's tuition, but he just couldn't bring himself to ask his boss for a loan. As Marvin thought about the situation, he realized how simple it would be for him to "borrow" some money from the company to help him through these rough times and pay it back before anyone noticed.

Marvin was responsible for all of the bookkeeping functions, plus opening the mail, counting the cash in the registers at the end of the day, and making the daily bank deposit. With these combined duties, Marvin found it fairly simple to give himself a "loan." He removed $2,500 in cash from the cash register and replaced it with a $2,500 cheque from the incoming mail that day. The cheque was from a customer who was paying his or her account in full. Marvin made a journal entry crediting *Accounts Receivable* to clear the customer's account, but rather than debiting Cash, he debited Inventory. Marvin knew that inventory was not counted and reconciled until year-end. This would give Marvin plenty of time to get the "loan" repaid before anyone noticed.

Requirements

1. What are the ethical considerations in this case?
2. Discuss the primary internal control weakness in this case that could have contributed to Marvin's actions.

Case 8. You are the controller for CrystalClean Services, a company that provides janitorial services to large commercial customers. The company has been very successful during its first two years of operations, but to expand its customer base the company is in need of additional capital to be used for equipment purchases. The two brothers who started the business, Chuck and Josh Wisher, invested their life savings in the business, so they have contacted a local bank about securing a loan for $150,000.

The bank has asked for a set of financial statements, and Chuck, being the businessperson that he is, knows that the bank is going to be looking for a growth in earnings each year. Although the company's earnings have increased, Chuck would like the past year to look better than it does now.

Chuck stops by your office late in the afternoon on December 31 to find out when the financial statements will be ready. You explain that you still have to close out the end of the year, but should have them ready by the end of the week. Chuck tells you that he is aware of a major contract that Josh is working on that will be signed on January 2, and asks you to delay the closing process a couple of days so the new contract can be included in this year's operating results. You attempt to explain to Chuck that you cannot do that, but you can tell that he is not listening to you. Chuck interrupts by saying, "I don't know why you accountants get so worked up over a couple of days. Let me just say that *it would be in your best interest* to include this contract in the current year's operating results." Chuck left your office in a hurry and you heard him mutter under his breath as he turned the corner, "That accountant—who does he think he is trying to tell me how to run my business."

Requirements

1. What are the accounting issues related to Chuck's request?
2. What is the ethical issue involved in this case?
3. What would be the appropriate course of action for you to take?

KNOW YOUR BUSINESS

FINANCIAL ANALYSIS

Purpose: To help familiarize you with the financial reporting of a real company to further your understanding of the chapter material you are learning.

The Bombardier Annual Report in MyAccountingLab contains much more information than what is reported in the financial statements and related notes. In this case, you will explore other information presented in the annual report to determine the responsibilities of both management and the independent auditors for the annual report content. In addition, you will investigate the respective roles of both management and the auditors in the company's internal control system.

Refer to the Bombardier Annual Report in MyAccountingLab. You will need to find and then read the following reports:

- Management's Responsibility for Financial Reporting
- Independent Auditors' Report to the Shareholders of Bombardier Inc.

Requirements

1. Who is responsible for the information in the consolidated financial statements and the annual report? How are these responsibilities fulfilled?

2. Who were the independent auditors? Under what standards did they conduct their audit? What was their opinion of the audited financial statements? Who do the auditors primarily interact with and report to?

3. Who is responsible for establishing and maintaining adequate internal control over financial reporting? Is the effectiveness of the internal controls ever reviewed? Do you think that internal control procedures are necessary? Why?

INDUSTRY ANALYSIS

Purpose: To help you understand and compare the performance of two companies in the same industry.

Find the Bombardier Annual Report located in MyAccountingLab and look for information regarding their internal control systems. Now access the 2010 annual report for The Boeing Company. To do this from the internet, go to their webpage for the Investor Relations at *http://www.boeing.com/companyoffices/financial/quarterly.htm* and, under annual reports, go to the 2010 Annual Report. You'll find a section (Item 9A) where they discuss the company's Controls and Procedures.

Requirement

1. Compare the two annual reports as they relate to their disclosure of internal control procedures and the system of internal control. (These are found on page 156 of the Bombardier report in the "Controls and Procedures" section, and on page 111 of The Boeing Company report under "Item 9A. Controls and Procedures.")

SMALL BUSINESS ANALYSIS

Purpose: To help you understand the importance of cash flows in the operation of a small business.

You're having a tough time figuring out why your actual cash is always coming up less than the amount that the general ledger says should be there. You would hate to think that any of your employees would be stealing from you, because they have all been with you since you opened the business five years ago. But maybe it's time to do a little investigative work. After all, cash is the lifeblood of the business, and if it's being misappropriated, you need to find out fast!

You start to think back over some of the observations you've made recently and some of the conversations you've overheard, and one startling conclusion is staring you in the face. Joe's been a good employee, but lately he's been bragging about his wild weekends and some of the gambling casinos he's been going to. Joe never used to be like that. You overheard one of his fellow employees ask him where he's getting all this money, and he said that his wife just got a really good raise at her job and they're celebrating. Then just last week, Joe drove to work in a new sports car and again you overheard him tell someone about the great deal his brother-in-law got for him on this car.

Joe is in charge of billing and collecting. Since your office is so small, you always felt like these two jobs could be done more efficiently by the same person. You also remember that Joe's uncle is one of your vendors and there was that situation last year where you discovered a double billing to his uncle's company. When you brought it to Joe's attention, he immediately admitted his error and took care of it.

Requirement

1. Respond to the following: You are wondering whether or not you should call Joe into your office and have a talk with him, or just observe a little bit more to see if you can discover any irregularities in Joe's area.

WRITTEN COMMUNICATION

You've been asked by your boss to write a brief description of what the control activities should be as part of the development of a strong internal control system in your office. You know that the office is small in terms of personnel, which does create some control problems. So your boss has also asked you to make some recommendations on ways to strengthen any weaknesses that you discover in the internal control system.

Self Check Answers
1. b 2. c 3. a 4. c 5. c 6. a 7. d 8. c 9. b 10. b

Appendix 4A

WHAT IS A PETTY CASH FUND?

A business may choose to keep a petty cash fund, which is a fund containing a small amount of cash used to pay for minor expenditures, such as the purchase of postage stamps or a shipment of a small package. Cash is easy to steal and the thief is often able to do so without leaving evidence. For this reason, petty cash funds need controls such as the following:

9 ▶ (Appendix 4A) Account for the petty cash fund

- Designate a custodian for the petty cash fund. This assigns responsibility for the fund.
- Establish the fund by keeping a specific, fixed amount of cash on hand so that any missing amount can be easily identified.
- Keep the fund in a safe, locked location and only allow the custodian to have access to the fund.
- Support all payments from the fund with a written record documenting the purpose and amount of the payment.

Setting Up the Petty Cash Fund

Businesses establish a petty cash fund by writing a cheque for the designated amount, usually between $200 and $500, depending on the size and the needs of the business. They typically make the cheque payable to Petty Cash, cash the cheque, and place the money in the fund. Every business may have its own form for documenting petty cash payments, but the form is usually signed by the recipient of the petty cash and the custodian to verify the transaction. *The cash in the fund plus the total of the payment forms should always equal the fund balance at all times*.

Suppose that Inland Equipment established a petty cash fund of $200 on June 1. The journal entry to record the creation of the fund is as follows:

DATE	ACCOUNTS	POST REF.	DR.	CR.
Jun 1	Petty Cash		200	
	Cash			200
	Establish the petty cash fund.			

Now imagine that on June 21 Suzanne Kimmel, the fund custodian, approved a cash payment from the petty cash fund to Jim Dirks to reimburse Jim for $25 of envelopes he purchased for the business. Suzanne prepared a record of the disbursement, much like the petty cash ticket in **Exhibit 4A-1**, and both she and Jim signed it. Suzanne kept the form in the fund as a replacement for the cash taken.

```
             PETTY CASH TICKET

Date  Jun 21
Amount   $25
For   Envelopes
Debit  Office Supplies
Received by  Jim Dirks        Fund Custodian  SK
```

Exhibit 4A-1 ▲

Replenishing the Petty Cash Fund

Payments deplete the petty cash fund, so periodically it must be replenished. On July 31 the petty cash fund of Inland Equipment holds the following:

- $108 cash on hand
- $90 in petty cash tickets: office supplies, $53; delivery expense, $37

Notice that when the $108 of cash on hand is added to the $90 of petty cash tickets, the total comes to $198, which is $2 less than the fund balance of $200. The $2 difference signifies that $2 was misplaced from the fund. The petty cash fund can be reconciled as follows:

Cash on Hand....................................	$108
+ Petty Cash Tickets	90
=	198
+ Cash Shortage	2
= Fund Balance	$200

To replenish the petty cash fund and make the cash on hand equal to $200 again, the company writes a cheque, payable to Petty Cash, for the $92 ($200 − $108) difference between the cash on hand and the fund balance. The fund custodian cashes this cheque and puts $92 back in the fund. Now the fund holds $200 cash as required. The following journal entry would be made to record the issuance of the cheque:

DATE	ACCOUNTS	POST REF.	DR.	CR.
Jul 31	Office Supplies Expense		53	
	Delivery Expense		37	
	Cash Short		2	
	Cash			92
	Replenish the petty cash fund.			

The accounts debited in the entry represent the expense accounts associated with what the petty cash funds were used to purchase. The cash shortage is debited to an expense account titled Cash Short. Notice that the journal entry included a credit to Cash, not Petty Cash. This is because the money to replenish the petty cash fund was taken from the Cash account. The Petty Cash account is only affected when

- the petty cash fund is established.
- the petty cash fund balance is increased or decreased.

Changing the Petty Cash Fund

Imagine that Inland Equipment wants to increase the size of its fund from $200 to $300 on August 1. The business writes a $100 cheque payable to Petty Cash, and the custodian cashes it and places the money in the fund. In this case, the journal entry to record this $100 increase will look like the following:

DATE	ACCOUNTS	POST REF.	DR.	CR.
Aug 1	Petty Cash		100	
	Cash			100
	Increase petty cash fund balance.			

ACCOUNTING PRACTICE

SHORT EXERCISES

S4A-1. Petty cash transactions (*Learning Objective 9*) 5–10 min.

Record the following petty cash transactions of Handy Dan in the journal; explanations are not required.

Nov	1	Established a petty cash fund with a $100 balance.
	30	The petty cash fund had $33 in cash and $67 in petty cash tickets that were issued to pay for postage. Replenished the fund with cash.

S4A-2. Petty cash transactions (*Learning Objective 9*) 5–10 min.

Record the following petty cash transactions of Xeno, Corp. in the journal; explanations are not required.

Jun	1	Established a petty cash fund with a $200 balance.
	30	The petty cash fund had $22 in cash and $174 in petty cash tickets that were issued to pay for office supplies ($104) and entertainment expense ($70). Replenished the fund.
	30	Increased the petty cash fund balance to $300.

EXERCISES (GROUP A)

E4A-1A. Petty cash transactions (*Learning Objective 9*) 10–15 min.

Jamie's Music School created a $200 petty cash fund on March 1. During the month, the fund custodian authorized and signed petty cash tickets as follows:

Petty Cash			
Ticket No.	Item	Account Debited	Amount
1	Delivery of programs to customers	Delivery Expense	$20
2	Mail package	Postage Expense	40
3	Newsletter	Supplies Expense	44
4	Key to closet	Miscellaneous Expense	16
5	Blank DVDs	Supplies Expense	30

Requirements

1. Record the journal entry to create the petty cash fund.
2. Assuming that the cash in the fund totals $45 on March 31, make the journal entry to replenish the petty cash fund.

E4A-2A. Petty cash transactions (*Learning Objective 9*) 10–15 min.

Hazelnut maintains a petty cash fund of $150. On November 30, the fund holds $7 cash, and petty cash tickets for office supplies, $90, and delivery expense, $50.

Requirements

1. Make the journal entry to replenish the petty cash fund.
2. Hazelnut decided to increase the petty cash fund by $100. Prepare the journal entry.

EXERCISES (GROUP B)

E4A-1B. Petty cash transactions (*Learning Objective 9*) 10–15 min.

Christine's Music School created a $220 petty cash fund on October 1. During the month, the fund custodian authorized and signed petty cash tickets as follows:

Petty Cash			
Ticket No.	Item	Account Debited	Amount
1	Delivery of programs to customers	Delivery Expense	$15
2	Mail package	Postage Expense	50
3	Newsletter	Supplies Expense	43
4	Key to closet	Miscellaneous Expense	19
5	Blank DVDs	Supplies Expense	10

Requirements

1. Record the journal entry to create the petty cash fund.
2. Assuming that the cash in the fund totals $55 on October 31, make the journal entry to replenish the petty cash fund.

E4A-2B. Petty cash transactions (*Learning Objective 9*) 10–15 min.

Maple maintains a petty cash fund of $250. On April 30, the fund holds $19 cash, petty cash tickets for office supplies, $185, and delivery expense, $40.

Requirements

1. Make the journal entry to replenish the petty cash fund.
2. Maple decided to increase the petty cash fund by $120. Prepare the journal entry.

EXERCISES (ALTERNATES 1, 2, AND 3)

These alternative exercise sets are available for your practice benefit at *www.myaccountinglab.com*

PROBLEMS (GROUP A)

P4A-1A. Petty cash transactions (*Learning Objective 9*) 10–15 min.

On July 1, Chi Kong creates a petty cash fund with a balance of $300. During July, Elise Sautter, the fund custodian, signs the following petty cash tickets:

Petty Cash Ticket Number	Item	Amount
101	Office supplies	$86
102	Cab fare for executive	25
103	Delivery of package across town	17
104	Dinner money for president and a potential customer	90

On July 31, prior to replenishment, the fund contains these tickets plus cash of $62. The accounts affected by petty cash payments are Office Supplies Expense, Travel Expense, Delivery Expense, and Entertainment Expense.

Requirements

1. Record the journal entry to create the petty cash fund.

2. Record the journal entry to replenish the petty cash fund on July 31. Do you have any concerns regarding the Over/Short account?

3. Make the August 1 entry to increase the fund balance to $350. Include an explanation, and briefly describe what the custodian does when the balance is increased.

PROBLEMS (GROUP B)

P4A-1B. Petty cash transactions (*Learning Objectives 9*) 10–15 min.

On March 1, Fab Kong creates a petty cash fund with a balance of $300. During March, Elise Sautter, the fund custodian, signs the following petty cash tickets:

Petty Cash Ticket Number	Item	Amount
101	Office supplies	$86
102	Cab fare for executive	27
103	Delivery of package across town	10
104	Dinner money for president and a potential customer	110

On March 31, prior to replenishment, the fund contains these tickets plus cash of $37. The accounts affected by petty cash payments are Office Supplies Expense, Travel Expense, Delivery Expense, and Entertainment Expense.

Requirements

1. Record the journal entry to create the petty cash fund.

2. Record the journal entry to replenish the petty cash fund on March 31. Do you have any concerns over the Over/Short account?

3. Make the entry on April 1 to increase the fund balance to $375. Include an explanation, and briefly describe what the custodian does when the balance is increased.

PROBLEMS (ALTERNATES 1, 2, AND 3)

These alternative problem sets are available for your practice benefit at
www.myaccountinglab.com

SCAN THIS

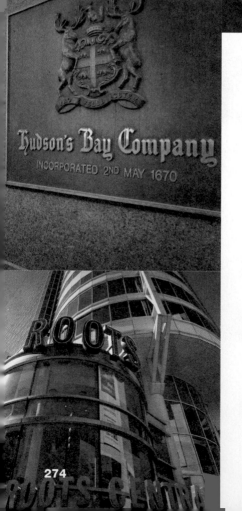

CHAPTER 5

Accounting for a Merchandising Business

LEARNING OBJECTIVES:

1. Describe the relationship among wholesalers, retailers, and customers

2. Define periodic and perpetual inventory systems

3. Journalize transactions for the purchase of inventory

4. Journalize transactions for the sale of inventory

5. Understand shipping terms, and journalize transactions for freight charges and other selling expenses

6. Prepare a multi-step income statement and a classified balance sheet

7. Compute the gross profit percentage and the current ratio

Although service businesses are the predominant type of business in Canada, they are not the only type. Canada also has a significant number of merchandising businesses. Maybe you are curious about how the accounting works for an organization that sells a product instead of a service? Do the financial statements that a merchandiser prepares differ from those of a service organization? In Chapter 5, you will discover the answers to these questions as we explore accounting for merchandise organizations.

CHAPTER OUTLINE:

WHAT IS THE RELATIONSHIP AMONG WHOLESALERS, RETAILERS, AND CUSTOMERS?

1 Describe the relationship among wholesalers, retailers, and customers

In this chapter, you will learn about the special accounting methods for a merchandising business. A merchandising business buys and sells products, called **merchandise inventory**, instead of services. Inventory is a very important asset to a merchandising business because it reflects the amount of goods the business has available to sell to its customers. Throughout the remainder of the book, we will refer to merchandise inventory simply as **inventory**.

A merchandising business can be either a wholesaler or a **retailer**. Wholesalers generally purchase large lots of products from manufacturers and resell them to retailers. Retailers buy goods from wholesalers and resell them to the final consumers, the general public. It is also possible for a retailer to purchase products directly from a manufacturer. **Exhibit 5-1** shows the relationship among manufacturers, wholesalers, retailers, and customers.

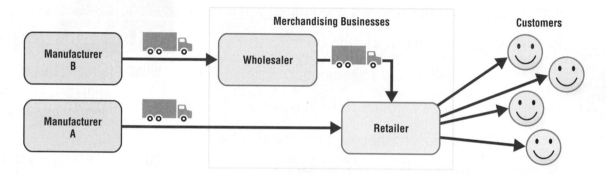

Exhibit 5-1 ▲

The discount chain Giant Tiger and the internet merchandiser Amazon.ca are familiar examples of retailers. In this chapter, a fictitious merchandiser named Cosmic Cellular, Inc. is used to illustrate merchandising operations. Cosmic Cellular is a mall retailer that sells cell phones and accessories. We will learn how Cosmic Cellular records entries related to purchases from its suppliers. In addition, we will learn the entries Cosmic uses to record sales of merchandise to its customers. We will also learn how the type of inventory tracking system chosen by Cosmic will impact the journal entries that it must make.

HOW DO PERIODIC AND PERPETUAL INVENTORY SYSTEMS DIFFER?

 Define periodic and perpetual inventory systems

Merchandisers use one of two inventory tracking systems:

- The **periodic inventory system** is a system of accounting for inventory that does *not* keep a continuous, running record of inventory as it is bought and sold. Instead, the business physically counts the goods in inventory at the end of the accounting period. It then multiplies the quantity of each item by its cost to get the total value of the ending inventory. Once the ending inventory has been determined, a business will calculate the cost of the inventory it has sold during the period. **Exhibit 5-2** shows the components of inventory activities, and the schedule of cost of goods sold is calculated using these components.

Historically, businesses that sold large quantities of relatively inexpensive goods used the periodic inventory system because it was too costly and time consuming to track the inventory items that were sold. Currently, thanks to innovations in inventory tracking technology, most businesses utilize a perpetual inventory system.

■ The **perpetual inventory system** is a system of accounting for inventory that keeps a running record of inventory as it is bought and sold. Every time the business engages in a transaction involving inventory, the balance in the inventory account is immediately updated. By doing this, the inventory balance is *perpetually* up-to-date. However, the business must still physically count inventory at least once a year to see whether any goods have been lost, damaged, or stolen. Just because the accounting records indicate that a certain amount of inventory exists, it doesn't mean that this amount is actually on hand. If the actual inventory count is different than the perpetual records indicate, the perpetual records are adjusted to reflect the physical count. The general ledger is also updated by debiting or crediting the inventory account as needed. The offsetting debit or credit is to the Cost of Goods Sold account. Technology makes it easier for almost any business to use the perpetual system. Usually, a cash register used in a perpetual system is connected to a bar code scanner. When an inventory item is scanned, not only is the sale recorded, but the inventory records are simultaneously updated.

Beginning Inventory
+ Purchases
_____
= Cost of Goods Available for Sale
− Ending Inventory
_____
= Cost of Goods Sold

Exhibit 5-2 ▲

DECISION GUIDELINES

Decision	Guideline	Analyze
Which inventory system should my business use?	This decision depends on whether or not you plan on utilizing a computer system to help with inventory management.	The *perpetual system* shows the current, correct amounts of inventory on hand and the cost of goods sold at all times. The *periodic system* requires that a physical count of the inventory be taken to know the correct balances of inventory and cost of goods sold. Before computers, only businesses that sold smaller quantities of higher cost items could use the perpetual method. Today, thanks to computers and other technology, most companies utilize the perpetual method even if they sell a high quantity of low-cost items.

HOW DO YOU ACCOUNT FOR THE PURCHASE OF INVENTORY?

Throughout the year, merchandisers engage in a number of inventory transactions with suppliers including cash purchases, credit purchases, **purchase returns and allowances**, and **purchase discounts**. Depending on the inventory system the merchandiser uses, the recording of the purchase of inventory and the sale of inventory are

 Journalize transactions for the purchase of inventory

accounted for differently. Since the periodic inventory does not require constant updating of the inventory level, we use separate accounts for recording purchases, purchase returns and allowances, transportation-in, and purchase discounts. On the other hand, the perpetual inventory system requires updating the inventory account balance, so when inventory is purchased, we need to increase inventory, and when inventory is sold, we also need to decrease inventory. Let's examine how Cosmic Cellular accounts for these types of transactions.

Cash and Credit Purchases

Cosmic Cellular purchases 300 cell phone cases from Accessories Unlimited on account at a cost of $25 each. Therefore, the total value of Cosmic's purchase is $7,500 (300 cases × $25). Cosmic Cellular receives the goods on February 1 and records this purchase as follows:

Perpetual Inventory System

DATE	ACCOUNTS	DR.	CR.
Feb 1	Inventory	7,500	
	Accounts Payable—Accessories Unlimited		7,500
	Record purchase of inventory on account.		

Periodic Inventory System

DATE	ACCOUNTS	DR.	CR.
Feb 1	Purchases	7,500	
	Accounts Payable—Accessories Unlimited		7,500
	Record purchase of inventory on account.		

Using the perpetual inventory system, the purchase of inventory on account increases both Cosmic Cellular's assets and liabilities. The Inventory account reflects the cost of goods purchased for resale. The balance increases every time inventory is purchased. Inventory is an asset until it is sold because, as discussed in Chapter 1, assets represent things of value that the business has. Using the periodic inventory system, the purchase of inventory does not increase assets, as the Inventory account is not updated. Instead, the purchases account, which is one of the cost of goods sold accounts, is increased. This amount will be used to calculate the overall cost of goods sold for the period.

Notice that the name of the supplier is listed in the journal entry following Accounts Payable. The supplier's name is used because the amount owed to each individual supplier will be posted to a **subsidiary ledger** in addition to the Accounts Payable account in the general ledger. The subsidiary ledger contains a record for each separate supplier. If everything has been posted correctly, the total of the account balances in the accounts payable subsidiary ledger will equal the Accounts Payable account balance in the general ledger. This way, a merchandiser can keep track of the amount of accounts payable owed to each individual supplier.

Some suppliers may require cash to be paid at the time of shipment. If Accessories Unlimited required cash payment for the 300 cell phone cases at the time of sale, Cosmic Cellular would record the cash purchase as follows:

Perpetual Inventory System

DATE	ACCOUNTS	DR.	CR.
Feb 1	Inventory	7,500	
	Cash		7,500
	Record purchase of inventory for cash.		

Periodic Inventory System

DATE	ACCOUNTS	DR.	CR.
Feb 1	Purchases	7,500	
	Cash		7,500
	Record purchase of inventory for cash.		

Purchase Returns and Allowances

Occasionally, merchandisers buy goods that are not satisfactory. In these cases, most suppliers allow the goods to be returned. Or, they may allow the merchandiser to keep the unsuitable goods and receive a deduction, or allowance, from the amount they owe for the merchandise. Both purchase returns and allowances decrease the merchandiser's cost of the inventory.

Suppose Cosmic Cellular buys 20 hands-free headsets for $20 each from Mega Mobile, and these headsets become damaged in shipment. If Cosmic returns the merchandise to Mega Mobile, it will issue a **debit memorandum**. A debit memorandum is a document that supports the return of goods to the supplier, as illustrated in **Exhibit 5-3**.

COSMIC CELLULAR

1471 Front St.
Toronto, Ontario

DEBIT MEMORANDUM #47

To: Mega Mobile
21 Dundas Street
Hamilton, Ontario

Date: April 5, 2013

We debit your account balance for the following:

20 T180 Headsets @ $20 each	**$400**

Exhibit 5-3 ▲

A debit memorandum gets its name from the fact that the issuer's Accounts Payable account will be debited as a result of the return of the goods. Upon issuing the debit memorandum, Cosmic will *debit*, or reduce, its Accounts Payable balance for the value of the merchandise returned. Cosmic will also reduce the inventory account by the amount of the return because it no longer has this inventory. Cosmic records the purchase return as follows:

Perpetual Inventory System

DATE	ACCOUNTS	DR.	CR.
Apr 5	Accounts Payable—Mega Mobile	400	
	Inventory		400
	Record inventory returned to manufacturer.		

Periodic Inventory System

DATE	ACCOUNTS	DR.	CR.
Apr 5	Accounts Payable—Mega Mobile	400	
	Purchase Returns and Allowances		400
	Record inventory returned to manufacturer.		

Purchase Discounts

Exhibit 5-4 on the following page illustrates Accessories Unlimited's invoice for Cosmic's $7,500 purchase of inventory. A **sales invoice** is a bill that documents the sale of goods to a business customer. The invoice includes **credit terms**, or the payment terms, for customers who buy on account. A customer may pay cash when it receives the goods or it may pay within a period of time following the receipt of those goods. Merchandisers use credit terms on sales to communicate to the customer when payment is due. Often, merchandisers will use the term **n/30**, which means that the sales price for the goods must be paid within 30 days after the date of the invoice. If the amount is due at the end of the month, the invoice will include the phrase **n/eom** or just **eom**.

All businesses want to have enough cash to pay their bills on time. Therefore, suppliers often offer merchandisers purchase discounts for early payment to improve their cash inflow.

ᎠᏨᏟᏋᎦᎦᎧᏒᎥᏋᎦ UNLIMITED		Invoice	
Accessories Unlimited P.O. Box 873 Windsor, Ont.		Date	Number
		2/1/13	644

Shipped to:	Cosmic Cellular 1471 Front St. Toronto, Ontario		Terms: 3/15, n/30	

Quantity	Item		Unit Price	Total
300 each	Cell phone cases		$ 25	$ 7,500

		Subtotal	$ 7,500
		Shipping Charge	–
		Tax	–
		Total	$ 7,500

Exhibit 5-4 ▲

By rewarding the merchandiser for paying amounts before the due date, these companies get cash sooner. The time period in which the merchandiser may pay and receive the discount is called the **discount period**. If the merchandiser takes advantage of this offer and pays early, then these discounts represent a reduction in the cost of the merchandise purchased.

Review Accessories Unlimited's invoice in Exhibit 5-4. Accessories Unlimited's credit terms of "3/15, n/30" mean that Cosmic Cellular may deduct 3% of the total amount due to Accessories Unlimited if it pays within 15 days of the invoice date. Otherwise, the full amount is due in 30 days. In this case, the discount period covers 15 days. However, if Accessories Unlimited listed terms of "n/30" instead of "3/15, n/30," it would mean that it was not offering a discount at all, and payment is due 30 days after the invoice date.

If Cosmic Cellular pays within the discount period, it will pay $7,275, or 97% of the purchase invoice amount of $7,500:

Invoice Total	$7,500	(100% of invoice amount)
– Purchase Discount	(225)	(3% of invoice amount, or .03 × $7,500)
= Cash Paid	$7,275	(97% of invoice amount, or .97 × $7,500)

Cosmic records its payment on February 13, which is within the discount period, as shown:

Perpetual Inventory System

DATE	ACCOUNTS	DR.	CR.
Feb 13	Accounts Payable—Accessories Unlimited	7,500	
	Cash		7,275
	Inventory		225
	Record payment of inventory purchases within the discount period.		

Periodic Inventory System

DATE	ACCOUNTS	DR.	CR.
Feb 13	Accounts Payable—Accessories Unlimited	7,500	
	Cash		7,275
	Purchase Discount		225
	Record payment of inventory purchases within the discount period.		

In the perpetual inventory system, the discount is credited to the Inventory account. This is because the discount decreases the cost of the cell phone cases that Cosmic Cellular bought from Accessories Unlimited. Using the periodic inventory system, the discount taken is credited directly to the Purchase Discount account, a contra purchases account. Note that the full invoice amount of the payable, $7,500, should be debited, rather than the net amount of $7,275; otherwise, the Accounts Payable—Accessories Unlimited account will show an outstanding amount of $225.

If Cosmic Cellular pays this invoice after the discount period, it pays the full amount of $7,500. In this case, it records the payment as follows:

Perpetual Inventory System

DATE	ACCOUNTS	DR.	CR.
Feb 13	Accounts Payable—Accessories Unlimited	7,500	
	Cash		7500
	Record payment of inventory purchases after the discount period.		

Periodic Inventory System

DATE	ACCOUNTS	DR.	CR.
Feb 13	Accounts Payable—Accessories Unlimited	7,500	
	Cash		7,500
	Record payment of inventory purchases after the discount period.		

It is important to note that discounts are not granted on any portion of a purchase that is returned to the supplier. For example, if Cosmic Cellular returned four damaged cell phone cases at $25 each to Accessories Unlimited on February 3, the balance owed to Accessories Unlimited on February 13 before the payment was made would be $7,400. Cosmic records the purchase returns on February 3 and payment on February 13, which is within the discount period, as shown:

Perpetual Inventory System

DATE	ACCOUNTS	DR.	CR.
Feb 3	Accounts Payable—Accessories Unlimited	100	
	Inventory		100
	Record inventory returned to manufacturer.		
Feb 13	Accounts Payable—Accessories Unlimited	7,400	
	Cash		7,178
	Inventory		222
	Record payment of inventory purchases within the discount period.		

Periodic Inventory System

DATE	ACCOUNTS	DR.	CR.
Feb 3	Accounts Payable—Accessories Unlimited	100	
	Purchase Returns and Allowances		100
	Record inventory returned to manufacturer.		
Feb 13	Accounts Payable—Accessories Unlimited	7,400	
	Cash		7,178
	Purchase Discount		222
	Record payment of inventory purchases within the discount period.		

Many companies take advantage of this discount, if they have cash or have access to cash to pay the invoice within 15 days. In fact, the effective interest rate is approximately 75%. This interest rate is calculated by taking $3 on the balance owing of $97; in other words, if $97 is not paid within 15 days, then there is a $3 interest charge for the additional 15 days. In fact, if companies can borrow money at a lower rate to pay for the purchase and pay back the borrowed amount by the 30th day, then they manage their cash flows and operations effectively.

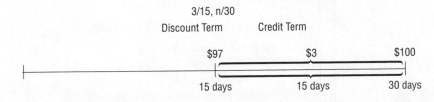

3/15, n/30

Discount Term   Credit Term

$97 $3 $100

15 days   15 days   30 days

$3 ÷ $97 = 3.09% for 15 days   3.09% ÷ 15 days = 0.206% per day
0.206% × 365 days = 75.26% per year

Period-End Cost of Goods Sold and Inventory Adjustments

Under the perpetual inventory system, we use the cost of goods sold and inventory accounts to account for all the purchases, purchase returns, sales, and sales returns; therefore, the cost of goods sold and inventory should be up to date, and there should be no need for period-end adjustments. However, under the periodic inventory system, the cost of goods sold and inventory accounts have not been updated for the entire accounting period. We need to calculate the cost of goods sold and to update the inventory account balance. For example, Cosmic Cellular's ledger shows the following account balances on December 31, 2013:

ACCOUNT #	ACCOUNT TITLE	DR.	CR.
1030	Inventory	35,800	
5020	Purchases	80,500	
5030	Purchases Returns and Allowances		7,500
5040	Purchase Discounts		2,500
5050	Transportation-in	12,000	

And the year-end inventory physical count shows the inventory is $28,000. The cost of goods sold is calculated as follows:

Beginning Inventory		$ 35,800
+ Purchases	$80,500	
− Purchase Returns and Allowances	(7,500)	
− Purchase Discounts	(2,500)	
+ Transportation-in	12,000	
= Total Cost of Goods Purchased		82,500
Goods Available for Sale		$118,300
− Ending Inventory		(28,000)
= Cost of Goods Sold		$ 90,300

Two period-end adjusting entries are required to close the beginning inventory and all purchase-related accounts to the Cost of Goods Sold account and to update the inventory balance. Once these two entries are recorded, both the Cost of Goods Sold account ($90,300) and Inventory ($28,000) accounts are updated.

Perpetual Inventory System

DATE	ACCOUNTS	DR.	CR.
Dec 31	No entry		

Periodic Inventory System

DATE	ACCOUNTS	DR.	CR.
Dec 31	Cost of Goods Sold	128,300	
	Inventory		35,800
	Purchases		80,500
	Transportation-in		12,000
	To close beginning Inventory, Purchases, and Transportation-in to the Cost of Goods Sold account		
Dec 31	Inventory	28,000	
	Purchase Returns and Allowances	7,500	
	Purchase Discounts	2,500	
	Cost of Goods Sold		38,000
	To update ending Inventory, close Purchase Returns and Allowance and Purchase Discount accounts to the Cost of Goods Sold account		

HOW DO YOU ACCOUNT FOR THE SALE OF INVENTORY?

Merchandisers engage in several different types of business transactions with customers:

4 ▶ Journalize transactions for the sale of inventory

- Cash sales: Goods are sold for cash.

- Credit sales: Goods are sold on account.

- Sales returns and allowances: Damaged goods are returned by a customer for a refund. However, sometimes the customer keeps the damaged goods and accepts an allowance (price reduction) on the goods.

- Sales discounts: Suppliers grant customers a reduction in the amount owed as an incentive for paying within a discount period.

Let's examine how Cosmic Cellular accounts for these types of transactions.

Cash Sales

Merchandisers, such as Cosmic Cellular, often receive cash at the time they sell merchandise. The journal entry to record a cash sale increases the asset Cash, and increases the revenue account, **Sales Revenue**. Sales Revenue is the account used by merchandisers to track the value of merchandise sold to customers at the price that the merchandiser charges those customers.

Using the periodic system, Cosmic Cellular only requires recording the sales, since the reduction of inventory is not updated. However, using the perpetual inventory system, Cosmic Cellular not only needs to account for the sales, but also to reduce the Inventory balance for the value of the merchandise sold. By doing this, the Inventory account is updated so that it always, or perpetually, reflects the current balance. The value of the merchandise sold is accounted for in the **Cost of Goods Sold** account. This income statement account reflects the cost of merchandise sold during the period. The Cost of Goods Sold is deducted from Sales Revenue as a step in determining the amount of net income or loss for the period.

Assume that on June 9, Cosmic Cellular sells $3,000 of merchandise to customers for cash. The goods that Cosmic sold its customers cost Cosmic $1,900. The journal entry to record the sale is as follows:

Perpetual Inventory System

DATE	ACCOUNTS	DR.	CR.
Jun 9	Cash	3,000	
	Sales Revenue		3,000
	Cost of Goods Sold	1,900	
	Inventory		1,900
	Record sale of inventory for cash.	1,900	

Periodic Inventory System

DATE	ACCOUNTS	DR.	CR.
Jun 9	Cash	3,000	
	Sales Revenue		3,000
	Record sale of inventory for cash.		

Using the perpetual inventory system, when a product is sold, a merchandiser recognizes the following:

❶ Sales revenue for the selling price of the product to the customer

❷ Cost of goods sold for the merchandiser's cost of the product

A journal entry that involves more than two accounts is called a compound journal entry. A compound entry may include more than one debit amount or more than one credit amount.

Some merchandisers allow customers to use credit cards and debit cards rather than currency. These transactions are treated as cash sales because the merchandiser receives cash from the credit/debit card company within a short period of time. The credit/debit card company then collects the amount due from the customer. The merchandiser, however, usually must pay a service charge to the credit/debit card company in exchange for its processing of the transactions. Accounting for debit and credit card sales is discussed in Chapter 7 in more detail.

Credit Sales

Many merchandisers establish charge accounts for their customers. Assume that Cosmic Cellular sold on account a cell phone and accessories to Jim Kahl on June 11 for $500. The goods cost Cosmic $290. The entry to record this transaction is similar to accounting for a cash sale except Accounts Receivable is debited instead of Cash. Cosmic records this sale on account as follows:

Perpetual Inventory System

DATE	ACCOUNTS	DR.	CR.
Jun 11	Accounts Receivable—Jim Kahl	500	
	Sales Revenue		500
	Cost of Goods Sold	290	
	Inventory		290
	Record sale of inventory on account, invoice no. 322.		

Periodic Inventory System

DATE	ACCOUNTS	DR.	CR.
Jun 9	Accounts Receivable—Jim Kahl	500	
	Sales Revenue		500
	Record sale of inventory on account, invoice no. 322.		

When Jim sends Cosmic his payment for this merchandise, Cosmic records the cash receipt on account as follows:

Perpetual Inventory System

DATE	ACCOUNTS	DR.	CR.
Jun 19	Cash	500	
	Accounts Receivable—Jim Kahl		500
	Record payment received on invoice no. 322.		

Periodic Inventory System

DATE	ACCOUNTS	DR.	CR.
Jun 19	Cash	500	
	Accounts Receivable—Jim Kahl		500
	Record payment received on invoice no. 322.		

Notice that the name of the customer is listed in the journal entry following Accounts Receivable. This is similar to what is done for Accounts Payable. A separate account is kept in an accounts receivable subsidiary ledger for each charge customer. Each entry affecting accounts receivable is posted to the customer's account in the subsidiary ledger as well as to the Accounts Receivable account in the general ledger. After all entries are posted, the total of the account balances in the accounts receivable subsidiary ledger will equal the Accounts Receivable account balance in the general ledger. This way, the merchandiser can keep track of the amount of accounts receivable owed by each individual customer.

Sales Returns and Allowances

Merchandisers may allow customers to return unwanted merchandise or they may let customers keep the goods and request an allowance. A business tracks these returns so that it can analyze and manage the causes behind the returns and measure the related costs to the business. To track returns accurately, the amount of returns is recorded in a contra-account called **Sales Returns and Allowances**. Remember from Chapter 3 that a contra-account is an account with a balance opposite of the account to which it is linked. Sales Returns and Allowances is linked to Sales Revenue, which has a credit balance. Therefore, Sales Returns and Allowances will have a debit balance. As we will see later, Sales Returns and Allowances appears on the income statement and is deducted from Sales Revenue to arrive at Net Sales.

Exhibit 5-5 illustrates a **credit memorandum**, a document that acknowledges the return of goods from a customer. The credit memo gets its name from the effect that it has on the balance of the customer's account. Because the credit memo decreases the amount due from the customer, the merchandiser *credits* the accounts receivable balance for that customer. The merchandiser sends a credit memorandum to the customer as notification that an adjustment has been made to the amount the customer owes the merchandiser.

COSMIC CELLULAR

1471 Front St.
Toronto, Ontario

CREDIT MEMORANDUM #14

To: Jill Harris   Date: August 15, 2013
     28 St. George St.
     Calgary, Alberta

We credit your account balance for the following:

3 car chargers @ $25 each	**$75**

Exhibit 5-5 ▲

Sales Returns

When a customer returns goods, the merchandiser will

- decrease net sales revenue by increasing Sales Returns and Allowances, and decrease the customer's Accounts Receivable account balance for the sales price of those goods.
- decrease Cost of Goods Sold and increase Inventory for the cost of the returned goods, if the perpetual inventory system is used. No inventory adjustment is required for the periodic inventory system, when the goods are returned. The adjustment will be done at the end of the accounting period, when the inventory physical count takes place.

Let's see how Cosmic records the return illustrated in the credit memo in Exhibit 5-5. The credit memo reflects the return of three car chargers, originally purchased for $75, by Jill Harris, a customer. The returned car chargers cost Cosmic $30. Cosmic Cellular records the sales return as follows:

Perpetual Inventory System

DATE	ACCOUNTS	DR.	CR.
Aug 15	Sales Returns and Allowances	75	
	Accounts Receivable—Jill Harris		75
	Inventory	30	
	Costs of Goods Sold		30
	Record receipt of returned goods, credit memo no. 14.		

Periodic Inventory System

DATE	ACCOUNTS	DR.	CR.
Aug 15	Sales Returns and Allowances	75	
	Accounts Receivable—Jill Harris		75
	Record receipt of returned goods, credit memo no. 14.		

Accounts Receivable decreases because the customer no longer owes Cosmic for the returned goods. In the perpetual system only, Cosmic also updates its inventory because its perpetual inventory system needs to reflect the increase to Inventory because of the return of the goods. Cosmic also decreases the Cost of Goods Sold because the goods are no longer sold.

Sales Allowances

Rather than return goods to the merchandiser, some customers may be willing to keep unwanted goods and accept an allowance. Assume Cosmic Cellular grants credit customer Bill Logan a $100 sales allowance for damaged goods. Cosmic records the sales allowance as follows:

Perpetual Inventory System

DATE	ACCOUNTS	DR.	CR.
Aug 15	Sales Returns and Allowances	100	
	Accounts Receivable—Bill Logan		100
	Record sales allowance for damaged goods, credit memo no. 15.		

Periodic Inventory System

DATE	ACCOUNTS	DR.	CR.
Aug 15	Sales Returns and Allowances	100	
	Accounts Receivable—Bill Logan		100
	Record sales allowance for damaged goods, credit memo no. 15.		

Notice that the journal entry for a sales allowance does not affect Inventory or Cost of Goods Sold because the customer did not return any goods to the merchandiser.

Sales Discounts

Do you recall the discount that Cosmic Cellular received from Accessories Unlimited for early payment? It is possible for Cosmic to offer discounts to its credit customers for early payment. Let's assume that Cosmic sells merchandise to Kelly Harding for $450. The sale is made on account with credit terms of 2/15, n/30. If Kelly chooses to pay the invoice within the 15-day discount period, she will get a 2%, or $9, discount on her $450 purchase ($450 × 0.02). Kelly will pay $441, or 98% of the invoice amount of $450. This discount represents a reduction in the value of sales to Cosmic.

Businesses track the amount of these sales discounts so they can measure the impact on their sales revenue. To do so, businesses record these discounts in a contra-account called **Sales Discounts**. Because Sales Discounts is linked to Sales Revenue, it will normally have a debit balance. The Sales Discounts account tracks decreases in sales revenue that result from a discount to customers. Similar to the treatment of Sales Returns and Allowances, Sales Discounts appears on the income statement and is deducted from Sales

CONCEPT CHECK

If a customer returned $2,500 of merchandise and the transaction was recorded by debiting Sales and crediting Accounts Receivable, instead of debiting Sales Returns and Allowances and crediting Accounts Receivable, would the net income on the income statement be incorrect?

Answer:

No. Let's assume that the company has $20,000 of total sales at the time the return is made and that this is the first time merchandise is returned during the period. If the transaction is recorded by debiting Sales, the Sales balance will be reduced to $17,500. Because there have been no other sales returns, the balance in the Sales Returns and Allowances will be zero. Therefore, the amount of net sales will be $17,500. If, instead of debiting Sales, the Sales Returns and Allowances account is debited, the Sales account will have a balance of $20,000 and the Sales Returns and Allowances account will have a balance of $2,500. Therefore, the amount of net sales will still be $17,500 ($20,000 – $2,500). If the amount of net sales is $17,500 regardless of which way the transaction is recorded, the net income will be the same. The reason for using the Sales Returns and Allowances account is simply to keep track of the amount of merchandise returned during the period. Managers often use this information to determine if there are quality issues with their products.

Revenue to arrive at net sales. Because the Sales Returns and Allowances and the Sales Discount accounts have debit balances, they will be closed along with the expense accounts at the end of the period.

Assume that Cosmic receives payment of $441 from Kelly on February 13 within the discount period. The journal entry to record the receipt of cash and the sales discount is as follows:

DATE	ACCOUNTS	DR.	CR.
Feb 13	Cash	441	
	Sales Discounts	9	
	Accounts Receivable—Kelly Harding		450

If Kelly fails to pay within the 15-day discount period, she will have to pay the full invoice price of $450. If Cosmic receives payment from Kelly on February 24, it records the payment as follows:

DATE	ACCOUNTS	DR.	CR.
Feb 24	Cash	450	
	Accounts Receivable—Kelly Harding		450

Notice that there is no entry for inventory because this is a receipt of payment from the customer.

HOW DO YOU ACCOUNT FOR FREIGHT CHARGES AND OTHER SELLING EXPENSES?

5 Understand shipping terms, and journalize transactions for freight charges and other selling expenses

In addition to purchases and sales transactions, a merchandiser also accounts for shipping costs and other selling expenses. Merchandisers often pay costs related to

- receiving goods from suppliers.
- delivering goods to customers.
- advertising and other selling costs.

When merchandisers order items, they often pay the cost of shipping the items to their place of business. These shipping costs are often referred to as **freight charges**.

ACCOUNTING IN YOUR WORLD

Have you ever purchased something online, or from a catalogue, and thought you received a really great deal until you received the bill and realized that the company charged you a significant amount for "shipping and handling"? The reason that you were required to pay these shipping charges is because the merchandise was sold with shipping terms of "FOB Shipping Point." Next time, you should purchase items from a company that offers "FOB Destination" shipping terms.

Buyers and sellers specify who pays shipping costs by agreeing to shipping terms. In addition to dictating who is responsible for paying shipping costs, shipping terms also specify the point at which ownership of the goods, or **title**, transfers from seller to buyer. Shipping terms may be **free on board (FOB) shipping point** or **free on board (FOB) destination**.

- Under free on board (FOB) shipping point, ownership transfers from the seller to the buyer at the point where the goods are *shipped*. Also, this term means that the buyer pays the shipping charges to have the merchandise delivered to their place of business. The buyer adds the shipping costs to inventory by debiting Inventory because these amounts increase the cost of the goods purchased.

■ Free on board (FOB) destination denotes the opposite arrangement. Ownership transfers from the seller to the buyer when the goods reach their *destination*. This term means that the seller must pay to ship goods to that point. The seller records the shipping costs with a debit to Delivery Expense.

Exhibit 5-6 summarizes FOB terms.

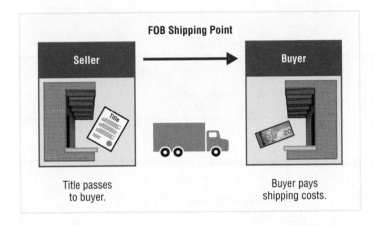
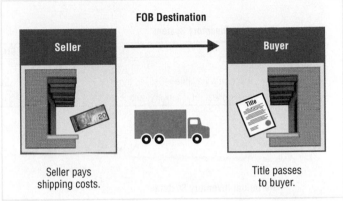

FOB Shipping Point

Seller → Buyer

Title passes to buyer.

Buyer pays shipping costs.

FOB Destination

Seller → Buyer

Seller pays shipping costs.

Title passes to buyer.

Exhibit 5-6 ▲

Costs Related to the Receipt of Goods from Suppliers

Let us see how Cosmic Cellular records shipping costs when it purchases goods. When it buys products under FOB shipping point, Cosmic either pays the shipping company directly or reimburses the seller for the freight charges if they have been prepaid by the seller. When Cosmic buys products under FOB destination, the supplier pays the freight charges.

FOB Shipping Point, Pay the Shipping Company

Suppose Cosmic Cellular incurs shipping costs related to the purchase of merchandise (FOB shipping point) from Accessories Unlimited. Cosmic pays $60 to the carrier for the February 1 shipment. Cosmic Cellular's entry to record payment of the shipping charge is as follows:

Perpetual Inventory System

DATE	ACCOUNTS	DR.	CR.
Feb 1	Inventory	60	
	Cash		60
	Record payment of shipping bill for the February 1 purchase.		

Periodic Inventory System

DATE	ACCOUNTS	DR.	CR.
Feb 1	Transportation-in	60	
	Cash		60
	Record payment of shipping bill for the February 1 purchase.		

Note that under the perpetual inventory system, the shipping cost is debited in the Inventory account, as the cost of the inventory is increased. However, under the periodic inventory system, the shipping cost is recorded in the Transportation-In account, which is one of the cost of goods sold accounts.

FOB Shipping Point, Repay the Seller for Prepaid Shipping Costs

Under FOB shipping point, the seller sometimes prepays the shipping costs as a convenience to the buyer. These costs are added to the invoice for the merchandise.

Let's see how Cosmic records the following purchase transactions. On July 15, Cosmic buys $1,000 of goods on account from CellTel, Inc. The terms of the purchase are 2/10, n/30, FOB shipping point. CellTel prepaid $80 of shipping costs and added the charges to the invoice for an invoice total of $1,080. Cosmic then returns $100 of these goods for credit on July 20. On July 25, Cosmic makes payment in full for the purchase.

First, Cosmic records the purchase of goods:

Perpetual Inventory System

DATE	ACCOUNTS	DR.	CR.
Jul 15	Inventory	1,080	
	Accounts Payable—CellTel, Inc.		1,080
	Record purchase of inventory on account.		

Periodic Inventory System

DATE	ACCOUNTS	DR.	CR.
Jul 15	Purchases	1,080	
	Accounts Payable—CellTel, Inc.		1,080
	Record purchase of inventory on account.		

Next, Cosmic records the return of inventory, as follows:

Perpetual Inventory System

DATE	ACCOUNTS	DR.	CR.
Jul 20	Accounts Payable—CellTel, Inc.	100	
	Inventory		100
	Record inventory returned to the manufacturer.		

Periodic Inventory System

DATE	ACCOUNTS	DR.	CR.
Jul 20	Accounts Payable—CellTel, Inc.	100	
	Purchase Returns and Allowances		100
	Record inventory returned to the manufacturer.		

Finally, it records the payment for the purchase by calculating the purchase discount and the balance due. Cosmic pays on July 25, which is within the 10-day discount period, so it receives a discount of $18: 2% of the $1,000 original cost of the goods minus $100 of returned goods, or $0.02 \times \$900$. Although shipping costs increase the invoice amount of the merchandise purchased, they are not included in the calculation of any purchase discount. The purchase discount is computed only on the amount due to the supplier for the goods purchased. The calculation of the payment amount is as follows:

Purchase Amount	$1,000
+ Shipping Costs	80
− Purchase Return	(100)
− Purchase Discount	(18) ($1,000 − $100 = $900; $900 × 0.02 = $18)
= Cash Paid	$ 962

The journal entry to record the cash payment is as follows:

Perpetual Inventory System

DATE	ACCOUNTS	DR.	CR.
Jul 25	Accounts Payable—CellTel, Inc.	980	
	($1,000 + $80 − $100)		
	Inventory [($1,000 − $100) × 0.02]		18
	Cash ($1,000 + $80 − $100 − $18)		962
	Record payment of inventory purchases within the discount period.		

Periodic Inventory System

DATE	ACCOUNTS	DR.	CR.
Jul 25	Accounts Payable—CellTel, Inc.	980	
	($1,000 + $80 − $100)		
	Purchase Discounts [($1,000 − $100) × 0.02]		18
	Cash ($1,000 + $80 − $100 − $18)		962
	Record payment of inventory puchases within the discount period.		

FOB Destination

Under FOB destination, the seller pays to ship the goods to the destination requested by the customer. If Cosmic Cellular purchased goods under these terms, it has no shipping costs to record because the supplier pays the freight.

Costs Related to Delivering Goods to Customers

The cost of shipping goods to customers is recorded in an expense account titled Delivery Expense. This cost occurs when the seller agrees to shipping terms of FOB destination. Delivery Expense is an expense on the income statement and, as an expense account, normally has a debit balance.

Let's see how the sale of goods and payment of shipping costs affect Cosmic Cellular in different situations. Rob Macklin, a frequent customer at Cosmic Cellular, has an account with the store. Rob buys a Bluetooth headset as a Christmas gift for his sister who lives in Vancouver. Cosmic purchases the head set for $45 and sells it to Rob for $100. Shipping costs to Vancouver total $15.

FOB Destination

Let's assume that Cosmic advertises that shipping costs are free with any purchase of $100 or more. Assume Rob buys the headset on November 30 and charges it to his account. He asks Cosmic to ship it to Vancouver. Cosmic records the sale and payment of shipping costs as follows:

Perpetual Inventory System

DATE	ACCOUNTS	DR.	CR.
Nov 30	Accounts Receivable—Rob Macklin	100	
	Sales Revenue		100
	Cost of Goods Sold	45	
	Inventory		45
	Record sale of inventory on account.		

Periodic Inventory System

DATE	ACCOUNTS	DR.	CR.
Nov 30	Accounts Receivable—Rob Macklin	100	
	Sales Revenue		100
	Record sale of inventory on account.		

Perpetual Inventory System

DATE	ACCOUNTS	DR.	CR.
Nov 30	Delivery Expense	15	
	Cash		15
	Record shipping on sale.		

Periodic Inventory System

DATE	ACCOUNTS	DR.	CR.
Nov 30	Delivery Expense	15	
	Cash		15
	Record shipping on sale.		

In this case, income from the sale is $40 ($100 – $45 – $15).

FOB Shipping Point

Now, let's assume that Cosmic does not offer free shipping. Because Cosmic sold the goods FOB shipping point, Rob pays for the shipping costs. Rob purchases the headset on November 30 and takes it home to wrap and send with another gift. Cosmic would record the sale as follows:

Perpetual Inventory System

DATE	ACCOUNTS	DR.	CR.
Nov 30	Accounts Receivable—Rob Macklin	100	
	Sales Revenue		100
	Cost of Goods Sold	45	
	Inventory		45
	Record sale of inventory on account.		

Periodic Inventory System

DATE	ACCOUNTS	DR.	CR.
Nov 30	Accounts Receivable—Rob Macklin	100	
	Sales Revenue		100
	Record sale of inventory on account.		

In this situation, income from the sale would be $55 ($100 – $45).

FOB Shipping Point, Seller Agrees to Prepay the Shipping Costs

Now assume that Rob buys the headset on November 30 and asks Cosmic to ship it to Vancouver for him. Again, because the goods are sold FOB shipping point, Rob is responsible for the shipping charges. In this case, Cosmic pays for shipping the goods and adds the cost to Rob's invoice. Cosmic records the sale, including the payment of shipping costs, as follows:

Perpetual Inventory System

DATE	ACCOUNTS	DR.	CR.
Nov 30	Accounts Receivable—Rob Macklin	100	
	Sales Revenue		100
	Cost of Goods Sold	45	
	Inventory		45
	Record sale of inventory on account.		

Periodic Inventory System

DATE	ACCOUNTS	DR.	CR.
Nov 30	Accounts Receivable—Rob Macklin	100	
	Sales Revenue		100
	Record sale of inventory on account.		

Perpetual Inventory System

DATE	ACCOUNTS	DR.	CR.
Nov 30	Accounts Receivable—Rob Macklin	15	
	Cash		15
	Record prepayment of shipping costs.		

Periodic Inventory System

DATE	ACCOUNTS	DR.	CR.
Nov 30	Accounts Receivable—Rob Macklin	15	
	Cash		15
	Record prepayment of shipping costs.		

Income from the sale is again $55 ($100 – $45). The $15 Cosmic paid to ship the headset to Vancouver is not an expense as it will be reimbursed by Rob. A comparison reveals that the income from the sale under FOB shipping point remains the same whether or not Cosmic prepays the shipping charges:

	FOB destination	FOB Shipping Point	FOB Shipping Point, Seller Prepays
Sales Revenue	$100	$100	$100
– Cost of Goods Sold	(45)	(45)	(45)
– Delivery Expense	(15)	—	—
= Income from Sale	$ 40	$ 55	$ 55

Other Selling Costs

Selling expenses represent the costs associated with advertising and selling inventory. Examples of selling expenses usually found on a merchandiser's income statement include the following:

- Sales salaries, wages, and commissions
- Advertising and promotion
- Depreciation for the use of stores, parking lots, counters, displays, shelves, vehicles of salespeople, and storage space (such as warehouses and refrigerators)
- Delivery of merchandise to customers

As we will see in the next section, selling expenses are a deduction when arriving at the net income of a merchandiser.

Exhibit 5-7 summarizes the comparison of the purchases-related journal entries using the perpetual inventory system and the periodic inventory system:

Perpetual Inventory System	DR.	CR.	Periodic Inventory System	DR.	CR.
Inventory	xxxx		Purchases	xxxx	
Accounts Payable		xxxx	Accounts Payable		xxxx
Record purchase of inventory on account.			Record purchase of inventory on account.		
Accounts Payable	xx		Accounts Payable	xx	
Inventory		xx	Purchase Returns and Allowances		xx
Record inventory returned to manufacturer.			Record inventory returned to manufacturer.		
Inventory	xx		Transportation-in	xx	
Cash		xx	Cash		xx
Record payment for transportation			Record payment for transportation		
Accounts Payable	xxxx		Accounts Payable	xxxx	
Inventory		xx	Purchase Discounts		xx
Cash		xxxx	Cash		xxxx
Record payment of inventory purchases within the discount period.			Record payment of inventory purchases within the discount period.		

Exhibit 5-7 ▲

Note that when using the perpetual inventory system, the Inventory account is used to record Purchases, Purchase Returns and Allowances, Purchase Discounts, and Transportation-in; when using the periodic inventory system, all the purchase-related activities are recorded in separate accounts.

Exhibit 5-8 summarizes the comparison of the sales-related journal entries using the perpetual inventory system and the periodic inventory system:

Step 1 Perpetual Inventory System AND Periodic Inventory System	DR.	CR.	Step 2 Perpetual Inventory System Only (Inventory Adjustments)	DR.	CR.
Accounts Receivable	xxxx		Cost of Goods Sold	xxxx	
Sales		xxxx	Inventory		xxxx
To record the sales of inventory			To record the purchase of inventory		
Sales Returns and Allowances	xx		Inventory	xx	
Accounts Receivable		xx	Cost of Goods Sold		xx
Record receipt of returned goods			Record receipt of returned goods		
			No entry if goods are defective		
Cash	xxxx				
Sales Discounts	xx				
Accounts Receivable		xxxx			
Record payment received					

Exhibit 5-8 ▲

Note that regardless of which inventory system is used, the seller has to record the first step—the sales-related activities. Only in the perpetual inventory system does the seller need to record the second step to update the inventory activities, such as the reduction of inventory when it is sold and the increase of inventory when it is returned by the customer.

CRITICAL THINKING

Take a minute to think about the impact of the following independent cases on each of the assets, liabilities, and shareholders' equity accounts, based on each of the scenarios. Examine the impact of the cost of the inventory only.

1. Using the periodic inventory method, the sale of inventory for $7,000 (with a cost of $5,000) on account was recorded, but the cost of inventory was not recorded.

2. Using the perpetual inventory method, the sale of inventory for $8,500 (with a cost of $6,200) on account was recorded, but the cost of inventory was not recorded.

3. Using the perpetual inventory method, the purchase of inventory with a term FOB shipping point, the shipping cost of $500 on account was recorded in the Shipping Expense account.

4. Using the perpetual inventory method, a purchase discount of $250 was recorded in the Purchase Discounts account.

Solutions:

Impact on Accounts			
Assets	Liabilities	Shareholders' Equity	Entry in Accounting Record
1. No	No	No	This is correct—no entry is required for the inventory update since the periodic system is used.
2. + 6,200	No	+ 6,200	Assets and Shareholders' Equity would be overstated because the change in inventory was not recorded. The correct entry should include: Cost of Goods Sold (Dr); Inventory (Cr) in the amount of $6,200.
3. – 500	No	– 500	Assets and Shareholders' Equity would be understated because the cost of the shipping should have been included in the inventory account rather than in a shipping expense account. To correct the entry, the buyer should record the adjusting entry: Inventory (Dr); Shipping Expense (Cr)
4. + 250	No	+ 250	Assets and Shareholders' Equity would be overstated because the discount should have reduced the Inventory account instead of going into a contra account against purchases. To correct the entry, the buyer should record the adjusting entry: Purchase Discounts (Dr); Inventory (Cr)

HOW DO YOU PREPARE A MERCHANDISER'S FINANCIAL STATEMENTS?

The Income Statement

In earlier chapters, you learned how to complete the financial statements for a service business. Most service businesses use a **single-step income statement**. The single-step income statement groups all revenues together and all expenses together. Then, the total expenses are subtracted from total revenues in a single step without calculating any subtotals. The advantage of the single-step format is that it clearly distinguishes revenues from expenses. Although Cosmic Cellular is a merchandiser, Exhibit 5-9 illustrates its income statement for the year ended December 31, 2013, prepared using the single-step format. We focus on the first part of the comprehensive income statement, Income Statement. The second part of the comprehensive income statement, Other Comprehensive Income, will be covered in higher-level accounting courses.

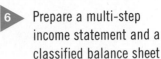

6 Prepare a multi-step income statement and a classified balance sheet

Cosmic Cellular, Inc. Income Statement Year Ended December 31, 2013		
Revenues:		
Net Sales Revenue		$167,900
Expenses:		
Cost of Goods Sold	$90,300	
Selling Expenses	1,200	
General and Administrative Expenses	19,650	
Interest Expense	1,100	
Total Expenses		112,250
Net Income		$ 55,650

Exhibit 5-9 ▲

Most merchandisers use a **multi-step income statement**. The multi-step income statement is prepared in steps. Important subtotals are computed as part of the calculation of net income or net loss. Investors prefer this format because it provides step-by-step information about the profitability of the business. This format makes it more useful for managers within the business as well as investors outside of the business. The multi-step income statement for most merchandisers will contain most, but not necessarily all, of the following items:

■ **Net Sales Revenue** is presented first, and is calculated by subtracting both Sales Returns and Allowances and Sales Discounts from Sales Revenue. Keep in mind that a company may not offer its customers any sales discounts. Also, even if sales discounts are offered, customers may not take advantage of them. Therefore, it is possible that no sales discounts will appear on a company's income statement.

■ The cost of the merchandise that is sold appears next as Cost of Goods Sold. Remember, with the perpetual inventory method, cost of goods sold is already known as this is recorded with the sales transactions; however, if the periodic inventory method is used, then cost of goods sold needs to be calculated.

- **Gross Profit**, also called **Gross Margin**, is a subtotal computed next. The gross profit equals Net Sales Revenue minus Cost of Goods Sold.

- **Operating Expenses** are the expenses, other than cost of goods sold, of operating the business. Operating Expenses are listed after Gross Profit. Many companies report operating expenses in two categories:

  1. Selling Expenses include sales salaries, commissions, advertising, promotion, depreciation for items used in sales, and delivery costs to customers.

  2. **General and Administrative Expenses** include office expenses, such as the salaries of the company president and office employees, depreciation of items used in administration, rent, utilities, and property taxes on the office building.

- On the multi-step income statement, Gross Profit minus Operating Expenses equals **Operating Income**, or **Income from Operations**. Operating income measures the results of the entity's primary, ongoing business activities.

- The last section of a multi-step income statement is **Other Revenues and Expenses**. This category reports revenues and expenses that fall outside of a business's main operations. Examples include interest revenue, interest expense, dividend revenue, and gains and losses on the sale of long-term assets. Because not every business has revenues and expenses outside its business operations, not all income statements will include this section.

- The last line of the multi-step income statement is Net Income or Net Loss. To calculate, add Other Revenues and subtract Other Expenses from Operating Income. The final results of operations, net income or net loss, is a company's *bottom line,* a commonly used business term.

Cosmic Cellular's multi-step income statement for the year ended December 31, 2013, appears in **Exhibit 5-10** along with the statement of retained earnings and the balance sheet.

After you review Cosmic Cellular's multi-step income statement in Exhibit 5-10, look again at its single-step version in Exhibit 5-9. Notice that in both formats net income is exactly the same. The format of the income statement does not change the net income or net loss of a business. It simply changes how the calculation of net income or net loss is presented.

DECISION GUIDELINES

Decision	**Guideline**	**Analyze**
I have an appointment at the bank to request a new loan. Which format of financial statement should I use?	The choice of the format for the statement depends on who the intended users of the financial statements are.	The *single-step format* shows the calculation of net income or net loss by subtracting all expenses from all revenues in a single step. The single-step format typically shows summary information and is intended for users who do not need much detail. This format would not be a good format for creditors or investors to use but it would be great to use in a press release or newspaper article.
		The *multi-step format* shows the calculation of net income or net loss in a series of steps with subtotals for *gross profit* and *operating income.* This format shows detailed information and is best suited for creditors and investors.

Cosmic Cellular, Inc.
Income Statement
Year Ended December 31, 2013

Sales Revenue		$171,300	
Less: Sales Returns and Allowances		3,400	
Net Sales Revenue			$167,900
Cost of Goods Sold			90,300
Gross Profit			77,600
Operating Expenses:			
Selling Expenses:			
Advertising	$ 1,000		
Delivery Expense	200	1,200	
General and Administrative Expenses:			
Wage Expense	10,200		
Rent Expense	7,300		
Insurance Expense	1,000		
Depreciation Expense, Office Equipment	600		
Supplies Expense	550	19,650	20,850
Operating Income			56,750
Other Revenues and (Expenses):			
Interest Expense			(1,100)
Net Income			$ 55,650

Cosmic Cellular, Inc.
Statement of Retained Earnings
Year Ended December 31, 2013

Retained Earnings, December 31, 2012	$ 20,900
Add: Net Income	55,650
Subtotal	76,550
Less: Dividends	55,900
Retained Earnings, December 31, 2013	$ 20,650

Cosmic Cellular, Inc.
Classified Balance Sheet
December 31, 2013

ASSETS			LIABILITIES		
Current Assets:			Current Liabilities:		
Cash	$ 3,150		Accounts Payable	$30,000	
Accounts Receivable	4,600		Wages Payable	400	
Supplies	100		Unearned Sales Revenue	700	
Inventory	39,700		Total Current Liabilities		$31,100
Prepaid Insurance	200		Long-Term Liabilities		
Total Current Assets		$47,750	Mortgage Payable		10,000
Long-Term Assets:			Total Liabilities		41,100
Office Equipment	32,000				
Less: Accumulated			SHAREHOLDERS'		
Depreciation, Office			EQUITY		
Equipment	3,000	29,000	Common Shares	15,000	
			Retained Earnings	20,650	
			Total Equity		35,650
			Total Liabilities &		
Total Assets		$76,750	Shareholders' Equity		$76,750

Exhibit 5-10 ▲

The Statement of Retained Earnings

A merchandiser's statement of retained earnings, which is one component of the Statement of Equity, looks exactly like that of a service business. Cosmic's statement of retained earnings is presented in Exhibit 5-10.

The Balance Sheet

To provide more useful information, merchandisers, as well as most service businesses, usually prepare a **classified balance sheet**. A classified balance sheet lists assets in classes in the order of their **liquidity**. Liquidity refers to how close an asset is to becoming cash or being used up. Similar to the assets, the liabilities are listed in classes based on how soon the obligation will be paid or fulfilled. By listing the assets and liabilities in these classes, financial statement users can better analyze the business's ability to pay its bills on time.

Assets

The most liquid assets are presented on a classified balance sheet in a class called Current Assets. Current Assets are assets that will be converted to cash, sold, or used up during the next 12 months or within a business's normal **operating cycle** if longer than one year.

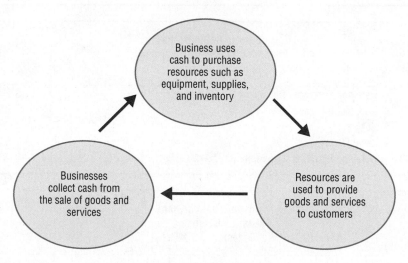

The Operating Cycle

For most businesses, the operating cycle is a few months. Cash, Accounts Receivable, Notes Receivable due within one year, and Prepaid Expenses are all current assets. If the business is a merchandiser, then the major difference between its balance sheet and that of a service business is that it also shows Inventory as a current asset.

All assets other than current assets are reported in a class called long-term assets. One category of long-term assets is called **plant assets** or **fixed assets**. This category is labelled on the balance sheet as **property, plant, and equipment**. Land, buildings, furniture, fixtures, and equipment are examples of these assets.

Liabilities

The debts or obligations of a business that must be paid for or fulfilled within one year (or within the entity's operating cycle if the cycle is longer than a year) are reported in a class called current liabilities. Accounts Payable, Notes Payable due within one year, Salary Payable, Interest Payable, and Unearned Revenue are current liabilities.

Obligations that extend beyond one year are reported as **long-term liabilities**. Often, a business owner signs a contract to repay a note or mortgage over several years. The portion of the note or mortgage that must be paid within one year is classified as a current liability. However, the remaining balance is a long-term liability.

The balance sheet for Cosmic Cellular is presented in Exhibit 5-10. Cosmic's balance sheet is presented in **account form**. The account form lists the assets on the left and the liabilities and shareholders' equity on the right, just as these accounts appear in the accounting equation. It is also acceptable to present the balance sheet in **report form**, which lists the assets at the top and the liabilities and shareholders' equity on the bottom.

FOCUS ON DECISION MAKING: RATIOS

The Gross Profit Percentage

Gross profit, also called gross margin, is a key tool in evaluating merchandising operations. Remember that gross profit is net sales revenue minus the cost of goods sold. Thus, gross profit is the amount left over from sales after deducting the cost of the merchandise sold. Merchandisers strive to maximize gross profit to help maximize net income. The **gross profit percentage**, also called the **gross margin percentage**, shows how well a merchandising business meets this goal. The gross profit percentage measures the relationship between gross profit and sales.

The gross profit percentage is one of the most carefully watched measures of profitability by investors and business managers. This information is used to compare changes in gross profit from year to year for the business. Also, it is used to compare the company to other businesses in the same industry. For most businesses, the gross profit percentage changes little from year to year. To investors, a significant change in the gross profit percentage signals a significant change in the business's operations meriting further investigation.

To compute the gross profit percentage, divide gross profit by net sales revenue. Based on information provided from the income statement in Exhibit 5-10, the gross profit percentage for Cosmic Cellular is 46.2%, calculated as follows:

7 ▸ Compute the gross profit percentage and the current ratio

$$\text{Gross Profit Percentage} = \frac{\text{Gross Profit}}{\text{Net Sales Revenue}} = \frac{\$77,600}{\$167,900} = 0.462 = 46.2\%$$

A 46.2% gross margin percentage means that each dollar of net sales generates 46.2 cents of gross profit. Every time Cosmic Cellular sells $1 of merchandise, it produces 46.2 cents of gross profit that hopefully covers operating expenses and generates net income.

The Current Ratio

The **current ratio** is one of the most widely used tools by investors, creditors, and suppliers. They use the current ratio to evaluate a company's ability to pay its obligations as they come due. The granting of credit is often based upon a company having a strong current ratio. The current ratio measures a company's ability to pay its current liabilities by comparing those liabilities to its current assets. The formula for calculating the current ratio is as follows:

$$\text{Current Ratio} = \text{Current Assets}/\text{Current Liabilities}$$

A high current ratio is desired because that means a company has plenty of current assets to pay its current liabilities. An increasing current ratio over time indicates improvement in a company's ability to pay current debts. A general benchmark is that a strong current ratio is 1.50. This indicates that the company has $1.50 in current assets for every $1.00 in current liabilities. A company with a current ratio of 1.50 would probably have little trouble paying its current liabilities. A current ratio below 1.00 is considered low.

Based on information provided from the balance sheet in Exhibit 5-10, the current ratio for Cosmic Cellular is 1.54, calculated as follows:

$$\text{Current Ratio} = \frac{\text{Current Assets}}{\text{Current Liabilities}} = \frac{\$47{,}750}{\$31{,}100} = 1.54$$

It appears that Cosmic Cellular should have no trouble paying its obligations as they come due.

DECISION GUIDELINES

Decision

As a supplier, I am looking at a new customer's financial statements to determine whether or not to grant credit for the customer to make purchases. What can I use to to evaluate the company's performance for this decision?

Guideline

Key ratios are often used as a quick way to measure a business's performance.

Analyze

The *gross profit percentage* helps analyze the profitability of a merchandiser. The gross profit percentage provides a measurement of how much of each sales dollar remains after covering the cost of the goods sold.

The *current ratio* can be used to determine a business's ability to pay its obligations as they come due. A current ratio that is above 1.5 is generally considered to be good. However, if a current ratio gets too high it can be an indicator that the business has too much tied up in current assets and, therefore, is not utilizing its assets as effectively as it could be.

FOCUS ON USERS

Concept	User	Why is this Important to this User?
Perpetual and Periodic Inventory		Management needs to know whether the inventory amounts that are showing in the general ledger are reliable for decision making. If the company uses a perpetual system, then the inventory account is continually updated and will only be missing any details for inventory that has disappeared but not been sold (stolen, damaged, etc.). If the company uses a periodic system, then a visual inspection or manual count of the inventory would be needed to know the amount in inventory.
Free On Board (FOB)		It is important to management to understand what is included in the ending inventory amounts so that management can plan for inventory purchases in the next month. For any purchases that have been sold and are in the process of being delivered, the FOB details need to be known to understand if these items are included in the ending inventory account. If the items were sold FOB destination, then the ending inventory amounts will still include these items even though they have been sold.
		Similar to managers, creditors need to understand the composition of the ending inventory, but creditors would want to know this information because the inventory may be used as collateral for loans.
Multi-Step Income Statement		Shareholders and potential investors will closely examine a multi-step income statement for details on gross profit. Gross profit shows how much the company has to contribute to expenses after the cost of the inventory sold is deducted. The gross profit percentage would be compared to other companies in the same industry, which can help determine the strategy of the company as either a high-volume low-price strategy (such as a dollar store or discount retailer) or as a low-volume high-price strategy (such as a high-quality brand retailer).
		Creditors would be interested in the operating income amount on a multi-step income statement as this gives an indication of how effectively the company operates its normal operations. For example, a pizza company that also has a warehouse that it rents to other companies would show how much it has earned in income from just making and selling pizzas in the operating income.

DEMO DOC

Transaction Analysis for a Merchandiser Using the Perpetual Inventory System

Spokane Paper Products, Inc. had the following transactions in March 2013:

Mar	1	Purchased $1,500 of inventory on account. Terms were 2/10, n/30, FOB destination.
	2	Sold inventory for cash, $800 (cost, $550).
	7	Returned $400 of the inventory purchased on March 1 because it was defective.
	9	Paid supplier for goods purchased on March 1.
	11	Purchased inventory for $1,800 on account. Terms were 3/15, n/30, FOB shipping point.
	14	Paid freight bill on merchandise purchased on March 11, $125.
	18	Sold inventory for $2,200 (cost, $1,500) on account. Terms were 2/10, n/30, FOB shipping point.
	24	Paid supplier for goods purchased on March 11.
	26	The customer from the March 18 sale returned $750 ($500 cost) of goods.
	28	Received cash in full settlement of its account from the customer who purchased inventory on March 18.

Requirement:

❶ Journalize these transactions by using the perpetual inventory system. Omit explanations.

Demo Doc Solution

Requirement ❶

Journalize these transactions. Omit explanations.

Part 1	Demo Doc Complete

Mar 1   Purchased $1,500 of inventory on account. Terms were 2/10, n/30, FOB destination.

The purchase of inventory causes the Inventory account to increase by $1,500. The Inventory account is an asset and is, therefore, increased with a debit. Because the purchase was made on account, Accounts Payable is increased (credited) by $1,500. The credit terms are not relevant until the *payment* is made to the supplier. The freight terms indicate that the supplier is responsible for paying the freight charges.

DATE	ACCOUNTS	POST REF.	DR.	CR.
Mar 1	Inventory		1,500	
	Accounts Payable			1,500

Mar 2   Sold inventory for cash, $800 (cost, $550).

Under the perpetual inventory method, the entry required to account for a sale requires two parts. The first part of the entry is required to record the recognition of revenue. Because the sale was a cash sale, the Cash account is increased (debited) by $800. When merchandise is sold (and delivered) to a customer, the company earns sales revenue. By selling merchandise, Spokane

Paper Products, Inc. has earned sales revenue of $800. Therefore, Sales Revenue is increased (credited) by $800.

The second part of the entry is required to record the cost of the goods sold. The Cost of Goods Sold account is increased (debited) for $550 (Spokane Paper Products' cost of the merchandise). Remember, Cost of Goods Sold is an *expense*. Because goods from inventory were given to the customer, the Inventory account is decreased (credited) by $550.

DATE	ACCOUNTS	POST REF.	DR.	CR.
Mar 2	Cash		800	
	Sales Revenue			800
	Cost of Goods Sold		550	
	Inventory			550

Mar 7   Returned $400 of the inventory purchased on March 1 because it was defective.

Because Spokane Paper Products, Inc. has not yet paid for the purchase, the return of the merchandise will result in a $400 decrease (debit) to Accounts Payable. Also, because the goods were returned to the supplier, the Inventory account will be decreased (credited) by $400.

DATE	ACCOUNTS	POST REF.	DR.	CR.
Mar 7	Accounts Payable		400	
	Inventory			400

Mar 9   Paid supplier for goods purchased on March 1.

Because the original purchase was made on account, we need to consider the credit terms, which were 2/10, n/30. Because Spokane Paper Products, Inc. is paying within the 10-day discount period, it is entitled to take a 2% discount. However, the discount does not apply to the $400 of goods that Spokane Paper Products, Inc. has returned. It only applies to the net account payable that Spokane Paper Products, Inc. owes after the return.

Original purchase price of goods	$1,500
Less amount of goods returned	$ 400
Net account payable................................	$1,100

The discount, and the amount of cash paid, is calculated as follows:

Net account payable.............	$ 1,100
Less 2% discount	$ (22) (2% × $1,100)
Total cash paid	$ 1,078

Accounts Payable is decreased (debited) by the remaining amount due of $1,100. The cash account will be decreased (credited) by the $1,078 of cash paid. The $22 difference is the discount and is treated as a reduction to the Inventory account because it represents a reduction in the cost of the inventory. So, Inventory is decreased (credited) by the $22 amount of the discount.

DATE	ACCOUNTS	POST REF.	DR.	CR.
Mar 9	Accounts Payable		1,100	
	Cash			1,078
	Inventory			22

Mar 11 Purchased inventory for $1,800 on account. Terms were 3/15, n/30, FOB shipping point.

The purchase of inventory causes the Inventory account to increase (debit) by $1,800. Because the purchase was made on account, Accounts Payable is increased by $1,800 with a credit. The credit terms are not relevant until the *payment* is made to the supplier. The freight terms indicate that the Spokane Paper Products, Inc. is responsible for paying the freight charges.

DATE	ACCOUNTS	POST REF.	DR.	CR.
Mar 11	Inventory		1,800	
	Accounts Payable			1,800

Mar 14 Paid freight bill on merchandise purchased on March 11, $125.

The shipping terms of FOB shipping point means that Spokane Paper Products, Inc. is responsible for paying the freight charges. Because the freight charges represent an increase in the cost of the inventory to Spokane Paper Products, the Inventory account will be increased (debited) by $125. Cash will be decreased (credited) by $125.

DATE	ACCOUNTS	POST REF.	DR.	CR.
Mar 14	Inventory		125	
	Cash			125

Mar 18 Sold inventory for $2,200 (cost, $1,500) on account. Terms were 2/10, n/30, FOB shipping point.

Remember, under the perpetual inventory method, the entry required to account for a sale requires two parts. The first part of the entry is required to record the recognition of revenue. Because the sale was on account, the Accounts Receivable account is increased (debited) by $2,200. Sales revenue is increased (credited) by $2,200. The second part of the entry is required to record the cost of the goods sold. The Cost of Goods Sold account is increased (debited) for $1,500 and Inventory is decreased (credited) by $1,500.

DATE	ACCOUNTS	POST REF.	DR.	CR.
Mar 18	Accounts Receivable		2,200	
	Sales Revenue			2,200
	Cost of Goods Sold		1,500	
	Inventory			1,500

Mar 24 Paid supplier for goods purchased on March 11.

Because the original purchase was made on account, we need to consider the credit terms, which were 3/15, n/30. Because Spokane Paper Products, Inc. is paying within the 15-day discount period, it is entitled to take a 3% discount. There were no returns related to this purchase so the discount, and the amount of cash paid, is calculated as follows:

Net account payable	$ 1,800
Less 3% discount (3% × $1,800)	$ (54)
Total cash paid	$ 1,746

Accounts Payable is decreased (debited) by the amount due of $1,800. The Cash account will be decreased (credited) by the $1,746 of cash paid. The $54 difference is the discount and is treated as a reduction to the Inventory account because it represents a reduction in the cost of the inventory. So, Inventory is decreased (credited) by the $54 amount of the discount.

DATE	ACCOUNTS	POST REF.	DR.	CR.
Mar 24	Accounts Payable		1,800	
	Cash			1,746
	Inventory			54

Mar 26 The customer from the March 18 sale returned $750 ($500 cost) of goods.

Just as the sale of goods under the perpetual inventory method requires a two-part entry, so does the return of goods from a customer. The first part of the entry "undoes" the sale and is recorded by increasing (debiting) the contra-account Sales Returns and Allowances by $750. The customer has not yet paid the account, so the return of the goods will result in a decrease (credit) to Accounts Receivable for $750. The second part of the entry will record the physical return of the goods. The Inventory account is increased (debited) by $500, the value of the goods returned and put back for resale. Because the goods were returned and were put back for resale, they are no longer "sold," so the Cost of Goods Sold account is decreased (credited) by $500.

DATE	ACCOUNTS	POST REF.	DR.	CR.
Mar 26	Sales Returns and Allowances		750	
	Accounts Receivable			750
	Inventory		500	
	Cost of Goods Sold			500

Mar 28 Received cash in full settlement of its account from the customer who purchased inventory on March 18.

Because the original purchase was made on account, we need to consider the credit terms, which were 2/10, n/30. Because the customer is paying within the 10-day discount period, he or she is entitled to take a 2% discount. However, the discount does not apply to the $750 of goods that the customer returned. It only applies to the net account receivable that the customer still owes to Spokane Paper Products, Inc. after the return.

Original sales price of goods....................	$2,200
Less amount of goods returned...............	$ 750
Net account receivable............................	$1,450

The discount, and the amount of cash Spokane Paper Products, Inc. receives, is calculated as follows:

Net account receivable............................	$ 1,450
Less 2% discount (2% × $1,450).............	$ (29)
Total cash received..................................	$ 1,421

The cash account will be increased (debited) by the $1,421 of cash received. The amount of the discount, $29, is recorded as an increase (debit) to the contra-account, Sales Discounts. Accounts Receivable is decreased (credited) by the net account receivable of $1,450.

DATE	ACCOUNTS	POST REF.	DR.	CR.
Mar 28	Cash		1,421	
	Sales Discounts		29	
	Accounts Receivable			1,450

Demo Doc Complete

Part 1	Demo Doc Complete

DECISION GUIDELINES

Accounting for a Merchandising Business

As a merchandiser, you might be faced with decisions such as the following:

Decision	**Guideline**	**Analyze**
Which inventory system should my business use?	This decision depends on whether or not you plan on utilizing a computer system to help with inventory management.	The *perpetual system* shows the current, correct amounts of inventory on hand and the cost of goods sold at all times. The *periodic system* requires that a physical count of the inventory be taken to know the correct balances of inventory and cost of goods sold. Before computers, only businesses that sold smaller quantities of higher cost items could use the perpetual method. Today, thanks to computers and other technology, most companies utilize the perpetual method even if they sell a high quantity of low cost items.
I have an appointment at the bank to request a new loan. Which format of financial statement should I use?	The choice of the format for the statement depends on the intended users of the financial statements.	The *single-step format* shows the calculation of net income or net loss by subtracting all expenses from all revenues in a single step. The single-step format typically shows summary information and is intended for users who do not need much detail. This format would not be a good format for creditors or investors to use but it would be great to use in a press release or newspaper article. The *multi-step format* shows the calculation of net income or net loss in a series of steps with subtotals for *gross profit* and *operating income*. This format shows detailed information and is best suited for creditors and investors.
As a supplier, I am looking at a new customer's financial statements to determine whether or not to grant credit for the customer to make purchases. What can I use to to evaluate the company's performance for this decision?	Key ratios are often used as a quick way to measure a business's performance.	The *gross profit percentage* helps analyze the profitability of a merchandiser. The gross profit percentage provides a measurement of how much of each sales dollar remains after covering the cost of the inventory. The *current ratio* can be used to determine a business's ability to pay its obligations as they come due. A current ratio that is above 1.5 is generally considered to be good. However, if a current ratio gets too high it can be an indicator that the business has too much tied up in current assets and, therefore, is not utilizing its assets as effectively as it could be.

ACCOUNTING VOCABULARY
THE LANGUAGE OF BUSINESS

Account form (p. 299) A balance sheet format that lists assets on the left of the report and liabilities and shareholders' equity on the right, just as those accounts appear in the accounting equation.

Classified balance sheet (p. 298) A balance sheet that separates assets and liabilities into current and long-term classes.

Cost of Goods Sold (p. 283) The cost of the inventory that the business has sold to customers.

Credit memorandum (p. 285) A document that supports the return of goods from the customer and the adjustment to the customer's account balance.

Credit terms (p. 279) The payment terms for customers who buy on account.

Current ratio (p. 299) The ratio of current assets to current liabilities; a key measure of liquidity.

Debit memorandum (p. 279) A document that supports the return of goods to the supplier and the adjustment to the balance owed to the supplier.

Discount period (p. 280) Period in which the buyer can make early payment for a purchase and receive a discount on that purchase.

eom (p. 279) Credit term specifying that payment for a purchase is due by the end of the month; also referred to as *n/eom*.

Fixed assets (p. 298) The long-lived assets of a business including land, buildings, furniture, fixtures, and equipment; also called *plant assets* and commonly shown on the balance sheet as property, plant, and equipment.

Free on board (FOB) destination (p. 288) A shipping term specifying that title to goods passes to the buyer when the goods are received at the buyer's destination; thus, the seller pays the cost of shipping the goods to this destination.

Free on board (FOB) shipping point (p. 288) A shipping term specifying that title to goods passes to the buyer when the goods are shipped at the seller's place of business; thus, the buyer pays the cost of shipping the goods to its location.

Freight charges (p. 288) The cost of shipping merchandise from the seller to the buyer.

General and Administrative Expenses (p. 296) Office expenses, such as the salaries of the company president and office employees, depreciation of items used in administration, rent, utilities, and property taxes on the office building.

Gross Margin (p. 296) Net sales revenue minus cost of goods sold; also called *gross profit*.

Gross margin percentage (p. 299) A measure of profitability equal to gross margin divided by net sales revenue; also called *gross profit percentage*.

Gross Profit (p. 296) Net sales revenue minus cost of goods sold; also called *gross margin*.

Gross profit percentage (p. 299) A measure of profitability equal to gross profit divided by net sales revenue; also called *gross margin percentage*.

Income from Operations (p. 296) Gross profit minus operating expenses; also called *operating income*.

Inventory (p. 276) Goods purchased for resale to customers in the normal course of merchandising operations; also called *merchandise inventory*.

Liquidity (p. 298) The ability to convert an asset to cash quickly.

Long-term liabilities (p. 299) Liabilities other than those that are current.

Merchandise Inventory (p. 276) Goods purchased for resale to customers in the normal course of merchandising operations; also called *inventory*.

Multi-step income statement (p. 295) Income statement format that calculates net income or net loss by listing important subtotals, such as gross profit and operating income.

n/30 (p. 279) Credit term specifying that payment for a purchase is due within 30 days after the date of the invoice.

n/eom (p. 279) Credit term specifying that payment for a purchase is due by the end of the month; also referred to as *eom*.

Net Sales Revenue (p. 295) Sales revenue less sales discounts and sales returns and allowances.

Operating cycle (p. 298) The time span during which the business obtains resources, uses them to sell goods and services to customers, and collects cash from these customers.

Operating expenses (p. 296) Expenses of operating a business other than cost of goods sold. Examples include depreciation, rent, salaries, utilities, advertising, delivery expense, property taxes, and supplies expense.

Operating Income (p. 296) Gross profit minus operating expenses. Also called *income from operations*.

Other Revenues and Expenses (p. 296) Revenues and expenses that fall outside the main operations of a business, such as interest expense and a loss on the sale of long-term assets.

Periodic inventory system (p. 276) An inventory system in which the business does not keep a continuous record of inventory on hand. At the end of the period, a physical count of inventory is taken and determines the inventory owned as well as the cost of the goods sold.

Perpetual inventory system (p. 277) An inventory system in which the business keeps a continuous record of inventory on hand and the cost of the goods sold.

Plant assets (p. 298) The long-lived assets of a business including land, buildings, furniture, fixtures, and equipment; also called *fixed assets* and commonly shown on the balance sheet as property, plant, and equipment.

Property, plant, and equipment (p. 298) A heading often seen on the balance sheet used to describe fixed, or plant, assets.

Purchase discount (p. 277) Discount received on purchases by paying early within a discount period.

Purchase returns and allowances (p. 277) A reduction in the amount owed for a purchase due to returning merchandise or accepting damaged goods.

Report form (p. 299) A balance sheet format that reports assets at the top of the report, followed by liabilities, and ending with shareholders' equity at the end of the report.

Retailers (p. 276) Businesses that buy goods from manufacturers or wholesalers and resell them to the general public.

Sales Discount (p. 286) Discount granted on sales for the customer's early payment within a discount period; a contra-account to Sales Revenue.

Sales invoice (p. 279) A bill that documents the sale of goods to a business customer.

Sales Returns and Allowances (p. 285) A reduction in the amount of sales due to customers returning merchandise or accepting damaged goods; a contra-account to Sales Revenue.

Sales revenue (p. 283) The amount that a retailer earns from selling its inventory.

Selling expenses (p. 292) Expenses related to advertising and selling products including sales salaries, sales commissions, advertising, depreciation on items used in sales, and delivery expense.

Single-step income statement (p. 295) Income statement format that groups all revenues together and lists all expenses together, subtracting total expenses from total revenues and calculating net income or net loss without computing any subtotals.

Subsidiary ledger (p. 278) An accounting record that contains details, such as a list of customers and the accounts receivable due from each, or a list of suppliers and the accounts payable due to each.

Title (p. 288) Ownership.

MyAccountingLab

Make the grade with MyAccountingLab. The exercises and problems in this chapter can be found on MyAccountingLab at www.myaccountinglab.com. You can practise them as often as you want, and they feature step-by-step guided solutions to help you find the right answer.

ACCOUNTING PRACTICE

DISCUSSION QUESTIONS

1. What accounts will appear on the financial statements of a merchandiser that will not appear on those of a service-oriented company?

2. What are some reasons why a merchandiser might prefer to use a perpetual inventory system over a periodic inventory system?

3. Why do businesses use subsidiary ledgers?

4. What do the terms 2/10, n/30 mean? If you were advising a company who bought goods under these terms, what would you advise it to do with respect to payment? Why?

5. How many accounts are involved in recording the sale of merchandise on credit?

6. What kind of account is Sales Returns and Allowances? Where would it appear on the financial statements?

7. What is a debit memorandum? What is a credit memorandum? Give an example of the types of transactions for which each would be used.

8. What does the term "free on board" mean? Why is this an important term to understand if you are involved in making decisions about the purchasing of inventory or the setting of prices for your products?

9. What is the difference between a single-step and multi-step income statement? For what type of business is a multi-step income statement most appropriate?

10. What situation might explain why a company's gross profit percentage went down from 60% to 40% from one year to the next?

SELF CHECK

1. Which account does a merchandiser use that a service company does not use?

   a. Cost of goods sold
   b. Inventory
   c. Sales revenue
   d. All of the above ·

2. The two main inventory accounting systems are the

   a. perpetual and periodic.
   b. purchase and sale.
   c. returns and allowances.
   d. cash and accrual.

3. Which of the following journal entries for the purchase of $900 of inventory on account, using the perpetual inventory system, is correct?

DATE	ACCOUNTS	POST REF.	DR.	CR.
a.	Cost of Goods Sold		900	
	Accounts Payable			900
b.	Inventory		900	
	Accounts Payable			900
c.	Accounts Payable		900	
	Inventory			900
d.	Inventory		900	
	Cash			900

4. Apex Electrical Supply, Inc. purchased inventory for $2,000 and also paid $125 freight to have the inventory delivered. Apex Electrical Supply, Inc. returned $500 of the goods to the seller and later took a 2% purchase discount. What is the final cost of the inventory that Apex Electrical Supply, Inc. kept?

   a. $2,083
   b. $2,085
   c. $1,595
   d. $1,593

5. Suppose Bonzai Boards, Inc. had sales of $180,000 and sales returns of $22,000. Cost of goods sold was $110,000. How much gross profit did Bonzai Boards, Inc. report?

   a. $48,000
   b. $70,000
   c. $92,000
   d. $158,000

6. Suppose Apex Electrical Supply's Inventory account showed a balance of $43,000. A physical count showed $41,800 of goods on hand. To adjust the inventory account, Apex Electrical Supply, Inc. would make which of the following entries:

DATE	ACCOUNTS	POST REF.	DR.	CR.
a.	Cost of Goods Sold		1,200	
	Inventory			1,200
b.	Accounts Payable		1,200	
	Inventory			1,200
c.	Inventory		1,200	
	Cost of Goods Sold			1,200
d.	Inventory		1,200	
	Accounts Payable			1,200

7. If Bonzai Boards, Inc. returned $3,600 of snowboards to a supplier it would record the transaction as which of the following?

DATE	ACCOUNTS	POST REF.	DR.	CR.
a.	Cost of Goods Sold		3,600	
	Inventory			3,600
b.	Accounts Payable		3,600	
	Sales Returns and Allowances			3,600
c.	Inventory		3,600	
	Accounts Payable			3,600
d.	Accounts Payable		3,600	
	Inventory			3,600

8. An asset is classified as current if it
  a. was purchased within the last six months.
  b. will become cash, be sold, or be used up within 12 months.
  c. was purchased with cash.
  d. will last longer than one year.

9. The income statement format that shows important subtotals is referred to as
  a. a classified income statement.
  b. a single-step income statement.
  c. a multi-step income statement.
  d. a subtotalled income statement.

10. Suppose Bonzai Boards, Inc. had sales of $210,000 and sales returns of $18,000. Cost of goods sold was $125,000. What was Bonzai Boards' gross profit percentage (rounded) for this period?
  a. 35%
  b. 54%
  c. 40%
  d. 32%

Answers are given after Written Communication.

SHORT EXERCISES

S5-1. Inventory methods (*Learning Objective 2*) 5–10 min.

The following characteristics are related to either periodic inventory or perpetual inventory systems.

a. A physical count of goods on hand at year end is required.

b. Inventory records are continuously updated.

c. Purchases of inventory are recorded in an asset account at the time of purchase.

d. Bar code scanners are often utilized when using this inventory system.

e. It is necessary to calculate the cost of goods sold at the end of the year with this inventory system.

Identify each characteristic as one of the following:

a. Periodic inventory.

b. Perpetual inventory.

c. Both periodic and perpetual inventory.

d. Neither periodic nor perpetual inventory.

S5-2. Adjusting inventory based on a physical count (*Learning Objective 2*) 5–10 min.

Charleston's Furniture uses the perpetual inventory method. At the end of the year, Charleston's Furniture's Inventory account had a ledger balance of $87,000. A physical inventory count revealed that the actual inventory on hand totaled $85,300.

Journalize the transaction necessary to adjust the Inventory account at the end of the year.

S5-3. Journalizing inventory purchases (*Learning Objective 3*) 5–10 min.

Suppose Sports-R-Us purchases $40,000 of sportswear on account from Pacific Trail on March 1, 2013. Credit terms are 2/10, net 30. Sports-R-Us pays Pacific Trail on March 8, 2013.

1. Journalize the transactions for Sports-R-Us on March 1, 2013, and March 8, 2013, using (1) the perpetual system and (2) the periodic inventory system.

2. What was the final cost of this inventory for Sports-R-Us?

S5-4. Inventory purchases and returns (*Learning Objective 3*) 5–10 min.

Sonny's Spas, Inc. purchased $8,000 worth of inventory from the Pool Warehouse on account, terms of 2/10, n/30. Some of the goods are damaged in shipment, so Sonny's Spas, Inc. returns $1,100 of the merchandise to the Pool Warehouse.

How much must Sonny's Spas, Inc. pay the Pool Warehouse

1. after the discount period?

2. within the discount period?

S5-5. Journalizing inventory purchases and returns (*Learning Objective 3*) 5–10 min.

Sonny's Spas, Inc. purchased $8,000 worth of inventory from the Pool Warehouse on account, terms of 2/10, n/30. Some of the goods are damaged in shipment, so Sonny's Spas, Inc. returns $1,100 of the merchandise to the Pool Warehouse.

Journalize the following transactions, using (1) the perpetual system and (2) the periodic inventory system, for Sonny's Spas, Inc. Explanations are not required.

a. Purchase of the goods

b. Return of the damaged goods

c. Payment for the goods within the discount period

S5-6. Journalizing inventory purchases and freight charges (*Learning Objectives 3 & 5*) 5–10 min.

Journalize the following transactions, using (1) the perpetual system and (2) the periodic inventory system, for the Jazz Man music store.

   a. Purchased $8,700 of merchandise on account, terms 2/10, n/30, FOB shipping point.

   b. Paid $175 to the freight company for the delivery of the merchandise purchased.

   c. Paid for the inventory purchased in Part a within the discount period.

S5-7. Journalizing sales transactions (*Learning Objective 4*) 5–10 min.

Journalize the following transactions for the Pool Warehouse. Explanations are not required.

   a. The Pool Warehouse sold $55,000 of merchandise to Sonny's Spas, Inc. on account, terms 2/15, n/30. The merchandise cost the Pool Warehouse $30,250.

   b. Received payment for the goods from Sonny's Spas, Inc. within the discount period.

S5-8. Journalizing sales and return transactions (*Learning Objective 4*) 5–10 min.

Suppose Peter's Hardware sells merchandise on account, terms 2/10, n/45, for $750 (cost of the inventory is $460) on May 17, 2013. Peter's Hardware later received $225 of goods (cost, $140) as sales returns on May 21, 2013. The customer paid the balance due on May 26, 2013.

Journalize the May, 2013 transactions, using (1) the perpetual system and (2) the periodic inventory system, for Peter's Hardware.

S5-9. Calculate income statement items (*Learning Objective 6*) 5–10 min.

Suppose Peter's Hardware sells merchandise on account, terms 2/10, n/45, for $750 (cost of the inventory is $460) on May 17, 2013. Peter's Hardware later received $225 of goods (cost, $140) as sales returns on May 21, 2013. The customer paid the balance due on May 26, 2013.

   1. Calculate net sales revenue for May 2013.

   2. Calculate gross profit for May 2013.

   3. Calculate the effective interest rate for the saving, if Peter's Hardware makes the payment within the discount period.

S5-10. Calculate classified balance sheet amounts (*Learning Objective 6*) 5–10 min.

Selected account balances for Jill's Java at the end of the month are listed below in random order:

Accounts Payable	$19,500
Unearned Revenue	2,000
Equipment	33,000
Inventory	37,000
Accounts Receivable	6,000
Wages Payable	1,500
Note Payable, Long-Term	28,000
Accumulated Depreciation, Equipment	4,500
Common Shares	25,000
Supplies	3,400
Building	87,000
Cash	5,200
Accumulated Depreciation, Building	24,000
Prepaid Rent	6,200
Retained Earnings	15,000

Identify or compute the following amounts for Jill's Java:

  a. Total current assets

  b. Total current liabilities

  c. Book value of plant assets

  d. Total long-term liabilities

S5-11. Prepare a multi-step income statement (*Learning Objective 6*) 10–15 min.

The accounting records for ADR, Inc. reflected the following amounts at the end of August 2013:

Cash	$3,500	Cost of Goods Sold	$19,500
Total Operating Expenses	3,700	Equipment, Net	6,100
Accounts Payable	4,500	Accrued Liabilities	1,900
Total Shareholders' Equity	5,200	Net Sales Revenue	28,000
Long-Term Notes Payable	2,300	Accounts Receivable	2,900
Inventory	1,700	Prepaid Rent	800
Wages Payable	1,100		

Prepare ADR's multi-step income statement for the fiscal year ended August 31, 2013.

S5-12. Prepare a classified balance sheet (*Learning Objective 6*) 10–15 min.

The accounting records for ADR, Inc. reflected the following amounts at the end of August 2013:

Cash	$3,500	Cost of Goods Sold	$19,500
Total Operating Expenses	3,700	Equipment, Net	6,100
Accounts Payable	4,500	Accrued Liabilities	1,900
Total Shareholders' Equity	5,200	Net Sales Revenue	28,000
Long-Term Notes Payable	2,300	Accounts Receivable	2,900
Inventory	1,700	Prepaid Rent	800
Wages Payable	1,100		

Prepare the ADR, Inc. classified balance sheet at August 31, 2013. Use the report format.

S5-13. Calculate gross profit and current ratio (*Learning Objective 7*) 10–15 min.

The accounting records for ADR, Inc. reflected the following amounts at the end of August, 2013:

Cash	$3,500	Cost of Goods Sold	$19,500
Total Operating Expenses	3,700	Equipment, Net	6,100
Accounts Payable	4,500	Accrued Liabilities	1,900
Total Shareholders' Equity	5,200	Net Sales Revenue	28,000
Long-Term Notes Payable	2,300	Accounts Receivable	2,900
Inventory	1,700	Prepaid Rent	800
Wages Payable	1,100		

Calculate the gross profit percentage and current ratio for 2013.

EXERCISES (GROUP A)

E5-1A. Adjusting inventory based on a physical count (*Learning Objective 2*) 5–10 min.

The Inventory account for McCormack Tire Company had a balance of $112,600 at the end of its fiscal year. A physical count taken at year end revealed that the value of inventory on hand amounted to $110,800.

Requirements

1. Journalize the adjustment for inventory shrinkage.

2. What could cause the inventory balance according to the physical count to be different from the ledger balance?

E5-2A. Journalizing inventory purchases, returns, and freight transactions (*Learning Objectives 3 & 5*) 10–15 min.

On June 15, 2013, Bailey's Department Store purchased $4,300 of inventory on account from one of its suppliers. The terms were 3/15, n/45, FOB shipping point. On June 18 Bailey's Department Store paid freight charges of $350 related to the delivery of the goods purchased on June 15. Upon receiving the goods, Bailey's Department Store checked the order and found $900 of unsuitable merchandise, which was returned to the supplier on June 20. Then, on June 28, Bailey's Department Store paid the invoice.

Requirement

1. Journalize all necessary transactions for Bailey's Department Store, using (1) the perpetual inventory system, and (2) the periodic inventory system. Omit explanations.

E5-3A. Journalizing inventory purchases, returns, and freight transactions (*Learning Objective 3 & 5*) 10–15 min.

Journalize the following transactions for Amazing Audio, Inc. that occurred during the month of March, using (1) the perpetual inventory system, and (2) the periodic inventory system. Omit explanations.

Mar	3	Purchased $4,600 of merchandise on account, terms 2/10, n/30, FOB shipping point. The supplier prepaid freight charges of $250 and added the amount to the invoice.
	6	Returned damaged goods to the supplier and received a credit memorandum in the amount of $600.
	12	Paid for the goods purchased on March 3.

E5-4A. Journalizing inventory sales, returns, and freight transactions (*Learning Objectives 4 & 5*) 10–15 min.

On September 14, 2013, C & T Machinery, Inc. sold $2,300 of inventory (cost is $1,350) on account to one of its customers. The terms were 1/10, n/30, FOB destination. On September 16, C & T Machinery, Inc. paid freight charges of $75 related to the delivery of the goods sold on September 14. On September 20, $900 of damaged goods (cost is $540) were returned by the customer. On September 23, C & T Machinery, Inc. received payment in full from the customer.

Requirement

1. Journalize all necessary transactions for C & T Machinery, Inc. using (1) the perpetual inventory system, and (2) the periodic inventory system. Omit explanations.

E5-5A. Journalizing inventory sales, returns, and freight transactions (*Learning Objectives 4 & 5*) 10–15 min.

Journalize the following transactions for Amazing Audio, Inc. that occurred during the month of November using (1) the perpetual inventory system and (2) the periodic inventory system. Omit explanations. Amazing Audio's cost of inventory is 65% of the sales price.

Nov	3	Sold $1,600 of merchandise on account, terms 2/15, n/45, FOB shipping point. Amazing Audio, Inc. prepaid $85 of shipping costs and added the amount to the customer's invoice.
	7	Issued a credit memo to the customer acknowledging the return of $250 of damaged goods.
	16	Received payment in full from the customer for the November 3 invoice.

E5-6A. Journalizing inventory purchases, sales, returns, and freight transactions (*Learning Objectives 3, 4, & 5*) 15–20 min.

The following transactions occurred during April 2013 for Angelo's Garden Centre, Inc.:

Apr	3	Purchased $3,500 of goods on account, terms 2/10, n/30, FOB shipping point.
	6	Returned $400 of defective merchandise purchased on April 3.
	8	Paid freight charges of $110 for delivery of goods purchased on April 3.
	11	Sold $4,300 of inventory to a customer on account, terms 3/15, n/45, FOB shipping point. The cost of the goods was $2,100.
	12	Paid amount owed on the April 3 purchase.
	18	Granted a $300 sales allowance on the April 11 sale because the goods were the wrong colour.
	25	Received payment in full from customer for the April 11 sale.

Requirement

1. Journalize all necessary transactions for Angelo's Garden Centre, Inc. using (1) the perpetual inventory system, and (2) the periodic inventory system. Omit explanations.

E5-7A. Calculate multi-step income statement items (*Learning Objective 6*) 10–15 min.

Consider the following incomplete table of a merchandiser's profit data:

Sales	Sales Discounts	Net Sales	Cost of Goods Sold	Gross Profit
$ (a)	$2,500	$ (b)	$68,300	$32,100
64,000	1,700	(c)	44,600	(d)
102,000	(e)	93,500	(f)	28,600
(g)	2,100	86,300	57,700	(h)

Requirement

1. Complete the table by computing the missing amounts.

E5-8A. Prepare a single-step income statement (*Learning Objective 6*) 10–15 min.

The account balances for Atlantis Aquatics, Inc. for the year ended December 31, 2013, are presented next in random order:

Cash.......................................	$ 3,700	Cost of Goods Sold..................	$136,400
Equipment..............................	13,700	Accumulated Depreciation,	
Accounts Payable...................	4,500	Equipment...........................	6,100
Common Shares....................	35,000	Unearned Revenues................	1,900
Long-Term Notes Payable......	10,000	Sales Revenue.........................	243,500
General Expenses...................	18,200	Accounts Receivable...............	3,200
Wages Payable.......................	1,100	Accumulated Depreciation,	
Supplies.................................	900	Building..............................	18,500
Building..................................	125,000	Mortgage Payable	
Sales Returns and		(Long-Term)......................	37,000
Allowances.........................	4,800	Dividends..............................	34,000
Prepaid Rent..........................	800	Sales Discounts.......................	2,200
Retained Earnings..................	13,800	Selling Expenses.....................	26,800
Inventory................................	1,700		

Quick solution:

1. Net Income = $55,100.

Requirements

1. Prepare Atlantis Aquatics' *single-step* income statement.
2. Would you recommend the use of the single-step income statement format by a merchandiser? Why?

E5-9A. Prepare a multi-step income statement; calculate gross profit percentage (*Learning Objectives 6 & 7*) 15–20 min.

Use the data for Atlantis Aquatics, Inc. from E5-8A.

Requirements

1. Prepare Atlantis Aquatics' *multi-step* income statement.
2. Calculate the gross profit percentage.
3. The gross profit percentage for 2012 was 38.7%. Did the gross profit percentage improve or deteriorate during 2013?

E5-10A. Prepare a classified balance sheet; calculate current ratio (*Learning Objectives 6 & 7*) 15–20 min.

Use the data for Atlantis Aquatics, Inc. from E5-8A.

Requirements

1. Prepare Atlantis Aquatics' classified balance sheet. Use the account format. The balance shown for retained earnings represents the balance prior to closing the temporary accounts for the year.

2. Calculate the current ratio.

3. The current ratio for 2012 was 1.25. Did the current ratio improve or deteriorate during 2013?

E5-11A. Calculate gross profit percentage and current ratio (*Learning Objective 7*) 10–15 min.

Apex, Inc. had sales revenue of $47 million, sales returns and allowances of $2 million, and sales discounts of $0.5 million in 2013. Cost of goods sold was $24 million, and net income was $7 million for the year. At December 31, the company had total assets of $36 million, of which total current assets amounted to $15 million. Apex's current liabilities were $9 million and its long-term liabilities were $4 million.

Requirement

1. Compute Apex's gross profit percentage and current ratio for 2013.

EXERCISES (GROUP B)

E5-1B. Adjusting inventory based on a physical count (*Learning Objective 2*) 5–10 min.

The Inventory account for Brady Company had a balance of $137,900 at the end of its fiscal year. A physical count taken at year end revealed that the value of inventory on hand amounted to $136,400.

Requirements

1. Journalize the adjustment for inventory shrinkage.

2. What could cause the inventory balance according to the physical count to be different from the ledger balance?

E5-2B. Journalizing inventory purchases, returns, and freight transactions (*Learning Objectives 3 & 5*) 10–15 min.

On November 15, 2013, Chandler's Department Store purchased $5,100 of inventory on account from one of its suppliers. The terms were 3/15, n/45, FOB shipping point. On November 18 Chandler's Department Store paid freight charges of $175 related to the delivery of the goods purchased on November 15. Upon receiving the goods, Chandler's Department Store checked the order and found $600 of unsuitable merchandise, which was returned to the supplier on November 20. Then, on November 28, Chandler's Department Store paid the invoice.

Requirement

1. Journalize all necessary transactions for Chandler's Department Store, using (1) the perpetual inventory system, and (2) the periodic inventory system. Omit explanations.

E5-3B. Journalizing inventory purchases, returns, and freight transactions (*Learning Objectives 3 & 5***) 10–15 min.**

Journalize the following transactions for Antique Furniture, Inc. that occurred during the month of January. Omit explanations using (1) the perpetual inventory system and (2) the periodic inventory system.

Jan	3	Purchased $5,700 of merchandise on account, terms 1/10, n/30, FOB shipping point. The supplier prepaid freight charges of $225 and added the amount to the invoice.
	6	Returned damaged goods to the supplier and received a credit memorandum in the amount of $500.
	12	Paid for the goods purchased on January 3.

E5-4B. Journalizing inventory sales, returns, and freight transactions (*Learning Objectives 4 & 5***) 10–15 min.**

On November 14, 2013, Amazing Sound, Inc. sold $3,100 of inventory (cost is $1,330) on account to one of its customers. The terms were 3/10, n/30, FOB destination. On November 16, Amazing Sound, Inc. paid freight charges of $65 related to the delivery of the goods sold on November 14. On November 20, $800 of damaged goods (cost is $420) were returned by the customer. On November 23, Amazing Sound, Inc. received payment in full from the customer.

Requirement

1. Journalize all necessary transactions for Amazing Sound, Inc. using (1) the perpetual inventory system and (2) the periodic inventory system. Omit explanations.

E5-5B. Journalizing inventory sales, returns, and freight transactions (*Learning Objectives 4 & 5***) 10–15 min.**

Journalize the following transactions for Antique Furniture, Inc. that occurred during the month of April using (1) the perpetual inventory system and (2) the periodic inventory system. Antique Furniture's cost of inventory is 70% of the sales price.

Apr	3	Sold $2,100 of merchandise on account, terms 1/15, n/45, FOB shipping point. Antique Furniture, Inc. prepaid $50 of shipping costs and added the amount to the customer's invoice.
	7	Issued a credit memo to the customer acknowledging the return of $225 of damaged goods.
	16	Received payment in full from the customer for the April 3 invoice.

E5-6B. Journalizing inventory purchases, sales, returns, and freight transactions (*Learning Objectives 3, 4, & 5***) 15–20 min.**

The following transactions occurred during April 2013, for Sandy Salon Products, Inc.:

Apr	3	Purchased $3,400 of goods on account, terms 1/15, n/30, FOB shipping point.
	6	Returned $500 of defective merchandise purchased on April 3.
	8	Paid freight charges of $130 for delivery of goods purchased on April 3.
	11	Sold $2,800 of inventory to a customer on account, terms 3/15, n/45, FOB shipping point. The cost of the goods was $1,600.
	12	Paid amount owed on the April 3 purchase.
	18	Granted a $225 sales allowance on the April 11 sale because the goods were the wrong colour.
	25	Received payment in full from customer for the April 11 sale.

Requirement

1. Journalize all necessary transactions for Sandy Salon Products, Inc. using (1) the perpetual inventory system, and (2) the periodic inventory system. Omit explanations.

E5-7B. Calculate multi-step income statement items (*Learning Objective 6*) 10–15 min.

Consider the following incomplete table of a merchandiser's profit data:

Sales	Sales Discounts	Net Sales	Cost of Goods Sold	Gross Profit
$ (a)	$1,700	$ (b)	$67,500	$37,700
89,600	2,900	(c)	55,700	(d)
103,000	(e)	94,300	(f)	31,500
(g)	1,400	88,000	51,900	(h)

Requirement

1. Complete the table by computing the missing amounts.

E5-8B. Prepare a single-step income statement (*Learning Objective 6*) 10–15 min.

The account balances for Great Gadget, Inc. for the year ended December 31, 2013, are presented next in random order:

Cash...	$ 9,300	Cost of Goods Sold................	$135,000
Equipment...............................	39,800	Accumulated Depreciation,	
Accounts Payable....................	6,300	Equipment.........................	13,700
Common Shares	25,000	Unearned Revenues	1,900
Long-Term Notes Payable.......	35,000	Sales Revenue........................	257,000
General Expenses...................	18,200	Accounts Receivable..............	4,500
Wages Payable........................	1,300	Accumulated Depreciation,	
Supplies	3,300	Building.............................	25,900
Building..................................	130,000	Mortgage Payable	
Sales Returns and		(Long-Term)	43,500
Allowances........................	2,900	Dividends..............................	41,000
Prepaid Rent	2,600	Sales Discounts	1,500
Retained Earnings..................	25,700	Selling Expenses...................	43,500
Inventory.................................	3,700		

Requirements

1. Prepare Great Gadget's *single-step* income statement.
2. Would you recommend the use of the single-step income statement format by a merchandiser? Why?

E5-9B. Prepare a multi-step income statement; calculate gross profit percentage (*Learning Objectives 6 & 7*) 15–20 min.

Use the data for Great Gadget, Inc. from E5-8B.

Requirements

1. Prepare Great Gadget's *multi-step* income statement.
2. Calculate the gross profit percentage.
3. The gross profit percentage for 2012 was 52.3%. Did the gross profit percentage improve or deteriorate during 2013?

E5-10B. Prepare a classified balance sheet; calculate current ratio (*Learning Objectives 6 & 7*) **15–20 min.**

Use the data for Great Gadget, Inc. from E5-8B.

Requirements

1. Prepare Great Gadget's classified balance sheet. Use the account format. The balance shown for retained earnings represents the balance prior to closing the temporary accounts for the year.

2. Calculate the current ratio.

3. The current ratio for 2012 was 3.62. Did the current ratio improve or deteriorate during 2013?

E5-11B. Calculate gross profit percentage and current ratio (*Learning Objective 7*) **10–15 min.**

Sunny Day Sunlamps, Inc. had sales revenue of $53 million, sales returns and allowances of $2 million, and sales discounts of $0.3 million in 2013. Cost of goods sold was $23 million, and net income was $12 million for the year. At December 31, the company had total assets of $33 million, of which total current assets amounted to $13 million. Sunny Day Sunlamps' current liabilities were $7 million and its long-term liabilities were $4 million.

Requirement

1. Compute Sunny Day Sunlamps' gross profit percentage and current ratio for 2013.

EXERCISES (ALTERNATES 1, 2, AND 3)

These alternative exercise sets are available for your practice benefit at **www.myaccountinglab.com**

PROBLEMS (GROUP A)

P5-1A. Journalizing inventory purchases, returns, and freight transactions (*Learning Objective 3 & 5*) **15–20 min.**

The following purchase-related transactions for Axiom, Inc. occurred during the month of February.

Feb	3	Purchased $5,400 of merchandise, paid cash.
	9	Purchased $650 of supplies on account from Supplies Unlimited, terms n/30, FOB destination.
	16	Purchased $6,800 of merchandise on account from A to Z, Inc., terms 2/15, n/30, FOB shipping point.
	22	Received a credit memo in the amount of $1,200 from A to Z, Inc. for damaged goods from the February 16 purchase that were returned.
	28	Paid for the supplies purchased on February 9.
	28	Paid A to Z, Inc. in full for the February 16 purchase.

Requirement

1. Journalize all necessary transactions for Axiom, Inc. using (1) the perpetual inventory system, and (2) the periodic inventory system. Omit explanations.

P5-2A. Journalizing inventory sales, returns, and freight transactions (*Learning Objectives 3 & 5*) 15–20 min.

The following sale-related transactions for PDR, Inc. occurred during the month of June.

Jun 3	Sold $3,200 (cost $2,100) of merchandise on account to J. Henderson, terms 2/15, n/45, FOB destination.
4	Paid $250 to ship the goods sold on June 3 to J. Henderson.
10	Sold $1,800 (cost $1,200) of merchandise to cash customers.
17	Received payment in full from J. Henderson for the June 3 sale.
22	Sold $4,700 (cost $3,100) of merchandise to M. Perez, terms 3/10, n/30, FOB shipping point.
26	Granted M. Perez a $600 allowance on the June 22 sale due to minor defects in the goods shipped.
30	Received payment in full from M. Perez for the June 22 sale.

Requirement

1. Journalize all necessary transactions for PDR, Inc. using (1) the perpetual inventory system, and (2) the periodic inventory system. Omit explanations.

P5-3A. Journalizing inventory purchases, sales, returns, and freight transactions (*Learning Objectives 3, 4, & 5*) 20–25 min.

The following transactions occurred between Kinzer Furniture and M & L Furniture Warehouse during May of the current year:

May 4	Kinzer Furniture purchased $5,800 of merchandise from M & L Furniture Warehouse on account, terms 2/15, n/30, FOB shipping point. The goods cost M & L Furniture Warehouse $3,300.
7	Kinzer Furniture paid a $125 freight bill for delivery of the goods purchased on May 4.
10	Kinzer Furniture returned $1,400 of the merchandise purchased on May 4. The goods cost M & L Furniture Warehouse $800.
18	Kinzer Furniture paid $2,000 of the May 4 invoice less the discount.
31	Kinzer Furniture paid the remaining amount owed on the May 4 invoice.

Requirements

1. Journalize all necessary transactions for Kinzer Furniture, using

   (a) The perpetual inventory system

   (b) The periodic inventory system

2. Journalize these transactions on the books of M & L Furniture Warehouse, using

   (a) The perpetual inventory system

   (b) The periodic inventory system

   Omit explanations.

P5-4A. Journalizing inventory purchases, sales, returns, and freight transactions; calculate gross profit (*Learning Objectives 3, 4, 5, & 6*) 25–30 min.

The following transactions for Liberty Tire, Co. occurred during October:

Oct	4	Purchased $5,900 of merchandise on account from Firerock Tire, terms 2/15, n/45, FOB shipping point. Firerock Tire prepaid the $300 shipping cost and added the amount to the invoice.
	7	Purchased $350 of supplies on account from Office Maxx, terms 2/10, n/30, FOB destination.
	9	Sold $950 (cost, $500) of merchandise on account to L. Simpson, terms 3/15, n/45, FOB destination.
	11	Paid $75 freight charges to deliver goods to L. Simpson.
	13	Returned $1,400 of the merchandise purchased on October 4 and received a credit.
	15	Sold $650 (cost, $350) of merchandise to cash customers.
	16	Paid for the supplies purchased on October 7.
	18	Paid Firerock Tire the amount due from the October 4 purchase in full.
	20	L. Simpson returned $175 (cost, $100) of merchandise from the October 9 sale.
	22	Purchased $2,100 of inventory. Paid cash.
	23	Received payment in full from L. Simpson for the October 9 sale.

Requirements

1. Journalize the transactions on the books of Liberty Tire, Co. using

   (a) The perpetual inventory system

   (b) The periodic inventory system.

2. What was Liberty Tire's gross profit for the month of October?

Quick solution:

2. Gross Profit for the month of October = $651.75.

P5-5A. Prepare a multi-step income statement; calculate gross profit percentage
   (*Learning Objectives 6 & 7*) **20–25 min.**

The adjusted trial balance for Sparky's Electrical Supply, Inc. as of November 30, 2013, is presented next:

		ACCOUNT	DEBIT	CREDIT
		Sparky's Electrical Supply, Inc.		
		Trial Balance		
		November 30, 2013		
		Cash	$ 15,000	
		Accounts Receivable	37,300	
		Inventory	18,500	
		Supplies	900	
		Equipment	68,000	
		Accumulated Depreciation, Equipment		$ 8,000
		Accounts Payable		12,900
		Unearned Sales Revenue		5,300
		Note Payable, Long-Term		15,000
		Common Shares		10,000
		Retained Earnings		73,300
		Dividends	22,000	
		Sales Revenue		193,200
		Sales Returns and Allowances	8,700	
		Sales Discounts	2,600	
		Cost of Goods Sold	103,400	
		Selling Expense	25,200	
		General Expense	16,100	
		Total	$317,700	$317,700

Requirements

1. Prepare the multi-step income statement for November for Sparky's Electrical Supply, Inc.

2. Calculate the gross profit percentage for November for Sparky's Electrical Supply, Inc.

3. What does Sparky's Electrical Supply Inc.'s gross profit percentage mean?

P5-6A. Prepare a multi-step income statement, a statement of retained earnings, and a classified balance sheet (Learning Objective 6) 25–30 min.

The account balances for the year ended December 31, 2013, for Williams Industries are listed next:

Sales Revenue	$322,800	Cost of Goods Sold	$158,400
Equipment	104,000	Accumulated Depreciation,	
Accounts Payable	16,500	Equipment	26,400
Sales Discounts	2,200	Unearned Sales Revenue	2,500
Advertising Expense	12,600	Prepaid Rent	1,200
Interest Expense	1,700	Office Salaries Expense	52,000
Wages Payable	1,600	Accumulated Depreciation,	
Accounts Receivable	6,900	Building	40,500
Building	140,000	Rent Expense	5,800
Sales Returns and		Dividends	14,000
Allowances	6,700	Cash	7,800
Common Shares	35,000	Retained Earnings	87,600
Utilities Expense	10,300	Delivery Expense	1,300
Inventory	16,400	Insurance Expense	5,700
Commission Expense	22,300	Mortgage Payable	
Supplies	600	(Long-Term)	37,000

Requirements

1. Prepare Williams' Industries' *multi-step* income statement.
2. Prepare Williams' Industries' statement of retained earnings.
3. Prepare Williams' Industries' classified balance sheet in *report form*.

P5-7A. Calculate gross profit percentage and current ratio (Learning Objective 7) 20–25 min.

The account balances for the year ended December 31, 2013, for Williams Industries are listed next:

Sales Revenue	$322,800	Cost of Goods Sold	$158,400
Equipment	104,000	Accumulated Depreciation,	
Accounts Payable	16,500	Equipment	26,400
Sales Discounts	2,200	Unearned Sales Revenue	2,500
Advertising Expense	12,600	Prepaid Rent	1,200
Interest Expense	1,700	Office Salaries Expense	52,000
Wages Payable	1,600	Accumulated Depreciation,	
Accounts Receivable	6,900	Building	40,500
Building	140,000	Rent Expense	5,800
Sales Returns and		Dividends	14,000
Allowances	6,700	Cash	7,800
Common Shares	35,000	Retained Earnings	87,600
Utilities Expense	10,300	Delivery Expense	1,300
Inventory	16,400	Insurance Expense	5,700
Commission Expense	22,300	Mortgage Payable	37,000
Supplies	600		

Requirements

1. Calculate the gross profit percentage for Williams Industries for the year.
2. The gross profit percentage for 2012 was 51.3%. Did the gross profit percentage improve or deteriorate during 2013?

3. Calculate the current ratio for Williams Industries.

4. The current ratio for 2012 was 1.47. Did the current ratio improve or deteriorate during 2013?

PROBLEMS (GROUP B)

P5-1B. Journalizing inventory purchases, returns, and freight transactions (*Learning Objectives 3 & 5*) 15–20 min.

The following purchase-related transactions for Lavery, Inc. occurred during the month of September.

Sep	3	Purchased $5,100 of merchandise, paid cash.
	9	Purchased $800 of supplies on account from Chandler Unlimited, terms n/30, FOB destination.
	16	Purchased $4,300 of merchandise on account from Garden Supplies, Inc., terms 3/15, n/30, FOB shipping point.
	22	Received a credit memo in the amount of $1,100 from Garden Supplies, Inc. for damaged goods from the Sep 16 purchase that were returned.
	30	Paid for the supplies purchased on Sep 9.
	30	Paid Garden Supplies, Inc. in full for the Sep 16 purchase.

Requirement

1. Journalize all necessary transactions for Lavery, Inc. using (1) the perpetual inventory system, and (2) the periodic inventory system. Omit explanations.

P5-2B. Journalizing inventory sales, returns, and freight transactions (*Learning Objectives 3 & 5*) 15–20 min.

The following sales-related transactions for Beautiful Decor, Inc. occurred during the month of April.

Apr	3	Sold $3,600 (cost $1,700) of merchandise on account to A. Klecans, terms 3/15, n/45, FOB destination.
	4	Paid $75 to ship the goods sold on April 3 to A. Klecans.
	10	Sold $2,700 (cost $1,200) of merchandise to cash customers.
	17	Received payment in full from A. Klecans for the April 3 sale.
	22	Sold $5,100 (cost $2,500) of merchandise to M. Perez, terms 2/10, n/30, FOB shipping point.
	26	Granted M. Perez a $200 allowance on the April 22 sale due to minor defects in the goods shipped.
	30	Received payment in full from M. Perez for the April 22 sale.

Requirement

1. Journalize all necessary transactions for Beautiful Decor, Inc. using (1) the perpetual inventory system, and (2) the periodic inventory system. Omit explanations.

P5-3B. Journalizing inventory purchases, sales, returns, and freight transactions (*Learning Objectives 3, 4, & 5*) 20–25 min.

The following transactions occurred between Retro Furniture and E & S Furniture Warehouse during October of the current year:

Oct 4	Retro Furniture purchased $8,000 of merchandise from E & S Furniture Warehouse on account, terms 1/15, n/30. FOB shipping point. The goods cost E & S Furniture Warehouse $2,900.
7	Retro Furniture paid a $200 freight bill for delivery of the goods purchased on October 4.
10	Retro Furniture returned $1,000 of the merchandise purchased on October 4. The goods cost E & S Furniture Warehouse $450.
18	Retro Furniture paid $2,000 of the October 4 invoice less the discount.
31	Retro Furniture paid the remaining amount owed on the October 4 invoice.

Requirements

1. Journalize all necessary transactions for Retro Furniture, using

   (a) The perpetual inventory system

   (b) The periodic inventory system

2. Journalize these transactions on the books of E & S Furniture Warehouse, using

   (a) The perpetual inventory system

   (b) The periodic inventory system

P5-4B. Journalizing inventory purchases, sales, returns, and freight transactions; calculate gross profit (*Learning Objectives 3, 4, 5, & 6*) 25–30 min.

The following transactions for Best Deal Tire, Co. occurred during May:

May 4	Purchased $5,400 of merchandise on account from Bargain Tire, terms 3/15, n/45, FOB shipping point. Bargain Tire prepaid the $125 shipping cost and added the amount to the invoice.
7	Purchased $375 of supplies on account from Office Maxx, terms 3/10, n/30, FOB destination.
9	Sold $950 (cost, $250) of merchandise on account to W. Furmick, terms 3/15, n/45, FOB destination.
11	Paid $25 freight charges to deliver goods to W. Furmick.
13	Returned $600 of the merchandise purchased on May 4 and received a credit.
15	Sold $900 (cost, $350) of merchandise to cash customers.
16	Paid for the supplies purchased on May 7.
18	Paid Bargain Tire the amount due from the May 4 purchase in full.
20	W. Furmick returned $175 (cost, $100) of merchandise from the May 9 sale.
22	Purchased $3,900 of inventory. Paid cash.
23	Received payment in full from W. Furmick for the May 9 sale.

Requirements

1. Journalize the transactions on the books of Best Deal Tire, Co. using (1) the perpetual inventory system, and (2) the periodic inventory system.

2. What was Best Deal Tire's gross profit for the month of May?

P5-5B. Prepare a multi-step income statement; calculate gross profit percentage (*Learning Objectives 6 & 7*) 20–25 min.

The adjusted trial balance for CED Electric, Inc. as of June 30, 2013, is presented next:

CED Electric, Inc.
Trial Balance
June 30, 2013

ACCOUNT	DEBIT	CREDIT
Cash	$ 13,600	
Accounts Receivable	32,600	
Inventory	19,600	
Supplies	2,600	
Equipment	69,000	
Accumulated Depreciation, Equipment		$ 13,700
Accounts Payable		5,100
Unearned Sales Revenue		2,800
Note Payable, Long-Term		40,000
Common Shares		25,000
Retained Earnings		68,200
Dividends	48,000	
Sales Revenues		197,500
Sales Returns and Allowances	4,800	
Sales Discount	3,100	
Cost of Goods Sold	101,400	
Selling Expense	37,000	
General Expense	20,600	
Total	$352,300	$352,300

Requirements

1. Prepare the multi-step income statement for June for CED Electric, Inc.

2. Calculate the gross profit percentage for June for CED Electric, Inc.

3. What does CED Electric Inc.'s gross profit percentage mean?

P5-6B. Prepare a multi-step income statement, a statement of retained earnings, and a classified balance sheet (*Learning Objective 6*) 25–30 min.

The accounts for the year ended March 31, 2013, for Clark Industries, Inc. are listed next:

Sales Revenue	$275,100	Cost of Goods Sold	$119,000
Equipment	27,000	Accumulated Depreciation,	
Accounts Payable	16,500	Equipment	13,000
Sales Discounts	2,500	Unearned Sales Revenue	2,500
Advertising Expense	11,500	Prepaid Rent	5,000
Interest Expense	700	Office Salaries Expense	54,000
Wages Payable	1,000	Accumulated Depreciation,	
Accounts Receivable	8,800	Building	52,500
Building	190,000	Rent Expense	5,200
Sales Returns and		Dividends	12,000
Allowances	4,900	Cash	22,500
Common Shares	35,000	Retained Earnings	112,800
Utilities Expense	14,000	Delivery Expense	1,200
Inventory	29,000	Insurance Expense	10,200
Commission Expense	31,700	Mortgage Payable	
Supplies	1,200	(Long-Term)	42,000

Requirements

1. Prepare Clark Industries' *multi-step* income statement.
2. Prepare Clark Industries' statement of retained earnings.
3. Prepare Clark Industries' classified balance sheet in *report form*.

P5-7B. Calculate gross profit percentage and current ratio (*Learning Objective 7*) 20–25 min.

The list of accounts and balances for Clark Industries at March 31, 2013, are presented next:

Sales Revenue	$275,100	Cost of Goods Sold	$119,000
Equipment	27,000	Accumulated Depreciation,	
Accounts Payable	16,500	Equipment	13,000
Sales Discounts	2,500	Unearned Sales Revenue	2,500
Advertising Expense	11,500	Prepaid Rent	5,000
Interest Expense	700	Office Salaries Expense	54,000
Wages Payable	1,000	Accumulated Depreciation,	
Accounts Receivable	8,800	Building	52,500
Building	190,000	Rent Expense	5,200
Sales Returns and		Dividends	12,000
Allowances	4,900	Cash	22,500
Common Shares	35,000	Retained Earnings	112,800
Utilities Expense	14,000	Delivery Expense	1,200
Inventory	29,000	Insurance Expense	10,200
Commission Expense	31,700	Mortgage Payable	
Supplies	1,200	(Long-Term)	42,000

Requirements

1. Calculate the gross profit percentage for Clark Industries for the year.
2. The gross profit percentage for 2012 was 39.1%. Did the gross profit percentage improve or deteriorate during 2013?
3. Calculate the current ratio for Clark Industries.
4. The current ratio for 2012 was 2.33. Did the current ratio improve or deteriorate during 2013?

PROBLEMS (ALTERNATES 1, 2, AND 3)

These alternative problem sets are available for your practice benefit at
www.myaccountinglab.com

CONTINUING EXERCISE

Let's continue our accounting for Graham's Yard Care, Inc. from Chapter 3. Starting in July, Graham's Yard Care, Inc. has begun selling plants that it purchases from a wholesaler. During July, Graham's Yard Care, Inc. completed the following transactions:

Jul	2	Completed lawn service and received cash of $500.
	5	Purchased 100 plants on account for inventory, $250, plus freight in of $10.
	15	Sold 40 plants on account, $400 (cost $104).
	17	Consulted with a client on landscaping design for a fee of $150 on account.
	20	Purchased 100 plants on account for inventory, $300.
	21	Paid on account, $100.
	25	Sold 100 plants for cash, $700 (cost $276).
	31	Recorded the following adjusting entries: Accrued salaries for the month of July equal $225 Depreciation on equipment $30 Physical count of plant inventory, 50 plants (cost $150)

Refer to the T-accounts for Graham's Yard Care, Inc. from the Continuing Exercise in Chapter 3.

Requirements

1. Journalize and post the July transactions., using the perpetual inventory system. Omit explanations. Compute each account balance, and denote the balance as *Bal*. Open additional accounts as necessary.

2. Prepare the July income statement of Graham's Yard Care, Inc. using the single-step format.

CONTINUING PROBLEM

In this problem, we continue the accounting for Aqua Elite, Inc. from Chapter 3. On August 1, Aqua Elite, Inc. expanded its business and began selling and installing swimming pools and spas. The post-closing trial balance for Aqua Elite, Inc. as of July 31, 2013, is presented next.

Aqua Elite, Inc. Trial Balance July 31, 2013		
ACCOUNT	**DEBIT**	**CREDIT**
Cash	$17,380	
Accounts Receivable	5,400	
Supplies	350	
Prepaid Rent	3,600	
Land	15,000	
Furniture	3,300	
Accumulated Depreciation, Furniture		$ 210
Equipment	4,700	
Accumulated Depreciation, Equipment		400
Vehicles	31,000	
Accumulated Depreciation, Vehicles		650
Accounts Payable		1,840
Salary Payable		675
Unearned Service Revenue		2,800
Notes Payable		31,000
Common Shares		38,500
Retained Earnings		4,655
Total	$80,730	$80,730

The following transactions occurred during the month of August:

Aug	2	Paid the receptionist's salary, which was accrued on July 31.
	3	Purchased $20,600 of merchandise on account from the Spa Superstore, terms 3/15, n/45, FOB shipping point.
	5	Purchased $750 of supplies. Paid cash.
	6	Paid freight charges of $475 related to the August 3 purchase.
	8	Sold a spa for $5,800 (cost, $3,600) on account to R. Tanaka, terms 2/15, n/30, FOB shipping point.
	10	Purchased office furniture for $1,200. Paid cash.
	11	Paid advertising expense, $625.
	12	Returned a defective spa, which was purchased on August 3. Received a $3,400 credit from the Spa Superstore.
	13	Sold a spa for $6,750 (cost, $3,360) to a cash customer.
	15	Granted R. Tanaka a $300 allowance because of imperfections she detected upon receiving her spa.
	16	Paid receptionist's salary, $675.
	17	Paid the Spa Superstore the amount due from the August 3 purchase in full.
	19	Purchased $12,100 of inventory on account from Pool Universe, terms 2/10, n/30, FOB destination.
	21	Sold an above-ground pool for $13,700 (cost, $8,500) on account to B. Wagoner, terms 2/10, n/30, FOB destination.
	22	Received payment in full from R. Tanaka for the August 8 sale.
	24	Paid freight charges of $560 to have the pool sold to B. Wagoner on August 21 delivered.
	25	Purchased equipment on account from Betterbuy, Inc. for $2,600, terms n/30, FOB destination.
	27	Received payment in full from B. Wagoner for the August 21 sale.
	28	Paid in full the invoice from the August 19 purchase from Pool Universe.
	30	Paid monthly utilities, $850.
	31	Paid sales commissions of $1,300 to the sales staff.

Requirements

1. Journalize the transactions that occurred in August, using the perpetual inventory system.

2. Using the four-column accounts from the continuing problem in Chapter 3, post the transactions to the ledger creating new ledger accounts as necessary; omit posting references. Calculate the new account balances.

3. Prepare the unadjusted trial balance for Aqua Elite, Inc. at the end of August.

4. Journalize and post the adjusting entries for August based on the following adjustment information.

   a. Record the expired rent, $1800.

   b. Supplies on hand, $445.

   c. Depreciation: $575 equipment, $380 furniture, $650 vehicles.

   d. A physical count of inventory revealed $13,387 of inventory on hand.

5. Prepare an adjusted trial balance for Aqua Elite, Inc. at the end of August.

6. Prepare the multi-step income statement, statement of retained earnings, and classified balance sheet for the month of August.

7. Prepare and post closing entries.

8. Prepare a post-closing trial balance for the end of the period.

APPLY YOUR KNOWLEDGE

ETHICS IN ACTION

Case 1. Tim Jackson works as a salesperson at Conway, Inc. In addition to a base monthly salary, Tim receives a commission that is based on the amount of sales that he makes during the month. Tim was hoping to have enough money for a down payment on a new car but sales have been low due to a downturn in the economy. Tim was aware that Conway, Inc. granted credit terms of 2/10, n/30 to its credit customers. In addition, Tim knew that Conway, Inc. had a "no questions asked" return policy. Based on this knowledge, Tim had an idea. Tim contacted a regular customer and convinced the customer to make a substantial purchase of merchandise so that he could earn the commission on the sale. Tim explained to the customer that they would not have to pay for the goods for thirty days and that they could return part, or all, of the goods prior to paying for them. However, Tim asked the customer not to return any of the goods until the following month to ensure that he would earn the full commission.

Requirements

1. Do you feel Tim acted unethically? Why or why not?

2. How can Conway, Inc. deter actions like Tim's?

Case 2. Tina Adams owns and operates the Cottage Café. Tina has requested a credit application from UMT, Inc., a major food supplier, that she hopes to begin purchasing inventory from. UMT, Inc. has requested that Tina submit a full set of financial statements for the Cottage Café with the credit application. Tina is concerned because the most recent balance sheet for the Cottage Café reflects a current ratio of 1.24. Tina has heard that most creditors like to see a current ratio that is 1.5 or higher. To increase the Cottage Café's current ratio, Tina has convinced her parents to loan the business $25,000 on an 18-month long-term note payable. Tina's parents are apprehensive about having their money "tied up" for over a year. Tina reassured them that even though the note is an 18-month note, the Cottage Café can, and probably will, repay the $25,000 sooner.

Requirements

1. Discuss the ethical issues related to the loan from Tina's parents.

2. Why do you think creditors like to see current ratios of 1.5 or higher?

KNOW YOUR BUSINESS

FINANCIAL ANALYSIS

Purpose: To help familiarize you with the financial reporting of a real company to further your understanding of the chapter material you are learning.

This case uses both the income statement (statement of operations) and the balance sheet of Bombardier Inc. in MyAccountingLab.

Requirements

1. What income statement format does Bombardier Inc. use? How can you tell?

2. Calculate the gross profit ratio for Bombardier Inc. for 2011 and 2010. Has the gross profit rate improved or deteriorated? (Hints on how this is calculated were provided in Chapter 2 questions.)

3. Does Bombardier Inc. report a classified balance sheet? How can you tell? Why do you think Bombardier reports the balance sheet in this manner?

INDUSTRY ANALYSIS

Purpose: To help you understand and compare the performance of two companies in the same industry.

Find the Bombardier Annual Report located in MyAccountingLab and go to the financial statements. Now access the 2010 annual report for The Boeing Company. To do this from the internet, go to their webpage for the Investor Relations at *http://www.boeing.com/companyoffices/financial/quarterly.htm* and, under Annual Report, go to the 2010 Annual Report.

Requirements

1. Calculate the current ratio for Boeing for 2010 and 2009. Has the current ratio improved or deteriorated? Comment on how Boeing determines what is in current? (Hint: See Note 1—Operating Cycle). Which balance sheet classification presentation do you find more useful: Boeing's or Bombardier's? Why?

2. Which of these companies is also involved in providing customer financing? How did you determine this? Which accounts on the consolidated balance sheets indicate this? Which accounts on the consolidated statements of income (or operations) might also indicate this?

SMALL BUSINESS ANALYSIS

Purpose: To help you understand the importance of cash flows in the operation of a small business.

The end of the year is approaching. You're going to meet with your CA next week to do some end-of-the-year tax planning, so in preparation for that meeting you look at your last month's income statement. You know that you've had a pretty good year, which means that you're going to have to pay some income taxes. But you know if you can get your taxable income down, you won't have to pay as much in income taxes.

You remember that one of your suppliers was offering a pretty good discount if you purchased from the company in bulk. The only problem is you have to pay for the purchases at the time of purchase. Knowing that you want to decrease your taxable income, you call up the supplier and place a large order and write the supplier a cheque.

At your meeting with the CA, you tell of the large inventory purchase for cash that you just made and how much income tax that will save you on this year's income tax return. The CA has a rather troubled look on his face; that look usually means you've made some kind of an error. So you pose this question to him:

"Steve, you got that look on your face right after I told you about the big inventory purchase that I made. Even though I used up a lot of my available cash, the reason I did it was to save money on my tax return. A big purchase like that has to knock down my taxable income pretty good, huh? And besides, I got these products for a really good price, which means I'll make more profit when I sell them. So why do you have that look? Did I mess up?"

Requirement

1. If you were the CA, how would you respond to this client? Is the large inventory purchase going to have any effect on his income statement? What about the fact that he paid for this large purchase in cash? Was that a good idea to use a large portion of available cash for a purchase like this? Keeping in mind that inventory can have a significant amount of carrying cost (storage, personnel, opportunity cost of the money, etc.) would you tell your client that this was a good thing that he did, or not?

WRITTEN COMMUNICATION

You just got a letter from one of your good customers complaining about the shipment of your product that he or she just received. Football season is approaching and the customer had ordered a large shipment of regulation size footballs. Instead, he or she received youth size footballs for half of the order. The customer is asking you what can be done about this mistake. Knowing that this client is located halfway across the country, it's not feasible to just have him or her drop by your facility and trade the footballs.

The customer also had a question about a line item on his or her invoice under shipping terms. It said FOB Destination and the customer noticed that he or she was charged freight, which the customer normally doesn't have to pay. The customer wants to know if that is correct.

Requirement

1. Write a letter to your customer explaining how you intend to handle this purchase return or this purchase allowance (you choose which one you're going to do). Explain the accounting forms that will need to be prepared to document this transaction. Also address the customer's concern about the shipping terms.

Self Check Answers
1. d 2. a 3. b 4. c 5. a 6. a 7. d 8. b 9. c 10. a

SCAN THIS

CHAPTER 6

Inventory

If you have ever worked in a retail establishment, it is very likely that you have witnessed, or maybe even participated in, the counting of inventory. If so, did you wonder why the inventory had to be counted or what would happen if the count was done incorrectly? Did you ever hear the term FIFO and wonder what it had to do with inventory? Let's explore the answers to these questions in Chapter 6 as we learn how to account for inventory.

CHAPTER OUTLINE:

WHAT INVENTORY COSTING METHODS ARE ALLOWED?

1 Describe the three different inventory costing methods

As discussed in Chapter 5, merchandise inventory represents the goods that a merchandiser has available to sell to its customers. A manufacturer also has goods it holds for sale to its customers. These goods are called **finished goods** inventory. In addition, a manufacturer maintains two other types of inventory: **raw materials** inventory, which it uses to produce the goods it sells, and **work in process** inventory, which represents partially completed goods. In other words, work in process inventory represents goods that are in the process of becoming finished goods. A more detailed discussion of the inventory accounts of a manufacturer will be left to a managerial or cost accounting course. In this chapter, we focus on managing and accounting for inventory in merchandise businesses. Inventory represents a key asset for a merchandiser and is probably the business's largest current asset.

Recall from Chapter 5 that most companies utilize a perpetual inventory system. Under a perpetual system, the cost of goods purchased is added to the Inventory account in the general ledger when goods are purchased. When the goods are sold, the cost of the goods is removed from the Inventory account and added to the Cost of Goods Sold account. Most merchandisers purchase large quantities of identical items. Due to inflation and other market forces, the cost the merchandiser pays for the items often differs from one purchase to the next. This raises an important accounting dilemma. If the goods are identical, but have different costs, how does the business know which costs to remove from the Inventory account and transfer to Cost of Goods Sold at the time merchandise is sold?

According to IFRS and Canadian ASPE, a business can assign costs using one of three different inventory costing methods. The three costing methods allowed by IFRS and Canadian ASPE are as follows:

❶ **Specific-identification** method—Assumes that the cost assigned to an inventory item when it is sold is the actual cost paid for that item. Therefore, the Cost of Goods Sold represents the actual cost of the items that were sold. Also, the Ending Inventory represents the actual cost of the goods remaining in inventory. Under specific-identification, the cost flow of the goods through the accounting records will *exactly* match the physical flow of the goods through the business.

❷ **First-in, first-out (FIFO)** method—Assumes that the earliest inventory costs are assigned to items as they are sold. The Cost of Goods Sold represents the oldest costs incurred to purchase inventory items. The Ending Inventory represents the most recent costs incurred to purchase inventory items.

❸ **Average cost** method—Assumes that an average cost per item of the entire inventory purchased is assigned to items as they are sold. Two types of average cost can be used, depending on whether the company utilizes a perpetual inventory system (moving average cost) or a periodic inventory system (weighted average cost). Both the Cost of Goods Sold and the Ending Inventory represent an average of the cost incurred to purchase inventory items. Under the average cost method, the Cost of Goods Sold does not match the physical flow of goods, but the method smooths the cost fluctuations.

ACCOUNTING IN YOUR WORLD

Does this taste funny to you?

Jill was at the grocery store the other day picking up a container of milk when she started thinking about FIFO, which she had been learning about in her accounting class. It did not make sense to her that any customer would want the company to use FIFO. After all, she reasoned, if the grocery store used FIFO, it would be selling milk that it purchased a while ago and would leave fresh milk on the shelves. Jill wonders how she can be sure that the container of milk she took off the shelf is fresh and not one that has been on the shelf for weeks, or even months.

Jill is confusing the flow of costs through the accounting records with the physical flow of inventory through a store. FIFO refers to the flow of costs through the accounting records and not to the physical flow of goods. The flow of costs through the accounting records can match, or be exactly opposite of, the physical flow of goods through a store. Jill can rest assured that even if the store uses FIFO, her milk is fresh.

Cost Flow Versus Physical Flow of Inventory

The inventory costing method (FIFO, weighted average, etc.) refers to the flow of costs through a merchandiser's accounting records rather than to the physical flow of the goods through the business. The physical flow of the goods through the business will depend on how the goods are stocked and in what order customers, or employees, remove the goods from the shelves when they are sold. The flow of the *costs* through the accounting records will depend upon which inventory costing method the business chooses.

Imagine that every inventory item that is purchased has a yellow sticky note attached to it with the price that was paid for the item written on the sticky note. Next, assume that when the business receives a shipment of inventory items, the sticky notes reflecting the cost of the items are removed from each item and given to the Accounting Department. The Accounting Department will keep track of the sticky notes for each separate purchase in what is referred to as an **inventory layer**. The quantity purchased of each item along with the purchase price is tracked as an inventory layer for every separate purchase.

The physical inventory will most likely be managed in a manner that causes the oldest inventory to be sold first, followed by more recent purchases, and so on. The physical flow of the inventory is maintained in this manner to prevent inventory items from spoiling if they are perishable, or to prevent having items that look outdated should the manufacturer choose to change the packaging of the items. The Accounting Department calculates the cost flow of the inventory without any consideration of the actual physical flow of the merchandise (unless the specific-identification inventory method is used). The Accounting Department only needs to know *how many* units were sold, not *which* units were sold. The Accounting Department then applies the cost flow method to the inventory layers that it has recorded. In other words, the inventory costs are assigned based on the layers of sticky notes. **Exhibit 6-1** demonstrates the difference between cost flow and physical flow.

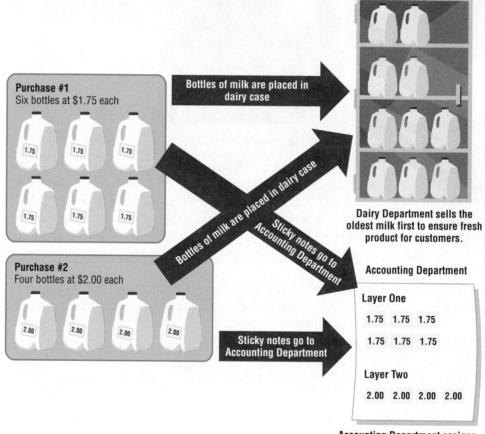

Exhibit 6-1 ▲

DECISION GUIDELINES

Decision	Guideline	Analyze
Decision	**Guideline**	**Analyze**

Decision

The cost of my products will determine the price that I can sell them for as well as impact other decisions. How do I determine the cost of the inventory I sell?

Guideline

The physical flow of the inventory and the cost flow of the inventory can be different. The cost assigned to the units sold may be based on one of the following three methods:

- Specific-identification
- First-in, first-out (FIFO)
- Average cost

Analyze

Specific-identification: Inventory items are specifically labelled or identified and the actual cost of each item sold is assigned to cost of goods sold.

First-in, first-out (FIFO): The first inventory costs incurred are the first costs to be assigned to cost of goods sold.

Average cost: After each purchase of inventory, a new weighted-average cost per unit is computed and assigned to cost of goods sold.

HOW ARE THE THREE INVENTORY COSTING METHODS APPLIED?

Inventory Cost Flows

Recollect from Chapter 5 that, in a perpetual inventory system, purchases of goods for resale increase the balance of the Inventory account, while sales of goods to customers decrease the account. The Inventory account also reflects purchase discounts, purchase returns and allowances, and shipping costs related to the purchase of goods:

> 2 Compute inventory costs using specific-identification; first-in, first-out (FIFO); and average cost methods and journalize inventory transactions

Inventory			
Bal	XX		
Purchases	XX	Purchase Discounts	XX
Shipping	XX	Purchase Returns and Allowances	XX
		Sales	XX
Bal	XX		

The cost of the inventory flows through the Inventory account as items are purchased and sold. The cost of the units on hand in inventory at the beginning of the period is added to the net cost of units purchased for the period to determine the **cost of goods available for sale**. The objective of tracking the inventory cost is to allocate the cost of the goods available for sale between the following:

- Units sold, which is recorded as Cost of Goods Sold and is subtracted from net sales revenue on the income statement to arrive at gross profit.
- Units on hand, or unsold, which is reflected as ending inventory, a current asset on the balance sheet.

Let's follow the September inventory activity for ski parkas sold by Northwest Outfitters, Inc. assuming the following:

Sep 1	One parka costing $40 is on hand, unsold from the previous month.
5	Purchased six parkas for $45 each.
15	Sold four parkas for $80 each.
26	Purchased seven parkas for $50 each.
30	Sold eight parkas for $80 each.
30	Two parkas are on hand, unsold.

During September, Northwest Outfitters had 14 parkas available for sale: 1 unit on hand in beginning inventory plus 13 units purchased during the month. Northwest Outfitters' goods available for sale would be calculated as follows:

Beginning Inventory	(1 @ $40)	= $ 40
+ Purchases	(6 @ $45) = $270	
	(7 @ $50) = 350	620
= Goods Available for Sale		$660

Of the 14 parkas available for sale, Northwest sold 12 parkas and still had 2 parkas on hand in ending inventory at the end of the month. What would be the cost of the goods sold for the month and the ending inventory balance for that month? The answer depends on which inventory costing method Northwest Outfitters elects to use. **Exhibit 6-2** illustrates the objective of calculating inventory costs for Northwest Outfitters.

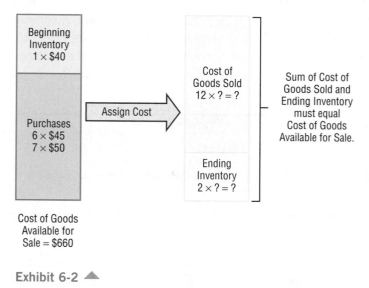

Exhibit 6-2 ▲

As we shall see, the various inventory costing methods produce different values for ending inventory and cost of goods sold.

Specific-Identification Method

The specific-identification method is also called the **specific-unit cost** method. This method values inventory according to the specific cost of each item of inventory. This method is used predominately by businesses that sell unique items with very different costs. Some examples are businesses that sell automobiles, houses, and artwork. For instance, an automobile dealer may have two vehicles on its car lot, a "basic" model that costs

$22,000 and a "fully-equipped" model that costs $29,000. Accordingly, the sales price of the basic model would be less than the sales price for the fully equipped model. It would not make sense for the dealer to assign the cost of the fully equipped model to the basic model when the basic model is sold. This would cause gross profit to be inaccurately stated because the higher cost of the fully equipped model would be subtracted from the lower selling price of the basic model. The dealer would want to specifically identify which model it sold and assign the actual cost of that model to the cost of goods sold. To utilize the specific-identification method, each inventory item must be able to be distinguished from other items with some identifying mark such as a serial number. Because the specific-identification method of inventory valuation is not widely used, we will focus on the more popular inventory costing methods. Let's see how to compute inventory amounts using the FIFO and average cost methods for Northwest Outfitters.

First-In, First-Out (FIFO) Method in a Perpetual Inventory System

Assume that Northwest Outfitters uses the FIFO method to account for its inventory. Under FIFO, the first inventory costs incurred by Northwest each period are the first costs to be assigned to cost of goods sold. *Simply put, FIFO assumes that the first inventory items Northwest purchased are the first inventory items it sold.* To efficiently track inventory costs, a **perpetual inventory record** is often utilized. The perpetual inventory record maintains the detail supporting the quantity of, and costs assigned to, the inventory items as they are purchased and sold. It also maintains a running balance of the inventory on hand. When preparing the perpetual inventory record, it is critical that the inventory "layers" are kept in the proper order. An inventory layer consists of the quantity of inventory and its purchase cost. **Exhibit 6-3** illustrates the FIFO perpetual inventory record for Northwest Outfitters, while **Exhibit 6-4** (on the next page) illustrates the flow of costs using FIFO.

Northwest began September with one parka that cost $40. After the September 5 purchase, the inventory on hand consists of seven units: one at $40 plus six at $45. On September 15, Northwest sold four units. Under FIFO, the cost of the first unit sold is the

Parkas									
	Purchases			**Cost of Goods Sold**			**Inventory on Hand**		
Date	**Quantity**	**Unit Cost**	**Total Cost**	**Quantity**	**Unit Cost**	**Total Cost**	**Quantity**	**Unit Cost**	**Total Cost**
Sep 1							1	$40	$ 40
5	6	$45	$270				1	$40	$ 40
							6	$45	$270
15				1	$40	$ 40			
				3	$45	$135	3	$45	$135
26	7	$50	$350				3	$45	$135
							7	$50	$350
30				3	$45	$135			
				5	$50	$250	2	$50	$100
30	13		$620	12		$560	2		$100

Exhibit 6-3 ▲

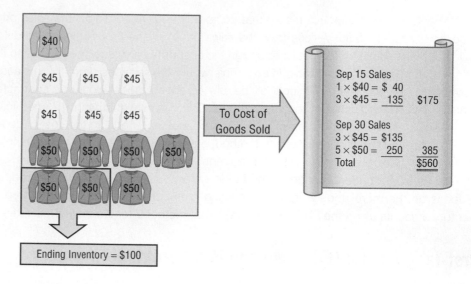

Exhibit 6-4 ▲

oldest cost, $40 per unit. The next three units sold come from the layer that cost $45 per unit. That leaves three units in inventory on hand, and those units cost $45 each. The remainder of the perpetual inventory record is completed in the same manner.

The FIFO monthly summary on September 30 is as follows:

- Cost of Goods Sold: 12 units that cost a total of $560
- Ending Inventory: 2 units that cost a total of $100

Look for these amounts in the last row of the perpetual inventory record in Exhibit 6-3 as well as in Exhibit 6-4. If Northwest uses the FIFO method, it will use these amounts for the cost of goods sold and inventory in its financial statements. Notice that the sum of the cost of goods sold plus ending inventory equals the cost of goods available for sale, $660 ($560 + $100).

Moving Average Cost Method in a Perpetual Inventory System

Suppose Northwest Outfitters uses the average cost method to account for its inventory of parkas. *With this method, the business computes a new, weighted-average cost per unit after each purchase* based on the number of items purchased at each price. Ending inventory and cost of goods sold are then based on the average cost per unit. **Exhibit 6-5** shows a perpetual inventory record for the average cost method. We round average unit cost to the nearest cent and total cost to the nearest dollar.

Parkas									
	Purchases			**Cost of Goods Sold**			**Inventory on Hand**		
Date	Quantity	Unit Cost	Total Cost	Quantity	Unit Cost	Total Cost	Quantity	Unit Cost	Total Cost
Sep 1							1	$40.00	$ 40
5	6	$45	$270				7	$44.29	$310
15				4	$44.29	$177	3	$44.29	$133
26	7	$50	$350				10	$48.30	$483
30				8	$48.30	$386	2	$48.30	$ 97
30	13		$620	12		$563	2		$ 97

Exhibit 6-5 ▲

In a perpetual inventory system, the average unit cost on September 5 is based on the cost of the unit on hand at the beginning of September plus the cost of the six units purchased on September 5 as follows:

		Number of Units	Unit Cost	Total Cost
Sep 1	Beginning Inventory	1	$40	$ 40
5	Purchase	6	$45	$270
Total		7		$310

Total Cost of Inventory on Hand ÷ Number of Units on Hand = Average Cost per Unit		
$310	7 Units	$44.29

The four items sold on September 15 are assigned a cost of $44.29 per unit and the remaining three units are carried forward at a cost of $44.29 each. Northwest then computes a new average cost after the September 26 purchase in the same manner.

The average cost monthly summary on September 30 is as follows:

- Cost of Goods Sold: 12 units that cost a total of $563
- Ending Inventory: 2 units that cost a total of $97

Once again, these amounts can be seen in the last row of the perpetual inventory record presented in Exhibit 6-5. If Northwest uses the average cost method, it will use these amounts to prepare its financial statements. Yet again, the sum of the cost of goods sold and ending inventory equals the cost of goods available for sale, $660 ($563 + $97).

FIFO and Average Cost Methods in a Periodic Inventory System

When using the FIFO method in a periodic inventory system, the method of calculating the cost of goods sold and ending inventory is different from that used in a perpetual inventory system. However, the amounts of both the cost of goods sold and the ending inventory are the same.

When using the average cost method in a periodic inventory system, the method of calculating the cost of goods sold and ending inventory is different from that used in a perpetual inventory system, and the amounts of both the cost of goods sold and the ending inventory are different as well. This is because in the periodic inventory system there is only one average cost, which we call a **weighted average cost**, while in the perpetual inventory system we have a new average cost every time we sell and/or purchase new inventory, which we call a **moving average**.

In a periodic inventory system, the inventory level is not updated until the end of the accounting period. Northwest would add the beginning inventory to all the purchases incurred during the accounting period. A physical count of inventory is conducted at the end of the accounting period. At this point, we need to assign the cost to the inventory. Using the FIFO costing method, the first costs incurred by the company are the first ones to get assigned to COGS; therefore, the ending inventory costs will come from the last inventory items purchased. Since nine parkas were purchased on different dates, we will need to get the purchase price from the most recent purchase and then go back to the previous purchase price, if needed.

	Unit	Cost $	Total $
Beginning Inventory, Sep 1	1	$40	$40
Purchase, Sep 5	6	$45	$270
Purchase, Sep 26	7	$50	$350
Goods Available for Sale	14		$660

Northwest will first assign $50 to the 2 unsold parkas, since these items are from the most recent purchase price. The following shows the calculations for the ending inventory and the cost of goods sold.

FIFO Method:

Ending Inventory	2 × $50 =	$100
		$100
Goods Available for Sale		$660
– Ending Inventory		100
= Cost of Goods Sold		$560

As you can see, even though Northwest used the periodic system instead of the perpetual system, the Ending Inventory and COGS amounts are the same as the results from the perpetual system.

Using the weighted average cost method in a periodic system, Northwest needs to find out the average cost per parka for the entire inventory. Since the goods available for sale is $660 for 14 parkas, the weighted average cost per parka is $47.14 ($660/14). This is the cost that Northwest will use to assign the cost of goods sold and ending inventory amounts.

Weighted Average Cost Method:

Ending Inventory	2 × $47.14 =	$94.28
Goods Available for Sale		$660.00
– Ending Inventory		94.28
= Cost of Goods Sold		$565.72

Journalizing Inventory Transactions

The journal entries to record the inventory transactions for Northwest Outfitters for the month of September are presented below. Exhibit 6-6 shows the journal entries using the perpetual inventory system, and Exhibit 6-7 shows the journal entries using the periodic inventory system. Assume the following information:

- All purchases and sales in September were made on account.
- The sales price of a parka charged to a customer was $80.

Notice that the journal entries to record the purchases of inventory on account are the same, regardless of the costing method chosen. *The differences occur in the second part of the sales entries that removes the cost of the parkas sold from the inventory account and transfers it to cost of goods sold.*

DATE	ACCOUNTS	Perpetual FIFO		Perpetual Moving Average	
		DR.	CR.	DR.	CR.
Sep 05	Inventory	270		270	
	Accounts Payable		270		270
	Purchase inventory on account				
	(6 parkas @ $45 each)				
15	Accounts Receivable	320		320	
	Sales Revenue		320		320
	Cost of Goods Sold	175		177	
	Inventory		175		177
26	Inventory	350		350	
	Accounts Payable		350		350
	Purchase inventory on account				
	(7 parkas @ $50 each)				
30	Accounts Receivable	640		640	
	Sales Revenue		640		640
	Cost of Goods Sold	385		386	
	Inventory		385		386

Exhibit 6-6 ▲

DATE	ACCOUNTS	Periodic FIFO		Periodic Moving Average	
		DR.	CR.	DR.	CR.
Sep 05	Purchases	270		270	
	Accounts Payable		270		270
	Purchase inventory on account				
	(6 parkas @ $45 each)				
15	Accounts Receivable	320		320	
	Sales Revenue		320		320
26	Purchases	350		350	
	Accounts Payable		350		350
	Purchase inventory on account				
	(7 parkas @ $50 each)				
30	Accounts Receivable	640		640	
	Sales Revenue		640		640
30	Cost of Goods Sold	560		565.72	
	Inventory (100 − 40), (94.28 − 40)	60		54.28	
	Purchases		620		620
	Adjusting entry to set up ending				
	inventory, clear out purchases account,				
	and record COGS.				

Exhibit 6-7 ▲

WHAT EFFECT DO THE DIFFERENT COSTING METHODS HAVE ON NET INCOME?

> **3** Compare the effects of the different costing methods on the financial statements

The choice of inventory costing method often has an effect on the amount of net income a company reports on its income statement.

Exhibit 6-8 compares the FIFO and average cost methods of costing inventory assuming that, over time, inventory costs are *increasing*. As you can see, different methods have different benefits. FIFO is the most popular inventory costing method.

Inventory Costing Method	Description	Benefit
First-In, First-Out (FIFO)	Cost of goods sold has older, lower costs. Ending inventory has the newer, higher costs.	Most closely matches actual flow of goods in most cases. Maximizes net income.
Average Cost	Averages costs in ending inventory and cost of goods sold.	A "middle-ground solution" for reporting net income and inventory.

Exhibit 6-8 ▲

Exhibit 6-9 summarizes the effect that rising and declining inventory cost have on the ending inventory, cost of goods sold, gross profit, and net income. In comparing FIFO to weighted average cost, when the cost of inventory is rising, using the FIFO method will show higher ending inventory cost than the weighted average method, which will result in higher gross income and net income. The reverse is true when the cost of inventory is declining.

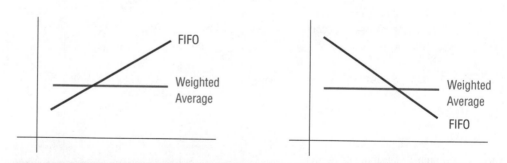

	Rising Cost of Inventory		Declining Cost of Inventory	
	FIFO	**WA**	**FIFO**	**WA**
Cost of Goods Sold	lower	higher	higher	lower
Ending Inventory	higher	lower	lower	higher
Gross Profit	higher	lower	lower	higher
Net Income	higher	lower	lower	higher

Exhibit 6-9 ▲

Exhibit 6-10 summarizes the results of the two inventory methods as used for Northwest Outfitters. It shows Sales Revenue, Cost of Goods Sold, and Gross Profit for FIFO and average cost. Net income is the highest under FIFO when inventory costs are rising.

	Perpetual FIFO	Periodic FIFO	Perpetual Moving Average	Periodic Weighted Average
Sales Revenue	$960.00	$960.00	$960.00	$960.00
Cost of Goods Sold	$560.00	$560.00	$563.00	$565.72
Gross Profit	$400.00	$400.00	$397.00	$394.28

Exhibit 6-10 ▲

Based upon the previous information, it appears that a business could "manage its income" by switching back and forth between costing methods depending upon the circumstances. This is not the case due to the **consistency** principle mandated by IFRS and Canadian ASPE. The consistency principle states that businesses should use the same accounting methods and procedures from period to period. The consistency principle does not mean that a company can never change its accounting methods, for instance changing from the average cost to FIFO inventory valuation method, but that it can only do so if it can justify the change. Also, any changes in accounting methods must be disclosed to the financial statement users.

Suppose you are analyzing a company's net income pattern over a two-year period and costs are rising. If the company switched from average cost to FIFO during that time, its net income likely increased significantly. The problem is that much, if not all, of the increase in income could be the result of the change in inventory method. If you were unaware of the change, you might believe that the company's income increased because of improved operations. Therefore, companies must report any changes in the accounting methods they use and they generally must retrospectively apply the impact of the change as an adjustment to beginning retained earnings, unless it is impractical to do so. Consistency helps investors compare a company's financial statements from one period to the next and make better decisions.

DECISION GUIDELINES

Decision

As a shareholder, I need to evaluate how well management has done in achieving goals for net income in order to award executive bonuses. How do inventory costing methods impact this decision?

Guideline

The combination of increasing or decreasing costs with inventory costing methods will create opportunities for affecting net income.

Analyze

When costs are rising

- FIFO reports the highest ending inventory value and lowest cost of goods sold and, therefore, the highest net income.

- average cost reports an average cost for the value of ending inventory and cost of goods sold. Average cost can be used to stabilize fluctuations in net income if inventory costs are continually fluctuating. This means that an unethical manager could simply change inventory costing methods and manipulate the net income. Evaluations for executives need to examine not only the results, but the methods that are chosen to achieve the results.

Value inventory using the lower of cost or net realizable value rule

Inventory is initially recorded at cost to comply with the cost principle. However, merchandisers are often faced with a situation where the cost of replacing an inventory item is lower than what was originally paid for the item. To take a conservative approach when these situations arise, businesses will often apply the **lower of cost or net realizable value (LCNRV) rule**. Net realizable value (NRV) is the estimated selling price less the estimated costs to complete the sale. The LCNRV rule requires businesses to report inventory in the financial statements at whichever is lower, the amount originally paid or the net realizable value, of each inventory item. The comparison of cost and net realizable value should be done on an item-by-item basis. If the net realizable value of inventory is less than its historical cost, a company writes down the inventory value by decreasing inventory and increasing cost of goods sold. In this way, net income is decreased in the period in which the decrease in the market value of the inventory occurred. However, if the circumstances change, and net realizable value has increased, then inventory that has been written down can be reversed up to cost.

Let's look at the process of valuing inventory according to the lower of cost or net realizable value rule for the inventory in **Exhibit 6-11**.

■ Prepare a table listing each inventory item, its quantity, unit cost, and net realizable value.

■ Calculate the total cost and total net realizable value for each item. Inventory Item 122A, for example, has a total cost of $2,000 (40 units × $50 cost per unit) and a total net realizable value of $2,080 (40 units × $52 market value per unit).

■ Place the lower of the cost or net realizable value for each item in the "LCNRV" (lower of cost or net realizable value) column. Item 122A would have a value of $2,000.

■ Add the amounts in each column to obtain the total cost, total net realizable value, and total lower of cost or net realizable value amounts.

■ Adjust the inventory balance to reflect the lower of cost or net realizable value amount. The total cost is $14,800 and the total LCNRV amount is $14,425, so a journal entry is made to reduce the inventory amount by the difference of $375 ($14,800 − $14,425).

The application of LCNRV is actually more complex than what is demonstrated in Exhibit 6-11; however, more in-depth coverage will be left to a more advanced accounting course. Application of the LCNRV rule is a continuation of the process of valuing inventory. Businesses using LCNRV will record inventory transactions, assigning a cost to each inventory item sold using the specific-identification, FIFO, or average cost method. Then, at the end of the accounting period, they will apply the LCNRV rule to the ending inventory. In this way, businesses report more prudent values for inventory and net income.

Inventory Item	Inventory Quantity	Unit Cost	Unit Net Realizable Value	Total Cost	Total Net Realizable Value	LCNRV
122A	40	$ 50	$ 52	$ 2,000	$ 2,080	$ 2,000
1587L	75	$ 80	$ 75	6,000	5,625	5,625
394CZ	68	$100	$101	6,800	6,868	6,800
				$14,800	$14,573	$14,425

Exhibit 6-11 ▲

Most businesses will report inventory on the balance sheet at the lower of cost or net realizable value; however, others will use the concept of materiality to decide whether inventory needs to be written down to its current replacement cost. The materiality concept states that a company must perform strictly proper accounting *only* for items that have a material effect on the company's financial statements. An item is considered to have a material effect when it would cause someone to change a decision; stated differently, a material amount is one large enough to make a difference to a user of the financial statements. For example, if the lower of cost or net realizable value comparison in Exhibit 6-11 resulted in a difference between total cost and total LCNRV of $3, the company would have been appropriate in ignoring any adjustment to inventory for the $3. Hence, the materiality concept frees accountants from having to report every account in strict accordance with IFRS or Canadian ASPE, yet still report items properly.

HOW IS INVENTORY REPORTED ON THE BALANCE SHEET?

Inventory is reported as a current asset and is often listed after receivables on the balance sheet. In addition to showing the inventory amount, a business must disclose the costing method used to value inventory (specific-identification, FIFO, or average cost) and whether the inventory is valued using LCNRV. This disclosure helps a business adhere to the **full-disclosure** principle. The full-disclosure principle requires that a company's financial statements report enough information for outsiders to make knowledgeable decisions about the company. To provide this information, accountants typically include a set of **footnotes** that accompany the financial statements. Footnote disclosures help ensure that companies report relevant, reliable, and comparable financial information. A common footnote related to inventory would look like this:

 Illustrate the reporting of inventory in the financial statements

> NOTE 2: Statement of Significant Accounting Policies:
> *Inventory*. Inventory is carried at the *lower of cost or net realizable value*. Cost is determined using the first-in, first-out method.

Suppose a banker is comparing two companies, one using average cost and the other FIFO. When prices are rising, the company using the FIFO inventory costing method reports higher net income, but only because it uses FIFO. Without knowledge of the accounting methods the companies are using, the banker could lend money to the wrong business, or lend the wrong amount of money to each.

Inventory Shrinkage

The perpetual inventory method keeps a continuous record of the inventory on hand at all times. However, the actual amount of inventory on hand may differ from the amount on hand according to the accounting records due to errors in recording inventory-related transactions or due to **inventory shrinkage**. Inventory shrinkage represents a loss of inventory. Inventory shrinkage is most often the result of employee theft, customer theft, and the damage, spillage, or spoilage of inventory items.

A physical inventory count is used to determine the amount of inventory actually on hand at the end of the accounting period. A number of commonly used procedures help ensure the accuracy of the count. It usually occurs when the store is closed. Individuals assigned to the count can use maps of inventory locations, pre-numbered count sheets, ink pens, and may count in pairs. The count may also involve prewritten inventory instructions and tags to identify merchandise to be counted, and is typically supervised. To save time and increase objectivity for the count, an outside inventory-taking firm may be used to take counts instead of, or in addition to, employees. If the entity has its financial statements audited, a representative of the audit firm will usually be present at the count to take test counts and determine whether inventory instructions are being adequately followed. This allows the auditor to evaluate whether inventory and cost of goods sold are fairly presented in the statements.

The inventory value derived from the physical inventory count is used as the inventory account balance on the balance sheet. The accounting records are adjusted for any difference between the inventory value determined by the count and the value according to the perpetual records. The Inventory account is debited or credited as necessary with a corresponding credit or debit to the Cost of Goods Sold account.

HOW DO INVENTORY ERRORS AFFECT THE FINANCIAL STATEMENTS?

6 Determine the effect of inventory errors on the financial statements

A correct count of the inventory items on hand is necessary to ensure the accurate reporting of the inventory's value. However, errors in the inventory count can and do occur such as the following:

- Improperly counting inventory
- Double counting inventory; for example, counting it in one location and then moving it to another location where it is counted again
- Not counting one section of the storeroom or excluding incoming goods shipped FOB shipping point
- Failure to recognize obsolete or damaged goods, resulting in failure to write down their value accordingly

What is the impact of a counting error? Remember that the inventory account balance is adjusted to reflect the value arrived at by the physical count. A wrong count will result in making a journal entry that causes both the Inventory balance and the Cost of Goods Sold to be incorrect.

To demonstrate, let's look at the income statements for a company for two consecutive years. To keep the example simple, we will assume that the company has a $20,000 balance in both beginning inventory and ending inventory for the first year. We will also assume that it has a $20,000 balance in ending inventory in the second year (remember that the beginning balance in the inventory account in year 2 is the ending inventory balance from year 1). We will also assume that the company made purchases of $75,000 and that it had sales of $160,000 and operating expenses of $40,000 in both years. In other words, the activity for both years is exactly the same. **Exhibit 6-12**, Panel A, illustrates the income statements for both years assuming that inventory was properly counted.

Panel A—Ending Inventory correctly stated	Year 1		Year 2	
Sales Revenue		$160,000		$160,000
Cost of Goods Sold:				
Beginning Inventory	$20,000		$ 20,000	
Purchases	75,000		75,000	
Cost of Goods Available for Sale	95,000		95,000	
Ending Inventory	20,000		20,000	
Cost of Goods Sold		75,000		75,000
Gross Profit		85,000		85,000
Operating Expenses		40,000		40,000
Net Income		$45,000		$45,000

Panel B—Ending Inventory overstated by $5,000				
Sales Revenue		$160,000		$160,000
Cost of Goods Sold:				
Beginning Inventory	$20,000		$ 25,000	
Purchases	75,000		75,000	
Cost of Goods Available for Sale	95,000		100,000	
Ending Inventory	25,000		20,000	
Cost of Goods Sold		70,000		80,000
Gross Profit		90,000		80,000
Operating Expenses		40,000		40,000
Net Income		$ 50,000		$ 40,000

Exhibit 6-12 ▲

Now, let's assume that the ending inventory was incorrectly valued at $25,000 (instead of the correct amount of $20,000) due to an error in the physical count. Exhibit 6-12, Panel B, illustrates the income statements for both years assuming that ending inventory was overstated by $5,000.

A comparison of the statements in Panel A and Panel B of Exhibit 6-12 reveals the following for year one.

- Cost of Goods Sold is understated by $5,000.
- Gross Profit is overstated by $5,000.
- Net Income is overstated by $5,000.
- Retained Earnings will be overstated because Net Income is closed into Retained Earnings.

Recall from Chapter 3 that Inventory, as an asset, is a permanent account that carries its balance over to the next period. So, one period's ending inventory becomes the next period's beginning inventory. Thus, the error in ending inventory in year 1 carries over as an error in the beginning inventory in year 2. A comparison of the statements in Panel A and Panel B of Exhibit 6-12 reveals the following for year 2.

- Cost of Goods Available for Sale is overstated by $5,000.
- Cost of Goods Sold is overstated by $5,000.
- Gross Profit is understated by $5,000.
- Net Income is understated by $5,000.
- Retained Earnings will now be correctly stated because the understatement in Net Income in year 2 will offset the overstatement from year 1 when the Net Income from year 2 is closed into Retained Earnings.

As you can see, the error cancels out after two periods. The total net income, $90,000, from Panel B for the two periods combined when there is an error is the same as it is in Panel A for the two periods when there are no errors. The effects of inventory errors are summarized in **Exhibit 6-13**.

	Year 1		Year 2	
	COGS	**Income**	**COGS**	**Income**
Ending inventory overstated in first year, correct in second year	understated	overstated	overstated	understated
Ending inventory understated in first year, correct in second year	overstated	understated	understated	overstated

Exhibit 6-13 ▲

We can use the following mathematical equation of the calculation of the cost of goods sold to explain the understatement or overstatement of the items in the income statement and the balance sheet:

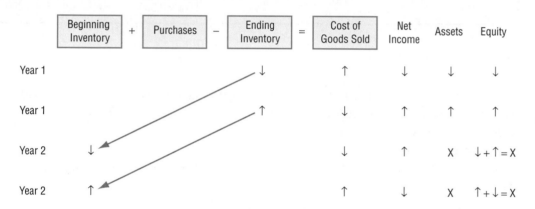

DECISION GUIDELINES

Decision

I just realized that the company that I hired to count my inventory missed a section that I forgot to tell them about. I'll make sure they count it correctly next time, so should I bother to inform the CEO about this error?

Guideline

In addition to causing an overstatement or understatement of Inventory on the balance sheet, a misstatement of ending inventory will cause an error on the income statement. You must inform the CEO about this error.

Analyze

If ending inventory is overstated, then
- Cost of Goods Sold is understated.
- Gross Profit is overstated.
- Net Income is overstated.

If ending inventory is understated, then
- Cost of Goods Sold is overstated.
- Gross Profit is understated.
- Net Income is understated.

Because ending inventory for one period becomes beginning inventory for the next period, the Cost of Goods Sold, Gross Profit, and Net Income of the next period are also misstated.

IS IT POSSIBLE TO ESTIMATE THE VALUE OF INVENTORY IF THE INVENTORY IS ACCIDENTALLY DESTROYED?

Often a business must estimate the value of its inventory. Suppose the company suffers a fire loss. To collect insurance, it must estimate the cost of the inventory destroyed, that is, it must estimate the ending inventory.

7 Use the gross profit method to estimate ending inventory

The **gross profit method** estimates inventory by using the format for the Cost of Goods Sold:

> Beginning Inventory
> \+ Purchases (Net of Discounts and Returns and Allowances,
>   Plus Shipping Costs)
> = Cost of Goods Available for Sale
> − Ending Inventory
> = Cost of Goods Sold

Rearranging ending inventory and cost of goods sold helps to estimate ending inventory. Let's look at an example. We can estimate ending inventory through the following steps and amounts, as shown in **Exhibits 6-14** and **6-15**:

Step 1 Calculate the cost of goods available for sale. Add the beginning balance of inventory and the net cost of purchases for the accounting period ($14,000 + $66,000 = $80,000).

Step 2 Estimate the cost of goods sold. Do you remember calculating the gross profit percentage in Chapter 5? The historical gross profit percentage of a business can be used to estimate the current period's gross profit. Calculate the estimated gross profit by multiplying the net sales revenue by the historical gross profit percentage ($100,000 × 40% = $40,000). Subtract the estimated gross profit from the net sales revenue to get the estimated cost of goods sold ($100,000 − $40,000 = $60,000).

Step 3 Estimate the ending inventory. Subtract estimated cost of goods sold from the cost of goods available for sale ($80,000 − $60,000 = $20,000).

Step 1	Beginning Inventory		$ 14,000
	+ Purchases (net)		66,000
	= Cost of Goods Available for Sale		80,000
Step 2	Estimated Cost of Goods Sold:		
	Net Sales Revenue	$100,000	
	− Estimated Gross Profit of 40% ($100,000 × 40%)	(40,000)	
	= Estimated Cost of Goods Sold		(60,000)
Step 3	Estimated Ending Inventory		$ 20,000

Exhibit 6-14 ▲

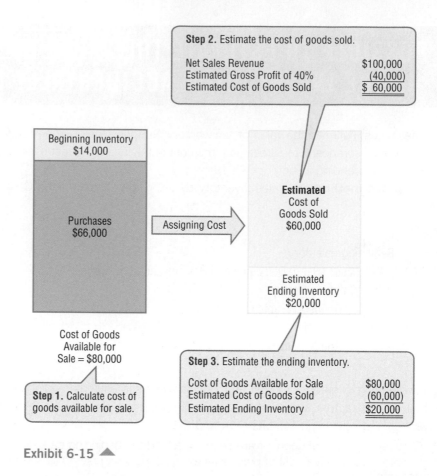

Step 2. Estimate the cost of goods sold.

Net Sales Revenue	$100,000
Estimated Gross Profit of 40%	(40,000)
Estimated Cost of Goods Sold	$ 60,000

Beginning Inventory
$14,000

Purchases
$66,000

Estimated
Cost of
Goods Sold
$60,000

Assigning Cost

Estimated
Ending Inventory
$20,000

Cost of Goods
Available for
Sale = $80,000

Step 3. Estimate the ending inventory.

Cost of Goods Available for Sale	$80,000
Estimated Cost of Goods Sold	(60,000)
Estimated Ending Inventory	$20,000

Step 1. Calculate cost of goods available for sale.

Exhibit 6-15 ▲

FOCUS ON DECISION MAKING: RATIOS

The Rate of Inventory Turnover

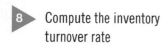

8 Compute the inventory turnover rate

Inventory is the most important asset for a merchandising business because it is often the largest current asset and the focus of a company's operations. Owners and managers strive to sell inventory quickly because inventory generates no profit until it is sold. The faster a business produces sales, the higher the sales revenue available to create income will be. **Inventory turnover**, the ratio of cost of goods sold to average inventory, measures the number of times a company sells, or *turns over*, its average level of inventory during a period. To demonstrate the inventory turnover we will use the financial statements for Cosmic Cellular from Exhibit 5-9 in Chapter 5. Cosmic Cellular's rate of inventory turnover is calculated as follows:

$$\text{Inventory Turnover} = \frac{\text{Cost of Goods Sold}}{\text{Average Inventory}} = \frac{\text{Cost of Goods Sold}}{(\text{Beginning Inventory} + \text{Ending Inventory})/2}$$

$$= \frac{\$90,300}{(\$40,000^* + \$39,700)/2} = \text{2.27 Times Per Year}$$

*The $40,000 beginning inventory balance is the ending inventory balance for the prior period and is not shown in Exhibit 5-9.

Cosmic's inventory turnover rate shows that it is selling its merchandise inventory a little more than two times a year. Converting the inventory turnover rate into an amount that tells you how long the inventory is usually on hand before it is sold can help you understand how efficiently the inventory is being used. To do the conversion, you simply take 365 and divide by the inventory turnover rate as follows:

$$365 \div 2.27 = 160.8 \text{ days}$$

This means that, on average, the inventory is held for over 160 days before it is sold. For a product that is not perishable, having the inventory around for that long may be fine; however, the product might also go out of style or become obsolete if it is held onto for too long. For a product that is perishable, such as fresh fruit, it is obvious that having it on hand for 160 days would not be good. Analysis of the type of product is important for a full understanding of the days in inventory calculation.

Inventory turnover is usually computed for an annual period, so the cost of goods sold figure is the amount for the entire year. Average inventory is computed by adding the beginning inventory balance to the ending inventory balance, and dividing the total by two. Remember that balance sheet accounts, such as Inventory, carry their balances from one period to the next, so the ending inventory for one year becomes the beginning inventory for the next year. A high turnover rate is desirable because it indicates that the inventory is turning over, or being sold, fast; an increase in the turnover rate usually means increasing profits will result from increasing sales.

Regardless of the turnover rate, merchandisers need to keep sufficient levels of inventory on hand to meet sales demand. However, they also need to avoid purchasing too much inventory because more money will be needed to pay for the inventory and to store it until the goods are sold. These actions will increase interest expense if the funds needed are borrowed, and warehouse rent expense, if warehouse storage space is rented.

DECISION GUIDELINES

Decision

As a creditor, I have used a company's inventory as collateral towards its loan with my bank. How do I assess the company's management of its inventory?

Guideline

Use the inventory turnover ratios:

$$\text{Inventory Turnover} = \frac{\text{Cost of Goods Sold}}{\text{Average Inventory}}$$

$$\text{Days in Inventory} = \frac{365}{\text{Inventory Turnover}}$$

Analyze

The inventory turnover ratios can indicate that a business is poorly managing its inventory. For example, a turnover ratio that is low compared to the industry average or a turnover ratio that has declined from the prior year may indicate that the business has damaged or obsolete inventory. It is sometimes more clear to use the days in inventory calculation to determine how well the inventory is managed.

FOCUS ON USERS

Concept	User	Why is this Important to this User?
Inventory Costing Method		All users need to understand the inventory costing methods used and any changes in the costing methods since this can have a drastic impact on the COGS, net income, and ending inventory amounts that are reported by a company.
		Creditors would need to carefully consider the inventory costing methods for decisions regarding the value of the inventory for collateral purposes and the quality of the net income for representing a company's ability to generate sufficient income to support a loan.
		Shareholders need to be sure to understand the inventory amounts reported and how they impact net income (and therefore retained earnings and shareholders' equity).
		Since income can be manipulated by changes in inventory, government regulators and accounting regulators want to ensure that consistency is applied so that each year's financial statements are based on the same assumptions and cost flow methods. This will make comparison from one year to the next easier and help alleviate the chance of cost flow methods being changed simply to serve a specific purpose for the company (such as showing high income to attract investors).
		Unions are interested in the ways in which companies report their earnings because union negotiations will revolve around what the company can afford to do with salaries and other benefits to the employees. If changing the cost flow method can alter the net income and the COGS (and therefore the expenses) of the company, the union will want to make sure that the impact of the cost flow assumption is understood for their own purposes of negotiating for the best support of the employees.

DEMO DOC

Inventory Costing

Mackay Specialty Products, Inc., which uses the perpetual inventory method, had the following inventory information for the month of June, 2014:

MyAccountingLab

Visit MyAccountingLab at www. myaccountinglab.com to watch animated versions of these Demo Docs.

L.O.

Requirements:

❶ Without resorting to calculations, determine which costing method, FIFO or average cost, will result in the highest reported income for Mackay Specialty Products, Inc.

❷ Calculate the cost of goods sold and the value of ending inventory for Mackay Specialty Products, Inc. for the month of June 2014 under the following costing methods:

a. FIFO

b. Average cost

Jun	1	Beginning inventory was 200 units costing $9.00 per unit.
	3	Purchased 125 units at $9.25 per unit.
	7	Sold 180 units.
	13	Purchased 100 units at $9.40 per unit.
	18	Sold 115 units.
	25	Sold 65 units.

Demo Doc Solutions

Requirement ❶

Without resorting to calculations, determine which costing method, FIFO or average cost, will result in the highest reported income for Mackay Specialty Products, Inc.

Part 1	Part 2	Demo Doc Complete

To determine whether the FIFO or average cost costing method would result in the highest income, we must first look to see if the cost of inventory is increasing or decreasing. A review of the data indicates that the cost of inventory has steadily increased from $9.00 to $9.40 per unit during the month. To have the highest income possible, we must choose the inventory costing method that results in the lowest cost of goods sold. The FIFO costing method assumes that the earliest inventory costs become part of cost of goods sold, which leaves the most recent costs in ending inventory. The average cost smooths out the cost. Because the inventory costs for Mackay Specialty Products, Inc. have steadily increased, the earliest inventory costs are lower than the most recent purchases. Therefore, choosing the FIFO costing method will result in the highest income for Mackay Specialty Products, Inc. as it will result in the lowest cost of goods sold.

Requirement ❷

Calculate the cost of goods sold and the value of ending inventory for Mackay Specialty Products, Inc. for the month of June 2014 under the following costing methods:

Part 1	**Part 2**	Demo Doc Complete

a. FIFO

An easy way to determine the cost of goods sold and the value of ending inventory is to prepare a perpetual inventory record. The first entry necessary in the record records the beginning inventory of 200 units at $9.00 each for a total of $1,800.00. This information is entered in the inventory on hand columns of the record as follows:

Date	Purchases Quantity	Unit Cost	Total Cost	Cost of Goods Sold Quantity	Unit Cost	Total Cost	Inventory on Hand Quantity	Unit Cost	Total Cost
Jun 1							200	$9.00	$1,800.00

Next, we enter the June 3 purchase of 125 units costing $9.25 each for a total of $1,156.25 in the purchases columns of the record.

Date	Purchases Quantity	Unit Cost	Total Cost	Cost of Goods Sold Quantity	Unit Cost	Total Cost	Inventory on Hand Quantity	Unit Cost	Total Cost
Jun 1							200	$9.00	$1,800.00
Jun 3	125	$9.25	$1,156.25						

The inventory on hand columns are completed by carrying down the original layer of inventory (200 units at $9.00) and then adding the new layer (125 units at $9.25).

Date	Purchases Quantity	Unit Cost	Total Cost	Cost of Goods Sold Quantity	Unit Cost	Total Cost	Inventory on Hand Quantity	Unit Cost	Total Cost
Jun 1							200	$9.00	$1,800.00
Jun 3	125	$9.25	$1,156.25				200	$9.00	$1,800.00
							125	$9.25	$1,156.25

Next, we will enter the June 7 sale transaction. Under FIFO, costs are assigned to cost of goods sold based on the *oldest* units on hand (the *first* units in). The oldest units we have are the units in beginning inventory (200 units at $9.00 each). The 180 units sold are, therefore, assigned a cost of $9.00 each for a total of $1,620.00. This information is entered into the cost of goods sold columns of the record.

Date	Purchases Quantity	Unit Cost	Total Cost	Cost of Goods Sold Quantity	Unit Cost	Total Cost	Inventory on Hand Quantity	Unit Cost	Total Cost
Jun 1							200	$9.00	$1,800.00
Jun 3	125	$9.25	$1,156.25				200	$9.00	$1,800.00
							125	$9.25	$1,156.25
Jun 7				180	$9.00	$1,620.00			

The inventory on hand columns are completed next. Of the original 200 units in beginning inventory, only 20 (200 – 180) are left. We also still have the 125 units purchased on June 3 for $9.25 each.

Date	Purchases Quantity	Unit Cost	Total Cost	Cost of Goods Sold Quantity	Unit Cost	Total Cost	Inventory on Hand Quantity	Unit Cost	Total Cost
Jun 1							200	$9.00	$1,800.00
Jun 3	125	$9.25	$1,156.25				200	$9.00	$1,800.00
							125	$9.25	$1,156.25
Jun 7				180	$9.00	$1,620.00	20	$9.00	$ 180.00
							125	$9.25	$1,156.25

The June 13 purchase of 100 units at $9.40 each is entered into the purchases columns of the record.

Date	Purchases Quantity	Unit Cost	Total Cost	Cost of Goods Sold Quantity	Unit Cost	Total Cost	Inventory on Hand Quantity	Unit Cost	Total Cost
Jun 1							200	$9.00	$1,800.00
Jun 3	125	$9.25	$1,156.25				200	$9.00	$1,800.00
							125	$9.25	$1,156.25
Jun 7				180	$9.00	$1,620.00	20	$9.00	$ 180.00
							125	$9.25	$1,156.25
Jun 13	100	$9.40	$ 940.00						

The inventory on hand columns are now completed by carrying down the layers of inventory from June 7 and adding a layer consisting of the 100 units purchased on June 13.

Date	Purchases Quantity	Unit Cost	Total Cost	Cost of Goods Sold Quantity	Unit Cost	Total Cost	Inventory on Hand Quantity	Unit Cost	Total Cost
Jun 1							200	$9.00	$1,800.00
Jun 3	125	$9.25	$1,156.25				200	$9.00	$1,800.00
							125	$9.25	$1,156.25
Jun 7				180	$9.00	$1,620.00	20	$9.00	$ 180.00
							125	$9.25	$1,156.25
Jun 13	100	$9.40	$ 940.00				20	$9.00	$ 180.00
							125	$9.25	$1,156.25
							100	$9.40	$ 940.00

On June 18, 115 units are sold. Remember that under FIFO we must assign the oldest cost to cost of goods sold first. The oldest cost of inventory on hand is the 20 units at $9.00 each. Because we sold more than 20 units, we must look to the next inventory layer for the cost to assign to the remaining 95 units (115 – 20). These 95 units are assigned a cost of $9.25 each. The sale is entered into the cost of goods sold columns of the record as follows:

Date	Purchases Quantity	Purchases Unit Cost	Purchases Total Cost	Cost of Goods Sold Quantity	Cost of Goods Sold Unit Cost	Cost of Goods Sold Total Cost	Inventory on Hand Quantity	Inventory on Hand Unit Cost	Inventory on Hand Total Cost
Jun 1							200	$9.00	$1,800.00
Jun 3	125	$9.25	$1,156.25				200	$9.00	$1,800.00
							125	$9.25	$1,156.25
Jun 7				180	$9.00	$1,620.00	20	$9.00	$ 180.00
							125	$9.25	$1,156.25
Jun 13	100	$9.40	$ 940.00				20	$9.00	$ 180.00
							125	$9.25	$1,156.25
							100	$9.40	$ 940.00
Jun 18				20	$9.00	$ 180.00			
				95	$9.25	$ 878.75			

After this sale, all of the beginning inventory items are assumed to be sold as well as 95 of the units costing $9.25. Therefore, the remaining inventory is made up of 30 units (125 − 95) at $9.25 and 100 units at $9.40. These amounts are entered into the inventory on hand columns of the record.

Date	Purchases Quantity	Purchases Unit Cost	Purchases Total Cost	Cost of Goods Sold Quantity	Cost of Goods Sold Unit Cost	Cost of Goods Sold Total Cost	Inventory on Hand Quantity	Inventory on Hand Unit Cost	Inventory on Hand Total Cost
Jun 1							200	$9.00	$1,800.00
Jun 3	125	$9.25	$1,156.25				200	$9.00	$1,800.00
							125	$9.25	$1,156.25
Jun 7				180	$9.00	$1,620.00	20	$9.00	$ 180.00
							125	$9.25	$1,156.25
Jun 13	100	$9.40	$ 940.00				20	$9.00	$ 180.00
							125	$9.25	$1,156.25
							100	$9.40	$ 940.00
Jun 18				20	$9.00	$ 180.00	30	$9.25	$ 277.50
				95	$9.25	$ 878.75	100	$9.40	$ 940.00

In the last transaction on June 25, 65 units were sold. Of these 65 units, 30 are assumed to cost $9.25 and the remaining 35 (65 − 30) are assumed to cost $9.40.

Date	Purchases			Cost of Goods Sold			Inventory on Hand		
	Quantity	Unit Cost	Total Cost	Quantity	Unit Cost	Total Cost	Quantity	Unit Cost	Total Cost
Jun 1							200	$9.00	$1,800.00
Jun 3	125	$9.25	$1,156.25				200	$9.00	$1,800.00
							125	$9.25	$1,156.25
Jun 7				180	$9.00	$1,620.00	20	$9.00	$ 180.00
							125	$9.25	$1,156.25
Jun 13	100	$9.40	$ 940.00				20	$9.00	$ 180.00
							125	$9.25	$1,156.25
							100	$9.40	$ 940.00
Jun 18				20	$9.00	$ 180.00	30	$9.25	$ 277.50
				95	$9.25	$ 878.75	100	$9.40	$ 940.00
Jun 25				30	$9.25	$ 277.50			
				35	$9.40	$ 329.00			

After this sale, all units costing $9.25 are assumed to be sold as well as 35 of the units costing $9.40. Therefore, the remaining inventory is made up of 65 units (100 – 35) at $9.40. These amounts are entered into the inventory on hand columns of the record.

Date	Purchases			Cost of Goods Sold			Inventory on Hand		
	Quantity	Unit Cost	Total Cost	Quantity	Unit Cost	Total Cost	Quantity	Unit Cost	Total Cost
Jun 1							200	$9.00	$1,800.00
Jun 3	125	$9.25	$1,156.25				200	$9.00	$1,800.00
							125	$9.25	$1,156.25
Jun 7				180	$9.00	$1,620.00	20	$9.00	$ 180.00
							125	$9.25	$1,156.25
Jun 13	100	$9.40	$ 940.00				20	$9.00	$ 180.00
							125	$9.25	$1,156.25
							100	$9.40	$ 940.00
Jun 18				20	$9.00	$ 180.00	30	$9.25	$ 277.50
				95	$9.25	$ 878.75	100	$9.40	$ 940.00
Jun 25				30	$9.25	$ 277.50			
				35	$9.40	$ 329.00	65	$9.40	$ 611.00

The perpetual inventory record is completed by calculating the total quantity and total cost for the purchases, cost of goods sold, and inventory on hand columns and entering the results in the last row. Notice that the amounts in the inventory on hand columns only reflect the amounts that existed after the last transaction.

Date	Purchases Quantity	Unit Cost	Total Cost	Cost of Goods Sold Quantity	Unit Cost	Total Cost	Inventory on Hand Quantity	Unit Cost	Total Cost
Jun 1							200	$9.00	$1,800.00
Jun 3	125	$9.25	$1,156.25				200	$9.00	$1,800.00
							125	$9.25	$1,156.25
Jun 7				180	$9.00	$1,620.00	20	$9.00	$ 180.00
							125	$9.25	$1,156.25
Jun 13	100	$9.40	$ 940.00				20	$9.00	$ 180.00
							125	$9.25	$1,156.25
							100	$9.40	$ 940.00
Jun 18				20	$9.00	$ 180.00	30	$9.25	$ 277.50
				95	$9.25	$ 878.75	100	$9.40	$ 940.00
Jun 25				30	$9.25	$ 277.50			
				35	$9.40	$ 329.00	65	$9.40	$ 611.00
Jun 30	225		$2,096.25	360		$3,285.25	65		$ 611.00

We can double-check our calculations using the following formula:

Cost of Goods Sold = (Beginning Inventory + Purchases − Ending Inventory)

Using this formula, the cost of goods sold is $3,285.25 ($1,800.00 + $2,096.25 − $611.00). This agrees with the cost of goods sold total on the perpetual inventory record so our calculations are correct.

b. Average cost

We will now complete a perpetual inventory record using average cost. As we did for the FIFO inventory records, the first entry is to record the beginning inventory of 200 units costing $9.00 each.

Date	Purchases Quantity	Unit Cost	Total Cost	Cost of Goods Sold Quantity	Unit Cost	Total Cost	Inventory on Hand Quantity	Unit Cost	Total Cost
Jun 1							200	$9.00	$1,800.00

The entry for the first purchase of 125 units on June 3 is the same as for the FIFO inventory records.

Date	Purchases Quantity	Unit Cost	Total Cost	Cost of Goods Sold Quantity	Unit Cost	Total Cost	Inventory on Hand Quantity	Unit Cost	Total Cost
Jun 1							200	$9.00	$1,800.00
Jun 3	125	$9.25	$1,156.25						

Once a purchase is made, the average cost per unit must be calculated. The average cost per unit is calculated by dividing the total cost of inventory on hand by the total quantity of inventory on hand. The total cost of inventory equals $2,956.25 ($1,800.00 beginning inventory + $1,156.25 purchased on June 3). The total quantity of inventory on hand equals the 200 units in beginning inventory plus the 125 units purchased for a total of 325 units. The average cost per unit is calculated as follows:

$$\frac{\$2,956.25}{325} = \$9.10^* \text{ per unit}$$

*Rounded

The inventory on hand consists of 325 units at $9.10 each. This information is entered into the inventory on hand columns of the inventory record.

	Purchases			Cost of Goods Sold			Inventory on Hand		
Date	Quantity	Unit Cost	Total Cost	Quantity	Unit Cost	Total Cost	Quantity	Unit Cost	Total Cost
Jun 1							200	$9.00	$1,800.00
Jun 3	125	$9.25	$1,156.25				325	$9.10	$2,957.50

On June 7, 180 units are sold. The units in inventory have an average cost of $9.10 each, so the units sold are assigned a cost of $9.10 for a total of $1,638.00. This information is entered into the cost of goods sold columns of the record.

	Purchases			Cost of Goods Sold			Inventory on Hand		
Date	Quantity	Unit Cost	Total Cost	Quantity	Unit Cost	Total Cost	Quantity	Unit Cost	Total Cost
Jun 1							200	$9.00	$1,800.00
Jun 3	125	$9.25	$1,156.25				325	$9.10	2,957.50
Jun 7				180	$9.10	$1,638.00			

This transaction leaves 145 units (325 − 180) in inventory at $9.10 each. This information is now entered in the inventory on hand columns of the record.

	Purchases			Cost of Goods Sold			Inventory on Hand		
Date	Quantity	Unit Cost	Total Cost	Quantity	Unit Cost	Total Cost	Quantity	Unit Cost	Total Cost
Jun 1							200	$9.00	$1,800.00
Jun 3	125	$9.25	$1,156.25				325	$9.10	$2,957.50
Jun 7				180	$9.10	$1,638.00	145	$9.10	$1,319.50

The June 13 purchase of 100 units at $9.40 each is now entered into the purchases columns of the inventory record.

	Purchases			Cost of Goods Sold			Inventory on Hand		
Date	Quantity	Unit Cost	Total Cost	Quantity	Unit Cost	Total Cost	Quantity	Unit Cost	Total Cost
Jun 1							200	$9.00	$1,800.00
Jun 3	125	$9.25	$1,156.25				325	$9.10	$2,957.50
Jun 7				180	$9.10	$1,638.00	145	$9.10	$1,319.50
Jun 13	100	$9.40	$ 940.00						

Because another purchase has been made, the average cost per unit must be recalculated. The total cost of inventory equals $2,259.50 ($1,319.50 June 7 remaining inventory + $940.00 purchased on June 13). The total quantity of inventory on hand equals the 145 units remaining in inventory on June 7 plus the 100 units purchased for a total of 245 units. The average cost per unit is calculated as follows:

$$\frac{\$2,259.50}{245} = \$9.22^* \text{ per unit}$$

*Rounded

The inventory on hand consists of 245 units at $9.22 each. This information is entered into the inventory on hand columns of the inventory record.

Date	Purchases Quantity	Purchases Unit Cost	Purchases Total Cost	Cost of Goods Sold Quantity	Cost of Goods Sold Unit Cost	Cost of Goods Sold Total Cost	Inventory on Hand Quantity	Inventory on Hand Unit Cost	Inventory on Hand Total Cost
Jun 1							200	$9.00	$1,800.00
Jun 3	125	$9.25	$1,156.25				325	$9.10	$2,957.50
Jun 7				180	$9.10	$1,638.00	145	$9.10	$1,319.50
Jun 13	100	$9.40	$ 940.00				245	$9.22	$2,258.90

On June 18, 115 units are sold. The units in inventory have an average cost of $9.22 each, so the units sold are assigned a cost of $9.22 for a total of $1,060.30. This information is entered into the cost of goods sold columns of the record.

Date	Purchases Quantity	Purchases Unit Cost	Purchases Total Cost	Cost of Goods Sold Quantity	Cost of Goods Sold Unit Cost	Cost of Goods Sold Total Cost	Inventory on Hand Quantity	Inventory on Hand Unit Cost	Inventory on Hand Total Cost
Jun 1							200	$9.00	$1,800.00
Jun 3	125	$9.25	$1,156.25				325	$9.10	$2,957.50
Jun 7				180	$9.10	$1,638.00	145	$9.10	$1,319.50
Jun 13	100	$9.40	$ 940.00				245	$9.22	$2,258.90
Jun 18				115	$9.22	$1,060.30			

This transaction leaves 130 units (245 − 115) in inventory at $9.22 each. This information is now entered in the inventory on hand columns of the record.

Date	Purchases Quantity	Purchases Unit Cost	Purchases Total Cost	Cost of Goods Sold Quantity	Cost of Goods Sold Unit Cost	Cost of Goods Sold Total Cost	Inventory on Hand Quantity	Inventory on Hand Unit Cost	Inventory on Hand Total Cost
Jun 1							200	$9.00	$1,800.00
Jun 3	125	$9.25	$1,156.25				325	$9.10	$2,957.50
Jun 7				180	$9.10	$1,638.00	145	$9.10	$1,319.50
Jun 13	100	$9.40	$ 940.00				245	$9.22	$2,258.90
Jun 18				115	$9.22	$1,060.30	130	$9.22	$1,198.60

The last transaction on June 25 was for the sale of 65 units. Because there have been no purchases since the last transaction, there is no need to recalculate the average cost per unit. So the cost assigned to the 65 units will be $9.22 each. This information is entered into the cost of goods sold columns of the record.

Date	Purchases Quantity	Purchases Unit Cost	Purchases Total Cost	Cost of Goods Sold Quantity	Cost of Goods Sold Unit Cost	Cost of Goods Sold Total Cost	Inventory on Hand Quantity	Inventory on Hand Unit Cost	Inventory on Hand Total Cost
Jun 1							200	$9.00	$1,800.00
Jun 3	125	$9.25	$1,156.25				325	$9.10	$2,957.50
Jun 7				180	$9.10	$1,638.00	145	$9.10	$1,319.50
Jun 13	100	$9.40	$ 940.00				245	$9.22	$2,258.90
Jun 18				115	$9.22	$1,060.30	130	$9.22	$1,198.60
Jun 25				65	$9.22	$ 599.30			

This transaction leaves 65 units (130 – 65) in inventory at $9.22 each. This information is now entered in the inventory on hand columns of the record.

Date	Purchases Quantity	Purchases Unit Cost	Purchases Total Cost	Cost of Goods Sold Quantity	Cost of Goods Sold Unit Cost	Cost of Goods Sold Total Cost	Inventory on Hand Quantity	Inventory on Hand Unit Cost	Inventory on Hand Total Cost
Jun 1							200	$9.00	$1,800.00
Jun 3	125	$9.25	$1,156.25				325	$9.10	$2,957.50
Jun 7				180	$9.10	$1,638.00	145	$9.10	$1,319.50
Jun 13	100	$9.40	$ 940.00				245	$9.22	$2,258.90
Jun 18				115	$9.22	$1,060.30	130	$9.22	$1,198.60
Jun 25				65	$9.22	$ 599.30	65	$9.22	$ 599.30

As we did with FIFO, the perpetual inventory record is completed by calculating the total quantity and total cost for the purchases, cost of goods sold, and inventory on hand columns and entering the results in the last row. Notice that the amounts in the inventory on hand columns only reflect the amounts that existed after the last transaction.

Date	Purchases Quantity	Purchases Unit Cost	Purchases Total Cost	Cost of Goods Sold Quantity	Cost of Goods Sold Unit Cost	Cost of Goods Sold Total Cost	Inventory on Hand Quantity	Inventory on Hand Unit Cost	Inventory on Hand Total Cost
Jun 1							200	$9.00	$1,800.00
Jun 3	125	$9.25	$1,156.25				325	$9.10	$2,957.50
Jun 7				180	$9.10	$1,638.00	145	$9.10	$1,319.50
Jun 13	100	$9.40	$ 940.00				245	$9.22	$2,258.90
Jun 18				115	$9.22	$1,060.30	130	$9.22	$1,198.60
Jun 25				65	$9.22	$ 599.30	65	$9.22	$ 599.30
Jun 30	225		$2,096.25	360		$3,297.60	65		$ 599.30

Once again, we can double-check our calculations by calculating the cost of goods sold using the same formula that we used in steps a and b. Using this formula, the cost of goods sold is $3,296.95 ($1,800.00 + $2,096.25 – $599.30). The difference ($0.65) between this amount and the cost of goods sold found on our perpetual inventory record ($3,297.60) is due to rounding when calculating the average unit costs and is immaterial.

Demo Doc Complete

Part 1	Part 2	**Demo Doc Complete**

DECISION GUIDELINES

Inventories

If you own or work for a merchandiser, here are some decisions related to inventory that you may encounter.

Decision	Guideline	Analyze
The cost of my products will determine the price that I can sell them for as well as impact other decisions. How do I determine the cost of the inventory I sell?	The physical flow of the inventory and the cost flow of the inventory can be different. The cost assigned to the units sold may be based on one of the following three methods: • Specific-identification • First-in, first-out (FIFO) • Average cost	*Specific-identification*: Inventory items are specifically labelled or identified and the actual cost of each item sold is assigned to cost of goods sold. *First-in, first-out (FIFO)*: The first inventory costs incurred are the first costs to be assigned to cost of goods sold. *Average cost*: With the perpetual system, a new moving average cost per unit is computed after each purchase and assigned to cost of goods sold. With the periodic system, a new weighted-average cost per unit is calculated at the end of each period.
As a shareholder, I need to evaluate how well management has done in achieving goals for net income to award executive bonuses. How do inventory costing methods impact this decision?	The combination of increasing or decreasing costs with inventory costing methods will create opportunities for affecting net income.	When costs are rising • FIFO reports the highest ending inventory value and lowest cost of goods sold and, therefore, the highest net income. • average cost reports an average cost for the value of ending inventory and cost of goods sold. Average cost can be used to stabilize fluctuations in net income if inventory costs are continually fluctuating. This means that an unethical manager could simply change inventory costing methods to manipulate the net income. Evaluations for executives need to examine not only the results, but the methods that are chosen to achieve the results.

What is the effect of a misstatement of ending inventory?	In addition to causing an overstatement or understatement of Inventory on the balance sheet, a misstatement of ending inventory will cause an error on the income statement.	If ending inventory is overstated, then
		• Cost of Goods Sold is understated.
		• Gross Profit is overstated.
		• Net Income is overstated.
		
		If ending inventory is understated, then
		• Cost of Goods Sold is overstated.
		• Gross Profit is understated.
		• Net Income is understated.
		
		Because ending inventory for one period becomes beginning inventory for the next period, the Cost of Goods Sold, Gross Profit, and Net Income of the next period are also misstated.

As a creditor, I have used a company's inventory as collateral towards its loan with my bank. How do I assess the company's management of its inventory?	Use the inventory turnover ratios: $$\text{Inventory Turnover} = \frac{\text{Cost of Goods Sold}}{\text{Average Inventory}}$$ $$\text{Days in Inventory} = \frac{365}{\text{Inventory Turnover}}$$	The inventory turnover ratio can be an indicator that a business is poorly managing its inventory. For example, a turnover ratio that is low compared to the industry average or a turnover ratio that has declined from the prior year may indicate that the business has damaged or obsolete inventory. It is sometimes more clear to use the Days in Inventory calculation to determine how well the inventory is managed.

ACCOUNTING VOCABULARY
THE LANGUAGE OF BUSINESS

Average cost (p. 336) Inventory costing method where a new average cost per unit is computed and is used to value ending inventory and cost of goods sold. There are two types of average cost: (1) moving average, and (2) weighted average. Moving average is applied in a perpetual inventory system. Weighted average is applied in a periodic inventory system.

Consistency (p. 347) Accounting principle that states that a business should use the same accounting methods and procedures from period to period.

Cost of goods available for sale (p. 339) The cost of inventory on hand at the beginning of the period plus the net cost of inventory purchased during the period.

Finished goods (p. 336) Inventory of goods ready to sell.

First-in, first-out (FIFO) (p. 336) Inventory costing method in which the first inventory costs incurred are the first costs to be assigned to cost of goods sold; FIFO leaves in ending inventory the last, the most recent, costs incurred.

Footnotes (p. 349) Disclosures that accompany the financial statements.

Full disclosure (p. 349) Accounting principle that states that a company's financial statements should report enough information for users to make knowledgeable decisions about the company.

Gross profit method (p. 353) A way of estimating inventory by estimating gross profit, using estimated gross profit to estimate cost of goods sold, and using estimated cost of goods sold to estimate ending inventory.

Inventory layer (p. 337) A record of the quantity of and the cost of inventory items made in a single purchase.

Inventory shrinkage (p. 349) The loss of inventory.

Inventory turnover (p. 354) The ratio of cost of goods sold to average inventory.

Lower of cost or net realizable value (LCNRV) rule (p. 348) The rule that a business must report inventory in the financial statements at whichever is lower, the historical cost or the net realizable value, of each inventory item.

Moving average cost (p. 343) Inventory costing method where, after each purchase of inventory, a new average cost per unit is computed and is used to value ending inventory and cost of goods sold in the perpetual inventory system.

Perpetual inventory record (p. 341) A record that tracks the quantity of, and cost assigned to, inventory items as they are purchased and sold.

Raw materials (p. 336) Inventory items used in the production of goods.

Specific-identification (p. 336) Inventory costing method in which a business uses the specific cost of each unit of inventory; also called the *specific-unit cost* method.

Specific-unit cost (p. 340) Inventory costing method in which a business uses the specific cost of each unit of inventory; also called *specific-identification* method.

Weighted average cost (p. 343) Inventory costing method where the beginning inventory and all purchases of inventory are added and divided by the total number of units to get one average cost. This average cost is used to value ending inventory and cost of goods sold in the periodic system.

Work in process (p. 336) Inventory of partially completed goods.

ACCOUNTING PRACTICE

DISCUSSION QUESTIONS

1. The introduction to this chapter suggests that the chapter will explore the answers to some questions about inventory. Did you get the answers to those questions? Specifically,
   a. why does inventory need to be counted?
   b. what would happen if the count was done incorrectly?
   c. what does the term FIFO have to do with inventory?
2. How are the financial statements of a manufacturer different from those of a merchandiser with respect to inventory?

MyAccountingLab

Make the grade with MyAccountingLab. The exercises and problems in this chapter can be found on MyAccountingLab at www.myaccountinglab.com. You can practise them as often as you want, and they feature step-by-step guided solutions to help you find the right answer.

3. What is a cost-flow assumption? Why is a cost-flow assumption necessary in accounting for inventory?

4. If a company had two units that cost $1 each in its beginning inventory and purchased two more units for $2 each, what would be the cost of goods sold associated with a sale of three units under each of the following assumptions?
   a. FIFO
   b. Average cost

5. If a company had two units that cost $1 each in its beginning inventory and purchased two more units for $2 each, what would be the gross profit reported on the income statement under each of the following assumptions if three units were sold for $3 each?
   a. FIFO
   b. Average cost

6. In a period of rising prices, which cost-flow assumption would produce the highest net income? Why?

7. Let's say that two companies, identical in every way except that one used FIFO and one used average cost, went into a bank on the same day to get a loan to deal with the rising cost of acquiring inventory. Despite the fact that they both engaged in the same transactions at the same dollar values, one company reported higher net income and higher total assets on the financial statements. Which one was it? If the banker made the decision based on the company that would have better cash flow associated with the inventory costing method choice, which company would have received the loan?

8. Describe some business and economic conditions that might make the lower of cost or net realizable value more likely to be used.

9. Under which of the inventory methods, periodic or perpetual, would a company be better equipped to detect inventory shrinkage? Why?

10. If a company is having a harder time selling its products, even at discounted prices compared to last year, would this year's inventory turnover rate be higher or lower than last year's rate? What about the gross profit rate?

SELF CHECK

1. During February, Peter's Hardware made sales of $38,600 and ended the month with inventories totaling $5,400. Cost of Goods Sold was $23,200. Total operating expenses were $8,700. How much net income did Peter's Hardware earn for the month?
   a. $1,300
   b. $15,400
   c. $6,700
   d. $10,000

2. Which inventory costing method assigns the newest, most recent, costs incurred during the period to ending inventory?
   a. Specific-unit cost
   b. First-in, first-out (FIFO)
   c. Moving average cost
   d. Weighted average cost

3. Which inventory costing method results in the lowest net income during a period of declining inventory costs?
   a. Weighted average cost
   b. Specific-unit cost
   c. First-in, first-out (FIFO)
   d. Moving average cost

4. Assume HPC, Inc. began December with 60 units of inventory that cost a total of $720. During December, HPC, Inc. purchased and sold goods as follows:

Dec	6	Purchased 120 units @ $13 each
	15	Sold 145 units @ $28 each
	22	Purchased 100 units @ $15
	30	Sold 85 units @ $29 each

HPC, Inc. uses perpetual inventory. Under the FIFO inventory method, how much is HPC's cost of goods sold for the sale on December 15?

a. $455

b. $1,740

c. $1,860

d. $1,825

5. Assume HPC, Inc. began December with 60 units of inventory that cost a total of $720. During December, HPC, Inc. purchased and sold goods as follows:

Dec	6	Purchased 120 units @ $13 each
	15	Sold 145 units @ $28 each
	22	Purchased 100 units @ $15 each
	30	Sold 85 units @ $29 each

HPC, Inc. uses perpetual inventory. Under the FIFO inventory method, how much is HPC's cost of inventory on hand after the sale on December 30?

a. $645

b. $750

c. $600

d. $650

6. Assume HPC, Inc. began December with 60 units of inventory that cost a total of $720. During December, HPC, Inc. purchased and sold goods as follows:

Dec	6	Purchased 120 units @ $13 each
	15	Sold 145 units @ $28 each
	22	Purchased 100 units @ $15 each
	30	Sold 85 units @ $29 each

HPC, Inc. uses perpetual inventory. Under the average cost inventory method, how much is HPC's cost of goods sold for the sale on December 15? Round unit cost to the nearest cent.

a. $1,812.50

b. $1,837.15

c. $1,825.75

d. $1,934.30

7. Which of the following prevents a company from switching its inventory costing method to a different method each year?

a. Disclosure principle

b. Consistency principle

c. Lower of cost or net realizable value

d. Materiality concept

8. Which of the following is most closely linked to accounting conservatism?

a. Materiality concept

b. Consistency principle

c. Disclosure principle

d. Lower of cost or net realizable value

9. At December 31, 2014, Inland Equipment understated ending inventory by $2,800. How does this error affect cost of goods sold and net income for 2014?

a. Overstates cost of goods sold and understates net income

b. Understates costs of goods sold and overstates net income

c. Overstates both cost of goods sold and net income

d. Leaves both cost of goods sold and net income correct because the errors cancel each other

10. Suppose Ironman, Inc. lost all of its inventory in a flood. Beginning inventory was $43,000, net purchases totalled $524,000, and sales came to $875,000. Ironman's normal gross profit percentage is 44%. Use the gross profit method to estimate the cost of the inventory lost in the flood.

a. $308,000   **b.** $182,000

c. $77,000   **d.** $34,000

Answers are given after Written Communication.

SHORT EXERCISES

S6-1. Inventory methods (*Learning Objective 1*) 5 min.

Motion Auto would like to assign the newest costs of inventory items to its ending inventory.

Which inventory costing method should Motion Auto choose?

S6-2. Inventory methods (*Learning Objective 1*) 5–10 min.

Hamilton Furniture doesn't expect prices to change dramatically and wants to use a method that averages price changes.

Which inventory method would best meet Hamilton Furniture's goal? What if Hamilton Furniture wanted to expense out the older purchases of goods instead? Which inventory method would best meet that need?

S6-3. FIFO (*Learning Objective 2*) 5–10 min.

Mike's Powersports uses the FIFO inventory method. Mike's Powersports started August with 10 helmets that cost $54 each. On August 19, Mike's Powersports bought 15 helmets at $56 each. On August 28, Mike's Powersports sold 12 helmets. Four units were taken from the batch of the beginning inventory and 8 units from the purchase on August 19.

Prepare a perpetual inventory record for Mike's Powersports.

S6-4. Specific-identification (*Learning Objective 2*) 5–10 min.

Mike's Powersports uses the specific-identification inventory method. Mike's Powersports started August with 10 helmets that cost $54 each. On August 19, Mike's Powersports bought 15 helmets at $56 each. On August 28, Mike's Powersports sold 12 helmets. Four units were taken from the batch of the beginning inventory and 8 units from the purchase on August 19.

Calculate the cost of goods sold and ending inventory for Mike's Powersports.

S6-5. Average cost (*Learning Objective 2*) 5–10 min.

Mike's Powersports uses the average cost inventory method. Mike's Powersports started August with 10 helmets that cost $54 each. On August 19, Mike's Powersports bought 15 helmets at $56 each. On August 28, Mike's Powersports sold 12 helmets.

Prepare a perpetual inventory record for the average cost method. Round average cost per unit to the nearest cent and all other amounts to the nearest dollar.

S6-6. Recording inventory transactions (*Learning Objective 2*) 5–10 min.

Mike's Powersports uses the (perpetual) average cost inventory method. Mike's Powersports started August with 10 helmets that cost $54 each. On August 19, Mike's Powersports bought 15 helmets at $56 each. On August 28, Mike's Powersports sold 12 helmets.

1. The August 19 purchase of inventory was on account.

2. The August 28 sale of inventory was on account. Mike's Powersports sold each helmet for $95.

Prepare the required journal entries for the purchase and sale of inventory.

S6-7. FIFO versus average cost (*Learning Objective 2*) 5–10 min.

Consider the FIFO and average cost inventory costing methods. Answer the following questions assuming that inventory costs are increasing:

1. Which method of inventory costing will produce the lower cost of goods sold?

2. Which method of inventory costing will produce the higher cost of goods sold?

3. If prices had been declining instead of rising, which inventory method will produce the higher cost of goods sold?

S6-8. Terms (*Learning Objectives 4 & 5*) 5–10 min.

Match the terms with the definitions.

a. Full disclosure

b. Materiality

c. Consistency

d. Prudence

_____ 1. A company must perform strictly proper accounting only for items that are significant to the business's financial statements

_____ 2. Reporting the realistic figures in the financial statements

_____ 3. A business's financial statements must report enough information for users to make knowledgeable decisions about the company

_____ 4. A business should use the same accounting methods and procedures from period to period

S6-9. Lower of cost or net realizable value (*Learning Objective 4*) 5–10 min.

Assume that Bonsai Boards has the following FIFO perpetual inventory record for snowboards for the month of November:

			Snowboards	
Date	Purchases	Cost of Goods Sold	Inventory on Hand	
Nov 1			$1,320	
8	$ 840		$2,160	
19		$1,640	$ 520	
30	$1,130		$1,650	

At November 30, the accountant for Bonsai Boards determines that the current replacement cost of the ending inventory is $1,615. Make any adjusting entry needed to apply the lower of cost or net realizable value rule. Inventory would be reported on the balance sheet at what value on November 30?

S6-10. Reporting inventory on the balance sheet (*Learning Objective 5*) 5–10 min.

At the end of the current year, Cuppa Joes' inventory account balance was $12,600. A physical count of the inventory revealed that inventory on hand totaled $12,200.

What amount should Cuppa Joes report on its balance sheet?

S6-11. Inventory principles and terminology (*Learning Objectives 1, 4, & 5*) 5–10 min.

Match the accounting terms on the left with the corresponding definitions on the right.

___ 1. Prudence	a. Assigns the most recent inventory costs to ending inventory.
___ 2. Full disclosure	
___ 3. Moving average cost	b. Inventory costing method where a new weighted average cost per unit is computed and is used to value ending inventory and cost of goods sold.
___ 4. FIFO	
___ 5. Consistency	
___ 6. Materiality	c. This is the basis for using lower of cost or net realizable value.
___ 7. Specific identification	d. Principle that prevents a company from using a different inventory costing method each year.
	e. Identifies exactly which inventory item was sold. Usually used for unique inventory items.
	f. Requires that a company report enough information for outsiders to make decisions.
	g. Principle that states significant items must conform to IFRS and Canadian ASPE.

S6-12. Inventory errors (*Learning Objective 6*) 5–10 min.

Bonsai Board's income statement data for the year ended December 31, 2014, follow.

Sales Revenue	$237,500
Cost of Goods Sold	142,800
Gross Profit	$ 94,700

Assume that the ending inventory was accidentally overstated by $3,300.

What are the correct amounts for cost of goods sold and gross profit?

S6-13. Inventory errors (*Learning Objective 6*) 10–15 min.

Bonsai Board's income statement data for the year ended December 31, 2014, follow.

Sales Revenue	$237,500
Cost of Goods Sold	142,800
Gross Profit	$ 94,700

Assume that the ending inventory was accidentally overstated by $3,300. How would the inventory error affect Bonsai Boards' cost of goods sold and gross profit for the year ended December 31, 2015, if the error is not corrected in 2014?

S6-14. Estimating ending inventory (*Learning Objective 7*) 10–15 min.

Inland Lumber began the year with inventory of $52,200 and made purchases of $316,700 during the year. Sales for the year are $503,800, and Inland Lumber's gross profit percentage is 42% of sales.

Compute Inland Lumber's estimated cost of ending inventory using the gross profit method.

S6-15. Inventory turnover (*Learning Objective 8*) 5–10 min.

Mackay Industries' sales for the year ended December 31, 2014, were $1,287,000 and cost of goods sold amounted to $707,000. Beginning inventory was $58,000 and ending inventory was $77,000.

Compute Mackay Industries' rate of inventory turnover for the year ended December 31, 2014. Round answer to the nearest tenth.

EXERCISES (GROUP A)

E6-1A. FIFO (*Learning Objective 2*) 10–15 min.

Austin's Jewelers carries a line of waterproof watches. Austin's Jewelers uses the FIFO method and a perpetual inventory system. The sales price of each watch is $175. Company records indicate the following activity for waterproof watches for the month of March:

Date	Item	Quantity	Unit Cost
Mar 1	Balance	3	$ 96
7	Purchase	10	$ 98
11	Sale	12	
19	Purchase	15	$104
28	Sale	10	

Requirements

1. Prepare a perpetual inventory record for the waterproof watches to determine the amount Austin's Jewelers should report for ending inventory and cost of goods sold using the FIFO method.

2. Journalize Austin's Jewelers' inventory transactions using the FIFO method. Assume that all purchases and sales are on account.

E6-2A. Specific-identification (*Learning Objective 2*) 10–15 min.

Refer to the data for E6-1A. However, instead of the FIFO method, assume Austin's Jewelers uses the specific-identification method, assuming the following for each sale:

March 11 Sale: 2 units from the beginning inventory, and the rest from the March 7 purchase.

March 19 Sale: all units are from the March 19 purchase.

Requirements

1. Prepare a perpetual inventory record for the watches on the specific-identification basis to determine the cost of ending inventory and cost of goods sold for the month.

2. Journalize Austin's Jewelers' inventory transactions using the perpetual specific-identification method. Assume that all purchases and sales are on account.

E6-3A. Average cost (*Learning Objective 2*) 10–15 min.

Refer to the data for E6-1A. However, instead of the FIFO method, assume Austin's Jewelers uses the average cost method.

Requirements

1. Prepare a perpetual inventory record for the watches on the average cost basis to determine the cost of ending inventory and cost of goods sold for the month. Round average cost per unit to the nearest cent and all other amounts to the nearest dollar.

2. Journalize Austin's Jewelers' inventory transactions using the perpetual average cost method. Assume that all purchases and sales are on account.

E6-4A. FIFO versus average cost (*Learning Objective 2*) 10–15 min.

Assume that Midway Cycles bought and sold a line of mountain bikes during May as follows:

Date	Item	Quantity	Unit Cost
May 1	Balance	10	$243
5	Sale	5	
12	Purchase	12	$252
21	Sale	7	
30	Sale	6	

Midway Cycles uses the perpetual inventory system.

Requirements

1. Compute the cost of ending inventory under FIFO.
2. Compute the cost of ending inventory under average cost.
3. Which method results in higher cost of ending inventory?

E6-5A. FIFO versus average cost (*Learning Objective 2*) 10–15 min.

Refer to the data for Midway Cycles in E6-4A.

Requirements

Quick solution: 1. FIFO cost of goods sold = $4,446; 2. Weighted average cost of goods sold = $4,456

1. Compute the cost of goods sold under FIFO.
2. Compute the cost of goods sold under average cost.
3. Which method results in the higher cost of goods sold?

E6-6A. FIFO versus average cost (*Learning Objectives 2 & 3*) 15–20 min.

Assume that a Firestone Tire Store completed the following perpetual inventory transactions for a line of tires.

Beginning Inventory	34 tires @ $ 82
Purchase	25 tires @ $ 88
Sale	40 tires @ $134

Requirements

1. Compute cost of goods sold and gross profit under FIFO.
2. Compute cost of goods sold and gross profit using average cost. Round average cost per unit to the nearest cent and all other amounts to the nearest dollar.
3. Which method results in the larger gross profit and why?

E6-7A. Lower of cost or net realizable value (*Learning Objective 4*) 10–15 min.

GDL Enterprises has the following account balances at December 31, 2014. The inventory balance was determined using FIFO.

Inventory		Cost of Goods Sold		Sales Revenue	
Beg Bal 26,500					
End Bal 31,800		Bal 106,000			Bal 176,000

GDL Enterprises has determined that the replacement cost (current market value) of the December 31, 2014, ending inventory is $32,400.

Requirements

1. What value would GDL Enterprises report on the balance sheet at December 31, 2014, for inventory assuming the company uses the lower of cost or net realizable value rule?

2. Prepare any adjusting journal entry required from the information given.

E6-8A. Reporting inventory on the balance sheet (*Learning Objective 5*) 5–10 min.

Eagle Eye Sunglasses had the following FIFO perpetual inventory record at June 30, the end of the fiscal year.

	Purchases			Cost of Goods Sold			Inventory on Hand		
Date	Quantity	Unit Cost	Total Cost	Quantity	Unit Cost	Total Cost	Quantity	Unit Cost	Total Cost
Jun 1							200	$9.00	$1,800.00
Jun 3	125	$9.25	$1,156.25				200	$9.00	$1,800.00
							125	$9.25	$1,156.25
Jun 7				180	$9.00	$1,620.00	20	$9.00	$ 180.00
							125	$9.25	$1,156.25
Jun 13	100	$9.40	$ 940.00				20	$9.00	$ 180.00
							125	$9.25	$1,156.25
							100	$9.40	$ 940.00
Jun 18				20	$9.00	$ 180.00	30	$9.25	$ 277.50
				95	$9.25	$ 878.75	100	$9.40	$ 940.00
Jun 25				30	$9.25	$ 277.50			
				35	$9.40	$ 329.00	65	$9.40	$ 611.00
Jun 30	225		$2,096.25	360		$3,285.25	65		$ 611.00

A physical count of the inventory performed at year end revealed $587.00 of inventory on hand.

Requirements

1. Journalize the adjusting entry for inventory, if any is required.

2. What could have caused the value of the ending inventory based on the physical count to be lower than the amount based on the perpetual inventory record?

E6-9A. Inventory errors (*Learning Objective 6*) 10–15 min.

Motion Auto reported sales revenue of $138,000 and cost of goods sold of $76,000.

Requirements

1. Compute Motion Auto's correct gross profit assuming the company's ending inventory is overstated by $1,300. Show your work.

2. Compute Motion Auto's correct gross profit assuming the company's ending inventory is understated by $2,700. Show your work.

E6-10A. Inventory errors (*Learning Objective 6*) 10–15 min.

Hanson's Furniture Outlet reported the following comparative income statement for the years ended June 30, 2014 and 2013.

	2014		**2013**	
Hanson's Furniture Outlet				
Comparative Income Statement				
For the Years Ended December 31, 2014 and 2013				
Sales Revenue		$187,600		$164,000
Cost of Goods Sold:				
Beginning Inventory	$ 12,300		$ 9,100	
Net Purchases	114,500		101,600	
Cost of Goods Available	126,800		110,700	
Ending Inventory	14,600		12,300	
Cost of Goods Sold		112,200		98,400
Gross Profit		75,400		65,600
Operating Expenses		32,900		26,700
Net Income		$ 42,500		$ 38,900

During 2014, Hanson's Furniture Outlet discovered that the 2013 ending inventory, as previously reported, was understated by $2,100.

Requirements

1. Prepare the corrected comparative income statement for the two-year period, complete with a heading for the statement.

2. What was the effect of the error on net income for the two years combined? Explain your answer.

E6-11A. Estimating ending inventory (*Learning Objective 7*) 5–10 min.

Totally Tunes sells and installs audio equipment. During a recent fire that occurred at its warehouse, Totally Tunes' entire inventory was destroyed. Totally Tunes' accounting records reflect the following information.

Beginning Inventory	$ 46,400
Net Purchases	243,900
Net Sales	404,000
Gross Profit Rate	35%

Requirement

1. Use the gross profit method to estimate the amount of Totally Tunes' inventory loss.

E6-12A. Inventory turnover (*Learning Objective 8*) 10–15 min.

Gibson's Nursery has the following information as of December 31, 2014:

Sales Revenue...		$1,287,500
Cost of Goods Sold:		
Beginning Inventory..	$ 44,300	
Net Purchases..	750,600	
Cost of Goods Available	794,900	
Ending Inventory...	48,700	
Cost of Goods Sold		746,200
Gross Profit..		541,300
Operating Expenses		388,700
Net Income		$ 152,600

Requirements

1. Compute the rate of inventory turnover for Gibson's Nursery for the year ended December 31, 2014. Round the result to two decimal places.

2. The rate of inventory turnover for Gibson's Nursery was 17.36 in 2013. Has the rate improved or deteriorated?

E6-13A. FIFO versus average cost and inventory turnover (*Learning Objectives 2, 3, & 8*) 20–25 min.

Kimco's sales for the year 2014 were $575,000 ($230/unit). On January 1, 2014, Kimco's beginning inventory showed 450 units, costing $40,500. During 2014, Kimco purchased 2,650 units at $95 each. Kimco's income statement is as follows.

Income Statement
Inventory Costing Method

	Units	FIFO	Weighted Average
Sales	_____	_____	_____
Cost of Goods Sold:			
Beginning Inventory	_____	_____	_____
Purchases	_____	_____	_____
Goods Available for Sale	_____	_____	_____
Ending Inventory	_____	_____	_____
Cost of Goods Sold	_____	_____	_____
Gross Profit		_____	_____
Operating Expenses		$265,000	$265,000
Operating Income		_____	_____
Income Tax Expense (30%)		_____	_____
Net Income		_____	_____

Requirements

1. Complete the income statement for Kimco, using FIFO and weighted average cost methods.

2. Calculate the inventory turnover, using FIFO and weighted average cost methods.

3. Which method shows higher profit and inventory turnover? Explain.

EXERCISES (GROUP B)

E6-1B. FIFO (*Learning Objective 2*) 10–15 min.

Underwater Way carries a line of waterproof watches. Underwater Way uses the FIFO method and a perpetual inventory system. The sales price of each watch is $188. Company records indicate the following activity for waterproof watches for the month of August:

Date	Item	Quantity	Unit Cost
Aug 1	Balance	4	$106
7	Purchase	13	$110
11	Sale	16	
19	Purchase	18	$112
28	Sale	11	

Requirements

1. Prepare a perpetual inventory record for the waterproof watches to determine the amount Underwater Way should report for ending inventory and cost of goods sold using the FIFO method.

2. Journalize Underwater Way's inventory transactions using the FIFO method. Assume that all purchases and sales are on account.

E6-2B. Specific-identification (*Learning Objective 2*) 10–15 min.

Refer to the data for E6-1B. However, instead of the FIFO method, assume Underwater Way uses the specific-identification method, assuming the following for each sale:

August 11 Sale: 3 units from the beginning inventory, and the rest from the August 7 purchase.

August 28 Sale: all units are from the August 19 purchase.

Requirements

1. Prepare a perpetual inventory record for the watches on the specific identification basis to determine the cost of ending inventory and cost of goods sold for the month.

2. Journalize Underwater Way's inventory transactions using the perpetual specific-identification method. Assume that all purchases and sales are on account.

E6-3B. Average cost (*Learning Objective 2*) 10–15 min.

Refer to the data for E6-1B. However, instead of the FIFO method, assume that Underwater Way uses the average cost method.

Requirements

1. Prepare a perpetual inventory record for the watches on the average cost basis to determine the cost of ending inventory and cost of goods sold for the month. Round average cost per unit to the nearest cent and all other amounts to the nearest dollar.

2. Journalize Underwater Way's inventory transactions using the perpetual average cost method. Assume that all purchases and sales are on account.

E6-4B. FIFO vs. average cost (*Learning Objective 2*) 10–15 min.

Assume that Cycle Guys bought and sold a line of mountain bikes during December as follows:

Date	Item	Quantity	Unit Cost
Dec 1	Balance	12	$225
5	Sale	6	
12	Purchase	10	$220
21	Sale	8	
30	Sale	6	

Cycle Guys uses the perpetual inventory system.

Requirements

1. Compute the cost of ending inventory under FIFO.

2. Compute the cost of ending inventory under average cost.

3. Which method results in a higher cost of ending inventory?

E6-5B. FIFO versus average cost (*Learning Objective 2*) 10–15 min.

Refer to the data for Cycle Guys in E6-4B.

Requirements

1. Compute the cost of goods sold under FIFO.

2. Compute the cost of goods sold under average cost.

3. Which method results in a higher cost of goods sold?

E6-6B. FIFO versus average cost (*Learning Objectives 2 & 3*) 15–20 min.

Assume that RB Tire Store completed the following perpetual inventory transactions for a line of tires.

Beginning Inventory..	32 tires @ $ 73
Purchase...	37 tires @ $ 67
Sale...	38 tires @ $154

Requirements

1. Compute cost of goods sold and gross profit under FIFO.

2. Compute cost of goods sold and gross profit using average cost. Round average cost per unit to the nearest cent and all other amounts to the nearest dollar.

3. Which method results in the larger gross profit and why?

E6-7B. Lower of cost or net realizable value (*Learning Objective 4*) 10–15 min.

Clarmont Resources has the following account balances at October 31, 2014. The inventory balance was determined using FIFO.

Inventory		Cost of Goods Sold		Sales Revenue	
Beg Bal 22,400					
End Bal 35,500		Bal 114,000			Bal 188,000

Clarmont Resources has determined that the replacement cost (current market value) of the October 31, 2014, ending inventory is $38,000.

Requirements

1. What value would Clarmont Resources report on the balance sheet at October 31, 2014, for inventory assuming the company uses the lower of cost or net realizable value rule?

2. Prepare any adjusting journal entry required from the information given.

E6-8B. Reporting inventory on the balance sheet (*Learning Objective 5*) 5–10 min.

Ray Blocker Sunglasses had the following FIFO perpetual inventory record at April 30, the end of the fiscal year.

Date	Purchases Quantity	Purchases Unit Cost	Purchases Total Cost	Cost of Goods Sold Quantity	Cost of Goods Sold Unit Cost	Cost of Goods Sold Total Cost	Inventory on Hand Quantity	Inventory on Hand Unit Cost	Inventory on Hand Total Cost
Apr 1							150	$9.00	$1,350.00
Apr 3	150	$9.50	$1,425.00				150	$9.00	$1,350.00
							150	$9.50	$1,425.00
Apr 7				110	$9.00	$ 990.00	40	$9.00	$ 360.00
							150	$9.50	$1,425.00
Apr 13	110	$9.70	$1,067.00				40	$9.00	$ 360.00
							150	$9.50	$1,425.00
							110	$9.70	$1,067.00
Apr 18				40	$9.00	$ 360.00	90	$9.50	$ 855.00
				60	$9.50	$ 570.00	110	$9.70	$1,067.00
Apr 25				90	$9.50	$ 855.00			
				35	$9.70	$ 339.50	75	$9.70	$ 727.50
Apr 30	260		$2,492.00	335		$3,114.50	75		$ 727.50

A physical count of the inventory performed at year-end revealed $672.50 of inventory on hand.

Requirements

1. Journalize the adjusting entry for inventory, if any is required.

2. What could have caused the value of the ending inventory based on the physical count to be lower than the amount based on the perpetual inventory record?

E6-9B. Inventory errors (*Learning Objective 6*) 10–15 min.

Boston Auto reported sales revenue of $160,000 and cost of goods sold of $90,000.

Requirements

1. Compute Boston Auto's correct gross profit assuming the company's ending inventory is overstated by $1,400. Show your work.

2. Compute Boston Auto's correct gross profit assuming the company's ending inventory is understated by $2,400. Show your work.

E6-10B. Inventory errors (*Learning Objective 6*) 10–15 min.

Healthy Bite Mart reported the following comparative income statement for the years ended November 30, 2014 and 2013.

Healthy Bite Mart
Comparative Income Statements
For the Years Ended November 30, 2014 and 2013

		2014		2013	
Sales Revenue			$137,000		$120,000
Cost of Goods Sold:					
Beginning Inventory	$15,500			$11,000	
Net Purchases	70,000			69,000	
Cost of Goods Available	85,500			80,000	
Ending Inventory	18,500			15,500	
Cost of Goods Sold			67,000		64,500
Gross Profit			70,000		55,500
Operating Expenses			24,000		20,000
Net Income			$ 46,000		$ 35,500

During 2014, Healthy Bite Mart discovered that the 2013 ending inventory, as previously reported, was understated by $2,500.

Requirements

1. Prepare the corrected comparative income statement for the two-year period, complete with a heading for the statement.

2. What was the effect of the error on net income for the two years combined? Explain your answer.

E6-11B. Estimating ending inventory (*Learning Objective 7*) 5–10 min.

Speaker Shop sells and installs audio equipment. During a recent fire that occurred at its warehouse, Speaker Shop's entire inventory was destroyed. Speaker Shop's accounting records reflect the following information.

Beginning Inventory	$ 47,500
Net Purchases	288,500
Net Sales	440,000
Gross Profit Rate	30%

Requirement

1. Use the gross profit method to estimate the amount of Speaker Shop's inventory loss.

E6-12B. Inventory turnover (*Learning Objective 8*) 10–15 min.

Pete's Plants has the following information as of October 31, 2014:

Sales Revenue		$1,345,000
Cost of Goods Sold:		
Beginning Inventory	$ 30,000	
Net Purchases	840,600	
Cost of Goods Available	870,600	
Ending Inventory	41,000	
Cost of Goods Sold		829,600
Gross Profit		515,400
Operating Expenses		109,000
Net Income		$ 406,400

Requirements

1. Compute the rate of inventory turnover for Pete's Plants for the year ended October 31, 2014. Round the result to two decimal places.

2. The rate of inventory turnover for Pete's Plants was 21.96 in 2013. Has the rate improved or deteriorated?

E6-13B. FIFO versus average cost and inventory turnover (*Learning Objectives 2, 3, & 8*) 20–25 min.

Calco's sales for the year 2014 were $115,000 ($92/unit). On January 1, 2014, Calco's beginning inventory showed 120 units, costing $4,800. During 2014, Calco purchased 1,420 units at $38 each. Calco's income statement is as follows

	Income Statement Inventory Costing Method		
	Units	**FIFO**	**Weighted Average**
Sales			
Cost of Goods Sold:			
Beginning Inventory			
Purchases			
Goods Available for Sale			
Ending Inventory			
Cost of Goods Sold			
Gross Profit			
Operating Expenses		$25,000	$25,000
Operating Income			
Income Tax Expense (30%)			
Net Income			

Requirements

1. Complete the income statement for Calco, using FIFO and weighted average cost methods.

2. Calculate the inventory turnover, using FIFO and weighted average cost methods.

3. Which method shows higher profit and inventory turnover? Explain.

EXERCISES (ALTERNATES 1, 2, AND 3)

These alternative exercise sets are available for your practice benefit at *www.myaccountinglab.com*

PROBLEMS (GROUP A)

P6-1A. Computing FIFO and journalizing inventory transactions (*Learning Objectives 1 & 2*) 15–20 min.

Inland Equipment sells hand-held engine analyzers to automotive service shops. Inland Equipment started April with an inventory of 85 units that cost a total of $12,750. During the month, Inland Equipment purchased and sold merchandise on account as follows:

Apr 6	Purchased 125 units @ $160
13	Sold 110 units @ $310
19	Purchased 130 units @ $168
25	Sold 80 units @ $310
29	Sold 75 units @ $310

Inland Equipment uses the FIFO method. Cash payments on account totalled $21,700. Operating expenses for the month were $12,000, with two-thirds paid in cash and the rest accrued as Accounts Payable.

Requirements

1. Which inventory method (excluding specific-unit) most likely mimics the physical flow of Inland Equipment's inventory?

2. Prepare a perpetual inventory record, using FIFO cost, for this merchandise.

3. Journalize all transactions using FIFO. Record the payments on account and the operating expenses on the 30th.

P6-2A. Computing average cost and journalizing inventory transactions (*Learning Objectives 2 & 5*) 15–20 min.

Refer to the data for Inland Equipment in P6-1A. However, assume Inland Equipment uses the average cost method.

Requirements

1. Prepare a perpetual inventory record using average cost. Round the average unit cost to the nearest cent and all other amounts to the nearest dollar.

2. Prepare a multi-step income statement for Inland Equipment for the month of April.

P6-3A. FIFO and average cost (*Learning Objectives 2 & 3*) 15–20 min.

MAC Industries completed the following inventory transactions during the month of August:

Date	Item	Quantity	Unit Cost
Aug 1	Balance	25	$80
4	Purchase	40	$78
12	Sale	52	
22	Purchase	30	$77
31	Sale	22	

Requirements

1. Without resorting to calculations, determine which inventory method will result in MAC Industries paying the lowest income taxes.

2. Prepare a perpetual inventory record using FIFO.

3. Prepare a perpetual inventory record using average cost.

P6-4A. Lower of cost or net realizable value (*Learning Objective 4*) 10–15 min.

Titan Offroad Equipment uses the FIFO inventory method and values its inventory using the lower of cost or net realizable value rule. Titan Offroad Equipment has the following account balances at December 31, 2014, prior to releasing the financial statements for the year:

Inventory			Cost of Goods Sold			Sales Revenue	
Beg Bal 54,300							
End Bal 61,100			Bal 258,600				Bal 419,500

The accountant for Titan Offroad Equipment has determined that the replacement cost (current market value) of the ending inventory as of December 31, 2014, is $58,300.

Requirements

1. Which accounting principle or concept is most relevant to Titan Offroad Equipment's decision to utilize LCNRV?
2. What value would Titan Offroad Equipment report on the balance sheet at December 31, 2014, for inventory?
3. Prepare any adjusting journal entry required from the information given.

P6-5A. Lower of cost or net realizable value (*Learning Objective 4*) 10–15 min.

Due to a nationwide recession, PC World's merchandise inventory is gathering dust. It is now December 31, 2014, and the $162,000 that PC World paid for its ending inventory is $14,000 higher than current replacement cost. Before any adjustments at the end of the period, PC World's Cost of Goods Sold account has a balance of $628,000. PC World uses lower of cost or net realizable value to value its ending inventory.

Requirements

1. What amount should PC World report for inventory on the balance sheet?
2. What amount should PC World report for cost of goods sold?
3. Journalize any required entries.

P6-6A. Inventory errors (*Learning Objective 6*) 20–25 min.

A & R Industrial Supply shows the following financial statement data for 2012, 2013, and 2014. Prior to issuing the 2014 statements, auditors found that the ending inventory for 2012 was understated by $8,000 and that the ending inventory for 2014 was overstated by $9,000. The ending inventory at December 31, 2013, was correct.

(In thousands)	2014		2013		2012	
Sales Revenue		$210		$191		$186
Cost of Goods Sold:						
Beginning Inventory	$ 12		$ 18		$ 15	
Net Purchases	143		121		128	
Cost of Goods Available	155		139		143	
Ending Inventory	16		12		18	
Cost of Goods Sold		139		127		125
Gross Profit		71		64		61
Operating Expenses		46		43		42
Net Income		$ 25		$ 21		$ 19

Requirements

1. State whether each year's net income before corrections is understated or overstated and indicate the amount of the understatement or overstatement.

2. Prepare corrected income statements for the three years.

3. What is the impact on the 2014 income statement if the 2012 inventory error is left uncorrected?

P6-7A. Estimating ending inventory (*Learning Objective 7*) 15–20 min.

Amtran Enterprises lost its entire inventory in a hurricane that occurred on May 31, 2014. Over the past five years, gross profit has averaged 32% of net sales. The company's records reveal the following data for the month of May:

Beginning Inventory	$ 38,600
Net Purchases	341,900
Sales	530,400
Sales Returns and Allowances	12,300
Sales Discounts	6,500

Requirements

1. Estimate the May 31 inventory using the gross profit method.

2. Prepare the May income statement through gross profit for Amtran Enterprises.

Quick solution: *1. May 31 estimated inventory = $32,612; 2. Gross Profit = $163,712*

P6-8A. Inventory turnover (*Learning Objective 8*) 10–15 min.

Motion Auto has the following information for the years ending December 31, 2014 and 2013:

(In thousands)	2014		2013	
Sales Revenue		$242		$239
Cost of Goods Sold:				
Beginning Inventory	$ 22		$ 38	
Net Purchases	152		144	
Cost of Goods Available	174		182	
Ending Inventory	13		22	
Cost of Goods Sold		161		160
Gross Profit		81		79
Operating Expenses		55		54
Net Income		$ 26		$ 25

Requirements

1. Compute the rate of inventory turnover for Motion Auto for the years ended December 31, 2014 and 2013. Round the result to two decimal places.

2. What is a likely cause for the change in the rate of inventory turnover from 2013 to 2014?

P6-9A. Inventory turnover (*Learning Objective 8*) **20–25 min.**

Luson's manager is quite concerned about its inventory turnover and would like to improve the turnover. The following is the financial information for the past two years:

	2013	**2014**
Sales	$360,000	$378,000
Inventory	42,500	33,100

Luson's financial objective is to continue with the same growth rate in sales for 2015. Its cost of goods sold is 60% of the sales.

Requirements

1. What is the inventory turnover for 2014?

2. What are the projected sales in 2015?

3. With the projected growth in sales in 2015, if Luson wants to increase inventory turnover to 5.5 times, what should the inventory be?

P6-10A. Computing FIFO, specific-identification, average cost, and journalizing inventory transactions (*Learning Objectives 2 & 3*) **40–45 min.**

Silverin Gifts, Inc. had the following transactions related to purchases and sales of merchandise for the last month. The selling price of silver plates was $120 each, with a credit term of 2/10, n/30. All purchases were on credit, with a term of 2/10, n/30.

Mar 5   Purchased 25 silver plates at $55 each.

Mar 7   Sold 15 silver plates to Botan, Inc.

Mar 10   Purchased 20 silver plates at $58 each.

Mar 15   Sold 10 silver plates to Zenith Co.

Mar 17   Zenith returned 5 silver plates to Silverin.

Mar 21   Purchased 40 silver plates at $60 each.

Mar 25   Sold 12 silver plates to Raj Co.

Mar 30   Sold 15 silver plates to Kito Co.

On March 1, Silverin had 5 silver plates in inventory, with a total cost of $260.

Requirements

1. Calculate the ending inventory and cost of goods sold, using a perpetual inventory system:

    (a) FIFO

    (b) Average cost (round the average unit cost to the nearest cent and all other amounts to the nearest dollar.)

2. Calculate the ending inventory and cost of goods sold, using a periodic inventory system:

    (a) FIFO

    (b) Average cost (round the average unit cost to the nearest cent and all other amounts to the nearest dollar.)

3. Prepare the journal entries, using a perpetual inventory system:

    (a) FIFO

    (b) Average cost (round the average unit cost to the nearest cent and all other amounts to the nearest dollar.)

4. Calculate the ending inventory and cost of goods sold, assuming Silverin uses the specific-identification method. Silverin provided the following additional information:

- Mar 7 sale: all units were taken from the Mar 5 purchase.
- Mar 15 sale: 5 units were taken from the beginning inventory, 5 units from the Mar 10 purchase
- Mar 17 sales return: 5 units were returned to the March 10 purchase
- Mar 25 sale: all units were taken from the Mar 21 purchase
- Mar 30 sale: all units were taken from the Mar 21 purchase

P6-11A. Correcting inventory errors (*Learning Objective 6*) 20–25 min.

Raj Trading reported the following amounts in its financial statements:

	Financial Statement for Year Ended Dec. 31		
	2014	2015	2016
(a) Cost of Goods Sold	$ 715,000	$ 847,000	$ 735,000
(b) Net Income	275,000	220,000	292,000
(c) Total Current Assets	865,000	764,000	847,000
(d) Shareholders' Equity	1,287,000	1,169,000	1,232,000

In making the physical count of inventory, the following errors were made:

(1) Inventory on Dec. 31, 2014: included $25,000 of goods that were on consignment from a friend of the owner.

(2) Inventory on Dec. 31, 2015: did not count a section of inventory, $42,000.

Requirements

For each of the preceding financial statement items—(a), (b), (c), and (d)—prepare a schedule and show the adjustments that would have been necessary to correct the reported amounts.

Cost of Goods Sold	2014	2015	2016
Reported			
Adjustments for (1)			
Adjustments for (2)			
Corrected			

Total Current Assets	2014	2015	2016
Reported			
Adjustments for (1)			
Adjustments for (2)			
Corrected			

Net Income	2014	2015	2016
Reported			
Adjustments for (1)			
Adjustments for (2)			
Corrected			

Shareholders' Equity	2014	2015	2016
Reported			
Adjustments for (1)			
Adjustments for (2)			
Corrected			

PROBLEMS (GROUP B)

P6-1B. Computing FIFO and journalizing inventory transactions (Learning Objectives 1 & 2) 15–20 min.

Builder Bee Equipment sells hand-held engine analyzers to automotive service shops. Builder Bee Equipment started April with an inventory of 45 units that cost a total of $5,760. During the month, Builder Bee Equipment purchased and sold merchandise on account as follows:

Apr 6	Purchased 115 units @ $142
13	Sold 100 units @ $300
19	Purchased 80 units @ $152
25	Sold 40 units @ $300
29	Sold 75 units @ $300

Builder Bee Equipment uses the FIFO method. Cash payments on account totalled $20,000. Operating expenses for the month were $15,000, with two-thirds paid in cash and the rest accrued as Accounts Payable.

Requirements

1. Which inventory method (excluding specific-unit) most likely mimics the physical flow of Builder Bee Equipment's inventory?

2. Prepare a perpetual inventory record using FIFO cost for this merchandise.

3. Journalize all transactions using FIFO. Record the payments on account and the operating expenses on the 30th.

P6-2B. Computing average cost and journalizing inventory transactions (Learning Objectives 2 & 5) 15–20 min.

Refer to the data for Builder Bee Equipment in P6-1B. However, assume Builder Bee Equipment uses the average cost method.

Requirements

1. Prepare a perpetual inventory record using average cost. Round the average unit cost to the nearest cent and all other amounts to the nearest dollar.

2. Prepare a multi-step income statement for Builder Bee Equipment for the month of April.

P6-3B. FIFO and average cost (Learning Objectives 2 & 3) 15–20 min.

Widget, Corp. completed the following inventory transactions during the month of January:

Date	Item	Quantity	Unit Cost
Jan 1	Balance	15	$50
4	Purchase	55	$55
12	Sale	66	
22	Purchase	35	$58
31	Sale	24	

Requirements

1. Without resorting to calculations, determine which inventory method will result in Widget, Corp. paying the lowest income taxes.

2. Prepare a perpetual inventory record using FIFO.

3. Prepare a perpetual inventory record using average cost.

P6-4B. Lower of cost or net realizable value (*Learning Objective* 4) 10–15 min.

Richmond Sporting Goods uses the FIFO inventory method and values its inventory using the lower of cost or net realizable value (LCNRV) rule. Richmond Sporting Goods has the following account balances at May 31, 2014, prior to releasing the financial statements for the year:

Inventory		Cost of Goods Sold		Sales Revenue	
Beg Bal 41,800					
End Bal 68,900		Bal 206,000		Bal 303,000	

The accountant for Richmond Sporting Goods has determined that the replacement cost (current market value) of the ending inventory as of May 31, 2014, is $54,000.

Requirements

1. Which accounting principle or concept is most relevant to Richmond Sporting Goods' decision to utilize LCNRV?

2. What value would Richmond Sporting Goods report on the balance sheet at May 31, 2014, for inventory?

3. Prepare any adjusting journal entry required from the information given.

P6-5B. Lower of cost or net realizable value (LCNRV) (*Learning Objective* 4) 10–15 min.

Due to a nationwide recession, Amesbury Systems' merchandise inventory is gathering dust. It is now October 31, 2014, and the $163,300 that Amesbury Systems paid for its ending inventory is $18,500 higher than current replacement cost. Before any adjustments at the end of the period, Amesbury Systems' Cost of Goods Sold account has a balance of $695,000. Amesbury Systems uses lower of cost or net realizable value to value its ending inventory.

Requirements

1. What amount should Amesbury Systems report for inventory on the balance sheet?

2. What amount should Amesbury Systems report for cost of goods sold?

3. Journalize any required entries.

P6-6B. Inventory errors (*Learning Objective* 6) 20–25 min.

Lally Industries shows the following financial statement data for 2012, 2013, and 2014.

(In thousands)	2014		2013		2012	
Net Sales Revenue		$205		$170		$175
Cost of Goods Sold:						
Beginning Inventory	$ 12		$ 27		$ 24	
Net Purchases	138		103		126	
Cost of Goods Available	150		130		150	
Ending Inventory	21		12		27	
Cost of Goods Sold		129		118		123
Gross Profit		76		52		52
Operating Expenses		47		31		36
Net Income		$ 29		$ 21		$ 16

Prior to issuing the 2014 statements, auditors found that the ending inventory for 2012 was understated by $5,000 and that the ending inventory for 2014 was overstated by $12,000. The ending inventory at December 31, 2013, was correct.

Requirements

1. State whether each year's net income before corrections is understated or overstated and indicate the amount of the understatement or overstatement.
2. Prepare corrected income statements for the three years.
3. What is the impact on the 2014 income statement if the 2012 inventory error is left uncorrected?

P6-7B. Estimating ending inventory (*Learning Objective 7*) 15–20 min.

Olympic Village Enterprises lost its entire inventory in a hurricane that occurred on July 31, 2014. Over the past five years, gross profit has averaged 30% of net sales. The company's records reveal the following data for the month of July:

Beginning Inventory	$ 37,100
Net Purchases	294,600
Sales	540,100
Sales Returns and Allowances	72,200
Sales Discounts	8,300

Requirements

1. Estimate the July 31 inventory using the gross profit method.
2. Prepare the July income statement through gross profit for Olympic Village Enterprises.

P6-8B. Inventory turnover (*Learning Objective 8*) 10–15 min

Hulu's Hybrids has the following information for the years ending January 31, 2014 and 2013:

(In thousands)	2014		2013	
Sales Revenue		$235		$213
Cost of Goods Sold:				
Beginning Inventory	$ 23		$ 33	
Net Purchases	141		147	
Cost of Goods Available	164		180	
Ending Inventory	6		23	
Cost of Goods Sold		158		157
Gross Profit		77		56
Operating Expenses		59		42
Net Income		$ 18		$ 14

Requirements

1. Compute the rate of inventory turnover for Hulu's Hybrids for the years ended January 31, 2014 and 2013. Round the result to two decimal places.
2. What is a likely cause for the change in the rate of inventory turnover from 2013 to 2014?

P6-9B. Inventory turnover (*Learning Objective 8*) 20–25 min.

Taiping's owner thinks he manages his inventory quite well. However, his accountant advises him that the industry average of inventory turnover is 9 times. The following is the financial information for the past two years:

	2013	2014
Sales	$360,000	$378,000
Inventory	42,500	33,100

Taiping's financial objective is to continue with the same growth rate in sales for 2015. Its cost of goods sold is 70% of the sales.

Requirements

1. What is the inventory turnover for 2014?

2. What are the projected sales in 2015?

3. With the projected growth in sales in 2015, if Taiping wants to increase inventory turnover to 9 times, what should the inventory be?

P6-10B. Computing FIFO, specific-identification, average cost, and journalizing inventory transactions (Learning Objectives 2 & 3) 40–45 min.

Hamada Hand Tools, Inc. (HHT) had the following transactions related to purchases and sales of merchandise for the last month. The selling price of hand tools was $80 each, with a credit term of 2/10, n/30. All purchases were on credit, with a term of 2/10, n/30.

May 2	Purchased 30 hand tools at $45 each.
May 6	Sold 15 hand tools to CAT Construction, Inc.
May 10	Purchased 25 hand tools at $42 each.
May 14	Sold 20 hand tools to Max Tools.
May 16	Max Tools returned 2 hand tools to HHT.
May 18	Sold 12 hand tools to Parker Co.
May 22	Purchased 40 hand tools at $44 each.
May 27	Sold 25 hand tools to Bibby Co.

On May 1, HHT had 10 hand tools in inventory, with a total cost of $480.

Requirements

1. Calculate the ending inventory and cost of goods sold using a perpetual inventory system:

   (a) FIFO

   (b) Average cost (round the average unit cost to the nearest cent and all other amounts to the nearest dollar.)

2. Calculate the ending inventory and cost of goods sold using a periodic inventory system:

   (c) FIFO

   (d) Average cost (round the average unit cost to the nearest cent and all other amounts to the nearest dollar.)

3. Prepare the journal entries using a perpetual inventory system:

   (a) FIFO

   (b) Average cost (round the average unit cost to the nearest cent and all other amounts to the nearest dollar.)

4. Calculate the ending inventory and cost of goods sold, assuming HHT is using the specific-identification method. HHT provided the following additional information:

   • May 6 sale: all units were taken from the May 2 purchase.

   • May 14 sale: 10 units were taken from the beginning inventory and 10 units from the May 10 purchase

- May 16 sales return: 2 units were returned to the beginning inventory cost
- May 18 sale: all units were taken from the May 10 purchase
- May 27 sale: all units were taken from the May 22 purchase

P6-11B. Correcting inventory errors (*Learning Objective 6*) 20–25 min.

Suresh Import, Inc. reported the following amounts in its financial statements:

	Financial Statement for Year Ended Dec. 31		
	2014	2015	2016
(a) Cost of Goods Sold	$425,000	$369,000	$406,000
(b) Net Income	128,000	240,000	148,000
(c) Total Current Assets	465,000	547,000	527,000
(d) Shareholders' Equity	782,000	896,000	876,000

In making the physical count of inventory, the following errors were made:

(1) Inventory on Dec. 31, 2014: did not count a section of inventory, $45,000.

(2) Inventory on Dec. 31, 2015: included $32,000 of goods that were sold and set aside to be shipped the next day.

Requirements

For each of the preceding financial statement items—(a), (b), (c), and (d)—prepare a schedule and show the adjustments that would have been necessary to correct the reported amounts.

Cost of Goods Sold	2014	2015	2016
Reported			
Adjustments for (1)			
Adjustments for (2)			
Corrected			

Total Current Assets	2014	2015	2016
Reported			
Adjustments for (1)			
Adjustments for (2)			
Corrected			

Net Income	2014	2015	2016
Reported			
Adjustments for (1)			
Adjustments for (2)			
Corrected			

Shareholders' Equity	2014	2015	2016
Reported			
Adjustments for (1)			
Adjustments for (2)			
Corrected			

PROBLEMS (ALTERNATES 1, 2, AND 3)

These alternative problem sets are available for your practice benefit at
www.myaccountinglab.com

CONTINUING EXERCISE

This exercise continues the Graham's Yard Care, Inc. exercise begun in Chapter 1. Consider the July transactions for Graham's Yard Care that were presented in Chapter 5. (Cost data have been removed from the sale transactions.)

Jul	2	Completed lawn service and received cash of $500.
	5	Purchased 100 plants on account for inventory, $250, plus freight in of $10.
	15	Sold 40 plants on account, $400.
	17	Consulted with a client on landscaping design for a fee of $150 on account.
	20	Purchased 100 plants on account for inventory, $300.
	21	Paid on account, $100.
	25	Sold 100 plants for cash, $700.
	31	Recorded the following adjusting entries:
		Accrued salaries for the month of July equal $225
		Depreciation on equipment $30
		Physical count of plant inventory, 50 plants

Refer to the T-accounts for Graham's Yard Care, Inc. from the continuing exercise in Chapter 3.

Requirements

1. Prepare perpetual inventory records for July for Graham's Yard Care, Inc. using the FIFO method.

2. Journalize and post the July transactions using the perpetual inventory record created in Requirement 1. Omit explanations. Key all items by date. Compute each account balance, and denote the balance as *Bal*.

3. Journalize and post the adjusting entries. Denote each adjustment amount as *Adj*.

4. Journalize and post closing entries. After posting all closing entries, prove the equality of debits and credits in the ledger.

CONTINUING PROBLEM

This continues our accounting for Aqua Elite, Inc. As stated in the continuing problem in Chapter 5, Aqua Elite, Inc. began selling pools and spas in August. For this problem, we will focus on the purchase and sales of spas during the month of September. The purchases and sales of spa inventory for the month of September are as follows:

Spa Inventory		
	Unit @ Cost	Total Cost
August 31 balance	3 units @ $1,800/each	$ 5,400
September 5 purchase	5 units @ $2,000/each	$10,000
September 11 sale	4 units	
September 17 purchase	6 units @ $2,100/each	$12,600
September 21 sale	5 units	
September 25 purchase	5 units @ $2,200/each	$11,000
September 29 sale	4 units	

Requirements

1. Assuming that Aqua Elite, Inc. uses the FIFO inventory cost flow assumption, what is the September 30 ending spa inventory balance and September cost of goods sold for spas?

2. Assuming that Aqua Elite, Inc. uses the average cost inventory cost flow assumption, what is the September 30 ending spa inventory balance and September cost of goods sold for spas?

APPLY YOUR KNOWLEDGE

ETHICS IN ACTION

Case 1. Julie Robertson recently went to work for K & K Enterprises as the accounting manager. At the end of the year, Jeffrey Baker, the CEO, called Julie into his office for a meeting. Mr. Baker explained to Julie that K & K Enterprises was in the midst of obtaining a substantial investment of cash by a major investor. Mr. Baker explained that he was concerned that the investor would decide not to invest in K & K Enterprises when it saw the current year's results of operations. Mr. Baker then asked Julie to revise the current year's financial statements by increasing the value of the ending inventory in order to decrease cost of goods sold and increase net income. Mr. Baker tried to reassure Julie by explaining that the company is undertaking a new advertising campaign that will result in a significant improvement in the company's income in the following year. Julie is concerned about the future of her job, as well as others within the company, if the company does not receive the investment of cash.

Requirements

1. What would you do if you were in Julie's position?
2. If Julie increases the value of the current year's ending inventory, what will be the effect on the following year's net income?

Case 2. Inland Standard Equipment, which sells industrial handling equipment, values its inventory using FIFO. During the recent year, Inland Standard Equipment has experienced a significant decrease in the cost of its inventory items. Although the net income for the current year has been fairly good, Roberta Hill, the company president, wishes it was higher because the company has been considering borrowing money to purchase a new building. Mrs. Hill has heard that a company's choice of inventory valuation method can impact the net income of the company. Mrs. Hill has asked the controller, Vicki Simpson, to explore the possibility of changing the company's inventory valuation method.

Requirement

1. If you were in Vicki's position how would you respond to Mrs. Hill? Address potential ethical implications and applicable accounting principles in your answer.

KNOW YOUR BUSINESS

FINANCIAL ANALYSIS

Purpose: To help familiarize you with the financial reporting of a real company to further your understanding of the chapter material you are learning.

The Bombardier Annual Report, Year Ended January 31, 2011 is included in MyAccountingLab. Access the annual report and answer the following questions.

Requirements

1. Which note discusses the inventory costing method used by Bombardier Inc.? What types of costs are included in inventories?
2. Which note discloses the types of inventories held by Bombardier? Describe the types of inventory that Bombardier has and why? What are the Advances and Progress Billings and why are these deducted in determining inventories? What is included in "Finished Products"?
3. What is the amount of inventories recognized in cost of sales for 2011? What is the gross inventory balance (before taking the deduction for the Advances and Progress Billings) for 2011? Using these two numbers, calculate an inven-

tory turnover ratio for 2011. Why might an inventory turnover ratio not be very relevant or useful in the case of Bombardier?

INDUSTRY ANALYSIS

Purpose: To help you understand and compare the performance of two companies in the same industry.

Now access The Boeing Company's 2010 Annual Report. To do this from the internet, go to their webpage for the Investor Relations at *http://www.boeing.com/companyoffices/financial/quarterly.htm* and, under Annual Report, go to the 2010 Annual Report.

Requirement

1. Calculate the inventory turnover for both companies (calculate the turnover for January 31, 2011 for Bombardier and for December 31, 2010 for Boeing). For both companies, use the inventory balances before the deduction for Advances and Progress Billings in calculating the turnover ratio. Who has the highest inventory turnover? Is that good or bad? Is it better to have a high inventory turnover or a low inventory turnover?

SMALL BUSINESS ANALYSIS

Purpose: To help you understand the importance of cash flows in the operation of a small business.

It's the end of the year and your warehouse manager just finished taking a physical count of the inventory on hand. Because you are utilizing the perpetual inventory method with a relatively sophisticated inventory software program, you expect that the ending inventory balance will be pretty close to the balance on your general ledger. In the past, you've had to make some pretty large adjustments for inventory shrinkage, but with the new security measures you've installed to safeguard your inventory, you're expecting that any shrinkage adjustment this year will be minimal. At least you hope that's the case, because your net income can't take many more adjustments. This year's financial statements are very important to your banker because of the loan renewal coming up early next year.

You look at the amount from the final inventory count and it reads $467,450. You go to the general ledger Merchandise Inventory account and it reads $498,500. You look at the preliminary income statement, which doesn't reflect any of these adjustments yet, and the net income is $128,400. You remember that the banker said that he really wanted to see a net income of at least $100,000 this year.

Requirements

1. Calculate the effect that the required inventory adjustments will have on the net income for the year. Would your banker be happy or not so happy when you presented the financial statements to him after these adjustments?

2. If the adjustment you made for inventory shrinkage last year was about $10,000, should that cause you any concern for the amount of adjustment you have to make this year?

3. In addition to the impact that the inventory adjustment might have on your loan renewal, what effect did it have on your cash flow during the year?

WRITTEN COMMUNICATION

You just got off the telephone with one of your clients who has decided to expand her business by beginning to offer some merchandise for sale. Previously the company had only been a consulting business, but now it has an opportunity to sell some product from a new line offered by one of its clients.

The client's question to you seems rather simple, at least in her eyes. Which inventory costing method should the client use that will give the highest amount of net income? Because the consulting part of the business has not been doing very well lately, the company wants to have a lot of net income from this new side of the business so that the income statement will look good at the end of the year. The company has heard that either average cost or FIFO will result in higher net income, but it is not certain which it is. Plus, the company definitely plans to always sell the oldest merchandise first, so will this have any impact on which method it chooses? The question does seem simple, but is the answer simple?

Requirement

1. Respond to your client either with a memo, a letter, or an email.

Self Check Answers
1. c 2. b 3. c 4. d 5. b 6. b 7. b 8. d 9. a 10. c

COMPREHENSIVE PROBLEM

THE ACCOUNTING CYCLE FOR A MERCHANDISER INCLUDING INVENTORY VALUATION

Wild Wheels, Inc. wholesales a line of custom mountain bikes. Wild Wheels' inventory as of November 30, 2014, consisted of 20 bikes costing $550 each. Wild Wheels' trial balance as of November 30 appears as follows:

Wild Wheels, Inc. Trial Balance November 30, 2014		
ACCOUNT	**DEBIT**	**CREDIT**
Cash	$ 9,150	
Accounts Receivable	12,300	
Inventory	11,000	
Supplies	900	
Office Equipment	18,000	
Accumulated Depreciation, Office Equipment		3,000
Accounts Payable		1,325
Note Payable, Long-Term		5,000
Common Shares		8,500
Retained Earnings		21,425
Dividends	4,250	
Sales Revenues		93,500
Sales Returns and Allowances	1,700	
Sales Discounts	1,275	
Cost of Goods Sold	46,750	
Sales Commissions	11,300	
Office Salaries Expense	7,425	
Office Rent Expense	5,500	
Shipping Expense	3,200	
Total	$132,750	$132,750

During the month of December 2014 Wild Wheels, Inc., had the following transactions:

Dec	4	Purchased 10 mountain bikes for $575 each from Slickrock Bicycle, Co. on account, terms 2/15, n/45, FOB destination.
	6	Sold 14 mountain bikes for $1,100 each on account to Allsport, Inc., terms 3/10, n/30, FOB destination.
	8	Paid $175 freight charges to deliver goods to Allsport, Inc.
	10	Received $6,200 from Cyclemart as payment on a November 17 purchase. Terms were n/30.
	12	Purchased $350 of supplies on account from Office Maxx, terms 2/10, n/30, FOB destination.
	14	Received payment in full from Allsport, Inc. for the Dec 6 sale.
	16	Purchased 15 mountain bikes for $600 each from Slickrock Bicycle, Co. on account, terms 2/15, n/45, FOB destination.
	18	Paid Slickrock Bicycle, Co. the amount due from the December 4 purchase in full.
	19	Sold 18 mountain bikes for $1,125 each on account to Bikeworld, Inc., terms 2/15, n/45, FOB shipping point.
	20	Paid for the supplies purchased on December 12.
	22	Paid sales commissions, $875.
	30	Paid current month's rent, $500.

Requirements

1. Using the transactions listed above, prepare a perpetual inventory record for Wild Wheels, Inc. for the month of December. Wild Wheels, Inc. uses the FIFO inventory costing method.

2. Open four-column general ledger accounts and enter the balances from the November 30 trial balance.

3. Record each transaction in the general journal. Explanations are not required. Post the journal entries to the general ledger, creating new ledger accounts as necessary. Omit posting references. Calculate the new account balances.

4. Prepare an unadjusted trial balance as of December 31, 2014.

5. Journalize and post the adjusting journal entries based on the following information, creating new ledger accounts as necessary:

   a. Depreciation expense on office equipment, $1,650.

   b. Supplies on hand, $125.

   c. Accrued salary expense for the office receptionist, $675.

6. Prepare an adjusted trial balance as of December 31, 2014. Use the adjusted trial balance to prepare Wild Wheels, Inc.'s multi-step income statement, statement of retained earnings, and classified balance sheet for the year ending December 31, 2014.

7. Journalize and post the closing entries.

8. Prepare a post-closing trial balance at December 31, 2014.

SCAN THIS

CHAPTER 7

Sales and Receivables

LEARNING OBJECTIVES:

1 ▶ Identify the different types of sales and receivables and discuss related internal controls for accounts receivable

2 ▶ Use the allowance method to account for uncollectible accounts

3 ▶ Report accounts receivable on the balance sheet

4 ▶ Account for notes receivable

5 ▶ Calculate the quick ratio and accounts receivable turnover

If you ever have the opportunity of owning your own business or working in upper management, you will quickly learn how important cash is to a business. The need for cash can make the decision of whether or not to grant credit to customers a critical decision. If you do grant credit, how do you account for customers that fail to pay the amount they owe? Should your company accept debit and credit cards as forms of payment? In Chapter 7, we will explore the issues surrounding these important decisions as we study sales, receivables, and bad debt.

CHAPTER OUTLINE:

In earlier chapters we have seen that net income is the result of deducting all of a business's expenses from its revenues. Therefore, it makes sense that to increase net income a business must either reduce its expenses or increase its revenues. The choice of what methods of payment a business is willing to accept from its customers can have a significant effect on the amount of revenues it is able to generate. The method of payment a business accepts is determined by the type of sales it makes.

HOW DO YOU ACCOUNT FOR REVENUE?

Accounting for the sale of goods is similar under IFRS and Accounting Standards for Private Enterprises (ASPE). The seller recognizes sales revenue when goods and ownership are transferred to the buyers and the seller has no control over the goods. The transfer of ownership or the title is usually specified in the sales contract or the invoice. In Chapter 5, we discussed FOB shipping point and FOB destination. The point of delivery specifies when the ownership passes on to the buyer. This also has an impact on the inventory count.

Service companies recognize revenue when they have performed services for the client. There are also situations when companies can record revenues at other points in the process of selling a product or service. The guidelines according to IFRS and the Accounting Standards for Private Enterprises are similar in that both guidelines stipulate that revenue is recognized when: (a) the risks and rewards of ownership are passed to the buyer; (b) the revenues can be reasonably measured; and, (c) collection from the customer is reasonably assured. The IFRS guidelines also add that the costs associated with the goods sold should be able to be measured reliably and the seller no longer has control or managerial influence over the item to a degree that would be normally associated with ownership. We can find the specific revenue recognition principles and policies that the companies used in the notes to their financial statements.

Accounting for Revenue in Long-Term Contracts

Long-term projects such as construction of a cruise ship or building may take more than one year to complete. If the company waited to record revenue until the delivery of the cruise ship or passing the ownership of the building when the project was completed, then the company would show only expenses and no revenues during the years when the projects were being constructed and show a huge revenue during the year of delivery. This method is called the **completed contract method**; however, this method distorts the company's economic activities. Under IFRS, the completed contract method is prohibited. Instead, the revenue from long-term contracts must be recognized using the **percentage of completion method**, if percentage of completion can be used reliably. Canadian ASPE provides an option to use the percentage of completion or completed contract method.

Under the percentage of completion method, the total revenues and expenses are estimated. Then, the revenue for the first year is recognized based on the percentage of expenses incurred during the year over the total expenses of the project. For example, Kidel Constructions, Inc. estimated total revenue for a new office building of $25 million and total expenses of $20 million. During the first year of the project, Kidel incurred $8 million of expenses, which is 40% of the contract expenses ($8 million ÷ $20 million). Kidel will recognize 40% of revenue, which is $10 million. During the second year of the project, Kidel incurred $7 million, and the total expenses incurred to date were $15 million. If the total estimated expenses were not expected to change, then the total expenses incurred to date were 75% of the total estimated expenses. The revenue for the second year is $8.75 million, calculated by taking 75% of the total estimated revenue and subtracting the revenue that has been recognized in the previous year, as shown in Exhibit 7-1:

	Year 1	Year 2
Expenses Incurred to Date	$ 8,000,000	$15,000,000
Total Estimated Expenses	$20,000,000	$20,000,000
Percentage of Completion	40%	75%
Revenue Recognized to Date	$10,000,000	$18,750,000
Revenue Recognized for the Year	$10,000,000	$ 8,750,000

Exhibit 7-1 ▲

The revenue to be recognized in following years would work in the same way as the second year, until the long-term project was complete.

WHAT ARE THE DIFFERENT TYPES OF SALES?

Cash Sales

Cash sales are the most desirable form of sales because the business receives cash immediately upon delivering goods or services. Cash sales are also the easiest type to track because customers give currency or a cheque at the time of sale. The business does not need to keep records of the individual customers. As demonstrated in earlier chapters, a cash sale is recorded as follows (assume the sale amount is $500):

 Identify the different types of sales and receivables and discuss related internal controls for accounts receivable

DATE	ACCOUNTS	POST REF.	DR.	CR.
	Cash		500	
	Sales			500

Although cash sales are easy to account for, businesses may limit their sales potential by not providing options for customers to buy now and pay later.

Credit Card Sales

An alternative that helps businesses attract more customers is the acceptance of credit cards. There are two main types of credit cards:

- Credit cards issued by a financial institution such as a bank or a credit union, such as Scotiabank or Bank of Montreal. The most common types of these cards are Visa and MasterCard.
- Credit cards issued by a credit card company on behalf of a retail store or other corporation, such as MBNA or Hudson's Bay Company.

One of the primary benefits of credit cards is that they allow customers to buy now and pay later. Retailers who accept credit card payments do not have to worry about collecting from the customer or keeping accounts receivable records because the entity that issued the card bears the responsibility of collecting the amounts due from the customers. Instead of collecting cash from the customer, the retailer will receive payment from the issuer of the card. Another benefit of credit card sales is that they facilitate purchases made via telephone or online due to the fact that no cash has to change hands at the time of sale. One drawback to accepting credit card payments is that retailers typically pay a service fee to cover the cost of processing the transaction.

Debit Card Sales

Businesses can also attract customers by accepting debit card payments in addition to cash and credit card payments. From the retailer's perspective, debit cards are nearly identical to credit cards and have the same benefits and drawbacks. The primary difference between a debit card and a credit card is how and when the cardholder must pay the card issuer.

Credit/Debit Card Processing

Most businesses hire a third party processor to process credit and debit card transactions. Transactions are typically entered into an electronic terminal that is often rented from the processor. Businesses may also purchase a terminal if they would rather own the terminal than rent it. As previously discussed, there is a fee associated with credit and debit card transactions. The fees vary depending on the type of card processed and depending upon the specific agreement the business has with the card processor. The agreement also specifies when and how fees are paid. The most common methods of fee payment follow:

- The fees are deducted from the proceeds of each sale at the time the sale proceeds are deposited into the business's bank account.
- The fees for all transactions processed are deducted from the business's bank account on a monthly basis.

Proceeds from credit and debit card transactions are typically deposited into a business's bank account within a one- to three-day period. Therefore, credit and debit card sales are journalized in a manner similar to cash sales. Assume a business has a credit/debit card sale of $500, with a cost of the product being $350. The customer paid by credit card. The business pays $8 of processing fees, which are deducted from the proceeds. The journal entry to record the card sale is as follows:

DATE	ACCOUNTS	POST REF.	DR.	CR.
Mar 31	Cash		492	
	Credit Card Expense		8	
	Sales			500
	Cost of Goods Sold		350	
	Inventory			350

The expense associated with processing the transactions is recorded at the same time the sale proceeds are recorded. Now, assume that instead of having the processing fees deducted from the sales proceeds, the business has the fees deducted from its bank account at the end of each month. The journal entry to record the day's card sales would now look like this:

DATE	ACCOUNTS	POST REF.	DR.	CR.
Mar 31	Cash		500	
	Sales			500
	Cost of Goods Sold		350	
	Inventory			350

Notice that this entry is exactly the same as the entry required for cash sales. The expense associated with processing the transactions will be recorded at the time a statement is received from the processor or at the time the monthly bank reconciliation is prepared.

Sales on Account

In Chapter 5, we discussed sales of merchandise on account. When businesses agree to sell on credit, sales increase, but so does the risk of not being able to collect what is owed as a result of these sales. Accordingly, companies bear the risk of **bad debts**, or **uncollectible accounts**, which occur when a customer does not pay for the goods or services they received. Regardless of its size, a business must manage its customer relationships to avoid bad debts.

HOW DO YOU ACCOUNT FOR RECEIVABLES?

Types of Receivables

Companies often make sales on account that create a receivable from the customer. The two major types of receivables are accounts receivable and notes receivable. Remember from Chapter 1 that a business's accounts receivable are current assets that reflect the amounts due from customers for credit sales of goods or services. Also recall from Chapter 2 that notes receivable are written promises by customers to pay an amount of cash to the business in the future. Notes receivable are more formal and usually longer in term than accounts receivable. Notes also usually include a charge for interest. A detailed discussion of Notes Receivable will follow later in the chapter.

A company may also have other receivables, such as loans to employees and interest receivable. These other receivables may be either current or long-term assets, depending on if they are due within one year or less.

Internal Control over Accounts Receivable

Most companies have a Credit Department to evaluate customers' credit applications. The extension of credit requires a balancing act. The company wants to avoid receivables that will never be collected while at the same time granting credit to as many customers as possible. Also, companies that sell on credit often receive the related payment by mail, so internal control over collections is important. Remember, a critical element of internal control is the separation of cash-handling and cash-accounting duties.

Good internal control over Accounts Receivable dictates that the granting of credit, the receipt of cash, and the recording of Accounts Receivable transactions is done by different individuals preferably from different departments. For example, if the employee who handles the daily cash receipts also records the Accounts Receivable transactions, the company would have no separation of duties. The employee could pocket money received from a customer. He or she could then label the customer's account as uncollectible, and the company would **write off** the account receivable, as discussed in the next section. The company would stop billing that customer, and the employee would have covered his or her theft. For this reason, separation of duties is important.

Accounting for Uncollectible Accounts Receivable

Unfortunately, when a business chooses to sell goods or services on account, there will likely be customers who fail to pay the amount owed. When this happens, the customer's account is referred to as an uncollectible account. Uncollectible accounts reflect a cost associated with selling goods and services on account. Companies who make sales on account expect that the benefit of granting credit to customers outweighs the cost.

- **The benefit:** Increased revenues and profits from making sales to a wider range of customers.
- **The cost:** Some customers don't pay, and that creates an expense called **bad debt expense**.

HOW DO YOU ACCOUNT FOR BAD DEBTS?

Accounting for Bad Debts

When businesses agree to sell on credit, sales increase, but so does the risk of not being able to collect what is owed as a result of these sales. The amount of bad debt is unknown when the sales are made. Therefore, the bad debt amount needs to be estimated. This amount is used to reduce the income and also to reduce the accounts receivable, and this amount needs to be recorded at the end of an accounting period.

The Direct Write-Off Method

2 ▶ Use the allowance method to account for uncollectible accounts

The simplest way to account for uncollectible accounts is to use the **direct write-off method**. Under the direct write-off method, at the time it is determined the business will not collect from a specific customer, the business writes off that customer's Account Receivable. The Account Receivable is written off by debiting Bad Debt Expense and crediting the customer's Account Receivable. However, this method is not accepted for financial reporting purposes because it does not show the realizable value of accounts receivable.

The Allowance Method

The **allowance method** is a method of accounting for bad debts in which bad debt expense is recorded in the same period as sales revenue. Under the allowance method, a business will use an adjusting entry at the end of the period to record the bad debt expense for the period. Since the business does not know which customers will eventually not pay them, it must estimate the amount of bad debt expense based on past experience. This expense must be recognized during the same period when the credit sales are generated. The debit side of the adjusting entry will be to the Bad Debt Expense account. However, instead of crediting Accounts Receivable, a contra-account called **Allowance for Doubtful Accounts (AFDA)** will be credited. The Allowance for Doubtful Accounts is "tied" to the Accounts Receivable account and serves to reduce the **net realizable value** of the Accounts Receivable. The adjusting entry will look like this:

DATE	ACCOUNTS	POST REF.	DR.	CR.
Dec 31	Bad Debt Expense		XXX	
	Allowance for Doubtful Accounts			XXX
	To record estimated bad debts.			

The Allowance for Doubtful Accounts is utilized because the specific customers who will ultimately not pay are unknown at the time the adjusting entry is made. Companies usually create the Accounts Receivable **control account** in the general ledger. Each customer has an account in the accounts receivable subsidiary account, under the Accounts Receivable control account. To reduce Accounts Receivable, the specific customer would have to be known so that his or her Account Receivable could be reduced in the subsidiary ledger. As we will demonstrate later in the chapter, once it is known that a specific customer's account is uncollectible, his or her Account Receivable will be written off. The offset to this entry will be to reduce the Allowance for Doubtful Accounts by an equal amount.

Estimating the Amount of Uncollectible Accounts

In order to estimate the amount of Bad Debt Expense, a company will use its past bad debt experience to make an educated guess of how much will be uncollectible. The state of the economy, the industry the business operates in, and other variables are also used to arrive at the best estimate possible. There are two basic ways to estimate the amount of uncollectible accounts:

- Percentage of sales method or income statement method
- Aging method or balance sheet method

Percentage of Sales Method The **percentage of sales method** or the income statement method computes the estimated amount of uncollectible accounts as a percentage of **net credit sales**. This amount is the bad debt amount. As both sales and bad debt expense are income statement accounts, this method of estimating the amount is also called the **income statement method**. To demonstrate, let's assume that Allied Enterprises has the following selected account balances as of December 31, 2013, prior to adjusting for bad debts:

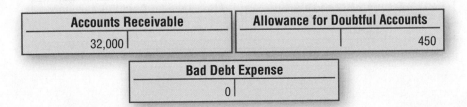

Accounts Receivable		Allowance for Doubtful Accounts	
32,000			450

Bad Debt Expense	
0	

It is important to note that when using the allowance method, the Allowance for Doubtful Accounts will almost always have a balance at the end of the period. The balance in the account may have a debit or a credit balance depending on the amount of the adjusting entry from the prior period and the amount of uncollectible accounts that have been written off during the current period. Also note that the Bad Debt Expense account will always have a zero balance. This is because, as an expense account, it was closed at the end of the prior period.

Now, let's assume that Allied Enterprises estimates Bad Debt Expense to be 1/2 of 1% of net credit sales, which totalled $300,000 during 2013. The estimated amount of bad debts is $1,500 ($300,000 × 0.005). Under the percentage of sales method, once the estimated amount of uncollectible accounts has been determined, the adjusting entry is made for that amount. The required journal entry at December 31, 2013, would be as follows:

DATE	ACCOUNTS	POST REF.	DR.	CR.
Dec 31	Bad Debt Expense		1,500	
	Allowance for Doubtful Accounts			1,500
	To record estimated bad debts.			

After posting the adjusting entry, Allied Enterprises' accounts would look like this:

Accounts Receivable	
32,000	

Allowance for Doubtful Accounts	
	450
	1,500
	1,950

Bad Debt Expense	
0	
1,500	
1,500	

The net realizable value of Allied Enterprises' Accounts Receivable is $30,050 at December 31, 2013 ($32,000 A/R less $1,950 Allowance for Doubtful Accounts). Notice that Bad Debt Expense reflects the calculated amount of uncollectible accounts ($1,500), whereas Allowance for Doubtful Accounts reflects a different amount ($1,950). This reflects why this method is also called the income statement approach. This method focuses more on the income statement than on the balance sheet. After the adjusting entry has been posted, the income statement account (Bad Debt Expense) reflects the calculated amount of uncollectible accounts rather than the balance sheet account (Allowance for Doubtful Accounts).

Aging Method The other method for estimating uncollectible accounts is the **aging method**. Once again, let's assume Allied Enterprises had the following account balances at December 31, 2013, prior to adjusting for bad debts.

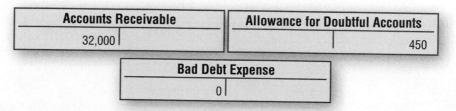

Accounts Receivable	
32,000	

Allowance for Doubtful Accounts	
	450

Bad Debt Expense	
0	

When using the aging method, a schedule is created that reflects all of the company's individual credit customers with their account balances broken down based on how long they've been outstanding. This is known as an Accounts Receivable aging report. **Exhibit 7-2** reflects the Accounts Receivable aging report for Allied Enterprises at December 31, 2013.

	Customer	Balance	Current	1–30	31–60	61–90	91–180	> 181
						Days Past Due		
1	B. Ashford	$ 450		150	300			
2	L. Clark	875	875					
32	M. Reynolds	575	575					
33	R. Turlock	225						225
34	K. Wilson	950				125	825	
	Total	$32,000	26,850	2,800	475	325	1,250	300

Exhibit 7-2 ▲

Once the aging has been prepared, an estimated percentage of bad debts is determined for each age category. This percentage is then multiplied by the balance for each age category to determine the estimated bad debts for that category. These amounts are then added together to arrive at the total estimated amount of bad debts for the period. The calculation for Allied Enterprises would look like this:

Account Age	Balance	Estimated Percent Uncollectible	Estimated Uncollectible Amount
Current	$26,850	2%	$ 537
1–30	2,800	5%	140
31–60	475	20%	95
61–90	325	40%	130
91–180	1,250	50%	625
> 181	300	80%	240
Total	$32,000		$1,767

Now that we know the total estimated amount of bad debts, $1,767, we are ready to make the adjusting entry. The most significant difference between the two methods is that, unlike when using the percentage of sales method, we do not simply take the calculated amount of bad debts and use this as the amount of the journal entry. Instead, we must look at the existing balance in Allowance for Doubtful Accounts and perform a calculation to determine the amount to use in the adjusting entry. When using the aging method, the goal is for Allowance for Doubtful Accounts to reflect the calculated amount of bad debts *after* the adjusting entry has been recorded and posted. The easiest way to determine the correct amount of the required adjusting entry is to do a T-account analysis of Allowance for Doubtful Accounts as follows:

Allowance for Doubtful Accounts	
	450
	?
	1,767

The first step in the analysis is to enter the Allowance for Doubtful Accounts balance that existed prior to making the adjusting entry. Next, skip a line and enter the desired ending balance in the T-account. This balance will be the calculated amount of the bad debts, $1,767. The question mark represents the adjusting entry amount that is required. This amount is determined by calculating the credit needed to bring the ending balance up to the desired amount. It is very important to pay attention to whether the Allowance for Doubtful Accounts balance that existed prior to making the adjusting entry was a debit or a credit. Also, remember that the ending balance in the account will always be a credit balance. By looking at the T-account analysis, we can see that the required adjusting entry amount is $1,317 ($1,767 − $450). The required journal entry at December 31, 2013, would be as follows:

DATE	ACCOUNTS	POST REF.	DR.	CR.
Dec 31	Bad Debt Expense		1,317	
	Allowance for Doubtful Accounts			1,317
	To record estimated bad debts.			

After posting the adjusting entry, Allied Enterprises' accounts would look like this:

Accounts Receivable	
32,000	

Allowance for Doubtful Accounts	
	450
	1,317
	1,767

Bad Debt Expense	
0	
1,317	
1,317	

The net realizable value of Allied Enterprises' Accounts Receivable is $30,233 at December 31, 2013 ($32,000 A/R less $1,767 Allowance for Doubtful Accounts). Notice that Allowance for Doubtful Accounts reflects the calculated amount of bad debts ($1,767) whereas Bad Debt Expense reflects a different amount ($1,317). This reflects why this method is also called the **balance sheet method**. This method focuses more on the balance sheet than on the income statement. After the adjusting entry has been posted, the balance sheet account (Allowance for Doubtful Accounts) reflects the calculated amount of bad debts rather than the income statement account (Bad Debt Expense).

Writing Off Bad Debts Under the Allowance Method

The entry to write off a customer's account under the allowance method begins with a credit to Accounts Receivable to remove it from the company's books with a debit made to Allowance for Doubtful Accounts. Assume that on March 5, 2014, Allied Enterprises determined that Bill Johnson's $400 Account Receivable was uncollectible. The entry to write off Bill Johnson's account under the allowance method would be as follows:

DATE	ACCOUNTS	POST REF.	DR.	CR.
Mar 5	Allowance for Doubtful Accounts		400	
	Accounts Receivable—Bill Johnson			400
	Wrote off Bill Johnson's account.			

Remember that the expense related to writing off Bill Johnson's account was recognized in 2013 when Allied Enterprises made the adjusting entry to record the estimated bad debts.

CONCEPT CHECK

Will writing off Bill Johnson's $400 account reduce the net realizable value of Allied Enterprises' Accounts Receivable?

Answer

No, the write off of uncollectible receivables has no impact on the net realizable value of Accounts Receivable. Remember that the net realizable value of Accounts Receivable equals the balance in the Accounts Receivable account less the balance in the related contra account, Allowance for Doubtful Accounts. When Bill Johnson's account was written off, the asset account, Accounts Receivable, was reduced by $400. However, the Allowance for Doubtful Accounts was also reduced by $400 so the total change in the net realizable value of the Accounts Receivable is zero.

Allowance Method: Recovery of Accounts Previously Written Off

Entries are required to record the receipt of cash from a customer whose account was previously written off. First, the customer's Account Receivable is reinstated. Then, the payment on the account is recorded. Let's assume once again that on August 10, 2014, Bill Johnson unexpectedly sent Allied Enterprises a cheque for $250 as payment on his previously written-off account. Allied Enterprises would first reinstate the Account Receivable as follows:

DATE	ACCOUNTS	POST REF.	DR.	CR.
Aug 10	Accounts Receivable—Bill Johnson		250	
	Allowance for Doubtful Accounts			250
	Reinstated Bill Johnson's account.			

Notice again that the accounts debited and credited in this entry are exactly opposite of those used in the entry to write off the account. Allied Enterprises now records the receipt of cash as follows:

DATE	ACCOUNTS	POST REF.	DR.	CR.
Aug 10	Cash		250	
	Accounts Receivable—Bill Johnson			250
	Collected cash on account.			

Exhibit 7-3 summarizes the transactions that cause changes in Accounts Receivable and Allowance for Doubtful Accounts, and the entries required when using the allowance method.

Cash	
Dr (+)	**Cr (−)**
(2) Collection of credit sales	
(6) Collection of written-off AR	

Accounts Receivable	
Dr (+)	**Cr (−)**
(1) Sales on credit	(2) Collection of credit sales
	(4) Write-off of uncollectable AR
(5) Recovery of previously written-off AR	(6) Collection of written-off AR

Allowance for Doubtful Accounts	
Dr (−)	**Cr (+)**
	(3) Adj. estimated uncollectable amount
(4) Write-off of uncollectable AR	
	(5) Recovery of previously written-off AR

Bad Debt Expense	
Dr (+)	**Cr (−)**
(3) Adj. estimated uncollectable amount	

Sales	
Dr (−)	**Cr (+)**
	(1) Sales on credit

Event	Journal Entries	DR.	CR.
(1) Sales	Accounts Receivable	XXXX	
	Sales		XXXX
(2) Collection of Credit Sales	Cash	XXXX	
	Accounts Receivable		XXXX
(3) Period-end adjusting entry	Bad Debt Expense	XXXX	
	Allowance for Doubtful Accounts		XXXX
(4) Entry to write off customer account	Allowance for Doubtful Accounts	XXXX	
	Accounts Receivable—Customer Name		XXXX
(5) and (6) Entries to record receipt of payment on an account previously written off	Accounts Receivable—Customer Name	XXXX	
	Allowance for Doubtful Accounts		XXXX
	Cash	XXXX	
	Accounts Receivable—Customer Name		XXXX

Exhibit 7-3 ▲

HOW ARE ACCOUNTS RECEIVABLE REPORTED ON THE BALANCE SHEET?

Accounts receivable are reported at "net realizable value" in the current assets section of the balance sheet. There are two ways to show Accounts Receivable at net realizable value. For example, assume that at December 31, 2013, Allied Enterprises' Accounts Receivable balance is $32,000 and its Allowance for Doubtful Accounts balance is $1,767. Allied Enterprises could report its accounts receivable in either of the two ways shown here:

3 Report accounts receivable on the balance sheet

Allied Enterprises **Balance Sheet (partial):** December 31, 2013	
Accounts Receivable	$32,000
Less: Allowance for Doubtful Accounts	1,767
Accounts Receivable, Net	$30,233

Allied Enterprises **Balance Sheet (partial):** December 31, 2013	
Accounts Receivable, Net of Allowance for Doubtful Accounts of $1,767	$30,233

Most companies use the second method, but either is acceptable. The key is to show Accounts Receivable at net realizable value.

CRITICAL THINKING

Take a minute to think about the impact of the following independent cases on the assets and net income, based on each of the scenarios.

1. When the company determined an uncollectible accounts receivable of $1,200, the journal entry was recorded as debit to Bad Debt Expense $1,200 and credit to Accounts Receivable $1,200.

2. When the company determined an uncollectible accounts receivable of $900, the journal entry was recorded as debit to Allowance for Doubtful Accounts $900 and credit to Accounts Receivable $900.

3. When the company determined an uncollectible accounts receivable of $2,500, the journal entry was recorded as debit to Allowance for Doubtful Accounts $2,500 and credit to Accounts Receivable $2,500. As the result, the balance of the Allowance for Doubtful Accounts has a debit balance of $2,000.

Solutions:

Impact on Account		
Assets	**Net Income**	**Entry in Accounting Record**
1. −1,200	−1,200	Assets and Net Income would be understated. The correct entry should be: Allowance for Doubtful Accounts (Dr); Accounts Receivable (Cr).
2. NE	NE	This is the correct entry. There is no impact on accounts for the subsequent accounting period when the allowance method is used.
3. NE	NE	Assets and Net Income would not be impacted. However, the debit balance of Allowance for Doubtful Accounts indicates that the estimation for bad debts was too low for this period.

DECISION GUIDELINES

Decision

As an entrepreneur, I am in the process of setting up my first business. Should I use the direct write-off method or the allowance method to account for bad debts?

Guideline

Both IFRS and ASPE dictate the use of the allowance method.

Analyze

Because the allowance method matches bad debt expense with the credit sales that resulted in the bad debts, it is generally viewed as the preferred method. The allowance method also reports accounts receivable at its net realizable value, which is a better indicator of the amount of cash that will ultimately be collected from the receivables.

HOW DO YOU ACCOUNT FOR NOTES RECEIVABLE?

Notes receivable are more formal than accounts receivable. The debtor signs a promissory note as evidence of the transaction. Before launching into the accounting, let's define the terms related to notes receivable.

> **4** Account for notes receivable

- **Promissory note**: A written promise to pay a specified amount of money on a particular future date.
- **Maker of a note** (debtor): The entity that signs the note and promises to pay the required amount; the maker of the note is the **debtor**.
- **Payee of a note** (creditor): The entity to whom the maker promises future payment; the payee of the note is the **creditor**.
- **Principal:** The amount loaned out by the payee and borrowed by the maker of the note.
- **Interest:** The amount charged for loaning money. Interest is expense to the debtor and income to the creditor.
- **Interest rate:** The percentage rate of interest specified by the note. Interest rates are almost always stated for a period of one year. A 10% note means that the amount of interest for *one year* is 10% of the note's principal.
- **Maturity date:** This is the date when final payment of the note is due. Also called the **due date**.
- **Maturity value:** The sum of the principal plus interest due at maturity.
- **Note term:** The period of time during which interest is earned. It extends from the original date of the note to the maturity date.

Exhibit 7-4 illustrates a promissory note. As you study the promissory note, look for the items mentioned previously.

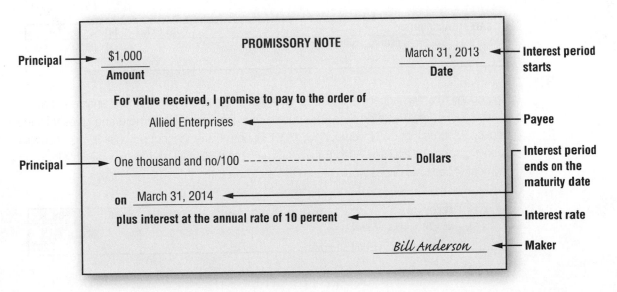

Exhibit 7-4 ▲

Identifying Maturity Date

Some notes specify the maturity date. For example, March 31, 2014, is the maturity date of the note shown in Exhibit 7-4. Other notes state the period of the note in days or months. When the period is given in months, the note's maturity date falls on the same day of the month as the date the note was issued. For example, a three-month note dated March 1, 2013, would mature on June 1, 2013.

When the period is given in days, the maturity date is determined by counting the actual days from the date of issue. A 180-day note dated February 16, 2013, matures on August 15, 2013.

When counting the days for a note term remember to

- count the maturity date.
- omit the date the note was issued.

Origination of Notes Receivable

Notes receivable typically originate from a company doing one of the following:

- Lending money
- Providing goods or services in exchange for a promissory note
- Accepting a promissory note as payment on an account receivable

Assume that on August 1, 2013, Allied Enterprises lent $800 to Kim Simmons on a six-month, 8% promissory note. The journal entry to record the note would be as follows:

DATE	ACCOUNTS	POST REF.	DR.	CR.
Aug 1	Note Receivable—K. Simmons		800	
	Cash			800

Next, assume that on September 5, Allied Enterprises sells goods for $2,500 to Don Hammond. Hammond signs a nine-month promissory note at 10% annual interest. Allied Enterprises' entry to record the sale is as follows:

DATE	ACCOUNTS	POST REF.	DR.	CR.
Sep 5	Note Receivable—D. Hammond		2,500	
	Sales			2,500

A company may also accept a note receivable from a credit customer who is unable to pay his or her account receivable on time. The customer signs a promissory note and gives it to the creditor. Assume that on November 18, 2013, Sandra Fisher cannot pay her $1,200 account when it comes due and that Allied Enterprises accepts a 60-day, 12% note receivable in lieu of payment. Allied Enterprises would record this as follows:

DATE	ACCOUNTS	POST REF.	DR.	CR.
Nov 18	Note Receivable—S. Fisher		1,200	
	Accounts Receivable—S. Fisher			1,200

Computing Interest on a Note

The formula for computing the interest is as follows:

> Amount of interest = Principal × Interest rate × Time

In the formula, multiplying by "Time" adjusts for the fact that the interest rate represents a year's worth of interest. The "Time," or time period, represents the portion of a year for which interest has accrued on the note. It may be expressed as a fraction of a year in months (x/12) or a fraction of a year in days (x/360 or x/365). When the interest period is stated in days, interest may be computed based on either a 360-day year or a 365-day year. Using the data in Exhibit 7-4, Allied Enterprises computes interest revenue for one year as follows:

> Amount of interest = Principal × Interest rate × Time
>
> $100   = $1,000 ×   0.10   × 12/12

The maturity value of the note is $1,100 ($1,000 principal + $100 interest). The time element is 12/12 or 1 because the note's term is 1 year.

    Interest on a $2,000 note at 6% for nine months is computed as follows:

> Amount of interest = Principal × Interest rate × Time
>
> $90   = $2,000 ×   0.06   × 9/12

Interest on a $4,000 note at 8% for 90 days (assuming a 360-day year) is computed as follows:

> Amount of interest = Principal × Interest rate × Time
>
> $80   = $4,000 ×   0.08   × 90/360

Accruing Interest Revenue

Notes receivable are often outstanding at the end of an accounting period. The interest revenue earned on the notes up to year-end should be recorded as part of that year's earnings. Recall that interest revenue is earned over time, not just when cash is received. We want to record the earnings from notes in the year in which they were earned.

    Let's continue with the Allied Enterprises note receivable from Exhibit 7-4. Allied Enterprises' accounting period ends December 31.

■ How much of the total interest revenue does Allied Enterprises earn in 2013 (from March 31 through December 31, 2013)?

> Amount of interest = Principal × Interest rate × Time
>
> $75   = $1,000 ×   0.10   × 9/12

Allied Enterprises makes the following adjusting entry at December 31, 2013:

DATE	ACCOUNTS	POST REF.	DR.	CR.
Dec 31	Interest Receivable		75	
	Interest Revenue			75
	Accrue interest revenue.			

- How much interest revenue does Allied Enterprises earn in 2014 (from January 1 through March 31, 2014)?

$$\text{Amount of interest} = \text{Principal} \times \text{Interest rate} \times \text{Time}$$
$$\$25 \qquad = \$1{,}000 \times \quad 0.10 \quad \times 3/12$$

On the note's maturity date, Allied Enterprises makes the following entry:

DATE	ACCOUNTS	POST REF.	DR.	CR.
Mar 31	Cash (Maturity Value)		1,100	
	Note Receivable—B. Anderson			1,000
	Interest Receivable			75
	Interest Revenue			25
	Record repayment of note at maturity.			

Earlier we determined that total interest on the note was $100 ($1,000 × 0.10 × 12/12). These entries assign the correct amount of interest to each year.

$$2013 = \$\ 75$$
$$2014 = \underline{\$\ 25}$$
$$\text{Total Interest} = \$100$$

FOCUS ON DECISION MAKING: RATIOS

Quick Ratio

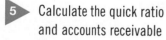

5 Calculate the quick ratio and accounts receivable turnover

In Chapter 4, we discussed the current ratio, which measures the ability to pay current liabilities with current assets. A more stringent measure of a company's ability to pay current liabilities is the **quick ratio**. The quick ratio, also called the **acid-test ratio**, compares a company's **quick assets** to its current liabilities. The quick ratio reveals whether the entity could pay all of its current liabilities if they were to become due immediately. The formula for the quick ratio is as follows:

$$\text{Quick ratio} = \frac{\text{Cash} + \text{Net current receivables} + \text{Short-term investments}}{\text{Total current liabilities}}$$

Let's assume that Mackay Industries has the following current asset information for December 31, 2013: cash, $3,100; net current receivables, $2,500; inventory, $6,300; and short-term investments, $1,600. Current liabilities are $4,300. The quick ratio for Mackay Industries is calculated as follows:

$$\text{Quick ratio} = \frac{\$3,100 + \$2,500 + \$1,600}{\$4,300} = 1.67$$

Notice the $6,300 of inventory was not considered in the calculation of the quick ratio. This is because, although inventory is a current asset, it is not considered to be a "quick" asset.

The higher the quick ratio, the more able the business is to pay its current liabilities. Mackay Industries has a very strong quick ratio. Mackay Industries' quick ratio of 1.67 means that it has $1.67 of quick assets to pay each $1 of current liabilities.

What is an acceptable quick ratio? The answer depends on the industry. Walmart operates smoothly with a quick ratio of less than 0.20. Several things make this low ratio possible: Walmart collects cash rapidly and has almost no receivables. The quick ratios for most department stores cluster around 0.80, while travel agencies average 1.10. In general, a quick ratio of 1.00 is considered safe.

DECISION GUIDELINES

Decision	**Guideline**	**Analyze**
As a supplier, I need to determine whether or not to extend credit to customers. As part of this assessment, I need to look at how easily the company can pay its short-term debts. What is the best way to assess this?	Utilize the quick ratio.	The quick ratio provides an indicator of a business's ability to pay its obligations as they come due. Although the quick ratio takes into account a business's short-term investments, the primary components are cash and receivables. A quick ratio that is below 1.0 is generally an indicator that a business has an inadequate amount of cash and receivables on hand. If too many liabilities come due at once, the business is likely to encounter cash flow problems.

Accounts Receivable Turnover

Accounts receivable turnover measures the ability to collect cash from credit customers. The higher the ratio, the more successful the business is in collecting cash. However, an accounts receivable turnover that is too high may indicate that a company is not extending credit freely enough to make sales to all potentially good customers. Accounts receivable turnover is calculated as follows:

$$\text{Accounts receivable turnover} = \frac{\text{Net Credit Sales}}{\text{Average net Accounts Receivable}}$$

Assume that Mackay Industries has net credit sales for the year of $486,000, beginning net Accounts Receivable of $64,000, and ending net Accounts Receivable of $52,000. Mackay Industries would calculate the accounts receivable turnover for the year as follows:

$$\text{Accounts receivable turnover} = \frac{\$486,000}{\$58,000} = 8.38$$

The average net Accounts Receivable, $58,000, is figured by adding the beginning Accounts Receivable balance of $64,000 to the ending balance of $52,000 and dividing the result by two. The determination of whether a company's accounts receivable turnover rate is good or bad depends on the company's credit terms. If Mackay Industries grants 30-day credit terms, its 8.38 accounts receivable turnover rate would be viewed as poor. With 30-day credit terms, you would expect a ratio of closer to 12 (360 days divided by 30 days). If Mackay Industries grants 45-day credit terms, its 8.38 accounts receivable turnover rate would be viewed as good. With 45-day credit terms, you would expect a ratio of closer to 8 (360 days divided by 45 days).

DECISION GUIDELINES

Decision	Guideline	Analyze
As a manager, I would like to know if I need to make changes in our credit terms for our customers. What can I examine to help with this decision?	Utilize the accounts receivable turnover ratio.	A low accounts receivable turnover ratio is often an indicator that a business is not properly managing its credit accounts. A low ratio is usually the result of credit accounts becoming delinquent. This can adversely affect a company because it negatively impacts cash flows.
		However, an accounts receivable turnover that is too high may also be an indicator that accounts receivable is being poorly managed. This often occurs when credit is not granted freely enough, resulting in lost sales.

FOCUS ON USERS

Concept	User	Why is this Important to this User?
Revenue Recognition		The point at which revenue is recognized is critically important to all users as this has a significant impact on the amount of revenues that are recognized by a company in any period. This will affect the company's net income and performance measures and impact decisions that revolve around income such as shareholders purchasing shares, creditors loaning funds, unions negotiating for additional benefits, competitors developing strategies, etc. The rules around revenue recognition are subjective, which means that different people would come up with different responses to how much should be recorded for revenues in the period. This can lead to the potential for unethical practices, so users of financial statements need to understand the principles that were used to create the statements.
Net Accounts Receivable		Competitors are interested in a company's accounts receivable for a number of different reasons. A competitor would examine the accounts receivable and net accounts receivable to determine the amount recorded in the Allowance for Doubtful Accounts. This would provide a competitor with an idea of how much another company in the same industry is experiencing bad debts to know whether its own level of bad debts is similar, larger, or smaller. A competitor would also calculate the accounts receivable turnover to determine how long it takes to collect the accounts on average. Again this would provide a competitor with a comparison figure, particularly for how quickly its competitors pay their accounts in relation to the credit terms that the company offers.

DEMO DOC

Accounts Receivable

Advantage Cycle accounts for its bad debts using the allowance method. Advantage Cycle had the following account balances as of September 1:

MyAccountingLab

Visit MyAccountingLab at www. myaccountinglab.com to watch animated versions of these Demo Docs.

L.O. **2**

Accounts Receivable		Allowance for Doubtful Accounts	
Bal	32,000	Bal	1,700

During the month of September, Advantage Cycle had the following transactions:

a. Made $57,000 of sales on account.

b. Collected $49,000 on account from credit customers.

c. Wrote off $2,300 of Accounts Receivable as uncollectible.

d. Unexpectedly collected $250 of Accounts Receivable that had previously been written off.

Requirements:

❶ Journalize Transactions a–d (because information about individual customers has not been given, record all entries as summary entries to the Accounts Receivable control account). Post the entries to the Accounts Receivable and Allowance for Doubtful Accounts T-accounts and calculate the account balances.

❷ Assume that on September 30, based on an aging of its accounts receivable, Advantage Cycle estimates that $2,100 of Accounts Receivable will be uncollectible. Journalize the entry to record Bad Debt Expense for the month of September. What is the net realizable value of Accounts Receivable at September 30?

❸ Ignoring Requirement 2, assume instead that Advantage Cycle estimates that Accounts Receivable equal to 3% of all credit sales will eventually be uncollectible. Journalize the entry to record Bad Debt Expense for the month of September. What is the net realizable value of Accounts Receivable at September 30?

Demo Doc Solutions

Requirement ❶

Journalize Transactions a–d.

| Part 1 | Part 2 | Part 3 | Demo Doc Complete |

a. Made $57,000 of sales on account.

Because the sales were on account, Accounts Receivable is increased (debited) by $57,000. Sales is also increased (credited) by $57,000.

DATE	ACCOUNTS	POST REF.	DR.	CR.
	Accounts Receivable		57,000	
	Sales			57,000
	Sold merchandise on account.			

b. Collected $49,000 on account from credit customers.

When cash is collected from customers, Cash is increased (debited) by $49,000 and Accounts Receivable is decreased (credited) by $49,000.

DATE	ACCOUNTS	POST REF.	DR.	CR.
	Cash		49,000	
	Accounts Receivable			49,000
	Received cash on account.			

c. Wrote off $2,300 of Accounts Receivable as uncollectible.

When receivables are uncollectible, they no longer have value. Therefore, they are no longer considered to be valid assets so Accounts Receivable needs to be decreased (credited) by $2,300. Because Advantage Cycle uses the allowance method, the debit side of the entry is made to Allowance for Doubtful Accounts. Remember that under the allowance method, the Allowance for Doubtful Accounts is created when the period-end adjusting entry is made to record the estimated Bad Debt Expense.

DATE	ACCOUNTS	POST REF.	DR.	CR.
	Allowance for Doubtful Accounts		2,300	
	Accounts Receivable			2,300
	Wrote off uncollectible accounts.			

d. Unexpectedly collected $250 of Accounts Receivable that had previously been written off.

When an account is written off, it is removed from the accounting records. If it is subsequently collected, it must first be put back into the accounting records. To reinstate the receivable, we must reverse the entry that removed the account. In other words, we must debit the accounts that were originally credited and credit the accounts that were originally debited. The entry to write off accounts receivable debits the allowance and credits the accounts receivable (as in Transaction c). To reverse this entry, we must do the opposite: Debit the accounts receivable and credit the allowance by $250.

DATE	ACCOUNTS	POST REF.	DR.	CR.
	Accounts Receivable		250	
	Allowance for Doubtful Accounts			250
	Reinstated Accounts Receivable.			

Once this journal entry has been made, the cash collection is recorded as usual. Cash is increased (debited) by $250 and Accounts Receivable is decreased (credited) by $250.

DATE	ACCOUNTS	POST REF.	DR.	CR.
	Cash		250	
	Accounts Receivable			250
	Received cash on account.			

Post the entries to the Accounts Receivable and Allowance for Doubtful Accounts T-accounts and calculate the account balances.

The entries are posted to the T-accounts and the ending balances are calculated as follows:

Accounts Receivable				Allowance for Doubtful Accounts			
Bal	32,000	b.	49,000	c.	2,300	Bal	1,700
a.	57,000	c.	2,300			d.	250
d.	250	d.	250	Bal	350		
Bal	37,700						

Requirement ❷

Assume that on September 30, based on an aging of its accounts receivable, Advantage Cycle estimates that $2,100 of Accounts Receivable will be uncollectible. Journalize the entry to record Bad Debt Expense for the month of September. What is the net realizable value of Accounts Receivable at September 30?

Part 1	**Part 2**	Part 3	Demo Doc Complete

The phrase "based on an aging of its accounts receivable" tells us that Advantage Cycle is using the accounts receivable aging method to determine its Allowance for Doubtful Accounts. Under the aging method, the ending balance in the allowance account should equal the estimated amount of bad debts that was determined based on the aging of accounts receivable ($2,100).

What do we need to do to bring the allowance account to a balance of $2,100? By inserting the desired ending balance into the allowance account's T-account, we can determine how much we must credit the account for in order to bring its balance to $2,100.

Allowance for Doubtful Accounts			
c.	2,300	Bal	1,700
		d.	250
Bal	350		?
		Bal	2,100

The question mark represents the required credit to the account. Notice that the account has a debit balance prior to making the adjusting entry. This is because the amount of accounts written off during the period exceeds the balance that was in the allowance account at the beginning of the period. Remember, it is possible for the allowance account to have either a debit or a credit balance prior to making the period-end adjusting entry. It is very important to pay attention to whether the account has a debit or a credit balance as this has an impact on the calculation of the required adjusting entry.

To bring the account from a debit balance of $350 to a credit balance of $2,100 we must credit the account for a total of $2,450 ($350 + $2,100). This represents a credit of $350, which brings the account to a zero balance, plus an additional credit of $2,100, which brings the account to the desired $2,100 balance. The debit side of the entry is to Bad Debt Expense.

DATE	ACCOUNTS	POST REF.	DR.	CR.
Sep 30	Bad Debt Expense		2,450	
	Allowance for Doubtful Accounts			2,450
	Record estimated uncollectible accounts.			

The net realizable value of Accounts Receivable is calculated by subtracting the ending Allowance for Doubtful Accounts balance from the ending balance of Accounts Receivable calculated in Requirement 1.

Accounts Receivable	$37,700
− Allowance for Doubtful Accounts	(2,100)
= Accounts Receivable, Net	$35,600

Requirement ❸

Ignoring Requirement 2, assume instead that Advantage Cycle estimates that Accounts Receivable equal to 3% of all credit sales will eventually be uncollectible. Journalize the entry to record Bad Debt Expense for the month of September. What is the net realizable value of Accounts Receivable at September 30?

Part 1	Part 2	**Part 3**	Demo Doc Complete

The phrase "that Accounts Receivable equal to 3% of all credit sales will eventually be uncollectible" tells us that Advantage Cycle is using the percentage of sales method to determine its Allowance for Doubtful Accounts. From Requirement 1, Transaction a, we know that credit sales were $57,000 for the month. The amount of estimated bad debts is calculated as follows:

$$\text{Estimated uncollectible accounts} = 3\% \text{ of credit sales}$$
$$\$1,710 = 3\% \times \$57,000$$

Unlike with the aging method, it is not necessary to consider the Allowance for Doubtful Accounts balance to determine the amount of the required period-end adjusting entry. Once the estimated amount of bad debts has been calculated, that amount is used as the debit to Bad Debt Expense and the credit to Allowance for Doubtful Accounts as follows:

DATE	ACCOUNTS	POST REF.	DR.	CR.
Sep 30	Bad Debt Expense		1,710	
	Allowance for Doubtful Accounts			1,710
	Record estimated uncollectible accounts.			

Before we can calculate the net realizable value of Accounts Receivable we need to post the adjusting entry to the allowance account and calculate the ending balance.

Allowance for Doubtful Accounts

c.	2,300	Bal	1,700
		d.	250
Bal	350	Adj	1,710
		Bal	1,360

The net realizable value of Accounts Receivable can now be calculated as in Requirement 2.

Accounts Receivable	$37,700
− Allowance for Doubtful Accounts	(1,360)
= Accounts Receivable, Net	$36,340

Demo Doc Complete

Part 1	Part 2	Part 3	**Demo Doc Complete**

DECISION GUIDELINES

What decisions might you encounter while accounting for cash and receivables within your business?

Decision	Guideline	Analyze
As an entrepreneur, I am in the process of setting up my first business. Should I use the direct write-off method or the allowance method to account for bad debts?	Both IFRS and ASPE dictate the use of the allowance method.	Because the allowance method matches bad debt expense with the credit sales that resulted in the bad debts, it is generally viewed as the preferred method. The allowance method also reports accounts receivable at its net realizable value, which is a better indicator of the amount of cash that will ultimately be collected from the receivables.
As a supplier, I need to determine whether or not to extend credit to customers. As part of this assessment, I need to look at how easily the company can pay its short-term debts. What is the best way to assess this?	Utilize the quick ratio.	The quick ratio provides an indicator of a business's ability to pay its obligations as they come due. Although the quick ratio takes into account a business's short-term investments, the primary components are cash and receivables. A quick ratio that is below 1.0 is generally an indicator that a business has an inadequate amount of cash and receivables on hand. If too many liabilities come due at once, the business is likely to encounter cash flow problems.
As a manager, I would like to know if I need to make changes in our credit terms for our customers. What can I examine to help with this decision?	Utilize the accounts receivable turnover ratio.	A low accounts receivable turnover ratio is often an indicator that a business is not properly managing its credit accounts. A low ratio is usually the result of credit accounts becoming delinquent. This can adversely affect a company because it negatively impacts cash flows. However, an accounts receivable turnover that is too high may also be an indicator that accounts receivable is being poorly managed. This often occurs when credit is not granted freely enough, resulting in lost sales.

ACCOUNTING VOCABULARY
THE LANGUAGE OF BUSINESS

Accounts receivable turnover (p. 417) Net Credit Sales divided by net average Accounts Receivable; it measures a company's ability to collect cash from its credit customers.

Acid-test ratio (p. 416) Ratio that reveals how well the entity can pay its current liabilities. Also called the *quick ratio.*

Aging method (p. 406) The method of estimating bad debts that focuses on accounts receivable; the accountant calculates the end-of-period allowance balance based on an aging of the Accounts Receivable; also called the *balance sheet approach.*

Allowance for Doubtful Account (AFDA) (p. 405) A contra-asset account that holds the estimated amount of bad debts receivable.

Allowance method (p. 404) The method of accounting for bad debts that estimates these amounts and uses an allowance account so that the balance sheet shows the net amount of Accounts Receivable expected to be collected in the future.

Bad debt (p. 403) An account receivable that is unable to be collected; also called an *uncollectible account.*

Bad debt expense (p. 404) Selling expense caused by bad debts that reduce operating income.

Balance sheet method (p. 408) The method of estimating bad debts that focuses on accounts receivable. The accountant calculates the end-of-period allowance balance based on an aging of the Accounts Receivable; also called the *aging method*.

Completed contract method (p. 400) Under this method, revenues, costs, and gross profit are recognized only after the project is fully completed.

Control account (p. 405) An account in the general ledger that summarizes the details of an account balance.

Creditor (p. 413) The entity to whom the debtor promises future payment; also called the *payee of a note*.

Debtor (p. 413) The entity that promises future payment; also called the *maker of a note*.

Direct write-off method (p. 404) The method of accounting for bad debts in which a customer's account is written off as uncollectible when the business determines that the customer will not pay.

Due date (p. 413) The date when final payment of the note is due; also called the *maturity date*.

Income statement method (p. 405) The method of estimating bad debts that focuses on net credit sales; also called the *percentage of sales method*.

Interest (p. 413) The fee for using money; revenue to the creditor for loaning money; expense to the debtor for borrowing money.

Interest rate (p. 413) The percentage rate of interest specified by the note; almost always stated for a period of one year.

Maker of a note (p. 413) The entity that promises future payment; also called the *debtor*.

Maturity date (p. 413) The date when final payment of a note is due; also called the *due date*.

Maturity value (p. 413) The sum of the principal of a note plus interest due at maturity.

Net credit sales (p. 405) The total credit sales less sales discounts and sales returns and allowances related to the credit sales.

Net realizable value (p. 405) The net amount that the business expects to collect; the net realizable value of receivables is calculated by subtracting Allowance for Doubtful Accounts from Accounts Receivable.

Note term (p. 413) The time span of the note during which interest is computed; it extends from the original date of the note to the maturity date.

Payee of a note (p. 413) The entity to whom the debtor promises future payment; also called the *creditor*.

Percentage of completion method (p. 400) Under this method, revenues and gross profit are recognized each period based on the percentage of expenses incurred, or the percentage of completion to date.

Percentage of sales method (p. 405) The method of estimating bad debts that focuses on net credit sales; also called the *income statement method*.

Principal (p. 413) The amount loaned out by the payee and borrowed by the maker of the note.

Promissory note (p. 413) A written promise to pay a specified amount of money at a particular future date.

Quick assets (p. 416) Highly liquid assets used to calculate the quick ratio, including cash and cash equivalents, short-term investments, and net accounts receivable.

Quick ratio (p. 416) Ratio that reveals how well the entity can pay its current liabilities; also called the *acid-test ratio*.

Uncollectible account (p. 403) An Account Receivable that is unable to be collected; also called a *bad debt*.

Write off (p. 404) Removing a customer's receivable from the accounting records because it is considered uncollectible.

ACCOUNTING PRACTICE

DISCUSSION QUESTIONS

1. What are the different types of sales? Explain the difference between gross sales and net sales.

2. What is the benefit of using the percentage of net credit sales to estimate the bad debt expense? What is the benefit of using the aging method to estimate the bad debt expense?

MyAccountingLab

Make the grade with MyAccountingLab. The exercises and problems in this chapter can be found on MyAccountingLab at www.myaccountinglab.com. You can practise them as often as you want, and they feature step-by-step guided solutions to help you find the right answer.

3. What would be the surest way to eliminate the possibility of having any bad debts? Why don't companies operate this way if it could help them eliminate this costly expense?

4. Why does the allowance method of accounting for bad debts conform to IFRS and Canadian ASPE while the direct write-off method does not?

5. How is Allowance for Doubtful Accounts reported on the financial statements? Why is it important for companies to report net realizable value of Accounts Receivable on the balance sheet?

6. Why is the percentage of sales method called the "income statement approach" while the aging method is called the "balance sheet approach"?

7. Under which method, percentage of sales or aging, would the balance in Allowance for Doubtful Accounts just before the adjusting entry affect the amount of the adjusting entry? Why?

8. How would the net realizable value of Accounts Receivable change when an account is written off under the allowance method?

9. If a company with a 12/31 year-end lends money in the form of a 6-month note on 11/1, which accounts will be credited when the note is paid off on 4/30?

10. When in a deep recession, what would be the expected effect of the recession on accounts receivable turnover ratios?

SELF CHECK

1. ADI Company's ledger shows the following balances on December 31: Sales $365,000, Accounts Receivable, $146,000, Allowance for Doubtful Accounts $7,300, Sales Returns and Allowances $3,650, Sales Discounts $5,475, and Credit Card Expense $4,380. Calculate the amount of net sales reported on the income statement.
   a. $355,875
   b. $351,495
   c. $348,575
   d. $211,700

2. Which type of sales will not increase the company's operating expenses?
   a. Cash sales
   b. Debit card sales
   c. Credit card sales
   d. Sales on account

3. Which of the following statements is true when a company has a debit balance for the Allowance for Doubtful Accounts?
   a. The company over-estimated the bad debt expense.
   b. The bad debt is smaller than the allocated amount for the Allowance for Doubtful Accounts.
   c. The company should not record bad expense for the current year.
   d. None of the above.

4. GIA Company's net credit sales for the year were $468,000, Accounts Receivable, $192,000, Allowance for Doubtful Accounts, $3,600 (Dr.). GIA uses 5% of net credit sales as the bad debt expense. The amount of the bad debt expense to be recorded is
   a. $13,200
   b. $19,800
   c. $23,400
   d. $27,000

5. What is the impact on the quick ratio of recording the bad debt expense adjusting entry?

   a. Increase
   b. Decrease
   c. Remain the same
   d. Cannot be determined

6. Uncollectible accounts are the same as

   a. bad debts.
   b. notes receivable.
   c. both a and b.
   d. none of the above.

7. Which method of estimating uncollectible receivables focuses on net credit sales?

   a. Aging approach
   b. Percentage-of-sales approach
   c. Net realizable value approach
   d. All of the above

8. Your business uses the allowance method to account for uncollectible receivables. At the beginning of the year, Allowance for Doubtful Accounts had a credit balance of $1,100. During the year you wrote off bad receivables of $2,100 and recorded Bad Debt Expense of $2,000. What is your year-end balance in Allowance for Doubtful Accounts?

   a. $1,000   **b.** $2,000   **c.** $3,100   **d.** $3,200

9. Niko Company's net credit sales for the year were $480,000 and the average accounts receivable was $96,000. To improve accounts receivable turnover to 6 times, what should the average accounts receivable be, if the net credit sales are expected to increase by 10%?

   a. $86,400
   b. $87,273
   c. $88,000
   d. $105,600

10. On December 31, you have a $10,000 note receivable from a customer. Interest of 8% has also accrued for six months on the note. What will your financial statements report for this situation?

   a. Nothing will be reported because you haven't received the cash yet.
   b. The balance sheet will report the note receivable of $10,000.
   c. The balance sheet will report the note receivable of $10,000 and interest receivable of $400.
   d. The income statement will report a note receivable of $10,000.

   Answers are given after Written Communication.

SHORT EXERCISES

S7-1. Reporting net sales with sales returns and allowances and sales discounts (*Learning Objective 1*) 10 min.

The total sales for April were $265,000, of which 60% was on credit. One percent of the total sales was defective and returned. Two percent of the net credit sales were sales discounts. What are the amount of sales returns and allowance, sales discounts, and net sales?

S7-2. Missing information (*Learning Objective 2*) 15 min.

The following data were selected from Chow's ledger. Chow's accounting policy related to estimated bad debt expense is to keep the same relation between the Accounts Receivable and Allowance for Doubtful Accounts.

Accounts Receivable			
	42,000	(2)	?
(1)	252,000	(3)	226,800
	58,500		

Allowance for Doubtful Accounts			
(2)	?		3,360
		(4)	?
			4,680

Sales		
	(1)	252,000

Requirements

1. Calculate the missing information.
2. What is the percentage used to estimate the bad debts?
3. Explain the transactions (1) to (4).

S7-3. Comparing two methods of estimating bad debts (*Learning Objective 2*) 15 min.

Gupta Electronic recorded $425,000 of credit sales during its first year of operation. Gupta reported $102,000 (Dr.) in Accounts Receivable and $2,800 (Dr.) in Allowance for Doubtful Accounts before the adjustments at the end of the year. The Accounts Receivable account has $65,000 that is current and $37,000 that is 30 days or older. The accountant is wondering which method to use to estimate the bad debts. She has two options:

(1) 3% of credit sales

(2) aging of accounts receivable: 1% of current Accounts Receivable, 20% of 30+.

Requirements

1. Calculate the bad debt expense using (1) the percentage of credit sales, and (2) the aging of accounts receivable.
2. Prepare the adjusting journal entry to record bad debt expense using the two different methods.
3. Explain the main differences between the two methods of estimating bad debts.

S7-4. Receivable terms (*Learning Objectives 1 & 2*) 5–10 min.

Match the term with its definition by placing the corresponding letter in the space provided:

__c__	Example: Amounts owed to a business by another business or individual	a. Creditor
		b. Debtor
___ 1.	A contra-account, related to accounts receivable, that holds the estimated amount of uncollectible receivables	c. Receivables
		d. Bad Debt Expense
___ 2.	A method of accounting for uncollectible receivables in which the company waits until a specific customer's account receivable is uncollectible before recording Bad Debt Expense	e. Allowance method
		f. Allowance for Doubtful Accounts
___ 3.	A method of recording receivable losses on the basis of estimates instead of waiting to see which customers the company will not collect from	g. Percentage of sales method
		h. Aging method
___ 4.	The party to a credit transaction who sells goods or a service and obtains a receivable	i. Direct write-off method

5. A way to estimate bad debts by analyzing individual accounts receivable according to the length of time they have been receivable

6. The party to a credit transaction who makes a purchase and has a payable

7. Cost to the seller of credit sales; arises from the failure to collect from credit customers

8. A method of estimating uncollectible receivables that calculates Bad Debt Expense based on net credit sales

S7-5. Allowance method (*Learning Objective 2*) 5–10 min.

Antonio Galvan, an attorney, uses the allowance method to account for uncollectible receivables. On August 31, Galvan's accounts receivable were $8,000. During September, he earned service revenue of $20,000 on account and collected $22,000 from clients on account. He also wrote off uncollectible receivables of $2,000. What is Galvan's balance of Accounts Receivable on September 30? Does he expect to collect this entire amount? Why or why not?

S7-6. Percentage of sales allowance method (*Learning Objectives 2 & 3*) 5–10 min.

During its first year of operations, Atlas Travel earned revenue of $400,000 on account. Industry experience suggests that Atlas Travel's bad debts will amount to 2% of revenues. On December 31, 2013, accounts receivable total $90,000. The company uses the allowance method to account for uncollectibles.

Journalize Atlas Travel's Bad Debt Expense using the percentage of sales method. Show how Atlas should report Accounts Receivable on its balance sheet on December 31, 2013.

S7-7. Percentage of sales allowance method (*Learning Objective 2*) 5–10 min.

Atlas Travel ended 2012 with Accounts Receivable of $90,000 and an Allowance for Doubtful Accounts balance of $8,000. During 2013, Atlas Travel had the following activity:

a. Service revenue earned on account, $600,000.

b. Collections on account, $580,000.

c. Write-offs of uncollectibles, $15,000.

d. Bad Debt Expense, estimated as 2% of service revenue.

Journalize Atlas Travel's activity for 2013.

S7-8. Aging of accounts receivable allowance method (*Learning Objective 2*) 5–10 min.

Gorav Dental Group started 2013 with Accounts Receivable of $120,000 and an Allowance for Doubtful Accounts balance of $6,000. The following information relates to Gorav Dental's 2013 operations:

a. Credit sales, $400,000.

b. Collections on account, $320,000.

c. Write-offs of uncollectibles, $15,000.

d. At December 31, the aging of accounts receivable showed that Gorav will probably *not* collect $5,000 of its accounts receivable.

Journalize Gorav's 2013 transactions based on the information provided. Prepare a T-account for the Allowance for Doubtful Accounts to show your computation of Bad Debt Expense for the year.

S7-9. Aging of accounts receivable allowance method (*Learning Objective 2*)
5–10 min.

Limo.com had the following balances on December 31, 2013, before the year-end adjustments:

Accounts Receivable		Allowance for Doubtful Accounts	
104,000			1,300

The aging of receivables yields these data:

	1–30 Days	31–60 Days	61–90 Days	Over 90 Days	Total Receivables
			Age of Accounts		
Accounts Receivable	$70,000	$20,000	$10,000	$4,000	$104,000
Estimate Percentage Uncollectible	×1%	×2%	×5%	×50%	

Journalize Limo.com's entry to adjust the allowance account to its correct balance on December 31, 2013.

S7-10. Internal controls—credit sales (*Learning Objective 1*) 10–15 min.

Claire Billiot, the office manager of a local office supply company, is designing its internal control system. Billiot proposes the following procedures for credit checks on new customers, sales on account, cash collections, and write-offs of uncollectible receivables:

a. The Credit Department runs a credit check on all customers who apply for credit. When an account proves uncollectible, the Credit Department authorizes the write-off of the account receivable.

b. Cash receipts come into the Credit Department, which separates the cash received from the customer remittance slips. The Credit Department lists all cash receipts by customer name and amount of cash received.

c. The cash goes to the treasurer for deposit in the bank. The remittance slips go to the Accounting Department for recording of the collections.

d. The controller compares the daily deposit slip to the total amount of the collections recorded. Both amounts must agree.

For each of the four procedures, indicate whether the procedure includes an internal control weakness. Explain how employee fraud could occur because of the weakness. What can Claire do to strengthen the internal control system?

S7-11. Notes receivable terms (*Learning Objective 4*) 10–15 min.

Match the term with its definition by placing the corresponding letter in the space provided:

_____ 1. A written promise to pay a specified amount of money at a particular future date

_____ 2. The date when final payment of the note is due; also called the due date

_____ 3. The percentage rate of interest specified by the note for one year

_____ 4. The entity to whom the maker promises future payment

_____ 5. The period of time during which interest is earned

_____ 6. The amount loaned out by the payee and borrowed by the maker of the note

a. Interest

b. Note term

c. Interest rate

d. Maker of the note

e. Maturity date

f. Maturity value

g. Payee of the note

h. Principal

i. Promissory note

.... 7. The sum of the principal plus interest due
at maturity

.... 8. The entity that signs the note and promises to
pay the required amount

.... 9. The revenue to the payee for loaning money;
the expense to the debtor

S7-12. Accounting for notes receivable (*Learning Objective 4*) 10–15 min.

For each of the following notes receivable, compute the amount of interest revenue
earned during 2013. Use a 360-day year, and round to the nearest dollar.

	Principal	Interest Rate	Interest Period During 2013
Note 1	$100,000	8%	6 months
Note 2	30,000	12%	75 days
Note 3	20,000	9%	60 days
Note 4	50,000	10%	3 months

S7-13. Accounting for notes receivable (*Learning Objective 4*) 10–15 min.

Bank of Montreal lent $100,000 to Christine Kleuters on a 90-day, 8% note.
Record the following transactions for Bank of Montreal (explanations are not
required):

1. Lending the money on June 12.

2. Collecting the principal and interest at maturity. Specify the date. For the computation of interest, use a 360-day year.

S7-14. Quick ratio (*Learning Objective 5*) 5–10 min.

Calculate the quick assets and the quick ratio for each of the following companies:

	Jaxon	Kilborn
Cash..	$10,000	$ 25,000
Short-term Investments..	5,000	15,000
Net Receivables...	45,000	52,000
Current Liabilities...	45,000	100,000

S7-15. Accounts receivable turnover (*Learning Objective 5*) 5–10 min.

Calculate accounts receivable turnover for the following two companies.

	Moore	Noel
Net Credit Sales	$73,000	$45,625
Net Accounts Receivable, Beginning..	12,000	23,000
Net Accounts Receivable, Ending..	13,000	21,000

EXERCISES (GROUP A)

E7-1A. Reporting net sales with sales returns and allowances and sales discounts (*Learning Objective 1*) 10–15 min.

Cheng Enterprises completed the following transactions during May. Cheng uses the periodic inventory system in accounting for inventory.

May	4	Sold merchandise to a customer for $2,500. Customer paid with a credit card. The credit card company charged a 2% service fee.
	6	Sold merchandise worth $6,200 to Wang on account, with terms of 2/10, n/30, FOB shipping point.
	8	Wang returned $300 of merchandise.
	12	Sold merchandise worth $4,800 to Jung on account, with terms of 2/10, n/30, FOB shipping point.
	15	Received payment from Wang.
	22	Received payment from Jung.

Requirements

1. Calculate the net sales for May.

2. Prepare the journal entries to record the transactions that occurred in May.

E7-2A. Bad Debt Write-Offs and Cash Collections (*Learning Objective 2*) 10–15 min.

Sun's ledger shows the following account balances on December 31:

	2013	2012
Accounts Receivable	$ 530,000	$ 450,000
Allowance for Doubtful Accounts	26,500	18,000
Sales	3,500,000	2,700,000

During 2013, Sun wrote off $12,500 of uncollectible accounts receivable, and reinstated $1,500 of previously written-off accounts receivable.

Requirements

1. Calculate the bad debt expense for 2013.

2. Calculate cash collections from accounts receivable, assuming that all sales were on credit.

E7-3A. Allowance method (*Learning Objective 2*) 5–10 min.

Allied Industries uses the allowance method to account for bad debts. Record the following transactions that occurred during the year:

Feb 3	Provided $600 of services to Bill Hanson on account.
Aug 8	Wrote off Bill Hanson's $600 account as uncollectible.
Nov 10	Unexpectedly collected $400 from Bill Hanson on the account that had been written off. Allied Industries does not expect to collect the remaining balance.

E7-4A. Percentage of sales allowance method (*Learning Objective 2*) 10–15 min.

Rice Automotive ended December 2012 with Accounts Receivable of $30,000 and Allowance for Doubtful Accounts of $1,500. During January 2013, Rice Automotive completed the following transactions:

- Sales of $180,000, which included $120,000 in credit sales and $60,000 of cash sales.
- Cash collections on account, $90,000.
- Write-offs of uncollectible receivables, $1,200.
- Bad debt expense, estimated as 2% of credit sales.

Requirements

1. Prepare journal entries to record sales, collections, writeoffs of uncollectibles, and Bad Debt Expense by the percentage-of-sales method.

2. Calculate the ending balances in Accounts Receivable, Allowance for Doubtful Accounts, and net Accounts Receivable at January 31. How much does Rice Automotive expect to collect?

E7-5A. Aging of accounts receivable allowance method (*Learning Objective 2*) 15–20 min.

On December 31, 2013, the Accounts Receivable balance of Alterations Express is $300,000. The Allowance for Doubtful Accounts has a $3,900 credit balance. Alterations prepares the following aging schedule for its accounts receivable:

	Age of Accounts			
	1–30 Days	31–60 Days	61–90 Days	Over 90 Days
Accounts Receivable..............................	$140,000	$80,000	$70,000	$10,000
Estimated Percentage Uncollectible........	0.5%	1.0%	6.0%	50%

Requirements

1. Journalize the year-end adjusting entry for bad debts on the basis of the aging schedule. Calculate the resulting ending balance of the Allowance account based on the account aging. Show the T-account for the Allowance on December 31, 2013.

2. Assume that instead of a $3,900 credit balance, there is a $1,300 debit balance in the Allowance account prior to adjustment. Journalize the year-end adjusting entry for bad debts on the basis of the aging schedule. Calculate the resulting ending balance of the Allowance account based on the account aging. Show the T-account for the Allowance on December 31, 2013.

E7-6A. Percentage of sales and aging of accounts receivable allowance methods (*Learning Objective 2*) 15–20 min.

Inland Equipment uses the allowance method to account for bad debts. On December 31, 2013, Allowance for Doubtful Accounts has a $600 credit balance. Journalize the year-end adjusting entry for bad debts assuming the following *independent* scenarios:

1. Inland Equipment estimates bad debts as ½ of 1% of net credit sales. Net credit sales for the year equal $550,000.

2. Based on an aging of Accounts Receivable, Inland Equipment estimates that bad debts will equal $2,575.

E7-7A. Sales, bad debt write-offs, and cash collections (*Learning Objectives 1 & 2*) 20–25 min.

Momo Industries began operations on January 1, 2013. During the next two years, the company completed a number of transactions involving credit sales, accounts receivable collections, and bad debts. Momo uses a perpetual inventory system, and the gross margin is 40% of the sales. These transactions are summarized as follows:

2013

   a. Sold merchandise on credit for $1,500,000, terms n/30.

   b. Wrote off uncollectible accounts receivable in the amount of $20,000.

   c. Received cash of $720,000 in payment of outstanding accounts receivable.

   d. December 31, Momo estimated that 3.5% of the outstanding accounts receivable would become uncollectible.

2014

   e. Sold merchandise on credit for $1,750,000 terms n/30.

   f. Wrote off uncollectible accounts receivable in the amount of $28,000.

   g. Received cash of $1,250,000 in payment of outstanding accounts receivable.

   h. Momo uses the same method as in 2013 to estimate and record the uncollectible accounts receivable.

Requirements

   1. Prepare the journal entries to record the transactions that occurred in 2013 and 2014, and the adjusting entries to record bad debt expense at the end of each year.

   2. Is the estimated amount for the bad debt expense sufficient?

E7-8A. Accounting for notes receivable (*Learning Objective 4*) 15–20 min.

On April 30, 2013, Scotiabank loaned $100,000 to Grant Hughes on a one-year, 6% note.

Requirements

   1. Compute the interest for the years ended December 31, 2013 and 2014, on the Hughes note.

   2. Which party has

   a. a note receivable?

   b. a note payable?

   c. interest revenue?

   d. interest expense?

   3. How much in total would Hughes pay the bank if he pays off the note early—say, on November 30, 2013?

E7-9A. Accounting for notes receivable (*Learning Objective 4*) 15–20 min.

Journalize the following transactions of Cramer, Inc., which ends its accounting year on June 30:

Apr 1	Loaned $20,000 cash to R. Simpson on a one-year, 8% note.
Jun 6	Sold goods to Friday, Corp., receiving a 90-day, 10% note for $3,000.
30	Made a single compound entry to accrue interest revenue on both notes. Use a 360-day year for interest computations.

E7-10A. Accounting for notes receivable (*Learning Objective 4*) 15–20 min.

Gorman Enterprises sells on account. When a customer account becomes four months old, Gorman converts the account to a note receivable. During 2013, Gorman completed these transactions:

Jun 29	Sold goods on account to I. Happy, $10,000.
Nov 1	Received a $10,000, 60-day, 9% note from I. Happy in satisfaction of his past-due account receivable.
Dec 31	Collected the I. Happy note at maturity.

Requirement

1. Record the transactions in Gorman Enterprises' journal.

E7-11A. Quick ratio (*Learning Objective 5*) 15–20 min.

Consider the following data:

	A	B	C	D
Cash..................................	$ 92,000	$ 64,000	$23,000	$107,000
Short-term Investments.................	70,000	28,000	15,000	53,000
Net Receivables............................	125,000	110,000	52,000	140,000
Current Liabilities..........................	205,000	101,000	60,000	350,000

Requirements

1. Calculate the quick assets and the quick ratio for each company.
2. Which of the companies should be concerned about its liquidity?

E7-12A. Quick ratio and accounts receivable turnover (*Learning Objective 5*) 15–20 min.

Vision Equipment reported the following items on February 28, 2013 (amounts in thousands, with last year's amounts also given as needed):

Accounts Payable........................	$ 449	Accounts Receivable, Net:	
Cash...	215	February 28, 2013..................	$ 220
Inventory:		February 28, 2012..................	150
February 28, 2013..................	190	Cost of Goods Sold.....................	1,200
February 28, 2012..................	160	Short-term Investments..............	165
Net Credit Sales.........................	1,930	Other Current Assets..................	90
Long-term Assets.......................	410	Other Current Liabilities..............	145
Long-term Liabilities...................	10		

Requirements:

1. Compute Vision Equipment's (a) quick ratio and (b) accounts receivable turnover for 2013.
2. Evaluate each ratio value as strong or weak. Assume Vision Equipment sells on terms of net 30.

EXERCISES (GROUP B)

E7-1B. Reporting net sales with sales returns and allowances and sales discounts
(*Learning Objective 1*) 10–15 min.

Wu International completed the following transactions during July. Wu uses the periodic inventory system in accounting for inventory.

Jul	2	Sold merchandise worth $4,500 to Hung on account, with terms of 2/15, n/30, FOB shipping point.
	7	Sold merchandise worth $7,800 to Lee on account, with terms of 2/15, n/30, FOB shipping point.
	8	Lee returned $300 of merchandise.
	14	Sold merchandise to a customer for $2,500. Customer paid with a credit card. The credit card company charged a 2% service fee.
	17	Received payment from Hung.
	21	Received payment from Lee.

Requirements

1. Calculate the net sales for July.
2. Prepare the journal entries to record the transactions that occurred in July.

E7-2B. Bad Debt Write-Offs and Cash Collections (*Learning Objective 2*) 10–15 min.

Moto's ledger shows the following account balances on December 31:

	2013	2012
Accounts Receivable	$ 720,000	$ 540,000
Allowance for Doubtful Accounts	36,000	24,000
Sales	3,600,000	2,970,000

During 2013, Moto reinstated $2,500 of previously written-off accounts receivable, and recorded $21,000 bad debt expense.

Requirements

1. Calculate the written-off accounts receivable for 2013.
2. Calculate cash collections from accounts receivable, assuming that all sales were on credit.

E7-3B. Allowance method (*Learning Objective 2*) 5–10 min.

White Top Rafters uses the allowance method to account for bad debts. Record the following transactions that occurred during the year:

May 3	Provided $970 of services to Sam Martin on account.
Nov 8	Wrote off Sam Martin's $970 account as uncollectible.
Dec 10	Unexpectedly collected $200 from Sam Martin on the account that had been written off. White Top Rafters does not expect to collect the remaining balance.

E7-4B. **Percentage of sales allowance method** (*Learning Objective 2*) 10–15 min.

Ortiz Automotive ended December 2012 with Accounts Receivable of $20,000 and Allowance for Doubtful Accounts of $5,900. During January 2013, Ortiz Automotive completed the following transactions:

- Sales of $260,000, which included $160,000 in credit sales and $100,000 of cash sales.
- Cash collections on account, $54,000.
- Write-offs of uncollectible receivables, $2,500.
- Bad debt expense estimated as 4% of credit sales.

Requirements

1. Prepare journal entries to record sales, collections, write-offs of uncollectibles, and Bad Debt Expense by the percentage-of-sales method.

2. Calculate the ending balances in Accounts Receivable, Allowance for Doubtful Accounts, and net Accounts Receivable at January 31. How much does Ortiz Automotive expect to collect?

E7-5B. **Aging of accounts receivable allowance method** (*Learning Objective 2*) 15–20 min.

On July 31, 2013, the Accounts Receivable balance of Questor Application, Inc. is $320,000. The Allowance for Doubtful Accounts has a $6,400 credit balance. Questor prepares the following aging schedule for its accounts receivable:

	Age of Accounts			
	1–30 Days	31–60 Days	61–90 Days	Over 90 Days
Accounts Receivable..............................	$175,000	$70,000	$60,000	$15,000
Estimated Percentage Uncollectible........	0.8%	3.0%	5.0%	60%

Requirements

1. Journalize the year-end adjusting entry for uncollectible accounts on the basis of the aging schedule. Calculate the resulting ending balance of the Allowance account based on the account aging. Show the T-account for the Allowance on July 31, 2013.

2. Assume that instead of a $6,400 credit balance, there is a $500 debit balance in the Allowance account prior to adjustment. Journalize the year-end adjusting entry for uncollectible accounts on the basis of the aging schedule. Calculate the resulting ending balance of the Allowance account based on the account aging. Show the T-account for the Allowance on July 31, 2013.

E7-6B. **Percentage of sales and aging of accounts receivable allowance methods** (*Learning Objective 2*) 15–20 min.

Cotton, Corp. uses the allowance method to account for uncollectible accounts. On May 31, 2013, Allowance for Doubtful Accounts has a $1,300 credit balance. Journalize the year-end adjusting entry for Doubtful Accounts assuming the following *independent* scenarios:

1. Cotton, Corp., estimates Doubtful Accounts as ¾ of 1% of net credit sales. Net credit sales for the year equal $750,000.

2. Based on an aging of Accounts Receivable, Cotton, Corp., estimates that Doubtful Accounts will equal $3,120.

E7-7B. Sales, bad debt write-offs, and cash collections (*Learning Objectives 1 & 2*) 20–25 min.

Vihn Luggage Manufacturing began operations on January 1, 2013. During the next two years, the company completed a number of transactions involving credit sales, accounts receivable collections, and bad debts. Vihn uses a perpetual inventory system, and the gross margin is 30% of the sales. These transactions are summarized as follows:

2013

   a. Sold merchandise on credit for $850,000, terms n/30.

   b. Wrote off uncollectible accounts receivable in the amount of $15,000.

   c. Received cash of $320,000 in payment of outstanding accounts receivable.

   d. December 31, Vihn estimated that 2% of the outstanding accounts receivable would become uncollectible.

2014

   e. Sold merchandise on credit for $920,000, terms n/30.

   f. Wrote off uncollectible accounts receivable in the amount of $20,000.

   g. Received cash of $480,000 in payment of outstanding accounts receivable.

   h. Vihn uses the same method as in 2013 to estimate and record the uncollectible accounts receivable.

Requirements

   1. Prepare the journal entries to record the transactions that occurred in 2013 and 2014, and the adjusting entries to record bad debt expense at the end of each year.

   2. Is the estimated amount for the bad debt expense sufficient?

E7-8B. Accounting for notes receivable (*Learning Objective 4*) 15–20 min.

On June 30, 2013, Nature Bank loaned $2,000,000 to Gary Simon on a one-year, 7% note.

Requirements

   1. Compute the interest for the years ended December 31, 2013 and 2014, on the Simon note.

   2. Which party has

      a. a note receivable?

      b. a note payable?

      c. interest revenue?

      d. interest expense?

   3. How much in total would Simon pay the bank if he pays off the note early— say, on January 31, 2014?

E7-9B. Accounting for notes receivable (*Learning Objective 4*) 15–20 min.

Journalize the following transactions of Coral, Inc., which ends its accounting year on April 30:

Feb 1	Loaned $15,000 cash to Carroll Fadal on a one-year, 10% note.
Apr 6	Sold goods to Lawn Pro, receiving a 90-day, 4% note for $6,000.
30	Made a single compound entry to accrue interest revenue on both notes. Use a 360-day year for interest computations.

E7-10B. Accounting for notes receivable (*Learning Objective 4*) 15–20 min.

Professional Enterprises sells on account. When a customer account becomes four months old, Professional converts the account to a note receivable. During 2013, Professional completed these transactions:

Mar 29	Sold goods on account to Montclair, Inc., $21,000.
Aug 1	Received a $21,000, 60-day, 5% note from Montclair, Inc., in satisfaction of its past-due account receivable.
Sep 30	Collected the Montclair, Inc. note at maturity.

Requirement

1. Record the transactions in Professional Enterprises' journal.

E7-11B. Quick ratio (*Learning Objective 5*) 15–20 min.

Consider the following data:

	A	B	C	D
Cash..	$ 93,000	$ 67,000	$23,000	$111,000
Short-term Investments..................	75,000	27,000	18,000	49,000
Net Receivables.............................	126,000	110,000	54,000	144,000
Current Liabilities...........................	335,000	280,000	35,000	220,000

Requirements

1. Calculate the quick assets and the quick ratio for each company.

2. Which of the companies should be concerned about its liquidity?

E7-12B. Quick ratio and accounts receivable turnover (*Learning Objective 5*) 15–20 min.

Algonquin Equipment reported the following items on November 30, 2013 (amounts in thousands, with last year's amounts also given as needed):

Accounts Payable.........................	$ 434	Accounts Receivable, Net:	
Cash..	210	November 30, 2013	$200
Inventory:		November 30, 2012	110
November 30, 2013	170	Cost of Goods Sold..........................	800
November 30, 2012	130	Short-term Investments..................	170
Net Credit Sales	2,450	Other Current Assets........................	30
Long-term Assets	410	Other Current Liabilities...................	170
Long-term Liabilities...................	60		

Requirements

1. Compute Algonquin Equipment's (a) quick ratio and (b) accounts receivable turnover for 2013.

2. Evaluate each ratio value as strong or weak. Assume Algonquin Equipment sells on terms of net 30.

EXERCISES (ALTERNATES 1, 2, AND 3)

These alternative exercise sets are available for your practice benefit at *www.myaccountinglab.com*

PROBLEMS (GROUP A)

P7-1A. Prepare journal entries for various types of sales (*Learning Objective 1*) 20–25 min.

Ace Party Supplies, Ltd. completed the following transactions during December. Ace uses the perpetual inventory system in accounting for inventory.

Dec	2	Sold party supplies for $1,800 to Goody Bags on account, with terms of 2/10, n/30, FOB shipping point. The cost of the sale was $1,125.
	4	Sold party supplies to a customer for $500, with cost of $350. Customer paid with a credit card. The credit card company charged a 2% service fee.
	6	Sold party supplies for $1,200 to Party Queen on account, with terms of 2/10, n/30, FOB shipping point. The cost of the sale was $750.
	12	Party Queen returned $200 of the party supplies. The cost of the returned products was $125. These products were returned to the warehouse for resale.
	15	Sold party supplies to customer for $320 cash. The cost of the sale was $200.
	16	Received payment from Party Queen, less returns and discount.
	23	Sold party supplies to a customer for $400, with cost of $280. Customer paid with a debit card. The bank charged a 2% of service fee.
	31	Received payment from Goody Bags.

Requirements

1. Record the transactions in the journal.
2. What are the amounts for total sales, sales returns and allowances, and sales discounts to be reported in the income statement?

P7-2A. Allowance method and accounts receivable reporting (*Learning Objectives 2 & 3*) 20–25 min.

On August 31, Pro Tennis Equipment had a $150,000 debit balance in Accounts Receivable ($70,000 current, $55,000 30 to 60 days, $35,000 60+). During September, Pro Tennis Equipment had the following transactions:

- Sales of $500,000, all on credit.
- Collections on account, $550,000.
- Write-offs of uncollectible receivables, $7,000.

Requirements

1. Assume that Pro Tennis Equipment uses the allowance method to account for doubtful accounts and that there was a $9,000 credit balance in the allowance account on August 31. Prepare journal entries to record sales, collections on account, and write-offs of Doubtful Accounts for the month of September. Next, assuming that Doubtful Accounts expense is estimated at 2% of credit sales, prepare the adjusting journal entry to record bad debts expense. Enter the beginning balances and post all September activity in T-accounts for Accounts Receivable, Allowance for Doubtful Accounts, and Bad Debt Expense.

2. Suppose that instead of the percentage of sales method, Pro Tennis Equipment uses the aging of accounts receivable method. The estimated bad debt is as follows: 1% of current A/R, 5% of A/R 30–60 days, 20% of A/R 60+ days. Prepare journal entries to record sales, collections on account, and write-offs of Doubtful Accounts for the month of September. Enter the beginning balances and post all September activity in T-accounts for Accounts Receivable and Bad Debt Expense.

3. What amount of Bad Debt Expense would Pro Tennis Equipment report on its September income statement under each of the two methods?

4. What amount of net accounts receivable would Pro Tennis Equipment report on its September 30 balance sheet under each of the two methods?

P7-3A. **Aging of accounts receivable allowance method** (*Learning Objectives 2 & 3*)
15–20 min.

Regents Supply completed the following selected transactions during the year:

Jan 17	Sold inventory to Abe Gomez, $600, on account. Ignore cost of goods sold.
Jun 29	Wrote off the Abe Gomez account as uncollectible after repeated efforts to collect from him.
Aug 6	Received $200 from Abe Gomez, along with a letter stating his intention to pay within 30 days. Reinstated his account in full.
Sep 4	Received the balance due from Abe Gomez.
Dec 31	Made a compound entry to write off the following accounts as uncollectible: Bernard Clark, $700; Marie Montrose, $300; and Terry Forman, $600.
Dec 31	Based on an aging of accounts receivable, estimated uncollectible accounts as $2,300.

Requirements

1. Open T-accounts for Allowance for Doubtful Accounts and Bad Debt Expense. These accounts have beginning balances of $1,800 (Cr.) and 0, respectively.

2. Record the transactions in the journal, and post to the two T-accounts.

3. The December 31 balance of Accounts Receivable is $139,000. Show how Accounts Receivable would be reported on the balance sheet at that date.

Quick solution: 2. Adjusting journal entry amount to record bad debts expense = $2,100; Allowance for Doubtful Accounts ending balance = $2,300; Bad Debt Expense ending balance = $2,100

P7-4A. **Aging of accounts receivable allowance method** (*Learning Objectives 2 & 3*)
30–35 min.

Goto Foods International, Inc. uses the aging of accounts receivable method to account for bad debts at the end of each year. All of its customers are on account with the credit terms 2/10, n/30. Accounts receivable are grouped into three aging periods: (1) current—within the current month, (2) 31 to 60 days, and (3) 61+ days. Goto's accounting policy for estimating the uncollectible accounts receivable is calculated based on (1) 5% on the current, (2) 10% on the 2nd aging period, and (3) 30% on the 3rd aging period.

At December 31, Goto Foods' accounts receivable was $92,800, and the unadjusted Allowance for Doubtful Accounts was $3,200 (Cr.). The following is a list of the accounts receivable subsidiary ledger for five customers:

Date	Document	Debit	Credit	Balance
	Bua Foods			
Oct 28	Invoice 337	$ 6,850		$ 6,850
Nov 28	Invoice 395	4,750		11,600
Dec 5	Receipt Inv 337		3,360	8,240
Dec 23	Invoice 456	7,240		15,480
	Nitesh Grocers			
Oct 08	Invoice 263	6,500		6,500
Oct 10	Credit Memo 105		700	5,800
Oct 17	Receipt Inv 263		5,800	0
Oct 30	Invoice 346	12,500		12,500
	Pusan Export, Inc.			
Nov 18	Invoice 279	30,200		30,200
	Vuong Company			
Oct 22	Invoice 302	8,520		8,520
Dec 10	Invoice 418	3,400		11,920
	Wang Enterprise			
Oct 26	Invoice 328	8,600		8,600
Nov 05	Receipt Inv 328		4,300	4,300
Dec 30	Invoice 468	18,400		22,700

Requirements

1. Prepare the customer aging schedule based on the three aging groups.

2. Calculate the estimated uncollectible accounts for the year.

3. Prepare the journal entry for the bad debt expense.

4. Which company has taken the sales discounts? What was the amount of the sales discounts taken?

P7-5A. Sales and bad debt write-offs (*Learning Objectives 1 & 2*) 20–25 min.

MinTech Computer Supplies, Inc.'s accounting data show the following balances for 2013 and 2014:

	2013	2014
Sales (40%—Cash, 60%—Credit)	$280,000	$322,000
Sales Returns and Allowances	5,600	6,400
Accounts Receivable written off during the year	2,700	11,000
Accounts Receivable, December 31	84,000	108,000
Allowance for Doubtful Accounts (credit balance), December 31	4,200	5,400

The accountant also provided the following additional information:

1. MinTech uses the perpetual inventory system and its gross margin is 40% of the sales.

2. During 2014, there was a large writeoff of $11,000 due to an unexpected bankruptcy of a major customer.

3. During 2014, $500 of the previously written-off amount was collected in full.

Requirements

1. Calculate the bad debt expense for the year ended December 31, 2014.

2. Calculate the cash collections from accounts receivable for 2014.

3. Prepare journal entries to record all the transactions for MinTech in 2014.

4. What is the impact on each of Assets, Shareholders' Equity, and Net Income, when the uncollectible accounts are written off? Please identify as increase (I), decrease (D), or no effect (NE).

P7-6A. Accounting for notes receivable (*Learning Objective 4*) 20–25 min.

The Bailey Insurance Agency received the following notes during 2013:

Note	Date	Principal Amount	Interest Rate	Term
(1)	Dec 23	$13,000	9%	1 year
(2)	Nov 30	12,000	12%	6 months
(3)	Dec 7	9,000	10%	30 days

Requirements

1. Identifying each note by number, compute interest using a 360-day year, and determine the due date and maturity value of each note.

2. Journalize a single adjusting entry on December 31, 2013, to record accrued interest revenue on all three notes. Explanations are not required.

3. For note (1), journalize the collection of principal and interest at maturity. Explanations are not required.

P7-7A. Accounting for notes receivable (*Learning Objective 4*) 20–25 min.

Record the following transactions in the journal of Bingham Phone Accessories. Explanations are not required.

2012
Dec 19   Received a $3,000, 60-day, 12% note on account from Arnold Collins.
    31   Made an adjusting entry to accrue interest on the Collins note.
    31   Made a closing entry for interest revenue.
2013
Feb 17   Collected the maturity value of the Collins note.
Jun 1   Loaned $10,000 cash to Electra Mann, receiving a six-month, 11% note.
Oct 31   Received a $1,500, 60-day, 12% note from Mark Phillips on his past-due account receivable.
Dec 1   Collected the maturity value of the Electra Mann note.

P7-8A. Quick ratio and accounts receivable turnover (*Learning Objective 5*) 20–25 min.

The comparative financial statements of Bien Taco Restaurants for 2013, 2012, and 2011 include the following selected data:

	(In Thousands)		
	2013	2012	2011
Balance Sheet			
Current Assets:			
Cash	$ 82	$ 80	$ 60
Short-term Investments	140	174	122
Receivables, Net of Allowance for Doubtful Accounts of $6, $6, and $5 respectively	257	265	218
Inventory	429	341	302
Prepaid Expenses	21	27	46
Total Current Assets	929	887	748
Total Current Liabilities	$ 680	$ 700	$ 600
Income Statement			
Sales Revenue	$5,189	$4,995	$4,206
Cost of Goods Sold	2,734	2,636	2,418

Requirements

1. Compute these ratios for 2013 and 2012:

   a. Quick ratio.

   b. Accounts receivable turnover. Assume all sales are credit sales.

2. Write a memo explaining to the company owner which ratios improved from 2012 to 2013, which ratios deteriorated, and which items in the financial statements changed and caused changes in some ratios. Discuss whether this conveys a favourable or an unfavourable impression about the company.

PROBLEMS (GROUP B)

P7-1B. Prepare journal entries for various types of sales (*Learning Objective 1*) 20–25 min.

Bill Building Supplies, Ltd. completed the following transactions during June. Bill uses the perpetual inventory system in accounting for inventory.

Jun	2	Sold plumbing supplies to a customer for $1,100, with cost of $660. Customer paid with a credit card. The credit card company charged a 2% service fee.
	6	Sold building supplies for $2,600 to Goh Development on account, with terms of 2/15, n/30, FOB shipping point. The cost of the sale was $1,560.
	12	Goh Development returned $600 of the building supplies. The cost of the returned products was $360. These products were returned to the warehouse for resale.
	15	Sold building supplies for $1,800 to Lum Contractors on account, with terms of 2/15, n/30, FOB shipping point. The cost of the sale was $1,080.
	16	Sold building supplies to a customer for $820 cash. The cost of the sale was $500.
	21	Received payment from Goh Development, less returns and discount.
	23	Sold building supplies to a customer for $1,400, with cost of $840. Customer paid with a debit card. The bank charged a 2% service fee.
	30	Received payment from Lum Contractors, less discount.

Requirements

1. Record the transactions in the journal.

2. What are the amounts for total sales, sales returns and allowances, and sales discounts to be reported in the income statement?

P7-2B. Allowance method and accounts receivable reporting (*Learning Objectives 2 & 3*) 20–25 min.

On March 31, Daisy Tennis Equipment had a $165,000 debit balance in Accounts Receivable ($80,000 current, $65,000 30 to 60 days, $20,000 60+). During April, Daisy Tennis Equipment had the following transactions:

- Sales of $490,000, all on credit.
- Collections on account, $425,000.
- Write-offs of uncollectible receivables, $6,000.

Requirements

1. Assume that Daisy Tennis Equipment uses the allowance method to account for doubtful accounts and that there was an $8,000 credit balance in the allowance

account on March 31. Prepare journal entries to record sales, collections on account, and write-offs of Doubtful Accounts for the month of April. Next, assuming that Bad Debt Expense is estimated at 2% of credit sales, prepare the adjusting journal entry to record bad debts expense. Enter the beginning balances and post all April activity in T-accounts for Accounts Receivable, Allowance for Doubtful Accounts, and Bad Debt Expense.

2. Suppose that instead of the allowance method, Daisy Tennis Equipment uses the aging of accounts receivable method. The estimated bad debt is as follows: 0.5% of current A/R, 5% of A/R 30–60 days, 30% of A/R 60+ days. Prepare journal entries to record sales, collections on account, and write-offs of Doubtful Accounts for the month of April. Enter the beginning balances and post all April activity in T-accounts for Accounts Receivable and Bad Debt Expense.

3. What amount of Bad Debt Expense would Daisy Tennis Equipment report on its April income statement under each of the two methods?

4. What amount of net accounts receivable would Daisy Tennis Equipment report on its April 30 balance sheet under each of the two methods?

P7-3B. Aging of accounts receivable allowance method (*Learning Objectives 2 & 3*) 15–20 min.

Beta Supply completed the following selected transactions during the year:

Jan 17	Sold inventory to Abe Gomez, $800 on account. Ignore cost of goods sold.
Jun 29	Wrote off Abe Gomez's account as uncollectible after repeated efforts to collect from him.
Aug 6	Received $250 from Abe Gomez, along with a letter stating his intention to pay within 30 days. Reinstated Gomez's account in full.
Sep 4	Received the balance due from Abe Gomez.
Dec 31	Made a compound entry to write off the following accounts as uncollectible: Brian Kemper, $1,000; Marie Montrose, $200; and Tanya Wayne, $900.
Dec 31	Based on an aging of accounts receivable, estimated uncollectible accounts as $2,600.

Requirements

1. Open T-accounts for Allowance for Doubtful Accounts and Bad Debt Expense. These accounts have beginning balances of $1,500 (Cr.) and 0, respectively.

2. Record the transactions in the journal, and post to the two T-accounts.

3. The December 31 balance of Accounts Receivable is $133,000. Show how Accounts Receivable would be reported on the balance sheet at that date.

P7-4B. Aging of accounts receivable allowance method (*Learning Objectives 2 & 3*) 30–35 min.

Yangzi International, Inc. uses the aging of accounts receivable method to account for uncollectible accounts at the end of each year. All of its customers are on account with the credit terms 2/10, n/30. Accounts receivable are grouped in three aging periods: (1) current—within the current month, (2) 31 to 60 days, and (3) 61+ days. Yangzi's accounting policy for estimating the uncollectible accounts receivable is calculated based on (1) 5% on the current, (2) 10% on the 2nd aging period, and (3) 40% on the 3rd aging period.

On March 31, the end of this fiscal year, Yangzi's accounts receivable was $130,600, and the unadjusted Allowance for Doubtful Accounts was $5,800 (credit). The following is a list of the accounts receivable subsidiary ledger for five customers:

Date	Document	Debit	Credit	Balance
Chen Enterprise				
Jan 8	Invoice 121	26,500		26,500
Jan 10	Credit Memo 52		1,200	25,300
Jan 21	Invoice 130	14,600		39,900
Feb 7	Receipt Inv 121		25,300	14,600
Dong Gifts				
Jan 22	Invoice 132	25,800		25,800
Feb 21	Receipt Inv 132		15,480	10,320
Mar 10	Invoice 158	32,400		42,720
Mar 15	Receipt Inv 132		5,320	37,400
Jeevan Export, Inc.				
Jan 28	Invoice 145	12,400		12,400
Feb 28	Invoice 159	8,600		21,000
Mar 5	Receipt Inv 145		6,400	14,600
Mar 25	Invoice 178	32,400		47,000
Prasad Trades Company				
Jan 18	Invoice 128	13,200		13,200
Zhou International				
Jan 26	Invoice 143	7,500		7,500
Feb 5	Receipt Inv 143		7,500	0
Mar 30	Invoice 168	18,400		18,400

Requirements

1. Prepare the customer aging schedule based on the three aging groups.
2. Calculate the estimated uncollectible accounts for the year.
3. Prepare the journal entry for the bad debt expense.
4. Which company has taken the sales discounts? What was the amount of the sales discounts taken?

P7-5B. Sales and bad debt write-offs (Learning Objectives 1 & 2) 20–25 min.

ATel Electronics, Inc.'s accounting data show the following balances for 2013 and 2014:

	2013	2014
Sales (40%—Cash, 60%—Credit)	$420,000	$546,000
Sales Returns and Allowances	12,600	13,650
Accounts Receivable written off during the year	5,200	15,800
Accounts Receivable, December 31	128,000	164,000
Allowance for Doubtful Accounts (credit balance), December 31	6,400	8,200

The accountant also provided the following additional information:

1. ATel Electronics uses the perpetual inventory system and its gross margin is 40% of the sales.
2. During 2014, there was a large writeoff of $15,800 due to an unexpected bankruptcy of a major customer.
3. During 2014, $1,200 of the previously written-off amount was collected in full.

Requirements

1. Calculate the bad debt expense for the year ended December 31, 2014.
2. Calculate the cash collections from accounts receivable for 2014.
3. Prepare journal entries to record all the transactions for ATel in 2014.

4. What is the impact on each of Assets, Shareholders' Equity and Net Income, when the uncollectible accounts are written off? Please identify as increase (I), decrease (D), or no effect (NE).

P7-6B. Accounting for notes receivable (*Learning Objective 4*) 20–25 min.

The Buffalo Insurance Agency received the following notes during 2013:

Note	Date	Principal	Interest Rate	Term
(1)	Oct 23	$13,000	8%	1 year
(2)	Sep 30	8,000	11%	2 months
(3)	Oct 7	10,000	12%	45 days

Requirements

1. Identifying each note by number, compute interest using a 360-day year, and determine the due date and maturity value of each note.

2. Journalize a single adjusting entry on October 31, 2013, to record accrued interest revenue on all three notes. Explanations are not required.

3. For note (1), journalize the collection of principal and interest at maturity. Explanations are not required.

P7-7B. Accounting for notes receivable (*Learning Objective 4*) 20–25 min.

Record the following transactions in the journal of Birds Eye Music. Explanations are not required.

2012

Dec 19 Received a $6,000, 60-day, 12% note on account from AVC Company.
    31 Made an adjusting entry to accrue interest on the AVC Company note.
    31 Made a closing entry for interest revenue.

2013

Feb 17 Collected the maturity value of the AVC Company note.
Jun 1 Loaned $12,000 cash to Lincoln Music, receiving a 6-month, 11% note.
Oct 31 Received a $5,500, 60-day, 13% note from Ying Yang Music on its past-due account receivable.
Dec 1 Collected the maturity value of the Lincoln Music note.

P7-8B. Quick ratio and accounts receivable turnover (*Learning Objective 5*) 20–25 min.

The comparative financial statements of Perfection Taco Restaurants for 2013, 2012, and 2011 include the following selected data:

	(In Thousands)		
	2013	**2012**	**2011**
Balance Sheet			
Current Assets:			
Cash	$ 82	$ 80	$ 55
Short-term Investments	130	178	125
Receivables, Net of Allowance for			
Doubtful Accounts of $7, $6,			
and $4, respectively	290	305	256
Inventory	434	335	315
Prepaid Expenses	24	30	55
Total Current Assets	960	928	806
Total Current Liabilities	$ 780	$ 800	$ 625
Income Statement			
Sales Revenue	$5,223	$5,039	$4,250
Cost of Goods Sold	2,768	2,650	2,490

Requirements

1. Compute these ratios for 2013 and 2012:
   a. Quick ratio.
   b. Accounts receivable turnover. Assume all sales are credit sales.

2. Write a memo explaining to the company owner which ratios improved from 2012 to 2013, which ratios deteriorated, and which items in the financial statements changed and caused changes in some ratios. Discuss whether this change conveys a favourable or an unfavourable impression about the company.

PROBLEMS (ALTERNATES 1, 2, AND 3)

These alternative problem sets are available for your practice benefit at
www.myaccountinglab.com

CONTINUING EXERCISE

In this exercise, we continue our accounting for Graham's Yard Care, Inc. from Chapter 6. Refer to the Continuing Exercise from Chapter 6. On August 18, Graham's Yard Care, Inc. received $250 on account from Jim Henderson related to his July 15 purchase. On October 12, Jim notified Graham's Yard Care, Inc. that he was filing for bankruptcy and that he would not be able to pay the remaining amount owed.

Requirement

1. Journalize the entry to record the payment from Jim and to record the writeoff of Jim's uncollectible account. Assume that Graham's Yard Care, Inc. uses the allowance method to account for Doubtful Accounts.

CONTINUING PROBLEM

In this problem, we continue our accounting for Aqua Elite, Inc. from Chapter 6. Refer to the Continuing Problem in Chapters 5 and 6. Assume that all 13 of the spas Aqua Elite, Inc. sold in September were sold on account for $4,000 each. At September 30, Aqua Elite, Inc. estimates that 5% of the sales will not be collected.

Requirements

1. Calculate the ending balance in Accounts Receivable at September 30.

2. Journalize the entry to record Aqua Elite's Bad Debt Expense for September.

3. How will Accounts Receivable be reflected on Aqua Elite's balance sheet at September 30?

APPLY YOUR KNOWLEDGE

ETHICS IN ACTION

Case 1. Ed Hanson is the controller of Casey's Collectibles. The business uses the accrual method of accounting and recognizes sales revenue in the period in which the sale is made. As a result, the Accounts Receivable balance at year-end was $92,480, which was net of the Allowance for Doubtful Accounts of $1,260. Ed was completing the year-end financial statements for the business to apply for a much needed business loan when he saw a letter from a district court. The letter was to inform him as controller of Casey's Collectibles that Charlie Smith had declared bankruptcy. As it turned out, Charlie was Casey's Collectibles' largest customer and his account receivable balance was $24,295, which the bankruptcy notification letter stated was never going to be paid. When Ed looked over the account receivable aging schedule he saw that Charlie's account was more than 90 days past due, and even though Ed had been suspicious, he still hoped that Charlie would pay his account balance. Ed looked at his balance sheet and thought that if he wrote off Charlie's account, the bank would become concerned about all of the accounts receivable listed. He then thought that had he not been so quick to open the mail, he would have not known that Charlie was bankrupt, and the balance sheet he was about to present to the bank would be fine. Knowing how potentially damaging this new information could be, Ed decided to just ignore it for the moment and simply go ahead with the balance sheet he had originally planned to give to the bank.

Should Ed provide the bank with a new balance sheet that reflects this new information? Would Ed have been fine with the original balance sheet had he simply waited to open his mail? Are any ethical issues involved with updating financial statement information for subsequent events? Did Ed not properly use the allowance method as he only had a balance for doubtful accounts totaling $1,260? Would Ed need to inform the bank had the bankruptcy letter been from a customer with an account receivable balance of $120?

Case 2. Bob and Larry were finishing the financial statements for their business when they saw the net income for the year was not going to be as high as they had hoped. Concerned that the bank would question the lower reported net income, Bob suggested that they reduce the percentage used to estimate Doubtful Accounts for the current year from 5% of credit sales to 1% of credit sales. Larry quickly pointed out that for the last seven years, the bad debts always approximated 5% of the total credit sales. Bob then said that the key was simply that an "estimate" was used to compute the bad debt expense, so why not simply change the percentage from the "5% estimate" to a "1% estimate"? Larry was concerned because the change was not due to new business information; rather it was due to pressure to increase the current year profit by reducing the amount of bad debt expense currently included in the income statement. He told Bob that the current year credit sales were $6,587,000 and the Bad Debt Expense should be 5% or $329,350, not 1% or $65,870, because they could expect that over the next fiscal year approximately $329,000 of Accounts Receivable would end up as uncollectible. Bob pointed out, however, that by only using a 1% estimate the current year net income would be much higher since the amount of Bad Debt Expense would only be $65,870 instead of the larger $329,350. He also noted that the allowance account would also be reduced so the net Accounts Receivable on the balance sheet would be larger as well. Besides, Bob told Larry that they could worry about it in the next fiscal year. Larry told Bob that the bank would find out what they had done, to which Bob said there would be no problem; they could just say they made a mistake in their estimate.

Would it be unethical to change the percentage used to compute the current year's Bad Debt Expense? Would it be acceptable to change the percentage amount if the change was disclosed? Would it be acceptable if they compromised and used 3%? If they had used a new screening method to determine the creditworthiness of customers and, as a result, they were certain that the bad debts would be drastically reduced, could they change the percentage amount used? What do you think would happen if they used the 1% of credit sales for the current year financial statements? What would you recommend?

KNOW YOUR BUSINESS

FINANCIAL ANALYSIS

Purpose: To help familiarize you with the financial reporting of a real company to further your understanding of the chapter material you are learning.

This case will address the accounts receivable reflected on Bombardier Inc.'s balance sheet. We will once again refer to the annual report for Bombardier Inc. located in MyAccountingLab to answer some questions related to Bombardier Inc.'s receivables.

Requirements

1. What was the Accounts Receivable balance as of January 31, 2011? What was the Accounts Receivable balance as of January 31, 2010? Did the amount of accounts receivable increase or decrease during the year?

2. Refer to the note on Accounts Receivables (Note 4). What types of receivables are included in Accounts Receivable?

3. How much of the trade accounts receivable is estimated not likely to be collected? How much of the trade receivables are impaired and how does the company determine impairment? How much of the receivables are past due but not impaired?

INDUSTRY ANALYSIS

Purpose: To help you understand and compare the performance of two companies in the same industry.

Find the Bombardier Annual Report, Year Ended January 31, 2011 located in MyAccountingLab. Now access the The Boeing Company's 2010 Annual Report. To do this from the internet, go to their webpage for the Investor Relations at http://www.boeing.com/companyoffices/financial/quarterly.htm and under Annual Report, go to the 2010 Annual Report.

Requirement

1. Calculate the accounts receivable turnover for Bombardier for 2011 and Boeing for 2010 using the gross trade receivable amounts for each company. Who has the highest accounts receivable turnover? Is that good or bad? Is it better to have a high accounts receivable turnover or a low accounts receivable turnover? Explain your answer.

SMALL BUSINESS ANALYSIS

Purpose: To help you understand the importance of managing accounts receivable of a small business.

Louise was horrified when she realized, too late, that it was only five days until the end of the month, and there was insufficient cash available to pay all her employees and the rent. What happened? The last 4 weeks had been a whirlwind of activity, as her small software training company had been immersed in the biggest, most profitable training initiative of the firm's existence, during which time she had ignored her usual weekly activity of calling clients whose accounts receivable was 3 days overdue, to remind them to process the invoice for payment.

Since the firm typically sent out dozens of invoices weekly for training completed, but customers often needed reminding to send the invoices to their accounts payable department for processing, Louise had found from past experience that it was necessary to follow up by phone on approximately thirty percent of invoices, or else they would not get processed.

Requirements

1. What happened? Why did Louise find she wouldn't have enough cash to pay all her employees and the rent at month end?

2. If the accounts receivable were not collected, what happens to the accounts receivable turnover?

WRITTEN COMMUNICATION

You're pretty excited about your cash balance at the end of the month because this was the month you were going to take the big bonus from the business and make a down payment on a new house. You were waiting on a big cheque to come in from a client who has owed you for several months. You had considered writing it off because you had heard through some business associates that the company had been experiencing some financial difficulties. However, after your telephone call to the company the first of the week, the cheque finally arrived. You rushed the cheque down to the bank and deposited it. A couple days later, you access your account online at the bank to figure out how much of a bonus cheque you can afford to write yourself. After depositing the $30,000 from your client, you expect to have a balance of at least $40,000 and since you always like to keep a balance of at least $10,000 in your account as a buffer, you figure you can easily write a bonus check for $25,000 for your down payment. After reviewing your account, you're really concerned when you see that your bank balance is only $9,500! What happened? You scroll down through the screen for an explanation and you see the following:

NSF cheque—Burns & Associates, Inc.—$30,000.00
Return cheque charge $200.00
Monthly service charge $300.00

Prepare an email to the owner of Burns & Associates, Inc., explaining the situation with the returned cheque and the charge that the bank applied to your account for processing the returned cheque. Also request payment for this entire amount, as it is now several months overdue. However, keep in mind that the tone of the e-mail might have some bearing on whether or not Burns continues to utilize your services or not.

Self Check Answers
1. a 2. a 3.d 4. c 5. b 6. a 7. b 8. a 9. c 10. c

SCAN THIS

CHAPTER 8

Long-Term Assets

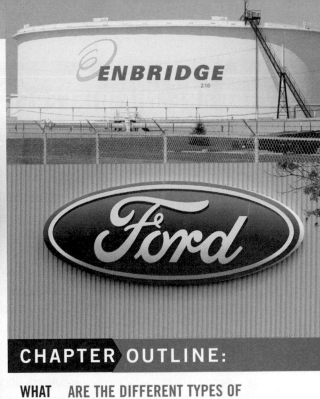

Regardless of whether you work for (or own) a service business, a merchandising business, or a manufacturing business, that business will likely own long-term assets. Many questions often arise with regard to long-term assets. What different types of long-term assets are there? How do you account for these assets? How do the different methods of accounting for these assets affect the financial statements? What happens when a long-term asset is sold? In this chapter, we will learn the answers to these and other questions as we study long-term assets.

WHAT ARE THE DIFFERENT TYPES OF LONG-TERM ASSETS?

1 Describe the difference between plant assets, intangible assets, and natural resources

Most businesses will own at least one of the following types of long-term assets:

- **Plant assets.** Plant assets, also called fixed assets, are "physical assets"—meaning they can be seen, touched, or held. This includes assets such as land, buildings, vehicles, desks, and equipment. Plant assets are also sometimes referred to as **tangible assets**.

- **Intangible assets.** Patents, trademarks, brands, and goodwill are examples of **intangible assets**. Unlike plant assets, intangible assets cannot be seen, touched, or held. For example, even though there may a piece of paper that provides written evidence of a patent, the paper is not the patent. The patent (the intangible asset) is actually the specific rights that are conveyed to the owner of the patent. Similarly, a logo, such as the Maplewood Equestrian Centre logo below, identifies a brand, and is an intangible element of creating the image of the company that is recognizable by customers and the public at large.

- **Natural resources.** Assets that come from the earth and can ultimately be used up are called **natural resources**. Timber, oil, minerals, and coal are all examples of natural resources.

As we learned in Chapter 3, the cost of a long-term asset must be allocated to an expense as the asset is used up. Although the process of cost allocation is similar for the different types of assets, the terminology used to describe the process is different for each type of asset. **Exhibit 8-1** summarizes the different asset types and the cost allocation terminology used with each.

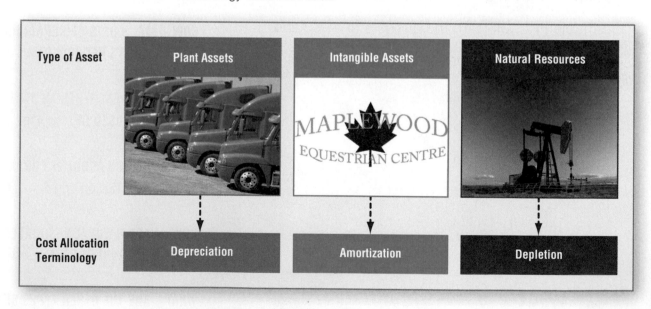

Exhibit 8-1 ▲

The cost allocation methods for each type of asset will be covered later in the chapter.

Companies may also own long-term assets that are classified as *other long-term assets*. Other long-term assets typically consist of long-term investments made by a business. These will be discussed near the end of the chapter.

HOW IS THE COST OF A PLANT ASSET CALCULATED?

Both IFRS and Canadian ASPE require that the *cost principle,* which we learned about in Chapter 1, be applied when determining the cost of a plant asset. Therefore, the actual amount paid for an asset is to be used as the asset's cost. The amount paid for an asset should include all amounts paid to acquire the asset and to prepare it for its intended purpose. These costs vary depending on the type of plant asset being purchased, so let's discuss each asset type individually.

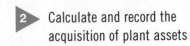

2 Calculate and record the acquisition of plant assets

Land and Land Improvements

The cost of land includes, but is not limited to, the following amounts paid by the purchaser:

- Purchase price
- Realtor commissions
- Survey and legal fees
- Unpaid property taxes owed on the land
- Fees associated with transferring the ownership (title) on the land
- Cost of clearing the land and removing unwanted buildings

The cost of land does *not* include the following costs:

- Fencing
- Paving
- Sprinkler systems
- Lighting
- Signs

These costs are recorded as separate plant assets called **land improvements**.

Suppose that Apex Industries purchases land for $75,000 by signing a note payable for the same amount. Apex Industries also pays cash as follows: $2,500 in realtor commission, $1,200 in transfer fees, a $1,700 survey fee, $4,500 to remove an old building, $2,200 to have the land graded and levelled, $6,300 to have the land fenced, $1,300 for a sprinkler system, and $2,700 for outdoor lighting. What amount would Apex Industries record as the cost of the land? How much would Apex record as land improvements? Apex Industries would assign the costs to land and land improvements as follows:

Cost Incurred	Land	Land Improvements
Purchase price	$75,000	
Realtor commission	2,500	
Transfer fees	1,200	
Survey fee	1,700	
Building removal	4,500	
Grading	2,200	
Fencing		$ 6,300
Sprinkler system		1,300
Lighting		2,700
Total cost	$87,100	$10,300

The purchase of the land and the subsequent cash payments are recorded as follows:

DATE	ACCOUNTS	POST REF.	DR.	CR.
	Land		75,000	
	Note Payable			75,000
	Purchased land on a note payable.			
	Land		12,100	
	Land Improvements		10,300	
	Cash			22,400
	Paid cash for land and land improvements.			

We would say that Apex Industries *capitalized* the cost of the land at $87,100 ($75,000 + $12,100) and the land improvements at $10,300. **Capitalized** means that an asset account is debited (increased) for the cost of an asset. Notice that Land and Land Improvements are two entirely separate assets. Land is a special plant asset because it is never really used up. Therefore, land is not depreciated. However, the cost of land improvements *is* depreciated over the useful life of the improvements.

Buildings

The cost of a building depends on whether the building is constructed or whether an existing building is purchased. If a building is constructed, the cost of the building includes the following:

- Architectural fees
- Building permit fees
- Contractor charges
- Payments for material, labour, and overhead

The time to complete a building can be months, even years. If a company constructs its own assets, the cost of a building may also include interest charged during the time of construction on any borrowed money.

If a company purchases an existing building, the cost of the building includes the following:

- Purchase price
- Realtor commissions
- Survey and legal fees
- Unpaid property taxes owed on the building
- Fees associated with transferring the ownership (title) on the building
- Costs of repairing and renovating the building for its intended use

Machinery and Equipment

The cost of machinery and equipment includes the following:

- Purchase price (less any discounts)
- Transportation (delivery) charges
- Insurance while in transit
- Sales and other taxes
- Purchase commission

- Installation costs
- Cost of testing the asset before it is used

After the asset is up and running, the company no longer debits insurance, taxes, and maintenance costs to the Equipment account. From that point on, insurance, taxes, repairs, and maintenance costs are recorded as expenses.

Furniture and Fixtures

Furniture and fixtures include desks, chairs, file cabinets, display racks, shelving, and so forth. The cost of furniture and fixtures includes the basic cost of each asset (less any discounts), plus all other costs to ready the asset for its intended use. For example, for a desk, this may include the costs to ship the desk to the business and the cost paid to a handyman to assemble the desk.

Exhibit 8-2 summarizes the costs associated with the different types of plant assets.

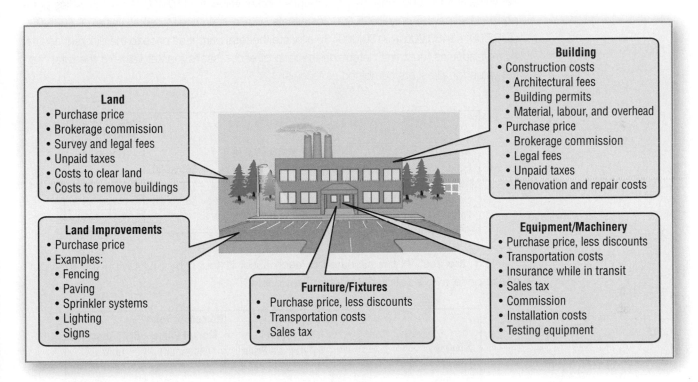

Land
- Purchase price
- Brokerage commission
- Survey and legal fees
- Unpaid taxes
- Costs to clear land
- Costs to remove buildings

Building
- Construction costs
  - Architectural fees
  - Building permits
  - Material, labour, and overhead
- Purchase price
  - Brokerage commission
  - Legal fees
  - Unpaid taxes
  - Renovation and repair costs

Land Improvements
- Purchase price
- Examples:
  - Fencing
  - Paving
  - Sprinkler systems
  - Lighting
  - Signs

Furniture/Fixtures
- Purchase price, less discounts
- Transportation costs
- Sales tax

Equipment/Machinery
- Purchase price, less discounts
- Transportation costs
- Insurance while in transit
- Sales tax
- Commission
- Installation costs
- Testing equipment

Exhibit 8-2 ▲

Lump-Sum (Basket) Purchase of Assets

When a company pays a single price for several assets as a group it is referred to as a **lump-sum purchase**, or **"basket" purchase**. For example, Apex Industries may pay one price ($625,000) for land, a building, and equipment. For accounting, the company must allocate a portion of the total cost to each individual asset, as shown in the following diagram:

The total cost is allocated to the different assets based on their relative market values. Let's assume that an appraisal revealed that the land's market value is $75,000, the building's market value is $480,000, and the equipment's market value is $130,000. Apex Industries got a good deal, paying only $625,000 for assets with a combined market value of $685,000 ($75,000 + $480,000 + $130,000). To allocate the total purchase price to the different assets, Apex Industries must first determine the ratio of each asset's market value to the total market value for all assets combined as follows:

Asset	Market Value		Percent of Total Market Value (Rounded)
Land	$ 75,000	÷ $685,000	11%
Building	480,000	÷ $685,000	70%
Equipment	130,000	÷ $685,000	19%
Total	**$685,000**		**100%**

Next, the cost that is allocated to each asset is found by multiplying the total purchase price by the ratios determined previously.

Asset	Total Purchase Price	×	Percent of Total Market Value (Rounded)	Cost Allocated to Asset
Land	$625,000	×	11%	$ 68,750
Building	$625,000	×	70%	437,500
Equipment	$625,000	×	19%	118,750
Total			**100%**	**$625,000**

If we assume that Apex Industries purchased the combined assets on a note payable, the purchase is recorded as follows:

DATE	ACCOUNTS	POST REF.	DR.	CR.
	Land		68,750	
	Building		437,500	
	Equipment		118,750	
	Note Payable			625,000
	Purchased land, building, and equipment on a note payable.			

How Are Costs Measured?

Asset values should be measured based on the amount of cash that is exchanged. However, in some situations, companies do not pay cash for their assets; instead, companies may issue shares in exchange for assets. In the case of a share-based payment, if the asset value can be reliably determined, then the fair value of the asset should be used; otherwise, the fair value of the shares given in exchange should be used. If a company's shares are publicly traded, then the fair value of the shares is easily obtainable and verifiable. Therefore, the share value given up should be used. If it is a private company whose shares are not traded, then it is more reliable to use the fair value of the asset acquired.

DECISION GUIDELINES

Decision	Guideline	Analyze
How do I determine the cost of an asset?	All costs associated with acquiring an asset, and preparing it for its intended use, should be considered as part of the cost of the asset.	It is tempting to treat costs related to the purchase of an asset (delivery fees, taxes, set up costs, etc.) as current period expenses. However, if these costs are expensed in the current period, then the cost of the asset does not reflect all of thecosts that are necessary for the asset to be able to be used. This causes the current period's net income to be understated and future periods' net income to be overstated.

HOW ARE PLANT ASSETS DEPRECIATED?

As we saw in Exhibit 8-1, the process of allocating a plant asset's cost to expense over its useful life is referred to as depreciation. In accounting, the "using up" of a plant asset is also referred to as depreciation. For example, a delivery truck can only go so many kilometres before it is worn out, or used up. As the truck is driven, it depreciates, or is used up. Physical factors, like age and weather, will also contribute to the depreciation of assets. So, depreciation refers to the "using up" of a plant asset as well as to the process of allocating the asset's cost to expense over the asset's useful life.

 3 Calculate and record the depreciation of plant assets

Both IFRS and Canadian ASPE require companies to develop a componentization policy. **Componentization** is to group assets into separate component parts, where the cost of each of these components is significant in relation to the total cost of the asset. Each of the component parts is recognized and depreciated separately. For example, an aircraft can be grouped into several components, such as engine, cabin interior modifications, and the aircraft itself.

Let's contrast this with what depreciation is **not**.

- **Depreciation is not a process of valuation.** Businesses do not record depreciation based on changes in the asset's market (sales) value.

- **Depreciation does not mean that the business sets aside cash to replace an asset when it is used up.** Depreciation has nothing to do with cash.

ACCOUNTING IN YOUR WORLD

Have you ever bought a new car, or know someone who has? If so, then you have probably heard people comment on how much the car "depreciated" the minute it was driven off the car lot. These people were referring to the fact that the resale value of the car was most likely less than what had been paid for it. In everyday life, the term depreciation is commonly used to describe a decrease in the market value of an asset, such as a car. However, from an accounting point of view, the car had not depreciated merely because it was driven off the lot. In accounting, depreciation refers to the allocation of the cost of an asset to expense during the life of the asset rather than to a decline in the market value of the asset.

Measuring Depreciation

Depreciation of a plant asset is based on three factors:

1 Cost

2 Estimated useful life

3 Estimated residual value

Cost is known and, as mentioned earlier in this chapter, includes all amounts incurred to prepare the asset for its intended purpose. The other two factors are estimates.

Estimated **useful life** represents the expected life of an asset during which it is anticipated to generate revenues. Useful life may be measured in years, or in units of output. For example, a building's life is usually stated in years, a truck's in the number of kilometres it can be driven, and a photocopier's in the number of copies it can make. For each asset, the goal is to define the estimated useful life that best matches the "using up" of the asset.

Some assets, such as computers and software, may become obsolete before they wear out. An asset is obsolete when a newer asset can perform the job more efficiently. As a result of obsolescence, an asset's useful life may be determined to be shorter than its physical life. In all cases, an asset's cost is depreciated over its useful life.

Estimated **residual value**—also called salvage value—is the asset's expected cash value at the end of its useful life. A delivery truck's useful life may be 150,000 kilometres. When the truck has driven that distance, the company will sell or scrap it. The expected cash value at the end of the truck's life is the truck's estimated residual value. Because the estimated residual value represents a portion of the asset's cost that will be recovered, it is not depreciated. The residual value is subtracted from the cost of the asset to arrive at the asset's **depreciable cost**.

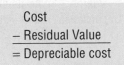

Cost
− Residual Value
= Depreciable cost

A business will use past experience as well as information obtained from other sources to make the best estimates it can of useful life and residual value.

Depreciation Methods

The most commonly used depreciation methods are as follows:

- Straight-line
- Units-of-production
- Declining-balance

These methods work differently in *how* the yearly depreciation amount is calculated, but they all result in the same total depreciation over the useful life of the asset. To demonstrate the different depreciation methods, let's assume that Apex Industries purchased and placed in service a new delivery truck on January 1. The data related to Apex Industries' new delivery truck is presented next:

Purchase price (cost).. $43,000
Estimated residual (salvage) value.. $ 4,000
Estimated useful life.. 5 years

Straight-Line Method The **straight-line (SL) depreciation method** allocates an equal amount of depreciation to each year. Apex Industries might want to use this method for the truck if it thinks time is the best indicator of the truck's depreciation. The equation to find yearly depreciation using straight-line depreciation is as follows:

$$\text{Straight-line depreciation} = \frac{\text{Cost} - \text{Residual value}}{\text{Estimated useful life in years}} = \text{Depreciation per year}$$

The yearly depreciation expense for Apex Industries' delivery truck is as follows:

$$\frac{\text{Cost} - \text{Residual value}}{\text{Estimated useful life}} = \frac{\$43,000 - \$4,000}{5} = \$7,800 \text{ per year}$$

Because Apex Industries purchased the delivery truck on January 1, an entire year's worth of depreciation will be recorded for the first year as follows on December 31:

DATE	ACCOUNTS	POST REF.	DR.	CR.
Dec 31	Depreciation Expense, Vehicles		7,800	
	Accumulated Depreciation, Vehicles			7,800
	Record yearly depreciation.			

Exhibit 8-3 demonstrates a straight-line depreciation schedule that has been prepared for Apex Industries' delivery truck.

Year	Asset Cost	Yearly Depreciation	Accumulated Depreciation	Book Value
0	$43,000			$43,000
1		$7,800	$ 7,800	35,200
2		7,800	15,600	27,400
3		7,800	23,400	19,600
4		7,800	31,200	11,800
5		7,800	39,000	4,000

Exhibit 8-3 ▲

The final column shows the asset's *book value*, which is its cost less accumulated depreciation.

Notice that as an asset is depreciated, its accumulated depreciation increases and its book value decreases. Observe the Accumulated Depreciation and Book Value columns in Exhibit 8-3. At the end of its useful life, the asset is said to be **fully depreciated**. Once an asset has been fully depreciated its final book value should equal its residual value, $4,000 in this case.

Units-of-Production (UOP) Method The **units-of-production (UOP) depreciation method** allocates a fixed amount of depreciation to each unit of output as follows:

$$\text{Units-of-production depreciation} = \frac{\text{Cost} - \text{Residual value}}{\text{Estimated useful life in units}} = \text{Depreciation per unit}$$

Assume that instead of straight-line, Apex Industries depreciates its delivery truck using units-of-production depreciation. Apex Industries might want to use UOP depreciation for the truck if it thinks kilometres are the best measure of the truck's depreciation. The delivery truck is estimated to be driven 35,000 kilometres the first year, 30,000 the second, 30,000 the third, 20,000 the fourth, and 15,000 during the fifth (for a total of 130,000 kilometres). The UOP depreciation each period varies with the number of units (kilometres, in the case of the truck) the asset produces. The depreciation per unit for Apex Industries' delivery truck is calculated as follows:

$$\frac{\text{Cost} - \text{Residual value}}{\text{Estimated useful life in units}} = \frac{\$43,000 - \$4,000}{130,000 \text{ kilometres}} = \$0.30 \text{ per kilometre}$$

Apex Industries would record $10,500 (35,000 kilometres × $0.30) of depreciation at December 31, of the first year as follows:

DATE	ACCOUNTS	POST REF.	DR.	CR.
Dec 31	Depreciation Expense, Vehicles		10,500	
	Accumulated Depreciation, Vehicles			10,500
	Record yearly depreciation.			

A depreciation schedule similar to the one prepared for straight-line depreciation is presented in **Exhibit 8-4** for units-of-production depreciation.

Year	Asset Cost	Yearly Depreciation			Depreciation Expense	Accumulated Depreciation	Book Value
		Number of Units		Depreciation Per Unit			
0	$43,000						$43,000
1		35,000 km	×	$0.30	=	$10,500	$10,500	32,500
2		30,000 km	×	$0.30	=	9,000	19,500	23,500
3		30,000 km	×	$0.30	=	9,000	28,500	14,500
4		20,000 km	×	$0.30	=	6,000	34,500	8,500
5		15,000 km	×	$0.30	=	4,500	39,000	4,000

Exhibit 8-4 ▲

Notice once again that the ending book value of the delivery truck, $4,000, equals its residual value as it did with straight-line depreciation.

Double-Declining-Balance Method The **double-declining-balance (DDB)** method is known as an **accelerated depreciation method**. An accelerated depreciation method writes off more depreciation near the start of an asset's life and less at the end. The use of DDB by Apex Industries would be appropriate if Apex anticipates the delivery truck will be significantly more productive in its early years. The DDB method multiplies the asset's decreasing book value by a constant rate that is twice the straight-line depreciation rate. DDB amounts can be computed using the following formula:

$$\text{Double-declining-balance depreciation} = \frac{1}{\text{Estimated useful life in years}} \times 2 \times \text{Book value} = \text{Depreciation per year}$$

Note that residual value is not included in the formula. Unlike with straight-line and units-of-production, with double-declining-balance depreciation, residual value is ignored until the end of an asset's life.

For the first year of the delivery truck, the calculation would be as shown here:

$$\frac{1}{5} \times 2 = \frac{2}{5}$$

$$\frac{2}{5} \times \$43,000 = \$17,200$$

Exhibit 8-5 reflects a depreciation schedule for the delivery truck using double-declining-balance depreciation.

Year	Asset Cost	Yearly Depreciation			Depreciation Expense	Accumulated Depreciation	Book Value
		DDB Rate*		Book Value			
0	$43,000						$43,000
1		2/5	×	$43,000	=	$17,200	$17,200	25,800
2		2/5	×	25,800	=	10,320	27,520	15,480
3		2/5	×	15,480	=	6,192	33,712	9,288
4		2/5	×	9,288	=	3,715**	37,427	5,573
5						1,573***	39,000	4,000

*1/5 × 2 = 2/5
**rounded
***5,573 − 4,000 = 1,573

Exhibit 8-5 ▲

Under double-declining-balance, the depreciation schedule is altered in the final years to prevent the asset from being depreciated below the residual value. In the case of Apex Industries' delivery truck, the residual value was given as $4,000. In the DDB schedule in Exhibit 8-5, notice that after year 4, the truck's book value is $5,573. Depreciation expense calculated using DDB would reduce the book value below the residual value. Therefore, in the final year, the depreciation expense is reduced to $1,573, which is the book value of $5,573 less the $4,000 residual value. If the residual value is high enough, it is possible that the second to last year's depreciation expense could be reduced and there would be no depreciation in the final year.

Some companies change to the straight-line method during the last years of an asset's life to "level-off" the yearly depreciation expense in the final years. The yearly depreciation when switching to straight-line is calculated as follows:

$$\frac{\text{Remaining book value} - \text{Residual value}}{\text{Remaining useful life}} = \text{Depreciation per year}$$

Exhibit 8-6 reflects a depreciation schedule for the delivery truck using double-declining-balance depreciation with a switch to straight-line after year 3.

Year	Asset Cost	Yearly Depreciation			Accumulated Depreciation	Book Value
		DDB Rate*	Book Value	Depreciation Expense		
0	$43,000					$43,000
1		2/5 ×	$43,000 =	$17,200	$17,200	25,800
2		2/5 ×	25,800 =	10,320	27,520	15,480
3		2/5 ×	15,480 =	6,192	33,712	9,288
4				2,644*	36,356	6,644
5				2,644*	39,000	4,000

*(9,288 – 4,000) ÷ 2 = 2,644

Exhibit 8-6 ▲

Comparing Depreciation Methods

Let's compare the depreciation methods. Annual amounts vary, but total accumulated depreciation equals $39,000 for all three methods.

Year	Depreciation per Year		
	Straight-Line	Units-of-Production	Double-Declining-Balance
1	$ 7,800	$10,500	$17,200
2	7,800	9,000	10,320
3	7,800	9,000	6,192
4	7,800	6,000	3,715
5	7,800	4,500	1,573
Total Depreciation	$39,000	$39,000	$39,000

Which method is best? That depends on the asset. A business should match an asset's expense against the revenue that the asset produces. Following are some guidelines:

- **Straight-Line.** For an asset that generates revenue evenly over time, the straight-line method will demonstrate the even usage of the asset over time as well.
- **Units-of-Production.** The UOP method works best for an asset whose use varies from year to year. More use causes greater depreciation. For example, UOP might be good for depreciating copy machines, vehicles, and machinery.
- **Double-Declining-Balance.** The DDB method works best for assets that produce more revenue in their early years and less in their later years. Higher depreciation in the early years is matched against the greater revenue. For example, DDB would be good for depreciating computers.

Partial Year Depreciation

In the examples for Apex Industries' delivery truck, it was assumed that the truck was purchased on January 1 and used for an entire year. However, most assets are not purchased on the first day of the year and used for the entire year. When an asset is not used for an entire year, the depreciation expense for that year must be prorated for the number of months the asset was actually used during the year. If an asset is in service for more than one half of the month, it is considered to be in service for the entire month. The formula for prorating the depreciation expense is as follows:

$$\text{Depreciation expense for the entire year} \times \frac{\text{\# of months asset was used}}{12} = \text{Prorated yearly depreciation expense}$$

Let's return to our example using Apex Industries' delivery truck. Assume that instead of purchasing the delivery truck on January 1, Apex Industries purchased the delivery truck on May 1. **Exhibits 8-7** and **8-8** reflect new depreciation schedules for Apex Industries' delivery truck using straight-line and double-declining-balance depreciation respectively.

Year	Asset Cost	Yearly Depreciation	Accumulated Depreciation	Book Value
0	$43,000			$43,000
1		$7,800 × 8/12* = $5,200	$ 5,200	37,800
2		7,800	13,000	30,000
3		7,800	20,800	22,200
4		7,800	28,600	14,400
5		7,800	36,400	6,600
6		$7,800 × 4/12** = 2,600	39,000	4,000

*Prorated for May through December
**Prorated for January through April

Exhibit 8-7 ▲

Notice that both schedules now reflect six years even though the delivery truck has a five-year life. Because the truck was only depreciated for eight months in the first year instead of twelve, the sixth year is added to "pick up" the final four months of depreciation. With units-of-production depreciation, there is no need to prorate the depreciation for partial years. This is because UOP is based on the quantity of units produced by an asset, regardless of how many months the asset was in service during the year.

Year	Asset Cost	Yearly Depreciation			Accumulated Depreciation	Book Value
		DDB Rate	Book Value	Depreciation Expense*		
0	$43,000					$43,000
1		2/5	× $43,000	= $17,200 × 8/12** = $11,467	$11,467	31,533
2		2/5	× 31,533	= 12,613	24,080	18,920
3		2/5	× 18,920	= 7,568	31,648	11,352
4		2/5	× 11,352	= 4,541	36,189	6,811
5		2/5	× 6,811	= 2,724	38,913	4,087
6				(4,087 − 4,000) = 87	39,000	4,000

*Rounded
**Prorated for May through December

Exhibit 8-8 ▲

Changing the Useful Life of a Depreciable Asset

Estimating the useful life and residual value of a plant asset can be difficult. Sometimes, as the asset is used, a business may determine that it needs to revise the useful life and/or the residual value of the asset. For example, at the end of year 3, Apex Industries may find that its delivery truck is expected to last seven years instead of five. Accounting changes like this are not uncommon because the original estimates are not based on perfect foresight. The formula used to calculate the new yearly depreciation amount if the useful life or residual value is changed looks like this:

$$\frac{(\text{Remaining book value} - \text{New residual value})}{(\text{New estimated useful life} - \text{Number of years already depreciated})} = \text{Revised annual depreciation}$$

In effect, the asset's remaining depreciable book value is spread over the asset's remaining life.

Let's return to our Apex Industries' example. If we look back at Exhibit 8-3, we see that the remaining book value for Apex Industries' delivery truck after year 3 is $19,600. Now let's suppose that in addition to revising the estimated useful life from five to seven years, the residual value is also revised from $4,000 to $3,000. Apex Industries would calculate the new yearly depreciation as follows:

$$\frac{(\$19,600 - \$3,000)}{(7 \text{ years} - 3 \text{ years})} = \frac{\$16,600}{4} = \$4,150$$

A new straight-line depreciation schedule reflecting the changes in estimates appears in **Exhibit 8-9**.

Year	Yearly Depreciation	Accumulated Depreciation	Book Value
0			$43,000
1	$7,800	$ 7,800	35,200
2	7,800	15,600	27,400
3	7,800	23,400	19,600
4	4,150	27,550	15,450
5	4,150	31,700	11,300
6	4,150	35,850	7,150
7	4,150	40,000	3,000

Exhibit 8-9 ▲

Using Fully-Depreciated Assets

As explained earlier in the chapter, a fully-depreciated asset is one that has reached the end of its *estimated* useful life. No more depreciation is recorded for the asset. If the asset is no longer useful, it is disposed of. If the asset is still useful, the company may continue using it. The asset account and its accumulated depreciation remain on the books, but no additional depreciation is recorded. In short, the asset never goes below residual value.

Capital Cost Allowance

When companies calculate income taxes to be paid each year, the calculations need to be based on a declining balance formula but with specific rates as assigned for each capital cost allowance category. For example, most passenger vehicles would be in Class 10 and a 30% rate would be used to calculate the depreciation for capital cost allowance purposes. Although coverage of capital cost allowance will be left to a more advanced financial accounting course, it is important to understand that companies must calculate capital cost allowance for income tax purposes rather than using the depreciation calculation that they use for external financial reporting.

DECISION GUIDELINES

Decision	**Guideline**	**Analyze**
I'm a new business owner and have made numerous purchases of capital assets to begin my operations. Which depreciation method is the best for my assets?	The choice of depreciation method depends upon the specific asset being depreciated as well as what the intended use of that asset is. The best method is one that most closely matches the cost of an asset against the future revenues it helps generate.	Straight-line depreciation is best for assets that will be used evenly throughout their lives and that will incur repair and maintenance cost evenly. Units-of-production depreciation is best for assets that will be utilized on an irregular basis throughout their lives. Double-declining-balance depreciation is best for assets that will be utilized significantly more in the early years of their lives. It is also best for assets that will require significantly more repair and maintenance expenditures in the later years of the asset's life.

HOW ARE COSTS OF REPAIRING PLANT ASSETS RECORDED?

When a business has to repair an existing plant asset, the method of accounting for the expenditure is determined by the type of repair that occurred. Repairs are generally broken down into three types:

 4 Account for repairs to plant assets

- Ordinary repairs
- Extraordinary repairs
- Betterments

Ordinary Repairs

Expenditures incurred to maintain an asset in proper working order are called **ordinary repairs**. For example, the cost of repairing the radiator, changing the oil and filter, or replacing the tires on a company vehicle would be considered to be ordinary repairs. Ordinary repairs do not extend the useful life of an asset beyond its original useful life nor do they increase the productivity of the asset. They simply keep the asset running. Ordinary repairs are recorded as an expense (usually by debiting Repairs and Maintenance Expense) in the period in which they are incurred. Ordinary repairs are also called **revenue expenditures** because the repair expense is matched against the revenues for the period.

Extraordinary Repairs

When an expenditure extends the useful life of an asset, it is called an **extraordinary repair**. Replacing the engine on a four-year-old company vehicle is an example of an extraordinary repair. This extraordinary repair would extend the vehicle's useful life past its original expected life. Extraordinary repairs are not expensed when they are incurred because they provide value beyond the current period. Instead, the expenditure is capitalized by debiting the cost of the repair to an asset account. The asset is then depreciated over its remaining useful life. For this reason, extraordinary repairs are also called **capital expenditures**.

Betterments

Expenditures that increase an asset's capacity or productivity are called **betterments**. An addition to an existing building is an example of a betterment. As with extraordinary repairs, betterments are capital expenditures that provide value that extends beyond the current period. The cost of a betterment is capitalized (debited to an asset account) and depreciated over the life of the betterment.

Treating a capital expenditure as an expense, or vice versa, creates an accounting error. Suppose Mackay Machine Works replaces the engine in a company vehicle. This would be an extraordinary repair because it increases the vehicle's life. If Mackay Machine Works expenses the cost by debiting Repair and Maintenance Expense, rather than capitalizing it (debiting an asset), Mackay Machine Works makes an accounting error. This error would

- overstate Repair and Maintenance Expense.
- understate Net Income and therefore, Retained Earnings.
- understate Assets on the balance sheet.

Incorrectly capitalizing an expense creates the opposite error. Assume a minor repair, such as replacing the alternator on a vehicle, was incorrectly debited to an asset account. The error would result in expenses being understated and Net Income (and therefore Retained Earnings) being overstated. Furthermore, the balance sheet would overstate assets by the amount of the repair bill. Knowingly capitalizing an ordinary repair or expensing a capital expenditure is a violation of proper ethical behaviour!

Changes in Cost and Estimates

As a result of repairing assets or changes of estimates of the useful life and/or residual value, calculations of depreciation will have to change accordingly. For example, Apex Industries' delivery truck was purchased for $43,000, on January 1, with an estimated residual value of $4,000 after 5 years of useful life. Apex uses the straight-line depreciation method. On July 1, year 3, Apex overhauled the engine with a cost of $5,000. As a result of the overhaul, Apex estimated its residual value would increase by $500 and its useful life would increase by 1.5 years.

New Depreciable Amount = Cost − Accum. Depreciation

New Depreciable Amount − New Residual Value

$$\frac{\text{\textbf{Cost}}\atop{\text{Initial + Additional}} - {\text{\textbf{Accum. Depreciation}}\atop{\text{Up to date}}} - {\text{\textbf{New Residual Value}}\atop{\text{Initial + Additional}}}}{\text{\textbf{Useful Life}}\atop{\text{Initial + Additional − Used}}}$$

In the second half of the third year, the depreciation amount is calculated as follows:

Year 3: January 1 to June 30 = $7,800 ÷ 2 = $3,900
Year 3: July 1 to December 31 = $6,000 ÷ 2 = $3,000

$$\frac{{\text{\textbf{Cost}}\atop{\$43,000 + \$5,000}} \quad {\text{\textbf{Accum. Depreciation}}\atop{\$7,800 + \$7,800 + \$3,900}} - {\text{\textbf{New Residual Value}}\atop{\$4,000 + \$500}}}{\text{\textbf{Useful Life}}\atop{\text{5 years + 1.5 years − 2.5 years}}}$$

Total depreciation expense for Year 3 is $6,900

Exhibit 8-10 shows the new straight-line depreciation schedule reflecting the changes in estimates:

Year	Cost	Yearly Depreciation	Accumulated Depreciation	Book Value
0	$43,000			$43,000
1	43,000	$7,800	$7,800	35,200
2	43,000	7,800	15,600	27,400
3	$48,000	6,900	22,500	25,500*
4	48,000	6,000	28,500	19,500
5	48,000	6,000	34,500	13,500
6	48,000	6,000	40,500	7,500
6.5	48,000	3,000	43,500	4,500

*Year 3 book value = ($43,000 + $5,000) − ($15,600 + $6,900)

Exhibit 8-10 ◤

DECISION GUIDELINES

Decision	Guideline	Analyze
Decision	**Guideline**	**Analyze**
Should I expense the cost of repairing my assets?	The effect of the repair and whether or not it betters the asset will determine when the cost of the repair should be expensed.	Ordinary repairs are repairs that simply maintain an asset in a state of operation. The cost of ordinary repairs is expensed in the period incurred because no future benefit is expected to arise from the repair.
		If a repair extends the useful life of an asset or makes it more efficient, it is known as an extraordinary repair. The cost of the repair should be capitalized and depreciated over the remaining life of the asset because it will provide future benefits.
		If an extraordinary repair is incorrectly expensed in the current period, the net income for that period will be understated and the net income for future periods will be overstated.

WHAT HAPPENS WHEN AN ASSET IS DISPOSED OF?

 Account for the disposal of plant assets

In addition to acquiring and depreciating plant assets, businesses often dispose of plant assets. This may happen before, or after, the asset has reached the end of its useful life. The following are the most common ways that plant assets are disposed of.

❶ The asset is discarded (thrown out).

❷ The asset is sold.

❸ The asset is exchanged for another asset. This occurs most often when an asset is used as a trade-in toward the purchase of another asset.

Regardless of the method of disposal, it is important to ensure that depreciation expense on the asset is up to date prior to recording the disposal. Therefore, for any asset that has not been fully depreciated, a business must record the current period's depreciation expense before recording the disposal of the asset. In many cases, the depreciation needs to be prorated because the asset is not in service for the entire year in which it is disposed of. Prorating depreciation was covered earlier in the chapter in the discussion of partial-year's depreciation.

Once depreciation is up to date, the disposal of an asset is recorded using the following steps.

Step 1 *Record "what you got."* In other words, if you received any cash as part of the disposal transaction, then you would debit Cash for the amount of cash received. If you received a piece of equipment, then you would debit the Equipment account for the cost of the equipment you received.

Step 2 *Record "what you gave up."* You need to remove the asset that was disposed of from your books by debiting Accumulated Depreciation and crediting the Asset account (i.e., Office Equipment) for the respective amounts associated with the disposed of asset. Then, if you paid out any cash you would credit Cash. If you gave a note payable, you would credit Notes Payable.

Step 3 *Record any gain or loss recognized on the transaction*. You will recognize (debit) a loss if the value of "what you got" in the transaction is less than "what you gave up." You will recognize (credit) a gain if the value of "what you got" is more than the value of "what you gave up" in the transaction. In effect, the debit or credit needed in this part of the entry will equal the amount necessary to make the entire entry balance.

Let's demonstrate asset disposals by once again using the Apex Industries' delivery truck as an example. At the end of its useful life, the delivery truck is represented in the books as follows:

Truck		Accumulated Depreciation, Truck	
43,000			39,000

Consider these three situations in which Apex Industries disposes of the delivery truck. All disposals are assumed to take place after the delivery truck has been fully depreciated.

Situation A: The truck is completely worthless and is scrapped for $0. Let's apply the three steps for disposal outlined previously to demonstrate this:

Step 1 Record "what you got." In this case Apex Industries received nothing for the truck so there will be nothing to record.

Step 2 Record "what you gave up." In this case, Apex Industries gave up the old delivery truck and should remove it from the books. To remove the asset, we must zero out both the Asset and Accumulated Depreciation accounts. To do this we will need to debit the Accumulated Depreciation account for $39,000 and credit the Truck account for $43,000.

Step 3 Record any gain or loss on the transaction. This is a loss on disposal because Apex Industries received nothing for a truck that had a net book value (cost minus accumulated depreciation) of $4,000. Apex Industries will debit Loss on Disposal for $4,000.

Apex Industries will record the disposal as follows:

DATE	ACCOUNTS	POST REF.	DR.	CR.
	Accumulated Depreciation, Truck		39,000	
	Loss on Disposal of Truck		4,000	
	Truck			43,000
	Record discarding of truck.			

Notice that the debit to the loss account equals the amount needed to bring the entire entry into balance.

Situation B: Apex Industries sells the truck for $5,000 cash. The three steps for disposal outlined previously can be applied to this situation as follows:

Step 1 Record "what you got." In this case Apex Industries received $5,000 for the truck so Cash will be debited for $5,000.

Step 2 Record "what you gave up." Once again, Apex Industries gave up the old delivery truck and should remove it from the books. Accumulated Depreciation is debited for $39,000 and the Truck account is credited for $43,000.

Step 3 Record any gain or loss on the transaction. This is a gain on sale because Apex Industries received $5,000 for a truck that had a net book value (cost – accumulated depreciation) of $4,000. Apex Industries will credit Gain on Sale for $1,000.

Apex Industries will record the disposal as follows:

DATE	ACCOUNTS	POST REF.	DR.	CR.
	Cash		5,000	
	Accumulated Depreciation, Truck		39,000	
	Truck			43,000
	Gain on Sale of Truck			1,000
	Record sale of truck.			

Observe that the credit to the gain account equals the amount needed to bring the entire entry into balance.

Situation C: Apex Industries trades the delivery truck in on a new truck that costs $48,000. Apex is granted a trade-in allowance of $5,500 and pays for the difference in cash. Here again we will apply the three-step process to record the disposal.

Step 1 Record "what you got." In this transaction, Apex Industries received a $48,000 new truck. So, Truck (new) will be debited for $48,000.

Step 2 Record "what you gave up." As in the previous situations, Apex Industries gave up the old delivery truck and should remove it from the books. Accumulated Depreciation is debited for $39,000 and the Truck (old) account is credited for $43,000. In addition to giving up the truck, Apex Industries paid cash in the amount of $42,500 so Cash is also credited for $42,500. With a trade-in, the amount of cash paid is determined by subtracting the trade-in allowance from the purchase price of the new asset. So, the $48,000 cost of the new truck less the $5,500 trade-in allowance equals the $42,500 cash paid. This same process is used to determine the amount of a note payable if a note is given instead of cash.

Step 3 Record any gain or loss on the transaction. A gain on the exchange occurs because Apex Industries received $48,000 of equipment for assets worth $46,500 (a truck that had a net book value of $4,000 plus cash of $42,500). Apex Industries will credit Gain on Exchange for $1,500.

Apex Industries will record the disposal as follows:

DATE	ACCOUNTS	POST REF.	DR.	CR.
	Truck (New)		48,000	
	Accumulated Depreciation, Truck		39,000	
	Truck (Old)			43,000
	Cash			42,500
	Gain on Exchange of Assets			1,500
	Record trade-in of old truck on a new truck.			

Once again, the gain equals the amount necessary to bring the entry into balance.

HOW DO YOU ACCOUNT FOR INTANGIBLE ASSETS?

As we saw earlier, *intangible assets* have no physical form. Instead, in most cases, these assets convey special rights to their owner. Intangible assets include patents, copyrights, trademarks, and other creative works. The process of allocating the cost of an intangible asset to expense is called **amortization**. Amortization applies to intangible assets exactly as depreciation applies to plant assets and depletion to natural resources.

Amortization is computed over the intangible asset's estimated useful life—usually by the straight-line method. The residual value of most intangible assets is zero. Also, obsolescence can sometimes cause an intangible asset's useful life to be shortened from its original expected length. Amortization expense for an intangible asset is usually credited directly to the asset account instead of using an accumulated amortization account.

> 6 ▸ Account for intangible assets

Specific Intangibles

Patents A **patent** is an intangible asset that is a federal government grant conveying an exclusive 20-year right to produce and sell an invention. The patent may cover a product, process, or technology. The useful life of a patent is often much less than 20 years because newer, better products and processes are invented, rendering the patent obsolete. As an international example, from 1993 to 2007, IBM was granted over 38,000 U.S. patents, more than any other U.S. company. When an intangible asset is acquired, the acquisition cost is debited to an asset account.

Suppose Apex Industries pays $160,000 on January 1 to acquire a patent on a new manufacturing process. Apex Industries believes this patent's useful life is only five years, because it is likely that a new, more efficient process will be developed within that time. Amortization expense is $32,000 per year ($160,000/5 years). The acquisition and year-end amortization entries for this patent are as follows:

DATE	ACCOUNTS	POST REF.	DR.	CR.
Jan 1	Patents		160,000	
	Cash			160,000
	Purchase patent.			
Dec 31	Amortization Expense		32,000	
	Patents ·			32,000
	Record yearly amortization.			

At the end of the first year, Apex Industries will report this patent at $128,000 ($160,000 minus first-year amortization of $32,000), the next year at $96,000, and so forth. Each year for five years the value of the patent will be reduced by $32,000 until the end of its five-year life, at which point its net book value will be $0.

Copyrights A **copyright** is the exclusive right to reproduce and sell a book, musical composition, film, or other work of art or intellectual property. Copyrights also protect computer software programs such as Microsoft Vista™. Copyrights are issued by the federal government and extend 50 years beyond the author's life, although the useful life of most copyrights is relatively short. A copyright is accounted for in the same manner as a patent.

Trademarks and Brand Names **Trademarks** and **brand names** (also known as **trade names**) convey the exclusive right to utilize a symbol, slogan, or name that represents a distinctive product or service such as Sony's Blu-ray Disc™, Intel's Centrino®, and RIM's BlackBerry PlayBook. The cost of a trademark or trade name is amortized over its useful life.

Franchises and Licenses **Franchises** and **licenses** are privileges granted by a private business or a government to sell goods or services under specified conditions. The Toronto Blue Jays baseball team is a franchise granted by Major League Baseball. Subway restaurants and Midas Muffler centres are well-known business franchises. The acquisition cost of a franchise or license is amortized over its useful life.

Goodwill *Goodwill* in accounting has a different meaning from the everyday phrase "goodwill among men." In accounting, **goodwill** refers to the excess of the cost to purchase another company over the market value of its net assets (assets minus liabilities).

Suppose Apex Industries acquires Mackay Machine Works for $1,350,000. At the time of the purchase, the market value of Mackay Machine Works' assets is $1,750,000 and its liabilities total $500,000. In this case, Apex Industries pays $100,000 above the value of Mackay Machine Works' net assets of $1,250,000 ($1,750,000 – $500,000). The extra $100,000 is considered to be goodwill and is recorded as follows:

DATE	ACCOUNTS	POST REF.	DR.	CR.
	Assets (Cash, Accounts Receivable, Equipment, etc. recorded at market value)		1,750,000	
	Goodwill		100,000	
	Liabilities (Accounts Payable, Notes Payable, Accrued Liabilities, etc.)			500,000
	Cash			1,350,000
	To record purchase of Mackay Machine Works.			

Goodwill has some unique features from other intangible assets.

❶ Goodwill is recorded only by an acquiring company when it purchases another company. An outstanding reputation may create goodwill, but that company never records goodwill for its own business.

❷ Intangible assets with indefinite lives are not subject to amortization. Goodwill is not amortized; however, companies are required to apply an impairment test. Under IFRS, the companies should test **impairment** on an annual basis, while under Canadian ASPE, companies need to test impairment when events or changes occur that indicate impairment. If the goodwill has increased in value, there is nothing to record. But if goodwill's value has decreased, or become impaired, then the company records a loss and writes the goodwill down. For example, suppose Apex Industries' goodwill—which it acquired in the purchase of Mackay Machine Works—is worth only $80,000 a year after the purchase. In this case, Apex Industries would make the following entry:

DATE	ACCOUNTS	POST REF.	DR.	CR.
	Loss on Goodwill		20,000	
	Goodwill ($100,000 – $80,000)			20,000
	To record decrease in value of goodwill.			

Apex Industries would then report this goodwill at its reduced current value of $80,000.

Accounting for Research and Development Costs

Research and Development Research and development (R&D) costs are the lifeblood of companies such as RIM, Bombardier, Apple, and Ford. Companies should charge all research costs to expense accounts. Development costs may be capitalized but only after a new product is commercially feasible for sale or use. If a company cannot separate the research phase from the development phase, the company should treat the expenditure as if it were incurred in the research phase only, and expense the cost.

HOW ARE NATURAL RESOURCES ACCOUNTED FOR?

Natural resources are assets that come from the earth. Examples include minerals, oil, natural gas, precious metals, coal, and timber. As stated earlier in the chapter, the process of allocating the cost of a natural resource to an expense is called **depletion**. Depletion expense is that portion of the cost of a natural resource that is used up in a particular period. Depletion expense is computed in a manner almost identical to units-of-production depreciation. The formula used to calculate the depletion per unit of a natural resource is as follows:

Account for natural resources

$$\text{Depletion per unit of natural resource} = \frac{\text{Cost}}{\text{Estimated total units of natural resource}} = \text{Depletion expense per unit}$$

Notice that, unlike UOP depreciation, there is no residual value in the calculation of depletion expense. This is because when a natural resource is used up, there is nothing left to sell.

To illustrate, let's assume that Pegasus Gold owns gold reserves that cost $8,500,000. A geological study estimates that the reserves hold 20,000 (Troy) ounces of gold. Pegasus Gold would calculate the depletion per ounce of gold as follows:

$$\frac{\$8,500,000}{20,000 \text{ ounces}} = \$425 \text{ per ounce}$$

If 600 ounces of gold are removed during the month, depletion is $255,000 (600 ounces × $425 per ounce) and would be recorded as follows:

DATE	ACCOUNTS	POST REF.	DR.	CR.
	Inventory or Depletion Expense		255,000	
	Accumulated Depletion—Gold Reserves			255,000
	Record monthly depletion.			

Accumulated Depletion is a contra-account similar to Accumulated Depreciation. It is deducted from the cost of the natural resource to determine the net book value of the natural resource.

The depletion of natural resources can be recorded as depletion expense or be recorded in the Inventory account. When the gold is sold, the inventory will be reduced and the cost of inventory will be transferred to cost of goods sold.

WHAT ARE THE OTHER TYPES OF LONG-TERM ASSETS?

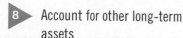

8 ▶ Account for other long-term assets

Other long-term assets may consist of any assets a business owns that we have not already discussed. Two common long-term assets that a business might own are real estate (land or buildings) that are being held for resale rather than for use, and investments in marketable securities. Marketable securities are investments, such as shares, also known as equity securities, and bonds, also called debt securities. Bonds will be discussed more in Chapter 9, but basically buying bonds is a way of loaning money to an entity. Marketable securities are classified as current assets if management intends to sell them, or they mature within a year. However, if they are not intended to be sold, or they do not mature within a year, they are shown as other long-term assets.

A company investing in marketable securities earns income when it receives dividends on shares or interest on bonds that it holds. Also, changes in the value of a security can impact a company's income in two ways:

- Realized gains and losses occur when a security is sold for an amount different from its cost.

- Unrealized gains and losses occur when a security's market value changes while the company still owns it. These are considered "unreal" because the company won't actually gain or lose money until it sells the investment.

Accounting for marketable securities depends on the type of investment and on management's intention for the investment. Marketable securities are classified as trading securities, held-to-maturity securities, or available-for-sale securities.

- Trading securities include equity or debt securities that are actively managed to maximize profit as a result of short-term changes in price. These are shown as current assets on the balance sheet at their market value as of the balance sheet date. Any increase or decrease in price during the period is shown as an unrealized gain or loss on the income statement. Any interest or dividends earned during the period are reported as income on the income statement.

- Held-to-maturity securities are debt securities that a company intends and is able to hold until they mature. These are valued at their cost on the balance sheet as either current or long-term assets based on their maturity date. Any interest income earned on these securities is reported on the income statement.

- Available-for-sale securities include equity or debt securities that cannot be classified as trading or held-to-maturity securities. These are valued at their current market value on the balance sheet date. Any interest or dividends earned during the period is included in net income on the income statement. However, increases or decreases in value during the period are not reported as part of net income on the income statement. Instead, they are shown as separate changes in shareholders' equity for the period.

If the assets are classified as an investment, such as real estate, then the initial cost of acquisition, under both IFRS and Canadian ASPE, is to be recorded based on the cost principle. However, after the acquisition, a company needs to make an accounting policy as to how to treat the investment property. A company has two choices—to record the investment property at cost or fair value. If a company chooses to record the investment at cost, it has to disclose the fair value information or describe why it cannot reliably obtain the fair value in the notes to the financial statements. On the other hand, if a company chooses to record the investment at fair value, it will need to adjust the value of the assets by recording the unrealized gains or losses in either net income or in other comprehensive income. The details of this topic will be covered in higher level accounting courses.

HOW ARE LONG-TERM ASSETS REPORTED ON THE BALANCE SHEET?

In Chapter 5, we learned that current assets appear first on a classified balance sheet. Following the current assets, a business will report its long-term assets. Fixed assets are usually the first long-term asset reported and are often shown as "Property, Plant, and Equipment." Property, Plant, and Equipment includes the original cost, accumulated depreciation, and book value of assets such as land, buildings, and equipment. Natural resources are typically shown after the fixed assets and include the original cost, accumulated depletion, and book value of any natural resources the business owns. A business may choose to show only the net book value of fixed assets and natural resources on the balance sheet. In this case, the business will disclose the costs and accumulated depreciation or depletion for each asset group in the financial statement footnotes.

 9 Report long-term assets on the balance sheet

When a business has intangible assets, the balance sheet will typically show the amount after the fixed assets and the natural resources. The footnotes to the financial statements will include a description of the intangible asset and its estimated useful life. Other long-term assets are typically shown last in the long-term assets section of a balance sheet. **Exhibit 8-11** illustrates a typical long-term assets section of a balance sheet:

Total Current Assets		$ 165,000
Property, Plant, and Equipment:		
Land	$ 175,000	
Buildings	680,000	
Equipment	240,000	
	1,095,000	
Less: Accumulated Depreciation	385,000	
Net Property, Plant, and Equipment		710,000
Gold Reserves, Net of Accumulated Depletion of $260,000		620,000
Patents		80,000
Other Long-Term Assets		145,000
Total Assets		$1,720,000

Exhibit 8-11 ▲

Both IFRS and Canadian ASPE require the initial acquisition on property, plant and equipment, as well as investment properties to be recorded based on the cost principle. However, after the acquisition, when reporting the value of assets in the financial statements, a company, depending on whether it is publicly accountable (uses IFRS) or a private enterprise (uses ASPE), can choose among various cost methods, depending on whether IFRS or Canadian ASPE is applied. **Exhibit 8-12** summarizes the differences:

	IFRS	Canadian ASPE
Initial Acquisition		
Property, Plant, Equipment	Cost	Cost
Investment Property	Cost	Cost
After Acquisition		
Property, Plant, Equipment	Cost or Revaluation	Cost
Investment Property	Cost or Fair Value	Cost

Exhibit 8-12 ▲

As shown in Exhibit 8-2, under Canadian ASPE, companies do not re-measure property, plant, and equipment and investment property at fair value. Property, plant, and equipment is only measured at fair value if it is lower than the original cost of the asset, as a result of an impairment loss. Under IFRS, companies can choose to report their property, plant, and equipment either at cost and depreciation, or at fair value using the **revaluation model** and depreciation. The revaluation model can be used only if the asset's fair value can be measured reliably. In the revaluation model, any increase from fair value is recognized in Revaluation Surplus under Other Comprehensive Income in the statement of changes in equity. Since this increase goes directly to equity, it does not impact the current year's income statement. If in a subsequent year the fair value decreases, then we will first reduce the Revaluation Surplus. If the amount of decrease goes below the Revaluation Surplus, then we will record the decrease in the income statement. In essence, revaluations often do not impact the income statement and are recognized in shareholders' equity; however, when the revaluation decreases an asset below its original cost, the loss from the revaluation will be recognized in the income statement.

Asset Impairment

When an asset's carrying value is greater than its recoverable amount, we say that the asset is impaired. The **recoverable amount** is the higher of the future discounted cash flow that the asset can provide (or **value in use**) and the amount it can be disposed for. Unlike inventory, we don't apply the lower of cost and net realizable value, because property, plant, and equipment is expected to be used in operations for a long period of time. Instead, we will need to perform an impairment test. Some indications of asset impairment include market value declines; negative changes in technology, economy or laws; physical damage of the asset; or worse economic performance than expected. Similar to goodwill, IFRS requires that assets be tested for impairment at the end of each reporting period, while Canadian ASPE requires the test only when events and changes in circumstances indicate that an asset's carrying amount may not be recoverable.

For example, in the fifth year after the initial purchase by Apex Industries and the overhauling of the engine, the accountant obtains the following amounts: fair value of the truck $12,000, the value in use $14,000, and the carrying value $13,500.

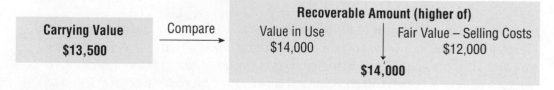

There is no impairment, because the carrying value is less than the recoverable amount. However, if the accountant obtains the following: fair value of the truck $12,000, value in use $12,500, and carrying value $13,500, then the impairment loss is $1,000 ($13,500 – $12,500).

Carrying Value		Recoverable Amount (higher of)	
	Compare →	Value in Use	Fair Value – Selling Costs
$13,500		$12,500	$12,000
		$12,500	

The journal entry to record the impairment is as follows:

Dec 31	Loss on Impairment	1,000	
	Accumulated Impairment Losses		1,000

FOCUS ON USERS

Concept	User	Why is this Important to this User?
Depreciation		Since depreciation expense impacts the income statement and also the balance sheet through both assets and retained earnings, depreciation and the choices that are made regarding the various depreciation methods and estimations are important to all users of financial statements. For a user of financial statements who is interested in the amount of net income (for example, a union representative would want to know the quality of the earnings on the statement and the impact on the cash holdings of the company, and a competitor would want to make comparisons of performance), a net loss may be able to be explained through the use of an accelerated depreciation schedule by the company. For a user of financial statements who is interested in the amount of assets that are shown on the balance sheet (for example, shareholders would want to know what it is that they would have rights to should the company be liquidated, and creditors would want to know what might be used for collateral), the book value of the assets can be deceiving as this is not reflective of what the assets are actually worth. An good understanding of the recording of assets is essential for being able to make decisions that are based on the assets owned by the company.
Goodwill		Shareholders will need to pay attention to goodwill and changes in goodwill. Goodwill cannot be created within a company, but can be recorded when another company is purchased. However, quite often the amount paid to acquire another company is too high and impairments of goodwill are recorded in the years following the purchase.
		Acquisitions of companies can signal movements in new strategies (for example, a company may purchase one of its own suppliers to have more control over the quality of the materials going into the manufacture of a product, or a company may purchase a competitor in order to facilitate growth).

DEMO DOC

Depreciation and Disposal of Depreciable Assets

Jensen, Inc. purchased a colour laser printer for $100,000 on January 1, 2014. The printer
was expected to last for six years and to print 180,000 pages during that time. The printer
has a residual value of $10,000.

Jensen, Inc. printed 50,000 pages in 2014, 20,000 in 2015, and 40,000 in 2016.

Requirements:

❶ Prepare a depreciation table showing depreciation calculations for the years 2014,
2015, and 2016 under the following depreciation methods: (a) straight-line, (b) units-
of-production, and (c) double-declining-balance.

❷ On May 1, 2017, Jensen, Inc. sold the printer for $60,000 cash. Assume that Jensen,
Inc. was using the straight-line method of depreciation. Journalize all transactions
on this date.

Demo Doc Solutions

Requirement ❶

Prepare a depreciation table showing depreciation calculations for the years 2014,
2015, and 2016 under the following depreciation methods: (a) straight-line,
(b) units-of-production, and (c) double-declining-balance.

Part 1	Part 2	Demo Doc Complete

Straight-Line

Refer to the straight-line depreciation table as shown in Exhibit 8-3. On the printer's purchase
date (January 1, 2014), the printer's cost of $100,000 must be input. Because no deprecia-
tion has been taken yet, the book value is the same as the original cost.

Date	Asset Cost	Yearly Depreciation	Accumulated Depreciation	Book Value
Jan 1, 2014	$100,000			$100,000
Dec 31, 2014				
Dec 31, 2015				
Dec 31, 2016				

Remember that,

$$\text{Straight-line depreciation} = \frac{\text{Cost} - \text{Residual value}}{\text{Estimated useful life in years}} = \frac{\$100,000 - \$10,000}{6} = \$15,000 \text{ per year}$$

So for each year, the depreciation expense will be $15,000:

Date	Asset Cost	Yearly Depreciation	Accumulated Depreciation	Book Value
Jan 1, 2014	$100,000			$100,000
Dec 31, 2014		$15,000		
Dec 31, 2015		15,000		
Dec 31, 2016		15,000		

Accumulated depreciation is all of the depreciation expense that has *ever* been taken. So, to calculate accumulated depreciation, we take the previous year's accumulated depreciation and add on the current year's depreciation expense.

The first year of the printer's life is 2014, so in that year no prior depreciation has accumulated. Therefore, accumulated depreciation at December 31, 2014, is the same as the depreciation expense for 2014: $15,000.

For 2015, the accumulated depreciation is the December 31, 2014, accumulated depreciation plus the 2015 depreciation expense. Accumulated depreciation at December 31, 2015, is as follows:

$$\$15,000 + \$15,000 = \$30,000$$

For 2016, the accumulated depreciation is the December 31, 2015, accumulated depreciation plus the 2016 depreciation expense. So accumulated depreciation at December 31, 2016, is as follows:

$$\$30,000 + \$15,000 = \$45,000$$

Date	Asset Cost	Yearly Depreciation	Accumulated Depreciation	Book Value
Jan 1, 2014	$100,000			$100,000
Dec 31, 2014		$15,000	$15,000	
Dec 31, 2015		15,000	30,000	
Dec 31, 2016		15,000	45,000	

The book value of the printer is its cost minus its accumulated depreciation. So to calculate the book value for each year, subtract the accumulated depreciation from the total cost of $100,000.

Book Value at December 31, 2014 = $85,000 ($100,000 − $15,000)
Book Value at December 31, 2015 = $70,000 ($100,000 − $30,000)
Book Value at December 31, 2016 = $55,000 ($100,000 − $45,000)

Date	Asset Cost	Yearly Depreciation	Accumulated Depreciation	Book Value
Jan 1, 2014	$100,000			$100,000
Dec 31, 2014		$15,000	$15,000	85,000
Dec 31, 2015		15,000	30,000	70,000
Dec 31, 2016		15,000	45,000	55,000

Units-of-Production

Refer to the units-of-production depreciation table as shown in Exhibit 8-4. As with straight-line, the cost and starting book value of the printer are both $100,000.

| Date | Asset Cost | Yearly Depreciation | | | Accumulated Depreciation | Book Value |
		Number of Units	Depreciation Per Unit	Depreciation Expense		
Jan 1, 2014	$100,000					$100,000
Dec 31, 2014						
Dec 31, 2015						
Dec 31, 2016						

Remember that,

$$\text{Units of production depreciation per unit} = \frac{\text{Cost} - \text{Residual value}}{\text{Estimated useful life in units}} = \frac{\$100,000 - \$10,000}{180,000 \text{ pages}} = \$0.50 \text{ per page}$$

Each year, the depreciation expense is calculated as the depreciation cost per page multiplied by the number of pages printed.

$$2014 \text{ Depreciation Expense} = \$0.50 \text{ Depreciation expense per page} \times 50,000 \text{ Pages printed}$$
$$= \$25,000$$

$$2015 \text{ Depreciation Expense} = \$0.50 \text{ Depreciation expense per page} \times 20,000 \text{ Pages printed}$$
$$= \$10,000$$

$$2016 \text{ Depreciation Expense} = \$0.50 \text{ Depreciation expense per page} \times 40,000 \text{ Pages printed}$$
$$= \$20,000$$

| Date | Asset Cost | Yearly Depreciation | | | | | Accumulated Depreciation | Book Value |
		Number of Units		Depreciation Per Unit		Depreciation Expense		
Jan 1, 2014	$100,000							$100,000
Dec 31, 2014		50,000	×	$0.50	=	$25,000		
Dec 31, 2015		20,000	×	$0.50	=	$10,000		
Dec 31, 2016		40,000	×	$0.50	=	$20,000		

Accumulated depreciation and book value are calculated in the same manner as was used for straight-line.

$$\text{Accumulated Depreciation at December 31, 2014} = \$0 + \$25,000 = \$25,000$$
$$\text{Book Value at December 31, 2014} = \$100,000 - \$25,000 = \$75,000$$

$$\text{Accumulated Depreciation at December 31, 2015} = \$25,000 + \$10,000 = \$35,000$$
$$\text{Book Value at December 31, 2015} = \$100,000 - \$35,000 = \$65,000$$

$$\text{Accumulated Depreciation at December 31, 2016} = \$35,000 + \$20,000 = \$55,000$$
$$\text{Book Value at December 31, 2016} = \$100,000 - \$55,000 = \$45,000$$

The completed table would look as follows:

Date	Asset Cost	Number of Units		Depreciation Per Unit		Depreciation Expense	Accumulated Depreciation	Book Value
				Yearly Depreciation				
Jan 1, 2014	$100,000							$100,000
Dec 31, 2014		50,000	×	$0.50	=	$25,000	$25,000	75,000
Dec 31, 2015		20,000	×	$0.50	=	$10,000	35,000	65,000
Dec 31, 2016		40,000	×	$0.50	=	$20,000	55,000	45,000

Double-Declining-Balance

Refer to the double-declining-balance (DDB) depreciation table as shown in Exhibit 8-5. As with straight-line and units-of-production, the cost and starting book value of the printer are both $100,000.

Date	Asset Cost	DDB Rate*		Book Value		Depreciation Expense	Accumulated Depreciation	Book Value
				Yearly Depreciation				
Jan 1, 2014	$100,000							$100,000
Dec 31, 2014								
Dec 31, 2015								
Dec 31, 2016								

The DDB depreciation rate is calculated as follows:

$$\text{Double-declining-balance depreciation} = \frac{1}{\text{Estimated useful life in years}} \times 2 = 1/6 \times 2 = 2/6 \text{ or } 1/3$$

Each year, the depreciation rate is multiplied by the book value of the printer *at the beginning of the year*. So for 2014, the depreciation expense is as follows:

$$\$100,000 \times 1/3 = \$33,333$$

Accumulated depreciation and book value at the end of the year are calculated as under straight-line and units-of-production.

$$\text{Accumulated Depreciation at December 31, 2014} = \$0 + \$33,333 = \$33,333$$
$$\text{Book Value at December 31, 2014} = \$100,000 - \$33,333 = \$66,667$$

Date	Asset Cost	DDB Rate*		Book Value		Depreciation Expense*	Accumulated Depreciation	Book Value
				Yearly Depreciation				
Jan 1, 2014	$100,000							$100,000
Dec 31, 2014		1/3	×	$100,000	=	$33,333	$33,333	66,667
Dec 31, 2015								
Dec 31, 2016								

*Rounded

Depreciation expense for 2015 is the book value of the printer *at the beginning* of 2015 multiplied by the depreciation rate. So for 2015, the depreciation expense is as follows:

$$\$66{,}667 \times 1/3 = \$22{,}222$$

Accumulated Depreciation at December 31, 2015 = $33,333 + $22,222 = $55,555
Book Value at December 31, 2015 = $100,000 − $55,555 = $44,445

Date	Asset Cost	Yearly Depreciation DDB Rate*		Book Value		Depreciation Expense*	Accumulated Depreciation	Book Value
Jan 1, 2014	$100,000							$100,000
Dec 31, 2014		1/3	×	$100,000	=	$33,333	$33,333	66,667
Dec 31, 2015		1/3	×	66,667	=	22,222	$55,555	44,445
Dec 31, 2016								

*Rounded

Depreciation expense for 2016 is the book value of the printer *at the beginning* of 2016 multiplied by the depreciation rate. So for 2016, the depreciation expense is as follows:

$$\$44{,}445 \times 1/3 = \$14{,}815$$

Accumulated Depreciation at December 31, 2016 = $55,555 + $14,815 = $70,370
Book Value at December 31, 2016 = $100,000 − $70,370 = $29,630

The completed table would look like this:

Date	Asset Cost	Yearly Depreciation DDB Rate*		Book Value		Depreciation Expense*	Accumulated Depreciation	Book Value
Jan 1, 2014	$100,000							$100,000
Dec 31, 2014		1/3	×	$100,000	=	$33,333	$33,333	66,667
Dec 31, 2015		1/3	×	66,667	=	22,222	$55,555	44,445
Dec 31, 2016		1/3	×	44,445	=	14,815	$70,370	29,630

*Rounded

Requirement ❷

On May 1, 2017, Jensen, Inc. sold the printer for $60,000 cash. Assume that Jensen, Inc. was using the straight-line method of depreciation. Journalize all transactions on this date.

Part 1	**Part 2**	Demo Doc Complete

Before Jensen, Inc. can record the disposal of the printer, it must update the depreciation on the printer. Depreciation represents use of an asset and because the asset was used for four months of 2017 (January, February, March, and April), four months of depreciation expense must be recorded.

From Requirement 1, we know that the annual depreciation expense on the printer under the straight-line method is $15,000 per year (12 months). To adjust for only four months we must multiply by the fraction of 4/12.

Depreciation Expense for 2017 is as follows:

$$\$15,000 \times 4/12 = \$5,000$$

This depreciation expense must now be recorded in a journal entry. Depreciation Expense is increased (debit) by $5,000, and Accumulated Depreciation is increased (credit) by $5,000.

DATE	ACCOUNTS	POST REF.	DR.	CR.
May 1	Depreciation Expense, Printer		5,000	
	Accumulated Depreciation, Printer			5,000
	To record four months' depreciation on printer.			

Now that this journal entry is made, we can calculate the balance in Accumulated Depreciation immediately before the disposal.

The transactions that have affected the Accumulated Depreciation account are the depreciation expense recorded in each year (2014, 2015, 2016, and 2017). We can add the 2017 depreciation expense to the Accumulated Depreciation balance from the prior year (2016).

Printer		Accumulated Depreciation, Printer	
Bal 100,000		Dec 31, 2016 Bal	45,000
		May 1, 2017	5,000
		May 1, 2017 Bal	50,000

Now we are ready to journalize the disposal of the printer.

Jensen, Inc. is receiving cash, so Cash increases (debit) by the $60,000 of cash received.

The printer is being sold, so the Printer asset will be decreased (credit) by its original cost of $100,000 (the amount in the printer T-account).

If the printer is sold, it no longer makes sense to have the accumulated depreciation on the printer. This account must be removed as well. Remember that Accumulated Depreciation is a contra-account, and so it goes wherever its associated asset goes. If we remove the printer from the accounting records, then the accumulated depreciation on that printer goes with it and is removed as well. We will, therefore, decrease Accumulated Depreciation (debit) by its balance of $50,000.

So far for the journal entry we have the following:

DATE	ACCOUNTS	POST REF.	DR.	CR.
May 1	Cash		60,000	
	Accumulated Depreciation, Printer		50,000	
	Printer			100,000

To complete the journal entry, we need to record the gain or loss on the sale of the printer. Remember that the amount of gain or loss can be calculated by comparing "what you got" to "what you gave up." In this case, Jensen got $60,000 for a printer with a book value of $50,000 ($100,000 − $50,000), so it had a $10,000 ($60,000 − $50,000) gain. The amount of the gain or loss can also equal the amount required to balance the journal entry. So far, the total debits in this entry are $110,000 ($60,000 + $50,000), and the total credits are $100,000. So a credit of $10,000 ($110,000 − $100,000) is needed to balance the entry.

Because the balancing amount is a credit, it is *similar* to revenue in that it will increase net income (be a positive number on the income statement). Therefore, it is a gain, so we will credit Gain on Sale of Printer for $10,000.

DATE	ACCOUNTS	POST REF.	DR.	CR.
May 1	Cash		60,000	
	Accumulated Depreciation, Printer		50,000	
	Printer			100,000
	Gain on Sale of Printer			10,000
	Record sale of printer.			

Demo Doc Complete

Part 1	Part 2	**Demo Doc Complete**

DECISION GUIDELINES

Long-Term Assets

If your company has long-term assets, you will likely encounter one or more of the following decisions with regard to those assets:

Decision	**Guideline**	**Analyze**
How do I determine the cost of an asset?	All costs associated with acquiring an asset, and preparing it for its intended use, should be considered as part of the cost of the asset.	It is tempting to treat costs related to the purchase of an asset (delivery fees, taxes, set up costs, etc.) as current period expenses. However, if these costs are expensed in the current period, then the cost of the asset does not reflect all of the costs that are necessary for the asset to be able to be used. This causes the current period's net income to be understated and future periods' net income to be overstated.
I'm a new business owner and have made numerous purchases of capital assets to begin my operations. Which depreciation method is the best for my assets?	The choice of depreciation method depends upon the specific asset being depreciated as well as what the intended use of that asset is. The best method is one that most closely matches the cost of an asset against the future revenues it helps generate.	Straight-line depreciation is best for assets that will be used evenly throughout their lives and that will incur repair and maintenance cost evenly.
		Units-of-production depreciation is best for assets that will be utilized on an irregular basis throughout their lives.
		Double-declining-balance depreciation is best for assets that will be utilized significantly more in the early years of their lives. It is also best for assets that will require significantly more repair and maintenance expenditures in the later years of the asset's life.
Should I expense the cost of repairing my assets?	The effect of the repair and whether or not it betters the asset will determine when the cost of the repair should be expensed.	Ordinary repairs are repairs that simply maintain an asset in a state of operation. The cost of ordinary repairs is expensed in the period incurred because no future benefit is expected to arise from the repair.
		If a repair extends the useful life of an asset or makes it more efficient, it is known as an extraordinary repair. The cost of the repair should be capitalized and depreciated over the remaining life of the asset because it will provide future benefits.
		If an extraordinary repair is incorrectly expensed in the current period, the net income for that period will be understated and the net income for future periods will be overstated.

ACCOUNTING VOCABULARY
THE LANGUAGE OF BUSINESS

Accelerated depreciation method (p. 463) A depreciation method that writes off more of the asset's cost near the start of its useful life than the straight-line method does.

Amortization (p. 473) Systematic reduction of an intangibles asset's carrying value on the books. An expense that applies to intangibles in the same way depreciation applies to plant assets and depletion to natural resources.

Basket purchase (p. 457) Purchase of multiple assets for one price; also called a *lump-sum purchase*.

Betterment (p. 468) Expenditure that increases the capacity or efficiency of an asset.

Brand names (p. 474) Assets that represent distinctive identifications of a product or service; also called *trade names*.

Capital expenditure (p. 468) Expenditure that increases the capacity or efficiency of an asset or extends its useful life. Capital expenditures are debited to an asset account.

Capitalized (p. 456) The process of debiting (increasing) an asset account for the cost of an asset.

Componentization (p. 459) To take the cost of an asset and divide it between its separate component parts, where the cost of each of these components is significant in relation to the total cost of the asset.

Copyright (p. 473) Exclusive right to reproduce and sell a book, musical composition, film, other work of art, or computer program. Issued by the federal government, copyrights extend 50 years beyond the author's life.

Depletion (p. 475) Systematic reduction of a natural resource's carrying value on the books. Expense that applies to natural resource in the same way depreciation applies to plant assets and amortization to intangible assets. It is computed in the same way as units-of-production depreciation.

Depreciable cost (p. 461) The cost of a plant asset minus its estimated residual value.

Double-declining-balance (DDB) method (p. 463) An accelerated depreciation method that computes annual depreciation by multiplying the asset's decreasing book value by a constant percent that is two times the straight-line rate.

Extraordinary repair (p. 468) Repair work that extends the life of an asset.

Franchises (p. 474) Privileges granted by a private business or a government to sell a product or service under specified conditions.

Fully-depreciated asset (p. 462) An asset that has reached the end of its estimated useful life. No more depreciation is recorded for the asset.

Goodwill (p. 474) Excess of the cost of an acquired company over the sum of the market values of its net assets (assets minus liabilities).

Impairment (p. 474) An asset is impaired when its carrying amount exceeds its recoverable amount, which is the future undiscounted cash flow that the asset can provide and be disposed for.

Intangible assets (p. 454) Assets with no physical form. They are valuable because of the special rights they carry. Examples include patents and copyrights.

Land improvements (p. 455) Depreciable improvements to land, such as fencing, sprinklers, paving, signs, and lighting.

Licenses (p. 474) Privileges granted by a private business or a government to sell a product or service under specified conditions.

Lump-sum purchase (p. 457) Purchase of multiple assets for one price; also called a *basket purchase*.

Natural resources (p. 454) Assets that come from the earth. Examples include minerals, gas, oil, and timber.

Obsolete (p. 460) [to come]

Ordinary repair (p. 468) Repair work that is necessary to maintain an asset in normal operating condition.

Patent (p. 473) An intangible asset that is a federal government grant conveying an exclusive 20-year right to produce and sell a process or formula.

Recoverable amount (p. 478) The higher of the future discounted cash flow that the asset can provide and the amount it can be disposed for.

Residual value (p. 460) Expected cash value of an asset at the end of its useful life; also called *salvage value*.

Revaluation model (p. 478) Under IFRS, property, plant and equipment can be revalued to the fair value if the value can be reliably measured.

Revenue expenditure (p. 468) Expenditure that is debited to an expense account.

Straight-line (SL) depreciation method (p. 461) Depreciation method in which an equal amount of depreciation expense is assigned to each year of asset use.

Tangible assets (p. 454) Assets that are physical in form. They can be seen, touched, or held.

Trade names (p. 474) Assets that represent distinctive identifications of a product or service; also called *brand names*.

Trademarks (p. 474) Assets that represent distinctive identifications of a product or service.

Units-of-production (UOP) depreciation method (p. 462) Depreciation method by which a fixed amount of depreciation is assigned to each unit of output produced by an asset.

Useful life (p. 460) The expected life of an asset during which it is anticipated to generate revenues. May be expressed in years or units of output.

Value in use (p. 478) The discounted future cash flows expected to arise from the continuing use of an asset and from its disposal at the end of its useful life.

MyAccountingLab

Make the grade with MyAccountingLab. The exercises and problems in this chapter can be found on MyAccountingLab at **www.myaccountinglab.com**. You can practise them as often as you want, and they feature step-by-step guided solutions to help you find the right answer.

ACCOUNTING PRACTICE

DISCUSSION QUESTIONS

1. When a company makes an expenditure, it can either capitalize or expense the cost, depending on the nature of the expenditure. What does it mean to capitalize an expenditure? What determines whether an expenditure can be capitalized?

2. If a company were to purchase a piece of land with a building on it that it demolishes to make room for its new building, in which account would the cost of demolition be recorded (land, building, demolition expense, or something else)? Why?

3. What is a lump-sum purchase of assets? How does a company determine how much to allocate to each asset purchased in a lump-sum purchase?

4. What is depreciation and why is it used in accounting?

5. Are useful life and physical life the same thing relative to plant assets? Provide some examples that illustrate your answer.

6. Which depreciation method would be most appropriate for each of the following assets?
   a. This machine is used as a backup to the other machines in the production process. As a result there are some years where it sees a lot of action and others where it is seldom used. It is not a high-tech machine. It will not become obsolete in the foreseeable future.
   b. Typically this machine will work very effectively and with few repairs for the first three years, but will be down for maintenance quite a bit during its final four years of use.
   c. This machine is expected to run constantly over the entire period it is used. It requires regular maintenance over its lifetime to maintain its expected steady level of production.

7. What makes a repair "extraordinary" (as opposed to ordinary)? Give an example of an extraordinary and an ordinary repair. What is the financial statement effect of recording a repair as an extraordinary repair instead of an ordinary repair?

8. What is the book value of an asset? How is gain or loss on disposal of assets calculated?

9. If a machine that cost $10,000 was estimated to have a salvage value of zero after a useful life of 10 years and was sold for $4,500 after it had been owned for 6 complete years, what would be the amount of gain or loss recognized on the sale?

10. Complete the following analogies. What are some similarities and differences between the two concepts involved in each?
    a. Depreciation is to plant assets as _____ is to intangible assets.
    b. Depreciation is to plant assets as _____ is to natural resources.

SELF CHECK

1. Which cost is *not* recorded as part of the cost of a building?

   a. Construction materials, labour, and overhead
   b. Annual building maintenance
   c. Real estate commission paid to buy the building
   d. Earthmoving for the building's foundation

2. Orbit Airways bought two used Boeing 707 airplanes. Each plane was worth $35 million, but Orbit bought the combination for $60 million. How much is Orbit Airways' cost of each plane?

   a. $30 million
   c. $60 million
   b. $35 million
   d. $70 million

3. How should a capital expenditure be recorded?

   a. Debit capital
   c. Debit a liability
   b. Debit an expense
   d. Debit an asset

4. Which depreciation method usually produces the most depreciation in the first year?

   a. Straight-line
   b. Units-of-production
   c. Double-declining-balance
   d. All produce the same amount of depreciation for the first year.

5. A FedEx airplane costs $50 million and is expected to fly 500 million miles during its 10-year life. Residual value is expected to be zero because the plane was used when acquired. If the plane travels 20 million miles the first year, how much depreciation should FedEx record under the units-of-production method?

   a. $2 million
   b. $5 million
   c. $10 million
   d. Cannot be determined from the data given

6. Which depreciation method will result in lower net income in the first years of the asset's life? Why?

   a. Straight-line, because it is simplest
   b. Units-of-production, because it best tracks the asset's use
   c. Double-declining-balance, because it gives the most total depreciation over the asset's life
   d. Double-declining-balance, because it gives higher depreciation deductions in earlier years

7. A copy machine cost $40,000 when new and has accumulated depreciation of $37,000. Suppose Copies R Us junks this machine, receiving nothing in return. What is the result of the disposal transaction?

   a. Gain of $3,000
   c. Gain of $37,000
   b. Loss of $3,000
   d. Loss of $40,000

8. Using information from the preceding question, suppose Copies R Us sold the machine for $5,000. What is the result of this disposal transaction?

   a. Gain of $2,000
   c. Gain of $3,000
   b. Loss of $2,000
   d. Gain of $5,000

9. Depletion is calculated in a manner similar to which depreciation method?

   a. Accelerated method
   c. Units-of-production method
   b. Straight-line method
   d. Double-declining-balance method

10. Which intangible asset is recorded only as part of the acquisition of another company?

   a. Copyright
   c. Franchise
   b. Patent
   d. Goodwill

Answers are given after Written Communication.

SHORT EXERCISES

S8-1. Long-term asset terms (*Learning Objective 1*) 5–10 min.

Identify each of the following assets as a plant asset (P) or an intangible asset (I):

_____ 1. Franchises
_____ 2. Vehicles
_____ 3. Buildings
_____ 4. Furniture
_____ 5. Patents
_____ 6. Copyrights
_____ 7. Trademarks
_____ 8. Land improvements

S8-2. Long-term asset terms *(Learning Objective 1)* 5–10 min.

For each of the following long-term assets, identify the type of expense that will be incurred to allocate the asset's cost as depreciation expense (DR), depletion expense (DL), amortization expense (A), or none of these (NA).

_____ 1. Franchises
_____ 2. Land
_____ 3. Buildings
_____ 4. Furniture
_____ 5. Patents
_____ 6. Copyrights
_____ 7. Trademarks
_____ 8. Land improvements
_____ 9. Gold ore deposits

S8-3. Land or land improvements (*Learning Objective 2*) 5–10 min.

Identify each of the following as land (L) or land improvements (LI):

_____ 1. Survey fees
_____ 2. Fencing
_____ 3. Lighting
_____ 4. Clearing land
_____ 5. Parking lot

S8-4. Lump-sum purchase (*Learning Objective 2*) 5–10 min.

Johnson purchased land having a current market value of $80,000, a building with a market value of $64,000, and equipment with a market value of $16,000. Journalize the lump-sum purchase of the three assets purchased for a total cost of $120,000 in exchange for a note payable.

S8-5. Errors in accounting for long-term assets (*Learning Objective 2*) 5–10 min.

Orbit Airways repaired one of its Boeing 767 aircraft at a cost of $600,000, which Orbit Airways paid in cash. Orbit Airways erroneously capitalized this cost as part of the cost of the plane.

Journalize both the incorrect entry the accountant made to record this transaction and the correct entry that the accountant should have made. How will this accounting error affect Orbit Airways' net income? Ignore depreciation.

S8-6. Concept of depreciation *(Learning Objective 3)* 10–15 min.

Jessica Brooks just slept through the class in which Professor Dominguez explained the concept of depreciation. Because the next test is scheduled for Wednesday, Jessica Brooks telephones Hanna Svensen to get her notes from the lecture. Hanna Svensen's notes are concise: "Depreciation—Sounds like Greek to me." Jessica Brooks next tries Tim Lake, who says he thinks depreciation is what happens when an asset wears out. David Coe is confident that depreciation is the process of building up a cash fund to replace an asset at the end of its useful life. Explain the concept of depreciation for Jessica Brooks. Evaluate the explanations of Tim Lake and David Coe. Be specific.

S8-7. Depreciation methods *(Learning Objective 3)* 10–15 min.

At the beginning of the year, Orbit Airways purchased a used Boeing aircraft at a cost of $45 million. Orbit Airways expects the plane to remain useful for five years (3 million kilometres) and to have a residual value of $5 million. Orbit Airways expects the plane to be flown 750,000 kilometres the first year and 1.5 million kilometres the second year.

Compute Orbit Airways' first-year depreciation on the plane using the following methods:

  a. Straight-line

  b. Units-of-production

  c. Double-declining-balance

Show the airplane's book value at the end of the first year under the straight-line method.

S8-8. Depreciation methods *(Learning Objective 3)* 10–15 min.

Refer to the data for S8-7. Compute second-year depreciation on the plane using the following methods:

  a. Straight-line

  b. Units-of-production

  c. Double-declining-balance

S8-9. Straight-line depreciation method *(Learning Objective 3)* 5–10 min.

On March 31, 2014, Orbit Airways purchased a used Boeing aircraft at a cost of $45 million. Orbit Airways expects to fly the plane for five years and to have a residual value of $5 million. Compute Orbit Airways' depreciation on the plane for the year ended December 31, 2014, using the straight-line method.

S8-10. Straight-line depreciation method *(Learning Objective 3)* 5–10 min.

Big Boy's Hot Dogs purchased a hotdog stand for $40,000 with an estimated useful life of eight years and no residual value. Suppose that after using the hotdog stand for four years, the company determines that the asset will remain useful for only two more years. Record Big Boy's Hot Dogs' depreciation on the hotdog stand for year 5 by the straight-line method.

S8-11. Capitalized versus expensed costs for long-term assets *(Learning Objectives 2 & 4)* 10–15 min.

Classify each of the following expenditures as a capital expenditure (CAP) or a revenue expenditure (REV):

  a. Purchase price

  b. Ordinary recurring repairs to keep the machinery in good working order

  c. Lubrication of the machinery before it is placed in service

d. Periodic lubrication after the machinery is placed in service

e. Major overhaul to extend useful life by three years

f. Sales tax paid on the purchase price

g. Transportation and insurance while machinery is in transit from seller to buyer

h. Installation

i. Training of personnel for initial operation of the machinery

S8-12. Disposition of long-term assets *(Learning Objective 5)* 5–10 min.

Orbit Airways purchased a baggage-handling truck for $41,000. Suppose Orbit Airways sold the truck on December 31, 2014, for $28,000 cash, after using the truck for two full years and accumulating depreciation of $16,000. Make the journal entry to record Orbit Airways' sale of the truck.

S8-13. Goodwill *(Learning Objective 6)* 15–20 min.

When one media company buys another, goodwill is often the most costly asset acquired. World Media paid $700,000 to acquire the *Dandy Dime*, a weekly advertising paper. At the time of the acquisition, the *Dandy Dime's* balance sheet reported total assets of $1,200,000 and liabilities of $600,000. The fair market value of the *Dandy Dime's* assets was $800,000.

How much goodwill did World Media purchase as part of the acquisition of the *Dandy Dime*? Journalize World Media's acquisition of the *Dandy Dime*.

S8-14. Amortization *(Learning Objective 6)* 5–10 min.

On April 1, Keystone Applications paid $500,000 to acquire a patent on software. Keystone Application expects the patent to have a useful life of five years.

Journalize the entry to record the purchase of the patent on April 1. Journalize the entry to record amortization on December 31.

S8-15. Depletion *(Learning Objective 7)* 5–10 min.

Kent Oil, a small Texas oil company, holds huge reserves of oil and gas assets. Assume that at the end of 2014, Kent Oil's cost of mineral assets totalled approximately $18 million, representing 2.4 million barrels of oil and gas reserves in the ground.

Calculate Kent Oil's depletion expense per barrel of oil. Suppose Kent Oil removed 0.8 million barrels of oil during 2015 and sold all of these barrels during the year. Record Kent Oil's depletion expense for 2015.

S8-16. Other long-term assets *(Learning Objective 8)* 5–10 min.

Classify each of the following as:

Trading security (T)

Available-for-sale security (A)

Held-to-maturity security (H)

None of the above (N)

1. A bond that management plans on owning until it is repaid. Management does not believe it will need to sell the bond to generate cash before the bond's scheduled maturity date.

2. Land that management is holding as an investment.

3. Intel shares that company management plans on selling quickly, as soon as its price is 10% more than what the company paid at the time it purchased the shares.

4. Ford Motor Company shares. Management does not actively manage these shares and intends to sell them only if they need to generate cash.

    5. A bond that management plans on owning until it is repaid. However, management believes it may have to sell the bond within the year to provide enough cash for operations.

    6. Inventory that management intends to sell within the year.

S8-17. Other long-term assets (*Learning Objective 8*) 5–10 min.

Specify how each of the following items would be reported in the financial statements of Tanaka Enterprises for its current fiscal year. Also specify the amount that would appear on the statement. Some items may be reported on more than one financial statement. In these cases, specify the amount that would appear on each statement.

Income Statement (IS)

Balance Sheet (BS)

Change in Shareholders' Equity (SE)

1. Tanaka Enterprises received $55 of dividends during the year on shares it owned in Jasper, Inc.

2. At year-end, Tanaka Enterprises owned a $1,000 Canada Savings Bond.

3. Tanaka Enterprises sold shares for $110 cash that had been held as an available-for-sale security. The shares had been purchased for $90 and hadn't changed in value until the time of their sale.

4. Shares that Tanaka Enterprises purchased for $90 during the year as an available-for-sale security have a market value of $110 at the year-end balance sheet date.

5. Shares that Tanaka Enterprises purchased for $90 during the year as a trading security had a market value of $110 at the year-end balance sheet date.

6. Earned $75 of interest on a bond that Tanaka Enterprises purchased from the province of Quebec.

EXERCISES (GROUP A)

E8-1A. Capitalized costs for long-term assets (*Learning Objective 2*) 10–15 min.

Bozeman Systems purchased land, paying $80,000 cash as a down payment and signing a $120,000 note payable for the balance. In addition, Bozeman Systems paid delinquent property tax of $2,100, title insurance costing $2,500, and a $10,400 charge for levelling the land and removing an unwanted building. The company constructed an office building on the land at a cost of $800,000. It also paid $51,000 for a fence around the property, $15,000 for the company sign near the entrance, and $6,000 for special lighting of the grounds.

Requirements

1. Determine the cost of the company's land, land improvements, and building.

2. Which of the assets will Bozeman depreciate?

Quick solution:
Land = $215,000; Land Improvements = $72,000; Building = $800,000

E8-2A. Capitalized costs for long-term assets (*Learning Objective 2*) 10–15 min.

Lynch Brothers manufactures conveyor belts. Early in January 2015, Lynch Brothers constructed its own building at a materials, labour, and overhead cost of $900,000. Lynch Brothers also paid for architect fees and building permits of $72,000.

Requirements

1. How much should Lynch Brothers record as the cost of the building in 2015?

2. Record Lynch Brothers' transactions related to the construction of the building.

E8-3A. Capitalized costs for long-term assets *(Learning Objective 2)* 10–15 min.

Tonya's Tanning Salon bought three tanning beds in a $10,000 lump-sum purchase. An independent appraiser valued the tanning beds as follows:

Tanning Bed	Appraised Value
1	$3,000
2	5,000
3	4,000

Tonya's Tanning Salon paid $5,000 in cash and signed a note payable for $5,000. Record the purchase in the journal, identifying each tanning bed's cost by number in a separate Tanning Bed account. Round decimals to three places.

E8-4A. Errors in accounting for long-term assets *(Learning Objective 2)* 15–20 min.

Assume that early in year 1, Mariposa Company purchased equipment at a cost of $500,000. Management expects the equipment to remain in service for five years, with zero residual value. Mariposa Company uses the straight-line depreciation method. Through an accounting error, Mariposa Company accidentally expensed the entire cost of the equipment at the time of purchase.

Requirement

1. Prepare a schedule to show the overstatement or understatement in the following items at the end of each year over the five-year life of the equipment.

   a. Equipment, net

   b. Net income

E8-5A. Depreciation methods *(Learning Objective 3)* 15–20 min.

Memorial Medical Centre bought equipment on January 2, 2014, for $30,000. The equipment was expected to remain in service for four years and to perform 1,000 operations. At the end of the equipment's useful life, Memorial estimates that its residual value will be $6,000. The equipment performed 100 operations the first year, 300 the second year, 400 the third year, and 200 the fourth year.

Requirements

1. Prepare a schedule of depreciation expense per year for the equipment under the three depreciation methods. After two years under double-declining-balance depreciation, the company switched to the straight-line method. Show your computations.

2. Which method tracks the wear and tear on the equipment most closely?

3. Which method would result in the lowest net income over the first few year's of the asset's life? Why?

E8-6A. Straight-line depreciation *(Learning Objective 3)* 10–15 min.

LHD Freight purchased a building for $700,000 and depreciated it on a straight-line basis over a 40-year period. The estimated residual value was $100,000. After using the building for 15 years, LHD realized that wear and tear on the building would force the company to replace it before 40 years. Starting with the sixteenth year, LHD began depreciating the building over a revised total life of 30 years and increased the estimated residual value to $175,000. Record depreciation expense on the building for years 15 and 16.

E8-7A. Straight-line depreciation and long-term asset disposal *(Learning Objectives 3 & 5)* **15–20 min.**

On January 2, 2014, Bright Lights purchased showroom fixtures for $10,000 cash, expecting the fixtures to remain in service for five years. Bright Lights has depreciated the fixtures on a straight-line basis, with zero residual value. On September 30, 2015, Bright Lights sold the fixtures for $5,000 cash. Record both the depreciation expense on the fixtures for 2015 and the sale of the fixtures on September 30, 2015.

E8-8A. Disposition of long-term assets *(Learning Objective 5)* **10–15 min.**

Assume that Henson Corporation's comparative balance sheet reported these amounts:

	December 31	
	2013	**2012**
Plant and Equipment..	$ 600,000	$ 595,000
Less: Accumulated Depreciation.................................	145,000	135,000
Net Plant and Equipment..	$ 455,000	$ 460,000

Requirement

1. Assume that on January 2, 2014, Henson sold 1/10 of its plant and equipment for $75,500 in cash. Journalize this transaction for Henson.

E8-9A. Trade-in on purchase of new asset *(Learning Objectives 3 & 5)* **15–20 min.**

Mesilla Valley Transport is a large trucking company. Mesilla Valley Transport uses the units-of-production (UOP) method to depreciate its trucks. In 2013, Mesilla Valley Transport acquired a Mack truck costing $350,000 with a useful life of 10 years or 1 million kilometres. Estimated residual value was $100,000. The truck was driven 80,000 kilometres in 2013, 120,000 kilometres in 2014, and 160,000 kilometres in 2015. After 40,000 kilometres in 2016, Mesilla Valley Transport traded in the Mack truck for a new Freightliner that cost $480,000. Mesilla Valley Transport received a $275,000 trade-in allowance for the old truck and paid the difference in cash. Journalize the entry to record the purchase of the new truck.

E8-10A. Patents *(Learning Objective 6)* **10–15 min.**

Part 1. Millennium Printing manufactures high-speed printers. Millennium Printing recently paid $1 million for a patent on a new laser printer. Although it gives legal protection for 20 years, the patent is expected to provide a competitive advantage for only 8 years. Using the straight-line method of amortization, make journal entries to record (a) the purchase of the patent and (b) amortization for year 1.

Part 2. After using the patent for 4 years, Millennium Printing learns at an industry trade show that another company is designing a more efficient printer. On the basis of this new information, Millennium Printing decides, starting with year 5, to amortize the remaining cost of the patent over 2 remaining years, giving the patent a total useful life of 6 years. Record amortization for year 5.

E8-11A. Goodwill *(Learning Objective 6)* **10–15 min.**

Rutherford, Corp. aggressively acquired other companies. Assume that Rutherford, Corp. purchased Lancer, Inc. for $11 million cash. The market value of Lancer's assets is $15 million, and it has liabilities of $10 million.

Requirements

1. Compute the cost of goodwill purchased by Rutherford, Corp.
2. Record the purchase of Lancer, Inc. by Rutherford, Corp.

E8-12A. Depletion *(Learning Objective 7)* 10–15 min.

Asarco Mining paid $398,500 for the right to extract mineral assets from a 200,000-tonne mineral deposit. In addition to the purchase price, Asarco Mining also paid a $500 filing fee, a $1,000 license fee to the Yukon Territory, and $60,000 for a geological survey of the property. Because the company purchased the rights to the minerals only, the company expected the asset to have zero residual value when fully depleted. During the first year, Asarco Mining removed 40,000 tonnes of minerals. Using the Mineral Assets account, make journal entries to record the following:

a. Purchase of the mineral rights

b. Payment of fees and other costs

c. Depletion for the first year (none of the minerals were sold during the year)

E8-13A. Balance sheet disclosure of long-term assets *(Learning Objective 9)* 10–15 min.

At the end of 2014, Zeman, Corp. had total assets of $25 million and total liabilities of $13 million. Included in the assets were property, plant, and equipment with a cost of $9 million and accumulated depreciation of $3 million. During 2014, Zeman, Corp. earned total revenues of $20 million and had total expenses of $17 million. Show how Zeman, Corp. reported property, plant, and equipment on its balance sheet on December 31, 2014. What was the book value of property, plant, and equipment on that date?

E8-14A. Depreciation methods *(Learning Objective 3)* 10–15 min.

Oteda purchased a machine on January 1 for $11,500. Oteda expected the machine will be used for 4 years and will have a residual value of $2,500. Oteda expects the machine to be used for 25,000 hours: first year, 5,200 hours; second year, 7,500 hours; third year, 8,600 hours; and the fourth year, 3,700 hours.

Requirement:

Compute the annual depreciation amount using three different depreciation methods by filling in the following table:

	Straight-Line	Units-of-Production	Double Declining
Year 1			
Year 2			
Year 3			
Year 4			
Total			

E8-15A. Identify asset impairment *(Learning Objective 8)* 10–15 min.

Gupta Ltd. has four assets. You are an accounting assistant who is in charge of identifying the recoverable amount and determining whether each of the assets is impaired. If so, what is the amount that should be recorded?

	Carrying Value	Value in Use	Fair Value	Recoverable Amount	Is Asset Impaired?	Impairment Amount
1. Equipment	$ 21,000	$ 18,000	$ 18,500			
2. Goodwill	150,000	80,000	75,000			
3. Building	560,000	620,000	750,000			
4. Patent	25,000	16,000	16,500			

E8-16A. Amortization (*Learning Objectives 2 and 6*) 10–15 min.

Trinh Technologies Company (TTC) has two intangible assets at the end of the year.

1. Signed a 5-year lease for an office on March 1. TTC immediately spent $35,000 for leasehold improvements. TTC estimated the leasehold improvements would last for 7 years. TTC moved into the office on April 1, after the improvements were completed.

2. TTC purchased a patent for $6,000 on June 1. The patent was registered with the Canadian Intellectual Property Office 8 years ago. TTC estimated that it would keep the patent for 8 years.

Requirements

1. Record the acquisition of the two intangible assets.

2. Calculate the amortization of each intangible asset at December 31.

3. Record the year-end adjusting entries.

4. What is the carrying value of each asset reported in the balance sheet?

EXERCISES (GROUP B)

E8-1B. Capitalized costs for long-term assets (*Learning Objective 2*) 10–15 min.

Ogden Systems purchased land, paying $110,000 cash as a down payment and signing a $140,000 note payable for the balance. In addition, Ogden Systems paid delinquent property tax of $1,500, title Insurance costing $3,500, and a $10,400 charge for levelling the land and removing an unwanted building. The company constructed an office building on the land at a cost of $600,000. It also paid $46,000 for a fence around the property, $7,000 for the company sign near the entrance, and $5,000 for special lighting of the grounds.

Requirements

1. Determine the cost of the company's land, land improvements, and building.

2. Which of the assets will Ogden depreciate?

E8-2B. Capitalized costs for long-term assets (*Learning Objective 2*) 10–15 min.

White Brothers manufactures conveyor belts. Early in May 2015, White Brothers constructed its own building at a materials, labour, and overhead cost of $970,000. White Brothers also paid for architect fees and building permits of $76,000.

Requirements

1. How much should White record as the cost of the building in 2015?

2. Record White Brothers' transactions related to the construction of the building.

E8-3B. Capitalized costs for long-term assets (*Learning Objective 2*) 10–15 min.

Amy's Tanning Salon bought three tanning beds in a $20,000 lump-sum purchase. An independent appraiser valued the tanning beds as follows:

Tanning Bed	Appraised Value
1	$ 7,000
2	8,000
3	11,000

Amy's Tanning Salon paid $10,000 in cash and signed a note payable for $10,000. Record the purchase in the journal, identifying each tanning bed's cost by number in a separate Tanning Bed account. Round decimals to three places.

E8-4B. Errors in accounting for long-term assets (*Learning Objective 2*) 15–20 min.

Assume that early in year 1, Marginal Company purchased equipment at a cost of $520,000. Management expects the equipment to remain in service for five years, with zero residual value. Marginal Company uses the straight-line depreciation method. Through an accounting error, Marginal Company accidentally expensed the entire cost of the equipment at the time of purchase.

Requirement

1. Prepare a schedule to show the overstatement or understatement in the following items at the end of each year over the five-year life of the equipment:
   a. Equipment, net
   b. Net income

E8-5B. Depreciation methods (*Learning Objective 3*) 15–20 min.

General Medical Centre bought equipment on January 2, 2014, for $18,000. The equipment was expected to remain in service for four years and to perform 400 operations. At the end of the equipment's useful life, General estimates that its residual value will be $4,000. The equipment performed 40 operations the first year, 120 the second year, 160 the third year, and 80 the fourth year.

Requirements

1. Prepare a schedule of depreciation expense per year for the equipment under the three depreciation methods. After two years under double-declining-balance depreciation, the company switched to the straight-line method. Show your computations.
2. Which method tracks the wear and tear on the equipment most closely?
3. Which method would result in the lowest net income over the first few year's of the asset's life? Why?

E8-6B. Straight-line depreciation (*Learning Objective 3*) 10–15 min.

Chapin Freight purchased a building for $800,000 and depreciated it on a straight-line basis over a 30-year period. The estimated residual value was $110,000. After using the building for 15 years, Chapin realized that wear and tear on the building would force the company to replace it before 30 years. Starting with the sixteenth year, Chapin began depreciating the building over a revised total life of 20 years and increased the estimated residual value to $170,000. Record depreciation expense on the building for years 15 and 16.

E8-7B. Straight-line depreciation and long-term asset disposal (*Learning Objectives 3 & 5*) 15–20 min.

On January 2, 2014, Shine Lights purchased showroom fixtures for $18,000 cash, expecting the fixtures to remain in service for five years. Shine Lights has depreciated the fixtures on a straight-line basis, with zero residual value. On March 31, 2015, Shine Lights sold the fixtures for $5,000 cash. Record both the depreciation expense on the fixtures for 2015 and the sale of the fixtures on March 31, 2015.

E8-8B. Disposition of long-term assets (*Learning Objective 5*) 10–15 min.

Assume that Hector Corporation's comparative balance sheet reported these amounts:

	December 31	
	2013	2012
Plant and Equipment	$ 610,000	$ 583,000
Less: Accumulated Depreciation	160,000	120,000
Net Plant and Equipment	$ 450,000	$ 463,000

Requirement

1. Assume that on January 2, 2014, Hector sold 1/2 of its plant and equipment for $237,000 in cash. Journalize this transaction for Hector.

E8-9B. Trade-in on purchase of new asset *(Learning Objectives 3 & 5)* 15–20 min.

Regional Highway Transport is a large trucking company. Regional Highway Transport uses the units-of-production (UOP) method to depreciate its trucks. In 2013, Regional Highway Transport acquired a Mack truck costing $410,000 with a useful life of 10 years or 1,250,000 kilometres. Estimated residual value was $10,000. The truck was driven 85,000 kilometres in 2013, 110,000 kilometres in 2014, and 150,000 kilometres in 2015. After 10,000 kilometres in 2016, Regional Highway Transport traded in the Mack truck for a new Freightliner that costs $524,400. Regional Highway Transport received a $314,400 trade-in allowance for the old truck and paid the difference in cash. Journalize the entry to record the purchase of the new truck.

E8-10B. Patents *(Learning Objective 6)* 10–15 min.

Part 1. Mayflower Printing manufactures high-speed printers. Mayflower Printing recently paid $9 million for a patent on a new laser printer. Although it gives legal protection for 20 years, the patent is expected to provide a competitive advantage for only 15 years. Using the straight-line method of amortization, make journal entries to record (a) the purchase of the patent and (b) amortization for year 1.

Part 2. After using the patent for 7 years, Mayflower Printing learns at an industry trade show that another company is designing a more efficient printer. On the basis of this new information, Mayflower Printing decides, starting with year 8, to amortize the remaining cost of the patent over 2 remaining years, giving the patent a total useful life of 9 years. Record amortization for year 8.

E8-11B. Goodwill *(Learning Objective 6)* 10–15 min.

Richardson, Corp. aggressively acquired other companies. Assume that Richardson, Corp. purchased Lawrence, Inc. for $14 million cash. The market value of Lawrence's assets is $22 million, and it has liabilities of $14 million.

Requirements

1. Compute the cost of goodwill purchased by Richardson, Corp.

2. Record the purchase of Lawrence, Inc. by Richardson, Corp.

E8-12B. Depletion *(Learning Objective 7)* 10–15 min.

McKenzie Mining paid $831,600 for the right to extract mineral assets from a 600,000-tonne mineral deposit. In addition to the purchase price, McKenzie Mining also paid a $600 filing fee, a $2,800 license fee to the province of Quebec, and $65,000 for a geological survey of the property. Because the company purchased the rights to the minerals only, the company expected the asset to have zero residual value when fully depleted. During the first year, McKenzie Mining removed 75,000 tonnes of minerals. Using the Mineral Assets account, make journal entries to record the following:

a. Purchase of the mineral rights

b. Payment of fees and other costs

c. Depletion for the first year (none of the minerals were sold during the year)

E8-13B. Balance sheet disclosure of long-term assets (*Learning Objective 9*) 10–15 min.

At the end of 2014, Zaney, Corp. had total assets of $26 million and total liabilities of $15 million. Included in the assets were property, plant, and equipment with a cost of $14 million and accumulated depreciation of $5 million. During 2014, Zaney, Corp. earned total revenues of $24 million and had total expenses of $15 million. Show how Zaney, Corp. reported property, plant, and equipment on its balance sheet on December 31, 2014. What was the book value of property, plant, and equipment on that date?

E8-14B. Depreciation methods (*Learning Objective 3*) 10–15min.

Wilson Mining (WM) purchased a truck on April 1 for $98,500. WM expected the truck will be used for 5 years and to have a residual value of $3,500. WM expects the truck to be used for 125,000 kilometres: first year, 23,000 km; second year, 28,500 km; third year, 26,400 km; the fourth year, 24,500 km; and the fifth year, 22,600 km.

Requirement:

Compute the annual depreciation amount using three different depreciation methods by filling in the following table:

	Straight-Line	Units-of-Production	Double Declining
Year 1			
Year 2			
Year 3			
Year 4			
Year 5			
Total			

E8-15B. Identify asset impairment (*Learning Objective 8*) 10–15min.

TaoYuen Ltd. has four assets. You are an accounting assistant who is in charge of identifying the recoverable amount and determining whether each of the assets is impaired. If so, what is the amount that should be recorded?

	Carrying Value	Value in Use	Fair Value	Recoverable Amount	Is Asset Impaired?	Impairment Amount
1. Truck	$52,000	$48,000	$45,000			
2. Franchise	45,000	52,000	$55,000			
3. Machine	60,000	52,000	$50,000			
4. Patent	12,000	16,000	$16,500			

E8-16B. Amortization (*Learning Objectives 2 and 6*) 10–15min.

Lakeshore Company has two intangible assets at the end of the year.

1. On July 1, Lakeshore joined a franchise business and paid $60,000 for a 5-year franchise agreement.

2. On October 1, Lakeshore purchased a copyright for $26,000. The copyright had 25 years of legal life remaining; however, Lakeshore estimated that the copyright will have no value after 20 years.

Requirements

1. Record the acquisition of the two intangible assets.

2. Calculate the amortization of each intangible asset at December 31.

3. Record the year-end adjusting entries.

4. What is the carrying value of each asset reported in the balance sheet?

EXERCISES (ALTERNATES 1, 2, AND 3)

These alternative exercise sets are available for your practice benefit at
www.myaccountinglab.com

PROBLEMS (GROUP A)

P8-1A. Long-term asset costs and partial year depreciation *(Learning Objectives 2 & 3)*
20–25 min.

Gegax Manufacturing incurred the following costs in acquiring land, making land improvements, and constructing and furnishing a new building.

a.	Purchase price of four acres of land..	$200,000
b.	Additional dirt and earthmoving	8,100
c.	Fence around the boundary of the property..	17,600
d.	Attorney fee for title search on the land..	1,000
e.	Unpaid property taxes on the land to be paid by Gegax............................	5,900
f.	Company signs at the front of the property..	4,400
g.	Building permit for the building...	500
h.	Architect's fee for the design of the building	22,500
i.	Labour to construct the building	709,000
j.	Materials used to construct the building	224,000
k.	Landscaping...	6,400
l.	Parking lot and concrete walks..	29,700
m.	Lights for the parking lot and walkways	10,300
n.	Salary of construction supervisor (85% to building; 15% to parking lot and concrete walks)	40,000
o.	Furniture for the building..	107,100
p.	Transportation and installation of furniture	2,100

Gegax Manufacturing depreciates buildings over 40 years, land improvements over 20 years, and furniture over 8 years, all on a straight-line basis with zero residual value.

Requirements

1. Set up columns for Land, Land Improvements, Building, and Furniture. Show how to account for each cost by listing the cost under the correct account. Determine the total cost of each asset.

2. All construction was complete and assets were placed in service on May 1. Record partial-year depreciation for the year ended December 31. Round to the nearest dollar.

P8-2A. Journalize long-term asset transactions *(Learning Objectives 2, 3, & 5)*
20–25 min.

Regal Freightway provides freight service. The company's balance sheet includes Land, Buildings, and Motor-Carrier Equipment. Regal Freightway uses a separate accumulated depreciation account for each depreciable asset. During 2014, Regal Freightway completed the following transactions:

Jan 1	Traded in motor-carrier equipment with accumulated depreciation of $90,000 (cost of $130,000) for new equipment with a cash cost of $176,000. Regal Freightway received a trade-in allowance of $70,000 on the old equipment and paid the remainder in cash.
Jul 1	Sold a building that cost $550,000 and had accumulated depreciation of $250,000 through December 31 of the preceding year. Depreciation is computed on a straight-line basis. The building has a 40-year useful life and a residual value of $50,000. Regal Freightway received $100,000 cash and a $600,000 note receivable.
Oct 31	Purchased land and a building for a cash payment of $300,000. An independent appraisal valued the land at $115,000 and the building at $230,000.
Dec 31	Recorded depreciation as follows: New motor-carrier equipment has an expected useful life of 1 million kilometres and an estimated residual value of $26,000. Depreciation method is the units-of-production method. During the year, Regal Freightway drove the truck 150,000 kilometres. Depreciation on buildings is straight-line. The new building has a 40-year useful life and a residual value equal to $20,000.

Requirement

1. Record the transactions in Regal Freightway's journal.

P8-3A. Capitalize long-term asset costs and several depreciation methods (Learning Objectives 2, 3, & 9) 20–25 min.

On January 3, 2015, Jose Rojo, Inc. paid $224,000 for equipment used in manufacturing automotive supplies. In addition to the basic purchase price, the company paid $700 transportation charges, $100 insurance for the equipment while in transit, $12,100 sales tax, and $3,100 for a special platform on which to place the equipment in the plant. Jose Rojo, Inc. management estimates that the equipment will remain in service for five years and have a residual value of $20,000. The equipment will produce 50,000 units the first year, with annual production decreasing by 5,000 units during each of the next four years (i.e. 45,000 units in year 2; 40,000 units in year 3; and so on for a total of 200,000 units). In trying to decide which depreciation method to use, Jose Rojo, Inc. requested a depreciation schedule for each of the three depreciation methods (straight-line, units-of-production, and double-declining-balance).

Requirements

1. For each depreciation method, prepare a depreciation schedule showing asset cost, depreciation expense, accumulated depreciation, and asset book value. For the units-of-production method, round depreciation per unit to three decimal places.

2. Show how Jose Rojo, Inc. would report equipment on the December 31, 2015, balance sheet for each depreciation method.

P8-4A. Disposing of an asset (Learning Objective 5) 15–20 min.

Atco Industries had a piece of equipment that cost $25,000 and had accumulated depreciation of $23,000.

Requirement

1. Record the disposition of the equipment assuming the following independent situations:

   a. Atco discarded the equipment, receiving $0.

   b. Atco sold the equipment for $3,000 cash.

   c. Atco traded the equipment in on a new piece of equipment costing $30,000. Atco was granted a $5,000 trade-in allowance for the old equipment and paid the difference in cash.

Quick solution: a. $2,000 loss; b. $1,000 gain; c. $3,000 gain; d. $1,000 loss

d. Atco traded the equipment in on a new piece of equipment costing $20,000. Atco was granted a $1,000 trade-in allowance for the old equipment and signed a note payable for the difference.

P8-5A. Goodwill *(Learning Objective 6)* 15–20 min.

Benny's Restaurants acquired Hungry Boy Diners. The financial records of Hungry Boy Diners included the following:

Book Value of Assets	$2.4 million
Market Value of Assets	2.7 million
Liabilities..	2.2 million

Requirements

1. Make the journal entry to record Benny's Restaurants' purchase of Hungry Boy Diners for $3 million cash, including any goodwill.

2. How should Benny's Restaurants account for this goodwill after acquiring Hungry Boy Diners? Explain in detail.

P8-6A. Depletion *(Learning Objective 7)* 20–25 min.

Wright Oil Company's balance sheet includes three assets: Natural Gas, Oil, and Coal. Suppose Wright Oil Company paid $2.8 million in cash for the right to work a mine with an estimated 100,000 tonnes of coal. Assume the company paid $60,000 to remove unwanted buildings from the land and $45,000 to prepare the surface for mining. Further, assume that Wright Oil Company signed a $30,000 note payable to a company that will return the land surface to its original condition after the mining ends. During the first year, Wright Oil Company removed 40,000 tonnes of coal, which it sold on account for $39 per tonne. Operating expenses for the first year totalled $252,000, all paid in cash.

Requirements

1. Record all of Wright Oil Company's transactions, including depletion, for the year.

2. Prepare the company's income statement for its coal operations for the year.

P8-7A. Lump-sum basket purchase of long-term assets *(Learning Objective 2)* 20–25 min.

On March 1, Taikin Manufacturing Ltd. purchased a factory with a lot of land and a machine for $818,000. Taikin paid legal fees of $2,000 for this purchase, renovation costs on the building of $27,000, and the $8,000 cost of overhauling the machine. The appraisal value for the land was $225,000, for the building was $585,000, and for the machine was $90,000.

Taikin estimated that the building's useful life was 15 years with a residual value of $20,000 and the machine's production hours would be 43,000 machine hours, with a residual value of $4,000. Taikin uses the straight-line method to depreciate buildings and the units-of-production method to depreciate machines. Taikin's year-end is December 31. Taikin used the machine 3,600 hours for the first year and 4,500 hours for the second year.

Requirements

1. Apportion the cost of the factory on the basis of the appraised value. Show your calculations.

2. Record the journal entry for the purchase of the building, land, and machine.

3. Record the adjusting entry for the depreciation for the first year.

4. What would be the carrying value of each asset at the end of the first year and the second year?

P8-8A. Changes in estimates and disposal (*Learning Objectives 3 & 5*) 20–25 min.

On January 1, 2014, Nami Inc.'s ledger shows its capital asset of $79,000 (at cost) and accumulated depreciation of $28,125. When the capital asset was purchased, Nami estimated that its useful life would be 12 years. On July 1, 2014, Nami paid $18,000 for property betterment and, as a result, it estimated its residual value had increased from $4,000 to $6,000; as well, the useful life had increased by 2.5 years. Nami uses straight-line amortization. On October 1, 2016, Nami sold the capital asset for $45,000.

Requirements

1. What was the age of the capital asset as of Janary 1, 2014? What was the annual depreciation amount?
2. Prepare the journal entry to record the betterment.
3. Prepare the adjusting entry for the depreciation expense at the end of the year.
4. What is the impact on the income statement after the betterment has been completed?
5. Prepare the journal entry to record the disposal of the capital asset.

P8-9A. Natural resources and depletion (*Learning Objective 7*) 20–25 min.

Golden Gate Mining (GGM) purchased a mineral deposit for $1,350,000 in May, 2014. In June, GGM spent $50,000 to prepare for the exploitation. The mineral deposit was ready for exploitation on July 1. GGM estimated 800,000 ounces of minerals could be economically extracted and sold. On January 2, 2016, GGM spent $80,000 for further development cost. As a result, GGM estimated an additional 110,000 ounces of mineral could be extracted and sold. The amount of mineral extracted for 2014, 2015, and 2016 is as follows:

Year	Ounces
2014	72,000
2015	88,000
2016	75,000

Requirements

1. Calculate the acquisition cost of the minerals and record the journal entry for the acquisition in 2014.
2. Record the journal entries for the depletion expense for 2014 and 2015.
3. What is the carrying value for the mineral deposit on December 31, 2015?
4 Record the journal entry for additional development cost in 2016.
5. Calculate the depletion expense for 2016 and record the journal entry for the depletion on December 31, 2016.

P8-10A. Disposal of assets (*Learning Objective 5*) 20–25 min.

Qasim Manufacturing Ltd. has three assets. Their costs, estimated residual value, useful life in years, and their carrying value on January 1, 2014, are listed in the following table:

	Cost	Residual Value	Useful Life	Carrying Value
Equipment A	$125,000	$5,000	8	$ 46,250
Equipment B	224,000	8,000	15	101,600
Equipment C	86,000	2,000	12	38,750

During 2014, Qasim completed the following transactions related to asset retirement:

April 1	Sold Equipment A for $42,500 cash.
July 31	Sold Equipment B for $112,500; received $12,500 cash and an interest-bearing (6%) note receivable for the remainder due on July 31, 2015.
October 2	Sold Equipment C for $30,000; received $20,000 and a note receivable due on December 31, 2014.

Requirements

1. What is the age of each asset on January 1, 2014?
2. Prepare all journal entries related to the disposal of each of the assets in 2014.
3. Record adjusting entries on December 31, 2014.
4. What is the total gain or loss from the disposal of these three assets?

P8-11A. Journalize long-term asset transactions (_Learning Objectives 2, 3, & 5_) 25–30 min.

On October 1, 2014, Lyndon, Inc. purchased a computer system for $86,000 from AIT Systems. The computer system had an estimated life of 5 years and residual value of $3,000. Lyndon paid $2,820 for shipping and insurance and hired an engineering company to install and set up the computer system for $7,500. AIT asked for $20,000 cash payment immediately; in addition, AIT accepted a one-year note payable of $50,000 plus 6% interest due on September 30, 2015. The remaining $16,000 is due in 30 days; however, AIT allowed a 2% discount on this $16,000 if Lyndon makes a payment by October 15. Lyndon paid the invoice on October 31. Lyndon uses the straight-line depreciation method.

On July 1, 2016, Lyndon replaced a hard drive costing $12,000 and, as a result, the useful life of the computer system increased by 2 years.

On January 10, 2017, the computer system experienced irreparable damage. Lyndon made a claim to the insurance company. Subsequently, Lyndon received $40,000 cash on January 31, 2017.

Requirements

1. Calculate the acquisition cost of the computer system.
2. Prepare all journal entries for 2014, 2015, 2016, and 2017.

P8-12A. Lump-sum basket purchase of long-term assets, depreciation, and disposal (_Learning Objectives 2, 3, & 5_) 30–35 min.

On July 1, 2014, Park and Kim, Ltd. purchased a factory, including factory building, land, machine, and fixtures, for $825,000. Park and Kim hired an appraiser to provide the appraisal value for each asset: building $600,000, land $120,000, machine $420,000, and fixtures $60,000. To prepare the factory for use in production, Park and Kim spent $21,250 to renovate the factory building and $5,250 to overhaul the machine. The following table shows the estimates and the method of depreciation for each of the assets:

	Method	Life	Residual Value
Building	Straight-Line	15 years	$13,750
Machine	Unit-of-Production	20,000 hours	10,000
Fixtures	Double-Declining	5 years	6,250

The machine was used 2,000 hours in 2014 and 3,000 hours in 2015.

Park and Kim had several transactions related to maintaining and upgrading the assets. On April 15, 2015, Park and Kim spent $1,200 to repair the fixtures, and on January 5, 2016, Park and Kim spent $49,500 to overhaul the engine. As a result, the total remaining machine hours were estimated at 21,000 hours. The machine was used 2,400 hours in 2016.

On January 2, 2017, Park and Kim sold the factory for $785,000.

Requirements

1. Apportion the cost of the factory on the basis of the appraisal value. Show your calculations.

2. Calculate the depreciation expense for each asset for 2014, 2015, and 2016:

	Building	Machine	Fixtures
2014			
2015			
2016			
Total			

3. Record all journal entries for 2014, 2015, and 2016. Park and Kim's year-end is December 31.

4. Record the sale of the factory on January 2, 2017.

PROBLEMS (GROUP B)

P8-1B. Long-term asset costs and partial year depreciation *(Learning Objectives 2 & 3)*
20–25 min.

Zed's Manufacturing incurred the following costs in acquiring land, making land improvements, and constructing and furnishing a new building.

a.	Purchase price of four acres of land	$192,000
b.	Additional dirt and earthmoving	8,800
c.	Fence around the boundary of the property	16,200
d.	Attorney fee for title search on the land	1,100
e.	Unpaid property taxes on the land to be paid by Zed's	6,300
f.	Company signs at the front of the property	5,000
g.	Building permit for the building	700
h.	Architect's fee for the design of the building	24,100
i.	Labour to construct the building	691,000
j.	Materials used to construct the building	217,000
k.	Landscaping	6,600
l.	Parking lot and concrete walks	28,700
m.	Lights for the parking lot and walkways	10,700
n.	Salary of construction supervisor (85% to building; 15% to parking lot and concrete walks)	80,000
o.	Furniture for the building	106,100
p.	Transportation and installation of furniture	2,300

Zed's Manufacturing depreciates buildings over 50 years, land improvements over 25 years, and furniture over 12 years, all on a straight-line basis with zero residual value.

Requirements

1. Set up columns for Land, Land Improvements, Building, and Furniture. Show how to account for each cost by listing the cost under the correct account. Determine the total cost of each asset.

2. All construction was complete and the assets were placed in service on November 1. Record partial-year depreciation for the year ended December 31. (Round to the nearest dollar.)

P8-2B. Journalize long-term asset transactions *(Learning Objectives 2, 3, & 5)* **20–25 min.**

Russell Freightway provides freight service. The company's balance sheet includes Land, Buildings, and Motor-Carrier Equipment. Russell uses a separate accumulated depreciation account for each depreciable asset. During 2014, Russell Freightway completed the following transactions:

Jan 1	Traded in motor-carrier equipment with accumulated depreciation of $83,000 (cost of $136,000) for new equipment with a cash cost of $136,000. Russell received a trade-in allowance of $63,000 on the old equipment and paid the remainder in cash.
Jul 1	Sold a building that cost $565,000 and had accumulated depreciation of $265,000 through December 31 of the preceding year. Depreciation is computed on a straight-line basis. The building has a 40-year useful life and a residual value of $45,000. Russell received $90,000 cash and a $620,000 note receivable.
Oct 31	Purchased land and a building for a cash payment of $400,000. An independent appraisal valued the land at $140,000 and the building at $310,000.
Dec 31	Recorded depreciation as follows: New motor-carrier equipment has an expected useful life of 1 million kilometres and an estimated residual value of $24,000. Depreciation method is the units-of-production method. During the year, Russell drove the truck 180,000 kilometres. Depreciation on buildings is straight-line. The new building has a 40-year useful life and a residual value equal to $20,000.

Requirement

1. Record the transactions in Russell Freightway's journal. (Round your depreciation expense to the nearest whole dollar.)

P8-3B. Capitalize long-term asset costs and several depreciation methods *(Learning Objectives 2, 3, & 9)* **20–25 min.**

On January 7, Red Tucker, Inc. paid $254,700 for equipment used in manufacturing automotive supplies. In addition to the basic purchase price, the company paid $500 transportation charges, $300 insurance for the equipment while in transit, $12,000 sales tax, and $2,500 for a special platform on which to place the equipment in the plant. Red Tucker, Inc. management estimates that the equipment will remain in service for five years and have a residual value of $30,000. The equipment will produce 60,000 units the first year, with annual production decreasing by 5,000 units during each of the next four years (i.e., 55,000 units in year 2, 50,000 units in year 3, and so on for a total of 250,000 units). In trying to decide which depreciation method to use, Red Tucker, Inc. requested a depreciation schedule for each of the three depreciation methods (straight-line, units-of-production, and double-declining-balance).

Requirements

1. For each depreciation method, prepare a depreciation schedule showing asset cost, depreciation expense, accumulated depreciation, and asset book value. For the units-of-production method, round depreciation per unit to three decimal places.

2. Prepare the balance sheet disclosure for Red Tucker's equipment at December 31 of the first year.

P8-4B. Disposing of an asset *(Learning Objective 5)* 15–20 min.

Mackay Industries had a piece of equipment that cost $32,000 and had accumulated depreciation of $28,000.

Requirement

1. Record the disposition of the equipment assuming the following independent situations:

   a. Mackay discarded the equipment receiving $0.

   b. Mackay sold the equipment for $6,000 cash.

   c. Mackay traded the equipment in on a new piece of equipment costing $35,000. Mackay was granted a $5,000 trade-in allowance for the old equipment and paid the difference in cash.

   d. Mackay traded the equipment in on a new piece of equipment costing $25,000. Mackay was granted a $3,000 trade-in allowance for the old equipment and signed a note payable for the difference.

P8-5B. Goodwill *(Learning Objective 6)* 15–20 min.

Tico's Restaurants acquired Tin Bus Diners. The financial records of Tin Bus Diners included the following:

Book Value of Assets	$2,300,000
Market Value of Assets	2,750,000
Liabilities	2,250,000

Requirements

1. Make the journal entry to record Tico's Restaurants' purchase of Tin Bus Diners for $3,200,000 cash, including any goodwill.

2. How should Tico's Restaurants account for this goodwill after acquiring Tin Bus Diners? Explain in detail.

P8-6B. Depletion *(Learning Objective 7)* 20–25 min.

Airheart Oil Company's balance sheet includes three assets: Natural Gas, Oil, and Coal. Suppose Airheart Oil Company paid $1,900,000 cash for the right to work a mine with an estimated 200,000 tonnes of coal. Assume the company paid $68,000 to remove unwanted buildings from the land and $45,000 to prepare the surface for mining. Further, assume that Airheart Oil Company signed a $33,000 note payable to a company that will return the land surface to its original condition after the mining ends. During the first year, Airheart Oil Company removed 41,000 tonnes of coal, which it sold on account for $36 per ton. Operating expenses for the first year totalled $248,000, all paid in cash.

Requirements

1. Record all of Airheart Oil Company's transactions, including depletion, for the year.

2. Prepare the company's income statement for its coal operations for the year.

P8-7B. Lump-sum basket purchase of long-term assets *(Learning Objective 2)* 20–25 min.

On May 1, Chippewa Brewery, Ltd. purchased a bottling factory including land and equipment for $920,000. Chippewa paid legal fees of $20,000, renovation costs on the building of $38,000, and the $18,000 cost of overhauling the equipment. The appraisal value for the land was $300,000, for the building was $780,000, and for the equipment was $120,000.

Chippewa estimated that the building's useful life was 20 years with a residual value of $16,000 and that the equipment would produce 2,000,000 bottles of beer, with a residual value of $2,000. Chippewa uses the straight-line method to depreciate buildings and the units-of-production method to depreciate equipment. Chippewa's year-end is December 31. The equipment produced 350,000 bottles for the first year and 420,000 bottles for the second year.

Requirements

1. Apportion the cost of the factory on the basis of the appraised value. Show your calculations.

2. Record the journal entry for the purchase of the factory, land, and machine.

3. Record the adjusting entry for the depreciation for the first year.

4. What would be the carrying value of the asset at the end of the first year and the second year?

P8-8B. Changes in estimates and disposal (*Learning Objectives 3 & 5*) 20–25 min.

On July 1, 2014 Yama Inc.'s ledger shows its capital assets at $144,000 (at cost) and accumulated depreciation of $55,000. When the capital assets were purchased, Yama estimated that their useful life would be 7 years. On October 1, 2014, Yama paid $26,000 for additional investment on the capital assets, and as a result, it estimated its residual value had increased from $4,000 to $8,000, and the useful life had increased by 2 years. Yama uses straight-line amortization. On April 1, 2016, Yama sold these capital assets for $60,000. Yama's year-end date is June 30.

Requirements

1. What was the age of the capital assets? What was the annual depreciation amount?

2. Prepare the journal entry to record the betterment.

3. Prepare the adjusting entry for the depreciation expense at the end of the year.

4. What is the impact on the income statement after the betterment has been completed?

5. Prepare the journal entry to record the disposal of the capital assets.

P8-9B. Natural resources and depletion (*Learning Objective 7*) 20–25 min.

TinTin Mining (TTM) purchased a mineral deposit for $2,480,000 in June, 2014. In July, TTM spent $120,000 to prepare for the exploitation. The mineral deposit was ready for exploitation on August 1. TTM estimated $1,300,000 ounces of minerals could be economically extracted and sold. On January 2, 2016, TTM spent $62,000 for further development. As a result, TTM estimated an additional 121,000 ounces of minerals could be extracted and sold. The amount of minerals extracted for 2014, 2015, and 2016 are as follows:

Year	Ounces
2014	65,000
2015	156,000
2016	180,000

Requirements

1. Calculate the acquisition cost of the mineral deposit and record the journal entry for the acquisition in 2014.

2. Record the journal entries for the depletion expense for 2014 and 2015.

3. What is the carrying value for the mineral deposit on December 31, 2015?

4. Record the journal entry for additional development costs in 2016.

5. Calculate the depletion expense for 2016 and record the journal entry for the depletion on December 31, 2016.

P8-10B. Disposal of assets (*Learning Objective 5*) 25–30 min.

Aslam Manufacturing Ltd. has three assets. Aslam's year-end is June 30. The assets' costs, estimated residual value, useful life, and their carrying value on July 1, 2014 are listed in the following table:

	Cost	Residual Value	Useful Life	Carrying Value
Machine 1	$228,000	$ 4,000	7	$ 52,000
Machine 2	426,000	12,000	12	210,375
Machine 3	332,000	8,000	9	161,000

During 2014, Aslam completed the following transactions related to asset retirement:

August 1	Sold Machine 2 for $200,000; received $50,000 cash and an interest-bearing (6%) note receivable for the remainder, due on July 31, 2015.
December 31	Sold Machine 1 for $50,000 cash.
February 2, 2015	The engine of Machine 3 broke down and was determined irreparable. The insurance company agreed to compensation of $120,000; and sent a cheque for $20,000 and a note receivable for the remaining $100,000, due on February 28, 2015.

Requirements

1. What is the age of each asset on July 1, 2014?

2. Prepare all journal entries related to the disposal of each of the assets in 2014 and 2015.

3. What is the total gain or loss from the disposal of these three assets?

P8-11B. Journalize long-term asset transactions (*Learning Objectives 2, 3, & 5*) 25–30 min.

On July 1, 2014, Seto, Inc. purchased a fire extinguisher system for $130,000 from MTI Systems. The fire extinguisher system had an estimated life of 15 years and residual value of $2,800. Seto paid $4,500 for shipping and insurance, and hired an engineering company to install and set up the fire extinguisher system for $12,500. MTI asked for $80,000 cash payment upon purchase, $10,000 is due on July 31, 2014, with a 2% discount if Seto makes the payment by July 10, and a $40,000 one-year note payable plus 6% interest due on June 30, 2015. Seto paid the invoice on July 31. Seto uses the straight-line depreciation method.

On January 1, 2016, Seto replaced a valve component costing $38,700, and as a result, the useful life of the fire extinguisher system increased by 3 years.

On September 3, 2017, the fire extinguisher system was destroyed by a factory fire. Seto made a claim to the insurance company. Subsequently, Seto received $125,000 cash on September 30, 2017.

Requirements

1. Calculate the acquisition cost of the fire extinguisher system.

2. Prepare all journal entries for 2014, 2015, 2016, and 2017.

P8-12B. Lump-sum basket purchase of long-term assets, depreciation, and disposal (Learning Objectives 2, 3, & 5) 30–35 min.

On April 1, 2014, KD Candies, Ltd. purchased a candy factory, including building, computer system, and equipment for $550,000. KD Candies hired an appraiser to provide the appraisal value for each asset: building $350,000, computer system $150,000, and equipment $125,000. To prepare the factory for use in production, KD Candies spent $30,000 to renovate the factory facilities, $23,000 to upgrade the computer system, and $25,000 to upgrade the equipment. The following table shows the estimates and the method of depreciation for each of the assets:

	Method	Life	Residual Value
Building	Straight-Line	12 years	$14,000
Computer System	Double-Declining	5 years	5,000
Equipment	Units-of-Production	25,000 hours	15,000

The machine was used 3,800 hours in 2014 and 5,200 hours in 2015.

KD Candies had several transactions related to maintaining and upgrading the assets. On July 1, 2015, KD Candies spent $6,500 to upgrade the computer system, and on January 5, 2016, KD Candies spent $13,200 to upgrade the equipment. As a result, the total remaining machine hours were estimated at 20,000 hours. The machine was used 6,500 hours.

On January 2, 2017, KD Candies sold the factory for $350,000.

Requirements

1. Apportion the cost of the factory on the basis of the appraisal value. Show your calculations.

2. Calculate the depreciation expense for each asset for 2014, 2015, and 2016:

	Building	Computer System	Equipment
2014			
2015			
2016			
Total			

3. Record all journal entries for 2014, 2015, and 2016. KD Candies' year-end is December 31.

4. Record the sale of the factory on January 2, 2017.

PROBLEMS (ALTERNATES 1, 2, AND 3)

These alternative problem sets are available for your practice benefit at *www.myaccountinglab.com*

CONTINUING EXERCISE

This exercise continues our accounting for Graham's Yard Care Inc. from previous chapters. In this exercise, we will account for the annual depreciation expense for Graham's Yard Care, Inc. In the Continuing Exercise in Chapter 2 we learned that

Graham's Yard Care, Inc. had purchased a lawn mower and a weed whacker on June 3 and that they were expected to last four years.

Requirements

1. Calculate the annual depreciation expense amount for each asset assuming both assets are using straight-line depreciation for both assets.

2. Record the entry for the partial year's depreciation for 2014. Date it December 31, 2014. Assume that no depreciation has been recorded yet in 2014.

CONTINUING PROBLEM

This problem continues our accounting for Aqua Elite, Inc. from Chapter 7. During 2014, Aqua Elite made the following purchases:

- On May 3, Aqua Elite, Inc. purchased a copy machine for $4,700 cash. The copy machine has an estimated useful life of four years and no salvage value. Aqua Elite uses double-declining-balance depreciation for the copy machine.

- On May 18, Aqua Elite, Inc. purchased a $31,000 truck financed by a note payable bearing 8% annual interest. The truck has an estimated useful life of 200,000 kilometres and a residual value of $3,000. The truck was driven 28,000 kilometres in 2014 and is depreciated using the units-of-production method.

- On June 2, Aqua Elite, Inc. paid $15,000 for land.

- On June 22, $3,300 of furniture was purchased on account. The furniture has a five-year life and a residual value of $500. Furniture is depreciated using straight-line depreciation.

- On August 10, $1,200 of furniture was purchased. The furniture has a four-year life and no residual value, and is depreciated using straight-line depreciation.

- On September 1, Aqua Elite, Inc. purchased a building for $85,000 financed by a mortgage bearing 6% annual interest. The building has an estimated salvage value of $10,000 and is being depreciated over 25 years using the straight-line method.

Requirements

1. Calculate the depreciation expense as of December 31, 2014, for all assets purchased in 2014.

2. Assuming these are Aqua Elite's only assets, how will fixed assets be reflected on the balance sheet at December 31, 2014?

APPLY YOUR KNOWLEDGE

ETHICS IN ACTION

Case 1. Larry Johnson owns Larry's Limousine, which operates a fleet of limousines and shuttle buses. Upon reviewing the most recent financial statements, he became confused over the recent decline in net income. He called his accountant and asked for an explanation. The accountant told Larry that the numerous repairs and maintenance expenses, such as oil changes, cleaning, and minor engine repairs, had totalled up to a large amount. Further, because several drivers were involved in accidents, the fleet insurance premiums had also risen sharply. Larry told his accountant to simply capitalize all the expenses related to the vehicles rather than expensing them. These capitalized repair costs could then be depreciated over the next 10 or 20 years. By capitalizing those expenses, the net income would be higher, as would property and equipment assets; therefore, both the income statement and balance sheet would look better. His accountant, however, disagreed because the costs were clearly routine maintenance and because they did not extend the fleet's useful life. Larry then told his accountant that the estimated useful life of the vehicles needed to be changed from 5 years to 20 years to lower the amount of depreciation expense. His accountant responded that capitalizing costs that should be expensed and extending the estimated lives of assets just to increase the reported net income was unethical and wrong. Larry said that it was his business and, therefore, demanded that the financial statements be changed to show more net income. As a result, the accountant told Larry to pick up his files and find another accountant. What ethical concerns did the accountant have? If the total amount of repairs and maintenance were so large, couldn't a case be made that the amount should be capitalized? Is it unethical to change the estimated life of an asset? Was it unethical for the accountant to sever the business relationship? Do you have any suggestions?

Case 2. Table Corporation purchased Chairs Unlimited for $10 million. The fair market value of Chairs' net assets at the time was $8 million, so Table Corporation recorded $2 million of goodwill. Also included in the purchase was a patent valued at $1 million with an estimated remaining life of 10 years. To comply with accounting guidelines, the goodwill was not amortized, but the patent was amortized over the remaining 10-year life. However, the Chairs Unlimited business was not as profitable as anticipated and, as a result, the accountant for Table Corporation stated that the goodwill needed to be written off. Further, the accountant discovered that the remaining life of the patent was only 6 years and that it should be amortized over the remaining 6-year life rather than the 10-year life originally estimated. The CEO became concerned because these adjustments would cause net income to be extremely low for the year. As a result, he told the accountant to wait before writing off the goodwill because of the possibility that the purchase could be profitable in the future. Also, he argued, the life of the patent should be left alone because it was originally based upon what was thought to be a 10-year life. After much debate, the CEO then agreed with the accountant as long as the amount of goodwill was not completely written off in the current year. What ethical concerns are involved? Should the accountant change the amortizable life of an intangible asset? Should the accountant completely write off the goodwill account in the current year? Does the CEO's concern for higher net income create any ethical problems when the accountant agrees to not completely write off the goodwill? Do you have any other thoughts?

KNOW YOUR BUSINESS

FINANCIAL ANALYSIS

Purpose: To help familiarize you with the financial reporting of a real company to further your understanding of the chapter material you are learning.

This case addresses the long-term assets of Bombardier Inc. The majority of these assets consist of tangible assets and intangible assets. In the text, you learned how most long-term tangible assets used in business are capitalized and depreciated over their estimated useful lives. Further, you learned that certain intangible assets are amortized over time while others are not. In this case, you will not only see and understand the classification and presentation of these assets, but also explore the methods used by Bombardier Inc. to depreciate and amortize them. Refer to Bombardier Inc.'s financial statements in MyAccountingLab. Also consider the information presented in Note 7, under the heading Property, Plant, and Equipment, and in Note 8 titled Intangible Assets.

Requirements

1. What were the balances of Property, Plant, and Equipment on January 31, 2011 and January 31, 2010? Did the amount of ending Property, Plant, and Equipment increase or decrease? Assume Bombardier Inc. removed fully

depreciated equipment having a cost of $357 (million) in 2011. What effect would this have on the value of the Property, Plant, and Equipment balance? Explain your answer.

2. What kinds of tangible assets does Bombardier Inc. have? What kinds of intangible assets does Bombardier Inc. have? Which intangible assets are amortized by Bombardier Inc. and which are not? Why?

3. What was the percentage of tangible assets compared to the total assets on January 31, 2011? What was the percentage of tangible assets compared to the total assets on January 31, 2010? Did the percentage increase or decrease during the year?

4. What depreciation policies does the Bombardier use for its Property, Plant, and Equipment? How much amortization was expensed during the year related to its property, plant, and equipment?

5. For the intangible assets, how much was acquired from third parties and how much was internally generated during 2011?

INDUSTRY ANALYSIS

Purpose: To help you understand and compare the performance of two companies in the same industry.

Find the Bombardier Annual Report, Year Ended January 31, 2011, located in MyAccountingLab and go to the Notes to Consolidated Financial Statements on page 170. Now access The Boeing Company's 2010 Annual Report. To do this from the internet, go to their webpage for the Investor Relations at *http://www.boeing.com/companyoffices/ financial/quarterly.htm* and, under Annual Report, go to the 2010 Annual Report.

Requirement

1. Find the section in the notes for each company where the company discusses its Property, Plant, and Equipment, net. Also find the section where the company discusses Intangible Assets. Compare the two and note any major differences. Also examine the depreciation and amortization policies used by the two companies. What are some differences between these two companies related to these policies?

SMALL BUSINESS ANALYSIS

Purpose: To help you understand the importance of cash flows in the operation of a small business.

You've made an appointment to take your year-end financial statements down to the bank. You know that your banker is usually concerned about two things, your net income and the amount of cash you have. You are a little concerned because you know that your current year net income was down a little bit from the prior year. You figure that a significant cause for the decline was due to a large equipment purchase you made early in the year, which resulted in a lot of depreciation expense. However, as you look at your balance sheet, it says that cash increased from last year to this year. That's a little puzzling, but you're hoping the banker can figure it out.

A couple of days later, you get a call from the banker. You're expecting him to tell you the bank won't be able to extend any more credit to you because your net income has declined. Imagine your surprise when he tells you how pleased he is with your financial performance this year, and that he doesn't anticipate any problems extending more credit to you. You want to know what he saw in your financial statements that you didn't see so you say to him, "Bob, thanks for the good news and the good report on my financial condition, even though our cash increased this year. I was afraid that the decline in our income might cause you some concern. How come it didn't?"

Requirement

1. What kind of response do you think that you might get from the banker regarding your net income as it relates to cash flow?

WRITTEN COMMUNICATION

A client of yours notified you that she just closed a deal to purchase an existing business. It's a pretty hefty purchase. As part of the purchase of the business, she received the land, the building, all the equipment, and the entire merchandise inventory of the company purchased. Your client emailed you a copy of the closing statement along with the breakdown of the purchase price shown below. In the email, your client expressed concern about how the $1,500,000 paid for the land and building should be accounted for. She also wanted to know the proper way to account for the merchandise inventory and the goodwill that was purchased.

Asset List	
Description	**Amount**
Land and Building	$1,500,000
Equipment..	675,000
Inventory...	425,000
Goodwill..	1,400,000
Total Purchase Price	$4,000,000

Requirement

1. Prepare an email to your client explaining how the $1,500,000 should be allocated between the land and building as well as how the merchandise inventory and goodwill should be accounted for.

Self Check Answers
1. b 2. a 3. d 4. c 5. a 6. d 7. b 8. a 9. c 10. d

SCAN THIS

CHAPTER 9

Current Liabilities and Long-Term Debt

LEARNING OBJECTIVES:

1 ▶ Distinguish among known, estimated, and contingent liabilities and provisions

2 ▶ Account for current liabilities of a known amount

3 ▶ Account for liabilities of an uncertain amount

4 ▶ Account for contingent liabilities and provisions

5 ▶ Account for long-term debt

6 ▶ Report liabilities on the balance sheet

7 ▶ Compute the debt ratio

In the past few chapters, we have examined the assets that most businesses have including Cash, Accounts Receivable, Inventory, and Long-Term Assets. We have seen how important it is to value assets properly, and to report them correctly in the financial statements. It is equally important, if not more important, for a business to properly value its liabilities and to report them correctly in the financial statements. When discussing liabilities, several questions may come to mind such as what different types of liabilities do most businesses have? Or, what happens if a company knows that a liability exists but doesn't know the amount of the liability? These, and other important questions, are answered here in Chapter 9 as we take a closer look at liabilities.

CHAPTER OUTLINE:

WHAT IS THE DIFFERENCE BETWEEN KNOWN, ESTIMATED, AND CONTINGENT LIABILITIES AND PROVISIONS?

Distinguish among known, estimated, and contingent liabilities and provisions

Both IFRS and Canadian ASPE have similar definitions of liabilities. Liabilities are the present obligations of an entity that arise from past events and require future settlement using the entity's resources. Liabilities can generally be broken down into three categories as follows:

- **Known liabilities:** The majority of a company's liabilities fall into this category. Known liabilities can be defined as known obligations of known amounts. In other words, the business knows that it owes something and it knows how much it owes. Examples of known liabilities include accounts payable, notes payable, unearned revenues, and accrued liabilities such as interest or taxes payable.
- **Estimated liabilities:** An estimated liability is defined as a known obligation of an unknown amount. A business will sometimes encounter a situation where it knows that a liability exists but it does not know the exact amount of the liability. In these situations, the amount of the liability must be estimated. A typical example is estimated warranties payable, which is common for companies that manufacture or sell products (such as RIM's BlackBerry or Bombardier's aircraft).
- **Contingent liabilities and provisions: Contingent liabilities** and **provisions** are unique liabilities that differ from all other types of liabilities. These liabilities arise because of a *past* event, but they are dependent upon the outcome of a *future* event. In other words, whether or not a company has an obligation depends upon the result of an event that has not yet occurred. In addition, the amount of a contingent liability may be either known or unknown. Current or pending litigation is an example of a contingent liability.

As we learned in Chapter 4, a liability is classified as a current liability if the related obligation will be settled within one year. All liabilities not classified as current liabilities are classified as long-term debt. It is possible for known, unknown, or contingent liabilities and provisions to be classified as either current or long term. We will begin our discussion of accounting for liabilities by looking at current liabilities of a known amount.

HOW DO YOU ACCOUNT FOR CURRENT LIABILITIES OF A KNOWN AMOUNT?

Account for current liabilities of a known amount

A large portion of liabilities for most companies will be made up of known liabilities that are due within one year. In the following paragraphs, we will learn how to account for the majority of the types of current liabilities of a known amount that most companies are likely to encounter.

Accounts Payable

As we have learned in previous chapters, amounts owed for purchases on account are known as accounts payable. Since accounts payable are typically due in 30 to 45 days, they are classified as current liabilities. The largest portion of accounts payable for most merchandising companies is related to the purchase of inventory on account. Merchandising and service businesses also incur accounts payable when they purchase items such as supplies, electricity, or telephone service on account. Accounts payable transactions are recorded by debiting the related asset or expense account and crediting Accounts Payable. For example, assume that Mackay Industries receives a utility bill for $680. The bill represents prior electricity usage and is not due for 30 days. Mackay Industries would record the receipt of the bill as follows:

DATE	ACCOUNTS	POST REF.	DR.	CR.
	Utilities Expense		680	
	Accounts Payable			680
	Record utility bill due in 30 days.			

When Mackay Industries pays the utility bill, it will record the payment on account as follows:

DATE	ACCOUNTS	POST REF.	DR.	CR.
	Accounts Payable		680	
	Cash			680
	Record payment on account.			

Notes Payable

When a business borrows money, usually from a financial institution, the signing of a promissory note is generally required. Businesses also often finance purchases of long-term assets through the use of notes payable. Any note payable that must be paid within one year from the balance sheet date is classified as a current liability. All notes not classified as a current liability are classified as long-term debt (discussed later in the chapter).

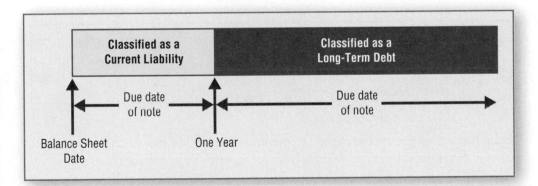

In Chapter 7 we learned about promissory notes when we studied notes receivable. The terms and concepts we learned about then will also apply to notes payable. However, we are now learning about the promissory note transaction from the opposite perspective. To illustrate a note payable, assume that on September 1, 2014, Mackay Industries borrows $8,000 from First National Bank on a nine-month, 6% note payable. Mackay Industries would record the transaction as follows on September 1:

DATE	ACCOUNTS	POST REF.	DR.	CR.
Sep 1	Cash		8,000	
	Notes Payable			8,000
	Record 6%, nine-month note.			

At December 31, 2014, it is necessary for Mackay Industries to accrue interest expense for the four months from September to December. The accrued interest is recorded as follows:

DATE	ACCOUNTS	POST REF.	DR.	CR.
Dec 31	Interest Expense		160*	
	Interest Payable			160
	Accrue four months' interest expense.			

*$160 = ($8,000 × 0.06 × 4/12)

The interest accrual at December 31, 2014, allocated $160 of the interest on this note to 2014. The remaining $200 ($8,000 × 0.06 × 5/12) of interest expense on this note will be allocated to 2015 at the time the note is paid off as follows:

DATE	ACCOUNTS	POST REF.	DR.	CR.
Jun 1, 2015	Notes Payable		8,000	
	Interest Payable		160	
	Interest Expense		200	
	Cash			8,360
	Repay 6%, nine-month note.			

Notice that the $160 debit to Interest Payable zeros out the amount that was accrued in the liability account at December 31, 2014. The $8,000 debit to Notes Payable removes the note from Mackay Industries' books. The $200 debit to Interest Expense records the interest expense for 2015. In addition, the $8,360 credit to Cash reflects the payment of the entire maturity value of the note. If the term of the note had not spanned the end of the period, no adjusting entry to accrue interest would have been necessary. If this had been the case for Mackay Industries in the previous example, the final entry to repay the note would look like this:

DATE	ACCOUNTS	POST REF.	DR.	CR.
	Notes Payable		8,000	
	Interest Expense		360	
	Cash			8,360
	Repay 6%, nine-month note.			

Notice that Interest Expense is debited for the full amount of the interest on the note, $360. There is also no debit to Interest Payable because no interest had been accrued on the note.

Sales Tax Payable

Most provinces levy harmonized sales tax (HST) or provincial sales tax (PST), and goods and services tax (GST) on retail sales. Retailers collect the sales tax from their customers in addition to the price of the item sold. The sales tax collected must then be remitted, or paid, to the Canada Revenue Agency (CRA) on a periodic basis, usually monthly or quarterly. Sales Tax Payable is a current liability because the retailer must pay the CRA in less than a year. Let's apply this to Mackay Industries.

Suppose December's taxable sales for Mackay Industries totalled $22,000. Assume that Mackay Industries is required to collect an additional 13% of sales tax (HST), which would equal $2,860 ($22,000 × 0.13). Mackay Industries would record December sales as follows:

DATE	ACCOUNTS	POST REF.	DR.	CR.
	Accounts Receivable or Cash		24,860	
	Sales Revenue			22,000
	HST Payable			2,860
	Record December sales.			

To determine how much needs to be paid to the CRA for the HST collected, Mackay Industries also needs to incorporate the amount of HST that Mackay has paid out on purchases. The amount of HST paid on purchases is deducted from the amount of HST collected from customers to determine the amount that needs to be remitted to the government. Assume that Mackay Industries paid $13,200 for merchandise in the same period as the sales recorded above, and also paid 13% HST. Mackay Industries would record the December purchase as follows:

DATE	ACCOUNTS	POST REF.	DR.	CR.
	Inventory		13,200	
	HST Paid on Purchases		1,716	
	Accounts Payable			14,916
	Record December inventory purchases..			

The entry recorded when Mackay Industries remits the HST to the government looks like this:

DATE	ACCOUNTS	POST REF.	DR.	CR.
	HST Payable		2,860	
	HST Paid on Purchases			1,716
	Cash			1,144
	Remit HST.			

Accrued Expenses (Accrued Liabilities)

In Chapter 3, we learned that an accrued expense is any expense that has been incurred but has not yet been paid. That's why accrued expenses are also called accrued liabilities. Most businesses will often have accrued liabilities for one or more of the following:

- Interest
- Salaries and wages
- Payroll
- Income taxes

Payroll liabilities are employees deductions withheld by employers, such as Canada Pension Plan (CPP), employment insurance (EI), and employee income tax. Employers must remit these deductions to appropriate government agencies. In addition, if employees participate in any additional benefits, such as pension plans, union dues, or extended health plans, then the employers have to deduct these fees and remit them to appropriate agencies.

So, in addition to salary expense, employers also incur employee benefits expenses, which include employers' contributions to CPP, EI, private pension plans, extended health plans, etc. Employers have to pay CPP contributions in the same amount as the employees' deduction, but must pay 1.4 times the EI contribution of employees. For example, in December, Mackay Industries' gross pay, or salary expense, was $10,000. Mackay Industries would make two transactions to record (1) salary expense and payroll deductions, and (2) employee benefits expense and payroll payable:

DATE	ACCOUNTS	POST REF.	DR.	CR.
	Salary Expense		10,000	
	CPP Payable – Employees			495
	EI Payable – Employees			175
	Income Taxes Payable			2,500
	Union Dues Payable			25
	Salary Payable			6,805
	To record payroll and employee deductions for the month of December.			

DATE	ACCOUNTS	POST REF.	DR.	CR.
	Employee Benefits Expense		740	
	CPP Payable – Employer			495
	EI Payable – Employer			245
	To record employer's payroll costs for the month of December.			

Suppose Mackay Industries remits the payroll payable to Canadian Revenue Agency (CRA) on January 15. It would record the following entry:

DATE	ACCOUNTS	POST REF.	DR.	CR.
	CPP Payable – Employees		495	
	CPP Payable – Employer		495	
	EI Payable – Employees		175	
	EI Payable – Employer		245	
	Income Taxes Payable		2,500	
	Cash			3,910
	To record December payroll payable remittance to CRA.			

Notice that the Union Dues Payable is not included in the payment to the CRA. The union dues payable will be paid to the employees' union organization, which is separate from CRA. It is worth noting that CPP and EI deductions from the employees' paycheque is the employees' expense, while the employer portion of CPP and EI is the employer's payroll expense, in addition to the salary expense.

Accrued liabilities are recorded by debiting the related expense account and crediting a liability account. For example, the entry to record $7,000 of accrued corporate income tax would be as follows:

DATE	ACCOUNTS	POST REF.	DR.	CR.
	Corporate Income Tax Expense		$7,000	
	Corporate Income Tax Payable			$7,000
	Record accrued income tax expense.			

Unearned Revenues

As we saw in Chapter 3, unearned revenues, also called deferred revenues, arise when a business receives cash in advance of providing goods or services. As a result, the business has an obligation to provide goods or services to the customer in the future.

Unearned revenues are typically classified as current liabilities because customers do not usually pay for more than one year's worth of goods or services in advance.

Current Portion of Long-Term Debt

Many long-term debt obligations (discussed later in the chapter) are paid in instalments. The principal amount of these obligations, due within one year from the balance sheet date, is referred to as **current portion of long-term debt**. Because it is due within one year from the balance sheet date, the current portion of long-term debt is classified as a current liability on the balance sheet. Let's assume that Mackay Industries signs a $30,000, 6% note payable on June 1, 2014. The note requires that annual instalments of $6,000, plus interest, be paid on June 1 of each of the next five years. On Mackay Industries' December 31, 2014, balance sheet, what amount will be reflected as current portion of long-term debt? Because the $6,000 payment that is due on June 1, 2015, is due within one year from the balance sheet date, it will be classified as current portion of long-term debt. The remaining $24,000 ($30,000 – $6,000) will be classified as long term.

CONCEPT CHECK

Jill and Alan both work in the Accounting Department of a large retail business that has a significant amount of long-term debt. Jill was commenting to Alan how important it is to ensure that the current portion of the company's long-term debt be properly classified as such on the balance sheet. Alan argued that it really didn't matter how the debt was classified as long as the correct total amount of debt was included somewhere on the balance sheet. Is Alan's point of view correct?

Answer

No, Jill's point of view is correct. In Chapter 4 we learned that the current ratio is one of the most widely used tools investors, creditors, and suppliers use to evaluate a company's ability to pay its obligations as they come due. So, even though a company includes the correct amount of total liabilities on the balance sheet, if the liabilities are not properly classified as current versus long-term, the current ratio will not be correct. As a result, investors, creditors, and suppliers will be unable to correctly assess the ability of a business to pay its obligations as they come due. Therefore, it is very important for a business to analyze all of its long-term debt at the end of each accounting period to ensure that it is being properly classified as current versus long-term.

HOW DO YOU ACCOUNT FOR CURRENT LIABILITIES OF AN UNCERTAIN AMOUNT?

A business may know that a liability exists but not know the exact amount of the liability. It cannot simply ignore the liability. The liability must be reported on the balance sheet. Although there are other types of estimated liabilities, the most common example occurs when a company guarantees its products or services against defects under a **warranty** agreement. Therefore, we will focus our attention on accounting for estimated warranties.

 3 Account for liabilities of an uncertain amount

Estimated Warranty Liability

It is common for companies to provide either 90-day or 1-year warranties on the goods or services they provide. When a sale is made, it is reasonable to assume that there is the potential for a warranty claim to be made. Without recognizing this potential expense (and liability), the financial statements will not accurately reflect the true nature of the sale. The expense, therefore, is incurred when sales are made, not when warranty claims are settled. At the time of sale, the company does not know how many warranty claims will be filed. Therefore, the amount of warranty expense for a period is unknown and must be estimated.

Assume that Mackay Industries makes sales of $75,000 during the month of August and that Mackay Industries extends its customers a 90-day warranty on all products sold. Mackay Industries estimates that its products will require warranty repairs at a rate of 2% of the sales amounts. The company would record sales and warranty expense for the month of August as follows:

DATE	ACCOUNTS	POST REF.	DR.	CR.
	Accounts Receivable or Cash		75,000	
	Sales Revenue			75,000
	Record monthly sales.			
	Warranty Expense		1,500	
	Estimated Warranty Payable			1,500
	Record estimated warranty expense.			

Now assume that during September Mackay Industries paid $450 to settle warranty claims filed by customers. Mackay would make the following entry to record payment of the warranty claims:

DATE	ACCOUNTS	POST REF.	DR.	CR.
	Estimated Warranty Payable		450	
	Cash			450
	Settled warranty claims.			

If, instead of paying cash to settle the warranty claims, Mackay Industries had replaced the defective goods with new items, the entry would have been as follows:

DATE	ACCOUNTS	POST REF.	DR.	CR.
	Estimated Warranty Payable		450	
	Inventory			450
	Settled warranty claims.			

Estimated liabilities are generally current liabilities. However, if the estimated liability is expected to be settled more than one year from the balance sheet date, it would be classified as long term.

DECISION GUIDELINES

Decision

What should I do if I do not know the exact amount of a liability?

Guideline

Use professional judgment and estimate the amount.

Analyze

To properly reflect the true financial position and the results of operations of a company, it is important that all obligations of the business be recorded. When the exact amount of a liability is unknown, an estimate of the amount owed should be made. It is important to use professional judgment to estimate a reasonable amount.

HOW DO YOU ACCOUNT FOR CONTINGENT LIABILITIES AND PROVISIONS?

As stated earlier, although contingent liabilities and provisions arise as the result of a past event, they are dependent upon the outcome of a future event. Therefore, contingent liabilities or provisions represent potential, rather than actual obligations.

4 Account for contingent liabilities and provisions

There are differences in terminology used between IFRS and Canadian ASPE. Under IFRS, a *provision* is a liability that has uncertain timing or uncertain amount, while a *contingent liability* is a possible obligation that will be confirmed by uncertain future events. Under Canadian ASPE, there is no specific definition for provisions. A contingency is an uncertain situation that will involve a possible gain or loss to a company. The outcome of the future event will determine whether or not a company will incur an obligation. Examples of contingent liabilities are as follows:

- Pending, or actual, legal action
- Potential fines resulting from investigations conducted by regulatory agencies
- Loan guarantees that occur when one entity co-signs a note payable for another entity

One example of a provision is an asset retirement obligation. Companies may be required to clean up pollution, or remove or dismantle an asset at the end of its useful life. This is a present obligation and will require future outflow of resources to fulfil the obligation; however, the timing and the amount of resources required is uncertain.

Suppose Mackay Industries guarantees a note for Tucker Enterprises. If Tucker Enterprises fails to pay the note when it comes due, Mackay Industries would be obligated to pay the amount due. This represents a contingent liability to Mackay Industries. Although Mackay Industries cosigned the note (a past event), it will only incur an obligation if Tucker Enterprises fails to pay the note (the future event).

The accounting treatment of a contingent liability or a provision depends on the likelihood of an actual obligation occurring. **Exhibit 9-1** outlines the accounting treatment of contingent liabilities.

Likelihood of Obligation Occurring	Accounting Treatment
Remote (very unlikely)	No action is necessary.
Possible (it could occur)	Disclose the existence of the contingent liability in the financial statement footnotes. An explanation of the circumstances related to the contingent liability should be included in the footnote.
Probable (more likely than not)	If the amount of the potential obligation is known (or can be reasonably estimated), the contingent liability should be recorded. The circumstances related to the contingent liability should also be disclosed in the financial statement footnotes.
	If the amount of the obligation is not known and cannot be reasonably estimated, then only footnote disclosure is required.

Exhibit 9-1 ▲

Exhibit 9-2 shows the comparison of the measurement and accounting treatment of contingent liabilities and provisions under IFRS and Canadian ASPE.

	IFRS	Canadian ASPE
Likelihood of Outcome (Measurement) Accounting Treatment	Virtually Certain > 95% Recognize	Virtually Certain > 95% Recognize
Likelihood of Outcome (Measurement) Accounting Treatment	Probable: 50% - 95% Recognize	Likely: 70%–95% Disclose
Likelihood of Outcome (Measurement) Accounting Treatment	Possible: 5% - 50% Disclose	Possible: 5%–70% No Disclosure Required
Likelihood of Outcome (Measurement) Accounting Treatment	Remote: < 5% No Disclosure Required	Remote: < 5% No Disclosure Required

Exhibit 9-2 ▲

Let's return to our earlier example of the loan guarantee. As long as Tucker Enterprises is in sound financial condition, the likelihood of Mackay Industries being required to pay the loan is remote and, therefore, no action is required. If Mackay Industries becomes aware of the fact that Tucker Enterprises is experiencing financial difficulties, it is now possible that Mackay Industries will be obligated to repay the loan. In this case, Mackay Industries would be required to disclose the contingent liability in the notes to its financial statements. If Tucker Enterprises files for bankruptcy or defaults on the loan, it is probable that Mackay Industries will be obligated to repay the loan. Now, in addition to disclosing the contingent liability in the financial statement footnotes, Mackay Industries will have to record the contingent liability in the financial statements. The contingent liability would be recorded by debiting a loss account and crediting a liability account. Contingent liabilities and provisions are classified as current versus long-term based upon when the liability is expected to be paid.

CRITICAL THINKING

Take a minute to think about each of the following cases. What is the appropriate accounting treatment for each case—report a liability on the financial statement, recognize a provision, or not report the situation? What is the impact on the company's financial statements?

Cases	Accounting Treatment	Impact on Financial Statements
1. Star Café sells hot beverages. The owner of Star Café is concerned about the hot temperature of the hot beverages that it sells. She is wondering whether to book a $500,000 provision in the liability.		
2. DIT is a chemical company that sells pesticides. The auditor of DIT recently found that DIT has leaked a small quantity of the chemical in the nearby river. The cleanup of the chemical is likely to cost $1 million to $2 million.		
3. Dia Mine, Inc. mines diamonds. Under provincial law, the company must clean up any pollution at the end of operations. Current estimates indicate that the cleanup will cost up to $3 million.		

Solutions:

Cases	Accounting Treatment	Impact on Financial Statements
1. Star Café sells hot beverages. The owner of Star Café is concerned about the hot temperature of the hot beverages that it sells. She is wondering whether to book a $500,000 provision in the liability.	No Disclosure Required • No past event and no current obligation • No potential future outflow of assets due to past events and current obligations	No impact on the financial statements
2. DIT is a chemical company that sells pesticides. The auditor of DIT recently found that DIT has leaked a small quantity of the chemical in the near-by river. The cleanup of the chemical is likely to cost $1 million to $2 million.	Recognize • Past event—chemical leak—caused the current obligation to clean up the river • The future outflow of $1 million or $2 million is required	Expense and Provision will reduce income and increase liabilities
3. Dia Mine, Inc. mines diamonds. Under provincial law, the company must clean up any pollution at the end of operations. Current estimates indicate that the cleanup will cost up to $3 million.	Disclose • Dia Mine has not polluted the environment in the past. However, under provincial law the company will likely have a cash outflow of up to $3 million.	No impact on the financial statements

HOW DO YOU ACCOUNT FOR LONG-TERM DEBT?

5 Account for long-term debt

The long-term debt of most companies is comprised of the following types of obligations:

- Notes payable
- Bonds payable
- Leases payable

There are many similarities in the accounting for these different obligations. However, there are also some unique differences. Therefore, we will examine each of the three separately.

Notes Payable

As discussed previously, a note payable is a debt obligation that is supported by a promissory note. Notes payable that are due to be repaid more than one year from the balance sheet date are classified as long-term debt. Most long-term notes payable represent loans taken out for the purchase of land, buildings, or both that are repaid over a long-term period. A note payable used to purchase land or buildings is a special type of note called a **mortgage**. A mortgage is an example of a secured note because it gives the lender the right to take specified assets, called **collateral**, if the borrower is unable to repay the loan.

ACCOUNTING IN YOUR WORLD

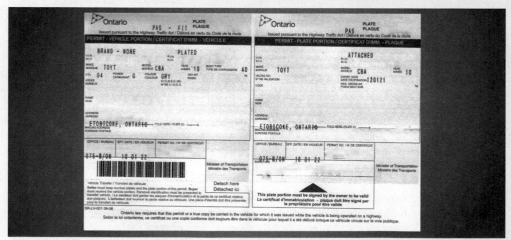

If you have ever borrowed money to purchase a car, then you probably know that you do not get the title to the car until the loan has been paid off. The vehicle title represents legal ownership of the vehicle. Lenders often secure car loans by using the car as collateral for the loan and placing a lien on the title. This means that the lender gets the title to the car (and has legal ownership of the car) until the loan is repaid. If the borrower fails to repay the loan, the lender has the right to repossess, or take back, the car to compensate it for the unpaid loan. Once the loan has been repaid, the lender will release the lien on the title by "signing it over" to the borrower. This transfers legal ownership of the car to the borrower.

A mortgage is typically paid off through instalment payments that include both principal and interest. The entries required to record mortgage note transactions are similar to those for note payable transactions. Let's assume that Mackay Industries signed a $155,000, 8%, 20-year mortgage note on January 1, 2014, to finance the purchase of a new building. Payments of $7,831 on the mortgage will be made semiannually on June 30 and December 31 of each year. The purchase of the building is recorded as follows:

DATE	ACCOUNTS	POST REF.	DR.	CR.
Jan 1	Buildings		155,000	
	Mortgage Payable			155,000
	Issued mortgage to purchase building.			

In order to keep track of the portion of each payment that is allocated to principal and to interest, an amortization schedule is usually prepared. **Exhibit 9-3** illustrates an amortization schedule for the first four years of Mackay Industries' mortgage:

	A	B	C	D
		Interest	Principal	Loan Balance
Date	Payment	(D × .08 × 1/2)*	(A – B)	(D – C)
1/01/2014				$155,000
6/30/2014	$7,831	$6,200	$1,631	153,369
12/31/2014	7,831	6,135	1,696	151,673
6/30/2015	7,831	6,067	1,764	149,909
12/31/2015	7,831	5,996	1,835	148,074
6/30/2016	7,831	5,923	1,908	146,166
12/31/2016	7,831	5,847	1,984	144,182
6/30/2017	7,831	5,767	2,064	142,118
12/31/2017	7,831	5,685	2,146	139,972

*Rounded

Column B is calculated by multiplying the loan balance from the prior period (column D) by the interest rate (8%) and then multiplying by 1/2 to account for the fact that the payment is made semiannually.

Column C is calculated by subtracting the interest (column B) from the payment (column A).

Column D is calculated by subtracting the principal portion of the payment (column C) from the loan balance from the prior period (column D).

Exhibit 9-3 ▲

Based on information found in Exhibit 9-3, Mackay Industries will record the June 30, 2014, loan payment as follows:

DATE	ACCOUNTS	POST REF.	DR.	CR.
Jun 30	Interest Expense		6,200	
	Mortgage Payable		1,631	
	Cash			7,831
	Record semiannual loan payment.			

As discussed previously in the chapter, the principal portion of any mortgage payments due within one year from the balance sheet date will be classified under current portion of long-term debt on the balance sheet.

Bonds Payable

In addition to using notes payable to aquire needed cash, a business may obtain money by issuing **bonds payable**. Bonds payable are long-term, interest-bearing notes that are issued to multiple lenders, called bondholders. By issuing bonds, it is often possible for a business to borrow hundreds of thousands (or even millions) of dollars. Instead of depending on one large loan from a single bank or lender, with bonds, a large number of smaller amounts are borrowed from different investors. For example, Mackay Industries could raise $1,000,000 by borrowing $1,000 each from 1,000 different investors.

Before we move on, let's explore some of the terminology associated with bonds.

- **Term bonds** all mature at the same specified time. For example, $500,000 of term bonds may all mature 10 years from today. With term bonds, the company issuing the bonds will have to repay all $500,000 at the same time.

- **Serial bonds** are bonds from the same bond issuance that mature at different times. For example, a $1,500,000 serial bond issuance may specify that one-third of the bonds mature in 10 years, one-third mature in 15 years, and one-third mature in 20 years.

- **Secured bonds** are bonds that are backed with some form of collateral. Secured bonds give the bondholders the right to take specified assets of the issuer if the issuer fails to pay principal or interest.

- **Unsecured bonds** are bonds that are not backed by any assets. They are backed only by the general credit of the company issuing the bond. Unsecured bonds are also called **debentures**.

- **Convertible bonds** are bonds that give the bondholder the option of exchanging the bond for common shares in the company.

- **Callable bonds** are bonds that may be bought back and retired (called) by the bond issuer at a pre-arranged price.

- **Principal amount** is the amount the borrower must pay back to the bondholders on the maturity date. The principal amount is also called **maturity value**, or **par value**.

- **Maturity date** is the date on which the borrower must repay the principal amount to the bondholders.

- **Stated interest rate**, or coupon rate, determines the amount of cash interest the bond issuer pays each year. The stated interest rate is printed on the bond and *does not change* from year to year. For example, if a $1,000 bond has a stated interest rate of 9%, the bond issuer pays $90 of interest annually on the bond.

- **Market interest rate**, or yield, is the rate of interest investors are willing to pay for similar bonds of equal risk at the current time. Bonds are often issued with a stated interest rate that differs from the market interest rate. This is due to the time gap between when the stated rate is determined and when the bonds are actually issued.

Bond Prices

A bond can be issued (sold) at a price that is equal to the par value of the bond, below the par value of the bond, or above the par value of the bond. Whether a bond sells at par, below par, or above par depends on the relationship between the stated interest rate on the bond and the current market rate of interest at the time the bond is sold. Bonds sold at a price equal to par value are said to be sold "at par." Bonds sold at a price below par are said to be sold "at a **discount**," and bonds sold at a price above par are said to be sold "at a

premium." Regardless of the amount the company receives on the issuance date, on the maturity date, the company has to pay back the principal amount, or par value.

To illustrate, let's assume that Mackay Industries issues 6% bonds when the market rate for similar bonds of equal risk is higher, say 6.5% or 7%. Mackay Industries will have a hard time attracting investors to buy its bonds when investors can earn higher returns on bonds of other companies. Therefore, to attract investors, Mackay Industries will offer to sell its bonds at a price less than maturity value, or at a discount. So, for example, Mackay Industries may offer to sell its $1,000, 6% bonds for only $920 each. Mackay Industries will pay the investors yearly interest payments equal to $60 ($1,000 par value × 6% stated interest) on each bond. However, because the investors only paid $920 for each bond, the $60 interest payment represents a return of approximately 6.5% ($60 interest/$920 invested).

On the other hand, if the market interest rate is 5% or 5.5%, Mackay Industries's 6% bonds will be so attractive that investors will pay more than maturity value, or a premium, for them. So, for example, Mackay Industries may offer to sell its $1,000, 6% bonds for $1,085 each. Mackay Industries will still pay the investors yearly interest payments equal to $60 ($1,000 par value × 6% interest) on each bond. However, because the investors paid $1,085 for each bond, the $60 interest payment represents a return of approximately 5.5% ($60 interest/$1,085 invested). The actual price of a bond represents a price that makes the return on the bond effectively the same as the market rate of interest at the time the bond is sold. **Exhibit 9-4** illustrates the relationship between the stated interest rate and the market interest rate and how it affects the sales price of a bond.

Relationship of Stated Interest Rate to Current Market Interest Rate	Bond Is Sold At	Why?
Stated rate = Market rate	Par	Investors are willing to pay the full maturity value for the bond because it offers the same interest rate as similar bonds with equal risk.
Stated rate < Market rate	Discount	Investors demand a lower price for the bond because they will receive a lower return from this bond than from similar bonds with equal risk.
Stated rate > Market rate	Premium	Investors are willing to pay a higher price for the bond because they will receive a higher return from this bond than from similar bonds with equal risk.

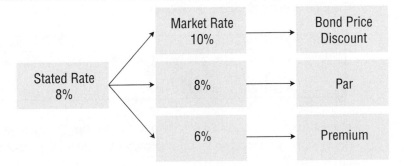

Exhibit 9-4 ▲

The issue price of a bond determines the amount of cash the company receives when it issues the bond. However, the issue price of a bond does not affect the required payment at maturity. A company must always pay the maturity value (par value) of the bonds when they mature.

After bonds have been issued, investors may buy and sell them on the bond market just as they buy and sell shares on the stock market.

Bond prices are quoted as a percentage of maturity value. For example,

- a $1,000 bond quoted at 100 is bought or sold for 100% of maturity value, ($1,000 × 1.00).
- a $1,000 bond quoted at 96.4 has a price of $964 ($1,000 × 0.964).
- a $1,000 bond quoted at 102.8 has a price of $1,028 ($1,000 × 1.028).

Issuing Bonds Payable at Par

The journal entry to record the issuance of bonds payable depends on whether the bond is issued at par, at a discount, or at a premium. Let's assume that on April 1, 2014, Mackay Industries issues $500,000 of 8% bonds payable that mature in 10 years. The bonds will pay interest semiannually on March 31 and September 30 of each year. First, let's assume that the market rate of interest on April 1, 2014, is 8%. Because the stated interest rate equals the market interest rate, Mackay Industries will issue these bonds at maturity (par) value. The calculation of cash receipt for the bond is the sum of present value of the bond at maturity ($500,000) and the present value of the twenty interest payments ($20,000). The concept of present value is discussed in Appendix B. The present value of interest factors are in Table B-3 and Table B-4 of Appendix B. We will use the market rate, or yield, to discount the principal and interest payment amounts, and use the stated rate, or coupon rate, to calculate the interest payment. The cash receipt is calculated as follows:

Facts:
Principal: $500,000
Interest payments: $500,000 × 8% ÷ 2 = $20,000
Period: 10 years × 2 payments per year = 20 periods
Yield: 8% ÷ 2 = 4%

Cash Receipt:
Present value of Principal: $500,000 × PVIF$_{(4\%, 20)}$ = $500,000 × 0.4563 = $228,150
Present value of Interest Payments: $20,000 × PVIFA$_{(4\%, 20)}$ = $20,000 × 13.5903 = $ 271,806
                                                                        Cash Receipt = $500,000

The journal entry to record the receipt of cash and issuance of bonds payable is as follows:

DATE	ACCOUNTS	POST REF.	DR.	CR.
Apr 1	Cash		500,000	
	Bonds Payable			500,000
	Issued bonds at par.			

Interest payments occur March 31 and September 30 each year. Mackay Industries' first semiannual interest payment on September 30, 2014, is journalized as follows:

DATE	ACCOUNTS	POST REF.	DR.	CR.
Sep 30	Interest Expense		20,000*	
	Cash			20,000
	Paid semiannual interest.			

*$500,000 × 0.08 × 1/2

Each semiannual interest payment made until the bonds mature will be the same as the September 30, 2014, entry.

At maturity on March 31, 2024, after making the journal entry to record the final interest payment, Mackay Industries will record the repayment of the bonds as follows:

DATE	ACCOUNTS	POST REF.	DR.	CR.
2024				
Mar 31	Bonds Payable		500,000	
	Cash			500,000
	Repaid bonds at maturity.			

Now let's look at how bonds issued at a discount are accounted for.

Issuing Bonds Payable at a Discount

Suppose the market rate of interest is higher than 8% on April 1, 2014, when Mackay Industries issues the $500,000 of bonds. Remember from our previous discussion, if the market rate of interest is higher than the stated rate of interest, bonds will sell at a discount. Suppose the market rate of interest is 10% on April 1, 2014. The cash receipt and discount on bonds payable are calculated as follows:

Facts:

Principal: $500,000

Interest payments: $500,000 × 8% ÷ 2 = $20,000

Periods: 10 years × 2 payments per year = 20 periods

Yield: 10% ÷ 2 = 5%

Cash Receipt:

Present value of Principal: $500,000 × PVIF$_{(5\%, 20)}$ = $500,000 × 0.3769 = $188,450

Present value of Interest Payments: $20,000 × PVIF$_{(5\%, 20)}$ = $20,000 × 12.4622 = 249,244

Cash Receipt = $437,694

Bonds Payable at Maturity = $500,000

Discount on Bonds Payable = $(62,306)

Mackay Industries receives $437,694, instead of $500,000. The difference ($62,306) is the discount on bonds payable. Mackay Industries receives less money on the issuance date. However, at the maturity date, Mackay Industries will pay bondholders the whole $500,000. Mackay Industries makes the following journal entry to record the issuance of the bonds at a discount:

DATE	ACCOUNTS	POST REF.	DR.	CR.
Apr 1	Cash		437,694	
	Discount on Bonds Payable		62,306	
	Bonds Payable			500,000
	Issued bonds at discount.			

After posting, the bond accounts have the following balances:

Bonds Payable		Discount on Bonds Payable	
	500,000	62,306	

Discount on Bonds Payable is a contra account to Bonds Payable and, therefore, has a debit balance. Bonds payable *minus* the discount gives the **carrying amount** of the bonds. The carrying amount of the bonds represents the "net" bond liability that is carried on the company's books. The carrying value of Mackay Industries' bonds immediately after issue would be as follows:

Bonds Payable	$500,000
Less, Discount on Bonds Payable	52,306
Carrying Value of Bonds Payable	$437,694

Issuing Bonds Payable at a Premium

To illustrate a bond premium, let's change the Mackay Industries example. Suppose the market rate of interest is 6% on April 1, 2014, when Mackay Industries issues the $500,000 of bonds. Mackay Industries' 8% bonds are attractive when the market interest rate is less than 8% so investors will pay a premium to acquire them. In this case, Mackay Industries receives $574,400 cash upon issuance. The cash receipt and premium on bonds payable are calculated as follows:

Facts:

Principal: $500,000

Interest payments: $500,000 $\times$ 8% $\div$ 2 = $20,000

Periods: 10 years $\times$ 2 payments per year = 20 periods

Yield: 6% $\div$ 2 = 3%

Cash Receipt:

Present value of Principal: $500,000 $\times$ PVIF$_{(3\%, 20)}$ = $500,000 $\times$ 0.5537 = $276,850

Present value of Interest Payments: $20,000 $\times$ PVIF$_{(3\%, 20)}$ = $20,000 $\times$ 14.8775 = $\underline{297,550}$

Cash Receipt = $574,400

Bonds Payable at Maturity = $500,000

Premium on Bonds Payable = $\underline{\$~74,400}$

Mackay Industries receives $574,400, instead of $500,000. The difference ($74,400) is the premium on bonds payable. Mackay Industries receives more money on the issuance date. However, at the maturity date, Mackay Industries will pay bondholders the whole $500,000. Mackay Industries makes the following journal entry to record the issuance of the bonds at a premium:

DATE	ACCOUNTS	POST REF.	DR.	CR.
Apr 1	Cash		574,400	
	Premium on Bonds Payable			74,400
	Bonds Payable			500,000
	Issued bonds at premium.			

After posting, the bond accounts have the following balances:

Bonds Payable	Premium on Bonds Payable
500,000	74,400

Notice that Bonds Payable and Premium on Bonds Payable each have a credit balance. The Premium on Bonds Payable account is known as an **adjunct account**. Like a contra account, an adjunct account is a companion account to another account. However, unlike a contra account, an adjunct account serves to "add to" instead of "take away from" its companion account. Therefore, we add the Premium on Bonds Payable to Bonds Payable to determine the bond carrying value. The carrying value of the Mackay Industries' bonds immediately after issuance is as follows:

Bonds Payable	$500,000
Plus, Premium on Bonds Payable	74,400
Carrying Value of Bonds Payable	$574,400

Interest Expense on Bonds Payable with a Discount

When Mackay Industries issued the bonds, it received $437,694 but it still must repay $500,000 when the bonds mature. The $62,306 difference between what it received and what it must pay back (the discount) ultimately represents additional interest expense to Mackay Industries. This additional interest effectively raises Mackay Industries' true interest rate on the bonds to the market interest rate, 10%, which was higher than the stated interest rate of 8%. The discount is allocated to interest expense through the process of amortization.

The interest expense is calculated by taking the bond carrying value (borrowed amount) and multiplying by the market rate or yield. The interest payment is calculated by taking the par value and multiplying by the stated rate. The interest expense amount is not the same as the interest payment. The difference is the amortization amount. This method of calculating the amortization of discount on bonds payable is called the **effective interest method**. This is the preferred method because interest expense is calculated based on the amount owed.

Interest Expense Carrying Amount × Market Rate	−	**Interest Payment** Par Value × Stated Rate	=	**Amortization Amount**
($500,000 − $62,306) × 10% × ½	−	$500,000 × 8% × ½	=	$1,885

Using the effective interest method, Mackay Industries' first semi-annual interest payment is recorded as follows:

DATE	ACCOUNTS	POST REF.	DR.	CR.
Sep 30	Interest Expense		21,885	
	Discount on Bonds Payable			1,885
	Cash			20,000
	Paid semi-annual interest.			

However, Canadian private enterprises may choose to use *straight-line amortization*, if the amortization amount is not significantly different. The straight-line method is similar to the amortization of intangible assets, like patents, which we learned about in Chapter 8. Under straight-line amortization, the discount on bonds payable is divided by the number of periods; therefore, an equal amount of the discount is allocated to interest expense at the time of each semi-annual interest payment.

In our example, the discount on bonds payable is $62,306, and there are 20 semi-annual interest periods during the bonds' 10-year life. Therefore, 1/20 of the $62,306 bond discount ($3,115) is amortized each interest period. As a result, the interest expense is the sum of the amortization amount and interest payment.

Using the straight-line method, Mackay Industries' first semi-annual interest payment is recorded as follows:

DATE	ACCOUNTS	POST REF.	DR.	CR.
Sep 30	Interest Expense		23,115	
	Discount on Bonds Payable			3,115
	Cash			20,000
	Paid semi-annual interest.			

Discount on Bonds Payable has a debit balance. Therefore, when the bond discount is amortized, the Discount on Bonds Payable is credited to reduce its balance. As the balance in the discount account is reduced, the carrying value of the bonds increases. After 20 amortization entries, the discount will be reduced to zero and the carrying amount of the bonds payable will be $500,000.

Bonds Payable	$500,000
Less, Discount on Bonds Payable	-0-
Carrying Value of Bonds Payable	$500,000

At maturity, after making the journal entry to record the final interest payment, Mackay Industries will record the repayment of the bonds as follows:

DATE	ACCOUNTS	POST REF.	DR.	CR.
2024				
Mar 31	Bonds Payable		500,000	
	Cash			500,000
	Repaid bonds at maturity.			

Notice that the entry to record the repayment of the bonds is the same as it was for bonds that were issued at par. This is because, at maturity, the carrying value of the bonds is equal to the par value of the bonds.

Interest Expense on Bonds Payable with a Premium

When Mackay Industries issued the bonds it received $574,400 but it must pay back only $500,000 at maturity. The $74,400 difference between what it received and what it must pay back (the premium) ultimately represents a reduction of interest expense to Mackay Industries. This reduced interest effectively lowers Mackay Industries' true interest rate on the bonds to the market interest rate that was lower than the stated interest rate of 8%. As with a discount, a premium is allocated to interest expense through the process of amortization. Only, in the case of a premium, the amortization decreases interest expense over the life of the bonds.

Using the effective interest method, Mackay Industries' interest expense and the amortization of premium on bonds payable for the first 6 months is calculated as follows:

Interest Expense Carrying Amount × Market Rate	−	Interest Payment Par Value × Stated Rate	=	Amortization Amount
($500,000 + $74,400) × 6% × ½	−	$500,000 × 8% × ½	=	$(2,768)

Mackay Industries' first semi-annual interest payment is recorded as follows:

DATE	ACCOUNTS	POST REF.	DR.	CR.
Sep 30	Interest Expense		17,232	
	Premium on Bonds Payable		2,768	
	Cash			20,000
	Paid semi-annual interest.			

In our example, the premium on bonds payable is $74,400, and there are 20 semi-annual interest periods during the bonds' 10-year life. Therefore, using the straight-line method, 1/20 of the $74,400 bond premium ($3,720) is amortized each interest period. As a result, the interest expense is the sum of the amortization amount and interest payment.

Using the straight-line method, Mackay Industries' first semi-annual interest payment is recorded as follows:

DATE	ACCOUNTS	POST REF.	DR.	CR.
Sep 30	Interest Expense		16,280	
	Premium on Bonds Payable		3,720	
	Cash			20,000
	Paid semi-annual interest.			

As the balance in the premium account is reduced, the carrying value of the bonds decreases. At maturity on March 31, 2024, the bond premium will have been fully amortized (it will have a zero balance), and the bond's carrying amount will be $500,000 (the amount in the Bonds Payable account). Therefore, the entry to record the repayment of the bonds will be the same as it was when the bonds were issued at par or at a discount.

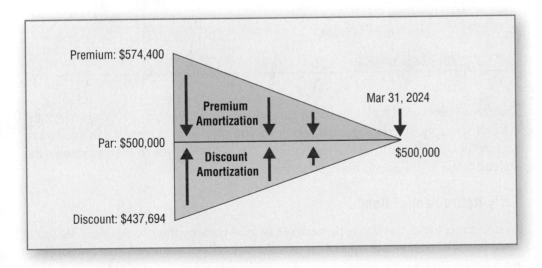

Exhibit 9-5 ▲

Adjusting Entries for Bonds Payable

Interest payments on bonds seldom occur on December 31, so interest expense must be accrued at year end. The accrual entry should also amortize any related bond discount or premium. Let's return to our Mackay Industries example where Mackay Industries sold $500,000 of bonds at a discount for $437,694 on April 1, 2014. Mackay Industries made an interest payment on September 30, 2014. Using the effective interest method, Mackay Industries' interest expense and the amortization of discount on bonds payable for three months is calculated as follows:

Interest Expense Carrying Amount × Market Rate	−	Interest Payment Par Value × Stated Rate	=	Amortization Amount
[($500,000 − ($62,306 − $1,885)] × 10% × 3/12	−	$500,000 × 8% × 3/12	=	$989

The balance of discount on bonds payable is $60,421 ($62,306 − $1,885) after the first interest payment on September 30. Therefore, the bond carrying value ($439,579) is higher than on the issuance date ($437,694). Since the bond carrying value, or the borrowed amount, is higher, thus, the interest expense is higher.

On December 31, Mackay Industries accrues interest and amortizes bond discount for three months (October, November, and December) as follows:

DATE	ACCOUNTS	POST REF.	DR.	CR.
Dec 31	Interest Expense		10,989	
	Discount on Bonds Payable			989
	Interest Payable			10,000
	Accrued three months interest expense.			

Interest payable is credited for the three months of interest owed to the bondholders, $10,000. The next semiannual interest payment occurs on March 31, 2015, and Mackay Industries makes the following journal entry:

DATE	ACCOUNTS	POST REF.	DR.	CR.
Mar 31	Interest Expense		10,989	
	Interest Payable		10,000	
	Discount on Bonds Payable			989
	Cash			20,000
	Paid semiannual interest.			

The interest expense of $10,989 and the discount on bonds payable of $989 are half of the 6-month amounts. Interest payable is debited for $10,000 to reflect the fact that the amount accrued at December 31, 2014, is being paid. The $20,000 credit to cash represents the stated interest that is paid to the bondholders.

Early Retirement of Bonds

As discussed earlier, the bonds principal will be paid back by the maturity date. However, some bonds may come with special features, such as offering the bond issuer or bondholders an option to retire the entire or part of the outstanding bonds before the bond maturity date. These are callable (redeemable) bonds. Companies might choose to retire their bonds early if the yield is significantly lower than the coupon rate. They can issue new bonds at the new yield and pay a lower interest rate than they are currently paying, and thus save on the interest payment.

Suppose the yield drops to 6% on April 1, 2020 from a yield of 10% when the bonds were issued on April 1, 2014 (with a stated rate of 8%). If Mackay Industries decides to call the bonds and issue new ones at the current yield, the semi-annual interest payment on $500,000 would be reduced from $20,000 to $15,000 ($500,000 × 6% × ½). Mackay Industries would save $5,000 every six months for 4 years until the maturity date. This means that Mackay Industries would save $35,098 ($5,000 × PVIFA$_{(3\%,\ 8)}$) on April 1, 2020.

Another option is for Mackay Industries to retire its bonds in the open market. Once Mackay Industries owns the bond it can retire it; however, it must offer to pay a price for the bonds that is attractive to the bondholders. This price is stated as a percentage of the par value. In this case, Mackay Industries decides to retire its bonds in the open market at 95½ (that is, 95.5% of par value). Mackay Industries needs to calculate whether there is a gain or loss as a result of the early retirement. The gain or loss on bond retirement is calculated as follows:

Carrying value of Bonds Payable on April 1, 2020:
Principal: $500,000
Interest payments: $500,000 × 8% ÷ 2 = $20,000
Periods remaining: 4 years × 2 payments per year = 8 periods
Yield on the issuing date (April 1, 2014): 10% ÷ 2 = 5%

Present value of Principal:	$500,000 × PVIF$_{(5\%,\ 8)}$ = $500,000 × 0.6768 = $338,400
Present value of Interest Payments:	$20,000 × PVIFA$_{(5\%,\ 8)}$ = $20,000 × 6.4632 = <u>129,264</u>
	Bonds Carrying Value on April 1, 2020 = $467,664
	Bonds Payable at Maturity = $500,000
	Discount on Bonds Payable on April 1, 2010 = <u>$(32,336)</u>

Cash payment for bonds retirement: $500,000 × 95½% = $477,500

Cash payment	$(477,500)
Carrying value of Bonds Payable	<u>467,664</u>
Loss on Bonds Retirement	<u>$ (9,836)</u>

Mackay Industries makes the following journal entry to record the bonds retirement:

DATE	ACCOUNTS	POST REF.	DR.	CR.
Apr 1, 2020	Bonds Payable		500,000	
	Loss on Bonds Retirement		9,836	
	Discount on Bonds Payable			32,336
	Cash			477,500
	Retired bonds at a loss.			

DECISION GUIDELINES

Decision	Guideline	Analyze
What should I do if my business needs more cash than the bank will lend me?	Consider issuing bonds.	With notes payable, a business typically borrows a large sum of money from one lender, usually a bank. With bonds, a business borrows smaller amounts, often in $1,000 increments, from many different investors. By utilizing bonds payable, a business can often borrow very large sums of money because no single investor is exposed to a significant amount of risk.

Lease Liabilities

A lease is an agreement in which one party (the lessee) agrees to pay another party (the lessor) for the use of an asset. Many businesses enter into leases for

- equipment such as computers, phone systems, and manufacturing equipment.
- vehicles, such as automobiles and delivery trucks.
- real estate, such as offices or warehouses.

Leases may be divided into two categories: operating leases and financial (capital) leases. The accounting treatment is different for each type of lease.

Operating Leases

An **operating lease** is basically a rental agreement. An operating lease grants the use of an asset to the lessee for the duration of the lease in exchange for regular payments. At the end of the lease, the lessee must return the leased asset to the lessor. The title (ownership) of the asset remains with the lessor. The lease payments are treated as an expense by the lessee and as revenue by the lessor. For example, assume that Mackay Industries entered into a lease agreement for the use of a copy machine. The agreement was an operating lease that required monthly payments of $250 for a three-year period. Mackay Industries would make the following entry to record the monthly lease payments:

DATE	ACCOUNTS	POST REF.	DR.	CR.
	Lease (or Rent) Expense		250	
	Cash			250
	Record monthly lease payment.			

At the end of the lease, Mackay Industries will return the copy machine to the lessor.

Financial or Capital Leases

A **financial** or **capital lease** is treated as a financed purchase. In other words, it is treated as if the lessee borrowed money to purchase the asset. IFRS and Canadian ASPE have similar accounting treatments for non-operating leases; however, the terminology used is different. For example, IFRS uses the term financial lease and Canadian ASPE uses the term capital lease. If a lease meets any one of the following criteria, it is classified as a financial or capital lease:

❶ Title (ownership) of the leased asset is transferred to the lessee at the end of the lease term.

❷ The lease contains a bargain purchase option. In other words, the lessee has the option to purchase the asset at a price significantly less than fair market value at the end of the lease term.

❸ The duration of the lease is a major portion of the economic life of the leased asset. IFRS does not provide quantitative thresholds, but the general practice in Canada is to use 75% or more of the estimated useful life of the leased asset as the major portion of the economic life.

❹ The present value of the lease payments equals substantially all of the fair value of the leased property at the inception of the lease. Ninety percent or more of the market value of the leased asset is usually used by Canadian companies. The concept of present value is discussed in Appendix B at the end of the book.

⑤ The leased assets are specialized so that only the lessee can use them without significant modifications.

Because a capital lease is treated as a financed purchase, the lessee will record the lease by debiting an asset account and crediting Lease Payable at the time the lease is entered into. For example, assume that Mackay Industries leases a delivery truck for a five-year period. The lease calls for monthly payments of $825 and has a bargain purchase option. Assume also that the liability under this capital lease is determined to be $38,000. (The calculation of the amount due under a financial or capital lease will be covered in more advanced accounting courses.) Mackay Industries would record the lease as follows:

DATE	ACCOUNTS	POST REF.	DR.	CR.
	Delivery Truck		38,000	
	Lease Payable			38,000
	Acquired truck under a capital lease.			

Lease payments made under a financial or capital lease agreement are similar to repayments of mortgage notes payable. The lessee allocates the lease payment between interest and principal, as demonstrated earlier in our discussion of accounting for mortgage note payments. Depreciation expense is recorded on a leased asset as it is for any other asset, as described in Chapter 8. As with mortgages, the principal portion of capital lease payments due within one year from the balance sheet date will be classified under current portion of long-term debt on the balance sheet.

DECISION GUIDELINES

Decision	**Guideline**	**Analyze**
When leasing an asset, am I better off with an operating lease or a capital lease?	Evaluate the costs and benefits associated with both types of leases.	The total lease payments made under an operating lease often seem to be expensive, especially considering that the asset must be returned at the end of the lease. However, operating leases are often attractive because they can take away some of the risks associated with owning an asset. Under an operating lease, the cost of repairing and maintaining the asset is often borne by the lessor. This helps the lessee budget his or her cash outflows knowing that they will not incur any unexpected repair bills. Also, with an operating lease, the risk of obsolescence of the asset is borne by the lessor.

HOW ARE LIABILITIES REPORTED ON THE BALANCE SHEET?

In Chapter 4, we learned how to prepare a classified balance sheet. Throughout the chapter, we have seen how all of a company's liabilities are classified as either current liabilities or long-term liabilities. This classification determines where the liabilities are reported on the company's classified balance sheet. An example of what the liabilities section of Mackay Industries' balance sheet might look like is presented in **Exhibit 9-6** on the following page.

 6 Report liabilities on the balance sheet

Mackay Industries Balance Sheet—Partial		
Current Liabilities:		
Accounts Payable		$ 2,200
Salaries Payable		8,700
Payroll Taxes Payable		2,610
Interest Payable		1,850
Sales Tax Payable		975
Estimated Warranty Payable		1,310
Unearned Revenue		1,400
Income Tax Payable		6,200
Current Portion of Long-Term Debt		11,700
Total Current Liabilities		36,945
Long-Term Debt		
Mortgage Payable		85,000
Bonds Payable, Net of $20,350 Discount		479,650
Lease Payable		36,650
Total Long-Term Debt		601,300
Total Liabilities		$638,245

Exhibit 9-6 ▲

Proper accounting for liabilities can also pose an ethical challenge. Classifying current liabilities as long-term, or vice versa, can have a big impact on a company's current ratio. Owners and managers may also be tempted to overlook expenses and their related liabilities at the end of the accounting period in an effort to make a business look more profitable. For example, a company might neglect to accrue warranty expense and the related warranty liability. This will cause reported liabilities and total expenses to be understated. Net income will also be overstated.

Provisions or contingent liabilities also pose an ethical challenge. Because contingencies are based on the outcome of a future event, they are easier to overlook. However, a contingency can turn into a real liability and can significantly change the company's financial position. Successful people refuse to play games with their accounting. Falsifying financial statements can result, and has resulted, in a prison term.

FOCUS ON DECISION MAKING: RATIOS

 7 Compute the debt ratio

In Chapter 4 we learned how the current ratio is used to analyze a business's ability to pay its obligations as they come due. The **debt ratio** also uses liabilities to help examine a business; however, instead of focusing on current liabilities, the debt ratio focuses on the total liabilities of an organization. The debt ratio is found by dividing the total liabilities (debt) of an organization by the total assets:

$$\text{Debt ratio} = \frac{\text{Total liabilities}}{\text{Total assets}}$$

The debt ratio reveals what percentage of a company's assets would be required to pay off all of its liabilities. The debt ratio is an indicator of a company's solvency. It is also a good indicator of a company's ability to incur, or take on, more debt. Let's assume that Mackay Industries has assets totalling $685,000, total liabilities of $425,000, and total shareholders' equity of $260,000. Mackay Industries' debt ratio is as follows:

$$\text{Debt ratio} = \frac{\text{Total liabilities}}{\text{Total assets}} = \frac{\$425,000}{\$685,000} = 62\% \text{ (rounded)}$$

Mackay Industries' debt ratio of 62% indicates that 62% of Mackay Industries' assets would be required to pay off all of its liabilitites. Another way of looking at it is that after paying off all liabilities, 38% of Mackay Industries' assets would be left for the shareholders. The higher the debt, the higher the leverage, and thus the higher the business risk. The average debt ratio for most companies ranges from 57% to 67%, with relatively little variation from company to company. Mackay Industries' debt ratio falls right in the middle of the range of industry averages.

FOCUS ON USERS

Concept	User	Why is this Important to this User?
Payroll liabilities		The union will be very interested in the recording of payroll liabilities to ensure that the elements that are removed from employees' paycheques are ultimately forwarded to the correct agencies and that they are recorded at the correct amounts. It could create quite a problem if pension amounts were recorded and accounted for incorrectly and not noticed until the employees retire.
Leases		The manager of a department needs to understand the difference between capital leases and operating leases to ensure that the lease is recorded properly. Each one has its own benefits and drawbacks and they are recorded very differently with significant impact on the financial statements depending on the type of lease. With the choice of lease type having an impact on the financial statements, this means that ultimately the net income and balance sheet items will be different between the two alternatives.
Debt ratio		The debt ratio will be watched by creditors as this ratio is a good indication of the long-term ability of the organization to pay its debt. A high ratio is not necessarily a bad thing because the debt ratio is very industry-dependent. Some industries will rely heavily on debt financing, while others may have very little debt financing, with each debt structure being a valid way of financing an organization. Competitor comparisons become quite important when examining the debt ratio and assessing whether or not the amount that was calculated is an indication of a strength or a weakness of the organization.

DEMO DOC

MyAccountingLab

Visit MyAccountingLab at www.
myaccountinglab.com to watch
animated versions of these Demo Docs.

L.O.

Known and Estimated Current Liabilities

Advantage Audio, Inc. began operations on January 1, 2014, selling personal music players. Each player comes with a one-year warranty included in the selling price. Advantage Audio, Inc. also sells digital songs that owners can download to their players. Customers prepay $100 for 100 songs and can download them whenever they wish.

During 2014, Advantage Audio, Inc. had the following information:

Sales revenue from sale of music players sold to customers	$100,000
Purchase cost of music players sold to customers.................................	$ 40,000
Sales tax rate (sales tax charged on player sales only)	7%
Music downloads purchased by customers..	20,000 songs
Songs downloaded by customers..	6,000 songs
Repairs made to players under warranty...	$ 1,200

Advantage Audio, Inc. estimates that the repairs it will have to make to music players under the warranty provided will cost 2% of the selling price. Advantage Audio, Inc. has made an upfront cash payment to contract with a local repair shop to service any players as required.

At December 31, 2014, Advantage Audio, Inc. estimated that of the remaining prepaid music downloads, 10,000 songs would be downloaded in 2015, with the rest downloaded in 2016.

Requirements:

❶ **Journalize the following transactions:**

   a. The sale of all music players in 2014 (assume cash sales)

   b. Payment of the year's sales taxes to the Canada Revenue Agency

   c. The sale of music downloads in 2014 (assume cash sales)

   d. Song downloads in 2014

   e. Repairs made under warranty in 2014

❷ **Are the following liabilities current or long-term for Advantage Audio, Inc.?**

   a. Sales Tax Payable

   b. Unearned Music Downloads Revenue

   c. Estimated Warranty Payable

Demo Doc Solutions

Requirement ❶

Journalize the following transactions:

Part 1	Part 2	Demo Doc Complete

   a. **The sale of all music players in 2014 (assume cash sales)**
      When the players are sold, a number of accounts are affected. First, Advantage Audio, Inc. must record the sales revenue and cash collected. We are told in the problem that $100,000 of music players were sold, so "Sales Revenue—Players" increases (credit) by $100,000.

Cash also increases, but is $100,000 the *only* amount the customers paid? No, in addition to the selling price, customers must also pay sales tax when they buy a player. The total cash paid by customers was $107,000 [$100,000 + ($100,000 × 7%)]. So, Cash is increased (debit) by $107,000.

The extra $7,000 ($100,000 × 7%) collected by Advantage Audio, Inc. *does not belong* to it. It belongs to the government and must be paid to the CRA at a future date. A future payment (or *obligation*) is a liability. Therefore, Advantage Audio, Inc. must record (credit) a Sales Tax Payable of $7,000.

DATE	ACCOUNTS	POST REF.	DR.	CR.
	Cash ($100,000 × 1.07)		107,000	
	Sales Revenue—Players			100,000
	Sales Tax Payable ($100,000 × 7%)			7,000
	Record sales for cash.			

In addition to recording the sales revenue, Advantage Audio, Inc. must record the cost of the players sold. The players cost $40,000 to purchase, so we must record (debit) Cost of Goods Sold for $40,000. As the players are sold, Inventory is also decreased (credit) by $40,000.

DATE	ACCOUNTS	POST REF.	DR.	CR.
	Cost of Goods Sold		40,000	
	Inventory			40,000
	Record cost of sales.			

One other issue must be addressed when recording the sales of the players: the warranties included in the selling price. Warranty costs are recorded at the time of sale so that the liabilities and the expenses are accurately reflected in the financial statements.

Advantage Audio, Inc. estimates that the warranty costs will be 2% of selling price, so Advantage Audio, Inc. must record (debit) Warranty Expense for $2,000 ($100,000 × 2%). Advantage Audio, Inc. is now *obligated* to pay for these repairs when customer players break down. In accounting, *a future obligation is a liability*. So, Advantage Audio, Inc. must record an Estimated Warranty Payable liability (credit) of $2,000.

DATE	ACCOUNTS	POST REF.	DR.	CR.
	Warranty Expense ($100,000 × 0.02)		2,000	
	Estimated Warranty Payable			2,000
	Record estimated warranty expense.			

b. Payment of the year's sales taxes to the CRA

The sales taxes must be sent to the government. When this payment is made, Sales Tax Payable is decreased (debit) by $7,000 and Cash is decreased (credit) by $7,000.

DATE	ACCOUNTS	POST REF.	DR.	CR.
	Sales Tax Payable		7,000	
	Cash			7,000
	Record payment of sales tax collected.			

Notice that this entry is nearly identical to the entry to record payment of general accounts payable.

c. The sale of music downloads in 2014 (assume cash sales)

The customer pays for the music downloads before he or she receives them. In other words, Advantage Audio, Inc. has received the cash but has not provided the songs yet. So, Advantage Audio, Inc. has an *obligation* (a liability) to provide these songs to the customer.

Advantage Audio, Inc. *has not yet earned* the download revenue because it has not yet provided the songs to customers. Revenue will be earned as customers download their songs.

With 20,000 songs prepaid for $1 per song, we must record Unearned Music Download Revenue (credit) of $20,000 (20,000 × $1). We must also record an increase in Cash (debit) of $20,000.

DATE	ACCOUNTS	POST REF.	DR.	CR.
	Cash		20,000	
	Unearned Music Download Revenue			20,000
	Record cash received for music downloads in advance of providing songs.			

d. Song downloads in 2014

Once songs are downloaded, Advantage Audio, Inc. earns the revenue from the sale of the songs. Then, it records "Sales Revenue—Music Downloads" of $6,000 (6,000 × $1). Because Advantage Audio, Inc. is now meeting its obligation to its customers by providing songs, the Unearned Music Download Revenue account is decreased (debit) by $6,000.

DATE	ACCOUNTS	POST REF.	DR.	CR.
	Unearned Music Download Revenue		6,000	
	Sales Revenue—Music Downloads (6,000 × $1)			6,000
	Record downloads revenue earned.			

After this transaction is recorded, the Unearned Revenue and related Sales Revenue accounts are as follows:

Unearned Music Download Revenue		
	(Downloads prepaid)	20,000
(Songs downloaded) 6,000		
	Dec 31 Bal	14,000

Sales Revenue—Music Downloads	
	6,000

e. Repairs made under warranty in 2014

When repairs are made under warranty, Advantage Audio's obligation to pay for these repairs is being met. This causes Estimated Warranty Payable to decrease (debit) by $1,200.

The repairs are being paid for in cash, so Cash is also decreased (credit) by $1,200.

DATE	ACCOUNTS	POST REF.	DR.	CR.
	Estimated Warranty Payable		1,200	
	Cash			1,200
	Record payment of warranty claims.			

Notice that warranty expense is *not* affected by this transaction! The expense was *already* recorded back when the players were sold (see Transaction a). To record warranty expense now would be double-counting the expense.

After this transaction is recorded, the warranty-related accounts are as follows:

Estimated Warranty Payable		
	(Players sold)	2,000
(Repairs made) 1,200		
	Dec 31 Bal	800

Warranty Expense
2,000

Requirement ❷

Are the following liabilities current or long-term for Advantage Audio, Inc.?

Part 1	**Part 2**	Demo Doc Complete

a. Sales Tax Payable

Governments usually do not want to wait long for their money. Most sales taxes are remitted to the government within one month (or sooner) of being collected. In this example, Advantage Audio, Inc. already remitted the 2014 sales taxes before the end of the year. A real company could send sales tax collections to the CRA once a month. Because sales tax liabilities are paid well within one year, the Sales Tax Payable account is a current liability.

b. Unearned Music Downloads Revenue

The prepaid music downloads are unearned revenue. But when will that revenue be earned? In 2014, 6,000 songs were downloaded, and Advantage Audio, Inc. expects that another 10,000 will be downloaded in 2015, with the remaining 4,000 songs (20,000 − 6,000 − 10,000) being downloaded in 2016.

At December 31, 2014, Advantage Audio, Inc. has an Unearned Music Download Revenue liability of $14,000 for 14,000 songs (see Transaction d). Of this $14,000, $10,000 is a current liability (because it will be earned during the next year of 2015 as songs are downloaded) and $4,000 is a long-term liability (for songs downloaded after 2015).

c. Estimated Warranty Payable

Warranties can cover many years, so it is possible that an Estimated Warranty Payable liability could have both current and long-term portions (as Advantage Audio's Unearned Revenue does). However, the warranties Advantage Audio, Inc. provides are only one year long, so we know that all obligations under the warranty will be met within one year. Therefore, the entire Estimated Warranty Payable is a current liability.

Demo Doc Complete

Part 1	Part 2	**Demo Doc Complete**

DECISION GUIDELINES

Accounting for Current Liabilities and Long-Term Debt

Within your business, you will likely encounter some, or all, of these decisions related to liabilities:

Decision	Guideline	Analyze
What should I do if I do not know the exact amount of a liability?	Use professional judgment and estimate the amount.	In order to properly reflect the true financial position and results of operations of a company, it is important that all obligations of the business be recorded. When the exact amount of a liability is unknown, an estimate of the amount owed should be made. It is important to use professional judgment to estimate a reasonable amount.
What should I do if my business needs more cash than the bank will lend me?	Consider issuing bonds.	With notes payable, a business typically borrows a large sum of money from one lender, usually a bank. With bonds, a business borrows smaller amounts, often in $1,000 increments, from many different investors. By utilizing bonds payable, a business can often borrow very large sums of money because no single investor is exposed to a significant amount of risk.
When leasing an asset, am I better off with an operating lease or a capital lease?	Evaluate the costs and benefits associated with both types of leases.	The total lease payments made under an operating lease often seem to be expensive, especially considering that the asset must be returned at the end of the lease. However, operating leases are often attractive because they can take away some of the risks associated with owning an asset. Under an operating lease, the cost of repairing and maintaining the asset is often borne by the lessor. This helps the lessee budget his or her cash outflows knowing that they will not incur any unexpected repair bills. Also, with an operating lease, the risk of obsolescence of the asset is borne by the lessor.

ACCOUNTING VOCABULARY

THE LANGUAGE OF BUSINESS

Adjunct account (p. 535) An account that is linked to another account (a companion account). An adjunct account will have a normal balance that is the same as its companion account.

Bonds payable (p. 530) Long-term, interest-bearing notes payable issued to multiple lenders called bondholders.

Callable bonds (p. 530) Bonds that the issuer may call or pay off at a specified price whenever the issuer wants.

Capital lease (p. 540) A term used by Canadian ASPE. A lease agreement that is treated as a financed purchase.

Carrying amount (p. 533) Bonds payable *minus* the discount or *plus* the premium.

Collateral (p. 528) Assets pledged to secure repayment of a loan. In the case of nonpayment by the borrower, the lender has the right to take the collateral.

Contingent liability (p. 518) A potential liability that depends on the outcome of a future event.

Convertible bonds (p. 530) Bonds that may be converted into the common shares of the issuing company at the option of the investor.

Current portion of long-term debt (p. 523) The principal portion of a long-term liability that is payable within one year.

Debentures (p. 530) Unsecured bonds backed only by the good faith of the borrower; also called *unsecured bonds*.

Debt ratio (p. 542) The ratio of a company's total liabilities (debt) to its total assets.

Discount (p. 530) Excess of a bond's maturity value over its issue price; also called a *bond discount*.

Effective interest method (p. 535) The calculation of interest on a bond based on the amount that is owed to bondholders.

Financial lease (p. 540) A term used by IFRS. A lease agreement that is treated as a financed purchase.

Market interest rate (p. 530) Interest rate investors are willing to pay for similar bonds of equal risk at the current time. Also called *yield*.

Maturity date (p. 530) The date on which the bond issuer (the borrower) must repay the principal amount to the bondholders.

Maturity value (p. 530) The amount a borrower must pay back to the bondholders on the maturity date; also called *principal amount* or *par value*.

Mortgage (p. 528) A long-term note payable that is secured by real estate.

Operating lease (p. 540) A lease (rental) agreement that grants the use of an asset to the lessee for the duration of the lease in exchange for regular payments.

Par value (p. 530) The amount a borrower must pay back to the bondholders on the maturity date; also called *principal amount* or *maturity value*.

Premium (p. 531) Excess of a bond's issue price over its maturity value; also called *bond premium*.

Principal amount (p. 530) The amount a borrower must pay back to the bondholders on the maturity date; also called *par value* or *maturity value*.

Provision (p. 518) A liability that that has uncertain timing or uncertain amount.

Secured bonds (p. 530) Bonds that give bondholders the right to take specified assets of the issuer if the issuer fails to pay principal or interest.

Serial bonds (p. 530) Bonds from the same bond issuance that mature at different times.

Stated interest rate (p. 530) Interest rate that determines the amount of cash interest the borrower pays and the investor receives each year. Also called the *coupon rate*.

Term bonds (p. 530) Bonds that all mature at the same time.

Unsecured bonds (p. 530) Bonds that are backed only by the general credit of the company issuing the bond; also called *debentures*.

Warranty (p. 523) A guarantee that a product or service is free from defect.

ACCOUNTING PRACTICE

DISCUSSION QUESTIONS

1. Provide an example of a known liability, an estimated liability, and a contingent liability or provision.

2. If a company with a 12/31 year-end were to borrow money in the form of a four-month note on 11/1, what accounts would be debited on 3/1 when it pays the note off?

3. What journal entry is made when unearned revenue is earned?

4. What is the difference between a current liability for an uncertain amount and a contingent liability? Give an example of each and demonstrate how they differ with respect to the difference that you identified in the first part of this question.

5. What is the distinguishing feature of each of the following types of bonds:
   a. Convertible   b. Callable   c. Secured
   d. Unsecured   e. Serial   f. Term

6. What do we know about the relationship between the market rate of interest and the stated interest rate for a particular bond when the bond is sold at
   a. par?   b. a premium?   c. a discount?

7. Will interest expense be greater than, less than, or equal to the interest payment made on bonds when the bonds are sold at
   a. par?   b. a premium?   c. a discount?

MyAccountingLab

Make the grade with MyAccountingLab. The exercises and problems in this chapter can be found on MyAccountingLab at www.myaccountinglab.com. You can practise them as often as you want, and they feature step-by-step guided solutions to help you find the right answer.

8. What happens to the difference between the carrying amount of bonds and the principal amount of the bonds over time?

9. What are the differences between an operating lease and a capital lease?

10. What are some ways that companies might use improper recording of liabilities to manipulate financial statements?

SELF CHECK

1. Known liabilities of uncertain amounts should be
   a. estimated and accrued when they occur.
   b. ignored; record them when they are paid.
   c. reported on the income statement.
   d. described in the notes to the financial statements.

2. On January 1, 2014, you borrowed $10,000 on a five-year, 8% note payable. At December 31, 2014, you should record a journal entry that includes which of the following?
   a. Note Payable of $10,000
   b. Nothing; the note has already been recorded
   c. Interest Payable of $800
   d. Cash receipt of $10,000

3. Your company sells $100,000 of goods and you collect sales tax of 3%. What current liability does the sale create?
   a. Accounts Payable of $3,000
   b. Unearned Revenue of $3,000
   c. Sales Revenue of $103,000
   d. Sales Tax Payable of $3,000

4. Sony owed Estimated Warranty Payable of $1,000 at the end of 2013. During 2014, Sony made sales of $100,000 and expects product warranties to cost the company 3% of the sales. During 2014, Sony paid $2,500 for warranties. What is Sony's Estimated Warranty Payable at the end of 2014?
   a. $1,500   b. $2,500   c. $3,000   d. $3,500

5. What is the term used to describe an unsecured bond?
   a. Debenture bond   b. Mortgage bond   c. Serial bond   d. Callable bond

6. Which interest rate on a bond determines the amount of the semiannual interest payment?
   a. Market rate   b. Effective rate   c. Stated rate   d. None of the above

7. Plavix Corporation's bonds payable carry a stated interest rate of 7%, and the market rate of interest at the time of issuance is 8%. Plavix Corporation's bonds will be sold at
   a. a premium.   b. a discount.   c. par value.   d. maturity value.

8. Bonds issued at a premium always have
   a. interest expense less than the interest payments.
   b. interest expense greater than the interest payments.
   c. interest expense equal to the interest payments.
   d. none of the above.

9. Milton's bonds pay interest semiannually on July 1 and January 1. If its fiscal year ends on September 30, which statement is *true* of Milton's year-end adjusting journal entry for bond interest?
   a. Milton must record three month's accrued interest expense and amortize three month's discount or premium.
   b. Milton will record nine month's accrued interest expense and amortize nine month's discount or premium.
   c. Milton must record three month's accrued interest expense only.
   d. Milton will record nine month's accrued interest expense and amortize three month's discount or premium.

10. A company recognizes a lease as a capital lease when

a. the lease term is less than a major portion of the estimated useful life of the leased asset.

b. the lease has no option to purchase the asset at the end of the lease term.

c. the lease transfers title of the leased asset to the lessee at the end of the lease term.

d. the present value of the lease payments is less than a significant portion of the market value of the leased asset.

Answers are given after Written Communication.

SHORT EXERCISES

S9-1. Accounting for notes payable (*Learning Objective 2*) 5–10 min.

On June 30, 2014, Harper, Co. purchased $9,000 of inventory for a one-year, 9% note payable. Journalize the following for the company:

  1. Accrual of interest expense on December 31, 2014

  2. Payment of the note plus interest on June 30, 2015

S9-2. Accounting for notes payable (*Learning Objective 2*) 5–10 min.

On September 30, 2014, Tucker, Co. borrowed $15,000 on a one-year, 7% note payable. What amounts would Tucker, Co. report for the note payable and the related interest payable on its balance sheet at December 31, 2014, and on its income statement for the year ended December 31, 2014?

S9-3. Warranties (*Learning Objective 3*) 5–10 min.

Lake Country Boats guarantees its boats for three years or 1,500 hours, whichever comes first. Past experience of other boat makers indicates that Lake Country can expect warranty costs will equal 6% of sales. Assume in its first year Lake Country Boats had sales totalling $600,000, receiving cash for 30% of sales and notes receivable for the remainder. Warranty payments totalled $22,000 during the year.

  1. Record the sales, warranty expense, and warranty payments for Lake Country Boats.

  2. Post relevant portions of the journal entries to the Estimated Warranty Payable T-account. At the end of the first year, how much in estimated warranty payable does Lake Country owe its customers?

  3. What amount of warranty expense will Lake Country report during its first year of operations? Does the warranty expense for the year equal the year's cash payments for warranties?

S9-4. Commitments and contingencies (*Learning Objective 4*) 5–10 min.

Phatboy Motorcycles, Inc., a motorcycle manufacturer, included the following note in its annual report:

Notes to Consolidated Financial Statements

9: Commitments and Contingencies

The Company self-insures its product liability losses in Canada up to $2.5 million.

Catastrophic coverage is maintained for individual claims in excess of $2.5 million up to $25 million.

  1. Why are product liability losses considered contingent liabilities?

  2. How can a contingent liability become a real liability for Phatboy Motorcycles?

S9-5. Accounting for mortgages (*Learning Objective 5*) 10–15 min.

Ling Company issued a $200,000, 8%, 30-year mortgage on January 1, 2014, to purchase a building. Payments of $8,840 are made semiannually. Complete the following amortization schedule (partial) for Ling Company.

Date	Payment	Interest	Principal	Loan Balance
Jan 1, 2014				$200,000
Jun 30, 2014	$8,840			
Dec 31, 2014				
Jun 30, 2015				
Dec 31, 2015				

S9-6. Accounting for mortgages (*Learning Objective 5*) 5–10 min.

Apex, Co. issued a $225,000, 9% mortgage on January 1, 2014. Payments of $10,900 are made semiannually on June 30 and December 31 each year. Calculate and record the journal entries for (a) issuance of the mortgage on January 1, 2014, and (b) the first semiannual payment on June 30, 2014.

S9-7. Bond terms (*Learning Objective 5*) 5–10 min.

Match the following terms with the correct definition.

.... 1. Bonds that all mature at the same time.

.... 2. Interest rate investors are willing to pay for similar bonds of equal risk.

.... 3. Unsecured bonds backed only by the good faith of the borrower.

.... 4. Amount of a bond's issue price over its maturity value.

.... 5. Bonds that may be converted into the common shares of the issuing company at the option of the investor.

.... 6. Amount of a bond's maturity value over its issue price.

.... 7. Interest rate that determines the amount of cash interest the borrower pays and the investor receives.

.... 8. Bonds in the same bond issuance that mature at different times.

.... 9. Bonds that the issuer may call or pay off at a specified price whenever the issuer wants.

a. Convertible bonds

b. Premium on bond

c. Callable bonds

d. Debentures

e. Term bonds

f. Serial bonds

g. Discount on bond

h. Stated interest rate

i. Market interest rate

S9-8. Determining the issue price for bonds (*Learning Objective 5*) 5–10 min.

Determine whether the following bonds payable will be issued at par, at a premium, or at a discount:

a. The market interest rate is 7%. Owens, Corp. issues bonds payable with a stated rate of 8 1/2%.

b. Bakers, Inc. issued 7% bonds payable when the market rate was 7 1/2%.

c. Saratoga Corporation issued 8% bonds when the market interest rate was 8%.

d. Tacoma Company issued bonds payable that pay cash interest at the stated rate of 7%. At the date of issuance, the market interest rate was 8 1/4%.

S9-9. Analyzing bond terms (*Learning Objective 5*) 10–15 min.

All Star Amusements is planning to issue long-term bonds payable to borrow for a major expansion. For each of the following questions, identify whether the bond price involves a discount, a premium, or par value.

   a. The stated interest rate on the bonds is 7%, and the market interest rate is 8%. What type of price can All Star Amusements expect for the bonds?

   b. All Star Amusements could raise the stated interest rate on the bonds to 9% (market rate is 8%). In that case, what type of price can All Star Amusements expect for the bonds?

   c. At what type of bond price will All Star Amusements have total interest expense equal to the cash interest payments?

   d. At which type of price will All Star Amusements' total interest expense be less than the cash interest payments?

   e. At which type of price will All Star Amusements' total interest expense be greater than the cash interest payments?

S9-10. Accounting for bonds (*Learning Objective 5*) 15–20 min.

Delta, Corp. issued 6%, five-year bonds payable with a maturity value of $5,000 on January 1, 2014. Journalize the following transactions and include an explanation for each entry. The market rate of interest equalled the stated rate at the date of issuance.

   a. Issuance of the bonds payable at par on January 1, 2014.

   b. Payment of semiannual interest on July 1, 2014.

   c. Payment of the bonds payable at maturity. (Give the date.)

S9-11. Accounting for bonds (*Learning Objective 5*) 15–20 min.

Hastings, Corp. issued 6%, five-year bonds payable with a maturity value of $5,000 at a price of $4,570 when the market rate was 8% on January 1, 2014. Journalize the following transactions for Hastings, Corp. Include an explanation for each entry.

   a. Issuance of the bonds payable on January 1, 2014.

   b. Payment of semiannual interest and amortization of bond discount on July 1, 2014. (Use the effective interest method to amortize the discount.)

S9-12. Accounting for bonds (*Learning Objective 5*) 15–20 min.

Hastings, Corp. issued 6%, five-year bonds payable with a maturity value of $5,000 at a price of $5,460 when the market rate was 4% on January 1, 2014. Journalize the following transactions for Hastings, Corp. Include an explanation for each entry.

   a. Issuance of the bonds payable on January 1, 2014.

   b. Payment of semiannual interest and amortization of bond premium on July 1, 2014. (Use the effective interest method to amortize the premium.)

S9-13. Accounting for bonds (*Learning Objective 5*) 15–20 min.

Hastings, Corp. issued 6%, five-year bonds payable with a maturity value of $5,000 at par on May 1, 2014. Assume that the fiscal year ends on December 31. Journalize the following transactions and include an explanation for each entry.

   a. Issuance of the bonds payable on May 1, 2014.

   b. Payment of the first semiannual interest amount on November 1, 2014.

   c. Accrual of semiannual interest expense on December 31, 2014.

S9-14. Classification of liability accounts as current or long-term. (*Learning Objective 6*) 5–10 min.

Identify the section of the balance sheet in which the following accounts would be located: Current Assets (CA), Long-Term Assets (LTA), Current Liabilities (CL), or Long-Term Liabilities (LTL).

_____ 1. Bonds Payable

_____ 2. Interest Payable

_____ 3. Leased Equipment

_____ 4. Discount on Bonds Payable

_____ 5. Accumulated Depreciation on Leased Equipment

_____ 6. Lease Payable (due in four years)

_____ 7. Mortgage Notes Payable

S9-15. Balance sheet disclosure of long-term liabilities (*Learning Objective 6*) 5–10 min.

FastTrack Magazine, Inc. includes the following selected accounts in its general ledger at December 31, 2014:

Mortgage Notes Payable	$100,000	Accounts Payable	$19,000
Lease Payable, Long-Term	20,000	Discount on Bonds Payable	6,000
Bonds Payable	350,000		
Interest Payable (due next year)	7,000		

Prepare the liabilities section of FastTrack Magazine's balance sheet at December 31, 2014, to show how the company would report these items. Report a total for current liabilities.

EXERCISES (GROUP A)

E9-1A. HST payable (*Learning Objective 2*) 5–10 min.

Make journal entries to record the following transactions. Explanations are not required.

Mar 31	Recorded cash sales of $200,000 for the month, plus HST of 13% collected for the Province of Ontario.
Apr 6	Sent March HST to CRA.

E9-2A. Accounting for notes payable (*Learning Objective 2*) 5–10 min.

Record the following note payable transactions of Lisbon, Corp. in the company's journal. Explanations are not required.

2014

May 1	Purchased equipment costing $15,000 by issuing a one-year, 6% note payable.
Dec 31	Accrued interest on the note payable.

2015

May 1	Paid the note payable at maturity.

E9-3A. Subscriptions (*Learning Objective 2*) 5–10 min.

Ozark Publishing Company completed the following transactions during 2014:

Nov 1	Sold a six-month subscription, collecting cash of $180, plus sales tax of 5%.
Dec 15	Remitted the sales tax to the CRA.
31	Made the necessary adjustment at year-end to record the amount of subscription revenue earned during the year.

Requirements

1. Journalize these transactions. Explanations are not required.

2. What amounts would Ozark Publishing Company report on the balance sheet at December 31, 2014?

E9-4A. Warranties (*Learning Objective 3*) 5–10 min.

The accounting records of Osgood Carpets showed a balance of $3,000 in Estimated Warranty Payable at December 31, 2013. In the past, Osgood's warranty expense has been 5% of sales. During 2014, Osgood made sales of $300,000 on account and paid $12,000 to satisfy warranty claims.

Quick solution: 2. December 31, 2014 balance in Estimated Warranty Payable = $6,000

Requirements

1. Journalize Osgood's sales, warranty expense, and cash payments made to satisfy warranty claims during 2014. Explanations are not required.

2. What balance of Estimated Warranty Payable will Osgood report on its balance sheet at December 31, 2014?

E9-5A. Accounting for mortgages (*Learning Objective 5*) 10–15 min.

Orbit, Corp. issued a $400,000, 10%, 15-year mortgage on January 1, 2014, to purchase warehouses.

Date	Payment	Interest	Principal	Loan Balance
Jan 1, 2014				$400,000
Jun 30, 2014	$26,021			
Dec 31, 2014				
Jun 30, 2015				
Dec 31, 2015				
Jun 30, 2016				

Requirements

1. Complete the amortization schedule for Orbit, Corp. assuming payments are made semiannually.

2. Record the journal entries for (a) issuance of mortgage on January 1, 2014, and (b) the first semiannual payment on June 30, 2014.

E9-6A. Accounting for bonds (*Learning Objective 5*) 15–20 min.

Pluto Corporation issued 8%, 20-year bonds payable with a maturity value of $500,000 on March 31. The bonds were issued at par and pay interest on March 31 and September 30. Record (a) issuance of the bonds on March 31, (b) payment of interest on September 30, and (c) accrual of interest on December 31.

E9-7A. Accounting for bonds (*Learning Objective 5*) 15–20 min.

On January 1, Quizmo, Corp. issues 8%, 20-year bonds payable with a maturity value of $100,000. The bonds sell at 98 and pay interest on January 1 and July 1. Quizmo, Corp. amortizes any bond discount or premium by the straight-line method. Record (a) the issuance of the bonds on January 1, and (b) the semian-nual interest payment and amortization of any bond discount or premium on July 1.

E9-8A. Accounting for bonds (*Learning Objective 5*) 15–20 min.

Datil, Inc. issued $100,000 of 10-year, 6% bonds payable on January 1. Datil, Inc. pays interest each January 1 and July 1 and amortizes any discount or premium by the straight-line method. Datil, Inc. can issue its bonds payable under various conditions:

a. Issuance at par value

b. Issuance at a price of $90,000 when the market rate was 7%

c. Issuance at a price of $105,000 when the market rate was 5.5%

Requirements

1. Journalize Datil's issuance of the bonds and first semiannual interest payment for each situation. Explanations are not required.

2. Which condition results in the most interest expense for Datil, Inc.? Explain in detail.

E9-9A. Classifying notes payable as current or long-term (*Learning Objective 5 & 6*) 10–15 min.

Carruthers Medical Group borrowed $300,000 on July 1, 2014, by issuing a 9% long-term note payable that must be paid in three equal annual instalments plus interest each July 1 for the next three years.

Requirement

1. Insert the appropriate amounts to show how Carruthers would report its current and long-term liabilities.

	December 31		
	2014	**2015**	**2016**
Current Liabilities:			
Current Portion of Long-Term Note Payable	$	$	$
Interest Payable			
Long-Term Liabilities:			
Long-Term Note Payable			

E9-10A. Balance sheet disclosure of liabilities (*Learning Objective 6*) 15–20 min.

At December 31, Deming Drapes owes $50,000 on accounts payable, plus salary payable of $14,000 and income tax payable of $8,000. Deming Drapes also has $300,000 of bonds payable that require payment of a $30,000 instalment next year and the remainder in later years. The bonds payable also require an interest payment of $7,000 at the end of each year. Report Deming Drapes' liabilities on its year-end classified balance sheet.

E9-11A. Debt ratio (*Learning Objective 7*) 5–10 min.

Appleway Company had the following balances as of December 31, 2014:

Total Current Assets	$ 87,000
Total Long-Term Assets	358,000
Total Current Liabilities	42,000
Total Long-Term Liabilities	217,000
Total Shareholders' Equity	186,000

Requirement

1. Calculate Appleway Company's debt ratio as of December 31, 2014. Does it appear that Appleway Company is in a position to take on more debt?

E9-12A. Accounting for bonds (*Learning Objective 5*) 20–25 min.

Jung Inc. issued $500,000 of 10-year, 7% bonds payable on April 1, when the market rate was 8%. Jung, Inc. pays interest each September 30 and March 31 and amortizes any discount or premium by the effective interest method. Jung's year-end is December 31.

Requirements

1. Calculate the cash receipt for the bond issuance.

2. Journalize Jung's issuance of the bonds.

3. Journalize Jung's first semiannual interest payment, year-end adjustment, and the second semi-annual interest payment. Explanations are not required.

E9-13A. Accounting for bonds and bonds retirement (*Learning Objective 5*) 20–25 min.

Yamada Inc. issued $1,000,000 of 5-year, 5% bonds payable on January 1, 2014, when the market rate was 6%. Yamada Inc. pays interest each June 30 and December 31 and amortizes any discount or premium by the effective interest method. On July 1, 2017, Yamada retired 60% of its bonds at 99.5 in the open market.

Requirements

1. Calculate the cash receipt for the bond issuance.

2. Calculate the bond carrying value on July 1, 2017.

3. Calculate the gain or loss on bond retirement.

4. Journalize Yamada's issuance of the bonds on January 1, 2014 and bond retirement on July 1, 2017.

E9-14A. Accounting for payroll payable (*Learning Objective 2*) 15–20 min.

The following is Kiten's payroll information on employees' deductions for December:

Gross Pay	EI	CPP	Income Tax	Union Dues
52,000	910	2,574	10,400	520

Kiten pays its employees at the end of each month, and is required to remit employees' deductions and payroll payable to CRA by January 15.

Requirements

1. Record the journal entries for the salary expense and employee benefit expense on December 31.

2. Record the journal entry for the remittance to CRA on January 15.

E9-15A. Accounting treatment of provisions and contingent liabilities (*Learning Objective 3*) 10–15 min.

Wulai Company is facing the following situations, and the owner of the company needs your help in identify the accounting treatment:

1. A customer sued Wulai for selling a defective product. The time that the customer took to fix the defective product caused the customer's company productivity loss, which was estimated around $30,000. Wulai claimed that the product was not defective, but was misused by the customer. Wulai's lawyer is confident that the court will dismiss the case.

2. A competitor sued Wulai for infringing their patent for one of Wulai's best-selling smart phones. The court has awarded the plantiff $1 million. The owner of Wulai is appealing the case and believes that the company will win the lawsuit, but the lawyers believe that it could lose the appeal.

Requirements

Determine the appropriate accounting treatment. Based on your analysis, identify whether the company should (1) recognize a provision, (2) disclose a provision liability, or (3) determine no disclosure is required.

EXERCISES (GROUP B)

E9-1B. Sales tax payable (*Learning Objective 2*) 5–10 min.

Make journal entries to record the following transactions. Explanations are not required.

Aug 31	Recorded cash sales of $770,000 for the month, plus sales tax of 7% collected for the Province of Alberta.
Sep 6	Sent August sales tax to the CRA.

E9-2B. Accounting for notes payable (*Learning Objective 2*) 5–10 min.

Record the following note payable transactions of Concilio, Corp. in the company's journal. Explanations are not required.

2014	
Oct 1	Purchased equipment costing $8,000 by issuing a one-year, 8% note payable.
Dec 31	Accrued interest on the note payable.

2015	
Oct 1	Paid the note payable at maturity.

E9-3B. Subscriptions (*Learning Objective 2*) 5–10 min.

TransWorld Publishing Company completed the following transactions during 2014:

Aug 1	Sold a six-month subscription, collecting cash of $3,000, plus sales tax of 4%.
Dec 15	Remitted the sales tax to the provincial tax authority.
31	Made the necessary adjustment at year-end to record the amount of subscription revenue earned during the year.

Requirements

1. Journalize these transactions. Explanations are not required.

2. What amounts would TransWorld Publishing Company report on the balance sheet at December 31, 2014?

E9-4B. Warranties (*Learning Objective 3*) 5–10 min.

The accounting records of Atkinson Books showed a balance of $2,000 in Estimated Warranty Payable at December 31, 2013. In the past, Atkinson's warranty expense has been 6% of sales. During 2014, Atkinson made sales of $329,000 on account and paid $6,000 to satisfy warranty claims.

Requirements

1. Journalize Atkinson's sales, warranty expense, and cash payments made to satisfy warranty claims during 2014. Explanations are not required.
2. What balance of Estimated Warranty Payable will Atkinson report on its balance sheet at December 31, 2014?

E9-5B. Accounting for mortgages (*Learning Objective 5*) 10–15 min.

Jupiter, Corp. issued a $500,000, 8%, 15-year mortgage on January 1, 2014, to purchase warehouses.

Date	Payment	Interest	Principal	Loan Balance
Jan 1, 2014				$500,000
Jun 30, 2014	$28,915			
Dec 31, 2014				
Jun 30, 2015				
Dec 31, 2015				
Jun 30, 2016				

Requirements

1. Complete the amortization schedule for Jupiter, Corp. assuming payments are made semiannually.
2. Record the journal entries for (a) issuance of the mortgage on the January 1, 2014, and (b) the first semiannual payment on June 30, 2014.

E9-6B. Accounting for bonds (*Learning Objective 5*) 15–20 min.

Daffy Corporation issued 4%, 20-year bonds payable with a maturity value of $330,000 on January 31. The bonds were issued at par and pay interest on January 31 and July 31. Record (a) issuance of the bonds on January 31, (b) payment of interest on July 31, and (c) accrual of interest on December 31.

E9-7B. Accounting for bonds (*Learning Objective 5*) 15–20 min.

On January 1, Danvers, Corp. issues 5%, four-year bonds payable with a maturity value of $110,000. The bonds sell at 94 and pay interest on January 1 and July 1. Danvers, Corp. amortizes any bond discount or premium by the straight-line method. Record (a) the issuance of the bonds on January 1, and (b) the semiannual interest payment and amortization of any bond discount or premium on July 1.

E9-8B. Accounting for bonds (*Learning Objective 5*) 15–20 min.

Jefferson, Inc. issued $200,000 of 10-year, 4% bonds payable on January 1. Jefferson, Inc. pays interest each January 1 and July 1 and amortizes any discount or premium by the straight-line method. Jefferson, Inc. can issue its bonds payable under various conditions:

a. Issuance at par value
b. Issuance at a price of $130,000 when the market rate is 6.2%

c. Issuance at a price of $250,000 when the market rate is 3.2%

Requirements

1. Journalize Jefferson's issuance of the bonds and first semiannual interest payment for each situation. Explanations are not required.

2. Which condition results in the most interest expense for Jefferson, Inc.? Explain in detail.

E9-9B. Classifying notes payable as current or long-term (*Learning Objective 5 & 6*) 10–15 min.

Bon Secour Medical Group borrowed $600,000 on July 1, 2014, by issuing a 14% long-term note payable that must be paid in three equal annual instalments plus interest each July 1 for the next three years.

Requirement

1. Insert the appropriate amounts to show how Bon Secour would report its current and long-term liabilities.

	December 31		
	2014	**2015**	**2016**
Current Liabilities:			
Current Portion of Long-Term Note Payable	$	$	$
Interest Payable			
Long-Term Liabilities:			
Long-Term Note Payable			

E9-10B. Balance sheet disclosure of liabilities (*Learning Objective 6*) 15–20 min.

At December 31, Trumpette Drapes owes $59,000 on accounts payable, plus salary payable of $15,000 and income tax payable of $13,000. Trumpette Drapes also has $270,000 of bonds payable that require payment of a $25,000 instalment next year and the remainder in later years. The bonds payable also require an interest payment of $5,500 at the end of each year. Report Trumpette Drapes' liabilities on its year-end classified balance sheet.

E9-11B. Debt ratio (*Learning Objective 7*) 5–10 min.

Pine City Company had the following balances as of December 31, 2014:

Total Current Assets	$154,000
Total Long-Term Assets	501,000
Total Current Liabilities	95,000
Total Long-Term Liabilities	195,000
Total Shareholders' Equity	365,000

Requirement

1. Calculate Pine City Company's debt ratio as of December 31, 2014. Does it appear that Pine City Company is in a position to take on more debt?

E9-12B. Accounting for bonds (*Learning Objective 5*) 20–25 min.

Yip Inc. issued $800,000 of 8-year, 9% bonds payable on October 1, when the market rate was 8%. Yip Inc. pays interest each March 31 and September 30 and amortizes any discount or premium by the effective interest method. Yip's year-end is December 31.

Requirements

1. Calculate the cash receipt for the bond issuance.

2. Journalize Yip's issuance of the bonds.

3. Journalize Yip's first semiannual interest payment, year-end adjustment, and the second semiannual interest payment. Explanations are not required.

E9-13B. Accounting for bonds and bonds retirement (*Learning Objective 5*) 20–25 min.

Tran Inc. issued $1,500,000 of 8-year, 7% bonds payable on July 1, 2014 when the market rate was 6%. Tran Inc. pays interest each June 30 and December 31 and amortizes any discount or premium by the effective interest method. On January 1, 2019, Tran retired 50% of its bonds at 101.5 in the open market.

Requirements

1. Calculate the cash receipt for the bond issuance.

2. Calculate the bond carrying value on January 1, 2019.

3. Calculate the gain or loss on bond retirement.

4. Journalize Tran's issuance of the bonds on January 1, 2014, and bond retirement on January 1, 2019.

E9-14B. Accounting for payroll payable (*Learning Objective 2*) 15–20 min.

The following is Hoshi's payroll information on employees' deductions for March:

Gross Pay	EI	CPP	Income Tax	Extended Health Insurance
68,000	1,190	3,366	16,320	1,360

Hoshi pays its employees at the end of each month, and is required to remit employees' deductions and payroll payable to CRA by April 15.

Requirements

1. Record the journal entries for the salary expense and employee benefit expense on March 31.

2. Record the journal entry for the remittance to CRA on April 15.

E9-15B. Accounting treatment of provisions and contingent liabilities (*Learning Objective 3*) 10–15 min.

Chemco Company is facing the following situations, and the owner of the company needs your help in identify the accounting treatment:

1. In making one of Chemco's products, Chemco leaked out waste into a nearby lake. Under provincial law, Chemco has to clean the polluted lake and also pay a fine. The total estimates for the incident would likely be about $3 million.

2. A customer purchased pesticides from Chemco. The customer was injured due to inappropriate handling of the pesticides. The customer is suing Chemco $100,000 for his damage.

Requirements

Determine the appropriate accounting treatment. Based on your analysis, identify whether the company should (1) recognize a provision, (2) disclose a provision liability, or (3) determine no disclosure is required.

EXERCISES (ALTERNATES 1, 2, AND 3)

These alternative exercise sets are available for your practice benefit at
www.myaccountinglab.com

PROBLEMS (GROUP A)

P9-1A. Accounting for several current liabilities (*Learning Objectives 2 & 3*) 20–25 min.

The following transactions of My Dollar stores occurred during 2014 and 2015:

2014	
Feb 3	Purchased equipment for $10,000, signing a six-month, 9% note payable.
28	Recorded the week's sales of $51,000, one-third for cash, and two-thirds on account. All sales amounts are subject to a 5% sales tax.
Mar 7	Sent last week's sales tax to the CRA.
Apr 30	Borrowed $100,000 on a four-year, 9% note payable that calls for annual payments of interest each April 30.
Aug 3	Paid the six-month, 9% note at maturity.
Nov 30	Purchased inventory at a cost of $7,200, signing a three-month, 8% note payable for that amount.
Dec 31	Accrued warranty expense, which is estimated at 3% of total sales of $260,000.
31	Accrued interest on all outstanding notes payable. Accrued interest for each note separately.
2015	
Feb 28	Paid off the 8% inventory note, plus interest, at maturity.
Apr 30	Paid the interest for one year on the long-term note payable.

Requirement

1. Record the transactions in the company's journal. Explanations are not required.

P9-2A. Accounting for several current and long-term liabilities (*Learning Objectives 2, 3, & 5*) 20–25 min.

Following are pertinent facts about events during the current year at Greely Snowboards.

a. December sales totalled $404,000, and Greely collected sales tax of 5%. The sales tax will be sent to Ontario early in January.

b. Greely owes $75,000 on a long-term note payable. At December 31, 6% interest for the year plus $25,000 of principal are payable within one year.

c. On August 31, Greely signed a six-month, 6% note payable to purchase a machine costing $80,000. The note requires payment of principal and interest at maturity.

d. Sales of $909,000 were covered by the Greely product warranty. At January 1, estimated warranty payable was $11,300. During the year, Greely recorded warranty expense of $27,900 and paid warranty claims of $30,100.

e. On October 31, Greely received cash of $2,400 in advance for the rent on a building. This rent will be earned evenly over six months.

Requirement

1. For each item, indicate the account and the related amount to be reported as a current liability on Greely's December 31 balance sheet.

P9-3A. Accounting for mortgages (*Learning Objective 5*) 20–25 min.

Jordan, Corp. completed the following transactions in 2014:

Jan 1	Purchased a building costing $100,000 and signed a 10-year, 10% mortgage note payable for the same amount.
Jun 30	Made the first semiannual payment on the mortgage note payable.
Dec 1	Signed a five-year lease to rent a warehouse for $7,000 per month due at the end of each month. The lease is considered an operating lease.
31	Paid for one month's rent on the warehouse.
31	Purchased 10 copiers and signed a $40,000, four-year lease with the option to buy the copiers at the end of the fourth year at a bargain price.
31	Made the second semiannual payment on the mortgage note payable.

Requirements

1. Complete the following amortization schedule for the first four mortgage payments on the $100,000 mortgage note, assuming semiannual payments of $8,024.

Date	Payment	Interest	Principal	Loan Balance
Jan 1, 2014				$100,000
Jun 30, 2014	$8,024			
Dec 31, 2014				
Jun 30, 2015				
Dec 31, 2015				

2. Record the journal entries for the 2014 transactions.

3. Prepare the long-term liabilities section of the balance sheet on December 31, 2014.

P9-4A. Analyzing bond terms and accounting for bonds (*Learning Objective 5*) 20–25 min.

Assume that on April 1, 2014, Roland, Corp. issues 8%, 10-year bonds payable with a maturity value of $400,000. The bonds pay interest on March 31 and September 30. Roland's fiscal year-end is December 31.

Requirements

1. If the market interest rate is 7 1/2% when Roland, Corp. issues its bonds, will the bonds be priced at par, at a premium, or at a discount? Explain.

2. If the market interest rate is 9% when Roland, Corp. issues its bonds, will the bonds be priced at par, at a premium, or at a discount? Explain.

3. Assume that the issue price of the bonds is $404,000. Journalize the following bonds payable transactions, first using the straight-line method and second using the effective interest method (Note: you will need a financial calculator to calculate the market rate for the effective interest method):

   a. Issuance of the bonds on April 1, 2014.

   b. Payment of interest and amortization of premium on September 30, 2014.

   c. Accrual of interest and amortization of premium on December 31, 2014.

   d. Payment of interest and amortization of premium on March 31, 2015.

P9-5A. Analyzing bond terms and accounting for bonds (*Learning Objective 5*) 20–25 min.

On January 1, 2014, Cave Creek Golf Club issued $600,000 of 20-year, 9% bonds payable. The bonds were sold for $600,000. The bonds pay interest each June 30 and December 31 and any discount or premium is amortized using effective interest amortization.

Requirements

1. Fill in the blanks to complete these statements:

   a. Cave Creek Golf Club's bonds are priced at (express the price as a percentage) _____.

   b. When Cave Creek Golf Club issued its bonds, the market interest rate was (higher than, lower than, or equal to) _____ 9%.

   c. The amount of bond discount or premium is $ _____.

2. Record the following transactions:

   a. Issuance of the bonds payable on January 1, 2014.

   b. Payment of interest (and amortization of discount or premium, if any) on June 30, 2014.

   c. Payment of interest (and amortization of discount or premium, if any) on December 31, 2014. Explanations are not required.

3. At what amount will Cave Creek Golf Club report the bonds on its balance sheet at December 31, 2014?

Quick solution: Total current liabilities = $153,000; total long-term liabilities = $383,000

P9-6A. Balance sheet disclosure of long-term liabilities (*Learning Objective 6*) 15–20 min.

The accounting records of Stokes, Corp. include the following items at December 31, 2014:

Salary Payable	$32,000	Accounts Payable	$ 60,000
Bonds Payable,		Mortgage Note Payable,	
Current Portion	25,000	Long-Term	90,000
Discount on Bonds Payable	7,000	Interest Payable	20,000
Income Tax Payable	16,000	Bonds Payable	300,000

Requirement

1. Report these liabilities on Stokes' balance sheet at December 31, 2014, including headings.

P9-7A. Calculation of debt ratio (Learning Objective 7) 10–15 min.

The classified balance sheet for Tipke, Inc. as of December 31, 2014, is presented next.

Tipke, Inc.
Balance Sheet
December 31, 2014

Current Assets:			Current Liabilities:	
Cash		$ 17,500	Accounts Payable	$ 1,100
Accounts Receivable		5,400	Salary Payable	2,400
Supplies		400	Unearned Service Revenue	650
Prepaid Rent		3,600	Note Payable	10,000
Total Current Assets		26,900	Total Current Liabilities	14,150
Fixed Assets:			Long-Term Debt:	
Land		55,000	Mortgage Note Payable	10,000
Equipment	38,000		Bonds Payable	140,000
Less Accumulated			Total Long-Term Debt	150,000
Depreciation, Equipment	8,000	30,000		
			Shareholders' Equity:	
Building	225,000		Common Shares	20,000
Less Accumulated			Retained Earnings	122,750
Depreciation, Building	30,000	195,000	Total Shareholders' Equity	142,750
Total Fixed Assets		280,000	Total Liabilities and	
Total Assets		$306,900	Shareholders' Equity	$306,900

Requirements

1. Calculate Tipke's debt ratio as of December 31, 2014.
2. What percentage of Tipke's assets belong to the shareholders?
3. Would you be willing to extend credit to Tipke, Inc.? Why or why not?

P9-8A. Accounting for bonds (Learning Objective 5) 30–35 min.

Misan Inc. is planning to issue $2,000,000, 5-year, 6% bonds. Interest is payable semiannually each June 30 and December 31. All of the bonds will be sold on July 1, 2014; they mature on June 30, 2019. Misan's year-end is December 31.

Requirements

1. Compute the issue (sale) price on July 1, 2014, if the yield is:
   (a) 6%
   (b) 8%
   (c) 4%
2. Prepare all journal entries for the above three cases in 2014.
3. Prepare all journal entries for the above three cases in 2015, using the effective interest method.
4. Show how the bond interest expense and the bonds payable, for each case, should be reported on the annual financial statements for 2014 and 2015.

P9-9A. Accounting for bonds, year-end adjustment, and bond retirement (Learning Objective 5) 30–35 min.

Lamon Inc. issued $1,000,000, 5-year, 7% bonds on March 1, 2014, when the yield was 6%. Interest is payable semiannually each August 31 and February 28. All of the bonds were sold on March 1, 2014; they mature on February 28, 2019. Lamon's year-end is December 31.

Requirements

1. Compute the issue (sale) price on March 1, 2014.

2. Record all journal entries for 2014. Lamon used the effective interest method.

3. Record the journal entry for the interest payment on February 28, 2015.

4. Assume on September 1, 2016, Lamon retired 70% of its bonds at 102.75. What is the carrying value of the bonds payable? Calculate the gain or loss on the bond retirement.

5. Record the journal entry for the bond retirement on September 1, 2016.

P9-10A. Accounting for various short-term and long-term liabilities and their impact on the debt ratio (*Learning Objectives 2, 3, 6, & 7*) 30–35 min.

Binco Inc. completed the following transactions during month of December. The company's fiscal year ends on December 31. The HST of 13% is included on all purchases and sales. Cost of goods sold is 60% of the sales.

December	1	Borrowed $50,000 from the PC Bank by signing a five-year note at 6% interest rate. The interest is paid monthly on the 1st of the month.
	3	Purchased merchandise inventory on credit for $50,850, terms 2/10, n/30. Binco uses a perpetual inventory system.
	8	Sold merchandise on credit for $14,125, including HST, terms 2/10, n/30.
	15	Leased a photocopier with a fair value of $50,000. The present value of the monthly payments, $500 for 5 years, represents a major portion of the fair value of the photocopier.
	17	Received a cheque from a customer who purchased merchandise on December 8.
	20	Purchased merchandise inventory on credit for $40,680, (including HST) terms 2/10, n/30.
	24	Received a $300 deposit for back-ordered merchandise to be shipped at the beginning of the new year.
	31	Salary Expense for the month was $10,000, of which employees deductions included CPP, $450; EI, $160; and income tax, $2,400. Binco also recorded the employee benefits expense.

Requirements

1. Record all journal entries, including adjusting entries, for the month of December.

2. Show the liability section of the balance sheet on December 31.

3. Identify the impact on the debt ratio—(1) no change, (2) increase, or (3) decrease, after each transaction is complete. Identify each transaction as an independent case, rather than a cumulative effect. Assume that the debt ratio is at 50% and current ratio is 1.5 before considering each transaction.

PROBLEMS (GROUP B)

P9-1B. Accounting for several current liabilities (*Learning Objectives 2 & 3*)
20–25 min.

The following transactions of Crazy Craft stores occurred during 2014 and 2015:

2014

Feb 3	Purchased equipment for $11,000, signing a six-month, 8% note payable.
28	Recorded the week's sales of $93,000, one-third for cash, and two-thirds on account. All sales amounts are subject to a 5% sales tax.
Mar 7	Sent last week's sales tax to the CRA.
Apr 30	Borrowed $110,000 on a four-year, 10% note payable that calls for annual payment of interest each April 30.
Aug 3	Paid the six-month, 8% note at maturity.
Nov 30	Purchased inventory at a cost of $6,000, signing a three-month, 5% note payable for that amount.
Dec 31	Accrued warranty expense, which is estimated at 4% of total sales of $250,000.
31	Accrued interest on all outstanding notes payable. Accrued interest for each note separately.

2015

Feb 28	Paid off the 5% note, plus interest, at maturity.
Apr 30	Paid the interest for one year on the long-term note payable.

Requirement

1. Record the transactions in the company's journal. Explanations are not required.

P9-2B. Accounting for several current and long-term liabilities (*Learning Objectives 2, 3, & 5*) 20–25 min.

Following are pertinent facts about events during the current year at Laughton Snowboards.

  a. December sales totalled $405,000, and Laughton collected sales tax of 5%. The sales tax will be sent to Alberta early in January.

  b. Laughton owes $70,000 on a long-term note payable. At December 31, 6% interest for the year plus $45,000 of principal are payable within one year.

  c. On August 31, Laughton signed a six-month, 6% note payable to purchase a machine costing $78,000. The note requires payment of principal and interest at maturity.

  d. Sales of $101,000 were covered by a Laughton product warranty. At January 1, estimated warranty payable was $11,100. During the year, Laughton recorded warranty expense of $27,800 and paid warranty claims of $30,050.

  e. On October 31, Laughton received cash of $3,990 in advance for the rent on a building. This rent will be earned evenly over six months.

Requirement

1. For each item, indicate the account and the related amount to be reported as a current liability on Laughton's December 31 balance sheet.

P9-3B. Accounting for mortgages (*Learning Objective 5*) 20–25 min.

Franco, Corp. completed the following transactions in 2014:

Jan 1	Purchased a building costing $140,000 and signed a 10-year, 11% mortgage note payable for the same amount.
Jun 30	Made the first semiannual payment on the mortgage note payable.
Dec 1	Signed a five-year lease to rent a warehouse for $9,000 per month due at the end of each month. The lease is considered an operating lease.
31	Paid for one month's rent on the warehouse.
31	Purchased 10 copiers and signed a $32,000, four-year lease with the option to buy the copiers at the end of the fourth year at a bargain price.
31	Made the second semiannual payment on the mortgage note payable.

Requirements

1. Complete the following amortization schedule for the first four mortgage payments on the $140,000 mortgage note, assuming semiannual payments of $9,633.

Date	Payment	Interest	Principal	Loan Balance
Jan 1, 2014				$140,000
Jun 30, 2014	$9,633			
Dec 31, 2014				
Jun 30, 2015				
Dec 31, 2015				

2. Record the journal entries for the 2014 transactions.

3. Prepare the long-term liabilities section of the balance sheet on December 31, 2014.

P9-4B. Analyzing bond terms and accounting for bonds (*Learning Objective 5*) 20–25 min.

Assume that on February 1, 2014, Atlantic, Corp. issued 9%, 10-year bonds payable with maturity value of $800,000. The bonds pay interest on January 31 and July 31. Atlantic's fiscal year-end is October 31.

Requirements

1. If the market interest rate is 8.5% when Atlantic, Corp. issues its bonds, will the bonds be priced at par, at a premium, or at a discount? Explain.

2. If the market interest rate is 10% when Atlantic, Corp. issues its bonds, will the bonds be priced at par, at a premium, or at a discount? Explain.

3. Assume that the issue price of the bonds is $832,000. Journalize the following bonds payable transactions, first using the straight-line method and second using the effective interest method (Note: you will need a financial calculator to calculate the market rate for the effective interest method):

   a. Issuance of the bonds on February 1, 2014.

   b. Payment of interest and amortization of premium on July 31, 2014.

   c. Accrual of interest and amortization of premium on October 31, 2014.

   d. Payment of interest and amortization of premium on January 31, 2015.

P9-5B. Analyzing bond terms and accounting for bonds (*Learning Objective 5*)
20–25 min.

On January 1, 2014, De La Terre Bistro issued $700,000 of 15-year, 7% bonds
payable. The bonds were sold for $725,000. The bonds pay interest each
June 30 and December 31.

Requirements

1. Fill in the blanks to complete these statements:

   a. De La Terre Bistro's bonds are priced at (express the price as a percentage)
   ....

   b. When De La Terre Bistro issued its bonds, the market interest rate was
   (higher than, lower than, or equal to) .... 7%.

   c. The amount of bond discount or premium is $............ .

2. Record the following transactions, first using the straight-line method and second using the effective interest method (Note: you will need a financial calcula-
   tor to calculate the market rate for the effective interest method):

   a. Issuance of the bonds payable on January 1, 2014. Explanations are
   not required.

   b. Payment of interest (and amortization of discount or premium, if any) on
   June 30, 2014. Explanations are not required.

   c. Payment of interest (and amortization of discount or premium, if any) on
   December 31, 2014. Explanations are not required.

3. At what amount will De La Terre Bistro report the bonds on its balance sheet
   at December 31, 2014?

P9-6B. Balance sheet disclosure of long-term liabilities (*Learning Objective 6*)
15–20 min.

The accounting records of Green, Corp. include the following items at
December 31, 2014:

Salary Payable..........................	$10,000	Accounts Payable...................	$ 52,000
Bonds Payable,		Mortgage Note Payable,	
Current Portion	17,000	Long-Term	120,000
Discount on Bonds Payable	13,000	Interest Payable	16,000
Income Tax Payable	8,000	Bonds Payable	220,000

Requirement

1. Report these liabilities on Green's balance sheet at December 31, 2014,
   including headings.

P9-7B. Calculation of debt ratio (*Learning Objective 7*) 10–15 min.

The classified balance sheet for Thorn, Inc. as of December 31, 2014, is presented next.

Thorn, Inc.
Balance Sheet
December 31, 2014

ASSETS			LIABILITIES	
Current Assets:			**Current Liabilities:**	
Cash		$ 6,600	Accounts Payable	$ 10,200
Accounts Receivable		10,100	Salary Payable	1,900
Supplies		1,300	Unearned Service Revenue	17,700
Prepaid Rent		2,800	Note Payable	10,000
Total Current Assets		$ 20,800	Total Current Liabilities	39,800
Fixed Assets:			**Long-Term Debt:**	
Land		55,000	Mortgage Note Payable	30,000
Equipment	$ 40,000		Bonds Payable	110,000
Less: Accumulated			Total Long-Term Debt	140,000
Depreciation, Equipment	14,000	26,000		
Building	225,000		**SHAREHOLDERS' EQUITY**	
Less: Accumulated			Common Shares	8,000
Depreciation, Building	90,000	135,000	Retained Earnings	49,000
Total Fixed Assets		216,000	Total Shareholders' Equity	57,000
			Total Liabilities and	
Total Assets		$236,800	Shareholders' Equity	$236,800

Requirements

1. Calculate Thorn's debt ratio as of December 31, 2014.
2. What percentage of Thorn's assets belong to the shareholders?
3. Would you be willing to extend credit to Thorn, Inc.? Why or why not?

P9-8B. Accounting for bonds (*Learning Objective 5*) 30–35 min.

Sansen Inc. is planning to issue $5,000,000, 8-year, 4% bonds. Interest is payable semiannually each June 30 and December 31. All of the bonds will be sold on July 1, 2014; they mature on June 30, 2022. Sansen's year-end is December 31.

Requirements

1. Compute the issue (sale) price on July 1, 2014, if the yield is:
   (a) 4%
   (b) 6%
   (c) 2%

2. Prepare all journal entries for the above three cases in 2014.
3. Prepare all journal entries for the above three cases in 2015 using the effective interest method.
4. Show how the bond interest expense and the bonds payable, for each case, should be reported on the annual financial statements for 2014 and 2015.

P9-9B. Accounting for bonds, year-end adjustment, and bond retirement
(*Learning Objective 5*) **30–35 min.**

Chura Inc. issued $5,000,000, 10-year, 5% bonds on February 1, 2014, when the yield was 6%. Interest is payable semiannually each July 31 and January 31. All of the bonds were sold on February 1, 2014; they mature on January 31, 2024. Chura's year-end is December 31. The effective interest method is used.

Requirements

1. Compute the issue (sale) price on February 1, 2014.

2. Record all journal entries for 2014.

3. Record the journal entry for the interest payment on January 31, 2015.

4. Assume on February 1, 2021, Chura retired 60% of its bonds at 96.75. What is the carrying value of the bonds payable? Calculate the gain or loss on the bond retirement.

5. Record the journal entry for the bond retirement on February 1, 2021.

P9-10B. Accounting for various short-term and long-term liabilities and their impact on the debt ratio (*Learning Objectives 2, 3, 6, & 7*) 30–35 min.

Budai Inc. completed the following transactions during the month of December. The company's fiscal year ends on December 31. The HST of 13% is included in all purchases and sales. Cost of goods sold is 50% of the sales.

December	1	Leased an automobile with a fair value of $50,000. The present value of the monthly payments, $600 for 4 years, represents a major portion of the fair value of the automobile. At the end of the 4th year, Budai can purchase the automobile for $1,000, which will be significantly lower than the fair value at the end of the 4th year.
	3	Purchased merchandise inventory on credit for $28,250, terms 2/10, n/30. Budai uses a perpetual inventory system.
	10	Sold merchandise on credit for $18,080, terms 2/10, n/30.
	12	Paid the invoice for the purchase on December 3.
	16	Borrowed $30,000 from the CT Bank by signing a three-year note at 4% interest rate. The interest is paid monthly on the 15th of the month.
	19	Received a cheque from a customer who purchased merchandise on December 10.
	23	Purchased merchandise inventory on credit for $47,460, terms 2/10, n/30.
	28	Received a $500 deposit for back-ordered merchandise to be shipped at the beginning of the new year.
	31	Salary Expense for the month was $25,000, of which employee deductions included CPP, $1,230; EI, $430; and income tax, $6,250. Budai also recorded the employee benefits expense.

Requirements

1. Record all journal entries, including adjusting entries, for the month of December.

2. Show the liability section of the balance sheet on December 31.

3. Identify the impact on the debt ratio and current ratio—(1) no change, (2) increase, or (3) decrease, after each transaction is complete. Identify each transaction as an independent case, rather than a cumulative effect. Assume that the debt ratio is at 40% and current ratio is 0.75 before considering each transaction.

PROBLEMS (ALTERNATES 1, 2, AND 3)

These alternative problem sets are available for your practice benefit at
www.myaccountinglab.com

CONTINUING EXERCISE

In this exercise we will continue the accounting for Graham's Yard Care, Inc. Assume that on September 1, 2014, Graham's Yard Care, Inc. borrowed $5,000 from First National Bank, signing a nine-month, 10% note.

Requirement

1. Prepare the journal required on September 1, 2014, December 31, 2014, and May 31, 2015, to record the transactions related to the note.

CONTINUING PROBLEM

This continues the Aqua Elite, Inc. example from the Continuing Problem in Chapter 8. Aqua Elite, Inc. purchased some of its fixed assets during 2014 using long-term debt. The following table summarizes the nature of this long-term debt.

Date	Item	Annual Interest Rate	Amount	Payment Terms
May 18	Note payable	8%	$31,000	Five equal annual payments of principal plus accrued interest are due on May 18 of each year.
Sep 1	Mortgage payable	6%	$85,000	Semiannual payments of $3,677 due on March 1 and September 1 of each year.

Requirements

1. Calculate the interest expense that Aqua Elite, Inc. should accrue as of December 31, 2014.

2. Prepare the balance sheet presentation for all long-term debt indicating the portion that should be classified as current and the portion that should be classified as long-term.

APPLY YOUR KNOWLEDGE

ETHICS IN ACTION

Case 1. The Transmission Shop was the largest company in Ontario specializing in rebuilding automobile transmissions. Every transmission rebuilt by the business was covered by a six-month warranty. The owner, Ron Wood, was meeting with his accountant to go over the yearly financial statements. In reviewing the balance sheet, Ron became puzzled by the large amount of current liabilities being reported, so he asked his accountant to explain them. The accountant said that most of the current liabilities were the result of accruals, such as the estimated warranty payable, some additional wages payable, and interest accrued on the note owed to the bank. The employees were not actually paid until the first week of the new year, so some of their wages had to be recorded and properly matched against revenues in the current period. Also, several months of interest expense had to be accrued on a bank loan, but the largest amount of the accrued liabilities was due to the estimated warranty expense. Ron asked whether the wages payable and the interest payable could be removed because they would be paid off shortly after the year ended. The accountant stated that accrued liabilities had to be properly recognized in the current accounting period, and, thus, they could not be removed. Ron agreed but then asked about the large accrued liability based upon the estimated warranty amounts. Again, the accountant stated that in previous years actual warranty cost had been about 5% of the total sales and, therefore, in the current year the estimate was accrued at 5%. Ron then informed the accountant that a new conditioning lubricant had been added to each transmission rebuilt, which dramatically reduced the amount of rebuilt transmissions being returned under warranty. As a result, Ron strongly felt that the warranty estimate should be reduced to only 2% of total sales and, thereby, the accrued warranty liability and related expense would also be reduced. The accountant argued that the only reason Ron wanted to reduce the estimated percentage was to improve the financial statements, which would be unethical and inappropriate.

Requirements

1. What is the impact of accrued liabilities on the financial statements? Should the accrued liabilities for wages and interest payable be removed from the balance sheet?

2. Does Ron have a valid reason for wanting to reduce the estimated warranty liability? Are the concerns expressed by the accountant valid?

3. What ethical issues are involved?

Case 2. Sam Gray, the CEO of Steele Corporation, was meeting with the company controller to discuss a possible major lease of a new production facility. Steele Corporation had a large amount of debt, and Sam was concerned that adding more debt to acquire the production facility would worry the shareholders. Sam knew that if the production facility could be classified as an operating lease rather than a capital lease, the lease obligation would not have to be reported on the balance sheet. Thus, the company could have a new production facility without having to report any additional debt. The accountant told Sam that if the title to the production facility transferred automatically to Steele at the end of the lease term, then the lease would have to be classified as a capital lease. Also, if the lease had a bargain purchase option, such that Steele Corporation could simply purchase the facility at the end of the lease term for a small option amount, it would also be classified as a capital lease. Sam said not to worry because he would make sure that the lease contract would not contain any title transfer or bargain purchase option. The accountant then said that the facility had a 20-year life and the lease was for 16 years, which was more than 75% of the economic life of the asset, so it would have to be classified as a capital lease. Sam then said he would change the lease term to 14 years so the lease term would be less than the 75% of the economic life of the facility. The accountant then computed the present value of all the lease payments, and the total was more than 90% of the market value of the facility. Again, Sam said he would make any needed changes so that the total present value of the lease payments would be 89% of the current market value of the facility. At this point the accountant became frustrated and told Sam that the rules of accounting used to determine the proper classification of a lease were not meant to be used to misclassify a leased asset and, thereby, provide misleading information. Sam then said the rules simply served as a guide for structuring the lease and that he was merely using the rules to allow the lease to be classified as an operating lease and, thus, the lease obligation would not have to be recorded. The accountant said that intentionally avoiding the rules was unethical and wrong.

Requirements

1. Why does Sam want to have the lease classified as an operating lease rather than a capital lease?

2. Does the accountant have a legitimate argument? Does Sam have a legitimate argument?

3. What ethical issues are involved?

4. Do you have any other thoughts?

KNOW YOUR BUSINESS

FINANCIAL ANALYSIS

Purpose: To help familiarize you with the financial reporting of a real company to further your understanding of the chapter material you are learning.

This case focuses on the liabilities of Bombardier Inc. Current liabilities are those obligations that will become due and payable within the next year or operating cycle (whichever is longer), while long-term liabilities are those that are due and payable more than one year from the balance sheet date. It is important to properly classify and report these liabilities because they affect liquidity. We will now consider the current and long-term liabilities of Bombardier Inc. Refer to the Bombardier Inc. financial statements found in MyAccountingLab. Also, consider Note 12 and Note 13 in the footnotes included in the annual report.

Requirements

1. What was the balance of Accounts Payable and Accrued Liabilities at January 31, 2011 and January 31, 2010? Did the amount increase or decrease over the year?

2. Why does Bombardier not disclose current liabilities separately from non-current liabilities?

3. What do the Advances on Aerospace Programs represent?

4. How much is owed for long-term debt at January 31, 2011? Look at the financing activities section of the Consolidated Statements of Cash Flows. What is the amount of proceeds from issuance of long-term debt over the last year? What is the amount of repayments of long-term debt over the last year? Does it appear that Bombardier Inc. is borrowing more than it repays or repaying more than it borrows? From Note 13, determine how much of the long-term debt must be repaid in the next twelve months, i.e., during the year ended January 31, 2012?

5. What are the total liabilities that Bombardier owes at January 31, 2011? What type of liabilities represents the highest percentage of total liabilities and what is this percentage for 2011 and 2010? Is the amount of total shareholders' equity more than or less than the total of all the liabilities at January 31, 2011? What does this result mean?

INDUSTRY ANALYSIS

Purpose: To help you understand and compare the performance of two companies in the same industry.

Find the Bombardier Annual Report, Year Ended January 31, 2011, located in MyAccountingLab and go to the Financial Statements. Now access The Boeing Company's 2010 Annual Report. To do this from the internet, go to their webpage for the Investor Relations at *http://www.boeing.com/companyoffices/financial/quarterly.htm* and under Annual Report, go to the 2010 Annual Report.

Requirement

1. Calculate the debt to total asset ratio (total liabilities to total assets) for both companies for the past two years. Generally speaking, what does this ratio tell you? Using these calculations, what comments can you make about these two companies?

SMALL BUSINESS ANALYSIS

Purpose: To help you understand the importance of cash flows in the operation of a small business.

Your business has been doing pretty well since you first opened the doors five years ago. You've been thinking for the last six months or so about expanding the business. There is some property right next door that would work well into your expansion plans. It would take some renovations to the building, but to continue to grow, you know you're going to need more room. But here's the problem. How are you going to pay for the building and the renovations? Your cash account is in pretty good shape, but you remember the sage advice of the business consultant who helped you when you were just getting started. That advice was to always have enough available cash to cover three months' worth of expenses just in case of some unexpected business interruption. Your available cash and short-term investments of $100,000 is right at that benchmark.

Some preliminary investigation into the property next door indicates that the existing owner would probably be willing to accept $200,000 for the property. You also have a discussion with a contractor associate who tells you that the renovations to your specifications would cost about $50,000. So your dilemma is how are you going to come up with $250,000? You figure the best place to start is with a visit to your banker.

At that meeting with the banker, he tells you something like this:

"Frank, we would be pleased to help you out with your expansion plans. We would require you to take out a mortgage on the building and we would need a 20% down payment of the total amount up front. So the balance that we would be lending you would be 80% of the total you need, or $200,000. Your down payment amount would be $50,000. At 8% for 20 years, your monthly payments would be $1,672.88."

You are somewhat pleased with the outcome of the meeting, but you tell the banker you will get back to him in a day or two. You know that this is a big step and a long-term investment for the business.

Requirements

1. After considering the details of the plan the banker gave you, what are your thoughts? Since the down payment is going to use up about half of your available cash, how does that concern you? What about the long-term commitment of 20 years?

2. Assuming you go ahead with the mortgage and the purchase and renovation of the property, journalize the transactions to acquire the property and make the renovations. Where will the building and the renovations show up on your financial statements? Where will the mortgage show up on your financial statements? If the interest portion of your first payment is going to be $1,333.33, journalize the transaction to make your first mortgage payment.

WRITTEN COMMUNICATION

Your boss has just asked you to write a short note to one of his clients that had expressed some concerns about the difference between liabilities that are of an unknown amount versus contingent liabilities. The client is in the midst of a lawsuit with a governmental agency that its attorney thinks has about a 50-50 chance of winning. However, if the company loses, it could cost a substantial amount of money. The client is wondering if it needs to account for the lawsuit, and if so, how?

Requirement

1. Write a note to the client explaining the difference between a liability of an unknown amount and a contingent liability. Also, make a suggestion as to how this particular situation might need to be accounted for.

SCAN THIS

Self Check Answers

1. a 2. c 3. d 4. a 5. a 6. c 7. b 8. a 9. a 10. c

CHAPTER **10**

Corporations: Share Capital and Retained Earnings

GOLDCORP

Goldcorp 2010
Annual General Meeting of Shareholders

LEARNING OBJECTIVES:

1 ▶ **Review the characteristics of a corporation**

2 ▶ **Describe the two sources of shareholders' equity and the classes of shares**

3 ▶ **Journalize the issuance of shares**

4 ▶ **Account for cash dividends**

5 ▶ **Account for stock dividends and stock splits**

6 ▶ **Account for treasury shares**

7 ▶ **Report shareholders' equity**

8 ▶ **Evaluate return on shareholders' equity and return on common shareholders' equity**

Throughout the book, we have focused on the corporate form of business organization. We have made journal entries to record investments by shareholders in a corporation. We have also learned how to record the payment of dividends to shareholders. Maybe you've wondered, "Is issuing shares and paying dividends as simple as we have learned so far?" or, "How does a business actually become a corporation anyway?" You might have heard of stock dividends or stock splits and wondered what they are. As we explore corporations in greater detail in this chapter we will uncover the answers to these questions.

CHAPTER OUTLINE:

HOW ARE CORPORATIONS ORGANIZED?

1 Review the characteristics of a corporation

A corporation is a separate legal entity from its owners. Corporations in Canada are established as a result of an application to either the federal government or to a particular provincial government. The process of becoming a corporation is known as incorporating. To incorporate, an organization's founders file an application to the appropriate government authorities, specifying information including the name of the corporation, the type of business, the location of the business, the number and types of shares to be authorized, and so forth.

Once the organization has become a corporation, it is authorized to sell individuals an ownership interest, or shares, in the corporation. When you invest in a corporation, you may call yourself a shareholder, or stock holder. Different classes of shares may be issued, but it is the "common shareholders" who actually own the company.

It is important to distinguish between a private corporation and a public corporation. A public corporation has its shares listed for trading in a stock market such as the Toronto Stock Exchange (TSX). Many large Canadian corporations, including companies like Research in Motion, Loblaws, Shoppers Drug Mart, and Tim Hortons, have their shares listed on the TSX. Private corporations, on the other hand, are typically, though not always, smaller companies, and usually only have a small number of shareholders, and the shares are not "liquid," that is, the shares are not easily traded, or transferred from one person to another.

While other forms of business activity such as proprietorships and partnerships are very numerous in Canada, it is the corporate form of ownership that dominates.

A corporation has a separate legal existence from its common shareholders, and may act independently of its owners. It may sue and be sued, must pay taxes as a separate entity and, crucially, enables the limited liability of its shareholders. This means that creditors cannot generally make a claim against individual shareholders for liabilities associated with the corporation.

Exhibit 10-1 summarizes some of the advantages and disadvantages of the corporate form of business.

	Advantages		Disadvantages
1.	Shareholders have limited liability because the corporation is a separate legal entity.	1.	Government regulation is cumbersome and expensive.
2.	Corporations can raise more money than a proprietorship or partnership.	2.	Double taxation.
3.	A corporation has a continuous life.		
4.	The transfer of corporate ownership is easy.		

Exhibit 10-1 ▲

WHAT MAKES UP THE SHAREHOLDERS' EQUITY OF A CORPORATION?

Recall from Chapter 1 that the shareholders' equity of a corporation is divided into two categories:

2   Describe the two sources of shareholders' equity and the classes of shares

- Share capital (also called contributed capital) represents amounts received from the shareholders. Common shares, discussed in Chapter 1, are the main source of share capital. This is *externally* generated capital and results from transactions with outsiders.

- Retained earnings is capital earned by profitable operations. This is *internally* generated capital and results from internal corporate decisions and earnings.

Shareholders' Rights

There are four basic rights a shareholder may have:

1. **Vote.** Shareholders participate in management by voting on corporate matters. This is the only way in which a shareholder can help to manage the corporation. Normally, each common share carries one vote.

2. **Dividends.** Shareholders receive a proportionate part of any dividend. Each share receives an equal dividend so, for example, a shareholder who owns 1% of the total shares in the company receives 1% of any dividend.

3. **Liquidation.** Shareholders receive their proportionate share of any assets remaining after the corporation pays its debts and liquidates (goes out of business).

4. **Preemption.** Shareholders can maintain their proportionate ownership in the corporation. Suppose you own 5% of a corporation's shares. If the corporation issues 100,000 new shares, it must offer you the opportunity to buy 5% (5,000) of the new shares. For most companies, preemptive rights are the exception rather than the rule.

Classes of Shares

Every corporation must issue common shares, which represent the basic ownership of the corporation. The real "owners" of the corporation are the common shareholders. Some companies issue Class A common shares, which carry the right to vote, and Class B common shares, which are non-voting. There must be at least one voting "class" of shares. However, there is no limit to the number or types of classes of shares that a corporation may issue. Each class of shares has a separate account.

In addition to common shares, a corporation may also issue **preferred shares**. Preferred shares give their owners certain advantages over the owners of common shares. Most notably, preferred shareholders receive dividends before the common shareholders. They also receive assets before common shareholders if the corporation liquidates. Corporations pay a fixed dividend on preferred shares, which is printed on the face of the preferred share certificate. Investors usually buy preferred shares to earn those fixed dividends. With these advantages, preferred shareholders take less investment risk than common shareholders.

Owners of preferred shares may also have the four basic shareholder rights, unless a right is withheld. The right to vote, however, is usually withheld from preferred shares. Companies may issue different series of preferred shares (Series A and Series B, for example). Each series is recorded in a separate account.

Par Value

Shares may carry a par value, a stated value, or they may be no-par shares. **Par value** is an arbitrary amount assigned by a company to a share.

Shares that have a face value printed on the share certificate were called "par value." Typically, this value represented the amount for which the shares had originally been issued by the corporation. However, immediately after the issue of the shares, the marketplace would set the new value of the shares which made the par value meaningless. Therefore, under the Canada Business Corporations Act (CBCA), shares must be no par value.

HOW IS THE ISSUANCE OF SHARES RECORDED?

 Journalize the issuance of shares

Corporations such as RIM and Canadian Tire need huge quantities of money to operate. They cannot finance all their operations through borrowing, so they raise capital by issuing shares. A company can sell its shares directly to shareholders or it can use the services of an **underwriter**, such as the brokerage firms RBC Dominion and TD Waterhouse. An underwriter usually agrees to buy all the shares it cannot sell to its clients.

The price that the corporation receives from issuing shares is called the **issue price**. We use Mackay Industries to show how to account for the issuance of shares.

Issuing Common Shares

How does a company record the issuance of shares? Let's assume that the shares for Mackay Industries were trading at $15 per share on January 1. Remember that we do not need to refer to these shares as "no-par shares" because all Canadian shares are no-par value. The entry to record the issuance of 500,000 shares for $15 per share would be as follows:

DATE	ACCOUNTS	POST REF.	DR.	CR.
Jan 1	Cash (500,000 × $15)		7,500,000	
	Common Shares			7,500,000
	Issued 500,000 common shares for $15 per share.			

Issuing Shares for Assets Other Than Cash

A corporation may issue shares for assets other than cash. It records the assets received at their current market value and credits the share accounts accordingly. The assets' prior book value is irrelevant. Now let's reconsider the January 1 entry for Mackay Industries. Assume that, instead of cash, Mackay Industries received a building worth $7,500,000 in exchange for the 500,000 shares of its $15 common shares on January 1. How would the entry change?

Under IFRS and Canadian ASPE, non-monetary exchanges, such as shares exchanged for an asset, should be measured at the more reliable measure of the fair value of the asset received. However, if the value of the shares can be more reliably measured, for instance when the share price can be easily obtained from the stock market, then the asset exchanged should be recorded at the fair value of the share price. If Mackay Industries is not a publicly traded company, the fair market value of the building is a more reliable measure, which would make the value of each share $15 ($7,500,000 / 500,000 shares = $15 per share). If Mackay Industries is a publicly traded company, the share value given up will also be valued at $15 per share (500,000 × $15 = $7,500,000).

DATE	ACCOUNTS	POST REF.	DR.	CR.
Jan 01	Building (fair market value)		7,500,000	
	Common Shares ($15 × 500,000)			7,500,000
	Issued 500,000 common shares in exchange for a building.			

Issuing Preferred Shares

Accounting for preferred shares is similar to the process illustrated for issuing common shares. Let's assume that Mackay Industries decides to issue 10,000 of its 10% preferred shares on February 15 for $25 per share. The entry to record the issuance would be as follows:

DATE	ACCOUNTS	POST REF.	DR.	CR.
Feb 15	Cash (10,000 × $25)		250,000	
	Preferred Shares (10,000 × $25)			250,000
	Issued 10,000 preferred shares for $25 per share.			

HOW ARE CASH DIVIDENDS ACCOUNTED FOR?

As discussed in Chapter 1, a profitable corporation may distribute cash to the shareholders in the form of *dividends*. Dividends cause a decrease in both Assets and Shareholders' Equity (Retained Earnings). Companies are prohibited from using share capital for dividends. Accountants, therefore, use the term **legal capital** to refer to the portion of shareholders' equity that cannot be used for dividends. Corporations declare cash dividends from Retained Earnings and then pay them with cash.

4 ▶ Account for cash dividends

Dividend Dates

A corporation declares a dividend before paying it. There are three dates associated with the declaration and payment of a cash dividend.

1. **Declaration date.** On the declaration date—say, March 5—the board of directors announces the intention to pay the dividend. The declaration of a cash dividend creates an obligation (liability) for the corporation.

2. **Date of record.** Those shareholders holding the shares at the end of business on the date of record—usually a week or two after declaration, say, March 19—will receive the dividend cheque.

3. **Payment date.** Payment of the dividend usually follows the record date by a week or two—say, March 31.

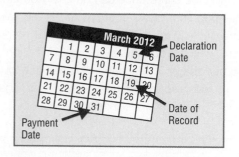

Declaring and Paying Dividends

The annual dividend rate on *preferred shares* is expressed as a flat dollar amount per share, such as $2 per share. Let's look at how to compute preferred dividends, using Mackay Industries' 10,000 outstanding preferred shares.

Outstanding shares	×	flat dividend rate	=	preferred dividend
10,000 shares	×	$2 per share	=	$20,000

Cash dividends on *common shares* are computed the same way.

Remember from Chapter 3 that the Dividends account is closed to Retained Earnings at the end of the year. So, instead of using the Dividends account, companies may record the declaration of a dividend by debiting the Retained Earnings account instead of Dividends. In this case, there will be no entry required at year-end to close the Dividends account. To account for Mackay Industries' declaration of a cash dividend we debit Retained Earnings and credit Dividends Payable on the date of declaration as follows:

DATE	ACCOUNTS	POST REF.	DR.	CR.
Mar 5	Retained Earnings		20,000	
	Dividends Payable			20,000
	Declared a cash dividend.			

On the date of record, no journal entry is required. On the payment date, Mackay Industries will record the payment of the dividend as follows:

DATE	ACCOUNTS	POST REF.	DR.	CR.
Mar 31	Dividends Payable		20,000	
	Cash			20,000
	Paid cash dividend.			

When a company has issued only common shares, the common shareholders will receive any dividend that is declared. However, if both preferred and common shares are issued, the preferred shareholders get their dividends first. The common shareholders receive dividends only if the total dividend declared is larger than the amount of the annual preferred dividend. In other words, the common shareholders get the leftovers. Let's see how dividends are divided between preferred and common shareholders.

Dividing Dividends Between Preferred and Common Shareholders

Assume that Mackay Industries has 500,000 common shares outstanding and 10,000 preferred shares outstanding. We calculated earlier that Mackay Industries' annual preferred dividend was $20,000. So, total declared dividends must exceed $20,000 for the common shareholders to get anything. **Exhibit 10-2** shows the division of dividends between preferred and common for two situations.

Situation A—Total Dividend of $15,000:		
Preferred dividend (the full $15,000 goes to the preferred shareholders because the annual preferred dividend is $20,000)		$15,000
Common dividend (none because the total dividend did not cover the preferred annual dividend)		0
Total dividend		$15,000
Situation B—Total Dividend of $30,000:		
Preferred dividend (10,000 shares × $2 per share)		$20,000
Common dividend ($30,000 − $20,000)		10,000
Total dividend		$30,000

Exhibit 10-2 ▲

If Mackay Industries' dividend is large enough to cover the preferred dividend (Situation B), the preferred shareholders get their regular dividend ($20,000), and the common shareholders get the remainder ($10,000). But if the year's dividend falls below the annual preferred amount (Situation A), the preferred shareholders will receive the entire dividend, and the common shareholders get nothing that year.

Dividends on Cumulative and Noncumulative Preferred Shares

Preferred shares can be either

- cumulative.
- noncumulative.

Preferred shares are assumed to be cumulative unless they are specifically designated as noncumulative. Most preferred shares are cumulative. Let's see what effect the cumulative versus noncumulative designation has on the payment of dividends.

As we saw with Mackay Industries in Situation A in Exhibit 10-2, a corporation may fail to pay the entire annual preferred dividend. This may happen if, for example, the company does not have enough cash to fund the entire dividend. This is called *passing the dividend*, and the dividends are said to be in **arrears**. **Cumulative preferred shares** shareholders must receive all dividends in arrears before the common shareholders get any dividend.

The preferred shares of Mackay Industries are cumulative. How do we know this? Because it is not labelled as noncumulative.

Suppose Mackay Industries passed the entire 2014 preferred dividend of $20,000. Before paying any common dividend in 2015, Mackay Industries must first pay preferred dividends of $20,000 for 2014 and $20,000 for 2015, a total of $40,000. In 2015, Mackay Industries declares a $75,000 dividend. How much of this dividend goes to preferred? How much goes to common? The allocation of this $75,000 dividend is as follows:

Total dividend...	$75,000
Preferred shareholders get:	
2014 dividend (10,000 × $2 per share)............................... $20,000	
2015 dividend (10,000 × $2 per share)................................ 20,000	
Total to preferred..	40,000
Common shareholders get the remainder................................	$35,000

If Mackay Industries declared the $75,000 dividend on November 10, 2015, it would make the following entry:

DATE	ACCOUNTS	POST REF.	DR.	CR.
Nov 10	Retained Earnings		75,000	
	Dividends Payable—Preferred			40,000
	Dividends Payable—Common			35,000
	Declared a cash dividend.			

If the preferred shares are *noncumulative*, the corporation is not required to pay any dividends in arrears. Suppose Mackay Industries' preferred shares were noncumulative and the company passed the 2014 dividend. The preferred shareholders would lose the 2014 dividend of $20,000 forever. Then, before paying any common dividends in 2015, Mackay Industries would only have to pay the 2015 preferred dividend of $20,000, which would leave $55,000 for the common shareholders.

Dividends in arrears are *not* a liability. A liability for dividends arises only after the board of directors declares a dividend. It is possible that the board may never declare another dividend in the future. However, a corporation does report cumulative preferred dividends in arrears in the notes to the financial statements. This shows the common shareholders how big the declared dividend will need to be for them to get any dividends in the future.

DECISION GUIDELINES

Decision	Guideline	Analyze
As a member of the Board of Directors, I make decisions on when to declare dividends, how much to declare, and whether they will be cash dividends or something else. When making these decisions, when is a cash dividend appropriate?	Consider the amount of available cash as well as the balance in Retained Earnings.	A cash dividend is a distribution of earnings to the company's shareholders. So, a company cannot declare and distribute dividends unless the balance in retained earnings (counting the current year's earnings) exceeds the amount of the desired dividend. In addition, the company must have the cash available to pay the dividend if it is declared. A business should carefully analyze its future cash needs so that it does not deplete its cash with a dividend and end up with cash flow issues in the future.

HOW ARE STOCK DIVIDENDS AND STOCK SPLITS ACCOUNTED FOR?

Stock Dividends

A **stock dividend** is a distribution of a corporation's own shares to its shareholders. Unlike cash dividends, stock dividends do not give any assets to the shareholders. Stock dividends

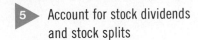

5 ▶ Account for stock dividends and stock splits

- affect only shareholders' equity accounts (including Retained Earnings and Common Shares).
- have no effect on total shareholders' equity.
- have no effect on assets or liabilities.

A corporation distributes stock dividends to shareholders in proportion to the number of shares they already own. Suppose you own 5,000 shares of Mackay Industries' common shares. If Mackay Industries distributes a 5% stock dividend, you would receive 250 (5,000 × 0.05) additional shares. You would now own 5,250 shares. All other Mackay Industries' shareholders also receive additional shares equal to 5% of the amount of shares they currently have. Because the amount of shares every shareholder has increases by 5%, the shareholders would all own the same percentage share of Mackay Industries' shares as they did before the stock dividend.

Companies issue stock dividends for several reasons including

1. to continue a history of declaring dividends while conserving cash. A company may wish to continue dividends to keep shareholders happy but needs to keep its cash for operations. A stock dividend is a way to do so without using any cash.

2. to reduce the market price of its shares. A stock dividend will usually cause the company's share price to fall. This happens because after the stock dividend there will be more shares representing the same amount of value. Suppose that Mackay Industries' shares traded at $40 recently. Increasing the shares outstanding by issuing a 10% stock dividend would likely drop Mackay Industries' shares market price to around $36 per share. The objective behind a stock dividend is to make the shares less expensive and, therefore, more available and attractive to investors.

3. to reward investors. Investors often feel like they've received something of value when they get a stock dividend.

Recording Stock Dividends

As with a cash dividend, there are three dates associated with a stock dividend:

- Declaration date
- Date of record
- Distribution date

The board of directors announces the stock dividend on the declaration date. The date of record determines who will receive the additional shares. The distribution date is the date the additional shares are distributed to the shareholders. Unlike with a cash dividend, the declaration of a stock dividend does *not* create a liability. This is because the corporation is not obligated to distribute any assets to the shareholders. (Recall that a liability is a claim on assets.) With a stock dividend, the corporation has simply declared its intention to distribute more of its shares. A stock dividend affects the following accounts:

- Retained Earnings is reduced (debited) by an amount equal to the number of shares being distributed times the current market price of the company's shares.
- Common Shares is increased (credited) by an amount equal to the number of shares being distributed times the value of the share. If the company declares a stock dividend of an amount that is less than 20% of the total number of shares outstanding, then the market value of the shares will be used. If the company declares a stock dividend of more than 20%, then the average share price will be used.

The net effect of a stock dividend is to transfer an amount equal to the market value of the dividend from Retained Earnings into share capital.

Assume that Mackay Industries has the following shareholders' equity on June 1, prior to declaring a stock dividend:

Mackay Industries, Inc. Shareholders' Equity June 1	
Share Capital:	
Preferred Shares, 500,000 shares authorized, 10,000 shares issued	$ 250,000
Common Shares, 2,000,000 shares authorized, 500,000 shares issued	7,500,000
Total Share Capital	7,750,000
Retained Earnings	2,000,000
Total Shareholders' Equity	$9,750,000

Now, assume Mackay Industries declares a 5% stock dividend on June 15 when the market value of Mackay Industries common shares is $40 per share. Once Mackay declares the stock dividend, the Retained Earnings account is reduced or debited; however, this is not the date to distribute the additional shares. Mackay will need to credit an account called Stock Dividends Distributable. The Stock Dividends Distributable account is one of the shareholders' equity accounts and is increased when stock dividends are declared and decreased when stock dividends are distributed to shareholders. Mackay would record the declaration and distribution of the stock dividend as follows:

DATE	ACCOUNTS	POST REF.	DR.	CR.
Jun 15	Retained Earnings (500,000 × 5% × $40)		1,000,000	
	Stock Dividends Distributable			1,000,000
	Declared 5% common share dividend.			

DATE	ACCOUNTS	POST REF.	DR.	CR.
Jun 30	Stock Dividends Distributable		1,000,000	
	Common Shares			1,000,000
	Distributed 5% common share dividend.			

As we did with cash dividends, we debited Retained Earnings directly instead of using a dividend account. Remember that a stock dividend does not affect assets, liabilities, or total shareholders' equity. A stock dividend merely rearranges the balances in the equity accounts, leaving total equity unchanged. Immediately after the stock dividend, Mackay Industries' shareholders' equity looks like this:

		Mackay Industries, Inc. Shareholders' Equity June 30	
		Share Capital:	
		Preferred Shares, 500,000 shares authorized,	
		10,000 shares issued	$ 250,000
		Common Shares, 2,000,000 shares authorized,	
		525,000 shares issued	8,500,000
		Total Share Capital	8,750,000
		Retained Earnings	1,000,000
		Total Shareholders' Equity	$9,750,000

Note that the number of outstanding shares is now 525,000 [500,000 + (500,000 × 0.05)]. Note also that total shareholders' equity is still $9,750,000. The effect of the stock dividend was simply to transfer $1,000,000 from retained earnings to share capital.

Stock Splits

When a company's share price is too high, the board of directors may consider reducing the share price in the market by splitting (dividing) the shares. The effect of a stock split is to increase the total number of shares and reduce the share price. The purpose of a stock split is to increase the liquidity of the shares in the market. Many shareholders do not like or have the ability to buy high-priced stock. The illiquidity of share trading in the stock market is not good for companies. Although a stock split does not change the total value of a company, many investors interpret a stock split as a positive sign. In general, shares perform well after a company announces a stock split.

On the other hand, when a company's share price is too low, the board of directors may consider increasing the share price in the market by a reverse stock split. For example, a 1-for-2 reverse stock split will result in a reduction of number of shares outstanding by half. Since the total share capital does not change, the share price will double.

Both a stock dividend and a **stock split** will increase the number of shares outstanding. However, a stock split is fundamentally different from a stock dividend. A stock split increases not only the number of outstanding shares, but also the number of authorized and issued shares. For example, if Mackay Industries splits its common shares 2-for-1, the number of outstanding shares is doubled.

Assume the market price of a common share of Mackay Industries has been approximately $40. If Mackay Industries initiates a 2-for-1 split of its common shares on August 1, the market price per share will drop to around $20. A 2-for-1 stock split means that Mackay Industries will have twice as many shares authorized and outstanding after the split as before. **Exhibit 10-3** on the following page shows the before and after of how a 2-for-1 split affects Mackay Industries' shareholders' equity.

	Mackay Industries, Inc. Shareholders' Equity—Before Split August 1	
	Share Capital:	
	Preferred Shares, 500,000 shares authorized, 10,000 shares issued and outstanding	$ 250,000
	Common Shares, 2,000,000 shares authorized, 525,000 shares issued and outstanding	8,500,000
	Total Share Capital	8,750,000
	Retained Earnings	1,000,000
	Total Shareholders' Equity	$9,750,000

	Mackay Industries, Inc. Shareholders' Equity—After Split August 1	
	Share Capital:	
	Preferred Shares, 500,000 shares authorized, 10,000 shares issued and outstanding	$ 250,000
	Common Shares, 4,000,000 shares authorized, 1,050,000 shares issued and outstanding	8,500,000
	Total Share Capital	8,750,000
	Retained Earnings	1,000,000
	Total Shareholders' Equity	$9,750,000

Exhibit 10-3 ▲

Study the exhibit and you'll see that a 2-for-1 stock split does the following:

- Doubles the shares authorized and issued
- Leaves all account balances and total equity unchanged

Because the stock split does not affect any account balances, no formal journal entry is needed to record a stock split. Instead, the split is recorded in a **memorandum entry**, a journal entry that "notes" a significant event, but which has no debit or credit amount. Following is an example of a memorandum entry:

DATE	ACCOUNTS	POST REF.	DR.	CR.
Aug 1	Split the common stock 2-for-1.			
	OLD: 2,000,000 shares authorized; 525,000 shares issued			
	NEW: 4,000,000 shares authorized; 1,050,000 shares issued			

ACCOUNTING IN YOUR WORLD

Robert invited three friends over to watch a football game and share a "take-and-bake" pizza he had purchased. On game day, Robert pulled the pizza out of the oven and was just about to slice it into eight pieces (two slices for each of them) when he began to wonder if there was enough pizza. Robert had an idea. He figured that if he cut the pizza into twelve slices instead of eight slices, each person would get three slices of pizza instead of two. Robert knew that each person would still receive the same amount of pizza but he figured that his friends would feel more satisfied if they received three slices instead of only two slices. It worked; no one complained that they did not get enough to eat.

The logic behind a stock split is similar to the logic behind Robert slicing the pizza into more pieces. When a company splits its shares, each shareholder still owns the same amount of the company (think the whole pizza). However, the shareholders' ownership is now represented by more shares (think slices of pizza). For example, after a 3-for-2 stock split, each shareholder would own the same amount of the company. Each shareholder would just own three shares now for every two shares he or she used to own.

Stock Dividends and Stock Splits Compared

Stock dividends and stock splits have some similarities and some differences. Exhibit 10-4 summarizes the effects of each on shareholders' equity. Cash dividends have also been included in the exhibit for comparison purposes.

Event	Common Shares	Share Capital	Retained Earnings	Total Shareholders' Equity
Cash dividend	No effect	No effect	Decrease	Decrease
Stock dividend	Increase	Increase	Decrease	No effect
Stock split	Increase	Increase	No effect	No effect

Exhibit 10-4 ▲

DECISION GUIDELINES

Decision

I am a member of the Board of Directors and we are having difficulty selling our shares on the stock market. We've been told that our share price is too high because the company has been performing very well. To decrease the market price of a company's shares, is it better to use a stock dividend or a stock split?

Guideline

The amount by which a company wishes to reduce the market price of the shares influences the decision to use a stock dividend or a stock split.

Analyze

Because both a stock dividend and a stock split increase the number of outstanding shares (with no increase in the company's Shareholders' Equity), they both reduce the market value of a company's shares. A stock split usually increases the number of outstanding shares by a larger amount than a stock dividend. Therefore, it tends to have a bigger impact on the market price of the shares and should be used when a significant decrease in the market price is desired. For example, a 2-for-1 split will typically reduce the market price of a company's shares by 50%.

HOW ARE TREASURY SHARES ACCOUNTED FOR?

 Account for treasury shares

After a company has issued shares, it is possible for that company to reacquire, or buy back, some of its shares at a later date. In general, when a company buys back its own shares, it cancels these shares and the number of common shares and the balance of the common share account are reduced. However, if a company buys back its own shares and holds these shares, then the reacquired shares are called **treasury shares** because they are, in effect, held in the company's treasury. A corporation such as Mackay Industries may purchase treasury shares for several reasons:

❶ Management hopes to buy the shares when the price is low and sell them when the price goes higher.

❷ Management wants to support the company's share price.

❸ Management wants to avoid a takeover by an outside party. If the company purchases the available shares, the shares are not available for others to purchase.

❹ Management wants to reward valued employees with shares. Treasury shares can be given to employees as a reward.

Treasury share transactions are common among larger corporations.

Treasury Share Basics

Before we see how treasury shares are accounted for, let's review some basic concepts related to treasury shares:

■ The Treasury Shares account is a contra-equity account. Therefore, Treasury Shares has a debit balance, which is the opposite of the other equity accounts.

- Treasury shares are recorded at average cost
- The Treasury Shares account is reported beneath Retained Earnings on the balance sheet as a reduction to total shareholders' equity.

Although treasury shares are still considered to be issued shares, they decrease the company's shares that are outstanding. This is because the shares are no longer held by outsiders (the shareholders). We compute outstanding shares as follows:

> Outstanding shares = Issued shares – Treasury shares

Outstanding shares are important because only outstanding shares have voting rights and receive cash dividends. Treasury shares don't have voting rights, and they get no dividends. Now let's illustrate how to account for treasury shares, continuing with Mackay Industries.

Purchase of Treasury Shares

Assuming that there was no stock split or stock dividend, Mackay Industries' shareholders' equity on August 1, the same as on June 30, is shown in **Exhibit 10-5**.

Mackay Industries, Inc. Shareholders' Equity August 1	
Share Capital:	
Preferred Shares, 500,000 shares authorized,	
10,000 shares issued	$ 250,000
Common Shares, 2,000,000 shares authorized,	
500,000 shares issued	7,500,000
Total Share Capital	7,750,000
Retained Earnings	2,000,000
Total Shareholders' Equity	$9,750,000

Exhibit 10-5 ▲

Assume that on August 10, Mackay Industries purchased 5,000 treasury shares (common shares). If cash paid is less than the average cost of the shares, then the Contributed Surplus account will be increased to record the difference. If cash paid is more than the average cost of the shares, then Retained Earnings should be reduced. For example, Mackay Industries pays $12 per share to purchase back 5,000 of its shares. Mackay would record the purchase as follows:

DATE	ACCOUNTS	POST REF.	DR.	CR.
Aug 10	Treasury Shares ($7,500,000 ÷ 500,000) × 5,000		75,000	
	Contributed Surplus			15,000
	Cash			60,000
	Purchased 5,000 treasury shares.			

Suppose MacKay purchases another 10,000 shares at $17 per share on October 1. Since the purchase price per share is higher than the average price, MacKay needs to reduce the contributed surplus to zero. If the balance in the Contributed Surplus account is not enough, then MacKay needs to reduce retained earnings. The entry for the October 1 purchase follows:

DATE	ACCOUNTS	POST REF.	DR.	CR.
Oct 1	Treasury Shares ($7,500,000 ÷ 500,000) × 10,000		150,000	
	Contributed Surplus		15,000	
	Retained Earnings		5,000	
	Cash			170,000
	Purchased 10,000 treasury shares.			

After posting the entry, the Treasury Shares account would look like this:

Treasury Shares		
8/10	75,000	
10/1	150,000	
	225,000	

CRITICAL THINKING

Take a minute to think about each of the following cases. What would be the impact from the company's perspective and the shareholders' perspective?

Cases	Impact on Company	Impact on Shareholders
(1) Sida's shares are trading at $100. Sida's management thinks that the share price is too high and is considering three courses of action: (1) 4-for-1 stock split, (2) 20% stock dividend, or (3) $10 cash dividend. What is your recommendation?		
	Recommendation:	
(2) Darcy's has 1,000,000 shares outstanding and the shares are trading at $10. Darcy's management thinks that the share price is too low and is considering two courses of action: (1) purchase back 500,000 shares, or (2) 1-for-2 reverse stock split. What is your recommendation?		
	Recommendation:	

Solutions:

Cases	Impact on Company	Impact on Shareholders
(1) Sida's shares are trading at $100. Sida's management thinks that the share price is too high and is considering three courses of actions: (1) 4-for-1 stock split, (2) 20% stock dividend, or (3) $10 cash dividend. What is your recommendation?	(1) The number of shares will quadruple and the share price will drop to approximately $25. (2) The number of shares will increase by 20% and the share price will be approximately $83.33. (3) The number of shares is unchanged and the share price will drop to approximately $90.	(1) The number of shares increases but not the value of their investment. However, a 4-for-1 stock split sends a positive signal to investors that usually results in the shares performing well. (2) The number of shares increases but not the value of their investment. (3) The number of shares is unchanged but the investors receive cash in their account.

Recommendation:

All three actions will reduce the share price. However, the 4-for-1 stock split has the biggest impact on share price reduction and a potential benefit of better share performance.

Cases	Impact on Company	Impact on Shareholders
(2) Darcy's has 1,000,000 shares outstanding and the shares are trading at $10. Darcy's management thinks that the share price is too low and is considering two courses of action: (1) purchase back 500,000 shares, or (2) 1-for-2 reverse stock split. What is your recommendation?	(1) The company's cash will be reduced by $5,000,000, and the number of shares outstanding will reduce to 500,000 shares. But the share price will remain approximately unchanged. (2) The company's shares will be reduced by 500,000 shares, but the total share capital remains unchanged. Therefore, the share price will approximately double to $20 per share.	(1) The share price does not change; however, those shareholders who keep their shares see their percentage ownership stake in the company double. (2) The number of shares owned by each shareholder is cut in half, but the share price approximately doubled. Therefore, the ownership stake in the company does not change.

Recommendation:

Since the goal is to increase the share price, the reverse stock split achieves that goal. However, a share buyback often sends a positive signal to investors, which may result in a small increase in share price.

HOW IS SHAREHOLDERS' EQUITY REPORTED?

The components of Shareholders' Equity include two major categories:

 7 Report shareholders' equity

❶ Contributed Capital: the items included in this category are Share Capital, such as Common and Preferred Shares, and Contributed Surplus.

❷ Earned Capital: the items included in this category are Retained Earnings and Accumulated Other Comprehensive Income.

Accumulated Other Comprehensive Income (AOCI) is the cumulative change in equity related to other comprehensive income that bypasses net income. Under IFRS, companies need to present the following items as Other Comprehensive Income (OCI):

1 Foreign currency translation adjustments

2 Changes in the fair value of available-for-sale financial assets

3 Revaluations of property, plant, and equipment

4 Changes in the fair value of a financial instrument in a cash flow hedge

Under IFRS, companies need to prepare a Statement of Comprehensive Income and Statement of Changes in Equity showing every account, including Accumulated Other Comprehensive Income. This statement is used to show investors the significant changes in all of the equity categories that occurred during the year. An example of a statement of shareholders' equity is presented in **Exhibit 10-6**.

	Preferred Shares	Common Shares	Contributed Surplus	Retained Earnings	Other Comprehensive Income	Total
Example Company						
Statement of Shareholders' Equity						
Year Ended December 31, 2014						
Balance, December 31, 2013	$250,000	$5,000,000	$15,000	$450,000	$35,000	$5,750,000
Increase in OCI					5,000	5,000
Issue of Preferred Shares	100,000					100,000
Purchase of Common Shares		(75,000)	(15,000)			(90,000)
Stock Dividend		50,000		(50,000)		0
Cash Dividend:						0
Preferred				(25,000)		(25,000)
Common				(50,000)		(50,000)
Balance, December 31, 2014	$350,000	$4,975,000	$ 0	$325,000	$40,000	$5,690,000

Exhibit 10-6 ▲

FOCUS ON DECISION MAKING: RATIOS

8 Evaluate return on shareholders' equity and return on common shareholders' equity

Investors are constantly evaluating companies' profits to determine performance. Two important ratios to use for comparison are return on shareholders' equity and return on common shareholders' equity.

Rate of Return on Shareholders' Equity

Rate of return on shareholders' equity, or **return on equity**, shows the relationship between net income and the average shareholders' equity. The numerator is net income and the denominator is average shareholders' equity. Let's assume Mackay Industries has the following data:

Net income for 2014	$136,000
Total shareholders' equity, 12/31/2014...	$943,000
Total shareholders' equity, 12/31/2013...	$825,000

Mackay Industries' rate of return on shareholders' equity for 2014 is computed as follows:

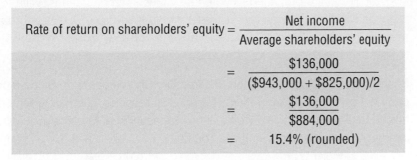

$$\text{Rate of return on shareholders' equity} = \frac{\text{Net income}}{\text{Average shareholders' equity}}$$

$$= \frac{\$136,000}{(\$943,000 + \$825,000)/2}$$

$$= \frac{\$136,000}{\$884,000}$$

$$= 15.4\% \text{ (rounded)}$$

Rate of Return on Common Shareholders' Equity

Rate of return on common shareholders' equity, or **return on common equity**, shows the relationship between the net income available to the common shareholders and their average shareholders' equity. The numerator is net income minus preferred dividends. The preferred dividends are subtracted because they represent part of the net income that is unavailable to the common shareholders. The denominator is average common shareholders' equity (total shareholders' equity minus preferred share capital). Let's assume Mackay Industries has the following data:

Net income for 2014	$136,000
Preferred dividends for 2014	$ 18,000
Common shareholders' equity, 12/31/2014	$847,000
Common shareholders' equity, 12/31/2013	$723,000

Mackay Industries' rate of return on common shareholders' equity for 2014 is computed as follows:

$$\text{Rate of return on common shareholders' equity} = \frac{\text{Net income} - \text{preferred dividends}}{\text{Average common shareholders' equity}}$$

$$= \frac{\$136,000 - 18,000}{(\$847,000 + \$723,000)/2}$$

$$= \frac{\$118,000}{\$785,000}$$

$$= 15.0\% \text{ (rounded)}$$

Return on equity can be compared to returns that can be earned from other investments such as investments in other companies, or even investments in money market accounts or certificates of deposit. Returns on equity between 13% and 15% are generally considered to be good returns. Mackay Industries' return on equity of 15.4% and return on common equity of 15.0% are both strong.

FOCUS ON USERS

Concept	User	Why is this Important to this User?
Dividends		Shareholders are able to receive a financial benefit from owning shares in two ways: the value of the share increasing and receiving dividends. As an investor, if you are preparing to purchase some shares, you may wish to examine the financial statements to determine the history of dividend payments. This will provide an indication of what you may expect in the way of dividends should you decide to purchase the shares.
Treasury Shares		Shareholders will want to watch the Treasury Shares account. Since a company will purchase its own shares for specific reasons, such as to fend off a hostile take-over, the appearance of new treasury shares can signal some interesting developments with the company.
Stock Splits		Competitors will want to watch the market for actions such as stock splits. A stock split can be used when the share price for a company has become high and perhaps a little too expensive for the average investor to make the stock more affordable. A stock split could indicate that the company is expecting further good results for the company or that the company may be looking to raise funds by issuing more shares. Raising additional funds is usually a sign that the company will be expanding or going through a growth phase and requires funds to support this action. If a competitor can read these signs and have an idea of the competition's movements before they happen, then the competitor can plan its own strategy to deal with the changes in the market too.

DEMO DOC

MyAccountingLab

Visit MyAccountingLab at www. myaccountinglab.com to watch animated versions of these Demo Docs.

L.O. 3 – 6

Equity Transactions

At January 1, 2014, Sara, Corp. had 2,000 common shares outstanding, $20,000. During 2014, Sara had the following transactions:

Jan 31	Issued 500 common shares for $10 cash per share.
Mar 31	Declared cash dividends of $0.40 per common share.
May 31	Paid the cash dividends declared in March.
Jul 31	Purchased 300 treasury shares for $11 cash per share.
Sep 30	Declared and distributed a 5% stock dividend when the market price was $12 per share.
Dec 31	Declared 2-for-1 stock split.

Requirement:

❶ **Journalize all of Sara's equity transactions for 2014. After each transaction determine how many common shares are outstanding.**

Demo Doc Solutions

Requirement ❶

Journalize all of Sara's equity transactions for 2014. After each transaction determine how many common shares are outstanding.

Part 1	Demo Doc Complete

Jan 31   Issued 500 common shares for $10 cash per share.

Issuing common shares means that brand new share certificates were printed by Sara and sold to outside investors. It means an increase (credit) to Common Shares.

Sara receives $10 cash per share, so Cash is increased (debit) by $5,000 (500 shares × $10 per share), and Common Shares increase (credit) by $5,000.

DATE	ACCOUNTS	POST REF.	DR.	CR.
Jan 31	Cash (500 shares × $10)		5,000	
	Common Shares (500 shares × $10)			5,000
	Issued shares.			

Selling common shares to outside investors increases the number of outstanding shares. So after this transaction, Sara has 2,500 (2,000 + 500) common shares outstanding.

Mar 31   Declared cash dividends of $0.40 per common share.

DATE	ACCOUNTS	POST REF.	DR.	CR.
Mar 31	Retained Earnings		1,000	
	Dividends Payable (2,500 shares × $0.40)			1,000
	Declared cash dividends.			

Declaring cash dividends decreases Retained Earnings (debit) and increases Dividends Payable (credit) by the amount to be paid. Sara declares $1,000 (2,500 shares outstanding × $0.40 per share) in cash dividends.

Declaring cash dividends does not change the number of outstanding shares, so 2,500 common shares remain outstanding after this transaction.

May 31   Paid the cash dividends declared in March.

When the dividends are paid, the Dividends Payable account is decreased (debit), in this case by $1,000, and Cash is also decreased (credit) by $1,000.

DATE	ACCOUNTS	POST REF.	DR.	CR.
May 31	Dividends Payable		1,000	
	Cash			1,000
	Paid cash dividends.			

Paying cash dividends does not change the number of outstanding shares, so 2,500 common shares remain outstanding after this transaction.

Jul 31   Purchased 300 treasury shares for $11 cash per share.

When treasury shares are purchased, the Treasury Shares account is increased by the cost of the treasury shares. Treasury Shares is a *contra-equity* account, which means that it has a balance *opposite* to normal equity accounts. Most equity accounts have credit balances, so Treasury Shares has a debit balance. *Treasury shares decrease equity.* Cash is also decreased because Sara is *buying* (that is, paying for) the treasury shares.

In this case, the Treasury Shares account is increased (debit) by $3,000 (300 shares × $10 average cost per share), Retained Earnings is reduced (debit) by $300, and Cash is decreased (credit) by $3,300.

DATE	ACCOUNTS	POST REF.	DR.	CR.
Aug 10	Treasury Shares (300 shares × $10)		3,000	
	Retained Earnings		300	
	Cash			3,300
	Purchased 300 treasury shares.			

Treasury shares are *no longer outstanding*. Because they are held by the company, they no longer have votes at shareholder meetings nor do they receive dividends. So the number of outstanding shares is now 2,200 (2,500 − 300).

Sep 30 Declared and distributed a 5% stock dividend when the market price was $12 per share.

Stock dividends are similar to cash dividends except that a stock dividend is distributed in shares instead of paid in cash. The stock dividend will issue brand new common shares to investors who already own shares of the corporation.

Dividends (both shares and cash) only apply to *outstanding* shares. The treasury shares are considered inactive and *do not* receive dividends of any kind.

Just as with cash dividends, stock dividends decrease Retained Earnings. Retained Earnings is decreased by the *market value* of the new shares issued. Retained Earnings is decreased (debit) by $1,320 (2,200 shares × 5% × $12 per share), and the Common Shares account is increased by $1,320.

The remainder of the entry is similar to the entry to issue common shares. The only difference between this transaction and the one on January 31 is that Retained Earnings is debited *instead of* Cash.

DATE	ACCOUNTS	POST REF.	DR.	CR.
Sep 30	Retained Earnings (2,200 × 5% × $12)		1,320	
	Common Shares (2,200 × 5% × $12)			1,320
	Declared and distributed a stock dividend.			

Because the stock dividend increases the number of common shares held by outside investors, it increases the number of outstanding common shares by 110 shares (2,200 shares × 5%). So after this transaction, Sara has 2,310 (2,200 + 110) common shares outstanding.

Dec 31 Declared 2-for-1 stock split.

A stock split does not affect any account balances, and no journal entry is required. However, a note disclosure is necessary. Sara, Corp. would state that on December 31, the board of directors declared a 2-for-1 common stock split. The total number of common shares outstanding after the split is 4,620 shares.

Demo Doc Complete

Part 1	Demo Doc Complete

DECISION GUIDELINES

Corporations: Contributed Capital and Retained Earnings

The corporate form of business organization is very popular. You will possibly work for a corporation someday. Or, you may even have an opportunity to organize your own corporation. If you do, you will most likely encounter the following decisions.

Decision	Guideline	Analyze
As a member of the Board of Directors, I make decisions on when to declare dividends, how much to declare, and whether they will be cash dividends or something else. When making these decisions, when is a cash dividend appropriate?	Consider the amount of available cash as well as the balance in Retained Earnings.	A cash dividend is a distribution of earnings to the company's shareholders. So a company cannot declare and distribute dividends unless the balance in retained earnings (counting the current year's earnings) exceeds the amount of the desired dividend. In addition, the company must have the cash available to pay the dividend if it is declared. A business should carefully analyze its future cash needs so that it does not deplete its cash with a dividend and end up with cash flow issues in the future.
I am a member of the Board of Directors and we are having difficulty selling our shares on the stock market. We've been told that our share price is too high because the company has been performing very well. To decrease the market price of a company's shares is it better to use a stock dividend or a stock split?	The amount by which a company wishes to reduce the market price of the shares influences the decision to use a stock dividend or a stock split.	Because both a stock dividend and a stock split increase the number of outstanding shares (with no increase in the company's Shareholders' Equity), they both reduce the market value of a company's shares. A stock split usually increases the number of outstanding shares by a larger amount than a stock dividend. Therefore, it tends to have a bigger impact on the market price of the shares and should be used when a significant decrease in the market price is desired. For example, a 2-for-1 split will typically reduce the market price of a company's shares by 50%.

ACCOUNTING VOCABULARY
THE LANGUAGE OF BUSINESS

Accumulated other comprehensive income (p. 594) The cumulative change in equity that is due to the revenues and expenses, and gains and losses derived from non-shareholder transactions.

Arrears (p. 583) A cumulative dividend on preferred shares that has not been paid for the year.

Cumulative preferred shares (p. 583) Preferred shares whose owners must receive all dividends in arrears before the corporation pays dividends to the common shareholders.

Issue price (p. 580) The price the shares initially sell for the first time they are sold.

Legal capital (p. 581) The portion of shareholders' equity that cannot be used for dividends.

Memorandum entry (p. 588) A journal entry that "notes" a significant event, but which has no debit or credit amount.

Par value (p. 580) Arbitrary amount assigned to a share.

Preferred shares (p. 579) Shares that gives their owners certain advantages over common shareholders, such as the right to receive dividends before the common shareholders and the right to receive assets before the common shareholders if the corporation liquidates.

Rate of return on common shareholders' equity (p. 595) Net income minus preferred dividends, divided by average common shareholders' equity. It is a measure of profitability; also called *return on common equity*.

Rate of return on shareholders' equity (p. 594) Net income divided by average shareholders' equity. It is a measure of profitability; also called *return on equity*.

Return on common equity (p. 595) Net income minus preferred dividends, divided by average common shareholders' equity. It is measure of profitability; also called *rate of return on common shareholders' equity*.

Return on equity (p. 594) Net income divided by average shareholders' equity. It is a measure of profitability; also called *rate of return on shareholders' equity*.

Stock dividend (p. 585) A distribution by a corporation of its own shares to shareholders.

Stock split (p. 587) An increase in the number of outstanding shares coupled with a proportionate reduction in the value of the shares.

Treasury shares (p. 590) A corporation's own shares that it has issued and later reacquired.

Underwriter (p. 580) A firm, such as TD Waterhouse, that usually agrees to buy all the shares a company wants to issue if the firm cannot sell the shares to its clients.

MyAccountingLab

Make the grade with MyAccountingLab. The exercises and problems in this chapter can be found on MyAccountingLab at www.myaccountinglab.com. You can practise them as often as you want, and they feature step-by-step guided solutions to help you find the right answer.

ACCOUNTING PRACTICE

DISCUSSION QUESTIONS

1. What are the four basic rights of shareholders?

2. Assume that you are a CFO of a company that is attempting to raise additional capital to finance an expansion of its production facility. You are considering either issuing bonds or additional shares. What are some of the differences in the two options?

3. What accounts, if any, are involved in the journal entries to record the events associated with each of the following dates associated with cash dividends?
   a. Declaration date
   b. Date of record
   c. Payment date

4. With which type of shares would dividends in arrears be associated? Why?

5. What accounts are affected by the declaration and distribution of a stock dividend? What is the effect of a stock dividend on
   a. Total Shareholders' Equity?
   b. Total Assets?
   c. Total Liabilities?
   d. Cash?

6. What are some of the reasons for issuing a stock dividend?

7. What kind of account is Treasury Shares? What is its normal balance? Where would it be reported on the financial statements?

8. What could you reasonably conclude if a company reports more shares issued than outstanding?

9. Why are preferred dividends subtracted from the numerator in calculating the return on common equity ratio?

SELF CHECK

1. Which characteristic of a corporation is considered to be an advantage?

   a. Ease of transferring ownership
   b. Indefinite life
   c. Limited shareholder liability
   d. All of the above

2. Which of the following is a disadvantage of organizing as a corporation?

   a. Separate legal entity
   b. Limited ability to raise capital
   c. Double taxation
   d. Limited shareholder liability

3. What are the two basic sources of corporate capital?

   a. Share capital and retained earnings
   b. Shares and bonds
   c. Common shares and preferred shares
   d. Retained earnings and dividends

4. Which of the following statements is correct?

   a. A stock split results in a transfer of retained earnings while a stock dividend does not
   b. A stock dividend changes the proportion of ownership while a stock split does not
   c. While a stock split does not require any journal entries, it does require disclosure in the notes to the financial statements
   d. None of the above

5. Chewning Corporation has 10,000 shares of 5%, $10, cumulative preferred shares and 50,000 common shares outstanding. Chewning Corporation declared no dividends in 2014. In 2015, Chewning Corporation declares a total dividend of $25,000. How much of the dividends goes to the common shareholders?

   a. $ 5,000
   c. $15,000
   b. $10,000
   d. None; it all goes to preferred.

6. Techster Company has 10,000 common shares outstanding, which Techster Company issued at $5 per share. Techster Company also has retained earnings of $80,000. How much is Techster Company's total shareholders' equity?

   a. $ 50,000
   c. $ 90,000
   b. $ 80,000
   d. $130,000

7. What is the term for a company's own shares that it has issued and repurchased?

   a. Issued shares
   b. Stock dividend
   c. Outstanding shares
   d. Treasury shares

8. What does a stock dividend do?

   a. Increases Common Shares
   b. Has no effect on total equity
   c. Decreases Retained Earnings
   d. All of the above

9. What happens with a stock split?

   a. Increases the number of shares issued
   b. Reduces Retained Earnings
   c. Both a and b
   d. None of the above

10. Assume that Pier 1 Imports pays $10 per share to purchase 1,000 of its common shares as treasury shares. What is the effect of purchasing the treasury shares?

    a. Decreases total shareholders' equity by $1,000
    b. Decreases total shareholders' equity by $10,000

c. Increases total shareholders' equity by $1,000

d. Increases total shareholders' equity by $10,000

Answers are given after Written Communication.

SHORT EXERCISES

S10-1. Shareholders' equity terminology (*Learning Objectives 1 & 2*) 10–15 min.

Match the following terms with the correct definition.

a. Common shares	_____ **1.** Share capital plus Retained Earnings.
b. Share capital	_____ **2.** Capital from investments by the shareholders.
c. Dividends	_____ **3.** Capital earned through profitable operation of the business.
d. Legal capital	
e. Outstanding shares	_____ **4.** The basic form of capital shares.
f. Preferred shares	_____ **5.** Shares in the hands of shareholders.
g. Retained earnings	_____ **6.** Distributions by a corporation to its shareholders.
h. Treasury shares	
i. Shareholders' equity	_____ **7.** Shares that give their owners certain advantages over common shareholders, such as the right to receive dividends before the common shareholders.
	_____ **8.** The portion of shareholders' equity maintained for the protection of creditors.
	_____ **9.** A corporation's own shares that it reacquires.

S10-2. Shares issuance (*Learning Objectives 3, 4, & 7*) 15–20 min.

Tricor, Corp. was incorporated on January 20, 2014. During 2014, Tricor had the following transactions related to share capital:

1. Issued 300,000 common shares for $3 million.
2. Issued 20,000 cumulative preferred shares for $25 per share, with $1.50 dividend per share.
3. Tricor showed a $35,000 net loss.

Requirements

1. Prepare journal entries.
2. Prepare the shareholders' equity section of the balance sheet at December 31, 2014.
3. Assuming that you are a preferred shareholder, would you expect to receive a dividend in 2014? Explain.

S10-3. Issuance of shares for cash and noncash assets (*Learning Objective 3*) 10–15 min.

This exercise shows the similarity and the difference between two ways to acquire plant assets.

Case A—Issue shares and buy the assets in separate transactions:

Atar, Inc. issued 10,000 common shares for cash of $700,000. In a separate transaction, Atar, Inc. purchased a building for $500,000 and equipment for $200,000. Journalize the two transactions.

Case B—Issue shares to acquire the assets:

Atar, Inc. issued 10,000 common shares to acquire a building valued at $500,000 and equipment worth $200,000. Journalize this single transaction.

Compare the balances in all accounts after making both sets of entries. Are the account balances similar or different?

S10-4. Share issuance (*Learning Objectives 2 & 3*) 5–10 min.

The Kingston Company reported the following on its balance sheet at December 31, 2014:

	Common Shares, 500,000 shares authorized,		
	350,000 shares issued and outstanding		$ 473,000
	Retained Earnings		2,500,000

1. Assume Kingston Company issued all of its shares during 2014. Journalize the company's issuance of the shares for cash.

S10-5. Analyzing shareholders' equity (*Learning Objectives 2 & 3*) 5–10 min.

At December 31, 2014, Kingston Company reported the following on its comparative balance sheet, which included 2013 amounts for comparison:

	December 31	
	2014	**2013**
Common Shares, 500,000 shares authorized, 350,000 shares issued and outstanding in 2014; 349,000 shares in 2013	$ 473,000	$ 439,250
Retained Earnings	2,500,000	2,250,000

1. How much did Kingston Company's total share capital increase during 2014? What caused total share capital to increase? How can you tell?

2. Did Kingston Company have a profit or a loss for 2014? How can you tell?

S10-6. Shares issuance (*Learning Objectives 2 & 3*) 5–10 min.

Bruner Corporation has two classes of shares, common shares and preferred shares. Journalize Bruner's issuance of the following:

a. 1,000 common shares for $50 per share

b. 1,000 preferred shares for a total of $32,000

Explanations are not required.

S10-7. Accounting for cash dividends (*Learning Objective 4*) 10–15 min.

Midas Company earned net income of $85,000 during the year ended December 31, 2014. On December 15, 2014, Midas Company declared the annual cash dividend on its 6% preferred shares ($100,000) and a $0.50 per share cash dividend on its common shares (50,000 shares outstanding). Midas Company then paid the dividends on January 4, 2015.

Journalize for Midas Company

a. declaring the cash dividends on December 15, 2014.

b. paying the cash dividends on January 4, 2015.

S10-8. Accounting for cash dividends (*Learning Objective 4*) 10–15 min.

Holiday.com prepared the following shareholders' equity section as of December 31, 2014.

Shareholders' Equity	
Share Capital:	
Preferred Shares, 5%, 5,000 shares authorized,	
400 shares issued and outstanding	$ 40,000
Common Shares, 20,000 shares authorized,	
5,000 shares issued and outstanding	120,000
Total Share Capital	$160,000
Retained Earnings	90,000
Total Shareholders' Equity	$250,000

Answer the following questions about Holiday.com's dividends:

1. How much in dividends must Holiday.com declare each year before the common shareholders get any cash dividends for the year?

2. Suppose Holiday.com declares cash dividends of $20,000 for 2014. How much of the dividends goes to preferred? How much goes to common?

3. Are Holiday.com's preferred shares cumulative or noncumulative? How can you tell?

4. Suppose Holiday.com passed the preferred dividend in 2015 and 2016. In 2017, the company declares cash dividends of $9,000. How much of the dividends goes to preferred? How much goes to common?

S10-9. Accounting for stock dividends (*Learning Objective 5*) 10–15 min.

Transtech, Inc. has 200,000 common shares outstanding. Transtech, Inc. declares and distributes a 5% stock dividend when the market value of its shares is $10 per share.

1. Journalize Transtech's declaration and distribution of the stock dividend on September 30. An explanation is not required.

2. What is the overall effect of the stock dividend on Transtech's total assets? On total shareholders' equity?

S10-10. Comparing cash and stock dividends (*Learning Objectives 4 & 5*) 10–15 min.

Compare and contrast the accounting for cash dividends and stock dividends. In the space provided, insert either "Cash dividends," "Stock dividends," or "Both" to complete each of the following statements:

1. _____ increase share capital by the same amount that they decrease retained earnings.

2. _____ decrease both total assets and total shareholders' equity.

3. _____ decrease retained earnings.

4. _____ have no effect on a liability.

S10-11. Accounting for stock splits (*Learning Objective 5*) 5–10 min.

Suppose Pier 1 Imports has common shares, 500,000 shares authorized, and 100,000 shares issued and outstanding. The book value of the common shares is $500,000. The company decided to split its common shares 2-for-1 to decrease the market price of its shares. The company's shares were trading at $20 immediately before the split. The common shares account balance was $100,000 prior to the split.

1. Show how the common shareholders' equity would appear in the shareholders' equity section of Pier 1 Imports' balance sheet after the stock split.

2. Which account balances changed after the stock split? Which account balances were unchanged?

S10-12. Accounting for treasury shares (*Learning Objective 6*) 10–15 min.

Classic Corporation began operations in 2014. After issuing its common shares to the public, Classic Corporation completed the following treasury shares transaction:

a. Purchased 2,000 shares of the company's $1 average price common shares as treasury shares, paying cash of $5 per share.

Journalize the transaction. Explanations are not required. Show how Classic Corporation will report treasury shares on its December 31, 2014 balance sheet. In reporting the treasury shares, focus solely on the Treasury Shares account. You may ignore all other accounts.

S10-13. Balance sheet disclosure of shareholders' equity (*Learning Objective 7*) 5–10 min.

The financial statements of Nason Corporation reported the following accounts (in thousands):

Contributed Surplus	$170	Net Sales	$1,080
Cost of Goods Sold	588	Accounts Payable	60
Common Shares, 400 shares		Retained Earnings	166
issued and outstanding	400	Other Current Liabilities	52
Cash	240	Operating Expenses	412
Long-Term Debt	76	Total Assets	?

Prepare the shareholders' equity section of Nason Corporation's balance sheet. Net income has already been closed to Retained Earnings.

S10-14. Analyzing shareholders' equity (*Learning Objective 7*) 10–15 min.

Use the statement of shareholders' equity in Exhibit 10-6 to answer the following questions:

1. Make journal entries to record the declaration and payment of cash dividends during 2014.

2. How much cash did the issuance of preferred shares bring in during 2014?

3. What was the cost of the treasury shares that were purchased during 2014?

EXERCISES (GROUP A)

E10-1A. Shares issuance (*Learning Objective 3*) 10–15 min.

Stanley Systems completed the following shares issuance transactions:

Apr 19	Issued 1,000 common shares for cash of $10.50 per share.
May 3	Sold 300 shares of $4.50, preferred shares for $15,000 cash.
11	Received inventory valued at $23,000 and equipment with a market value of $11,000. Issued 3,000 common shares in exchange.

Requirement

1. Journalize the transactions. Explanations are not required.

E10-2A. Share issuance (*Learning Objectives 3 & 7*) 10–15 min.

The charter for Zycor, Inc. authorizes the company to issue 100,000 preferred shares and 500,000 common shares. During its start-up phase, Zycor, Inc. completed the following transactions:

2014

Aug	6	Issued 500 common shares to the promoters who organized the corporation, receiving cash of $15,000.
	12	Issued 300 preferred shares for cash of $20,000.
	14	Issued 1,000 common shares in exchange for land valued at $26,000.

Requirements

1. Record the transactions in the journal.

2. Prepare the shareholders' equity section of Zycor's balance sheet at December 31, 2014. Assume that the company earned net income of $25,000 during this period.

E10-3A. Share issuance and financial statement presentation (*Learning Objectives 3 & 7*) 15–20 min.

BiBa Manufacturing's charter authorized the company to issue an unlimited number of common shares and 750,000 preferred shares. The following transactions occurred during BiBa's first year of business:

Jan 10	Issued 5,000 common shares to the firm's promoters for the work done to set up the corporation. This work has an estimated value of $60,000.
May 21	40,000 shares were issued for cash of $15 per share.
July 25	15,000 preferred shares were issued for cash totalling $225,000.
Oct 1	50,000 common shares in total were issued for land, buildings, and equipment with appraised values of $250,000, $380,000, and $170,000 respectively.

Requirements

1. Prepare journal entries for all the transactions.

2. Prepare the shareholders' equity section of the balance sheet at December 31, 2014

E10-4A. Issuance of shares for cash and noncash assets (*Learning Objective 3*) 10–15 min.

Victor, Co. recently organized. The company issued common shares to an attorney in exchange for his patent with a market value of $40,000. In addition, Victor, Co. received cash for 2,000 of its $50 preferred shares, and 26,000 of its common shares sold at $10 per share. Retained Earnings at the end of the first year was $70,000.

Requirement

1. Without making journal entries, determine the total share capital created by these transactions.

E10-5A. Accounting for cash dividends (*Learning Objective 4*) 10–15 min.

Horizon Communications has the following shareholders' equity:

Quick solution:

2014 dividends = $15,000 preferred, $0 common; 2015 dividends = $17,000 preferred, $33,000 common

Horizon Communications Shareholders' Equity	
Share Capital:	
Preferred Shares, 8%, unlimited number of shares authorized,	
20,000 shares issued and outstanding	$ 200,000
Common Shares, 500,000 shares authorized,	
300,000 shares issued and outstanding	750,000
Total Share Capital	$ 950,000
Retained Earnings	150,000
Total Shareholders' Equity	$1,100,000

Requirement

1. Assume the preferred shares are cumulative. Compute the amount of dividends to preferred and common shareholders for 2014 and 2015 if total dividends are $15,000 in 2014 and $50,000 in 2015.

E10-6A. Accounting for cash dividends (*Learning Objective 4*) 10–15 min.

The following elements of shareholders' equity are adapted from the balance sheet of Scribner Corporation.

Shareholders' Equity	$ Thousands
Preferred Shares, cumulative, $0.40, 50,000 shares issued and outstanding	$100
Common Shares, 9,000,000 shares issued and outstanding	900

Scribner Corporation paid no preferred dividends in 2014 but paid the designated amount of cash dividends per share to preferred shareholders in all prior years.

Requirement

1. Compute the dividends to preferred and common shareholders for 2015 if total dividends are $150,000.

E10-7A. Accounting for stock dividends (*Learning Objectives 5 & 7*) 10–15 min.

The shareholders' equity for Blade, Inc. on December 31, 2013, follows:

Shareholders' Equity	
Share Capital:	
Common Shares, 100,000 shares authorized,	
50,000 shares issued and outstanding	$450,000
Total Share Capital	$450,000
Retained Earnings	120,000
Total Shareholders' Equity	$570,000

On April 30, 2014, the market price of Blade's common shares was $16 per share and the company distributed a 10% stock dividend.

Requirements

1. Journalize the declaration and distribution of the stock dividend.

2. Prepare the shareholders' equity section of the balance sheet after the stock dividend.

E10-8A. Accounting for cash and stock dividends (*Learning Objectives 4 & 5*) 10–15 min.

Rolly Racing Motors is authorized to issue an unlimited number of common shares. The company issued 80,000 shares at $4 per share, and all 80,000 shares are outstanding. When the market price of common shares was $5 per share, Rolly Racing Motors declared and distributed a 10% stock dividend. Later, Rolly Racing Motors declared and paid a $0.50 per share cash dividend.

Requirements

1. Journalize the declaration and distribution of the stock dividend.

2. Journalize the declaration and the payment of the cash dividend.

E10-9A. Accounting for stock splits (*Learning Objectives 5 & 7*) 10–15 min.

Lipton Travel, Inc. had the following shareholders' equity at May 31:

Shareholders' Equity	
Share Capital:	
Common Shares, 200,000 shares authorized, 50,000 shares issued and outstanding	$600,000
Total Share Capital	$600,000
Retained Earnings	200,000
Total Shareholders' Equity	$800,000

On June 30, Lipton Travel, Inc. split its common shares 2-for-1.

Requirement

1. Make any necessary entries to record the stock split.

2. Prepare the shareholders' equity section of the balance sheet immediately after the split.

E10-10A. Accounting for shares issuance, splits, and treasury shares (*Learning Objectives 3, 5, & 6*) 20–25 min.

Consider each of the following transactions separately from every other transaction:

a. Issuance of 50,000 common shares at $15.

b. Purchase of 1,000 treasury shares (average price is $0.50) at $5 per share.

c. Issuance of a 10% stock dividend. Before the dividend, 500,000 common shares were outstanding; market value was $7 at the time of the dividend.

d. Split shares 3-for-1. Prior to the split, 60,000 common shares were outstanding.

Requirement

1. Identify whether each transaction increased, decreased, or did not change total shareholders' equity.

E10-11A. Accounting for treasury shares (*Learning Objectives 3 & 6*) 10–15 min.

Journalize the following transactions of Goddard Sports, Inc., a chain of sports stores:

Feb	4	Issued 20,000 common shares at $15 per share.
Apr	22	Purchased 1,000 treasury shares at $14 per share.
Jun	20	Purchased 2,000 treasury shares at $16 per share.

E10-12A. Accounting for treasury shares (*Learning Objectives 6 & 7*) 20–25 min.

Franklin, Inc. had the following shareholders' equity on November 30:

Shareholders' Equity	
Share Capital:	
Common Shares, unlimited number of shares authorized,	
50,000 shares issued and 45,000 shares outstanding	$400,000
Contributed Surplus (purchase of treasury shares, June 30)	10,000
Retained Earnings	520,000
Less: 5,000 Treasury Shares	(40,000)
Total Shareholders' Equity	$890,000

On December 30, Franklin, Inc. purchased another 8,000 treasury shares at $10 per share.

Requirement

1. What is the average price per common share? What is the amount paid to purchase treasury shares on June 30?

2. Journalize the purchases of the treasury shares on June 30 and December 30.

3. Prepare the shareholders' equity section of the balance sheet at December 31.

E10-13A. Balance sheet disclosure of shareholders' equity (*Learning Objective 7*) 10–15 min.

Casey Manufacturing, Co. has the following selected account balances at June 30, 2014.

Common Shares, unlimited number of shares authorized, 100,000 shares issued and outstanding	$100,000	Inventory	$112,000
		Machinery and Equipment	109,000
		Preferred Shares, 5%, 20,000 shares authorized, 5,000 shares issued and	
Accumulated Depreciation, Machinery and Equipment	62,000	outstanding	190,000
Retained Earnings	110,000	Cost of Goods Sold	81,000

Requirement

1. Prepare the shareholders' equity section of the company's balance sheet.

E10-14A. Accounting for various shareholders' equity transactions (*Learning Objectives 3, 4, 5, 7, & 8*) 20–25 min.

Smart Tech Inc.'s shareholders' equity on December 31, 2013, was as follows:

Shareholders' Equity	
Share Capital:	
Preferred Shares, $1 accumulated deferred dividends,	
150,000 shares authorized, 50,000 issued and outstanding	$1,000,000
Common Shares, unlimited number of shares authorized,	
100,000 shares issued and outstanding	$2,000,000
Retained Earnings	450,000
Total Shareholders' Equity	$3,450,000

During 2014, the following transactions occurred.

Jan	2	10,000 preferred shares were issued at $22.00 per share.
Feb	1	12,000 common shares were issued in exchange for a building with a fair value of $300,000.
Nov	25	Declared preferred dividends to be paid on December 23.
Dec	27	Declared 5% common stock dividend, when the market price was $25, to be distributed on January 30, 2015
Dec	31	Net income for the year was $520,000.

Requirements

1. Journalize the above transactions.
2. Prepare the shareholders' equity section of the Smart Tech Inc. balance sheet as of December 31, 2014.

E10-15A. Accounting for cash, stock dividends, and stock split (*Learning Objectives 4 & 5*) 20–25 min.

Try-Fly Corp. had the following shares outstanding and retained earnings as of December 31, 2014:

Preferred shares, 6%, 5,000 shares outstanding	$150,000
Common shares, with 50,000 shares outstanding	$550,000
Retained earnings	$160,000

No dividends have been paid since 2012. The board is considering a cash dividend to both the preferred and the common shareholders.

Requirements

1. Assume that the total amount of dividends is $27,000:
   a. What is the amount of dividends distributed to preferred shareholders and common shareholders if the preferred shares are noncumulative?
   b. What is the amount of dividends distributed to preferred shareholders and common shareholders if the preferred shares are cumulative?
2. Assuming that the total amount of dividends is $57,000, what is the amount of dividends distributed to preferred shareholders and common shareholders?

E10-16A. Calculating return on equity (*Learning Objective 8*) 10–15 min.

Assume that Apex, Inc. has the following data:

Net income for 2014	$ 127,000
Preferred dividends for 2014	23,000
Total shareholders' equity, 12/31/2014	1,627,000
Total shareholders' equity, 12/31/2013	1,589,000
Common shareholders' equity, 12/31/2014	1,484,000
Common shareholders' equity, 12/31/2013	1,392,000

Requirements

1. Calculate Apex's return on equity for 2014.

2. Calculate Apex's return on common equity for 2014.

3. Comment on Apex's performance during 2014.

EXERCISES (GROUP B)

E10-1B. Share issuance (*Learning Objective 3*) 10–15 min.

Sierra Systems completed the following share issuance transactions:

Sep 19	Issued 1,300 common shares for cash of $10.00 per share.
Oct 3	Sold 500 preferred shares for $25,000 cash.
11	Received inventory valued at $21,000 and equipment with a market value of $16,000. Issued 12,000 common shares in exchange.

Requirements

1. Journalize the transactions. Explanations are not required.

E10-2B. Share issuance (*Learning Objectives 3 & 7*) 10–15 min.

The charter for Zerron, Inc. authorizes the company to issue 500,000 preferred shares and 700,000 common shares. During its start-up phase, Zerron, Inc. completed the following transactions:

2014	
Jul 6	Issued 575 common shares to the promoters who organized the corporation, receiving cash of $17,250.
12	Issued 650 preferred shares for cash of $23,000.
14	Issued 1,200 common shares in exchange for land valued at $19,000.

Requirements

1. Record the transactions in the journal.

2. Prepare the shareholders' equity section of Zerron's balance sheet at December 31, 2014. Assume that the company earned net income of $37,000 during this period.

E10-3B. Share issuance and financial statement presentation (*Learning Objectives 3 & 7*) 15–20 min.

HoShi Electronics' charter authorized the company to issue an unlimited number of common shares and 250,000 preferred shares. The following transactions occurred during Hoshi's first year of business:

Mar 10	Issued 3,000 common shares to the firm's promoters for the work done to set up the corporation. This work has an estimated value of $90,000.
July 21	20,000 shares were issued for cash of $32 per share.
Sep 1	12,000 preferred shares were issued for cash totalling $300,000.
Dec 11	27,000 common shares in total were issued for land, buildings, and equipment with appraised values of $225,000, $450,000, and $270,000 respectively.

Requirements

1. Prepare journal entries for all the transactions.
2. Prepare the shareholders' equity section of the balance sheet at December 31, 2014.

E10-4B. Issuance of shares for cash and noncash assets (*Learning Objective 3*) 10–15 min.

Arilla, Co. recently organized. The company issued common shares to an attorney in exchange for his patent with a market value of $52,000. In addition, Arilla, Co. received cash for 1,000 shares of its $60 preferred shares and for 30,000 common shares sold at $15 per share. Retained Earnings at the end of the first year was $88,000.

Requirement

1. Without making journal entries, determine the total share capital created by these transactions.

E10-5B. Accounting for cash dividends (*Learning Objective 4*) 10–15 min.

Eastern Communications has the following shareholders' equity:

Eastern Communications Shareholders' Equity	
Share Capital:	
Preferred Shares, 15%, unlimited number of shares authorized	
28,000 shares issued and outstanding	$ 280,000
Common Shares, 500,000 shares authorized	
320,000 shares issued and outstanding	710,000
Total Share Capital	990,000
Retained Earnings	160,000
Total Shareholders' Equity	$1,150,000

Requirement

1. Assume the preferred shares are cumulative. Compute the amount of dividends to preferred and common shareholders for 2014 and 2015 if total dividends are $36,000 in 2014 and $51,000 in 2015.

E10-6B. Accounting for cash dividends (*Learning Objective 4*) 10–15 min.

The following elements of shareholders' equity are adapted from the balance sheet of Sacchetti Corporation.

Shareholders' Equity	$ Thousands
Preferred Shares, cumulative, $0.75, 45,000 shares issued and outstanding	$225
Common Shares, 8,750,000 shares issued and outstanding	875

Sacchetti Corporation paid no preferred dividends in 2014 but paid the designated amount of cash dividends per share to preferred shareholders in all prior years.

Requirement

1. Compute the dividends to preferred and common shareholders for 2015 if total dividends are $185,000.

E10-7B. Accounting for stock dividends (*Learning Objectives 5 & 7*) 10–15 min.

The shareholders' equity for Pondwood, Inc. on December 31, 2013, follows:

Shareholders' Equity	
Share Capital:	
Common Shares, 350,000 shares authorized,	
40,000 issued and outstanding	$200,000
Total Share Capital	200,000
Retained Earnings	360,000
Total Shareholders' Equity	$560,000

On September 30, 2014, the market price of Pondwood's common shares was $11 per share and the company distributed a 30% stock dividend.

Requirements

1. Journalize the declaration and distribution of the stock dividend.
2. Prepare the shareholders' equity section of the balance sheet after the stock dividend.

E10-8B. Accounting for cash and stock dividends (*Learning Objectives 4 & 5*) 10–15 min.

Artistic Expression is authorized to issue an unlimited number of common shares. The company issued 71,000 shares at $4 per share, and all 71,000 shares are outstanding. When the market price of common shares was $12 per share, Artistic Expression declared and distributed a 20% stock dividend. Later, Artistic Expression declared and paid a $0.45 per share cash dividend.

Requirements

1. Journalize the declaration and distribution of the stock dividend.
2. Journalize the declaration and the payment of the cash dividend.

E10-9B. Accounting for stock splits (*Learning Objectives 5 & 7*) 10–15 min.

Clubhouse Landing, Inc. had the following shareholders' equity at May 31:

Shareholders' Equity	
Share Capital:	
Common Shares, 30,000 shares authorized,	
10,000 issued and outstanding	$ 30,000
Total Share Capital	30,000
Retained Earnings	700,000
Total Shareholders' Equity	$730,000

On June 30, Clubhouse Landing, Inc. split its common shares 5-for-1.

Requirements

1. Make any necessary entries to record the stock split.
2. Prepare the shareholders' equity section of the balance sheet immediately after the split.

E10-10B. Accounting for shares issuance, splits, and treasury shares (*Learning Objectives 3, 5, & 6*) 20–25 min.

Consider each of the following transactions separately from every other transaction:

a. Issuance of 57,000 common shares at $13.
b. Purchase of 1,800 treasury shares at $8 per share.
c. Issuance of a 10% stock dividend. Before the dividend, 500,000 common shares were outstanding; market value was $9 at the time of the dividend.
d. Split shares 3-for-1. Prior to the split, 120,000 common shares were outstanding.

Requirement

1. Identify whether each transaction increased, decreased, or did not change total shareholders' equity.

E10-11B. Accounting for treasury shares (*Learning Objectives 3 & 6*) 10–15 min.

Journalize the following transactions of Goddard Sports, Inc., a chain of sports stores:

Mar	4	Issued 30,000 common shares at $12 per share.
Jul	22	Purchased 3,000 treasury shares at $14 per share.
Oct	20	Purchased 2,000 treasury shares at $11 per share.

E10-12B. Accounting for treasury shares (*Learning Objectives 6 & 7*) 20–25 min.

Southern, Inc. had the following shareholders' equity on November 30:

Shareholders' Equity	
Share Capital:	
Common Shares, unlimited number of shares authorized,	
40,000 shares issued and 30,000 outstanding	$480,000
Contributed Surplus (purchase of treasury shares, May 30)	20,000
Retained Earnings	520,000
Less: 10,000 Treasury Shares	(120,000)
Total Shareholders' Equity	$900,000

On December 10, Southern purchased 5,000 treasury shares at $15 per share.

Requirement

1. What is the average price per common share? What is the amount paid to purchase treasury shares on May 30?

2. Journalize the purchases of the treasury shares on May 30 and December 10.

3. Prepare the shareholders' equity section of the balance sheet at December 31.

E10-13B. **Balance sheet disclosure of shareholders' equity** (*Learning Objective 7*) **10–15 min.**

Bretton Manufacturing, Co. has the following selected account balances at April 30, 2014.

Common Shares, 140,000 shares authorized, issued, and outstanding.....	$560,000	Inventory.................................	$ 55,000
		Machinery and Equipment	77,000
Accumulated Depreciation, Machinery and Equipment...	14,000	Preferred Shares, 5%, 20,000 shares authorized, 6,000 shares issued and	
Retained Earnings...................	150,000	outstanding	102,000
		Cost of Goods Sold................	76,000

Requirement

1. Prepare the shareholders' equity section of the company's balance sheet.

E10-14B. **Accounting for various shareholders' equity transactions** (*Learning Objectives 3, 4, 5, 7, & 8*) **20–25 min.**

Shohei Inc.'s shareholders' equity on December 31, 2013 was as follows:

Shareholders' Equity	
Share Capital:	
Preferred Shares, $0.75 accumulated deferred dividends, 500,000 shares authorized, 100,000 issued and outstanding	$1,000,000
Common Shares, unlimited number of shares authorized, 250,000 shares issued and outstanding	$4,000,000
Retained Earnings	750,000
Total Shareholders' Equity	$5,750,000

During 2014, the following transactions occurred.

Jan	2	10,000 preferred shares were issued at $22.00 per share.
Feb	1	12,000 common shares were issued in exchange for a building with a fair value of $300,000.
Nov	25	Declared preferred dividends to be paid on December 23.
Dec	27	Declared 5% common stock dividend, when the market price was $25, to be distributed on January 30, 2015
Dec	31	Net income for the year was $520,000.

Requirements

1. Journalize the above transactions.

2. Prepare the shareholders' equity section of the Shohei Inc. balance sheet as of December 31, 2014.

E10-15B. Accounting for cash, stock dividends and stock split (*Learning Objectives 4 & 5*) 20–25 min.

Dragonfly Corp. had the following shares outstanding and retained earnings as of December 31, 2014:

Preferred shares, 5%, 10,000 shares outstanding	$200,000
Common shares, with 80,000 shares outstanding	$720,000
Retained earnings	$125,000

No dividends have been paid since 2012. The board is considering a cash dividend to both the preferred and the common shareholders.

Requirements

1. Assume that the total amount of dividends is $30,000:

   a. What is the amount of dividends distributed to preferred shareholders and common shareholders if the preferred shares are noncumulative?

   b. What is the amount of dividends distributed to preferred shareholders and common shareholders if the preferred shares are cumulative?

2. Assume that instead of a cash dividend, the company gave the common shareholders a 15% stock dividend when the common shares were trading at $10 each. Prepare the shareholders' equity section of the balance sheet before and after the dividend. Describe what has happened to the total and each account.

E10-16B. Calculating return on equity (*Learning Objective 8*) 10–15 min.

Assume that Skippito, Inc. has the following data:

Net income for 2014	$ 223,000
Preferred dividends for 2014	23,000
Total shareholders' equity, 12/31/2014	1,009,000
Total shareholders' equity, 12/31/2013	1,384,000
Common shareholders' equity, 12/31/2014	987,000
Common shareholders' equity, 12/31/2013	1,207,000

Requirements

1. Calculate Skippito's return on equity for 2014.

2. Calculate Skippito's return on common equity for 2014.

3. Comment on Skippito's performance during 2014.

EXERCISES (ALTERNATES 1, 2, AND 3)

These alternative exercise sets are available for your practice benefit at *www.myaccountinglab.com*

PROBLEMS (GROUP A)

P10-1A. Shares issuance (*Learning Objectives 3 & 7*) 10–15 min.

Partners Dempsey and Perry wish to avoid the unlimited personal liability of the partnership form of business, so they are incorporating the company as D & P Services, Inc. The charter from Ontario authorizes the corporation to issue 10,000 shares of 6%, preferred shares and 250,000 common shares. In its first month, D & P Services, Inc. completed the following transactions:

Jan	3	Issued 6,300 common shares to Dempsey and 3,800 shares to Perry, both for cash of $10 per share.
	12	Issued 1,100 preferred shares to acquire a patent with a market value of $110,000.
	22	Issued 1,500 common shares to other investors for $10 cash per share.

Requirements

1. Record the transactions in the journal.

2. Prepare the shareholders' equity section of the D & P Services, Inc. balance sheet at December 31. The ending balance of Retained Earnings is $40,000.

P10-2A. Analyzing shareholders' equity (*Learning Objectives 2, 3, 4, & 7*) 20–25 min.

Gamma Corporation was organized in 2013. At December 31, 2013, Gamma Corporation's balance sheet reported the following shareholders' equity:

Shareholders' Equity	
Share Capital:	
Preferred Shares, $2, 50,000 shares authorized, none issued	$ 0
Common Shares, 100,000 shares authorized,	
10,000 shares issued and outstanding	50,000
Total Share Capital	50,000
Retained Earnings (deficit)	(5,000)
Total Shareholders' Equity	$45,000

Requirements

Answer the following questions and make journal entries as needed:

1. What does the $2 mean for the preferred shares? After Gamma Corporation issues preferred shares, how much in annual cash dividends would Gamma Corporation expect to pay on 1,000 shares?

2. At what price per share did Gamma Corporation issue the common shares during 2013?

3. Were first-year operations profitable? Give your reason.

4. During 2014, the company completed the following selected transactions. Journalize each transaction. Explanations are not required.

   a. Issued for cash 5,000 preferred shares at $10 per share.

   b. Issued for cash 1,000 common shares at a price of $7 per share.

5. Prepare the shareholders' equity section of the Gamma Corporation balance sheet at December 31, 2014. Assume net income for the year is $50,000.

P10-3A. Analyzing shareholders' equity (*Learning Objectives 2, 3, & 4*) 20–25 min.

Radisson, Inc. included the following shareholders' equity on its year-end balance sheet at December 31, 2014, with all dollar amounts adapted and in millions:

Shareholders' Equity	$ Millions
Share Capital:	
Preferred Shares, 6% cumulative	$ 65
Common Shares, 650,000,000 shares authorized,	
236,000,000 shares issued and outstanding	306
Total Share Capital	371
Retained Earnings	247
Total Shareholders' Equity	$618

Requirements

1. Identify the different issues of shares Radisson, Inc. has outstanding.

2. Give the two entries to record issuance of the Radisson, Inc. shares. Assume that all the shares were issued for cash. Explanations are not required.

3. Assume that preferred dividends are in arrears for 2013 and 2014. Record the declaration of a $50 million cash dividend on December 30, 2015. Use separate Dividends Payable accounts for preferred and common shares. Round to the nearest $1 million. An explanation is not required.

P10-4A. Accounting for cash dividends (*Learning Objective 4*) 15–20 min.

Klammer Consulting, Inc. has 10,000 shares of $4.50 preferred shares and 50,000 common shares outstanding. Klammer Consulting, Inc. declared and paid the following dividends during a three-year period: 2012, $20,000; 2013, $100,000; and 2014, $200,000.

Requirements

1. Compute the total dividends to preferred shareholders and to common shareholders for each of the three years if

   a. preferred is noncumulative.

   b. preferred is cumulative.

2. For case 1(b), journalize the declaration of the 2014 dividends on December 28, 2014, and the payment of the dividends on January 17, 2015. Use separate Dividends Payable accounts for preferred and common shares.

P10-5A. Accounting for various shareholders' equity transactions (*Learning Objectives 4, 5, & 6*) 20–25 min.

Ralston Sports Corporation completed the following selected transactions during 2014:

Jan 6	Declared a cash dividend on the 10,000 $2.25 preferred shares outstanding. Declared a $0.20 per share dividend on the 10,000 common shares outstanding. The date of record is January 17, and the payment date is January 20.
Jan 20	Paid the cash dividends.
Mar 21	Split the common shares 2-for-1 by calling in the 10,000 common shares and issuing new shares in their place.
Apr 18	Declared and distributed a 10% stock dividend on the common shares. The market value of the common shares was $27 per share.
Jun 18	Purchased 2,000 treasury common shares at $25 per share.

Requirement

1. Record the transactions in the journal.

P10-6A. Accounting for stock split, stock dividends, and reporting shareholders' equity on the balance sheet (*Learning Objectives 5, 6, & 7*) 20–25 min.

Mingu Inc. had the following balances in its shareholders' equity accounts at December 31, 2014:

Share Capital

Common Shares, unlimited number of shares authorized,
30,000 shares issued and outstanding $4,500,000

Retained Earnings 625,000

Total Shareholders' Equity $5,125,000

During 2014, Mingu completed the following selected transactions related to shareholders' equity:

Feb 15	Purchased and retired 2,500 common shares at $130 per share.
Jun 28	Purchased and retired 3,500 common shares at $160 per share.
Dec 18	Declared a 3-for-2 stock split effective on this date.
Dec 30	Mingu reported net income for the year of $150,000

Requirements

1. Prepare journal entries to account for the transactions during 2014.

2. Assume that instead of a 3-for-2 split, the board of directors declared a 5% stock dividend when the market price was $165. The stock dividends were to be distributed on January 15, 2015. Prepare the journal entry to account for the stock dividend.

3. Prepare the company's shareholders' equity section at December 31, 2014 for (a) the stock split and (b) the stock dividend.

P10-7A. **Accounting for various shareholders' equity transactions (*Learning Objective 3, 4, 5, & 7*) 30–35 min.**

At December 31, 2013, Eaton Corp. reported the following shareholders' equity:

Shareholders' Equity	
Share Capital:	
Common Shares, 240,000 shares authorized,	
120,000 shares issued and 100,000 outstanding	$1,440,000
Contributed Surplus (purchase of treasury shares)	20,000
Retained Earnings	730,000
Less: 20,000 Treasury Shares	(240,000)
Total Shareholders' Equity	$1,950,000

During 2014, Eaton Corp. completed these transactions and events:

Jan 15	Paid cash dividends of $0.50 per share, which were declared on December 15, 2013.
Apr 1	Issued 50,000 common shares at $15 per share.
Jun 30	Declared a 10% stock dividend to be distributed on July 31. The market price was $16.
July 31	Distributed stock dividend.
Dec 20	Declared a 2-for-1 stock split.
Dec 31	Net income for the year was $200,000.

Requirements

1. Prepare journal entries to record the above transactions.

2. Prepare Eaton's shareholders' equity section of the balance sheet at December 31, 2014.

3. Prepare Eaton's statement of changes in equity for 2014.

P10-8A. Accounting for various shareholders' equity transactions (*Learning Objective 3, 4, 5, & 7*) 30–35 min.

After the books have been closed, the ledger of Suki Corporation at December 31, 2014, contains the following shareholders' equity accounts:

Preferred Shares (10,000 shares issued)	$1,100,000
Common Shares (400,000 shares issued)	1,850,000
Contributed Capital—purchase of common shares	10,000
Common Stock dividend distributable	110,000
Retained Earnings	2,390,000

A review of the accounting records reveals the following:

a. Both the common and preferred shares have no par value and unlimited number of shares authorized.

b. The preferred shares are noncumulative with an $11 dividend. The 10,000 shares were issued on January 15, 2012. No dividend was paid to the preferred shareholders in 2012 or 2013.

c. The January 1 balance in Retained Earnings was $2,250,000.

d. On January 15, the firm purchased 20,000 common shares for $4 cash per share and cancelled these shares.

e. On October 1, 100,000 common shares were sold for cash at $5 per share.

f. A cash dividend of $650,000 was declared and properly allocated to Preferred Shares and Common Shares on November 1.

g. On December 31, a 5% stock dividend was declared for common shares.

Requirements

1. Calculate the allocation of the cash dividend to preferred and common shareholders.

2. Calculate (a) the initial common share issuing price per share, (b) the net income, and (c) market price for the common shares on December 31.

3. Prepare all necessary journal entries for Suki Corporation in 2014.

4 Prepare a statement of shareholders' equity for the year ended December 31, 2014.

PROBLEMS (GROUP B)

P10-1B. Shares issuance (*Learning Objectives 3 & 7*) 10–15 min.

Partners Meeks and Olsen wish to avoid the unlimited personal liability of the partnership form of business, so they are incorporating the company as M & O Services, Inc. The charter from Alberta authorizes the corporation to issue 15,000 shares of 7%, preferred shares and 220,000 common shares. In its first month, M & O Services, Inc. completed the following transactions:

Jan 3	Issued 6,200 common shares to Meeks and 3,700 shares to Olsen, both for cash of $12 per share.
12	Issued 1,200 preferred shares to acquire a patent with a market value of $180,000.
22	Issued 1,700 common shares to other investors for $12 cash per share.

Requirements

1. Record the transactions in the journal.

2. Prepare the shareholders' equity section of the M & O Services, Inc. balance sheet at December 31. The ending balance of Retained Earnings is $59,000.

P10-2B. Analyzing shareholders' equity (*Learning Objectives 2, 3, 4, & 7*) 20–25 min.

Robert Corporation was organized in 2013. At December 31, 2013, Robert Corporation's balance sheet reported the following shareholders' equity:

Shareholders' Equity	
Share Capital:	
Preferred Shares, 6%, 35,000 shares authorized, none issued	$ 0
Common Shares, 120,000 shares authorized,	
11,000 shares issued and outstanding	44,000
Total Share Capital	44,000
Retained Earnings (deficit)	(5,000)
Total Shareholders' Equity	$39,000

Requirements

Answer the following questions and make journal entries as needed:

1. What does the 6% mean for the preferred shares? After Robert Corporation issues preferred shares, how much in annual cash dividends would Robert Corporation expect to pay on 1,000 shares?

2. At what price per share did Robert Corporation issue the common shares during 2013?

3. Were the first-year operations profitable? Give your reasons.

4. During 2014, the company completed the following selected transactions. Journalize each transaction. Explanations are not required.

   a. Issued for cash 2,000 preferred shares at $10 per share.

   b. Issued for cash 1,500 common shares at a price of $5 per share.

5. Prepare the shareholders' equity section of the Robert Corporation balance sheet at December 31, 2014. Assume net income for the year was $65,000.

P10-3B. Analyzing shareholders' equity (*Learning Objectives 2, 3, & 4*) 20–25 min.

Madison Hotel, Inc. included the following shareholders' equity on its year-end balance sheet at December 31, 2014, with all dollar amounts in millions:

Shareholders' Equity	$ Millions
Share Capital:	
Preferred Shares, 6.5% cumulative	$ 45
Common Shares; 500,000,000 shares authorized,	
176,000,000 shares issued and outstanding	228
Total Share Capital	273
Retained Earnings	142
Total Shareholders' Equity	$415

Requirements

1. Identify the different issues of shares Madison Hotel, Inc. has outstanding.

2. Give the two entries to record issuance of the Madison Hotel, Inc. shares. Assume all the shares were issued for cash. Explanations are not required.

3. Assume that preferred dividends are in arrears for 2013 and 2014. Record the declaration of a $37 million cash dividend on December 30, 2015. Use separate Dividends Payable accounts for preferred and common shares. Round to the nearest $1 million. An explanation is not required.

P10-4B. Accounting for cash dividends (*Learning Objective 4*) 15–20 min.

Krystal Consulting, Inc. has 13,000 shares of $4.00 preferred shares and 90,000 common shares outstanding. Krystal declared and paid the following dividends during a three-year period: 2012, $24,000; 2013, $115,000; and 2014, $230,000.

Requirements

1. Compute the total dividends to preferred shareholders and to common shareholders for each of the three years if

    a. preferred is noncumulative.

    b. preferred is cumulative.

2. For case 1(b), journalize the declaration of the 2014 dividends on December 28, 2014, and the payment of dividends on January 17, 2015. Use separate Dividends Payable accounts for preferred and common shares.

P10-5B. Accounting for various shareholders' equity transactions (*Learning Objectives 4, 5, & 6*) 20–25 min.

Triton Triathlete Corporation completed the following selected transactions during 2015:

Jan 6	Declared a cash dividend on the 7,000 shares of $3.00, preferred shares outstanding. Declared a $0.10 per share dividend on the 15,000 common shares outstanding. The date of record is January 17, and the payment date is January 20.
Jan 20	Paid the cash dividends.
Mar 21	Completed a 2-for-1 stock split on common shares by calling in the 15,000 common shares and issuing new shares in their place.
Apr 18	Declared and distributed a 15% stock dividend on the common shares. The market value of the common shares was $34 per share.
Jun 18	Purchased 2,000 treasury shares at $31 per share.

Requirement

1. Record the transactions in the journal.

P10-6B. Accounting for stock split, stock dividends, and reporting shareholders' equity on the balance sheet (*Learning Objectives 5, 6, & 7*) 20–25 min.

Fuken Inc. had the following balances in its shareholders' equity accounts at December 31, 2014:

Share Capital	
Common Shares, unlimited number of shares authorized,	
50,000 shares issued and outstanding	$8,000,000
Retained Earnings	750,000
Total Shareholders' Equity	$8,750,000

During 2014, Fuken completed the following selected transactions related to shareholders' equity:

Mar 15	Purchased and retired 4,500 common shares at $150 per share.
Jul 21	Purchased and retired 3,500 common shares at $170 per share.
Dec 28	Declared a 2-for-1 stock split effective on this date.
Dec 30	Fuken reported net income for the year of $325,000

Requirements

1. Prepare journal entries to account for the transactions during 2014.

2. Assume that instead of a 2-for-1 split, the board of directors declared a 5% stock dividend when the market price was $175. The stock dividends were to be distributed on January 31, 2015. Prepare the journal entry to account for the stock dividend.

3. Prepare the company's shareholders' equity section at December 31, 2014 for (a) the stock split and (b) the stock dividend.

P10-7B. Accounting for various shareholders' equity transactions (*Learning Objective 3, 4, 5, & 7*) 30–35 min.

At December 31, 2013, Maloney, Corp. reported the following shareholders' equity.

Shareholders' Equity	
Share Capital:	
Common Shares, unlimited number of shares authorized,	
200,000 shares issued and 180,000 outstanding	$5,600,000
Stock Dividends Distributable	270,000
Retained Earnings	690,000
Less: 20,000 Treasury Shares	(560,000)
Total Shareholders' Equity	$6,000,000

During 2014, Maloney, Corp. completed these transactions and events:

Jan 20	Distributed stock dividends (5% of outstanding common shares), which were declared on December 1, 2013.
May 1	Issued 21,000 common shares at $31 per share.
Sep 30	Declared cash dividends of $1 per share.
Oct 31	Paid cash dividends declared on September 30.
Dec 20	Declared a 2-for-1 stock split.
Dec 31	Net income for the year was $240,000.

Requirements

1. What is the market price per share on December 1, 2013?

2. Prepare journal entries to record the above transactions.

3. Prepare Maloney's shareholders' equity section of the balance sheet at December 31, 2014.

4. Prepare Maloney's statement of shareholders' equity for 2014.

P10-8B. Accounting for various shareholders' equity transactions (*Learning Objective 3, 4, 5, & 7*) 30–35 min.

After the books have been closed, the ledger of Rotan Corporation at December 31, 2014, contains the following shareholders' equity accounts:

Preferred Shares (20,000 shares issued)	$2,000,000
Common Shares (500,000 shares issued)	3,325,000
Contributed Capital—purchase of common shares	15,000
Common Stock dividend distributable	175,000
Retained Earnings	3,150,000

A review of the accounting records reveals the following:

a. Both the common and preferred shares have an unlimited number of shares authorized.

b. The preferred shares are noncumulative with a $10 dividend. The 20,000 shares were issued on January 15, 2012. No dividend was paid to the preferred shareholders in 2012 or 2013.

c. The January 1 balance in Retained Earnings was $ 2,950,000.

d. On February 20, the firm purchased 30,000 common shares for $6 cash per share and cancelled these shares.

e. On October 15, 150,000 common shares were sold for cash at $7 per share.

f. A cash dividend of $780,000 was declared and properly allocated to preferred shares and common shares on November 1.

g. On December 31, a 5% common stock dividend was declared.

Requirements

1. Calculate the allocation of the cash dividend to preferred and common shareholders.

2. Calculate (a) the initial common share issuing price per share, (b) the net income, (c) market price for the common shares on December 31.

3. Prepare all necessary journal entries for Rotan Corporation in 2014.

4 Prepare a statement of shareholders' equity for the year ended December 31, 2014.

PROBLEMS (ALTERNATES 1, 2, AND 3)

These alternative problem sets are available for your practice benefit at *www.myaccountinglab.com*

CONTINUING EXERCISE

This exercise continues our accounting for Graham's Yard Care, Inc. from Chapter 9. In this exercise, we will account for the declaration and issuance of a cash dividend by Graham's Yard Care, Inc. On October 15, 2014, Graham's Yard Care, Inc. declared a $5,000 dividend. The dividend was payable to all common shareholders of record on October 31 and was paid on November 15, 2014.

Requirements

1. Journalize the entries related to the dividends.

2. What was the effect of the dividend on the following?

- Cash
- Retained Earnings
- Total Shareholders' Equity

CONTINUING PROBLEM

This problem continues our accounting for Aqua Elite, Inc. from Chapter 9. Aqua Elite, Inc. has been authorized to sell 500,000 common shares and 100,000 8% preferred shares. During the year, Aqua Elite had the following transactions related to shareholders' equity:

May 5	Issued 5,700 common shares to Mike Hanson in exchange for $15,000 cash and a truck valued at $13,500.
Jun 13	Issued an additional 2,000 shares to Mike Hanson for $10,000 cash.
Jul 18	Sold 4,000 common shares to investors for $45,000.
Aug 6	Sold 1,500 preferred shares to investors for $20,000.
Oct 22	Purchased 1,000 common shares for $12 per share to hold in the company's treasury.
Nov 14	Declared a $5,000 dividend payable on December 15 to shareholders on record on December 1. Used separate payable accounts for preferred and common dividends.
Dec 15	Paid the dividend.

Requirements

1. Record the transactions in the journal. Explanations are not required.

2. Prepare the shareholders' equity section of the balance sheet at December 31, 2014, assuming Aqua Elite, Inc. earned $96,000 of net income during the year. In addition to the dividends paid on December 15, $3,400 of dividends were paid earlier in the year.

APPLY YOUR KNOWLEDGE

ETHICS IN ACTION

Case 1. Ted was a wealthy, 20% shareholder of TDS Corporation. He was looking over the financial statements of the corporation and saw that TDS Corporation was in need of a large loan. Furthermore, he knew that December sales were weaker than expected and that the yearly financial statements would show a lower net income than anticipated. He then decided to loan the company $3 million at 5% interest and also become a customer and purchase $250,000 of merchandise. By Ted becoming a customer, it would increase the business's December sales and net income, and give the company sufficient cash to meet expenses. When approached with the ideas, the CEO objected, stating that the "loan" would have to be recorded as additional capital because a shareholder could not loan money to a company. Ted stated that as long as the money was treated as a loan with interest and the expectation of repayment, it should be allowed. The CEO then stated that it would be unethical for the company to "borrow" money from a shareholder. Also, it would be unethical for the company to "sell" merchandise to a shareholder, because it would merely be done to improve the December sales. Ted stated that the loan agreement and 5% interest would make the arrangement reasonable. He stated that if the interest rate were 25%, then the CEO might have a valid ethical concern. Ted also argued that the sale of merchandise to him was completely ethical, because he was not going to return the merchandise. He further contended that it should not matter whether he was a shareholder because in these transactions he would be a lender and a customer, which would not involve any ethical issues.

Can a shareholder ethically lend money to the corporation? What potential ethical issues would be involved? Can a shareholder ethically become a customer to make purchases just to improve the sales and net income? Does the amount of the purchase matter? Why do you think the CEO was concerned?

Case 2. The board of directors for Atlantic Corporation met in January to address growing concerns about the declining share price of the firm. Because the price per share was so low, the board decided that the company would buy back 10 million outstanding shares. During the year, Atlantic Corporation repurchased the shares at a total cost of $62 million. With fewer shares in the hands of shareholders, the board of directors declared and paid a dividend on only those remaining shares outstanding. As a result of these activities, the price per share rose dramatically in only 10 months. The board of directors then felt it best to reissue the treasury shares at the highest per share price possible. Accordingly, Atlantic Corporation reissued the 10 million shares for $142 million. When the board of directors looked over the yearly financial statements, however, it could not find the $80 million "gain" from the treasury shares sale, equal to the reissue price of $142 million less the purchase cost of $62 million. The accountant had recorded the excess as "Additional Share Capital" rather than as a gain on sale. The board of directors met with the accountant and demanded that a gain be recorded; the board wanted more revenue to be included on the income statement. It argued that shares had been sold at a price higher than they were purchased for, and, therefore, it really did not matter whether the shares were Atlantic Corporation shares or any other company's shares, because all share sales result in either a gain or loss.

Why does the board of directors want to recognize the $80 million excess from the treasury share transactions as a gain? Why does the accountant want to recognize the $80 million as an increase in total equity? Who is right and are any ethical issues involved? Does the board of directors have a strong argument that it does not matter whether the shares were Atlantic Corporation shares or any other company since all shares are the same? Do you have any additional thoughts?

KNOW YOUR BUSINESS

FINANCIAL ANALYSIS

Purpose: To help familiarize you with the financial reporting of a real company in order to further your understanding of the chapter material you are learning.

This case continues our examination of Bombardier Inc. We will now study the shareholders' equity of Bombardier Inc. Refer to the Bombardier Inc. financial statements found in MyAccountingLab. Look for the Consolidated Balance Sheets as well as the Consolidated Statements of Changes in Equity and Note 14.

Requirements

1. What was the balance of total shareholders' equity at January 31, 2011 and January 31, 2010? Did the amount of ending total shareholders' equity increase or decrease? What seems to be the main reason for the change in total shareholders' equity? What is the largest component of total shareholders' equity? (Hint: Look at the Consolidated Statements of Changes in Equity to help answer this last question.)

2. Does Bombardier Inc. have any preferred shares authorized? Issued? Describe the preferred shares: voting or non-voting; cumulative or non-cumulative; redeemable (at what price) or not redeemable and their dividend rates.

3. Describe the classes of common shares that Bombardier has authorized and issued. How many common shares are issued and outstanding at the end of the 2011 fiscal year for each class? How many shares were issued and outstanding at the beginning of the year?

4. Look at the consolidated statements of shareholders' equity. Did Bombardier Inc. declare any dividends in 2011? Can you determine whether Bombardier Inc. has been repurchasing its common shares? If so, has the amount of share repurchases been increasing or decreasing?

5. Examine the Statements of Cash Flows. How much cash was required to repurchase shares during 2011?

INDUSTRY ANALYSIS

Purpose: To help you understand and compare the performance of two companies in the same industry.

Find the Bombardier Annual Report, Year Ended January 31, 2011, located in MyAccountingLab and go to the Financial Statements. Now access the The Boeing

Company's 2010 Annual Report. To do this from the internet, go to their webpage for the Investor Relations at *http://www.boeing.com/companyoffices/financial/quarterly.htm* and, under Annual Report, go to the 2010 Annual Report.

Requirement

1. On the Consolidated Balance Sheets for each company, look at the Shareholders' Equity section. What type or class of shares has each company issued? What is the book value per common share outstanding for each company? How might this compare to the market value per share?

SMALL BUSINESS ANALYSIS

Purpose: To help you understand the importance of cash flows in the operation of a small business.

You are the chief operating officer (COO) of a small public corporation. The company just completed its fiscal year, and the annual meeting is just a few weeks away. Your company has had a pretty good year despite the rough economic climate your industry has been weathering. In spite of that, the share price has maintained its high level. But here's the dilemma: The corporation has paid out a cash dividend every year since its inception, but this year you have some concerns about continuing that tradition. Cash flows during the latter part of the year have been slow because your customers are taking longer to pay than they normally do. There's also the concern about the lump sum payment on the mortgage that is due in a couple of months. You've got to have sufficient cash for that. You've already had some inquiries from shareholders about the amount of the dividend that the company will be paying out this year. You've answered all the inquiries with a very positive tone, but the whole while you're wondering if there will even **be** a dividend this year. You're certain that the important shareholders would understand if the corporation had to forego paying a dividend this year. Or would they? You decide to have a meeting with the controller to discuss the situation.

Requirement

1. What would be the most viable suggestion that your controller might make to you as an alternative to paying out a cash dividend this year? What are the implications of your recommendation?

WRITTEN COMMUNICATION

You just got off the telephone with one of your clients who is wanting to start a new business as a corporation. His question to you was concerning the different types of shares that can be issued to the potential shareholders of this new corporation. You had explained it to him during the telephone call, but you thought you should follow up your conversation with a letter.

Requirement

1. Prepare a letter to your client explaining the different types or classes of shares that can be issued, and the characteristics of each different type.

Self Check Answers
1. d 2. c 3. a 4. c 5. c 6. d 7. d 8. d 9. a 10. b

SCAN THIS

CHAPTER 11

The Cash Flow Statement

LEARNING OBJECTIVES:

1 ▶ Identify the purposes of the cash flow statement

2 ▶ Differentiate among cash flows from operating, investing, and financing activities

3 ▶ Prepare the cash flow statement using the indirect method

4 ▶ Prepare the cash flow statement using the direct method

5 ▶ Evaluate a company's performance with respect to cash

Throughout this book you have examined many different types of transactions businesses encounter each day. Did you notice how many of those transactions involved cash? Cash is a significant asset for most businesses and is important to their success. Because of this, business owners and managers, as well as investors and creditors, often have questions about a company's cash, such as "Where did the company get the cash it needed for the year?" and, "Where did all of the company's cash go?" The answers to these questions can be found in the cash flow statement, which we will learn about in this chapter.

CHAPTER OUTLINE:

WHAT IS THE CASH FLOW STATEMENT?

1 Identify the purposes of the cash flow statement

Cash is often considered to be the "life blood" of a business. As we have seen throughout the book, the balance sheet reports the amount of cash a business has at the end of the accounting period. Remember from Chapter 4, this cash balance typically includes cash as well as cash equivalents. When a comparative balance sheet is presented, the balance of cash the business has at the end of two consecutive periods is reported. The comparative balance sheet shows whether cash increased or decreased from one period to the next. However, the comparative balance sheet does not show *why* cash increased or decreased. Therefore, a **cash flow statement** is usually prepared to show why the cash amount changed during the year. The cash flow statement reports

- all sources of cash during the period. In other words, it shows where a company got its cash during the year.
- all uses of cash during the period. In other words, it shows where a company spent its cash during the year.

ACCOUNTING IN YOUR WORLD

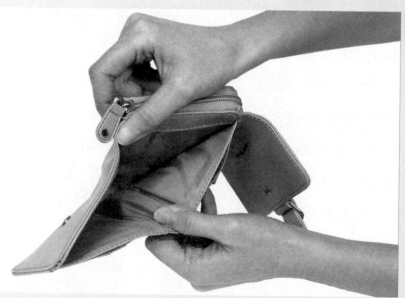

Have you ever taken a weekend road trip with some of your friends? If so, you probably went to the bank to get some cash before you took off. Then, at least once, you probably had to find an ATM to get a little more cash. When you got home, you probably looked in your wallet to see how much money you had left. Upon realizing that you had very little money left, you probably wondered "Where did all my money go?" At this point, you might have taken out a piece of paper and written down how much money you started with and how much additional cash you got along the way (your sources of cash). Then, you probably recorded all the things you spent money on, such as gas $120, food $73, movies $28, etc. (your uses of cash). Finally, you subtracted all of your uses of cash from your sources of cash and, sure enough, it equalled the amount of money left in your wallet. In essence, you prepared a cash flow statement for the period of your road trip.

The cash flow statement helps investors and creditors do the following:

1. **Predict future cash flows.** Past cash receipts and payments help predict future cash flows.

2. **Evaluate management decisions.** Wise investment decisions help the business prosper. Unwise decisions cause problems. Investors and creditors use cash-flow information to evaluate managers' decisions.

3. **Predict ability to pay debts and dividends.** Lenders want to know whether they'll collect on their loans. Shareholders want dividends on their investments. The cash flow statement helps make these predictions.

The cash flow statement also helps financial statement users understand why net income as reported on the income statement does not equal the change in cash according to the balance sheet. This is especially helpful for small business owners as they often do not trust the Net Income figure on the income statement. This is because Net Income often shows that the business made money at a time when there is little cash to show for it. Or the opposite may occur. Net Income may reflect that the business made little or no money at a time when the business has a lot of cash. In essence, the cash flow statement is the communicating link between the accrual-based income statement and the cash reported on the balance sheet. **Exhibit 11–1** illustrates the relationships among the balance sheet, the income statement, and the cash flow statement.

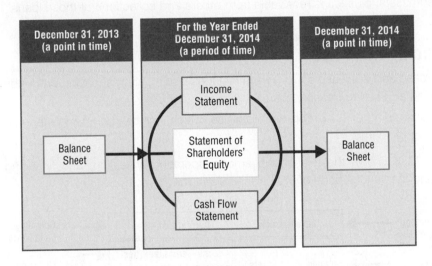

Exhibit 11-1 ▲

To provide more useful information, the cash flow statement reports the sources and uses of cash for three different types of business activities:

- Operating activities
- Investing activities
- Financing activities

WHAT IS THE DIFFERENCE AMONG OPERATING, INVESTING, AND FINANCING ACTIVITIES?

2 ▶ Differentiate among cash flows from operating, investing, and financing activities

The cash flow statement is broken down into different sections based on three types of business activities; **operating activities**, **investing activities**, and **financing activities**. Let's explore each of the three types of activities.

Operating Activities

- Reflect the day-to-day operations of an organization.
- Create revenues, expenses, gains, and losses.
- Affect net income on the income statement.
- Affect current assets and current liabilities on the balance sheet.

Investing Activities

- Increase and decrease long-term assets, which includes purchases and sales of fixed assets, plus loans receivable from others and collections of those loans.

Financing Activities

- Increase and decrease equity, which includes issuing shares, paying dividends, and buying and selling treasury shares.
- Increase and decrease long-term liabilities, which includes borrowing money and paying off loans.

Exhibit 11-2 shows the relationship among operating, investing, and financing cash flows and the various parts of the balance sheet they affect.

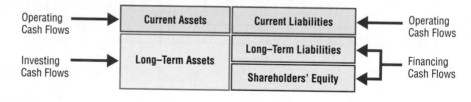

Exhibit 11-2 ▲

As you can see, operating cash flows affect the current accounts. Investing cash flows affect the long-term assets. Financing cash flows affect long-term liabilities and equity.

Two Formats for Operating Activities

There are two ways to format operating activities on the cash flow statement:

- The **direct method** shows all cash receipts and all cash payments from operating activities. The direct method restates each (accrual-based) item on the income statement on a cash basis.

- The **indirect method** starts with net income and adjusts it to net cash provided by operating activities.

  The direct and indirect methods

- produce the same amount of cash flow from operations through the use of different computations.
- have no effect on investing activities or financing activities.

DECISION GUIDELINES

Decision	Guideline	Analyze
As a creditor, the way a business manages its cash can make a difference between having a loan repaid or not. How do I determine how cash is being managed by a business?	Review the cash flow statement.	The cash flow statement shows all of the sources and all of the uses of cash for the period. The sources and uses of cash are reported separately for the operating activities, the investing activities, and the financing activities of the business. If a business is to remain successful, operating activities must be the main source of its cash over the long run.

HOW IS THE CASH FLOW STATEMENT PREPARED USING THE INDIRECT METHOD?

Most businesses prefer to use the indirect method because its format makes it easier to reconcile net income to the change in cash for the period. To prepare the cash flow statement you will need to have the other financial statements as well as some supplemental information about the company's operations. The format for the indirect method cash flow statement for Mackay Industries is presented in **Exhibit 11-3** on the following page.

Mackay Industries' financial statements are presented in **Exhibit 11-4**, also on the following two pages. The Cash account shows an increase of $7,000 from 2013 to 2014 in Mackay Industries' balance sheet. The cash flow statement is to show where this increase of $7,000 came from, through three business activities. Please note that the sum of the three business activities subtotals should equal the difference in the Cash account.

3 Prepare the cash flow statement using the indirect method

Mackay Industries, Inc.
Cash Flow Statement
Year Ended December 31, 2014

Cash flows from operating activities:				
Net Income				
Adjustments to reconcile net income to net cash				
provided by operating activities:				
+ Depreciation / amortization expense				
+ Loss on sale of long-term assets				
− Gain on sale of long-term assets				
− Increases in current assets other than cash				
+ Decreases in current assets other than cash				
+ Increases in current liabilities				
− Decreases in current liabilities				
Net cash provided by operating activities				
± **Cash flows from investing activities:**				
+ Cash receipts from sales of long-term assets				
(investments, land, building, equipment, and so on)				
− Purchases of long-term assets				
Net cash provided by (used for) investing activities				
± **Cash flows from financing activities:**				
+ Cash receipts from issuance of shares				
+ Sale of treasury shares				
− Purchase of treasury shares				
+ Cash receipts from issuance of notes or bonds				
payable (borrowing)				
− Payment of notes or bonds payable				
− Payment of dividends				
Net cash provided by (used for) financing activities				
= **Net increase (decrease) in cash during the year**				
+ Cash at December 31, 2013				
= Cash at December 31, 2014				

Exhibit 11-3 ▲

Mackay Industries, Inc.
Income Statement
Year Ended December 31, 2014

Revenue:			
Sales Revenue	$268,000		
Interest Revenue	13,000		
Dividend Revenue	5,000		
Total Revenues		$286,000	
Expenses:			
Cost of Goods Sold	$137,000		
Salaries Expense	48,000		
B Depreciation Expense	18,000		
Other Operating Expense	12,000		
Interest Expense	11,000		
Income Tax Expense	9,000		
C Loss on Sale of Plant Assets	3,000		
Total Expenses		238,000	
A Net Income		$ 48,000	

Exhibit 11-4 ▲

Mackay Industries, Inc.
Statement of Retained Earnings
Year Ended December 31, 2014

	Retained Earnings, December 31, 2013	$121,000
	Add: Net Income for the Year	48,000
	Subtotal	169,000
M	Less: Dividends	23,000
	Retained Earnings, December 31, 2014	$146,000

Mackay Industries, Inc.
Balance Sheet
December 31, 2013 and 2014

			2014	2013	SOURCE (USE) OF CASH
		ASSETS			
		Current:			
		Cash	$ 18,000	$ 11,000	($ 7,000)
D		Accounts Receivable	76,000	93,000	17,000
E		Inventory	132,000	124,000	(8,000)
		Total Current Assets	226,000	228,000	
H/I		Plant Assets, Net	385,000	315,000	(70,000)
		Total Assets	$611,000	$543,000	
		LIABILITIES			
		Current:			
F		Accounts Payable	$ 84,000	$ 96,000	$(12,000)
G		Accrued Liabilities	12,000	8,000	4,000
		Total Current Liabilities	96,000	104,000	
J/K		Long-Term Notes Payable	147,000	98,000	49,000
		Total Liabilities	243,000	202,000	
		SHAREHOLDERS' EQUITY			
L		Common Shares	240,000	220,000	20,000
A/M		Retained Earnings	146,000	121,000	25,000
N		Less Treasury Shares	(18,000)	(0)	(18,000)
		Total Shareholders' Equity	368,000	341,000	
		Total Liabilities and Shareholders' Equity	$611,000	$543,000	
		Totals			0

Exhibit 11-4 ▲ (*continued*)

Identifying Sources and Uses of Cash

Before we prepare the cash flow statement, it is important to understand the sources of cash (i.e., cash inflow) and uses of cash (i.e., cash outflow) as a result of the changes in each account in the balance sheet. We will use the accounting equation to illustrate the impact on cash as the change in each type of account:

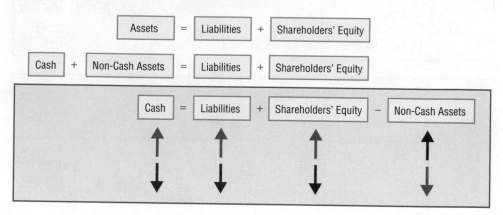

First, on the assets side, we separate cash and noncash assets. Then, we move non-cash assets to the right side of the equation. By doing so, we isolate the cash account, and now we can observe how changes in the balances in each type of account will impact the cash account.

The cash account will increase if liabilities accounts increase, if shareholders' equity accounts increase, or if a noncash assets account decreases. For example, a company will receive cash if it borrows money from the bank (e.g., note payable increases), issues more shares (e.g., share capital increases), or sells some noncash assets (e.g., equipment decreases). A company will reserve cash if it does not pay its accounts payable (e.g., accounts payable increases).

On the other hand, the balance in the cash account will decrease if liabilities accounts decrease, if shareholders' equity accounts decrease, or if a noncash assets account increases. For example, a company will use cash to pay down its debt (e.g., accounts payable decreases), pay dividends (e.g., retained earnings decreases), or purchase non-cash assets (e.g., inventory increases). A company will tie up cash, in other words, no cash inflow when accounts receivable increases.

Liabilities		+	Shareholders' Equity		−	Noncash Assets	
Dr (−)	**Cr (−)**		**Dr (−)**	**Cr (−)**		**Dr (−)**	**Cr (−)**
Use of Cash	Source of Cash		Use of Cash	Source of Cash		Use of Cash	Source of Cash

Now, let's prepare Mackay Industries' cash flow statement one section at a time. To make things easier to follow, each item on the cash flow statement has been cross referenced to the financial statements by a letter.

Cash Flows from Operating Activities

The operating activities section of Mackay Industries' cash flow statement would look like this:

		Cash flows from operating activities:		
A		Net Income		$48,000
		Adjustments to reconcile net income to net cash		
		provided by operating activities:		
B		Depreciation Expense	$ 18,000	
C		Loss on sale of plant assets	3,000	
D		Decrease in Accounts Receivable	17,000	
E		Increase in Inventory	(8,000)	
F		Decrease in Accounts Payable	(12,000)	
G		Increase in Accrued Liabilities	4,000	22,000
		Net cash provided by operating activities		70,000

Operating cash flows begin with net income, taken from the income statement.

A Net Income

The cash flow statement—indirect method—begins with net income because revenues and expenses, which affect net income, produce cash receipts and cash payments. Revenues bring in cash receipts and expenses must be paid. But net income is accrual based and the accrual basis of revenues and expenses don't always equal the cash flows (cash basis net income). For example, sales *on account* are revenues that increase net income, but the company hasn't yet collected cash from those sales. Accrued expenses decrease your net income, but you haven't paid cash *if the expenses are accrued*.

To go from net income to cash flow from operations, we must make some adjustments to net income on the cash flow statement. These additions and subtractions follow net income and are labelled "Adjustments to reconcile net income to net cash provided by operating activities." There are three items to be adjusted: (1) noncash items from the income statement, such as depreciation, (2) non-operating items from the income statement, such as a gain or loss from the sale of fixed assets, and (3) noncash working capital accounts from the balance sheet.

B Depreciation, Depletion, and Amortization Expenses

These expenses are added back to net income to reconcile it to cash flows from operations. Let's see why. Depreciation is recorded as follows:

DATE	ACCOUNTS	POST REF.	DR.	CR.
	Depreciation Expense		18,000	
	Accumulated Depreciation			18,000

You can see that depreciation does not affect cash because there's no Cash account in the journal entry. However, depreciation, like all the other expenses, decreases net income. Therefore, to go from net income to cash flows, we must add the depreciation back to net income.

Example: Suppose you had only two transactions during the period:

- $50,000 cash sale
- Depreciation expense of $20,000

Accrual basis net income is $30,000 ($50,000 – $20,000). But cash flow from operations is $50,000. To reconcile the net income of $30,000 to the cash flow from operations of $50,000, add back the $20,000 of depreciation expense. You would also add back depletion and amortization expenses because they are noncash expenses similar to depreciation.

C Gains and Losses on the Sale of Assets

Sales of long-term assets such as land and buildings are investing activities. The total cash proceeds from these sales are included in the investing section of the cash flow statement. However, these sales usually result in a gain or a loss, which is included in net income. Gains and losses do not represent cash flows. They are simply a function of the difference between the cash proceeds and the book value of the asset. Therefore, gains and losses must be removed from net income on the cash flow statement.

Mackay Industries' income statement includes a loss on the sale of plant assets. During 2014, Mackay Industries sold equipment resulting in a loss of $3,000 on the sale. Because the loss reduces net income, it is added back to net income to arrive at cash flows from operating activities. On the other hand, a gain on the sale of plant assets would increase net income. So, it would be subtracted from net income to arrive at cash flows from operating activities. The impact on cash from the sale of a capital asset will be properly calculated in the cash flow from the investing activities section.

D, E, F, & G Changes in the Current Assets and the Current Liabilities

Most current assets and current liabilities result from operating activities. For example,

- accounts receivable result from sales,
- inventory and accounts payable relate to cost of goods sold,
- prepaid assets and accrued liabilities relate to operating expenses, and so on.

Changes in the current asset and current liability accounts create adjustments to net income on the cash flow statement, as follows:

1. **A decrease in a current asset other than cash causes an increase in cash.** Mackay Industries' Accounts Receivable decreased by $17,000 **D**. What caused the decrease? During the year, Mackay Industries must have collected more cash from credit customers than the current year's credit sales. This means that $17,000 more was collected from customers than what is represented by the Revenues on the income statement. Therefore, the $17,000 decrease in Accounts Receivable is added to net income to arrive at cash flows from operating activities. A decrease in any current asset other than cash will be added to net income to arrive at cash flows from operating activities. The last column in Exhibit 11-4 also shows that this decrease in accounts receivable represents a "source" or inflow of cash.

2. **An increase in a current asset other than cash causes a decrease in cash.** It takes cash to acquire assets. If Accounts Receivable, Inventory, or Prepaid Expenses increase, then Cash decreases. Therefore, subtract the increase in the current asset from net income to get cash flow from operations. For example, Mackay Industries' Inventory went up by $8,000 **E**. The $8,000 increase in inventory is not reflected in Cost of Goods Sold on the Income Statement. However, this increase required the payment of cash so it is deducted from net income to arrive at cash flows from operating activities. An increase in any current asset other than cash will be subtracted from net income to arrive at cash flows from operating activities. The last column in Exhibit 11-4 also shows that this increase in inventory represents a "use" or outflow of cash.

3. **A decrease in a current liability causes a decrease in cash.** Mackay Industries'
   Accounts Payable went down $12,000 **F**. This means that Mackay Industries
   paid $12,000 more on its payables than it charged during the current year.
   However, the amount that Mackay Industries charged on its payables is what is
   reflected in Cost of Goods Sold and Operating Expenses on the income statement. So, the $12,000 decrease in Accounts Payable is subtracted from net
   income to arrive at cash flows from operating activities. A decrease in any current
   liability will be subtracted from net income to arrive at cash flows from operating
   activities. The last column in Exhibit 11-4 also shows that this decrease in
   accounts payable represents a "use" or outflow of cash.

4. **An increase in a current liability causes an increase in cash.** Mackay Industries'
   Accrued Liabilities increased by $4,000 **G**. This means that $4,000 of the operating expenses on the income statement have not yet been paid for. Accordingly,
   even though net income was reduced by the $4,000, cash was not reduced.
   Therefore, the $4,000 increase in current liabilities is added to net income to arrive
   at cash flows from operations. An increase in any current liability will be added to
   net income to arrive at cash flows from operating activities. The last column in
   Exhibit 11-4 also shows that this increase in accrued liabilities payable represents a
   "source" or inflow of cash.

During 2014, Mackay Industries' operations provided net cash flow of $70,000. This
amount exceeds net income (due to the various adjustments discussed previously).
However, to fully evaluate a company's cash flows, we must also examine its investing
and financing activities.

Cash Flows from Investing Activities

As shown in Exhibit 11-2, investing activities affect long-term assets, such as Plant
Assets and Investments. The investing section of Mackay Industries' cash flow statement
is presented next:

		Cash flows from investing activities:		
	H	Acquisition of plant assets	$(195,000)	
	I	Proceeds from sale of plant assets	104,000	
		Net cash used in investing activities		(91,000)

Computing Acquisitions and Sales of Plant Assets

Companies usually keep a separate account for each type of plant asset. However, for
computing investing cash flows, it is helpful to combine all the plant assets into a single
Plant Assets account. We subtract Accumulated Depreciation from the assets' cost to
work with a single net figure for plant assets, such as Plant Assets, Net . . . $385,000.
This simplifies the computations.

To illustrate, observe that Mackay Industries' financial statements presented in
Exhibit 11-4 show the following:

- The balance sheet reports plant assets, net of depreciation, of $385,000 at the end
  of 2014 and $315,000 at the end of 2013.
- The income statement shows depreciation expense of $18,000 and a $3,000 loss
  on sale of plant assets.

The increase in the net amount of plant assets tells us that Mackay Industries acquired plant assets during 2014. Let's assume that Mackay Industries' acquisitions of plant assets during 2014 consisted of $195,000 of cash purchases. The $195,000 of cash used to purchase the plant assets will be reported as a cash outflow (item **H**) in the investing section of the cash flow statement. If any portion of the purchase of plant assets is financed with notes payable, the amount financed is not included in the cash outflow.

The loss on sale of assets reported on the income statement indicates that Mackay Industries sold some older plant assets. This gives us an incomplete T-account as follows:

Plant Assets, Net			
12/31/13 Bal	315,000	2014 Depr exp	18,000
Acquisitions	195,000	Sales	?
12/31/14 Bal	385,000		

We can now solve for the net book value of the assets that were sold as follows:

12/31/2013 Balance + Acquisitions − Depreciation Expense − Sales? = 12/31/2014 Balance

$315,000	+ $195,000	−	$ 18,000	− Sales? =	$385,000
			$492,000	− Sales? =	$385,000
				Sales =	$107,000

Our completed T-account now looks like this:

Plant Assets, Net			
12/31/13 Bal	315,000	2014 Depr exp	18,000
Acquisitions	195,000	Sales	107,000
12/31/14 Bal	385,000		

Once we know the book value of the assets sold, we can calculate the amount of cash received from selling plant assets by using the journal entry approach:

DATE	ACCOUNTS	POST REF.	DR.	CR.
	Cash		??????	
	Loss on Sale of Plant Assets		3,000	
	Plant Assets, Net			107,000

So, we compute the cash receipt from the sale as follows:

Cash = Plant assets, net − loss
Cash = $107,000 − $3,000
Cash = $104,000

The cash receipt from the sale of plant assets of $104,000 is shown as item **I** in the investing activities section of the cash flow statement. **Exhibit 11-5** on the following page summarizes the computation of the investing cash flows from the acquisition and sale of plant assets. Items to be computed are shown in blue.

The investing section of the cash flow statement will also include cash outflows for the purchase of investments and for any amounts lent to others under long-term notes receivable. Cash inflows reported in the investing section of the cash flow statement will

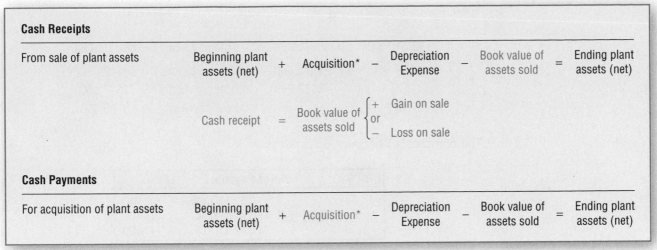

Cash Receipts						
From sale of plant assets	Beginning plant assets (net)	+ Acquisition*	− Depreciation Expense	− Book value of assets sold	= Ending plant assets (net)	

$$\text{Cash receipt} = \text{Book value of assets sold} \begin{cases} + & \text{Gain on sale} \\ \text{or} & \\ - & \text{Loss on sale} \end{cases}$$

Cash Payments						
For acquisition of plant assets	Beginning plant assets (net)	+ Acquisition*	− Depreciation Expense	− Book value of assets sold	= Ending plant assets (net)	

*Any portion of the acquisition that is financed by a note payable must be deducted from the amount of cash paid.

Exhibit 11-5 ▲

include proceeds from the sale of investments and any payments received on long-term notes receivable.

As we can see, Mackay Industries used $91,000 in investing activities. Now let's examine the financing section of the cash flow statement.

Cash Flows from Financing Activities

As shown in Exhibit 11-2, financing activities affect the liability and shareholders' equity accounts, such as Long-Term Notes Payable, Bonds Payable, Common Shares, and Retained Earnings. The financing section of Mackay Industries' cash flow statement is presented next:

	Cash flows from financing activities:		
J	Proceeds from issuance of notes payable	$ 75,000	
L	Proceeds from issuance of common shares	20,000	
K	Payment of notes payable	(26,000)	
M	Payment of dividends	(23,000)	
N	Purchase of treasury shares	(18,000)	
	Net cash provided by financing activities		28,000

Computing Issuances and Payments of Long-Term Notes Payable

The beginning and ending balances of Notes Payable or Bonds Payable are found on the balance sheet. If either the amount of new issuances or payments is known, the other amount can be computed. For Mackay Industries, Inc., let's assume that during 2014, $75,000 was borrowed on a long-term note payable. We can use the amount of the note proceeds and the beginning and ending balances of Notes Payable from Mackay Industries' balance sheet in Exhibit 11-4 to create the following incomplete T-account:

Notes Payable			
		12/31/13 Bal	98,000
Note payments	?	New notes	75,000
		12/31/14 Bal	147,000

Then, solve for the missing payments value:

> 12/31/13 Bal + New notes issued − Note payments? = 12/31/14 Bal
>
> $98,000 + $ 75,000 − Note payments? = $147,000
>
> $173,000 − Note payments? = $147,000
>
> Note payments = $ 26,000

The completed T-account looks like this:

Notes Payable			
		12/31/13 Bal	98,000
Note payments	26,000	New notes	75,000
		12/31/14 Bal	147,000

The $75,000 cash received is reflected as a cash inflow (item **J**) in the financing section of the cash flow statement. The payment of $26,000 is reflected as a cash outflow (item **K**) in the financing section of the cash flow statement. The difference between $75,000 and $26,000 is the net cash inflow showing in Exhibit 11-4 as "source" of $49,000.

Computing Issuances of Shares

Cash flows for these financing activities can be determined by analyzing the share accounts. We can see from looking at the data in Exhibit 11-4 that the balance in the Common Shares account increased by $20,000. Since we were not told about any shares retirements, we can assume there were none. Therefore, the $20,000 change in the Common Shares balance must be due to new share issuances. We will assume the shares were issued in exchange for cash so the $20,000 will be reflected as a cash inflow (item **L**) in the financing section of the cash flow statement.

Computing Dividend Payments

The amount of dividends that were declared during the year can be found on the statement of retained earnings. From the statement of retained earnings in Exhibit 11-4, we see that Mackay Industries declared $23,000 of dividends during 2014. Remember, a stock dividend has *no* effect on Cash and is, therefore, *not* reported on the cash flow statement. We will assume that all of Mackay Industries dividends were cash dividends. Because there were no beginning or ending balances in Dividends Payable on the balance sheet, we can conclude that the entire $23,000 (and no more) was paid during 2014. Therefore, the $23,000 will be reflected as a cash outflow (Item **M**) in the financing section of the cash flow statement.

   If the statement of retained earnings is unavailable, the amount of dividends can be computed by analyzing the Retained Earnings account. Remember, Retained Earnings increases when companies earn net income. Retained Earnings also decreases when companies have a net loss and when they declare dividends. We can use the amount of the Net Income and the beginning and ending balances of Retained Earnings (from Mackay Industries' financial statements in Exhibit 11-4) to create the following incomplete T-account:

Retained Earnings			
		12/31/13 Bal	121,000
Dividends	?	Net income	48,000
		12/31/14 Bal	146,000

Then, solve for the missing amount of dividends declared:

$$12/31/13 \text{ Bal} + \text{Net income} - \text{Dividends?} = 12/31/14 \text{ Bal}$$

$$\$121,000 + \$48,000 - \text{Dividends?} = \$146,000$$

$$\$169,000 - \text{Dividends?} = \$146,000$$

$$\text{Dividends} = \$23,000$$

The completed T-account looks like this:

Retained Earnings			
		12/31/13 Bal	121,000
Dividends	23,000	Net income	48,000
		12/31/14 Bal	146,000

Another way to determine the amount of dividends declared is to compare the net income and the amount of increase in the Retained Earnings account. Exhibit 11-4 shows that there is a "source" or inflow of cash of $25,000. However, Mackay Industries reported a net income of $48,000. The difference of $23,000 was declared as dividends.

Purchases and Sales of Treasury Shares

The last item that changed on Mackay Industries' balance sheet was Treasury Shares. Since we were not told that any Treasury Shares were sold, we must assume that 100% of the account change represents new acquisitions of Treasury Shares. So, $18,000 is shown as a cash outflow in the financing section of the cash flow statement for purchase of treasury shares (item **N**).

Net Change in Cash and Cash Balances

The cash provided by or used in operating, investing, and financing activities is totalled to arrive at the net increase of $7,000 in cash. Next, the beginning cash of $11,000 from December 31, 2013 is listed. The net increase of $7,000 is added to the beginning cash of $11,000 to get the ending cash balance on December 31, 2014 of $18,000. The completed cash flow statement for Mackay Industries, Inc. is presented in **Exhibit 11-6** on the following page.

You can see why the cash flow statement is so valuable. It explains why the cash balance for Mackay Industries increased by only $7,000, even though the company reported net income for the year of $48,000.

Noncash Investing and Financing Activities

The operating, investing, and financing sections of the cash flow statement only reflect activity that results from the exchange of cash; however, companies may make investments that do not require cash. They may also obtain financing for other reasons than to acquire cash. These types of transactions are called noncash investing and financing activities. Although these transactions do not affect cash, they still affect the long-term assets, long-term liabilities, and equity of a business. To provide financial statement users with complete information, all noncash investing and financing activities are reported. Noncash investing and financing activities can be reported in a separate schedule that accompanies the cash flow statement or they can be disclosed in a financial statement footnote.

Mackay Industries
Cash Flow Statement
Year Ended December 31, 2014

	Cash flows from operating activities:			
A	Net Income			$ 48,000
	Adjustments to reconcile net income to net cash provided by operating activities:			
B	Depreciation Expense		$ 18,000	
C	Loss on sale of plant assets		3,000	
D	Decrease in Accounts Receivable		17,000	
E	Increase in Inventory		(8,000)	
F	Decrease in Accounts Payable		(12,000)	
G	Increase in Accrued Liabilities		4,000	22,000
	Net cash provided by operating activities			70,000
	Cash flows from investing activities:			
H	Acquisition of plant assets		(195,000)	
I	Proceeds from sale of plant assets		104,000	
	Net cash used in investing activities			(91,000)
	Cash flows from financing activities:			
J	Proceeds from issuance of notes payable		75,000	
L	Proceeds from issuance of common shares		20,000	
K	Payment of notes payable		(26,000)	
M	Payment of dividends		(23,000)	
N	Purchase of treasury shares		(18,000)	
	Net cash provided by financing activities			28,000
	Net increase in cash:			7,000
	Cash balance, December 31, 2013			11,000
	Cash balance, December 31, 2014			$ 18,000

Exhibit 11-6 ▲

Our Mackay Industries example did not include noncash transactions because the company did not have any transactions of this type during the year. So, to illustrate the reporting of noncash transactions, let's consider the following three noncash transactions for Tucker Enterprises.

❶ Tucker Enterprises issues $450,000 of common shares in exchange for a building. The journal entry to record the purchase would be as follows:

DATE	ACCOUNTS	POST REF.	DR.	CR.
	Building		450,000	
	Common Shares			450,000
	Exchanged shares for a building.			

The purchase of the building is an investing activity. The issuance of common shares is a financing activity. However, this transaction is not reported in the investing and financing sections of the cash flow statement because no cash is exchanged. Instead, this transaction is reported as a *noncash investing and financing activity.*

❷ Tucker Enterprises acquired $120,000 of land by issuing a note. The journal entry to record the purchase would be as follows:

DATE	ACCOUNTS	POST REF.	DR.	CR.
	Land		120,000	
	Notes Payable			120,000
	Purchased land.			

The purchase of the land is an investing activity. The issuance of the note is a financing activity. Once again, this transaction is not reported in the investing and financing sections of the cash flow statement because no cash is exchanged. Instead, this transaction is reported as a *noncash investing and financing activity*.

❸ Tucker Enterprises issued $100,000 of common shares to pay off a debt. The journal entry to record the payment would be as follows:

DATE	ACCOUNTS	POST REF.	DR.	CR.
	Notes Payable		100,000	
	Common Shares			100,000
	Paid note with shares.			

The payment on the note and the issuance of the common shares are both financing activities. But, because no cash is involved, this transaction will not be reported in the financing section of the cash flow statement. It is reported as a *noncash investing and financing activity*.

Exhibit 11-7 illustrates how the noncash investing and financing activities for Tucker Enterprises would be presented.

Tucker Enterprises Cash Flow Statement—Partial Year Ended December 31, 2014		
Noncash investing and financing activities:		
Issued 10,000 common shares in exchange for a building		$450,000
Issued a note in exchange for land		120,000
Issued 1,800 common shares as repayment of note		100,000

Exhibit 11-7 ▲

CONCEPT CHECK

Alpine Manufacturing purchased a new piece of equipment costing $45,000. Alpine paid $5,000 cash down and signed a note for the remainder. What types of activities (operating, financing, or investing) are represented by this transaction? How would this transaction be reported in Alpine Manufacturing's cash flow statement?

Answer

Because this transaction involves both the purchase of new plant assets and the issuance of a note payable, it represents both an investing activity and a financing activity. However, on Alpine Manufacturing's cash flow statement, only $5,000 will be reflected in the investing section as an outflow of cash for the purchase of plant assets. The remaining $40,000 will be reflected as a noncash investing and financing activity in a separate schedule.

HOW IS THE CASH FLOW STATEMENT PREPARED USING THE DIRECT METHOD?

4 ▶ Prepare the cash flow statement using the direct method

Although most companies utilize the indirect method of reporting cash flows from operating activities, the IFRS and the Canadian ASPE prefer the direct method. This is one instance when companies choose to use an accounting method that is contrary to the general rules. But since most companies use the indirect method, the discrepancy is overlooked. The direct method provides clearer information about the sources and uses of cash than the indirect method. Investing and financing cash flows are presented exactly the same under both direct and indirect methods.

To illustrate how the operating section of the cash flow statement differs for the direct method, we will be using the Mackay Industries, Inc. data we used with the indirect method. The format for the direct method cash flow statement for Mackay Industries is presented in **Exhibit 11-8**.

Mackay Industries, Inc. Cash Flow Statement Year Ended December 31, 2014		
Cash flows from operating activities:		
Receipts:		
Collections from customers		
Interest received		
Dividends received on investments		
Total cash receipts		
Payments:		
To suppliers		
To employees		
For interest and income tax		
Total cash payments		
Net cash provided by operating activities		
± **Cash flows from investing activities:**		
+ Cash receipts from sales of long-term assets (investments, land, building, equipment, and so on)		
− Purchases of long-term assets		
Net cash provided by (used for) investing activities		
± **Cash flows from financing activities:**		
+ Cash receipts from issuance of shares		
+ Sale of treasury shares		
− Purchase of treasury shares		
+ Cash receipts from issuance of notes or bonds payable (borrowing)		
− Payment of notes or bonds payable		
− Payment of dividends		
Net cash provided by (used for) financing activities		
= **Net increase (decrease) in cash during the year**		
+ Cash at December 31, 2013		
= Cash at December 31, 2014		

Exhibit 11-8 ▲

Mackay Industries' completed direct method cash flow statement for 2014 is presented in Exhibit 11-9.

	Mackay Industries **Cash Flow Statement** Year Ended December 31, 2014			
	Cash flows from operating activities:			
	Receipts:			
A	Collections from customers	$ 285,000		
B	Interest received	13,000		
C	Dividends received	5,000		
	Total cash receipts		$ 303,000	
	Payments:			
D	To suppliers	(165,000)		
E	To employees	(48,000)		
F	For interest	(11,000)		
G	For taxes	(9,000)		
	Total cash payments		(233,000)	
	Net cash provided by operating activities		70,000	
	Cash flows from investing activities:			
	Acquisition of plant assets	(195,000)		
	Proceeds from sale of plant assets	104,000		
	Net cash used in investing activities		(91,000)	
	Cash flows from financing activities:			
	Proceeds from issuance of notes payable	75,000		
	Proceeds from issuance of common shares	20,000		
	Payment of notes payable	(26,000)		
	Payment of dividends	(23,000)		
	Purchase of treasury shares	(18,000)		
	Net cash provided by financing activities		28,000	
	Net increase in cash:		7,000	
	Cash balance, December 31, 2013		11,000	
	Cash balance, December 31, 2014		$ 18,000	

Exhibit 11-9 ▲

Now, we'll explain how we calculated each number.

Cash Flows from Operating Activities

In the indirect method, we start with net income and then adjust it to "cash-basis" through a series of adjusting items. In the direct method, we convert each line item on the income statement from accrual to cash basis. So, in essence, the operating activities section of the direct method cash flow statement is really just a cash-basis income statement.

Depreciation, Depletion, and Amortization Expense

Because these expenses do not require the payment of cash, they are **not** reported on the direct method cash flow statement.

Gains and Losses on the Sale of Plant Assets

The last item on the income statement is a loss on sale of plant assets of $3,000. Remember that gains and losses do not represent cash flows. The cash flow related to the sale of a plant asset equals the proceeds from the sale of the asset. As with the indirect method, the proceeds from the sale of the asset are reported in the investing section, not the operating section.

A Cash Collections from Customers

The first item on the income statement is Sales Revenue of $268,000. Sales Revenue represents the total of all sales, whether for cash or on account. The balance sheet accounts related to Sales Revenue are Accounts Receivable and Unearned Revenues. Accounts receivable decreased $17,000 from $93,000 at 12/31/13 to $76,000 at 12/31/14. A decrease in Accounts Receivable means that Mackay Industries collected more cash than it made in sales during the current year, as shown in Exhibit 11-4 source of cash of $17,000. This means that the cash receipts during the year are $17,000 greater than Sales Revenues. The balance sheet shows no unearned revenues so no adjustment is needed for unearned revenues. We can calculate the cash received from customers as follows:

Sales Revenue...	$268,000
Plus decrease in Accounts Receivable............	17,000
Cash receipts from customers........................	$285,000

B Cash Receipts of Interest

The second item on the income statement is Interest Revenue of $13,000. The balance sheet account related to Interest Revenue is Interest Receivable. Since there is no Interest Receivable account on the balance sheet, the Interest Revenue must have all been received in cash. So, the cash flow statement shows Interest Received of $13,000. Had there been Interest Receivable in either year, the accrual basis Interest Revenue would have been converted to cash basis in a manner similar to that used for Sales Revenue and Accounts Receivable.

C Cash Receipts of Dividends

Dividend Revenue of $5,000 is the third item reported on the income statement. The balance sheet account related to Dividend Revenue is Dividends Receivable. As with the interest, there is no Dividends Receivable on the balance sheet. Therefore, the Dividend Revenue must have all been received in cash. So, the cash flow statement shows cash received from dividends of $5,000.

D Payments to Suppliers

Payments to suppliers include all payments for

- inventory and
- operating expenses except employee compensation, interest, and income taxes.

Suppliers are those entities that provide the business with its inventory and essential services. The accounts related to payments to suppliers for inventory are Cost of Goods Sold, Inventory, and Accounts Payable. Cost of Goods Sold on the income statement was $137,000. Inventory increased from $124,000 at 12/31/13 to $132,000 at 12/31/14. The $8,000

($132,000 – $124,000) increase in Inventory means that Mackay Industries purchased more inventory than it sold during the year. This means that the total amount of inventory purchased during the year would be $145,000.

Cost of Goods Sold	$137,000
Plus increase in Inventory	8,000
Total inventory purchased	$145,000

Next we need to consider the change in Accounts Payable to determine the total cash payments for inventory purchased during the year. Accounts Payable decreased from $96,000 at 12/31/13 to $84,000 at 12/31/14. The $12,000 decrease ($96,000 – $84,000) in Accounts Payable means that Mackay Industries paid $12,000 more during the year than the amount of inventory purchased. So, the cash payments for inventory purchased during the year can be calculated as follows:

Total inventory purchased	$145,000
Plus decrease in Accounts Payable	12,000
Cash payments for inventory	$157,000

The accounts related to payments to suppliers for operating expenses are Operating Expenses, Prepaid Expenses, and Accrued Liabilities. Operating Expenses on the income statement were $12,000. There are no Prepaid Expenses on the balance sheet so no adjustment is needed for changes in prepaid expenses. Accrued Liabilities increased from $8,000 at 12/31/13 to $12,000 at 12/31/14. This means that Mackay Industries incurred more operating expenses than it paid for during the year. By subtracting the $4,000 ($12,000 – $8,000) from the operating expenses we get the amount of cash payments made to suppliers for operating expense:

Operating Expenses	$12,000
Less increase in Accrued Liabilities	4,000
Cash payments for operating expenses	$ 8,000

Finally, by adding the cash paid to suppliers for inventory to the cash paid to suppliers for operating expenses we get the total cash paid to suppliers of $165,000.

Cash payments for inventory	$157,000
Cash payments for operating expenses	8,000
Total cash payments to suppliers	$165,000

ᴇ Payments to Employees

This category includes payments for salaries, wages, and other forms of employee compensation. The accounts related to employee payments are Salaries Expense from the income statement and Salaries Payable from the balance sheet. Since there aren't any Salaries Payable on the balance sheet, the Salaries Expense account must represent all amounts paid in cash to employees. So, the cash flow statement shows cash payments to employees of $48,000. Had there been any Salaries Payable, the Salaries Expense account would have been adjusted to arrive at the cash paid to employees in a manner similar to how operating expenses were adjusted for accrued liabilities above.

▪F Payments for Interest Expense

These cash payments are reported separately from the other expenses. The accounts related to interest payments are Interest Expense from the income statement and Interest Payable from the balance sheet. Since there is no Interest Payable on the balance sheet, the Interest Expense from the income statement must represent all amounts paid in cash for interest. So, the cash flow statement shows cash payments for interest of $11,000.

▪G Payments for Income Tax Expense

Like interest expense, these cash payments are reported separately from the other expenses. The accounts related to income tax payments are Income Tax Expense from the income statement and Income Tax Payable from the balance sheet. Again, since there is no Income Tax Payable on the balance sheet, the Income Tax Expense from the income statement must represent all amounts paid in cash for income tax. Therefore, the cash flow statement shows cash payments for income tax of $9,000.

Net Cash Provided by Operating Activities

To calculate net cash provided by operating activities using the direct method, we add all the cash receipts and cash payments described previously and find the difference. For Mackay Industries, Inc., total Cash receipts were $303,000. Total Cash payments were $233,000. So, net cash provided by operating activities is $70,000. If you refer back to the indirect method cash flow statement shown in Exhibit 11-6, you will find that it showed the same $70,000 for net cash provided by operating activities—only the method by which it was calculated was different.

The remainder of Mackay Industries' cash flow statement is exactly the same as what we calculated using the indirect method (see Exhibit 11-6).

Exhibit 11-10 summarizes the operating activities using indirect and direct methods:

Method	Indirect Method	Direct Method
Financial Statements	Start with Income Statement, then go to Balance Sheet	Look at both Income Statement and Balance Sheet simultaneously

Steps:	Net Income Adjustments:
	+ (1) Non-cash items: Depreciation
	± (2) Non-operating items: Loss/Gain on sale of asset or retirement of debt
	± (3) Non-cash working capital accounts: source or (use) of cash for each current asset and current liability account
		Cash receipt from customers:
		    Sales + △AR + △Unearned Revenue
		Cash paid to suppliers:
		    (Cost of Goods Sold) + △Inventory + △Accounts Payable
		Cash paid to employees:
		    (Salary Expense) + △Salary Payable
		Cash paid for other expenses:
		    (Other Expense) + △Prepayment + △Accrued Liabilities
		Cash paid for interest expenses:
		    (Interest Expense) + △Interest Payable
		Cash paid for income tax expense:
		    (Income Tax Expense) + △Income Tax Payable

Exhibit 11-10 ▲

CRITICAL THINKING

Take a minute to think about the following items. How do companies record journal entries for each of these items? What do they do in preparing the cash flow statement?

- Premium on bonds payable
- Discount on bonds payable
- Warranty Expense
- Bad Debt Expense
- Contributed surplus

Solution:

		DR.	CR.	CASH FLOW STATEMENT
1	Interest Expense	XXX		Need to subtract this amount from net income to get cash amount paid for interest.
	Premium on Bonds Payable	XX		
	Cash		XXX	
2	Interest Expense	XXX		Need to add this amount to net income to get cash amount paid for interest.
	Discount on Bonds Payable		XX	
	Cash		XXX	
3	Warranty Expense	XXX		This is a noncash item. This amount needs to be added back to net income
	Estimated Warranty Liabilities		XXX	
4	Bad Debt Expense	XXX		This is a noncash item. This amount needs to be added back to net income
	Allowance for Doubtful Accounts		XXX	
5	Common Shares	XXX		Need to subtract this amount from the changes in the Common Shares account to get total cash amount paid to buy back Common Shares
	Contributed Surplus		XX	
	Cash		XXX	

DECISION GUIDELINES

Decision

I just started my own business and I want to make sure that I report things properly. Should the direct or indirect method be used to prepare the cash flow statement?

Guideline

Although the direct method is preferred by IFRS and Canadian ASPE, most financial statement users find the indirect method more useful.

Analyze

Because the indirect method reconciles net income as reported on the income statement to net cash provided by operating activities, it is more useful to most financial statements users. It helps answer the questions "How can the company have so much income when it has so little cash?" or "How can the company have so much cash when it made so little income?"

FOCUS ON DECISION MAKING: FREE CASH FLOW AND THE CASH CONVERSION CYCLE

Free Cash Flow

5 Evaluate a company's performance with respect to cash

The cash flow statement is a useful tool for examining the sources and uses of cash during an accounting period. However, investors may want to know how much cash a company anticipates it can "free up" for new opportunities. **Free cash flow** is the amount of anticipated cash available from operations after paying for planned investments in long-term assets and paying dividends. Free cash flow can be computed as follows:

$$\text{Free cash flow} = \begin{array}{c}\text{Anticipated net}\\\text{cash provided by}\\\text{operating activities}\end{array} - \begin{array}{c}\text{Cash payments planned for}\\\text{investments in plant, equipment,}\\\text{and other long-term assets}\end{array} - \begin{array}{c}\text{Anticipated cash}\\\text{payments for dividends}\end{array}$$

Many companies use free cash flow to manage their operations. Suppose Tucker Enterprises expects net cash provided by operations of $160,000 during the next year. Tucker Enterprises also plans to spend $85,000 to purchase new equipment and anticipates paying another $15,000 in dividends. In this case, Tucker Enterprises' free cash flow would be $60,000 ($160,000 – $85,000 – $15,000). If a good investment opportunity comes along (or an anticipated need for cash), Tucker Enterprises should have $60,000 of free cash available.

Cash Conversion Cycle

The **cash conversion cycle** represents the time it takes a company to sell its inventory and collect its receivables less the time it takes the company to pay its payables. In other words, the cash conversion cycle represents the number of days a company's cash is "tied up" in the operations of the business. The cash conversion cycle is calculated as follows:

$$\text{Cash conversion cycle} = \text{Inventory turnover (in days)} + \begin{array}{c}\text{Accounts receivable}\\\text{turnover (in days)}\end{array} - \begin{array}{c}\text{Accounts payable}\\\text{turnover (in days)}\end{array}$$

The inventory turnover in days can be found by dividing 365 by the inventory turnover (discussed in Chapter 6). Alternatively, it can be found using the following formula:

$$\text{Inventory turnover in days} = \text{Average inventory} \div \text{Cost of goods sold} \times 365$$

The accounts receivable turnover in days can be found by dividing 365 by the accounts receivable turnover (discussed in Chapter 7). Alternatively, it can be found by using the following formula:

$$\text{Accounts receivable turnover in days} = \text{Average net accounts receivable} \div \text{Net credit saies} \times 365$$

The accounts payable turnover in days is calculated as follows:

$$\text{Accounts payable turnover in days} = \text{Average accounts payable} \div \text{Cost of goods sold} \times 365$$

Let's assume that Tucker Enterprises has an inventory turnover of 52 days, an accounts receivable turnover of 34 days, and an accounts payable turnover of 39 days. Tucker Enterprises' cash conversion cycle would equal 47 days (52 + 34 − 39). This means that, on average, Tucker Enterprises' cash is tied up for 47 days. Generally, the lower the cash conversion cycle the healthier the company. This is because cash is the life blood of a business and the less amount of time it is "tied up" the better. Over time, if the cash conversion cycle for a business grows longer, it can be a sign that the business may be facing a pending cash flow "crunch."

DECISION GUIDELINES

Decision

As the manager of a department, I would like to have renovations done on my retail area. Does the company have sufficient cash available?

Guideline

Calculate the company's free cash flow and its cash conversion cycle.

Analyze

For a business to be able to take advantage of unforeseen opportunities, it is important that it has "free cash" available. A lack of "free cash" will probably not negatively impact a business's normal operations but it will most likely result in lost income due to forgone opportunities.

The cash conversion cycle indicates how long a company's cash is being "tied up" in its operations. The longer cash is tied up, the more likely it is that the company will encounter cash flow problems in the future. A company with a long cash conversion cycle should consider obtaining a line of credit to provide some insurance against cash flow problems.

FOCUS ON USERS

Concept	User	Why is this Important to this User?
Cash Flow Statement		All users of financial statements will spend a great deal of time examining the cash flow statement for the signals that it will send. For example, a new company may not have sufficient sales to generate positive cash flows from operations because the company will be purchasing inventory, selling to customers on credit, but paying for their purchases and expenses such as payroll; investing activities will also likely be a use of cash because the company needs to purchase the assets that will make the company productive; and, in order to support the operating and investing activities, a new company would need to have significant cash inflows from financing activities by selling shares, acquiring long-term debt, or both.
		A company that has been around long enough to be in its mature phase will likely have positive cash flows from operations that are significant enough to support any new purchases of capital assets in the investing activities (to replace older equipment), and uses of cash in the financing activities for paying down debt and paying dividends to shareholders.

(continued)

Concept	User	Why is this Important to this User?
Cash Flow Statement (*cont.*)		Each combination of sources and uses of cash in the three areas of activities will tell a story of how the company is performing. Since cash is the most important asset of an organization (because a company cannot exist without sufficient cash to satisfy its needs), understanding where a company is receiving cash and where a company uses its cash is critical for understanding its long-term potential. The cash flow needs to be understood in combination with the other financial statements and other information, though. For example, negative cash flows from a company's operating activities without understanding that this company is a start-up organization, could lead to a misinterpretation of how the organization is performing.
		Overall, the cash flow statement can provide users with important information for analysing whether creditors want to extend credit, competitors want to adjust their own strategies, investors want to purchase shares, or management needs to adjust their priorities for cash.

DEMO DOC

MyAccountingLab

Visit MyAccountingLab at www.myaccountinglab.com to watch animated versions of these Demo Docs.

L.O. 3

Preparing the Cash Flow Statement Using the Indirect Method

Cassidy, Inc. has the following information for 2014:

Cassidy, Inc.
Income Statement
Year Ended December 31, 2014

Sales Revenue		$550,000
Cost of Goods Sold		320,000
Gross Profit		230,000
Operating Expenses:		
Salary Expense	$165,000	
Depreciation Expense	21,000	
Insurance Expense	19,000	
Total Operating Expense		205,000
Income from Operations		25,000
Other items:		
Gain on Sale of Furniture		3,000
Net Income		$ 28,000

Cassidy, Inc.
Balance Sheet
December 31, 2014 and 2013

ASSETS	2014	2013	LIABILITIES	2014	2013
Current:			Current:		
Cash	$ 28,000	$ 33,000	Accounts Payable	$ 20,000	$ 23,000
Accounts Receivable	26,000	15,000	Salary Payable	10,000	8,000
Prepaid Insurance	30,000	42,000	Total Current		
Total Current Assets	84,000	90,000	Liabilities	30,000	31,000
Furniture, net	90,000	74,500	Notes Payable	40,000	50,000
			SHAREHOLDERS'		
			EQUITY		
			Common Shares	4,000	3,500
			Retained Earnings	100,000	80,000
			Total Liabilities and		
Total Assets	$174,000	$164,500	Shareholders' Equity	$174,000	$164,500

During 2014 Cassidy

- sold furniture with a book value of $15,000 for cash. New furniture was purchased for cash.
- repaid notes payable with a principal value of $22,000. Issued new notes for cash.
- issued new common shares for cash.
- paid cash dividends.

Requirement:

1 **Prepare Cassidy's cash flow statement using the indirect method.**

Demo Doc Solution

Requirement **1**

Prepare Cassidy's cash flow statement using the indirect method.

Part 1	Demo Doc Complete

Operating Activities

As with income statements and balance sheets, every cash flow statement needs a proper title. The first line of the title is the company name, next is the name of the statement (cash flow statement), and last is the date (year ended December 31, 2014). Put all together, the title is as follows:

Cassidy, Inc.
Cash Flow Statement
Year Ended December 31, 2014

The first section of the cash flow statement is operating activities. This section begins with net income. We can find net income on the income statement. According to Cassidy's income statement, net income for the year is $28,000.

Items are added or subtracted on the cash flow statement based on their impact to cash. In this case, net income increases cash, so it is added on the cash flow statement.

Next, we must take a quick look through the income statement and look for any non-cash items. Noncash items are *not* part of cash flows, so any noncash items in net income must be removed.

The most frequent noncash item on the income statement is depreciation expense. Depreciation expense is subtracted to arrive at net income (if you look at the income statement, you will see a subtraction for depreciation expense), so to *remove* its impact, the *opposite* must be done: Depreciation expense of $21,000 must be added back to net income.

The other noncash item that you will see on many income statements is gains/losses on sale of assets. In this example, Cassidy has a gain on sale of furniture of $3,000. As you can see on the income statement, this gain was added to arrive at net income. To *remove* its effect, we do the *opposite*: subtract it. So the gain of $3,000 is subtracted.

Now that we have gotten all necessary information from the income statement, we can turn to the balance sheet.

Operating activities deal with everyday transactions of the business, the kind of things the company normally does to earn a profit. What kinds of accounts do businesses deal with on a daily basis? Some accounts are Accounts Receivable, Accounts Payable, Inventory, and so forth. In other words, they are the current assets and current liabilities of the company. Changes in the balances of these accounts impact income differently than they impact cash flows. So, adjustments must be made to reconcile net income to the cash flows for the period.

Other than Cash (which we are trying to analyze in preparing the cash flow statement), what is the first current asset on the balance sheet? It is Accounts Receivable. What happened to Accounts Receivable during the year? It increased from $15,000 to $26,000. This means that $11,000 ($26,000 – $15,000) of the revenues on the income statement have not yet been collected in cash. So the $11,000 increase to Accounts Receivable is subtracted from net income on the cash flow statement.

The other current asset is Prepaid Insurance. This account decreased from $42,000 to $30,000. A decrease to Prepaid Insurance indicates that part of the expenses for the period were not paid for with cash. Instead, we used something we had prepaid—that is something we had already paid for in an earlier period. So, the decrease of $12,000 ($42,000 – $30,000) will be added to net income on the cash flow statement.

So far, operating activities show the following information:

Cash flows from operating activities:		
Net Income		$28,000
Adjustments to reconcile net income to net cash provided by operating activities:		
Depreciation Expense	$ 21,000	
Gain on sale of plant assets	(3,000)	
Increase in Accounts Receivable	(11,000)	
Decrease in Prepaid Insurance	12,000	

Now that we have looked at the current assets, we can look at the current liabilities. The first current liability is Accounts Payable. During the year, Accounts Payable decreased from $23,000 to $20,000. This means that $3,000 ($23,000 – $20,000) more was paid for during the current year than was charged on account. So, the $3,000 will be subtracted from net income on the cash flow statement.

The other current liability is Salary Payable. During the year, Salary Payable increased from $8,000 to $10,000. The increase in this payable account means that part of the current year's salaries expense was not paid for with cash. So $2,000 ($10,000 – $8,000) will be added to net income on the cash flow statement.

Now that we have looked at all of the current assets and liabilities, we can total the operating activities section:

Cash flows from operating activities:		
Net Income		$28,000
Adjustments to reconcile net income to net cash provided by operating activities:		
Depreciation Expense	$ 21,000	
Gain on sale of plant assets	(3,000)	
Increase in Accounts Receivable	(11,000)	
Decrease in Prepaid Insurance	12,000	
Decrease in Accounts Payable	(3,000)	
Increase in Salary Payable	2,000	18,000
Net cash provided by operating activities		46,000

Investing Activities

Investing activities deal with long-term assets. The only long-term asset is Furniture. Unfortunately, we cannot just say "increase in Furniture" or "decrease in Furniture" and look at the overall change because Furniture is a major account. We must look at each significant transaction affecting the account.

From the additional information we were given with the question, we know that Cassidy purchased furniture and sold furniture during the year. Each of these transactions will be a separate line in investing activities.

Cash flows from investing activities:		
Acquisition of furniture	???	
Proceeds from sale of furniture	???	
Net cash used for investing activities		???

We do not know these totals, but we can calculate them with the information we already have.

First, we should analyze the Furniture, Net T-account. From the balance sheet, we know that in 2014, Furniture, Net has a beginning balance of $74,500 and an ending balance of $90,000. During the year, Furniture, Net increased and decreased.

Furniture, Net			
Beginning balance	74,500		
Increases	???	Decreases	???
Ending balance	90,000		

Furniture, Net increases when new furniture is purchased (acquisitions). Furniture, Net decreases by the book value of furniture sold and when depreciation expense is recorded. Depreciation expense of $21,000 can be obtained from the income statement (or the operating activities section of the cash flow statement). The book value of $15,000 for the assets sold was given in the problem. Putting these items into the T-account is shown next:

Furniture, Net			
Beginning balance	74,500	Depreciation	21,000
Acquisitions	X	Book value of assets sold	15,000
Ending balance	90,000		

We can use this information to calculate the cost of furniture purchased (acquisitions), X.

$$\$74{,}500 - \$21{,}000 - \$15{,}000 + X = \$90{,}000$$
$$X = \$90{,}000 - \$74{,}500 + \$21{,}000 + \$15{,}000$$
$$X = \$51{,}500$$

So acquisitions of furniture were $51,500. Purchasing furniture caused Cash to decrease, so the $51,500 will be subtracted on the cash flow statement.

We still need to determine the cash received when furniture was sold (proceeds). We can use the gain/loss formula for this calculation:

$$\text{Proceeds} = \quad \text{Book value of assets sold} \quad + \text{Gain, or} - \text{Loss}$$
$$\text{Proceeds} = \$15{,}000 \text{ Book value of assets sold} + \text{Gain of } \$3{,}000$$
$$\text{Proceeds} = \$18{,}000$$

So the proceeds from sale of furniture were $18,000. Selling furniture caused Cash to increase, so the $18,000 will be added on the cash flow statement. Filling this information into the investing activities, we have the following:

	Cash flows from investing activities:		
	Acquisition of furniture	$(51,500)	
	Proceeds from sale of furniture	18,000	
	Net cash used for investing activities		$(33,500)

Financing Activities

Financing activities deal with long-term liabilities (debt financing) and equity (equity financing).

Cassidy only has one long-term liability: Notes Payable. As with Furniture, we know that we must report the major transactions in this account separately.

From the additional information we were given with the question, we know that Cassidy paid off notes payable and issued new notes payable during the year. Each of these transactions will be a separate line in financing activities.

	Cash flows from financing activities:	
	Proceeds from issuance of long-term notes payable	???
	Payment of long-term notes payable	???

We need to calculate the value of new notes issued. As we did with furniture, we can make this calculation by analyzing the T-account. In 2014, Notes Payable had a beginning balance of $50,000 and an ending balance of $40,000.

Notes Payable			
		Beginning balance	50,000
Decreases	???	Increases	???
		Ending balance	40,000

Notes Payable is increased when new notes are issued and is decreased when notes are paid off. From the additional information given in the problem, we know that $22,000 of notes were paid off. Putting this information into the T-account, we have the following:

Notes Payable			
		Beginning balance	50,000
Payments	22,000	Issuance of new notes payable	X
		Ending balance	40,000

We can use this information to calculate the value of new notes issued:

$$\$50,000 - \$22,000 + X = \$40,000$$
$$X = \$40,000 - \$50,000 + \$22,000$$
$$X = \$12,000$$

So, issuance of new notes payable was $12,000. Because issuing notes payable increased Cash, $12,000 will be added on the cash flow statement.

Putting this information into the financing activities section, we have the following:

	Cash flows from financing activities:		
	Proceeds from issuance of long-term notes payable	$ 12,000	
	Payment of long-term notes payable	(22,000)	

Now that we have examined the long-term liabilities, we only have equity remaining. The first account in equity is Common Shares. From the additional information, we know that new common shares were issued during the year. Because this is the only transaction affecting Common Shares, we know that the change in the Common Shares account represents the issuance of these shares. Using the T-account we have the following:

Common Shares		
	Beginning balance	3,500
	Issuance of new shares	X
	Ending balance	4,000

We use this information to calculate the value of new common shares issued, X.

$$\$3,500 + X = \$4,000$$
$$X = \$4,000 - \$3,500$$
$$X = \$500$$

So issuance of common shares (proceeds) was $500. Because issuing common shares increases Cash, $500 will be added on the cash flow statement.

The last account in equity is Retained Earnings. This account changed during 2014. Looking at the T-account we have the following:

Retained Earnings			
		Beginning balance	80,000
Decreases	???	Increases	???
		Ending balance	100,000

Retained Earnings is increased when the company earns net income and is decreased when the company declares dividends. If we put the net income from the income statement into the T-account, we have the following:

Retained Earnings			
		Beginning balance	80,000
Dividends	X	Net income	28,000
		Ending balance	100,000

We use this information to calculate the amount of cash dividends declared, X.

$$\$80,000 + \$28,000 - X = \$100,000$$
$$X = \$80,000 + \$28,000 - \$100,000$$
$$X = \$8,000$$

So, since there were no dividends payable, the cash dividends declared and paid were $8,000. Because the payment of dividends decreased Cash, $8,000 will be subtracted on the cash flow statement.

Notice that we *do not record net income* in the financing activities (even though it affects Retained Earnings), because net income was already accounted for in the operating activities section.

Putting all of this information into the financing activities section, we have the following:

	Cash flows from financing activities:		
	Proceeds from issuance of long-term notes payable	$ 12,000	
	Payment of long-term notes payable	(22,000)	
	Proceeds from issuance of common shares	500	
	Payment of dividends	(8,000)	
	Net cash used for financing activities		$(17,500)

Finishing the Cash Flow Statement

Now that we have completed the three main sections of the cash flow statement, we can add the totals of the three sections together to determine cash flow (the net change in cash).

Net change in cash = Cash provided by operating activities − Cash used for investing activities − Cash used for financing activities

Net change in cash =	$46,000	−	$33,500	−	$17,500

Net change in cash = $(5,000)

Because the change in cash is negative, we know that it means a net *decrease* in cash.

The statement began with net income (from the income statement). Now we tie it to the balance sheet to bring cash flows full circle. We add the decrease of $5,000 in cash to the cash balance at the beginning of the year of $33,000 (from Cassidy's balance sheet). This gives us the cash balance at the end of the year of $(5,000) + $33,000 = $28,000.

Putting this information in cash flow statement format, we have the following:

Net decrease in cash	$ (5,000)
Cash balance, December 31, 2013	33,000
Cash balance, December 31, 2014	$28,000

This section of the statement is also a nice check to ensure that our calculations are correct. The $28,000 calculated *is the number reported for cash* on the balance sheet at December 31, 2014.

To finish the cash flow statement, we just put all of these pieces together:

<table>
<tr><td colspan="3" align="center">**Cassidy, Inc.**
Cash Flow Statement
Year Ended December 31, 2014</td></tr>
<tr><td>**Cash flows from operating activities:**</td><td></td><td></td></tr>
<tr><td>Net Income</td><td></td><td>$ 28,000</td></tr>
<tr><td>Adjustments to reconcile net income to net cash
    provided by operating activities:</td><td></td><td></td></tr>
<tr><td>Depreciation Expense</td><td>$ 21,000</td><td></td></tr>
<tr><td>Gain on sale of plant assets</td><td>(3,000)</td><td></td></tr>
<tr><td>Increase in Accounts Receivable</td><td>(11,000)</td><td></td></tr>
<tr><td>Decrease in Prepaid Insurance</td><td>12,000</td><td></td></tr>
<tr><td>Decrease in Accounts Payable</td><td>(3,000)</td><td></td></tr>
<tr><td>Increase in Salary Payable</td><td>2,000</td><td>18,000</td></tr>
<tr><td>   Net cash provided by operating activities</td><td></td><td>$ 46,000</td></tr>
<tr><td>**Cash flows from investing activities:**</td><td></td><td></td></tr>
<tr><td>Acquisition of furniture</td><td>(51,500)</td><td></td></tr>
<tr><td>Proceeds from sale of furniture</td><td>18,000</td><td></td></tr>
<tr><td>   Net cash used for investing activities</td><td></td><td>(33,500)</td></tr>
<tr><td>**Cash flows from financing activities:**</td><td></td><td></td></tr>
<tr><td>Proceeds from issuance of long-term notes payable</td><td>12,000</td><td></td></tr>
<tr><td>Payment of long-term notes payable</td><td>(22,000)</td><td></td></tr>
<tr><td>Proceeds from issuance of common shares</td><td>500</td><td></td></tr>
<tr><td>Payment of dividends</td><td>(8,000)</td><td></td></tr>
<tr><td>   Net cash used for financing activities</td><td></td><td>(17,500)</td></tr>
<tr><td>**Net decrease in cash**</td><td></td><td>$ (5,000)</td></tr>
<tr><td>Cash balance, December 31, 2013</td><td></td><td>33,000</td></tr>
<tr><td>Cash balance, December 31, 2014</td><td></td><td>$ 28,000</td></tr>
</table>

Demo Doc Complete

Part 1	**Demo Doc Complete**

DECISION GUIDELINES

The Cash Flow Statement

As you examine the performance of a company (perhaps someday even your own) you may encounter some of the following decisions related to cash:

Decision	Guideline	Analyze
As a creditor, the way a business manages its cash can make a difference between having a loan repaid or not. How do I determine how cash is being managed by a business?	Review the cash flow statement.	The cash flow statement shows all of the sources and all of the uses of cash for the period. The sources and uses of cash are reported separately for the operating activities, the investing activities, and the financing activities of the business. For a business to remain successful, operating activities must be the main source of its cash over the long run.
I just started my own business and I want to make sure that I report things properly. Should the direct or indirect method be used to prepare the cash flow statement?	Although the direct method is preferred by IFRS and Canadian ASPE, most financial statement users find the indirect method more useful.	Because the indirect method reconciles net income as reported on the income statement to net cash provided by operating activities, it is more useful to most financial statements users. It helps answer the questions "How can the company have so much income when it has so little cash?" or "How can the company have so much cash when it made so little income?"
As the manager of a department, I would like to have renovations done on my retail area. Does the company have sufficient cash available?	Calculate the company's free cash flow and its cash conversion cycle.	For a business to be able to take advantage of unforeseen opportunities, it is important that it has "free cash" available. A lack of "free cash" will probably not negatively impact a business's normal operations but it will most likely result in lost income due to foregone opportunities.
		The cash conversion cycle indicates how long a company's cash is being "tied up" in its operations. The longer cash is tied up, the more likely it is that the company will encounter cash flow problems in the future. A company with a long cash conversion cycle should consider obtaining a line of credit to provide some insurance against cash flow problems.

ACCOUNTING VOCABULARY

THE LANGUAGE OF BUSINESS

Cash conversion cycle (p. 652) A measurement of the amount of time a company's cash is tied up in its operations.

Cash flow statement (p. 630) A financial statement that shows all of the sources and all of the uses of cash for an accounting period.

Direct method (p. 632) Format of the operating activities section of the cash flow statement; it lists the cash receipts and cash payments resulting from a company's day-to-day operations.

Financing activities (p. 632) Activities related to the issuance of, and repayment of, long-term debt or to the issuance of shares and the payment of dividends; it's a section of the cash flow statement.

Free cash flow (p. 652) The anticipated amount of cash available from operations after paying for planned investments in long-term assets and paying dividends.

Indirect method (p. 633) Format of the operating activities section of the cash flow statement; it starts with net income and reconciles to net cash provided by operating activities.

Investing activities (p. 632) Activities that increase or decrease long-term assets; it's a section of the cash flow statement.

Operating activities (p. 632) Activities that create revenue or expense in the entity's major line of business; it's a section of the cash flow statement. Operating activities affect the income statement.

ACCOUNTING PRACTICE

DISCUSSION QUESTIONS

1. What are some of the reasons why a cash flow statement may be important to users of financial statements?

2. A company used cash to build a new factory and received cash when it sold off the machines in the old factory. In which section of the cash flow statement would the cash flows from these activities be reported?

3. A company used cash to pay employees and received cash from performing services. In which section of the cash flow statement would the cash flows from these activities be reported?

4. A company issued bonds during the year. Would this be reported as a source or use of cash on the cash flow statement? In which section would it be reported?

5. Why is net income a good place to start when attempting to determine the cash flows from operating activities using the indirect method? Why is it not the same as the cash flows from operating activities?

6. When using the indirect method, why are gains on the sale of plant assets subtracted from net income in the operating activities section of the cash flow statement? Why are losses on the sale of plant assets added to net income?

7. How does an increase in accounts receivable during the year affect the cash flow statement (if at all)? Why?

8. Why would a decrease in accounts payable be shown as a decrease in cash when using the indirect method of calculating the cash flows from operating activities?

9. How would the sale of treasury shares that were acquired three years ago appear in the cash flow statement (if at all)?

10. A company's cash conversion cycle increased from 55 days in Year 1 to 68 days in Year 3. What are the implications of this increase? What do you think happens to the cash conversion cycles of companies during a recession?

SELF CHECK

1. The three main categories of cash flows are

a. direct, indirect, and hybrid.

b. current, long-term, and fixed.

c. operating, investing, and financing.

d. short-term, long-term, and equity.

2. The purpose of the cash flow statement is to

a. predict future cash flows.

b. evaluate management decisions.

c. predict ability to make payments to lenders.

d. All of the above

3. Financing activities are most closely related to

a. current assets and current liabilities.

b. long-term assets.

c. long-term liabilities and shareholder's equity.

d. net income and dividends.

4. Which item does not appear on a cash flow statement prepared by the indirect method?

a. Collections from customers

b. Net income

c. Depreciation

d. Gain on sale of land

5. Advanced Robotics earned net income of $60,000 after deducting depreciation of $4,000 and all other expenses. Current assets increased by $3,000 and current liabilities decreased by $5,000. Using the indirect method, how much was Advanced Robotics' cash flows from operating activities?

a. $48,000

b. $50,000

c. $52,000

d. $56,000

6. The Plant Assets account of Betterbuilt, Inc. shows the following:

Plant Assets, Net			
Beginning balance	100,000	Depreciation	30,000
Purchase	400,000	Sale	?
Ending balance	420,000		

Betterbuilt, Inc. sold plant assets at a $10,000 gain. How much should Betterbuilt, Inc. report for the sale?

a. Cash flows from investing activities, $40,000

b. Cash flows from investing activities, $50,000

c. Cash flows from investing activities, $60,000

d. Cash flows from investing activities, $10,000

7. Widget Corporation borrowed $15,000, issued common shares of $10,000, and paid dividends of $25,000. What was Widget Corporation's net cash provided or used by financing activities?

a. $0

b. $25,000

c. $(25,000)

d. $50,000

8. Which item appears on a cash flow statement prepared by the indirect method?

a. Net income

b. Payment to suppliers

c. Collections from customers

d. Payment of income tax

9. Structural Systems, Inc. had accounts receivable of $20,000 at the beginning of the year and $50,000 at year-end. Revenue for the year totalled $100,000. How much cash did Structural Systems collect from customers?

   a. $170,000　　　　　　　　**b.** $150,000
   c. $120,000　　　　　　　　**d.** $70,000

10. Allied Enterprises had operating expenses of $40,000. At the beginning of the year, Allied Enterprises owed $5,000 on accrued liabilities. At year-end, accrued liabilities were $8,000. How much cash did Allied Enterprises pay for operating expenses?

    a. $35,000　　　　　　　　**b.** $37,000
    c. $43,000　　　　　　　　**d.** $45,000

Answers are given after Written Communication.

SHORT EXERCISES

S11-1. Purpose of the cash flow statement *(Learning Objective 1)* 5–10 min.

Describe how the cash flow statement helps investors and creditors perform each of the following functions:

1. Predict future cash flows
2. Evaluate management decisions
3. Predict the ability to make debt payments to lenders and pay dividends to shareholders

S11-2. Basics of the cash flow statement *(Learning Objectives 2 & 3)* 5–10 min.

Answer these questions about the cash flow statement:

1. What is the "check figure" for the cash flow statement? Where do you get this check figure?
2. List the categories of cash flows in order of importance.
3. What is the first dollar amount reported using the indirect method?

S11-3. Purpose of the cash flow statement *(Learning Objective 1)* 5–10 min.

Intermountain, Inc. experienced an unbroken string of 10 years of growth in net income. Nevertheless, the business is facing bankruptcy. Creditors are calling all of Intermountain's outstanding loans for immediate payment, and Intermountain, Inc. has no cash available to make these payments because managers placed undue emphasis on net income and gave too little attention to cash flows.

Write a brief memo in your own words to explain to the managers of Intermountain, Inc. the purposes of the cash flow statement.

S11-4. Classification of items as operating, investing, or financing *(Learning Objective 2)* 10–15 min.

Identify each of the following transactions as one of the following:

- Operating activity (O)
- Investing activity (I)
- Financing activity (F)
- Noncash investing and financing activity (NIF)

For each item, indicate whether it represents an increase (+) or a decrease (–) in cash. The indirect method is used to report cash flows from operating activities.

____ a. Cash sale of land

____ b. Issuance of long-term note payable in exchange for cash

____ c. Depreciation of equipment

____ d. Purchase of treasury shares

____ e. Issuance of common shares for cash

____ f. Increase in Accounts Payable

____ g. Net income

____ h. Payment of cash dividend

____ i. Decrease in Accrued Liabilities

____ j. Loss on sale of land

____ k. Acquisition of building by issuance of notes payable

____ l. Payment of long-term debt

____ m. Acquisition of building by issuance of common shares

____ n. Decrease in Accounts Receivable

____ o. Decrease in Inventory

____ p. Increase in prepaid expenses

S11-5. Classification of items as operating, investing, or financing *(Learning Objectives 2 & 3)* **10–15 min.**

Indicate whether each of the following transactions would result in an operating activity, an investing activity, a financing activity, or a transaction that does not affect cash for a cash flow statement prepared by the indirect method.

DATE	ACCOUNTS	POST REF.	DR.	CR.
a.	Equipment		18,000	
	Cash			18,000
b.	Cash		7,200	
	Long-Term Investment			7,200
c.	Bonds Payable		45,000	
	Cash			45,000
d.	Building		164,000	
	Notes Payable, Long-Term			164,000
e.	Loss on Disposal of Equipment		1,400	
	Equipment			1,400
f.	Dividend Payable		16,500	
	Cash			16,500
g.	Cash		81,000	
	Common Shares			81,000
h.	Treasury Shares		13,000	
	Cash			13,000
i.	Cash		60,000	
	Sales Revenue			60,000
j.	Land		87,700	
	Cash			87,700
k.	Depreciation		9,000	
	Accumulated Depreciation			9,000

S11-6. Operating activities—indirect method *(Learning Objective 3)* **10–15 min.**

C. Kirk Corporation reported the following data for 2014:

Income statement:	Net Income	$50,000
	Depreciation	8,000
Balance sheet:	Increase in Accounts Receivable	6,000
	Decrease in Accounts Payable	4,000

Compute C. Kirk Corporation's net cash provided by operating activities according to the indirect method.

S11-7. Operating activities—indirect method *(Learning Objective 3)* 10–15 min.

Inland Equipment's accountants assembled the following data for the year ended June 30, 2014.

Net Income	$60,000	Purchase of equipment	$40,000
Proceeds from issuance of		Decrease in	
common shares	20,000	current liabilities	5,000
Payment of dividends	6,000	Payment of note payable	30,000
Increase in current assets		Proceeds from	
other than cash	30,000	sale of land	60,000
Purchase of treasury shares	5,000	Depreciation Expense	15,000

Prepare Inland Equipment's cash flow statement for the year ended June 30, 2014 using the indirect method. The cash balance for Inland Equipment, Inc. at June 30, 2013 was $12,000.

S11-8. Operating activities—direct method *(Learning Objective 4)* 5–10 min.

Uhura Health Spas began 2014 with cash of $104,000. During the year, Uhura earned service revenue of $600,000 and collected $590,000 from customers. Expenses for the year totalled $420,000, of which Uhura paid $410,000 in cash to suppliers and employees. Uhura also paid $140,000 to purchase equipment and paid a cash dividend of $50,000 to its shareholders during 2014. Prepare the company's cash flow statement for the year ended December 31, 2014. Format cash flows from operating activities by the direct method.

S11-9. Operating activities—direct method *(Learning Objective 4)* 5–10 min.

Inland Equipment, Inc. assembled the following data related to its cash transactions for the year ended June 30, 2014:

Payment of dividends	$ 6,000
Proceeds from issuance of shares	20,000
Collections from customers	200,000
Proceeds from sale of land	60,000
Payments to suppliers	80,000
Purchase of equipment	40,000
Payments to employees	70,000
Payment of note payable	30,000

Prepare Inland Equipment's cash flow statement for the year ended June 30, 2014 using the direct method. Inland Equipment's cash balance at June 30, 2013 was $12,000.

S11-10. Calculate certain operating information for direct method *(Learning Objective 4)*
5–10 min.

McCoy Medical Company reported the following financial statements for 2014:

McCoy Medical Company Income Statement Year Ended December 31, 2014		
Revenue:		
Sales Revenue		$710
Expenses:		
Cost of Goods Sold	$340	
Depreciation Expense	60	
Other Expenses	200	
Total Expense		600
Net Income		$110

McCoy Medical Company
Comparative Balance Sheet
December 31, 2014 and 2013

(in thousands) ASSETS	2014	2013	LIABILITIES	2014	2013
Current:			Current:		
Cash	$ 19	$ 16	Accounts Payable	$ 47	$ 42
Accounts Receivable	54	48	Salary Payable	23	21
Inventory	80	84	Accrued Liabilities	8	11
Prepaid Expenses	3	2	Long-Term Notes Payable	66	68
Long-Term Investments	75	90			
Plant Assets, Net	225	185	**SHAREHOLDERS' EQUITY**		
			Common Shares	40	37
			Retained Earnings	272	246
			Total Liabilities and		
Total Assets	$456	$425	Shareholders' Equity	$456	$425

Use the information in McCoy Medical Company's financial statements to compute
the following:

1. Collections from customers

2. Payments for inventory

S11-11. Calculate certain investing and financing information from financial
statements *(Learning Objective 3)* **10–15 min.**

Use the McCoy Medical Company data in S11-10 to compute the amount of plant
assets acquired by McCoy Medical Company, assuming McCoy sold no plant
assets in 2014.

S11-12. Calculate certain investing and financing information from financial statements *(Learning Objective 3)* **10–15 min.**

Use the McCoy Medical Company data in S11-10 to compute the following amounts for 2014:

1. Borrowing or payment of long-term notes payable, assuming McCoy had only one long-term note payable transaction during the year

2. Issuance of common shares, assuming McCoy had only one common shares transaction during the year

3. Payment of cash dividends

EXERCISES (GROUP A)

E11-1A. Operating activities—indirect method *(Learning Objective 3)* **10–15 min.**

The accounting records of Rising Star Talent Agency reveal the following:

Net Income	$22,000
Depreciation	12,000
Sales Revenue	9,000
Decrease in current liabilities	20,000
Loss on sale of land	5,000
Increase in current assets other than Cash	27,000
Acquisition of land	37,000

Requirements

1. Compute cash flows from operating activities by the indirect method. Use the format of the operating activities section shown in Exhibit 11-3.

2. Evaluate the operating cash flow of Rising Star Talent Agency. Give the reason for your evaluation.

E11-2A. Operating activities—indirect method *(Learning Objective 3)* **10–15 min.**

The March accounting records of Jackson & Associates include these accounts:

Cash			
Mar 1	5,000	Payments	448,000
Receipts	447,000		
Mar 31	4,000		

Accounts Receivable			
Mar 1	18,000	Collections	447,000
Sales	443,000		
Mar 31	14,000		

Inventory			
Mar 1	19,000	Cost of goods sold	335,000
Purchases	337,000		
Mar 31	21,000		

Accounts Payable			
Payments	332,000	Mar 1	14,000
		Purchases	337,000
		Mar 31	19,000

Accumulated Depreciation			
		Mar 1	52,000
		Depreciation	3,000
		Mar 31	55,000

Retained Earnings			
Dividends	18,000	Mar 1	64,000
		Net income	69,000
		Mar 31	115,000

Requirement

1. Compute Jackson & Associates' net cash provided by operating activities during March. Use the indirect method.

E11-3A. Prepare cash flow statement—indirect method (Learning Objective 3)
20–25 min.

The income statement and additional data of Specialized Services, Inc. follow:

Specialized Services, Inc.
Income Statement
Year Ended June 30, 2014

Revenues:			
	Sales Revenue	$229,000	
	Dividend Revenue	8,000	
	Total Revenues		$237,000
Expenses:			
	Cost of Goods Sold	$103,000	
	Salary Expense	45,000	
	Depreciation Expense	28,000	
	Advertising Expense	12,000	
	Interest Expense	2,000	
	Income Tax Expense	9,000	
	Total Expenses		199,000
Net Income			$ 38,000

Additional data follow:

a. Acquisition of plant assets totalled $116,000. Of this amount, $101,000 was paid in cash and a $15,000 note payable was signed for the remainder.

b. Proceeds from sale of land totalled $24,000. No gain was recognized on the sale.

c. Proceeds from issuance of common shares totalled $30,000.

d. Payment of long-term note payable was $15,000.

e. Payment of dividends was $11,000.

f. Data from the comparative balance sheet follow:

June 30	2014	2013
Current Assets:		
Cash	$26,000	$20,000
Accounts Receivable	43,000	58,000
Inventory	92,000	85,000
Current Liabilities:		
Accounts Payable	$35,000	$22,000
Accrued Liabilities	13,000	21,000

Requirements

1. Prepare Specialized Services' cash flow statement for the year ended June 30, 2014, using the indirect method.

2. Evaluate Specialized Services' cash flows for the year. In your evaluation, mention all three categories of cash flows and give the reason for your evaluation.

E11-4A. Calculate certain investing and financing information from financial statements *(Learning Objective 3)* **10–15 min.**

Compute the following items for the cash flow statement:

1. The beginning and ending Retained Earnings balances are $45,000 and $73,000, respectively. Net income for the period is $62,000. How much are cash dividends?

2. The beginning and ending Plant Assets, Net, balances are $103,000 and $107,000, respectively. Depreciation for the period is $16,000, and acquisitions of new plant assets total $27,000. Plant assets were sold at a $1,000 loss. What were the cash proceeds of the sale?

Quick solution:

1. Cash dividends = $34,000;

2. Cash proceeds from sale = $6,000

E11-5A. Operating activities—direct method *(Learning Objective 4)* **10–15 min.**

The accounting records of The Fenceman, Inc. reveal the following:

Net Income	$ 22,000	Payment of	
Payment of income tax	13,000	salaries and wages..............	$34,000
Collection of		Depreciation............................	12,000
dividend revenue...............	7,000	Payment of interest..................	16,000
Payment to suppliers	54,000	Payment of	
Collections from customers...	102,000	dividends............................	7,000

Requirements

1. Compute cash flows from operating activities by the direct method.

2. Evaluate the operating cash flow of The Fenceman, Inc. Give the reason for your evaluation.

E11-6A. Prepare cash flow statement—direct method *(Learning Objective 4)* **20–25 min.**

The income statement and additional data of Specialized Services, Inc. follow:

Specialized Services, Inc. Income Statement Year Ended June 30, 2014		
Revenues:		
Sales Revenue	$229,000	
Dividend Revenue	8,000	
Total Revenues		$237,000
Expenses:		
Cost of Goods Sold	$103,000	
Salary Expense	45,000	
Depreciation Expense	28,000	
Advertising Expense	12,000	
Interest Expense	2,000	
Income Tax Expense	9,000	
Total Expenses		199,000
Net Income		$ 38,000

Additional data follow:

a. Collections from customers are $15,000 more than sales.

b. Payments to suppliers are the sum of cost of goods sold plus advertising expense.

c. Payments to employees are $2,000 more than salary expense.

d. Dividend revenue, interest expense, and income tax expense equal their cash amounts.

e. Acquisition of plant assets for cash is $101,000.

f. Proceeds from sale of land total $24,000.

g. Proceeds from issuance of common shares for cash total $30,000.

h. Payment of long-term note payable is $15,000.

i. Payment of dividends is $11,000.

j. Cash balance, June 30, 2013, was $20,000.

Requirement

1. Prepare Specialized Services' cash flow statement for the year ended June 30, 2014. Use the direct method.

E11-7A. Calculate certain information for direct method (Learning Objective 4) 10–15 min.

Compute the following items for the cash flow statement:

1. The beginning and ending Accounts Receivable balances are $22,000 and $18,000, respectively. Credit sales for the period total $81,000. How much are cash collections?

2. Cost of Goods Sold is $90,000. Beginning Inventory balance is $25,000, and ending Inventory balance is $21,000. Beginning and ending Accounts Payable are $11,000 and $8,000, respectively. How much are cash payments for inventory?

E11-8A. Calculate certain information for direct method (Learning Objective 4) 20–25 min.

Top Ten Corporation, a nationwide insurance chain, reported the following selected amounts in its financial statements for the year ended August 31, 2014 (adapted, in millions):

Income Statement

	2014	2013
Net Sales	$24,623	$21,207
Cost of Goods Sold	18,048	15,466
Depreciation Expense	269	230
Other Expenses	4,883	4,248
Income Tax Expense	537	486
Net Income	886	777

Balance Sheet

	2014	2013
Cash and Cash Equivalents	$ 17	$ 13
Accounts Receivable	798	615
Inventories	3,482	2,831
Property and Equipment, Net	4,345	3,428
Accounts Payable	1,547	1,364
Accrued Liabilities	938	848
Long-Term Liabilities	478	464
Common Shares	676	446
Retained Earnings	4,531	3,788

Requirement

1. Determine the following for Top Ten Corporation during 2014. (Enter all amounts in millions.)

a. Collections from customers

b. Payments for inventory

c. Payments of operating expenses

d. Acquisitions of property and equipment; no sales were made during 2014

e. Long-term borrowing, assuming Top Ten made no payments on long-term liabilities

f. Proceeds from issuance of common shares

g. Payment of cash dividends

EXERCISES (GROUP B)

E11-1B. Operating activities—indirect method *(Learning Objective 3)* **10–15 min.**

The accounting records of Rodeo Talent Agency reveal the following:

Net Income	$30,000
Depreciation	6,000
Sales Revenue	10,000
Decrease in current liabilities	24,000
Loss on sale of land	6,000
Increase in current assets other than Cash	15,000
Acquisition of land	42,000

Requirements

1. Compute cash flows from operating activities by the indirect method. Use the format of the operating activities section shown in Exhibit 11-3.

2. Evaluate the operating cash flow of Rodeo Talent Agency. Give the reason for your evaluation.

E11-2B. Operating activities—indirect method *(Learning Objective 3)* **10–15 min.**

The October accounting records of Morrison & Associates include these accounts:

Cash			
Oct 1	12,000	Payments	400,000
Receipts	394,000		
Oct 31	6,000		

Accounts Receivable			
Oct 1	16,000	Collections	394,000
Sales	391,000		
Oct 31	13,000		

Inventory			
Oct 1	20,000	Cost of goods sold	309,000
Purchases	321,000		
Oct 31	32,000		

Accounts Payable			
Payments	319,000	Oct 1	19,000
		Purchases	321,000
		Oct 31	21,000

Accumulated Depreciation			
		Oct 1	49,000
		Depreciation	10,000
		Oct 31	59,000

Retained Earnings			
Dividends	24,000	Oct 1	67,000
		Net income	50,000
		Oct 31	93,000

Requirement

1. Compute Morrison & Associates' net cash provided by operating activities during October. Use the indirect method.

E11-3B. Prepare cash flow statement—indirect method *(Learning Objective 3)*
20–25 min.

The income statement and additional data of Rayborn Services, Inc. follow:

Rayborn Services, Inc. Income Statement Year Ended April 30, 2014		
Revenues:		
Sales Revenue	$262,000	
Dividend Revenue	11,000	
Total Revenues		$273,000
Expenses:		
Cost of Goods Sold	$107,000	
Salary Expense	60,000	
Depreciation Expense	18,000	
Advertising Expense	14,000	
Interest Expense	9,000	
Income Tax Expense	8,000	
Total Expenses		216,000
Net Income		$ 57,000

Additional data follow:

a. Acquisition of plant assets totalled $116,000. Of this amount, $101,000 was paid in cash and a $15,000 note payable was signed for the remainder.

b. Proceeds from the sale of land totalled $22,000. No gain was recognized on the sale.

c. Proceeds from issuance of common shares total $34,000.

d. Payment of long-term note payable was $15,000.

e. Payment of dividends was $14,000.

f. Data from the comparative balance sheet follow:

June 30	2014	2013
Current Assets:		
Cash	$30,000	$21,000
Accounts Receivable	42,000	57,000
Inventory	89,000	83,000
Current Liabilities:		
Accounts Payable	$38,000	$31,000
Accrued Liabilities	12,000	20,000

Requirements

1. Prepare Rayborn Services' cash flow statement for the year ended April 30, 2014, using the indirect method.

2. Evaluate Rayborn Services' cash flows for the year. In your evaluation, mention all three categories of cash flows and give the reason for your evaluation.

E11-4B. Calculate certain investing and financing information from financial statements *(Learning Objective 3)* 10–15 min.

Compute the following items for the cash flow statement:

1. The beginning and ending Retained Earnings balances are $47,000 and $71,000, respectively. Net income for the period is $93,000. How much are cash dividends?

2. The beginning and ending Plant Assets, Net, balances are $104,000 and $113,000, respectively. Depreciation for the period is $13,000, and acquisitions of new plant assets total $30,000. Plant assets were sold at a $6,000 loss. What were the cash proceeds of the sale?

E11-5B. Operating activities—direct method *(Learning Objective 4)* **10–15 min.**

The accounting records of Fence Up, Inc. reveal the following:

Net Income	$ 64,000	Payment of	
Payment of income tax	20,000	salaries and wages	$30,000
Collection of		Depreciation.............................	15,000
dividend revenue...............	7,000	Payment of interest..................	18,000
Payment to suppliers	36,000	Payment of	
Collections from customers...	113,000	dividends.............................	7,000

Requirements

1. Compute cash flows from operating activities by the *direct* method.

2. Evaluate the operating cash flow of Fence Up, Inc. Give the reason for your evaluation.

E11-6B. Prepare cash flow statement—direct method *(Learning Objective 4)* **20–25 min.**

The income statement and additional data of Rayborn Services, Inc. follow:

Rayborn Services, Inc. Income Statement Year Ended April 30, 2014		
Revenues:		
Sales Revenue	$262,000	
Dividend Revenue	11,000	
Total Revenues		$273,000
Expenses:		
Cost of Goods Sold	$107,000	
Salary Expense	60,000	
Depreciation Expense	18,000	
Advertising Expense	14,000	
Interest Expense	9,000	
Income Tax Expense	8,000	
Total Expenses		216,000
Net Income		$ 57,000

Additional data follow:

a. Collections from customers are $15,000 more than sales.

b. Payments to suppliers are the sum of cost of goods sold plus advertising expense.

c. Payments to employees are $7,000 more than salary expense.

d. Dividend revenue, interest expense, and income tax expense equal their cash amounts.

e. Acquisition of plant assets for cash is $101,000.

f. Proceeds from sale of land total $22,000.

g. Proceeds from issuance of common shares for cash total $34,000.

h. Payment of long-term note payable is $15,000.

i. Payment of dividends is $14,000.

j. Cash balance, April 30, 2013, was $21,000.

Requirement

1. Prepare Rayborn Services' cash flow statement for the year ended April 30, 2014. Use the direct method.

E11-7B. Calculate certain information for direct method *(Learning Objective 4)* 10–15 min.

Compute the following items for the cash flow statement:

1. The beginning and ending Accounts Receivable balances are $18,000 and $22,000, respectively. Credit sales for the period total $115,000. How much are cash collections?

2. Cost of Goods Sold is $76,000. Beginning Inventory balance is $26,000, and ending Inventory balance is $28,000. Beginning and ending Accounts Payable are $15,000 and $12,000, respectively. How much are cash payments for inventory?

E11-8B. Calculate certain information for direct method *(Learning Objective 4)* 20–25 min.

A-One Corporation, a nationwide insurance chain, reported the following selected amounts in its financial statements for the year ended March 31, 2014 (adapted, in millions):

Income Statement

	2014	2013
Net Sales...	$24,859	$21,099
Cost of Goods Sold...	18,026	15,497
Depreciation Expense...	270	230
Other Expenses...	4,801	4,460
Income Tax Expense...	539	488
Net Income	1,223	424

Balance Sheet

	2014	2013
Cash and Cash Equivalents	$ 30	$ 28
Accounts Receivable...	804	626
Inventories...	3,484	3,264
Property and Equipment, Net..	4,225	3,825
Accounts Payable..	1,543	1,373
Accrued Liabilities...	939	848
Long-Term Liabilities...	450	445
Common Shares	675	575
Retained Earnings...	4,936	4,502

Requirement

1. Determine the following for A-One Corporation during 2014. (Enter all amounts in millions.)

a. Collections from customers

b. Payments for inventory

c. Payments of operating expenses

d. Acquisitions of property and equipment; no sales were made during 2014

e. Long-term borrowing, assuming A-One made no payments on long-term liabilities

f. Proceeds from issuance of common shares

g. Payment of cash dividends

EXERCISES (ALTERNATES 1, 2, AND 3)

These alternative exercise sets are available for your practice benefit at
www.myaccountinglab.com

PROBLEMS (GROUP A)

P11-1A. Prepare cash flow statement—indirect method *(Learning Objective 3)*
20–25 min.

O'Malley Corporation accountants assembled the following data for the year ended
December 31, 2014:

O'Malley Corporation		
December 31	**2014**	**2013**
Current Assets:		
Cash and Cash Equivalents	$85,000	$22,000
Accounts Receivable	69,200	64,200
Inventory	80,000	83,000
Current Liabilities:		
Accounts Payable	$57,800	$55,800
Income Tax Payable	14,700	16,700

Transaction Data for 2014:	
Net Income	$ 57,000
Purchase of treasury shares	14,000
Issuance of common shares for cash	41,000
Loss on sale of equipment	11,000
Payment of cash dividends	18,000
Depreciation Expense	21,000
Issuance of long-term note payable in exchange for cash	34,000
Purchase of building for cash	125,000
Retirement of bonds payable by issuing common shares	65,000
Sale of equipment for cash	58,000

Requirement

1. Prepare O'Malley Corporation's cash flow statement using the indirect method
to report operating activities. List noncash investing and financing activities on
an accompanying schedule.

Quick solution:

*1. Cash provided by operating
activities = $87,000;
Cash used for investing
activities = ($67,000);
Cash provided by financing
activities = $43,000*

P11-2A. Prepare cash flow statement—indirect method *(Learning Objective 3)*
20–25 min.

Data from the comparative balance sheet of Izzie Company at March 31, 2014, follow:

March 31	2014	2013
Current Assets:		
Cash and Cash Equivalents	$ 6,200	$ 4,000
Accounts Receivable	14,900	21,700
Inventory	63,200	60,600
Current Liabilities:		
Accounts Payable	$30,100	$27,600
Accrued Liabilities	10,700	11,100
Income Tax Payable	8,000	4,700

Izzie Company's transactions during the year ended March 31, 2014, included the following:

Payment of cash dividend........	$30,000	Depreciation Expense...............	$17,300
Purchase of		Purchase of	
equipment for cash	78,700	building for cash	47,000
Issuance of long-term		Net Income	70,000
note payable in exchange		Issuance of	
for cash.............................	50,000	common shares	11,000

Requirements

1. Prepare Izzie Company's cash flow statement for the year ended March 31, 2014, using the indirect method to report cash flows from operating activities.

2. Evaluate Izzie's cash flows for the year. Mention all three categories of cash flows and give the reason for your evaluation.

P11-3A. Prepare cash flow statement—indirect method *(Learning Objective 3)* 20–25 min.

The 2014 comparative balance sheet and income statement of A. Karev Medical Supplies follow:

A. Karev Medical Supplies Comparative Balance Sheet December 31, 2014 and 2013			
	2014	**2013**	**INCREASE (DECREASE)**
Current Assets:			
Cash and Cash Equivalents	$ 6,700	$ 5,300	$ 1,400
Accounts Receivable	25,300	26,900	(1,600)
Inventory	91,800	89,800	2,000
Plant Assets:			
Land	89,000	60,000	29,000
Equipment, Net	53,500	49,400	4,100
Total Assets	$266,300	$231,400	$ 34,900
Current Liabilities:			
Accounts Payable	$ 30,900	$ 35,400	$ (4,500)
Accrued Liabilities	30,600	28,600	2,000
Long-Term Liabilities:			
Notes Payable	75,000	100,000	(25,000)
Shareholders' Equity:			
Common Shares	88,300	64,700	23,600
Retained Earnings	41,500	2,700	38,800
Total Liabilities and Shareholders' Equity	$266,300	$231,400	$ 34,900

A. Karev Medical Supplies
Income Statement
Year Ended December 31, 2014

Revenues:		
Sales Revenue	$213,000	
Interest Revenue	8,600	
Total Revenues		$221,600
Expenses:		
Cost of Goods Sold	$ 70,600	
Salary Expense	27,800	
Depreciation Expense	4,000	
Other Operating Expenses	10,500	
Interest Expense	11,600	
Income Tax Expense	29,100	
Total Expenses		153,600
Net Income		**$ 68,000**

A. Karev Medical Supplies had no noncash investing and financing transactions during 2014. During the year, A. Karev Medical Supplies made no sales of land or equipment, no issuance of notes payable, no retirement of shares, and no treasury share transactions.

Requirements

1. Prepare the 2014 cash flow statement, formatting operating activities by the indirect method.

2. How will what you learned in this problem help you evaluate an investment in A. Karev Medical Supplies?

P11-4A. Prepare cash flow statement—direct method (*Learning Objective 4*)
20–25 min.

The accounting records for R. Webber Associates, Inc. for the year ended April 30, 2014, contain the following information:

a. Purchase of plant assets for cash, $59,400

b. Proceeds from issuance of common shares, $8,000

c. Payment of dividends, $48,400

d. Collection of interest, $4,400

e. Payment of salaries, $93,600

f. Proceeds from sale of plant assets, $22,400

g. Collections from customers, $620,500

h. Cash receipt of dividend revenue, $4,100

i. Payments to suppliers, $368,500

j. Depreciation expense, $59,900

k. Proceeds from issuance of long-term notes, $19,600

l. Payments of long-term notes payable, $50,000

m. Interest expense and payments, $13,300

n. Income tax expense and payments, $37,900

o. Cash balances: April 30, 2013, $39,300; April 30, 2014, $47,200

Requirement

1. Prepare R. Webber Associates' cash flow statement for the year ended April 30, 2014. Use the direct method for cash flows from operating activities.

P11-5A. Prepare cash flow statement—direct method (*Learning Objective 4*)
20–25 min.

Use the A. Karev Medical Supplies data from P11-3A. The cash amounts for Interest Revenue, Salary Expense, Interest Expense, and Income Tax Expense are the same as the accrual amounts for these items.

Requirements

1. Prepare the 2014 cash flow statement by the direct method.

2. How will what you learned in this problem help you evaluate an investment in A. Karev Medical Supplies?

P11-6A. Prepare cash flow statement—direct method (*Learning Objective 4*)
20–25 min.

To prepare the cash flow statement, accountants for C. Yang, Inc. summarized 2014 activity in the Cash account as follows:

Cash			
Beginning balance	53,600	Payment on accounts payable	399,100
Receipts of interest	17,100	Payment of dividends	27,200
Collections from customers	673,700	Payment of salaries and wages	143,800
Issuance of common shares	47,300	Payment of interest	26,900
		Payment for equipment	10,200
		Payment of operating expenses	34,300
		Payment of notes payable	67,700
		Payment of income tax	18,900
Ending balance	63,600		

Requirement

1. Prepare the cash flow statement of C. Yang, Inc. for the year ended December 31, 2014, using the direct method for operating activities.

P11-7A. Prepare cash flow statement—indirect and direct methods
(*Learning Objectives 3 & 4*) 25–30 min.

Comparative selected account balances and an unclassified income statement for
THK Company follow:

THK Company Account Balances as at December 31		
	2014	**2013**
Cash	$28,400	$ 4,700
Accounts Receivable	35,200	18,600
Inventory	15,000	21,000
Accounts Payable	15,500	21,000
Wages Payable	3,500	1,200

THK Company Income Statement For the Year Ended December 31, 2014		
Sales		$241,800
Cost of Goods Sold	$180,000	
Wages	43,500	
Supplies	4,800	
Property Taxes	2,400	
Utilities	1,600	
Loss on Disposal of Equipment	5,000	
Depreciation of Capital Assets	3,200	240,500
Net Income		$ 1,300

In addition, the following information is available:

- Accounts Payable balances resulted from merchandise inventory purchases.
- The book value of the equipment was $13,000.
- Signed a 6%, 10-year note payable in exchange for a building with a market
  value of $80,000.
- Issued 2,000 new common shares at $10 per share.

Requirements

1. Prepare a cash flow statement for THK, using the indirect method.
2. Prepare the cash flow from operating activities section by using the direct
   method.

P11-8A. Identify source or use of cash and prepare cash flow statement—indirect and direct methods (*Learning Objectives 2, 3, & 4*) 30–35 min.

The following is the financial information for TinTing School Supplies, Ltd.:

	TinTing School Supplies, Ltd. **Balance Sheet** As of December 31			
		2014	**2013**	**SOURCE/** **(USES)**
Current Assets:				
	Cash	$ 3,600	$ 6,500	
	Accounts Receivable	23,600	21,400	
	Packaging Supplies	1,300	1,600	
	Prepaid Insurance	1,400	2,340	
	Inventory	12,100	10,400	
	Total Current Assets	42,000	42,240	
Capital Assets				
	Store Equipment	27,000	18,200	
	Accumulated Depreciation, Store Equipment	(5,400)	(3,640)	
	Delivery Trucks	168,000	116,500	
	Accumulated Depreciation, Delivery Trucks	(33,600)	(23,300)	
	Total Capital Assets	156,000	107,760	
Total Assets		$198,000	$150,000	
Current Liabilities				
	Accounts Payable	$ 23,700	$ 14,200	
	Income Tax Payable	4,030	3,500	
	Total Current Liabilities	27,730	17,700	
Long-term Liabilities				
	Long-Term Note Payable	36,250	31,000	
	Bank Loan	71,300	45,300	
	Total Long-Term Liabilities	107,550	76,300	
Shareholders' Equity				
	Common Shares	35,000	35,000	
	Retained Earnings	27,720	21,000	
	Total Shareholders' Equity	62,720	56,000	
Total Liabilities & Shareholders' Equity		$198,000	$150,000	

	TinTing School Supplies, Ltd. **Income Statement** For the Year Ended December 31, 2014		
	Revenues:		$125,000
	Cost of Goods Sold		50,000
	Gross Profit		75,000
	Operating Expenses		
	Depreciation Expense	$12,060	
	Wages Expense	35,000	
	Other Expenses	8,240	
	Total Operating Expenses		55,300
	Income Before Taxes		19,700
	Income Taxes (40%)		7,880
	Net Income		$ 11,820

Additional information:

1. Store equipment was purchased by signing a two-year long-term note payable.

2. Additional bank loan was borrowed as a partial payment for the purchase of delivery trucks.

3. TinTing declared and paid dividends on December 28, 2014.

4. TinTing's net income was $11,820.

Requirements

1. Identify source and use of cash for each account in the Balance Sheet.

2. Prepare a cash flow statement, using the indirect method.

3. Prepare the cash flow from operating activities section by using the direct method.

P11-9A. Identify source or use of cash and prepare cash flow statement—indirect and direct methods (*Learning Objectives 2, 3, & 4*) 35–40 min.

ShinFu Electronic, Inc.'s income statement and comparative balance sheets appear as follows:

ShinFu Electronic, Inc. Income Statement For the Year Ended December 31, 2014		
Sales Revenue		$610,000
Cost of Goods Sold		(366,000)
		244,000
Depreciation Expense — Patent	$ 1,500	
Depreciation Expense — Equipment	15,200	
Salaries Expense	62,000	
Other Operating Expenses	83,300	
Interest Expense	14,500	
Loss on Sale of Equipment	12,500	189,000
Income Before Income Taxes		55,000
Income Tax Expense		16,500
Net Income		$ 38,500

ShinFu Electronic, Inc.
Balance Sheet
As of December 31

	2014	2013	SOURCE/ (USE)
Cash	$ 12,500	$ 15,200	
Accounts Receivable	32,500	43,500	
Inventory	72,700	68,400	
Prepaid Expenses	4,100	2,600	
Equipment	189,800	145,200	
Accumulated Depreciation	(45,000)	(67,200)	
Land	183,000	135,000	
Patents	11,000	12,500	
Total	$460,600	$355,200	
Accounts Payable	48,600	36,200	
Accrued Liabilities	26,200	58,900	
Salaries Payable	14,500	10,200	
Dividends Payable	8,600	7,200	
Interest Payable	12,200	18,000	
Income Tax Payable	32,000	24,200	
Mortgage	20,000	0	
Common Shares	240,000	170,000	
Retained Earnings	58,500	30,500	
Total	$460,600	$355,200	

Additional information related to business activities during 2014:

1. All accounts payable pertain to inventory purchases, and accrued liabilities pertain to other operating expenses.

2. The original cost of the equipment sold was $80,400. New equipment was purchased and 5,000 common shares at $14 per share were issued as a partial payment.

3. ShinFu purchased some land and borrowed $20,000 from a mortgage company as a partial payment.

4. ShinFu declared a dividend on December 15 to be paid on January 15, 2015.

Requirements

1. Identify source and use of cash for each account in the Balance Sheet.

2. Calculate the cash receipt from the sale of equipment and the cost of the new equipment, using T-accounts to show your calculations.

3. Calculate the amount of cash dividend declared and cash dividend paid, using T-accounts to show your calculations.

4. Prepare a cash flow statement, using the indirect method.

5. Prepare the cash flow from operating activities section by using the direct method.

P11-10A. Identify source or use of cash and prepare cash flow statement—indirect and direct methods (Learning Objectives 2, 3, & 4) 35–40 min.

Sawada Trades, Inc.'s income statement and comparative balance sheets appear as follows:

Sawada Trading Company Income Statement For the Year Ended December 31, 2014		
Sales Revenue		$420,000
Cost of Goods Sold		(252,000)
		168,000
Depreciation Expense — Equipment	$25,500	
Salaries Expense	52,000	
Other Operating Expenses	65,000	
Interest Expense	12,000	
Loss on Sale of Equipment	9,500	164,000
Income Tax Expense		1,600
Net Income (Loss)		$ 2,400

Sawada Trading Company Balance Sheet As of December 31			
	2014	**2013**	**SOURCE/ (USE)**
Cash	$ 7,600	$ 9,200	
Accounts Receivable	20,200	13,400	
Inventory	25,600	22,000	
Prepaid Expenses	3,600	4,400	
Equipment	170,000	148,000	
Accumulated Depreciation	(33,000)	(28,000)	
Total	$194,000	$169,000	
Accounts Payable	$ 21,600	$ 18,200	
Unearned Revenue	4,000	2,600	
Salaries Payable	15,500	12,000	
Interest Payable	7,700	6,200	
Income Tax Payable	12,000	23,200	
Common Shares	85,000	60,000	
Retained Earnings	48,200	46,800	
Total	$194,000	$169,000	

Additional information related to business activities during 2014:

1. All accounts payable pertain to inventory purchases, and accrued liabilities pertain to other operating expenses.

2. The original cost of the equipment sold was $43,000. New equipment was purchased and 5,000 common shares at $5 per share were issued as a partial payment.

3. Sawada declared and paid a dividend on December 30.

Requirements

1. Identify source and use of cash for each account in the Balance Sheet.

2. Calculate the cash receipt from the sale of equipment and the cost of the new equipment, using T-accounts to show your calculations.

3. Prepare a cash flow statement, using the indirect method.

4. Prepare the cash flow from operating activities section by using the direct method.

PROBLEMS (GROUP B)

P11-1B. Prepare cash flow statement—indirect method *(Learning Objective 3)*
20–25 min.

Morgensen Corporation accountants assembled the following data for the year ended December 31, 2014:

Morgensen Corporation		
December 31	**2014**	**2013**
Current Assets:		
Cash and Cash Equivalents	$85,000	$23,000
Accounts Receivable	69,600	64,700
Inventory	80,900	83,500
Current Liabilities:		
Accounts Payable	$57,700	$55,600
Income Tax Payable	14,800	16,400

Transaction Data for 2014:	
Net Income	$ 57,800
Purchase of treasury shares	14,500
Issuance of common shares for cash	36,200
Loss on sale of equipment	11,000
Payment of cash dividends	18,100
Depreciation Expense	21,900
Issuance of long-term note payable in exchange for cash	34,500
Purchase of building for cash	122,000
Retirement of bonds payable by issuing common shares	62,000
Sale of equipment for cash	57,000

Requirement

1. Prepare Morgensen Corporation's cash flow statement using the indirect method to report operating activities. List noncash investing and financing activities on an accompanying schedule.

P11-2B. Prepare cash flow statement—indirect method *(Learning Objective 3)*
20–25 min.

Data from the comparative balance sheet of Johnson Company at March 31, 2014, follow:

March 31	**2014**	**2013**
Current Assets:		
Cash and Cash Equivalents	$13,400	$ 4,600
Accounts Receivable	14,800	21,400
Inventory	54,300	53,600
Current Liabilities:		
Accounts Payable	$29,000	$28,400
Accrued Liabilities	14,600	16,200
Income Tax Payable	8,300	4,800

Johnson Company's transactions during the year ended March 31, 2014, included the following:

Payment of cash dividend........	$33,500	Depreciation Expense..............	$17,500
Purchase of		Purchase of	
equipment for cash	78,300	building for cash	47,800
Issuance of long-term		Net Income	73,500
note payable in exchange		Issuance of	
for cash.............................	56,000	common shares	13,000

Requirements

1. Prepare Johnson Company's cash flow statement for the year ended March 31, 2014, using the indirect method to report cash flows from operating activities.

2. Evaluate Johnson Company's cash flows for the year. Mention all three categories of cash flows and give the reason for your evaluation.

P11-3B. Prepare cash flow statement—indirect method (Learning Objective 3)
20–25 min.

The 2014 comparative balance sheet and income statement of Goldman Medical Supplies follow:

Goldman Medical Supplies
Comparative Balance Sheet
December 31, 2014 and 2013

	2014	2013	INCREASE (DECREASE)
Current Assets:			
Cash and Cash Equivalents	$ 6,700	$ 5,400	$ 1,300
Accounts Receivable	25,200	26,800	(1,600)
Inventory	91,500	89,600	1,900
Plant Assets:			
Land	89,200	60,300	28,900
Equipment, Net	53,200	49,200	4,000
Total Assets	$265,800	$231,300	$ 34,500
Current Liabilities:			
Accounts Payable	$ 30,200	$ 35,400	$ (5,200)
Accrued Liabilities	30,400	28,100	2,300
Long-Term Liabilities:			
Notes Payable	72,000	100,000	(28,000)
Shareholders' Equity:			
Common Shares	88,900	64,700	24,200
Retained Earnings	44,300	3,100	41,200
Total Liabilities and Shareholders' Equity	$265,800	$231,300	$ 34,500

Goldman Medical Supplies
Income Statement
Year Ended December 31, 2014

Revenues:			
	Sales Revenue	$217,000	
	Interest Revenue	8,500	
	Total Revenues		225,500
Expenses:			
	Cost of Goods Sold	$ 70,700	
	Salary Expense	27,400	
	Depreciation Expense	4,400	
	Other Operating Expenses	10,400	
	Interest Expense	11,100	
	Income Tax Expense	29,700	
	Total Expenses		153,700
Net Income			$ 71,800

Goldman Medical Supplies had no noncash investing and financing transactions during 2014. During the year, Goldman Medical Supplies made no sales of land or equipment, no issuance of notes payable, no retirement of shares, and no treasury share transactions.

Requirements

1. Prepare the 2014 cash flow statement, formatting operating activities by the indirect method.

2. How will what you learned in this problem help you evaluate an investment in Goldman Medical Supplies?

P11-4B. Prepare cash flow statement—direct method *(Learning Objective 4)*
20–25 min.

The accounting records for L. Lee Associates, Inc. for the year ended April 30, 2014, contain the following information:

a. Purchase of plant assets, $55,400

b. Proceeds from issuance of common shares, $45,000

c. Payment of dividends, $44,400

d. Collection of interest, $8,500

e. Payments of salaries, $93,600

f. Proceeds from sale of plant assets, $27,000

g. Collections from customers, $630,000

h. Cash receipt of dividend revenue, $4,600

i. Payments to suppliers, $374,800

j. Depreciation expense, $58,500

k. Proceeds from issuance of long-term notes, $46,100

l. Payments of long-term notes payable, $39,000

m. Interest expense and payments, $14,000

n. Income tax expense and payments, $45,000

o. Cash balance: April 30, 2013, $39,400; April 30, 2014, $134,400

Requirement

1. Prepare L. Lee Associates' cash flow statement for the year ended April 30, 2014. Use the direct method for cash flows from operating activities.

P11-5B. Prepare cash flow statement—direct method *(Learning Objective 4)*
20–25 min.

Use the Goldman Medical Supplies data from P11-3B. The cash amounts for Interest Revenue, Salary Expense, Interest Expense, and Income Tax Expense are the same as the accrual amounts for these items.

Requirements

1. Prepare the 2014 cash flow statement by the direct method.

2. How will what you learned in this problem help you evaluate an investment in Goldman Medical Supplies?

P11-6B. Prepare cash flow statement—direct method *(Learning Objective 4)*
20–25 min.

To prepare the cash flow statement, accountants for H. Laurie, Inc. summarized 2014 activity in the Cash account as follows:

Cash			
Beginning balance	91,700	Payment on accounts payable	347,400
Receipts of interest	15,100	Payment of dividends	30,000
Collections from customers	492,300	Payment of salaries and wages	63,500
Issuance of common shares	90,000	Payment of interest	21,100
		Payment for equipment	11,000
		Payment of operating expenses	21,100
		Payment of notes payable	77,000
		Payment of income tax	18,900
Ending balance	99,100		

Requirement

1. Prepare the cash flow statement of H. Laurie, Inc. for the year ended December 31, 2014, using the direct method for operating activities.

P11-7B. Prepare cash flow statement—indirect and direct methods
(Learning Objectives 3 & 4) **25–30 min.**

Comparative selected account balances and an unclassified income statement for KTA Company follow:

KTA Company Account Balances As at December 31		
	2014	**2013**
Cash	$22,800	$30,100
Accounts Receivable	27,600	42,800
Inventory	15,000	21,000
Prepaid Insurance	3,600	1,400
Accounts Payable	26,000	18,000
Accrued Liabilities	14,200	16,800
Tax Payable	4,600	1,800

KTA Company Income Statement For the Year Ended Dec 31, 2014		
Sales		$338,000
Cost of Goods Sold	$219,700	
Salary Expense	52,600	
Other Operating Expenses	22,800	
Gain on Disposal of Equipment	(6,000)	
Depreciation of Capital Assets	6,400	295,500
Income Taxes		2,400
Net Income		$ 40,100

In addition, the following information is available:

- Accounts Payable balances resulted from merchandise inventory purchases.
- The book value of the equipment was $24,000.
- Declared and paid $25,000 dividends.
- Purchased a truck costing $100,000 by issuing a long-term note payable of $20,000 as a partial payment.

Requirements

1. Prepare a cash flow statement for KTA using the indirect method.
2. Prepare the cash flow from operating activities section by using the direct method.

P11-8B. Identify source or use of cash and prepare cash flow statement—indirect and direct methods (Learning Objectives 2, 3, & 4) 30–35 min.

The following is the financial information for Shine Hair Supplies, Ltd.:

Shine Hair Supplies, Ltd. Balance Sheet As of December 31			
	2014	**2013**	**SOURCE/ (USES)**
Current Assets:			
Cash	$ 5,400	$ 2,700	
Accounts Receivable	8,600	10,300	
Store Supplies	1,800	1,200	
Prepaid Insurance	1,020	1,920	
Inventory	12,900	10,400	
Total Current Assets	29,720	26,520	
Capital Assets			
Store Equipment	16,500	12,000	
Accumulated Depreciation, Store Equipment	(3,300)	(2,400)	
Delivery Trucks	72,600	37,600	
Accumulated Depreciation, Delivery Trucks	(14,520)	(7,520)	
Total Capital Assets	71,280	39,680	
Total Assets	$101,000	$66,200	
Current Liabilities			
Accounts Payable	16,600	10,800	
Interest Payable	2,800	1,700	
Total Current Liabilities	19,400	12,500	
Long-Term Liabilities			
Long-Term Note Payable	21,500	17,000	
Bank Loan	27,500	7,500	
Total Long-Term Liabilities	49,000	24,500	
Shareholders' Equity			
Common Shares	15,000	15,000	
Retained Earnings	17,600	14,200	
Total Shareholders' Equity	32,600	29,200	
Total Liabilities & Shareholders' Equity	$101,000	$66,200	

Shine Hair Supplies, Ltd.
Income Statement
For the Year Ended December 31, 2014

Revenues:		$86,000
Cost of Goods Sold		34,400
Gross Profit		51,600
Operating Expenses:		
Depreciation Expense	$ 7,900	
Wages Expense	26,000	
Other Expenses	6,000	
Total Operating Expenses		39,900
Interest Expense		2,450
Income Before Taxes		9,250
Income Taxes (40%)		3,700
Net Income		$ 5,550

Additional information:

1. Store equipment was purchased by signing a two-year long-term note payable.

2. Additional bank loan of $35,000 was obtained for the purchase of delivery trucks.

3. Shine Hair declared and paid dividends on December 24, 2014.

Requirements

1. Identify source and use of cash for each account in the Balance Sheet.

2. Prepare a cash flow statement, using the indirect method.

3. Prepare the cash flow from operating activities section by using the direct method.

P11-9B. Identify source or use of cash and prepare cash flow statement—indirect and direct methods (*Learning Objectives 2, 3, & 4*) 35–40 min.

DelTek, Inc.'s income statement and comparative balance sheets appear as follows:

DelTek, Inc.
Income Statement
For the Year Ended December 31, 2014

Sales Revenue		$212,000
Cost of Goods Sold		(84,800)
		127,200
Depreciation Expense — Patent	$ 1,200	
Depreciation Expense — Equipment	12,600	
Salaries Expense	52,500	
Other Operating Expenses	37,500	
Interest Expense	9,000	
Gain on Sale of Equipment	(2,600)	110,200
Income Before Income Taxes		17,000
Income Tax Expense		5,100
Net Income		$ 11,900

DelTek, Inc.
Balance Sheet
As of December 31

	2014	2013	SOURCE/ (USE)
Cash	$ 8,000	$ 5,200	
Accounts Receivable	12,500	16,800	
Inventory	36,700	42,600	
Prepaid Expenses	2,500	4,300	
Equipment	143,500	86,700	
Accumulated Depreciation	(41,000)	(34,600)	
Land	83,000	35,000	
Patents	4,800	6,000	
Total	$250,000	$162,000	
Accounts Payable	24,300	16,200	
Accrued Liabilities	6,700	8,900	
Salaries Payable	14,500	10,200	
Dividends Payable	8,600	9,200	
Interest payable	12,200	18,000	
Income Tax Payable	3,600	4,800	
Mortgage	20,000	0	
Common Shares	130,000	70,000	
Retained Earnings	30,100	24,700	
Total	$250,000	$162,000	

Additional information related to business activities during 2014:

1. All accounts payable pertain to inventory purchases, and accrued liabilities pertain to other operating expenses.

2. The original cost of the equipment sold was $19,600. New equipment was purchased and 6,000 common shares at $10/share were issued as a partial payment.

3. DelTek purchased some land and borrowed $20,000 from a mortgage company as a partial payment.

4. DelTek declared a dividend on December 24 to be paid on January 24, 2015.

Requirements

1. Identify source and use of cash for each account in the balance sheet.

2. Calculate the cash receipt from the sale of equipment and the cost of the new equipment, using T-accounts to show your calculations.

3. Calculate the amount of cash dividend declared and cash dividend paid, using T-accounts to show your calculations.

4. Prepare a cash flow statement, using the indirect method.

5. Prepare the cash flow from operating activities section by using the direct method.

P11-10B. **Identify source or use of cash and prepare cash flow statement—indirect and direct methods (*Learning Objectives 2, 3, & 4*) 35–40 min.**

Kenji International, Inc.'s income statement and comparative balance sheets appear as follows:

Kenji International, Inc. Income Statement For the Year Ended December 31, 2014		
Sales Revenue		$160,000
Cost of Goods Sold		(64,000)
		96,000
Depreciation Expense — Equipment	$14,500	
Salaries Expense	48,500	
Bad Debt Expense	2,400	
Other Operating Expenses	35,200	
Interest Expense	6,000	106,600
Operating Income (Loss)		(10,600)
Gain on Sale of Equipment		3,500
Net Loss		($ 7,100)

Kenji International, Inc. Balance Sheet As of December 31			
	2014	**2013**	**SOURCE/ (USE)**
Cash	$ 2,800	$ 4,800	
Accounts Receivable	26,000	12,800	
Allowance for Doubtful Accounts	(3,600)	(1,200)	
Inventory	24,500	27,800	
Prepaid Expenses	4,800	2,100	
Equipment	167,000	85,000	
Accumulated Depreciation	(37,500)	(42,500)	
Total	$184,000	$88,800	
Accounts Payable	10,400	7,200	
Salaries Payable	4,000	6,400	
Interest Payable	3,500	2,000	
Long-Term Note Payable	100,000	0	
Common Shares	50,000	50,000	
Retained Earnings	16,100	23,200	
Total	$184,000	$88,800	

Additional information related to business activities during 2014:

1. All accounts payable pertain to inventory purchases, and accrued liabilities pertain to other operating expenses.

2. The original cost of the equipment sold was $38,000. New equipment was purchased by issuing a 6%, $100,000, 5-year long-term note payable as a partial payment.

Requirements

1. Identify source and use of cash for each account in the Balance Sheet.

2. Calculate the cash receipt from the sale of equipment and the cost of the new equipment, using T-accounts to show your calculations.

3. Prepare a cash flow statement, using the indirect method.

4. Prepare the cash flow from operating activities section by using the direct method.

PROBLEMS (ALTERNATES 1, 2, AND 3)

These alternative problem sets are available for your practice benefit at
www.myaccountinglab.com

CONTINUING EXERCISE

This exercise continues the accounting for Graham's Yard Care, Inc. from the Continuing Exercise in Chapter 10. Assume that Graham's Yard Care, Inc. had the following comparative balance sheet at the end of 2015, its second year of operations.

Graham's Yard Care, Inc.
Comparative Balance Sheet
December 31, 2015 and 2014

	2015	2014
ASSETS		
Cash	$1,500	$6,480
Accounts Receivable	2,200	150
Lawn Supplies	150	70
Equipment	4,900	1,400
(Less Accumulated Depreciation)	(495)	(146)
Total Assets	$8,255	$7,954
LIABILITIES		
Accounts Payable	$ 350	$1,400
Notes Payable		5,000
SHAREHOLDERS' EQUITY		
Common Shares	2,000	1,000
Retained Earnings	5,905	554
Total Liabilities and Sharesholders' Equity	$8,255	$7,954

Requirement

1. Prepare the cash flow statement for Graham's Yard Care, Inc. for 2015 using the indirect method. The following additional information applies to 2015:

■ Common shares were issued.

■ No dividends were declared or paid during the year.

■ No equipment was sold during the year and all purchases of equipment were for cash.

CONTINUING PROBLEM

In this problem, we continue our accounting for Aqua Elite, Inc. from Chapter 10. We will assume that Aqua Elite, Inc. is now in its second year of operations.

Assume that the comparative balance sheet for Aqua Elite, Inc. at July 31, 2015, and the income statement for the month ended July 31, 2015, are as follows.

Aqua Elite, Inc. Comparative Balance Sheets July 31 and June 30, 2015		
	July 31	June 30
ASSETS		
Cash	$ 5,333	$3,270
Accounts Receivable, net	2,280	1,000
Inventory	4,175	180
Supplies	105	125
Total Current Assets	11,893	4,575
Fixed Assets	67,250	2,250
Less: Accumulated Depreciation	(352)	(47)
Net Fixed Assets	66,898	2,203
Total Assets	$78,791	$6,778
LIABILITIES		
Accounts Payable	$ 1,805	$ 450
Unearned Revenue	5,800	2,000
Salary Payable	950	900
Interest Payable	375	17
Payroll Taxes Payable	188	—
Dividend Payable	500	—
Current Portion of Long-Term Debt	4,410	2,000
Total Current Liabilities	14,028	5,367
Notes Payable	20,000	—
Mortgage Payable	42,590	—
Total Liabilities	76,618	5,367
SHAREHOLDERS' EQUITY		
Common Shares	1,000	1,000
Retained Earnings	1,173	411
Total Shareholders' Equity	2,173	1,411
Total Liabilities & Shareholders' Equity	$78,791	$6,778

Aqua Elite, Inc.
Income Statement
Month Ended July 31, 2015

Revenue		$6,300
Expenses:		
Cost of Goods Sold		1,080
Depreciation Expense		305
Bad Debt Expense		220
Interest Expense		375
Insurance Expense		150
Supplies Expense		210
Salary Expense		2,400
Payroll Taxes Expense		268
Bank Service Fees		30
Net Income*		$1,262

*Income taxes ignored

Additional information follows:

Aqua Elite, Inc. purchased a $20,000 truck financed with a note payable; it purchased a $45,000 building site financed with a mortgage payable; and it did not sell any fixed assets during the month.

Requirement

1. Prepare the cash flow statement using the indirect method for the month of July.

APPLY YOUR KNOWLEDGE

ETHICS IN ACTION

Case 1. Design Incorporated experienced a downturn in December sales. To make matters worse, many of the recent sales were on account and because many customers were not paying on their accounts, the ending balance of Accounts Receivable at December 31 was higher than the beginning balance. Because the business had a dramatic need for cash, a prime piece of land owned by the company was sold for cash in December at a substantial gain. Design had purchased the land 10 years earlier and properly classified it as a long-term investment. The CEO, Jim Shady, was looking over the financial statements and saw the company's weak operating cash flows. He approached the accountant to ask why the December cash flows provided from operations were so weak, given that the land had been sold. The accountant explained that because the indirect method was used in preparing the cash flow statement, certain adjustments to net income were required. To begin with, the increase in accounts receivable was a decreasing adjustment made in arriving at the net cash provided from operating activities. Next, the large gain recognized on the sale of land had to be adjusted by subtracting it from the net income in arriving at the cash provided by operating activities. These large negative adjustments drastically reduced the reported cash provided from that category of cash flows. The accountant then explained that all the cash proceeds from the land sale were included as cash inflows in the investing activities section.

Jim became worried because he remembered the bank telling him about the importance of strong operating cash flows, so he told the accountant to redo the statement but not to reduce the net income by the accounts receivable increase or the gain on the land sale. The accountant refused because these adjustments were necessary to properly arrive at the net cash provided from operating activities. If these adjustments were not made, then the net change in cash could not be reconciled. Jim finally agreed but then told the accountant to just include the cash proceeds from the sale of land in the operating activities rather than in the investing activities. The accountant said that would be wrong. Besides, everyone would know that proceeds from the sale of land should be an investing activity. Jim then suggested listing it as "other" in the operating section so no one would ever know that it wasn't an operating cash flow.

Why didn't Jim want the accountant to decrease the net income by the increase in accounts receivable and the gain on the land sale? Why do you think Jim finally agreed with the accountant? Could the operating cash flows be increased by including the cash proceeds from the sale but listing them as "other" rather than as land sale proceeds? What ethical concerns are involved? Do you have any other thoughts?

Case 2. Kevin Sailors, the CEO of Candle Corporation, was discussing the financial statements with the company accountant. Weak cash flows had resulted in the company borrowing a lot of money. Kevin wanted to know why the money borrowed was included as cash inflows in the financing section of the cash flow statement but the interest paid on the amounts borrowed was not. The accountant replied that the interest paid on loans was an expense included in the calculation of net income, which was in the operating activities section. Kevin then asked why the dividends Candle Corporation paid to shareholders were included as an outflow of cash in the financing section. The accountant then explained that dividends paid, unlike interest paid, were a return to shareholders and not an expense; therefore, it would not be included in net income, nor would it appear in the operating activities section. Kevin replied that he did not care, and instructed the accountant to include both the interest paid and the dividends paid in the financing section. The accountant said that such a move would not be proper. Kevin then said to not provide the cash flow statement at all because too many people would see the weakening operating cash flows. He further stated that investors and creditors who really analyzed the income statements and balance sheets would be able to understand the company without the need for a cash flow statement spelling out the net changes in cash flows.

Why would Kevin want the interest paid to be included in the financing activities section? Why would the accountant state that interest paid should not be included in the financing activities section? Can the cash flow statement be omitted? What ethical issues are involved? Do you have any additional thoughts?

KNOW YOUR BUSINESS

FINANCIAL ANALYSIS

Purpose: To help familiarize you with the financial reporting of a real company to further your understanding of the chapter material you are learning.

This case focuses on the cash flows of Bombardier Inc. Recall that inflows and outflows of cash are classified as operating activities, investing activities, or financing activities. The cash flow statement presents cash flows from each of these three activities. It is, therefore, important to understand the information provided in this revealing financial statement. The cash flow statement and additional related information for Bombardier Inc. are disclosed in its annual report found in MyAccountingLab.

Requirements

1. Look at the operating activities section of the Consolidated Statements of Cash Flows. Compare the net cash provided by operating activities to the net income for each of the two years presented. Are the net income amounts reported on the cash flow statement the same as on the income statement? How does the total cash flows provided by operating activities compare to the net income? Why do they differ? Is this difference good or bad? Have the cash flows provided from operations been increasing or decreasing? On average,

what is the largest non-cash adjustment item in the operating cash flows section? Why is this amount added back each year?

2. Review Note 21. Explain what it means when receivables show a negative cash flow in 2011 and a positive cash flow in 2010. Explain what it means when the accounts payable and accrued liabilities have positive cash flows for both 2011 and 2010.

3. Look at the investing activities section of the Consolidated Statements of Cash Flows. What has created the largest outflow of cash related to investing activities? Did investing activities provide or use cash for the two years presented? Is this good or bad for the company?

4. Look at the financing activities section of the Consolidated Statements of Cash Flows. Did financing activities provide or require cash for the two fiscal years presented? What is the significance of this information? What was the largest item in the financing section for the 2011 year-end?

5. How do you feel about the overall sufficiency of cash flows? Does the cash provided from operations cover the cash required for investing activities?

6. What was the net change in cash and cash equivalents for the most recent fiscal year? Does the ending cash and cash equivalents amount agree with the cash and cash equivalents reported on the balance sheet? Do you have any other observations about the cash flow statement?

7. What was the amount of cash actually paid for interest in 2011? Why does the cash paid for interest not agree with the financing expense for the year?

INDUSTRY ANALYSIS

Purpose: To help you understand and compare the performance of two companies in the same industry.

Find the Bombardier Annual Report, Year Ended January 31, 2011, located in MyAccountingLab and go to the Consolidated Cash Flows. Now access The Boeing Company's 2010 Annual Report. To do this from the internet, go to their webpage for the Investor Relations at *http://www.boeing.com/companyoffices/financial/quarterly.htm* and under Annual Report, go to the 2010 Annual Report.

Requirement

1. Which method (direct or indirect) does each of these companies use to prepare its cash flow statement? How can you tell? Which activities provided cash for each of the companies? Which activities used cash for each of these companies? What conclusions can you draw from these results?

SMALL BUSINESS ANALYSIS

Purpose: To help you understand the importance of cash flows in the operation of a small business.

You just received your year-end financial statements from your accountant. Although receiving the year-end financial package is important every year for your financing institutions and your investors, it is especially important this year because of the potential investment opportunity that just became available to you. Yesterday you got a telephone call from one of your competitors with whom you have been discussing the possibility of a merger. The gist of the conversation was that the board of directors wanted to sell outright to you instead of merging. You're pretty happy about that except for the fact that it could create some potential cash flow problems. The other company wants $1,000,000 cash and it wants to do it soon or the deal is off. You've got that amount of cash and cash equivalents available right now, but you know there are some cash commitments coming up soon for capital expenditures and dividend payments. You decide to call one of your financial investors. He or she suggests that you calculate free cash flow from the end of the year to determine if that amount of cash is available to complete the deal.

You look at your cash flow statement from the financial statements and see that cash flows from operations was $1,725,000 and you expect that same amount for this year. From the capital budget, anticipated capital expenditures in the short term are $550,000. And from the board of director's minutes of the last meeting, the cash dividend approved for payout next month is $275,000.

Requirement

1. Define free cash flow and calculate it based on the information previously provided. With your understanding of free cash flow, is this new investment something that this company should pursue?

WRITTEN COMMUNICATION

You have been asked by your accounting professor to prepare a paper outlining the importance of the cash flow statement, the details of what is included in each of the three sections of the statement, and how it provides a link between the income statement and the balance sheet.

Self Check Answers
1. c 2. d 3. c 4. a 5. d 6. c 7. a 8. a 9. d 10. b

SCAN THIS

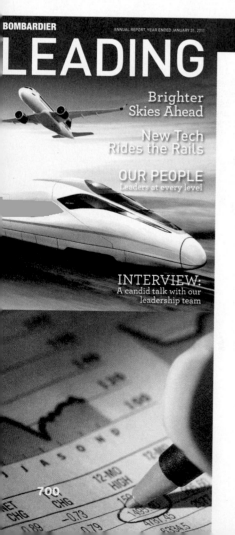

LEARNING OBJECTIVES:

1. Understand items on corporate income statements

2. Perform a horizontal analysis of financial statements

3. Perform a vertical analysis of financial statements

4. Compare one company to another using common-size financial statements and benchmarking

5. Compute various financial ratios

Throughout the book you have learned about the process of accounting. You have learned how to account for the transactions of a business and how to report the results of those transactions in the financial statements. However, have you ever wondered how the financial statements are utilized by managers, investors, and creditors to assess the performance of a business? In Chapter 12 you will learn several tools that can be applied to the financial statements to help assess a company's performance.

CHAPTER OUTLINE:

In Chapter 1, we learned that the study of accounting is important because it teaches us about the "language of business." In this chapter we will learn that another important reason to study accounting is that it teaches us how to use financial information to make better decisions. Managers, investors, and creditors can all benefit from being able to make better decisions regarding the performance of a company. As we begin our discussion of financial statement analysis, there are several important points that should be considered.

❶ Financial statement analysis usually does not indicate that a problem definitely exists within a company. Also, even if a problem does exist, financial statement analysis generally will not identify what the specific problem is. Instead, financial statement analysis indicates that a problem may exist and it gives clues as to what the problem might be.

❷ A company's performance is best evaluated by examining more than one year's data. This is why most financial statements cover at least two periods. In fact, most financial analysis covers trends of up to five years.

❸ A company's performance is best evaluated by comparing it against the following:

- Its own past performance
- The performance of competitors
- Industry averages for the industry the company is in

ACCOUNTING IN YOUR WORLD

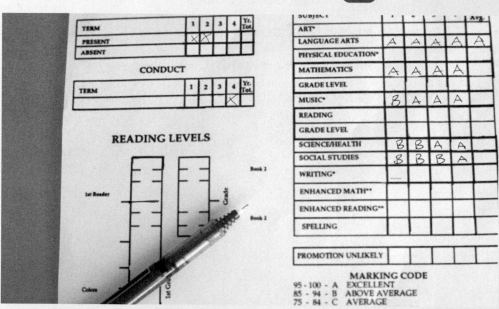

So just how badly did you do on that test?

Have you ever received a test or an assignment back and, after looking at your score, you were sure you failed? Then you found out your score wasn't so bad after all because there were only 80 points possible. Or perhaps you found out that your score, although low, was higher than the class average. Until you had a point of reference, your raw score did not tell the whole story about your performance. The results of financial statement analysis are similar. The results of financial statement analysis have minimal value without a point of reference. This is why, when conducting financial statement analysis, a company's performance is compared to past performance and industry averages.

There are three main ways to analyze financial statements:

- Horizontal analysis
- Vertical analysis
- Ratio analysis

Before we begin our discussion of financial statement analysis, let's take a closer look at the income statements of a corporation.

WHAT IS THE DIFFERENCE BETWEEN OPERATING INCOME AND NET INCOME ON THE INCOME STATEMENT?

In Chapter 4 we examined the multi-step income statement format. Recall that the multi-step format provides detailed information about the items comprising net income so that financial statement users can make more informed decisions about a company's results of operations. Corporate income statements often contain additional items that are reported to better inform users about a company's results of operations. The income items we will examine are as follows:

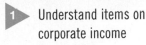

1 Understand items on corporate income statements

- Continuing operations
- Discontinued operations
- Effects of changes in accounting principles

For illustration purposes, refer to the income statement for Best Way, Inc. presented in **Exhibit 12-1** on the following page.

Income from Continuing Operations

In Exhibit 12-1, the top-most section reports income from continuing operations. Continuing operations consist of business activities that will most likely continue from period to period. Reporting income from continuing operations, therefore, helps investors make predictions about a company's future earnings. The continuing operations of Best Way, Inc. include two items that need explanation:

- *Other income (expense)* includes items that, although a normal part of business operations, fall outside of a company's core business activities. Therefore, these items are not included in sales, cost of goods sold, or operating expenses but are instead reported separately. Gains and losses on the sale of fixed assets as well as interest income and interest expense are examples of items reported as part of other income (expense). Best Way, Inc. reported interest expense of $32,000 and a loss on the sale of fixed assets of $14,000.
- *Income tax expense* reflects the income tax expense that is assessed on the company's operating income. Best Way, Inc. was assessed $72,000 of income tax on its operating income.

After continuing operations, an income statement may include the following items:

- Discontinued operations
- Cumulative effects of changes in accounting principles

Best Way, Inc. Income Statement Year Ended December 31, 2014		
Net Sales Revenue		$1,877,000
Cost of Goods Sold		1,145,000
Gross Profit		732,000
Operating Expenses (detailed)		423,000
Operating Income		309,000
Other income (expense):		
Interest Expense		(32,000)
Loss on Sale of Fixed Assets		(14,000)
Income from continuing operations before income tax		263,000
Income tax expense		72,000
Income from continuing operations		191,000
Income from discontinued operations, net of income tax of $11,000		26,000
Net Income		$ 217,000
Earnings per common share (100,000 shares outstanding):		
Income from continuing operations	$	1.91
Income from discontinued operations		0.26
Net Income	$	2.17

Exhibit 12-1 ▲

Discontinued Operations

Corporations often consist of many different business segments. A business segment is a distinguishable part of a business that is subject to a different set of risks and returns than other parts of the business. Information on any of the company's segments that have been sold (or otherwise discontinued) is reported separately from the results of continuing operations. This is because the discontinued segment will not be part of the company's operations in the future. The results of discontinued operations are generally reported net of income tax expense (or income tax savings in the case of a loss). Best Way, Inc. reported net income from discontinued operations of $26,000. This amount represents income of $37,000 less income tax expense of $11,000.

Effects of Changes in Accounting Principles

Occasionally, a company will change from the application of one accounting principle to another. For example, a business may change from weighted average to FIFO inventory valuation. Both IFRS and ASPE require retrospective application to account for the effects of most changes in accounting principles. Retrospective application means that a change in accounting principle is accounted for by restating comparative financial statements to reflect the new method as though it had been applied all along.

Earnings per Share

The final segment of a corporate income statement reports the company's earnings per share, abbreviated as EPS. Earnings per share reports the amount of net income for each share of the company's *outstanding common shares.* The computation of EPS is discussed later in the chapter. Corporations report a separate EPS figure for each element of income. Some corporations must report two sets of EPS figures, as follows:

- Basic EPS—EPS based on outstanding common shares.
- Diluted EPS—EPS based on outstanding common shares plus the additional common shares that would arise if convertible preferred shares (or other dilutive items) were exchanged for common shares. Diluted EPS is always lower than basic EPS.

Best Way, Inc. had no convertible (dilutive) items and therefore reported only one set of EPS figures for each element of income.

Now let's examine financial statement analysis. As previously discussed, the three most popular forms of financial statement analysis are horizontal analysis, vertical analysis, and ratio analysis. We will begin our discussion with horizontal analysis.

WHAT IS HORIZONTAL ANALYSIS?

The study of percentage changes in the line items on comparative financial statements is called **horizontal analysis**. Although it can be useful to know if individual financial statement amounts (such as sales, wages expense, or accounts receivable) have increased or decreased from the prior period, the *percentage change* is often more relevant and, therefore, more helpful to know. For example, sales may have increased by $80,000, but considered alone, this fact is not very helpful. For some companies, an $80,000 increase in sales would be significant while for others, it would be minor. It is better to know by what percentage sales have increased from the prior year. For instance, knowing that sales have increased by 15% is more meaningful than knowing sales increased by $80,000.

To compute the percentage change in the line items on comparative financial statements

 2 Perform a horizontal analysis of financial statements

❶ compute the dollar amount of the change from the earlier period to the later period.

❷ divide the dollar amount of change by the earlier period amount and multiply by 100. We call the earlier period the base period.

To illustrate horizontal analysis, let's consider the comparative income statement and balance sheet for Tucker Enterprises presented in **Exhibits 12-2** and **12-3**.

Tucker Enterprises, Inc.
Income Statement
Years Ended December 31, 2014 and 2013

(in thousands)	2014	2013
Net Sales	$824	$596
Cost of Goods Sold	375	277
Gross Profit	449	319
Operating Expenses:		
Selling, General, and Administrative	213	167
Other	48	34
Income Before Income Tax	188	118
Income Tax Expense	33	21
Net Income	$155	$ 97

Exhibit 12-2 ▲

Tucker Enterprises, Inc.
Balance Sheet
December 31, 2014 and 2013

(in thousands)	2014	2013
Assets		
Current Assets:		
Cash and Cash Equivalents	$ 36	$ 47
Accounts Receivable, Net	61	52
Inventory	144	116
Total Current Assets	241	215
Property, Plant, and Equipment, Net	319	179
Total Assets	$560	$394
Liabilities		
Current Liabilities:		
Accounts Payable	$121	$ 74
Accrued Liabilities	24	33
Total Current Liabilities	145	107
Long-Term Liabilities	173	104
Total Liabilities	318	211
Shareholders' Equity		
Common Shares	35	30
Retained Earnings	207	153
Total Shareholders' Equity	242	183
Total Liabilities and Shareholders' Equity	$560	$394

Exhibit 12-3 ▲

The increase in sales is computed as follows:

Step 1 Compute the dollar amount of change in sales from 2013 to 2014:

$$\frac{\text{2014 Amount}}{\$824} - \frac{\text{2013 Amount}}{\$596} = \frac{\text{Dollar Change}}{\$228}$$

Step 2 Compute the percentage change for the period by dividing the dollar amount of change by the base-period (2013) amount and multiplying the result by 100:

$$\text{Percentage change} = \frac{\text{Dollar change}}{\text{Base period amount}} \times 100 = \frac{\$228}{\$596} \times 100 = 38.3\% \text{ (rounded)}$$

The percentage changes in the remaining items are computed in the same manner. The completed horizontal analyses for Tucker Enterprises' financial statements are shown in **Exhibits 12-4** below and **12-5** on the next page.

Horizontal Analysis of the Income Statement

Tucker Enterprises' comparative income statement reveals strong growth during 2014. The 38.3% increase in Sales coupled with only a 35.4% increase in Cost of Goods Sold resulted in an increase in Gross Profit of 40.8%. The item on Tucker Enterprises' income statement with the lowest growth rate is Selling, General, and Administrative Expense, with an increase of only 27.5%. Even though Other Operating Expenses and Income Tax Expense increased by 41.2% and 57.1% respectively, they were the smallest dollar amounts on the income statement. So, on the bottom line, Net Income grew by a very respectable 59.8%.

Horizontal Analysis of the Balance Sheet

Tucker Enterprises' comparative balance sheet also shows significant growth with total assets increasing by 42.1%. Accounts Receivable and Inventory increased 17.3% and 24.1% respectively. These increases are likely related to the increase in Sales during the year. Cash actually decreased by 23.4%, which could be a concern for Tucker Enterprises' management. If a decrease in cash becomes a trend, the company could face cash flow problems in the future. Tucker Enterprises' Property, Plant, and Equipment also grew notably at a rate of 78.2%.

Total liabilities increased by 50.7%. Accounts Payable increased notably at a rate of 63.5%, however, Accrued Liabilities actually decreased by 27.3%. The 66.3% increase in Long-Term Liabilities is probably not a concern for management as it is most likely

				INCREASE (DECREASE)	
Tucker Enterprises, Inc. Income Statement Years Ended December 31, 2014 and 2013					
(in thousands)	**2014**	**2013**	**AMOUNT**	**PERCENTAGE**	
Net Sales	$824	$596	$228	38.3%	
Cost of Goods Sold	375	277	98	35.4	
Gross Profit	449	319	130	40.8	
Operating Expenses:					
Selling, General, and Administrative	213	167	46	27.5	
Other	48	34	14	41.2	
Income Before Income Tax	188	118	70	59.3	
Income Tax Expense	33	21	12	57.1	
Net Income	$155	$ 97	58	59.8%	

Exhibit 12-4 ▲

Tucker Enterprises, Inc.
Balance Sheet
December 31, 2014 and 2013

(in thousands)	2014	2013	INCREASE (DECREASE)	
			AMOUNT	PERCENTAGE
Assets				
Current Assets:				
Cash and Cash Equivalents	$ 36	$ 47	$ (11)	(23.4)%
Accounts Receivable, Net	61	52	9	17.3
Inventory	144	116	28	24.1
Total Current Assets	241	215	26	12.1
Property, Plant, and Equipment, Net	319	179	140	78.2
Total Assets	$560	$394	$166	42.1 %
Liabilities				
Current Liabilities:				
Accounts Payable	$121	$ 74	$ 47	63.5
Accrued Liabilities	24	33	(9)	(27.3)
Total Current Liabilities	145	107	38	35.5
Long-Term Liabilities	173	104	69	66.3
Total Liabilities	318	211	107	50.7
Shareholders' Equity				
Common Shares	35	30	5	16.7
Retained Earnings	207	153	54	35.3
Total Shareholders' Equity	242	183	59	32.2
Total Liabilities and Shareholders' Equity	$560	$394	$166	42.1 %

Exhibit 12-5 ▲

related to the increase in Property, Plant, and Equipment. The strong growth in Net Income for the year helped Tucker Enterprises achieve a 32.2% increase in total shareholders' equity during 2014.

Trend Percentages

Trend percentages are a form of horizontal analysis. Trends indicate the direction a business is taking. How have sales changed over a five-year period? What trend does net income show? These questions can be answered by looking at trend percentages over a period of time, such as three to five years. To calculate trend percentages, a base year must first be selected. The base-year amounts are then set equal to 100%. Next, the amounts for each subsequent year are expressed as a percentage of the base-year amount. To compute trend percentages, divide each item for the years following the base year by the base-year amount and multiply the result by 100.

$$\text{Trend percentage} = \frac{\text{Any year } \$}{\text{Base year } \$} \times 100$$

Let's assume Tucker Enterprises' Net Sales were $387,000 in 2010 and rose to $824,000 in 2014. To illustrate trend analysis, let's review the trend of Net Sales during 2010–2014, with dollars in thousands. The base year is 2010, so that year's percentage is set equal to 100. We compute the trend percentages by dividing each year's net sales amount by the 2010 net sales amount and multiplying the result by 100.

(in thousands)	2014	2013	2012	2011	2010
Net Sales	$ 824	$ 596	$ 467	$ 411	$387
Trend Percentage	212.9%	154.0%	120.7%	106.2%	100%

The trend analysis shows that Tucker Enterprises' Net Sales increased moderately from 2010 to 2012 and then more significantly in 2013 and substantially in 2014. You can perform a trend analysis on any one, or multiple items, you consider important. Trend analysis is widely used to predict future performance.

WHAT IS VERTICAL ANALYSIS?

In addition to a horizontal analysis, a **vertical analysis** can also be performed to help evaluate a company's performance. A vertical analysis of a financial statement reflects each item on the financial statement as a percentage of another item (the base amount) on the financial statement. The vertical analysis percentages are calculated as follows:

3 ▸ Perform a vertical analysis of financial statements

$$\text{Vertical analysis percentage} = \frac{\text{Financial statement item \$}}{\text{Base amount \$}} \times 100$$

On the income statement, net sales is used as the base amount and is shown as 100%. On the balance sheet, total assets is used as the base amount and is shown as 100%. The completed vertical analysis of Tucker Enterprises' 2013 and 2014 income statement and balance sheet is presented in Exhibits 12-6 and 12-7.

Tucker Enterprises, Inc. Income Statement Years Ended December 31, 2014 and 2013				
(in thousands)	2014	PERCENT	2013	PERCENT
Net Sales	$824	100.0%	$596	100.0%
Cost of Goods Sold	375	45.5	277	46.5
Gross Profit	449	54.5	319	53.5
Operating Expenses:				
Selling, General, and Administrative	213	25.8	167	28.0
Other	48	5.8	34	5.7
Income Before Income Tax	188	22.8	118	19.8
Income Tax Expense	33	4.0	21	3.5
Net Income	$155	18.8%	$ 97	16.3%

Exhibit 12-6 ▲

Tucker Enterprises, Inc.
Balance Sheet
December 31, 2014 and 2013

(in thousands)	2014	PERCENT	2013	PERCENT
Assets				
Current Assets:				
Cash and Cash Equivalents	$ 36	6.4%	$ 47	11.9%
Accounts Receivable, Net	61	10.9	52	13.2
Inventory	144	25.7	116	29.4
Total Current Assets	241	43.0	215	54.6
Property, Plant, and Equipment, Net	319	57.0	179	45.4
Total Assets	$560	100.0%	$394	100.0%
Liabilities				
Current Liabilities:				
Accounts Payable	$121	21.6%	$ 74	18.8%
Accrued Liabilities	24	4.3	33	8.4
Total Current Liabilities	145	25.9	107	27.2
Long-Term Liabilities	173	30.9	104	26.4
Total Liabilities	318	56.8	211	53.6
Shareholders' Equity				
Common Shares	35	6.3	30	7.6
Retained Earnings	207	37.0	153	38.8
Total Shareholders' Equity	242	43.2	183	46.4
Total Liabilities and Shareholders' Equity	$560	100.0%	$394	100.0%

Exhibit 12-7 ▲

A Note About Rounding

An interesting issue often arises when preparing vertical analyses of financial statements. This issue occurs when the calculated percentage amounts are added or subtracted from each other in the same manner that was used to prepare the financial statements (i.e. the Cost of Goods Sold percentage is subtracted from the Net Sales percentage to get the Gross Profit percentage, etc.). Some of the percentage amounts arrived at in this manner often differ slightly from the percentage amounts that were initially calculated when doing the vertical analysis. For example, in Exhibit 12-6 for 2014, if the calculated percentages for Operating Expenses are subtracted from the calculated percentage for Gross Profit, the result is 22.9 (54.5–25.8–5.8). This amount differs from the 22.8 which was calculated when preparing the vertical analysis of the Income statement. These differences are the result of the rounding that took place when calculating the percentages for the vertical analysis. These differences are insignificant and will be ignored for purposes of our discussion of vertical analysis. All of the amounts in the vertical analyses that are performed in this textbook will be the result of the calculated percentages.

Vertical Analysis of the Income Statement

The vertical analysis reveals that Tucker Enterprises' 2014 cost of goods sold is 45.5% of net sales compared to 46.5% in 2013. The fact that Tucker Enterprises was able to decrease the Cost of Goods Sold as a percent of Net Sales while increasing Net Sales by over $200,000 is a positive sign. The analysis also indicates that Tucker Enterprises was able to decrease Selling, General, and Administrative Expenses from 28.0% of Net

Sales in 2013 to only 25.8% in 2014. This indicates that Tucker Enterprises' management appears to be doing a good job of controlling these expenses. We also see that Tucker Enterprises' 2014 Net Income is 18.8% of Net Sales. In other words, Tucker Enterprises earned $188 for every thousand dollars of net sales it had.

Vertical Analysis of the Balance Sheet

The vertical analysis of Tucker Enterprises' balance sheet reveals several things that warrant discussion. First, Cash and Cash Equivalents decreased from 11.9% of total assets to only 6.4% of total assets. This should concern management as it could indicate a potential cash flow problem in the future. In addition to Cash and Cash Equivalents, Accounts Receivable and Inventory also decrease as a percent of total assets. As a result, total current assets decreased from 54.6% of total assets to 43.0% of total assets. However, as we saw in the horizontal analysis, the current assets actually increased in total from 2013 to 2014. So, the decrease of current assets as a percentage of total assets was not due to a decrease in total current assets. It was actually the result of the significant increase in Property, Plant, and Equipment during the year. Also, total liabilities increased from 53.6% to 56.8% of total liabilities and shareholders' equity while total shareholders' equity decreased from 46.4 % to 43.2%. This indicates that creditors have claims to a higher percentage of Tucker Enterprises' assets in 2014 than they did in 2013.

HOW DO WE COMPARE ONE COMPANY WITH ANOTHER?

Horizontal and vertical analyses are useful tools to assess a company's performance. However, they only evaluate a company's performance against itself. To better assess a company's performance, it is often useful to compare the company against other companies. To compare Tucker Enterprises to another company we can use common-size statements. A **common-size statement** reports only percentages—the same percentages that appear in a vertical analysis. Common-size statements make it easier to compare companies of different sizes. By only reporting percentages, it removes **dollar value bias** when comparing the companies. Dollar value bias is the bias one sees from comparing numbers in absolute (dollars) rather than relative (percentages) terms. For example, it may appear that one company performed better than another because it had higher net income. However, the company with the lower net income might actually have been the better performer of the two companies in relative (percentage) terms.

To illustrate, let's assume that Tucker Enterprises, Inc. and Mackay Industries, Inc. compete in the same industry. Which company achieves a higher gross margin? Which company earns a higher percentage of revenues as profits for its shareholders? We can use a common-size income statement to compare the two companies and answer these questions. **Exhibit 12-8** on the next page gives both companies' common-size income statements for 2014 so that we may compare them on a relative, not absolute, basis. The figures for Tucker Enterprises are taken from the vertical analysis in Exhibit 12-6 and the figures for Mackay Industries are assumed.

Exhibit 12-8 shows that in 2014, Tucker Enterprises was more profitable than Mackay Industries. Tucker Enterprises' gross profit percentage is 54.5%, compared to 52.8% for Mackay Industries. This means that Tucker Enterprises is getting more profit from every dollar of net sales than Mackay Industries. And, more importantly, Tucker Enterprises'

 4 Compare one company to another using common-size financial statements and benchmarking

Tucker Enterprises, Inc. Versus Mackay Industries, Inc.
Common-Size Income Statement
Year Ended December 31, 2014

(in thousands)	TUCKER ENTERPRISES	MACKAY INDUSTRIES
Net Sales	100.0%	100.0%
Cost of Goods Sold	45.5	47.2
Gross Profit	54.5	52.8
Operating Expenses:		
Selling, General, and Administrative	25.8	26.3
Other	5.8	4.9
Income Before Income Tax	22.8	21.6
Income Tax Expense	4.0	3.7
Net Income	18.8%	17.9%

Exhibit 12-8 ▲

percentage of net income to net sales is 18.8%. That means that nearly one-fifth of Tucker Enterprises' net sales end up as profits for the company's shareholders. On the other hand, although close, Mackay Industries' percentage of net income to net sales is 17.9%. Both percentages are good; however, the common-size statement highlights Tucker Enterprises' advantage over Mackay Industries.

A common-size balance sheet can also be prepared to compare the two companies' balance sheets. **Exhibit 12-9** gives both companies' common-size balance sheets for

Tucker Enterprises, Inc. Versus Mackay Industries, Inc.
Common-Size Balance Sheet
December 31, 2014

(in thousands)	TUCKER ENTERPRISES	MACKAY INDUSTRIES
Assets		
Current Assets:		
Cash and Cash Equivalents	6.4%	11.1%
Accounts Receivable, Net	10.9	9.3
Inventory	25.7	26.5
Total Current Assets	43.0	46.9
Property, Plant, and Equipment, Net	57.0	53.1
Total Assets	100.0%	100.0%
Liabilities		
Current Liabilities:		
Accounts Payable	21.6%	20.7%
Accrued Liabilities	4.3	6.4
Total Current Liabilities	25.9	27.1
Long-Term Liabilities	30.9	32.2
Total Liabilities	56.8	59.3
Shareholders' Equity		
Common Shares	6.3	5.2
Retained Earnings	37.0	35.5
Total Shareholders' Equity	43.2	40.7
Total Liabilities and Shareholders' Equity	100.0%	100.0%

Exhibit 12-9 ▲

2014 so that we may compare them. The figures for Tucker Enterprises are taken from the vertical analysis in Exhibit 12-7 and the figures for Mackay Industries are assumed.

As we can see from the figures in Exhibit 12-9, Tucker Enterprises' cash represents only 6.4% of its total assets compared to 11.1% for Mackay Industries. This might concern Tucker Enterprises' managers as it could indicate cash flow issues for Tucker Enterprises in the future. We can also see that Tucker Enterprises' total liabilities represents 56.8% of the total liabilities and shareholders' equity compared to 59.3% for Mackay Industries. This means that a higher percentage of assets are financed by creditors rather than shareholders for Mackay Industries.

Benchmarking

The practice of comparing a company with other leading companies is known as **benchmarking**. The common-size financial statements presented in Exhibits 12-8 and 12-9 represent benchmarking against a key competitor. Mackay Industries, Inc. is a good company to use to benchmark Tucker Enterprises' performance because the two companies compete in the same industry. As we saw in the common-size income statement, Tucker Enterprises is slightly more profitable than Mackay Industries.

It is also possible to utilize industry averages as a benchmark for evaluating a company. An industry comparison would show how Tucker Enterprises is performing alongside the average for the industry it operates in. A popular source for industry averages is *Annual Statement Studies* published by The Risk Management Association. You can even find industry averages online at BizStats.com. To compare Tucker Enterprises, Inc. to the industry average, simply insert the industry average common-size financial statements in place of Mackay Industries in Exhibits 12-8 and 12-9.

DECISION GUIDELINES

Decision	**Guideline**	**Analyze**
As the CEO, I need to present the performance of the organization to the Board of Directors. I know that we had a bad year, but I also know that we are in a good position compared to our competitors. How do I show this comparison to competitors that are all different sizes?	Utilize common-size financial statements.	Common-size financial statements can be utilized to compare two different companies even if they are of dissimilar sizes. This is because common-size financial statements report financial statement items as percentages instead of as dollar amounts. The percentages for the two companies can be compared to see which company has the higher gross profit percentage and the lower expense percentages.
		Common-size financial statements can also be used to compare a company against the best companies in the industry. This is known as benchmarking. A business may not be able to achieve the same results as the industry leader, but benchmarking gives a company a goal to shoot for.

WHAT IS RATIO ANALYSIS?

 5 Compute various financial ratios

Ratio analysis is a form of financial statement analysis in which items on the financial statements are expressed as ratios of one number to another. These ratios are then compared to ratios from prior years, ratios of other companies, or industry average ratios to evaluate a company's performance. Remember, however, that no single ratio tells the whole picture of any company's performance. Different ratios explain different aspects of a company. The ratios we discuss in this chapter may be classified as follows:

- *Liquidity ratios* measure a company's ability to meet short-term obligations with current assets.
- *Asset management ratios* measure how efficiently a company utilizes its operating assets.
- *Solvency ratios* measure a company's ability to meet its long-term obligations or take on more debt.
- *Profitability ratios* measure a company's ability to generate profits.
- *Market analysis ratios* are used to evaluate a company's stock market performance.

In earlier chapters, we introduced many of these ratios. In this chapter, we will review previously introduced ratios and examine new ratios. To illustrate ratio analysis, we will return to the comparative income statement and balance sheet for Tucker Enterprises, which were presented in Exhibits 12-2 and 12-3. Let's start by discussing liquidity ratios.

Liquidity Ratios
Working Capital

Working capital is defined as current assets less current liabilities. Working capital measures the amount of current assets that are left over after settling all current liabilities. Tucker Enterprises' working capital is $96,000 in 2014 and $108,000 in 2013 calculated as follows:

$$\text{Working capital} = \text{Current assets} - \text{Current liabilities} = \begin{array}{l} \textbf{2014}\ \$241,000 - 145,000 = \$\ \ 96,000 \\ \textbf{2013}\ \$215,000 - 107,000 = \$108,000 \end{array}$$

Current Ratio

The **current ratio** is the most widely used liquidity ratio. The current ratio is calculated by dividing current assets by current liabilities. Tucker Enterprises' current ratio for 2014 and 2013 is calculated as follows:

		2014	2013
$\text{Current ratio} = \dfrac{\text{Current assets}}{\text{Current liabilities}} =$		$\dfrac{\$241,000}{\$145,000} = 1.66$	$\dfrac{\$215,000}{\$107,000} = 2.01$

A high current ratio indicates that the business has sufficient current assets to pay its current liabilities as they come due. But, what is an acceptable current ratio? The answer depends on the industry. For companies in most industries, a good current ratio is around 1.50, as reported by The Risk Management Association. Tucker Enterprises' current ratio of 1.66 in 2014 and 2.01 in 2013 are both strong. However, the decrease in the current ratio from 2013 to 2014 may be a cause for concern. Keep in mind that a current ratio that is too high would also be a cause for concern. This would indicate that the company is too liquid and, therefore, is not using its assets effectively.

Acid-Test Ratio

The **acid-test ratio** (or **quick ratio**) tells us whether the entity could pay all its current liabilities if they came due immediately. Inventory and prepaid expenses are *not* included in the acid-test ratio because they are not available to pay current liabilities. To compute the acid-test ratio, we add cash, short-term investments, and net current receivables (accounts and notes receivable, net of allowances) and divide this sum by current liabil-ities. Tucker Enterprises' acid-test ratios for 2014 and 2013 follow:

$$\text{Acid-test (Quick) ratio} = \frac{\text{Cash} + \text{Short-term investments} + \text{Net current receivables}}{\text{Current liabilities}}$$

	2014	**2013**
	$\dfrac{\$97{,}000}{\$145{,}000} = 0.67$	$\dfrac{\$99{,}000}{\$107{,}000} = 0.93$

The company's acid-test ratio declined from 0.93 in 2013 to 0.67 in 2014. An acid-test ratio of 0.90 to 1.00 is acceptable in most industries. Therefore, although it appears that Tucker Enterprises' acid-test ratio was acceptable in 2013, it is somewhat low in 2014.

DECISION GUIDELINES

Decision	**Guideline**	**Analyze**
As a supplier, how can I check a customer's ability to pay their obligations as they come due in order to know whether or not to extend them credit?	Utilize liquidity ratios: • Working capital • Current ratio • Acid-test ratio	Monitoring a business's liquidity ratios can often provide an indi-cator that the business may experience cash flow problems. Action should be taken so that the business does not encounter difficulty meeting its obligations as they come due. For most businesses, a current ratio that drops below 1.50 or an acid-test ratio that drops below 0.90 may be cause for concern.

It is not only important for a company to have good liquidity ratios. It is also important that a company manage its operations effectively. There are three ratios we will look at that measure how well a company manages its inventory and accounts receivable.

Asset Management Ratios

Inventory Turnover

The **inventory turnover** measures the number of times a company sells its average level of inventory during a year. A high rate of turnover indicates ease in selling inventory; a low rate indicates difficulty. A value of 6 means that the company sold its average level of inventory six times, or once every two months, during the year. To compute inventory turnover, we divide cost of goods sold by the average inventory for the period. We use the cost of goods sold—not sales—because both cost of goods sold and inventory are stated *at cost.* Tucker Enterprises' inventory turnover for 2014 and 2013 is calculated as follows:

$$\text{Inventory turnover ratio} = \frac{\text{Cost of goods sold}}{\text{Average inventory}} = \begin{array}{c} \textbf{2014} \\ \dfrac{\$375,000}{(\$116,000 + \$144,000)/2} = 2.88 \\ \textbf{2013} \\ = \dfrac{\$277,000}{(\$68,000^* + \$116,000)/2} = 3.01 \end{array}$$

*2012 inventory is $68,000.

Cost of goods sold comes directly from the income statement. Average inventory is calculated by adding the beginning inventory to the ending inventory and dividing by two.

When calculating any ratio, if one number is taken from the income statement and the other number is taken from the balance sheet, then the balance sheet number to be used has to be an average number. This is because the income statement number is accumulated for the whole year, while the balance sheet number is on a specific date. The balance sheet number may be skewed on the last day of the accounting period; therefore, we need to use the average number.

Inventory turnover varies widely with the nature of the business. For example, the inventory turnover ratio for a heavy equipment dealer will be significantly lower than that for a grocery store. Because of the high profit margin on heavy equipment, it is not necessary to turn the inventory over as many times and still be profitable. Let's assume the industry average inventory turnover ratio in Tucker Enterprises' industry is 2.5. In this case, Tucker Enterprises turnover ratio would be considered to be good in both 2013 and 2014. However, the decrease in the turnover from 2013 to 2014 should be investigated as it could be an indicator that Tucker Enterprises has some obsolete inventory.

Days' Sales in Inventory

The **days' sales in inventory** also measures how long it takes a company to turn its inventory into sales. To compute, we divide 365 by the preceding inventory turnover. It is more intuitive for users of financial statements to understand the number of days it takes to turn inventory to sales, rather than the number of times it turns over in a year. Tucker Enterprises' days' sales in inventory for 2014 and 2013 is calculated as follows:

$$\text{Days' sales in inventory} = \frac{365}{\text{Inventory turnover}} = \begin{array}{c} \textbf{2014} \\ \dfrac{365}{2.88} = 127 \text{ days} \\ \textbf{2013} \\ = \dfrac{365}{3.01} = 122 \text{ days} \end{array}$$

Accounts Receivable Turnover

The **accounts receivable turnover** measures the ability to collect cash from credit customers. The higher the ratio, the faster the company collects cash. However, a receivable turnover ratio that is too high may indicate that credit is too tight, causing the loss of sales to good customers. To compute accounts receivable turnover, net credit sales is divided by average net accounts receivable. Average net accounts receivable is calculated by adding the beginning and ending balances in net accounts receivable together and dividing the result by two. We will assume that all of Tucker Enterprises' sales were on account. Tucker Enterprises' accounts receivable turnover for 2014 and 2013 is computed as follows:

$$\text{Accounts receivable turnover ratio} = \frac{\text{Net credit sales}}{\text{Average net accounts receivable}} = \begin{array}{c} \textbf{2014} \\ \dfrac{\$824,000}{(\$52,000 + \$61,000)/2} = 14.58 \\[4pt] \textbf{2013} \\ \dfrac{\$596,000}{(\$43,000^* + \$52,000)/2} = 12.55 \end{array}$$

*2012 Accounts Receivable is $43,000.

Tucker Enterprises' receivable turnover of 14.58 in 2014 is an improvement over the 12.55 turnover in 2013. Considering Tucker Enterprises' credit terms are 2/10, n/30, it appears that Tucker Enterprises is doing a good job of collecting its receivables.

Days' Sales in Receivables

The **days' sales in receivables** also measures the ability to collect receivables. Days' sales in receivables tell us how many days' sales remain in Accounts Receivable. To compute, we divide 365 by the preceding accounts receivable turnover. Tucker Enterprises' days' sales in receivables for 2014 and 2013 is calculated as follows:

$$\text{Days' sales in receivables} = \frac{365}{\text{Accounts receivable turnover}} = \begin{array}{c} \textbf{2014} \\ \dfrac{365}{14.58} = 25 \text{ days} \\[4pt] \textbf{2013} \\ \dfrac{365}{12.55} = 29 \text{ days} \end{array}$$

An alternate method of calculating the days' sales in receivables is to do the following:

❶ Divide net sales by 365 days to figure average sales for one day.

❷ Divide this average day's sales amount into the average net accounts receivable.

Tucker Enterprises' ratio tells us that on average, 25 days' sales remain in Accounts Receivable in 2014 compared to 29 days in 2013. As with the accounts receivable turnover, this is an indicator that Tucker Enterprises has improved its ability to collect its accounts.

Fixed Asset Turnover

In addition to measuring how efficient the company is in managing its working capital accounts, we can also measure the company's operating efficiency by evaluating the company's **fixed asset turnover ratio**. The fixed asset turnover measures a company's ability to generate sales from fixed asset investments, specifically property, plant, and equipment (PPE). A higher turnover ratio shows that the company is more effective in using the investment in fixed assets to generate sales. Tucker Enterprises' fixed asset turnover for 2014 and 2013 is calculated as follows:

$$\text{Fixed asset turnover} = \frac{\text{Net sales}}{\text{Average net fixed assets}}$$

2014
$$= \frac{\$824,000}{(\$179,000 + \$319,000)/2} = 3.31$$

2013
$$= \frac{\$596,000}{(\$165,000^* + \$179,000)/2} = 3.47$$

*2012 Fixed Assets is $165,000.

Total Asset Turnover

Another asset management ratio is total asset turnover. The **total asset turnover ratio** measures the ability of a company to utilize its assets to generate sales. The higher the ratio, the more efficient the company is in generating sales. Tucker Enterprises' total asset turnover for 2014 and 2013 is calculated as follows:

$$\text{Total asset turnover} = \frac{\text{Net sales}}{\text{Average total assets}}$$

2014
$$= \frac{\$824,000}{(\$394,000 + \$560,000)/2} = 1.73$$

2013
$$= \frac{\$596,000}{(\$318,000^* + \$394,000)/2} = 1.67$$

*2012 Fixed Assets is $318,000.

DECISION GUIDELINES

Decision	**Guideline**	**Analyze**
As the manager, how do I determine if the Inventory and Accounts Receivable are being managed effectively?	Utilize assets management ratios: • Inventory turnover • Accounts receivable turnover • Days' sales in receivables	Monitoring the asset management ratios can provide an indicator that a business is not managing its inventory and accounts receivables effectively. A decrease in the inventory turnover may indicate that a business has obsolete inventory or that it is purchasing too much inventory. Carrying high levels of inventory results in decreased profits due to the increased costs associated with maintaining the increased inventory levels. A decrease in the Accounts Receivable turnover may be due to poor collection practices related to past due accounts. This can result in decreased profits for the business due to increased bad debts expense. The longer a receivable is past due, the less likely it is to be collected.

Solvency Ratios

The ratios discussed so far yield insight into a company's ability to pay current liabilities and manage its assets. Most businesses also have long-term debt. Solvency ratios help assess a business's ability to pay long-term liabilities and evaluate its capital structure. These ratios are good indicators of a business's financial risks.

Debt Ratio

The **debt ratio** shows the relationship between total liabilities and total assets. In other words, it shows the proportion of assets financed with debt. If the debt ratio is 1, then all the assets are financed with debt. A debt ratio of 0.50 means that half the assets are financed with debt and the other half are financed by the owners of the business. The higher the debt ratio, the higher the company's financial risk. The debt ratios for Tucker Enterprises at the end of 2014 and 2013 follow:

$$\text{Debt ratio} = \frac{\text{Total liabilities}}{\text{Total assets}} = \overset{\textbf{2014}}{\frac{\$318,000}{\$560,000}} = 0.57 \quad \overset{\textbf{2013}}{\frac{\$211,000}{\$394,000}} = 0.54$$

Tucker Enterprises' debt ratio in 2014 of 0.57 is slightly higher than the 2013 debt ratio of 0.54. However, neither ratio is considered to be very high. The Risk Management Association reports that the average debt ratio for most companies ranges from 0.57 to 0.67, with relatively little variation from company to company. Tucker Enterprises appears to be very solvent and in a position to take on more debt should the need arise.

Debt to Equity Ratio

The **debt to equity ratio** shows the relationship between total liabilities and total equity. A high debt to equity ratio means that a company has been aggressive in financing its growth with debt, in other words, the company is more leveraged. Generally, companies with higher ratios are thought to be more risky because they have more liabilities and less equity. Tucker Enterprises' debt to equity ratio for 2014 and 2013 is calculated as follows:

$$\text{Debt to equity ratio} = \frac{\text{Total liabilities}}{\text{Total shareholders' equity}} = \overset{\textbf{2014}}{\frac{\$318,000}{\$242,000}} = 1.31$$

$$= \overset{\textbf{2013}}{\frac{\$211,000}{\$183,000}} = 1.15$$

Times-Interest-Earned Ratio

The **times-interest-earned ratio**, also known as **interest-coverage ratio**, indicates a company's ability to continue to service its debt. It measures the number of times operating income can cover (pay) interest expense. A high ratio means that a company is able to meet its interest obligations because earnings are significantly greater than annual interest obligations. A low ratio indicates that a company may encounter difficulty meeting its obligations. To compute this ratio, we divide operating income by interest expense. Before we can calculate the times-interest-earned ratio for Tucker Enterprises, we must calculate its operating income. If Tucker Enterprises' interest expense was $28,000 and $17,000 in 2014 and 2013 respectively, we can calculate operating income for the two years as follows:

$$\text{Operating income} = \text{Income before income tax} + \text{Interest expense}$$
$$2014 = \$188,000 + \$28,000 = \$216,000$$
$$2013 = \$118,000 + \$17,000 = \$135,000$$

Next, we can calculate the times-interest-earned ratios as follows:

		2014		2013	
Times-interest-earned ratio $= \dfrac{\text{Operating income}}{\text{Interest expense}} =$		$\dfrac{\$216,000}{\$28,000} =$	7.7 times	$\dfrac{\$135,000}{\$17,000} =$	7.9 times

Tucker Enterprises' times-interest-earned ratio has declined slightly from 7.9 in 2013 to 7.7 in 2014. However, the norm, as reported by The Risk Management Association, falls in the range of 2.0 to 3.0. So, it appears that Tucker Enterprises will have little difficulty servicing its debt in the future.

DECISION GUIDELINES

Decision	**Guideline**	**Analyze**
As an entrepreneur, the long-term health of my company revolves around making my debt payments. Will my business be able to service (pay off) its long-term debt?	Utilize solvency ratios: • Debt ratio • Times-interest-earned	Monitoring a company's solvency ratios can provide an indicator that the company may have difficulty servicing its long-term debt. In addition to creditors, a company's shareholders should pay attention to the solvency ratios. If a company is unable to pay back its creditors, there will be no value left in the company for the shareholders.

Now let's look at how the profitability of a business can be evaluated. We will examine four profitability ratios.

Profitability Ratios
Rate of Return on Net Sales

The **rate of return on net sales**, or simply **return on sales**, shows the portion of each dollar of net sales that a firm is able to turn into income. Tucker Enterprises' rate of return on sales is calculated as follows:

		2014		2013	
Rate of return on sales $= \dfrac{\text{Net income}}{\text{Net sales}} =$		$\dfrac{\$155,000}{\$824,000} = 18.8\%$		$\dfrac{\$97,000}{\$596,000} = 16.3\%$	

Companies strive for a high rate of return on sales. The higher the rate of return, the more sales dollars end up as profit. The increase in Tucker Enterprises' return on sales from 16.3% in 2013 to 18.8% in 2014 is a good sign.

Rate of Return on Total Assets

The **rate of return on total assets**, or simply **return on assets**, measures a company's effectiveness in using assets to generate earnings. In other words, it gives investors an idea of how well the company is converting its assets into income. The assets of a company are financed by both debt and equity. The creditors have loaned money to the company and they earn interest. The shareholders have invested in shares and their return is net income. Therefore, the sum of interest expense and net income is added together when calculating the return to the two groups. The sum of these amounts is then divided by the average total assets to determine the return on assets. Average total assets is calculated by adding the beginning and ending total assets for the year together and dividing by two. Tucker Enterprises' return on assets for 2014 and 2013 is calculated as follows:

$$\text{Rate of return on total assets} = \frac{\text{Net income} + \text{Interest expense}}{\text{Average total assets}} = \begin{array}{c} \mathbf{2014} \\ \dfrac{\$155{,}000 + \$28{,}000}{(\$394{,}000 + \$560{,}000)/2} = 38.4\% \\ \mathbf{2013} \\ = \dfrac{\$97{,}000 + \$17{,}000}{(\$318{,}000^* + \$394{,}000)/2} = 32.0\% \end{array}$$

*2012 Total Assets is $318,000.

Remember from our discussion of the times-interest-earned ratio that Tucker Enterprises' interest expense was $28,000 and $17,000 in 2014 and 2013 respectively. Investors would like Tucker Enterprises' return on assets for both years as they generally look for a return on assets that is high and growing.

Rate of Return on Common Shareholders' Equity

The **rate of return on common shareholders' equity**, often shortened to **return on common equity**, is another popular measure of profitability. The return on common equity shows the amount of net income returned as a percentage of common shareholders' equity.

To compute this ratio, we first subtract preferred dividends from net income to get net income available to the common shareholders. Because Tucker Enterprises has no preferred shares issued, preferred dividends are zero. The net income available to common shareholders is then divided by average common equity during the year. Common equity is total shareholders' equity minus preferred shareholders' equity. Average equity is the average of the beginning and ending balances.

The 2013 and 2014 rate of return on common shareholders' equity for Tucker Enterprises follows:

$$\begin{array}{c} \text{Rate of return on common} \\ \text{shareholders' equity} \end{array} = \frac{\text{Net income} - \text{Preferred dividends}}{\text{Average common shareholders' equity}} = \begin{array}{c} \mathbf{2014} \\ \dfrac{\$155{,}000 - \$0}{(\$183{,}000 + \$242{,}000)/2} = 72.9\% \\ \mathbf{2013} \\ = \dfrac{\$97{,}000 - \$0}{(\$165{,}000^* + \$183{,}000)/2} = 55.7\% \end{array}$$

*2012 Total common shareholders' equity is $165,000.

As we can see, the return on equity was higher than 50% for both years, which is exceptional. The significant increase from 2013 to 2014 is sure to make the shareholders happy.

Earnings per Share of Common Shares

Perhaps the most widely quoted of all financial statistics is **earnings per share of common shares**, or simply *earnings per share* (EPS). EPS is the only ratio that is required to be shown on the income statement. EPS is the amount of net income earned for each of the company's outstanding common shares.

Earnings per share is computed by dividing net income available to common shareholders by the number of common shares outstanding during the year. As with return on equity, preferred dividends are subtracted from net income because the preferred share-holders have a prior claim to dividends. Tucker Enterprises has no preferred shares outstanding and, therefore, paid no preferred dividends. To calculate earnings per share, we must know the number of common shares outstanding. Tucker Enterprises had 15,000 common shares outstanding in 2013 and 17,000 shares outstanding in 2014. Tucker Enterprises' earnings per share is calculated as follows:

$$\text{Earnings per common share} = \frac{\text{Net income} - \text{Preferred dividends}}{\text{Number of common shares outstanding}}$$

2014
$$\frac{\$155,000 - \$0}{17,000} = \$9.12$$

2013
$$\frac{\$97,000 - \$0}{15,000} = \$6.47$$

Tucker Enterprises' EPS increased by \$2.65 from 2013 to 2014. This represents a 41% increase in the EPS. This is a good sign for Tucker Enterprises' shareholders; however, they should not expect this much increase in EPS every year. Most companies strive to increase EPS by 10% to 15% annually, and leading companies do so. But even the most successful companies have an occasional bad year.

DuPont Analysis

The financial ratios show the company's performance; however, they may not pinpoint where the problems are. For example, if the company shows a low rate of return on total assets, it would be difficult to know whether the problem lies with a low return, which is related to operations, or lies with the total assets, which is related to asset management. In the 1920s, DuPont Corporation started using the decomposed formula of the return on assets (ROA) ratio to help analyze performance so that management could improve results. **Exhibit 12-10** shows the decomposed formula:

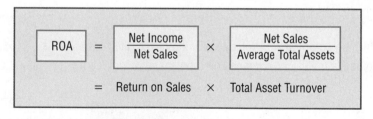

Exhibit 12-10 ▲

Companies can achieve a higher return on assets (ROA) by increasing the net income through better management of costs, or decreasing the average total assets through eliminating non-productive assets.

CRITICAL THINKING

Take a minute to think about the following case, using the DuPont analysis to help you analyze the case:

• BJ Enterprises just finished its second year of operations. The CEO of the company is pleased with the profit margin or return on sales, as it had a slightly better performance than its competitor. The asset management ratios, in particular related to the working capital accounts, also showed the company was doing a fair job in managing its current assets. However, the CEO was disappointed by the low return on assets. What would you recommend the company to investigate? What would you recommend the company do to improve the return on assets?

Solution:

Return on Assets can be examined in two parts: (1) return on sales (or profit margin), and (2) total asset turnover. If the return on sales does not show a problem, then the problem must reside with the total asset turnover. However, BJ was able to manage its current assets well; therefore, the only possible problem is related to long-term assets. This may mean that BJ has a lot of non-productive fixed assets, and was not able to effectively utilize these fixed assets to generate a sales level that met the desired return on assets.

DECISION GUIDELINES

Decision	**Guideline**	**Analyze**
As an investor, how do I assess the profitability of a company that I'm interested in?	Utilize profitability ratios: • Return on sales • Return on assets • Return on common equity • Earnings per share	The profitability of a business over the long run is critical to the survival of the business. By monitoring the profitability ratios, potential problems can be detected early and steps can be taken to prevent business failure. Many companies that have failed have shown warning signs well in advance of the company's collapse.

Market Analysis Ratios

Investors purchase shares with the hope of earning a return on their investments. There are two ways that investors earn returns on their shares. They have gains (or losses) from selling shares at prices above or below what they paid for them. They also may receive distributions of cash in the form of dividends from the company. The following tools are used to help people evaluate share investments.

Price/Earnings Ratio

The **price/earnings ratio** is the ratio of the market price of a common share to the company's earnings per share. This ratio, abbreviated P/E, shows how much investors are willing to pay per dollar of earnings. The market prices of common shares for publicly traded companies can be found in *The Globe and Mail*, or online from sources such as www.tmx.com. The market price of Tucker Enterprises' common shares was $67 at the end of 2014 and $44 at the end of 2013. Tucker Enterprises' P/E ratios for 2014 and 2013 are calculated as follows.

$$\text{Price/earnings ratio} = \frac{\text{Market price per share}}{\text{Earnings per share}}$$

	2014	2013
	$\dfrac{\$67.00}{\$9.12} = 7.35$	$\dfrac{\$44.00}{\$6.47} = 6.80$

Tucker Enterprises' P/E ratio increased slightly from 2013 to 2014. This indicates that investors are willing to pay more for $1 of earnings in 2014 than in 2013.

Dividend Yield

The ratio of dividends per share to a share's market price per share is called the **dividend yield**. This ratio measures the percentage of a share's market value that is returned annually as dividends. Dividend yield may be calculated on common shares, preferred shares, or both, depending on what type of shares a company issues. Because *preferred* shareholders invest primarily to receive dividends, they should pay special attention to dividend yield.

Tucker Enterprises paid annual cash dividends on common shares of $3.50 per share in 2014 and $2.25 in 2013. Remember, Tucker Enterprises has no preferred shares. As noted previously, market prices of the company's common shares were $67 in 2014 and $44 in 2013. Tucker's dividend yield on common shares for 2014 and 2013 is calculated next.

$$\text{Dividend yield} = \frac{\text{Dividend per share}}{\text{Market price per share}}$$

	2014	2013
	$\dfrac{\$3.50}{\$67.00} = 5.2\%$	$\dfrac{\$2.25}{\$44.00} = 5.1\%$

Based on the dividend yield, investors who buy Tucker Enterprises' common shares can expect to receive about 5% of their investment in the form of cash dividends.

Red Flags in Financial Statement Analysis

As stated earlier in the chapter, financial statement analysis usually will not indicate that a problem definitely exists with a company. Also, even if a problem does exist, financial statement analysis generally will not identify what the specific problem is. Instead, financial statement analysis generates *red flags* that may signal financial trouble. Recent accounting scandals highlight the importance of these red flags. The following conditions may be cause for concern.

- **Decreased Cash Flow.** Cash flow validates net income. Is cash flow from operations consistently lower than net income? If so, the company is in trouble. Are the sales of plant assets a major source of cash? If so, the company may face a cash shortage.

- **Inability to Collect Receivables.** Are days' sales in receivables growing faster than for competitors? A cash shortage may be looming.

- **Buildup of Inventories.** Is inventory turnover too slow? If so, the company may have obsolete inventory, or it may be overstating inventory.

- **Movement of Sales, Inventory, and Receivables.** Sales, receivables, and inventory generally move together. Increased sales lead to higher receivables and require more inventory to meet demand. Unexpected or inconsistent movements among sales, inventory, and receivables make the financial statements look suspect.

- **Earnings Problems.** Has net income decreased significantly for several years in a row? Has income turned into a loss? Most companies cannot survive consecutive losses year after year.

- **Too Much Debt.** How does the company's debt ratio compare to that of major competitors? If the debt ratio is too high, the company may be unable to pay its debts.

Based on our financial statement analysis of Tucker Enterprises, the company appears to be in a strong financial condition. The only area of concern could be the company's cash position. Tucker Enterprises should monitor its cash position to ensure that it does not encounter any cash flow problems in the future.

Exhibit 12-11, on the next page, summarizes the ratios we have learned in this chapter.

DEMO DOC

Horizontal and Vertical Analysis

Cassidy, Inc. has the following information for 2014 and 2013:

MyAccountingLab

Visit MyAccountingLab at **www. myaccountinglab.com** to watch animated versions of these Demo Docs.

L.O.

			2014	2013
		Cassidy, Inc. **Income Statement** Years Ended December 31, 2014 and 2013		
	Sales Revenue		$550,000	$600,000
	Cost of Goods Sold		320,000	350,000
	Gross Profit		230,000	250,000
	Salary Expense		165,000	158,000
	Depreciation Expense		21,000	16,000
	Insurance Expense		19,000	23,000
	Income from Operations		25,000	53,000
	Gain on Sale of Furniture		3,000	0
	Net Income		$ 28,000	$ 53,000

Cassidy, Inc.
Balance Sheet
December 31, 2014 and 2013

ASSETS	2014	2013	LIABILITIES	2014	2013
Current:			Current:		
Cash	$ 28,000	$ 33,000	Accounts Payable	$ 20,000	$ 23,000
Accounts Receivable	26,000	15,000	Salary Payable	10,000	8,000
Prepaid Insurance	30,000	42,000	Total Current Liabilities	30,000	31,000
Total Current Assets	84,000	90,000	Notes Payable	40,000	50,000
Furniture, Net	90,000	74,500			
			SHAREHOLDERS' EQUITY		
			Common Shares	4,000	3,500
			Retained Earnings	100,000	80,000
			Total Liabilities and		
Total Assets	$174,000	$164,500	Shareholders' Equity	$174,000	$164,500

Liquidity Ratios	To measure a company's ability to meet short-term obligations with current assets.
Working Capital	Current assets − Current liabilities
Current Ratio	$\dfrac{\text{Current assets}}{\text{Current liabilities}}$
Acid-test (Quick) Ratio	$\dfrac{\text{Cash} + \text{Short-term investments} + \text{Net current receivables}}{\text{Current liabilities}}$
Asset Management Ratios	To measure how efficiently a company utilizes its operating assets.
Inventory Turnover	$\dfrac{\text{Cost of goods sold}}{\text{Average inventory}}$
Days' Sales in Inventory	$\dfrac{365}{\text{Inventory turnover ratio}}$
Accounts Receivable Turnover	$\dfrac{\text{Net credit sales}}{\text{Average net accounts receivable}}$
Days' Sales in Receivable	$\dfrac{365}{\text{Accounts receivable turnover ratio}}$
Fixed Asset Turnover	$\dfrac{\text{Net sales}}{\text{Average net fixed assets}}$
Total Asset Turnover	$\dfrac{\text{Net sales}}{\text{Average total assets}}$
Solvency Ratios	To measure a company's ability to meet its long-term obligations or take on more debt.
Debt Ratio	$\dfrac{\text{Total liabilities}}{\text{Total assets}}$
Debt to Equity Ratio	$\dfrac{\text{Total liabilities}}{\text{Total equity}}$
Times-interest-earned Ratio	$\dfrac{\text{Operating income}}{\text{Interest expense}}$
Profitability Ratios	To measure a company's ability to generate profits.
Return on Sales	$\dfrac{\text{Net income}}{\text{Net sales}}$
Return on Assets	$\dfrac{\text{Net income} + \text{Interest expense}}{\text{Average total assets}}$
Return on (Common Shareholder's) Equity	$\dfrac{\text{Net income} - \text{Preferred dividends}}{\text{Average common shareholders' equity}}$
Earnings per (Common) Share	$\dfrac{\text{Net income} - \text{Preferred dividends}}{\text{Number of common shares outstanding}}$
Market Analysis Ratio	To measure company's stock market performance.
Price/Earnings Ratio	$\dfrac{\text{Market price per share}}{\text{Earnings per share}}$
Dividend Yield	$\dfrac{\text{Dividend per share}}{\text{Market price per share}}$

Exhibit 12-11 ▲

Requirements:

❶ Prepare a horizontal analysis of Cassidy's income statement and balance sheet for 2014.

❷ Prepare a vertical analysis of Cassidy's income statement and balance sheet for 2014.

Demo Doc Solutions

Requirement ❶

Prepare a horizontal analysis of Cassidy's income statement and balance sheet for 2014.

Part 1	Part 2	Demo Doc Complete

Horizontal analysis goes across the rows of each financial statement, looking at one account and how it has changed from the prior year.

To prepare a horizontal analysis, we need to calculate the dollar amount of change and the percentage change for every number on the income statement and balance sheet.

> Dollar amount of change = This year's amount (balance) − Last year's amount (balance)

For example, the dollar amount of change for Sales Revenue and Accounts Receivable would be as follows:

> Sales Revenue = $550,000 − $600,000 = $(50,000) Change
> Accounts Receivable = $26,000 − $15,000 = $11,000 Change

Notice that the parentheses around the change in Sales Revenue indicate that it decreased, whereas the positive value of the change in the amount of Accounts Receivable indicates that it increased.

Expenses are assumed to be negative numbers on the income statement, in that they are subtracted to calculate net income. However, we use the absolute value of the expenses (ignoring the fact that they are already negative numbers) to calculate the dollar amount of change. So the dollar amount of change of Depreciation Expense and Insurance Expense would be as follows:

> Depreciation Expense = $21,000 − $16,000 = $5,000 Change
> Insurance Expense = $19,000 − $23,000 = $(4,000) Change

The positive amount of change indicates that Depreciation Expense increased and the negative amount of change indicates that Insurance Expense decreased.

$$\text{Percentage change} = \frac{\text{Dollar amount of change}}{\text{Base-year amount}}$$

The base-year amount is last year's amount (balance).

Using this formula, the percentage changes in Sales Revenue and Accounts Receivable would be as follows:

$$\text{Percentage Change in Sales Revenue} = \frac{\$(50,000)}{\$600,000}$$
$$= (8.3)\% \text{ Change}$$

$$\text{Percentage Change in Accounts Receivable} = \frac{\$11,000}{\$15,000}$$
$$= 73.3\% \text{ Change}$$

Notice that the percentage change numbers are negative for Sales Revenue (which had a dollar amount decrease for 2014) and positive for Accounts Receivable (which had a dollar amount increase for 2014).

The percentage changes of Depreciation Expense and Insurance Expense would be as follows:

$$\text{Percentage Change in Depreciation Expense} = \frac{\$5,000}{\$16,000}$$
$$= 31.3\% \text{ Change}$$

$$\text{Percentage Change in Insurance Expense} = \frac{\$(4,000)}{\$23,000}$$
$$= (17.4)\% \text{ Change}$$

If an account did not exist in the prior year (such as the Gain on Sale of Furniture in this example), then horizontal analysis is irrelevant and a percentage change cannot be calculated. Extending these calculations to all of the accounts on the income statement and balance sheet appear as follows:

| | | | | | INCREASE (DECREASE) | |
			2014	2013	AMOUNT	PERCENTAGE
		Sales Revenue	$550,000	$600,000	$(50,000)	(8.3)%
		Cost of Goods Sold	320,000	350,000	(30,000)	(8.6)%
		Gross Profit	230,000	250,000	(20,000)	(8.0)%
		Salary Expense	165,000	158,000	7,000	4.4 %
		Depreciation Expense	21,000	16,000	5,000	31.3 %
		Insurance Expense	19,000	23,000	(4,000)	(17.4)%
		Income from Operations	25,000	53,000	(28,000)	(52.8)%
		Gain on Sale of Furniture	3,000	0	3,000	—
		Net Income	$ 28,000	$ 53,000	$(25,000)	(47.2)%

Cassidy, Inc.
Income Statement
Years Ended December 31, 2014 and 2013

			2014	2013	INCREASE (DECREASE)	
					AMOUNT	PERCENTAGE
	ASSETS					
	Current:					
		Cash	$ 28,000	$ 33,000	$ (5,000)	(15.2)%
		Accounts Receivable	26,000	15,000	11,000	73.3 %
		Prepaid Insurance	30,000	42,000	(12,000)	(28.6)%
		Total Current Assets	84,000	90,000	(6,000)	(6.7)%
	Furniture, Net		90,000	74,500	15,500	20.8 %
	Total Assets		$174,000	$164,500	9,500	5.8 %
	LIABILITIES					
	Current:					
		Accounts Payable	$ 20,000	$ 23,000	$ (3,000)	(13.0)%
		Salary Payable	10,000	8,000	2,000	25.0 %
		Total Current Liabilities	30,000	31,000	(1,000)	(3.2)%
	Notes Payable		40,000	50,000	(10,000)	(20.0)%
	Total Liabilities		70,000	81,000	(11,000)	(13.6)%
	SHAREHOLDERS' EQUITY					
	Common Shares		4,000	3,500	500	14.3 %
	Retained Earnings		100,000	80,000	20,000	25.0 %
	Total Shareholders' Equity		104,000	83,500	20,500	24.6 %
	Total Liabilities and					
	Shareholders' Equity		$174,000	$164,500	$ 9,500	5.8 %

Table title (above): **Cassidy, Inc. / Balance Sheet / December 31, 2014 and 2013**

Requirement ❷

Prepare a vertical analysis of Cassidy's balance sheet and income statement for 2014.

Part 1	**Part 2**	Demo Doc Complete

Vertical analysis compares every number on a financial statement to all others in the same year (that is, down the columns of the financial statements).

To prepare a vertical analysis, we need to calculate the vertical analysis percentage for each account.

Income Statement

On the income statement, each number is calculated as a percentage of net sales revenues.

$$\text{Vertical analysis \% (Income statement)} = \frac{\text{Income statement amount}}{\text{Net sales revenue}}$$

So in the case of Gross Profit, it is as follows:

$$\text{Vertical analysis \% (2014 Gross Profit)} = \frac{\$230,000}{\$550,000}$$
$$= 41.8\%$$

This figure means that $0.418 of gross profit resulted from every dollar of sales revenue.

The calculation is the same for expenses. The vertical analysis percentages for Depreciation Expense and Insurance Expense would be as follows:

$$\text{Vertical analysis \% (2014 Depreciation Expense)} = \frac{\$21,000}{\$550,000}$$
$$= 3.8\%$$

$$\text{Vertical analysis \% (2014 Insurance Expense)} = \frac{\$19,000}{\$550,000}$$
$$= 3.5\%$$

Balance Sheet

On the balance sheet, each number, whether it be for an asset, a liability, or an equity account, is calculated as a percentage of total assets.

$$\text{Vertical analysis \% (Balance Sheet)} = \frac{\text{Balance sheet amount}}{\text{Total assets}}$$

So in the case of Accounts Receivable, we have the following:

$$\text{Vertical analysis \% (2014 Accounts Receivable)} = \frac{\$26,000}{\$174,000}$$
$$= 14.9\%$$

In other words, approximately 15% of all the assets are Accounts Receivable.

Extending these calculations to all of the accounts on the income statement and balance sheet gives us the following:

Cassidy, Inc.
Income Statement
Years Ended December 31, 2014 and 2013

	2014		2013	
	AMOUNT	PERCENTAGE	AMOUNT	PERCENTAGE
Sales Revenue	$550,000	100.0%	$600,000	100.0%
Cost of Goods Sold	320,000	58.2%	350,000	58.3%
Gross Profit	230,000	41.8%	250,000	41.7%
Salary Expense	165,000	30.0%	158,000	26.3%
Depreciation Expense	21,000	3.8%	16,000	2.7%
Insurance Expense	19,000	3.5%	23,000	3.8%
Income from Operations	25,000	4.5%	53,000	8.8%
Gain on Sale of Furniture	3,000	0.5%	0	0.0%
Net Income	$ 28,000	5.1%	$ 53,000	8.8%

Cassidy, Inc.
Balance Sheet
December 31, 2014 and 2013

	2014		2013	
	AMOUNT	PERCENTAGE	AMOUNT	PERCENTAGE
Assets				
Current:				
Cash	$ 28,000	16.1%	$ 33,000	20.1%
Accounts Receivable	26,000	14.9%	15,000	9.1%
Prepaid Insurance	30,000	17.2%	42,000	25.5%
Total Current Assets	84,000	48.3%	90,000	54.7%
Furniture, Net	90,000	51.7%	74,500	45.3%
Total Assets	$174,000	100.0%	$164,500	100.0%
Liabilities				
Current:				
Accounts Payable	$ 20,000	11.5%	$ 23,000	14.0%
Salary Payable	10,000	5.7%	8,000	4.9%
Total Current Liabilities	30,000	17.2%	31,000	18.8%
Notes Payable	40,000	23.0%	50,000	30.4%
Total Liabilities	70,000	40.2%	81,000	49.2%
Shareholders' Equity				
Common Shares	4,000	2.3%	3,500	2.1%
Retained Earnings	100,000	57.5%	80,000	48.6%
Total Shareholders' Equity	104,000	59.8%	83,500	50.8%
Total Liabilities and Shareholders' Equity	$174,000	100.0%	$164,500	100.0%

Demo Doc Complete

Part 1	Part 2	**Demo Doc Complete**

DECISION GUIDELINES

Financial Statement Analysis

The following guidelines can help you determine how best to analyze the financial statements of different companies.

Decision	**Guideline**	**Analyze**
As the CEO, I need to present the performance of the organization to the Board of Directors. I know that we had a bad year, but I also know that we are in a good position compared to our competitors. How do I show this comparison to competitors that are all different sizes?	Utilize common-size financial statements.	Common-size financial statements can be utilized to compare two different companies even if they are of dissimilar sizes. This is because common-size financial statements report financial statement items as percentages instead of as dollar amounts. The percentages for the two companies can be compared to see which company has the highest gross profit percentage and the lowest expense percentages. Common-size financial statements can also be used to compare a company against the best companies in the industry. This is known as benchmarking. A business may not be able to achieve the same results as the industry leader, but benchmarking gives a company a goal to shoot for.
As a supplier, how can I check a customer's ability to pay their obligations as they come due in order to know whether or not to extend them credit?	Utilize liquidity ratios: • Working capital • Current ratio • Quick ratio	Monitoring a business's liquidity ratios can often provide an indicator that the business may experience cash flow problems. Action should be taken so that the business does not encounter difficulty meeting its obligations as they come due. For most businesses, a current ratio that drops below 1.50 or a quick ratio that drops below 0.90 may be cause for concern.
As the manager, how do I determine if the Inventory and Accounts Receivable are being managed effectively?	Utilize asset management ratios: • Inventory turnover • Accounts receivable turnover • Days' sales in receivables	Monitoring the asset management ratios can provide an indicator that a business is not managing its inventory and accounts receivables effectively. An decrease in the inventory turnover may indicate that a business has obsolete inventory or that it is purchasing too much inventory. Carrying high levels of inventory results in decreased profits due to the increased costs associated with maintaining the increased inventory levels. A decrease in the Accounts Receivable turnover may be due to poor collection practices related to past due accounts. This can result in decreased profits for the business due to increased bad debts expense. The longer a receivable is past due, the less likely it is to be collected.
As an entrepreneur, the long-term health of my company revolves around making my debt payments. Will my business be able to service (pay off) its long-term debt?	Utilize solvency ratios: • Debt ratio • Times-interest-earned	Monitoring a company's solvency ratios can provide an indicator that the company may have difficulty servicing its long-term debt. In addition to creditors, a company's shareholders should pay attention to the solvency ratios. If a company is unable to pay back its creditors, there will be no value left in the company for the shareholders.
As an investor, how do I assess the profitability of a company that I'm interested in?	Utilize profitability ratios: • Return on sales • Return on assets • Return on common equity • Earnings per share	The profitability of a business over the long run is critical to the survival of the business. By monitoring the profitability ratios, potential problems can be detected early and steps can be taken to prevent business failure. Many companies that have failed have shown warning signs well in advance of the company's collapse.

ACCOUNTING VOCABULARY
THE LANGUAGE OF BUSINESS

Accounts receivable turnover (p. 716) Measures a company's ability to collect cash from credit customers. To compute accounts receivable turnover, divide net credit sales by average net accounts receivable.

Acid-test ratio (p. 715) Quick assets (cash, short-term investments, and net current receivables) divided by current liabilities. It measures a company's ability to pay its current liabilities if they came due immediately; also called the *quick ratio*.

Benchmarking (p. 713) The practice of comparing a company with other companies that are leaders.

Common-size statement (p. 711) A financial statement that reports only percentages (no dollar amounts).

Current ratio (p. 714) Current assets divided by current liabilities. Measures a business's ability to meet its short-term obligations with its current assets.

Days' sales in inventory (p. 716) Measures a company's ability to turn inventory to sales. To compute the ratio, divide 365 by the inventory turnover.

Days' sales in receivables (p. 717) Measures a company's ability to collect receivables. To compute the ratio, divide 365 by the accounts receivable turnover.

Debt ratio (p. 719) Total liabilities divided by total assets. It measures a business's ability to pay long-term liabilities.

Debt to equity ratio (p. 719) Total liabilities divided by total equity. It measures a business's financial leverage and indicates what proportion of equity and debt the company is using to finance its assets.

Dividend yield (p. 724) Ratio of dividends per share to the share's market price. Tells the percentage of a share's market value that the company returns to shareholders annually as dividends.

Dollar value bias (p. 711) The bias one sees from comparing numbers in absolute (dollars) rather than relative (percentages) terms.

Earnings per share of common shares (p. 721) Reflects the net income earned for each share of the company's outstanding common shares.

Fixed asset turnover ratio (p. 717) Measures a company's ability to generate sales from fixed asset investments, specifically property, plant, and equipment (PPE).

Horizontal analysis (p. 705) Study of dollar amount and percentage changes in comparative financial statements.

Interest-coverage ratio (p. 719) Ratio of income from operations to interest expense. It measures the number of times that

operating income can cover interest expense; also called the *times-interest-earned ratio*.

Inventory turnover (p. 715) Measures the number of times a company sells its average level of inventory during a year.

Price/earnings ratio (p. 723) Ratio of the market price of a common share to the company's earnings per share. It measures the value that the stock market places on $1 of a company's earnings.

Quick ratio (p. 715) Quick assets (cash, short-term investments, and net current receivables) divided by current liabilities. It measures a company's ability to pay its current liabilities if they came due immediately; also called the *acid-test ratio*.

Rate of return on common shareholders' equity (p. 721) Ratio of net income minus preferred dividends to common shareholders' equity. It is a measure of profitability; also called *return on common equity*.

Rate of return on net sales (p. 720) Ratio of net income to net sales. It is a measure of profitability; also called *return on sales*.

Rate of return on total assets (p. 720) Ratio of net income plus interest expense to total assets. It measures a company's effectiveness in using assets to generate earnings; also called *return on assets*.

Ratio analysis (p. 714) A form of financial statement analysis in which items on the financial statements are expressed as ratios of one number to another.

Return on assets (p. 720) Ratio of net income plus interest expense to total assets. It measures a company's effectiveness in using assets to generate earnings; also called *rate of return on total assets*.

Return on common equity (p. 721) Ratio of net income minus preferred dividends to common shareholders' equity. It is a measure of profitability; also called *rate of return on common shareholders' equity*.

Return on sales (p. 720) Ratio of net income to net sales. It is a measure of profitability; also called *rate of return on net sales*.

Times-interest-earned ratio (p. 719) Ratio of income from operations to interest expense. It measures the number of times that operating income can cover interest expense; also called the *interest-coverage ratio*.

Total asset turnover ratio (p. 718) Measures a company's ability to generate sales from its total assets, including current assets, investments, fixed assets, etc.

Trend percentages (p. 708) A form of horizontal analysis in which percentages are computed by selecting a base year and then expressing amounts for following years as a percentage of the base-year amounts.

Vertical analysis (p. 709) Analysis of a financial statement that reveals the relationship of each statement item to a specified base amount, which is the 100% figure.

Working capital (p. 714) Current assets minus current liabilities. It measures a business's ability to meet its short-term obligations with its current assets.

ACCOUNTING PRACTICE

DISCUSSION QUESTIONS

1. How is percentage change calculated?

2. Which amount is the base amount for vertical analysis on the income statement?

3. Which amount is the base amount for vertical analysis on the balance sheet?

4. What is the purpose of common-size financial statements?

5. The Accounting Standards Board (AcSB) and the International Accounting Standards Board have identified the goal of comparability of financial statements as one toward which all companies should strive and consistency as the means toward achieving that goal. How are these characteristics important to horizontal and vertical analysis?

6. What is benchmarking? What should a company that wishes to use benchmarking look for in establishing benchmarks?

7. What are the major goals of each of the following types of ratios:

   a. Liquidity ratios   **b.** Asset management ratios
   c. Solvency ratios   **d.** Profitability ratios
   e. Market analysis ratios

8. How would you expect a recession to affect asset management ratios?

9. What is a "red flag" with respect to financial statement analysis?

10. A company has experienced increases in accounts receivable and inventory turnover ratios and has cash flows from operations that exceed net income. All other things constant, what could you conclude about the company's performance this year relative to last year?

SELF CHECK

1. Net income was $245,000 in 2012, $240,000 in 2013, and $276,000 in 2014. The change from 2013 to 2014 is an

   a. increase of 5%.   **b.** increase of 10%.
   c. increase of 15%.   **d.** increase of 20%.

2. Horizontal analysis of a financial statement shows

   a. the relationship of each statement item to a specified base.
   b. percentage changes in comparative balance sheets.
   c. percentage changes in comparative income statements.
   d. both b and c.

3. A statement that reports only percentages is called

   a. a comparative statement.   **b.** a common-size statement.
   c. a condensed statement.   **d.** a cumulative statement.

4. Working capital is

a. a measure of the ability to meet short-term obligations with current assets.
b. defined as current assets minus current liabilities.
c. defined as current assets divided by current liabilities.
d. both a and b.

5. Cash is $15,000, net accounts receivable amount to $6,000, inventory is $10,000, prepaid expenses total $4,000, and current liabilities are $20,000. What is the quick ratio?

a. 1.05   **b.** 1.55
c. 1.25   **d.** 1.75

6. Days' sales in receivables is computed by

a. dividing net sales by 365.
b. dividing 365 by accounts receivable turnover.
c. dividing sales by average net accounts receivable.
d. dividing accounts receivable turnover ratio by 365.

7. Rubble Company is experiencing a severe cash shortage due to its inability to collect accounts receivable. Which of the following would most likely identify this problem?

a. Current ratio
b. Working capital
c. Accounts receivable turnover
d. Return on sales

8. Which of the following statements is *true* of financial statement analysis?

a. Horizontal analysis expresses all items on a financial statement as percentages of a common base.
b. Vertical analysis involves comparing amounts from one year's financial statements to another year's statements.
c. Ratio analysis is more important than either horizontal or vertical analysis.
d. None of the above

9. Which statement is most likely to be *true*?

a. An increase in inventory turnover indicates that inventory is not selling as quickly as it was.
b. A decrease in inventory turnover indicates that inventory is not selling as quickly as it was.
c. A change in inventory turnover cannot be accurately assessed without considering the change in profit margin.
d. None of the above

10. How are financial ratios used in decision making?

a. They eliminate uncertainty regarding cash flows.
b. They can be used as a substitute for consulting financial statements.
c. They are only used in evaluating business liquidity.
d. They help to identify reasons for business success and failure.

Answers are given after Written Communication.

SHORT EXERCISES

S12-1. Corporate financial statements (*Learning Objective 1*) 5–10 min.

Identify whether each of the following items would be classified as:

■ Income from continuing operations (C)

■ Income from discontinued operations (D)

■ A change in accounting principle (P)

.... a. $2,500 gain on the sale of office furniture.

.... b. $18,000 increase in income as a result of changing from DDB depreciation to straight-line depreciation.

.... c. Income tax expense

.... d. $85,000 loss incurred as a result of closing the Coeur d'Alene, Quebec store location.

.... e. $4,600 loss incurred as a result of a company vehicle being involved in an accident.

S12-2. Horizontal analysis (*Learning Objective 2*) 10–15 min.

Aztec, Inc. had net sales of $250,000 and cost of goods sold of $150,000 in 2012, net sales of $275,000 and cost of goods sold of $165,000 in 2013, and net sales of $300,000 and cost of goods sold of $177,000 in 2014.

1. Find the percentage change in net sales from 2012 to 2013 and from 2013 to 2014.

2. Find the percentage change in gross profit from 2012 to 2013 and from 2013 to 2014.

S12-3. Vertical analysis (*Learning Objective 3*) 10–15 min.

The 2014 accounting records of Star Records showed the following: Cash, $15,000; Net Accounts Receivable, $8,000; Inventory, $5,000; Prepaid Expenses, $4,000; Net Plant and Equipment, $18,000.

Construct a vertical analysis of the asset section of Star Records' balance sheet for 2014.

S12-4. Ratio definitions (*Learning Objective 5*) 10–15 min.

Match the following terms to their definitions:

.... 1. Tells whether a company can pay all its current liabilities if they become due immediately

.... 2. Measures a company's success in using assets to earn income

.... 3. The practice of comparing a company with other companies that are leaders

.... 4. Indicates how rapidly inventory is sold

.... 5. Shows the proportion of a company's assets that is financed with debt

.... 6. Tells the percentage of a share's market value that the company returns to shareholders annually as dividends

.... 7. A measure of profitability

.... 8. Measures a company's ability to collect cash from credit customers

a. Inventory turnover

b. Return on sales

c. Quick ratio

d. Dividend yield

e. Return on assets

f. Accounts receivable turnover

g. Benchmarking

h. Debt ratio

S12-5. Purpose of select ratios (*Learning Objective 5*) 10–15 min.

Identify each of the following financial ratios as follows:

■ Profitability ratio (P)

■ Asset management ratio (A)

■ Liquidity ratio (L)

■ Solvency ratio (S)

.... a. Inventory turnover

.... b. Debt ratio

.... c. Return on equity

.... d. Days' sales in receivables

.... e. Quick ratio

.... f. Return on assets

.... g. Return on sales

.... h. Receivables turnover

.... i. Current ratio

.... j. Earnings per share

.... k. Times-interest-earned ratio

S12-6. Accounts receivable turnover, days' sales in accounts receivable, and inventory turnover (*Learning Objective 5*) 10–15 min.

The 2013 and 2014 balance sheets for Jackson and Sons showed net accounts receivable of $10,000 and $14,000, respectively, and inventory of $8,000 and $6,000, respectively. The company's 2014 income statement showed net sales of $109,500 and cost of goods sold of $70,000. Compute the following ratios for 2014:

1. Accounts receivable turnover

2. Days' sales in receivables

3. Inventory turnover

S12-7. Current ratio and quick ratio (*Learning Objective 5*) 10–15 min.

In addition to the information from S12-6, assume that cash on the 2014 balance sheet was $20,000 and current liabilities totaled $24,000. Compute the following ratios for 2014:

1. Current ratio

2. Quick ratio

S12-8. Return on sales, return on assets, return on common equity, times-interest-earned ratio, and debt ratio (*Learning Objective 5*) 10–15 min.

The 2014 financial statements for Country Cousin Stores show total assets of $490,000, total liabilities of $290,000, net sales of $1,800,000, net income of $450,000, income from operations of $520,000, cost of goods sold of $1,080,000, preferred dividends of $225,000, and interest expense of $20,000. Total assets and total liabilities for 2013 were $430,000 and $270,000, respectively. Preferred equity for both years is $35,000. Compute the following ratios for 2014:

1. Return on sales

2. Return on assets

3. Return on common equity

4. Times-interest-earned ratio

5. Debt ratio

S12-9. EPS and price/earnings ratio (*Learning Objective 5*) 10–15 min.

Using the information from S12-8, a market price of $25 per common share, and 100,000 common shares outstanding, compute the following for 2014:

1. Earnings per share

2. Price/earnings ratio

S12-10. Dividend yield (*Learning Objective 5*) 10–15 min.

In 2014, common shareholders received $2 per share in annual dividends. The market price per share for common shares was $12. Compute the dividend yield for common shares.

EXERCISES (GROUP A)

E12-1A. Horizontal analysis (*Learning Objective 2*) 15–20 min.

What were the dollar and percentage changes in Axel's Pawn Shop's working capital during 2013 and 2014? Is this trend favourable or unfavourable?

	2014	2013	2012
Total Current Assets	$410,000	$380,000	$360,000
Total Current Liabilities	250,000	217,000	240,000

E12-2A. Horizontal analysis (*Learning Objective 2*) 15–20 min.

Prepare a horizontal analysis of the following comparative income statement of R. Hanson, Inc. Round percentage changes to the nearest tenth of a percent.

R. Hanson, Inc. Comparative Income Statement Years Ended December 31, 2014 and 2013		
	2014	2013
Revenue	$492,000	$447,600
Expenses:		
Cost of Goods Sold	242,000	226,000
Selling and General Expenses	117,600	111,600
Interest Expense	8,000	5,000
Income Tax Expense	50,500	44,600
Total Expenses	418,100	387,200
Net Income	$ 73,900	$ 60,400

Requirement

1. Why did net income increase by a higher percent than total revenues increased during 2014?

E12-3A. Horizontal analysis (*Learning Objective 2*) 15–20 min.

Compute trend percentages for net sales and net income for the following five-year period, using year 1 as the base year:

	Year 5	Year 4	Year 3	Year 2	Year 1
Net Sales.................	$2,405	$2,185	$2,125	$2,005	$2,045
Net Income	717	714	683	671	685

Requirement

1. Which grew faster during the period, net sales or net income?

E12-4A. Vertical analysis (*Learning Objective 3*) 15–20 min.

Lori's Boutique requested that you perform a vertical analysis of its balance sheet to determine the component percentages of its assets, liabilities, and shareholders' equity. Round to the nearest tenth of a percent.

Lori's Boutique Balance Sheet December 31, 2014			
ASSETS		**LIABILITIES**	
Current Assets	$108,000	Current Liabilities	$ 87,000
Long-Term Investments	52,500	Long-Term Debt	177,000
Property, Plant, and		Total Liabilities	264,000
Equipment, Net	325,500		
		SHAREHOLDERS' EQUITY	
		Shareholders' Equity	222,000
		Liabilities and	
Total Assets	$486,000	Shareholders' Equity	$486,000

E12-5A. Common-size income statement (*Learning Objective 4*) 15–20 min.

Prepare a comparative common-size income statement for R. Hanson, Inc. using the 2014 and 2013 data of E12-2A. Round percentages to the nearest tenth of a percont.

E12-6A. Current ratio, quick ratio, inventory turnover, accounts receivable turnover, and days' sales in accounts receivable (*Learning Objective 5*) 15–20 min.

The financial statements of Hernandez & Sons, Inc. include the following items:

	Current Year	Previous Year
Balance Sheet		
Cash	$ 27,000	$ 33,000
Short-Term Investments	22,000	28,000
Accounts Receivable, Net	54,000	72,000
Inventory	65,000	42,000
Prepaid Expenses	7,000	9,000
Total Current Assets	175,000	184,000
Total Current Liabilities	87,500	92,000
Income Statement		
Net Credit Sales	$554,800	
Cost of Goods Sold	331,700	

Requirement

1. Compute the following ratios for the current year: (a) current ratio, (b) quick ratio, (c) inventory turnover, (d) accounts receivable turnover, and (e) days' sales in accounts receivable.

E12-7A. Current ratio, quick ratio, debt ratio, times-interest-earned ratio (*Learning Objective 5*) 15–20 min.

Brandy Pitts Winery requested that you determine whether the company's ability to pay its current liabilities and long-term debts improved or deteriorated during 2014. To answer this question, compute the following ratios for 2014 and 2013: (a) current ratio, (b) quick ratio, (c) debt ratio, and (d) times-interest-earned ratio. Summarize the results of your analysis.

	2014	2013
Cash	$ 32,000	$ 45,000
Short-Term Investments	35,000	–
Accounts Receivable, Net	130,000	142,000
Inventory	340,000	360,000
Prepaid Expenses	15,000	12,000
Total Assets	580,000	560,000
Total Current Liabilities	220,800	245,600
Long-Term Liabilities	24,200	29,400
Income From Operations	185,000	179,000
Interest Expense	42,000	44,000

E12-8A. Financial statement analysis (*Learning Objective 5*) 15–20 min.

For 2013 and 2014, compute the four ratios that measure the ability to earn profits for Fabulous Fashions, Inc., whose comparative income statement follows:

Fabulous Fashions, Inc. Income Statement Years Ended December 31, 2014 and 2013			
		2014	2013
	Net Sales	$261,000	$237,000
	Cost of Goods Sold	140,000	132,000
	Gross Profit	121,000	105,000
	Selling and General Expenses	72,000	65,000
	Income From Operations	49,000	40,000
	Interest Expense	32,000	15,000
	Income Before Income Tax	17,000	25,000
	Income Tax Expense	5,000	8,000
	Net Income	$ 12,000	$ 17,000

Additional data follow:

	2014	2013	2012
Total Assets	$320,000	$292,000	$282,000
Common Shareholders' Equity	$148,000	$140,000	$132,000
Preferred Dividends	$ 4,000	$ 4,000	
Number of Common Shares Outstanding	25,000	25,000	

Requirement

1. Did the company's operating performance improve or deteriorate during 2014?

E12-9A. Financial statement analysis (*Learning Objective 5*) 15–20 min.

Evaluate the common shares of TomCat Incorporated as an investment. Specifically, use the two market analysis ratios to determine whether the shares increased or decreased in attractiveness during the past year. Assume that TomCat Incorporated paid the full amount of preferred dividends.

	2014	2013
Net Income	$ 87,000	$ 83,000
Total Dividends	48,000	48,000
Common Shareholders' Equity at Year-End (100,000 shares)	780,000	750,000
Preferred Shareholders' Equity, 6%, at Year-End (3,000 shares)	300,000	300,000
Market Price of Common Shares at Year-End	$ 15.18	$ 11.63

Quick solution:

Price/earnings ratio = 22 in 2014 and 17.9 in 2013; Dividend yield = 2.0% in 2014 and 2.6% in 2013

E12-10A. Complete financial statement given certain information (*Learning Objective 5*) 15–20 min.

The following data (dollar amounts in millions) are adapted from the financial statements of Valco, Inc.:

Total Current Assets	$12,201
Accumulated Depreciation	1,738
Total Liabilities	14,755
Preferred Shares	10
Debt Ratio	55.145%
Current Ratio	2.1

Requirement

1. Complete the following condensed balance sheet. Report amounts rounded to the nearest $1 million:

Current Assets		$?
Property, Plant, and Equipment	$?	
Less: Accumulated Depreciation	(?)	?
Total Assets		$?
Current Liabilities		$?
Long-Term Liabilities		?
Shareholders' Equity		?
Total Liabilities and Shareholders' Equity		$?

EXERCISES (GROUP B)

E12-1B. Horizontal analysis (*Learning Objective 2*) 15–20 min.

What were the dollar and percentage changes in Hillary's Hair Salon's working capital during 2013 and 2014? Is this trend favourable or unfavourable?

	2014	2013	2012
Total Current Assets	$600,000	$320,000	$270,000
Total Current Liabilities	479,000	232,000	190,000

E12-2B. Horizontal analysis (*Learning Objective 2*) 15–20 min.

Prepare a horizontal analysis of the following comparative income statement of Zinkowski, Inc. Round percentage changes to the nearest tenth of a percent.

	2014	2013
Zinkowski, Inc. Comparative Income Statement Years Ended December 31, 2014 and 2013		
Revenue	$480,000	$411,100
Expenses:		
Cost of Goods Sold	$254,000	$226,000
Selling and General Expenses	110,000	105,500
Interest Expense	6,500	2,000
Income Tax Expense	46,600	45,000
Total Expenses	417,100	378,500
Net Income	$ 62,900	$ 32,600

Requirement

1. Why did net income increase by a higher percent than total revenues increased during 2014?

E12-3B. Horizontal analysis (*Learning Objective 2*) 15–20 min.

Compute trend percentages for net sales and net income for the following five-year period, using year 1 as the base year:

	Year 5	Year 4	Year 3	Year 2	Year 1
Net Sales..................	$2,332	$2,310	$2,266	$2,244	$2,200
Net Income	755	717	659	640	640

Requirement

1. Which grew faster during the period, net sales or net income?

E12-4B. Vertical analysis (*Learning Objective 3*) 15–20 min.

Mary's Gift Store requested that you perform a vertical analysis of its balance sheet to determine the component percentages of its assets, liabilities, and shareholders' equity. Round to the nearest tenth of a percent.

Mary's Gift Store Balance Sheet December 31, 2014			
ASSETS		**LIABILITIES**	
Total Current Assets	$192,000	Total Current Liabilities	$120,000
Long-Term Investments	38,500	Long-Term Debt	155,000
Property, Plant, and		Total Liabilities	275,000
Equipment, Net	330,500		
		SHAREHOLDERS' EQUITY	
		Total Shareholders' Equity	286,000
		Total Liabilities and	
Total Assets	$561,000	Shareholders' Equity	$561,000

E12-5B. Common-size income statement (*Learning Objective 4*) 15–20 min.

Prepare a comparative common-size income statement for Zinkowski, Inc. using the 2014 and 2013 data of E12-2B. Round percentages to the nearest tenth of a percent.

E12-6B. Current ratio, quick ratio, inventory turnover, accounts receivable turnover, and days' sales in accounts receivable (*Learning Objective 5*) 15–20 min.

The financial statements of Vacation, Inc. include the following items:

	Current Year	Previous Year
Balance Sheet		
Cash	$ 25,000	$ 37,000
Short-Term Investments	10,000	24,000
Accounts Receivable, Net	64,000	86,000
Inventory	80,000	47,000
Prepaid Expenses	4,000	16,000
Total Current Assets	183,000	210,000
Total Current Liabilities	95,000	90,000
Income Statement		
Net Credit Sales	$475,000	
Cost of Goods Sold	325,500	

Requirement

1. Compute the following ratios for the current year: (a) current ratio, (b) quick ratio, (c) inventory turnover, (d) accounts receivable turnover, and (e) days' sales in accounts receivable.

E12-7B. Current ratio, quick ratio, debt ratio, times-interest-earned ratio (*Learning Objective 5*) 15–20 min.

Hudson Crowe Winery requested that you determine whether the company's ability to pay its current liabilities and long-term debts improved or deteriorated during 2014. To answer this question, compute the following ratios for 2014 and 2013: (a) current ratio, (b) quick ratio, (c) debt ratio, and (d) times-interest-earned ratio. Summarize the results of your analysis.

	2014	2013
Cash	$ 41,000	$ 49,000
Short-Term Investments	50,000	—
Accounts Receivable, Net	90,000	156,000
Inventory	320,000	395,000
Total Assets	570,000	650,000
Total Current Liabilities	250,000	244,700
Long-Term Liabilities	30,200	32,000
Income From Operations	145,000	203,000
Interest Expense	46,000	40,000

E12-8B. Financial statement analysis (*Learning Objective 5*) 15–20 min.

For 2013 and 2014, compute the four ratios that measure the ability to earn profits for Waldorf Fashions, Inc. whose comparative income statement and additional data follow:

Waldorf Fashions, Inc. Income Statement Years Ended December 31, 2014 and 2013		
	2014	**2013**
Net Sales	$320,000	$298,000
Cost of Goods Sold	134,000	139,000
Gross Profit	186,000	159,000
Selling and General Expenses	66,000	68,000
Income from Operations	120,000	91,000
Interest Expense	32,000	19,000
Income Before Income Tax	88,000	72,000
Income Tax Expense	10,000	7,000
Net Income	$ 78,000	$ 65,000

Additional data follow:

	2014	**2013**	**2012**
Total Assets	$330,000	$286,000	$290,000
Common Shareholders' Equity....................................	$150,000	$142,000	$134,000
Preferred Dividends	$ 6,000	$ 6,000	
Number of Common Shares Outstanding	45,000	45,000	

Requirement

1. Did the company's operating performance improve or deteriorate during 2014?

E12-9B. Financial statement analysis (*Learning Objective 5*) 15–20 min.

Evaluate the common shares of Shamrock Incorporated as an investment. Specifically, use the two market analysis ratios to determine whether the shares increased or decreased in attractiveness during the past year. Assume that Shamrock Incorporated paid the full amount of preferred dividends.

	2014	**2013**
Net Income	$117,000	$113,000
Total Dividends	30,000	30,000
Common Shareholders' Equity at Year-End (130,000 shares)	887,000	800,000
Preferred Shareholders' Equity, 4%, at Year End (3,700 shares)	370,000	370,000
Market Price of Common Shares at Year-End...............................	$ 9.40	$ 11.63

E12-10B. Complete financial statement given certain information (*Learning Objective 5*)
15–20 min.

The following data (dollar amounts in millions) are adapted from the financial statements of Drawler, Inc.

Total Current Assets..	$11,983
Accumulated Depreciation	1,429
Total Liabilities..	15,200
Preferred Shares..	8
Debt Ratio...	77.79%
Current Ratio...	1.4

Requirement

1. Complete the following condensed balance sheet. Report amounts rounded to the nearest $1 million:

Current Assets		$?
Property, Plant, and Equipment	$?	
Less: Accumulated Depreciation	(?)	?
Total Assets		$?
Current Liabilities..		$?
Long-Term Liabilities		?
Shareholders' Equity		?
Total Liabilities and Shareholders' Equity..........................		$?

EXERCISES (ALTERNATES 1, 2, AND 3)

These alternative exercise sets are available for your practice benefit at
www.myaccountinglab.com

PROBLEMS (GROUP A)

P12-1A. Horizontal and vertical analysis (*Learning Objectives 2 & 3*) 20–25 min.

Net sales, net income, and total assets for Gene Blue Clothing Emporium for a four-year period follow:

(in thousands)	2014	2013	2012	2011
Net Sales..	$381	$357	$321	$331
Net Income	31	23	16	24
Ending Total Assets	193	177	165	148

Requirements

1. Compute trend percentages for each item for 2011–2014. Use 2011 as the base year.

2. Compute the rate of return on net sales for 2012–2014, rounding to three decimal places. In this industry, rates of 6% are average, rates above 8% are considered good, and rates above 10% are viewed as outstanding.

3. How does Gene Blue Clothing Emporium's return on net sales compare with the industry?

P12-2A. **Common-size financial statements and profitability ratios (***Learning Objectives 4 & 5***) 20–25 min.**

Love Bug Used Auto Sales asked for your help in comparing the company's profit performance and financial position with the average for the auto sales industry. The proprietor has given you the company's income statement and balance sheet as well as the industry average data for retailers of used autos.

Love Bug Used Auto Sales Income Statement Compared with Industry Average Year Ended December 31, 2014		
	LOVE BUG	**INDUSTRY AVERAGE**
Net Sales	$521,000	100.0%
Cost of Goods Sold	331,000	62.1%
Gross Profit	190,000	37.9%
Operating Expenses	110,000	27.8%
Operating Income	80,000	10.1%
Other Expenses	3,000	0.4%
Net Income	$ 77,000	9.7%

Love Bug Used Auto Sales Balance Sheet Compared with Industry Average December 31, 2014		
	LOVE BUG	**INDUSTRY AVERAGE**
Current Assets	$230,000	70.9%
Plant Assets, Net	49,000	23.6%
Intangible Assets, Net	3,000	0.8%
Other Assets	15,000	4.7%
Total Assets	$297,000	100.0%
Current Liabilities	$136,000	48.1%
Long-Term Liabilities	41,000	16.6%
Shareholders' Equity	120,000	35.3%
Total Liabilities and Shareholders' Equity	$297,000	100.0%

Requirements

1. Prepare a two-column, common-size income statement and a two-column, common-size balance sheet for Love Bug Used Auto Sales. The first column of each statement should present Love Bug Used Auto Sales' common-size statement and the second column should show the industry averages.

2. For the profitability analysis, examine Love Bug Used Auto Sales' (a) ratio of gross profit to net sales, (b) ratio of operating income to net sales, and (c) ratio of net income to net sales. Compare these figures with the industry averages. Is Love Bug's profit performance better or worse than the industry average?

3. For the analysis of financial position, examine Love Bug Used Auto Sales' (a) ratio of current assets to total assets, and (b) ratio of shareholders' equity to total assets. Compare these ratios with the industry averages. Is Love Bug Used Auto Sales' financial position better or worse than the industry average?

P12-3A. Current ratio, debt ratio, EPS (*Learning Objective 5*) 20–25 min.

Financial statement data of Barb Wired Fencing, Inc. include the following items:

Cash...	$ 17,000
Short-Term Investments...	22,000
Accounts Receivable, Net...	103,000
Inventory..	119,000
Prepaid Expenses...	10,000
Total Assets	660,000
Short-Term Notes Payable...	45,000
Accounts Payable...	105,000
Accrued Liabilities...	40,000
Long-Term Notes Payable...	158,000
Other Long-Term Liabilities	33,000
Net Income	75,000
Number of Common Shares Outstanding	35,000 shares

Requirements

1. Compute Barb Wired Fencing's current ratio, debt ratio, and earnings per share. Assume that the company had no preferred shares outstanding. Round all ratios to two decimal places.

2. Compute each of the same three ratios after evaluating the effect of each transaction that follows.

   a. Purchased merchandise of $38,000 on account, debiting Inventory.

   b. Issued 2,000 common shares, receiving cash of $80,000.

   c. Borrowed $80,000 on a long-term note payable.

   d. Received cash on account, $22,000.

Quick solution:

1. Current ratio = 1.43;
debt ratio = 0.58;
earnings per share = $2.14

P12-4A. Calculate various ratios for analysis (*Learning Objective 5*) 20–25 min.

Comparative financial statement data of Lounge Around Furniture Company follow:

Lounge Around Furniture Company **Income Statement** Years Ended December 31, 2014 and 2013		
	2014	**2013**
Net Sales	$482,000	$457,000
Cost of Goods Sold	238,000	229,000
Gross Profit	244,000	228,000
Operating Expenses	140,000	138,000
Income from Operations	104,000	90,000
Interest Expense	12,000	14,000
Income Before Income Tax	92,000	76,000
Income Tax Expense	28,000	23,000
Net Income	$ 64,000	$ 53,000

Lounge Around Furniture Company
Balance Sheet
December 31, 2014 and 2013
(Selected 2012 amounts given for computation of ratios)

	2014	2013	2012
Current Assets:			
Cash	$ 98,000	$ 99,000	
Accounts Receivable, Net	108,000	112,000	$104,000
Inventory	164,000	154,000	185,000
Prepaid Expenses	28,000	20,000	
Total Current Assets	398,000	385,000	
Property, Plant, and Equipment, Net	191,000	180,000	
Total Assets	$589,000	$565,000	
Total Current Liabilities	$208,000	$228,000	
Long-Term Liabilities	121,000	117,000	
Total Liabilities	329,000	345,000	
Preferred Shareholders' Equity, 8%	100,000	100,000	
Common Shareholders' Equity	160,000	120,000	100,000
Total Liabilities and Shareholders' Equity	$589,000	$565,000	

Other information follows:

  a. Market price of common shares was $48 at December 31, 2014, and $30.75 at December 31, 2013.

  b. Common shares outstanding were 10,000 during 2014 and 9,000 during 2013.

  c. All sales were made on credit.

  d. The full amount of preferred dividends was paid.

Requirements

  1. Compute the following ratios for 2014 and 2013:

    a. Current ratio

    b. Inventory turnover

    c. Accounts receivable turnover

    d. Times-interest-earned ratio

    e. Return on common shareholders' equity

    f. Earnings per share of common shares

    g. Price/earnings ratio

  2. Decide (a) whether Lounge Around Furniture Company's financial position improved or deteriorated during 2014 and (b) whether the investment attractiveness of its common shares appears to have increased or decreased.

  3. How will what you learned in this problem help you evaluate an investment?

P12-5A. Calculate various ratios for analysis (*Learning Objective 5*) 20–25 min.

Assume you are purchasing an investment and decide to invest in a company in the home remodelling business. You narrow the choice to Build It Right, Inc. or Structurally Sound, Corp. You assemble the following selected data:

Selected income statement data for the current year follow:

	Build It Right, Inc.	Structurally Sound, Corp.
Net Sales (all on credit)..................................	$298,000	$223,000
Cost of Goods Sold..	155,000	125,000
Income from Operations................................	83,000	47,000
Interest Expense	13,000	—
Net Income	43,000	29,000

Selected balance sheet and market price data at the end of the current year follow:

	Build It Right, Inc.	Structurally Sound, Corp.
Current Assets:		
Cash...	$ 12,000	$ 13,000
Short-Term Investments	11,000	12,000
Accounts Receivable, Net..........................	28,000	25,000
Inventory...	60,000	52,000
Prepaid Expenses.....................................	2,000	1,000
Total Current Assets.................................	113,000	103,000
Total Assets	197,000	159,000
Total Current Liabilities	59,000	65,000
Total Liabilities..	79,000	65,000
Preferred Shares, 5%....................................	20,000	
Common Shares, 6,000 Shares		6,000
3,000 Shares	7,500	
Total Shareholders' Equity	118,000	94,000
Market price per share of common shares.....	$ 67	$ 31

Selected balance sheet data at the beginning of the current year follow:

	Build It Right, Inc.	Structurally Sound, Corp.
Accounts Receivable, Net	$ 29,000	$ 24,000
Inventory	53,000	56,000
Total Assets	162,000	155,000
Preferred Shares, 5%, 200 shares	20,000	
Common Shares, 6,000 Shares		6,000
3,000 Shares	7,500	
Total Shareholders' Equity	76,000	71,000

Your investment strategy is to purchase the shares of the company that has a low price/earnings ratio but appears to be in good shape financially. Assume that you analyzed all other factors and your decision depends on the results of the ratio analysis to be performed.

Requirement

1. Compute the following ratios for both companies for the current year and decide which company's shares better fits your investment strategy.

   a. Quick ratio

   b. Inventory turnover

   c. Days' sales in receivables

   d. Debt ratio

e. Earnings per share of common shares

f. Price/earnings ratio

P12-6A. Financial statement ratio analysis (*Learning Objective 5*) 20–25 min.

You have been hired as an investment analyst at McNeice Securities, Inc. It is your job to recommend investments for your client. The only information you have are the following ratio values for two companies in the video game industry.

Ratio	Tomb Crater, Co.	Resident Upheaval, Inc.
Days to collect receivables	46	52
Inventory turnover	8	10
Gross profit percentage	67%	59%
Net income as a percent of sales	15%	21%
Times-interest-earned ratio	16	12
Return on equity	35%	26%
Return on assets	13%	18%

Requirement

1. Write a memo to your client recommending the company you believe to be a more attractive investment. Explain the reasons for your recommendation.

PROBLEMS (GROUP B)

P12-1B. Horizontal and vertical analysis (*Learning Objectives 2 & 3*) 20–25 min.

Net sales, net income, and total assets for Armanix Clothing Emporium for a four-year period follow:

(in thousands)	2014	2013	2012	2011
Net Sales	$386	$357	$324	$337
Net Income	31	26	12	22
Ending Total Assets	196	177	170	152

Requirements

1. Compute trend percentages for each item for 2011–2014. Use 2011 as the base year.

2. Compute the rate of return on net sales for 2012–2014, rounding to three decimal places. In this industry, rates of 6% are average, rates above 8% are considered good, and rates above 10% are viewed as outstanding.

3. How does Armanix Clothing Emporium's return on net sales compare with the industry?

P12-2B. **Common-size financial statements and profitability ratios (*Learning Objectives 3 & 4*) 20–25 min.**

Verifine Used Auto Sales asked for your help in comparing the company's profit performance and financial position with the average for the auto sales industry. The proprietor has given you the company's income statement and balance sheet as well as the industry average data for retailers of used autos.

			VERIFINE	INDUSTRY AVERAGE
Verifine Used Auto Sales				
Income Statement Compared with Industry Average				
Year Ended December 31, 2014				
Net Sales			$548,000	100.0%
Cost of Goods Sold			348,528	62.1%
Gross Profit			199,472	37.9%
Operating Expenses			122,752	27.8%
Operating Income			76,720	10.1%
Other Expenses			1,096	0.4%
Net Income			$ 75,624	9.7%

			VERIFINE	INDUSTRY AVERAGE
Verifine Used Auto Sales				
Balance Sheet Compared with Industry Average				
December 31, 2014				
Current Assets			$229,034	70.9%
Plant Assets, Net			50,830	23.6%
Intangible Assets, Net			8,970	0.8%
Other Assets			10,166	4.7%
Total Assets			$299,000	100.0%
Current Liabilities			$118,105	48.1%
Long-Term Liabilities			50,830	16.6%
Shareholders' Equity			130,065	35.3%
Total Liabilities and Shareholders' Equity			$299,000	100.0%

Requirements

1. Prepare a two-column, common-size income statement and a two-column, common-size balance sheet for Verifine Used Auto Sales. The first column of each statement should present Verifine Used Auto Sales' common-size statement and the second column should show the industry averages.

2. For the profitability analysis, examine Verifine Used Auto Sales' (a) ratio of gross profit to net sales, (b) ratio of operating income to net sales, and (c) ratio of net income to net sales. Compare these figures with the industry averages. Is Verifine Used Auto Sales' profit performance better or worse than the industry average?

3. For the analysis of financial position, examine Verifine Used Auto Sales' (a) ratio of current assets to total assets and (b) ratio of shareholders' equity to total assets. Compare these ratios with the industry averages. Is Verifine Used Auto Sales' financial position better or worse than the industry average?

P12-3B. Current ratio, debt ratio, EPS (*Learning Objective 5*) 20–25 min.

Financial statement data of ABC Fencing, Inc. include the following items:

Cash..	$ 21,000
Short-Term Investments..	25,000
Accounts Receivable, Net..	102,000
Inventory..	121,000
Prepaid Expenses...	15,000
Total Assets	660,500
Short-Term Notes Payable	45,000
Accounts Payable..	106,000
Accrued Liabilities...	44,000
Long-Term Notes Payable..	160,000
Other Long-Term Liabilities	37,000
Net Income	77,000
Number of Common Shares Outstanding	37,000 shares

Requirements

1. Compute ABC Fencing's current ratio, debt ratio, and earnings per share. Assume that the company had no preferred shares outstanding. Round all ratios to two decimal places.

2. Compute each of the same three ratios after evaluating the effect of each transaction that follows:

   a. Purchased merchandise of $40,000 on account, debiting Inventory.

   b. Issued 2,000 common shares, receiving cash of $78,000.

   c. Borrowed $78,000 on a long-term note payable.

   d. Received cash on account, $18,000.

P12-4B. Calculate various ratios for analysis (*Learning Objective 5*) 20–25 min.

Comparative financial statement data of Danfield Furniture Company follow:

Danfield Furniture Company Income Statement Years Ended December 31, 2014 and 2013		
	2014	**2013**
Net Sales	$483,000	$458,000
Cost of Goods Sold	244,000	234,000
Gross Profit	239,000	224,000
Operating Expenses	145,000	137,000
Income from Operations	94,000	87,000
Interest Expense	14,000	24,000
Income Before Income Tax	80,000	63,000
Income Tax Expense	28,000	24,000
Net Income	$ 52,000	$ 39,000

		2014	2013	2012
Current Assets:				
	Cash	$ 95,000	$ 98,000	
	Accounts Receivable, Net	104,000	114,000	$107,000
	Inventory	161,000	151,000	193,000
	Prepaid Expenses	38,000	28,000	
	Total Current Assets	398,000	391,000	
Property, Plant, and Equipment, Net		196,000	175,000	
Total Assets		$594,000	$566,000	
Total Current Liabilities		$212,000	$228,000	
Long-Term Liabilities		129,000	116,000	
Total Liabilities		341,000	344,000	
Preferred Shareholders' Equity, 8%		99,000	99,000	
Common Shareholders' Equity		154,000	123,000	97,000
Total Liabilities and Shareholders' Equity		$594,000	$566,000	

Danfield Furniture Company
Balance Sheet
December 31, 2014 and 2013
(Selected 2012 amounts given for computation of ratios)

Other information follows:

1. Market price of common shares was $48.50 at December 31, 2014, and $31.75 at December 31, 2013.

2. Common shares outstanding were 17,000 during 2014 and 15,000 during 2013.

3. All sales were made on credit.

4. The full amount of preferred dividends was paid.

Requirements

1. Compute the following ratios for 2014 and 2013:

   a. Current ratio

   b. Inventory turnover

   c. Accounts receivable turnover

   d. Times-interest-earned ratio

   e. Return on common shareholders' equity

   f. Earnings per share of common shares

   g. Price/earnings ratio

2. Decide (a) whether Danfield Furniture Company's financial position improved or deteriorated during 2014 and (b) whether the investment attractiveness of its common shares appears to have increased or decreased.

3. How will what you learned in this problem help you evaluate an investment?

P12-5B. Calculate various ratios for analysis (*Learning Objective 5*) 20–25 min.

Assume you are purchasing an investment and decide to invest in a company in the home remodelling business. You narrow the choice to Bob's Home Repair, Inc. or Stellar Stability, Corp. You assemble the following selected data.

Selected income statement data for the current year follow:

	Bob's Home Repair, Inc.	Stellar Stability, Corp.
Net Sales (all on credit)	$282,000	$226,000
Cost of Goods Sold	158,000	129,000
Income from Operations	88,000	48,000
Interest Expense	15,000	—
Net Income	44,000	24,000

Selected balance sheet and market price data at the end of the current year follow:

	Bob's Home Repair, Inc.	Stellar Stability, Corp.
Current Assets:		
Cash	$ 13,000	$ 14,000
Short-Term Investments	12,000	15,000
Accounts Receivable, Net	30,000	25,000
Inventory	69,000	50,000
Prepaid Expenses	5,000	4,000
Total Current Assets	129,000	108,000
Total Assets	201,000	166,000
Total Current Liabilities	54,000	68,000
Total Liabilities	80,000	71,000
Preferred Shares, 5%, 180 shares	18,000	
Common Shares, 7,000 Shares		7,000
4,000 Shares	10,000	
Total Shareholders' Equity	121,000	95,000
Market price per common share	$ 43.12	$ 30.87

Selected balance sheet data at the beginning of the current year follow:

	Bob's Home Repair, Inc.	Stellar Stability, Corp.
Accounts Receivable, Net	$ 29,000	$ 26,000
Inventory	52,000	62,000
Total Assets	162,000	157,000
Preferred Shares, 5% (180 shares)	18,000	
Common Shares, 7,000 Shares		7,000
4,000 Shares	10,000	
Total Shareholders' Equity	77,000	72,000

Your investment strategy is to purchase the shares of the company that has a low price/earnings ratio but appears to be in good shape financially. Assume that you analyzed all other factors and your decision depends on the results of the ratio analysis to be performed.

Requirement

1. Compute the following ratios for both companies for the current year and decide which company's shares better fit your investment strategy.

   a. Quick ratio

   b. Inventory turnover

   c. Days' sales in receivables

    d. Debt ratio

    e. Earnings per share of common shares

    f. Price/earnings ratio

P12-6B. Financial statement ratio analysis (*Learning Objective 5*) 20–25 min.

You have been hired as an investment analyst at Harriet Winston Company. It is your job to recommend investments for your client. The only information you have are the following ratio values for two companies in the video game industry.

Ratio	Mario and Luco, Co.	Witches and Warlocks, Inc.
Days to collect receivables	60	54
Inventory turnover	10	8
Gross profit percentage	69%	75%
Net income as a percent of sales	17%	11%
Times-interest-earned ratio	14	18
Return on equity	37%	45%
Return on assets	15%	13%

Requirement

    1. Write a memo to your client recommending the company you believe to be a more attractive investment. Explain the reasons for your recommendation.

PROBLEMS (ALTERNATES 1, 2, AND 3)

These alternative problem sets are available for your practice benefit at
www.myaccountinglab.com

CONTINUING EXERCISE

This concludes the accounting for Graham's Yard Care, Inc. that we began in Chapter 1. For this exercise, refer to the comparative balance sheet that was presented in the Continuing Exercise in Chapter 11.

    Requirements

    1. Prepare a horizontal analysis of the balance sheet for Graham's Yard Care, Inc.

    2. Prepare a vertical analysis of the balance sheet for Graham's Yard Care, Inc.

CONTINUING PROBLEM

In Chapter 11, we prepared a cash flow statement for Aqua Elite, Inc. Now, we will analyze Aqua Elite's financial statements using the tools we learned in this chapter.

Following are the balance sheets for the months ended July 31 and June 30, 2015 and the income statement for the month ended July 31, 2015, for Aqua Elite, Inc.

Aqua Elite, Inc.
Comparative Balance Sheets
July 31 and June 30, 2015

			JULY 31	JUNE 30
		Assets		
		Cash	$ 5,333	$3,270
		Accounts Receivable, Net	2,280	1,000
		Inventory	4,175	180
		Supplies	105	125
		Total Current Assets	11,893	4,575
		Fixed Assets	67,250	2,250
		Less: Accumulated Depreciation	(352)	(47)
		Net Fixed Assets	66,898	2,203
		Total Assets	$78,791	$6,778
		Liabilities		
		Accounts Payable	$ 1,805	$ 450
		Unearned Revenue	5,800	2,000
		Salary Payable	950	900
		Interest Payable	375	17
		Payroll Taxes Payable	188	—
		Dividend Payable	500	—
		Current Portion of Long-Term Debt	4,410	2,000
		Total Current Liabilities	14,028	5,367
		Notes Payable	20,000	—
		Mortgage Payable	42,590	—
		Total Liabilities	76,618	5,367
		Shareholders' Equity		
		Common Shares	1,000	1,000
		Retained Earnings	1,173	411
		Total Shareholders' Equity	2,173	1,411
		Total Liabilities & Shareholders' Equity	$78,791	$6,778

Aqua Elite, Inc.
Income Statement
Month Ended July 31, 2015

	Revenue		$6,300
	Expenses:		
	Cost of Goods Sold		1,080
	Depreciation Expense		305
	Bad Debt Expense		220
	Interest Expense		375
	Insurance Expense		150
	Supplies Expense		210
	Salary Expense		2,400
	Payroll Taxes Expense		268
	Bank Service Fees		30
	Net Income*		$1,262

*Income taxes ignored

Requirements

1. Prepare a vertical analysis of the income statement using a multi-step income statement.

2. Calculate the current ratio for Aqua Elite, Inc. at July 31, 2015.

3. Calculate the quick ratio for Aqua Elite, Inc. at July 31, 2015.

4. Why do you think the current and quick ratios are unfavourable? Do you believe that this is a temporary problem or a long-term problem?

APPLY YOUR KNOWLEDGE

ETHICS IN ACTION

Case 1. Robin Peterson, the CEO of Teldar Incorporated, was reviewing the financial statements for the first three months of the year. He saw that sales and net income were lower than expected. Because the reported net income and the related earnings per share were below expectations, the price of the shares declined. Robin held a meeting with top management and expressed his concerns over the declining trend in sales and income. He stated that the reduced profitability meant that he needed to formulate a plan to somehow increase the earnings per share. The vice president of marketing suggested that more advertising might help sales increase. Robin stated that spending more money on advertising would not guarantee an increase in sales. Then he announced that the excess company cash would instead be used to buy back outstanding common shares; this move would help increase the earnings per share because fewer shares would be outstanding. Robin reminded everyone that the yearly financial statements would be analyzed and the current year would be compared to previous years' results. He then stated that the treasury shares would lower the total shareholders' equity, which could then provide a stronger EPS so the current year would not look as bad. Finally, Robin reminded everyone that with fewer shares outstanding, the dividend per share could be increased and that would help make Teldar shares more attractive. The CFO argued that buying back shares merely to increase performance measures such as EPS was manipulative and unethical, and financial analysts would easily see what Teldar was trying to do.

Why did the CEO want to repurchase shares of Teldar common shares? Would the repurchase of common shares really have any impact on the financial ratios? Would an investor or financial analyst be able to see that financial performance measures were improved because of the share repurchase? Are any ethical issues involved? Were the concerns expressed by the CFO valid? Do you have any other thoughts?

Case 2. Crane Corporation was in the process of completing the financial statements for the latest fiscal year. Susan Randal, Crane's CEO, was reviewing the comparative financial statements and expressed some concerns. In comparing the current year income statement against those of the prior years, she noticed that total sales had decreased slightly. Further, the salary expense had increased while the advertising and research and development expenses had decreased. Although the total operating expenses were essentially the same, Susan was concerned that the increased salary expense would be questioned by the investors and financial analysts in light of the decreases in advertising and research and development. She knew that the lower sales would be blamed on reduced advertising and less spending on research and development. As a result, Susan ordered the accountants to issue a condensed income statement that would present all operating expenses as a single amount. Also, during the year Crane Corporation had purchased another company for a price higher than the total fair market value of the purchased business. Crane properly recorded the excess cost as goodwill, but the total amount of goodwill had increased substantially because of this purchase. Susan was concerned that this rather large increase in goodwill would be seen as an unnecessary purchase and investors and analysts would become upset. Thus, Susan ordered that the goodwill be lumped in with the other assets rather than listed separately on the balance sheet where it could easily be seen. The accountants argued that attempting to hide these items from investors and analysts would be unethical. They further argued that IFRS and Canadian ASPE required full disclosure, and that if Susan insisted on providing condensed statements, details would need to be provided in the footnotes anyway. Susan reluctantly agreed to the disclosure, knowing that often footnotes are not read.

Why would Susan want all the operating expenses lumped together? Why would Susan want the goodwill included as other assets? Were the ethical concerns raised by the accountants valid? Are any ethical issues involved in providing condensed information with the details included in the footnotes? Do you have any additional thoughts?

KNOW YOUR BUSINESS

FINANCIAL ANALYSIS

Purpose: To help familiarize you with the financial reporting of a real company to further your understanding of the chapter material you are learning.

This case focuses on the financial statement analysis of Bombardier Inc. Recall from the chapter that stakeholders use numerous ways to analyze and, thus, better understand the financial position and results of operations of a company. Tools such as vertical and horizontal analyses are available. In addition, financial ratios can be used to gain further insight into areas such as liquidity and profitability. Other measures include earnings per share and ratios that consider the share price of the company. Finally, nonfinancial information provides additional insights into the performance and financial position of the company. We will now apply some of the analytical tools contained in the chapter. Refer to the Bombardier Annual Report, Year Ended January 31, 2011, found in MyAccountingLab.

Requirements

1. Perform a vertical analysis on the income statements (Consolidated Statements of Operations). Discuss your results. What benefit do you see in performing this analysis? Perform a horizontal analysis of the balance sheets (Consolidated Balance Sheets). Discuss your results. What benefit do you see in performing this analysis?

2. Look at the income statements (Consolidated Statements of Income). Can you find the Basic EPS for each fiscal year presented? Has the Basic Earnings per Share increased or decreased each year? Why do you think the Basic EPS has been changing?

3. Compute the return on assets and the return on equity ratios for 2011 and 2010. Use only the ending amount for shareholders' equity instead of the average to calculate ROE for both years. Has Bombardier Inc.'s profitability improved or deteriorated?

INDUSTRY ANALYSIS

Purpose: To help you understand and compare the performance of two companies in the same industry.

Find the Bombardier Annual Report, Year Ended January 31, 2011 located in MyAccountingLab. Now access The Boeing Company's 2010 Annual Report. To do this from the internet, go to their webpage for the Investor Relations at *http://www.boeing.com/companyoffices/financial/quarterly.htm* and under Annual Report, go to the 2010 Annual Report.

Requirement

1. In your opinion and based on what you have learned from this chapter, to which company would you offer a short-term loan? And based on these data, which company would you invest in?

SMALL BUSINESS ANALYSIS

Purpose: To help you understand the importance of financial statement analysis in the operation of a small business.

You just returned from a meeting with your bank loan officer and you were a little taken aback by his comments. You've been doing business with this bank for a number of years and he always seemed happy with your company's performance. This is why you can't understand the bank's hesitation to continue extending credit to your company. At this meeting, you had supplied him with the current year's financial information and even ran some of the financial ratios that you know the bank asks about. You thought the numbers looked decent for the current year, maybe not the best, but decent. Sure, sales had fallen a little bit since the previous year, but they were still pretty good. So when the discussion turned to a comparison of the last couple of year's financial information with this year's, you had to question what that has to do with anything. "Why shouldn't each and every year stand by itself?" you asked the banker. His comments to you were, "A company's performance is best evaluated by examining more than one year's data. This is why most financial statements cover at least two periods. In fact, most financial analysis covers trends of up to five years." He also said that a company's performance is best evaluated by comparing it against its own past performance, the performance of competitors, and the industry averages for the industry the company is in.

Requirement

1. Below are some selected financial data from the last four years. Calculate the trend percentages using 2011 as the base year and the return on sales for these four years and see if you can figure out what the concern is that the banker has for the financial health of your company.

	2014	2013	2012	2011
Total Sales	1,010,000	1,050,000	1,080,000	1,000,000
Total Expenses	896,000	888,000	880,000	800,000
Net Income	114,000	162,000	200,000	200,000

WRITTEN COMMUNICATION

Below are selected financial data for your client for the current year and corresponding data for the client's industry.

	Company	Industry
Return on Sales	12.5%	10.0%
Return on Assets	23.0%	20.0%
Current Ratio	1.6	1.5
Inventory Turnover	8.5	7.1
Accounts Receivable Turnover	8.5	11.0
Days Sales in Receivables	42.9	33.2
Debt Ratio	0.6	0.5

Requirement

1. Write a memo to your client comparing his or her business to the industry averages and explain to the client the value of common-size financial statements.

Self Check Answers

1. c 2. d 3. b 4. d 5. a 6. b 7. c 8. d 9. b 10. d

COMPREHENSIVE PROBLEM FOR CHAPTERS 11–12

ANALYZING A COMPANY FOR ITS INVESTMENT POTENTIAL

In its annual report, BALLI Supply includes the following five-year financial summary:

BALLI Supply, Inc. Five-Year Financial Summary (partial)					
(Dollar Amounts in Thousands Except per Share Data)	**2014**	**2013**	**2012**	**2011**	**2010**
Net Sales	$244,524	$217,799	$191,329	$165,013	$137,634
Net Sales Increase	12%	14%	16%	20%	17%
# of Store Increase	5%	6%	5%	8%	9%
Other Income, Net	$ 2,001	$ 1,873	$ 1,787	$ 1,615	$ 1,391
Cost of Goods Sold	191,838	171,562	150,255	129,664	108,725
Selling, General, and					
Administrative Expenses	41,043	36,173	31,550	27,040	22,363
Interest Costs:					
Interest Expense	1,063	1,357	1,383	1,045	803
Interest Income	(138)	(171)	(188)	(204)	(189)
Net Income	8,039	6,671	6,295	5,377	4,430
Per Share of Common Shares:					
Net Income	1.81	1.49	1.41	1.21	0.99
Dividends	0.30	0.28	0.24	0.20	0.16
Financial Position					
Current Assets	$ 30,483	$ 27,878	$ 26,555	$ 24,356	$ 21,132
Inventories at FIFO Cost	24,891	22,614	21,442	19,793	17,076
Net Property, Plant, and Equipment	51,904	45,750	40,934	35,969	25,973
Total Assets	94,685	83,527	78,130	70,349	49,996
Current Liabilities	32,617	27,282	28,949	25,803	16,762
Long-Term Debt	19,608	18,732	15,655	16,674	9,607
Shareholders' Equity	39,337	35,102	31,343	25,834	21,112
Financial Ratios					
Current ratio	0.9	1.0	0.9	0.9	1.3
Return on assets	9.2%	8.5%	8.7%	9.5%	9.6%
Return on shareholders' equity	21.6%	20.1%	22.0%	22.9%	22.4%

Requirement

1. Analyze the company's financial summary for the fiscal years 2010–2014 to decide whether to invest in the common shares of BALLI. Include the following sections in your analysis, and fully explain your final decision.

   a. Trend analysis for net sales and net income (use 2010 as the base year)

   b. Profitability analysis

   c. Measuring ability to sell inventory

   d. Measuring ability to pay debts

   e. Measuring dividends

SCAN THIS

Appendix A

BOMBARDIER ANNUAL REPORT FOR YEAR ENDED JANUARY 31, 2011

MyAccountingLab

The Financial and Industry Analysis questions at the end of each chapter feature one company, Bombardier, allowing students to see how chapter concepts are connected. The financial statements for Bombardier can be found on MyAccountingLab at www.myaccountinglab.com.

Appendix B

TIME VALUE OF MONEY—FUTURE AND PRESENT VALUE CONCEPTS

Money earns income over time, a fact called the **time value of money.** The time value of money idea is based on the thought that $1 today is worth more than $1 in the future. This is because $1 today can be invested and earn interest and therefore become worth more than $1 at a later date.

FUTURE VALUE

Future value refers to the amount that a given sum of money will be "worth" at a specified time in the future assuming a certain interest rate. The main application of future value is calculating the future value of an amount invested today (a present value) that earns a constant rate of interest over time. For example, assume that you invest $4,545 and it earns 10% interest per year. After one year, the $4,545 invested grows to a future value of $5,000, as shown next.

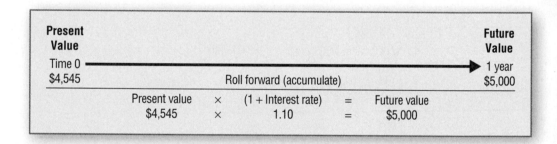

If the money were invested for five years, you would have to perform five such calculations. You would also have to consider the compound interest your investment is earning. **Compound interest** is the interest you earn not only on your principal amount, but also on the interest to date. Most business applications include compound interest. The following table shows the interest calculations for the first two years:

End of Year	Interest	Future Value
0	—	$4,545
1	$4,545 × 0.10 = $455	5,000
2	5,000 × 0.10 = 500	5,500

Earning 10%, a $4,545 investment grows to $5,000 at the end of one year, to $5,500 at the end of two years, and so on. (Throughout this discussion, we round dollar amounts to the nearest dollar.)

Future-Value Tables

Mathematical tables make computing a future value easy. Table B-1 shows the table used to calculate the future value of $1 for various interest rates over various time periods. Future value depends on three factors:

❶ The amount of the investment

❷ The length of time the amount is invested

❸ The interest rate

The heading in **Table B-1** states that the future value of $1 is being calculated. Future-value and present-value tables are based on $1 because $1 is so easy to work with. Look at the period and look at the interest rate columns from 4% to 16%.

| | | | | | | | Future value of $1 per period at i% for n periods, FVIF$_{(i,n)}$ | | | | | | | | | | | | | |
n	1%	2%	3%	3.5%	4%	4.5%	5%	6%	7%	8%	9%	10%	11%	12%	13%	14%	15%	16%	18%	20%	25%
1	1.0100	1.0200	1.0300	1.0350	1.0400	1.0450	1.0500	1.0600	1.0700	1.0800	1.0900	1.1000	1.1100	1.1200	1.1300	1.1400	1.1500	1.1600	1.1800	1.2000	1.2500
2	1.0201	1.0404	1.0609	1.0712	1.0816	1.0920	1.1025	1.1236	1.1449	1.1664	1.1881	1.2100	1.2321	1.2544	1.2769	1.2996	1.3225	1.3456	1.3924	1.4400	1.5625
3	1.0303	1.0612	1.0927	1.1087	1.1249	1.1412	1.1576	1.1910	1.2250	1.2597	1.2950	1.3310	1.3676	1.4049	1.4429	1.4815	1.5209	1.5609	1.6430	1.7280	1.9531
4	1.0406	1.0824	1.1255	1.1475	1.1699	1.1925	1.2155	1.2625	1.3108	1.3605	1.4116	1.4641	1.5181	1.5735	1.6305	1.6890	1.7490	1.8106	1.9388	2.0736	2.4414
5	1.0510	1.1041	1.1593	1.1877	1.2167	1.2462	1.2763	1.3382	1.4026	1.4693	1.5386	1.6105	1.6851	1.7623	1.8424	1.9254	2.0114	2.1003	2.2878	2.4883	3.0518
6	1.0615	1.1262	1.1941	1.2293	1.2653	1.3023	1.3401	1.4185	1.5007	1.5869	1.6771	1.7716	1.8704	1.9738	2.0820	2.1950	2.3131	2.4364	2.6996	2.9860	3.8147
7	1.0721	1.1487	1.2299	1.2723	1.3159	1.3609	1.4071	1.5036	1.6058	1.7138	1.8280	1.9487	2.0762	2.2107	2.3526	2.5023	2.6600	2.8262	3.1855	3.5832	4.7684
8	1.0829	1.1717	1.2668	1.3168	1.3686	1.4221	1.4775	1.5938	1.7182	1.8509	1.9926	2.1436	2.3045	2.4760	2.6584	2.8526	3.0590	3.2784	3.7589	4.2998	5.9605
9	1.0937	1.1951	1.3048	1.3629	1.4233	1.4861	1.5513	1.6895	1.8385	1.9990	2.1719	2.3579	2.5580	2.7731	3.0040	3.2519	3.5179	3.8030	4.4355	5.1598	7.4506
10	1.1046	1.2190	1.3439	1.4106	1.4802	1.5530	1.6289	1.7908	1.9672	2.1589	2.3674	2.5937	2.8394	3.1058	3.3946	3.7072	4.0456	4.4114	5.2338	6.1917	9.3132
11	1.1157	1.2434	1.3842	1.4600	1.5395	1.6229	1.7103	1.8983	2.1049	2.3316	2.5804	2.8531	3.1518	3.4785	3.8359	4.2262	4.6524	5.1173	6.1759	7.4301	11.6415
12	1.1268	1.2682	1.4258	1.5111	1.6010	1.6959	1.7959	2.0122	2.2522	2.5182	2.8127	3.1384	3.4985	3.8960	4.3345	4.8179	5.3503	5.9360	7.2876	8.9161	14.5519
13	1.1381	1.2936	1.4685	1.5640	1.6651	1.7722	1.8856	2.1329	2.4098	2.7196	3.0658	3.4523	3.8833	4.3635	4.8980	5.4924	6.1528	6.8858	8.5994	10.6993	18.1899
14	1.1495	1.3195	1.5126	1.6187	1.7317	1.8519	1.9799	2.2609	2.5785	2.9372	3.3417	3.7975	4.3104	4.8871	5.5348	6.2613	7.0757	7.9875	10.1472	12.8392	22.7374
15	1.1610	1.3459	1.5580	1.6753	1.8009	1.9353	2.0789	2.3966	2.7590	3.1722	3.6425	4.1772	4.7846	5.4736	6.2543	7.1379	8.1371	9.2655	11.9737	15.4070	28.4217
16	1.1726	1.3728	1.6047	1.7340	1.8730	2.0224	2.1829	2.5404	2.9522	3.4259	3.9703	4.5950	5.3109	6.1304	7.0673	8.1372	9.3576	10.7480	14.1290	18.4884	35.5271
17	1.1843	1.4002	1.6528	1.7947	1.9479	2.1134	2.2920	2.6928	3.1588	3.7000	4.3276	5.0545	5.8951	6.8660	7.9861	9.2765	10.7613	12.4677	16.6722	22.1861	44.4089
18	1.1961	1.4282	1.7024	1.8575	2.0258	2.2085	2.4066	2.8543	3.3799	3.9960	4.7171	5.5599	6.5436	7.6900	9.0243	10.5752	12.3755	14.4625	19.6733	26.6233	55.5112
19	1.2081	1.4568	1.7535	1.9225	2.1068	2.3079	2.5270	3.0256	3.6165	4.3157	5.1417	6.1159	7.2633	8.6128	10.1974	12.0557	14.2318	16.7765	23.2144	31.9480	69.3889
20	1.2202	1.4859	1.8061	1.9898	2.1911	2.4117	2.6533	3.2071	3.8697	4.6610	5.6044	6.7275	8.0623	9.6463	11.5231	13.7435	16.3665	19.4608	27.3930	38.3376	86.7362
25	1.2824	1.6406	2.0938	2.3632	2.6658	3.0054	3.3864	4.2919	5.4274	6.8485	8.6231	10.8347	13.5855	17.0001	21.2305	26.4619	32.9190	40.8742	62.6686	95.3962	264.6978
30	1.3478	1.8114	2.4273	2.8068	3.2434	3.7453	4.3219	5.7435	7.6123	10.0627	13.2677	17.4494	22.8923	29.9599	39.1159	50.9502	66.2118	85.8499	143.3706	237.3763	807.7936
35	1.4166	1.9999	2.8139	3.3336	3.9461	4.6673	5.5160	7.6861	10.6766	14.7853	20.4140	28.1024	38.5749	52.7996	72.0685	98.1002	133.1755	180.3141	327.9973	590.6682	2,465.1903
40	1.4889	2.2080	3.2620	3.9593	4.8010	5.8164	7.0400	10.2857	14.9745	21.7245	31.4094	45.2593	65.0009	93.0510	132.7816	188.8835	267.8635	378.7212	750.3783	1,469.7716	7,523.1638
50	1.6446	2.6916	4.3839	5.5849	7.1067	9.0326	11.4674	18.4202	29.4570	46.9016	74.3575	117.3909	184.5648	289.0022	450.7359	700.2330	1,083.6574	1,670.7038	3,927.3569	9,100.4382	70,064.9232

Table B-1 ▲

In business applications, interest rates are always stated for a one-year period unless specified otherwise. However, an interest rate can be stated for any period, such as 3% per quarter or 5% for a six-month period. For example, an investment may offer a return of 3% per quarter for two years. In that case, you would be working with 3% interest for eight periods (two years multiplied by four quarters per year). It would be incorrect to use 3% for two years because the interest in this case is 3% compounded quarterly, and different future values would result. Take care when calculating future-value and present-value problems to select the proper interest rate and the appropriate number of periods.

Let's demonstrate using the tables in Table B-1. The future value of $1.00 invested at 8% for one year is $1.08 ($1.00 × 1.0800, which appears at the intersection of the 8% column and the Period 1 row). The figure 1.0800 includes both the principal (1.000) and the compound interest for one period (0.0800).

Suppose you deposit $5,000 in a savings account that pays annual interest of 8%. The account balance at the end of one year will be $5,400. To compute the future value of $5,000 at 8% for one year, multiply $5,000 by 1.0800 to get $5,400.

Now suppose you invest $5,000 in a 10-year, 8% certificate of deposit (CD). What will be the future value of the CD at maturity? To compute the future value of $5,000 at 8% for 10 periods, multiply $5,000 by 2.1589 (from Table B-1) to get $10,795. This future value of $10,795 indicates that $5,000 earning 8% interest compounded annually grows to $10,795 at the end of 10 years. You can find any present amount's future value at a particular future date.

Future Value of an Annuity

In the preceding example, we made an investment of a single amount. Other investments, called **annuities**, include multiple investments of an equal periodic amount at fixed intervals over the length of the investment. Consider the Gomez family members investing for their child's education. Let's assume the Gomez family can invest $4,000 annually to accumulate a college fund for 15-year-old Daniel. The investment can earn 7% annually until Daniel turns 18—a three-year investment. How much will be available for Daniel on the date of the last investment? The investment will have a future value of $12,860 as calculated next.

End of Year	Annual Investment +	Interest =	Increase for the Year	Future Value of Annuity
0	—	—	—	0
1	$4,000	—	$4,000	$ 4,000
2	4,000	+ ($4,000 × 0.07 = $280) =	4,280	8,280
3	4,000	+ ($8,280 × 0.07 = $580) =	4,580	12,860

As with the Future Value of $1 table, mathematical tables make calculating the future value of annuities much easier. **Table B-2**, Future Value of Annuity of $1, gives the future value of a series of investments, each of equal amount, made at regular intervals.

	Future value of an ordinary annuity of $1 per period at i% for n periods, $\text{FVIFA}_{(i,n)}$																				
n	1%	2%	3%	3.5%	4%	4.5%	5%	6%	7%	8%	9%	10%	11%	12%	13%	14%	15%	16%	18%	20%	25%
1	1.0000	1.0000	1.0000	1.0000	1.0000	1.0000	1.0000	1.0000	1.0000	1.0000	1.0000	1.0000	1.0000	1.0000	1.0000	1.0000	1.0000	1.0000	1.0000	1.0000	1.0000
2	2.0100	2.0200	2.0300	2.0350	2.0400	2.0450	2.0500	2.0600	2.0700	2.0800	2.0900	2.1000	2.1100	2.1200	2.1300	2.1400	2.1500	2.1600	2.1800	2.2000	2.2500
3	3.0301	3.0604	3.0909	3.1062	3.1216	3.1370	3.1525	3.1836	3.2149	3.2464	3.2781	3.3100	3.3421	3.3744	3.4069	3.4396	3.4725	3.5056	3.5724	3.6400	3.8125
4	4.0604	4.1216	4.1836	4.2149	4.2465	4.2782	4.3101	4.3746	4.4399	4.5061	4.5731	4.6410	4.7097	4.7793	4.8498	4.9211	4.9934	5.0665	5.2154	5.3680	5.7656
5	5.1010	5.2040	5.3091	5.3625	5.4163	5.4707	5.5256	5.6371	5.7507	5.8666	5.9847	6.1051	6.2278	6.3528	6.4803	6.6101	6.7424	6.8771	7.1542	7.4416	8.2070
6	6.1520	6.3081	6.4684	6.5502	6.6330	6.7169	6.8019	6.9753	7.1533	7.3359	7.5233	7.7156	7.9129	8.1152	8.3227	8.5355	8.7537	8.9775	9.4420	9.9299	11.2588
7	7.2135	7.4343	7.6625	7.7794	7.8983	8.0192	8.1420	8.3938	8.6540	8.9228	9.2004	9.4872	9.7833	10.0890	10.4047	10.7305	11.0668	11.4139	12.1415	12.9159	15.0735
8	8.2857	8.5830	8.8923	9.0517	9.2142	9.3800	9.5491	9.8975	10.2598	10.6366	11.0285	11.4359	11.8594	12.2997	12.7573	13.2328	13.7268	14.2401	15.3270	16.4991	19.8419
9	9.3685	9.7546	10.1591	10.3685	10.5828	10.8021	11.0266	11.4913	11.9780	12.4876	13.0210	13.5795	14.1640	14.7757	15.4157	16.0853	16.7858	17.5185	19.0859	20.7989	25.8023
10	10.4622	10.9497	11.4639	11.7314	12.0061	12.2882	12.5779	13.1808	13.8164	14.4866	15.1929	15.9374	16.7220	17.5487	18.4197	19.3373	20.3037	21.3215	23.5213	25.9587	33.2529
11	11.5668	12.1687	12.8078	13.1420	13.4864	13.8412	14.2068	14.9716	15.7836	16.6455	17.5603	18.5312	19.5614	20.6546	21.8143	23.0445	24.3493	25.7329	28.7551	32.1504	42.5661
12	12.6825	13.4121	14.1920	14.6020	15.0258	15.4640	15.9171	16.8699	17.8885	18.9771	20.1407	21.3843	22.7132	24.1331	25.6502	27.2707	29.0017	30.8502	34.9311	39.5805	54.2077
13	13.8093	14.6803	15.6178	16.1130	16.6268	17.1599	17.7130	18.8821	20.1406	21.4953	22.9534	24.5227	26.2116	28.0291	29.9847	32.0887	34.3519	36.7862	42.2187	48.4966	68.7596
14	14.9474	15.9739	17.0863	17.6770	18.2919	18.9321	19.5986	21.0151	22.5505	24.2149	26.0192	27.9750	30.0949	32.3926	34.8827	37.5811	40.5047	43.6720	50.8180	59.1959	86.9495
15	16.0969	17.2934	18.5989	19.2957	20.0236	20.7841	21.5786	23.2760	25.1290	27.1521	29.3609	31.7725	34.4054	37.2797	40.4175	43.8424	47.5804	51.6595	60.9653	72.0351	109.6868
16	17.2579	18.6393	20.1569	20.9710	21.8245	22.7193	23.6575	25.6725	27.8881	30.3243	33.0034	35.9497	39.1899	42.7533	46.6717	50.9804	55.7175	60.9250	72.9390	87.4421	138.1085
17	18.4304	20.0121	21.7616	22.7050	23.6975	24.7417	25.8404	28.2129	30.8402	33.7502	36.9737	40.5447	44.5008	48.8837	53.7391	59.1176	65.0751	71.6730	87.0680	105.9306	173.6357
18	19.6147	21.4123	23.4144	24.4997	25.6454	26.8551	28.1324	30.9057	33.9990	37.4502	41.3013	45.5992	50.3959	55.7497	61.7251	68.3941	75.8364	84.1407	103.7403	128.1167	218.0446
19	20.8109	22.8406	25.1169	26.3572	27.6712	29.0636	30.5390	33.7600	37.3790	41.4463	46.0185	51.1591	56.9395	63.4397	70.7494	78.9692	88.2118	98.6032	123.4135	154.7400	273.5558
20	22.0190	24.2974	26.8704	28.2797	29.7781	31.3714	33.0660	36.7856	40.9955	45.7620	51.1601	57.2750	64.2028	72.0524	80.9468	91.0249	102.4436	115.3797	146.6280	186.6880	342.9447
25	28.2432	32.0303	36.4593	38.9499	41.6459	44.5652	47.7271	54.8645	63.2490	73.1059	84.7009	98.3471	114.4133	133.3339	155.6196	181.8708	212.7930	249.2140	342.6035	471.9811	1,054.7912
30	34.7849	40.5681	47.5754	51.6227	56.0849	61.0071	66.4388	79.0582	94.4608	113.2832	136.3075	164.4940	199.0209	241.3327	293.1992	356.7868	434.7451	530.3117	790.9480	1,181.8816	3,227.1743
35	41.6603	49.9945	60.4621	66.6740	73.6522	81.4966	90.3203	111.4348	138.2369	172.3168	215.7108	271.0244	341.5896	431.6635	546.6808	693.5727	881.1702	1,120.7130	1,816.6516	2,948.3411	9,856.7613
40	48.8864	60.4020	75.4013	84.5503	95.0255	107.0303	120.7998	154.7620	199.6351	259.0565	337.8824	442.5926	581.8261	767.0914	1,013.7042	1,342.0251	1,779.0903	2,360.7572	4,163.2130	7,343.8578	30,088.6554
50	64.4632	84.5794	112.7969	130.9979	152.6671	178.5030	209.3480	290.3359	406.5289	573.7702	815.0836	1,163.9085	1,668.7712	2,400.0182	3,459.5071	4,994.5213	7,217.7163	10,435.6488	21,813.0937	45,497.1908	280,255.6929

Table B-2 ▲

What is the future value of an annuity of three investments of $1 each that earn 7%? The answer, 3.2149, can be found in the 7% column and across from period 3 in Table B-2. This amount can be used to compute the future value of the investment for Daniel's education, as follows:

Amount of Each Periodic Investment	×	Future Value of Annuity of $1 (Table B-2)	=	Future Value of Investment
$4,000	×	3.2149	=	$12,860

You can compute the future value of any investment consisting of equal periodic amounts at regular intervals. Businesses make periodic investments to accumulate funds for plant expansion and other uses.

PRESENT VALUE

Often a person knows a future amount and needs to know the related **present value**. Present value is the value on a given date of a future amount, adjusted to reflect the time value of money. Suppose an investment promises to pay you $5,000 at the *end* of one year. How much would you pay *now* to acquire this investment? You would be willing to pay the present value of the $5,000 future amount.

Present value also depends on three factors:

❶ The amount of the future payment (or receipt)

❷ The time span between investment and future payment (or receipt)

❸ The interest rate

Computing a present value is called **discounting** because the present value is *always less* than the future value.

In our example, the future receipt is $5,000. The investment period is one year. Assume that you demand an annual interest rate of 10% on your investment. With all three factors specified, you can compute the present value of $5,000 at 10% for one year as follows:

$$\frac{\text{Future Value}}{(1 + \text{Interest Rate})} = \frac{\$5,000}{1.10} = \$4,545$$

By turning the data around into a future-value problem, we verify the present-value computation:

Amount Invested (present value)	$4,545
Expected Earnings ($4,545 × 0.10)...	455
Amount to Be Received One Year from Now (future value)....................................	$5,000

This example illustrates that present value and future value are based on the same equation:

$$\text{Present Value} \times (1 + \text{Interest Rate}) = \text{Future Value}$$

$$\frac{\text{Future Value}}{(1 + \text{Interest Rate})} = \text{Present Value}$$

If the $5,000 is to be received two years from now, you will pay only $4,132 for the investment, as shown next:

By turning the data around, we verify that $4,132 accumulates to $5,000 at 10% for two years:

Amount Invested (present value)	$4,132
Expected Earnings for First Year ($4,132 × 0.10)	413
Amount of Investment after One Year	4,545
Expected Earnings for Second Year ($4,545 × 0.10)	455
Amount to Be Received Two Years from Now (future value)	$5,000

You would pay $4,132, the present value of $5,000, to receive the $5,000 future amount at the end of two years at 10% per year. The $868 difference between the amount invested, $4,132, and the amount to be received, $5,000, is the return on the investment; it is the sum of the two interest receipts: $413 + $455 = $868.

Present-Value Tables

We have shown the simple formula for computing present value. However, calculating present value this way for investments spanning many years is tedious. Present-value tables ease our work. Let's reexamine our examples of present value by using **Table B-3**, Present Value of $1.

Present value of $1 per period at $i\%$ for n periods, $PVIF_{(i,n)}$

n	1%	2%	3%	3.5%	4%	4.5%	5%	6%	7%	8%	9%	10%	11%	12%	13%	14%	15%	16%	18%	20%	25%
1	0.9901	0.9804	0.9709	0.9662	0.9615	0.9569	0.9524	0.9434	0.9346	0.9259	0.9174	0.9091	0.9009	0.8929	0.8850	0.8772	0.8696	0.8621	0.8475	0.8333	0.8000
2	0.9803	0.9612	0.9426	0.9335	0.9246	0.9157	0.9070	0.8900	0.8734	0.8573	0.8417	0.8264	0.8116	0.7972	0.7831	0.7695	0.7561	0.7432	0.7182	0.6944	0.6400
3	0.9706	0.9423	0.9151	0.9019	0.8890	0.8763	0.8638	0.8396	0.8163	0.7938	0.7722	0.7513	0.7312	0.7118	0.6931	0.6750	0.6575	0.6407	0.6086	0.5787	0.5120
4	0.9610	0.9238	0.8885	0.8714	0.8548	0.8386	0.8227	0.7921	0.7629	0.7350	0.7084	0.6830	0.6587	0.6355	0.6133	0.5921	0.5718	0.5523	0.5158	0.4823	0.4096
5	0.9515	0.9057	0.8626	0.8420	0.8219	0.8025	0.7835	0.7473	0.7130	0.6806	0.6499	0.6209	0.5935	0.5674	0.5428	0.5194	0.4972	0.4761	0.4371	0.4019	0.3277
6	0.9420	0.8880	0.8375	0.8135	0.7903	0.7679	0.7462	0.7050	0.6663	0.6302	0.5963	0.5645	0.5346	0.5066	0.4803	0.4556	0.4323	0.4104	0.3704	0.3349	0.2621
7	0.9327	0.8706	0.8131	0.7860	0.7599	0.7348	0.7107	0.6651	0.6227	0.5835	0.5470	0.5132	0.4817	0.4523	0.4251	0.3996	0.3759	0.3538	0.3139	0.2791	0.2097
8	0.9235	0.8535	0.7894	0.7594	0.7307	0.7032	0.6768	0.6274	0.5820	0.5403	0.5019	0.4665	0.4339	0.4039	0.3762	0.3506	0.3269	0.3050	0.2660	0.2326	0.1678
9	0.9143	0.8368	0.7664	0.7337	0.7026	0.6729	0.6446	0.5919	0.5439	0.5002	0.4604	0.4241	0.3909	0.3606	0.3329	0.3075	0.2843	0.2630	0.2255	0.1938	0.1342
10	0.9053	0.8203	0.7441	0.7089	0.6756	0.6439	0.6139	0.5584	0.5083	0.4632	0.4224	0.3855	0.3522	0.3220	0.2946	0.2697	0.2472	0.2267	0.1911	0.1615	0.1074
11	0.8963	0.8043	0.7224	0.6849	0.6496	0.6162	0.5847	0.5268	0.4751	0.4289	0.3875	0.3505	0.3173	0.2875	0.2607	0.2366	0.2149	0.1954	0.1619	0.1346	0.0859
12	0.8874	0.7885	0.7014	0.6618	0.6246	0.5897	0.5568	0.4970	0.4440	0.3971	0.3555	0.3186	0.2858	0.2567	0.2307	0.2076	0.1869	0.1685	0.1372	0.1122	0.0687
13	0.8787	0.7730	0.6810	0.6394	0.6006	0.5643	0.5303	0.4688	0.4150	0.3677	0.3262	0.2897	0.2575	0.2292	0.2042	0.1821	0.1625	0.1452	0.1163	0.0935	0.0550
14	0.8700	0.7579	0.6611	0.6178	0.5775	0.5400	0.5051	0.4423	0.3878	0.3405	0.2992	0.2633	0.2320	0.2046	0.1807	0.1597	0.1413	0.1252	0.0985	0.0779	0.0440
15	0.8613	0.7430	0.6419	0.5969	0.5553	0.5167	0.4810	0.4173	0.3624	0.3152	0.2745	0.2394	0.2090	0.1827	0.1599	0.1401	0.1229	0.1079	0.0835	0.0649	0.0352
16	0.8528	0.7284	0.6232	0.5767	0.5339	0.4945	0.4581	0.3936	0.3387	0.2919	0.2519	0.2176	0.1883	0.1631	0.1415	0.1229	0.1069	0.0930	0.0708	0.0541	0.0281
17	0.8444	0.7142	0.6050	0.5572	0.5134	0.4732	0.4363	0.3714	0.3166	0.2703	0.2311	0.1978	0.1696	0.1456	0.1252	0.1078	0.0929	0.0802	0.0600	0.0451	0.0225
18	0.8360	0.7002	0.5874	0.5384	0.4936	0.4528	0.4155	0.3503	0.2959	0.2502	0.2120	0.1799	0.1528	0.1300	0.1108	0.0946	0.0808	0.0691	0.0508	0.0376	0.0180
19	0.8277	0.6864	0.5703	0.5202	0.4746	0.4333	0.3957	0.3305	0.2765	0.2317	0.1945	0.1635	0.1377	0.1161	0.0981	0.0829	0.0703	0.0596	0.0431	0.0313	0.0144
20	0.8195	0.6730	0.5537	0.5026	0.4564	0.4146	0.3769	0.3118	0.2584	0.2145	0.1784	0.1486	0.1240	0.1037	0.0868	0.0728	0.0611	0.0514	0.0365	0.0261	0.0115
25	0.7798	0.6095	0.4776	0.4231	0.3751	0.3327	0.2953	0.2330	0.1842	0.1460	0.1160	0.0923	0.0736	0.0588	0.0471	0.0378	0.0304	0.0245	0.0160	0.0105	0.0038
30	0.7419	0.5521	0.4120	0.3563	0.3083	0.2670	0.2314	0.1741	0.1314	0.0994	0.0754	0.0573	0.0437	0.0334	0.0256	0.0196	0.0151	0.0116	0.0070	0.0042	0.0012
35	0.7059	0.5000	0.3554	0.3000	0.2534	0.2143	0.1813	0.1301	0.0937	0.0676	0.0490	0.0356	0.0259	0.0189	0.0139	0.0102	0.0075	0.0055	0.0030	0.0017	0.0004
40	0.6717	0.4529	0.3066	0.2526	0.2083	0.1719	0.1420	0.0972	0.0668	0.0460	0.0318	0.0221	0.0154	0.0107	0.0075	0.0053	0.0037	0.0026	0.0013	0.0007	0.0001
50	0.6080	0.3715	0.2281	0.1791	0.1407	0.1107	0.0872	0.0543	0.0339	0.0213	0.0134	0.0085	0.0054	0.0035	0.0022	0.0014	0.0009	0.0006	0.0003	0.0001	0.0000

Table B-3 ▲

For the 10% investment for one year, we find the intersection of the 10% column and the first row of the period column. The figure 0.9091 is computed as follows: 1/1.10 = 0.9091. In preparing the table, this work has been done for us, so only the resulting present values are given in the table. The heading in Table B-3 states that the present value of $1 is being determined. To calculate present value for $5,000, we multiply $5,000 by 0.9091. The result is $4,545, which matches the result we obtained previously by hand.

For the two-year investment, we read down the 10% column and across the period 2 row. We multiply 0.8264 by $5,000 and get $4,132, which confirms our preceding computation of $4,132. Using the table, we can compute the present value of any single future amount.

Present Value of an Annuity

Let's return to the investment example that provided the investor with only a single future receipt of $5,000 at the end of two years. Annuity investments provide multiple receipts of an equal amount at fixed intervals over the investment's length.

Consider an investment that promises annual cash receipts of $10,000 to be received at the end of each of three years. Assume that you demand a 12% return on your investment. What is the investment's present value? What would you pay today to acquire the investment? The investment spans three periods, and you would pay the sum of three present values. The computation follows:

Year	Annual Cash Receipt	×	Present Value of $1 at 12% (Table B-3)	=	Present Value of Annual Cash Receipt
1	$10,000	×	0.8929	=	$ 8,929
2	10,000	×	0.7972	=	7,972
3	10,000	×	0.7118	=	7,118
			Total Present Value of Investment =		$24,019

The present value of this annuity is $24,019. By paying this amount today, you will receive $10,000 at the end of each of the three years while earning 12% on your investment.

The example illustrates repetitive computations of the three future amounts. One way to ease the computational burden is to add the three present values of $1, 0.8929 + 0.7972 + 0.7118, and multiply their sum of 2.4019 by the annual cash receipt of $10,000 to obtain the present value of the annuity, $24,019 ($10,000 × 2.4019).

An easier approach is to use a present value of an annuity table. Table B-4 shows the present value of $1 to be received at the end of each period for a given number of periods. The present value of a three-period annuity at 12% is 2.4018, the junction of the period 3 row and the 12% column. Thus, the present value of $10,000 received annually at the end of each of three years, discounted at 12%, is $24,018 ($10,000 × 2.4018). The difference is due to rounding in the present value table.

Present value of an annuity of $1 per period at i% for n periods, $PVIFA_{(i,n)}$

n	1%	2%	3%	3.5%	4%	4.5%	5%	6%	7%	8%	9%	10%	11%	12%	13%	14%	15%	16%	18%	20%	25%
1	0.9901	0.9804	0.9709	0.9662	0.9615	0.9569	0.9524	0.9434	0.9346	0.9259	0.9174	0.9091	0.9009	0.8929	0.8850	0.8772	0.8696	0.8621	0.8475	0.8333	0.8000
2	1.9704	1.9416	1.9135	1.8997	1.8861	1.8727	1.8594	1.8334	1.8080	1.7833	1.7591	1.7355	1.7125	1.6901	1.6681	1.6467	1.6257	1.6052	1.5656	1.5278	1.4400
3	2.9410	2.8839	2.8286	2.8016	2.7751	2.7490	2.7232	2.6730	2.6243	2.5771	2.5313	2.4869	2.4437	2.4018	2.3612	2.3216	2.2832	2.2459	2.1743	2.1065	1.9520
4	3.9020	3.8077	3.7171	3.6731	3.6299	3.5875	3.5460	3.4651	3.3872	3.3121	3.2397	3.1699	3.1024	3.0373	2.9745	2.9137	2.8550	2.7982	2.6901	2.5887	2.3616
5	4.8534	4.7135	4.5797	4.5151	4.4518	4.3900	4.3295	4.2124	4.1002	3.9927	3.8897	3.7908	3.6959	3.6048	3.5172	3.4331	3.3522	3.2743	3.1272	2.9906	2.6893
6	5.7955	5.6014	5.4172	5.3286	5.2421	5.1579	5.0757	4.9173	4.7665	4.6229	4.4859	4.3553	4.2305	4.1114	3.9975	3.8887	3.7845	3.6847	3.4976	3.3255	2.9514
7	6.7282	6.4720	6.2303	6.1145	6.0021	5.8927	5.7864	5.5824	5.3893	5.2064	5.0330	4.8684	4.7122	4.5638	4.4226	4.2883	4.1604	4.0386	3.8115	3.6046	3.1611
8	7.6517	7.3255	7.0197	6.8740	6.7327	6.5959	6.4632	6.2098	5.9713	5.7466	5.5348	5.3349	5.1461	4.9676	4.7988	4.6389	4.4873	4.3436	4.0776	3.8372	3.3289
9	8.5660	8.1622	7.7861	7.6077	7.4353	7.2688	7.1078	6.8017	6.5152	6.2469	5.9952	5.7590	5.5370	5.3282	5.1317	4.9464	4.7716	4.6065	4.3030	4.0310	3.4631
10	9.4713	8.9826	8.5302	8.3166	8.1109	7.9127	7.7217	7.3601	7.0236	6.7101	6.4177	6.1446	5.8892	5.6502	5.4262	5.2161	5.0188	4.8332	4.4941	4.1925	3.5705
11	10.3676	9.7868	9.2526	9.0016	8.7605	8.5289	8.3064	7.8869	7.4987	7.1390	6.8052	6.4951	6.2065	5.9377	5.6869	5.4527	5.2337	5.0286	4.6560	4.3271	3.6564
12	11.2551	10.5753	9.9540	9.6633	9.3851	9.1186	8.8633	8.3838	7.9427	7.5361	7.1607	6.8137	6.4924	6.1944	5.9176	5.6603	5.4206	5.1971	4.7932	4.4392	3.7251
13	12.1337	11.3484	10.6350	10.3027	9.9856	9.6829	9.3936	8.8527	8.3577	7.9038	7.4869	7.1034	6.7499	6.4235	6.1218	5.8424	5.5831	5.3423	4.9095	4.5327	3.7801
14	13.0037	12.1062	11.2961	10.9205	10.5631	10.2228	9.8986	9.2950	8.7455	8.2442	7.7862	7.3667	6.9819	6.6282	6.3025	6.0021	5.7245	5.4675	5.0081	4.6106	3.8241
15	13.8651	12.8493	11.9379	11.5174	11.1184	10.7395	10.3797	9.7122	9.1079	8.5595	8.0607	7.6061	7.1909	6.8109	6.4624	6.1422	5.8474	5.5755	5.0916	4.6755	3.8593
16	14.7179	13.5777	12.5611	12.0941	11.6523	11.2340	10.8378	10.1059	9.4466	8.8514	8.3126	7.8237	7.3792	6.9740	6.6039	6.2651	5.9542	5.6685	5.1624	4.7296	3.8874
17	15.5623	14.2919	13.1661	12.6513	12.1657	11.7072	11.2741	10.4773	9.7632	9.1216	8.5436	8.0216	7.5488	7.1196	6.7291	6.3729	6.0472	5.7487	5.2223	4.7746	3.9099
18	16.3983	14.9920	13.7535	13.1897	12.6593	12.1600	11.6896	10.8276	10.0591	9.3719	8.7556	8.2014	7.7016	7.2497	6.8399	6.4674	6.1280	5.8178	5.2732	4.8122	3.9279
19	17.2260	15.6785	14.3238	13.7098	13.1339	12.5933	12.0853	11.1581	10.3356	9.6036	8.9501	8.3649	7.8393	7.3658	6.9380	6.5504	6.1982	5.8775	5.3162	4.8435	3.9424
20	18.0456	16.3514	14.8775	14.2124	13.5903	13.0079	12.4622	11.4699	10.5940	9.8181	9.1285	8.5136	7.9633	7.4694	7.0248	6.6231	6.2593	5.9288	5.3527	4.8696	3.9539
25	22.0232	19.5235	17.4131	16.4815	15.6221	14.8282	14.0939	12.7834	11.6536	10.6748	9.8226	9.0770	8.4217	7.8431	7.3300	6.8729	6.4641	6.0971	5.4669	4.9476	3.9849
30	25.8077	22.3965	19.6004	18.3920	17.2920	16.2889	15.3725	13.7648	12.4090	11.2578	10.2737	9.4269	8.6938	8.0552	7.4957	7.0027	6.5660	6.1772	5.5168	4.9789	3.9950
35	29.4086	24.9986	21.4872	20.0007	18.6646	17.4610	16.3742	14.4982	12.9477	11.6546	10.5668	9.6442	8.8552	8.1755	7.5856	7.0700	6.6166	6.2153	5.5386	4.9915	3.9984
40	32.8347	27.3555	23.1148	21.3551	19.7928	18.4016	17.1591	15.0463	13.3317	11.9246	10.7574	9.7791	8.9511	8.2438	7.6344	7.1050	6.6418	6.2335	5.5482	4.9966	3.9995
50	39.1961	31.4236	25.7298	23.4556	21.4822	19.7620	18.2559	15.7619	13.8007	12.2335	10.9617	9.9148	9.0417	8.3045	7.6752	7.1327	6.6605	6.2463	5.5541	4.9995	3.9999

Table B-4 ▲

ACCOUNTING VOCABULARY

The Language of Business

Annuities (p. 764) Multiple investments of an equal periodic amount at fixed intervals over the length of the investment.

Compound interest (p. 762) Interest earned not only on principal but also on the interest to date.

Discounting (p. 765) Computing a present value.

Future value (p. 762) The amount that a given sum of money will be "worth" at a specified time in the future assuming a certain interest rate.

Present value (p. 765) The value on a given date of a future amount, adjusted to reflect the time value of money.

Time value of money (p. 762) The concept that states that a dollar today is worth more than a dollar received in the future.

MyAccountingLab

Make the grade with MyAccountingLab. The exercises n this Appendix can be found on MyAccountingLab at **www.myaccountinglab.com**. You can practise them as often as you want, and they feature step-by-step guided solutions to help you find the right answer.

ACCOUNTING PRACTICE

Exercises

EB-1A. Calculate present and future values. 10–15 min.

Presented next are four independent situations related to future and present values.

Requirement

1. Using the tables in this appendix, calculate the future or present value of each item as needed.

   a. $5,000 is deposited in the bank today for a period of eight years. Calculate the value of the $5,000 at the end of eight years assuming it earns 5% interest.

   b. How much must you invest today to receive $1,500 at the end of each year for the next four years, assuming you can earn 7% interest?

   c. $3,500 will be invested at the end of each year for a period of five years. Calculate the value of the investment at the end of five years, assuming it earns 9% interest.

   d. The company you work for wants to purchase a new piece of equipment that is estimated to cost $18,000 ten years from now. How much must it invest today to have the $18,000 necessary to purchase the equipment if it can earn 8% interest?

EB-2A. Future value concepts. 15–20 min.

Allen Hamilton is considering two plans for building an education fund for his children.

Plan A—Invest $2,000 each year for six years. This investment will earn 10% annual interest.

Plan B—Invest $10,000 now, earning 8% annual interest for six years.

Requirement

1. Before making any calculations, which plan would you expect to provide the larger future amount? Using the tables provided in this appendix, calculate the future value of each plan. Which plan provides the larger amount at the end of six years?

EB-3A. Present value concepts. 15–20 min.

Aztec Electronics, Inc. needs new manufacturing equipment. Two companies can provide similar equipment but under different payment plans:

a. Fancher Manufacturing offers to let Aztec Electronics, Inc. pay $60,000 at the end of each year for five years. The payments include interest at 12% per year.

b. Phoenix, Corp. will let Aztec Electronics, Inc. make a single payment of $400,000 at the end of five years. This payment includes both principal and interest at 12%.

Requirements

1. Calculate the present value cost of each payment plan.

2. In addition to the present value cost of the equipment, what other factors should Aztec Electronics consider when deciding which company to purchase the equipment from?

EB-4A. Present value concepts. 10–15 min.

Your tenant, Sandra, has just signed a one-year lease to rent the apartment from you at $850 per month, payable at the end of each month. However, you are short of cash and offer to accept a single payment now from Sandra of only $8,500. Sandra has been saving her money carefully for some time now, and has a large bank balance of more than $15,000, so has the money available to make the single payment now. If Sandra believes she can earn interest at a rate of 2% per month, should she take your offer, or not?

EB-5A. Future value concepts. 10–15 min.

Chan just won the grand prize at the city lottery, which consists of $100,000 at the end of one year, $200,000 at the end of two years, and $300,000 at the end of three years. The city lottery commission offers Chan the option of receiving a single payment of $700,000 at the end of five years, as an alternative to the three annual payments. If Chan believes that 8% is the right interest rate for borrowing or lending in the coming years, should Chan stick with the three payments or accept the single payment of $700,000? What if the annual interest rate is reduced to 4%?

EB-6A. Future value concepts. 10–15 min.

Hussain wants to buy a new car, which will cost him $23,000, tax included. Hussain has only $18,000 in his bank account, and does not like the idea of borrowing. He has decided to delay buying the car until he has enough money to do so. If Hussain is able to deposit $500 per month at the end of each month into his account, and if the money in his account earns interest at the rate of 2% per month, how long will Hussain have to wait until he can buy his new car?

EB-7A. Present value concepts. 10–15 min.

Rachel borrowed $10,000 and agreed to pay back the loan with five consecutive annual payments, with the first payment occurring in one year. If the annual interest rate is 5%, what is the amount of her annual payment?

EB-8A. Present value concepts. 10–15 min.

Hua Tran financed a new automobile by paying $7,500 cash and agreeing to make 40 monthly payments of $500 each, the first payment to be made one month after the purchase. The loan bears interest at an annual rate of 12%. What was the cost of the automobile?

EB-9A. Future value concepts. 10–15 min.

Miko Yamada desires to accumulate $1 million in 20 years using her money market fund balance of $20,000. At what interest rate must her investment compound annually?

EB-10A. Future value concepts. 10–15 min.

Mingteh Inc. has recently issued a $35 million, 20-year bond, and is committed to make annual sinking fund deposits of $600,000. The deposits are made on the last day of each year and yield a return of 10%. Will the fund at the end of 20 years be sufficient to retire the bonds? If not, what will the excess or deficiency be?

Glossary

Visit *MyAccountingLab* at **www.myaccountinglab.com** *to find Glossary Flashcards.*

A

Accelerated depreciation method. A depreciation method that writes off more of the asset's cost near the start of its useful life than the straight-line method does.

Account form. A balance sheet format that lists assets on the left of the report and liabilities and shareholders' equity on the right, just as those accounts appear in the accounting equation.

Accounting. The information system that measures business activity, processes the results of activities into reports, and communicates the results to decision makers.

Accounting cycle. The sequence of steps used to record and report business transactions.

Accounting period. Generally, the time period reflected by a set of financial statements.

Accounting Standards for Private Enterprises (ASPE). A set of guidelines that have replaced the original Canadian Generally Accepted Accounting Principles (GAAP), but specifically used for private enterprises.

Account. The basic summary device of accounting; the detailed record of all the changes in a specific asset, liability, or shareholders' equity item as a result of transactions.

Accounts payable. A liability backed by the general reputation and credit standing of the debtor.

Accounts receivable. An asset representing amounts due from customers to whom the business has sold goods or for whom the business has performed services.

Accounts receivable turnover. Net Credit Sales divided by net average Accounts Receivable; it measures a company's ability to collect cash from its credit customers. To compute accounts receivable turnover, divide net credit sales by average net accounts receivable.

Accrual basis accounting. An accounting system that records the business event based on when it occurs, not when cash is exchanged.

Accruals. Revenues earned or expenses incurred before cash has been exchanged.

Accrued expenses. Expenses that have been incurred prior to being paid for.

Accumulated depreciation. A contra-asset account that reflects all of the depreciation recorded for an asset to date.

Accumulated other comprehensive income. The cumulative change in equity that is due to the revenues and expenses, and gains and losses derived from non-shareholder transactions.

Acid-test ratio. Ratio that reveals how well the entity can pay its current liabilities. Quick assets (cash, short-term investments, and net current receivables) divided by current liabilities. It measures a company's ability to pay its current liabilities if they came due immediately Also called the *quick ratio*.

Adjunct account. An account that is linked to another account (a companion account). An adjunct account will have a normal balance that is the same as its companion account.

Adjusted trial balance. A list of all the accounts of a business with their adjusted balances.

Adjusting entries. Journal entries made at the end of the accounting period to measure the period's income accurately and bring the related asset and liability accounts to correct balances before the financial statements are prepared.

Aging method. The method of estimating uncollectible accounts that focuses on accounts receivable; the accountant calculates the end-of-period allowance balance based on an aging of the Accounts Receivable; also called the *balance sheet approach*.

Allowance for Doubtful Accounts. A contra-asset account that holds the estimated amount of uncollectible accounts receivable.

Allowance method. The method of accounting for uncollectible accounts that estimates these amounts and uses an allowance account so that the balance sheet shows the net amount of Accounts Receivable expected to be collected in the future.

Amortization. Systematic reduction of an intangible asset's carrying value on the books. An expense that applies to intangibles in the same way depreciation applies to plant assets and depletion to natural resources.

Annuities. Multiple investments of an equal periodic amount at fixed intervals over the length of the investment.

Arrears. A cumulative dividend on preferred stock that has not been paid for the year.

Assets. Items of value that a business possesses; also referred to as the economic resources or properties owned by the business that will provide future benefits to the business.

Audit. An examination of a company's financial statements performed to determine their fairness.

Audit trail. A trail of business documents and records that provides evidence of transactions.

Average cost method. Inventory costing method where a new average cost per unit is computed and is used to value ending inventory and cost of goods sold. There are two types of average cost: (1) moving average, and (2) weighted average. Moving average is applied in a perpetual inventory system. Weighted average is applied in a periodic inventory system.

B

Bad debt. An account receivable that is unable to be collected; also called an *uncollectible account*.

Bad debt expense. Selling expense caused by uncollectible accounts that reduce operating income.

Balance. The difference between an account's total debit and total credit amounts; the ending value of an account.

Balance sheet. Summary of an entity's assets, liabilities, and shareholders' equity as of a specific date; also called the *statement of financial position*.

Balance sheet method. The method of estimating uncollectible accounts that focuses on accounts receivable. The accountant calculates the end-of-period allowance balance based on an aging of the Accounts Receivable; also called the *aging method*.

Bank balance. The balance in the company's bank account according to the bank.

Bank collections. Collection of money by the bank on behalf of a depositor.

Bank reconciliation. A document that identifies and explains the differences between a depositor's record of a cash account and a bank's record of the same cash account.

Bank statement. A document the bank prepares to report the changes in the depositor's cash account for a period of time. It shows the beginning bank account balance, lists the month's cash transactions, and shows the ending bank account balance.

Basket purchase. Purchase of multiple assets for one price; also called a *lump-sum purchase*.

Benchmarking. The practice of comparing a company with other companies that are leaders.

Betterments. Expenditures that increase the capacity or efficiency of an asset.

Bonds payable. Long-term, interest-bearing notes payable issued to multiple lenders called bondholders.

Book balance. The balance in a company's bank account according to the company's accounting records, or books.

Book value. The asset's cost minus its accumulated depreciation; also called *carrying value*.

Brand names. Assets that represent distinctive identifications of a product or service; also called *trade names*.

Bribes. The payment of money to influence the conduct of a person.

Businesses. Organizations that sell products or services to customers.

C

Callable bonds. Bonds that the issuer may call or pay off at a specified price whenever the issuer wants.

Canadian Accounting Standards for Private Enterprises. Accounting rules, created by the Accounting Standards Board (AcSB), that govern how accountants measure, process, and communicate financial information for Canadian private enterprises.

Capital expenditures. Expenditures that increase the capacity or efficiency of an asset or extend its useful life. Capital expenditures are debited to an asset account.

Capital lease. A term used by Canadian ASPE. A lease agreement that is treated as a financed purchase.

Capitalized. The process of debiting (increasing) an asset account for the cost of an asset.

Carrying amount. Bonds payable *minus* the discount or *plus* the premium.

Carrying value. The asset's cost minus its accumulated depreciation; also called *book value*.

Cash. Coin, currency, cheques, petty cash, chequing accounts, payroll accounts, money orders, traveller's cheques, and anything the bank will accept as a deposit.

Cash and cash equivalents. The balance sheet item used to describe cash and items so closely resembling cash that they are presented as cash.

Cash conversion cycle. A measurement of the amount of time a company's cash is tied up in its operations.

Cash equivalents. Highly liquid, highly safe investments that so closely resemble cash that they may be shown with cash on the balance sheet.

Cash flow statement. A financial statement that shows all of the sources and all of the uses of cash for an accounting period.

Cash register schemes. A fraud scheme in which an employee steals cash by processing false refunds.

Cash-basis accounting. Accounting method that records revenues when cash is received and expenses when cash is paid.

Chart of accounts. A list of all the accounts of a business and the numbers assigned to those accounts.

Cheque tampering. A fraud scheme in which an employee writes a fraudulent cheque and makes the cheque payable to him- or herself, or obtains a cheque intended for an outside party, endorses the cheque, and then cashes it.

Classified balance sheet. A balance sheet that separates assets and liabilities into current and long-term classes.

Closing entries. Journal entries that are prepared at the end of the accounting period. Closing entries zero out the revenue, expense, and dividends accounts so that accounting can begin for the next period.

Code of ethics. A formal written document that contains broad statements intended to guide proper ethical decision making.

Collateral. Assets pledged to secure repayment of a loan. In the case of nonpayment by the borrower, the lender has the right to take the collateral.

Collusion. Two or more individuals working together to commit fraud.

Common shares. Represents the investment of assets made by shareholders into a corporation. The most typical kind of stock. Owners usually have voting rights, the rights to receive dividends, and the right to receive assets if the company liquidates.

Common-size statements. A financial statement that reports only percentages (no dollar amounts).

Comparability. One of the qualitative characteristics of accounting information that should enable users to compare one company's accounting information to another company's accounting information and to its own previous year's results.

Completed contract method. Under this method, revenues, costs, and gross profit are recognized only after the project is fully completed.

Componentization. To take the cost of an asset and divide it between its separate component parts, where the cost of each of these components is significant in relation to the total cost of the asset.

Compound interest. Interest earned not only on principal but also on the interest to date.

Compound journal entries. A journal entry affecting more than two accounts; an entry that has more than one debit and/or more than one credit.

Conceptual framework. A theoretical foundation that helps accounting standard setters develop consistent and coherent standards, and helps accountants determine the appropriate treatment of the events in the absence of specific guidance, so that financial information can be properly communicated to the users.

Consistency principle. Accounting principle that states that a business should use the same accounting methods and procedures from period to period.

Contingent liabilities. A potential liability that depends on the outcome of a future event.

Contra-accounts. An account that is linked to another account. A contra-account will have a normal balance opposite of the account it is linked to.

Contributed surplus. This account represents any excess of the average share price over cash paid to purchase back treasury shares.

Control account. An account in the general ledger that summarizes the details of an account balance.

Control activities. The policies and procedures implemented in an internal control system.

Control environment. The overall attitude, awareness, and actions of management and staff regarding the internal control system and its importance to the business.

Controller. The individual in an organization responsible for the accounting system and financial statements.

Convertible bonds. Bonds that may be converted into the common shares of the issuing company at the option of the investor.

Copyright. Exclusive right to reproduce and sell a book, musical composition, film, other work of art, or computer program. Issued by the federal government, copyrights extend 50 years beyond the author's life.

Corporation. A business owned by shareholders that is an entity legally separate from its owners.

Cost of goods available for sale. The cost of inventory on hand at the beginning of the period plus the net cost of inventory purchased during the period.

Cost of goods sold. The cost of the inventory that the business has sold to customers.

Cost–benefit. An analysis of what one option costs and what its benefits are to determine whether to implement the action or not.

Credit memorandum. A document that supports the return of goods from the customer and the adjustment to the customer's account balance.

Credit terms. The payment terms for customers who buy on account.

Credit. The right side of any account; an entry made to the right side of an account.

Creditor. The entity to whom the debtor promises future payment; also called the *payee of a note*.

Cumulative preferred shares. Preferred shares whose owners must receive all dividends in arrears before the corporation pays dividends to the common shareholders.

Current assets. Assets that are expected to be converted to cash, sold, or consumed within one year or the business's operating cycle if the cycle is longer than a year.

Current cost. The amount required to purchase the asset today.

Current liabilities. Debts due to be paid with cash or fulfilled with goods and services within one year or the entity's operating cycle if the cycle is longer than a year.

Current portion of long-term debt. The principal portion of a long-term liability that is payable within one year.

Current ratio. The ratio of current assets to current liabilities; a key measure of liquidity. Measures a business's ability to meet its short-term obligations with its current assets.

D

Days' sales in inventory. Measures a company's ability to turn inventory to sales. To compute the ratio, divide 365 by the inventory turnover.

Days' sales in receivables. Measures a company's ability to collect receivables. To compute the ratio, divide 365 by the accounts receivable turnover.

Debentures. Unsecured bonds backed only by the good faith of the borrower; also called *unsecured bonds*.

Debit. The left side of any account; an entry made to the left side of an account.

Debit memorandum. A document that supports the return of goods to the supplier and the adjustment to the balance owed to the supplier.

Debt ratio. The ratio of a company's total liabilities (debt) to its total assets. It measures a business's ability to pay long-term liabilities.

Debt to equity ratio. Total liabilities divided by total equity. It measures a business's financial leverage and indicates what proportion of equity and debt the company is using to finance its assets.

Debtor. The entity that promises future payment; also called the *maker of a note*.

Deferrals. Cash received or paid before revenues have been earned or expenses have been incurred. *See also* Adjusting entries

Deferred expenses. Amounts that are assets of a business because they represent items that have been paid for but will be used later. Also called *prepaid expenses*.

Deferred revenues. A liability created when a business collects cash from customers in advance of providing goods or services; also called *unearned revenue*.

Depletion. Systematic reduction of a natural resource's carrying value on the books. Expense that applies to natural resources in the same way depreciation applies to plant assets and amortization to intangible assets. It is computed in the same way as units-of-production depreciation.

Deposits in transit. Deposits that have been recorded by a company but not yet by its bank.

Depreciable cost. The cost of a plant asset minus its estimated residual value.

Depreciation. Allocation of the cost of a long-term asset to expense over its useful life.

Direct method. Format of the operating activities section of the cash flow statement; it lists the cash receipts and cash payments resulting from a company's day-to-day operations.

Direct write-off method. The method of accounting for uncollectible accounts in which a customer's account is written off as uncollectible when the business determines that the customer will not pay.

Disbursement schemes. A form of employee embezzlement in which an employee tricks a company into giving up cash for an invalid reason. Examples include cheque tampering, cash register schemes, and expense schemes.

Discount period. Period in which the buyer can make early payment for a purchase and receive a discount on that purchase.

Discount. Excess of a bond's maturity value over its issue price; also called a *bond discount*.

Discounting. Computing a present value.

Dividend yield. Ratio of dividends per share to the share's market price per share. Tells the percentage of a share's market value that the company returns to shareholders annually as dividends.

Dividends. Distribution of earnings by a corporation to its shareholders.

Dollar value bias. The bias one sees from comparing numbers in absolute (dollars) rather than relative (percentages) terms.

Double-declining-balance (DDB). An accelerated depreciation method that computes annual depreciation by multiplying the asset's decreasing book value by a constant percent that is two times the straight-line rate.

Double-entry accounting. The rule of accounting that specifies that every transaction involves at least two accounts and is recorded with equal amounts of debits and credits.

Due date. The date when final payment of the note is due; also called the *maturity date*.

E

Earnings per share of common shares. Reflects the net income earned for each share of the company's outstanding common shares.

Effective interest method. The calculation of interest on a bond based on the amount that is owed to bondholders.

Electronic data interchange (EDI). Direct electronic communication between suppliers and retailers.

Electronic funds transfer (EFT). System that transfers cash by electronic communication rather than by paper documents.

Employee embezzlement. Fraud where employees steal from employers by taking assets, bribes, or kickbacks, or engaging in disbursement schemes to steal cash.

Entity. An organization or a section of an organization that, for accounting purposes, stands apart as a separate economic unit.

eom. Credit term specifying that payment for a purchase is due by the end of the month; also referred to as *n/eom*.

Ethics. Principles of socially responsible behaviour.

Expense scheme. A fraud scheme in which an employee overcharges the company for travel and other business-related expenses, such as lunches, hotels, air travel, parking fees, and cab fares.

Expenses. Decreases to retained earnings caused by using resources to deliver goods or provide services to customers.

External audit. An audit of financial statements performed by public accountants.

Extraordinary repair. Repair work that extends the life of an asset.

F

Financial accounting. A process used to track business transactions and to provide financial information about a business to external users.

Financial lease. A term used by IFRS. A lease agreement that is treated as a financed purchase.

Financial statements. Financial information prepared according to IFRS or Canadian Accounting Standards for Private Enterprises, that communicates an entity's performance or financial position.

Financing activities. Activities related to the issuance of, and repayment of, long-term debt or to the issuance of shares and the payment of dividends; it's a section of the cash flow statement.

Finished goods. Inventory of goods ready to sell.

First-in, first-out (FIFO) method. Inventory costing method in which the first inventory costs incurred are the first costs to be assigned to cost of goods sold; FIFO leaves in ending inventory the last, the most recent, costs incurred.

Fiscal year. Any consecutive 12-month period that a business adopts as its accounting year.

Fixed asset turnover ratio. Measures a company's ability to generate sales from fixed asset investments, specifically property, plant, and equipment (PPE).

Fixed assets. The long-lived assets of a business including land, buildings, furniture, fixtures, and equipment; also called plant assets and commonly shown on the balance sheet as property, plant, and equipment.

Footnotes. Disclosures that accompany the financial statements.

Franchises. Privileges granted by a private business or a government to sell a product or service under specified conditions.

Fraud. Deceit or trickery involving intentional actions that cause harm to a business, its stakeholders, or both.

Fraud triangle. The combination of perceived pressure, rationalization, and perceived opportunity necessary to commit fraud.

Free cash flow. The anticipated amount of cash available from operations after paying for planned investments in long-term assets and paying dividends.

Free on board (FOB) destination. A shipping term specifying that title to goods passes to the buyer when the goods are received at buyer's destination; thus, the seller pays the cost of shipping the goods to this destination.

Free on board (FOB) shipping point. A shipping term specifying that title to goods passes to the buyer when the goods are shipped at the seller's place of business; thus, the buyer pays the cost of shipping the goods to its location.

Freight charges. The cost of shipping merchandise from the seller to the buyer.

Full-disclosure principle. Accounting principle that states that a company's financial statements should report enough information for users to make knowledgeable decisions about the company.

Fully-depreciated assets. An asset that has reached the end of its estimated useful life. No more depreciation is recorded for the asset.

Fundamental accounting equation. The basic tool of accounting that measures the resources of a business and the claims to those resources: Assets = Liabilities + Shareholders' Equity.

Future value. The amount that a given sum of money will be "worth" at a specified time in the future assuming a certain interest rate.

G

General and administrative expenses. Office expenses, such as the salaries of the company president and office employees, depreciation of items used in administration, rent, utilities, and property taxes on the office building.

General journal. The chronological accounting record of the transactions of a business.

General ledger. The accounting record summarizing, in accounts, the transactions of a business.

Going-concern principle. The assumption that the business entity will continue in operation for the foreseeable future.

Goodwill. Excess of the cost of an acquired company over the sum of the market values of its net assets (assets minus liabilities).

Gross margin. Net sales revenue minus cost of goods sold; also called *gross profit*.

Gross margin percentage. A measure of profitability equal to gross margin divided by net sales revenue; also called *gross profit percentage*.

Gross profit. Net sales revenue minus cost of goods sold; also called *gross margin*.

Gross profit method. A way of estimating inventory by estimating gross profit, using estimated gross profit to estimate cost of goods sold, and using estimated cost of goods sold to estimate ending inventory.

Gross profit percentage. A measure of profitability equal to gross profit divided by net sales revenue; also called *gross margin percentage*.

H

Historical cost. Actual cost of assets and services acquired.

Horizontal analysis. Study of dollar amount and percentage changes in comparative financial statements.

I

Impairment. An asset is impaired when its carrying amount exceeds its recoverable amount, which is the future undiscounted cash flow that the asset can provide and be disposed for.

Income from operations. Gross profit minus operating expenses; also called *operating income*.

Income statement. Summary of a business's revenues, expenses, and net income or net loss for a specific period.

Income statement method. The method of estimating uncollectible accounts that focuses on net credit sales; also called the *percentage of sales method*.

Indirect method. Format of the operating activities section of the cash flow statement; it starts with net income and reconciles to net cash provided by operating activities.

Intangible assets. Assets with no physical form. They are valuable because of the special rights they carry. Examples include patents and copyrights.

Interest. The fee for using money; revenue to the creditor for loaning money; expense to the debtor for borrowing money.

Interest rate. The percentage rate of interest specified by the note; almost always stated for a period of one year.

Interest-coverage ratio. Ratio of income from operations to interest expense. It measures the number of times that operating income can cover interest expense; also called the *times-interest-earned ratio*.

Internal audit. Assessment of a company's compliance with laws and regulations, operations, and policies and procedures performed by employees of the company.

Internal control. A system implemented within an organization to safeguard assets, operate efficiently and effectively, report financial information properly, and comply with applicable laws and regulations.

International Financial Reporting Standards (IFRS). A set of internationally accepted reporting standards that guide how business activities should be recognized, measured, and recorded, and how financial information should be reported. IFRS were developed by the International Accounting Standards Board.

Inventory layer. A record of the quantity of and the cost of inventory items made in a single purchase.

Inventory shrinkage. The loss of inventory.

Inventory turnover. The ratio of cost of goods sold to average inventory. Measures the number of times a company sells its average level of inventory during a year.

Inventory. Goods purchased for resale to customers in the normal course of merchandising operations; also called *merchandise inventory*.

Investing activities. Activities that increase or decrease long-term assets; it's a section of the cash flow statement.

Issue price. The price the shares initially sell for the first time they are sold.

J

Journalize. Entering a transaction in a journal; also called *record*.

K

Kickbacks. The return of part of a sum received because of a confidential agreement.

L

Land improvements. Depreciable improvements to land, such as fencing, sprinklers, paving, signs, and lighting.

Legal capital. The portion of shareholders' equity that cannot be used for dividends.

Liabilities. Third party or creditor claims to the assets of a business; the debts owed by the business entity to third parties, which will reduce the future assets of a business or require future services or products.

Licenses. Privileges granted by a private business or a government to sell a product or service under specified conditions.

Liquidity. The ability to convert an asset to cash quickly.

Lock-box system. A system in which customers send payments to a post office box of a business. The bank collects payments from the box and deposits them into the business's account.

Long-term assets. Long-lived, tangible assets such as land, buildings, equipment, and furniture lasting for more than a year used in the operation of a business. *See also* Plant assets on balance sheet.

Long-term liabilities. Liabilities other than those that are current.

Lower of cost and net realizable value (LCNRV) rule. The rule that a business must report inventory in the financial statements at whichever is lower, the historical cost or the net realizable value of each inventory item.

Lump-sum purchase. Purchase of multiple assets for one price; also called a *basket purchase*.

M

Maker of a note. The entity that promises future payment; also called the *debtor*.

Management fraud. Management's intentional misstatement of the financial statements, driven by greed or the pressure to show that a business is more profitable than it really is.

Managerial accounting. A branch of accounting involved in the process of gathering cost information, budgeting, planning, performance evaluation, etc. for internal users.

Manufacturing business. A business that makes its own products that are sold to the final customer or to other companies.

Market interest rate. Interest rate investors are willing to pay for similar bonds of equal risk at the current time. Also called *yield*.

Materiality. This is a measure of whether or not something is relevant to a decision. If an analysis leads to a response that something is significant or that it will change an opinion, then this is material, or of enough significance or size to matter.

Maturity date. The date when final payment of a note is due. The date on which the bond issuer (the borrower) must repay the principal amount to the bondholders; also called the *due date*.

Maturity value. The sum of the principal of a note plus interest due at maturity. The amount a borrower must pay back to the bondholders on the maturity date; also called *principal amount* or *par value*.

Memorandum entry. A journal entry that "notes" a significant event, but which has no debit or credit amount.

Merchandise inventory. Goods purchased for resale to customers in the normal course of merchandising operations; also called *inventory*.

Merchandising business. Businesses that sell products made by another company; also called *wholesale* and *retail companies*.

Mortgage. A long-term note payable that is secured by real estate.

Moving average cost. Inventory costing method where, after each purchase of inventory, a new average cost per unit is computed and is used to value ending inventory and cost of goods sold in the perpetual inventory system.

Multi-step income statement. Income statement format that calculates net income or net loss by listing important subtotals, such as gross profit and operating income.

N

n/30. Credit term specifying that payment for a purchase is due within 30 days after the date of the invoice.

n/eom. Credit term specifying that payment for a purchase is due by the end of the month; also referred to as *eom*.

Natural resources. Assets that come from the earth. Examples include minerals, gas, oil, and timber.

Net credit sales. The total credit sales less sales discounts and sales returns and allowances related to the credit sales.

Net income. The excess of total revenues over total expenses; also called *profit*.

Net loss. The excess of total expenses over total revenues.

Net realizable value. The net amount that the business expects to collect; the net realizable value of receivables is calculated by subtracting Allowance for Doubtful Accounts from Accounts Receivable.

Net sales revenue. Sales revenue less sales discounts and sales returns and allowances.

Net value. The amount found by subtracting the balance of a contra-account from the balance of the account it is linked to.

Non-current asset. An asset that will be held for more than one year or longer than the operating cycle.

Non-current liability. A liability that is expected to be paid after more than one year or after the period of one operating cycle.

Nonsufficient funds (NSF) cheques. A cheque drawn against a bank account that has insufficient money to pay the cheque.

Normal balance. The balance that appears on the side of an account where increases are recorded; the expected balance of an account.

Note payable. A written promise of future payment made by the business.

Note term. The time span of the note during which interest is computed; it extends from the original date of the note to the maturity date.

O

On account. Buying or selling on credit.

Operating activities. Activities that create revenue or expense in the entity's major line of business; it's a section of the cash flow statement. Operating activities affect the income statement.

Operating cycle. The time span during which the business obtains resources, uses them to sell goods and services to customers, and collects cash from these customers.

Operating expenses. Expenses of operating a business other than cost of goods sold. Examples include depreciation, rent, salaries, utilities, advertising, delivery expense, property taxes, and supplies expense.

Operating income. Gross profit minus operating expenses. Also called income from operations.

Operating leases. A lease (rental) agreement that grants the use of an asset to the lessee for the duration of the lease in exchange for regular payments.

Ordinary repairs. Repair work that is necessary to maintain an asset in normal operating condition.

Other revenues and expenses. Revenues and expenses that fall outside the main operations of a business, such as interest expense and a loss on the sale of long-term assets.

Outstanding cheques. Cheques that have been issued by a company and recorded in its books but have not yet been paid by its bank.

Owner's capital. The amount invested in a sole proprietorship or a partnership by an individual in exchange for ownership of the business.

P

Par value. The amount a borrower must pay back to the bondholders on the maturity date; also called *principal amount* or *maturity value*. Arbitrary amount assigned to a common share.

Partnership. A business with two or more owners.

Patent. An intangible asset that is a federal government grant conveying an exclusive 20-year right to produce and sell a process or formula.

Payee of a note. The entity to whom the debtor promises future payment; also called the *creditor*.

Perceived opportunity. An element of the fraud triangle in which the employee believes a chance exists to commit fraud, conceal it, and avoid punishment.

Perceived pressure. An element of the fraud triangle in which the employee feels a need to obtain cash or other assets.

Percentage of completion. Under this method, revenues and gross profit are recognized each period based on the percentage of expenses incurred, or the percentage of completion to date.

Percentage of sales method. The method of estimating uncollectible accounts that focuses on net credit sales; also called the *income statement method*.

Periodic inventory systems. An inventory system in which the business does not keep a continuous record of inventory on hand. At the end of the period, a physical count of inventory is taken and determines the inventory owned as well as the cost of the goods sold.

Permanent accounts. The asset, liability, and shareholders' equity accounts; these accounts are not closed at the end of the period.

Perpetual inventory record. A record that tracks the quantity of, and cost assigned to, inventory items as they are purchased and sold.

Perpetual inventory system. An inventory system in which the business keeps a continuous record of inventory on hand and the cost of the goods sold.

Petty cash. Fund containing a small amount of cash that is used to pay for minor expenditures.

Plant assets. The long-lived assets of a business including land, buildings, furniture, fixtures, and equipment; also called *fixed assets* and commonly shown on the balance sheet as property, plant, and equipment.

Post-closing trial balance. A list of the accounts and their balances at the end of the accounting period after closing entries have been journalized and posted.

Posting. Copying information from the general journal to accounts in the general ledger.

Posting reference. A notation in the journal and ledger that links these two accounting records together.

Preferred shares. Shares that give their owners certain advantages over common shareholders, such as the right to receive dividends before the common shareholders and the right to receive assets before the common shareholders if the corporation liquidates.

Premium. Excess of a bond's issue price over its maturity value; also called *bond premium*.

Prepaid expenses. Amounts that are assets of a business because they represent items that have been paid for but will be used later; also called *deferred expenses*.

Present value. The value on a given date of a future amount, adjusted to reflect the time value of money.

Price/earnings (P/E) ratio. Ratio of the market price of a common share to the company's earnings per share. It measures the value that the stock market places on $1 of a company's earnings.

Principal amount. The amount a borrower must pay back to the bondholders on the maturity date; also called *par value* or *maturity value*.

Principal. The amount loaned out by the payee and borrowed by the maker of the note.

Profit. The difference between the revenues (the sales price of the goods or services sold by the business) and expenses (the cost of the resources used to provide these goods and services); also called *net income*.

Promissory note. A written pledge to pay a fixed amount of money at a later date.

Property, plant, and equipment. A heading often seen on the balance sheet used to describe fixed, or plant, assets.

Provisions. A liability that has uncertain timing or uncertain amount.

Public accountant. A licensed accountant who serves the general public rather than one particular company.

Purchase discounts. Discount received on purchases by paying early within a discount period.

Purchase orders. A document showing details of merchandise being ordered from a supplier.

Purchase returns and allowances. A reduction in the amount owed for a purchase due to returning merchandise or accepting damaged goods.

Purchasing agents. The individual in an organization responsible for buying items for that organization.

Q

Quick assets. Highly liquid assets used to calculate the quick ratio, including cash and cash equivalents, short-term investments, and net accounts receivable.

Quick ratio. Ratio that reveals how well the entity can pay its current liabilities. Quick assets (cash, short-term investments, and net current receivables) divided by current liabilities. It measures a company's ability to pay its current liabilities if they came due immediately; also called the *acid-test ratio*.

R

Rate of return on common shareholders' equity. Net income minus preferred dividends, divided by average common shareholders' equity. It is a measure of profitability; also called *return on common equity*.

Rate of return on net sales. Ratio of net income to net sales. It is a measure of profitability; also called *return on sales*.

Rate of return on shareholder's equity. Net income divided by average shareholders' equity. It is a measure of profitability; also called *return on equity*.

Rate of return on total assets. Ratio of net income plus interest expense to total assets. It measures a company's effectiveness in using assets to generate earnings; also called *return on assets*.

Ratio analysis. A form of financial statement analysis in which items on the financial statements are expressed as ratios of one number to another.

Rationalization. An element of the fraud triangle in which the employee justifies his or her actions and convinces him- or herself that fraud is not wrong.

Raw materials. Inventory items used in the production of goods.

Realizable value. The amount that is likely to be received in exchange for an asset, factoring in any cash or other benefit, less any costs or expenses to sell or distribute the asset.

Receiving report. A document evidencing the receipt of goods purchased.

Record. Entering a transaction in a journal; also called *journalize*.

Recoverable amount. The higher of the future discounted cash flow that the asset can provide and the amount it can be disposed for.

Relevance. One of the qualitative characteristics of accounting information that makes a difference in a decision-making process. The information should be predictable and provide feedback in a timely manner.

Reliability. One of the qualitative characteristics of accounting information that it be verifiable, confirmable by any independent observer.

Report form. A balance sheet format that reports assets at the top of the report, followed by liabilities, and ending with shareholders' equity at the end of the report.

Residual value. Expected cash value of an asset at the end of its useful life; also called *salvage value*.

Retail business. A business that sells products purchased from another company to the final consumer,.

Retailers. Businesses that buy goods from manufacturers or wholesalers and resell them to the general public.

Retained earnings. Earnings of a business that are kept, or retained, in the business.

Return on assets. Ratio of net income plus interest expense to total assets. It measures a company's effectiveness in using assets to generate earnings; also called *rate of return on total assets*.

Return on common equity. Net income minus preferred dividends, divided by average common shareholders' equity. It is a measure of profitability; also called *rate of return on common shareholders' equity*.

Return on equity. Net income divided by average shareholders' equity. It is a measure of profitability; also called *rate of return on shareholders' equity*.

Return on sales. Ratio of net income to net sales. It is a measure of profitability; also called *rate of return on net sales*.

Revaluation model. Under IFRS, property, plant and equipment can be revalued to the fair value if the value can be reliably measured.

Revenue. Increases to retained earnings created by delivering goods or providing services to customers.

Revenue expenditures. Expenditure that is debited to an expense account.

Revenue recognition principle. Recording revenues when they are earned by providing goods or services to customers.

Risk assessment. The process of identifying risks and gauging the probability that they will occur.

S

Sales discount. Discount granted on sales for the customer's early payment within a discount period; a contra-account to Sales Revenue.

Sales invoice. A bill that documents the sale of goods to a business customer.

Sales returns and allowances. A reduction in the amount of sales due to customers returning merchandise or accepting damaged goods; a contra-account to Sales Revenue.

Sales revenue. The amount that a retailer earns from selling its inventory.

Salvage value. The estimated value at the end of a long-term asset's useful life; also called *residual value*.

Sarbanes-Oxley Act. A law passed in 2002 by the U.S. Congress in response to large-scale fraud in publicly owned companies.

Secured bonds. Bonds that give bondholders the right to take specified assets from the issuer if the issuer fails to pay principal or interest.

Selling expenses. Expenses related to advertising and selling products including sales salaries, sales commissions, advertising, depreciation on items used in sales, and delivery expense.

Serial bonds. Bonds from the same bond issuance that mature at different times.

Service business. A business that provides services to customers.

Share capital. Funds raised by the business entity in either cash or other consideration, and in exchange, the business entity issues ownership rights (preferred shares or common shares in a corporation) to the owner(s) who provided the funds.

Shareholder. A person who owns shares in a corporation.

Shareholders' equity. Represents the shareholders' ownership interest in the assets of a corporation.

Single-step income statement. Income statement format that groups all revenues together and lists all expenses together, subtracting total expenses from total revenues and calculating net income or net loss without computing any subtotals.

Sole proprietorship. A business with a single owner.

SOX. Acronym for the Sarbanes-Oxley Act.

Specific-identification method. Inventory costing method in which a business uses the specific cost of each unit of inventory; also called the *specific-unit cost* method.

Specific-unit cost. Inventory costing method in which a business uses the specific cost of each unit of inventory; also called the *specific-identification* method.

Stated interest rate. Interest rate that determines the amount of cash interest the borrower pays and the investor receives each year. Also called the *coupon rate*.

Statement of cash flows. Summary of the changes in a business's cash balance for a specific period. A financial statement that shows all of the sources and all of the uses of cash for an accounting period; also called the *cash flow statement*.

Statement of changes in equity. Summary of the changes in shareholders' equity during a period by providing information on common shares, retained earnings, and other comprehensive income.

Statement of comprehensive income. Summary of a business's revenues, expenses, and net income or net loss for a specific period, as well as other comprehensive income, such as unrealized gains or losses from holding assets. The income statement is one of the components included in the statement of comprehensive income.

Statement of financial position. Summary of business's assets, liabilities, and shareholders' equity as of a specific date; also called the *balance sheet*.

Stock dividends. A distribution by a corporation of its own shares to shareholders.

Stock splits. An increase in the number of outstanding shares coupled with a proportionate reduction in the value of the shares.

Straight-line depreciation. Depreciation method in which an equal amount of depreciation expense is assigned to each year of asset use. (Cost of the Asset – Salvage Value)/Useful Life of the Asset.

Subsidiary ledger. An accounting record that contains details, such as a list of customers and the accounts receivable due from each, or a list of suppliers and the accounts payable due to each.

T

T-account. An informal account form used to summarize transactions, where the top of the T holds the account title and the base divides the debit and credit sides of the account.

Tangible assets. Assets that are physical in form. They can be seen, touched, or held.

Temporary accounts. The revenue, expense, and dividend accounts; these accounts are closed at the end of the period.

Term bonds. Bonds that all mature at the same time.

Third party. People or organizations unrelated to the organization.

Time value of money. The concept that states that a dollar today is worth more than a dollar received in the future.

Timeliness. Having something done or information provided fast enough to make a difference in a decision.

Times-interest-earned ratio. Ratio of income from operations to interest expense. It measures the number of times that operating income can cover interest expense; also called the *interest-coverage ratio*.

Title. Ownership.

Total asset turnover ratio. Measures a company's ability to generate sales from its total assets, including current assets, investments, fixed assets, etc.

Trade names. Assets that represent distinctive identifications of a product or service; also called *brand names*.

Trademarks. Assets that represent distinctive identifications of a product or service.

Transaction. An event that has a financial impact on a business entity.

Treasurer. The individual in an organization responsible for the custody of assets, such as cash.

Treasury shares. A corporation's own shares that it has issued and later reacquired.

Trend percentages. A form of horizontal analysis in which percentages are computed by selecting a base year and then expressing amounts for following years as a percentage of the base year amounts.

Trial balance. A list of all the accounts of a business and their balances in the order of the statement of financial position; its purpose is to verify that total debits equal total credits.

U

Unadjusted trial balance. A trial balance that is prepared prior to the adjusting entries being made.

Uncollectible accounts. An Account Receivable that is unable to be collected; also called a *bad debt*.

Understandability. One of the qualitative characteristics of accounting information, that it be understandable for users.

Underwriter. A firm, such as TD Waterhouse, that usually agrees to buy all the shares a company wants to issue if the firm cannot sell the shares to its clients.

Unearned revenue. A liability created when a business collects cash from customers in advance of providing goods or services; also called *deferred revenue*.

Units-of-production (UOP) depreciation. Depreciation method by which a fixed amount of depreciation is assigned to each unit of output produced by an asset.

Unsecured bonds. Bonds that are backed only by the general credit of the company issuing the bond; also called *debentures*.

Useful life. The expected life of an asset during which it is anticipated to generate revenues. May be expressed in years or units of output.

V

Value in use. The discounted future cash flows expected to arise from the continuing use of an asset, and from its disposal at the end of its useful life.

Vertical analysis. Analysis of a financial statement that reveals the relationship of each statement item to a specified base amount, which is the 100% figure.

W

Warranty. A guarantee that a product or service is free from defect.

Weighted average cost. Inventory costing method where the beginning inventory and all purchases of inventory are added and divided by the total number of units to get one average cost. This average cost is used to value ending inventory and cost of goods sold in the periodic system.

Whistleblower. A person who reports unethical behaviour.

Wholesale business. A business that purchases products from a manufacturer and sells them to a retail business.

Withdrawals. Income that is removed from the company and distributed to the owner(s).

Work in process. Inventory of partially completed goods.

Working capital. Current assets minus current liabilities. It measures a business's ability to meet its short-term obligations with its current assets.

Write off. Removing a customer's receivable from the accounting records because it is considered uncollectible.

Index

Company Index

Credits